ZOLA: A LIFE

Frederick Brown, Professor of French Language and literature at the State University of New York at Stony Brook, is the author of *An Impersonation of Angels: A Biography of Jean Cocteau*, *Père Lachaise*, and *Theatre and Revolution*. He lives in New York City.

ALSO BY FREDERICK BROWN

An Impersonation of Angels: A Biography of Jean Cocteau (1968)
Père-Lachaise: Elysium as Real Estate (1973)
Theater and Revolution: The Culture of the French Stage (1980)

ZOLA
A LIFE

FREDERICK
BROWN

PAPERMAC

First published 1995 by Farrar, Straus & Giroux, New York,
and simultaneously in Canada by HarperCollins*CanadaLtd*

First published in Great Britain 1996 with corrections by Macmillan

This edition published 1997 by Papermac
an imprint of Macmillan Publishers Ltd
25 Eccleston Place, London SW1W 9NF
and Basingstoke

Associated companies throughout the world

ISBN 0 333 66212 1

The author gratefully acknowledges the kind permission to use illustrative material from the
following: Musée Carnavalet: illustrations nos 1, 9, 31, 42–44, 48–49, 52, 53, 64, 67 and 74. Musée
Zola: 2, 3, 11, 12, 17, 26, 32, 33, 34, 36, 37, 50, 51, 55, 57, 60, 70, 72 and 76. Musée de la Marine,
Chambre de Commerce et de l'Industrie de Marseille: 4. Bibliothèque Nationale de Paris: 8, 13,
14, 16, 18–25, 29, 30, 38, 39, 40, 45, 46, 54, 59, 61, 62, 65, 66, 69 and 75. Private collection: 10.
The Pierpont Morgan Library: 15, 41 and 63. The Bettmann Archive: 27, 28 and 68.
Collection Morin-Laborde: 35, 56, 58, 71. Madame Françoise LeBlond-Zola: 47.
Caisse Nationale des Monuments Historiques des Sites: 73.

Special thanks to Penguin Books Ltd for permission to reprint excerpts from *L'Assommoir*,
La Bête Humaine and *The Debacle* by Emile Zola, translated by Leonard W. Tancock; from *Nana*
by Emile Zola, translated by George Holden; from *The Earth* by Emile Zola, translated by Douglas
Parmée; and to Viking Penguin, a division of Penguin Books USA, for permission to reprint
from *Germinal* by Emile Zola, translated by Stanley and Eleanor Hochman.

1 3 5 7 9 8 6 4 2

A CIP catalogue record for this book is available from
the British Library

Printed and bound in Great Britain by
Mackays of Chatham plc, Chatham, Kent

FOR

RUTH

FOR

B. BERNIE
HERRON

ACKNOWLEDGMENTS

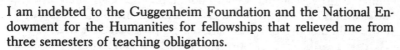

I am indebted to the Guggenheim Foundation and the National Endowment for the Humanities for fellowships that relieved me from three semesters of teaching obligations.

Invaluable help was provided by the staffs of the Melville Library at the State University of New York, Stony Brook; Butler Library at Columbia University; the New York City Public Library; Bobst Library at New York University; the Pierpont Morgan Library; the Centre d'Etudes sur Zola et le Naturalisme; the Bibliothèque Nationale; the Bibliothèque Méjane in Aix-en-Provence; and the Municipal Archives of Aix-en-Provence. I should like to thank them all, and to thank as well Bard Bakker, director of the Research Program on Zola and Naturalism at the University of Toronto, who will soon have shepherded through its tenth and final volume, a monumental edition of Zola's correspondence.

I thank Hilton Kramer and Frederick Morgan for publishing versions of five chapters in their journals, *The New Criterion* and *The Hudson Review*.

Colette Morin-Laborde and Danielle Coussot of the Centre d'Etudes sur Zola in Paris lightened the task of combing through indecipherable letters and performed essential tasks for me with great good humor. I owe them both debts of gratitude.

I am pleased to thank Jean-Claude Le Blond-Zola, who patiently answered my niggling queries, and Martine Le Blond-Zola, who was kind enough to furnish me with prints from the photographic collection of the Musée Zola at Médan. Professor Owen Morgan, one of the principal editors of the *Correspondance,* who knows his way around Zola's life as well as anyone, gave me some very useful pointers.

Encouragement from Professor Colette Becker, a distinguished Zola scholar, played an important part in helping me to get started, for which I am most grateful.

At every stage of the writing, this book has been tried out on friends, whose conversation and critical commentary have profited me more than I can say. I wish to thank Quentin Anderson, Miriam Arsham, my agent Georges Borchardt, Christopher Carduff, Phyllis Johnson, Johanna Kaplan, and Peter Shaw. Carol Blum, Benita Eisler, and Frances Taliaferro provided loyal and generous support year in and year out.

My special thanks go to Ruth Kozodoy, who in many ways helped me to persevere, and who read the manuscript with great care, giving every page of it the benefit of her critical acumen. It is a gift of time and talent that can't be adequately acknowledged.

Diane Mullen and Yoon-Il Auh helped the enterprise forward with word processing and printing. Jack Lynch did a superb job of copy editing. Ruth Elwell produced an admirably thorough index. And, at Farrar Straus and Giroux, Luba Ostashevsky assisted me efficiently in all the tasks that precede publication. I deeply appreciate their efforts.

Lastly, I wish to record my gratitude to a great editor, Elisabeth Sifton. But for her faith, enthusiasm, and sound advice, the book might not be. She was there throughout its history, from the first glimmer to the final formulation.

F.B.
New York, October 1994

CONTENTS

ILLUSTRATIONS

❧

CHRONOLOGY

1840: Emile Zola is born in Paris to Emilie Aubert and François Zola.

Abortive coup d'état by Louis Napoleon Bonaparte.
The ashes of Napoleon I are brought back to France from Saint Helena.

1843: The family settles in Aix-en-Provence.

Balzac publishes *Les Illusions perdues*.

The inauguration of the first major rail lines in France: Paris–Rouen and Paris–Orléans.

1847: The death of François Zola.

1851: The beginning of Emilie Zola's legal struggles with Jules Migeon.

Louis Napoleon's successful coup d'état; there are sporadic insurrections throughout France, including the Midi. Prominent republicans are exiled or executed.

1852: Zola enters the Collège Bourbon and forms a friendship with Paul Cézanne and Jean-Baptistin Baille.

The Empire is proclaimed at Paris's Hôtel de Ville.

1854: The Zola Canal is completed.
A cholera epidemic forces the Zolas to seek refuge in the countryside.

The Crimean War commences.

1857: Emilie Zola leaves for Paris to plead her cause before the Tribunal de Commerce.

Publication of *Madame Bovary*. Flaubert is indicted and brought to trial.

1858: Zola joins his mother in Paris; quarters are found on the rue Monsieur-le-Prince.
He enters the Lycée Saint-Louis as a scholarship student.

The reconstruction of Paris under Baron Haussmann begins in earnest.
Bernadette Soubirous's first vision at Lourdes.

1859: Zola twice fails the baccalauréat examination.

Napoleon III invades northern Italy; victories at Magenta and Solferino.
The government declares a general amnesty for political crimes.
Paris expands to include suburban villages between the customs wall and the fortifications, Montmartre among them.

1860: Zola works as a clerk in the Customs House on the Canal Saint-Martin.
He attends lectures on the rue de la Paix, writes verse, engages in an active correspondence with Cézanne and Baille.

Measures are taken to liberalize the regime.

1861: Zola claims French nationality.
He has a brief affair with a young woman known only as Berthe.
He searches in vain for employment after leaving the Customs House.
Cézanne and Baille arrive in Paris.

1862: The government recognizes Zola as a naturalized French citizen.
He is hired by Hachette and becomes director of its publicity department.

Students objecting to the denial of Christ's divinity interrupt Renan's inaugural lecture at the Collège de France.
A delegation of workers attends the Universal Exposition in London, under official auspices.

1864: Publication of *Les Contes à Ninon.*
Zola meets Gabrielle Alexandrine Meley.

Renan's *Vie de Jésus*, Flaubert's *Madame Bovary*, and Hugo's *Les Misérables* are placed on the papal Index.
The International Workingmen's Association (IWA) is founded in London, with a manifesto by Karl Marx.
Pius IX issues his encyclical *Syllabus of Errors.*

1865: Zola exchanges letters with the Goncourts, who publish *Germinie Lacerteux.*
He contributes regularly to the Lyon newspaper *Le Salut public* and publishes *La Confession de Claude.*
Thursday-evening gatherings become a regular event in the Zola household; attended by Pissarro as well as Zola's Aixois friends.
He sets up house with Alexandrine Meley.

Cholera epidemic in Paris claims more than 4,000 victims.
Inauguration of telegraph line between Paris and Lyon.

1866: Zola leaves Hachette to become a freelance journalist.
Villemessant hires him to write book reviews for *L'Evénement*.
Duranty introduces him to the Café Guerbois, where he meets Manet and the future Impressionists.
He reviews the annual Salon in seven articles that constitute a militant defense of Manet and the new "plein air" painting.
He and Alexandrine vacation at Bennecourt with Cézanne, Baille, Valabrègue, et al.
Publication of art and literary criticism in two volumes, *Mes Haines* and *Mon Salon,* and of a novel, *Le Voeu d'une morte.*

A senatus consultum gives the Legislative Body greater power.
France is afflicted with grave economic problems.
Prussia defeats Austria-Hungary at Sadowa.

1867: Publication of *Les Mystères de Marseille* and *Thérèse Raquin.*
Zola moves to the Right Bank. He frequents Manet's studio and has his portrait painted.

The Legislative Body acquires the right to summon and challenge ministers.
Collapse of the huge credit bank, Crédit Mobilier.
The prosecution of members of the French section of the IWA.
Jules Ferry publishes his pamphlet *Les Comptes fantastiques d'Haussmann.*
The French expeditionary force conquers Cochin China.
A Universal Exposition opens in Paris.

1868: Publication of *Madeleine Férat.*
Zola contributes regularly to *La Tribune.*
Monet's wife and son join Zola and Alexandrine in Bennecourt.
Zola dines for the first time at the Goncourts'.

A law is passed granting greater freedom of the press.
The Senate holds a debate on "materialist teachings" at the medical school.
Bismarck rejects the disarmament plan proposed by France.

1869: Zola submits the first master plan of *Les Rougon-Macquart* to Lacroix.
He writes a letter of self-introduction to Flaubert.
Paul Alexis makes Zola's acquaintance.
The Zolas sojourn frequently in Bennecourt.

The *Oeuvres complètes* of Balzac begin to appear.
Publication of Flaubert's *Education sentimentale.*
The Congress of the International League for Peace and Freedom meets in Lausanne, with Victor Hugo presiding.
The Empress Eugénie inaugurates the Suez Canal.
Miners strike in the Loire basin, at La Ricamarie, in the Aveyron, setting the stage for bloody confrontations with the army.

1870: The Franco-Prussian War breaks out, interrupting the serial publication of *La Fortune des Rougon.*
Zola and family flee to Marseille as German armies advance on Paris.
With Roux, he publishes a newspaper called *La Marseillaise.*
He leaves Marseille to seek employment with the wartime government in Bordeaux.

General von Moltke besieges Paris.
Gambetta escapes by balloon and establishes in Tours a delegation of the Government of National Defense.

1871: An armistice is declared in January, and elections are held to form a National Assembly. In March, Paris constitutes itself as a Commune. In May, the French army invades Paris under the command of Marshal MacMahon, and a week of bloody civil war known as *la semaine sanglante* ensues. Having fled Paris, Zola witnesses the aftermath of the massacre. Zola reports proceedings of the National Assembly to *La Cloche* and *Le Sémaphore de Marseille,* and continues to do so when the Assembly reconvenes at Versailles. Publication of *La Fortune des Rougon* as a volume; serialization of *La Curée.*

1872: Georges Charpentier becomes Zola's publisher.
A revised version of the master plan of *Les Rougon-Macquart* emerges.
Zola attends Flaubert's Sunday gatherings, where he meets Turgenev and Daudet.

Trials, executions, and deportations of Communards.

1873: Publication of *Le Ventre de Paris.*
Zola's stage adaptation of *Thérèse Raquin* is performed at the Théâtre de la Renaissance.
He writes for *L'Avenir national* and *Le Sémaphore de Marseille.*

Thiers resigns; MacMahon is elected president of the Republic and declares the need for "moral order."
The war indemnity is repaid; German troops evacuate French territory.
Monarchists make overtures to the Comte de Chambord.

1874: Publication of *La Conquête de Plassans* and *Nouveaux Contes à Ninon.*
Les Héritiers Rabourdin has a brief run at the Théâtre de Cluny.
The first "dinner of booed authors" takes place at the Café Riche.
Zola joins compatriots from Aix for a monthly dinner, called *le boeuf nature.*
He forms a friendship with Mallarmé.
Cézanne takes up residence in Auvers and works with Pissarro.

A revival of Bonapartism. In the National Assembly, Gambetta denounces high-ranking officials of the Second Empire.

1875: Publication of *La Faute de l'abbé Mouret.*
Zola begins a collaboration with a Saint Petersburg monthly, *The Eur-*

opean Herald.
He and Alexandrine vacation on the Channel coast, at Saint-Aubin.

The Wallon amendment passes by one vote, establishing the Republic in principle.
The foundation of the Sacré-Coeur is laid.

1876: Publication of *Son Excellence Eugène Rougon.*
Zola contributes regularly to *Le Bien public* (as drama critic), *The European Herald, Le Sémaphore de Marseille.*
Céard and Huysmans introduce themselves to him.
He seeks treatment for nervous disorders.
He and Alexandrine vacation at Piriac in Brittany.

Republicans win a majority in legislative elections. Jules Simon becomes the prime minister.
Worker congresses are held in Paris and Marseille (the latter under Guesde's sponsorship).
An end is put to the prosecution of cases connected with the Commune.

1877: Publication of *L'Assommoir.*
Céard, Huysmans, Alexis, Maupassant, Hennique, and Mirbeau stage a dinner at Chez Trapp to inaugurate the "naturalist school"; they invite Zola, Flaubert, and Goncourt.
The Zolas vacation at L'Estaque and visit Aix.
In Paris they move to the rue de Boulogne (now the rue Ballu).

The crisis of May 16: MacMahon dissolves the Assembly and 363 deputies protest.
Voters return a republican majority in October elections.

1878: Publication of *Une Page d'amour.*
Le Bouton de rose is staged at the Palais-Royal.
Zola acquires a cottage in Médan.
The publication in *Le Figaro* of Zola's article on contemporary novelists creates an uproar.
Zola becomes a regular contributor to *Le Voltaire.*
His friendship with Cézanne revives.

The Universal Exposition opens in Paris.
Republicans succeed in nationwide municipal elections.
Leo XIII is elected pope.
A socialist congress is broken up by police in Paris and Jules Guesde is arrested.

1879: Zola collaborates with William Busnach on stage adaptation of *L'Assommoir;* immensely successful run at the Ambigu.
The Zolas arrange longer sojourns at Médan; the cottage is enlarged and more property is acquired.

Grévy replaces MacMahon as president of the Republic.

1880: Publication of *Nana* and *Les Soirées de Médan*.
Zola's articles on the modern novel are brought out under the title *Le Roman expérimental*.
He breaks with Laffitte, publisher of the left-wing *Voltaire*, and decides to write for the conservative *Figaro*.
The deaths of Flaubert and of Emilie Zola.

Convicted Communards are granted full amnesty.
The government bans Jesuits and other unauthorized orders from teaching.
July 14 is decreed a national holiday.

1881: A stage adaptation of *Nana* is produced at the Ambigu.
Charpentier publishes collections of Zola's essays: *Le Naturalisme au théâtre, Nos auteurs dramatiques, Les Romanciers naturalistes*.
Zola leaves *Le Figaro*.
He dines at regular intervals with Daudet, Goncourt, Turgenev; frequently receives Huysmans, Céard, Alexis, et al. at Médan.

Public school education is made free in accordance with legislation drafted by Ferry, who serves as both prime minister and minister of public instruction.
Gambetta succeeds Ferry.

1882: Publication of *Pot-Bouille* and a collection of short stories, *Le Capitaine Burle*.
Much of the year is spent at Médan.
Zola's journalistic activity comes to a virtual halt.

An official circular forbids the display of religious symbols in schools.
The crash of the Union Générale.
Léon Gambetta dies.

1883: Publication of *Au Bonheur des Dames* and a collection of short stories entitled *Naïs Micoulin*.
A stage adaptation of *Pot-Bouille* is performed at the Ambigu.
The Zolas vacation at Bénodet in the Finistère (Brittany).
Deaths of Manet and of Turgenev.

The French military pursues colonial wars in Annam, Madagascar, North Africa.
A law is passed banishing from France pretenders to the throne.

1884: Publication of *La Joie de vivre*.
Research for and the writing of *Germinal* proceed.
Zola and Alexandrine seek relief for their ills at the spa of Mont-Dore.

Strikers at the coalfields of Anzin call for a nationwide closing of mines.
Colonial expansion continues in Southeast Asia.

1885: Publication of *Germinal*.
Zola collaborates with Busnach on a stage adaptation of *Germinal*,

which the official censor refuses to license.

The Zolas return to the spa of Mont-Dore for treatment of their ailments.

Cézanne visits Médan.

The death of Victor Hugo.

The Pantheon is secularized and dedicated to "great men of the nation."

1886: Publication of *L'Oeuvre*, leading to a permanent break with Cézanne.
Zola collaborates with Busnach on the stage adaptation of *Le Ventre de Paris*.
Fieldwork for *La Terre* takes him to the Beauce.
Zola and Alexandrine vacation at Royan on the Atlantic coast with the Charpentiers.

Boulanger is appointed minister of war.

1887: Publication of *La Terre*.
A violent diatribe against *La Terre* appears in *Le Figaro*, called the "Manifeste des Cinq."
Le Ventre de Paris is performed at the Théâtre de Paris.
The Zolas enjoy a long sojourn at Royan.

André Antoine founds the Théâtre Libre.
General Boulanger is reassigned to a provincial post. His supporters stage vehement demonstrations at the Gare de Lyon.
The decorations scandal erupts. Grévy resigns from the presidency and is replaced by Sadi Carnot.

1888: Publication of *Le Rêve*.
Zola makes the acquaintance of Alfred Bruneau, who will adapt *Le Rêve* for the operatic stage.
Lockroy names him a *chevalier* in the Legion of Honor.
Jeanne Rozerot enters Zola's life.
During a third sojourn at Royan he is introduced to photography.

Boulanger is forced to retire and is elected to the Chamber of Deputies; he proposes that the constitution be revised.
Clemenceau presides over the foundation of the Society of the Rights of Man and the Citizen.

1889: Preparations begin for *La Bête humaine*, including a trip from Paris to Le Havre on the Western Line with Jeanne Rozerot.
The Zolas move into a new apartment, at 21 bis, rue de Bruxelles.
The birth of Zola's daughter, Denise.
He makes the first of many futile bids for a seat in the French Academy.

The Universal Exposition opens, with the Eiffel Tower as its show-piece.
Boulanger flees France and is tried in absentia. The Boulangist movement collapses.

1890: Publication of *La Bête humaine.*
Half the year is spent at Médan, where the Bruneaus, the Charpentiers, and the Labordes are frequent houseguests.

First signs of the Catholic *Ralliement.* Cardinal Lavigerie urges acceptance of the Republic.

1891: Publication of *L'Argent.*
With Alexandrine, Zola retraces the itinerary of the 7th Army Corps from Courcelles to Sedan in preparing *La Débâcle.*
The birth of Zola's son Jacques.
Zola is elected president of the Société des Gens de Lettres.
He and Alexandrine travel through the Pyrenees, stopping at Lourdes.
An anonymous letter informs Alexandrine of Zola's secret family.

Leo XIII issues the encyclical *Rerum Novarum.*
France and Russia effect an *entente cordiale,* thus responding to the Triple Alliance of Germany, Austria, and Italy.
Boulanger commits suicide.
The Panama Scandal makes headlines.

1892: Publication of *La Débâcle.*
The Zolas travel across France, from Lourdes to Italy, stopping in Aix.

Outbreaks of anarchist violence terrorize Paris. Ravachol is arrested for bombings and murders, and executed.
Celebrations take place to mark the centenary of the proclamation of the Republic.

1893: Publication *Le Docteur Pascal.*
The completion of *Les Rougon-Macquart* is celebrated at the Chalet des Iles.
Zola receives a rosette on being promoted to the rank of officer in the Legion of Honor.
Bruneau's opera *L'Attaque du moulin,* based on Zola's short story, is performed at the Opéra-Comique.
Zola attends the congress of the English Institute of Journalists in London.
The death of Maupassant. Zola speaks at his funeral.

The death of Hippolyte Taine.
An anarchist bomb explodes in the Chamber of Deputies.
Trials take place in connection with the Panama Scandal; students riot in the Latin Quarter.

1894: Publication of *Lourdes,* first volume of the trilogy *Les Trois Villes.*
Zola reads excerpts of *Lourdes* to an audience of four thousand at the Trocadéro.
His novel is placed on the papal Index.
He spends six weeks in Italy with Alexandrine, gathering material for *Rome.*

More anarchist bombs wreak havoc in Paris; in Lyon an Italian anarchist assassinates the president of the Republic, Sadi Carnot.
Captain Alfred Dreyfus is arrested and court-martialed.

1895: The Société des Gens de Lettres reelects Zola president.
He signs a contract to write a series of articles for *Le Figaro*.
Alexandrine travels alone to Italy, the first of many such sojourns without Zola.

A workers' congress in Limoges leads to the formation of the Confédération Générale du Travail (CGT).
Alfred Dreyfus is transported to Devil's Island.

1896: Publication of *Rome*.
Zola publishes sixteen articles in *Le Figaro*, including "Pour les juifs."
The death of Edmond de Goncourt. Zola delivers a funeral oration.
Alexandrine sojourns a second time alone in Italy. On her return, Zola joins her in Marseille.

Colonel Picquart apprises General de Boisdeffre of his suspicions. He is reassigned to North Africa.

1897: *Messidor* is produced at the Opera.
Jeanne Rozerot and the children spend the summer months at Verneuil-sur-Seine, downriver from Médan.
Zola is invited to lunch by Scheurer-Kestner and begins his journalistic campaign on behalf of Dreyfus.

A fire at the Bazar de la Charité incinerates 117 people, mainly women of the aristocracy. High government officials attend a funeral ceremony at Notre-Dame Cathedral.
Anti-Semitic riots break out in France and Algeria.

1898: Publication of *Paris*.
J'accuse appears in *L'Aurore* and leads to Zola's being tried for slander.
He flees to England after an appeals court upholds the lower court's conviction.
Zola takes up residence in Surrey. Jeanne and Alexandrine visit him by turns.

The death of Stéphane Mallarmé.

1899: Publication of *Fécondité*, first volume of the tetralogy *Les Quatre Evangiles*.
The High Court of Appeals grants Dreyfus a second court-martial.
Zola returns to France.

Dreyfus's second court-martial takes place, in Rennes. He is reconvicted, and pardoned by the president of the Republic.

1901: Publication of *Travail*.
Fasquelle publishes a collection of Zola's articles on the Dreyfus Affair called *La Vérité en marche*.

1902: Zola dies of asphyxiation in his apartment on the rue de Bruxelles. Anatole France delivers the funeral oration at Montmartre Cemetery.

1903: Posthumous publication of *Vérité*.

1908: Zola's remains are transferred to the Pantheon.

ZOLA: A LIFE

I

❧

A BIRTH AND A DEATH

IN FEBRUARY 1847, François Zola, a civil engineer who left his native Italy soon after the 1820 uprisings against Austria, had good reason to feel jubilant, for on the fourth day of that month work finally began on a project he fully expected would make him rich. At fifty-one he was director of a joint-stock company authorized by the French government to build a dam across the Infernets gorge east of Aix-en-Provence that would channel water through the perennially drought-stricken countryside below. Since 1838, when Aix's municipal council first signed an agreement with him, there had been many turns at which a less obstinate man might have despaired of ever seeing the venture brought to a material conclusion. His proposal had spent seasons in the fastness of the French bureaucracy and would have perished there had not the Council of State saved it from the ministry of the interior. A squire over whose property the canal was to run had frustrated Monsieur Zola with legal maneuvers that wheeled around and around the issue of *commodo et incommodo*. Investors had grown impatient, ready to pull up stakes as the economy struggled through the second decade of Louis Philippe's reign before entering a full-scale depression in 1845. But that was in the past now, and the problems yet to be solved did not intimidate Zola. Blasting open the mountain announced a new era for him. Once water started to course into the fountains of Aix-en-Provence three or four years hence, he would satisfy the creditors who had maintained him during this long ordeal.

François Zola never repaid his debts. On the mountain where in February bitter winds knife down from the Massif Central, he caught a cold that became progressively worse as he shuttled without respite between Aix, the dam site, and the office of contractors in Marseille. He was at a small hotel in Marseille when, on March 27, 1847, it all ended for him. The doctor summoned by his wife attributed the death to pleurisy.

Although funeral arrangements were made at short notice, François Zola was buried with all the pomp and ceremony Aix could improvise for a citizen on whom had devolved something of the magical power that Provençaux formerly invested in rainmaking saints. At the Place de la Rotonde, outside the city wall, a delegation of clergy met the wagon draped in black cloth that brought his corpse up from Marseille, thirty miles to the south. Surrounded by the mayor, the subprefect, an eminent Paris lawyer named Alexandre Labot, and the district engineer, each holding a corner of the pall, François Zola was borne to the Cathedral of Saint-Sauveur and given absolution before Monsignor Rey, bishop of Saint-Denis. Afterward, the funeral cortege, at whose head were Zola's young widow and his seven-year-old son, Emile, proceeded through crowds that had gathered in the narrow streets of the old quarter to pay homage. Labot eulogized Zola as a heroic figure who united the virtue of antiquity and the scientific animus of modern times. "He fell on arriving at the goal. Just as he was about to crown his work, he succumbed in the prime of life, without having gathered the fruit of his long and painful labors. . . . To the literary renown of the city of Aix and to its judicial glory, Zola was intent on adding the glitter of industrial prosperity. . . . He will never witness this brilliant future. There he lies today in his coffin. But he will survive in the memory of the inhabitants of this city." One week later the newspaper *La Provence*, which outdid its rival *Le Mémorial d'Aix* in necrological embellishments and paired Zola with Moses, opened a subscription fund to raise money for a tombstone that would express the public's gratitude until such time as an operative canal entitled him to some "more splendid" monument.

Given the civic pride of Aix's official mourners, Labot did not belabor the point that a life so congenial to the age had begun and ended in cities for which nineteenth-century Europe could find no great or useful purpose. François Zola was born Francesco Zolla on August 7, 1795, in Venice, whose republic the Zolla family had provided with a succession of military officers and civil servants: Francesco's grandfather, Antonio, who hailed from Brescia, spent years as an infantry captain in the Levantine provinces; his father, Carlo, after serving in the Corps of Engineers, was appointed Inspector General of Public Buildings in Venice; and his older brother, Marco, followed suit.

The political upheavals that began with Napoleon's invasion of Venetia in 1797 did not interrupt the family tradition, though they were eventually to drive Francesco from the family fold. In 1810 he entered the military academy at Pavia. Two years later he was commissioned a second lieutenant in the Imperial Army—Napoleon having meanwhile whittled out of Lombardy-Venetia a puppet state called the Kingdom of Italy and made his stepson, Eugène de Beauharnais, viceroy. Then came Waterloo. When the Allied Powers met at the Congress of Vienna to redesign Europe, Metternich claimed Venice for Austria, and Francesco found himself serving the Hapsburgs in an Italian regiment. During this period of explosive calm, he petitioned the military governor of the Venetian provinces for leave to study at the University of Padua. His request was granted. "About one year ago I obtained, through your benevolence, permission to complete my mathematical studies at the university," he wrote by way of dedicating to his sponsor, Baron de Lattermann a dissertation published in 1818 under the title *Trattato di livellazione topografica.* "As soon as I had completed them I undertook, without neglecting my military duties, to examine the most delicate geodetic operations of the engineer. From this examination has come a little book that combines, I believe, well-established principles and several new ideas on the theory and practice of land surveying." Equipped with a doctorate in mathematics that would be his bridge back to civilian life, Lieutenant Zolla spent only two more years soldiering. In 1820, when the bastinado was introduced as punishment for military insubordination, he resigned from the 26th Regiment of Austrian infantry. In 1821 he departed Italy and never lived there again.

Unlike thousands of intellectuals hounded into exile after the uprisings of 1820, Francesco left of his own free will. Did he sympathize with fellow officers who went underground, or have clandestine associations with them? It would be remarkable if Metternich's attempt to make Italy a mere "geographical expression," as he called it, by incriminating all signs of cultural self-esteem never stirred in Francesco the impulse to join some such secret society as the Adelfi. He was young, and from Vienna a flock of bewigged officials had descended on Lombardy-Venetia with the message that youth was suspect. He had ambitions, and under the rigid Austrian bureaucracy forward movement became anathema. To be sure, Hapsburg rule saved Venetia from economic ruin, but with secret police agents everywhere and censorship exercised even on the works of Dante, a Venetian could hardly forget that he was a prisoner in his own land. As one observer put it, Italians "ate Austria in their bread."

While political fugitives scattered to England, Switzerland, Holland, Spain, Corsica, and Greece, Francesco Zolla went where opportunity beckoned, to Austria itself, spurning the advice of his cautious brother, Marco, who viewed the prospect of rewards to be won in the outside world as the jack-o'-lantern that leads fools astray. By 1824 Francesco had become associated with a project for which his expertise in surveying particularly qualified him—the construction of a rail line between Linz, on the Danube, and Budweis, on the Moldau. This route paralleled the *goldener Steig*, or "golden road," along which mule trains carried salt from mines high in the Salzkammergut range to a state-controlled market in Bohemia. Since the fourteenth century, plans for more expeditious transportation, of which there had been many, had always revolved around the idea of digging a canal through the hilly, forested terrain that separated the two great rivers. Then in 1813 an Austrian engineer named Franz-Josef von Gerstner suggested the railway, with horse-drawn cars, as a plausible alternative to an artificial watercourse, and eight years later his son, also an engineer, pursued the theory. After visiting Great Britain, which was unique in having towns linked by iron track, Franz Anton von Gerstner felt confident that English technology could be applied at Linz–Budweis. He thus founded the Erste österreichische Eisenbahn-Gesellschaft, with Francesco Zolla among his original recruits.

Had he left well enough alone, Gerstner would have built a railroad. But during the winter of 1826–27 he visited England once again, taking Zolla with him, and he came home a convert to the new steam-driven locomotive. This irresistible vision of the future estranged him from the company directors, who had only just woken to the novelties of his first scheme when they found themselves urged to approve its modernization. Diplomacy was not Gerstner's strong suit, as one might expect of a man professionally obsessed by the swiftest route between two points. He made enemies even of the engineers he hired, and fought alone during a bitter struggle that resulted in his dismissal.

Long before Gerstner came to grief, Zolla had left the Eisenbahn-Gesellschaft to organize a company of his own. Having figured out how the Linz–Budweis line could be run uphill as far as the salt mines near Gmunden, he brought to bear on rich acquaintances that power of persuasion which would almost always enable him to fund the ventures his active mind conceived. By June 1829, when Franz I granted him an imperial charter—one article of which required him to lay five miles of track within two years or forfeit his license—the preparatory work was already done. Zolla had surveyed the terrain, plotted a course, purchased land, ordered rails, and foreseen every contretemps save the unimaginable possibility that Austria might rescind its state monopoly on the sale of salt to Bohemia. This, however, is what the Austrian government did, several months after construction had begun in earnest. Nothing could have hurt Zolla more. Capital fled from an enterprise whose future suddenly seemed murky, and, to keep it afloat, he was obliged to go public. Here again the government visited disaster upon him, for it authorized incorporation, but not until time had caught him short. The Zola Railroad Company (Zola with only one l) was as good as dead at birth. Once it became clear that an effort to postpone the due date specified in his agreement would fail, Zola resigned. Directors of the Eisenbahn-Gesellschaft, who may have orchestrated this outcome, lost no time claiming the vacant concession. In 1832 they began work on the Gmunden line where Zola had left off, with Zola's plans to guide them. By then he himself had quit Austria and served a year in the French Foreign Legion.

There had presumably been no question of his going home, if he still considered Venice home. What Nathaniel Hawthorne wrote some years later during a European tour taken with his family, that "it was really like passing from death into life, to find ourselves in busy, cheerful, effervescing France, after living for so long between asleep and awake in sluggish Italy," pictures the scene much as Zola must have beheld it in 1831: life against death, progress versus retrogression. When France overthrew the Bourbon king in 1830 to set its course with a constitutional monarch who allowed bourgeois energies free play, a chill ran down Europe's spine from Berlin to Vienna to Rome and stiffened the powers-that-were against opinion inimical to established authority. Such opinion was seen to include not only liberties that Pope Gregory XVI denounced in his encyclical *Mirari Vos* (above all, freedom of conscience) but also the economic principles of List, Ricardo, and Say, which had won support among businessmen throughout those countries sheltering from change in their Holy Alliance. Anyone who would argue the need for better roads, steam navigation, insurance companies, modern banks, or uniform coinage exposed himself to a charge of subversion. And where liberal minds convened, as in Romagnosi's journal *Annali universali di statistica,* Austrian censors kept close watch. "All the movements which have been shaking Northern and Central Europe do not cross the Apennines," wrote Ivan Turgenev, who deplored "the feigned sanctity, the systematic enslavement, the absence of real life" he saw during his first trip to Italy in 1840.

Feeling out of joint with a world inhospitable to the creed that nurtured his adventurous and lofty sense of what men should be about, Zola made for Paris, along with a multitude of Poles, Italians, Germans, and Belgians who had become personae non gratae at home after the revolutions of 1830. A portrait from this period shows us a slight figure nothing like the portly bourgeois whom Emile Zola knew as his father. He was far from handsome, yet his gaze, which holds us at a genial, faintly ironic distance, suggests that he might have thought himself so, or given the matter little thought. The mustache he grew in middle age had not yet disguised the purposeful set of his mouth.

France welcomed refugees who would help man her North African outposts, eager as she was to extend herself beyond Europe in the quest for markets, raw materials, and glory, but with a male population numerically depleted by the Napoleonic campaigns. A survey of employment opportunities told Zola that military skill afforded the penniless immigrant more immediate credit than experience as an engineer, and so he joined the Foreign Legion, which was then a few months old. His dossier, supplemented with plans he had drawn up for an ingenious system of fortifications to be deployed around Paris, did not earn him the captaincy he felt was his due, though it elicited praise from one war office general. A lieutenant eleven years earlier, he became a lieutenant once again, in Algiers, under the name François Zola.

Its first volunteers contracted to serve at least three years in the Foreign Legion. Zola resigned after one as the result of a strange imbroglio that would perhaps be forgotten today (or at all events would concern us only for what it says about his character) had not a muckraker intent on compromising Emile Zola brought it to light sixty-seven years later, in 1898, during the Dreyfus Affair. According to the Duke de Rovigo, the general in command of the French occupation force, whose report dates to September 1832, François Zola mysteriously vanished from his regiment one day. Garments recognized as belonging to him were found on a beach near Algiers, which prompted speculation that he had either drowned himself for love of his mistress, one Madame Fischer, who had just left Algeria with her husband, or else joined them in a ménage à trois. It was decided to seize and search the vessel on which the Fischers were sailing, after close scrutiny of regimental accounts under Zola's management revealed a deficit. "Zola was not on board," wrote Rovigo, "but [among the Fischers' effects] were 4,000 francs. At first they claimed that the sum rightfully belonged to them, then confessed that a portion of it, 1,500 francs, had been deposited by Zola. They were taken ashore and led to prison." Soon thereafter, Zola, who apparently fled as soon as it dawned on him that he had played the stooge in an embezzlement scheme, made it known from his hiding place that he would cover the loss provided there be no prosecution. Needing money more than it needed another deserter, the Legion's administrative council agreed to this bargain. So it came about that on October 30, 1832, François Zola was given an honorable discharge and early in the following year embarked for Marseille, still determined at age thirty-seven to find purchase in his country of adoption.

Marseille offered easy purchase. The observation of an eighteenth-century merchant that "although Marseille be situated in France, one may regard it as little Turkey, little Italy, little Barbary, and an epitome of all the best and worst in those lands" was no less true in 1833 than in 1725. Since Napoleon's fall, many more ingredients had been added to the stew of nations mixing there. When its status as a free port was restored, the Greek colony grew larger. From across the Italian border there arrived fugitive Carbonari, including the most vociferous of all, Giuseppe Mazzini, who soon outspoke his welcome. Legionnaires bound for Algeria whiled away their last hours on European soil at dockside brothels. All the winds of war, trade, and social discontent that promoted movement in the Mediterranean basin brought human waves to Marseille, and now mechanical power brought them faster. Its population increased by half during Louis Philippe's regime as the steamship, together with the railroad, came of age.

Marseille was for a civil engineer what Byzantium must have been for a voluptuary. Wherever he chanced to look, opportunities abounded. The dark streets inspired Zola, three months after he arrived, to float a joint-stock company for manufacturing gas of the kind used since 1832 in the illumination of Paris. The woefully insufficient water supply needed urgent attention, and in due course Zola would devise a plan for tapping the Huveaune River. Crowded conditions within the city created a real estate boom outside it, where Zola acquired parcels of land that proved more remunerative than his planned gasworks. Above all, there was the question of a new harbor, to which he gave the better part of his life from about 1835—when records indicate he employed three draftsmen and two apprentices at his office on the Canebière—until 1839.

By then the old harbor, or Vieux-Port, which had choked on traffic even before French warships began mooring there for the Algerian expedition, was generally recognized as being incommensurate with the role that Marseille hoped to play in Mediterranean affairs of the nineteenth century. "It is astonishing," wrote Zola, "that so rich and prosperous a city does not yet possess a suitable establishment which, in facilitating commercial operations, warehousing merchandise, expediting its passage through customs and shipment, would—by its structure, by the grandiose idea that will have presided over its execution, by the real advantages it will offer commerce—be an eternal monument to the power of our resources and our energy." His orotund prospectus accompanied a blueprint he sent to the Marseille municipal council after bureaucratic machinery for building a new dock had finally been set in motion. Though there were those who found it rather too grandiose, Zola's strategy offered such a cogent solution to the navigational problems posed by reefs and contrary winds that on March 5, 1835, the municipal council moved to adopt it.

Presently we find him in Paris, where the ultimate task of obtaining government sanction would keep him for months at a stretch. Toward the end of May the *Moniteur universel* noted under its court rubric that "M. Zola, engineer-architect-topographer," had had an audience with the king's son, the Prince de Joinville, who perused "the plans of his masterful work, recently adopted by Marseille, for the creation of a harbor to be called the Joinville Docks." Other such auspicious signs flashed from above, and when, on September 26, a naval commission seconded the endorsement of the municipal council, success was finally at hand. Not for nothing—or so it must have seemed—had Zola exhorted the government "to accord us the tutelary protection which alone induces general confidence, . . . to reward the labors of genius by granting it exclusive ownership of its inventions, . . . to encourage capitalists and inventors with large concessions in order that they may direct their common energies toward the honorable goal of raising industrial France to the highest degree of perfection." This agenda, with a vocabulary that strongly suggests he had read Claude Henri de Saint-Simon on the technocratic utopia, explained his affinities with several prominent gentlemen who befriended him in Paris, among them Alexandre Labot.

Success, like a cruel flirt leading on her suitor for the pleasure of finally saying no, eluded Zola once again. In the long run, neither the boldness of his ideas, nor the intercession of his friends, nor even the putative sponsorship of the Prince de Joinville could thwart the campaign waged by a rival engineer named Eugène Flachat. Zola was prepared to show that Flachat's design for the Marseille waterfront had been lifted in almost every particular from technical books about the new port at London (where Flachat had lived), but reason alone did not avail against an old-boy network of French engineers whose influence permeated the public and private sectors. Such was the situation as described in a letter Marco Zolla wrote on February 26, 1837, to acknowledge receipt of documents that bore on Flachat's intrigues:

> Councillor Francesconi stopped here . . . en route to Vienna after his honorable mission to England and France. . . . He told me he had met you several times and acquainted you with his fear that, despite the justice of your cause, you may be undone by national jealousy, . . . that a new project may be adopted which would be yours in substance but not in name. . . . Nothing must surprise you in this blind world, given the fact that you have until now been the unrivaled victim of all-powerful blindness. Your ideas, which carried the day over those of 13 French engineers [in the competition for Marseille's port], are known to the entire civilized world.

Marco advised that he withdraw from the fray, live in Marseille, and quietly prosper there while his misguided foes learned the error of their ways. Once again, brother ignored brother's advice. What might have made some impression on a less pugnacious man glanced off this egoist, who would never have left Venice had he not been inclined to go for broke where great dreams were at stake. Two years later he had indeed gone broke, gambling his last sou on a favorable decision. "I have spent three years in Paris without income and have, besides, contracted 20,000 francs' worth of debts using every means to bring off this important enterprise," he told his sister, who had dunned him for money. "I hope that during this session [early 1839] the ministry will place before parliament the law relating to my project; I shall then be able to breathe a little, but there will be no definitive result for another 8 or 10 months."

All the same, there lurked an *homme moyen sensuel* in François Zola, or enough of one to persuade him that he should finally organize his life around a wife and a hearth. When everything else was hanging in the balance, he married a young woman named Emilie Aubert, whose family had come to Paris sometime after 1819, the year she was born, from the town of Dourdan, near Chartres. "He first noticed her as she was coming out of church, and her beauty and charm did the rest; he did not marry her for the sake of a portion, since she had none," wrote Emile Zola. In a metropolis where most people went hungry every day, the Auberts coped, but with no wide margin between themselves and indigence. Emilie's mother worked as a seamstress, her father as a housepainter and glazier. Of her four brothers none ever escaped this precarious existence, and François found himself called upon at times to help them out. That he could do so compensated for his being twenty-four years older than Emilie. Even if she had imagined her prince arriving in some other guise, which we know nothing about, a dowerless girl of twenty chosen by a man who numbered among his well-wishers a once and future prime minister, Adolphe Thiers, was bound to regard herself as greatly fortunate.

They were married in a civil ceremony on March 16, 1839, and again, eleven months later, at the Church of Saint-Germain-l'Auxerrois. It appears that the couple lived near the Louvre with Emilie's brother, Adolphe Aubert, until they found more suitable quarters near the Bourse, at 10, rue Saint-Joseph, in a handsome new building flanked by dilapidated tenements and mansions formerly belonging to the aristocracy. Until 1796, when a church from which the street got its name used one corner of it as burial ground, quiet must have reigned on the rue Saint-Joseph, but the graveyard had long since become a marketplace that overflowed with peddlers and behind it ran another narrow passage, the rue du Croissant, where printing presses, newspaper offices, and *camelots* hawking the daily editions raised a constant din. Here Emilie was only several blocks away from her par-

ents on the rue de Cléry, a fact that surely dictated the Zolas' choice
of neighborhood, for they knew beforehand that in the large flat they
had rented four floors above street level she would soon want the
comfort of a mother as well as the expertise of a midwife. At 11 p.m.
on April 2, 1840, Emilie gave birth to a boy, who was christened Emile
Edouard Charles Antoine.

Emile Zola entered this world trailing names that evoked a line of
Venetian ancestors, yet François's pious resolve to commemorate the
dead family did not influence him to keep the living one abreast of
events in his life. Since January 1839 he had not once corresponded
with his brother or sister, and they feared the worst until a letter from
him arrived in August 1840. "At last I've read you and I thank the
Almighty for such a favor," answered his sister. "Your long silence had
plunged us into anguish and we began wondering if you were still alive.
Whatever your occupations may have been, you would have comforted
your relatives by giving them fifteen minutes of your time. . . . You
have written and we are happy. I rejoice in your marriage and your
paternity. I should like with all my heart to meet your new wife, but
you forgot to tell me her name." Whereas Marco Zolla cherished a
dream that the whole family would someday knit together again, François's strongest impulse was to let the past unravel behind him, as he
advanced in life weaving a new fabric for himself out of the material
offered by France and science and Emilie Aubert. Perhaps his silence
during this momentous period gratified the same need to vanish, or
feign death, that overcame him on the beach at Algiers, just as the
omission of his wife's name may have answered some unconscious
wish to protect his own identity. The self-made man in whom François
manifested such pride made the expanse between Paris and Venice
terra incognita. So complete was this void (which, like "the self-made
man," became a theme with infinite variations in his son's life and
work) that Emile Zola would reach late middle age before meeting his
paternal kin. Half French and half Italian, he grew up deprived of
Italian roots and of French citizenship.[1]

Marco, who died in 1840, urged François one last time to seek the
easy commissions available in Marseille, declaring that "you must curb
your fantasy and devote yourself to your domestic duties and the
peaceful exercise of your profession," but what François hoped to obtain from the power brokers whose favor he had curried did not allow
him to relinquish just yet his seat beside them, least of all in 1840,
when Thiers was appointed prime minister. Ideas for one venture or
another tumbled down the rue Saint-Joseph and optimistically spread

[1]To enjoy French citizenship he would have to apply for it on attaining his majority, which he did.

out across Paris. Since the government had been roused by war fever over the "Eastern Question" to do something about the capital's fortification, François sent a new draft of his old plan to Louis Philippe. It got no farther than it had nine years earlier, and he consoled himself with the invention of a mechanical shovel that was eventually used in digging moats near Clignancourt. The year 1840 also marked the outbreak in Algeria of Abd-el-Kader's jihad, or holy war. On October 10, 1840, during the bloody battles being waged throughout the Mitidja region, François wrote the president of the council of ministers proposing that France charter in Algeria a kind of East India Company, to be capitalized at a hundred million francs and granted a ninety-nine-year concession over territory wrested from the Arabs. This enterprise, which argued its author's Saint-Simonian vision of a state run as a private corporation by businessmen and engineers, would have given these new aediles (had it found support) sovereign responsibility for protecting European settlers, directing their operations, building their villages, and furnishing them with provisions.

However important in itself, such activity made François think about something other than the Aix-en-Provence dam and canal on which his greatest hopes of success had rested for two years, when an agreement with Aix was first drawn up. He kept beating the devil's tattoo as he waited for the government to issue a decree of *utilité publique*, without which his contract remained ineffective; the government showed no disposition whatever to rush ahead. "It really seems that a curse hangs over this project: we lost eight months in the bureau of the Prefecture and now ten weeks more [awaiting a report drafted for the ministry of public works]," he lamented in March 1840. Round and round the project shuffled, with captious functionaries partnering it in an aimless two-step, until the stubborn Zola grew desperate. By 1842 a reasonably favorable decision emerged from the ministry of the interior, whereupon Zola, who had weak lungs, fell gravely ill. His presence was now required in Aix more than in Paris, but three months passed before he could consider moving south. He arrived in March 1843; his wife and child followed.

Emile Zola's earliest memory of a house took him back to 6, rue Silvacanne, where his parents settled after they familiarized themselves with Aix. Situated almost in the shadow of the Cathedral of Saint-Sauveur but just outside the ruins of a city wall, the house abutted town and country. Overlooking its own large garden with windows that, when shuttered, gave it the characteristically blank look of Provençal *bastides*, it had space far beyond the Zolas' immediate needs. It also had historical, or pseudo-historical, importance, for this square, whitewashed villa owned by a marquise named Henriette Félix-d'Ollières was reputed, mistakenly, to be the house in which Adolphe Thiers had lived during his law-school days.

For a while Aix seemed unbearable to the Zolas, and in a letter she wrote to Madame Aubert toward the end of June 1843, Emilie, a homesick Parisienne lost beneath a Provençal sky, described her tribulations. Foremost among them was the precarious health of her son, over whom she had anxiously watched ever since he fell into a death-like swoon at age two from what physicians diagnosed as "brain fever." Some mysterious illness kept him bedridden for weeks, but no sooner did he recover than François in turn began to ail. With everyone wilting around her, sickness colored Emilie's view of the world outside. The sun shed jaundice over Aix's antique charms. It bleached the hills and darkened her skin. It killed the crops and reduced her family to a monotonous diet of omelettes and lamb. "As you see, since our separation from you we have not known happiness," she told her mother. "I wish we could be reunited; if we were, I assure you that I believe it would improve our well-being here, since boredom has taken firm hold of me." All she had for diversion was a view of mountains, and she felt surrounded by them "as by the walls of a prison." In two years she never once took a stroll, which suggests that they eschewed the Cours, the wide main avenue of Aix where every Sunday Aixois paraded under the acacias in their finery—common people on the north side and aristocrats on the south. François could hardly walk through town without peasants badgering him with questions about when they might expect water. For Emilie this was "a land of savages."

Such hardships were endured with the idea constantly in mind that Zola, the lifelong arriviste, would soon arrive. "Our mayor promised him that the day water flows there will be a great celebration paid for by the city," wrote Emilie. In May 1844, King Louis Philippe at last set his seal on a decree of public utility which confirmed the agreement Zola had won from Aix, and fifteen months later papers were notarized that gave legal existence to a joint-stock company called the Société du Canal Zola, with headquarters in Paris. As director, he received several hundred shares, each worth five hundred francs. What is more, his seventy-year concession stipulated that he be paid between thirty and forty-five thousand francs yearly, depending on the volume of water needed by the city. In an era when two francs represented a day's wage for the average worker and thirty thousand the annual stipend of a senator, Zola stood to join France's plutocratic elite.

This led him to indulge his generous nature more freely, as one deduces from the account he opened with an expensive Paris tailor, who fitted out his entire family (father-in-law included), and from the considerable bill for jewelry purchased at Girard's on the rue d'Alger. "My father had lived in a comfortable style, without thought of saving money," is how Zola remembered it. Having so often been brought low, however, he was mindful of the formidable responsibilities his wife would find thrust upon her if she unexpectedly became a widow. Since Emilie had married Zola without benefit of a contract, the court could award creditors whatever she inherited, and creditors there were aplenty, even after he reduced their number by pledging away all but a hundred and twenty-one of his shares. He therefore made arrangements, during a long sojourn in Paris, to reconstitute his marriage under the regime known as *séparation des biens*, which meant dissolving their joint estate. This legal ceremony took place on November 12, 1846, or five months before it proved to have been a rehearsal for the definitive separation.

Eventually, details of that separation found their way into one of Zola's novels, *Une Page d'amour*, where Hélène Mouret pictures the grief she felt on emerging alone from the large, bare hotel room in which she had spent a week nursing her doomed husband. But among the many episodes of *Les Rougon-Macquart*, nowhere is there transfigured one particular incident that must have borne home on young Emile a sense of the majestic void left by his father. It was related in *La Provence* on July 29, 1847:

> Yesterday . . . Monsieur Thiers, along with Messieurs Aude, mayor of Aix; Borély, attorney general; Boyrand, deputy mayor; Lyder, justice of the peace; and several other notabilities, unexpectedly went to visit the construction site of the Zola Canal, on the Infernets heights. They were received amid noisy detonations which the workers, who were alerted at the last minute, had prepared for their benefit. . . . The director availed himself of the opportunity to introduce to Monsieur Thiers the young son of M. Zola. The illustrious orator welcomed with utmost grace the child as well as the widow of a man whose name will live among those of the region's benefactors.

Standing on the heights amid people who would honor him as someone great in his own right became for Emile not just an achievable goal but an imperative fraught with the underlying terror that its achievement might cost him his life. "My father passes like a shadow through memories of my early childhood," he later wrote, and indeed, François Zola had cast a very long shadow, against which he was to measure himself thenceforth. It would accompany him every morning, when he entered his own study as an intruder, to engage in what he described as "a continual exercise of will over doubt." Of that he did not yet know anything. He knew only that a boy bereft of his father was radically different from other children.

II

UNDER THE MOUNTAIN

HAVING ESTABLISHED THEMSELVES in Aix two years before François Zola died, Emilie's parents were able to give her and Emile emotional support during their mourning. Madame Henriette Félicité Aubert came of Beauceron peasant stock. Unlike her daughter—who was subject, even before tragedy befell her, to nervous fits accompanied by partial loss of memory, muscular convulsions, and globus hystericus—she presented a sturdy figure at the age of sixty, being "very lively, very gay, very round." As Zola told his first biographer, Paul Alexis, penury brought out the best in her. From a lifetime spent between rocks and hard places she had mastered the art of making do with little. While Emilie showed a strong disposition to sue for financial independence in courts of law, Madame Aubert felt at ease in milieux that called upon her ability to stretch, pare, and mend. "When circumstances demanded that they get what they could for the last remnants of the luxury they formerly enjoyed, it was Mama Aubert, a bold and crafty woman, who haggled with the secondhand merchants," wrote Alexis. About her husband, Louis-Etienne, few anecdotes exist, and it may be that he played the part of compliant male in a household run by women. Four years older than Henriette and rather the worse for wear, he contributed to the matriarchy an affectionate presence that endeared him to his grandson.

In 1847, Emilie could not entertain the thought that the techniques for survival which Madame Aubert had learned in Dourdan and in the poor neighborhoods of Paris might be useful in Aix. Although the

16

notary's inventory made after François Zola's death indicates how little he had bequeathed (aside from his substantial wardrobe), she relied on a briefcase stuffed with paper to gird herself against fears of destitution. Her 121 shares in the Zola Canal Company entitled her to 12 percent of its profits. Furthermore, the majority stockholder, a Jules Migeon, owed her some 150,000 francs for the 300 shares he had bought on option from François Zola when the company was first organized. That sum would provide her a comfortable annuity.

Emilie's struggles with Migeon were to assume epic proportions and trap every member of her family in a *machine infernale* that ultimately crushed them. By 1848 the canal project had already gone awry. Migeon and several other investors delayed payment of the balance owed on shares they had subscribed to, and the contractor halted work until they gave him his due. For two years the dam site lay forsaken while Emilie joined the director, Marius Daime, whom it had been her statutory right to appoint, in mobilizing sentiment against the delinquent parties. This campaign was onerous: not only her husband's venture but economic life in general had ground to a halt while France puzzled herself out again after the revolution that swept Louis Philippe from power. Everyone felt shaken, and the predicament of a widow with no income save a small pension granted by the company did not weigh heavily in the balance.

Before long Migeon's strategy became clear. In 1851, Marius Daime declared unpaid shares forfeit and moved to have them sold on the Paris Stock Exchange, whereupon Migeon countered with a demand that the company be dissolved. He had his way, for on January 19, 1852, the commercial court of Aix ruled that the company had gone bankrupt, which led the civil court, in a subsequent ruling, to order it sold at auction. Migeon was never held financially responsible by the official liquidator (whose clemency must have earned him more than gratitude), and although the imperial court of Aix found against him a year or so later, the sum at which it assessed his obligation to the bankrupt enterprise was a fraction of his real debt. Then, on May 10, 1853, Zola's canal company became Migeon's firm in bidding that saw it knocked down for the bargain price of 251,000 francs. Aix, which had meanwhile rescinded its original agreement, hastened to sign another one with Migeon, overlooking his sins because his power covered the multitude of them. Migeon was triumphant. In 1850, under the Second Republic, he had won election to the Legislative Assembly from Alsace, and he kept his seat after Louis Napoleon's coup d'état of December 2, 1851, when, under the Empire, Bonapartists endorsed his candidacy. There is no saying whether some previous regime might eventually have called him to account, but it is certain that with Napoleon III's accession, a golden age had dawned for swindlers such as he.[1]

In January 1851, Emilie had initiated legal action against Migeon to recover the 150,000 francs. That suit dragged on for some time, with Migeon leading her a merry chase through procedural thickets where she felt lost and he perfectly at home. The toll it took on her meager resources was calamitous. To make matters worse, bankruptcy relieved the canal company of any obligation to continue Emilie's allowance. Still, she persisted, and after winning eligibility for legal aid, renewed hostilities against her nemesis. By 1854, even those whom she trusted had grown weary of it all. Labot urged her to obtain an out-of-court settlement if she could or, failing that, to seek employment. "The prefect of Marseille would have helped you secure a tobacco or stamp concession. . . . Can't you find a job in some large business concern at Marseille?" he wrote, with an edge of impatience that suggests he knew from experience how reluctant she was to heed his advice. Like François Zola ignoring his brother's animadversions against "fantasy," Emilie went for broke, spurning as unworthy of her a more modest estate than she had come to anticipate. Implacable once the battle was joined, she sought not only her just portion but redress of the greater wrong life had done her when she found herself widowed at the age of twenty-seven and cast from "respectable" society. Had she made peace with Migeon, she could have made peace with misfortune. Instead she fought it, and created a substitute for marriage in litigation that became her raison d'être as she went on pleading year after year despite the odds against her suit being adjudicated in her favor. Why in the future Emile Zola's novels often featured a young man enamored of a woman whom he ultimately rescues from the ghost or demonic spirit to which she feels bound is not altogether mysterious. Rescue fantasies in which he figured as the rescuer were the boy's daily fare long before books and theater acquainted him with the various forms such fantasies took as a convention of romantic literature and of melodrama. He found his most important model at Aix-en-Provence, where Emilie held fast, like the old woman in *Bleak House* who lives right beside High Chancery Court with her caged birds, waiting for an end to the endless Jarndyce Case.

Caged was how nineteenth-century memoirists often portrayed themselves in Aix. Indeed, a wall three kilometers long, overgrown with ivy and gillyflowers, ran around the town. It served no practical

[1]The woes Migeon brought on himself in due course were only an instance of what often happened during the Second Empire to swindlers who swindled the swindler, rather than of justice vindicating the virtuous. He declared himself an independent, and the government, enraged by his ingratitude, arraigned him on charges of fraudulently assuming the title of Count.

purpose, of course, but when councilmen ridiculed it in 1848 as an excrescence, traditionalists rallied against those who would defile the city's sacred past. To them the wall was all that stood between their dream life and reality, between an *ancien régime* they kept embalmed and forces astir in the world outside. "It is not love of work we lack, or intelligence," observed one Aixois in 1840. "What we lack is desire for material development, for the implementation of practical ideas." Among the gentry, such unstriving had become a mark of honor that distinguished Aixois from vulgar Marseillais. As Marseille waxed into a great commercial hub, Aix waned into a backwater whose few energetic citizens did their best to advance the unlikely proposition that, given some encouragement, the city might yet be roused from sleep. Encouragement was not given. Every major railroad line across Provence skirted Aix; and its numerous hostelries, which showed the position it had once occupied as a nexus of trade routes in southeastern France, closed one by one, or survived on the clientele whose circulatory ailments brought them to its hot springs.

This eclipse left Aix without the capacity to replenish itself: in mid-century its death rate rose well above its birth rate. Had Napoleon I visited total war on another generation, the effect could not have been much more grievous. Country girls found employment in Aix's rich households, but young men, unless they fancied working as tanners or picking tobacco leaves and almonds or skinning rabbits for felt, migrated south to Marseille. Monastic orders, every variety of which had a chapter there, did not lack initiates, and widows eking out small lives abounded. A stillness hung over the city, an air of dereliction especially remarkable in the aristocratic neighborhood, where impoverished old nobles still had themselves carried to one another's town houses in sedan chairs. "It is a curious experience, standing at the entrance of a mansion where a soirée is in progress," wrote a student at Aix's famous law school in the 1830s. "Sedan chairs crowd the street, one more bizarre than the next, and all of them painted with cupids, nosegays, and shepherdesses which have faded since the eighteenth century. The first time I witnessed this spectacle, I wondered if I might not be at the door to some hospital." On entering Aix one entered the time frame of litigants and the moribund. It waited out each season much as it had the season before, under the immutable hulk of Mont Sainte-Victoire, which derived its name from Notre-Dame de la Victoire. A new arrival or the slightest alteration in the town's physiognomy made news, and *Le Mémorial d'Aix* had front-page copy when the councilmen of 1848 decided to condemn eight of the ten city gates.

Emilie lived outside the wall until 1853. Several years after François died she left her house on the rue Silvacanne, which had become too expensive, and found another at a tiny hamlet called Pont-de-Béraud, a kilometer or so northeast of Aix, where Emile had fields to wander in. Stricken during the winter of 1846–47 by some illness grave enough to have required the application of plasters, he looked a weakling, pale and slender, with one droopy eyelid. Madame Aubert and Emilie, who recognized this tic for what it was, tried to mitigate the effects of the terrible blow he had received by cosseting him. Their own isolation in this province that usually ridiculed northerners, or "Franciots," made them all the more aware of abuse to which his Parisian accent and a slight speech defect (he pronounced s as t) might subject him at school, so they kept him out.[2] Emile had turned eight and had not yet learned even the rudiments of reading and writing before they could bring themselves to enroll him at the Pension Notre-Dame, a small boarding school presumably stronger in catechism than in other subjects, whose master, Monsieur Isoard, did, however, wean him on La Fontaine.

Of his term at Isoard's establishment Zola later recalled only how he often played truant to join two friends named Philippe Solari and Marius Roux on frolics through the countryside. In 1851 another dislocation occurred when Emilie, pursuing justice to its seat, had him accompany her to Paris, where they spent some months with her brother Adolphe Aubert, who was the concierge at a building on the rue Monsieur-le-Prince. By now it had become obvious that Emile, for all his alertness, would vegetate unless taken firmly in hand, but proper schooling at a *lycée* or a *collège* required money, and the tuition that barred 95 percent of French children from higher education was beyond Madame Zola's means, especially after the canal company discontinued her stipend. She therefore entered him at the Collège Bourbon, in Aix, with some hope of being able in due course to exploit the goodwill François Zola had stored up for her among influential men. "The mayor read a request from Madame Zola, widow of the engineer who . . . planned the canal that bears his name," read the municipal council minutes of July 22, 1854. "She solicits a scholarship to secondary school on behalf of his son and hopes, she writes, that the council will show its benevolence by awarding it as posthumous compensation for services her husband rendered to the city of Aix." Whatever pain it cost her to go begging, at least Zola would not have this experience to draw upon for proof of his observation that "in the provinces people show fallen families no mercy." Aix's municipal council came through with a scholarship.

Emile entered the Collège Bourbon as a boarding student. Madame

[2]Paul Alexis wrote: "In early childhood he had a linguistic defect, less a pronounced stutter than a laziness in articulating certain consonants, principally the c and the s which came out as t: *tautitton* for *saucisson*. One day, however, when he was about four and a half, during a childish tantrum, he unleashed a superb '*Cochon!*' which delighted his father so much that he gave him a hundred sous."

Zola yielded him reluctantly to his new world (for, as she often told him, he was "her only consolation") and took modest quarters on the rue Bellegarde, quite near the school, so that she could see him every day in a parlor reserved for such interviews. Emile was now cast among forty other boarders, each with a little iron bed and footlocker in a group dormitory. As he soon discovered, the educational theory that held sheer discomfort to be a sine qua non of the tempering process whereby boys become young men had its exponents at the Collège Bourbon, which had formerly housed nuns. In winter his own body heat was all he had to keep him warm, and classroom recitations generated clouds of vapor. Nor did it promote a sense of well-being to study below street level in ill-lit rooms, *salles d'étude* where humidity stripped whitewash off the walls. Worst of all for Emile, whose emotional balance would always hinge as much on what he ate as on what he wrote, the food dished out was so unpalatable that his fellow inmates occasionally rioted over it. "Ah, what cuisine! Even now I feel nauseated to think of it," he reminisced many years later. "I remember horrible dishes, before which I stoically munched my dry bread, and, among others, a strange codfish stew that poisoned the mold. . . . We made up for it with bread, we stuffed crusts in our pocket and ate them in class and on the playground. During the six years I remained there, I was hungry."

However disagreeable, the Collège Bourbon had nothing like the barracks grayness of Paris *lycées*. Four plane trees shaded the main courtyard, where on warm days the boys splashed about in a large basin as noisily as the twittering sparrows that nested overhead. Next door were gardens from which the more audacious stole fruit to supplement their grim diet. A certain *laisser-aller* prevailed, or what Paul Alexis, who attended the same school, called "a paternalistic discipline [that] allowed each pupil his qualities and his vices." Serious punishment was likely to consist of copying five hundred lines of Boileau rather than the whipping administered in Jesuit schools, and the boy sent home because he had hurled spitballs at a portrait of Christ might have stayed had he been content to demonstrate his impiety in the quiet, snickering way countenanced by the authorities. Few took religious instruction to heart—so few, indeed, that the resident chaplain, a man imbued with his own insignificance, prudently ran through chapel service at full tilt.

Those of Emile's classmates who came from Aix were likely to be the children of notaries or lawyers, since aristocratic families traditionally bound their young over to the Jesuit order. They struck him as an indolent lot puffed with assurance that no matter how poorly they acquitted themselves at school, "they would graduate directly from our benches to the old family armchair and sit behind a desk where some

ancestor had begun his fortune." The greater number of pupils were
country boys, typically the sons of rich peasants eager to have them
acquire some polish, who arrived in hobnailed boots, like Charles Bovary, from the Var region or the Basses-Alpes, wondering why, and
never finding an answer. "Almost all of them had skulls harder than
the rocks on which they had grown," wrote Zola. "Many exhibited a
true horror of books. I knew one in particular whose brain could not
be made to hold three straight ideas. He spent days in the calm and
ponderous attitude of an ox digesting food, with big, vacant eyes that
would fix on the teacher as if he understood, when in fact his mind
was absent. Not everyone was quite so stupid, but intelligent boys were
the exception." After several years at the Collège Bourbon, they would
leave Aix imperceptibly less cloddish for having been invited to model
themselves on the ideal of human excellence drawn by Plutarch and
Corneille.

An honor roll posted in the room where she met with him told
Madame Zola that her son regularly achieved distinction as one of the
school's best students. Having entered somewhat behind his age group,
he won high marks during his first year and advanced a form.
What hopes and expectations rested on this academic enterprise were
made quite clear to Emile, who, although by no means without humor,
already mantled himself in the deep seriousness that became his usual
demeanor. "My mother and grandmother had taken me more and
more into their confidence as I grew up, acquainting me with their
many worries; and besides, I could see for myself that the poverty of
our home was always increasing, and that I should some day be entirely
dependent on my own efforts." While hardships at home nurtured in
him the idea that he must shoulder his father's burden, even without
Madame Zola having to articulate it (which she did), at school a tacit
bargain required that he prove himself worthy of the dispensation
granted him by the municipality because he was his father's son. On
other boys, who never questioned their inheritance, the past had conferred proprietary rights to a world that awaited them, like the armchair in the office. Where Emile was concerned, the past had receded,
leaving him stranded in a harsh moral environment with nothing that
was his except a wrack of debts for which he felt—and would indeed
always feel—responsible.[3]

We can imagine how frail Zola's self-esteem must have been during
his orphaned childhood from the despair that engulfed him much
later, following the death of a literary father-surrogate, Flaubert—
when everything he himself had accomplished suddenly seemed

[3]Thirty and forty years later, Aixois from whom Emilie had borrowed money to
pay the baker and other merchants hounded Zola for repayment.

worthless. His predicament brought him small sympathy at school, however, and an abundant literature testifies to the unkind treatment scholarship boys received from classmates, who were keenly aware of all social and economic insignia. To be sure, in his one consequential memoir on the Collège Bourbon, which appeared soon after the great success he had had with *L'Assommoir*, Zola saw fit to remember life there as a kind of Darwinian free-for-all that toughened him for the contests Paris held in store. Social station, he wrote, was forgotten in a "democratic" melee where physical strength decided rank, and the brawny yokel rather than the young patrician ended up lording it over the playground. "Nothing can replace this communal education that transforms the child into a man. Let him beat and be beaten, let him suffer and mete out punishment, let him do what must be done to acquire solid limbs and a strong heart. . . . Boys raised at home in their mothers' skirts remain girls. . . . The *collège* fortifies well-constituted natures." But what the playground democracy hid, if it hid anything at all, was a snobbish society that ragged the *boursier* for living on alms. Zola's own friend Marius Roux made much of this in a novel entitled *Eugénie Lamour*, and his knowledge came from Aix, of course, where in 1857 the inspector general, after visiting the Collège Bourbon, observed that "the regrettable facility with which parents place significant sums of money at the disposal of students" undermined the headmaster's ability to exercise his moral custodianship.

Thus, at unguarded moments, when Zola dared part the curtain he had drawn, a radically different picture emerges, in which the virile initiation he later glorified is seen as a psychological ordeal that scored deep wounds. More painful even than the undemocratic taunts hurled at him—"beggar," "parasite"—were assaults on his modesty by rough-necks who lost no time discovering how shy he was and making him the butt of jokes. "Let us remember how it was at secondary school. Vices had fertile ground, so that one lived in true Roman putrescence. Any cloistered association of people who belong to the same sex is morally reprehensible," he wrote in 1870, and the Goncourts report him lamenting on one occasion that "I had a perverted youth in a wretched provincial school. Yes, a rotten childhood!"

Since the Collège Bourbon was surely neither Sparta in its glory nor Rome in its decline, an incident that took place long before Zola entered the school will perhaps explain something of what compelled him to reflect upon his experience in such drastic terms. It is described in a report filed by the Marseille police on April 3, 1845: "We conducted to the Palace of Justice a person named Mustapha, twelve years old, a native of Algiers and a domestic in the service of Monsieur Zola, civil engineer, number 4, rue de l'Arbre, who committed indecent assault [*attentat à la pudeur*] on the young Emile Zola, five years old."

Did this ugly event, which may have occurred on his birthday, impress him with a sense of the punishment society reserved for sexual miscreants?[4] It would seem so. Zola's moralistic lashing out at adolescence suggests that the guardian his father had been to him in life became, after death, the prosecutor from whose indignation Emile drew strength, even as he turned that indignation against himself. Robbed of masculine assurance when his father died, he found manliness in rectitude, which obliged him to stand aloof and incriminate any complex or sympathetic feeling aroused in him by the hurly-burly of his schoolmates. This conflict reached into every corner of his life. In time, as we shall see, it shaped Zola into a paradoxical figure haunted by catastrophic visions of libido on the loose; who rejoiced in his power yet suffered from paralyzing stage fright, who created erotic cynosures only to destroy them, who kept himself hidden while craving love. But the outsider locked outside himself was already present at the age of twelve. "My years in *collège* were a time of tears," says the hero of his strongly autobiographical novel *La Confession de Claude*. "I had in me the pride of loving natures. I was not loved because I was not known and I refused to make myself known." One witness remembered Zola as "the stubbornly unsocial, melancholy sort other kids detest."

What saved Emile from the plight of his tearful character Claude was a friendship he made, soon after he arrived at the Collège Bourbon, with a large, ungainly boy fourteen months older than he named Paul Cézanne. Cézanne was quick to detect a kindred spirit in the pariah everyone else mocked for speaking Parisian French. "Opposed by nature, but drawn to each other by secret affinities, by the force of a common ambition, by the awakening in them of a superior intelligence for which the mob of dunces regularly thrashed them," Zola would write in *L'Oeuvre*, "they instantly formed a permanent bond." This vulnerable pair became a less vulnerable threesome when in due course they won the allegiance of another schoolmate, Jean-Baptistin Baille, whose parents ran a hotel on the Cours Sextius that catered to patrons of the thermal baths next door.

Although all the afflictions that originated in François Zola's death encouraged Emile to feel peculiarly the victim of malign fate, his friendship with Paul Cézanne taught him that having a father, and even a rich father, could be as onerous as losing one. Louis-Auguste Cézanne, who came from a long line of Provençal artisans, had begun his fortune in the felt-hat trade at Aix, where rabbits were far more

---

[4]It may also have furnished material for the novel *Thérèse Raquin*, where a "bestial" half-Algerian helps her equally bestial lover drown the mother's boy she married.

numerous than people. After apprenticing with a Parisian hatter during the early 1820s, he joined two Aixois in business and soon established his reputation as a shrewd merchant for whom François Guizot's commandment, *"Enrichissez-vous!,"* was worth the Decalogue. Resentful of Aix's privileged class, he saw to it that doors shut against him would be double-bolted by declaring himself a republican, but this exclusion did not harm the firm of Martin, Coupin, and Cézanne, which made him rich. In 1845, three years after he and his partners went their separate ways, history vindicated Louis-Auguste. The failure of Aix's one bank in the economic debacle that attended the 1848 revolution gave him an opportunity to have his idle fortune work him up another fortune (estimated at 1,200,000 francs): with local entrepreneurs facing ruin for want of credit, the hat exporter became a financier and did inordinately well at it, even before France's resurgence under Napoleon III.

Because, as a typical crotchet, he wore untanned leather boots to spare himself the expense and trouble of having them polished, some contemporaries saw in him a Père Grandet, and indeed, like Balzac's miser, Louis-Auguste held his family in a tight fist. Begrudging them title not only to his name and money but to civil dignity, he did not marry the woman by whom he had already sired two children until 1844, when Paul was five and Marie three. That this nonconformist behavior isolated the family in a town whose inhabitants piously clucked over it served both to justify his aversion from society and to reinforce his authority in the household. He closely monitored every transaction with the outside world, and marriage inspired no essential reform, as one gathers from what is generally taken to be a portrayal of the Cézannes in Zola's *La Conquête de Plassans:*

> Marthe loved her husband with a sober unimpassioned love, but with her affection was mingled considerable fear of his jokes and pleasantries, his perpetual teasing. She was hurt, too, by his selfishness, and the loneliness in which he left her; she felt a vague grudge against him for the quietude in which she lived—that very manner of life she said made her happy. When she spoke of him, she said, "He is very good to us. You've heard him, I daresay, get angry at times, but that arises from his passion for wanting everything in order, which he often carries to an almost ridiculous extreme. He gets quite vexed if he sees a flowerpot a little out of place in the garden or a plaything lying about on the floor; but in other matters he does quite right in pleasing himself. I know he is not very popular, because he has managed to accumulate some money and still goes on doing a good stroke of business now and then; but he only laughs at what people say about him."

With his passion for order, Louis-Auguste proved adept at getting the goods on those around him, whether kin or client. As we shall see, he regularly intercepted letters.

Paul's sensibility did not earn him high marks from Cézanne *père*. The earliest manifestations of it were greeted with such derision that he sought refuge near his mother, Elisabeth (born Aubert, curiously enough), a young woman capable of recognizing that certain endeavors were worthwhile even if their principal reward lay elsewhere than in the acquisition of money or power. Though she herself had not had any formal schooling, she nonetheless managed to blunt the edge of her husband's aggressive materialism. Paul grew up betwixt and between. "A quiet and docile student, he worked hard; he had a good mind, but did not reveal any remarkable qualities," his sister recalled. "He was criticized for his weakness of character; probably he allowed himself to be influenced too easily." Being unable on the one hand to square his mind with the values his father promoted and on the other to keep himself from craving legitimation, he could do nothing to avoid Louis-Auguste's terrible barbs. Far more grievous than the social disrepute that afflicted him at birth was this sense of internecine failure, which before long would compel him to make repeated, foredoomed, and humiliating overtures to the Salon jury. Submission followed by rage and then by self-doubt became his lifelong curriculum; every departure from Aix ended with his coming home again, like a prisoner at the end of a rope, to collect his allowance and to lay his unsuccess before Louis-Auguste, as if in hostile tribute. "Cézanne has many spells of discouragement. Despite the scorn he affects for glory, I see that he desires to succeed. When he does badly, he speaks of . . . returning to Aix and making himself a clerk in a commercial house," Zola observed in 1861, during Cézanne's first such venture abroad. Zola also had occasion to note, early in their friendship, how quickly the impressionable stuff of which Paul was made could harden under criticism and form a shell. Indeed, around his "faults" he built his most durable defenses. His dishevelment, for example, brought him frequent reprimands, but unkempt he remained, and the mess a painter makes may have been for him a secretly compelling attraction of his trade.

Paul and Emile found little understanding among the men who taught them at the Collège Bourbon. Both boys demonstrated such facility in the classical program, winning highest honors, Paul in Latin, Emile in French narration, that it would have required a sharp eye to see them as desperately wanting emotional support, and the typical high school teacher in Second Empire France was not recruited on the basis of discernment. "[Masters] taught four hours a day and had no other relationship with the students," wrote Zola. Whatever a schoolmaster thought and observed outside school, during those four hours for which the state paid him meager wages, he was as anachronistic as a Roman *grammaticus,* with the inevitable result that many of them, unless they could manage a double life, lost either their intellectual curiosity or their livelihood. "In the provinces the intellectual level of masters is rather low," Zola went on to say in the late 1870s, when such issues were publicly discussed.

> They drift along in the classical routine and know nothing beyond it. The machine functions and it works today because it worked yesterday. . . . [My masters] had gone gray repeating their own knowledge and they instructed us in much the same way I imagine our grandfathers had been taught. Wandering in their heads were three or four ideas on which they made do from October to July. Immured in their little town, they hardly knew what was happening outside. . . . For all that, the ones I recall were remarkable men who cannot be faulted for the narrowness of their horizon and their blind submission to programs.

Had blame been fairly apportioned, the major share would have fallen on a system that made teachers regard themselves as clocklike agents of central authority. When they strayed from a curriculum—devised by functionaries who seemed to believe that school should keep young minds ignorant of the modern world, and the teacher ignorant of young minds—an inspector called them to account. In consequence of this, wrote Zola, they acquired, especially in the provinces, the ponderous deportment of people who turn everlastingly in the same circle, "like horses at a riding academy." Resentment at having been buried in a remote province or hypersensitivity born of the ingratitude children showed them for the task they performed gave a distinctive coloration to those whom Zola could recall. "[One master] nursed a mortal grudge against me because one day, when I hadn't learned my Greek grammar lesson, I dared explain to him, with a schoolboy's candor, that Greek served no purpose in life. I'm not sure where that came from, but our pedagogue was in high dudgeon and persecuted me all year long for my unfortunate reflection."

Since his unfortunate reflection ran counter to dogma around which the bourgeoisie chose to groom its young, Emile received condign punishment. The more acquisitive and mobile French society became, the more anxiously did the haute bourgeoisie insist on classical humanities as a prerequisite for admission to the cultural body politic. Thus we find Louis Napoleon's minister of public instruction, Hippolyte Fortoul, declaring in the early 1850s that the explication of Latin and Greek authors, on which all French literary studies were based, remained "the essential part" of classwork; to it one owed every spare moment. Never had it seemed more urgent than during the aftermath of revolution, when Bonapartist skipjacks joined forces with an older establishment against "socialism," that this pedagogical strategy be enforced. Its raison d'être derived in some degree from its very hermeticism. Children bred on the ancients would ultimately merit high office for having acquired not only France's cultural patrimony but a style that was thought to be as essential to the character of a notable as the gloss or *fini* in academic painting was to images of authority. "The ruling classes will always be the ruling classes because they know Latin," wrote a militant bishop named Félix Dupanloup, and many beside him embraced the view that Latin constituted a patent of nobility. "In Latin . . . they have conversed with none but men of genius, they know only the language of Cicero and Virgil, along with that of Plato and Homer . . . Indeed, they know them at their most elevated and generous, so that their compositions necessarily show the effects of it and attain such perfection as they cannot attain in French, but which subsequently infiltrates French itself." The alarm raised by conservative Aixois fearful of what might visit them once the ancient city wall fell down was echoed in the hue and cry let out by conservatives throughout France over measures taken to institute a scientific baccalauréat. Classics sanctified privilege, just as science stood sponsor for almost every doctrine or movement that urged social reform.

An unusually enlightened inspector general wrote in the 1850s that a physics course given at the Collège Bourbon "sins on the experimental side, owing partly to the dearth of scientific facilities," corroborating Zola's memory of an education that did not, on principle, address material realities too familiarly. A wedge was driven there; and the same wedge that kept them aloof from nature served to discourage them from holding conversation with a baser or intimate self. Hence the importance of oratorical exercises modeled after the Roman progymnasmata, in which students imitated "great men." Emile playing a patriotic envoy who argues the case for Greek independence or François I who writes the queen a letter fraught with stoic sentiments after his defeat at Pavia underwent much the same therapy that edified boys in Paris and Rennes and Bordeaux. "To write an oration was to put noble words in the mouths of great personages," explains one historian.

Maximian writes to Diocletian imploring him not to renounce the Empire, François I to Charles V complaining of his imprisonment, et cetera. The subject who spoke was always a great one: king or emperor, saint, learned man, or poet. And what did one have these personages say? To be sure, nothing one might have happened to hear in everyday life but, rather, sturdy aphorisms. As in Corneille and Bossuet—who became classics for this very reason—one exhaled only great sentiments. . . . Honor, dignity, nobility, virtue, courage, sacrifice, repudiation of the world: on those heroic heights generosity was the air one breathed.

Ancient Rome furnished most of the exemplars, but even exemplars sometimes fell short of themselves, so that schoolmen had recourse to excerpta or they skirted trouble altogether by producing texts such as *De viris illustribus,* which conveyed a certain ideal of classical virtue more exactly than the genuine literature. When they trained their high-mindedness on French, what came of it was a syllabus containing no work written before the seventeenth century or since the eighteenth. For his baccalauréat examination Emile would need only Bossuet, Fénelon, Massillon, Montesquieu, Voltaire, Corneille, Racine, Boileau, and La Fontaine, and nothing even by these authors that the ministry of public instruction deemed risqué. Thus, pious regard for the classics did not extend to Racine's profane theater, to Montesquieu's *Persian Letters,* to Voltaire's philosophical tales.

In Paris, a boy could hardly walk to a *lycée* (or, if he boarded there, escape for a day) without having images of the modern world imprinted on his mind. But it was quite different at Aix, where, after Louis Napoleon's coup d'état in December 1851, which had excited rebellion in villages throughout Provence, a gerontocracy pettifogging under cover of civic idealism administered municipal business as if it were Latin class. How matters stood may be judged from the address delivered by Mayor Rigaud in honor of Louis Napoleon, whose state visit on September 29, 1852, occasioned a 101-gun salute, general cries of *Vive l'empereur,* and a spectacle of medieval pageantry that must surely have made some considerable impression on Emile, newly enrolled at the Collège Bourbon. "The city of Aix, which you deign to visit, was formerly the capital of Provence, the abode of a king, and the fatherland of valiant knights and troubadours," Rigaud declared when a Provençal drum corps had finished taboring its rendition of *Partant pour la Syrie.*[5] "Having fallen from its former splendor, it consoled itself with scholarship and love for arts and letters. It remained all the while faithful to the ideas of order, of authority, and of power. Prince, today you are the representative of these ideas in France; the national will has on two solemn occasions summoned you to the government of the country. We are happy to have maintained these fine feelings in our heart so as to lay them at your feet in tribute." *Le*

[5]A march associated with Louis Napoleon's mother, Queen Hortense, and played as a national anthem on all imperial occasions.

Mémorial d'Aix quoted this speech as evidence that Aix, if it could not rival Marseille in the opulence of its salutation, at any rate welcomed the prince-president with greater "calm" and "dignity."

In 1789 Aix had lost its high court and didn't get it back until Bonaparte seized power ten years later. The city relied on its judicial administration as much as any company town on its mine or mill, and sooner than risk another such loss—for what rulers gave rulers could take away—Aixois made "order" a watchword. Thus, Louis Napoleon had nothing to fear from this quarter, which behaved so obsequiously that even the prudent *Mémorial d'Aix* called attention to the fact on February 3, 1856, in an article whose author lamented: "If one wished to depict with exactitude its spiritual state, our city could fairly be compared to a dead sea where the tide of public spirit flows quiet beneath a leaden atmosphere that constricts blood vessels and dampens the will."

In the same way that schools of rhetoric had multiplied in Latin antiquity when forums of debate disappeared, the notable lack of public spirit in Second Empire Aix encouraged not only chicanery but a litigiousness far more confining than the city wall. Aix's lawyers, with their vested interest in the status quo, would have offered some local Daumier abundant material. They made their presence felt everywhere, clustering around the new Palais de Justice, which stood diagonally across a large square from the Eglise de la Madeleine, or flying toward their "cabinets," or gathering in black knots at cafés that had sprung up on the Cours, amid the larger population of students who attended Aix's law school and boarded all over town. If one lived in Aix, one lived one way or another by the law. So Louis-Auguste Cézanne, like many other fathers, decided that his son should someday practice it, and Emilie Zola was not the only litigant for whom the Palais de Justice had become a monument to blighted hopes.

The poet Frédéric Mistral claimed that behind closed doors, in the great mansions they had bought from ruined nobles, Aix's dynasts led a spirited social life, with balls and musicales and meetings of various professional or political *cercles*. Those who did not belong, however, tended to feel about Aix as Guinot had in 1837, when he observed that while curing their physical woes, patrons of the thermal establishment fell ill of boredom. Lucien Prévost-Paradol, the future academician whose distinguished career in letters included a brief stint at Aix's Faculté des Lettres during the 1850s, found the city's Lethe-like influence so powerful that the rejection of a manuscript, which ordinarily would have upset him, left him indifferent, and he could imagine himself being led down a "mossy path to extinction" in perfect numbness. On his successor at the Faculté des Lettres, J. J. Weiss, the anesthesia did not take effect quite so easily. "Nowhere outside Mazas [prison] can being be so dreary! I shall resign myself . . . but it will require mighty resignation or potent laziness." Had it been some other city, Weiss might have forgiven Aix's theater the dirty white walls that put Prévost-Paradol in mind of an assizes court, and the "Choral Society of Apollo" its off-pitch crooning, and the backwardness of an old dame who, to make ends meet, sold eggs from poultry in the garden of her eighteenth-century town house, where she lived among valuable antiques. As it was, they seemed so much of a piece with the general decrepitude that he could only wish himself gone from "this mausoleum" of the *ancien régime*.

Zola's recollections imply that during adolescence, in the shadow cast by François Zola's tombstone, which stood on a rise just beyond the city wall, he, too, found Aix inhospitable to the living. True, those recollections sometimes, almost apologetically, yield a vignette of Emile as a boy doing what normal boys did if they grew up in provincial France. His mother, who bore the Church no grudge, had him take Holy Communion. His principal, who decided that the Collège Bourbon should organize a little band, had him learn the clarinet, and Emile, tone-deaf, was to be heard tooting at official ceremonies, when some notable returned from Paris with the Legion of Honor, or when clergy paraded icons of therapeutic virgins during a cholera epidemic that swept through Aix in 1854.[6] Every June, after Pentecost, he joined other youths as they celebrated the *Fête-Dieu*, or Feast of the Holy Sacrament, in a suddenly vivid town whose buildings wore silk and brocade tapestries for the occasion and whose streets turned yellow with genista blossoms. And every August he would thrill to the prospect of summer vacation, which generally began with several first prizes being given him on commencement day and officials bidding restless children sententious farewells. "The children come forward when cited, offer their rosy cheeks to the parchment lips of elderly savants, and cross the podium still wearing laurel wreaths they had forgotten to remove in the excitement of the moment," wrote Zola. "Oh, what a day! The children fly off, in clouds, for two months! I have never since then experienced such absolute bliss."

But the images Zola drew in his fiction and essays are overwhelmingly ones of confinement or exile. Grass pushing up between the cobblestones, guards double-locking the massive wooden gates at 10 p.m. in winter and at 11 in summer, barricaded mansions, parish bells stirring the drowsy air every half hour, all evoke a moribund town where even the church stood on its last legs. To witness the *Fête-Dieu*, which featured a procession of citizens in the high, pointed hoods of

[6]Like many Aixois, Emile and his family soon fled to the countryside and spent three months there, possibly in a house belonging to the Bailles.

medieval penitents, was to see "a lame Catholicism dragging itself beneath the blue heaven of old beliefs." And nothing had replaced it, no faith or idea that could hoist men above the belfries and alert them to some new horizon. "Of course one finds serious students who read the papers and new books, and wax enthusiastic over new ideas, but they are so utterly lost in the crowd that one must consider them anomalous," Zola wrote in later years. "I speak here about the majority and this majority wallows satisfied in complete ignorance: no reading, no literary or philosophical passions, no interest in the ideas that preoccupy the modern world." Unless a stray spark ignited them, the young men who spent sodden hours playing cards at Les Deux Garçons would eventually become the older men who sat beside them playing a chronic game of dominoes. They would join a circle, parse *Le Mémorial d'Aix* or *La Provence* down to the last classified advertisement, and on Sunday after Vespers promenade along whichever side of the Cours best suited them. If they lived long enough, they would see the acacias uprooted for plane trees.

The ache of confinement begot rich fantasies of escape. Any nomad for whom Aix was just one more way station on the road to distant climes could serve as a Pied Piper, but gypsies above all. They lived in wagons near the rue Sylvacanne outside town, and Emile, who had heard tales warning against visiting them in their encampment, felt a lure compounded of dread, recalcitrance, and fascination. "I saw ravishingly beautiful creatures there," he wrote in an autobiographical section of *Nouveaux Contes à Ninon*. "We young scamps who didn't share the revulsion of proper folk would peek into the caravans where these people sleep during the winter, and I remember that one day, when my heart was heavy with some schoolboy grief, I dreamed of climbing into one of those departing wagons, of going off with those tall, beautiful girls whose black eyes scared me, of going far away, to the end of the earth, rolling forever along highways."

Highways brought another nomadic breed in the soldier. Beginning in 1854, when France and England joined forces against Russia on the Black Sea, soldiers filed through en route to Marseille and thence by ship to the Crimea. While peacetime traffic circumvented Aix, war offered it a grandstand view of the splendid army on whose exploits Louis Napoleon counted to legitimize his reign. In fact, most Aixois found this spectacle objectionable, for even if the government had not required as the price of admission that each citizen billet a man or two, regiments mustering at dawn cost them sleep. Lost sleep did not greatly trouble the young, however, and by 4 a.m. youths would be lined up along the Cours to watch a breathtaking sequence of cuirassiers, lancers, hussars, and dragoons. With the drumroll, they, too, moved forward, including Emile, who had ceased to be a boarder after his first year at the Collège Bourbon. "We'd follow them on the wide white roads," Zola wrote. "I remember walking for miles. We'd march in rhythm, our books cinched to our backs like cartridge pouches. We weren't supposed to accompany the soldiers beyond the gunpowder magazine, but we'd trespass as far as the bridge, then up a slope, then on to the next village." The family not only indulged him but even shared his pleasure, for the men invading Aix from every quarter of France gave it a cosmopolitan air and made them feel less foreign. When chance deposited at their doorstep some poor conscript who hailed from Madame Aubert's native province, she set the kitchen table for a feast *à la Beauceronne*.

Before long Emile no longer needed the license of patriotic fervor to venture abroad. As they reached mid-adolescence, he, Paul Cézanne, and Jean-Baptistin Baille, whom schoolmates dubbed "the inseparables," consolidated their threesome in excursions, hiking through the countryside or during the summer bathing nude in the Arc River where it meandered under dense foliage south of town. "These were flights far from the world . . . an unreasoning act of worship of trees, water, mountains which purchased us the boundless joy of being alone and free," he wrote in *L'Oeuvre*. The wild terrain his father had once surveyed became the playground in which Emile staked out his own claim on the world. Five miles up the Bibémus road and high above Aix he could encompass it all: an immense sky with sunlight glinting off the red earth, pine trees braced in grotesque postures against the mistral, chalk hills cupping a lake formed by the dam that finally stood complete eight years after its architect's death, and the dam itself, spanning the cleft of the Infernets gorge. Bibémus was one of their favorite itineraries. Another, to the south, took them along the Route du Tholonet as far as a lovely hamlet of that name, where they would pause for lunch and then resume their course down gullies or over the low walls that crisscrossed sheep meadows or the higher ones that surrounded an abandoned estate called the Domaine de Gallice, not far from Roquefavour. When game season came they packed guns, though no one among them could shoot straight and least of all Emile, who discovered at sixteen from not being able to read public notices how myopic he was. Their pleasure lay rather in the jaunt through lavender and gorse, in the expectant quiet of the hunter's blind, the crunch of chalk dust underfoot, the mutton roasted on a spit, the poems unfit for academic consumption of Hugo and Musset, which they declaimed to one another. Night would often overtake them before they saw Aix again and reduce Mont Sainte-Victoire to a spectral presence; its great limestone crop kept constant watch over the vagabonds, aligning and crowning every point of view.

Several decades later, when Zola had written novels that exhaled nostalgia for the Provençal *garrigue* and Cézanne was hauling his easel and colors up Bibémus road all year round in an obsessive tête-à-tête with the mountain, the importance of their earlier peregrinations could be better appreciated. Once Aix disappeared, so for the time being did humiliations and problems that lurked there. Nature reimbursed them for what town life exacted in self-esteem, as they shook off the image of misfits to cultivate a sense of their grandiose singularity. "With every return [we succumbed to] the delicious vacancy of fatigue, a triumphant boastfulness over having walked farther than the previous time, the rapture of feeling carried forward by [our] momentum and by the brisk cadence of some fierce soldiers' song, which rocked [us] as in the depths of a dream," was how Zola remembered this virile camaraderie. No doubt the experience derived some of its power to buoy him from associations with the soldier-engineer in whose paternal footsteps he felt himself "carried forward," like a sleepwalker. It's as if two fathers with discrete spheres of influence inhabited Emile, one holding him back, the other rallying him on, one emblemizing his frailty, the other making him vigorous. He could not predict which would gain the upper hand at any given moment, but his memoirs suggest that during such rambles the *chef de bande* in him began to stir. He celebrated friendship, he nattered about life, he read his own verse, he defended dreams and had enough left over to support the weak-kneed Paul when blackness, or what Zola called "the evil demon," lay hold of him. "When he says something hurtful, you must not blame his heart, but rather the evil demon that clouds his thought," Zola would caution Baille. "He has a heart of gold and is a friend who can understand us, for he is just as mad as we, and just as much a dreamer." So completely had their initial roles been reversed that Paul, standing head and shoulders taller than Emile, behaved like his silent shadow rather than his protector.

Paul's cruel outbursts proclaimed, among other things, his exasperation with his own silence, or with the authority he vested in Emile, and for once he found himself seconded by his father, who had a hunch that deferring to his bosom friend helped Paul secure independence. Emile, in turn, used the respect he was paid to redress the balance between Paul's material ease, which might otherwise have galled him, and his own humble circumstances. "Brotherhood," as the two described their friendship (in this they would have included Baille), was a commotion of the sublime and the unavowable. It often saw them stay together until dawn, feverishly sorting through ideas for some one eternal verity that would put everything right. It also armed them against fears they couldn't cope with alone, particularly the fear of women. "Timid and maladroit, they banned woman herself [from their excursions] and made their flaws out to be an austere virtue that marked them as superior," wrote Zola in *L'Oeuvre*, where Claude Lantier and Sandoz closely resemble Paul and himself. "For two years Claude was consumed with love for a milliner's apprentice, whom he trailed every evening and never had the courage to address. Sandoz nurtured dreams, women met on a journey, beautiful girls who would suddenly materialize in an unknown wood, yield themselves for the whole day, then dissipate at twilight like shadows." When, in manhood, Paul developed the phobias of a recluse—not suffering himself to be touched and shrinking back from nude female models—it became obvious that his pent-up instincts had wrought greater havoc than Emile's; but during adolescence, shy was shy. The same woods offered them refuge; the same stream and bed of hot sand appeased yearnings that their schoolmates contrived to satisfy with a maid, at a brothel, or alone; the same poet, Musset, reassured them that in flesh they would find the graveyard of nobility. Emile as well as Paul might have modeled for the lovelorn youngster adoring the milliner's apprentice from afar, and indeed, clues indicate that at sixteen or seventeen he was smitten by a dark-haired girl who never knew what reveries had once been embroidered around her barely nubile person unless, years after the fact, she recognized someone very like herself in *La Fortune des Rougon*. From afar, as he sat outside reciting Musset's poem "Rolla," which he did very often indeed, Emile may even have confused the dark-haired girl with the child prostitute of angelic appearance whom Rolla hires for one night in his farewell to this venal world.

Emile discovered modern verse either extracurricularly or through a young teacher from Paris whose acknowledgment of the romantic movement earned him a *succès de scandale* at the Collège Bourbon, but either way, Hugo and Musset came to walk beside the three boys as fourth and fifth companions. "We didn't amble alone. We had books in our pockets or in our game bags. For one entire year, Victor Hugo held absolute sway over us." The idea inculcated in nineteenth-century schoolboys that French literature was a classical tirade silenced by the 1789 revolution kept Hugo young beyond his age, or at any rate kept his youngest poetry from going stale in the syllabus alongside consecrated texts. *Les Orientales* and *Feuilles d'automne* had been written a generation earlier, but when high-strung children who were tuned for Boileau first heard such poems as "Les Djinns," "Mazeppa," and "Lord Byron en 1811," they felt themselves vibrate to some new diapason. Hugo's language promoted an emotional high, like the ones they sought outside Aix, and the hilltop on which Hugo ponders Napoleon in "A Joseph, Comte de S.," the sublime tower in "Soleils Couchants" where he sees the city open below him like an abyss, the metaphorical summit from which he scans his inner landscape as Moses scanned the Promised Land, all became paradigms of their own longing for transcendence. With Hugo in their game bag, walks up

Bibémus road seemed a mystic order of experience. His imagery glorified the mountain and the climb:

> Chaque homme, dans son coeur, crée à sa fantaisie
> Tout un monde enchanté d'art et de poésie.
> C'est notre Chanaan que nous voyons d'en haut.
> Restons où nous voyons. Pourquoi vouloir descendre
> Et toucher ce qu'on rêve, et marcher dans la cendre?[7]

These lines echo Hugo's preface to *Les Orientales*, where "good taste"
of the kind that sanctions only "beautiful literature drawn with a chalk
line" is brought up on charges of having tyrannized the artistic imagination. Here was a *parti pris* Emile found congenial.

Still, Hugo inspired nothing like as much affection as Alfred de Musset. While Hugo may have given them a lofty view, his rhetoric proved
more crushing than uplifting to young men beset with anxieties that
often made them feel unqualified for a heroic role in life, if not for
life itself. "We were born to literary consciousness after the December
coup d'état and knew about the battles of 1830 at second hand,
through stories told us by our elders," Zola wrote in 1879, just before
he issued a naturalist manifesto the effect of which was to carry the
war against good taste beyond territory that Hugo's generation had
conquered. "All that romantic heat had blown away and the exiled
Hugo stood on a distant pedestal. . . . We couldn't have said why his
verse did not move us as deeply as Musset's, but the mountainous
rhetoric was already chilling us, and Musset won our allegiance because the rhetorician in him doesn't obtrude: he goes straight to the
nerves."

Thus in 1879 it suited him to represent himself at sixteen as the
innocent delivering oracles sent from beyond, whose taste for Musset
was an expression of the Zeitgeist. "Brewing in our confused minds
was tomorrow's reaction, the new literary movement that must infal-
libly occur." During adolescence, however, his morbid sense of time
was governed by a past lost forever rather than by a brilliant future,
and Rolla's lament, "*Je suis venu trop tard dans un monde trop vieux*,"
might very well have been his own. Long before "1830" brought to
mind Victor Hugo, Théophile Gautier, Sainte-Beuve, et al. staging the
flamboyant birth of romanticism at the Comédie-Française, it marked
the year when Francesco Zolla entered France to wage battles that
became part of family lore. Victor Hugo on his distant pedestal in
Guernsey was not yet the literary patriarch against whom Emile would

---

[7]"In his heart every man creates as he fancies a whole enchanted world of art and
poetry. It is our Canaan we see from on high. Let us keep our vantage point. Why
should one wish to descend and touch one's dream, and walk in ashes?" From "A
mes amis L.B. et S.B."

measure himself at forty, but a surrogate for the Olympian father whose death had cast him adrift in time. Small, doubtful, and anachronistic is how Emile felt vis-à-vis the previous generation, and Musset understood better than anyone these sequelae of orphanhood. "Namouna," "Rolla," and "Les Nuits" expressed Emile's belief that a world in which great lungs sucked up so much oxygen could sustain only neurasthenic, self-conscious forms of life. Musset's waif, bantering while he weeps and committing suicide after one last quip, or mourning religious faith by debauching himself among its bare, ruined choirs, spoke to him as Jules Laforgue's Pierrot would speak to fin de siècle sensibilities. Where nothing seemed quite real except Mammon, consolation lay in arch parodies and quixotic shadow games that conferred a kind of elegance on adolescent despair. "We adored medieval decor, philtres, and sword thrusts: but we especially adored them in Musset's limber style, with its skepticism and mocking overtones," recalled Zola, who could not have enough of melodrama or of the Middle Ages, and who set out to write a romance about the Crusades. "We enthused over his ballad to the moon because it was for us the gauntlet a superior poet had thrown down to romantics as well as classics, the guffaw of an independent spirit in whom our entire generation recognized a brother." This guffaw, or stage laugh, resounds mirthlessly through the verse letters Paul was soon to write to Emile. It helped them make light of pain and keep the unruly self at a safe distance.

For under certain circumstances, Emile's self ran wild. Beginning in childhood, he developed a terror of thunderstorms, for example, and more than once his friends saw him shake uncontrollably when lightning flashed overhead. Obsessed with death, he relied on superstitious ceremonies to avert danger, which lay everywhere about him. In adolescence this obsession was not yet the full-blown tyrant it became years later, when Zola couldn't enter his study without first touching a particular tabletop, or hail a cab without assuring himself that its license number augured well, or encounter a funeral procession without taking it to be a black omen. Indeed, the sensible boy evoked by Paul Alexis in *Emile Zola, notes d'un ami* is remarkably unlike the writer whose fanatical orderliness girded him against the unforeseen:

I have often spoken about [his youth] with him, his mother, his former schoolmates. He was neither indolent nor given to swotting himself dizzy over books. An intelligent and practical boy . . . who, no sooner in the study hall or back at home, made for his desk, lost no time, courageously undertook his assignments, simplifying them as much as possible, and halted only when the task was done. Only then did he feel free and took full advantage of his freedom. In short, no excess of zeal, nothing except the indispensable and the necessary.

But inside the sensible boy was another whose burden of guilt and fear of punishment had already seen him create for himself a rich demonology, which fed on melodrama. It was not the sensible boy who regularly went to Aix's theater and sat enthralled by the hokum that road companies served up there, or who devoured the novels of Eugène Sue and Dumas and Emmanuel Gonzalès and Paul Féval. It was his imaginative alter ego, who feared that one misstep would send him over the edge into an abyss crackling with hellfire.

Emilie Zola encouraged these tendencies toward the melodramatic, as one gathers from a letter her son wrote to her on April 13, 1856.[8] Having joined several classmates in a minor rumpus at the Collège Bourbon, he was singled out for punishment by the headmaster, who announced that Madame Zola would duly receive a report of his misconduct. "You will receive a letter from the headmaster," Emile warned her:

> Believe me when I say that if I deserved to be punished it was only during a lapse in my thoughts about you, for if the thought that it might bring you grief had come to mind I assure you that I would have kept myself under rein. As I said, the headmaster will write to you but, above all, do not fret over it. He will tell you that I have become a bad student, but I shall be able to show him that if sometimes I do badly, at other times I surpass myself. You have often told me that I am your only consolation. I mean to remain just that. But do not grieve, I implore you, whatever my punishment may be. Come see me tomorrow at four, when I shall undoubtedly be free, and bring the letter with you. There is no point upsetting my grandparents. Farewell, I shall try to undo the harm I must have done you. Give it no more thought and you shall see that my future conduct will efface everything. I have written to you hoping thereby to temper somewhat the chagrin you will be feeling. . . . I remain the most devoted of sons and I shall make you forget everything. Farewell, you must bear in mind all the pain that this has caused me. The more you suffer, the greater my pain.

However lenient the Collège Bourbon may have been, misconduct often had serious consequences under a regime that did not gladly suffer insubordination: a year after this incident, five schoolmates who gave their monitor the slip during recreation period and fled singing through the countryside were expelled. Even so, what Emile wrote says more about the emotional climate Emilie fostered at home than

[8]Though described elsewhere as a "supervised day student" or *externe surveillé*, Zola, to judge from this letter, was still boarding at the school, at least during weekdays.

about harsh discipline at school, for at home the least contretemps spelled disaster. The mother hovered over the son, half awaiting a sign that nature had made him in the same breakable mold as her husband. It was incumbent on him to dispel such fears, and the grief Emile imagined would pour out when his headmaster's note reached her suggests how large they loomed. Equally large was his own fear that some untoward event might sever the only bond that kept him from falling into oblivion. Each constantly reassured the other, yet neither felt reassured, and Emile's vow to "efface everything," to make Emilie "forget everything," spoke against his deep knowledge that nothing he did could finally dry the tears shed by this *mater dolorosa*, or wipe clean the slate. A death having occurred, death married them both to hysteria. For Emile it prepared ambushes, it loosed lightning bolts, it filled the world with consternation.

Dared he succeed where François had failed? Dared he not? His quandary must have been more acute than usual in 1856, on the eve of a momentous decision he faced: whether to take a classical degree after the fourth form or work toward a scientific baccalauréat. That the choice existed at all was itself remarkable. Until 1852, plans for abolishing the integrated syllabus had consistently been beaten back by conservative opinion, which saw them as a Trojan horse devised to unleash upon France a utilitarian spirit incompatible with the national "genius." Educated men could still say *je perds mon grec* when they experienced a mental lapse, and those who took this expression seriously held the dropping of a Greek requirement for graduation to be symptomatic of social senility. Separate curricula would engender mongrel types. "For the first time in French society, those who intend to go into high positions in commerce and industry, the administration, science, medicine, or the learned professions . . . will be dispensed or rather excluded from the noble studies which have long cultivated and fortified the French genius," lamented one royalist newspaper. As Saint-Simonianism—the technocratic scheme for social reorganization propounded by the Comte de Saint-Simon—became quasi-official doctrine under Napoleon III, it bolstered the cause of modernism. We have seen how Hippolyte Fortoul, minister of public instruction, swore himself for Latin and Greek, lest old-guard Frenchmen dismayed by Napoleon's coup d'état think that the adventurer intended to reconstruct France without her lares and penates; nonetheless, science was legitimized through a system called "bifurcation," in which every third-former chose a curriculum preparing him for the *baccalauréat-ès-lettres* or else for the newly instituted *baccalauréat-ès-sciences*.

Unlike many children, Emile was keeping faith with family tradition when he chose science. However tedious he found the study of classical languages, to abandon Greek when defectors were generally urged to consider themselves second-rate would have been more difficult, had he not felt that piety endorsed his decision. "[Scientific education] is the seed of our future strength," he wrote twenty-two years later, and no doubt some such argument began to grow on him long before it reached maturity as this patriotic dictum. Perhaps the young Emile, who had after all sprung from François Zola's "seed," was already formulating around "science," "seed," and "future strength" a hereditary imperative that ghosted for the paternal wisdom he didn't enjoy. At any rate, the all-important promise of manhood inevitably came bound up with his idealized image of a father-scientist. Indeed, everything suggests that an oblique line led from the decision he made at this juncture to the grand finale of *Les Rougon-Macquart*, where Dr. Pascal, whose scientific notes have been wantonly destroyed, sires a son *in articulo mortis*.

Emilie was not reticent by nature, but what view she held in this matter is moot, for Zola never disclosed it in his recollections; it is equally plausible that a reverent widow encouraged her son to follow his father and that an ambitious plaintiff wanted him to get the *baccalauréat-ès-lettres* for a career in public administration or law. Emile himself juggled these alternatives even after he had presumably let one of them drop. "I want to do law; since a career one must have, the law is one I can happily square with my intellectual disposition," he told Baille later, in 1859, under circumstances he could not have foreseen. At any rate, his family's plight required him to do something more gainful than write poetry; how desperate it was may be inferred from a lease drawn up on November 28, 1855, between Emilie's confederate, Marius Daime, who had a baker's oven available for rent near the flour mill he owned in Aix, and Louis-Etienne Aubert, who at the age of seventy-two still possessed enough strength to knead dough, if not enough to start painting houses again. As her debts mounted (including one to a baker named Guien in the amount of 363 francs), Emilie found ever cheaper accommodations. From the flat on the rue Bellegarde she moved to a small house on the rue Roux-Alpheran, near the Collège Bourbon. In 1855 she and her parents established residence on the Cours de Minimes in a working-class neighborhood just outside the old quarter of Aix. Two years later they moved again, this time into two rooms facing the *barri* or alley that ran alongside the city wall.

Emilie spent little time in those dingy rooms. After a period of quiescence, in 1857 her brief against Jules Migeon had been revived when legal-aid authorities granted her permission to sue for a share in the canal company's assets, controlled by Migeon through a friend.[9] Since

---

[9] To block Emilie's application for legal aid, Migeon contended that her private life as well as her financial interests had long been bound up with those of the canal company manager, Marius Daime, implying that they were lovers.

the civil tribunal of the Seine would adjudicate her claim, she left Aix for Paris, where she soon found herself caught in procedures that offered no hope of a quick solution. Rebuffed by the civil tribunal, she sought redress at the Paris Tribunal de Commerce, and when it in turn handed down an unfavorable verdict, she appealed, hoping that legal aid would be renewed despite Migeon's obstructive tactics. It may have seemed during this wearisome contest that bad tidings could descend upon her only from the judicial bench, but on November 11, 1857, Emilie suddenly lost her mother, Henriette Aubert, who had made herself indispensable since François Zola's death. With destitution a very real prospect, the endgame being played out in court took precedence over everything else, and Emilie went back to Paris, where she hoped that men of influence such as Alexandre Labot would be disposed to help her. Aix, certainly, was not: the municipal council denied her request for a pension.

Emile's circle of friends, which included Cézanne, Baille, Philippe Solari, Marius Roux, and Louis Marguery, the son of a lawyer, did their best to fill out his shrunken world. They huddled around him as he waited through the Christmas holidays with his grandfather and entered the new year wondering what the future held in store. Weeks more passed before a letter arrived from Emilie. It did not announce the date of her return but instead informed him that there would be no return. Emile was told to raise money for third-class railway tickets for Paris by selling the furniture not already pawned and to join her as quickly as possible.

Paul, Jean-Baptistin, and Emile met for the last time in a room cluttered with schoolboy paraphernalia where they had spent many agreeable hours talking and rhyming three-act comedies and performing chemical experiments. They also planned excursions of farewell up the Bibémus road and along the windswept Route du Tholonet. Imagining life apart from one another made them choke, but it was agreed that Emile should consider himself a forerunner rather than an exile, in whose footsteps they would follow sooner or later. Without fail they would reassemble someday on the Left Bank, and perhaps the thought of their reunion kept Emile warm when, in February 1858, he and Louis Aubert boarded a train for Paris, which was still shaking from the bomb that had recently exploded around Louis Napoleon as his carriage drew up before the Opera House.[10]

---

[10]The fact that Emilie did not immediately give up her flat in Aix has led at least one scholar to conjecture that she may have expected to return after a favorable verdict. This may be so, but Zola always recalled his move as consciously irreversible, with the selling of the furniture. We have seen, moreover, how uncongenial Emilie Zola found Aix.

III

"THEIR CIRCLES WERE
PERFECTLY ROUND"

I N MID-NINETEENTH-CENTURY France, first-class railway carriages
came equipped with red and tan carpet beneath which ran an elaborate system of pipes containing hot water to warm the feet of well-
heeled passengers. Third-class offered only heat from bodies packed
together, and traveling eight hundred kilometers on a wooden bench
in wintertime required fortitude. "What a journey! Just thinking about
it three decades afterward, I can still feel my legs encased in icy fetters
and my stomach seized with cramps," wrote Zola's fellow Provençal
Alphonse Daudet. "Two days in a third-class carriage, dressed in thin
summer garb and frigid weather upon us; . . . I was literally dying!"
Those who made this voyage often did so on a one-way ticket, as the
lure of higher wages and of a fuller life attracted multitudes to Paris.
To be sure, some would go home again, like the Creusois stonemasons
who annually migrated north in the building season. But for many
people, that desolate expanse called "the zone," where city streets
trailed away into fields dotted with hovels and coal heaps before reaching the fortifications, constituted a boundary as definitive as the Ach-
eron. Year after year trains raced past it and ground to a halt under
the immense glass canopies of the Parisian termini, discharging provincials whose initiation took place at a table some yards longer than
the municipal banquet hall on which luggage was searched for taxable
goods. Every day omnibuses would draw up outside to collect the immigrant and deposit him in the congested center of town or in the
swelling *banlieue*.

Although Emile brought with him vivid memories of Paris, the city he saw at eighteen was markedly different from the one he had visited at eleven. In that decade, Louis Napoleon had not only crowned himself emperor but had gone some way toward implementing an imperial dream that began to obsess him as early as 1842, when, during his internment at the Ham prison fortress, he declared: "I want to be a second Augustus, because Augustus . . . made Rome a city of marble." Such aspirations may have appeared lunatic then. By 1856 they no longer seemed so. Road crews under the supervision of Louis Napoleon's indefatigable prefect of the Seine, Georges Haussmann, had been hard at work since 1855 prizing open the Latin Quarter to let traffic flow unimpeded, and vehicles that formerly crept uphill in the narrow aisle of medieval streets now moved along a wide, graded thoroughfare known as the "Boulevard de Sébastopol—rive gauche," which was soon to be renamed the Boulevard Saint-Michel after the statuary fountain installed near its intersection with the quai. At that intersection, even more dramatic changes revealed themselves, for across the Pont Saint-Michel, on the Ile de la Cité, a huge gap sprang to view where, shortly before, ten thousand members of Paris's lumpen proletariat had lived in unspeakable squalor. Gone were the dingy cabarets made famous by the popular novelist Eugène Sue in *Les Mystères de Paris,* the old morgue that Dickens found so oddly irresistible, the brothels along the rue Saint-Eloi, the maze of winding, fetid alleys that got a thorough bath only when the Seine flooded them. Around Notre-Dame Cathedral lay rubble-strewn earth, and from Quasimodo's vantage point one could clearly discern similar transformations on the Right Bank. There, cutting through the labyrinthine heart of revolutionary Paris, the Boulevard de Sébastopol met the rue de Rivoli, which now reached eastward far beyond its elegant sleeve of arcades. Neighborhoods sprawling between the Louvre and the Place de la Bastille no longer formed a lower-class stronghold ideally suited to the barricades of guerrilla warfare and the propagation of cholera morbus. With those salients they had lost their unbroken frontier and would, before long, be made to yield their inwardness as well.

People evicted by government decree were not alone in feeling bereft. While Louis Napoleon proudly saw his grand design unfold in the concentric rings, squares, circles, and radii that imposed logic on the higgledy-piggledy, nostalgia overcame writers and ideologues who regarded this geometric scheme as fatal to a world with which they had bonded. "I am a stranger to what beckons, to what is, as I am to these new, implacably straight boulevards . . . that no longer carry the scent of Balzac's world but announce some American Babylon," Jules de Goncourt noted on November 18, 1860. And three years later, as trouble brewed during legislative elections, Proudhon felt the spirit of 1848 pass through "Haussmann's new, monotonous, wearisome city with its rectilinear boulevards, its gigantic hotels, its magnificent but unvisited quais, its river sadly put to transporting sand and stone, . . . its squares, its theaters, its new barracks, its macadam, its legion of street sweepers and frightful dust: this cosmopolitan city where natives cannot be told from the Germans, Batavians, Americans, Russians, Arabs all about them." Socialist thus joined royalist against a "parvenu" unencumbered by the weight of history, whose ostentation bespoke his philistinism. Against *gai Paris*, which acquired that name at the 1855 World's Fair, when foreigners had indeed "invaded" the capital to admire it in the early stages of its metamorphosis, they kept alive the memory of *vieux Paris*, of a sacred place incubating itself without regard for the external world or for the future.

Despite it all, *vieux Paris* had not succumbed overnight, and the day Emile's mother led him and Louis Aubert to a small three-room flat at 63, rue Monsieur-le-Prince in the Latin Quarter, he discovered that life could still look seedy behind Paris's impressive new façades. On the rue Monsieur-le-Prince, which slants uphill from the Boulevard Saint-Germain to the Boulevard Saint-Michel, laundresses, shoemakers, dyers, weavers, hatters plied their trade side by side, jostling for space with publicans, some of whom may have come over from the Ile de la Cité along with the multitude of homeless rats. Scattered among them were restaurants where a vagrant clientele that otherwise went hungry ate on the cheap. This scene repeated itself along neighboring streets and, beyond the streets, in courtyards with shops and ateliers. Nor did business stop at street level, for high above the apartments occupied by bourgeois, another population was to be found sewing waistcoats, binding books, and stitching shoes, in cold, warren-like rooms only a few feet square. As demolition elsewhere proceeded, such rooms multiplied throughout the Latin Quarter. A cadastral survey shows that 63, rue Monsieur-le-Prince contained twenty of them, but some tenements contained nothing else, and these *maisons garnies*, whose grime Jules Vallès pictures so depressingly in *Le Bachelier*, became a last refuge for the poor artisan, the unskilled immigrant, the ex-scholar, the government clerk condemned never to make ends meet on twelve or fifteen hundred francs a year.

How matters stood with the Zolas may be gathered from a letter Emile wrote in March 1858 to his maternal uncle, Alfred Aubert, who had set up as a leather-goods merchant in Marseille and who, though impecunious himself, sent Father Aubert a fixed amount every quarter:

You must understand that our trip cost us dearly and that once in Paris we had to lay out more for lodging and household expenses. At the same time you know that the old man's allowance falls due on the 25th of this month. Well, he told me to tell you that it would please him if you could send him this right away. Several days sooner or later can't make much difference to you while the old man, who is destitute, will be greatly relieved by an advance payment. Do send it without delay . . . and be assured of my gratitude for having understood the difficult position in which we, and thus your father, find ourselves.

Three hundred sixty francs per annum was more rent than people who had no regular income could afford, but the family still lived, or half lived, on the illusory prospects bound up in Emilie's legal dossier, even after the Tribunal de Commerce dismissed yet another suit brought against Jules Migeon and company in January 1858. However obvious it was that further nagging would produce only further disappointment, the dream of restitution, which had kept plain, plump fact at bay since 1851, once again proved more cogent than evidence of its futility. Emilie set about reconstructing an objective basis for that dream and somewhere found material sufficient to have counsel introduce a new suit on her behalf at the Tribunal de Commerce. "Our legal business is going beautifully and the case will soon be adjudicated," Emile informed his uncle on June 30. "My mother has been assigned a first-rate lawyer, and those called upon to judge the matter have shown her nothing but sympathy. At last we near the goal toward which we have striven for so long."

One effect of this on Emile emerged several decades later, when a thirst for vengeance and official consecration drove him to importune the Académie Française as stubbornly as his mother had importuned the tribunal. Meanwhile, those hopes that did not await judgment day at court were vested in a future engineer. Around the time Emile left Aix, Madame Zola put the question of his schooling before Alexandre Labot, and the well-connected Labot, whose circle included Désiré Nisard, director of the Ecole Normale Supérieure, arranged to have him enter the Lycée Saint-Louis, which stood nearby, between the rue Monsieur-le-Prince and the Boulevard Saint-Michel.

If affiliation with a historical monument could do Emile good, hardly any could have done him better than affiliation with Saint-Louis. The Collège d'Harcourt, as it was formerly known, had occupied that cramped site for six hundred years, begetting clerics century after century until, in the 1600s, its Jansenist principal helped transform it from a theological seminary into a general academy much favored by members of the haute bourgeoisie. Among the illustrious men who boarded there during the *ancien régime* were Boileau, Racine, Perrault, Saint-Evremond, and Talleyrand. And since the Revolutionary period, when it became first a prison house, then a Napoleonic *lycée*, its honor roll had grown longer. Under Louis Philippe it acquired a reputation for breeding scientific talent by taking the mathematics prize in almost every Concours Général, which led Labot to assure Emile that success there would earn him free passage upward to the Ecole Polytechnique or to its civilian counterpart, the Ecole Centrale.

Had his move from provincial *collège* to Parisian *lycée* entailed only matters of agenda, syllabus, and pedagogical method, Emile might have negotiated it without a hitch. He knew beforehand that the same subjects would be taught at the same time of day in accordance with fastidious decrees Hippolyte Fortoul had promulgated in 1854. He also knew that in Saint-Louis as in the Collège Bourbon, lecturing teachers would deliver résumés for students to parrot or would assign them themes to elaborate during the study periods, when monitors stood guard. Taking dictation, memorizing, reciting formed a universal sequence in France, where the powers that were made sure, despite "bifurcation" (which did not last very long), that one model should prevail over the heuristic and utilitarian pedagogy reformers urged upon them.

But Saint-Louis was Parisian, for all the ploys adopted to keep reality outside its stone hulk, and the students Emile met possessed an urbanity that left him feeling woefully inept. "At first I was amazed by boys my age standing at the blackboard and reciting their lessons with elegance and ease, as if they themselves had assumed the role of professor," he wrote in 1877:

> They added to the lesson, embellished it with variants, demonstrated that they had gone beyond the syllabus. And what confounded me even more were the magnificent circles they drew on the blackboard in one swoop of chalk. Their circles were perfectly round. Alas, they put to shame our poor, flat, provincial circles, which resembled . . . deflated goatskins! When I ventured to draw one of them in Paris I felt the whole class snicker behind my back and that caused me intense humiliation. This business of circles seems inconsequential, but in reality it is a fitting emblem for both the Parisian schoolboy— brilliant, articulate, and nimble of hand as of tongue—and the provincial student, heavy and awkward, who can't find his words.

Even the fame Zola eventually enjoyed in greater measure than almost any other writer of his age never quite dispelled this image or stopped the trembling that afflicted him when he spoke in public. Audiences always stirred memories of his cruel initiation, just as the initiation itself brought back memories of older pain. Once again he heard a chorus mock him (though now, ironically, it substituted "Marseillais" for "Franciot"), and the pride he had won through friendship and scholastic achievement and cross-country jaunts knuckled under. If Stendhal fresh out of Grenoble found Paris alien because there were no mountains, how much more so did Emile, for whom the Infernets gorge bore witness not only to his own happiest experience but to François Zola's brief passage on earth. No longer could he fancy himself the son of an eponymous hero and expect those around him to recognize, just by looking up, what his father had wrought. In Paris, twenty-eight years after François Zola first came from Austria, Zola was another immigrant name lost among the many that crowded its civil register.

As an *externe surveillé*, or day student who ate lunch with boarders and attended study period until early evening, Emile soon floated up to the back bench of his classroom amphitheater. "Out of sixty children seated before him, a professor could profitably interest himself in fifteen at most," he observed. "The others did as they pleased with impunity, for in Paris punishment was rare. . . . Teachers taught but otherwise left to their own devices those who paid them no heed. I know whereof I speak, having become one such unreprimanded malingerer." During the 1830s or 1840s, discipline would in all likelihood have been enforced. Faculty still wore black robes and medieval toques, and the *lycée* was still a tight-knit community whose principal kept it under close surveillance. Indeed, keeping watch took precedence over teaching itself, and a schedule that had boarders parade soldierlike from dawn until dusk through the austere confines of dormitory, chapel, study hall, classroom, yard, and refectory made it difficult to escape notice. This quasi-hermetic world came undone when day students entered it in greater numbers (many of them coddled children of the rich). At Parisian *lycées*, which its detractors called "baccalauréat factories," there appeared between teacher and student a rift not unlike the one to be found between boss and worker in large-scale industry, where the paternalistic bonds traditionally maintained by French entrepreneurs had gone slack. "The professor forgot us; we simply didn't exist for him." That his reputation for brilliance in Aix should count for nothing in Paris was more than Emile could bear. "Being twentieth of sixty after being among the first in my class hurt me deeply. . . . I lost heart and became a very mediocre student," recalled Zola, who as a mature author seldom read what he had written the day before without feeling that overnight, by reverse alchemy, his gold had become lead.

An honorable mention in French composition did not assuage him. Belittled by Paris, he naturally visited this distraught perspective upon Aix, which now seemed smaller than it had been from its surrounding heights. But Aix also served as an emotional counterpoise, and throughout the 1860s Zola would vacillate between nostalgia and

scorn, sometimes chiding friends who settled there in provincial torpor, at other times prodding them to help him get a street named after
François Zola or to noise his own works around town. The vast indifference he encountered up north saw him lean homeward for consolation, for applause, and for reassurance that he had not fallen into
oblivion.

From such needs sprang a prolific correspondence with Baille and
Cézanne, in which the three strove to maintain their alliance. "Do you
swim? Do you party? Paint? Play the cornet? Versify? Well, what are
you doing? And your baccalauréat? Is work for it proceeding smoothly?
You'll floor all your examiners. Ah, we shall live it up, by Jove!" he
wrote on June 14, 1858, when Paul, to whom these questions and
prophecies were addressed, sat quaking at the approach of doomsday.
"As for me, I warrant you that I shall not have to stoop beneath the
weight of laurels. I may get a prize, the one in French composition,
and if so, that's all I'll get. Let's face it, not everyone has it in him to
shine. One finds oneself in good company among the dolts, so numerous are they." His letter, which followed several others long since
lost, shifted in tone from sententious to bantering, as he distanced
himself one way or the other from a predicament more anguishing
than he dared express outright:

> I see so much intellectual pretension here in young men who fancy
> themselves superior beings surrounded by creatures devoid of merit
> that I long for those endowed with genuine wit, for [my old compan-
> ions] who know that people in glass houses should not throw stones.
> Goodness, how solemn I am today. Forgive me such commonplace
> reflections but, you see, on close inspection the world seems so badly
> put together that one can't help playing philosopher. To hell with
> reason anyway and long live joy! What are you doing about your
> conquest? Have you spoken to her yet?

Framing this lament is an evocation of the Provençal countryside
which, with summer upon him, rose up in images and odors that gave
exile keener significance. On the rue Monsieur-le-Prince, where newspapers disclose that a terrible fire had recently sent billows of smoke
through the neighborhood, Emile pictured rock-strewn hills covered
with brambles and junipers, brilliant blue skies and limpid streams,
almond groves and flowering Judas trees. To Paul he wrote not about
local events or the perfect circles Parisian boys could draw, but about
sensual deprivation in a city unequipped to feed him all he wanted of
the pungent and colorful delights of southern cuisine. "Wait and I shall
vent my monstrous ideas [*idées biscornues*], wait until I come and I
shall fill your ears with them," he concluded, as if there were some

possibility that Paul might disappear before he revisited Aix in August.

Separation proved no less difficult for Paul, who also saw himself thrust into a comfortless world. "Since you've left Aix, my dear friend, I've been weighed down by sorrow, upon my word I have. I no longer recognize myself. I am heavy, dull, and slow," he wrote on April 9. Emile's departure would have hurt a year earlier or later, but especially during these final months at the Collège Bourbon he missed the support Emile had always given him. Ahead lay an examination fraught with tragic consequences, for passing it in order to enter law school was a prospect as grim as failure. No such dilemma troubled Jean-Baptistin Baille, who seems to have known already what path he would follow through life. Although Paul admired Baille, the narrow certitudes that guided him like tutelary spirits, producing an ideal, bourgeois design (he earned scientific recognition, married well, and became rich), made any very close relationship impossible, except *à trois*. Without Emile, to whom they wrote at least one note signed "Bacézanlle," each vexed the other, and this mating of names belied an incompatibility that grew deeper in time. Alone among intimate strangers, Paul felt panic-stricken, not to say freakish.

His letters do more than tell us how clever boys infatuated with Musset's banter must have entertained themselves when together. Underneath the rebuses, the drawings, the bawdry, and the mock-heroic alexandrines he showered upon Emile, but often leering through their wry surface, are obsessions that constitute a gloss on his emotional life. Above all, he feared judgment:

> Je frémis quand je vois toute la géographie,
> L'histoire, et le latin, le grec, la géométrie
> Conspirer contre moi: je les vois menaçants
> Ces examinateurs dont les regards perçants
> Jusqu'au fond de mon coeur portent un profond trouble.
> Ma crainte, à chaque instant, terriblement redouble!
> Et je me dis: Seigneur, de tous ces ennemis,
> Pour ma perte certaine, impudemment unis,
> Dispersez, confondez la troupe épouvantable,
> La prière, il est vrai, n'est pas trop charitable.
> Exaucez-moi pourtant, de grâce, mon Seigneur,
> Je suis de vos autels un pieux serviteur.[1]

---

[1] "I tremble when I see geography, history, Latin, Greek, geometry conspire against me. I see them threatening, those examiners whose gimlet eyes plant disquiet at the bottom of my heart. My fear redoubles from one minute to the next and I say to myself: Lord, disperse and confound these frightful enemies who have united to bring about my certain destruction. My prayer is not very charitable to be sure, but hear me, O Lord, I beg of you. I am a pious servant at your altar."

The baccalauréat exam was a trial held by a vice squad bent on exposing corruption, and punishment would damage him irreparably unless some superhuman agent disarmed enemies whom he pictured as mad with "rage." This scenario, in which Emile must have recognized both paternal scoffs and maternal prayers, haunted Paul beyond adolescence. No sooner did one examination end than another began for the sinner who, against his own better judgment, or against the anticlerical bias he acquired from his priest-baiting father, finally embraced religion. "Out of fear!" he told Paul Alexis in 1891, when the writer asked why he attended mass. "I feel that I have only a few days left on earth and then what? I believe I shall survive and I don't want to risk roasting *in aeternum.*" Acquaintances often heard him complain that "life is fearful."

To judge from his correspondence, hell at nineteen was a place where condign punishment took many forms, the most prominent being torture by visual impalement. In letter after letter, rectitude confronts depravity with knifelike eyes. The *regards perçants* of examiners recur in Paul's facetious poem about Catiline, whose "bloody dagger" proves ineffectual against Cicero's "venomous glances," which knock the traitor senseless. Another exercise of this sort has Hamilcar descend in dream upon a besotted Hannibal to scold him for losing consciousness during a feast and dishonoring the fatherland. Guilt induces prostration, culprits go limp, their substance liquefies. "For through the mighty swipe the hero gave the tablecloth, the wine spread pouring round" is how Hannibal disgraces himself:

> Les assiettes, les plats et les saladiers vides
> Roulèrent tristement dans des ruisseaux limpides
> De punch encore tout chaud, regrettable dégât!
> Se pouvait-il, messieurs, qu'Annibal gaspillât,
> Infandum, Infandum, le rhum de sa patrie![2]

On July 14, a date reminiscent of paternal government, Paul again used *infandum* (unspeakable), this time in connection with love, and the refrain provides further reason to surmise that what wastrels and squanderers did, unforgivably, was spill their seed. "After starting this letter on July 9," he wrote Emile, "it's appropriate that I should finish it today the 14, yet I cannot, alas, find the least little idea in my barren mind, with all we have to discuss, hunting, fishing, swimming, there's variety enough for you, and love, too (Infandum, let's not broach that

[2]"The plates, dishes, and empty salad bowls rolled sadly in the limpid streams of hot punch. A regrettable waste. Can it be, sirs, that Hannibal—oh, unspeakable, unspeakable act—squandered the rum of his fatherland?"

corrupting theme)." Had his parenthetical remark come from some other candidate fed up with Cicero, it might pass as a subversive giggle. Here it meant something more, for throughout these letters, his badinage harbors a fear of madness or impotence. Under no circumstances could Paul express love harmlessly, and he drank himself sodden rather than approach one particular woman whom he desired from afar. "Hang it all, I am reduced to uttering sighs, sighs that don't betray themselves to the outside world. . . . I wilt in silence, my love cannot burst out. A kind of boredom accompanies me everywhere and I forget my sorrow only after I've drowned it in drink. . . . I have gotten drunk and shall again unless, by some happy stroke, I should, God damn it, succeed! But I despair, I despair." Only Mother Church, to whom, in his despair, he eventually had recourse, kissed lepers and graduated fools.

When love did escape, it burst out like a convict warped by prison life. The profanity in his avowal voiced the same urge to degrade himself that saw him, years later, flaunt his expedition to a brothel, break paintbrushes in public, and skulk unwashed at the edge of Manet's circle in Les Batignolles. But foul language was also hair put on the naked child: it promoted an image of virility as grotesque as the threat of emasculation from which it derived its obsessive character. On April 9, Paul wrote Emile a letter that features this potent image in some doggerel about himself meeting a beautiful wood nymph. "Everything you have seems divine," he says. Then:

> Grâce à cette flatterie,
> Elle tombe en pamoison,
> Tandis qu'elle est engourdie,
> J'explore son mirliton
> O doux mirliton, etc.
> Puis revenant à la vie
> Sous mes vigoureux efforts,
> Elle se trouve ébahie
> De me sentir sur son corps.
> O doux mirliton, etc.
> Elle rougit et soupire
> Lève des yeux langoureux
> Qui semblaient vouloir me dire
> "Je me complais à ces jeux."
> Gentil mirliton, etc.
> Au bout de la jouissance
> Loin de dire: "C'est assez."
> Sentant que je recommence
> Elle me dit: "Enfoncez."

Gentil mirliton, etc.
Je retirera ma sapière,
Après dix ou douze coups—
Mais trémoussant du derrière:
"Pourquoi vous arrêtez-vous?"
Dit ce mirliton, etc.[3]

Between striking dumb and being dumbstruck lay the social milieu where Paul Cézanne had always felt lost. Home for him was a violent world filled with orators whose language imposed silence, with judges whose vision blinded, with satyrs whose lust brooked no resistance. And women in it happily yielded to force or stood contemptuously aloof, disqualifying one way or the other those decorous maneuvers men perform under the banner of courtship. "He had a celibate's passion for female beauty, an insane love for nudity desired but never possessed, and couldn't manage as man to satisfy himself or as creator to render palpable enough the beauty he dreamed of clasping in an ecstatic embrace," wrote Zola in the 1880s, when pictorial evidence for this observation abounded not only in Cézanne's various *Bathers* but in rape scenes showing snowy, voluptuous nudes overcome by Priapus.[4]

Akin to the compensations art offered him was the self-esteem he sought in friendship with men whose power or savoir vivre he envied. Seen through Paul's eyes, Emile had such qualities, and anticipating a summer together made him feel more robust. Besides the usual projects on their holiday agenda—dips in the Arc, cross-country walks, visits to favorite haunts like the Domaine de Gallice—he imagined one that would surely let his father know how he felt about law school. "I shall let my beard and mustache grow; I await you ad hoc. Tell me, do you wear a beard and mustache? Adieu, dear friend, I don't understand how I can be so stupid." His mind then traveled next door to the idea of writing a play about Bluebeard. "I have conceived the idea of a drama in five acts which we shall entitle (you and I): Henry

[3]"Thanks to this flattery she faints. While she lies benumbed I explore her pipe. O sweet pipe, etc. Then reviving under my vigorous efforts, she is startled to feel me on her body. O sweet pipe, etc. She blushes and sighs, lifts languorous eyes which seem to say: 'I take pleasure in this sport.' Gentle pipe, etc. After she has come, far from saying: 'Enough' as she feels me begin again, she says: 'Plunge it in.' Gentle pipe, etc. I withdraw my rapier after ten or twelve bouts. But wagging her behind, 'Why stop now?' says this pipe, etc."
[4]Had Zola reread this early correspondence for clues to Cézanne's enigma, he might have fixed on *mirliton*, whose meanings include "doggerel," "nose," "pipe," and by extension "phallus." When Cézanne has it signify the female sex as well, a strange picture emerges that puts one in mind of certain polymorphous nudes he later drew. In *Cézanne: His Life and Art*, Jack Lindsay points out a head which is unmistakably Zola's mounted on a voluptuous female body.

VIII of England. We'll do it together, during the vacation." Alone, Paul yearned for an elusive damsel, but with Emile in the offing hair began to sprout and wives to multiply. The Knight of the Sorrowful Countenance could suddenly picture himself the misogynous king of women.

What an 1861 photograph of Cézanne shows are sharp features, close-cropped hair, drooping mustachios, and, above all, large, malevolent eyes. In comparison Emile Zola looked like clemency itself as he met the world with a level gaze that owed something of its dark soulfulness to myopia. Measuring them against each other people might have found Emile runty, when in fact he stood taller, at five feet seven inches, than the average French male and carried himself on legs toughened by outdoor life. There is a Cézanne jingle that commemorates his athletic vigor, although that trait was destined to escape public recognition behind images of Zola wearing pince-nez and sitting foursquare amidst heavy period furniture. Except for the imperceptible droop of one eyelid, childhood illness had left him unscathed. Sturdily built, with thick, straight hair, a high forehead, a serious mouth, and a broad nose cleft at the tip, he needed only filling out to become the puggish figure who threw himself into frays. Like father, like son was Emilie's anthem, and his compact presence did indeed recall François Zola.

By June 1858, as the close of another school year brought him nearer the Polytechnique or the Centrale, that anthem rang hollow in Emile's mind. Though he dared not admit it, least of all to his mother, dwindling enthusiasm for science informs the letter he sent to Jean-Baptistin Baille late that month:

> Oh, my guardian angel, tell me what style I must employ. Shall I be stupid or just boring? In other words, shall I write in verse or in prose? I opt for the boring, so don't tremble, young Baille, I'll speak in ordinary language . . . But what can I tell a confrere in learned science? For heaven's sake, don't go soaring off, pen. You're not writing for the lettered Cézanne but for the scientific Baille (funny how scientific rhymes with soporific—no offense intended). Shall I discuss the trinomial $x + px + q + o$, or else study the variations of the function $ax + bx = c$, or demonstrate to him sine of a 45 degree arc equals cosec? The guardian angel replies: "Zola, my friend, you've got your nerve lecturing your superior! As far as the mysteries of science are concerned, be silent where you cannot be intelligent. Bow your head! Bite your tongue!!! And put yourself at ease by writing whatever pops into your head."

As his overwrought preamble suggests, Emile found himself baffled everywhere he turned in a conflict between piety and self-interest. To

study science was either to compete with a father he had already survived or to spend life eating humble pie at the table of a heroic progenitor who never toiled over logarithms. To desert science for
literature was to shirk responsibility (which may explain why the honor
one professor paid him in reading aloud an essay he had submitted on
the theme of "blind Milton dictating to his older daughter" goes unmentioned in his correspondence). No discernible path led around this
thicket. Nor could he seek help at home, where problems were more
plentiful than solutions. To be sure, there was always Paul out yonder,
but a soul mate who thought of himself as Hercules stuck at the crossroads of duty and pleasure hardly qualified as a guidance counsclor.

As soon as Emile saw Aix again, the notion of retrieving what
seemed in retrospect to have been a sunny childhood consoled him,
and knowing that Paul would need moral support—Paul whose nightmare had come true when he failed the baccalauréat examination in
July—truly brought back old times. They began where they had left
off six months earlier, on daylong tramps south toward the Pilon-du-
Roi and east toward Mont Sainte-Victoire. Emile laid up a store of
place names for novels not yet written while revisiting backcountry
villages, and inevitably their course took them past the immense white
slabs of François Zola's dam, which brimmed with water from the
rivers Cause and Bayon. They walked through fields of lavender and
shot at nothing in particular and swam in the Arc near a dilapidated
eighteenth-century manor known as the Jas de Bouffan, which was
soon to become the Cézanne estate. "My dear friend, I have delightful
news for you—I've plunged my body into the broad, broad, deep, deep
Seine," Emile had announced to Paul the previous June. "But what
are missing are a venerable old pine, a fresh spring to cool the blessed
bottle, and Cézanne's broad imagination and piquant, lively talk." He
would enjoy all these and have all he could eat of aioli and bouillabaisse
before the knell of the new school year called him back to Paris in
October. Whether his holiday afforded him less innocent delights is
open to conjecture. A year later he wrote a tale (it has since been lost)
about some inglorious escapade he had had together with Baille and
perhaps others in their crowd, which included one especially rakish
fellow named Edgard de Julienne. But it would be optimistic to imagine Aix as the scene of his deflowering. Any young man who knew
what country he inhabited knew that throughout it syphilis was often
the price paid for initiation by a grisette, and in Emile's case prudence
almost certainly joined powerful inhibitions to safeguard his virginity.
"Trammeled from an early age by habitual timidity, the sexual appetite
in Monsieur Zola has not been very expansive," Dr. Edouard Toulouse
observed much later in a "medico-psychological inquiry" to which Zola
lent himself. "Despite this shortcoming and perhaps because of it,

genital sensations have always had enormous repercussions in his psychic life."

The day after his return to Paris, Emile fell ill, and for weeks lay bedridden with high fever accompanied by nausea. There were delirious episodes, and when the fever subsided the typhoidlike disease attacked his mouth, inflicting painful sores and loosening his teeth so badly that he wrote messages rather than talk. October slipped away on a tide of dreams in which he felt himself teetering over empty space, whirling, falling, or struggling underground. "Time and again I dreamed that I was deep in the earth, far from everything, at the bottom of long, narrow underground passages where I had to creep relentlessly" is how he recalled it in notes entitled "Spring: Journal of a Convalescent":

> My legs got tangled in vines and unseen obstacles. My legs encountered debris I tried vainly to kick away. Bent double, my forehead banging against stone, my knees sinking into the loamy, slippery soil, I moved with incredible difficulty and anguish. At times, when the sickness tearing me apart became more acute, it seemed that the subterranean passages narrowed to the point of closing, whereupon I grew desperate in my efforts to pass beyond. I persisted and entered the obstacles suffocating me. I flailed until my bruised body seemed to have crossed this enormous glut of earth. Then, when the crisis was over, the gallery became wider and I could walk erect until another crisis laid me low in front of new rockfalls. . . . This underground trek, this struggle, this herculean labor lasted for days, weeks. I would always go straight ahead following the thousand twists of the dark corridor without ever entertaining the thought of turning around, for it was a fatal task that imposed itself, one that I had necessarily to accomplish.

Forty years later Zola wondered whether his illness had not made him the creator he became by "modifying" his brain. A more prosaic hypothesis says that during this siege his brain had been made to yield childhood memories and phantasms. Material usually kept hidden came up from the depths, and Zola revealed something of what it was all about in "Spring," in which the convalescent hovers at death's door through February and March (as François Zola had done) before learning on April 1 that he will survive. Since April 1 in the Zola family marked the eve of a birthday and the anniversary of a funeral, did the dream commemorate both events? Did Emile struggle underground to avoid a fate his fear of which inspired not only sagas such as *Germinal* and *La Terre* but the superstitious rituals that he believed enabled him to complete them? "Who can understand the soul torn apart by the prospect of being separated eternally from the work it conceived with love and leaves undone? Who can convey the cruel combat waged in the mind of this man between a heightened desire to execute something and the permanent impotence of death?" the author of François Zola's obituary notice had asked in *Le Mémorial d'Aix*, and these rhetorical questions haunted Emile. The thought that his near-fatal illness altered his "nature" and "afterlife" was perhaps reassuring. What hadn't killed him had reinvented him — which is to say that Zola characterized the disease itself as a kind of new father who gave him immunity against a curse laid upon him by the old. His sickness had made him new and naive.

Being cooped up with his mother in their small flat on the rue Monsieur-le-Prince also suffocated him, no doubt, especially after two months away. In that regard matters soon grew worse, for when Emile could walk again, Emilie took an even smaller flat at 241, rue Saint-Jacques, where five ramshackle tenements stood around a dark courtyard near the Val-de-Grâce Church. They were so poor by now that the extra twenty-centime stamp needed for Emile's longer letters constituted an extravagance; Paul, from whom he hid this dire state of affairs, teased him about mail arriving at Aix with insufficient postage. How they managed was known only to Emilie, who still held out hope, as she turned forty, that a deus ex machina would materialize. On February 28, 1859, the family rejoiced over news of Jules Migeon losing his parliamentary seat in connection with some electoral misdemeanor. "Things are going beautifully," Emile informed his uncle, Alfred Aubert. "Monsieur Migeon has just been drummed out of the legislature, the government is dead set against him, and at long last every new turn bodes well." But ultimately Migeon's disgrace did not promote Emilie's salvation. Several months later another adverse judgment forced her to concede at last that she would never be vindicated, and Aix followed by rejecting outright her appeal for financial support. That same month *La Provence* published a long poem entitled "Le Canal Zola," in which Emile celebrated his father's dam as the work of a Promethean figure who had brought order to a derelict corner of Creation, making "virgin nature" accept his design. It obviously fell on deaf ears, and with the mess François left behind him, perhaps Emile was himself unconvinced by his dithyramb.

Under pressure to set a straight course, he spent his last year at Saint-Louis, or what remained of it after he got up from his sickbed, in perfect agonies of indecision. On January 23 he had unburdened himself to Jean-Baptistin Baille, who had meanwhile breezed through two baccalauréat examinations and was preparing for the Polytechnique. In a parody of the rhetorical exercises that had become almost second nature with him, Emile staged his conflict as a dialogue between himself and a mentor:

"Life is a struggle," I said to myself. "Let us accept it and not succumb to weariness or vexation." I can take the scientific baccalauréat, get accepted to the Ecole Centrale, become an engineer. "Don't do it," a voice shouted at me from beyond. "The turtledove does not nest with the falcon, the butterfly does not gather honey from stinging nettles. For work to be fruitful, it must please; to make a painting, one needs colors. Your horizon is narrowing rather than broadening; you were no more born to study science than to be a functionary. Your mind will be forever leaving algebra to gambol elsewhere. Don't do it! Don't!" And when I asked in anguish what path I should take, the voice resumed, saying: "Listen, my choice may seem absurd and you will declare it would put you back instead of forward, but in this world, my child, there are idols to which everyone makes sacrifice . . . Shout as you may that you are a man of letters, people will not believe you unless you can produce your bachelor of letters diploma. Without diplomas, there is no salvation; they are the open sesame to all professions. . . . So get to work, my dear child! . . . To the rescue, Virgil and Cicero! Only a year or six months more of dogged labor and . . . you will be able to declare, as you wave the blessed parchment: 'I am a man of letters.' "

With a baccalauréat-ès-lettres he could enter law school, which was the lesser evil that seniors often chose as they marched fearfully toward graduation. "It is a career (since career there must be) that fits in very well with my ideas. I am therefore resolved to become a lawyer, though rest assured the toga will not muffle the writer." Indoctrinated by Madame Zola, Emile had grown up under the regime of her pleas and adjournments, and in that sense lawyering seemed a natural sequel to childhood. One can readily understand how the law "fit in well" with his ideas. (Indeed, *J'accuse* may have been as much a belated indictment of the rascals who had stolen his inheritance as it was a denunciation of those who framed Captain Dreyfus.) At the same time, nothing that provided adults a bourgeois livelihood quite suited him. He assured Baille, whose feat he hoped to duplicate, that he would try to get two diplomas. But when he had done whistling in the dark, he still regarded himself as a turtledove among falcons, unequal for all his bravado to the responsibility Emilie would have him assume. "I am no longer the person you formerly knew. . . . I am no longer that Zola who used to work, who loved science, who slogged away in the rut of our academic curriculum," he informed another friend from Aix, Louis Marguery, in June. "One lovely morning I noticed that the sky was blue, the grass heavy with dew, the birds chirping amorously and I began to

dream. I dream on. Will my life be the more bitter because I remain ignorant of the exact sciences? I think not. Dust to dust is our lot and we
might as well spend the pause between two nothingnesses as agreeably as
possible, which I shall strive to do . . . All this by way of telling you that
since I am idle, I shall fail the bac." His velleities call to mind the feckless
hero of *La Joie de vivre*, Lazare, who conceives one project after another
only to let them all dissipate in turn. On some level, Emile shared Paul's
view that graduation portended death.

Carpe diem was not a motto he could pleasurably exploit, and what
little we know about his extracurricular life suggests that during this
period he found it even harder to play than to work. In March, when
Mardi Gras came, he toured the festive city with a compatriot named
Aurélien Houchard, joining Parisians of every walk who heard Johann
Strauss lead an orchestra of 150 musicians at the Opera and thronged
to masquerades at honky-tonk dance halls near the customs gates. Two
joyless nights furnished him material for a sermon reminiscent of
Rousseau's meditation on the tawdry amusements that divert men
from nature. "If I weren't afraid that you would mock me, I would tell
you what thoughts crossed my eighteen-year-old heart as I watched all
those silly people hopping in front of one another and making a din
to numb themselves, to persuade themselves that they were having a
wonderful time," he told Baille. "Just as there are people who drown
their troubles in drink, so the ball seems to me a Lethe where the
woebegone immerse themselves frenziedly. . . . This is seen, I know,
from a poet's perspective, and people would guffaw if in the middle
of the joyous crowd they heard me clamor for my woods and dales.
Therefore I didn't; I observed and pretended to enjoy myself immensely." Several decades would pass until he became artist enough
to write *L'Assommoir* and *Nana*, but the naturalist reconnoitering Paris's lower depths was foreshadowed in this meek observer who hung
back from the feast. Surrounded by women of easy virtue, he girded
himself with bucolic fantasies and, like Jean-Jacques put off by a rav-
ishing courtesan's defective nipple, subjected one such woman to an
unexpectedly chaste holiday. "I even made the acquaintance of a
young working girl, as pink and dainty and sweet as can be, with a
name a poet might have chosen for her—Espérance," he confided to
Baille, whose approval he sought in almost everything, it seems.

Espérance, a name fit for a sylph. Alas, she frequents dance halls and
wears crinolines. Alas, she smokes and drinks punch. The sylph is
losing her wings and becoming dissipated. Poor poets. With good
reason is it said that they dream! No matter! Espérance is very pretty
and if I were Marguery, I would tell you that I had hope for one
whole night. I don't know if I'll see her again. She gave me the ad-

dress of the shop where she works. Shall I go or shan't I? Good Lord, Espérance is very pretty indeed!

Two years later another Espérance, with whom he would play the rescuer, found him less demure, if no less moralistic. Meanwhile, he waffled fretfully at the verge of manhood, unable as yet to choose a career or to take a woman.

Leaning backward, he also began inching forward, and his announcement that "I am no longer the person you formerly knew" was intended, in part, to safeguard what he perceived as a change for the better or the broader in himself. Regular intimacy with Paris was gradually loosening provincial attachments. At times he still felt overwhelmed by nostalgia, but nostalgia diminished as the metropolis caught him up in the excitement of its swift and unpredictable narrative. At the Collège Bourbon intellectual boys had paid scant attention to *Le Mémorial d'Aix*, which came out every Sunday like a stuffed shirt emerging for a stroll on the respectable side of the Cours. At Saint-Louis, newspapers were valuable contraband. "Boarders . . . had day students smuggle them in," wrote Zola, who could always, in a pinch, visit *cabinets de lecture* where residents of the Latin Quarter browsed through periodicals and borrowed books for three francs a month. "The daily edition was scoured during morning class, which put the *lycée* level with the street. Not an event took place in Paris but that echoes of it resounded through study hall. Crimes, political catastrophes, the death of celebrities all caused comment. As for fashionable novels, they circulated underground and gave the Parisian scholar a worldliness peculiar to him." He read George Sand and Jules Michelet, whose reflections on marriage and women in *L'Amour* impressed him deeply; also Rabelais and Montaigne, neither of whom was yet considered suitable for *lycéens*. This clandestine syllabus left him only odd moments in which to digest the literature a jury would want him to regurgitate at the baccalauréat examination.

In 1859 newspapers were more than usually pertinent as debate raged over the "Italian Question"; throughout that spring *lycéens* of conservative Catholic opinion held fast against a minority of anticlericals who, notwithstanding the repressive laws passed after a bomb thrown by one Felice Orsini had exploded near the imperial coach on January 14, 1858, felt that Napoleon III would redeem himself if he freed Italy from the Austrian and papal yoke.[5] What these young men

[5]A follower of Giuseppe Mazzini, Orsini had fought in the first war of Italian independence (1848) and been elected member of the short-lived Roman Constituent Assembly. Convinced that Napoleon III would remain Pius IX's mainstay, opposing emancipation from the papal autocracy, he recruited three fellow revolutionists to help him assassinate the emperor. He was executed on March 13, 1858. A year later, Napoleon III embraced his cause.

knew nothing about, of course, was that in a secret conference held at Plombières on July 20, 1858, the emperor and Count Cavour had laid plans for war in a trade requiring France to champion Italian unification under King Victor Emmanuel and Victor Emmanuel to enhance Napoleon's imperial position with a gift of Savoy and Nice. Diplomats wheeled around European capitals while Napoleon, who feigned interest in their maneuvers, sought the ideal casus belli. Austria did not disappoint him. It issued a belligerent ultimatum, and on May 3, 1859, France declared war. "France has drawn the sword not to conquer but to liberate," said Napoleon. "The purpose of this war is to give Italy to herself, not to make her change her master, and we shall have on our frontier a nation of friends who owes us its independence. We do not go to Italy to foment disorder or overthrow the power of the Holy Father . . . but to free him of that alien pressure which is weighing on the whole peninsula." The emperor's egress from Paris one week later in field uniform, tunic, and kepi was a triumphant procession through immense crowds singing *La Marseillaise* to cheer him on to the battlefields of Lombardy-Venetia, where Bonaparte once strode.

Before long people gathered again to celebrate the French victory at Magenta, and Emile, having closely followed newspaper reports of the campaign, joined the crowd on the Place de la Sorbonne. In his correspondence he professed revulsion for war. "Shall we talk about the war? Goodness gracious, no!" he wrote to Marguery. "We shouldn't consider that subject gayer than is seemly. I don't want to spoil the beautiful sun by reminding myself that at this very moment it is lighting an ugly battlefield littered with dead and wounded men." But the heavy-handed parallel Napoleon III drew between himself and Napoleon I when he stated that "we shall on that classic soil famed for so many victories find the traces left there by our fathers" was all Emile needed to draw a parallel of his own with the heroic age from which François Zola had sprung. On June 8 he sent the empress an ode entitled "To the Empress Eugénie, Regent of France" which develops the emperor's rhetorical figure:

> Pour délivrer du joug l'Italie opprimée
> Vers les Alpes on vit s'élancer notre armée;
> De roses sous ses pas on semait les chemins.
> Par de nombreux hourras l'accueillant au passage
> A sa noble valeur chacun rendait hommage,
> Et l'on battait de mains!
> Allez, Français, allez combattre sur ces terres
> Ou noblement jadis combattirent vos pères;
> Allez vaincre ceux-là qu'écrasa leur talon.

Allez! . . . Notre empereur nous quitte pour la gloire!
Comme autrefois, soldats, notre hymne de victoire.[6]

Certainly he had good reason to applaud this scenario. On the larger
stage it may have borne out Karl Marx's dictum that history repeats
itself first as tragedy, then as farce, but for Emile it became a personal
drama whose denouement would right the wrongs that made him sta-
teless in his own country. What mattered far more than Italy's unification was the dream he had of seeing lost fragments of his own
shattered world assembled in a coherent design, and Napoleon III following Napoleon I across Lombardy seemed to promise, for one brief
moment, that life could come full round.

It is another question whether Emile would have demonstrated
quite so much enthusiasm for this imperial reenactment if it had not
occurred just before his baccalauréat examination, when he felt guiltily
inclined to stray from his father's footsteps. In any event, his ode,
which he wrote with a *lycée* chum named George Pajot, who often
kept him company, brought him more jeers than ovations at Saint-
Louis. "Baille told me that your confreres . . . took it upon themselves
for some strange reason to criticize your poem to the empress," wrote
Paul in a letter that included rhymed vituperations against Emile's
detractors. "It raised my hackles and I belatedly hurl at them this diatribe, the terms of which don't do justice to such literary dodos. . . .
If you see fit to pass along my compliment, go right ahead, and say
furthermore that if they insist on answering me, I await them one and
all, ready to pummel the first who dares show up."

Emile's oral examination took place at the Sorbonne, where a jury
of university professors in academic regalia quizzed him rapid-fire on
mathematics, physics, chemistry, history, natural history, modern languages, and French literature. Questions certified by the ministry were
drawn at random from an urn containing more than six hundred slips,
and each examiner recorded his estimate of the candidate's performance with little balls colored white for pass and black for fail. Most
juries did what they could to coax along students, who had already
shown their mettle by passing a written test. But the solemn mise-en-
scène of this ceremony, the knowledge that one's professional fate
hung in the balance, the weeks of cramming, or *bachotage*, often resulted in a hopeless muddle.

[6]"To deliver oppressed Italy from its yoke we saw our army hasten toward the
Alps. Roses were strewn along the paths they took. With continuous hurrahs welcoming it along the way everyone paid homage to its noble quality and applauded.
Onward, Frenchmen, fight in those lands where your fathers nobly fought before
you. Go conquer those whom their heel crushed underfoot. Go! Our emperor
leaves us for glory as our victorious battle song did in former days."

Such was Emile's predicament. After scoring well in science, he came undone. Questions about the capitularies and Einhard's annals caught him unprepared. His German proved inadequate for translating a text by Schiller. His interpretation of La Fontaine did not impress the jurors. And so it went, from one embarrassment to another, until the black balls outnumbered the white. "In the brief time allotted him a student cannot reveal the true extent of his knowledge, and further-more the examination must restrict itself to questions on the slip he has drawn," Zola wrote in 1877, still vexed by the memory of it. "The baccalauréat is a lottery pure and simple. I have had occasion to see weak students pass it on luck, and the reverse." Everything we know about the emotional burden Emile carried at eighteen suggests that hard luck, which might have tripped him up under any circumstances, had a powerful accomplice in his desire to free himself from high expectations and be seen as a good boy no longer. Good boys don't vanish overnight, however, and failing in literature rather than in sci-ence may have been one way of giving piety its due. Another was to rant against the system, to curse the jinx by which he would always feel threatened, and to resolve to make amends at the earliest opportunity.

In August he traveled to Aix for a summer of convalescence with Jean-Baptistin, who entered the Ecole Polytechnique in 1861, and Paul, who had just completed one year of penance at law school after getting his baccalauréat diploma on a second try. Three months later, Emile took the examination again, in Marseille, where juries were re-puted to be lenient, and failed it even more decisively. It was late November before he returned to Paris from the Midi. He had no plans, no prospects, and was certain of nothing except the fact that for the second time in his life, an engineer had died in the city of Marseille.

IV

CLOSED DOORS AND FEARFUL
MYSTERIES

H AD EMILE JOINED Jean-Baptistin Baille at the Polytechnique, his
material future would have been assured, for Second Empire
France was the engineer's El Dorado. Napoleon III declared that
a government could get away with violating legality or even liberty but
would be short-lived unless it promoted civilization's "larger interests,"
and in a country where men inspired by Saint-Simon's technocratic
utopia now occupied high office, civilization's larger interests were
believed to coincide with those of the entrepreneurial class furiously
at work laying railroad track, stringing telegraph lines, digging canals,
mining coal, smelting ore, building factories, and opening markets far
beyond European frontiers.

Although captains of industry had received encouragement from
heads of state before 1851, not until Napoleon III's ascendancy did
government predicate its very raison d'être on the belief that capital
must at all costs flow, and flow wherever possible into public works of
a magnitude previously unimagined. "Government exists in order to
help society overcome the obstacles to its progress. . . . It is the beneficent mainspring of every social organism," said the emperor,
whose liberal philosophy reflected, in part, the animus of a bastard at
war with tradition. Recognizing that France's economic life could not
accommodate modern technology unless it burst the financial structure laid upon it by the old regime, he presided over a financial revolution that saw credit banks multiply. "Government loans of the old
regime had been taken up, right down to 1847, by private banking
firms, of which the Rothschilds were the most famous, and the use to

which the money might be put was limited by their interests—those of an international plutocracy in close touch with the old dynasties of Europe," observes J. M. Thompson. "It was for this purpose that in 1852 the Brothers Pereire—a name not unknown in the financial affairs of the Revolution—founded the first Crédit Mobilier, which did not limit itself to state loans, but laid itself out to finance industrial societies: and, in order to extend its influence beyond anything attainable by the old-fashioned family banks, offered its shares to the general public." The danger was of overexpansion, and when overexpansion led to a crisis, conservative financiers like the Rothschilds did not lose the opportunity to cluck. But for fifteen years, between 1852 and 1867, the Crédit Mobilier and its partner, the Crédit Foncier, together with the Comptoir d'Escompte and numerous Sociétés de Dépot, all backed by the Bank of France, financed industry and agriculture, making Paris the financial center of the continent.

What this revolution wrought was a state of affairs succinctly described in the bon mot of a contemporary wit: "Business? Why, it's very simple: business is other people's money." With other people's money, the Pereires amassed several hundred million francs financing the Austrian State Railroad, the Imperial Ottoman Bank, the Compagnie Générale Transatlantique, the Grand Hôtel, public utilities, the Louvre department store, transportation companies. Money borrowed from the Pereires or raised by public subscription enabled men like Haussmann and de Lesseps to reconstruct Paris and to dig a canal across the Isthmus of Suez. Credit also sponsored lesser visionaries than these and, indeed, thrived on dream, disproving King Lear's maxim that "nothing will come of nothing."

As portrayed by the novelists Jules and Edmond de Goncourt in their famous journal, Second Empire France was a nation remarkable for its venality, with everyone from members of the imperial entourage down to *chefs de bureau* on the take. "France is like Molière's miser, closing its fingers around dividends and property, ready to submit to any Praetorian or Caracalla . . . so long as its profits are safe," they wrote. "Orders and castes have disappeared in a rout where, like two armies fleeing helter-skelter, two kinds of men crush each other: those, the clever and the bold, who want money *per fas et nefas*, and the comfortable, who would keep their gain at any price." While the Goncourts were misanthropic snobs who often exaggerated a truth the better to legitimize their hatred of bourgeois society, it is undeniable that the industrial revolution bred not only industrialists but speculators who swam in great schools toward the lure of instant profit.

Conspicuous among the latter was Louis Napoleon's own brother, the Duc de Morny, a bon vivant utterly without scruple in peddling the influence he enjoyed at court. But Morny distinguished himself only by the extent and flagrancy of his peculations. Unlike General de Saint-Arnaud (whose debts Louis Napoleon canceled on hearing him protest that "Fould [the Jewish minister of finance] counts on the market's decline,' while I, who have confidence in your star, Sire, invest on the principle that it will go up"), Morny frankly honored greed above all sovereigns and seized every opportunity to prove it. It was characteristic of the man that after representing France at Tsar Alexander's coronation he should have brought home from Moscow a document granting Crédit Mobilier, in whose profits he shared, the right to construct a Russian railroad system. No sooner had Louis Napoleon produced his designs for a Roman capital in Paris than Morny built a Pompeian resort in Deauville, where courtiers loaded with money made on real estate ventures spent their summers gambling some portion of it away.

The gambling fever on which Deauville thrived was epidemic. It raged in cafés and restaurants where talk revolved around stocks, bonds, mortgages, debentures. It drove people who otherwise toiled eleven hours a day for five francs or less to queue up outside Parisian town halls on the eve of national loan subscriptions and stay there all night long hoping that their investment would treble their meager savings. It made itself felt in every quarter, but nowhere more deliriously than at the Bourse, from which there rose a din that could be heard until 10 p.m. by strollers on the Boulevard des Italiens, quite some distance away. "The steps and colonnade of the Bourse were black with the swarm of tailcoats, and from the wings, beneath the great clock, came the clamor of bids and offers, the tidal roar of speculation that drowned out the muffled noise of the city," Zola wrote many years later in *L'Argent*. "Passersby turned their heads out of desire and curiosity, baffled by what was happening there, by the mystery of financial operations which few French brains can fathom, by the ruins or sudden fortunes that emerged from the gesticulation and from the barbarous shouts."

What Zola sought to convey in *L'Argent* is the idea that gambling fever became a substitute for religious exaltation, the Bourse a pagan temple, the broker a priestlike figure invested with magical power, financial jargon an incantatory language, and the French a worshipful throng. Few quarreled with his metaphor, for tradition had unquestionably been dealt a serious blow by circumstances far beyond anybody's control. Where bourgeois tradition held that the virtuous man planned, labored, and saved, that he found the reward for all he begrudged himself in his children's advancement and thus set posterity an example of the golden rule—circumstances now invited men to believe that one shrewd guess might repeal the curse put on them at birth. Paris swarmed with immigrants from provincial France who had come by railroad seeking fortunes in the capital, only to end up in some squalid tenement outside the customs barrier eating dust all the days of their lives. But a gambler could always point to the parvenus who justified Alexis de Tocqueville's contention that "there is no longer a race of wealthy men just as there is no longer a race of paupers; the former emerge every day from the bosom of the crowd and constantly return to it." Not since Revolutionary days, when the Convention decreed 1792 Year I, had Frenchmen with nothing to lose but something to wager greeted so optimistically the prospect of losing their past. One such Frenchman even became emperor. When Louis Napoleon (whose patronymic was his first imposture) said, "We are all of us newcomers," he spoke as the emperor of opportunists.

To what extent sudden wealth fostered conspicuous consumption was most apparent on the Boulevard, the district that encompassed the large theaters, where high society converged to feast at the Café Anglais, the Café Riche, and the Maison d'Or. Europe's financial center soon became its gastronomic capital, and chefs like Dugléré recaptured a position France had lost under Louis Philippe. "The Second Empire was for French cuisine what the reign of François I was for the fine arts, a renaissance," explains one culinary historian. "Weary of the previous regime, the new court spent without counting in its pursuit of luxury and its infatuation with appearances. Important households made themselves known by sumptuous receptions where the table had pride of place. The court, ministries, embassies, and many town houses became the school at which great artists, exclusively French, received their training. All foreign courts were our tributaries."

In 1862 Baron Haussmann reported that if the municipal government were to feed every inhabitant who regularly went hungry or who sacrificed other necessities in order not to starve, 1.07 million out of the 1.7 million Parisians would qualify for help. The average worker spent between 35 and 63 percent of what he earned on bread alone, and inflation, which saw prices rise far more steeply than wages during Louis Napoleon's reign, narrowed his chances of survival. Gendarmes arrested 35,000 vagrants in one year as the population of those reduced to scavenging, begging, and whoring swelled. Without rations from the municipality, they made do on garbage from the imperial feast. "[Our maid] tells me that recently, while passing the Maison d'Or on the morning after a masquerade ball, she saw a nun collecting scraps in a little cart," Jules de Goncourt noted in February 1859. Every day, long before dawn, *chiffonniers*—ragpickers equipped with hooks, lanterns, and voluminous bags—fanned out through the city. As familiar a sight in Second Empire Paris as the child prostitute, the organ grinder, and the ill-clad errand boy posted at street corners, they scurried from rubbish bin to rubbish bin, along with rats crazed by the demolitions that had exposed their nests beneath the former Marché des Innocents. Homeless rats—they, too, casualties of Napoleon III's grand design—became a veritable scourge.

The Zolas were all but destitute. Needing cheaper accommodations, they left their small flat on the rue Saint-Jacques sometime during April 1860 to live at 35, rue Saint-Victor, just east of the Latin Quarter and quite near the Seine, where they had first a single room on the second floor, then a garret eight flights up. "[I shall enjoy] the highest vantage point in our neighborhood, with an immense terrace overlooking all of Paris," Emile informed Paul in June. "It is a delicious little room which I shall furnish in the latest style: divan, piano, hammock, pipes galore, Turkish hookah, etc. And flowers, and a birdcage, and a fountain. Pure enchantment." To save face, to console himself, and because he feared that the plain truth might dissuade Paul from coming north, Emile often embellished his dreary circumstances. Until 1855, the rue Saint-Victor had run obliquely through a poor, quiet parish favored by pensioned governesses, retired professors, and career soldiers who spent their waning years in boardinghouses and congregated on benches at the nearby Botanical Garden. But this district lost its villagelike character after road gangs descended upon it to gouge out the rue des Ecoles and the rue Monge. In the decade that followed, it became a slum scheduled for redevelopment, where old apartment buildings stood forlorn amid the rubble of demolished neighbors. All around 35, rue Saint-Victor were mud, noise, and dust billowing up as far as Emile's terrace on the eighth floor. (By 1864 that terrace had disappeared, together with the building itself.)

The prospect of job hunting tormented Emile, who knew full well that having a *lycée* education without a *lycée* diploma was, in the world's opinion, like being a child born out of wedlock. He was neither fish nor fowl, and to such indefinable types, society offered drudge work. "You must know that I am not exactly Fortune's favorite, and it hurts me seeing myself, a big boy twenty years old, still dependent on my family," he confided to Paul in January 1860. "I have therefore resolved to do something about earning the bread I eat. I think that in a fortnight at most I shall start work with the customs administration. You who know me and know how I value my freedom will understand that it's a willful resolution, but I believe that to act otherwise would be wicked." If failing the baccalauréat examination had been, at least in part, an unconscious strategy he hoped would set him free from expectations to which Madame Zola held him hostage, then taxing himself with failure and suffering its most unpleasant consequences may have assuaged his guilt.

Many letters dwell on this conflict. No sooner did the plucky Zola speak than the Zola whom Goncourt later described as "doleful" and "whining" felt overwhelmed by despair. "I haven't finished my studies, I can't even speak proper French, I am completely ignorant," he lamented several weeks after announcing his resolution. "There are days when I find myself bereft of intelligence, when I wonder how someone worth so little could have entertained such vainglorious dreams. . . . I doubt everything, myself foremost. No fortune, no métier, only discouragement. No one on whom to lean, no woman, no friends next door." Determined to earn his livelihood yet fearful that the strength to compete in a man's world would never be his unless bestowed upon him by a muse, a surrogate father, or the trio of comrades, Emile wavered between categorical imperatives and fantasies of escape. "All I want is a cave in the side of a mountain," he told Paul, who found such fantasies entirely congenial. "I shall live there dressed in sackcloth if need be, like a hermit, heeding neither the world nor its judgments. Don't mistake what I write for a poet's whimsy; I'm quite serious, and were it not that I have a mother, I would long ago have tried to enact my dream." Now that Provence was Arcadia for him, he constantly evoked the delights of exploring nature with Cézanne and Baille, as if remembering how life had been before the Fall. And he let his mind wander even farther afield, to an "Orient" where contemplation took precedence over acquisition. "The world is not my stock-in-trade, money is not my element," he proclaimed when it seemed inevitable that Alexandre Labot, on whom he could still rely, would place him at the Customs House. His trade was writing verse, for which he prepared himself, like a priest burning incense, by smoking his pipe. This "literary ablution," as he like to call it, "banished foul ideas."

All the same, one did not need a poet's soul to enter government service with grim forebodings. France treated her minor civil servants shabbily, and Edmond Texier denounced her for it in the opposition newspaper Le Siècle. "Want, real want, the kind that causes the most grievous suffering, is no longer to be found in society's lower depths but in a middle zone populated by pariahs of the bureaucracy and administration," he wrote on February 14, 1859. "It is all the more frightful there because it dares not speak out loud and plasters a smile on its famished lips; it doesn't appear in rags, it is even properly dressed and sometimes wears gloves. The poverty that goes begging is less horrible than this gloved destitution." Emile earned sixty francs a month (or less than the very poorest country vicar), which lends credence to a contemporary report that the salary of functionaries remained in 1857 what it had been in 1807. As living became dearer, existence became nightmarish for this despised class, whose members were asked to make an outward show of bourgeois *distinction*, though it bled them dry. Zola knew whereof he spoke when, many years later, in *Pot-Bouille,* he portrayed Jules Pichon never visiting the theater, never leaving town, never surprising his wife, never speaking except obsequiously. Like Pichon, lower-echelon functionaries nested under eaves, and the offices they pushed paper through bore further witness to their pariahdom. "Ministerial offices have their own peculiar odor," wrote one observer, "an indescribable and indefinable odor in which there mingle the most horrible exhalations, gruel cooking on the stove, the mouse that croaked between two files, the rotting debris of daily meals swept into corners, fetid breath, the sweat of clothes, the leather of shoes drying near the fire." Neglect was the air they breathed, and a fresh recruit who found himself stifled by it would have caused great consternation by throwing open a window.

During his brief period of employment at the Docks Napoléon, which began around mid-April 1860, Emile spent every spare minute gazing through the window. In a huge, vaguely neo-Romanesque warehouse where goods shipped up the Canal Saint-Martin underwent customs inspection, he felt like Jonah swallowed by Leviathan. Outwardly there must have been little to distinguish him from other young clerks as he sat among them slope-shouldered, with baggy pants and a fringe of beard he had grown since leaving Saint-Louis. And this resemblance hurt even more than the dull tasks that put him in mind of grade school *pensums.* "My life is still monotonous," he wrote to Paul on April 26, at midnight.

> When, bent over the desk and writing God knows what, I sleep with my eyes wide open, a fresh memory sometimes flashes by of our joyous parties or of some site we cherished, and my heart sinks. I look up and behold sad reality; the dusty room with old paper piled high in sheaves, and clerks—most of them quite stupid—crowding round; I hear the monotonous screech of pens, of harsh words, of terms that sound like gibberish to me. And over there, playing on the windowpane, are sunbeams that have come to announce, as if in mockery, that out yonder nature is on holiday, that birds have melodious songs, flowers intoxicating scents. I lean back in my chair, close my eyes, and for one instant I see you near me, you, my friends; I also see those women I loved without knowing it. Then everything vanishes. . . . I take up my pen again and feel close to tears. Oh, freedom! freedom!

Letters to Baille, of which one very long example bears the superscription "At the Docks, May 14, 3 p.m.," show him yearning for love. "I try vainly to clutch life; I want some kind of hope that would let me live from day to day, I want to live, in short. But before me stretches endless desert."

That Emile had helped bring his predicament upon himself was something he could not have recognized without admitting first that confinement meant safety, that prison, however onerous, saved him from the danger he saw in losses to be suffered and rewards to be won outside. As a rule, picturing himself the victim of unscrupulous men or the child of evil times was easier than coming clean. "The ill wind of our century," "the wound of our century"—such romantic slogans recur throughout his early correspondence, and when Baille called him to account, he declared, "My entire excuse is the age I live in." During adolescence Baille often heard him blame "the age" or fate or bad luck (*guigne*). Nurtured by his mother on a debilitating rationale of martyrdom, Emile was behaving as he had always done in finding explanations for his fecklessness outside himself. It was also outside himself that he sought an object for his rage. "Derision! I heard [the crowd] around me murmur odious surnames. I saw it step back and point at me. I bowed my head and wondered what crime I had committed," he wrote to Paul, recalling childhood. "But when I got to know the world better . . . I recognized myself as a giant among dwarfs. . . . Pride and scorn became my gods. I could have exonerated myself, but I chose not to stoop so low. Instead, I conceived another scheme, which was to crush them with my superiority and let envy . . . eat them alive. I addressed myself to poetry, that divine consolation." This Rousseauian brief against society left unimpeached his most severe judge: himself. Claiming superiority, he had nonetheless fallen flat before his baccalauréat jury. Declaring himself innocent, he arranged to languish in the prison house of the customs administration. Therein lay another paradox, or a cruel twist of fate, as Emile might have called it: it was certainly not lost upon him—he who detected the joker everywhere and mockery even in sunbeams—that François Zola's son sat stranded by a barge canal watching water flow past.

Watching water flow past (when, as he declared in his poem "Le Canal Zola," a *real* man made it spring from rocks) is how he characterized his inability to approach women and conquer them. "Your guiding principle is to let water flow by and rely on time and fate," he wrote, chiding Paul, a stand-in for himself. "You have already employed this strategy in love, waiting, you said, for the propitious moment and circumstance. You know better than I do that neither one nor the other ever arrived. The water flows on and the swimmer, waking up one day, is astounded to find nothing there but hot sand. . . . In many ways, our characters are alike." If we can believe what Jules Vallès claims in his *Souvenirs*, telling a grisette that one wrote poetry was the open sesame to her bedroom, and the Latin Quarter abounded in shopgirls. But nerve failed when a "propitious moment" arose. "For almost a fortnight I've been weaving a wildly platonic love," he confessed to Paul on June 13.

A florist, a young girl who is living next door, passes beneath my window twice a day, in the morning at 6:30 and in the evening at 8. She's a small blonde, utterly graceful and well turned; small hands, small feet, the nicest kind of grisette. When I know she is to pass by, I station myself at the window. She comes, lifts her eyes, we exchange a glance, even a smile—and that's all. My God, how crazy it is to love from afar the least cruel of Parisian beauties, a florist! Not to follow her, not to speak to her! I'll tell you straight out, laziness and dreaminess are what explain me. Living in this way rather than in the other takes much less effort: I await my adored one while smoking a pipe. . . . And not knowing her, I endow her with a thousand qualities. I can invent a thousand delirious adventures and see her and hear her talk through the prism of my imagination.

Emile seldom allowed anyone but Paul to see him quite so naked. Here he told a truth that ultimately furnished material for numerous scenes in his novels involving people who peer through windows and holes at absent mothers, unfaithful mistresses, unpossessable bodies, phantomatic lovers. As these scenes so often suggest, to venture beyond the window is to invite something even worse than failure. The adventurer might actually succeed, which meant to "forget himself" or "die," and in Emile's imagination (where his father lived on) such metaphors of sexual ecstasy signified literal punishments. Holding himself aloof preserved an inner distance where, for all the pain it cost him, he did not risk personal extinction. Obsessively conjuring up Provence may have served the same purpose. With remembered idylls he girded himself against dread temptations of the present moment.

In 1859, during his summer holiday at Aix, there had been another fetching blonde he never dared to court. The name he gave her was "L'Aérienne"—Aerial—and this sobriquet, which made her even more remote, served as the title of a poem he wrote in correct, high-flown alexandrines. "Un soir, je l'aperçus dans une ombreuse allée/ Onduler comme un rêve à la forme voilée," it begins.

> Son regard incertain qui, vague, par moment,
> Sans paraître rien voir, caresse doucement,
> Son pas harmonieux, sa démarche légère
> Qui semble dans un vol se détacher de terre
> Sa taille qui se plie au vent comme une fleur,
> Me la firent dans l'ombre, en poète rêveur,

Prendre pour une fée, une vierge sereine,
Et surnommer tout bas du nom d'Aérienne.[1]

Later he inquired after her when he felt lonely. "Should you see Aerial,
smile at her for me," he instructed Baille in December 1859, and in
August 1860 he wrote to Paul: "I wanted to ask you . . . to speak to
me in your spare moments about some beautiful nymph. . . . Speak
to me about Aerial, about someone, about something, in verse, and at
length." What warmth their reports afforded him was not always pleasurable, since they kept alive a burning memory of himself prowling
timorously around Aix for the chance to glimpse his inamorata. "I
should have done my utmost to see her alone, or, if that proved impossible, to write her a letter summarizing what I wanted her to know,"
he thought as he sat with his pipe in the Jardin des Plantes one evening
and ruminated about opportunities missed the year before.

Here is how I would have put it: "Mademoiselle, it isn't a lover writing to you, it is a brother. I feel terribly isolated in this world and
need a young heart that beats only for me, that pities and consoles
me, judges and encourages me. I neither want nor dare ask for your
love. It would profane the sentiment to imagine that it can spring
forth between two strangers. All I desire is your friendship, a friendship that will grow as we acquaint ourselves with each other's characters. If one day you should find me worthy of a more tender feeling,
we would question our hearts, and if they beat in unison, we would
then begin a new mode of life. Meanwhile, my hand shall press yours
fraternally . . . etc., etc. Your brother."

This monologue appeased him until Baille wrote in August that Aerial
was spoken for. "Allow me to declare myself innocent of several grave
accusations," he protested by return mail, as if the woman incarnate,
along with his own unfraternal flesh, had to be denied instantly. "It
isn't S. . . . I love and perhaps still love. It is Aerial, an ideal being who
existed less in my sighted eyes than in my dreams. What do I care if
a girl from here below, whom I courted for an hour, has a lover? Do
you think me mad enough to prevent the rose from loving every butterfly that caresses it?" Baille's letters have disappeared, so we cannot
know for certain what Emile took to be "grave accusations." They may

[1]"I saw her one evening in a shady lane undulating like a veiled, dreamlike form.
Her vague and uncertain glance, which at times sweetly caressed without appearing to see anything, and her harmonious movement, her light-footed carriage,
which gave the impression that her figure, bending in the wind like a flower, could
suddenly fly away, made me—a dreamy poet seated in the shadows—take her for
a fairy, a serene virgin, and under my breath give her the name Arielle."

have been innocuous digs. But his response was that of the voyeur who pleads innocent by reason of Platonism: the woman he admired from afar did not exist outside his mind except as a crude representation of the Idea. For someone with eyes turned upward, nature demonstrating its promiscuity in one amour after another made an inferior spectacle.

Sententiousness pervades his early correspondence. Such arguments, which left him feeling neither virile nor chaste, were the only soldiers he had to throw against his fear that no woman could love an orphan, a stray, a sport of nature. And he marshaled them in language bordering at times on the evangelical. "In this materialist age . . . when commerce absorbs everyone, when the sciences, which have grown so big and robust, render man vainglorious and make him forget the supreme intelligence, a holy mission awaits the poet: at every moment and everywhere to show the soul to those who think only about the body, and God to those in whom science has killed faith," he preached to Baille, whose cynicism irked him. A letter written several months earlier contains the same sermon. "Would not the high school boy who avowed a platonic love—in other words, a holy and poetic thing—be looked upon as mad? But . . . one cannot truthfully say that love is dead, that our age is all materialism. A great and beautiful task . . . a task I myself dare envisage on occasion, is to arrange man's return to woman." Disinherited in a world made for entrepreneurs and scientists, Emile liked to imagine himself lording it over them in a realm of impalpabilities. There, they would see their mundane knowledge eclipsed by the "supreme intelligence" and recognize in their physical possession of womankind an emptiness to be filled by the poet-cum-spiritual mediator.

Other remarks suggest that mediator was not the role he really sought, or, rather, that the spiritual mediator concealed a sexual usurper. "How beautiful it would be to create an expression of love in which the past would not intrude, to write beautiful verse in which the soul alone would speak its joys and torments without borrowing hackneyed images, uttering apostrophes to Nature, etc., etc.," he wrote on June 15. "In short, a love poetry . . . one might venture to recite at the feet of the woman one loves without fearing that she will burst into laughter." What emerges here, before Zola developed it in fictional plots, is an obsession with the visitant—with a man whose ghost inhabits the woman he deflowered and grips her so tyrannically that when he returns, which he always does, she will, despite herself, discard for him her faithful suitor, her devoted husband, her children, her *Moi*. This charismatic predecessor is another version of the literary antecedent that he feared would intrude upon and ruin the effect of his love song. Both indicate how cumbersome Emile found the father whom Madame Zola enshrined as a "divinity." And taken together, they reveal the extent of his erotic investment in language. Words, provided he wrote totally *original* verse, were an abracadabra that compelled women to yield themselves. A poet endowed with such incantatory power could, like a first lover, cast spells on them, or be the kind of priest Zola later portrayed in *La Conquête de Plassans*, Ovide Faujas, who becomes an erotic cynosure for his female parishioners.

From two books by Jules Michelet, *L'Amour* and *La Femme*, which he took to quoting chapter and verse, Emile extracted a view of relations between the sexes that helped him subdue his fears even as it encouraged his grandiosity. He was not alone in this: progressive young men had mustered behind the great historian ever since Napoleon III removed him from his chair at the Collège de France in 1852 for refusing to pledge allegiance to the regime. On whatever subject their culture hero spoke—birds, insects, tobacco, the sea—they listened. A volume no sooner appeared than it became the vade mecum of every Latin Quarter dissident, and his books about woman, which caused furious debate when Hachette published them in 1858 and 1859, were especially effective at sorting out ideological allegiances. The Republic would not have established itself on firm ground, according to Michelet, until society delivered woman from dogma that held her captive in bonds of guilt. A new era required a new Eve. When she was no longer subject to the Church's distortions but was understood biologically, her nature would blossom and marriage would function as a true union of souls for having been consecrated without benefit of clergy. Nothing would remain of the slave whom priests had taught to hate enlightened government. Free, she would mother institutions that safeguard freedom itself. "The wise and charming woman whose life constitutes this book [*La Femme*] foresees quite clearly the imminent future of European societies. Great and profound renewals will not fail to occur in them. It will be incumbent on women and families to change accordingly."

The assumption on which Michelet predicated his idea of freedom was that woman can achieve it only through marriage, in loving a man who answers her desire to merge with him and thus become a person. "You must make a person of her, have her join you more and more in your reflective life," he counseled husbands. "She will . . . feel freer through you, happy for having more to give, for having a will the better to lose herself in you." Consumed by jealous fantasies about the young wife he took in late middle age, Michelet solaced himself with a philosophy that brings to mind the Pygmalion myth, or Molière's *School for Wives*. "You are [your wife's] father, and day by day you will engender her mind," "It is for the husband alone to explain everything to his wife," "All is secure when one has created one's wife oneself—

one knows thoroughly only what one has made": such phrases abound in *L'Amour* and *La Femme*, as if Michelet could not coin enough of them to buy legitimacy for the paradox that woman's conjugal thralldom marks her liberation from nothingness. Being nothing in herself but an amorous receptacle, she stands empty until man fills her with children and ideas. What passed in mid-nineteenth-century France for the results of anatomical investigation were invoked to support the argument that even thinking women, who, after all, carry ideas implanted by men, are pregnant women. A female brain, he wrote, resembles a womb. "Such is the strength and happy fatality of love that a beloved object can impregnate woman, penetrate her to the point of her actually becoming the object, so that while she may grow in feminine grace, what constitutes her core is man."

Michelet's influence on Zola was to manifest itself in two early novels, *Thérèse Raquin* and *Madeleine Férat*. One also detects it in the hereditary thesis of the *Rougon-Macquart* saga, which operates throughout like a demon, laying hold of individuals, thwarting their attempts to exorcise what entered them at conception, and congratulating itself when the self—the character born of reason, of tutelage, of experience—comes undone. But before *La Femme* and *L'Amour* were grist for Zola's literary mill, they were bulk for his undernourished ego, and it must have given him somewhat the same satisfaction to cite Michelet as to smoke a pipe. Stuffing letters with large pronouncements made him feel weightier than a young man who might, in his own words, be thrown off balance by "a woman's glance, a mere trifle, a devouring thought that returns every day." If man is woman's substance, he could project himself into one such clone and not imagine that she harbored a fatal judgment in her mysterious depths.

Emile found his clerical work increasingly tedious. After two or three weeks, on May 5, he told Paul that he was fed up and described his office as a "putrid stable," with everyone wallowing in the dung of official paper. From 9 a.m. to 4 p.m. he recorded customs declarations, copied letters, yawned, paced the floor, read *Le Siècle*, consulted his watch, and suffered, until late June, when he suddenly bade adieu to fellow clerks, for many of whom this deadly rotation became a career. "You ask me for details about my material life," he answered Paul toward the end of July. "I've left the Docks. Was it a good move? A bad one? The question is relative and a matter of temperament. All I can say is that I couldn't stay there any longer and so I quit. What I have in mind to do now I shall tell you presently, after I've set about doing it." Such purposefulness belies the waffling that preceded his decision, and as soon as memories of the Customs House began to fade, he almost wished himself back there. "I know perfectly well that one must live, that in order to live one must eat, and that to eat one needs money," he wrote to Baille in October. "How does one attune the lyre to the clerk's pen or the worker's tool? Some job I can perform with my left hand just to cover living expenses, a job in no way calling upon the intellect, muck work for its own sake—that's my personal hell, my daily tribulation. . . . Any job will do." The only mention of his mother in this voluminous correspondence with Cézanne and Baille refers to her as "the best of mothers," which tells us nothing about the way she behaved under duress. Nor do we know if she herself sought employment before 1862. It is clear, however, that losing Emile's pittance reduced the family income by enough to make her wonder whether they would soon find themselves on the street or among the ragpickers who inhabited shantytowns in the *banlieue.*

For a reprieve from that "personal hell" Emile often went outside Paris on day trips, and before long he had grown as familiar with the city's rural fringe as with the wilderness outside Aix. To Vincennes via the Picpus gate and beyond the woods to Saint-Mandé was one itinerary. Another took him to Fontenay-aux-Roses, where roads led south through the Bois de Verrières and François-René de Chateaubriand's former domain, the Vallée aux Loups, which was planted with laurels from Grenada, magnolias, Jerusalem pines, cedars of Lebanon. Starting from his own neighborhood, he sometimes walked across the Saint-Marcel quarter and continued walking hour after hour until, near Vitry, the *banlieue* in all its ugliness receded behind a landscape of bluebottles and wheat fields. He wrote to Paul on June 13:

> The other day, on a beautiful morning, I wandered into the fields some eight or ten miles from Paris. Don't you love bluebottles, those little stars that twinkle in the wheat? . . . I picked a beautiful big bunch of them, just like a blithe convent girl modestly got up in white. My Lord, a very big bunch indeed. Running through the meadows, happy not to see any more houses, to walk in the dew, to imagine myself in Provence hunting, partying at [Baille's] country house. I was alone and enjoyed myself to the full, with no one there to spy on me and mock me.

Even though Vitry lay halfway between suburban railroad lines, Emile could not have gone far without encountering some of the Parisian horde laden with picnic baskets who, on a typical June Sunday, boarded trains to refresh themselves *en plein air.* "Sunday is . . . the day when, throwing care aside, the artisan, the shopman, or the clerk puts on his holiday coat and goes forth in search of pleasure: a morning spent in the pretty environs of the metropolis . . . is the mode in which most of our lively neighbors while away the day," explained the author of one English guidebook, and Zola himself was to claim that this exodus, which became even more numerous when tour boats, called *bateaux-mouches*, were launched in 1867, involved some half million people.

Emile gave Cézanne and Baille very little information about his social life, as though the picture of it he wanted them to see featured two empty spaces which they alone could fill. But an occasional anecdote suggests that Paris was not all darkness and woe. Student painters from Aix regularly traveled north to work at the atelier of Père Suisse on the Ile de la Cité or to attend the Ecole des Beaux-Arts, and one of them, Jean-Baptiste Chaillan, entered Emile's life as a stand-in for Cézanne, through whom they had met. "Last Sunday, Chaillan spent the whole day with me; we had lunch together, then dinner, chatting about you, smoking our pipes," he informed Paul on April 26. "He's a fine boy, but my God, what simplemindedness, what ignorance of the world! I should think it most improbable that he will ever succeed. On the other hand he will never be unhappy. . . . He'll retire to his village before it's too late, or be content to paint mediocre portraits for whatever price they'll fetch." Writing mock-heroic verse about a foolish classmate or a senescent teacher was a game Paul and Emile had enjoyed during their school days, when they themselves were objects of ridicule, and poor Chaillan became their latest victim. In all likelihood Emile felt angry at having to settle for the companionship of a yokel who retired at 9 p.m., wore a night bonnet, and spent hours every day copying masterpieces at the Louvre to as little effect as Charles Bovary poring over medical texts. "He showed me a copy he had done of Rubens's *Descent from the Cross*. Let me tell you, Chaillan-Rubens is a sorry sight. Luckily, night had fallen so I couldn't take in the full horror of this little canvas."

But Chaillan improved as warm weather roused in him a Provençal whose demonstrations of sentimentality Emile found endearing. Plied with a little wine, he vowed eternal friendship, and by way of friendship set to work on a mythological tableau for which Emile, dressed in a sheet and given a lyre, posed as Zeus's musician son, Amphion. From his account of how they disported themselves in the garret at 35, rue Saint-Victor, one gathers that Emilie Zola occupied separate quarters on a lower floor, with Father Aubert. "We've begun the painting of Amphion in my eighth-floor room, a paradise complete with terrace, where we survey all of Paris," he wrote to Paul late in July, when prospects for a summer reunion seemed dim.

Chaillan appears at around 1 o'clock. Pajot, a young man whom I've told you about, follows hard on his heels; we light our pipes and puff away until we can barely make out our faces. Then there's the noise—these gentlemen dance and sing and, upon my word, I imitate them. Are you looking around for bottles and glasses? Right you are, they're here on my desk, filled with a certain white wine called Saint-Georges, which bears some resemblance to the cooked variety, both in its delicious flavor and its treachery. The rogue took Chaillan unawares several days ago and dealt him such an underhanded blow that he sat painting every fly in sight and smoking tinder which he swore was excellent tobacco. As for me, I pose half naked—an inconvenience, but that's the sublime part of the spectacle. With glasses tinkling I dictate to Pajot whatever verse comes to mind, sometimes farcical stuff, at other times serious. . . . It's a real smoking den . . . and my only regret is that you're not here to join in the laughter.

On another occasion Pajot, whose normal behavior was decorous if not meek, climbed onto the roof and peed down a chimney. Zola told this anecdote twenty-five years later, in 1886, while reminiscing over dinner with Alphonse Daudet and Edmond de Goncourt. "[He said that] he had never been happier than in those days, despite his impoverishment," noted Goncourt, who knew better than to take him at his word. "He never doubted his future success. Not that he had any very clear idea how the future would turn out, but he felt certain that he would succeed, explaining . . . his self-confidence as follows: 'that if he lacked faith in his work, he believed in his effort.' " Had Pajot and Chaillon been present, the evening might have ended like *L'Education sentimentale*, with all of them sighing, *C'est là ce que nous avons eu de meilleur* ("Those were the days"). By then, Pajot had become a police commissioner, Chaillan had long since given up art to earn his livelihood as an itinerant merchant, and Zola had triumphed often enough to realize what he didn't tell his literary friends—that no degree of success would ever abolish his fear of suddenly going limp.

It flattered Emile to see Pajot record mere throwaway lines and Chaillan portray him as Amphion, but he was left wondering whether he really had a poetic vocation. Once he sobered up, doubts came back in force and undermined the small body of verse on which his self-esteem rested. "I know very well that I am still floundering, that I am not mature, that I am searching for the right path," he confessed to Paul in August 1860. "You write with your heart, I write with my mind. You firmly believe what you say, while for me it's often only a game, a brilliant lie." At the same time, we find him embracing a radically different view of himself in a letter to Baille. "Banish the clergy: I have no truck with them. Prayer is the only intermediary I accept between the Lord and myself. Banish commentators: I have my own idea of an eternal Power and worship it, without wishing to engage in theological quibbles." The feeling that his poems rang false,

which they did, and the assertion that his prayers were more effica-
cious than knowledge complemented each other. As a confidant of the
Lord or as an imposter unworthy of consideration by serious men,
Emile put himself too high or too low. Now abject, now grandiose, he
longed for paternal guidance but scorned paternal authority.

It seemed that only God the Father could rescue him, and it was a
man godlike in stature and remoteness whom he asked to legislate his
future when, on September 8, he wrote to the exiled Victor Hugo at
Hauteville House on Guernsey:

Sir,
 It is often said that the man of genius owes himself to youth, that
one of his most sacred duties is to encourage those who have received
the divine spark and to detain those who have taken the wrong path.
The young man writing this letter dares, then, to address his beloved
poet, the man of genius whose paternal solicitude for all things
young, free, and loving is common knowledge.

 When I left secondary school, alone in the world except for my
excellent mother, I wanted the opinions I formed in every matter to
be my own. Where literature was concerned, the directions one could
take were numerous. I explored every school and finally, having
thought it through, returned to your ideas on art, those eminently
true and pertinent ideas I had accepted in childhood with the faith
of enthusiasm.

 I am now twenty. As I detect within myself a faint echo of the
sublime voice that inspires you, I sometimes let my thoughts break
into song. But my lyre, still muffled, provokes neither jeers nor ovations. Alone and unknown, I stammer in the darkness . . .

 A day comes when this solitude begins to weigh. One understands
that one is not yet ready to face the public, yet one has grown weary
of hearing nothing but silence around oneself. One sits discouraged
and awaits the word of praise or criticism that will tell one whether
to advance or retreat, assuming there is still time for either. Such is
my predicament. Tired of walking in the dark . . . , I suddenly halted
and looked about for a torch to guide me. It was then, Sir, that I
thought of you . . . , the greatest and most celebrated poet of our
age. I see nothing out of the ordinary in this audacity. I come as a
student to his master, as a dreamy and passionate young man who
bows before the author of *Hernani* and *Les Feuilles d'automne*, as a
lover of liberty and of love who pays homage to the sublime cantor
of those two divinities. . . . May my feeble voice remind you that the
France you love so well still remembers her poet, and that young
hearts . . . are obliged to leave the fatherland and fly to your land of
exile.

 It remains for me, Sir, to excuse myself for importuning you and
sending you such a long poem. I know how much each of your mo-

ments counts for our literature and can only allege my fervent desire to be better known by you. It is no doubt a very flawed work . . . and has no bearing on present-day politics. To excite your interest in my hero, I can tell you that he is not a mere figment of my imagination but has been drawn from life. May he find favor with you. In all events, I am certain that you will winnow the wheat from the chaff . . . and I take the liberty to ask you for your precious advice.

To the twenty-year-old who felt out of joint with society, revealed truth came from the Channel Islands, and here again Emile followed where republican opinion led. One contemporary declared that in their reverence for Hugo, intellectuals under Napoleon III resembled half-pay officers glorifying the memory of Napoleon I after Waterloo. They swore by him apostolically, they read smuggled copies of *Les Châtiments,* and they called him "Le Père," as if to identify themselves as a distinct tribe. "I am nothing, . . . but the situation today is such that to utter my name is to protest, . . . to utter my name is to affirm liberty," Hugo told Jules Janin in 1856, when admirers already made regular pilgrimages to Guernsey, and sent him letters which a packet boat delivered by the armload. Most of these went unanswered.

Had Hugo read "Paolo," the seven-hundred-line poem on which Emile's fate was supposed to hinge, he would have recognized an imitation of "Rolla," with nothing of the wit and poignancy that distinguish Musset at his elegiac best. Where Musset made classical diction work for him by using it to play up the despair of would-be heroes in an unheroic age, the *style noble* as Emile practiced it was simply obsolete. His poems labor under the dead weight of expletives ("Alas!," "Ah!"), apostrophes ("Oh, gracious friend"), periphrases, euphemisms that he and every other rhymester who had been nurtured on seventeenth-century verse brought down from the attic like family heirlooms held in store for ceremonial occasions. Amid all this highly polished old furniture, even feelings that must have kept him awake at night come out sounding wooden:

> Ah! sois ma Béatrix, vierge aux pudiques voiles;
> Descends, viens d'ici-bas arracher ton amant;
> Et, le front couronné de rayons et d'étoiles,
> Quittons ce vil limon pour le bleu firmament.
> O vierge de seize ans, frêle bouton de rose,
> O fleur humide encore des baisers de la nuit.[2]

[2]"Ah! be my Beatrice, virgin of the modest veils. Descend, come here below to tear away your lover, and, your brow crowned with stars and rays of light, let us leave this vile clay for the blue firmament. O sixteen-year-old virgin, frail rosebud, O flower still moist from kisses of the night."

The three long poems he joined under the title *L'Amoureuse Comédie*—"Rodolpho," "L'Aérienne," "Paolo"—abound in such clichés, which were to journeymen verse of the period what figurative stereotypes were to Salon art. With enough of them, one always had material on hand to complete a pretty alexandrine, and embellishing thoughts that could not be seen naked characterized Emile's whole poetic effort. "My verse was very weak and decorative, if no worse than that of contemporaries who went on rhyming," he himself admitted years later. "The only thing in which I take some pride is the awareness I had of my mediocrity as a poet and the decision to do our century's heavy work with the rough-hewn tool of prose."

Yet obsessions that show through this rhetorical scrim turn out to be the same as those from which he would create much better poetry in the prose of *Les Rougon-Macquart*. We repeatedly find young men, for example, standing outside the world harboring an unavowable love or entering it only to suffer betrayal. Paolo never quite meets sixteen-year-old Marie as he hides behind pillars while she prays and gazes up at her lighted window:

> Depuis deux ans, Paolo suivait ainsi Marie;
> Depuis bientôt deux ans, le soleil le trouvait
> A la porte du vieil hôtel où la chérie,
> Dans son repos d'enfant, souriante, rêvait;
> Et l'étoile du soir, dans quelque recoin sombre,
> Le surprenait encore, caché, rêvant dans l'ombre,
> Les yeux sur la fenêtre ou, vague, par moment,
> Une forme aux longs plis glissait confusément.[3]

A lighted window also figures in "Rodolpho," whose titular hero, having witnessed his sixteen-year-old mistress betraying him with his best friend, impales them both, then commits suicide:

> Rodolpho s'accouda sur le balcon de pierre,
> D'un geste frémissant écartant le rideau,
> Tandis que, déjà sale et blanche de poussière,
> La couronne de fleurs tombait sur le carreau.
> "Hélas! murmura-t-il, c'était une chimère,
> Oh! Seigneur, qu'ai-je fait pour que vous, le Puissant,
> Vous laissiez éclater ainsi votre colère

[3]"For two years, Paolo thus followed Marie; for almost two years, the sun found him at the door of the old town house where the cherished one, smiling in her child's sleep, dreamed. And the evening star surprised him still there, hidden in some dark recess, dreaming, his eyes fixed on the window where, at times, a vague form in long folds was to be seen gliding confusedly."

Et la laissiez tomber sur un grain de poussière
Que le vent du matin pulvérise en passant.
Pitié! Seigneur, pitié! je ne suis qu'un enfant."
Et, là-bas, il voyait dans un fougueux désordre,
Rose aux bras d'un amant s'enlacer et se tordre.[4]

Almost every poem involves something hidden from view, half-seen or unmasked, and in "Religion" his paranoia, which conjured up numerous hobgoblins, led him to picture God as a secret agent delighting in obfuscation:

Toujours, toujours, ce Dieu se plaît à se voiler;
Même aux pages du Ciel je n'ai pu l'épeler[5]

God is inscrutable, language veils meaning, limpid water conceals muck, vague forms glide behind curtained windows. What Emile's poetry makes clear is made clearer still by his correspondence, where the antithesis between *être* and *paraître*, or reality and appearances, recurs so often as to suggest that it had become the principle on which he relied to organize thought itself. "The ground is covered with mud, the sky with clouds, the houses with ugly wash, the women with paint of every color," he wrote to Cézanne in January 1860. "Here [in Paris], there is always a mask before the face, and it is by no means certain that what you see when you unmask an object is the object itself. It may be a second mask." One such object was his own verse, which had deserted him to join the fashionable masquerade. "Something like a veil covers the ideas I want to express, my verse no longer has any strength or sharpness," he complained. And he laid his predicament at the doorstep of civilization, whose inherent duality rendered poets impotent: "The word civilization . . . signifies good and bad. Effeminate mores and always putting up a false front are the bad qualities to be found in civilized men. It is obvious that these qualities do not beget great poets." As far as we know, Emile had not yet read Rousseau's great work on this subject, *Lettre à d'Alembert sur les spectacles*, but his indictment of Parisian society for cultivating deceit, for intriguing, and for succumbing to the wiles of women is pure Rousseau.

[4]"Rodolpho rested his elbows on the stone balcony, parted the curtain tremulously while the wreath of flowers, already dirty and white with dust, fell to the floor. 'Alas!' he murmured, "it was a chimera. Oh, Lord, what have I done that you, the Almighty, should thus vent your anger on a grain of dust which the morning wind pulverizes in passing. Have pity! Lord, have pity! I am only a child!' . . . And over there, he saw, in passionate disorder, Rose twisting and entwining herself around a lover."
[5]"Ever and again this God takes pleasure in veiling himself. Even on the pages of Heaven, I couldn't decipher him."

Bound up with this perception of the universe as opaque was the ideal of perfect transparency, which also calls to mind Rousseau, who boasted that he would walk about in public even if his brain were made of glass, since his skull contained nothing but virtue. Only divine light could penetrate utter darkness, and "Paolo" describes how Emile imagined life would be when it did:

> Aussi viendra le temps où la seule prière
> Sera celle ou deux voix mêleront leurs accents,
> Où les bras enlacés, deux anges de la terre
> Offriront leur amour à Dieu comme un encens;
> Où le temple divin ne sera plus l'asile
> D'un pudeur à feindre et d'un vice à cacher;
> Où le corps pour forcer l'âme à ne point pécher
> N'ira plus lachement dans un cloître inutile,
> Alors la seule loi sera le grand Amour;
> Prières et baisers, hautement, en plein jour.[6]

Eight floors up, he happily spun gossamer reveries of marrying a female alter ego with God's benediction. The outsider thus became the anointed one, the cryptic world became legible, and the no-trespass sign posted before every desired object became a license to regard Creation as his earthly paradise. It is significant that Zola, whose novels often feature Edenic gardens, greatly admired Bernardin de Saint-Pierre's Rousseauian tale about two children on a tropical island, *Paul et Virginie*. An island where soul mates born for each other and chaperoned by Providence encounter nothing foreign or unfamiliar was where he himself sought refuge from the sense of being society's odd man out. "It is true," he wrote to Baille, "that the author ends up by having Virginie die. In my view he was wrong to do so, and I don't see why these fraternal lovers [*frères amants*] could not continue their idyll as spouses." The ambiguity raises the question whether his ideal woman legitimized certain homoerotic impulses. Something similar may lie behind the recurrent nightmare of a young man discovering the woman with whom he falls in love to have been deflowered and emotionally invested by some older friend of his: the shared woman serves as mediator, or passionate link. Emile's obsessive talk about

[6]"The time will come when the only prayer will be that in which two voices mingle, in which two arms intertwined—two angels of the earth—will offer their love to God like incense; in which the divine temple will no longer be the asylum for feigned modesty and hidden vice; in which the body will no longer have recourse to a useless cloister to force the soul not to sin. When that time comes, Love will be the only law, and it will manifest itself openly, in broad daylight, with prayers and kisses."

masks bespoke his own duplicity. Hidden from himself, lost between
être and *paraître*, he groped among chimeras of every description,
searching for a light to dispel them; but the luminous utopia he proposed was even more hermetic than his dark cave. Like the island
kingdom of Paul and Virginie, who are one person in their telepathic
intimacy, it let him live alone, with no "other" to judge him, to inhabit
him, to obstruct his view or curb his will:

> Le Seigneur, entendant, ainsi qu'un chant de lyre,
> Monter l'hymne sacré des amants en délire,
> Exaucera leurs voeux de paix, de liberté![7]

How far he traveled on that vision may best be judged from the historical sweep of the *Les Rougon-Macquart,* whose characters, in generation after generation, struggle against the ghosts inside them to
achieve identity.

Emile's flight from a hostile world into the dream of an island kingdom provided inspiration for several tales which he wrote during the
early 1860s and published as *Les Contes à Ninon* in 1864. The heroine
of "Soeur-des-Pauvres," for example, is a ten-year-old drudge mistreated by foster parents, who, having acquired from the Virgin an
amulet that lets her conjure up money at will, exercises her magic to
good effect throughout the poverty-stricken countryside, where she
becomes a vagabond queen followed by a horde of worshipful beggars.
"They saw the child halt on the crest of a hill; she stood still, contemplating the plains she had just enriched, and her tatters were silhou-
etted black against the twilit sky," wrote Emile in a scene that
curiously evokes his father, whom he had pictured standing godlike on
a mountain enriching or fertilizing the plain below. "The beggars gathered around her; they were a great somber mass quivering the way
restive crowds do. Then silence prevailed. Soeur-des-Pauvres, high in
the sky, smiled at seeing this multitude beneath her." The adolescent
duo in "Aventures du grand Sidoine et du petit Médéric," a dumb
giant with a brilliant midget perched in his ear, also loom large as they
walk the earth like Gargantua or Candide observing human folly from
their superior perspective. They at least acknowledge mankind. Elsewhere children are fugitives rather than picaresques. In the titular hero
of "Simplice," we have a prince disheartened by human corruption,
whose unmanly distaste for rough sport and carnal pleasure earns him
such contempt that he finds sanctuary in a forest. There the unsuccessful heir apparent becomes the filiarch of nature, living peacefully

[7]"The Lord, hearing, like the song of a lyre, the sacred hymn of delirious lovers,
will fulfill their wish for peace, for liberty!"

until a nymph named Fleur-des-Eaux reveals herself to him. Fate has it that she will die of her first kiss and so she does, along with him, when the two finally embrace. "Their lips united, their souls flew away." This denouement is not what might have been anticipated from one who faulted Bernardin de Saint-Pierre for cutting short Paul and Virginie's idyll, but the kiss that kills pubescent girls (as though puberty itself were the kiss of death) was to serve Zola again and again in *Les Rougon-Macquart*.

Emile descended from his lofty perch to keep abreast of events down below. It was a contentious time, when liberal reforms granted by Napoleon III were emboldening critics of his regime and *Le Siècle* found an ardent public in young men like Emile, who quoted its editorials.

On the far Left little papers multiplied as quickly as the censor could squash them, living only long enough to deliver a tirade against the Church or materialism. One such ephemerid, *Le Travail*, whose masthead featured the name Georges Clemenceau, published a long excerpt from "Rodolpho" in 1862. Another, started by alumni of Saint-Louis, brought Emile to the attention of judicial authorities, as we know from a report prepared by the attorney general after Emile's first novel appeared in 1865. "He began his studies in Aix and finished them in Paris at the Lycée Saint-Louis," it reads. "There he met that group of young men, hardly more than children, who, three years ago, edited *La Revue du Progrès*—Messieurs Xavier de Ricard, Racot, Paillon, Sallet, and Joubert, all five having been dealt with sternly by the law for audacities of every kind. He is still on intimate terms with most of them." The report put him nearer this clique than he actually stood, but it calls up a whole way of life that goes unmentioned in his letters to Baille and Cézanne: police spies keeping watch over the Latin Quarter, people vociferating at cafés and restaurants hospitable to radical opinion, or in the Jardin du Luxembourg, or on the street, where fistfights often broke out between *étudiants* (antiestablishment) and *calicots* (proregime).

It was a tight world. The latest word spread through it like wildfire, and a word to the wise sufficed to assemble its constituents for demonstrations against an objectionable play at the nearby state theater, the Odéon, or against the philosopher Ernest Renan, whose recently published *Vie de Jésus* believers considered blasphemous and atheists casuistic, when he gave his first lecture at the Collège de France. Did Emile join this chorus? In his memoir "The Days of My Youth," we see him doing solitary things. "If I did not find food for the stomach, I found it for the mind; for when I was not seeking work or exploring the banks of the Bièvre or the plain of Ivry, I roamed the quays of

Paris reading the second-hand books, which scores of dealers set out
for sale in little boxes on the parapets." Some part of him preferred
to hang back and record than to demonstrate on stage. But the intellectual commotion he felt all around excited a pride that let him rise
above his misery. "What harm is there in Paris being the intellectual
center; there is but one sun for countries of the earth and it lights and
heats them all," he declared to Baille in July 1860. "Paris is the star of
intelligence, sending its rays to the most distant provinces. Paris is the
head of France; the higher the head is raised, the taller the body grows.
. . . Since political decentralization has been rejected, why shouldn't
the same apply to literary decentralization?" Before long this chauvinistic feeling had become his settled view.

Emile eagerly snatched up ideas thrown out by the intelligentsia.
While his portrait of the young artist browsing through secondhand
bookstalls may have been designed to conceal this debt—to present
his intellectual baggage as material randomly acquired—the evidence
suggests that he read what *Le Siècle* recommended be read and propounded in his correspondence what he heard in lectures called "Les
Conférences de la rue de la Paix." The central figure here was one
Emile Deschanel, who organized the lecture series along with several
others known for their staunch commitment to the cause of free
thought. A brilliant teacher at the Ecole Normale Supérieure, he had
lost his post when his book *Catholicisme et Socialisme* appeared in
1850, and after Louis Napoleon's coup d'état found himself packed
off to Brussels, where he lived in exile, giving public courses attended
by both men and women (which outraged ecclesiastical authorities)
until the imperial government amnestied all political criminals on Assumption Day 1859. One year later, a fellow Normalien, Albert Le
Roy, proposed that the group exploit Napoleon's newfound lenience
to air their thoughts in public. "We do with the spoken word what the
newspaper does with the pen. The lecture is therefore, like the paper,
one of the instruments of progress, one of the forms of freedom," he
wrote. The purpose of the lectures, which covered not only science
and literature but geographical exploration, was to "spread knowledge,
stir ideas . . . , uplift souls mired in matter, coarse pleasure, and lucre,
rescue them from stupefaction and prejudices, from vices, ignorance,
and servitude." From December 1860 through the middle of 1862 they
held forth three times a week, arousing such controversy that the imperial administration finally silenced them. It was 1864 before the series resumed.

In an early lecture entitled "The Question of Physiology Applied to
Literary Criticism," Deschanel sounded the call for an attack on critical precepts widely held to be inviolable and on writers whose work
connived with church, state, and bourgeoisie. Just as the historian Hip-

polyte Taine declared that "virtue and vice are products, like vitriol and sugar," so Deschanel argued that the critic needed tools akin to the natural scientist's, literature being an outgrowth of material circumstances or deterministic forces. Properly analyzed, any literary fragment would, he told the audience, reveal its author's era, temperament, age, sex, profession, habitat. No one was exempt since no one had ever existed outside nature, and his positivist argument swept aside the claim to moral and aesthetic transcendence made on behalf of classical literature by those who wanted present-day realities, including the language that drove them home, excluded from literary discourse. "What one seeks in a piece of writing is a man," he stated. "The artist creates what he sees because he mingles with it: he fecundates it, transforms it, remakes it in his own image."

In this nineteenth-century sequel to the old debate between ancients and moderns, Deschanel's colleagues joined him in urging that artistic perception be set free from the prison house of consecrated models. Eugène Pelletan, who chose "progress" as his theme, traveled far and wide through European history to show how "one recognizes the true greatness of a people by the degree of freedom the spoken word enjoys among them." Léon Laurent-Pichat then joined the fray with a series of lectures on poetry in which academic verse was held up to ridicule. "Let the muse take off the worn hand-me-downs of another age; don't drag her to archaic masquerades, to the carnival of Olympus!" he exclaimed. Real art emerges when a "temperament" uninhibited by convention grasps the world it sees, hears, and feels:

> If I see a dreamer whom nothing moves, who writes without anger . . . , who laughs mirthlessly and rails unindignantly, an implacable artist who is heedless of those he passes on the street, who contemplates beauty but cares nothing for the soul, who feeds on cold symbols, a dervish of art, a marabout of poetry and plastic form who sings love by the book—to him I say: "You do not perform a function, all you do is ply a trade. You juggle words, you don't stir ideas. You scorn the crowd because you don't like humanity. . . . You lack the terrible audacity of the thinker who usurps and accepts the responsibility of creation!"

Some eighty years before Sartre popularized the term *littérature engagée*, it had its spokesmen on rue de la Paix, where newspapers like *La Réforme littéraire* recorded not only what was said but that which the police had denied Deschanel and others permission to say. Word thus spread from a small auditorium into the Latin Quarter and throughout Paris, kindling enthusiasm or rage among those who did not attend.

Several of Zola's well-known formulations lead us straight back to these lectures: "A work of art is a corner of Creation viewed through a temperament," for example, or "A work is simply the free and lofty manifestation of a personality." The change wrought in him by his contact with the intelligentsia can be inferred from his correspondence, as a new voice began to make itself heard above the clamor of adolescent affinities. Earlier on, in March 1860, he had expressed admiration for Ary Scheffer because this Salon painter was "a poet in every sense of the word, hardly ever painting the real, tackling the most sublime, the most delirious subjects." One year later, under Laurent-Pichat's influence, he declared that the artist must steer a middle course between romantic grotesquerie and Parnassian aestheticism. "Yes, one must drop the gutter muse, violent effects, lurid colors, heroes whose singularity resides in some physiological quirk. No, one must not go to the opposite extreme; no, poetry must not be devoid of life, must not be written for poets alone and speak only of love." Having formerly lapped up the poetry of Victor de Laprade, who did in verse what Scheffer did in paint, Emile now found it indigestible. "Man partakes of the brute and the angel and it is precisely this mixture that constitutes what, by common accord, we call the human element, it is from the eternal struggle between body and soul that morality is born," he wrote to Baille in a Montaigne-like reflection.[8]

> Always showing us heaven is very nice, but I am above all a living man and although I find commerce with the angels highly agreeable, I would like to encounter in [Laprade's] verse some familiar face on which to rest my eyes from the celestial light, a few fellow creatures whose feelings, joys, and tribulations move and interest me.

The poet should, he told Baille in July 1861, "study his contemporaries, their deeds and words." For a young man from a classical *lycée*, who once courted disaster when he dared to challenge the usefulness of Greek, this precept was not banal. It went against everything drummed into him since childhood and conferred upon Deschanel's group the dignity of heresiarchs. He must have felt that his new masters had, in some sense, begotten him anew by authorizing him to lower himself and look at people, at commonplace things, at his own body. On that level, he could manage without diplomas.

But if his not having a diploma hastened what in retrospect would

[8]Zola was immersing himself in Montaigne's essays, which had been the subject of a lecture by Deschanel, and absorbing his lessons on human nature. It should be noted that Montaigne, though widely read outside *lycées*, did not become required reading for the baccalauréat examination until 1860.

seem to have been a fortunate fall, it continued to hurt emotionally and materially. Seasons of dire want lay ahead. In February 1861 the Zolas left the rue Saint-Victor and rented separate quarters on the rue Neuve-Saint-Etienne-du-Mont, just behind the Pantheon, where narrow, shabby streets winding down from the top of Mont Sainte-Geneviève formed a labyrinthine ghetto. Again Emile's room looked out over Paris. "I really don't know what fate is at work in my choice of lodgings," he wrote to Cézanne on February 5, 1861.

As a child in Aix I lived in Thiers's house. I come to Paris and my first room is Raspail's. Now . . . I've moved out of my splendid eighth floor . . . and chosen another garret, the very one in which Bernardin de Saint-Pierre wrote most of his works. It's a real jewel, this little room: small to be sure, but cheered by sunlight and utterly novel. One gets to it by climbing up a spiral staircase and there are two windows, one facing north, the other south. In short, a belvedere, with the whole city as its horizon. I almost forgot to tell you that my new street is called Neuve-Saint-Etienne-du-Mont and that my new number is 24. But send your letters to me in care of my mother at number 21.

Bernardin de Saint-Pierre had indeed lived there and this local coincidence served Emile's need to bolster himself with famous antecedents, to believe that he went where greatness led, to adorn the plain truth that poverty rather than fate was the agent at work in his choice of lodgings. Eight or ten francs a month got him something like Rodolphe's belvedere in *Scènes de la vie de bohème*. It was a glass cage perched on the roof of an old tenement, with no fireplace. The two windows let wind whistle through, and in winter, which Emile spent bundled up in bed trying to write, frost completely shrouded his view of Paris. On the rue Saint-Victor he had learned how to cook and bake ("by way of reconciling the frugality that Baille preaches but doesn't practice and the gluttony he practices but doesn't preach," as he explained to Cézanne), but now there wasn't money enough for one proper meal a day. Unless his mother fed him he often went hungry, surviving on coffee and bread with two pennies' worth of cheese, some fried potatoes, or chestnuts bought from a street vendor.

His health suffered. Like his mother, he had a nervous stomach, which, even during years of plenty, was to incapacitate him at times with colic. It did not tolerate this meager diet, and anxiety over the future made matters worse. "My stomach and the future worry me," he confided in Baille on June 10, adding that physicians he had consulted could not explain to his satisfaction why his appetite should be by turns voracious and nonexistent. Nor could they diagnose symptoms that afflicted him when he felt especially bleak. "In the past several days I have had a bad attack of spleen. This illness presents peculiar characteristics: despondency mixed with restlessness, physical and emotional suffering. Everything seems wrapped in a dark veil; every part of me ails. I have an exaggerated sense of pain as well as of joy, and feel, moreover, almost completely indifferent to whether good or bad befalls me. My vision is impaired, my judgment infirm. An immense ennui bleaching and deflowering all my sensations, an ennui that burdens me wherever I go, wiping out the past and soiling the future." Lest Baille interpret his vague disorders as a malingerer's alibi, Emile assured him that he had not failed to secure employment for lack of trying. "Determined to earn my livelihood by any means, I can't even get routine clerical work." Not being a French citizen may have made some difference in this regard. On December 7, eight months after his twenty-first birthday, he applied for citizenship at the town hall of the fifth arrondissement but did not receive naturalization papers until October 1862.

The job hunt led him from office to office, at business firms and through the maze of Paris's government bureaucracy where *chefs de bureau* presided over *administrations* like faceless potentates, handing out clerkships as they saw fit. A typical interview earned him a predictable rebuff:

I enter, I find a gentleman dressed in black from head to toe, bent over a more or less cluttered desk. He goes on writing and my existence is as far from his mind as the idea of a white crow. At last, after quite some time, he raises his head, looks at me askance, and says brusquely: "What do you want?" I tell him my name, inform him of the application I made and the invitation I received to come for an interview. Then begins a series of questions and tirades, always the same: Do I have good penmanship? Do I know how to keep accounts? In what administration have I previously served? What aptitude do I have? He is deluged with applications, he has no opening in his office, everything is full and I must resign myself to looking elsewhere. And I beat a quick retreat, sad because I didn't succeed, but happy not to be working in that dreadful dump.

Rich in knowledge that counted for less than nothing among such people, he fulminated against a school system completely divorced from the real world. "I know a host of useless things and don't know what one ought to know." His upper-class education made a beggar of him, and increasingly he looked the part as his frayed black coat turned green, then yellow. At twelve hundred francs a year, which is what he deemed adequate to his needs, work was available for masons, not for rhetoricians.

Only when he touched bottom could he accept material aid from Baille, who figured as a gritty but dependable superego commanding his respect, unnerving him with injunctions to be practical, and coming unbidden to the rescue. "There is a delicate matter I wish to broach," Emile wrote in February.

> On several occasions, and again in your last letter, you seemed to place your purse at my disposal . . . which calls for a direct response: if you can . . . share what you have, if you can do so without pressuring your parents, I shall accept it as a loan. My silence in that regard might have offended you, and furthermore I feared that to refuse, after acquainting you with my straitened circumstances, might strike you as an expression of misplaced pride.

Eight months earlier, around the time Emile left the Customs House, a letter in which Baille held forth on the importance of seeking a "position" had provoked Emile to declare that he sounded like a rich, impossibly sententious grocer. "I've known you for seven years, I've rummaged through my memories looking for a folly, a passion that has rattled you and I can't find any. . . . You seem what you are, someone following a fixed idea straight to your goal, making it by dint of hard work without tripping over obstacles, laughing heartily but only in your spare time, measuring your smile, as you measure everything." Their friendship obviously survived this tantrum, and Baille, if he was disposed to keep accounts, could feel that Emile more than made up for the attack with entreaties such as: "Tell yourself, tell yourself every day, that I do not purposely wallow in apathy, that I would rather be a mason than remain idle."

By June, Madame Zola had written once again to Alexandre Labot in the hope that her credit with him was not yet exhausted. From a country estate where he spent summers, Labot, missing the note of urgency in her polite salutation, answered that he would look after her on his return. It then became Emile's chore to state the truth baldly. "August . . . is far off and our predicament requires prompt attention," he wrote on June 9. "Tired of the struggle and with nothing left after legal fees, my mother finds herself in a state bordering on indigence. Moreover, her father, who has been bedridden for the past few months, is dependent on her." What Madame Zola wanted was a small donation of several hundred francs from the government, which would buy her time to search out regular employment. Emile made requests for himself as well, explaining apologetically how fruitless his own search had been. Business firms offered unpaid apprenticeships, but he could not afford that investment. "My bent has always been in the direction of literature," he admitted, and went on to say that nothing would gratify him more than earning a livelihood with his pen. "My mother has often spoken to me, Sir, about two of your friends, Messrs. Ambert and Chevallon, and seems to recall that, being writers themselves, they have some influence at literary publications. What I should like then, Sir, is the address of these gentlemen, if they reside in Paris, and a letter of recommendation that will enable me to make their acquaintance."

There is reason to believe that Madame Zola found some sort of job, for in 1862 the cadastral register describes her as an *ouvrière*. And Emile's distress signal yielded him editorial work in the form of a manuscript that needed polishing. "I've tied up with an economist whose works I'm putting right, stylistically. For his part, he's trying to get me a publisher and plans on introducing me to certain writers," he reported to Baille in mid-July. These expedients kept them alive, but did not halt their descent into the lower depths of Latin Quarter society. While Emilie, who lost her father during the winter, moved from boardinghouse to boardinghouse, Emile left his belvedere for a furnished room on the rue Soufflot, which was, before Haussmann arrived, among the most squalid streets in that neighborhood. At number 11, separated from one another by paper-thin walls, lived a lumpen proletariat of students, shopgirls, drifters, and prostitutes whom the police visited periodically. Emile's attic room had none of the redeeming features that had allowed him to idealize his previous hovels. Oblong, "like a coffin," and with decrepit furniture painted bright red, it looked out on a sooty wall which he couldn't ignore, for lack of curtains. The place was dank all year round, as he learned during the year or so he spent there.

What makes this room noteworthy, besides the degradation it proclaimed, is that he shared it with a young woman of unknown origin named Berthe, whom apparently he had met while still living at 24, rue Neuve-Saint-Etienne-du-Mont; in a letter to Paul written on February 5 he gave every indication that the bloom had gone off the rose soon after their liaison began. "Real love has been a school of hard knocks for me and I'm so crushed that I can hardly think about anything else coherently. I'll have lots to tell you when you arrive." His mistress, he informed Baille, was a *fille à parties*, by which he meant that she walked the thin line between bohemian promiscuity and outright prostitution. "I can speak knowledgeably about the woman of easy virtue. Sometimes we get into our heads the crazy idea of restoring to goodness some wretched creature by loving her, by lifting her from the gutter. . . . On the one hand our vanity is at stake, on the other we recite high-flown phrases such as: love washes away all blemishes, it weighs as much in the balance as all defects. Alas! They sound lovely but they're false!"

In a society that took elaborate measures to keep proper young women chaste until they landed a mate, such temporary liaisons were commonplace, if not inevitable, and nineteenth-century literature offers abundant evidence of this in novels such as Alexandre Dumas *fils's La Dame aux camélias,* Alphonse Daudet's *Sapho,* and Paul Bourget's *La Physiologie de l'amour.* Impecunious students might visit a whorehouse, at their peril. Otherwise, they often made do with women who had arrived en masse from provincial France to staff the counters of department stores, to perform domestic labor, to sew for couturiers or on their own account. "We display prostitution in broad daylight and hide virginity from all eyes," Emile complained to Baille, after inveighing against a venal bourgeoisie that regarded the maidenhead as a commodity governed by laws of the marketplace. "[Parents] want their money's worth for the polite skills a demoiselle has been taught at school; they auction the young girl's lowered gaze, her childish and simpleminded air, and when they're done itemizing all her advantages, they cry out in the name of propriety: 'Sir, it will cost you this much: get married first, love will come later.' " Among women available for premarital relations, the doxy whom a young man could hope to set straight had greater appeal, he declared, than the widow with nothing to gain from him morally and nothing to learn sexually. "The widow is not the ideal of our dream: this free woman, older than we, frightens us. . . . We would rather take on vice in the form of a concubine than run up against painted virtue. We prefer a woman free as the result of willful emancipation to one who has been liberated by a sad accident. And finally, we would rather, in our youthful enthusiasm, do a good deed, join battle against debauchery than possess a deflowered woman whose love offers neither the difficulties nor the poetry of the other."

Why, even against his better judgment, moral purpose should have led him irresistibly downward is open to conjecture, but Freud's *Contributions to the Psychology of Love* sheds some light on the question. In an essay about men driven by fantasies of rescuing fallen women, he observed that the harlot invariably stands for the mother who "fell" when it dawned upon her son that she was a sexual creature with desires he never imagined she could have. His enlightenment awakens intense jealousy and the betrayed child recoups in dream what he lost in reality by fancying himself the sole object of her adulterous lust. Not only would he possess her: he seeks to "rescue" her. "The impulse to 'rescue' the beloved appears to stand merely in a loose and superficial relation, founded entirely on conscious grounds, to these phantasies that have gained control of the love-experiences of real life,"

Freud wrote. "Her propensity to fickleness and infidelity brings the loved woman into dangerous situations, so it is natural that the lover should do all he can to protect her by watching over her virtue and opposing her evil ways." Deeper down, where the unconscious mind plays fast and loose, Freud noted a compulsion in rescuers to equate the idea of saving life with that of giving life and inferred a hidden equation between the fantasy of stealing mother and that of fathering oneself on her. "The mother gave the child his life and it is not easy to replace this unique gift with anything of equal value. By a slight change of meaning . . . rescuing the mother acquires the significance of giving her a child or of making one for her—one like himself of course. . . . In the rescue phantasy . . . he identifies himself completely with the father."

Zola's fictionalized account of his first love affair, *La Confession de Claude,* informs us that it passed like a dream from which he sometimes awoke to find himself with a stranger whose slovenliness and foul language offended him. Rather than act upon this perception, he denied it, fearing above all the prospect of losing her. "When dirty words escape from her I pretend not to hear them," the hero tells himself. "If her chemisette parts, I see nothing, and treat her as a sister rather than a lover. . . . I seem unaware that an upstanding existence is not hers and go about imposing it on her so unaffectedly that she will end up doubting her past." This histrionic behavior, which calls to mind the therapy employed by eighteenth-century alienists who thought that madmen being made to feign a rational personality would sooner or later find their role quite natural, also served the puritan's dream of lording it over women, of controlling them like a puppeteer. Berthe would not be his until she surrendered her past.

The impulse to control was enmeshed with the feeling that he stood alone among people who hid behind masks, and the perfidious harlot occupied center stage in his fantasy of a malevolent, unknowable world. "I accuse the heavens of having so created us that the body always hides the soul," he wrote to Baille on March 17, 1861, using *J'accuse* in a context that explains more fully his eloquent denunciation thirty-seven years later.

My neighbor comes, honey-mouthed, to greet me . . . and I think that he has venom in his heart. My dog caresses me and I'm persuaded that he's ready to bite. My mistress kisses me and swears eternal tenderness, I wonder whether at that very moment she isn't thinking about some other man. What can I say? It's my daily torment; it seems to me that life would be bliss if the souls of those with whom I rub elbows were open to view. When my mistress is near me, I put my ear against her lips and listen to her breath; her breath tells me nothing, and I despair.

Emile never let it be known whether he, like the hero of *La Confession de Claude*, caught his mistress with another man (an older, more experienced man). If he did, then Berthe played her part to perfection and discovered that the moralist intent on lifting her up valued her the more for thwarting his efforts. "The more vile and soiled this woman, the more passionately I embrace her," says Claude. "I don't want an innocent, a white soul and pink face."

At first, the two may have gone on excursions to the countryside, like other lovers, but as time wore on, they understood that there was no reason, home, or sustenance for the relationship outside his furnished room. Pajot recalled Berthe shuffling about listlessly in a tattered dress "[waiting] for some external force to break her inertia," and he must have thought the same of Emile, who shuffled alongside her. Holding each other hostage, they ate less and less, and borrowed, and pawned, until, in midwinter, Emile had nothing left to wear except a bedsheet, which necessarily interrupted his quest for the job he didn't want. What he did want could not be found among men. "Her eyes followed me calmly as I walked back and forth in front of her," he wrote in *La Confession de Claude*. "I felt this look fixed on me and in my troubles I found it soothing. I am at a loss to explain the intimate and strange consolation I derived from knowing myself watched by a live being, by a woman." The stage had been set for a parody of Paul and Virginie running free on their island under God's watchful eye. Marooned on the rue Soufflot, Emile felt as lonesome as a castaway but now and then as safe as a babe cradled by an attentive mother. It seems extraordinary that this hunger-artist, once he broke his fast, should have become the writer who created a universe of characters, who made a fortune, gorged himself, filled a house with massive *objets*. And yet, quite early along, he himself enunciated the principle that united these extreme modes of being when he wrote to Baille in 1860: "As for the future, I don't know; if I undertake a literary career, I want to follow my motto: All or Nothing!" One ruled by encompassing all phenomena or one commanded a vacuum. Thus, even as he stared at the blank wall outside their window on the rue Soufflot, Emile thought about a poem to be called "La Chaîne des êtres," which would scientifically trace the evolution of humankind in three cantos, "Past," "Present," and "Future." He wrote eight lines.

This painful affair would not have meant quite so much to him or lasted quite so long if his obstinate dream of one day reintegrating the "trio" had not been dealt a serious blow in 1861. Paul Cézanne came north that year, and the experience proved to be more than he could handle.

———

Luring Cézanne north required infinite patience on Emile's part. He often found himself at odds not only with Cézanne *père* but with Paul himself, who, being terrified of failure, vacillated between the desire to pursue art as a career and unwillingness to overcome the obstacles his father placed in his path. Every step forward was followed by retreat as anger or depression gained the upper hand, and Emile, always aware that too much pressure might have contrary results, coached Paul from afar, urging his ego on while restraining his temper. "You must placate your father by studying law as diligently as possible, but you must also work hard and steadfastly at drawing," he wrote to him in March 1860, and he repeated this advice a month later: "Be firm without being disrespectful. Remember that your future hangs in the balance and your happiness depends on which way you go." Clearly, Emile believed that his own happiness depended on whether he could set Paul's mind in motion. But it was an unwieldy apparatus, driven by various masters, the least evident of whom was Paul himself. Sometimes cajolery seemed to work, but after numerous false starts Emile decided that perhaps strong language would ignite him. "Is painting nothing for you but a caprice that grabbed you by the hair one fine day when you were bored?" he exclaimed in a sharp remonstrance.

It is nothing but a pastime, a conversation piece, a pretext not to study law? If so, I understand your conduct: you are right not to push things to the limit and stir up your family. But if painting is your vocation, as I've always understood it to be—if you feel yourself capable of doing it well after working hard—then you become for me an enigma. . . . It's one of two things. Either you don't want it, and in that case you are achieving your purpose admirably; or else you do, in which case I am confounded. At times your letters give me a great deal of hope, at other times they take it all back and then some. In your last one you seem almost to bid farewell to your dreams, which you could transform into bright reality. There is in that letter a sentence I've tried vainly to understand: "I'm going to talk just for the sake of talking, for my conduct contradicts my words." I've constructed many hypotheses around the meaning of these words, none of which satisfies me. What is your conduct? That of a lazy person no doubt. But what's odd about that? You are forced to do work you find obnoxious, you want to ask your father to let you come to Paris to become an artist—I see no contradiction between this demand and your actions. You neglect the law, you go to the museum, painting is the only employment you can accept: that's what I call perfect harmony between your desires and your actions. . . . Shall I say it straight out? You must not take offense, but the fact is, you lack character. Whatever causes fatigue—whether intellectual labor or

physical—repels you. Your guiding principle is to let water flow and
to rely on time and chance. . . . I've thought it best to repeat one
last time here what I've often told you already and friendship sanctions my candor. In many respects our personalities are similar, but
by God, if I were in your place, I would want to speak my mind, risk
all for all and not drift between two such different futures, the atelier
and the bar. I pity you, because you must suffer from this incertitude,
which would be for me one more inducement to burst out.

Cézanne was told, in conclusion, to be one thing or another, "really
be a lawyer or really be an artist, but don't remain a nameless creature
wearing a toga soiled with paint."

All in all, admonitions such as this one had a positive effect on Paul,
who did not resume law school that fall but instead worked full-time
at painting, to Emile's immense delight. "The news charmed me because I deduce from your persistence your love of the arts and the
intensity of your devotion to work," he wrote on February 5, 1861,
when Paul told him that he hardly felt the bitter cold as he sat with a
sketch pad in the hills. On the other hand, drawing classes under Professor Gibert at Aix's Académie des Beaux-Arts, though they were infinitely preferable to lessons in tort law, left much to be desired. Paul's
description of a flaccid nude who wore a fig leaf while modeling
amused Emile. "Chaillan claims that here in Paris models are tolerable,
if not in their first bloom," he responded. "One draws them by day
and at night one caresses them (caress understates it). . . . As for the
fig leaf, it is unknown in ateliers. One undresses there unselfcons-
ciously, and the love of art veils what might otherwise prove too exciting in nudity. Come, you'll see." This curious invitation to get
undressed yet remain fully clothed suggests what made their bond so
strong. The thought that sexual pleasure might render him artistically
impotent had become an idée fixe with Emile. Those veils he saw
everywhere were the fabric of his own mind, and long intimacy had
taught him that Paul needed such protection as much as he did.

Worn down by his son's angry silence, Louis-Auguste Cézanne at
last consented to let Paul study painting in Paris. After months of
temporization, he, Paul, and Paul's sister, Marie, hastily departed for
the capital in April 1861 and arrived without having notified Emile,
who one Sunday morning heard a familiar voice calling up the stairwell
at 11, rue Soufflot. "I've seen Paul, . . . do you catch the whole melody
of those three words?" he announced jubilantly to Baille. "He came
this morning. . . . I was half asleep, I opened my door trembling with
joy and we embraced furiously. Then he reassured me on the score of
his father's antipathy toward me. He claimed that you exaggerated,
out of zeal no doubt." They immediately set out on a long walk

through Paris and sat in parks smoking pipes; they agreed to room together after Louis-Auguste went home. The reunion made Emile feel capable of great things, as in a dream he had had several weeks earlier, where his name, glittering like gold, was linked with Cézanne's on the title page of a book that manifested their genius. Each would work hard during the day and they would meet in the evening, he proposed. "Sundays we shall take flight and go several leagues from Paris; there are charming sites and, if it pleases you, you can throw on a piece of canvas the trees under which we will have lunched."

But independence did not sit well with Cézanne. Freed from his father's close supervision, he constructed a veritable cocoon, working all morning at the Atelier Suisse (where models were provided for a fixed monthly fee), spending afternoons drawing under the eye of an Aixois artist many years older than himself named Joseph-François Villevielle, eating supper, and retiring so early that his friend rarely saw him. When they met, Emile found that Paul stood far away, behind ramparts of distrust. "Paul is still the excellent and whimsical boy I knew in college," he lamented to Baille.

> As proof that he has lost nothing of his eccentricity, I need only tell you that he had no sooner arrived here than he started talking about returning to Aix. . . . Confronted by such a personality, by the unpredictable and irrational changes in his conduct, I am dumbstruck and muzzle my logic. Proving something to Cézanne is like trying to persuade the towers of Notre-Dame Cathedral to dance a quadrille. He may say yes, but won't budge an inch.

Age had increased his obstinacy without giving him subjects to be reasonably obstinate about, wrote Emile.

Paul's fragile sense of self may have been reason enough to justify his churlishness. In frustrating him, his father had also shielded him, for the amateur or would-be painter could always dismiss criticism as irrelevant. Now that art was his chosen profession, such criticism hit home. Bereft of the adversarial relationship with his father he felt naked, and sought cover from a world seemingly eager to remind him that he was made wrong. Emile continued:

> If, by chance, he advances an opposite opinion and you discuss it, he gets mad without wanting to examine the matter further, shouts that you understand nothing, and leaps to another subject. Try merely to converse with a boy of such temper and you will get nowhere. . . . I hoped that age would have worked some changes in him. But I find him to be the way I left him. My strategy is therefore very simple. I never thwart his fantasy. At most I offer very indirect

advice. I rely on his good nature to maintain the friendship. I never force his hand to shake mine. In a word, I efface myself completely, always welcoming him cheerfully, seeking him out without importuning him, and letting him decide how much or little intimacy should exist between us.

His strategy brought Paul around, and before long Emile reported that they were together six hours a day talking easily about art, Aix, women. These conversations took place in Paul's room while Emile modeled for him, or in museums, where the one did not entirely share the other's high opinion of Ary Scheffer, or in the Jardin du Luxembourg, which students regarded as their private preserve. But fair weather could suddenly disappear and black clouds eclipse the sun. Cézanne was always subject to fits of self-hatred, during which he professed contempt for worldly success and announced his resolve to become a clerk in some business firm down south. "I must then make long speeches proving that a return would be silly; he readily agrees and goes back to work," Emile told Baille. "But this idea gnaws at him; twice already he has been on the verge of leaving, and I fear that he will escape me from one minute to the next. If you write to him, try to portray our imminent reunion in the most seductive colors. It's the only way of keeping him here." At one point, Emile kept him in Paris by prevailing on him to paint his portrait. It was all but done when Cézanne destroyed it and swept up everything he owned for a frantic departure. "Paul may have the genius of a great painter, he will never have the genius to become one," wrote Emile, who must have sensed the murderous intention in this self-destructive act. "The least obstacle reduces him to despair. . . . Let him leave if he wishes to spare himself many troubles."

In September, five months after his arrival, Cézanne went home to the Jas de Bouffan, Louis-Auguste's new estate outside Aix. The two friends remained incommunicado for some time. Cézanne finally broke the silence, and Emile responded straightway, assuring him that he had no desire to examine what had gone amiss:

It's been a long time since I've written to you, I'm not quite sure why. Paris didn't do our friendship any good; perhaps it needs the sun of Provence to thrive. Some unfortunate misunderstanding threw a chill into our relations, some misconstrued circumstance or some nasty word blown out of all proportion. I don't know and I would just as well never know; in stirring muck one fouls one's hand. At all events, I still believe you to be my friend. I assume that you judge me incapable of a base action and esteem me as in the past.

He wrote this conciliatory letter on January 20, 1862. By then, Baille had traveled up to Paris and, wearing the uniform of a Polytechnique student, met Émile regularly twice a week, on Wednesdays and Sundays. With Baille, there was no guesswork in friendship.

Dire poverty and ill health afflicted Emile throughout the winter. On New Year's Day 1862 he was reduced to delivering greeting cards for a family friend, Professor Boudet of the Académie de Médecine, who gave him a twenty-franc gold piece. Such charitable improvisations helped him stave off hunger, but soon afterward Boudet did him a better turn: he secured Emile a clerkship at the Librairie Hachette, France's most distinguished publishing house. Emile began work there on March 1, packaging books for one hundred francs a month. This turn of events proved to be momentous.

V

SOMEONE TO RECKON WITH

FROM A SMALL SHOP at 12, rue Pierre-Sarrazin, where its founder opened for business in 1826, Hachette and Company had spread far beyond Paris. By 1862 it could claim preeminence among French publishers, with 139 employees working in buildings that occupied an entire square block near the intersection of the Boulevard Saint-Germain and the Boulevard Sébastopol (south). To have attended public school during the reign of Louis Philippe or in successive regimes was to have known this imprint since childhood. It figured on the textbooks used throughout France, on cheap editions of French and foreign classics, on sundry dictionaries and thesauri, on the scientific popularizations that became a best-selling genre after 1850. There were also the Joanne guides, whose fabulous success was an epiphenomenon of rail transportation. Hachette had something for everyone, from the common man who read its illustrated magazines to the intelligentsia who studied works by Michelet, Taine, or Littré, and contemporaries thought of it more as a quasi-official institution than as a merely private enterprise. "Twenty journals are produced there, one of which has, all by itself, a circulation that exceeds 100,000," noted Edmond About, a house author, referring to *Le Journal pour tous*. "The firm . . . covers 10,000 square meters. Seeing the crowd that tumbles out after work, one might take it to be the ministry of the book trade." Louis Hachette acquired the cognomen "emperor of publishing," which made peculiar sense in a nation ruled by a writer manqué, and present at Hachette's funeral in 1864 were members of the Academy, the minister of public instruction, and Napoleon III's personal representative, Marshal Vaillant.

Even in the mail room, where a large clock surmounted by a garlanded bust of Apollo hung overhead, it was impressed upon Hachette's employees that they served an *imperium in imperio*. During his brief stint wrapping parcels, Zola had occasion to learn something about his boss, and certainly registered the fact that he, too, had grown up fatherless. Educated at the Lycée Louis-le-Grand in the same class as Littré, Hachette had joined the elite corps who trained for pedagogical careers at the Ecole Normale Supérieure, and he might have spent his life teaching if the government of Louis XVIII, which held the basis of secondary school education to be "religion, monarchy, legitimacy, and the charter," had not thwarted him. In 1822 it denounced the Ecole Normale Supérieure as subversive and closed it down, scattering faculty and students. Private lessons gave Hachette a meager livelihood until, with some borrowed money, he purchased the stock of a Left Bank bookseller.

Determined to follow what he felt was his true calling, Hachette entered the classroom by another door. "I have found another way to teach," he told a former classmate, and 1830 vindicated him. The July Revolution brought about a regime that benefited merchants of the printed word, as France's reading public swelled in consequence of new laws requiring every parish with at least five hundred inhabitants to maintain a grade school and teachers to demonstrate minimal competence. Especially fortunate was Hachette, who cornered the market before other publishers could react. He edited not only textbooks for the classroom but journals for the pedagogue that were as effective as the state license in helping teachers forge a professional identity. His clientele made him even wealthier after 1850, when his company began churning out encyclopedias, almanacs, digests, surveys, demand for which reflected the soaring prestige of scientific knowledge and the layman's desire to keep abreast of it.

Part entrepreneur and part preacher, this conscientious bourgeois, after whom Zola would in some ways model himself, regarded books as moral commodities. "It behooves us to recognize that every man entering the world is entitled to sit at the social banquet," Hachette wrote in 1861. "Privileges have been abolished: the obstacles that once enclosed the lower classes behind insurmountable barriers have been removed. Such benefits do not suffice, however. Minds must be enlightened and made to see that physical and moral well-being, that social and political rights, cannot be exercised except by means of instruction and work." An abiding faith in self-improvement led him to create a collection called the Bibliothèque Populaire, which workers could acquire for one franc per volume, and to commission practical treatises on hygiene, moral deportment, domestic economy.

But liberalism never dulled Hachette's eye for the main chance. It was he who first realized that trains had begotten a captive audience and obtained the exclusive right to operate bookstands in railroad terminals. During Napoleon III's Italian campaign, he reaped immense profits with an illustrated newspaper reporting the progress of the war week by week. When opportunity beckoned, Hachette made haste, and the speed with which he marshaled his resources attested to innovations that gave the firm an edge over every other. Hydraulic conveyances, rational accounting procedures, special discounts for dealers who took books on consignment, and shorter hours for staff paid off handsomely. So did strategies devised to advertise the list, and here Zola became indispensable. Soon after joining Hachette he was put to work in the publicity department, which employed one other clerk. A superior, perhaps Louis Hachette himself or his son-in-law, had recognized that the well-spoken young man wrapping parcels would do better upstairs, writing copy for the *Bulletin du libraire et de l'amateur de livres.*

Every month the *Bulletin du libraire* was sent free of charge to regular clients, offering a list of Hachette's forthcoming titles and an extensive bibliography of material published under rival imprints. After March 1862, the format changed. Hachette's list came to occupy more space as one-line blurbs grew into long paragraphs describing the purpose and content of each book. For this alteration Zola was mainly responsible. "You ask me if I could send you, every month, brief reviews of noteworthy books published by Hachette," he replied in October 1863 to Géry-Legrand, founder of *La Revue de Paris.* "It's simple enough, since I edit a kind of bibliographic insert for the *Bulletin du libraire.*"

Six days a week, from 8:30 to 11:30 and again from 1 to 6, Zola sat at a table chewing whatever Hachette served up. His employer favored novels that had instructive denouements, and these were never in short supply with writers like Amédée Achard, Elie Berthet, and Louis Enault producing one exemplary tale after another. To have to tout such custom distressed Zola (he avenged himself years later, when he could risk it, in a piece entitled "Nos romanciers contemporains"), but Hachette's nonfiction compensated him for his drudgery. In July 1863 the company issued the first volume of Littré's monumental *Dictionnaire de la langue française,* and soon it brought out the lexicographer's homage to his mentor, *August Comte et la philosophie positive.* In January 1864 three volumes of Hippolyte Taine's *Histoire de la littérature anglaise* went on sale, with a preface that made "race, moment, and milieu" bywords for materialist doctrine. Several months later it was Emile Deschanel's turn; *Physiologie des écrivains et des artistes ou essai de critique naturelle* drove home the idea that art should be understood not moralistically but as a manifestation of natural forces and historical

circumstance. These seminal works, along with Jules Simon's sociological inquiry *L'Ouvrière,* bore fruit in Zola's *Rougon-Macquart.* His task
for the moment, however, was to help them reach every possible
reader.

Having gained a foothold, Zola lost no time calling attention to himself. He had been with the firm scarcely three months when Louis
Hachette received a long letter in which the novice proposed that his
patron launch a Bibliothèque des Débutants—a series reserved for previously unpublished authors. "I can tell you . . . that every young man
who writes, being intimidated by the reputation you enjoy, regards
your editorial department as an impregnable sanctuary and hesitates
before daring to submit his first work," Zola wrote. An offer of hospitality might bring in slush, but the reward would justify that
inconvenience:

> Is it not, Sir, a project meritorious enough to tempt a powerful pub-
> lisher, with great wealth and great credit? He would in a way place
> himself up front in the literary movement of the young generation.
> He would revolutionize established ideas and expose to ridicule me-
> diocrities who complain about going unrecognized. I venture to say
> that such an initiative would make him even more powerful and as-
> sure him a unique place among his confreres. He would be loved,
> and people would praise him for extending this helping hand to the
> young.

Several years earlier, under Michelet's influence, Zola had dreamed of
being the spiritual mediator who would "arrange man's return to
woman." Now, under the aegis of Michelet's publisher, he saw himself
interceding between estranged parties and prevailing upon father to
embrace son. Once again there came into play a fantasy that answered
his inveterate yearning for help from the man whose death had cost
him his inheritance. His letter, which features himself as both rescuer
and rescued—as Hachette's better nature and the voice of hapless
youth—may have been opportunistic, but it went far beyond opportunism in the hope it expressed that this powerful entrepreneur could
set matters right and give its writer a start in life. "Let a publisher
stand up then and . . . proclaim to young writers: 'All of you come
here, I shall read you, I shall judge you conscientiously, and if I detect
any talent, I shall facilitate your future.' "

Hachette did not heed Zola, whose own early fiction made a questionable case for the Beginners' Library. He did, however, reward initiative by appointing him advertising manager in October 1863, and
from that moment on Zola never again suffered total obscurity. Long
before he became famous, he won recognition among Hachette's

house authors, whom he kept informed of everything written about them. Taine, Deschanel, Edmond About, Prévost-Paradol paid regular visits, and smaller fry were constantly at his door. "How often, even now, when I mention some man of letters who is not exactly a household name . . . do I hear him exclaim: 'So and so? Why, I met him way back when, at Hachette,' " Pau! Alexis noted in 1882.

These men of letters included a great many literary journalists. At Hachette's direction, Zola set out to develop contacts throughout the burgeoning newspaper industry. In 1863, Moïse Millaud founded *Le Petit Journal,* a daily that cost only one sou and eschewed political reportage (on which Napoleon III's government levied a stamp tax) for "human interest" stories, lurid accounts of criminal mischief, serialized cliff-hangers, and practical advice. Such was its appeal, especially in the hinterland, where itinerant peddlers carried it from village to village, that its circulation topped a quarter million before any other paper's had reached 55,000. Success bred imitators as the market continued to expand. Presently *Le Petit Journal* found itself competing with a clone, *Le Petit Parisien,* and soon afterward came *La Petite presse quotidienne, Le Journal illustré, Le Nouvel illustré.* Widespread literacy, the railroad, the rotary press, the wireless telegraph all had a hand in this proliferation, which made newspapers irresistible to merchants wanting national exposure for their products. "I shall write to you anon about some company business," Zola informed Géry-Legrand in January 1864. "We would like our ads printed (gratis) in exchange for complimentary copies of our books, or some of them. . . . It's an arrangement we've worked out with all the major Parisian journals and I trust you will find it acceptable." At Christmas he again broached the matter of a quid pro quo:

> You propose to run a list ad of our gift books in *Le Populaire.* We much prefer book reviews. This very day you should receive Figuier's most recent volume, accompanied by a bibliographic notice. In addition, I am sending along a circular which informs provincial papers that we will give them free copies of *Le Ciel* and *Le Monde de la Mer* if they print our reviews.

Bartering became Zola's main occupation in 1864–65, and letters like these went out by the score. Indeed, his correspondence required so much time that he often sacrificed whole evenings to it. The result justified the ordeal, however, for what came of it was a web of influence that served him well long after he had left Hachette, when professional acquaintances would be called upon to boost his own latest work rather than Taine's or Figuier's.

One hundred francs a month, plus whatever Emilie may have

earned on her own, enabled the Zolas to survive, without any margin for whim or illness. In April 1862 they rented separate flats at 7, impasse Saint-Dominique (now called impasse Royer-Collard), where students, laborers, artists, and clerks were neighbors under the roof of a large, intricate tenement that had formerly been a convent house. Before the year was out they moved again and this time departed from the Latin Quarter, having found four cheap rooms—two of them equipped with fireplaces—just beyond Montparnasse Cemetery. Here, on the rue de la Pépinière (now rue Daguerre), which cut across the village of Montrouge, their neighbors regarded them as wayward bourgeois. Taverns, greasy spoons, and bottle shops that catered to wagoners entering Paris through the Denfert tollgate outnumbered houses in a squalid, working-class environment reminiscent of the one Zola later depicted in *L'Assommoir.*

In July 1863, when republican faithful were celebrating the dawn of a better day after dramatic gains in the recent legislative election, the Zolas moved back to Paris proper. By then Emile's salary had doubled, and the flat they took at 7, rue des Feuillantines, behind the Ecole Normale Supérieure, reflected this increment. Overlooking a quiet garden in a metropolis still topsy-turvy with reconstruction, it was by far the most agreeable niche they had been able to arrange for themselves since leaving Aix-en-Provence. But financial difficulties continued to plague them as the cost of living spiraled upward. "My mother must have acquainted you with the fact that I should like to borrow 100 francs, my salary not having sufficed this month to cover some small debts," he wrote on December 2, 1863, to an unknown correspondent. "She tells me that you kindly offered her hope of being able to procure this sum for us. Unfortunately the need is urgent. My IOUs fall due next Thursday." Even more onerous than IOUs was the quarterly rent deadline, which induced attacks of colic and a recurrent nightmare of bailiffs serving eviction notices. "I am ashamed to have to ask once again that you grant me a brief extension," Zola pleaded with his landlord on May 18, 1864:

> Since I would just as well not embarrass myself a second time by making promises I can't keep, I implore you to take no action until June 2. If by then I haven't been able to collect certain monies owing me, I shall pay you out of my salary for the month. . . . This business fills me with dismay. I feel perfectly at home in your-building and want to remain here at all costs, so I shall make certain that nothing of this sort happens again.

Monsieur Félix Masselin apparently turned a deaf ear to the entreaties of his delinquent tenant, for early in July Zola announced a new address around the corner from the rue des Feuillantines, on the rue Saint-Jacques.

Despite this familiar pattern, Paris no longer looked like a maze. Decisive changes had taken place in Zola's life, and the role of waif martyred by a philistine world was less compelling than before. To be sure, that role did not lose its appeal overnight (or, indeed, ever). But after 1862 Zola, who had unavailingly circulated his verse among literary reviews, stopped rhyming, and in correspondence he seldom voiced the nostalgia for Aix that had held him hostage to his poetic persona. "Someday . . . , in a year perhaps or in ten, it will be possible for me to take a trip through Provence," he confided to Baille and Cézanne in September 1862. "With what pleasure shall I behold again the tree in whose shade I once sat. . . . Old men, or at least men who have embarked upon a life of action, we shall live our former life for a month." Pleased with himself yet afraid of slipping backward (like so many of the congenitally doomed characters in the *Les Rougon-Macquart*), he saw Aix as a place to be visited only when the past had receded enough for immersion in it not to drown him. More time was what he felt would consecrate that interval, time and notoriety. "Where are those evenings of peaceful labor, when I found myself alone with my work, wondering whether it would ever see the light of day?" he asked a younger friend from Aix, Antony Valabrègue, whose own literary ambitions far exceeded his gifts and whose timorous, vacillating nature came increasingly to exasperate Zola. "Back then, I used to debate with myself, I used to hesitate. Now I must march, march no matter what. Whether the written page be good or bad, it must appear." His remarks call to mind a habit he had meanwhile acquired of counting doors, lampposts, and stairs as he walked, which one physician who knew about it dubbed "arithmomania." For all his rationalism, the superstitious young man could, at times, hardly stir without measuring the distance traversed, as if every errand in life, however routine, were evocative of a passage from "then" to "now," and numbers the magic that governed his perilous journey upward. Four pages a day, day after day, year after year, would never quite reassure him.

Making strides, writing prose, asserting masculinity became synonymous in Zola's rhetoric. "Today I must walk quickly, and rhyme would hinder me," he told Valabrègue. "We shall someday see whether this angered the Muse, and whether she didn't take another lover more naive and tender than I. I belong to prose and feel good about it." Prose was what virile men wrote. It lent itself to displays of power, and Zola trumpeted his with a version of the Catholic dictum *Hors de l'Eglise, point de salut.* "Outside prose, no salvation," he declared, repudiating almost too clamorously ideals he once held dear, in language that bespeaks religious fervor. The convert was determined to excommunicate adolescence and to have an "objective" structure of belief buttress him against the dreamer, the loser, the bohemian, the voyeur.

His declaration echoed the hosannas raised by men of positivist ideology, who felt confident that science, which had already fostered a new critical system in Hippolyte Taine's work, would revolutionize literature itself. "Poetry no longer suits the great conceptions of modern life" is how Gaston Bergeret put it in *La Revue du mois*, and contributors to Hachette's influential *Revue de l'instruction publique* chanted agreement. Before long poetry would celebrate what lay ahead instead of lamenting anachronisms, prophesied Arthur Arnauld; the imagination would "infer the consequences of generally accepted premises" instead of "naively inventing impossible facts or fictional beings." An article by Xavier de Ricard, "L'Urgence de la poésie scientifique," pictured future poets roaming through unexplored territory in search of "new problems that await a material solution." Science is so enmeshed with literature that their respective works can no longer be told apart, he exulted, and, indeed, the jargon of literary journalists might have led one to credit this egregious assertion. Abounding in terms taken from natural or medical science, it promoted the idea that a writer had not grown up until he donned a clinician's hat. "Doctor," "surgeon," "physiologist," "anatomist" stood for authoritativeness. Favorable notices described the praiseworthy author—whether critic, novelist, or playwright—as someone who performed operations in an amphitheater, who conducted experiments, who laid characters out on a slab and dissected them, who delved through innards. By the same token, his intellectual equipment was invariably likened to laboratory apparatus in metaphors that featured the scalpel, the microscope, the magnifying glass, and the retort. Thus, one critic discussing Taine's *La Fontaine et ses fables* in a December 1860 issue of *La Revue de l'instruction publique* evoked a surgeon-critic entering "a great amphitheater of literary dissection" with "kit in hand and apron at the ready," who "stoutly rolls up his sleeves and digs in [*se met à la besogne*]." Where positivism molded opinion, every word spoke against poetic license, even *besogne*, which served better than *travail* to make it understood that writing of the kind Taine did was not mere child's play but a muscular analysis of the physical world. And almost every such word entered Zola's vocabulary. "If I pride myself in one thing, it is in having acknowledged that I had no talent for verse and having courageously undertaken the labor of the century [*la besogne du siècle*] with the rough-hewn tool of prose," he noted years later, in 1881, when formulae with positivist implications had become second nature to him.

Zola first undertook the "labor of the century" as an occasional contributor to Géry-Legrand's newspaper *Le Journal populaire de Lille*, writing articles, the most important of which appeared on April 16, 1864, under the title "Du progrès dans les sciences et dans la poésie." In this confident, well-turned piece, he left no doubt of his resolve to go beyond the romantics who had shaped his literary sensibility and to embrace a new aesthetic order. "We must violently separate ourselves from the lyric school of 1830, or at least renew it, make it our own through some new inspiration," he argued. "Powerfully original," the poet of tomorrow would "draw only upon himself" for wisdom. And what would he say?

> I would bid farewell to the lovely lies of mythology; I would respectfully bury the last naiad and sylph; I would spurn myths and make truth my one-and-only. . . . In the depopulated heavens, I would show the Infinite presiding over worlds and the immutable laws that flow from it. Stripped of its cute adornments, the earth would be for me nothing but a harmonious whole through which the life force courses undiminished toward some mysterious goal. Need I say it? I would be a scientist and borrow from science its broad horizons . . . I would be a new Lucretius and commit to beautiful verse the philosophy of our knowledge.

Eight months later, in a review of Amédée Guillemin's *Le Ciel,* he again invoked "depopulated heavens" and boasted that fathers would bequeath to their sons "a sky purged of ghosts." The idea that scientific law had wiped the slate clean obviously delighted him. "It makes a marvelous, sublime spectacle—all of creation obedient to one force, all these spheres inseparably linked and moving in concert. . . . Laplace's universe was formed by such principles . . . and I know no grander poetry than that of this scientific genesis."

When Zola addressed the public at large, he spoke as François Zola's son, keeping alive a myth of heroic paternity while scorning mythopoeia. To create something significant required that one "draw only upon oneself," to be was to be "powerfully original," and this view had undergone no fundamental revision since he wrote his first published poem, "Le Canal Zola," where chaos is the material a demiurge informs with purpose. Nurtured on romantic literature, his mind found easy purchase at extremes, and it leapt from quaking reverence for magical forces to a belief in science holding sway over the universe. This is to say that Zola wavered between superstition and rationalism, between feelings of impotence and fantasies of omnipotence. What made him conceive the progenitor who masters virgin nature also made him sire those children, prisoners of heredity, who would soon crowd his novels.

But as François Zola assumed mythic proportions, it was inevitable that Emile should feel ambivalent about this ghost he could neither seize nor exorcise, by whose measure he often found himself wanting. On the one hand he stated that he would be a poet-scientist and borrow "science's broad horizons." On the other he counseled "violent" divorce from the generation of 1830, which surely included not only his literary fathers but the Italian engineer who established himself on French soil in 1830. Piety struggled with yearnings for an unencumbered self, and a "scientific genesis" helped to mute this conflict by whisking away the paterfamilias, substituting impersonal law for personal fatherhood. Without effacing François Zola outright, it let his son creep out from under. "Everyone can and wants to be the master," he declared in an essay on Taine.

Being the master is a theme that runs through several articles Zola contributed to *Le Salut public* between January and December 1865. Cocksure and authoritative in tone, these articles made Paris sit up, for although *Le Salut public* had the liberal bourgeoisie of Lyon as its main audience, it was a serious paper, a *grand journal* read wherever readers sought to keep abreast of developments in commerce, industry, and science. The editor-in-chief, who knew Zola from Hachette, allowed him ample space, and Zola filled it with commentary on art and letters, much of which would later reappear in a volume entitled *Mes Haines*.

Not every topic justified this combative title, but Proudhon's *Du Principe de l'art et de sa destination sociale* did indeed anger him. "An idealistic representation of nature and ourselves that serves to perfect the physical and moral character of our species" was how Proudhon defined art, and Zola vehemently took issue with the utopian philosopher, whom he saw as a tyrant formulating prescriptions for servitude. No social program should impose itself upon the creative mind. "I state it as fundamental that the work lives only by its originality; I must discern a man in each work, or the work leaves me cold," he wrote, and further along he declared art to be "a negation of society, an affirmation of the individual beyond all rules and social necessities." While Proudhon would have made his collective ideal the cynosure of all eyes, Zola, who found socialist dogmatism even more obnoxious than bourgeois conformism, glorified freedom of perception:

> I love . . . the free play of individual thought—what Proudhon calls anarchy. I love the Renaissance and our own age, these skirmishes among artists, these men all of whom pronounce words hitherto unheard. A work not made of blood and nerves . . . is one I reject, even if it should be the Venus de Milo.

A year earlier, the "poet of tomorrow" had occupied him. Now it was "the great painter of tomorrow" and, with Courbet in mind, he argued once again that greatness draws only upon itself, that "talent cannot be taught." Courbet's unmistakable signature illustrated the maxim on which Zola rested his case against Proudhon: "A work of art is a corner of creation seen through a temperament."

Phrases he first used in "Le Canal Zola," where the Provençal wilderness is a "corner of earth left intact and solitary," an "unfinished sketch of creation," make it quite clear that his maxim had deep personal roots. The new element, "temperament," had become a commonplace among literati sympathetic to modern art. It figures prominently in Baudelaire's *Curiosités esthétiques*; in an article Théophile Gautier wrote about Peter Cornelius; in *Manette Salomon*, where the Goncourts describe Delacroix as "a temperament all nerves, a sick man, a disturbed man." Ambitious for renown, Zola eagerly snatched up words that implied membership in an elite brotherhood. They were winks of complicity signaling mutual disdain for the *profanum vulgus*, which, by definition, feared "temperament." But disdain for the crowd had been with him since adolescence, and "a corner of creation seen through a temperament" harks back to the earlier idea that his insight would spark amorous recognition between man and woman. Making people see the world through Emile Zola occupied a prominent place in his imaginative life. What set great men apart was their power to create something from nothing and foist visions upon a credulous audience. "A work is simply the free and lofty manifestation of a personality. . . . What matters the crowd?" he exclaimed by way of praising the Goncourts' novel *Germinie Lacerteux*. "I serve my ideal when I anatomize with rigorous precision the subject under scrutiny. It is for me to penetrate an organism, to reconstruct an artistic temperament, to analyze a heart and an intelligence according to my own nature." Such manifestos often recur in *Le Salut public*, along with tirades against discipleship, and what he poured out for the newspaper filtered through his correspondence. "Schools have never produced a single great man. Quite the reverse is true, great men produce schools," he asserted to Valabrègue on August 18, 1864. "Artists of genius are born and grow freely, while disciples follow in their footsteps." Virtually the same words appear in a letter written in 1860, soon after he turned twenty: "I would rather not retrace anyone's footsteps."

Another name for the wilderness with no well-beaten paths and no God-given laws was anarchy, which he considered a desirable state of affairs insofar as it left him free to be himself. "Anarchy reigns and for me it is a curious and interesting spectacle," he noted halfway through a long article on Hippolyte Taine, whose relativistic views suited him.

Certainly I regret that the great man or dictator is absent, but observing all these kings wage war in a sort of republican state where each citizen rules his own roost gives me pleasure. Immense sums of energy are expended, life is feverish and excessive. The continual and obstinate birth-giving that marks our age has not elicited enough admiration. . . . Each artist holes up in his own corner and toils at the masterpiece that will decide which direction literature takes.

His introduction to *Mes Haines* contains a more ruthless picture of France's cultural scene, and here the would-be patriarch speaks decidedly louder than the republican. "Panting with anxiety, the age awaits those who will strike hardest and truest, whose fists will be strong enough to silence every other mouth, and within each new recruit lurks the vague hope that he will become our next dictator, our future tyrant." That he himself entertained such hopes may be further inferred from an anecdote told by the left-wing journalist Jules Vallès. Zola, whom he remembered as being a short man with olive skin, jet-black hair, and a supercilious mouth, must have felt that he could confide in him when he came to Hachette's publicity department on business, for during one chat he asked Vallès point-blank: "Do you believe you are someone to reckon with?" (*Sentez-vous que vous êtes une force?*) and defiantly volunteered, "I believe *I* am." He said this matter-of-factly, according to Vallès.

Strength might not have preyed upon his mind if he had had a more robust confidence, and he admitted as much in "M. H. Taine, Artiste," where the assurance Vallès found so disconcerting is shown for what it was. Zola openly identified with Taine as an intellectual conquistador who never left his mother, as a monk who wondered why society's handsome face always led him to investigate its "bestial and filthy rump," as a sensibility that sought refuge from private demons in scientific law. "One feels that the author [of *Voyage aux Pyrénées*] is our brother, that he is weak and naked, that he belongs to our century of nerves," wrote Zola. "His is a sickly and anxious nature, with passionate yearnings for strength and the free life. The splendid brutishness of those Saxons and Flemish whom he adulates [seems enviable to a man] who shivers, who has little appetite and a cramped stomach, who wears the dark, skimpy attire of our age." Although Taine the inflexible determinist made him squirm, for Taine the "artist" he had nothing but praise. Abidingly faithful to the ultimatum he gave himself at twenty, "All or Nothing," Zola found a kindred soul in this luminary, whose poor opinion of human nature led him to admire "naturals" who, without compunction, swallowed humanity whole.

"Out in the open countryside I would rather meet a sheep than a lion, but behind a gate I would rather see a lion than a sheep," is how

Taine put it in a book-length essay on Balzac from which Zola drew decisive lessons.

Art [wrote Taine] is this kind of gate: while removing the terror, it preserves the interest. Thanks to it, we can safely and painlessly contemplate the superb passions, the heartbreaks, the titanic struggles, all the sound and fury of human nature lifted out of itself by merciless clashes and unrestrained desire. Observed through art, strength moves and captivates us. It takes us out of ourselves; we transcend the vulgarity into which we are otherwise dragged by the meanness of our faculties and the timidity of our instincts.

He went on to proclaim that unless they live by some governing philosophy, scientists and artists are mere laborers and entertainers; a synthetic or panoramic view is the mark of a superior mind.

At home in the late nineteenth century, when men brought to learning the same monstrous appetite and digestive capacity they displayed around the banquet table, Zola was prone to believe that he would go hungry unless he went stuffed, that an all-inclusive store of knowledge argued unlimited power. In the projected long poem he had told Baille about, "The Chain of Being," three cantos were to describe the earth since its creation, mankind since the Stone Age, and the foreseeably more perfect future. "The first canto . . . will relate all the upheavals that have occurred on the globe, everything geology has taught us about regions laid waste and animals engulfed in the debris. The second will take humanity at birth . . . and lead it to civilized times; here I will resume what physiology tells us about physical man and philosophy about moral man. Finally, the third and last canto will be a magnificent divagation." Though he never wrote this positivist analogue of Hugo's *La Légende des siècles*, his essay on Taine leaves no doubt that the impulse to rise above the crowd and encompass something in its totality—if not all ages, then his own—held sway. Almost without exception, statements about art have *tout* or *entier* as their pivotal adjective, which makes for a kind of militant, bullying tone. "Everything alive is worth studying," "The doctor finds all illness relevant," "Every great artist gathers around him a generation of imitators," "[Every great artist] draws from his heart the cry of an entire age." Epic grandeur counted no less than truth, and by 1865, three years before he began his "natural history" of the Rougon-Macquart clan, it had already struck him that a merely honorable place in French letters would never do. As he waded through Balzac's *Comédie humaine*, he saw himself from afar on the throne reserved for "spiritual dictators" in whom race, moment, and milieu combined to "sum up a nation." Driven by ambition, Zola worked hard at seeking out those in positions of influence who could help him gain national exposure. "I should be very much in your debt if you were to guide me along this unfamiliar path where I'm afraid of stumbling," he wrote to an editor at *Le Petit Journal,* and to Alphonse Duchesne of *Le Figaro,* he put it even more bluntly: "I wish to improve my credentials without delay. In my haste, I thought of your paper as being the one most likely to bring me instant notoriety." There was no private time during the day, ten hours of which belonged to Hachette, and his fortnightly articles in *Le Salut public* kept him up late at night, but fresh opportunities were not to be missed for the sake of sleep. Success proved addictive, especially as it doubled his income. "You understand that I'm not writing all this prose out of love for the public," he assured the well-heeled Antony Valabrègue. "I am paid twenty francs an article by the *Le Petit Journal* and fifty to sixty by the *Le Salut public,* so that I earn about two hundred francs a month with my pen. Money is mainly what got me into all this, but I also regard journalism as a very powerful lever and do not in the least mind having to produce myself on an appointed day before a considerable number of readers."

Now that Cézanne had left Aix for a second sojourn in Paris, Valabrègue succeeded him as Zola's epistolary confidant and the object of his rough solicitude. Being admired by a young provincial poet after groveling for space in newspapers helped him walk taller. Obsequious with editors, he found it irresistible to swagger, to throw his weight around and preen before the tyro. "If only you knew, my poor friend, what a small part talent plays in success, you would drop pen and paper and begin to study the literary life, the thousand little skulduggeries that open doors, the art of exploiting other people's credit, the cruelty needed to walk on the bellies of one's dear confreres," he reflected in September 1865. "Come, I say; I know a lot and am at your disposal." Zola wanted a protégé up north, but he also wanted someone down south to beat the drums for him in Aix. Notwithstanding his scorn of France outside Paris, he thrived on fantasies of a triumphant return to the backwater from which he had fled under miserable circumstances, of its smug bourgeoisie brought low, of the family name emblazoned all over town. Such fantasies whet his appetite for success. "I have often let you know," he wrote to Valabrègue, "what I think of provincial life. The pity is, I still have memories residing in Aix and I hallow thoughts and deeds associated with former times. I therefore ponder this lost corner of earth more than I'd like. I don't exactly fret over their opinion of me, but I would as well they were kept informed of small favors fortune throws my way."

With his income rising, Zola could afford something better than an eighth-floor walk-up, which must have been arduous for Emilie. He made several moves between late 1864 and 1866, the first being to 142,

Boulevard du Montparnasse, a building of solid construction where a four-room flat that looked out onto the wide thoroughfare cost him 460 francs per annum. Like every neighborhood situated near a tollgate or customs station, this one, although it had acquired pavement and streetlights two decades earlier, was still half rural and abounded in penny arcades, garden restaurants, and dance halls frequented by working-class people. After a year or so, noise from a local shooting gallery proved to be more than Zola could take of the hurly-burly. He then established residence on the rue de l'Ecole-de-Médecine, quite near Hachette, but soon moved again, having found better quarters several blocks away at 10, rue de Vaugirard, which stood next door to the Odéon. "We have a big apartment here, with dining room, bedroom, salon, kitchen, guest room, terrace," he informed an Aixois painter friend named Numa Coste, who had been unlucky in the draw when young men drew lots to decide military service, and was stationed nearby. "It's a veritable palace, whose doors we shall throw wide open to you as soon as you return [from maneuvers]."

Offering hospitality was so agreeable that in 1863 he began to make a weekly ritual of it. Every Thursday evening friends gathered at his flat for potluck or tea (tea because his nervous stomach could not tolerate coffee) and talked until all hours. They were mostly men he knew from Aix: Cézanne, Baille, Marius Roux, Philippe Solari, Valabrègue. Indeed, George Pajot may have been the only Parisian among them. Before long, however, new faces materialized as one friend brought another and the *cénacle* came to include Camille Pissarro and Frédéric Bazille, whom Cézanne had met through an Atelier Suisse acquaintance. By 1870, when war with Prussia sent everyone scattering, the ritual loomed large in Zola's life. "Belonging to a band of friends all keen on the same idea delighted him," he wrote in his novel about bohemian Paris, *L'Oeuvre*, where he figures as the main character, Sandoz. "Though he was the same age as they, he swelled with paternal pride, with cheerful bonhomie when he saw them in his home, surrounding him, hands joined, drunk on hope." What declared itself here was a vocation for literary fatherhood that matured some fifteen years later in the naturalist movement, which saw younger writers wanting a leader and a cause flock to Zola at his country house near Paris. But literary fatherhood went hand in hand with literary childhood, and *L'Oeuvre* makes it clear that his Thursdays also promoted the dream of a mystical union binding him to kindred souls. "[Sandoz] envisioned Thursdays succeeding one another, all alike, all happy, down to the farthest reaches of time. . . . All eternally together, all having started out at the same moment and achieved the same victory." The traditional midweek school holiday, Thursday afternoon, became a symbolic receptacle for all those fraternal memories that had accumulated by 1858, when, having departed Aix involuntarily, he found himself cut off from his past. At once progressive and nostalgic, he spoke ad nauseam about marching forward yet nurtured a desire to transcend history with its deaths, rifts, and separations—to abolish loneliness altogether in an eternal return of Thursday.

Within the larger group, Paul Cézanne and Jean-Baptistin Baille still commanded his deepest affection. Since 1861 Cézanne had gone through ordeals that made it possible for him to embrace Zola again. After a period of expiation in the family bank, where he is said to have used ledgers as sketch pads, committing artistic suicide lost its appeal. He took evening classes at Aix's Ecole des Beaux-Arts and gradually worked up the courage to revisit Paris. "I wholeheartedly approve your idea of coming to work in Paris and then withdrawing to Provence," Zola had written on September 29, 1862, in answer to a letter that has since disappeared. "I believe that it is a way of skirting the influence of schools and developing one's originality, if one has any. If you come here, so much the better for you and for us. We shall regulate our life, spending two evenings a week together and working on every other."

Cézanne's second sojourn, which began in November 1862 and lasted until the middle of 1864, was happier than the first. For about ten francs a month he could paint or draw at the Atelier Suisse, fifteen minutes' distant from his room off the Jardin du Luxembourg, and he was usually there all morning and evening, as he had been before. But friendships with two fellow habitués of the atelier led him farther afield. Through a Spaniard named Francisco Oller he met Camille Pissarro, who had already started to ask those fundamental questions about light and color that would soon revolutionize landscape painting. Another new friend was Antoine Guillemet, the handsome and good-natured son of a rich wine merchant, who shepherded Cézanne, laden with his paraphernalia, on excursions through the countryside and introduced him to artists living in the Batignolles district, a hilly Right Bank neighborhood near Montmartre, which had been farmland in Napoleon's day. Cézanne thus made the acquaintance of Frédéric Bazille, Auguste Renoir (Bazille's studio mate), Alfred Sisley, and Armand Guillaumin. This network did wonders for his precarious self-esteem. Mocked by other students, he felt at ease with men who were all seen as constituting a lunatic fringe. "Didn't I judge rightly in 1861 when Oller and I went to see that odd Provençal at the Atelier Suisse where Cézanne's figure drawings were ridiculed by all the impotent artists, including the famous Jacquet, who declined ages ago into prettiness, and whose works fetch enormous sums?" Pissarro exulted thirty-two years after the fact (probably having mistaken by one year the date of their first encounter). Feeling at ease with women was out of the question, yet even here signs indicated that Cézanne liked himself enough to improve his appearance. "Cézanne has cut his beard and sacrificed the tufts on the altar of victorious Venus," Zola informed Valabrègue in April 1864. And three months later, when Cézanne returned to Aix, Valabrègue found him changed for the better: "[I often see Paul in the afternoon]," he wrote to Zola. "He who seemed your dumb servant now talks. He expounds theories, elaborates doctrines. Worst crime of all, he even allows one to engage in political discussion (on a theoretic level of course) and says the most frightful things about the tyrant." Furious denunciations of Napoleon III, who by then had half disarmed himself, were of a piece with the red waistcoat Cézanne sported around town and the coarse language he used for describing art, in which *couillard,* or "ballsy," signified approval.

Unexpectedly, Emile now followed where Paul led. In the belief that his shy, moody friend might burrow underground if left alone, Zola had prescribed a careful agenda which now gave way to an active social life. Together they frequented the studios of Les Batignolles, cultivating Renoir, Bazille, Fantin-Latour, Monet, and Degas: soon Zola told Valabrègue that he had virtually no conversation except with painters. They also saw much of Jean-Baptistin Baille, who would remain Zola's boon companion until 1870. As self-confident as ever, Baille resigned his military commission after graduating from the Polytechnique in 1863. He earned master's degrees in chemistry, physics, and mathematics and produced his doctoral thesis on a subject ("The refractive indices of lenses used in the construction of optical and photographic instruments") that made him eligible for the National Institute of France's Bordin Prize, which he won in December 1866. Two years later, Zola persuaded Hachette and Company to commission from Baille a science-for-the-layman book about electricity.

The influence exerted by Cézanne and Baille betrays itself in Zola's correspondence: especially pertinent is a long letter written to Valabrègue during the summer of 1864 in which visual and optical metaphors couch a theory of literature. "Every work of art is a window opening onto creation," he began.

> Mounted in the embrasure of the window is a kind of transparent screen, through which objects appear more or less distorted, their lines and color undergoing more or less perceptible change. These changes depend on the nature of the screen. One does not see creation portrayed exactly as it is but modified by the medium [*milieu*] its image traverses.

With Taine as his intellectual sponsor, Zola declared every aesthetic order to be worthy of consideration but voiced an emphatic preference for realism, on the grounds that it was less subjective in outlook than classicism and romanticism. "I fully accept its procedure, which would have us face nature unblinkingly and render it in its entirety, without reserve," he wrote only a year after Manet's *Le Déjeuner sur l'herbe* moved respectable people to derisive anger. "A work of art must, it seems to me, scan the whole broad horizon. . . . The screen I like best hugs reality closest and skews it no more than is necessary to let me feel the presence of a man in an image of creation."

Anxious to make his presence felt, Zola struggled against the voyeur in him who had on various occasions pictured himself at real and imaginary windows, yearning for some unpossessable woman or seeing her possessed by another man. The window that helped him formulate his doctrinal position often reappeared as a dreamlike fixture in his tales, and one such tale, "Celle qui m'aime," was published several months after he outlined the "screen" theory to Valabrègue. Its setting is a fairground where a young man becomes intrigued by the patter of a concessionaire who claims to have brought from India a magic mirror in which romantic fantasies spring to life. Hesitantly he enters the booth, queues up before a small round window, and peeping through it sees a lovely blonde dressed in flowing white muslin with a white veil secured to her hair by a crown of may. "At first glance I took her for a saint; at second, I perceived a decent sort, not at all prudish and very accommodating indeed." Smitten when she blows him kisses, he lingers near the booth until it closes, and his image of lugubrious innocence turns out to be an ordinary grisette plying a trade that pays better than needlework. "Opposite me, behind a little pane set in the partition, I continually see an eye that looks at me," she explains. "It is sometimes black, sometimes blue. Except for this eye, I would be perfectly happy. It spoils the job." Fantasy runs athwart reality, but two lines of dots at the end suggest that the disabused voyeur gains in flesh what he lost in dreams of erotic perfection.

"Celle qui m'aime," together with the other stories he had written since 1859, gave Zola enough material for a volume. During the spring of 1864 he undertook the laborious task of copying them and prevailed upon Emile Deschanel, whose public lectures he regularly summarized in the *Revue de l'instruction publique*, to find him a publisher. "I've won my first victory," he crowed to Valabrègue on July 6. "Hetzel has taken my volume of short stories, which will come out next October." The following agreement, as stated by Zola in a letter to Hetzel's associate, Albert Lacroix, had been reached four days earlier:

My volume of stories, bearing the title *Les Contes à Ninon*, will be published in the Hetzel and Lacroix list. There will be a first printing of 1,500 copies. Beyond this number, and in the event that you publish a second edition, I shall receive a royalty of 25 centimes per copy. To balance your initial expenses, I contract, in accordance with the

terms of my proposal, to place, in all newspapers, notices or advertisements worth at least as much as what it cost to print the work,
without M. Hetzel or you having to put yourselves to further
expense.

At Hachette, fiction normally appeared in first editions of three thousand copies, but elsewhere a thousand was considered the prudent
figure for unknowns, and in any event Hachette would not have offered Zola more than fifteen centimes per copy. Until then, publishers
had made a practice of paying authors flat fees in return for the right
to print as many copies as public demand warranted during a stipulated period, and to keep all profits from the sale. Thus, Flaubert
earned only 1,300 francs from *Madame Bovary* during its first five years
of existence, though Michel Lévy printed thirty-two thousand copies.
By 1870 royalties based on copies printed had become the rule, and
this convention obtained for the rest of Zola's lifetime.

With professional savoir faire, Zola launched a vigorous campaign
on behalf of *Les Contes à Ninon*, importuning magazine and newspaper editors to publish excerpts, to insert puffs, to review the book
or use reviews he himself had drafted. "Don't trouble to get one of
the stories placed in the *Le Journal littéraire*," he instructed Charles
Deulin, an editor at the *La Nouvelle Revue de Paris*. "I have an influential person there who has promised to publish whatever I wish, and
I prefer to use your credit for the *Nouvelle Revue*. So choose a story,
detach the pages you choose, and send back what remains. That way
I'll know your choice and submit the other elsewhere. I am offering
you my work's maidenhead." A more immodest appeal went to Géry-
Legrand, whom he called his literary godfather: "I hasten to send you
my *Contes à Ninon*. . . . You must continue to serve me, for a good
deed cannot be left half done. Kindly insert the brief note you will
find attached, and I beg you to publish as soon as possible an article
about my stories that one of my friends will be forwarding within the
next few days." The brief note to which he alluded read, in part:

> The author, M. Emile Zola, belongs to the literary family of free
> spirits, of passionate and subtly mocking temperaments; he proceeds
> from Mérimée, Voltaire, Alfred de Musset, Nodier, Murger, Heine.
> He is a storyteller who converses with his Muse as caprice dictates,
> whence this strange book, in which each narrative is born of a specific
> inspiration. *Les Contes à Ninon* is sure to succeed with people of
> taste.

At once reverent and self-aggrandizing, the young man who repeatedly
asserted that he would walk in no one else's footsteps found it expedient to parade behind illustrious forebears. Of the hundred-odd arti-

cles *Les Contes* generated, a good proportion were variations on this puff. To be sure, Gustave Vapereau used Zola's line against him in *La Revue française*, where he characterized the stories as pastiches written by a novice not yet sure of his own identity. But Zola had built up credit everywhere, and in the final reckoning yeas far outnumbered nays.

Like a ventriloquist half convinced that his thrown voice came from another person, he congratulated himself on *Les Contes à Ninon's* critical success, trying hard to forget that the edition had not sold out. "All in all the press has been benevolent: a concert of eulogies except for two or three discordant notes," he reflected in a letter to Valabrègue. "And note that those who inflicted slight wounds are the very people who thought they were tickling me most agreeably—they didn't read my stories and spoke about them obligingly but falsely so that their readers must imagine me to be the most insipid and mawkish of creatures. . . . I would have preferred that they savage me. I can't wait to publish a second volume. There's good reason to believe that the next one will almost establish my reputation." Valabrègue could not have known what volumes lay unborn in the word "almost," or predicted that every volume Zola wrote would feel to him like a botched performance for which he had to atone with another work. Although he always did his utmost to arrange fanfares, a shadow nonetheless fell over the victory celebration and darkened its joy. Disinheriting himself each time anew, like a man forever struggling free from childhood, he saw victory elude him even as he piled Pelion on Ossa. "Here are my stories," he announced in his dedication to Ninon, an imaginary woman who embodied Provence. "No longer raise your voice in me, the voice of memory that brings tears to my eyes. . . . Don't come back during my hours of struggle and sadden me with reminders of our lazy nights." Zola often warned Valabrègue against laziness, to which he feared that he himself would permanently succumb. Laziness meant impotence, and no accomplishment could dispel the threat.

A second volume was in fact more than half complete when *Les Contes à Ninon* appeared. Zola had begun what turned out to be his first novel soon after separating from Berthe, the young woman who had lived with him on the rue Soufflot, and *La Confession de Claude*, as he called it, relates that adventure. Overwhelmed by various responsibilities, he had put the manuscript in a drawer, where it lay until the demi-success of *Les Contes* prompted him to salvage it. Advice from an editor at Hetzel-Lacroix, who felt that he should invest his talent in something more substantial than short stories, may also have hit home. During much of 1865 every spare moment was reserved for the novel, which went into print in September, at which time Zola informed a prospective reviewer, "It is a rather harsh work—more virile, I believe, than my first one."

Fraught with melodramatic paradoxes, *La Confession de Claude* takes after certain Balzac novels in telling the story of an idealistic provincial whom Paris awakens to vice. But unlike Eugène de Rastignac's initiation, which exposes high society, Claude's reveals the lower depths. The lower depths inhabit a Latin Quarter *hôtel garni*, and Claude, a student boarder, begins his descent when he walks upstairs to help a destitute young whore named Laurence, who has fallen gravely ill. "The peaceful sleep of vice, of washed-out features imbued in their repose with angelic sweetness, cast some strange spell on me," he observes, adding, as he beholds her half-naked body: "I was ashamed for the young woman, I felt my virginity fly away in my glance." Before long his virginity flies away in his bedroom, where Laurence installs herself. Having nursed her back to health, Claude embarks on a gentle program of moral reform, hoping that she will become a different person. But in the end he finds himself abased by the woman he would elevate. His unregenerate concubine proves stronger than he, which is to say that the high-minded play he had devised for her salvation unmasks the not so high-minded playwright. Together they wallow in apathy, and as time passes, bonds other than this one become so tenuous that Claude no longer feels drawn by the world outside. His only commerce with it is through a pawnshop in which he hocks everything he owns, including his clothes, the better to remain sequestered *à deux*. First as savior, then as cynosure, he lives out a fantasy of omnipotence that reduces him to bondage.

Each has his foil inside the boardinghouse. Jacques is a callous philanderer whom Claude has known since boyhood. Marie is a good-hearted waif prematurely ravaged by the flesh trade. Marie's death brings Claude's story full circle, for while ministering to her he sees, projected against a wall outside her garret window, the silhouette of Laurence betraying him in Jacques's room below. Martyrdom began with a glance, and this image, which he finds painfully irresistible, accomplishes it. "My suspicions became flesh. At last I knew and saw, I found in my imagination certitudes fraught with painful delights." That the scenario had been written before their fatal encounter—that he would not have found Laurence if he hadn't sought both an instrument of self-punishment and a whipping girl—eludes the narrator. Virtuous but alone, Claude falls back upon two friends or "brothers" who have inspired his confession (*La Confession* is, in fact, dedicated to Cézanne and Baille). "I thought I was mature enough for the battle and I was only a naked and feeble child," he tells them. "Perhaps I shall always be a child."

No doubt Zola had Musset's *La Confession d'un enfant du siècle* very much in mind when he wrote *La Confession de Claude*. An inventory of likely models would also include Balzac's *Père Goriot* and *Les Illusions perdues*. But the novel shows Zola working imaginative material peculiar to him, on which he drew obsessively. The characters foreshadow innumerable men-children, sirens, rakes, and short-lived innocents in *Les Rougon-Macquart*. The boardinghouse stands as a prototype of the enclosure ripped apart by madness or inhumanity that assumes different guises in *La Conquête de Plassans, L'Assommoir, Une Page d'amour, La Joie de vivre, Pot-Bouille, Le Docteur Pascal*. And the triangle featuring a callow youth who yearns to possess an opaque woman would unfold at many more windows. Zola's Oedipal nightmare proved wonderfully fertile. He had already made it explicit in "Celle qui m'aime," where the narrator trembles lest the magic mirror reflect his dream of an old hag "thirsty for young blood." In *La Confession de Claude* that hag becomes yet another whore who seems to merge on one hallucinatory occasion with two others. "I looked at the three of them together," Claude recalls. "In my distraught state of mind, which made them appear larger than life, I saw them wavering strangely. . . . They conversed as sisters do, without a thought to the difference in age. My blurred vision confused their three heads so that I could no longer tell whose had white hair." In time he delivered himself of other such vampire mothers.

La Confession came out one year after *Les Contes*, and again Zola orchestrated a publicity campaign. In November 1865 letters begging for attention poured from his pen, along with this insert:

M. Emile Zola, whose maiden work, *Les Contes à Ninon*, was so well received, has just published, at the Librairie Internationale, a new book: *La Confession de Claude*. This one is a psychological and physiological study, a tale of blood and tears that has Fall and Redemption as its lofty and pure moral. The frightful narrative relates a virgin heart's passion for one of those girls to whom poets have given the sweet names Mimi Pinson and Musette. The author bares himself therein with a strange talent that combines exquisite delicacy and mad audacity. Some will applaud and others will jeer, but this drama fraught with anguish and terror will leave no one indifferent. Emanating from the work are an inexpressible pride, a passion and strength that herald a writer of unusual energy.

His letters vary in tone. To Ernest Chesneau, the fine arts editor of *Le Constitutionnel*, he presented himself as an orphan on bended knee to a foster parent who could help him "find his way." Elsewhere he struck an authoritative pose, or wheedled, or coached the prospective reviewer. "It is understood that I prefer a sincere slating to routine compliments," he told an acquaintance at the *La Gazette des étrangers,* who ultimately praised the book. "Have no fear, hit and hit hard." On instructions from Zola, Marius Roux wrote a piece for *Le Mémorial d'Aix* in which attention was drawn to the names of Baille and Cézanne. "It will please their families," Zola had explained.

The critical fraternity gave *La Confession* a mixed reception. Aside from praise of the kind Zola invited and scorned, several articles argue his case with real discernment. The majority, however, were reviews that upheld the verdict of Zola's printer, who refused at first to handle what he considered an immoral work, and moral indignation ran across party lines, exercising straitlaced republicans like Louis Ulbach as well as religious zealots like Barbey d'Aurevilly, founder of La *Revue du monde catholique.* The didactic purpose in which Zola clothed *La Confession*—that it would sober up young people intoxicated by the false enchantments of Henri Murger's *Scènes de la vie de Bohème*— fell on deaf ears. For some it showed the devil at work; for others it bespoke youthful perversity. "The psychological side of this study lacks general truth. One does not feel that the tortures of this conscience stifled for several months have any bearing on mankind's salvation," wrote Ulbach, whose Protestant high-mindedness did not make him a particular friend of the unconscious. "[Young people] are mistaken in believing that they must be eccentric in order to be original; they shy away from nothing and view taste and measure as snares." Barbey d'Aurevilly went much further, writing so abusively that Zola (who had savaged his novel *Un Prêtre marié*) felt compelled to defend himself in public. This bitter polemic echoed through editorial rooms all over Paris.

In private, he prosecuted himself more harshly than most of his critics. When the brouhaha died down, his ego began predictably to sag. *La Confession* was both adroit and clumsy, he told Valabrègue, but the virtues he could still recognize in it were disqualified and his previous evaluation of it reversed: "It's hard for me to answer your excessively good opinion of my book. It is weak in places and contains lots of infantile stuff . . . The work is not virile; it is the outcry of a child who sobs and rebels."

One review of *La Confession de Claude* that affected Zola profoundly never found its way into print. Its author was the attorney* general, who had been asked by the minister of justice to decide whether Zola's novel might be liable to prosecution on the grounds that it constituted "an outrage to public and religious morals." Sparing this writer the legal mortification to which Flaubert and Baudelaire had been subjected eight years earlier, in 1857, when *Madame Bovary* and *Les Fleurs du mal* were put on trial, he concluded that it was not punishable:

To be sure it inspires reservations from the point of view of good taste and because it violates the chastity of language with its crude images and cynical details. Obeying tendencies of the realist school, the author has on certain pages delighted too much in analyzing shameful passions. He has forgotten that it is not by sullying the imagination of youths that one must seek to purify their heart and that a book that purports to have a moral intention must avoid everything that might make it resemble a wicked book. Be that as it may, the premise of the work is not immoral. What the author set out to do was to turn young people away from those impure liaisons into which they let themselves be drawn on the faith of poets who have idealized the loves of bohemia.

His report offers detailed information on Zola's background, circumstances, and the journals in which he published. An investigation had taken place that led him to characterize Zola as a young man "without any definite political opinion," whose ambitions were safely limited to the realm of literature.

Although officialdom exonerated him, Zola lost face at Hachette, where employees who wrote novels that prompted visits from the attorney general were, it seems, viewed with extreme disfavor by Louis Hachette's son-in-law and successor, Emile Templier. Publicity of this kind shook the house, and Templier, who also disapproved of the ruckus over *La Confession de Claude*, may have felt no compunctions about letting him go or urging him to resign.

Urging was all Zola needed. It had become clear by 1866 that he ought to fend for himself. Except on bad days, when he anxiously wondered whether hubris would provoke the gods to push him off his narrow ledge, confidence in the future sustained him. "Today I am known, people fear me and insult me," he bragged to Valabrègue shortly before leaving Hachette. "Today I am ranked among those writers whose works cause trepidation. That took some doing." With ample experience in every relevant domain, he could easily manage a literary chronicle for some newspaper and, as letters show, the first paper he approached, *L'Evénement*, warmed to his proposal. He also won Templier's authorization to compose a trilogy in the positivist tradition, *Les Héroïsmes*, which would have seen him—if he had ever written it—digress upon "heroes of the family," "heroes of the nation," and "heroes of humanity." Above all, he knew that he had other novels stored up and wanted time to bring them forth. His imagination was where his fortune lay, he asserted in a letter that shows him still nursing wounds inflicted by the baccalauréat jury. "I am a great ignoramus, which doesn't sadden me in the least; but I must earn a livelihood with my heart and imagination alone." Something good came of failure. The ungraduated *lycéen* preferred to think of himself as having the virtues of a self-made man.

The year 1866 marked the beginning of the end for Napoleon III, as liberals exacting concessions at home and Bismarck outmaneuvering France abroad left him crippled and indecisive. It was also a fateful year for Zola. In January he underwent two rites of passage. Not only did he leave Hachette but he separated from his mother and set up house with a woman named Gabrielle Alexandrine Meley, whom he eventually married.

VI

A HEARTH, A CAFÉ, A CAUSE

THERE IS SOME REASON to believe that her illegitimate birth made it difficult for Gabrielle Meley ever to feel secure in the edifice of her respectability. Baptized Eléonore Alexandrine, she styled herself "Gabrielle" during adolescence but preferred, once her relationship with Zola became conjugal, that people call her Alexandrine, discarding the previous name like an unfashionable garment or keeping it only for intimate wear. Her looks belied her humble background. "Tall, dark-haired, distinguished, with the astonishing coal-black eyes of some Velásquez princess" is how the novelist J. K. Huysmans described her in 1877, and this portrait would have done her justice twelve years earlier, when, at twenty-five, she began to fix Zola's attention.

The little we know about her early life leaves no doubt that it had often been stormy. Born in 1839 to an eighteen-year-old hatter named Edmond Meley and a seventeen-year-old florist named Caroline Louise Wadoux, she survived childhood while depending for nurture on relatives more than on her parents, whose liaison was tenuous. In 1848, Edmond took a wife, and there is reason to believe that time spent under the dominion of this woman brought the little girl constant grief. Matters did not improve until her mother in turn married. Caroline set up house with Louis Deschamps, a riding master by profession, in the Sentier district, very near the rue Saint-Joseph, where François Zola had lived with Emilie Aubert. But their ménage lasted only six months, for in September 1849 Caroline suddenly died, leaving her daughter stranded between stepparents of whom one was a shrew and the other a virtual stranger. What happened then is open to conjecture. The most plausible scenario has it that she learned the flower business from Deschamps's sister, or became a dressmaker, and through some untold sequence of events fell in with painters whom Zola cultivated.[1]

Alexandrine and Emile were undoubtedly a match, but it seems that affection bound them together rather more than physical passion. Alexandrine, who wanted family above all else, found Zola worthy of her resourcefulness, her domestic skill, her energy, her loyal nature. In Alexandrine, Zola found, among other things, the manager on whom he could count to help him save his rich imagination for literature and produce books instead of dissipating himself in unprofitable escapades. Fascinated by low life, he stopped his ears to its siren call in choosing as his companion a woman rather like his mother. Both women had grown up poor in the same neighborhood. Both attained higher station through intellectually gifted men. And together they doted upon "Mimi," fretting over his ailments, satisfying his robust appetite, bolstering his precarious self-esteem, espousing his causes, and, from the outset, competing, sometimes quite rancorously, for pride of place. Along with Zola's trinity of friends went this ménage à trois, which reconstituted the matriarchal household he had known in Aix-en-Provence.

There was now a livelihood to be earned for three. One source of income dried up midway through December 1865, when Le Salut public informed Zola that its clientele could not tolerate long articles. Silenced, he returned three months later in a humbler role, but meanwhile Hippolyte de Villemessant kept him busy by hiring him to write a regular column for L'Evénement.

To associate with Hippolyte de Villemessant was to experience the daily hubbub that surrounded a man whom contemporaries dubbed the Barnum of French journalism. Jovial and munificent, this former ribbon merchant from Blois made himself at home in the fourth estate, where he first rose to prominence as a royalist during the Second Republic. Abusive rhetoric cost him several positions, but Louis Napoleon's coup d'état, which ushered in even stricter censorship, unexpectedly worked to his advantage. While the autocratic regime denied him political expression, it let him say what he would about café society, and "le Boulevard" was a gold mine that Villemessant exploited with phenomenal success in Le Figaro when the defunct weekly came alive under his management. Among disenfranchised Parisians, society gossip helped satisfy a craving for bread and circuses.

[1]The liaisons of her bohemian youth may have been another reason to slough off her first name.

"[*Le Figaro* figured as] the great official intelligencer of Parisian scandals, listening at doors, winkling out secrets, whispering indiscretions, telling the upper crust all about the demimonde, giving backstage intrigues the importance normally accorded political events, and thus wasting on foolishness energy that might have gone into serious thought," wrote one nineteenth-century critic. Duels and libel suits became regular occurrences as Villemessant, who broke new ground in the realm of defamation, often ventured too far. But from every such contretemps he emerged wealthier and more eager to pry behind respectable façades. At *Le Figaro* it did not much matter whether someone stood on the far Right or the far Left provided he stood outside the pale, and abetting Villemessant were writers chosen for their high color rather than their ideological hue. Himself a consummate opportunist, he favored militants, people goaded by bêtes noires, angry young men like Henri Rochefort and Jules Vallès, both of whom would, in due course, consecrate their polemical talent to the Paris Commune and suffer exile.

Having staked out the suburbs of political discourse, Villemessant multiplied there in publications such as *Le Figaro-Programme, La Gazette de Paris, Le Grand Journal, La Gazette rose, L'Autographe*. This little empire did not include a daily, however, and by 1865 it had become apparent that unless he created one to sell cheap, *Le Petit Journal* would gobble up the mass market. Hence *L'Evénement*, whose first issue appeared in November 1865 with bombastic self-acclaim. Its "phalanx," it declared, would rejoice as popular writers, or tyros bidding to achieve that status, swelled its ranks.

Tyros were paid handsomely, but Villemessant demanded his money's worth. Between February and November 1866, when the government banned *L'Evénement* for having dared to broach an issue outside its licensed subject matter, Zola wrote one hundred and ten articles under the rubric of "Livres d'aujourd'hui et de demain." After only a week on the job he excited controversy with the following manifesto:

No longer will I force myself to read through a book that irks me for the sole purpose of advising the public not to read it. I'm not sure how many people realize what is involved in the grueling task I've assigned myself. I read an average of three or four volumes a day and until now have read the good and the bad alike, so as not to speak about a work on slight acquaintance . . . Henceforth, when a book falls from my hands after the tenth page, I won't feel obliged to persevere. It will have been judged . . . and I shall merely announce its existence to my readers. Accordingly, I shall, if necessary, add an appendix to my articles, entitled: "Books not to read."

It was all he could do to remain current as new titles arrived pell-mell, and even those that escaped outright execution were given short shrift. "I beg readers to observe that my articles are merely conclusions," he explained. "I read the work, I discuss it with myself, and, since I have very little space, I can present only the verdict, not the pleas—whence a certain stiffness or dryness perhaps." Zola hurried them through three by three, rendering justice with an anecdote, a catchy phrase, a personal reminiscence, a quotation. Important works made him pause, notably Victor Hugo's *Travailleurs de la mer*, but for every such *livre de demain* there were dozens of *livres d'aujourd'hui*—popular biographies, travel literature, novels, criticism, books on homeopathic medicine, on cosmetics used in ancient Rome, on creatures of the deep. Much taken with his own virtuoso performance, he would occasionally interrupt it to point out that it involved risks, or to assure the public that what he sought was truth at any cost rather than mere notoriety. "It seems that telling the truth in the world of letters is called uncouthness and discourtesy," he boasted, like Molière's misanthrope.

> I am accused of not having those benevolent sentiments that should prevail in relationships among practitioners of the same trade. . . . People marvel at my candor and free speech as if they were monstrous aberrations; they tell me that I've gone astray and stand to make numerous enemies who will harm me later on. . . . Well, so be it. I am one who believes that highways are more direct than pathways and I shall continue to follow my own road, walking in sunlight, speaking out loud, as I believe I must.

As characteristic of him as the aggressiveness he demonstrated in print was the need he felt to legitimize the thrill of it with protestations of virtuous self-sacrifice.

Anyone who read "Livres d'aujourd'hui et de demain" beyond its first few installments would soon have mastered Zola's critical vocabulary. "Harsh," "violent," "analytical," "feverish" were compliments, and strung together they made his case for literature that featured what he liked to call "the human beast," meaning the primitive self held in strict quarantine by most novelists of the day (Zola found *la bête humaine* in Taine's *Notes sur l'Angleterre*). "I am sympathetic to these violent stories, when they spring from psychological and physiological analysis," he wrote of one novel. "The massacres committed by Ponson du Terrail's Rocambole make me laugh; they are puppet plays and I can see bran and wool oozing out of bullet holes. But show me the human beast in all its fury and I quake. Here blood flows, real blood. . . . The writer, through careful observation and authentic detail, brings his characters alive." Against well-bred fiction and history, Zola armed himself with a perverse credo according to which everything proper concealed impropriety and everyone famous some secret infamy. "I like historical indiscretions and nothing delights me more than the little facts of history, those that engender the big ones. Historians who solemnly record them neglect to lift the veil completely, so that we see the stage without seeing the wings." But this reductionism in no way tempered his enthusiasm for extravaganzas like Hugo's *Travailleurs de la mer*, where a bigger-than-life protagonist triumphs over nature. Nor, indeed, did one predilection contradict the other. Commuting as he did between sociopathic depths and an imaginative realm that nurtured fantasies of heroic transcendence, Zola found what he sought either above or beneath the pious universe of his confreres, in the pariahdom to which they consigned the irrational, the singular, the unsightly.

At stake was not only human truth but creative independence. Nothing irked him more than sententiousness (all except his own), and he regularly scolded those who used the novel as a pulpit for some ideological message or homily. Returning fiction to the storyteller became his refrain. "I'm not a disciple of art for art's sake; it's just that I like a novel to be a novel," is how he put it in a review of *Un Divorce*, by Madame Champceix, whose characters shuffle through the plot like men in sandwich boards with liberal agendas written all over them. "I would that the novelist told himself above all that he is a physiologist and a psychologist. Drama stops dead when politics or social science is dumped right into the path of action." Not even Hugo escaped scot-free, for Zola's tribute had a critical edge:

> Personally, I prefer the spectacle of the hero conquering the elements. Here the poet's heart and imagination run free. He no longer preaches, he no longer discusses. He is simply the great painter of human and natural forces. He is an artist pure, and I need not worry about his social theories or philosophical beliefs.

In the novel he saw a "virile" genre and in the novelist a demiurge illustrating "human and natural forces" or a sleuth uninhibited by moral strictures. Beyond good and evil was where his own future lay and on that height reigned the half-legendary father he hoped to equal, if not surpass. "Myself, I'm a rebel," he announced in the one review. "Ever since I burned my poems [which in fact he hadn't done], I have given myself over to reality with such passion that I can no longer swallow lies, however sweetly rhymed."

Since professions of faith shouted from a swiftly moving vehicle drew no crowds, he decided to go where people flocked, and in May they flocked to the annual state exhibition of painting and sculpture held at the Palace of Industry. This capital event, known as the Salon, was a plum that usually fell to seasoned critics who walked blindfold through the vast bazaar, genuflecting before work signed by eminences of the Academy. Had Villemessant played it safe he would have hired one such veteran, but the gambler or gadfly in him took over when a mere neophyte applied for the job. Zola, whose shy demeanor belied his pugnacity, got what he wanted, on condition that he use a pseudonym.

The Salon, like many another "bourgeois" institution, had royal origins. Conceived as a solemn occasion for showing art that promoted Louis XIV's cultural hegemony, it had been the preserve of academicians during the *ancien régime*. They alone might exhibit, and, indeed, membership in the Académie Royale de Peinture et de Sculpture required that they do so, until a jury was set up to limit submissions. The Terror dismantled this order. It declared every artist showworthy, and the Salon became an egalitarian ritual to be conducted without benefit of jury or Academy. All artists, French or foreign, members or not of the Académie de Peinture et de Sculpture, would be equally entitled to exhibit their work in that part of the Louvre assigned for that purpose, ran one decree. Wreaking havoc in institutional life did not, however, diminish the authority of the ancients. Classical models survived intact when Louis XVI fell, and under Jacques-Louis David's dictatorship they continued to hold sway.

This anachronistic backdrop, used by regicides as well as kings, readily found employment in nineteenth-century France, when the Ecole des Beaux-Arts was grooming artists who could serve the newly enriched and the precariously empowered by providing them with images that bespoke permanence. Taught like their *lycée*-bred counterparts to look backward, this establishment made modern life unwelcome at the Salon, where every spring brought forth lifeless foliage and, behind a coat of varnish, scenes from the Bible or Greek and Roman mythology or France's heroic past recurred year after year. As society became more mobile, official art became more sclerotic. Still, the modern world succeeded in wedging itself inch by inch through the temple gates. First to enter was Delacroix, of whom Théophile Gautier wrote in 1841 that "the future of painting is being realized on his canvases; he is the true child of this century and . . . every piece of contemporary poetry has cast its shadow on his palette." Along with him came painters of the Barbizon school, whose belief that nature should be rendered in its very midst produced works that classical landscapists found obnoxious. Corot and Daubigny met stubborn opposition from the Salon jury during Louis Philippe's reign. Twenty years later they themselves were jurors casting votes for Gustave Courbet.

The history of protest against a state apparatus that held imaginative work hostage to rigid convention included various one-man shows, the most dramatic of which had taken place at the 1855 World's Fair. There, in full view, Courbet built a private pavilion and exhibited masterpieces spurned by the Salon, charging people admission and issuing a catalogue that expounded his credo. "I have wanted quite simply to draw upon the total knowledge of tradition for a reasoned and independent sentiment of my own individuality," it read in part. "To know so as to have the power: that was my thought. To be equal to translating the manners, the ideas, the look of my age, in accordance with my own lights; to be not only a painter but a man as well; in a word, to create living art—that has been my goal."

No one dared imitate him, not right away, that is, for beyond the Salon lay a frontier where private galleries were still anomalous, where critics seldom ventured, and where the average patron, who regarded official consecration as a warranty of talent, felt quite lost. How matters stood became clear eight years after Courbet's fiasco, when Napoleon III, in a quixotic gesture that served to dampen the spirit of revolt, let rejected candidates exhibit their work at a Salon des Refusés. Many accepted the invitation, knowing that it would earn them public ridicule, and among these so-called *refusés* were not only the numerous drudges of art but also Pissarro, Fantin-Latour, Whistler, and Manet (with *Le Déjeuner sur l'herbe*). Any exposure was, they felt, better than proud obscurity. They also needed clients.

After 1863 officialdom prevailed upon Louis Napoleon to refrain from further intervention, and the Salon des Refusés was discontinued. It became a precedent invoked by disgruntled artists in their struggle against state censorship. One such artist was Paul Cézanne, who, with characteristic effrontery, laid his case before the Superintendent of Fine Arts, Count de Nieuwerkerke. "I have lately had the honor of writing to you about two canvases the jury has just refused," he protested in a letter dated April 19, 1866.

Since you have not yet answered, I feel compelled to dwell further on the motives that made me write it. As you have certainly received my letter, I need not repeat the arguments presented therein. I shall merely reiterate that I cannot accept the illegitimate judgment of confreres whom I myself have not entrusted with the mission of appraising my worth. I call upon you to support my demand. I wish to appeal directly to the public and exhibit nevertheless. I see nothing exorbitant in this wish, and if you questioned painters in my position, all would answer by repudiating the Jury and telling you that they want to participate one way or another in an exhibition which must, perforce, remain open to every serious worker.

May the Salon des Refusés therefore be reestablished. I would ardently wish to show my work, even if I were the lone exhibitor, in order that the crowd should know that I have no more desire to be confused with those gentlemen of the jury than they apparently have to be confused with me.

The same day Cézanne hoisted this petard, which had been formulated at Zola's weekly dinner, *L'Evénement* published a piece by Zola entitled "Un Suicide" under the pseudonym he was presently to adopt for his Salon articles—Claude. Calling attention to a painter of small repute named Jules Holtzapfel, who had shot himself after being rejected by the jury, he implied that juries inflicted capital punishment. "I wanted to see where the unhappy man committed suicide; I found out the address of his studio and have just now emerged from that sinister room, whose floor still shows large reddish spots," he wrote. "It gives me bitter satisfaction to note, even as I undertake my review of the Salon, that I have run smack against a tomb. I am thinking about those who will enjoy the crowd's applause, those whose works will be amply displayed in full light, and I see at the same time this poor man in his forlorn studio writing adieux and spending a whole night preparing himself for death."

Zola thus put readers on notice that he intended to avenge those whose art had been excluded from the Salon, and indeed his first articles, which appeared before the vernissage, constitute an indictment of the jury system. "Nowadays a Salon is not the work of artists but of a jury . . . [The jury] has created these long galleries, cold and livid, where a harsh light reveals all manner of timid nonentities and stolen reputations." His image of the Salon with its *tableaux morts* clearly foreshadows his portrayal in *Thérèse Raquin* of the city morgue, with its "livid" bodies aligned on marble slabs, which is to say that even as Paris began primping for a gala, Zola got dressed for a wake. It would be an excursion through some netherworld guarded by spirits who would sooner kill than admit color, light, and movement. "They mock truth and justice," he declared. "All-powerful, they show only the third or fourth part of what really exists; they amputate art and offer the crowd its mutilated corpse."

Zola habitually posed as a sacrificial victim, and the morbid eloquence he unleashed against the Salon jury had its source, no doubt, in hatred of juries past. It was an issue of injustice done not only to artists whose place had been taken by men with "stolen reputations" but to children robbed of their inheritance; rescuing artists from oblivion meant rescuing himself. Nothing illustrates this equation more transparently than a campaign he waged two years later in *Le Mémorial d'Aix*, when, as we shall see, much ink was spilled over the question of Aix having forgotten François Zola. "If the future treats me generously, if it amplifies my voice, the first cry I utter will be one of indignation against you. Then, in my own work, will my father have his name brilliantly enshrined," he prophesied. Altruistic boasts like these let Zola swagger without incurring divine wrath. Ambitious for fame but ever fearful that lightning would strike him dead, he could not assert himself except in a crusade for the derelict or exiled or anonymous, and it is remarkable how often he launched enterprises from beyond some grave. Just as Holtzapfel's suicide inaugurates the Salon, so the first novel of the *Les Rougon-Macquart* opens in a cemetery whose tenants had been dug up and carted away. To keep the dead alive was to keep alive the self-righteous anger that generated energy for writing.

His gorge might have risen even higher had he seen a memorandum written before the Salon des Refusés in which Louis Napoleon's administration fretted about déclassés seriously endangering society unless "a dike" was built to contain "so many individualities." But experience as a déclassé had familiarized him with the establishment's bugbears, and his own rhetoric shows it. "I hold that a work of art is . . . a personality, an individuality," he wrote after dispatching the jury.

> What I ask of an artist is . . . that he boldly assert a powerful and idiosyncratic mind, a nature that grasps the natural world and sets it plunk before our eyes . . . In short, I feel complete disdain for minor dexterities, for self-seeking blandishments, for what study has taught an artist and what dogged application has made routine, for all the theatrical stunts in history painting pulled off by this chap and all the perfumed daydreams of that one. But I have complete admiration for work that leaps spontaneously from a vigorous and singular hand. Here it is no longer a matter of pleasing or displeasing; it is a matter of being oneself, of baring one's heart, of energetically formulating an individuality.

His title for this pronouncement, "Le Moment artistique," informed the reader that he was, if not a hard-core positivist, a loyal fellow traveler. With the memory of baccalauréat examinations still rankling, Zola set out to wipe his slate clean. Against academic dogma he invoked natural science and let loose a barrage of metaphors calculated to make the prudish cringe. "Do you fear your own language that you toil so arduously over dead ones?" he sneered. "Art is a human product, a human secretion; it is our body that sweats the beauty of our works. Our body changes according to climate and custom, and secretions change likewise." Taine's influence is manifest here, but in characterizing mind as either creative or a mere receptacle for the pieties and prescriptions of schoolmen who swore by history painting, Zola went beyond his mentor. To create, he implied, was to behold a virgin world through uncouth eyes. To *be* was to exorcise despotic ghosts.

Villemessant soon understood that his protégé meant to exorcise the Salon itself. Where other critics saw images, Zola saw "dismal nullity," and when at last someone worthy of notice did materialize, it proved to be an artist with nothing on exhibition in 1866. "I liked him right away; since we first met, I've penetrated his talent," he stated in a piece devoted to Edouard Manet, whose *Olympia* had scandalized Paris the year before. "What certain confreres pass off as a depiction of nature impelled him, no doubt, to question reality on his own. He apparently rejected all the knowledge and experience of previous generations; he wanted to begin at the beginning, that is, to develop art from close observation of his material." The heroic truth seeker had found himself ostracized by subservient fantasists: "You know what effect Monsieur Manet's canvases produce at the Salon. They punch holes in the wall. Spread all around them are the wares of fashionable confectioners—sugarcane trees and pie-crust houses, gingerbread gents and whipped-cream ladies."

Like his characterization of realism as a clear window on life, Zola's image of holes punched in the wall assigns a virile function to the eye. Some eyes penetrate while some decorate. Some engage in child's play, some do yeoman work. Some devour flesh and some feast on pâtisserie (the stomach being yet another locus of virility for Zola, who ate with passion when he was not dyspeptic). "Monsieur Manet has a no-nonsense temperament, which cuts clean," he wrote. "He captures his figures alive, he does not shrink before nature's rowdiness, he lets objects assert themselves, detaching each from every other. His entire being compels him to see . . . in simple and energetic swatches. It could be said of him that he is satisfied to find the right tones and the right arrangement of them. What results is a strong, solid painting." Lest anyone so inclined tell himself that a man unconventional in his art must be immature in his way of life, Zola portrayed Manet as irreproachably bourgeois. "The waggish scapegrace imagined by the crowd . . . is married and leads the orderly life of a bourgeois. Furthermore, he works without respite, always searching, studying nature, posing questions, and following his own path."

Manliness, or "temperament," signified high praise from Zola (as from Cézanne). The word allowed him more freedom of movement than "realism," which felt too much like a straitjacket tailored by color-blind ideologues. And it let him attack officialdom low down, where he hoped a blow might cripple its authority. "Now there's a temperament, there's a man among eunuchs!" was how he introduced Claude Monet, whose *Camille* had somehow survived the otherwise efficient triage. "Glance at canvases all around it and you will see the pitiful show they make next to this window opened on nature. Here we have something more than a realist; we have a strong, subtle interpreter who has not gone wooden with his concern for detail." Did society's rulers pretend to lord it over Creation? Their artistic offspring were born sterile. Did a dynastic bourgeoisie that gloried in lines of succession urge itself on posterity? Posterity would instead heed men endowed with nothing but temperament—that is, the disinherited among whom Zola stood as fellow plaintiff. "I have tried to restore to M. Manet the place he owns, right up front," he declared. "People will perhaps mock the panegyrist as loudly as the painter. One day we will both be avenged . . . Temperaments alone live and alone dominate the ages."

Zola's view ultimately prevailed against academic fashion, of course, but in 1866 it took courage to thrash the jury and real discernment to single out Manet, Monet, and Pissarro. Jurors waxed wroth. Denunciatory letters flooded L'Evénement. "Lunatics tore up the paper in front of kiosks on the boulevard," wrote Alexis, and with one such lunatic Zola nearly fought a duel. Although Villemessant thrived on ballyhoo, so much of it was more than he had bargained for. Readers began canceling their subscriptions en masse, which prompted the publisher to muzzle his ferocious pup after three weeks. In a valedictory entitled "Adieux d'un critique d'art," Zola held nothing back. "I don't give a hoot about the French school!" he exclaimed.

> Me, I don't have any traditions; I don't discuss the fold of drapes, the attitude of limbs, the expression of faces. I don't grasp what people mean by a fault or a quality. I believe that a master's work is a coherent whole, the utterance of his heart and flesh. You can't change anything; you can only acknowledge genius and study it.

His exit line came next, and it sounded a note of truculent martyrdom. "I will always be on the side of the vanquished. There is open conflict between indomitable temperaments and the crowd. I am for temperaments, and I attack the crowd."

As bracing as he found the public outcry, applause from kindred spirits gave him greater satisfaction. Manet, for one, lost no time communicating his gratitude. Mutual friends had brought them together earlier that year, when The Fifer and The Tragic Actor were yet to be rejected by the jury. But until his Salon article appeared, Zola was for Manet a half-remembered face in the regular parade of late-afternoon visitors who trooped through his studio near Clichy. Only now, with Zola having shown his mettle, did they become fast friends. "Dear Monsieur Zola," Manet wrote on May 7. "I don't know where to find you so that I can shake your hand and tell you how happy and proud

The rue Saint-Joseph in Paris, where Zola was born. A photograph taken by Charles Marville in the 1850s, looking from the rue du Sentier toward the rue Montmartre.

Zola at the age of six, with his droopy eyelid. It is a face that seems to promise strong resolutions.

An anonymous painting of the Zola family done by an amateur in Aix-en-Provence. The mournful faces of mother and son are nearly identical.

An early-nineteenth-century lithograph of the Place des Quatre-Dauphins, in what was then the aristocratic quarter of Aix-en-Provence, the Quartier Mazarin. The fountain, showing four dolphins supporting an obelisk, which is surmounted by a pinecone, was erected in 1667. The Collège Bourbon abutted this square.

The entrance to one of Aix's aristocratic town houses, the Hôtel de Panisse-Passis, built in 1739.

One of the mountain paths on which Cézanne and Zola used to hike, as it enters a dense pine wood overlooking the Infernets gorge and the Zola dam.

The Zola dam, with Mont Sainte-Victoire in the distance.

The Lycée Saint-Louis was constructed at Napoleon Bonaparte's command and opened in 1820. Pictured here is the façade built in the 1850s, overlooking the newly traced Boulevard Saint-Michel.

Charles Marville's photograph of the leveled Châtelet district and the Châtelet Column being encased for removal dates to the 1850s, when Zola first arrived in Paris.

Paul Cézanne in 1861.

Zola in the early 1860s, when he was working as a clerk at the Customs House.

Zola in his mid-twenties, director of publicity at Hachette.

Edouard Manet, photographed by Nadar around 1865, when he was thirty-three.

Manet's portrait of Zola, exhibited at the 1868 Salon.

ÉMILE ZOLA

ÉD. MANET

ÉTUDE BIOGRAPHIQUE ET CRITIQUE
ACCOMPAGNÉE D'UN PORTRAIT D'ÉD. MANET PAR BRACQUEMOND
ET D'UNE EAU-FORTE D'ÉD. MANET
D'APRÈS OLYMPIA

PARIS
E. DENTU, ÉDITEUR
LIBRAIRE DE LA SOCIÉTÉ DES GENS DE LETTRES
PalaisRoyal, 17 et 19, Galerie d'Orléans
1867

The cover of Zola's 1867 brochure on Manet, published for the one-man show Manet organized after being excluded from the artistic section of the Universal Exposition.

A view of the Place de Clichy in June 1869, not long after Zola moved into the neighborhood.

An undated photograph of Alexandrine Meley Zola.

I am to be defended by a man of your talent. What a splendid article. Many, many thanks. Your previous piece ["Le Moment artistique"] was altogether remarkable and made a splash. I would like your opinion on some matter. Where can we meet? If it doesn't inconvenience you, I'm at the Café de Bade every day between 5:30 and 7:00."

Most people were either charmed or vexed by Manet, the son of a prominent magistrate whose demeanor offered no obvious clue to his artistic iconoclasm. At home in café society, he gravitated toward fashionable spots along the Boulevard des Italiens, where Zola, had their paths crossed, might have taken him for a typical Second Empire dandy idling life away. His banter, his manners, his wardrobe all bespoke privilege, and with them went a jauntiness that suggested immense self-confidence. "One evening . . . I was walking down the rue Pigalle when I saw approaching me a man of youthful appearance and distinguished carriage, dressed with elegant simplicity," recalled the painter Georges Jeanniot. "A blond wearing a fine silky beard, he had gray eyes, a straight nose, mobile nostrils, gloved hands, alert and nervous feet. It was Manet." The nonchalance of the gentleman expressed itself, too, in his aversion to theoretical debate. Those who knew him as a voluble and witty conversationalist could not easily draw him out on the subject of art. "Art is a circle," he would say. "One is born inside it or not, by happenstance."

That Manet sometimes wondered whether he himself belonged inside it or not may be inferred from Mallarmé's portrait of him lunging helter-skelter at the blank canvas, "as if he had never painted before." This apparently seamless figure was in fact a curious patchwork. Bold yet in some ways insecure, well bred but given to affecting the drawl of street arabs, staking out new artistic ground while producing art filled with quotations from Titian, Goya, Ingres, and Velásquez, he could neither do the conventional thing nor cease to value trophies society reserved for its pious sons. What Erik Satie once said about Ravel—"No matter that he spurns the Legion of Honor: his music accepts it"—would apply to Manet in reverse. Though his work violated every canon upheld by the Academy, he wanted a knight's cross all the same. "Anything that distinguishes one from the multitude is legitimate. . . . In this dog's life we lead, full of struggle, one can never be sufficiently well armed," he declared after Degas had done ridiculing some artist friend who made the honors list. Irony deserted him when recognition or the absence of it came into play. "It's no news to me how very bourgeois you are," rejoined Degas.

Degas knew full well that Manet wore many hats as he traveled from his flat to his studio to "the Boulevard," then home again. A plump, maternal Dutch woman named Suzanne Leenhoff, who bore him a son before they married in 1863, stood at either end of this itinerary, orienting her peripatetic spouse without hindering his movements. She was, so to speak, the ballast he carried on his daily flight into playland. "[Manet] has admitted to me that he adores café society and deep down takes sensual delight in the perfumed and luminous refinements of its nightlife," wrote Zola. "No doubt he is drawn to it by its broad and vivid color." But magnetic attraction worked both ways. Drawn to *le monde*, Manet in turn became a cynosure for young apostles like Fantin-Latour, confreres waffling between the old and the new, writers eking out a bare livelihood in the service of realism, financiers, theatrical impresarios, stray cocottes, notorious horizontals. People paid him impromptu visits, and if at 5:30 p.m. he did not appear all spruced up at the Café de Bade, he was often to be found at his studio entertaining a strange omnium-gatherum, which Zola made even stranger.

Certainly Manet and Zola had wider grounds for friendship than the transaction that gave one a visible platform and the other a stentorian voice. Soloists by nature, both men were jealous of their independence, and what Zola wrote about schools, implicitly justifying the distance he kept from literary ideologues, struck a sympathetic chord in Manet, who would snub the Impressionist exhibition organized several years later. To challenge dogma did not mean that either of them wished to plight his troth with a marginal heresy or to deny himself institutional insignia. Enamored of Paris, each sought to conquer it after the fashion of Balzac's Rastignac, and Manet hounding the Salon for recognition prefigured Zola obstinately campaigning for a seat in the Académie Française. Center stage held them spellbound. "It's criminal to live far from Paris in these times of fever and struggle," Zola exulted in a letter written on June 14, 1866, to Numa Coste.

His life shifted increasingly toward the Right Bank now that he saw more and more painters who inhabited Les Batignolles. Linked to central Paris by omnibuses called "Batignollaises," this urban village, where cottages survived among recently built tenements, became home for people needing cheap digs or wanting asylum from revolutionary turmoil. Its population had swelled after 1848 and continued to swell under Napoleon III, when widespread demolition of slums cast thousands adrift. Pensioned civil servants, retired shopkeepers, down-at-heel spinsters, and unemployed workers made do in an environment that also proved hospitable to young artists. Manet lived on the rue de Saint-Petersbourg (later renamed Leningrad); within hailing distance of him were Bazille, Sisley, Renoir, and Degas.

In 1867, Zola, too, found quarters in Les Batignolles. Meanwhile he showed up almost every week at a café just off the Place de Clichy where he was sure to find his painter friends assembled, especially on Friday afternoons, when they met in plenary session, knowing that Manet would join them. Until Manet "discovered" it, nothing distinguished the Café Guerbois except its trellised garden. Most habitués came for sport, and billiard balls colliding on tables in a dimly lit back room echoed through the saloon, which had mirrors and gingerbread to remind Manet of his beloved Boulevard. Here he matched wits with Degas while neighborhood folk, perplexed by their conversation, looked sideways at what they called "the artists' corner." It was a lively scene, if not bohemian in the way that the Café Momus had been when Charles Baudelaire, Gustave Courbet, and Gérard de Nerval gathered there during the 1840s. As Monet remembered years later:

> Nothing could have been more interesting than these talks, with their perpetual clashes of opinion. You kept your mind on the alert, you felt encouraged to do disinterested, sincere research, you laid in supplies of enthusiasm that kept you going for weeks and weeks, until a project you had in mind took definite form. You always left the café feeling hardened for the struggle, with a stronger will, a sharpened purpose, and a clearer head.

Consorting with porcupines like Degas and Duranty (a talented novelist who wrote art criticism) sometimes led to egos being punctured, but Monet's enthusiasm was generally shared, and as word of this *cénacle* spread, the few became more numerous. The Belgian painter Alfred Stevens, the great photographer Nadar, James Whistler all put in occasional appearances.

Zola seldom encountered Cézanne at the Guerbois. When Paul did go there he would arrive late, survey everyone warily, open his jacket, hitch up his pants like a cocksure street tough, then shake hands all around, except with Manet, to whom he'd doff his cap and say in the nasal twang of Provence: "I won't offer you my hand, Monsieur Manet, as it's been one week now since I've bathed." Torn between the need for companionship and an aversion to company that made him feel stupid, he frequently sat by himself, shunning the melee. More often than not his departure followed hard on his arrival. A queer look or a remark critical of some idea he cherished was a spark to tinder, and enough to propel him from the café without explanation. "They're a lot of bastards, they dress as smartly as solicitors," he told Antoine Guillemet. "Wit bores me shitless [*L'esprit m'emmerde*]."

Around the adolescent whose letters from Aix indicate how much he loved wit Cézanne had fabricated a caricature of oafishness, shielding himself behind this persona. Terror-ridden, he found shelter in the thicket of an unkempt beard and in the depths of a huge brown overcoat which turned green with age. Mortified by his body, he dressed as a scarecrow, flung obscenities at the world, and wherever he set up house wallowed in debris. "Last winter's ashes were still heaped up in front of the stove," Zola wrote in *L'Oeuvre*. "Apart from the bed, the little washstand and the divan, the only big pieces of furniture in the place were a dilapidated oak wardrobe and a huge deal table littered with brushes, tubes of paint, unwashed crockery, and a spirit stove crowned with a saucepan still dirty after being used for cooking noodles. The rest was a weird collection of battered old chairs and broken-down easels." Few people penetrated Cézanne's redoubt, especially when despair held him fast, and models who came, never came back. Indeed, the mess, like his scatological bluster, seemed calculated to prove that for women he could only be an object of revulsion or alarm. "I don't need a woman of my own," he protested. "She would complicate life. I don't even know what good it would do, and anyway I've always been afraid of trying."

Such behavior served above all to bolster him as he shuttled beggarlike between Aix and Paris and to help him vent anger accumulated since early childhood. Everything we know suggests that the artist who requested a Salon des Refusés from Nieuwerkerke spoke on behalf of the misbegotten son. Cézanne could hardly keep the two apart under any circumstances, least of all when up against paternal authority. Wanting approval yet inviting ostracism, he was, in the lifelong quarrel that yoked him to Louis-Auguste, by turns a bastard demanding his birthright and an heir flaunting the stigmata of illegitimate birth.

Rootless in Paris, Paul Cézanne counted on the Thursday-evening potluck dinner at Zola's flat. And so, with greater exuberance, did Zola, who, like his Freemason father, had a predilection for secret societies, mysterious covenants, bonds unsuspected by the profane. Sneering at his provincial past never prevented him from idealizing the memory of it, and while defending himself as a refugee from limbo, he addressed Paris as one whose homeland was his inner refuge. "Happy those with memories!" he exclaimed in *Mon Salon*, a pamphlet dedicated to Cézanne, which included the articles he had written for *L'Evénement*.

I feel profound joy, my friend, in talking privately with you. You wouldn't believe how I suffered during this quarrel I've just had with the crowd, with unknown people. I felt so misunderstood, I sensed so much hatred around me that I often let my pen drop in discouragement. But today I can offer myself the intimate satisfaction of resuming our ten-year-old conversation. What follows was written for you alone; I know that you will read it with your heart and that tomorrow you will love me all the more affectionately. Imagine us in some hidden culvert far from human strife: old friends who know each other to the core and communicate with mere glances. . . . I see you throughout my life as the pale boy Musset speaks about. You are my entire youth; I find you bound up with everything I've ever experienced of pain and pleasure. Our minds, fraternally united, grew side by side.

His preface let it be known that his work constituted a rumination à *deux* overheard by third parties, rather than an exercise in publicity-mongering. By addressing Cézanne, he conferred the virtue of inward-ness on articles born to provoke outrage or fetch applause. But this somewhat disingenuous manifesto was not without a basis in reality, for Zola disdained the Paris "scene," rarely lingering at *L'Evénement* and avoiding cafés where fellow writers liked to congregate. "I am surrounded by painters, I don't have a single literary conversational-ist," he informed Valabrègue. His competitive spirit would always make him wary. And hand in hand with competitiveness went a fear of exposure or humiliation from which he found relief at home, among Aixois whom he had known since childhood. Cézanne, Baille, Vala-brègue, Marius Roux, Philippe Solari were not just friends. They were family.

In June 1866, the clan, including Alexandrine, set up summer quar-ters in Gloton, near Bennecourt, a village of yellow-washed houses situated on a grassy bank of the Seine several miles upstream from Giverny, where Monet later settled and painted his famous water lilies. For three or four weeks, Zola brought himself to slack off. "I feel like an atom in the bosom of vast nature and want only to lose myself there, to surrender to these waters and clouds, to plunge into the well of this silence, . . . no longer nagged by doubt." Under the changeable Norman sky, the countryside rolled northward toward the valley of the Epte, and within easy walking distance was Tripleval, where the Seine ended its loop through great limestone bluffs reminiscent of the Pro-vençal *garrigue*. These inveterate hikers seldom moved except by row-boat, however. They spent their days swimming, fishing, or picnicking on thickly wooded islands, and, entranced by the Seine, took advantage of moonlight to glide among the water lilies. A blacksmith at his anvil woke them even before the morning Angelus tolled. They in turn kept villagers up past their usual bedtime with discussions that became stri-dent when, as often happened, one "ism" grated against another. Pre-sumably the racket they made was not intolerable, for Père Dumont, who let rooms over his grocery store, welcomed them back in the succeeding two years.

Although Zola had come quite a distance since January, hectoring him all the way were doubts which the therapeutic influence of nature could not banish. He would travel much further, and doubt would remain his faithful companion throughout the journey. "He is as am-bitious and domineering in the intellectual realm as he is soft and conciliatory in every other," Paul Alexis wrote fifteen years later. "He yields points grudgingly and never on the spot. Not being right causes him intense pain. So deeply rooted is this rivalrous spirit that it will seize the most trivial pretext to manifest itself. Thus, I have sometimes played chess with him and won. He confesses that, momentarily, his defeat irks him as much as if someone denied him literary talent." Zola turned victory itself into defeat by impugning his own achievement, which gave him little comfort. What he saw in taking stock of himself was not so much a young man on the rise as a climber who would fall very hard if he paused to rest or look backward. "I am impatient, I mean to advance more quickly," he confided to Numa Coste on July 26, soon after returning from vacation. "You can't imagine how subject one is to sudden spells of lassitude in the harsh métier I practice. I must produce almost an article a day. I must read, or at least riffle through, the works of every contemporary imbecile. I rest only by working a little at my own books." The conviction that he would lose his ability to write unless he wrote without respite, that his gift could, like his father, disappear at any moment, was an incontestable article of faith. Two days away from his desk made him writhe, noted Alexis. "After one week, he'd fall sick."

While laboring at "Livres d'aujourd'hui et de demain" he pondered ways of digging out from under the avalanche of ephemera, and one strategy saw him concentrate on famous men. That summer he made L'Evénement's front page with a profile of Hippolyte Taine. By February he had written seven more profiles and had mastered the genre, which suited his gift for caricature. Literary academicians were favorite subjects, and Zola, who (at first) hid behind the pseudonym "Simplice," showed them no mercy. Prévost-Paradol, Désiré Nisard, Edmond About, and Jules Janin—academicians all—found themselves held up to ridicule by a wag as dexterous as any in the Parisian art of drawing blood with bons mots. Villemessant applauded his performance.

Another avenue of escape from "Livres d'aujourd'hui et de demain" was popular fiction, which had become a regular feature of Parisian dailies when the dailies turned into commercial enterprises that depended chiefly on advertising for revenue. During Louis Philippe's reign, newspapermen needing material more seductive than mere news had found it in the roman-feuilleton, the serialized novel. This expedient worked magic. Circulation soared, and writers ingenious enough to keep disbelief suspended week after week with yarns of the most improbable complexity grew rich beyond their dreams. Eugène Sue sold Le Juif errant for 100,000 francs, or four times as much as had been paid for *Les Mystères de Paris*. Alexandre Dumas made a comparable fortune, some portion of which went to employees who helped him fabricate *Les Trois Mousquetaires* and *Le Comte de Monte-Cristo*. Lamenting the *roman-feuilleton*, Sainte-Beuve dubbed it "industrial literature," but his confrere Balzac heartily welcomed free-market competition. "Right now there's warfare over serials," he wrote in 1844.

> Véron has bought the *Le Constitutionnel*, knocked down the annual price to 48 francs, and is threatening to steal *Le Siècle*'s 45,000 sub-scribers with *Le Juif errant*, bought for 100,000 francs, and with a volume by G. Sand entitled Jeanne, bought, I hear, for 10,000 francs. *Les Débats* has yours truly, who, with *Les Petits Bourgeois*, guarantees them their strong position. Here's *Le Soleil* about to enter the lists and threaten both *Le Siècle* and *Le Constitutionnel*. This will make bidding even more frantic. . . . It's a money tournament. I'm free and shall try to exploit the situation.

Revolution pricked the bubble. After 1848, officialdom, which viewed a literature abounding in underworld fauna as subversive, levied a stamp tax on dailies that published *roman-feuilletons*. Writers' fees dropped precipitously. But serialization itself outlived Louis Napoleon's maneuver, and until 1914 the lower half of the front page (the "ground floor," in newspaper parlance) remained an important source of income for certain authors, Zola among them.

Confident that financial independence was his to win with the right formula, Zola spent August churning out a novel that features yet another lovelorn protagonist. In *Le Voeu d'une morte* this character bears the name Daniel, and his dolorous tale begins soon after he meets Blanche de Rionne, a woman some twelve years older than he, whose anonymous benefactions had saved him from the despond of orphanhood. At death's door, Blanche asks him in return to keep watch over her young daughter, Jeanne. Her wish explains the title. "He sacrificed everything without regret. He accepted an inferior position the better to look after the child. . . . [Jeanne] belonged to him like a legacy of love." Jeanne ultimately relives Blanche's drama by marrying an upper-class rake, but her guardian angel, who has meanwhile discovered that what he feels for her is not altogether platonic, allows neither the rake nor his own passion to thwart his mission. The rake dies, whereupon Daniel, with sublime self-renouncement, brings together Jeanne and his own bosom friend, George. Having thus accomplished Blanche de Rionne's wish, he may depart this world, which he does in an odor of sanctity, "always the brother, never the lover." Threadbare though it is, *Le Voeu d'une morte* was spun from the-

matic material that served Zola throughout his career. Daniel—an orphaned child and deracinated southerner—prefigures numerous exiles
wed to some faith, mission or opus whose idealism stifles their sex life.
Zola had already created one such character in *La Confession de
Claude*, and the paradigm announces itself at every turn. Like Claude,
Daniel is bewitched by a moribund woman who awakens rescue fantasies to which he sacrifices worldly ambition. Like Claude, Daniel
regards his inamorata as his mother or child, yearning for posthumous
union with the absent Blanche while hovering altruistically near the
untouchable Jeanne. And like Claude, he finds himself cast aside in
favor of a friend whose hands are free to possess. Incest is their common obsession, and it seems quite likely that what turns them against
themselves is what fathered the doubts, the phobias, the idées fixes
that would always make their author feel unequal to his public eminence. "Why this grief in the midst of such immense success?" Goncourt wondered some years later, when *Nana* appeared. Why, he might
have asked, did a man who gloried in power stock the *Les Rougon-
Macquart* with exemplars of nonentitlement and periodically curse his
lifelong enterprise for standing between him and erotic fulfillment? "I
will always be on the side of the vanquished," wrote Zola, as he set
forth to conquer.

Aside from the practice it gave him in narrative and dialogue, nothing came of *Le Voeu d'une morte*, not even adverse criticism: published
first as a *feuilleton* (between September 11 and September 26, 1866),
then as a book, it was twice consigned to oblivion. Zola bravely toiled
on, augmenting his income by writing a weekly version of "Livres
d'aujourd'hui et de demain" for *Le Salut public*. Together, *L'Evénement* and *Le Salut public* paid him six hundred francs a month, or
more than enough to support not only his wife but his mother, who
occupied separate quarters near the rue de Vaugirard.

Drudgery might have worn him down had he not kept himself in
fighting trim with a long article entitled "A New Manner in Painting:
M. Edouard Manet," which Arsène Houssaye accepted for his monthly
magazine, *La Revue du XIXe siècle*. Once again Zola took up arms
against the academic canon of beauty and praised a modernist intent
on capturing the world around him. "[Manet] paints neither history
nor the soul; what is called composition doesn't exist for him, and the
task he assigns himself is not to represent such and such a thought or
such and such a historical act," he wrote, drawing a parallel between
pure science and art emancipated from rhetorical conventions.

> Our modern landscape artists stand head and shoulders above history
> and genre painters because they have studied the countryside, ran-
> domly choosing any bit of nature as a fit object for portrayal. Edouard

Manet applies the same method to each of his works; while others rack their brains to invent a new "Death of Caesar" or "Socrates Drinking Hemlock," he calmly places several objects or people in a corner of his studio and begins to paint, analyzing it all with care. I repeat, he is an analyst; his work has far more significance than the plagiarisms of his confreres.

Why, asked Zola, did art that nineteenth-century spectators should have found congenial provoke outrage? "Originality, there's the great bugaboo," he answered. "We are all more or less creatures of habit who plod along the beaten path. And every new road terrifies us: we scent unknown precipices, we refuse to advance. . . . Directly a nonconformist appears, defiance and fright take command. We're like skittish horses bridling before a fallen tree because they can't explain the nature or cause of this obstacle and, furthermore, don't want explanations." People who secretly admire Manet, he went on, will join the derisive crowd sooner than endure its taunts. Force of habit sets them up for the coercion of prevailing taste. "In France, in this land of pluck and blithesomeness, we dread ridicule above all else," wrote Zola, seconding a view often expressed by another great outsider, Stendhal. "When at a meeting three people mock someone, the entire group laughs, and those inclined to defend the victim lower their eyes instead."

Manet had never had such attention lavished upon him and this well-wrought essay strengthened his resolve to organize an independent show at the Exposition of 1867. "You've made me a dandy New Year's gift with your remarkable article," he wrote on January 2, 1867, the day after it appeared.

It reaches me at the right moment, for I have been deemed unworthy of the advantage enjoyed by so many others of submitting my work to the Salon by list.[2] I expect nothing good from our judges and shall therefore send them nothing. They'd pull their usual stunt of taking only one or two and rejecting the rest as unfit for human consumption.

What I have in mind is a private show. There are at least forty canvases ready to exhibit. I've already been offered a plot of land very well situated near the Champs-de-Mars. I'll risk my all and, abetted by men such as yourself, I count on succeeding . . . Everyone here is enchanted by the article and instructs me to thank you.

[2]According to a new regulation, certain artists would have their work chosen on the basis of a list stating the size and subject of paintings.

As we shall see, Manet followed Courbet's audacious example. He built a pavilion on the Place de l'Alma in which visitors could see everything he had painted since 1859. Visitors could also obtain Zola's article, which went on sale there in the form of a brochure that included an etching after *Olympia*.

Before 1866 gave out, another occasion for self-advertisement presented itself, when the Congrès Scientifique de France invited Zola to read a paper at its session in Aix-en-Provence, the general topic being "The novel. Definition of this literary genre. What it was in antiquity and the early Christian era." Although unable to deliver the talk in person, he accepted with alacrity, and on December 10 informed Valabrègue:

> I can't explain at length the reasons that persuaded me to join. The fact is, I'm now a member of the Congrès . . . and yesterday posted some thirty pages entitled "A Definition of the Novel". I'm pleased, delighted, with this opuscule, in which I've broadly applied Taine's method. Blunt and audacious affirmations. I would like to be a fly on the wall of the auditorium where they declaim my prose.

No record exists of the impression it made, but in that solemn audience, some must have felt that they had been led astray. Dropping names culled from Victor Chauvin's *Les Romanciers grecs et latins*, Zola spent only as much time with the ancients as was necessary to dismiss their fiction wholesale (Petronius' *Satyricon* apart), or, rather, to establish a platform for the leap his argument takes across two millennia. Not until Balzac did fiction, emerging from chronic adolescence, yield a work comparable in stature to the Homeric epic. With *La Comédie humaine* it grew up, and the sign of its maturity was its newfound penchant for the close observation of nature. "When heaven came down to earth, when science killed the hobgoblins of night and unveiled the broad horizon of observation and method, when man turned his attention to humanity, when the drama of life came to assume different forms under different roofs, then the novel of mankind inevitably eclipsed the novel of gods and heroes." Like Rousseau in *L'Essai sur l'origine des langues*, Zola rigged up an antithesis between the public voice that made itself heard throughout the agora and the private language in which modern men converse. But bad for one author was good for the other. Where Rousseau saw secret councils as politically nefarious, Zola regarded the fragmentation of society as the very basis of novel writing. A hidden world is what inspires novelists, he affirmed, and if they accomplish their proper task, they will winkle out secrets harbored by the individual *en famille*. "Fabulation is less complicated now than hitherto; the first passerby is a sufficient hero; poke through him and you will find a simple drama that sets in motion all the cogwheels of sentiment and passion." As with painters, so with novelists, any bit of nature would do. The doctrine that set high art apart from stark reality and common knowledge was a sham.

Making ex cathedra pronouncements gave Zola immense satisfaction. Making them in Aix-en-Provence redoubled his pleasure, even if he had to experience it vicariously. "Ah! how nice you would be to sit in the little corner I myself can't occupy!" he importuned Valabrègue. "Could you do me that favor and then recount what you saw and heard? Truth to tell, I fear that my petard may fizzle, [as] provincial air is humid and usually extinguishes the mind's best fireworks." At twenty-seven, Zola was already a figure of consequence. The establishment loathed him, the avant-garde admired his courage, and Manet, in a letter asking him to pull strings at Hachette for two friends with unpublished manuscripts, wrote: "You are definitely regarded as a powerful man." But on some level Aix still loomed as large as Paris, which is to say that the name he acquired among movers and shakers in the capital would not feel altogether legitimate until it commanded respect from notables back home—until he rose high enough to cast a shadow over those who had, unforgivably, confiscated his birthright.

Zola might not have undertaken the arduous journey to Aix under any circumstances, but in December 1866 he could ill afford it. When the government had banned *L'Evénement* in November, Villemessant, undaunted, had converted *Le Figaro* into a daily, and Zola hoped to jump aboard. "How about my giving you, *only once a week*, a piece which would probe, discuss, or laud the most important work of the moment?" he inquired. "Not something ponderous, grave, hard on your readers, but an interesting study, dramatized if you will, and easily digestible." It soon became apparent, however, that *Le Voeu d'une morte*, the Salon, and innumerable installments of "Livres d'aujourd'hui et de demain" had sated Villemessant's appetite for Zola's prose. Thereafter he would publish him only fitfully.

A letter of dismissal from *Le Salut public* coincided with this misfortune, and Zola found himself wondering all over again how to earn a livelihood. "I must confess that I'm not very cheerful today," he told his young confidant, Valabrègue.

Nothing has panned out, and "the sky of the future" is singularly overcast.[3] In retrospect, last summer seems a golden age. The high spirits and splendid projects! Right now I feel like an idiot and as I

[3]"The sky of the future is overcast" (*Le ciel de l'avenir est noir*) was a favorite expression of Cézanne's.

write this letter the smell of ink nauseates me. One has slumps, and the worst of it is the pain they cause. Good God, no such thing as a smooth ride. My wretched machine has gone haywire and I'm not sure what's ailing me, my head or my stomach.

I can't say anything definite about my literary status, which changes from day to day. I'll write for several papers, but my most secure house, *Figaro,* is a shanty whose floor may collapse at any moment. You urge me to console myself by undertaking a serious work. Would that I could. I must scrounge a living and I'm peculiarly inept when it comes to that. I don't know the way out of this hellhole—I'm referring to my woes, for I'll never completely abandon journalism, which is the best available means of getting a message across.

The news that Jean-Baptistin Baille had won the Institute's Bordin Prize with a treatise on optics and was thus marked for success did not improve his mood. In despondency he turned to Cézanne, much as he had turned to him at the edge of a hostile playground. "Tell Paul to return without delay," he implored Valabrègue. "He will inject some courage into my life. I await him like a savior."

VII

"LA LITTÉRATURE PUTRIDE"

OLA'S MISFORTUNE redounded to the advantage of *Le Messager de Provence*, a regional newspaper with offices in Aix. Founded in 1861, it had shunned controversial issues so long as controversy made the government frown. But after 1866, when the moribund regime lost its zeal for prosecuting journalists openly critical of authority, Léopold Arnaud, who ran *Le Messager*, dared to occupy ground yielded by the censor. He attacked certain highly placed members of Marseille's clerical establishment in a campaign that would have been suicidal several years earlier. And on January 31, 1867, he announced his intention to publish a *roman-feuilleton* entitled *Les Mystères de Marseille*, describing this namesake of Eugène Sue's famous saga, *Les Mystères de Paris*, as "the true, palpitating, historical account of . . . knavish acts which have, all too often, and on every rung of the social ladder, afflicted or scandalized Marseille and Provence." Its author was Emile Zola.

How the idea for *Les Mystères de Marseille* originated is not known for sure. But we do know that Zola could not have written it without Marius Roux, his childhood friend. Roux spent weeks in the legal archives of Marseille laboriously copying records from which Zola, in Paris, spun one criminal episode after another. "My *feuilleton* appeared twice weekly. . . . Every afternoon, I would knock out seven or eight pages of *Les Mystères* in an hour." To earn two hundred francs a month at ten centimes a line, Zola had to flesh out his story with innumerable subplots, and this he did from March 1867 through January 1868, when a more congenial livelihood materialized. Arnaud published *Les Mystères* in three volumes.

Among the principals of the drama are a feckless but charming worker named Philippe Cayol, a local eminence named de Cazalis, and de Cazalis's sixteen-year-old niece and ward, Blanche. Seduced by Philippe, Blanche elopes with him. De Cazalis pursues them, hoping to thwart a marriage in order, as we subsequently learn, to retain control over Blanche's inheritance, which he has already plundered. The lovers are soon caught, and at a trial in Aix-en-Provence, Blanche's uncle makes her testify against Philippe. No sooner has de Cazalis put Philippe behind prison walls than he discovers that Blanche is with child. Closely guarded during her confinement, she atones for her betrayal by arranging to have Philippe's virtuous brother and sister-in-law, Marius and Fine, smuggle home the newborn infant, Joseph. There matters rest until 1848, when Philippe, who has meanwhile escaped from prison, becomes a revolutionary leader. The dramatis personae reunite in the war-torn streets of Marseille, where de Cazalis continues to hound Blanche's child amid workers building barricades against bourgeois. In due course all perish, except Joseph, Fine, and Marius. This makeshift family survives the hecatomb and, free at last from danger, lives harmoniously ever after.

Though virtue triumphs, myriad are the pitfalls it must avoid in a world where good never deteriorates and evil never improves. Haunted by one another, the good and the evil play hide-and-seek year after year, until doomsday stills them. Like Zola's later novels, *Les Mystères de Marseille* ends with a catastrophe that heralds a new order. The child born of strife fathers peace; Philippe, Blanche, and de Cazalis die, but die in order to produce a threesome who transcend class conflict and Oedipal rage.

Despite its contrivances, *Les Mystères* is fraught with incident, being a picaresque tale in which characters serve as vehicles for touring the underworld. While Claude and Daniel hankered after sainthood, here, on the contrary, we find a democracy of greed that encompasses the aristocrat and the hooligan, the notary and the loan shark, the priest and the harlot. They throng together awkwardly, and Zola, working from material sent by Roux, describes their felonies at length. Such commotion would have been unimaginable several years earlier. Then he couldn't plot a story without shrinking into the cocoon of some idée fixe. Now he let his mind browse through social strata. It seems clear that a more ambitious novelist had begun to stir in him, and one who stirred to the music of Honoré de Balzac. "Have you read all of Balzac?" Zola asked Valabrègue in May 1867. "What a man! I am rereading him at this moment. He crushes the entire century. For me, Victor Hugo and the others can't hold a candle to him. I'm thinking about writing a volume on the subject, a big study, a kind of real-life novel."

His enthusiasm for Balzac revealed itself elsewhere in an open letter he wrote to deny rumors that *Les Mystères* was a roman à clef each of whose characters had some identifiable model. It may have been a publicity stunt, with Zola denying a rumor the better to plant it; but the letter, published by *Le Messager*, also served as a manifesto. *"Les Mystères* is a contemporary historical novel insofar as all the facts contained therein derive from real life," he proclaimed.

> I have selected the necessary documents here and there, I have conflated twenty disparate stories into one tale, I have given a single character the traits of several people whom circumstances have allowed me to meet and study. I could thus produce a work in which everything is true . . . without it ever having been my intention to follow history step by step. I am above all a novelist; I do not assume the grave responsibility of the historian, who would expose himself to accusations of slander if he disturbed a fact or altered a specific personality. I did as I pleased with real events which have, so to speak, fallen into the public domain. Readers so inclined may ferret out my sources. As for me, I declare in advance that my characters are not portraits of so-and-so; these characters are types, not individuals.

He almost certainly had in mind the preface to *La Comédie humaine,* where Balzac declares that people, shaped as they are by the milieu they inhabit, form "social species" which the novelist classifies like a naturalist classifying members of the animal kingdom. In *La Duchesse de Langeais,* Balzac went one step further and argued that individual species can best be studied through typical specimens. "If, in any era, a nation contains a group with its own tribal identity, the historian can almost always single out some figure who epitomizes the virtues and faults of the aggregate to which he belongs: Coligny among the Huguenots, the Coadjutor of the Fronde, Marshal Richelieu under Louis XV, Danton during the Terror. That a man should bear an exact likeness to his historical cortege is in the nature of things." This idea was systematized by Hippolyte Taine, a devout Balzacian, in whose *Histoire de la littérature anglaise* the typical figure became the embodiment of "race, moment, and milieu." And thus did it take root among intellectuals eager to redefine literature for their age. When Zola wrote "types, not individuals," he implicitly disavowed the romanticism that brought forth heroes abounding in a sense of their absolute singularity. Heroes there were, but none who transcended kith and kin. Heroism would manifest itself, but not as the "column of flame and cloud without a base" that Paganini conjured up in Goethe's imagination.

Zola might as well have hitched a gig to a dray horse as used *Les Mystères de Marseille* to illustrate the tenets of realism. He knew what he was about in writing it and made no literary claims for himself in promoting it. "Be lenient," he asked Jules Claretie. "I know that it's a bad work. You will teach me nothing . . . by saying so in public, and you would thereby wrong the provincial paper which is publishing other parts of the novel right now. Go easy and emphasize that *Les Mystères* is appearing in *Le Messager,* at Marseille." Versions of this plea were sent to other book reviewers during the month of June 1867.

But a man whose faith in himself crumbled over trivial defeats couldn't suffer criticism even of a potboiler without feeling that his literary talent had been impugned, especially when criticism came from a friend like Antony Valabrègue. "Allow me . . . to tell you that you've judged the publication of *Les Mystères de Marseille* as a provincial," wrote Zola.

> If you were in our midst, if I could speak with you for ten minutes, you would immediately understand the raison d'être of this work. As you know, I obey exigencies and dictates. Unlike you, I am not at liberty to fall asleep, to enclose myself in an ivory tower on the pretext that the crowd is foolish. I need the crowd, I make overtures to it however I can, I try by every means to tame it. Right now there are two things I need most urgently: money and publicity. If you tell yourself that, you will understand why I accepted offers from the *Messager de Provence* . . . Give me a private income and I promise I will straightway cloister myself alongside you.

Vulnerable on the high ground of literary excellence, he chose a more strategic position on the battleground of commerce. Where Valabrègue practiced art for art's sake, Zola, who had not yet forgiven schoolmates born rich, glorified production for production's sake, setting the virile conqueror of crowds against the monk alone in an ivory tower. Did he take this line seriously? Not altogether. At once inclined to grant Valabrègue's point and afraid that doing so would paralyze him, he justified hackwork to himself by identifying with his entrepreneurial father. But identification was also perilous. "I labor over certain things and toss off others, trying to dig myself a hole as fast as I can shovel," he told the younger man. "Someday you'll find out how arduous it is to dig such a hole." Here his language confirms what he himself knew better than anyone, that ambition dwelt next door to death in his imagination. Building a canal would always mean digging a grave, just as conquering Marseille meant dying there.

Certainly *Les Mystères de Marseille* revived painful memories. In March, when there was still some reason to hope that the *feuilleton* might succeed, François Zola's career became the subject of a public debate occasioned by new plans for a protected harbor at Marseille submitted by an engineer named Paul Borde. Zola learned about this in the Lyon newspaper *Le Progrès* and took umbrage. "Your correspondent is mistaken when he says that the Zola project [submitted thirty years ago] was 'rejected,' " he wrote. "On the contrary, according to documents I possess, the municipal council . . . decreed that it served the public good. . . . I cannot explain what prevented its execution, though perhaps I shall one day find, in the intrigues of yesteryear, material for a high administrative comedy." Published simultaneously in *Le Progrès* and *Le Messager de Provence*, his letter elicited a response from Borde, who put the old project down as impractical. Zola then joined the battle in earnest. "The support this project was given in its day must convince you that it is both feasible and conscientious . . . Circumstances oblige me to let my father's plans compete against yours, in an official kind of way." With technical assistance, he would revise François Zola's plans, he said, and place them once again before the municipal council of Marseille. "[My father] toiled for Provence, for that cruel stepmother whom I still love, though she ruined me and made me an orphan."

Zola never went before the municipal council with blueprints in hand, but he enacted his fantasy of retribution through popular literature, hoping to hear himself talked about in Aix, indeed "all over the Midi." By June, when it was obvious that *Les Mystères* would not bring him fame or fortune, he had begun work on a theatrical adaptation, and he kept his fantasy alive several months longer with help from the director of Marseille's Théâtre du Gymnase, Bellevaut, who agreed to stage the play. "We must turn the novel upside down . . . if we want to avoid censorship," Zola instructed Roux. "I still see a prologue in which the birth of the two children is explained; two different paths —the path of vice and the path of virtue; in the end, virtue rewarded and vice punished. . . . Anyway, sketch it out. That will be the basis for our work. No priest in the drama, unless it's to flatter the Church."[1]

One after another letters sped between them as Zola, switching roles with his friend, threw out ideas from which Roux concocted dialogue. It took only six weeks to write an egregiously long melodrama, and on July 16 Zola announced that he had dispatched the last tableau. "There are several things I've rearranged to make our fat lies plausible. . . . Ah! my poor friend, what a creature we've whelped! Have it copied as quickly as possible and we'll unleash it upon the world. I'll invite you to supper one of these days, to celebrate our joyous delivery." A midsummer toast would have been premature, however, for Bellevaut,

---

[1]The play does not survive, but it's clear from these allusions that Roux and Zola introduced new characters, including a second child. Equally clear is the fact that the stage was subject to stricter censorship than newspapers.

whom Roux described as snarling mad, wanted their manuscript cut. Unable to face this adversary himself, Zola coached Roux in every detail of the negotiation. Cuts he could accept, so long as Bellevaut left intact the heart of their play. And if it was necessary to delay production until October, he could accept that too, provided Roux did not leave Marseille for Paris without first having wrung commitments from the director and the censor. "Bellevaut will doubtless tell you that he has time, that there's no rush," he warned his beleaguered collaborator, hammering home the instructions.

> Insist, force him to put his stamp on the play as it will be staged. Make the various corrections we've discussed, then collar the director and *oblige* him to review the work with you, to include necessary changes, in short to give the manuscript its definitive shape. This is of the utmost importance. Don't have the play copied until everything is settled. And to obtain this result, offer as your one and sufficient reason your imminent departure from Marseille. When the manuscript has fully ripened, hand it over to copyists . . . and secure the censor's approval.

Roux may have come to feel like an adjutant receiving general orders every day in the morning post. Zola overlooked nothing, and behaved as if the least oversight might spell disaster.

His anxiety fed, no doubt, on the hope that material relief lay at hand. Although a successful run would not have earned him as much in Marseille as in Paris, still, writing plays was everywhere far more lucrative than writing novels. This had already been true during Louis Philippe's reign, when Balzac told Madame Hanska: "My frightful production of books, which has generated masses of proof, will not make me solvent. I must resort to theater, where revenues far exceed what books bring in." It remained the state of affairs under Napoleon III, when theaters multiplied in response to a growing demand for "live" entertainment. The affluent society gravitated toward the Boulevard rather than the bookstore. More people were able to read serious fiction than during Louis Philippe's era, but proportionately fewer had the time or inclination, which led Edmond de Goncourt to note: "Theater is the only literature of many people, and superior people—scientists, lawyers, doctors—who, being entirely caught up in professional work, never open a volume that lies outside their competence." Perfect for short attention spans was the so-called *pièce bien faite*, the play ingeniously constructed around some topical issue such as real estate speculation, easy credit, or extramarital sex. Enough of them were written by Dumas *fils* and Emile Augier to keep crowds queueing up at theaters throughout France. And many ran long enough to enrich their authors. Our best informant here is Zola himself. "Let's say a play has one hundred performances, which defines success nowadays," he wrote years later in an essay about money in literature. "The theater takes in four thousand francs per performance on the average, or four hundred thousand francs altogether, with forty thousand going to the author if his contract allows him a ten percent share. A novelist collecting fifty centimes per copy would not earn that much from his novel unless it appeared in an edition of eighty thousand, and during the past half-century such editions can be counted on the fingers of one hand." Aware that Dumas *fils's La Dame aux camélias* had grossed far more than *Madame Bovary*, Flaubert tried his luck at playwriting. So, for the same reason, and with equally deplorable results, did almost every other major French novelist of the nineteenth century.

What hopes Zola brought to Marseille in October (he went at Roux's behest) were dashed overnight. Tinkering with *Les Mystères* continued until curtain time, yet nothing could make the contraption work as a dramatic vehicle. "People down here don't have faith in our genius, and they're quite right," he told Roux. Scheduled between two large-scale productions, Hugo's *Hernani* and Offenbach's *La Grande Duchesse de Gérolstein*, it opened on October 5 amidst publicity to the effect that the play fostered artistic independence from Paris, or "decentralization." It closed within a fortnight, despite this chauvinistic hoopla. "It seemed to me much too long, really tedious," Zola observed after its premiere, where scattered jeers rose above polite applause. "They began at 8 and finished at 1 a.m. The audience drooped. If we had attended rehearsals and made necessary cuts, we could have pulled it off. That's what everybody tells me. I've just seen Bellevaut to try to make cuts for this evening. It's apparently impossible. If the play doesn't fold they will be made for the third performance. Yesterday there were 1,200 francs in receipts." The alleged proponent of decentralization found fault, moreover, with a provincial theater that cramped his style. "What we need is a big stage like the Porte Saint-Martin's," he sighed.

Zola visited Cézanne in Aix, then went straight to Paris, where he and Roux lost no time conducting a postmortem. Their fiasco undoubtedly left them crestfallen, but not by any means hopeless. Soon afterward, Roux, who found employment at *Le Petit Journal*, began to write fiction. Zola in turn could look forward to the imminent appearance of a novel which had already been available in proof when he reached Marseille ten days earlier and which bore the title *Thérèse Raquin*.

Thérèse Raquin grew out of a short story Zola published in *Le Figaro* on December 24, 1866, "Un Mariage d'amour." Eager to orchestrate the theme, he sought encouragement from Arsène Houssaye, who presided over two literary journals, *L'Artiste* and *La Revue du XIXe siècle*. "I am certain that a masterly work can be drawn from this sketch," he argued. "I should like to attempt it, to write such a work with my heart and flesh, to make of it something vivid and poignant. Will you be the midwife? . . . Say yes and I shall forge ahead. I assume that it could be the great work of my youth. I'm possessed by the subject, I'm living with the characters. It will do both of us credit." Houssaye hesitated but decided finally that this game might be worth the candle and had his son, Henry, draft an affirmative response, which specified that *Un Mariage d'amour* would, come May, appear in three successive issues of *La Revue du XIXe siècle*.

Inspiration and desperation reinforced each other as Zola toiled all day long every day, saving mornings for *Un Mariage d'amour* and spending afternoons on *Les Mystères de Marseille*. By April he had written enough of the former to boast about it to Valabrègue. "I am very satisfied; *Un Mariage d'amour* is, I believe, my best effort to date; I even fear that the wine may have too much body, that Houssaye may back out at the last minute. . . . You see how quickly it goes. Last month I wrote part one, which means a third of the volume, and in addition a hundred pages of *Les Mystères*." Another, similarly phrased outburst of apprehensive self-congratulation came two months later, when the novel was almost done. "I am very pleased with the psychological and physiological novel I shall publish in *La Revue du XIXe siècle*," he informed Valabrègue on May 29. "This novel . . . will assuredly be my best work. I think my heart and flesh are in it. I even fear that I've put a bit too much flesh in it and may ruffle His Honor, the imperial prosecutor. Truth to tell, several months' imprisonment doesn't really scare me." Hewing to materialist doctrine as he had learned it from Hippolyte Taine, who taught that events of the mind report quirks of the body, Zola avoided, even in private, words fraught with religious significance. It was therefore his "flesh" he put into the book, rather than his soul.

It tried his soul, however, to endure the various mishaps that delayed publication of *Un Mariage d'amour* month after month. Houssaye rescheduled it for June or July when a preceding novel ran longer than anticipated, and the note he sent Zola barely concealed his discomfort with a work that invited prosecution on moral grounds. "My father," wrote Henry Houssaye, "instructs me to release you if you have some other journal or want the novel out in book form straightway; he would be very sorry, but does not consider he has the right to keep it against your will." In June three requests for galley proofs went unanswered. Worried by this lack of communication, which was causing him financial hardship, he learned at last that *La Revue du XIXe siècle* had lost its sponsor and would close on July 1. Houssaye did not rush to salvage

Un Mariage d'amour from the wreck; but ultimately honor vanquished fear, and beginning in August, he brought out the novel more or less uncut in his well-established review, *L'Artiste.* As the government made no prosecutorial move, Zola entered into negotiations with a book publisher. "I propose that *Thérèse Raquin,* the heroine's name, replace *Un Mariage d'amour,*" he wrote on September 13 to Albert Lacroix of Brussels, whose firm, the Librairie Internationale, published Hugo, Quinet, Louis Blanc, Michelet, Proudhon, and others on the Napoleonic index:

> Mystifying titles are a thing of the past and the public no longer has confidence in shop signs. I won't quarrel over this, however. I confess that I need money and would prefer to make the work your property for a fixed number of years if you can offer me, in return, some reasonable sum. . . . I should like an October publication date. Acquaint yourself with the work, let me choose a simple title, and state your own conditions. . . . We could strike a bargain very quickly, and so I hope we do.

He concluded by assuring Lacroix that the book was bound to be a *succès d'horreur.*

Horror is indeed what *Thérèse Raquin* portends from the first page, where Zola describes a narrow Parisian street or "passage" lined with shops and overhung by a dirt-encrusted glass roof through which daylight can barely filter. Living in this sepulchral milieu, above their haberdashery, are the Raquins—Thérèse, her husband, Camille, and her mother-in-law. Thérèse had joined the family long before her marriage. The illegitimate child of an Algerian woman fathered by Madame Raquin's brother, she had grown up alongside Camille and been reared to help Madame keep the sickly boy out of harm's way. Marriage, which she did not resist, consecrated her role as nurse. Repressing instincts that want satisfaction, she languishes until Camille brings home a friend named Laurent. Thereafter everything changes, for when Laurent enters, the "African" in her throws off her shackles. "Thérèse had never seen a man. Tall, strong, and ruddy, Laurent astonished her. She contemplated admiringly his low brow overgrown with thick, black hair, his full cheeks, his red lips, his regular features which bespoke a sanguine beauty. Her gaze rested for a moment on his neck; it was thick and short, fleshy and powerful." In due course they become lovers. Loath to sleep with her husband, Thérèse talks murder, and Laurent, a ne'er-do-well aroused as much by fantasies of being supported by two women as by Thérèse's sexual magic, resolves to commit it. On a Sunday excursion during which all three board a canoe, he hurls the feeble young man into the Seine, though not before Camille bites his neck. It is called a boating accident, the culprits go free, and Laurent, whose mock attempt to save his victim excited praise, diligently attends Madame Raquin. Punishment will come from within, or below. No sooner do Thérèse and Laurent abolish what stood between them than they discover that what stood between them bound them together, the act of murder having been the consummation of their lust. "By killing Camille, they managed to appease those wild desires they couldn't appease in each other's arms. The crime seemed an ultimate stab of pleasure. . . . Love no longer tempted them, their appetites were gone." Joined in marriage, they marry guilt and form a ménage à trois with the memory of Camille, who acquires enormous power, feeding on their flesh—almost literally, for the bite he inflicted won't heal. It eats away at Laurent like an insatiable mouth; it festers in his neck as desire once festered in his loins, and this displacement is gruesomely borne home when Laurent, now more or less impotent, makes Thérèse kiss the wound.[2] At length they reveal themselves for what they are to Madame Raquin, who has meanwhile suffered a stroke. Speechless, she cannot denounce them but watches as they sink lower day by day. When their degradation is complete, suicide follows. In a morbid betrothal, they die of poison swallowed from the same glass.

Seasoned by previous efforts, Zola came into his own with *Thérèse Raquin*, which illuminates "underground" Paris even as it dredges up monsters of the mind, and portrays a social milieu while engaging the reader on the level of dream discourse. After the murder, for example, Laurent repeatedly visits the morgue until at last he spies Camille's decomposed corpse. "The thin, bony, slightly swollen head wore a grimace; it leaned a little to one side with its hair slick against the temples, and its eyelids were raised, showing the pale orbit of the eyes." This image returns to haunt him later, when, unemployed, he tries his hand at painting.

Now his hand unconsciously traced those horrible lineaments the memory of which followed him everywhere. Little by little, the painter, who had fallen back on his couch, thought he saw the faces spring to life. There were five Camilles before him, five Camilles his own fingers had powerfully shaped and which, in some spooky way, assumed all ages and genders. . . . The thought that his fingers had the fatal and unconscious knack of incessantly reproducing Camille's portrait made him contemplate his hand with terror. He felt that this hand no longer belonged to him.

---

[2]Zola converted the literal meaning of "remorse"—"agenbite" as James Joyce put it—into a physical symptom.

Further along we read in connection with Laurent's wound that "he felt the seared portion of his neck no longer belonged to his body." Having created a virile ghost in destroying a sexless spouse, the brute with childish impulses comes undone. Estranged from him is his phallus-like neck but also his mind, which despite itself generates images of Camille. Here Zola tacitly introduced a theory known as "impregnation," whose proponents, among them Michelet, held that women are marked for life by their first lover, even to the extent of bearing children in his image years after separation. Not only does Laurent, as husband, sire no offspring on the woman he stole, but as artist, he fathers endless effigies of the man from whom he stole her. Unable to "fill" Thérèse, he himself becomes pregnant with Camille. "[An old acquaintance] contemplated Laurent, whose voice seemed softer than before, whose gestures had a kind of elegance," writes Zola in a chapter that describes Laurent's attempt to recover selfhood through art. "He couldn't guess what a frightful shock had changed him into someone with a woman's nerves experiencing delicate and acute sensations."

Laurent is otherwise seen as a puppet manipulated by guilt (at his easel he feels that his hand "no longer belonged to him"), and this motif reappears ironically in the dumbstruck Madame Raquin, who loses all capacity for independent movement. She, too, becomes a puppet, the puppet of distraught children who "dressed her, jerked her right and left, bent her to their every need and whim." Unlike Laurent, however, she achieves total self-possession, with her eyes assuming a body's power to grasp or to bite. "She used her eyes like a hand, like a mouth." While Laurent's eyes betray him, Madame Raquin's preserve life beyond the grave. And while Laurent delivers images of an alien, she gives birth to her son anew. "She felt in her moribund flesh a new being, pitiless and cruel, who wanted to bite her son's assassins." Physically indistinguishable from Camille, Madame Raquin, like some mythic crone suckling vengeance, emerges triumphant, with Thérèse and Laurent dead at her feet. "Their corpses lay all night long on the dining-room floor, twisted, arched, yellowish under the lamplight. And for almost twelve hours, till noon of the next day, Madame Raquin, stiff and mute, contemplated them at her feet, feeding her insatiable eyes, crushing them with her heavy gaze."

Zola's realism wasn't realistic enough for certain critics, and Sainte-Beuve was foremost among those to carp at his obvious distortions. "Your work is remarkable, conscientious, even epoch-making in the history of the contemporary novel, but . . . it goes beyond the limits and conditions of art," he wrote soon after the second edition appeared. "At the outset you describe the passage du Pont-Neuf, which I know as well as anybody for all the reasons that might compel a young man to want to loiter there. Well, your description isn't true to life, it's fantastic, it's like Balzac's rue Soli. The passage is drear, banal, ugly, above all narrow, but it doesn't have that utter blackness and those Rembrandtian hues you lend it. In this respect, among others, you are unfaithful." Aesthetically speaking, faithfulness for Zola implied something else—a creative exchange between nature and temperament, or between the observable world and the artist's imaginative life. His "passage du Pont-Neuf" is a case in point. Had Sainte-Beuve lived beyond 1869, he might have come to recognize it as the archetype of enclosed spaces that harbor violence or depravity throughout *Les Rougon-Macquart*. It prefigures the greenhouse in *La Curée*, the glass-roofed market in *Le Ventre de Paris*, the walled villa in *La Conquête de Plassans*, the derelict country church in *La Faute de l'abbé Mouret*, the apartment building in *Pot-Bouille*, the laundry in *L'Assommoir*, the underground maze in *Germinal*, the railroad barn in *La Bête humaine*. Like Balzac, Zola closely studied his various milieux. But what shapes each one is a fantasy of instinctual forces bursting through the structure that contains them and wreaking havoc. No sooner does *la bête humaine* rise up than order crumbles. Tree limbs poke into holy naves, well-laid gardens go to weed, locomotives race unmanned, water floods mine shafts, laundries overflow with dirty linen, male becomes female, and partitions of the mind fall in a reign of incest and madness. Zola, whose recurrent nightmare was of himself buried alive, could hardly conceive drama without a sacrificial victim or a denouement that expunges some character from humankind. Identity and enclosure, the self and an abode standing islandlike on the margin of some larger settlement are linked again and again in disaster.

When Zola asked Hippolyte Taine for a review (which Taine wouldn't write, explaining that polemics were not his strong point), the latter urged his young disciple to paint more panoramic pictures. *Thérèse Raquin* had impressed him deeply, but Zola's predilection for hermetic mise-en-scènes gave him pause. "There's a touch of lockjaw in the style and subject." Immuring readers in a "singular" tale, denying them doors and windows to escape from some "monster, madman or martyr to disease," makes them panicky, he warned. "They are often overcome with nausea; they rail against the author."

And rail they did. If his novel enjoyed infamous success, Zola had to thank most especially Louis Ulbach, a critic of note who under the pseudonym "Ferragus" wrote for *Le Figaro* a very long review in which opprobrium was heaped on *la littérature putride*. "In the past several years there has grown up a monstrous school of novelists which pretends to replace carnal eloquence with eloquence of the charnel house, which invokes the weirdest medical anomalies, which musters the plague-stricken so that we can admire their blotchy skin . . . and which makes pus squirt out of the conscience," he began. *"Germinie Lacer-teux, Thérèse Raquin, La Comtesse de Chalis,* and many other works that don't deserve special mention . . . will prove my point." His point was that good intentions pave the way to hell. Preaching in the style of high-minded *gauchistes* (an 1848 revolutionist, Ulbach had stead-fastly opposed Napoleon III), he characterized Zola and the Goncourts as errant reformers whose means subverted their ends, whose realism aroused lewd thoughts rather than a passion for redressing social wrongs.

Although motivated by republican idealism, Ulbach's broadside was as ferocious as any written by establishment critics in defense of the principle that "unsightly" things should be seen neither between covers, nor in frames, nor on stage. "Balzac . . . made a Madame Marneffe [in *La Cousine Bette*] to embody every corruption, every in-famy, but since he never put her in a position so grotesque or de-meaning that her image might provoke laughter or offend taste, she has been portrayed on stage," he argued. "I defy you to portray Ger-minie Lacerteux, Thérèse Raquin, all those impossible ghosts who ex-ude death without having breathed life, who are nothing but nightmares of reality." Nightmarish, too, were the women conjured up by Manet, whom Ulbach tarred with the same brush. "[Zola] sees woman as M. Manet paints her, mud-colored under pink makeup." Singling out one episode for praise—the nuptial night, which Laurent and Thérèse spend chastely in their torture chamber —licensed him to damn the rest as a compendium of all the sins of contemporary literature. "If this represented some individual fantasy I would have said nothing, but the disease is epidemic. Let us force novelists to display their talent instead of their pickings from the law court and the city dump." The blows he rained on *Thérèse Raquin* were accompanied by jabs at Zola himself. "M. Zola is said to be a young man of talent. All I know is that he has ardently been courting fame. Enthusiastic about smut, he published *La Confession de Claude,* which was the idyll of a student and a harlot. . . . Intolerant of criticism, he himself criticizes with intolerance, and at an age when desire is one's only rule, he entitles his so-called literary studies *Mes Haines!"* Desire being Zola's only rule, even the harsh sentence he had meted out to the adulterous couple served no moral purpose, for remorse seen as a physical affliction was pornography in another guise.

Zola counterattacked right away, and adroitly turned Ulbach's re-marks about theater into an indictment of the Parisian stage. He bludg-eoned Ulbach with Jacques Offenbach, mocking the idea that propriety forbade Germinie Lacerteux to show her work-worn face where chorus girls bared their gartered thighs. "Certainly not, one couldn't have Germinie Lacerteux occupy the boards on which Mlle Schneider cavorts," is how he put it, alluding to Offenbach's perennial star. "That 'sordid cook,' in your expression, would frighten the public that swoons over the Grand Duchess of Gérolstein's sluttish grins." Was Ulbach not just one more smug bourgeois addicted to "beautiful lies, ready-made sentiments, pat situations"? Pornography, wrote Zola, thrived not in the studios of realist painters but in the make-believe of Salon art and Boulevard theater. "It would not displease you too much, sir, if Germinie Lacerteux wore tights, provided she had well-turned legs. I begin to understand what you require: silken skin, firm and rounded contours, transparent gauze that barely veils treasures of voluptuousness. . . . Too bad Germinie isn't a courtesan; she's a poor woman cast into shame by the fatalities of her temperament." Denouncing in Ferragus a hypocrite whose squeamishness abetted the regime against which he had otherwise taken arms, Zola hoisted like a flag of liberty Stendhal's dictum that the novelist writes first for himself and then for the public. "Putrid" literature, he reassured Ulbach, did not enrich its authors.

When a second edition of *Thérèse Raquin* appeared several months later, it came with a preface that dismissed the moral issue in favor of a scientific agenda. "Where science is concerned, the accusation of immorality has no relevance," Zola now proclaimed. "I don't know if my novel is immoral, I confess that I never asked myself how chaste or unchaste it should be. What I do know is that smut detected in it by moral men is theirs rather than mine. Scientific truth was my touchstone for every scene, even the most febrile." As "analyst" or "surgeon," he had probed beneath character into the quick of human nature and investigated forces which hold us hostage to physiology. "He who reads the novel with care will see that each chapter explores a curious physiological phenomenon." Zola thus saw himself wielding the scalpel of Enlightenment against the pieties of men who ruled by Greek and Latin. "[My few congenial readers] will recognize in *Thérèse Raquin* the modern method, the instrument of universal inquiry with which our century is prying open the future. Whatever their final judgment, they will grant me my premise that circumstances and milieux work profound modifications upon an organism."

There can be no doubt that this credo, stated again and again, bespoke a missionary zeal. But Zola's image of the novelist performing experiments or dissecting flesh also served to impersonalize creative work, to distance him from childhood, to "objectify" unavowable fantasies and painful memories. One wonders, for example, how closely Thérèse Raquin was bound up with Mustapha, the Algerian houseboy whom François Zola had accused, in court, of molesting five-year-old Emile. That adolescent may well have been on Zola's mind when he pictured a sexually ambiguous woman from Algeria and when as writer-scientist he brought the hoyden to justice.

In April 1867, Louis Napoleon, who had been at work reinventing Paris ever since he had proclaimed himself Emperor Napoleon III fifteen years earlier, inaugurated a Universal Exposition that would attract more than six million people to his splendid new capital. Among those who came by special invitation were the tsar and the tsarina, the king of Prussia, the khedive of Egypt, the mikado's brother, the sultan of Turkey, the Hapsburg emperor, and the Prince of Wales. During seven months, hardly a week passed that Louis did not have occasion to greet some panjandrum alighting at a railroad depot and lead him in military pomp to the Tuileries Palace, where gala after gala preempted other, more banal affairs of state. Economic misery was rampant, but few looked backstage. All along the boulevards, theaters, restaurants, and boutiques drove a thriving trade as Paris mobilized its vast pleasure industry for visitors who arrived by the trainload or boatload.

"French is the language least heard on Paris streets," declared one chronicler, and this polyglot horde was indeed ubiquitous. It filled the Théâtre des Variétés when Offenbach's *La Grande Duchesse de Gérolstein* opened there on April 12. It fed its eyes on women high-kicking at dance halls like the Bal Mabille (to which it found its way by following a guide entitled *Parisian Cytheras*). It oohed at fireworks in the Tuileries Gardens and aahed at gorgeous carriages in the Bois de Boulogne, where Society paraded its wealth every afternoon. Gravitating to light, to movement, to fanfare, to novelty, it did not neglect Paris's venerable monuments, but often glimpsed them *en passant*, as did Mark Twain, who wrote in *The Innocents Abroad*: "We visited the Louvre at a time when we had no silk purchases in view, and looked at its miles of paintings by the old masters." Old masters couldn't quite compete against Blondin waltzing on a tightrope with blazing Catherine wheels fastened to his body. When the aerialist performed in a suburban pleasure garden, the horde of visitors flowed away from Paris like the sea at ebb tide. And when in October this horde left Paris for good, laden with silk from the great textile mills at Lyon, the image graven on its mind was more likely to be of machines in the Palace of Industry than of *Le Déjeuner sur l'herbe* in Manet's little pavilion.

The Palace of Industry occupied the Champ-de-Mars, where the Eiffel Tower was to rise on the occasion of another Exposition held twenty-two years later. Looming above gardens and grottoes laid out by Adolphe Alphand, architect of the Bois de Boulogne, this "bourgeois Colosseum" was an immense iron-and-glass oval whose bulk dwarfed the minarets, the pagodas, the domes, the cottages, the kiosks built to represent nation-states for the period of half a year. Unlike the Eiffel Tower, the Palace of Industry did not outlive abuse heaped on it by those who, with that French penchant for giving foreign names to native diseases, lamented France's "Americanization"; but while it stood, it advertised more completely than any American structure the materialist worldview to which Pope Pius IX had addressed himself in the encyclical *Syllabus of Errors.*

Had Pius ever seen the Palace, its six concentric galleries might have put him in mind of Dante's hell, especially by day, when a roar of machinery drowned the hubbub of the crowd and vapor from steam engines billowed toward the glass roof. To tour these mile-long galler-ies was, if one believed in progress, to rejoice in man's victory over nature or, if one did not, to witness the spectacle of pride running before a fall. Here industrial Europe displayed itself at its most vain-glorious. There were machines of every order and dimension: textile machines, compressed-air machines, coal-extracting machinery, rail-way equipment, electric dynamos, hydraulic lifts. There were loco-motives and large-scale models of those railroad stations that enshrined the nineteenth century's architectural befuddlement. There was a show on the History of Labor, where working-class visitors were given to understand that they did not lack basic necessities but had, on the contrary, earned enough since 1848 to afford the clothes, utensils, and gadgets laid before them in grotesque profusion. Beneath this glass roof nothing argued against Louis Napoleon's optimism, not even a fifty-eight-ton steel cannon made by Krupp of Essen for Wilhelm of Prussia. "A writer for the official bulletin wondered what earthly use it could have beyond frightening everyone to death. More offensive to Parisian sensibilities was that it was remarkably ugly, though in the end [the jury] did give the cannon a prize," notes one historian. With political reality suspended for the moment, inklings of doom were as unwelcome as paintings by the Batignolles renegades. Tourists pressed on heedlessly, orbiting through Wonderland until their journey led them to the outermost ring, where they restored themselves in cafés and restaurants, one more exotic than the next. At night the Palace's wall shimmered with gaslight, as women in native costumes brought out native dishes and scarlet-clad gypsy bands played czardas, and French flower girls selling Parma violets mingled with the crowd.

To Epicurus Rotundus, a pseudonymous Englishman writing in *Punch,* nothing about the Palace of Industry was so revealing of its nature and purpose as the garden around which it had been built. "My dear Sir, the heart of this garden, the center of all these monster rings, which made you feel as if you had got into Saturn, was a little money-changing office. I like this cynicism." Others reaped fortunes of irony from the fact that in Robespierre's day Parisians had gathered two hundred thousand strong to worship the Supreme Being on this same field. Where formerly there had stood a Revolutionary altar known as "the Sublime Mountain," now, like the hub of some immense carousel, stood the "Money Pavilion." Money, it said, made the world go round.

Zola could have walked Manet home after a day at the Exposition and not gone out of his way, for in April 1867 they became neighbors. Together with Alexandrine and Emilie, who would never live apart or far apart from her son, he moved into a four-room flat at 1, rue Moncey (now Dautencourt), near the Place de Clichy. Six hundred fifty francs a year was modest rent—indeed, more space for less money in quieter surroundings may have been one reason for the displacement—and around him dwelled people of modest means, mostly clerks and pensioners.

Stooped over his desk all day long, Zola felt bereft of friends. This feeling had already taken hold in February, when he told Valabrègue that he missed literary conversation, and that time spent at the Café Guerbois, where conversation was mostly about art, seemed to aggravate the feeling. "I seldom see Baille; it's desertlike for me up here on the heights of Batignolles," he lamented to Valabrègue on May 29. "When you return from Aix, I hope you will settle in my neighborhood." To Philippe Solari he wrote one week later: "I've wanted for quite some time to shake your hand, to congratulate you on your success at the Salon. Alas, we are now quartered so far from one another that I can't imagine when we'll get together. I would love to have the medal you struck of Gabrielle. . . . Paul leaves for Aix Saturday evening with his mother." A move that put the river between himself and the streets he had patrolled since adolescence might have caused him grief in any year. But 1867 was not just any year. Marking the tenth anniversary of his departure from Aix and the twentieth anniversary of his father's death, it evoked memories fraught with a sense of loss or abandonment. Now he found himself once again alone, *au désert.* Those who could have peopled the world for him were unavailable, and Aix still held prisoner a boon companion. "Two years in Aix must inevitably kill a man; there I have a settled opinion which will make me go on summoning you to Paris," he pleaded with Valabrègue. "Question Paul, question all our friends, and in all you will see the same terror of the provinces. Balzac has some admirable pages on the subject; read them."

Cézanne swooped unpredictably through Zola's life, coming north or going south as art, loneliness, or financial circumstances dictated. By 1867 he was quite well known in Aix-en-Provence, and not only on the Cours Mirabeau, where his hirsute figure made people gawk, but among students at the Conservatory, some of whom imitated his style.

"Paul has been an epidemic germ in Aix. Now all painters, even glass-makers, have begun to do impasto!" wrote a friend named Fortuné Marion. Their admiration, which must have been for portraits thickly larded with paint, did not buy him honor at home. Uplifted by fellow artists like Antoine Guillemet, who spent several months in Aix, he still felt downtrodden by his father, and swung as always from gran-diosity to self-hatred, from visions of himself painting huge canvases to black despair. Even old acquaintances were puzzled. "Paul is for me a veritable Sphinx," Roux reported in his correspondence with Zola, apparently during the summer of 1867.

> I contacted him soon after I arrived here. I saw him at his home, we chatted for quite some time. Several days ago he accompanied me on an overnight jaunt through the countryside. Again we had the opportunity to talk at length. Well, all I can tell you about him is . . . he's in good health! Not that I've forgotten our conversations, and I'll report them verbally. They need a translator like yourself, however; I myself am not equal to that task. You understand, it re-quires greater intimacy than I have with Paul to decipher the exact meaning of his words. My impression is that a holy flame still burns in him. He hasn't yet given up, but, although he has less enthusiasm for Aix than for painting, he will, I believe, prefer henceforth life here to life in Paris. He has been overcome by this . . . existence and reveres the paternal breadboard.

Something of what was hidden in Cézanne's cryptic language speaks more distinctly in a large oil Roux could not have missed seeing during his visit to the Jas de Bouffan. It shows Louis-Auguste reading *L'Evé-nement,* or Father learning about art from Zola. Dressed in rustic garb and seated in an armchair whose high back rises above the old man's dark skullcap, he looks, as Guillemet put it, like "a pope on his throne." Behind him, where an otherwise bare wall encloses the scene, hangs a still life by his son.

Zola continued to play big brother. When in April 1867 *Le Figaro* made fun of several canvases by "Monsieur Sésame," he wrote a vig-orous protest identifying Cézanne with "the analytic painters, the young school whose cause I have the honor to defend." This letter was read in Aix, and Valabrègue congratulated him effusively. "Paul is a child ignorant of life; you watch over him as guardian and guide. . . . His destiny is to paint pictures, yours to organize his life." But in fact the fraternal bond had gone somewhat slack. While Zola trotted out Cézanne for dedications, he never singled out Cézanne for notice. Extolling the friend, as if old friendship bespoke a purity of heart that validated his artistic judgment, he snubbed the artist. "I cannot give you the address of the painter you mention," he told Théodore Duret, an astute critic disposed to examine seriously work rejected by the establishment, who had heard rumors about the "eccentric" from Aix. "He shuts himself in a great deal; he is going through a period of groping. And, to my mind, he is right not to allow anyone in his studio. Wait until he has found himself." With his friend groping toward something he didn't understand, Zola may have feared not premature exposure but the possibility that Cézanne, once he found himself, would be unrecognizable, or that, once recognized, he would discredit the semi-fictional character he had become in a romance of childhood. Bound up with protectiveness was dominance, which made it difficult for Zola to help Paul achieve independence, to boost him, to let genius take its course.

Between them fell yet another shadow. Zola's mistress disliked Cézanne. His uncouthness embarrassed her, and embarrassment bred hostility as Gabrielle began to assume the bourgeois role of Alexandrine. Intent, moreover, on ordering life around shared experience, she saw in Cézanne a part of Zola that lay beyond her reach.

At twenty-seven, Zola looked older than his years. A dark mustache had sprouted above a dark beard and this growth, masking the lower face, set in relief his soft, mournful eyes. Nearsighted since adolescence, he wore pince-nez but as yet only for reading and writing. Despite the bookish life he led between sojourns at Bennecourt, he could still overeat with impunity. His frame was muscular enough to belie a nervous constitution that often sent him signals of distress. "You are doubtless aware that for thirty years I have been portrayed as an oaf, a plow horse with thick hide and coarse senses ponderously furrowing a straight line," he complained twenty-nine years later in a letter to Dr. Edouard Toulouse. "[In fact] I am a flayed man affected by every passing breeze, who never undertakes his daily task except in anguish and accomplishes it only after waging constant war against self-doubt." His nerves mocked the symptoms of cystitis and angina. Tight clothing sometimes produced a constriction in his chest. And around 1865 he began to suffer from pollakiuria, which would afflict him (as it had Jean-Jacques Rousseau) for the rest of his life. So persistent was his need to urinate, especially when writing, that he found it convenient to keep a chamber pot near his desk.

If he stopped writing, the family would starve, and in rough times, earning three or four hundred francs by his pen, which he managed to do almost every month, meant driving himself day after day. "Alas, you are quite right," he answered a nameless correspondent on January 30, 1867. "I'm running right and left under the whiplash of necessity. The day circumstances allow me to halt, the day I achieve an independent position, I shall try to satisfy you by writing a worthy, well-ripened novel." *Les Mystères de Marseille* had obviously not been that novel. Nor was it the source of an income equal to his expenses. The least delay in payment for work delivered could spell hardship, as temporizing publishers may not always have understood. "Your last letter announced the 600 francs I had been promised," he badgered Henry Houssaye in July. "The person who brought it gave me only 500 francs and said that I would shortly receive the balance. Would you kindly hand it over to my messenger?" When prospects were gloomiest, Alexandrine found some part-time work at Hachette, banding books.

We have seen how Zola banked on success with *Thérèse Raquin* to tide him over a lean year. A letter he wrote in September reiterates contractual terms set forth by Albert Lacroix. "You will print in 18 cm. format a first edition of 1,500 copies and I authorize you to bring out 200 over-copies, 150 of which you will give me for publicity," it begins.

> I shall collect a royalty of 10% on the catalogue price, which is to say 30 centimes per volume, the price of a volume in this first edition being 3 francs. The total sum I stand to collect will therefore be 450 francs, half of which will be paid me the day the edition goes on sale and half three months later. I concede the right of reproduction in newspapers, and if the work be translated into foreign languages, we shall evenly divide the fee for such translations.
>
> The work will be your property, you will be entitled to bring out new editions or reprints, provided I receive, the day they go on sale, 10% of the catalogue price for the totality of copies published. If, however, you decline to reprint the work after an edition has sold out, possession of it will revert to me after six months. . . . And finally, I shall have the right, ten years hence, to have *Thérèse Raquin* appear with my other works in a complete edition, should the opportunity arise.

Had *Thérèse Raquin* found a sizable public, this contract would have served him well—better, at any rate, than the customary arrangement whereby authors sold their work outright for a fixed period during which the publisher could market it as he saw fit. But *Thérèse Raquin* did not find a public of any consequence. Trade was sluggish in Paris, and the book's fate in rural France was sealed when the government commission that authorized such matters declined to let it be sold by licensed peddlers or *colporteurs* who traveled through regions that had no bookstores.

Zola would celebrate another birthday before his luck turned. As late as April 1868 he was still improvising a bare livelihood and found himself reduced to what he considered the desperate expedient of borrowing money from friends. "This pains me but as a last resort I must do what I should have liked to avoid in our relationship and that is ask you for a loan," he wrote on April 7 to Manet, who had recently done him another favor by painting his portrait. "Could you advance me . . . 600 francs? I'll reimburse you as soon as I receive my royalties, which should be June 15 at the latest. I've reached the end of my tether or else I wouldn't be addressing you. It would suit me better to shake your hand without the thought of money ever coming between us. There are sad necessities in life."

VIII

THE MASTER PLAN

B Y THE END of 1867, many parvenus felt decidedly old. The Universal Exposition that excited Paris all that year was in fact the last hurrah of a despotism weakened by political strife and economic disorder. Although gold flowed into the Banque de France, showing France's favorable balance of trade, there it accumulated as erstwhile borrowers became tightfisted observers, alert to what Napoleon III himself admitted were "black specks on the horizon." On the horizon loomed Prussia, which had made Europe tremble in 1866 by crushing Austria at the battle of Sadowa, and the sense of manifest destiny her victories brought home contrasted with the pall that hung over the Tuileries. "I hear from other persons besides Lord Cowley that the emperor is very much out of spirits," reported the British ambassador, Lord Lyons, in 1868. "It is even asserted that he is weary of the whole thing, disappointed at the contrast between the brilliancy at the beginning of his reign and the present gloom—and inclined, if it were possible, to retire into private life. This is no doubt a great exaggeration, but if he is really feeling unequal to governing with energy, the dynasty and the country are in great danger." Napoleon's poor health alarmed the financial community even more than his desperate improvisations. Stock prices climbed when he appeared on horseback and fell when a bout of illness conjured up the frightful image of Eugénie trying to govern France as regent. There was no market for long-term investment in a short-lived regime.

Napoleonic pillars collapsed one after another. First to fall was the Crédit Mobilier, half of whose capital disappeared overnight with the failure in 1866 of a Marseille real estate operation. The Banque de France would not shore it up, and patrician financiers led by Rothschild, who regarded Jacob and Isaac Pereire as reckless adventurers, delivered the coup de grâce, knocking down prices on the Bourse until a share of stock in Crédit Mobilier became a worthless memento. The next to topple was Baron Haussmann. In an exposé entitled *Les Comptes fantastiques d'Haussmann,* Jules Ferry, the future prime minister, laid bare an illicit scheme through which Haussmann had raised funds above and beyond what the legislature had sanctioned for his gigantic project.[1] Debate raged, Napoleon III made concessions enlarging the scope of parliamentary privilege, and Haussmann, whom Adolphe Thiers dubbed "vice-emperor," left office. Thus did the work of rebuilding Paris grind to a virtual halt, with disastrous consequences for some 100,000 people whose livelihood hinged on this enterprise.

Every morsel of freedom thrown to one class or another whetted its appetite for more, and the Empire fell not all at once but concession by concession as even formerly staunch Bonapartists rallied around Dame Liberty. When trade unions became legal in 1864, Louis Napoleon found soon enough that in attempting to buy quiescence he had licensed revolt. Strikes broke out, and strikes bred violence which profited the radical doctrine of ideologues like Auguste Blanqui. No less fruitless was Louis Napoleon's attempt to mollify a contentious legislature. In 1867 he made the government answerable for policy through the mechanism of interrogation or "interpellation," whereupon deputies, unmuzzled but not yet unleashed, bayed in chorus against a despot whose will remained law; forgetting—if they were old enough to remember—how easily France had traduced republican institutions fifteen years earlier.

The chorus of protest was amplified by the press, which spoke uninhibitedly after May 11, 1868, when a law went into effect permitting any Frenchman who had attained his majority and enjoyed his civil rights to publish a newspaper "without prior authorization." The law also reduced the stamp tax levied on papers read for political content, and forbade the much feared admonitions by which Napoleon had made independent-minded publishers heel. To be sure, such publishers would go on paying a steep price. Fines and prison sentences meted out as late as 1870 in courts of summary jurisdiction (*tribunaux correctionnels*) indicate how reluctant officialdom was to surrender its teeth. But criticism grew louder all the same. Hardly a week passed that did not see one or two new journals materialize, and by October 1868 the interior ministry counted ninety-seven in Paris alone, most of them anti-Bonapartist. "What we have is an unprecedented bur-

---

[1]The title of Ferry's exposé was inspired by *Les Contes fantastiques d'Hoffmann.*

geoning of newspapers," observed a journalist who apparently came of age after 1848, which had been equally fecund. "They are cramped for space in kiosks, and newspaper dealers, positively overwhelmed, don't know where to tuck the latest arrivals. Nowadays producing a paper is quite fashionable and one must be dead broke not to join the celebration. Fifty years hence every Frenchman will have a paper on his conscience." Among the dozen or so that survived their first temper tantrum, several established themselves as influential transmitters of republican opinion and gathered strength during the final days of Napoleon's empire.

This storm of print promised relief for drought-stricken journalists all over France. Even before May 11, however, Zola's future brightened somewhat thanks to a gentleman two years older than he named Théodore Duret, whom he met through Manet. Duret hailed from Saintes, near La Rochelle. Born to wealth, he had entertained political ambitions until the elections of 1863, when he ran last against Napoleon's candidate. Prevented from descending upon the capital as a liberal legislator, he traveled around the world as the representative of a cognac distillery and came home laden with Oriental objets d'art. Art rather than cognac was what impelled him to tour Iberia in 1865, where he made Manet's acquaintance. A year later he left Saintes for Paris, which captivated the aesthete but also reawakened the liberal. This tall, aristocratic young man, who looks Grecoesque in a portrait done by Manet, immediately cast his net wide. While frequenting the Café Guerbois, where he earned hospitality with a book sympathetic to Batignolles painters (*Les Peintres français en 1867*), he acquired friends among left-wing newspapermen, one of whom, Mille-Noé, founded *Le Globe* in January 1868. Duret became art critic for this daily, whose first issue announced that it was "the organ of democracy and the partisan of all freedoms." Zola, riding in on Duret's coattails, reviewed books and plays.

That he needed anybody's sponsorship is one measure of the ambiguous position he occupied vis-à-vis militant republicans. Whereas the latter held creative work accountable to political dogma, Zola viewed art and politics as inherently separate realms. "Proudhon would make me a citizen, I would make him an artist, [for] in my view art is a negation of society, an affirmation of the individual outside all rules and social imperatives," he had written at twenty-five, stating a belief that was to be reiterated time and again. As repugnant as he found the moral elevation that critics like Ulbach required of art, the conformity they expected of artists repelled him even more. Though he hated social injustice, he sided not with the crowd but with men who rose above it, who suffered its taunts or quickened its pulse. An engineer striking water from rocks, an artist braving convention, a visionary entrepreneur, a scientist plumbing unexplored depths, a Balzac measuring himself against Dante: these were his heroes, and for such heroism the sententious world of republican discourse had no room. What made him feel all the more dubious about that world was his own pessimism. Convinced that civilized man harbors an incorrigible savage screaming to be let out, he, like Taine, could travel only so far with idealists willfully ignorant of the part played in human affairs by *la bête humaine.*

Nothing daunted, Zola spoke his mind at *Le Globe* and reviewed works that lent themselves to a defense of naturalism or to an attack on religious superstition. "*Eugène Bastin* is not a novel . . . but a minute study of real life," he wrote in February. "The author has understood that greater moral rigor and livelier interest attaches to the true than to the fanciful. He took any old subject, a commonplace story, and studied human beings in their daily routine, in the facts of their existence, which could be your existence or mine." After an evening of bromidic theater, he called for the playwright who would someday "dramatize life in its reality, with virtues and vices we encounter on the street." Almost every other review made this same point, advocating now the legitimation of banal events, now the demystification of supernatural phenomena. "Supernatural," for example, was *Les Trésors du château de Crèvecoeur, épisode de l'affaire Frigard,* a book that recounted some rural hocus-pocus involving a peasant girl subject to divinatory trances. "Poor mankind, dreaming wide awake and soaring into madness on the wings of passion!" cried Zola. "Free minds have but one consolation, that being to ferret out the truth, to discover what lies behind the ecstasies of Saint Theresa and Léonie the somnambulist." These two names would, no doubt, have put readers in mind of a third, Bernadette Soubirous, whose vision at Lourdes ten years earlier had become grist for the anticlerical mill.

But *Le Globe* provided only temporary shelter. One month after Mille-Noé set it up the paper folded, and Zola, wondering if his vagrancy would ever end, once again went in search of regular employment. Not until spring did he find any. "I've saved the best for last," he informed Marius Roux on April 17. "[Adolphe Belot] has just started a cheap daily, *L'Evénement illustré,* under Adrien Marx's direction!!! They've offered me the Salon, which I took for want of something better. When you return I'll introduce you to Marx, and perhaps he'll let you write a column about Paris." This assignment, which generated seven articles, presented the piquant challenge of having to flatter his own image, with all due modesty. "Yesterday a friend asked me if I would comment on [Manet's portrait of me at the Salon]," he wrote. " 'Why not?' I answered. 'I'd like ten columns to repeat aloud what I thought in silence as I watched Edouard Manet during our sittings wrestle tenaciously with nature. Do you take me for a vain sort who delights in lecturing on his physiognomy? Yes, I shall discuss this portrait, and wags who make the most of it are simply imbeciles.'"

Scattered through the horde of indistinguishable genre scenes were more paintings by habitués of the Guerbois than had been the case in 1866, although they were usually "skyed," or hung high above eye level. Also present was a large sculpture by Philippe Solari, *Nègre endormi*, and Zola lavished praise on his old friend. "I find in Philippe Solari one of our few modern sculptors. . . . He has put behind him the dream of absolute beauty, he does not carve idols for a religion (that disappeared with the ancient Greeks). Beauty to him is the living expression of nature, the individual interpretation of the human body." With phrases flowing so effortlessly from his pen, he might have found a way of devoting some to another childhood friend. But nowhere in the review is mention made of Cézanne, whom the jury had rejected that year.

Meanwhile, Duret had remained on the alert for an opportunity to stake his claim in Paris's ebullient newspaper world. Opportunity knocked soon after the demise of *Le Globe* when he connected with Eugène Pelletan and André Lavertujon, two seasoned dissenters who were keen on founding a paper to boost the republican cause, as well as their own candidacies, in elections scheduled for 1869. By mid-April word of this project reached Zola. "Yesterday I saw Duret at Manet's," he wrote to Roux. "The venture is limping along. I think Pelletan may be as inept as Mille-Noé in business matters. No one is sure when *La Tribune* will appear, or whether it will appear at all." Roux, who had contributed several articles to *Le Globe* and thus knew Mille-Noé, responded in language that crudely expressed his low opinion of politicians on the left. "You think Pelletan has about as much brawn as [the flaccid] Mille-Noé? I believe democracy most definitely cannot be put right. Democracy is not strong. If it is, it is strong like a cheese that stinks but lacks consistency."[2]

Whatever Zola's qualms may have been, the new paper promised to give him more leeway than the unserious *Evénement illustré*. In any event he needed money, and need made Pelletan and company look more attractive with every passing day. As prospects of *La Tribune* materializing improved, Zola rose to the occasion. He badgered Pelletan through Duret until the future editor-in-chief granted him an interview. "I saw Pelletan this morning, and here is how our conversation went," he reported to Duret on May 8. "I'll do a causerie for *La Tribune*, a weekly chronicle about theaters, books, literary events.

---

[2] Zola and Roux would later break over the Dreyfus Affair when Roux was working for a fiercely anti-Dreyfusard newspaper, *Le Petit Journal*.

... We didn't discuss salary. I hope you'll be present when that issue is raised. ... Also, please see to it, I implore you, that they hire neither an art critic, nor a bibliographer, nor any other editor who might tread on my turf." Two weeks later he prodded Duret to settle the matter. "Has the salary question been thrashed out? It's a matter of grave importance. I miss working for a daily, which allowed me to earn what I need and live peacefully in an honorable family. I'm sick of *la petite presse* [popular journalism] with its more or less sleazy machinations. It diminishes people and kills them."

Duret let him know that his salary would be 4,000 francs per annum, but the situation remained unclear even after *La Tribune* had published its first issue. "I must apprise you of my conversation with M. Lavertujon," Zola wrote Duret on June 19.

> He seems quite well disposed but couldn't give me any assurances. In short, he doesn't think I can write an article every week because commitments have been made to too many people. ... I pleaded my cause by emphasizing Pelletan's promise and, *above all*, pointing out that a "causerie" is a chronicle that must absolutely appear in every issue. But what seemed to affect him most was my saying that I needed the work badly, with a mother to support and nothing to rely upon save my pen ... I told him furthermore how weary I am of popular journalism, how ardently I want safe haven at an upright and serious newspaper. "If *La Tribune* offered me 500 francs a month," I said, "I'd devote myself to it religiously."

In October, after producing a dozen causeries lauded by Pelletan, Zola was still apprehensive, and when Pelletan invited another literary journalist to write something for *La Tribune*, he assumed the worst. "I've learned that we shall soon be fellow collaborators at *La Tribune* and I'm delighted to see you enter a house where I am already settled," he warned Jules Claretie. "But rumor has it that you will share my task and write two of the four causeries I give the paper each month. As you know, I'm a poor devil. May I implore you—you on whom fortune smiles and who place articles just about everywhere—to leave intact my sole resource?" Claretie reassured him that the chronicle was not at stake and that he would have turned it down had it been offered. "I thank you for confiding in me, though I'm a bit peeved that you believed me capable of making cider from my neighbor's apples."

Zola's fear was not without a basis in reality. Pelletan had given him carte blanche only after overcoming doubts and overruling colleagues who thought the young man politically suspect. Thus in May, Duret had urged Zola to be "extra prudent" during negotiations. "You are under siege and attacked all around, so you'd better behave yourself. Everybody including some big names, some very big names indeed, will want to take your place. The first volleys have already been fired. What provokes such rage against you is the fact that you're not a democrat and certain democrats here fancy that they alone should write for it, even the literary articles." This antagonism persisted. Zola dared not lower his guard or speak his mind except in the company of literati like Jules and Edmond de Goncourt, and to them he spoke his mind rancorously at their first encounter in December 1868. "[I] would like to launch something big and not do these ignoble, infamous articles I must turn out for *La Tribune*, amidst people whose idiotic opinions I am compelled to share," they quote him as saying. "The truth of the matter is that this government with its indifference, its unawareness of talent and of everything that's being produced under its nose, thrusts us in our poverty upon opposition journals, which are the only ones prepared to offer us a livelihood!"

Eager to impress these supercilious novelists of whom he made so much and who in turn made so little of others, Zola may have thought it best to picture himself a journalist *malgré lui*. But his sixty-odd causeries, even when they invoke 1793, were not mere exercises in ideological ventriloquism. The voice that derided institutions, policies, and people week after week was unmistakably his own. Indeed, it became increasingly his, for he emerged from this ordeal broader in outlook and laden with enough subject matter to construct the fictional edifice already taking shape in his mind. What he wrote as *La Tribune*'s mordant chronicler foreshadows *Les Rougon-Macquart*.

Along with Dumas *fils* and the Goncourts, Zola waxed apocalyptic on the topic of degeneracy. His causeries abound in lurid anecdotes that demonstrate how France had become a nation devoid of pride, where men of high estate groveled before women of low repute. Obsessed by *la bête humaine*, he saw it consuming patrimonies, loosening family ties, tearing moral fabric, cheapening life altogether. His *bête* held sway over the moribund Empire like a nihilistic force that clouded memory and induced those born with noble patents or expectations of wealth to forget the past or bankrupt the future. "Ah! how many sinister dreams unfold in secret, how many men there are who cast off their black habit as if it were a mere costume, roll on the carpet like a dog, and beg for punishment!" he cried, with an image that was to become a major dramatic moment in *Nana*.

The quake of '89 followed hard on the scandals of the Regency and of Louis XV. I don't know what will follow our own age. I simply note that gentlemen send horses worth 25,000 francs a pair to trollops and fetch besotted women at the jailhouse. A kind of nervous erethism is unhinging our gilded youth. Aristocrats and scions live in lamebrained mirth. They applaud the cheap tunes ground out by Messieurs Offenbach and Hervé, they exalt wretched tightrope dancers cavorting on the legitimate stage. Their mistresses are street urchins who drag them down to their level of language and feeling.

This lament recurs throughout, and often, as here, in tandem with a diatribe against Offenbach, whose comic operas were all the rage. "*La Belle Hélène* amounts to nothing more than a grimace of convulsive gaiety, a display of gutter wit and gestures," he fumed when word reached France that *La Grande Duchesse de Gérolstein* had played to enthusiastic audiences in London. "The day some woman conceives the brilliant idea of running around a stage naked on all fours and acting the part of a stray bitch, that will be the day Paris cheers itself sick."

To ridicule the beau monde for worshipping base idols was also to condemn it for shunning spectacles of everyday life in the lower depths. The same people who lionized Offenbach found naturalism objectionable, and Zola concerned himself as much with their social blindness as with their pornographic voyeurism. "Walk around our working-class slums, strictly incognito," he wrote in a Montesquieu-like letter to Fatouma-Djombé, sultana of Mohéli, who obviously stood for the Empress Eugénie. "There you will see what it behooves a queen to see: lots of poverty, lots of courage, muffled rage against the idle and the wanton. There you will hear the great voice of the populace, growling for justice and bread." By September 1869, when Eugénie went south with her son, opposition to the regime had grown so openly vehement that Zola dared mock her in person. "At Toulon," he wrote, "mother and child were received with open arms. Among the first to greet the travelers were a dozen convicts, who broke their ban on this special occasion. . . . My only regret is that the empress did not feel compelled to have her son visit the casemates of Fort Lamalgue. Being a strong-minded woman who likes strong-armed tactics, she would, I'm sure, have enjoyed seeing the gloomy dungeon where her spouse had insurgents locked up in December 1851." Another blind eye belonged to Baron Haussmann, the architect of a capital from which thousands of workers had been driven by demolition crews and developers building flats they couldn't afford. "I know M. Haussmann doesn't like popular festivals. He has forbidden almost all those that once took place in the communes annexed to Paris [eight years ago, including Montmartre]. He relentlessly harasses street peddlers. In his dreams, he must see Paris as a gigantic chessboard, with geometrically perfect lines."

For his weekly prosecution of officialdom, Zola subpoenaed not only proscribed images but censored words. Censorship was, to be sure, no longer the weapon it had been during the "preliberal" Empire of the 1850s, when criticism of Napoleon's regime, however meek, prompted draconian reprisals from above, and when an obscenity charge awaited the author who led his reader astray. Not since Baudelaire and Flaubert stood trial for *"outrage aux bonnes moeurs"* in 1857 had the imperial prosecutor hauled up any writers of note. But many noted writers, Victor Hugo above all, still lived in exile, and the regime still employed a censor to guard its shrunken sphere of influence. "On some Wednesday morning, gain admittance if you can to the office where the censor works," Zola advised the aforementioned sultana of Mohéli. "Take a seat and listen. It's pure vaudeville. These gentlemen believe that there's a revolution taking place in the street. They subject thought to close inspection, sniffing every word for a scent of gunpowder, searching every phrase for a concealed bomb. They end up moving commas around and congratulating themselves on having saved the Empire."

Books were also scrutinized by a *commission de colportage,* whose purview encompassed bookstalls at railway stations and lending libraries as well as the countryside. A book could not be sold in such establishments or hawked from town to town unless it bore a prefectural stamp, and the commission furnished syllabi of approved works. This system having come under attack in parliament, Zola joined the fray with an epistolary tirade against mind control written on August 9, one month after *Thérèse Raquin* was judged immoral. The commission suppressed every plot that called traditional authority into question, and Zola cited as evidence a censored but otherwise undistinguished novel, *Madame Freinex,* whose titular heroine rebuffs her unscrupulous, politically ambitious husband. "I think I know what troubled you," he taunted.

> The author defends woman's freedom of conscience. You underlined the sentence in which Juliette tells her husband that she "has no master." However legitimate this declaration of freedom coming from the mouth of a woman whom a knave wishes to manipulate, it must have struck you as monstrous. Ah, pious young men that you are, you'll always remain true to your catechism! . . . I've said it before, you understand morality only at the most pedestrian level; the morality that transcends purely social duties and stands on truth and absolute justice escapes you and frightens you.

Framing an indictment of censorship around this example was especially meaningful in 1868, when *vieille France* felt threatened by measures that gave women greater intellectual scope. Louis Napoleon's courageous minister of public instruction, Victor Duruy, had just opened public secondary school courses to both sexes, and the Church, including even liberal clergy, protested vehemently. Conservatives and progressives alike viewed woman's mind as the field of Armageddon from which France would emerge Catholic or secular. "The Church intends to possess woman, and for that reason democracy must make it loosen its grip," Jules Ferry told an audience at the Sorbonne in May 1870. "Democracy must decide under pain of death whether woman will belong to Science or to the Church."

Another conflict in which Zola expressed republican sentiment was the one that marshaled pacifists favoring accommodation with Bismarck against nationalists spoiling for glory in a war with Prussia. Since Austria's defeat at Sadowa in 1866, every turn of events had brought Prussia nearer to the brink of war with France. Racked by disease, Louis Napoleon may have been unprepared to join battle, but he found himself caught between an iron chancellor in Germany who thwarted his diplomatic maneuvers and a military establishment at home that wanted a casus belli. Private life offered him no respite from this dilemma. While the emperor grew more indecisive, the empress, whose conviction it was that her son would never rule if her husband did not campaign, grew more belligerent. Sir Charles Oman described how matters stood in remembering a ceremony he witnessed as a child on holiday in France. "The Prince Imperial, then a boy of twelve, was a cadet, and was to drill a company of other cadets of his own age on the gravel in front of the Palace," he wrote in *Things I Have Seen.*

On a bench overlooking the gravel sat a very tired old gentleman, rather hunched together, and looking decidedly ill. I do not think I should have recognized him but for his spiky moustache. He was anything but terrifying in a tall hat and a rather loosely fitting frock coat . . . Behind him stood the Empress Eugénie, a splendid figure, straight as a dart, and to my young eyes the most beautiful thing that I had ever seen . . . wearing a zebra-striped black and white silk dress, with very full skirts, and a black and white bonnet. But it was the way she wore her clothes, and not the silks themselves, that impressed the beholder, young or old. . . . The Empress was a commanding figure, and dominated the whole group on the terrace—the Emperor, huddled in his seat, was a very minor show. She appeared extremely satisfied and self-confident as she watched the little manoeuvres below. Her son, the Prince Imperial, . . . drilled his little flock with complete success and not a single hitch or hesitation. His mother beamed down upon him. The boys marched off, and the spectators broke up after indulging in a little *Vive l'Empereur!*

Perhaps Louis Napoleon entertained strong suspicions that his army, compared with King Wilhelm's well-oiled and proven machine, loomed no larger than this diminutive band. An attempt at reform had produced a reserve, or *garde mobile*, preposterously unfit for battle. The general staff lacked cohesion. The legislature had cut war appropriations. But among patriots, a mystical belief in the Napoleonic legend and exorbitant faith in the new chassepot rifle outweighed evidence that counseled against force of arms. As such evidence mounted, war fever spread, until it seemed to young Charles Oman at least that France was one large parade ground. "In France there seemed to be bands and banners or military display almost every day . . . congresses of *Orphéonistes* with gorgeous lyres on their standards, or of *Pompiers* with magnificent brass helmets," he observed. "The soldier was everywhere, very conspicuous because of his various multicoloured and sometimes fantastic uniform . . . the trooper of the Cent Gardes—the hundred horsemen—in the brightest sky-blue, with cuirass and steel helmet . . . the bearskins of the grenadiers of the Imperial Guard . . . the white breeches and black gaiters of the original *grognards* of Napoleon I . . . the Zouaves of the Guard with their floppy tasselled headgear and immense baggy breeches, with yellow lace upon their absurdly small cut-away jackets."

Zola regularly interrupted the extravaganza to prophesy that unless France sobered up, this parti-colored cast of actors would soon be indistinguishable skeletons dancing a *danse macabre*. On All Souls' Day 1868 he mourned compatriots who had fallen in battle throughout Europe and pictured an old lady bereft of son or husband scanning the horizon for Sebastopol. The fallen were evoked again in July 1869, when workers began sprucing up the Champs-Elysées with oriflammes to celebrate the hundredth anniversary of Napoleon I's birth. "The administration should assemble not the quick but the dead," he proclaimed. "It should sound the call to arms all over Europe, in Italy, in Spain, in Austria, in Russia. And from all these battlefields, hordes would rise. Ah, what a festive gathering it would make, a gathering of the butchered. Paris would be too small. Never would an emperor have had before his arch of triumph so populous a nation." On the eve of Sedan, it must have seemed much longer than ten years since the battle of Magenta and the ode he had written then enjoining Frenchmen to "go fight where once your fathers fought so nobly." At nineteen he had identified himself as a "student of rhetoric from the Lycée Saint-Louis." Now he vilified a government that got young men drunk on fine phrases before sending them east to die.

Zola did not stay put very long on the rue Moncey. In April 1868 he moved nearer Clichy, having found, behind the apartment building at 23, rue Truffaut, a dollhouse-like pavilion that afforded him protection from the hubbub of a street crowded with shops and alive with women who gathered every day in the washhouse at number 26. A year later, when his newspaper articles were producing a comfortable income, he moved around the corner to a more "bourgeois" street, the rue de la Condamine, and rented another dollhouse, this one larger than the first but still so diminutive that its grandest room could not accommodate both a dinner table and an upright piano until a niche was hollowed out for the latter. Here he settled with his women, enjoying calm at the edge of pandemonium. There was a garden to putter in, and soon a big Newfoundland named Bertrand to receive the affection he lavished on dogs (dogs and other pets would follow Zola throughout his life). There were also friends constantly arriving from Aix to make it all feel even more provincial. "He had me talk at length about myself, my plans, about that Provence he still cherished after eleven years, a faint scent of which entered the house with me, no doubt," wrote Paul Alexis, who left Aix for Paris in 1869 and eventually became Zola's most intimate friend.

> More stay-at-home then than now, with fewer acquaintances and above all less money to spend ransacking antique and curio stores, not rich enough to afford a summer holiday outside Paris, he found a hygienic distraction in this little garden, which took the place of a café, a club, a country house, a chalet at Trouville. I can still see him in a sweater and an old pair of soil-stained pants, shod in big, fur-lined shoes.

Alexis would have known how his compatriot's love of Provence verged on blind hatred if he read *Le Mémorial d'Aix*, where in August 1868 Zola vituperated against the city that never gave François Zola his due. This jeremiad began obliquely enough, with an article deploring the misbehavior of some students who had offended two young ladies by singing ribald verse beneath their balcony and whose trial led to skirmishes on the Cours Mirabeau. "Such scandalous conduct could only have taken place at Aix, a barbarous town," he declared in *L'Evénement illustré*. "Where else but among stupid, churlish people would respectable women . . . unfortunate enough to be rich and beautiful arouse the jealousy of the entire feminine public and find themselves harassed by young men obeying nasty insinuations. . . . Times have changed since Aix fostered the first Courts of Love!"

His shaft hit the mark, and friends told him that indignant aldermen were bent on making him apologize. Before they could do so, however, he shifted ground to the real issue, which was one of name and fame. "My father, a civil engineer, died in 1847 after devoting his last years to a canal project that improved Aix's sanitation and fertilized the drought-stricken countryside," he wrote in *L'Evénement illustré* on July 28. "True to form, Aix has striven to forget the very name of someone who compromised his fortune and health on its behalf. I spent fifteen years there, my entire youth, and of its thirty thousand inhabitants, I can count three at most who haven't stoned me." He had been through the city a year before and found nothing graven on walls or published in papers to suggest that Aixois kept alive the memory of "their benefactor."

Le Mémorial dismissed the charge outright, but Zola attacked with redoubled fury, availing himself of an offer from Léopold Arnaud to bruit his case in Le Messager de Provence. Each side wrote ornately vicious letters, one longer than the next, until Le Mémorial announced that further debate would be pointless. After releasing a Parthian shot, on September 14 Zola turned to Aix's municipal council and, in the name of a grateful population, demanded "honorific recompense" for François Zola. "Deliver the letter and plead the cause, should it be necessary," he ordered Marius Roux, who, like Cézanne, shuttled between Aix and Paris. "It would be best if the mayor read it in your presence. Be sure to say that I couldn't indicate the exact nature of the recompense, but that naming a street after him seems appropriate. Go so far as to help him choose the street, if possible. I'm asking Arnaud to launch a campaign." When his request was heard six weeks later, the municipal council honored it with such alacrity that one member proposed commissioning a bust. They decided, instead, to rename Boulevard du Chemin-Neuf "Boulevard Zola" and notified Zola fils straightway. Soon afterward, Roux, Valabrègue, and other brethren from Aix gathered around the victors for a celebratory dinner in Les Batignolles. Emilie, now forty-nine, had at last won some measure of justice.

Zola did not let matters rest there. A letter sent to Marius Roux on December 4 reflects the ease with which he glided between opportunism and piety:

> I ask you first to find out why I haven't yet received a copy of the municipal council's minutes. Kindly see the mayor and tell him that I await them with rightful impatience. I thank you for worrying about the sale of my volumes in Aix. When you return and give me precise information, I shall know what to do. While you're at it, see if there might not be some way of slipping into Le Mémorial the review of Madeleine Férat [his latest novel]. Have I vexed Remondet to the point of not being able to count on his paper for publicity?

To make hometown notables honor Zola father and son remained his fixed goal. Belittling Aix only conferred on it the stature it had had for him during childhood, when names were won or lost down south rather than up north. He stoked his rage like a sacred fire and thus kept alive that youth who regularly climbed Les Infernets seeking the vantage point of his father's monument to lord it over those responsible for his mother's social disgrace. Whichever height he occupied in life, he always wanted Aix below.

Something of the same rage that inspired diatribes against *Le Mémorial* found expression in *Madeleine Férat*, a novel published serially as *La Honte* between September 2 and October 20, 1868. The story had been with him since 1865, when he wrote a three-act play entitled *Madeleine*, of which nothing came. Now, salvaging the framework, he improvised yet another vehicle for ideas that lent scientific credence to his private demonology.

Like Thérèse Raquin, Madeleine Férat, the daughter of a sixteen-year-old orphan and a self-made man of forty, is doomed *ab origine*. Her mother dies in childbirth and six years later her father, after suffering financial reverses, sails for America, never to reappear. Madeleine grows up with no one whom she can call family except her neglectful guardian, Lobrichon. The latter takes her home from boarding school when she turns fifteen, having conceived matrimonial designs upon the nubile redhead. He waits four years, then lecherously declares himself. Madeleine flees, wanders through Paris, and is offered shelter in the Latin Quarter by a young doctor, Jacques Berthier, to whom she makes love out of gratitude. They remain together several months until the army drafts him for service in the Far East; footloose womanizer that he is, he departs as if sprung from prison, leaving Madeleine mysteriously tethered to the relationship. "She never loved him deep down; rather, she received his imprint, she felt herself becoming him, she understood that he had taken complete possession of her flesh and her mind. She could never forget him."

No sooner does Jacques embark than Madeleine meets young Guillaume de Viargue, whose story is as fraught with Gothic incident as hers is with genetic hobgoblins. Zola conjures up a Norman castle, a reclusive father immersed in chemical experiments, a devoutly Calvinist housekeeper of great age named Geneviève. Fathered by Viargue senior on an adulterous bourgeoise, Guillaume was raised lovelessly between religion, which taught him to regard himself as the "child of sin," and science, which ignored him altogether. At school, where children mocked "the bastard," only one boy showed him kindness, and, despite their differences of nature and temperament, the two became fast friends. They had since gone separate ways. Always yearning for the perfect union, Guillaume drapes his fantasy on Madeleine as soon as chance throws them together; the strangers find refuge from history in a town house Guillaume acquires. "The lovers could imagine that the past had died. . . . Madeleine thought she had been born the day before." This beatific state is ruined when Madeleine discovers among

Guillaume's effects a photograph of Jacques, who turns out to be that childhood soul mate. Not even the news that Jacques has perished at sea, which breaks immediately afterward, can assuage her. Dead or alive, he lives on, like a devil impossible to exorcise. "She rediscovered him there, in her breast."

Five years later, the strangers are still together, having meanwhile married, begotten a daughter, and inherited the ancestral château. More Calvinist than ever, Geneviève, now a hundred years old, recites stories about destruction visited on lubricious women by "God the Father" as she challenges Madeleine for Guillaume's soul. But otherwise the couple feels safe. "The young woman luxuriated in the emptiness all around her; it seemed to isolate her more completely, to cushion her against wounds from the outside."

The implausibilities continue. While off attending to business, Guillaume encounters Jacques himself, who has not drowned after all, and joyously informs Madeleine that this long-lost brother, home from Cochin China, will join them for a night. Madeleine avoids her Nemesis but reveals the terrible truth to Guillaume, awakening his own worst fears. "The idea of having shared her with another, of having come second, was something he couldn't tolerate. . . . His wife's former liaison with the man he had considered a god during his youth seemed to him one of those abominations that confound human reason. He saw it as incestuous, as sacrilegious." A recovery from beyond the grave thus results in a fundamental loss, and Guillaume suddenly observes that his daughter resembles Jacques rather than himself. With no inner space they can call their own, he and Madeleine become fugitives shuttling between town and country but condemned to meet their master everywhere. In due course the tale comes full round. Madeleine finds her way to Jacques, yields her body somnambulistically, then learns that her child died at the moment of transgression. This preternatural coincidence tolls a denouement. "One after another all places had become uninhabitable," and Madeleine swallows poison concocted by M. Viargue years before. Stark raving mad, Guillaume dances around her corpse as Geneviève drily mutters: "God the Father did not pardon!"

Madeleine Férat was obviously patterned after *Thérèse Raquin*, with greater emphasis on the motif of "impregnation." Again there is a triangle involving a woman and two temperamentally antithetical lovers. Husband and wife are again effeminate and mannish. And again a ghost rises from the deep to destroy a haunted couple. Just as Camille's mother triumphs at the end of *Thérèse Raquin*, so in *Madeleine Férat* it is Guillaume's surrogate mother, Geneviève, who witnesses the final scene, interpreting what happens as condign punishment for original sin or innate lewdness. Each novel dramatizes the guilt that cannot plead extenuating circumstances to a rational jury. Though fathers are conspicuously absent from both, the fatherless inhabit a moral universe ruled by a patriarch vengeful in his justice, who manifests himself through widowed crones.

With all its melodramatic flummery and physiological humbug, *Madeleine Férat* translates the horror Zola saw in regression to a primitive state. Yearning for adulthood, Madeleine and Guillaume struggle against a force that pulls them backward or downward to where the identities they have acquired and the order they have built come undone. Once Jacques ruins their hermetic Eden by introducing consciousness of the past, they fall from grace. Ejected from themselves, the lawfully wed couple become partners in betrayal. "Guillaume's marriage proposal caused her singular revulsion, [for] it seemed to Madeleine that he was asking something impossible of her, that she was not self-possessed but the possession of another man," writes Zola. Such revulsion might appear excessive if the adulterous act were not experienced on some level as incestuous, and we have seen how incest eventually speaks its name. Bearing the "imprint" of the man who protected Guillaume in loco parentis, Madeleine plays Jocasta to her husband's Oedipus.

Their imbroglio is amplified and parodied in another triangular drama, which they observe unfolding next door under the nose of an old aristocrat named Rieux, whose wife, Hélène, has attached herself, after numerous liaisons, to a vulgar opportunist half her age named Tiburce Rouillard. Where Madeleine and Guillaume suffer for sins they didn't commit, Hélène and Tiburce fornicate without scruple, the one governed by lust, the other by ambition. Where history weighs upon Zola's guilt-ridden protagonists, his guiltless couple are savages unconscious of the past, trampling underfoot class distinctions and generational barriers as they dance naked before the aristocratic Rieux, who regards them scornfully. "Long contemplation of his wife had persuaded him that humans are mean, stupid marionettes. When he searched the wrinkled doll, he discovered, beneath her coquettish mask, infamies and fatuities that led him to consider her a beast good for whipping. Instead of whipping her, he amused himself by studying and despising her." An aristocrat marooned among Second Empire déclassés, a naturalist observing "the human beast" in its mindless progress toward self-degradation, and a puppeteer jerking lost souls, Rieux is, above all, one more avatar of the wrathful father exacting vengeance on the incestuous. This he does when at length Tiburce turns against Hélène. Rieux's final testament stipulates that the rapacious young man shall inherit his entire fortune, provided he marry the woman whom he now brutalizes. "My child, I have come to regard you as my son, I wish to assure your happiness," he says, and with these dying words arranges an infernal troth.

Although *Madeleine Férat* ran uncensored in *L'Evénement illustré*, shortly before its publication in book form authorities told its editor-in-chief, Edouard Bauer, that unless certain passages expounding the impregnation theory were cut from the book, he might be subject to prosecution. Distraught, Bauer informed Lacroix, the book publisher, and he, in turn, exerted pressure on Zola, who would not yield. "Let's reason this out, I beg of you," he answered.

What has been authorized on the street cannot be banished from the bookstore. . . . It seems the imperial prosecutor warned [Bauer] that although allowances had been made for him, with his powerful connections, it is unlikely that any would be made for me, an editor at *La Tribune*. There you have preventive censorship plain and simple, and instead of wanting me to purge my work, you should be helping me upbraid the public prosecutor. . . . I will therefore not approve the cuts you specify. For me it's a matter of law. Self-respect requires me to go forward and face this danger with which I'm threatened. If necessary, I shall relate the story out loud.

After an interview with the prosecutor, Zola devoted a long article to his predicament in *La Tribune*, invoking not only legal precedent but scientific authority. "The few lines they would expurgate contain the book's central thesis, which I took from Michelet and Dr. [Prosper] Lucas," he explained. "I dramatized it austerely and with conviction; good morals are not endangered by a medical study that serves, as I see it, a high human purpose." While the censor presumably saw in "impregnation" a physiological alibi for infidelity, Zola argued that if anything it bolstered the sacredness of marriage. "This study tends to accept the marriage bond as eternal from the physiological viewpoint. Religion and morality tell man: 'You will live with one woman'; and science says in turn: 'Your first wife will be your eternal wife.' " Calvinist in his depiction of woman struggling vainly against a cynical nature, Zola in his self-defense contrived to appear more Catholic than the pope.

He contrived as well to appear more beleaguered than he really was, or so said Lacroix in conversation many years later. The publisher and his author apparently manufactured publicity by staging quarrels and keeping literary chroniclers informed. Along with a legal writ that enjoined Lacroix to publish *Madeleine Férat*, Zola served him gossip for newspaper distribution. "Attached you will find the note that was supposed to run in *Le Figaro*. I find it so complete, so felicitous, that I cannot resolve to file it. Try then, for the love of God, to get it published somewhere. Feyrnet is back, I think. He could plant it in *Le Temps*. If he refuses, look elsewhere." When *Madeleine Férat* finally appeared, Zola referred to such gossip as evidence of literary martyrdom and sought help for this waif disinherited by its publisher. "I don't know if you still review books at *L'Artiste,* but I would greatly appreciate your inserting several lines about the attached volume," he entreated in a typical note. "The imperial prosecutor threatened its life before it was born, as you undoubtedly know from the newspapers. I hope that its misadventures will engage your sympathy."

In the end, the most sympathetic response may have come from Edouard Manet, to whom the novel was dedicated. "My dear friend," he wrote, "I am immersed in *Madeleine Férat* and don't want to wait until the end before sending you my compliments. Your portrait of the redhead makes me jealous, and for the love scenes you find expressions the mere reading of which would deflower a virgin." Otherwise, *Madeleine Férat* received a quiet burial. Obituaries noted either its harsh treatment of women or its abuse of the bourgeoisie.

Soon after *Madeleine Férat* appeared, Jules and Edmond de Goncourt first met Zola, and the figure they evoke in their journal leaps straight out of the novel. Powerful yet frail, burly but with finely chiseled features and waxen skin, he looked to them a dissipated intellectual "made in the mold of his characters, who, physically and emotionally, combine male and female." Never having seen him at table, where he thrived, or having been entertained *chez lui* by his latest pet, a short-tailed monkey named Rhunka, they describe their "admirer and student" as neurasthenic. "The dominant side, the sickly, ailing, ultranervous side, suggests someone afflicted with heart disease. An elusive being, deep, paradoxical in sum; pained, anxious, troubled, doubt-ridden." Doubt-ridden he certainly was, and inclined, moreover, to make himself an object of pity by dwelling on the financial obligations that bound him to Grub Street. But hand in hand with the childlike supplicant who invited help from prestigious elders went the gladiator fierce in his hunger for a success even greater than theirs. "Now and again recriminations, in which he told us repeatedly that he was only twenty-eight, sounded a note of bitter resolve and violent energy," they observed. Modest enterprises failed to excite him. He saw his future writ large, and on this occasion, with *Madeleine Férat* behind him, spoke about a ten-volume novel entitled *L'Histoire d'une famille.* He could accomplish it by the time he was thirty-four, he assured the skeptical brothers, if some publisher paid him thirty thousand francs over six years, or enough to live comfortably.

Thus did Zola announce a program destined to occupy him much longer than six years and to engender twenty volumes rather than ten. *L'Histoire d'une famille* was already in preparation when he visited the Goncourts. Mindful of Taine's dictum that no great novelist lacks a philosophy or system, he began acquiring one, and labored through recondite material at the Bibliothèque Impériale. Such treatises as *Leçons de physiologie* by Claude Bernard, *Traité des dégénérescences physiques, intellectuelles et morales de l'espèce humaine* by Bénédicte-August Morel, *Physiologie des passions* by Letourneau, and *De l'identité de l'état de rêve et de la folie* by Moreau de Tours figure prominently in the syllabus he assigned himself in 1868. But his chief inspiration came from the enormous work on which he had relied for *Madeleine Férat*, Dr. Prosper Lucas's *Traité philosophique et physiologique de l'hérédité naturelle*. "No need to indicate here all the works on physiology I consulted," he wrote years later. "I need cite only Dr. Lucas's *L'Hérédité naturelle*, where those who wonder about it can find the physiological system that helped me elaborate the genealogical tree of the Rougon-Macquart." Like a schoolboy given some monstrous *pensum*, he filled sixty pages with notes summarizing arguments, cataloguing hereditary permutations, citing examples, drawing social maps, and at last listing novels to be written.

It made no difference to him that savants considered *L'Hérédité naturelle* more fanciful than factual. This hodgepodge suggested a conceptual framework for *L'Histoire d'une famille* and at the same time bestowed scientific legitimacy on the creative enterprise by showing "how in procreation as in creation life obeys the laws of invention and imitation, which in procreation become the laws of innateness and heredity."[3] Science was what would distinguish his saga from Balzac's, he told himself in a brief memorandum entitled "Differences between Balzac and me":

> My work will be less social than scientific. Through 3,000 characters Balzac wants to write the history of manners; he bases this history on religion and royalty. His entire science resides in statements that there are lawyers, idlers, etc., as there are dogs, wolves, etc. In short, his work wants to be the mirror of contemporary society.

L'Histoire d'une famille, he continued, would be more limited in scope:

> I don't want to portray contemporary society but a single family and dramatize the interplay of race and milieu. *If I accept a historical frame, it is only in order to have a milieu that reacts* [emphasis Zola's]; professions being milieux as much as places of residence. It is especially important that I remain a naturalist, a physiologist. Rather than principles (royalty, Catholicism), I shall have laws (heredity, innate-

[3] In Lucas, *innéité*—translated here as "innateness"—signifies that which is the individual's own, apart from what is inherited.

ness). I don't want to be a politician, a philosopher or moralist, to imitate Balzac in telling men how to manage their affairs. It will suffice to be a scientist, to describe what is by searching for what lies underneath. No conclusion, moreover. A simple exposé of the facts of a family showing the inner mechanism that makes it run. I even admit the exception.

My characters need not return in particular novels.

Balzac says that he wants to depict men, women, and things. I, on the other hand, combine men and women while acknowledging natural differences, and I subject both to things.

What he envisaged, then, was a drama unfolding through successive generations, in which every conflict would have innateness warring against heredity, or the self challenging the demon within for possession of characters who, like Madeleine Férat, struggle to escape a native milieu, a tainted past, a script visited on them at birth. Whereas Balzac's personae reappear as live actors, his would carry ghosts. Whereas time in *La Comédie humaine* nurtures the dream of transcendence, in *L'Histoire d'une famille* it would conceal the threat of regression, with physiology operating like an idée fixe impervious to events. And finally, whereas Balzac intrudes upon his own stage, he, Zola, would play the impersonal voyeur.

L'Histoire d'une famille housed Zola's particular lares and penates, but it was also styled for family men who felt threatened from below or from outside. Just as evolutionary theory degraded mankind in general by linking it to bestial origins, so revolutionary doctrine raised the specter of a primitive horde subverting the middle class. One historian notes that this siege mentality gripped the Parisian bourgeoisie, who, "to disavow whatever elements of the primitive or the irrational survived in the civilization of their age," sought to "block from mind the provinces and rural life." While custodians of aesthetic order held proto-Impressionists responsible for corrupting morals, moralists held "provincials" or "foreigners" responsible for transforming a once virtuous capital into an Impressionist canvas. The villain was anyone who blurred social boundary lines, who skewed proportions, who celebrated fugitiveness, who glided through France as an epiphenomenon of the general havoc spread by railroads.

Many conservatives came to regard railroads as the preeminent instrument of an erotic force that would, unless stringent measures were taken, destroy the French family and substitute for France itself a mongrel pornocracy governed by queens all in the image of Manet's *Olympia*. "The railroads, exercising a bizarre influence on the intellectual as well as the economic state of society, pour into Paris every day a mobile but tightly packed mass of bustling provincials whose literary culture is, to say the least, slapdash and vagrant," wrote J. J. Weiss in *Theater and Manners*, referring to the exodus from rural France that saw Paris's population treble between 1830 and 1880. Dumas *fils* arraigned the railroad network in *Francillon*, where one character blames society's ills on "the invasion of women from abroad, the glorification of courtesans, the daily trainload of exotic mores that enter the city on every line, hastening local degenerations," and he reiterated this diagnosis in his preface to *La Dame aux camélias*:

> Railroads were created. The first rapid fortunes made by the first speculators seized upon pleasure, instantaneous love being one of the first needs . . . The new transportation facilities brought to Paris a host of rich young people from the provinces and from abroad. The newly enriched, most of whom had risen from the lowest classes, did not fear to compromise themselves with such and such a girl who had won herself a name at the Bal Mabille or the Château des Fleurs. It was necessary to provide for the sensual appetites of a progressing population, as well as for its physical nourishment.

"Invasion" often recurs in baleful prophecies inspired by women traveling unwed from the depths of society to the heights. "[The whore] has invaded society and knows it," wrote the Goncourts. "Nowadays she dictates manners, she muddies opinion, she nibbles iced chestnuts in the loge next to your wife, she has her own theater (Les Bouffes) and a world of her own—the Stock Exchange. . . . These are abnormal times. With its heart and mind so violently turned upside down . . . society cannot but explode."

If hereditary doubleness was to constitute the inner drama of *L'Histoire d'une famille*, its backdrop would be a world illustrating the confusion between high and low or the destructive survival of the primitive in modern man. "Characteristic of the modern movement is the . . . democratic thrust, the collapse of hierarchical order (whence the familiarity between fathers and sons, the mingling and shoulder-rubbing of different types)," Zola noted. "These are troubled times. It is the trouble of our times I portray. Take note: the greatness of the effort that propels the modern world forward I don't deny. I don't deny that we can come more or less close to freedom, to justice. But my belief tells me that men will always be men, animals good or bad as circumstances dictate." Using images then in fashion, he noted further that his family (whom he gave various hyphenated names before Rougon-Macquart) would end up a victim of speed, "unhinged" by its own frantic movement upward. "It will burn like matter devouring itself, it will exhaust itself in little more than a generation because it will have lived too fast."

No doubt Zola observed the motto he was later to engrave above his desk: *Nulla dies sine linea* ("No day without a sentence"), for at the beginning of 1869 a first volume had already been plotted chapter by chapter and nine more outlined, complete with characters forming a mature genealogical tree. Each novel would investigate some particular milieu, he explained in his proposal to Albert Lacroix, and one such would be the licentious Boulevard:

A novel whose milieu is café society and whose heroine is Louise Duval, daughter of the working-class couple. Offspring of both the Goiraud [Rougon] and the Bergasse [Macquart], one branch hungry for pleasure, the other eaten up by vice and poverty, she is at once a social misfit and a fungus harmful to society. Besides the hereditary effects, there is the fatal influence of the contemporary world. Louise is what is known as a "high-flyer." Picture of the world in which such doxies live. Poignant drama of a woman doomed by her appetite for luxury and facile satisfaction.

We shall see how *Nana* sprang from this seed twelve years later. But so did every other seed eventually bear fruit. *La Curée, La Faute de l'abbé Mouret, Son Excellence Eugène Rougon, L'Assommoir, L'Oeuvre, L'Argent, La Débâcle*—the first published in 1872, the last in 1892—were all conceived together in 1869.

Lacroix plumped for *L'Histoire d'une famille*, which soon became *Les Rougon-Macquart: l'histoire naturelle et sociale d'une famille sous le Second Empire*, and drew up a contract as original as the project itself. Expecting two novels a year, he offered in return five hundred francs a month, with the understanding that this stipend represented an advance against money earned from serialized publication. If income from *feuilletons* did not equal his investment, the difference would be obtained from book sales. Only after Lacroix had collected three thousand francs for each novel would the author collect royalties, and royalties meant eight sous, or somewhat less than half a franc, per copy sold.

As usual with Zola, necessity mothered invention. His causeries had been suspended after February 18, 1869, when *La Tribune* gave every line of type over to electoral issues, producing consternation in the Zola household. The causeries resumed on July 18 and Zola continued writing them throughout the year, but this weekly assignment, which someone else might have considered occupation enough, did not impede the progress of *Les Rougon-Macquart*. By September 1870 a first volume, entitled *La Fortune des Rougon*, had been sold to *Le Siècle*, where for months it waited its turn behind other *feuilletons*. The following spring, Zola, even before he finished *La Fortune*, set to work on the sketch of a second volume.

What leisure he had was enjoyed with friends on the rue de la Condamine or at the Café Guerbois, with family at Bennecourt, and with all comers at Manet's studio. Gingerly, however, he came to venture further afield and to reconnoiter circles dominated in person or in absentia by important literary figures.

There were people clustered around the playwright Paul Meurice, for example, the high priest of Hugo worship (he had once edited Hugo's *L'Evénement*). Looking distinctly ecclesiastical, Meurice held services every Monday evening, and in November 1868, after Zola had praised his work in *La Tribune*, he had sent the benevolent critic an invitation. "I would like to make your acquaintance. Now and again our mutual friend, Manet, spends Monday evenings with us; it would be nice if you accompanied him one day." Zola had attended more than one such soirée when word got out that Meurice and company were launching a newspaper with proceeds from Victor Hugo's latest novel, *L'Homme qui rit*. It was during the hiatus in Zola's employment at *La Tribune* and he lost no time jumping aboard. "I've heard much talk about *Le Rappel* recently and am told that you need chroniclers," he wrote Meurice. "If you haven't yet filled your quota, please keep me in mind. I'm behind you all the way. Perhaps you will want to consider at some point a novel in the series I discussed with you. I know that right now you have masterpieces on your plate." *Le Rappel* carried seven articles by Zola between May 1869 and May 1870, which is to say that Meurice welcomed him, but tentatively. While Zola's polemical verve commanded respect, his somber estimate of human nature vexed liberals who took their cues, literary and otherwise, from Victor Hugo. At *Le Rappel* as at *La Tribune*, *Thérèse Raquin* won no applause, and in due course relations became unpleasant. An encomium to Balzac on the occasion of Michel Lévy's publishing *La Comédie humaine* turned out to be his valedictory.

Altogether different were relations with Jules and Edmond de Goncourt, who, in one of the stranger literary partnerships of the nineteenth century, produced books that combined a mannered refinement of style and a passion for documentary rectitude. While writing at length about Fragonard and Watteau (in *L'Art au dix-huitième siècle*), they studied Paris's lower depths and declared in the preface to their novel *Germinie Lacerteux* that an age of universal suffrage could hardly continue to keep common people under a "literary interdict," or deem their obscure miseries unworthy of high fiction. Although it created nothing like the furor of *Madame Bovary*, this novel about the double life of a seemingly chaste maidservant figured importantly in the development of literary realism during the 1860s.

Zola had wooed the brothers before he met them and afterward proved even more assiduous in devising opportunities to promote their work.[4] "I have a request to make of you," he wrote on January 9, 1869. "Since January I have been contributing bibliographical articles to Le Gaulois and specialize in forthcoming books.[5] I should like to whisper something about your Madame Gervaisais, on condition that this indiscretion profit you . . . What must I reveal? In what way would you have me be indiscreet?" Gratitude was not the strong suit of such misanthropic peacocks as the Goncourts (least of all during this period, when syphilis had already gone some way toward undermining Jules in body and mind), but Zola's courtship, which they regarded as some small compensation for the neglect lavished upon them by a vulgar world, earned him invitations to the villa they had recently purchased near the Bois de Boulogne, in Auteuil.

It also earned him an introduction to Gustave Flaubert, whom he found disappointing at first. "I arrived with a preconceived Flaubert, a Flaubert whose works had made him the pioneer of our century, the painter and philosopher of our modern world," he remembered after Flaubert's death.

> I imagined him beating a new path, founding a regular state in the province conquered by romanticism, striding energetically and confidently toward the future. What I found instead . . . was a great strapping devil, a paradoxical spirit, an impenitent romantic who knocked me silly for hours with a barrage of stupefying theories. I'd go home sick, fagged out, dazed, telling myself that the man was not equal to the writer. I've since changed my mind, I've savored a temperament full of contradictions . . . and would not see my Flaubert altered a jot. But the first impression was nonetheless rude.

Zola met these writers of another generation just as their lives had started unraveling. They and their literary kinfolk were no longer numerous enough to surround a table at the restaurant Magny, where in 1862 Sainte-Beuve had assembled them for what became a ritual dinner. Sainte-Beuve died in 1869. In 1869 death also claimed Flaubert's lifelong friend, Louis Bouilhet. Then, on June 20, 1870, Edmond de Goncourt lost Jules after watching him rave through the tertiary stage of syphilis. Zola stumbled upon a wake and found himself clasped to the bosom of mourners shaken by intimations of their own mortality.

[4] Of their inseparability Jules wrote in 1866: "We are now like women who live together and whose states of health become confused with each other, who menstruate at the same time; we get migraine headaches on the same day."
[5] Zola contributed to this mildly liberal paper until October 1869, when the editor asked him to take no notice of "irreligious" books.

When fear subsided there would be time enough for Oedipal conflict. But in 1869–70, before they really knew one another, bereavement fostered closeness between arriviste and arrivés.

There were those in whose opinion Zola had already arrived. A steward to great men, he himself figured as a great man to certain compatriots and particularly to his newest friend, Paul Alexis. Seven years younger, Alexis first heard about Zola from Antony Valabrègue, his chum in the same schoolyard where Zola had once consorted with Cézanne. The exploits of this alumnus loomed large at the Collège Bourbon, and when *Les Contes à Ninon* appeared Alexis read it under cover, like a cult book. Bowing to parental pressure, he grudgingly studied law. He even finished law school, but a sense of literary vocation had meanwhile affirmed itself. Influenced by Marius Roux (who published some of his verse in *Le Figaro*, misrepresenting it as Baudelaire's) and at one remove by Zola, Alexis felt increasingly *dépaysé.* "The melancholy of [Aix's] promenades on Sunday brought tears to my eyes. Indifferent to stately old town houses blackened with age, to the hush of streets where grass sprouted between paving stones, I'd sometimes daydream, like Madame Bovary, before this word PARIS printed on the label of pomade jars." He concluded that poverty in the capital would suit him better than prosperity in the subprefecture, and after bootless appeals to his father, a rich notary, fled Aix with two hundred francs borrowed from Valabrègue. Valabrègue, who set Alexis up on the rue Cardinal-Lemoine in the Latin Quarter, lost no time shepherding him across Paris for an introduction to Zola, every detail of which remained graven in his mind. "Around September 15, 1869, at 8 p.m., I and my hometown friend, the poet Antony Valabrègue, boarded the top deck of an 'Odéon-Batignolles-Clichy' omnibus," he wrote.

> Having arrived in Paris several days earlier to "do" literature, but still quite young and with some verse in the style of Baudelaire as my only baggage, I was about to meet that Emile Zola whom I had never seen but whom I had heard much talk about since my fourteenth year. . . . We clambered down on reaching avenue de Clichy. A few steps beyond "the Fork" and we stood before 14, rue de la Condamine. My heart began pounding. The first words out of Zola's mouth were: "Ah! there you are, Alexis! I was expecting you." I felt that our initial handshake sealed a pact, that I had just yielded all my affection and could count on the staunch friendship of a kind of older brother.

Time proved him right. He would thenceforth serve Zola unwaveringly and be served in return.

One of the first services this "older brother" asked him to perform

did him honor, for on May 31, 1870, along with Paul Cézanne, Marius
Roux, and Philippe Solari, Alexis bore witness to Zola's marriage in
the town hall of Les Batignolles. Why Zola made an official commitment just then is not known, but some reasons seem obvious. After
five years of cohabitation, Alexandrine must have thought it high time
that she enjoy as much respectability as the dowager queen of the
ménage.[6] Her lover had turned thirty on April 2 and stood to earn a
predictable income from novel writing. No doubt Zola wanted to get
his house put in order for the immense enterprise he was undertaking.

Marriage may also have offered them security against the grim prospect of war. Since September 1868, when Queen Isabella of Spain fell
from power, relations between France and Prussia had seriously deteriorated as both sought to have a friendly candidate chosen for the
Spanish throne. Bismarck backed Leopold von Hohenzollern, though
he knew that Louis Napoleon would not countenance a Hapsburg on
his Pyrenean flank. No less dogged was France's parliament, where
talk of French honor rose above disclosures of imperial skulduggery.
To Louis Napoleon's tacit chagrin, each side wanted a casus belli and,
with patriotic rhetoric fanning indignation throughout the land, republicans stood alone in denouncing this savage conspiracy. Zola made
his voice heard as one such republican. Two years earlier he could not
have imagined himself Louis Ulbach's bedfellow, but bedfellows they
became when Ulbach founded *La Cloche* in December 1869; given
free rein, Zola took up where he had left off at the now defunct *Tribune*. Twenty-two articles spaced over seven months were so many
philippics against the Napoleonic regime, and its bloodthirstiness inspired the most eloquent of them. A law muzzling the press for reasons
of national security did nothing to quiet Zola. "Remember, France has
sown the world with far-flung cemeteries," he wrote on July 25, six
days after the outbreak of war.

> From China to Mexico, from the snows of Russia to the sands of
> Egypt, there isn't an acre under the sun that doesn't cradle some
> slaughtered Frenchman. Silent and forsaken cemeteries that slumber
> in the lush peace of the countryside. Most of them, nearly all, lie
> outside some desolate hamlet whose crumbling walls hold memories
> of terror. Waterloo was but a farm, Magenta had scarcely fifty houses.
> A tornado swept through these wee settlements, and their syllables,
> innocent the day before, acquired an odor of blood and powder such
> that humanity will forever shiver when pronouncing them.

[6]In a book on Zola's early career, Colette Becker points out that the Civil Code
then in effect required a son to obtain parental consent to marry until the age of
thirty. Her surmise is that Zola married Alexandrine two months after his thirtieth
birthday because Emilie Zola's consent had not previously been forthcoming.

Another article, in which he suggested that Napoleon III was France's true enemy, moved authorities to charge him with "inciting hatred and scorn of the government and provoking disobedience of the laws." National calamity invalidated the writ: just before his court appearance, Prussia won decisive victories on the Rhine. One month later there would be no empire to answer to.

As a widow's only son, and nearsighted into the bargain, Zola was doubly exempt from military service. But supporting his kin became problematical in a city under martial law. *Le Siècle* had already suspended publication of *La Fortune des Rougon* when on August 18 Ulbach shut down *La Cloche* for the interim. "With this frightful war, my pen falls from my hand. I'm like a soul in Purgatory. I roam the street," Zola lamented to Edmond de Goncourt. "An excursion to Auteuil would cheer up this poor devil of an unemployed novelist." On September 4, two days after Louis Napoleon passed into German captivity at Sedan, where he had watched General von Moltke's cannon pulverize General MacMahon's mousetrapped army, republican deputies formed a Government of National Defense. The Empire thus fell, and Zola decided to leave Paris, into which provisions for a siege were flowing, along with thousands of refugees terrified of the German onslaught. "If I left Paris I promised to let you know about it," he wrote Goncourt on September 7. "My wife is so frightened that I must take her away. I'll accompany her but if possible shall return in a few days to man my post. What an appalling business, this war!" If the bravado of his fellow journalists did not inspire him to join the Franc-tireurs-de-la-Presse (such private volunteer militia sprang up all over Paris), he felt required at least to make some excuse, it seems.

Two days after Victor Hugo's triumphant return from exile, Zola headed south with Emilie, Alexandrine, and dog Bertrand. He did not return until March 14, 1871.

IX

WARTIME IMPROVISATIONS

THE ZOLAS recovered themselves in L'Estaque, a village twenty miles from Marseille that lay half hidden between the Mediterranean and the deep pine-clad gorges of Provence's coastal mountain range. Already settled there was Paul Cézanne, who had flown south as soon as war broke out. In a small house rented for him by his mother they found him nesting amidst his usual paraphernalia, but not alone.

Little is known about Hortense Fiquet and the circumstances under which she became Cézanne's mistress. Born in the Jura on April 22, 1850, she had been raised in Paris, where her widowed father earned his livelihood as a bank clerk. Obliged early along to support herself, she stitched handmade books and occasionally posed for artists, which is, no doubt, how Cézanne met this strapping brunette with big, hooded eyes. "She seems to have been lively and quick-spirited, a volatile chatterbox interested superficially in people and things but with . . . no hint of intellect," writes one Cézanne biographer, Jack Lindsay, who surmises that "by some desperate act of submission" Paul allowed her to seduce him. "It says much for the easy warmth of Hortense, at least in those years of her youth, that she could get through his prickly defenses." It also says much for her masochism that the frightful humiliation those defenses caused her did not make her flee. In Hortense, tenacity was indistinguishable from inertia. Neither passionate enough to demand Cézanne's ardor nor venal enough to calculate his prospects nor inquisitive enough to ponder his conundrum, she drifted after him aimlessly, more his indentured servant than his companion. At L'Estaque began a life of semi-conjugal vagabondage.

Whatever positive changes it wrought, domestic life exacerbated the quarrel that had torn Cézanne apart since childhood. Though he vaunted his masculinity in paintings like *L'Enlèvement* and *Le Meurtre*, where brutes subjugate nude women, he could not overcome his fear of woman incarnate. The "ballsy style," as he called it, served to protect a guilt-stricken man for whom sex was a form of criminal conversation fraught with danger. Thus, sixteen years would pass before Hortense became Madame Cézanne. Unable either to tie himself down or to cut himself loose, Paul kept his mistress in purdah while surviving on doles from his father, under whose paternal roof he regularly sought refuge. "She became a burden in social and economic terms, but she seems not to have asserted her claims . . . in ways that would paralyze [him] with his fear of *grappins*," Lindsay observes.[1] By fits and starts did this sad liaison endure, and we may note that history came full round when in 1886 Cézanne's mother and sister prevailed on him to marry Hortense, for a witness at the ceremony was his fourteen-year-old child, also named Paul. Bastard father ended up legitimizing bastard son.

After a week or so the Zolas left L'Estaque, Alexandrine having meanwhile made it clear how much she was irritated by Hortense, whom she nicknamed *la Boule* ("the Ball"). Marseille was their next destination, and there, with no foreseeable income, they rented a fourth-floor apartment on the rue Haxo near the city's main thoroughfare, the Canebière.

When Napoleon III fell after the defeat at the battle of Sedan, his imperial regime shattered even more clamorously down south than in Paris. Heedless of the Government of National Defense, which postponed debate over France's political future lest factionalism undermine the war effort, Marseillais radicals ran riot, looting the arsenal to equip squads of worker-police and organizing committees to disinfect the army, the municipal administration, and the judiciary. This movement spread inland, and before long revolutionary communes throughout southeastern France banded together in a "Ligue du Midi," whose program called for taxes on the rich, freedom of the press, confiscation of the property of "traitors," separation of church and state, and the abolition of religious schools. "The Committee of Public Safety [which had enforced the Terror in 1792–94] is now the Ligue du Midi," declared one member. Such was the power it acquired that government functionaries dared not thwart its decision to expel Jesuits from Marseille and to silence a royalist newspaper. Indeed, one functionary, Alphonse Esquiros, helped found the Ligue, while another, Delpech, became prefect on September 24 and made himself its zealous instru-

---

[1] *Grappins*, meaning "hooks," was one of Cézanne's favorite expressions.

ment. At length Léon Gambetta, minister of the interior and of war, took matters in hand, sending as his plenipotentiary Alphonse Gent, who reached Marseille on November 2. Insurgents welcomed him with bayonets at the ready.

As a seasoned Parisian journalist, Zola might have induced some regional paper to let him write chronicles or causeries. He knew extremely well both Emile Barlatier of *Le Sémaphore de Marseille* and Lucien Arnaud of *Le Messager de Provence*. But it seems that Marseille galvanized the entrepreneur in him. National catastrophe was good business for those who reported it, and the idea of profiting from this trade captured his imagination. "What if we put out a small paper in Marseille during our enforced sojourn?" he asked Marius Roux, who had returned to Aix. "It would occupy our time *usefully*. Without you I can't risk it. With you, I believe it's feasible. We have supporters and fair conditions. Send me an immediate reply. If my proposition interests you, come visit me tomorrow." Roux leaped at the chance, whereupon Zola appointed Paul Alexis his Paris correspondent. "Roux and I are starting a little newspaper here in Marseille," he announced.

> What we'd like is this: *every day*, without worrying whether or not your letters get through, send us ten or twenty lines about important events, a simple résumé. The important thing is that we know what's happening daily. The letters may or may not arrive, that's our problem. Don't stamp them, to avoid the expense. The paper will succeed, and we'll settle accounts later. Agreed? We count on you absolutely.

He never heard from Alexis, for by then Paris, which Moltke and the German army had sealed tight in their victorious rush westward, needed birds and balloons to communicate with the outside world. "We have received news through a carrier pigeon that one of the postal balloons had reached Tours," wrote Labouchère of the London *Daily News* on September 26 (Tours was the government's extramural seat on the Loire, where Gambetta, who had been flown out of Paris to organize the war effort at the head of a "provincial delegation," held sway over unoccupied France). "We are told that balloons are to leave every evening." Balloonists under fire often jettisoned mail in order to gain altitude, and if Alexis had sent reports, as likely as not they would have landed unread on some fallow field. Zola did not yet know this in late September, when he launched *La Marseillaise*.

Though the name he chose obviously evoked a town and a hymn, it also put readers in mind of another paper, a Parisian *Marseillaise* whose chief editor, Henri Rochefort, had pilloried Napoleon III with abandon. On January 10, 1870, Prince Pierre Bonaparte shot dead one of Rochefort's young reporters, Victor Noir, by way of avenging the imperial family. More than 100,000 people had massed at the funeral service for Noir held in Neuilly, and Napoleon, fearful that the huge throng might invade Paris, led troops up the Champs-Elysées. Ultimately Pierre Bonaparte went free, but not so Henri Rochefort. The government jailed him for writing, among other diatribes: "I soft-headedly thought that a Bonaparte could be something other than an assassin. . . . After eighteen years of servitude to these bloody cut-throats, who, not content with slaughtering republicans on the street, ambush them at home, fellow Frenchmen, are you not fed up?" Workers smashed streetlamps all around Paris's east end, angry mobs swarmed through Marseille at night, and twelve more editors of *La Marseillaise* followed Rochefort to prison. The otherwise short-lived paper had fathered in Victor Noir a durable republican martyr.

Of Zola's *Marseillaise* one can say little more than that its name announced its radical agenda, as no copies survive. What promise it gave during its first weeks may be inferred from the contract Zola drew up ceding ownership to Gustave Naquet, who in 1869 had founded another left-wing journal, *Le Peuple*. In it a tough-minded businessman combines with a political opportunist:

> As of November 1, 1870, we cede to you ownership of *La Marseillaise*, a daily paper selling for 5 centimes, which has a circulation of about 10,000. All expenses are your responsibility. You will pay us each 300 francs a month so long as the circulation exceeds 6,000, but does not exceed 12,000. It is understood that we retain absolute control over the paper's fabrication. . . . M. Gustave Naquet reserves only the right to prevent us from publishing articles he considers dangerous, except where the forthcoming elections to the Constituent Assembly . . . are concerned.

Zola declared his intention to back the Republican Committee's list, with the proviso that "we shall feel free to substitute for candidates from Aix names of our own choosing. In that event, be it understood that we shall campaign against the candidate we've eliminated."

But gloom very quickly settled over the enterprise. Workers insisted on higher wages and created such havoc when management rebuffed them that there was some thought of having *Le Marseillaise* printed in Arles. After November its daily appearance became altogether problematical. Zola and Roux struggled to keep the paper alive, but with little encouragement from Naquet—who may have viewed it as a millstone around his neck or a rival *Le Peuple* could ill afford. The last issue appeared on December 16. Zola heard about its demise in Bordeaux, where, wasting no time on lost causes, he had, unknown to Naquet, gone in search of employment. "[Our printer] sorely regrets what happened," Roux informed him. "He had already designed new posters. He values us but, as I've told you, the workers made life impossible. . . . Sometimes none showed up for work, sometimes half the crew." The irony of a radical organ being sabotaged by its own proletariat did not escape them. Disorder, fumed Roux, was rampant throughout Marseille.

This fiasco led Zola to renounce journalism for the moment and try his luck in the Donnybrook Fair of French politics. Hankering after some administrative job, he petitioned Alexandre Glais-Bizoin, a founder of *La Tribune* who was now minister without portfolio under Gambetta:

> May I invoke my long collaboration at *La Tribune* to recommend myself to you? Under your orders I fought against the Empire; now I should like to place my energy and intelligence at the service of the Republic. Summoned to Aix by friends who would have had me run for the Constituent Assembly, I find myself at loose ends in the Midi and am ashamed of it. . . . Does the Republic have some post for me—a prefecture or subprefecture? I should not like to leave the Midi, where I am very well known and where my father rendered great public service. . . . Be so good, dear sir, as to recommend me to M. Gambetta, and kindly tell me whether an appointment depends on my visiting Tours.

Since *La Marseillaise* might have betrayed his erstwhile sympathy for the separatist movement organized by Alphonse Esquiros, he made it disappear. But his sleight of hand also revealed a dream that had meanwhile grown upon him irresistibly. If thirty-two-year-old Gambetta could rule free France as minister of the interior and of war, why shouldn't he, Zola, just two years younger, hope to govern Aix-en-Provence as subprefect? Recent developments there fortified this ambition. On September 4, at 10 p.m., when word of Napoleon's fall had reached Aix via telegraph, republicans had occupied the town hall, dismissed the mayor, and hurled a cast-iron bust of the emperor out the window. Overnight they elected a new municipal council whose roster included Jean-Baptistin Baille and Antony Valabrègue. "I observe the revolution march past," wrote Roux, tongue in cheek. "In the heap are to be found our admirable chums Baille and Valabrègue. Their exuberance amuses me no end. Can you fancy these two *francs-fileurs* from Paris sitting on the municipal council and urging military resistance? . . . They're really clownish."[2] The two worked hard for all that. While Valabrègue helped recruit National Guards, Baille, a young

---

[2]*Franc-fileur* is a play on the expression *franc-tireur*, meaning sniper. By substituting *fileur* for *tireur*, Roux made the "shooters" into "dodgers."

man with brilliant scientific credentials who until September had been assistant astronomer at the Paris Observatory, helped supervise public works. Baille may also have played some part in getting Paul Cézanne elected to a committee responsible for Aix's School of Design. If so, his campaign earned him no gratitude from the draft dodger. Given public recognition when all he wanted was complete anonymity, Cézanne seldom ventured beyond L'Estaque.

Zola also importuned Auguste Cabrol, private secretary to Marseille's prefect, Alphonse Gent, who encouraged him even as he made it clear that Aix was not his for the giving. Administrative plums, he explained, grew on ministerial trees and generally fell to those nearest the seat of power. But where did one find this seat? Early in December, Germany crushed French troops at Orléans, some seventy miles upstream from Tours. Realizing that his perch had become untenable, Gambetta decided to relocate the Government of National Defense, or the provincial delegation which he led. An exodus southward to Bordeaux began forthwith, ministry by ministry; close behind trooped office seekers, among them Zola, who left his family on December 11, boarded a train for the Gironde, and arrived twenty-four hours later in cold, wet weather.

Without a minute to lose or a franc to squander, he hurled himself at officialdom. "I immediately contacted M. Leuven, Crémieux's private secretary,"[3] he told Alexandrine and Emilie, who would receive progress reports every day, until they joined him on December 26. "As I feared, Cabrol has not yet written to him on my behalf. Moreover, there is absolutely nothing available in the judiciary, and replacing Martin [subprefect of Aix] will be very difficult. Leuven did, however, come through by sending me to Masure, editor-in-chief of L'Echo du Nord, where I published several pieces long ago." Now personnel director for the interior ministry, Gustave Masure shuffled prefectures and subprefectures, but dealt Zola a paltry hand:

He offered me Quimperlé in Brittany, which I refused: it's too far away and too grim. . . . He then proposed Lesparre, a little town several leagues from Bordeaux. Once again I refused, with the understanding that I may accept it later if I can't find better: the trip involved for you frightens me, and we don't have the money. Aix would be preferable. . . . Masure stands behind me foursquare; if it didn't hinge on Gent, he'd dismiss Martin today. At worst I'll leave Bordeaux with a letter for Gent, to whom he is closely tied.

[3]Born in 1796, Adolphe Crémieux was a Jewish lawyer who had been a member of the provisional government in 1848. As minister of justice in the Government of National Defense, and a Jew, he conferred French citizenship on Algerian Jews.

It soon became apparent that he was the shuttlecock in a game of battledore played by amicable functionaries who each wanted the other to sack an incumbent neither particularly liked. Fantasies of conquest then excited presentiments of doom, and after three days everything looked bleak. Would Aix, which had ruined his father, ruin him as well? "Your letters gave me great pleasure," he assured mother and wife. "You are in good health and await me. Well, you won't have long to wait, for I am in the throes of depression. . . . I am absolutely lost here. This Aix business will leave me destitute." Not that Zola didn't recognize for what it was the panic that often struck him when some obstacle intervened between a design and its execution. He also recognized that nothing could be accomplished overnight with the mail service unreliable, the government peripatetic, and people caught in tangled lines of authority. "I see I can't win a victory in several hours. The moment is too critical. Everyone's scared. . . . It would have been nice, I know, to be named emperor straightway; as it is, I might not get the job of game warden if I sought it." But for the most part reality fought at unequal odds against an impulse to blame himself or to hate those who denied him his due. Anger welled up in him along with the memory, no doubt, of his futile search for employment during adolescence. "I sometimes feel gusts of pride and tell myself that I am superior to all those people," he wrote. "What a sorry trade I ply, begging alms from the Republic! Just wait until they're all swept away; I'll still be around."

Taine in *Journeys Through France* called Bordeaux a "second Paris, gay and magnificent, with its wide streets, promenades, monuments, large mansions," but Zola took a more dismal view of the city as he spent his time quizzing fellow refugees under the arcade of the Grand-Théâtre or watching rain stream down the skylight of his tiny hotel room. "It rains continually," he complained. "I rise at eight and eat a small loaf. Then I run errands and loiter under the theater arcade until noon. At noon I lunch at the Chapon Fin, then sleep and read until dinnertime. At nine I retire. Not what you'd call a wildly gay existence." One brief boat trip up the Gironde was all the sightseeing he permitted himself. But if he didn't tour, neither did he write. Energy that would otherwise have generated prose found expression in a minute-by-minute review of dire alternatives or in an obsessive concern with money and food.

[Bordeaux] repels me, though of course . . . it doesn't show to its best advantage in this season. I've missed Marseille, which is saying something. I went to the Central Market to see what people eat hereabouts. Nothing extraordinary. The only novelty for me were little shellfish which don't look appetizing. On the other hand, this morning I had some first-rate oysters. They cost one franc twenty centimes the dozen. That's expensive, and I won't order any more unless I receive good news. Ten francs per day is a minimal budget. At that rate I'll survive one week.

Just as he punished his stomach for misfortune, so he rewarded it for minor victories. "Roux's telegram made me very happy and I treated myself to a dozen oysters," he wrote three days later on December 16, after learning that Cabrol had reconfirmed Gent's animus against Martin, whom he hoped to replace. "Furthermore, I'm saving money. I've given up coffee. After meals I walk up to my room, smoke a cigar, and concoct a grog from the remaining sugar and rum." These gastronomic bulletins were of vital interest to Alexandrine, who under normal circumstances fed Zola rather too well. "Enclosed are fifty francs, which will let you eat properly," she instructed him. "Do you hear me? If you have cold meals in such humid weather you'll get sick, and meals must be one of the distractions of your day, distractions being few, I gather."

Their correspondence reveals a tensely self-centered household in which Mother Zola hovered over Alexandrine and Emile, nursing the former with her neurasthenic illnesses and giving the latter matrimonial cues or political advice.[4] Among themselves Emile answered to "Mimi," Alexandrine to "Coco," Emilie to "Madame Canard." All three doted on the dog, Bertrand, as on a substitute child. But the affection that held them together seldom took wing. Zola's marriage was indeed almost fanatically earthbound, and never more so than during this difficult separation, when reckoning budgets became a kind of folie à deux. "I must tell you that you're not very good at arithmetic," chided Alexandrine. "You say three hundred francs but I can't make heads or tails of your account; here's mine and try if you can to let it sink in. On December 19, for the fortnight ending December 12, I paid Augustine [their maid] thirty francs plus thirty-two francs for supplies. That's sixty-two francs. I'm one week in arrears, I dismiss her the 22nd, which makes two days after the 19th to add to the week, or ten days in all at two francs per day, which makes twenty francs, as much for wood or a minimum of fifteen francs plus a dozen francs for supplies over those ten days, not including chamber pot and broken dishes. You see, your sum of sixty francs swells to ninety-seven. I sent

[4] "If M. Thiers is in Bordeaux, go see him," she urged. "It may be that he can't do anything just now but you don't know what lies ahead and . . . should the Orleanists return to power, which seems probable, he will remember your visit in the present circumstances. So don't hesitate. Present yourself as the son of Zola the engineer. . . . Recall for him all the sympathetic attention he accorded your father." Adolphe Thiers would indeed become chief executive of the provisional government in 1871.

you seventy-five francs, I kept twenty-five, which are now spent. Tomorrow I'll have to borrow twenty francs from Roux so we can manage until our departure." The imperiousness with which she marshaled numbers also showed in her scathing judgment of people who gave offense, especially Cézanne and Hortense. "Three days ago, Marie [Roux's mistress] saw the Ball walk by her apartment building and we've since learned through women from L'Estaque that Paul no longer resides there; it occurred to us that they may be hiding in Marseille," she informed Zola. "Naïs inquired after them, pretending to have an urgent message. As for us, we haven't yet seen them. Two fine-feathered specimens. Really thoughtful! Go ahead and worry yourself sick over those people. They're yet another pair who shouldn't exist for us." Zola humored Alexandrine, but ultimately these abrasive reflections frayed his bond with Paul.

It was December 17 before word from Marseille compelled Zola to give up all hope of obtaining the Aix subprefecture. He would have left Bordeaux right away had an interview with Glais-Bizoin not steeled his resolve. "He told me that he had received my letter, then led me to the telegraph office and train station. He runs like a hare. When we parted I said: 'I'm counting on you.' And he answered: 'Absolutely. I want you on board. This situation can't continue. I'll take charge of things.' " Old enough to have voted against the return of Napoleon's corpse from Saint Helena in 1840, this ebullient little man, whose political career spanned four regimes, had been nipping at authority since 1830 without ever quite inflicting serious damage, and his droll figure made him an easy mark for the caricaturist. "He has a bird's head and a birdlike vivacity," wrote one observer. "If not for his long tenure on the extreme Left, one might conclude that he can't sit still. He is small, thin, dark-skinned, bony, with eyes that glow like live coals under beetling brows. All quicksilver, he accurately records barometric pressure from the opposition." Dormant during the first twelve years of Napoleon III's reign, Glais-Bizoin had become active again in 1863, when his Flemish constituency elected him to the legislature at the age of sixty-four. As a minister under Gambetta he performed honorific functions, it being rumored that senility made him incapable of exercising good political judgment.

This rumor worried Zola. Afraid that the old trooper's mind might wander, never to be found again, he kept after him and in due course was rewarded for his persistence. "I have good news, but since the arrangement is not yet definitive, I hardly dare tell you about it," he announced on December 20.

> This morning . . . I stood for one full hour, in driving rain, at the door of his residence. He finally emerged with some big rascal of a Spaniard who claims he has a secret strategy for beating the Prus-

sians. I let them walk several steps, then accosted Glais-Bizoin as if by chance. He led me to a café and wanted to order me hot chocolate; since I know he's a tightwad, I refused, which must have pleased him. At length the Spaniard departed and I could talk. I said to him: "If you have offices, I'd ask for a little corner of them." He responded: "I have only one secretary, but he's in Vannes. Do you want his job?" At first I accepted without much enthusiasm. . . . It wasn't until this afternoon that I came to perceive all the advantages of such a position. Very little to do, no fixed hours (so he told me), and as boss a poor old man who is very decent.

As Glais-Bizoin's offer meant, of course, that he would remain in Bordeaux until the political situation clarified itself, Zola brought his two women from Marseille and arranged their trip with the obsessiveness of a logistics officer moving reinforcements from one front to another. Emilie and Alexandrine were issued quasi-military orders. "You will leave on the 10:10 p.m. convoy, which doesn't change at Tarascon," his instructions began. "You will arrive at Cette around about 4 a.m. There you catch the Bordeaux express. The day of your departure be sure to send . . . a telegram phrased as follows: 'This evening troops leave Midi; destination unknown.' Or something of the sort." While gathering information about schedule, fares, dog accommodations, and every possible contingency, he was obliged, in weather so frigid that ice halted river traffic, to search the overcrowded city for a proper flat. "I'm at the end of my tether," he wrote on Christmas Day. "The cold here is worse than anything I've ever experienced in Paris and I wander through the street like a tormented soul. As long as I had to fight I could endure our separation, but now that the fight is over you can't imagine how impatient I've grown." By December 27 they were together again, exhausted but grateful. Zola had had Alexandrine bruit his new title among acquaintances in Marseille lest anyone there remember him as a failed publisher or a common refugee. Among other satisfactions the new title offered was a letter from an ex-tutor at the Collège Bourbon, who, having subsequently studied law, asked Zola to help him secure a judgeship. No sooner did he begin to preen over such *marques d'estime*, however, than the political situation changed dramatically.

On January 17, 1871, the last French army corps patched together under Gambetta's provincial administration was defeated by General von Werder's troops near Belfort, in Alsace. After several weeks of clandestine shuttling between Paris and Versailles, where Bismarck had established German headquarters, Jules Favre, minister of foreign affairs, negotiated an armistice on January 28. Its central provision was that France would form in free elections a government with which

Germany could treat. When word of the armistice reached Bordeaux, Gambetta took umbrage. Instructed to announce elections for February 8, he obeyed, but in a spirit of defiance. "In place of the reactionary and cowardly Assembly of which the enemy dreams," ran one decree placarded on streets throughout Bordeaux, "let us install an Assembly that is truly national and republican, desiring peace, if peace assures our honor . . . but capable of willing war also, ready for anything rather than lend a hand in the murder of France." Except in Alsace-Lorraine and among working-class Parisians, implacable resistance to the Germans, or *la guerre à outrance*, was by then the position of only a small minority. Frenchmen wanted peace, and Gambetta, honoring what he acknowledged to be the general will, resigned his ministries. Up north wagons laden with food entered Paris, which surrendered its perimeter forts.

Zola may not have understood just how fortunate he had been until, during this lull, stories about the German siege of Paris reached him from the capital. After Moltke had encircled Paris on September 19, many writers and artists rallied to its defense by joining the National Guard, a formerly bourgeois militia that now accepted volunteers of every description. Manet was commissioned lieutenant and served in the artillery under the Academy painter Ernest Meissonier, who was famous for his battle scenes. Degas commuted between Montmartre and a gun emplacement in the outer fortifications ten miles away. Paul Alexis did guard duty at the Batignolles town hall. Philippe Solari performed inane drills on various parade grounds when not foraging for scraps to keep alive his young daughter and delicate wife. Trapped by an enemy they couldn't engage, all these men played at war but starved in carnest, along with several million other prisoners whose dreams of rescue became a martyrdom of hunger. "I spent all my time queuing up at the door of butchers, bakers, coal men, marching, standing at the fortifications," Solari recounted to Zola in February 1871. "What an existence! It's unbelievable, the suffering we endured and the things we ate. There was nothing left in Paris but black pudding and stringy horsemeat, expensive and dry, ever so dry. A potato was a miracle. . . . I almost ate a dog's head, which the butcher sold as veal." Once the quarter million sheep grazing in the Bois de Boulogne had been consumed, Parisians dined on rat pie, or if they had Victor Hugo's means, on bear and elephant slaughtered at the zoo.

Those who had not shared the common ordeal often felt stigmatized, morally diminished, or even unmanned, and Zola was the more susceptible to such feelings for having been exempt from military service. "How are you? How did you get through the siege?" he asked Paul Alexis in a letter of February 4. ". . . Now you are a man. The siege and its sufferings have made you a citizen of Paris. You are no

longer Aixois, and when we see each other again, I shall greet you as
a compatriot." We don't know how Alexis read this pompous accolade,
but certainly Zola wanted it understood that he himself had long since
undergone initiation, that his years of "struggle" in mufti equaled several months of resistance in uniform. To drive the point home, he
aggrandized his civilian status. "With Roux I founded, in Marseille, a
newspaper that survived two months. . . . Then, at the beginning of
December, I was summoned to the government delegation as private
secretary to Glais-Bizoin." Answering a call from above sounded impressive indeed. Furthermore, the word "summoned" (*appelé*) had a
military connotation.

As shame made him boastful, so the idea that he had lost face and
purchase in Paris sparked righteous indignation and he fumed when
Manet informed him that some refugees had been billeted in his quarters at 14, rue de la Condamine. "Tell me what shape things are in,"
he urged Alexis on February 17.

> I'll ask you several questions. Has the garden been ruined? Which
> rooms have been offered to the occupants? Is my study one of them?
> Has the furniture remained in place or been moved upstairs (which
> could have been done only through the windows)? If still in place,
> what does it look like? Have they respected the papers in my desk,
> my file case, and my secretary? Are there any broken dishes? Has
> anything been ransacked or stolen?

He went so far as to declare the billeting improper, if not actionable,
given that he was now a government official with "special" status:
"Please tell this to the concierge, to the landlord, to the mayor, to
everyone you see." Memories of squalid little pieds-à-terre one step
removed from the poorhouse still threatened him, no doubt. "What a
mess it must be, my poor study, where I began my *Rougon-Macquart*
in such high spirits." He longed for substance, and this questionnaire
conjures up not only the novelist amassing documentation but also the
collector gorging his future villa at Médan with ponderous antiques as
if to reassure himself, by the sheer weight of them, that he could never
again be taken lightly.

Early in February, Paris invaded Bordeaux, or so it seemed when
journalists, power brokers, actresses, boulevardiers flocked south, some
to observe the newly elected Assembly, which met at the Grand-
Théâtre, others to convalesce. Second Empire highlife resumed after
a morose intermission. "The streets swarmed with officers of every
rank and branch," wrote one witness, "with wheeler-dealers alert to
opportunity . . . with vendors hawking an illustrated newspaper whose
title, *La Victoire*, stung us in those days of defeat. Hotels were taken

by storm, theaters were booked solid every night. Bordeaux's population grew hourly, and almost all the deputies arrived before the inaugural meeting." One deputy who came late was Victor Hugo. Hailed en route from Paris by crowds shouting "Vive Victor Hugo! Vive la République!" Hugo met larger crowds in Bordeaux, where he, Louis Blanc, Pelletan, Gambetta, Clemenceau, *inter alios,* joined battle against rural conservatives eager to buy peace at any price. A minority within parliament, these republican stalwarts found support outside it among Bordelais whose demonstrations became so exuberant that light infantry and horse guards ended up patrolling the streets around the Grand-Théâtre. Horse guards were present in force on February 28, when Adolphe Thiers, elected chief executive ten days earlier with a mandate to negotiate a peace treaty at Versailles, set forth Bismarck's draconian terms. "Noon; a detachment of mounted police takes up position on the Place de la Comédie," noted Zola. "Soon cuirassiers arrive. . . . The crowd understands that the denouement is imminent. All of Bordeaux stands alert." By evening it was common knowledge that Germany wanted Alsace and Lorraine, in addition to five billion francs, a huge indemnity. On March 1, after hearing eloquent protests, the legislature yielded. "Today a tragic session," Hugo wrote in his diary. "First the Empire was executed, then, alas, France herself! They voted the Shylock-Bismarck treaty." Hugo spoke against the outrage, but Emile Kuss, an Alsatian representative who had served as Strasbourg's mayor since September 11, objected even more strenuously. He dropped dead.

Deader than Kuss was the Government of National Defense, and Zola quickly turned this circumstance to his advantage by offering *La Cloche* daily reports on the Assembly. "Would you like me to send you, *every day,* a sketch of the legislature, summarizing debates and providing sidelights?" he asked Louis Ulbach on February 10. "I'm at your disposal. All of France has its attention focused on what happens here. We can arrange the fee however you like." A response came without delay: "Your proposition is irresistible. Send me what you like or what you can, and I'll pay you as best I can."

Zola took his assignment seriously, giving *La Cloche* a vivid account of the issues that set Paris against the provinces, conservatives against republicans, moderate republicans against radical ones. When clashes occurred, he analyzed them. When parliamentary debate flagged, he noted talk of the town. When Thiers's sojourn in Versailles left Bordeaux free to conjecture about peace negotiations, he evoked the atmosphere of a citywide rumor mill. When he had done portraying major figures, he caricatured squireens in quaint headgear and unfashionable *paletots* who seemed to have emerged from a time warp for this one momentous conclave. "How many bald pates aglow under the great chandelier! I was scrutinizing them just now, studying the countenances of worried landowners."

Zola the novelist manifested himself right away in an article dated February 13 that showed his predilection for sinister mise-en-scènes:

> Imagine if you will a mortuary chapel. At 2 p.m., dazzled by sunlight, one falls into an auditorium lit by three chandeliers. Red plush seats below, and above on the stage, whose curtain is raised, a dais with purple bunting set in the midst of drawing-room decor. There's where France will be put to death. One searches dark corners for the hangman. In the loges, many women, a first-night audience. Gloved hands hold lorgnettes.

This image, which warned readers to expect a ritual drama performed by deputies, spectators, and journalists all feigning ignorance of the ineluctable denouement, became Zola's theme. "When I left the auditorium at nightfall the crowd stood in the gloaming, anxious and hungry for more news," he wrote ten days later, after Thiers divulged Bismarck's treaty terms. "I felt I had left a burial vault to mingle with grief-stricken people who had just conducted the funeral of their fatherland. Quiet, except for the number five billion and the names Metz and Strasbourg uttered like sobs. Ah! the sun has set this evening, and Bordeaux has put on mourning clothes."

Such language annoyed Ulbach, who took a moderate position, supporting Adolphe Thiers against deeper-dyed republicans. But on the whole he saw eye to eye with his reporter, and compliments certainly outnumbered cavils. "I can't accept your praise, as my dispatches are not all that I feel they should be," Zola wrote on March 8. "The postal service here disconcerts me. I have time neither to reflect nor to polish. Paris will be an altogether different matter. We'll talk about it." Ulbach had already assured him that he could, if he so desired, remain La Cloche's parliamentary correspondent once the Assembly moved north. With this prospect to buoy him and a second income expected from Le Sémaphore de Marseille, for which he would write some 1,800 articles during the 1870s, Zola left Bordeaux on March 13. At its penultimate meeting in the Grand-Théâtre, the Assembly, led by a conservative majority who feared Paris—where three revolutions had spawned since 1789—voted to reconvene on March 20 in yet another theater, the theater of the Palace of Versailles.

Versailles conveyed a political message that alarmed republicans, but of greater immediate consequence was the Assembly's decision to end two moratoria that had alleviated the suffering of trapped and unemployed Parisians since September 1870, one suspending payment due on promissory notes, the other deferring house rent. It could not have behaved more callously. When, impoverished by siege, Paris most needed a helping hand, rural France showed her a mailed fist, and survivors of Prussian cannon fire now found themselves condemned to bankruptcy, eviction, or both. "Very bravely but not with impunity had the Parisians suffered . . . the privations and emotions of the siege," wrote the Vicomte de Meaux, a prominent royalist. "At first we provincials couldn't reason with them. It seemed as if we did not even speak the same language and that they were prey to a kind of sickness, what we called 'fortress' fever." Like Monsieur de Meaux, who saw patriarchal order threatened by wild-eyed savages, many otherwise humane legislators did not let their humanity hinder them from abolishing the small stipend that fed National Guards or authorizing the State Pawnshop to sell material deposited during the siege. These callous measures, which promised further misery to several hundred thousand inhabitants of an economic wasteland, alienated the capital en masse. Debt-encumbered shopkeepers, idle workers, and artisans with tools in hock made common cause against an enemy all the more vengeful for being French. Indeed, German soldiers camped outside Paris became mere spectators as hatred of the foreigner turned inward.

To be sure, the legislature might not have been quite so stiff-necked had Paris not challenged its authority. After the elections of February 8, republicans in Paris presumed that the Assembly's provincial deputies would restore monarchical government, and their indignation voiced itself through the National Guard, which emerged as a quasi-political organism when on February 24 delegates from some two hundred National Guard battalions ratified statutes of federation. Swearing never to surrender arms or to recognize any commander-in-chief chosen by Thiers, this counter-Assembly held a kind of revival meeting at the Place de la Bastille, where beneath the monument lay workers killed exactly twenty-three years earlier, on February 24, 1848. Orators harangued large crowds and for three days National Guard bands played martial music, lowering their banners as they trooped past a Liberty draped in red cloth. Army regulars joined them, along with several thousand Parisian *mobiles*, who then sought to rally sailors at the naval barracks across town.

The authorities felt helpless in the whirlwind of what soon became a full-scale revolt. Policemen avoided working-class districts, where some been set upon violently. A mob forced the warden of Sainte-Pélagie to free demonstrators interned since January, and another raided the Gobelins police barracks for its stock of chassepot rifles. Pillaging spread throughout the city, which armed itself against invasion. Until Bismarck agreed not to occupy Paris, National Guards kept close watch at artillery parks situated on Montmartre and Belleville, ready to fire away, and rumors of a Prussian entry were announced by drummers beating *rappels*. Drums beat everywhere. But less ominous sounds also rent the air during this monthlong interregnum. Vendors appeared in their thousands as Paris came to resemble a huge kermis, half festive and half bellicose. "At one end of the square in front of City Hall, on the river side, besotted National Guards wearing immortelles in their buttonholes march to a tambour and salute the old monument with the cry of 'Vive la République,'" noted Edmond de Goncourt two days before the Bordeaux Assembly ratified treaty terms. "Along the rue de Rivoli, every imaginable product may be found displayed on the sidewalk, while vehicles transport death and replenishment in the street: hearses cross wagons laden with dried codfish."

Adolphe Thiers rode up from Bordeaux in high dudgeon, and his reappearance was a spark to tinder. Although this eloquent Provençal had fought hard against Napoleon III, working-class Frenchmen hated him for sins older than the Second Empire: he still bore the nickname "Père Transnonain" almost forty years after the "massacre of the rue Transnonain," when as Louis Philippe's interior minister he had ordered General Bugeaud to crush striking Lyonnais silk workers. People had also not forgotten his denunciation of the "vile multitude" in June 1848, when yet another massacre took place, nor his advocacy of an electoral law with residence requirements calculated to disenfranchise some two hundred thousand Parisians. Thiers may have shrunk since then, but the little man who had written volumes about Napoleon I had yielded nothing of his belief in the sacredness of private property. All five feet of him argued a political vision that impeached the nomad, the immigrant, the socialist, the crowd. "We have always desired freedom," he once proclaimed. "Not the freedom of factions but that which shelters affairs of state from the twofold influence of Courts and of Streets."

Far from seeking to assuage the National Guard or the Central Committee it elected midway through March, Thiers resolved to sweep aside this mutinous group with a *coup de main* and subjugate Paris before the Assembly reconvened in Versailles. His chief objective was the gun park atop Montmartre, where 171 cannon made a formidable battery. Early on the morning of March 18, General Paturel cordoned off lower Montmartre between Clichy and Pigalle, as troops led by General Lecomte marched south from Clignancourt. The operation ran smoothly until they seized the guns. It then became clear that since they were without equipment to transport heavy artillery downhill nothing had been accomplished, and time spent in summoning horse teams proved fatal. At dawn Montmartre was still asleep, but two hours later the army found itself marooned in a sea of villagers, among whom women greatly outnumbered men. "By the time a column of National Guards arrived the essential distance between troops and citizens had become gravely compromised," writes one historian.

Two National Guard officers stepped forward to parley with the line. The rest of the Guards and the soldiers who had already joined with them raised the butts of command. Women from the crowd thrust themselves between the two groups, shouting to the troops, "Will you fire on us? On your brothers? Our husbands? Our children?" Four times Lecomte vainly ordered his men to fire. In this expectant silence warrant officer Verdaguer called on his fellow soldiers to ground their arms and the crowd surged forward to embrace the troops, crying "Long live the line." The gendarmes were overrun and disarmed before they could fire, the officers were pulled off their horses and Lecomte himself was seized. By nine in the morning it was all over.

Neither the National Guard nor Montmartre's mayor, Georges Clemenceau, could control the mob, which vented its rage on Lecomte and on a retired general named Clément Thomas, whom curiosity had drawn to the Boulevard de Clichy. "Everyone was shrieking like wild beasts, without realizing what they were doing," Clemenceau recounted. "I observed then that pathological phenomenon which might be called blood lust." The bodies of both generals were found at nightfall riddled with bullets.

For Thiers, reports of troops breaking ranks all over town brought back memories of February 1848. On that occasion he had urged King Louis Philippe to leave Paris and recapture it from without. Louis Philippe had rejected his advice, but now God alone stood above Thiers. No sooner had he beaten a retreat than he issued general evacuation orders, spurning colleagues who felt that the army should entrench itself at the Ecole Militaire or in the Bois de Boulogne. Forty thousand men were thus marched out of Paris, never to serve again. Up from the provinces came fresh recruits "uncontaminated" by the capital, and before long 100,000 men occupied camps around Versailles. The day of reckoning was imminent, Thiers proclaimed on March 20, reassuring not only antirevolutionary Parisians stranded in a hostile environment but Bismarck as well, whose patience with quarrelsome Frenchmen had worn thin. Forty-eight hours later, Versailles took over where Germany had left off several months earlier, after the armistice. It declared Paris under siege once again.

In Paris, forsaken ministries were staffed by tyros who somehow improvised essential services.[5] The National Guard's Central Commit-

---

[5]One Paget-Lucipin, a self-styled Proudhonian and "medical student" in his fifties entered the ministry of education, found no one there, and made himself at home. "I took over the ministry, which nobody else was bothering about".

tee became, perforce, an alternative government, though its avowed program was to organize elections for a municipal council and then dissolve itself. "Obscure a few days ago, we will return to the obscurity of your ranks," it announced on March 20.

> The people of Paris, after having given since September 4 an undeniable and striking proof of their patriotism and devotion to the Republic; after having supported, with a courageous resignation beyond all praise, the suffering and struggles of a long and arduous siege, have again showed themselves to be equal to the present circumstances and unavoidable efforts that the country rightly expects of them. . . . The existing powers are essentially provisional, and will be replaced by an elected Communal Council. . . . We have only one hope, one goal: the safety of the country and the final triumph of the democratic Republic, one and indivisible.

The Central Committee sought approval of its mandate from beleaguered district mayors like Clemenceau in the naive belief that this would square Paris with Versailles, but councilmen elected on March 20 had no such scruples or illusions. Moderate republicans were few, and most resigned straightway, leaving the high ground to militants whose hatred of a government that had, they believed, traded honor for peace exacerbated visions of a new political and social order. "I am voting for the reddest of the reds, but in God's name, if I knew of something more radical than the red flag I would choose that instead," declared one resident of Belleville, a working-class neighborhood. Paris turned very red indeed the day it proclaimed itself a Commune in front of City Hall. Newly elected members all wore red sashes. They stood under a canopy surmounted by a bust of the Republic, draped in red. And overhead flew the red flag which had been hoisted on March 18. Forming up to music first heard during the great Revolution, National Guard battalions played *La Marseillaise* as people sang en masse and cannon fired salvos. It was, wrote Jules Vallès in *Le Cri du peuple*, "a revolutionary and patriotic festival, peaceful and joyous, a day of intoxication and solemnity, of grandeur and merriment, worthy of those witnessed by the men of '92 and one that compensated for twenty years of empire, six months of defeats and betrayals."

Had the Commune taken its own rhetoric seriously, it would have mobilized against the "criminals" organizing "a monarchist plot just beyond the city gates." What it did instead was abolish conscription and speak of martyred innocence when on April 2 two squadrons from Versailles captured a bridgehead at Courbevoie. "The royalist conspirators have *attacked*. Despite our moderate attitude, they have *attacked*. Unable to count on the French army, they have *attacked* with Pontifical Zouaves and the Imperial Police." Innocence cost the Commune far more dearly the next day. In a reckless counterattack it sent forth three columns of National Guards, or "federals," who were led to expect that the army would fraternize with them, as it had two weeks earlier. Accompanied by women and children, they entered the wooded country west of Paris like boisterous picnickers and made an easy target: many were slaughtered right away, others mercilessly hunted down, and several thousand herded through Versailles, where en route civilians beat them with canes and umbrellas. This disaster boosted Thiers's confidence, though not until late May did he enter Paris itself. Meanwhile the Commune reinstituted conscription on April 5 and decreed on April 6 that anyone suspected of complicity with Versailles would be arrested, tried, and if convicted held hostage. It decreed furthermore that three such hostages should die for every prisoner of war or "partisan of the regular government of the Paris Commune" executed by the enemy.

Zola may have seen something of the tumultuous demonstration that rocked Clichy on March 18, but events came much closer when he began to shuttle between Paris and Versailles as *La Cloche*'s legislative correspondent. On March 20 he was detained at the Gare Saint-Lazare by guards who undoubtedly knew that his editor-in-chief, Louis Ulbach, had earned an arrest warrant for denouncing the Central Committee. One day later he fell afoul of a minor official in Versailles, who took him to be an insurgent and had him jailed at the Orangerie until his credentials were verified. "Once again I almost missed the legislative session," he wrote. "This time I reached Versailles, but at the station exit an inspector sniffed danger all over me. The session had already begun when he gave me back my freedom . . . Harassed by the Central Committee yesterday, suspected by the Executive Power today, I'm pinching myself, anxiously probing my soul, and wondering if it wouldn't be wise to pack up. What comforts me is the knowledge that there isn't some third government to arrest me tomorrow."

Zola's "Lettres de Versailles" constitute a tirade against the intransigence of extremists dragging each other down the slippery slope. Those squireens he had mocked in Bordeaux continued to infuriate him. "Between the dissidents of City Hall and the blind bigots of the Assembly, France lies bleeding, cut to the quick," he wrote on March 23. "If one day history tells us how the insurrection pushed her over the edge, it will add that the regular and legitimate power did everything to make her plunge fatal." By then it was clear that a policy of conciliation with the Communards would find few friends right of center. Georges Clemenceau implored Versailles to hold municipal elections under its own auspices and thus blunt the Central Committee, but his plea went unheard. Given a choice between force and pragmatism, the legislature, which viewed any warning as a derogation from its authority, chose inaction. "Meeting follows meeting, and emptiness yawns ever wider," Zola despaired. "The majority will brook no mention of Paris. . . . This is a firm resolve: Paris doesn't exist for them, and its nonexistence sums up their political agenda." At the end of a report that describes the opprobrium heaped on district mayors who for the sake of unity had endorsed elections they couldn't forestall, he made common cause with Clemenceau. "I do not represent my paper, only myself, when I declare, as I do now, that tomorrow I shall vote." Like many republicans, Zola voted *against* civil war rather than *for* the Commune. No doubt he also voted *for* Paris against the venality and obscurantism that he remembered so well from his childhood in Aix-en-Provence.

La Cloche being one of twenty-eight Paris newspapers to declare the elections illegal, Ulbach might have given Zola notice or put him on a shorter leash, if not for Zola's loudly proclaimed faith in Adolphe Thiers's shrewdness and goodwill. Almost everyone knew that Thiers, with permission from Bismarck, was building up the French army. Zola, blinded by hope, at first interpreted this evidence of belligerent intentions as nothing more than a clever ploy. "What will M. Thiers's conduct be [now that the elections are over]?" he asked. "It is said in Versailles that he favors compromise, reasonable agreement. Rumor has it that he will wait until the Commune is legally installed and the government buttressed by a solid army before holding *pourparlers*, not because he intends ever to use force but because he understands how cogent its presence can be." Once he had adopted this view, Zola categorically dismissed every other. "As long as conciliation remains possible, it must be tried. That, furthermore, is M. Thiers's *absolute opinion*." The massacre of National Guards near Chatillon—or the jubilant air with which Thiers announced it—was what it took to make him doubt himself. "Toward the end of the session, M. Thiers gave the Chamber an account of the day's events," he wrote on April 4.

> I confess that this little speech, far from pleasing me, got my goat. Where I heard him express egotistical and bourgeois satisfaction, I would have preferred to hear him say: "Gentlemen, I am greatly aggrieved; today brothers have fought once again, and sorrow attends our victory. I beg you to be tolerant, to insist that this struggle cease right away. Above all, do not triumph, for every citizen who dies becomes an argument in favor of your dissolution."

Zola conceded at last that his picture of Thiers as a crypto-pacifist rattling a saber in order to quiet warmongers and intimidate revolutionaries had been fanciful. After April 6, the worst seemed inevitable. "Heartbroken, I must tell you," he informed readers of *La Cloche*, "conciliation is a pipe dream. In Versailles, Paris seems very far away, and people there imagine our poor metropolis swarming with bandits, all indiscriminately fit to gun down."

Paris needed no instruction from Versailles in the art of gross political caricature, and neutral parties had reason to observe that Communards were spoiling for Armageddon as fervently as right-wing deputies. A movement whose initial goal had been municipal independence soon consecrated the rift between the *ancien régime* and the new order. "The communal revolution . . . inaugurates a new era of scientific, positive, experimental politics," the Commune proclaimed on April 19 in a manifesto fraught with terms used elsewhere by writers like Zola to legitimize "naturalist" fiction.

> It's the end of the old governmental and clerical world, of militarism, of bureaucracy, of exploitation, of speculation, of monopolies, of privileges to which the proletariat owes its servitude and the nation its disasters. May this great, beloved fatherland deceived by lies and calumnies reassure itself! The struggle between Paris and Versailles is of a kind that cannot end in illusory compromises: the outcome will be unambiguous. Victory, pursued with irrepressible energy by the National Guards, is our aim and our due. We appeal to France!

Throughout April, decrees rained thick and fast. Rent unpaid since October 1870 was canceled. The grace period on overdue bills was extended three years. Night work for bakery workers was made illegal. A Labor and Exchange Commission authorized producers' cooperatives, of which forty-three had come into existence by May 14, to take over deserted ateliers. Mortmain property was nationalized when church was separated from state. And anticlericalism fostered secular education. "Religious or dogmatic instruction should . . . immediately and radically be suppressed, for both sexes, in all schools and establishments supported by the taxpayer," demanded Education Nouvelle, a group whose leader subsequently helped individual school districts reform their curricula. "Further, liturgical objects and religious images should be removed from public view. Neither prayers, nor dogma, nor anything that pertains to the individual conscience should be taught or practiced in common. Only one method should hold sway, the experimental or scientific, which is based upon the observation of facts, whatever their nature—physical, moral, intellectual." As priests and nuns were, of course, religious images incarnate, most removed themselves from the classroom (except in western Paris, where wealth defended tradition), forcing Edouard Vaillant, the Commune's commissioner of education, to open a recruitment center for teachers, or soi-disant teachers, at City Hall.

Little newspapers (some, like *Le Père Duchesne*, with names that evoked the first Revolution) multiplied as fast as cooperatives, but many big ones vanished overnight, for the Commune, despite its professed libertarianism, brooked no opposition from the bourgeois press. Freedom stopped where treason began, and treason began wherever an editor fought shy of direct democracy. First to disappear were *Le Figaro* and *Le Gaulois*. On April 14 the Comité de Sûreté Générale had *Paris-Journal*, *Le Journal des débats*, *Le Constitutionnel*, and *La Liberté* close shop. Two weeks later another purge silenced *La Cloche*, *Le Soir*, *Le Bien public*, and *L'Opinion nationale*, with the Sûreté explaining how dangerous it would be to countenance, in besieged Paris, "newspapers that openly preach civil war, give the enemy strategic information, and calumniate defenders of the Republic." Paranoia took command as Versailles crept closer, and on May 5, when *La Petite Presse*, *Le Petit Journal*, and *Le Temps* followed their brethren to the scaffold, they were dubbed "the most active auxiliaries of the enemies of Paris and the Republic."

While the Commune, which encompassed many ideological sects, tried in vain to convert the hydra-headed National Guard into a single-minded force, fifteen miles away Thiers was regularly assembling his generals, one of whom later wrote that the diminutive prime minister fancied himself Napoleon Bonaparte. The plan they laid called for a slow, methodical advance eastward toward Paris, and in due course 130,000 men accomplished the maneuver, first squeezing their foe inside the noose of the Seine, then tightening the noose at Neuilly, where every yard won cost several lives. Early in May artillery requisitioned from all over France opened fire on Issy and Vanves. Once these southwestern perimeter forts had been knocked out, no serious obstacle lay between Versailles and Saint-Cloud, which Thiers knew to be Paris's weakest gate. Less than three months after the German bombardment of the capital had ceased, an even more thunderous bombardment began. "This Sunday, Paris, without any other means of entertaining itself, spends the evening at the lower end of the Champs-Elysées watching the cannonade as though it were fireworks," noted Edmond de Goncourt, whose house in Auteuil took several hits from a gun at Mont-Valérien. "Otherwise the civil war continues unabated. Cannons boom and machine guns chatter. In the wet sky that stretches over leafless elms along the Champs-Elysées . . . a great cloud colored red by three new fires near Ternes billows upward. It's a lugubrious scene. From among shadowy groups one hears women curse the *Prussians of Versailles!*" Everything unstable crumbled under Versailles's relentless barrage, old structures but also the new government, which became frantic. A Jacobin majority threatened to arrest fellow Communards who dared oppose the formation of a committee of public safety. Further, it brought hostages before kangaroo courts or "juries of accusation" and impotently vented its rage against symbols. On May 15 Thiers's superb town house was wrecked. One day later, in a ceremony cheered by thousands, the Vendôme Column glorifying Napoleon I was sawed down.

After *La Cloche* fell silent Zola continued to send reports to *Le Sémaphore de Marseille,* and in this daily, unsigned "Lettre de Paris" lashed out at the Commune. Now that Versailles was inaccessible, City Hall commanded his attention. "Terror reigns supreme, individual freedom and the respect due to people's property are violated, the clergy is odiously hunted down, house searches and requisitions have become a form of government: such is the wretched, shameful truth," he declared on April 19. Excoriating ideologues who staged what he called an "abominable parody of '93" did not prevent him, however, from mourning humble *pères de famille* who died in battle and from pitying those who came back horribly disfigured. Nor did it stop him from denouncing the egotism of rich Parisians in western sections of the city. "Our implacable enemies of yesterday are called saviors by a segment of the population," he wrote. "I have heard Parisians say: 'Since Versailles can't come to our aid right away, let us address the Prussians'. . . . Terror is a sinister adviser: it drowns patriotism in personal interest." With France torn between bourgeois pledged to their material estate and "a cosmopolitan hard core" on the Left whose rootlessness begot "political adventurism," Zola saw Prussia emerging twice victorious. "At this moment, Prussia postures as the policeman of Europe. She is viewed by our neighbors as the guardian of public peace on our continent. She finds herself charged with the task of extinguishing the revolutionary fire, which burns only in Paris but which could spread beyond if the Prussian army together with the French do not form a cordon sanitaire around the great city."[6]

To escape from the great city without wearing a disguise, hiding in a trunk, swimming miles upstream, or joining a funeral procession, a young man needed a Prussian passport, and Zola somehow obtained one early in May, when it seemed quite possible that the National Guard might draft him unless the committee of public safety first took

---

[6]There are some vivid accounts of the city in "Souvenirs." For example, Zola describes Parisians crowding the heights of Montmartre to watch shells crash down on Neuilly as if the siege were a marvelous spectacle. "It's a magnificent amphitheater in which to watch from afar the battle being waged between Neuilly and Asnières. People brought folding chairs. Entrepreneurs even established benches and for two sous one was seated as in the orchestra of a theater."

him hostage.[7] Accompanied by Alexandrine, he left Paris on May 10 via the Gare du Nord, where trains ferried refugees to a transit camp at Saint-Denis, in territory occupied by the Germans. Two days later they summoned Emilie Zola, who had meanwhile stood guard over the house. No sooner had the local commandant issued them travel permits than the three made straight for Bennecourt. There they stayed a fortnight, missing the spectacle of butchery and arson that came to be known as the Bloody Week, *la semaine sanglante*.

It began on Monday, May 22, when troops poured through five gates and swept across western Paris in pincer columns. Had General MacMahon, who set up headquarters that same day at the Trocadéro, known that the Commune's only preparation for urban warfare was an immense barricade on the Place de la Concorde (built under the direction of a shoemaker named Napoleon Gaillard), his army might have taken City Hall by dusk. Instead it regrouped after its headlong advance, which gave the populous quarters time to improvise a fort. Montmartre, with cannons unmanned, fell almost immediately, but elsewhere resistance stiffened. Some two hundred barricades rose overnight, and the Versaillais fought their way eastward street by street, as fires set to impede them or to destroy obnoxious monuments raged out of control. The Tuileries Palace was soon ablaze, then the entire rue de Rivoli, the ministry of finance, the Palais de Justice, the prefecture of police, the three-hundred-year-old Hôtel de Ville. Paul Verlaine, who lived on the quai de la Tournelle, across the Seine from City Hall, witnessed this conflagration:

> [I saw] a thin column of black smoke come out of the campanile of the Hôtel de Ville, and after two or three minutes at most all the windows of the monument exploded, releasing enormous flames, and the roof fell in with an immense fountain of sparks. This fire lasted until the evening, and then assumed the form of a colossal brazier; this in its turn became, for days after, a gigantic smoldering ember. And the spectacle, horribly beautiful, was continued at night by the cannonade from the hills of Montmartre, which from nine that night to three in the morning provided a fireworks display such as had never been seen.

In due course spectators saw the July Column burning like a torch over the doomed Faubourg Saint-Antoine. By Saturday, May 27, all that remained unconquered of Paris was its proletarian northeast cor-

[7]Zola may also have felt apprehensive about possible reprisals by Versailles. Indeed, General Valentin, who became prefect of police, later declared that "the simple fact of having stayed in Paris under the Commune is a crime. Everyone there is to blame, and if I had my way everyone would be punished."

ner, where National Guards fought only to perish heroically. Caught between implacable Versaillais and German troops bivouacked just beyond the ramparts, many drew their last breath in Père-Lachaise Cemetery, which eventually housed Adolphe Thiers's remains. Those who didn't fall among the mausoleums were lined up against a wall known ever since as *le mur des fédérés*, shot, and thrown into a common pit.

Fifty-six hostages, including Archbishop Georges Darboy, died between May 22 and May 28, but the vengeance thus exacted by the Commune pales beside the carnage wrought by Versailles, whose army entered Paris intent on making it a killing field. When Montmartre fell, its residents paid dearly for the murder of Generals Lecomte and Thomas. "The massacres that were to grow more fearsome as the week advanced now began," writes one historian. "Forty-two men, three women and four children were shot in front of the wall where Lecomte and Clément Thomas had been killed. . . . A court-martial was improvised in the fatal house on the rue des Rosiers, and for the rest of the week batches of prisoners were brought there to be executed. Bareheaded, they were made to kneel down before the wall until their turn came." At least twenty-five thousand Parisians suffered the same fate, far more than had died during the Terror of 1793–94. Corpses lay strewn behind ruined barricades, on the riverbanks, against walls throughout the city, and their number grew even after May 28 as people taken prisoner in battle or denounced by neighbors (the government received some four hundred thousand anonymous letters) were brought before execution squads. A shallow grave dug in the Square Saint-Jacques overflowed with them. Blood ran down gutters there and elsewhere, coloring the Seine red.

Eager to give *Le Sémaphore de Marseille* eyewitness reports, or perhaps urged to do so by Barlatier, Zola came back from Bennecourt at week's end and surveyed the devastation while it still smelled of rotting flesh. "I managed to take a walk through Paris. It's atrocious," he wrote on May 27:

> All I want to tell you about are the corpses heaped high under the bridges. No, never will I forget the heartache I experienced at the sight of that frightful mound of bleeding human flesh, thrown haphazardly on the tow paths. Heads and limbs mingle in horrible dislocation. From the pile emerge convulsed faces. . . . There are dead who appear cut in two while others seem to have four legs and four arms. What a lugubrious charnel house!

Twenty thousand bodies, he estimated, lay unburied throughout the capital:

With warm days upon us, they will breed disease. I don't know if the troubled imagination plays a part here, but while loitering among ruins I smelled the heavy, noxious air that hangs over cemeteries in stormy weather. It all looks like a grim necropolis where fire hasn't purified death. Stale odors reminiscent of the morgue cling to sidewalks. Paris, which was called the boudoir or the hostel of Europe under the Empire, no longer gives off an aroma of truffles and rice powder, and one enters it holding one's nose, as in some foul sewer.

More of the same awaited him at Père-Lachaise Cemetery, which he visited hours after Versailles had wrested it from Communards. That Elysium for Paris's rich and famous was soaked with blood:

I remember a walk I took there three years ago. . . . I had gone to see Alfred de Musset's tomb on the anniversary of his death, to honor a poet I loved in adolescence. It was May and radiant sunlight bathed the young foliage. . . . But how appallingly different the place is now! Tombs are broken, flowers crushed by combatants. One would have thought that a tornado had funneled across this field of repose and killed the dead a second time . . . Cannon lie everywhere, tipped over on their sides or with their muzzles driven into the ground. From this vantage point they had hurled petrol bombs at central Paris day after day. How very strange that tombs should have served as an emplacement for the destruction of the living. This part of the cemetery, where men engaged in brutal hand-to-hand combat, is completely trampled down. Here and there are pools of blood, corpses that no one has even taken the trouble to collect. I saw a child of seventeen, stretched out on a white gravestone, his arms crossed, like one of those stiff gisants the Middle Ages put to bed on sarcophagi. Nearby, a National Guard had fallen on the sharp spikes of a gate and still hung there impaled, bent in two, horrible, like a carcass in a butcher's window. Blood had spurted over funeral wreaths and along the marble slabs there were bloody fingerprints, suggesting that some poor devil, mortally wounded, had clung to the edge before collapsing.

Every street spoke to the reality of a *bête humaine* trampling civilization underfoot, and evidence just as gruesome abounded in Versailles, where the Orangerie, the riding schools, and the stables became hell on earth for forty thousand prisoners. Crushed together, starved, and taunted by the locals, not a few ended up dashing out their brains or dying of disease before they could be court-martialed. "Measures taken against fugitive insurgents are more and more severe," wrote Zola, who was himself not yet prepared to grant them amnesty. "I fear that for quite some time people entering or leaving the city will need safe-conducts. Trains are to be reorganized, but as during the first days of the armistice, no one will board them unless furnished with a special permit. . . . We must not grumble, however. Given the heinous crimes that have just been perpetrated, every decent citizen should support this search for the guilty, even if it involves some inconvenience."

Images of this massacre haunted him for decades, and twenty years later they would furnish material for his novel about the Franco-Prussian War, *La Débâcle*. But a letter he wrote to Cézanne on July 4 suggests that in the immediate aftermath, yearning for business as usual, he, like many others, felt impelled to distance himself from what he had seen, or somehow to bracket the horror of it all: "I am now back in Batignolles, like someone roused from a bad dream. My little house is unchanged, my garden has not moved, neither furniture nor foliage has been damaged, and I can believe that those two sieges were nasty farces, invented to scare children." The fact that his pen had not been idle, he continued, made the resumption of normal life easier. "Twice I returned to Paris with more money than I had had when I left. *La Cloche* and *Le Sémaphore* . . . fed me each in turn, and fed me well. I tell you this so that you won't lament my fate. Never have I felt so hopeful or so eager to work. Paris is reviving. As I've often said, our reign will soon begin. . . . It's a pity all the imbeciles didn't die, but I console myself with the thought that not one of us has fallen by the wayside."

La Fortune des Rougon was to appear at last, after a long postponement, and correcting page proofs quickened his fantasy that this first chapter of *Les Rougon-Macquart* would rout his pious detractors. With war now over, he girded himself for peace.

X

NULLA DIES SINE LINEA

O NE CAN HARDLY imagine a naturalist agreeing with Stéphane Mallarmé that "everything in the world exists to result in a book," but after the French defeat at the battle of Sedan some such affirmation might have struck Zola as reasonable, for the same events that delayed *Les Rougon-Macquart* helped him round out its fictional scheme. "I had spent three years assembling documents . . . and the present volume was already written when Bonaparte's fall, which I needed artistically and saw as the inevitable last act though never dared to hope would occur so soon, furnished an awesome denouement," he wrote on July 1, 1871. "My work is now complete; it unfolds inside a closed circle; it becomes the tableau of a dead reign, of a strange era fraught with madness and shame." There was yet another benefit: disencumbered of Napoleon III, Zola, who once before had launched an important enterprise over someone's grave, no longer faced a competitor in *le devenir*—in ongoing history. Free to picture Second Empire France without being threatened by its officials or outmoded by its future, the guilt-ridden son intent on enshrining François Zola could survey this extinct world like the Lord of Creation.

Provence is where his fictional family of Rougons and Macquarts has its roots, and in *La Fortune des Rougon* Zola traces it through three generations, beginning in the eighteenth century with Adélaïde Fouque. An only child of prosperous peasants who own land just outside Plassans (Plassans being an alias for Aix), Adélaïde is orphaned at eighteen when her father dies insane. Marriage to an illiterate gardener named Rougon follows in 1790 or thereabouts and soon produces a

224

son, Pierre. Dogged by misfortune, Adélaïde, whose tainted heredity betrays itself in nervous fits, loses her husband three months after childbirth. Unable to live alone or to join society, which shuns her, she finds companionship with her reclusive neighbor, Macquart. As brutal as Adélaïde is meek, this hirsute drunkard, who survives by poaching and running contraband, fathers two bastards but dwells apart from the ménage in a windowless hovel. Pierre, Antoine, and Ursule grow up half wild. Of their mother Zola wrote that she "lacked all practical sense; the exact value of things and the necessity for order escaped her."

Evaluating things is, however, Pierre Rougon's dominant trait. Even as time makes Adélaïde increasingly naive, it awakens a shrewd proprietor in her firstborn, who at seventeen learns the distinction between legitimate and illegitimate. Kinfolk suddenly become for him strangers, if not indeed foes to be outwitted. "When Pierre . . . could understand Adélaïde's disorders and the peculiar situation of Antoine and Ursule, he seemed neither sad nor indignant but simply much preoccupied with the design that would best serve his interests." Tyrannizing his mother, he persuades her to sell her land, and with no one to oppose him—Macquart has meanwhile met a violent end, Antoine has been drafted, and Ursule has left for Marseille as the bride of a young hatter named Mouret—he pockets the 50,000 francs. Adélaïde entombs herself in Macquart's shack, but not until the wall around her family's former property has been razed does her unscrupulous son feel free of a past that would otherwise define him. "The party wall no longer existed, a plow uprooted the plantations, the Fouque farm was to become, as young Rougon wished, a half-remembered legend."

Pierre Rougon now enters Plassans, where social classes inhabit neighborhoods separated by walls no less monolithic for being invisible. Drawn to Félicité Puech, whose father trades in olive oil, he acquires—with the money stolen from his forsworn kin—not only a wife envious of those more fortunate than she but also a partnership. As climbers they are well matched. Pierre conceals his peasant origins, and Félicité harbors the secret knowledge that she is the illegitimate child of a marquis named Carnavant. Pierre has risen above himself, while Félicité demands her rightful elevation. "Félicité was a type of swarthy little woman not uncommon in Provence," writes Zola. "She resembled one of those dried-up, brown, strident cicadas that bash against the almond trees in sudden leaps. . . . Born unlucky, convinced that fortune had not given her her due, she never completely resigned herself to being a mere plain Jane. Her dream was to flaunt such happiness and wealth as would turn everyone green with envy." Once her father retires, his firm becomes the vehicle for Félicité's ambition, but bad luck, or what she calls *guignon*, continues to hold sway. Disappointed by Rougon, who can't make gold from olive oil, Félicité seeks salvation through the five children she has borne and more particularly through her three sons, all of whom settle in Plassans after studying in Paris.

Eugène, the oldest, is a *force de la nature* whose rough-hewn exterior belies his powerful, devious mind. Bored by the law, for which he has trained, he works desultorily, as if marking time or waiting for some turn of events to provide a forum more congenial than the local Palais de Justice. Very different is the youngest son, Aristide, Félicité's pet. Having inherited his mother's greed but not her mettle, he indulges himself with abandon and never finishes law school. A glorified clerkship affords him leisure to gamble away the modest dowry of a wife chosen for him by his father. "The Rougon tribe — thick, avid peasants with brutish appetites — had matured too quickly; its materialistic lust found full expression in Aristide." Yet another disappointment is the middle son, Pascal. Benevolent and intellectually gifted, he studies medicine, loves science for its own sake, and treats poor people gratis, which exasperates his mother, who is scornful of virtues that buy no admission to the Promised Land of social eminence. This mutant figures as the author-outsider who investigates the Rougons and Macquarts. "Heredity had preoccupied him for several years. He compared animal breeds with the human race, himself and his family being his point of departure. It yielded curious results." That his published results stir the scientific community abroad means nothing to hometown folk, who generally measure success by Félicité's venal standard.

Becalmed until 1848, the Rougons resume their piratical quest when revolution storms south from Paris. In Plassans, bourgeois fearful of being expropriated unite with aristocrats hopeful that disorder will ultimately enthrone Henri V, and Félicité becomes the muse of this conservative league. Her salon is where they gather every week to bolster one another, to curse the Republic, to monitor its rapid decline. Pierre Rougon exults, or would exult if not for a bête noire prowling nearby in the person of his loutish half brother Antoine Macquart. Long since returned from war, he has set up house with a hardworking woman who bears him three children — Lisa, Gervaise, and Jean. They all suffer abuse, but neither the blows Antoine rains upon them nor the liquor he guzzles will slake his desire to ruin Pierre for having left him destitute. When blackmail fails, Antoine embraces radical doctrine. "Every party has its freaks and knaves," writes Zola. "Filled with hatred and envy, dead set against all of society, Antoine Macquart welcomed the Republic as a blissful era in which permission would be given him to rifle his neighbor's safe and strangle the man if he so much as frowned. His café life, the newspaper articles he had read uncomprehendingly, had made him a formidable chatterbox."

Unlike Pascal, who finds biological determinism more rewarding than games of chance, his brothers stake their all on the red and black of French politics. Aristide becomes an ostentatious democrat and scourges priests in a newspaper called *L'Indépendant*. Eugène is quick to realize that France's "Prince-President," Louis Napoleon, will not content himself with what he has—constitutional power under a republic—and he becomes a Bonapartist secret agent. Shuttling between Paris and Plassans, he keeps his father informed of machinations underground. "The year was 1851. Rougon had received, every fortnight since mid-1849, a letter from his son Eugène. He'd read them in the bedroom, then stash them in an old secretary, the key to which he hid on his person." No sooner does Félicité unlock this correspondence than her stripes change. Her fellow royalists also Napoleonize themselves, and when the coup d'état takes place on December 2, all stand ready to perform a mock-heroic play that will make Pierre Rougon the "savior" of Plassans.

An insurrection against Louis Napoleon serves Pierre well. As republicans from villages near Plassans parade through town, he takes refuge in Adélaïde's hovel, having arranged to summon men and weapons when needed. The peasant army detaches one small group commanded by Antoine Macquart, who jubilantly occupies the mayor's office. Late at night, forty-one timorous conspirators follow Pierre into City Hall, and there they help him subdue Macquart in what is hailed as a gesture worthy of Corneille, a triumph of civic virtue over internecine loyalty.

Alone at last, Rougon sat in the armchair warmed by Macquart. He heaved a sigh, he wiped his brow. What an onerous task, conquering fortune and honors! But the goal had drawn near, he felt the mayor's soft armchair yield beneath him, he automatically caressed the ebony desk, which he found to be as smooth and delicate as the skin of a gentlewoman. . . . This room with faded drapes, reeking of petty business, of the trifles that loom large in a third-rate municipality, seemed a temple whose god he was becoming. He was entering something holy. He who didn't really much like priests remembered the thrill of his first communion, when he felt he had swallowed Jesus.

The legend of the nocturnal raid grows with each retelling. Acclaimed by grateful bourgeois, Pierre Rougon obtains a lucrative sinecure as well as a rosette. Antoine Macquart must flee France for his life.

Through this opportunistic saga Zola weaves another tale, a romance whose ill-fated hero is Silvère, the son of Ursule Mouret, née Macquart. Orphaned at five when her mother dies of consumption and her father hangs himself in despair, Silvère finds no one to nurture him except his grandmother, Adélaïde, and growing up beside her he rekindles life where darkness had fallen. Eventually the waif becomes a republican enthusiast. "He thought about horizons closed to him, he venerated things the hand couldn't touch, he worshipped great thoughts and big words for which he'd reach without always grasping them. . . . An innocent at the temple gates, he stood entranced by candles that looked to him, from afar, like stars. Such a mind sopped up republican ideas. . . . He read Rousseau over and over." Hungry for knowledge, Silvère also yearns for love, which materializes one day in the person of Marie Chantegreil, or "Miette," who has been cast adrift with wounds even more grievous than his own. Outside the town ruled by Mammon, these pubescent creatures—he is fifteen, she thirteen—awaken to nature even as they thrill to revolution. Budding desire speaks the language of political rebirth, and it will consummate itself tragically when girl joins boy in the festive march of the peasant army across Provence. Napoleon's henchmen shoot Miette dead and take Silvère prisoner. Brought to Plassans, he is executed there hours before Pierre and Félicité celebrate victory over a table laden with sweetmeats.

Playing insider against outcast, La Fortune's contrapuntal scheme is enhanced by images that recur in almost every episode, and most obviously by the image of the wall. Could Plassans exist otherwise than immured? Zola describes a settlement whose circumvallation has outlived its military raison d'être and has become a psychopathic defense:

> As if to isolate and seal itself more completely, the town stands surrounded by ancient ramparts that now serve only to make it darker and narrower. Thick with ivy and gillyflowers, this ludicrous fortification would crumble under rifle shots. At 11 p.m. in summer, at 10 in winter, the gates were bolted, [whereupon] the city, like a fainthearted maiden, could rest easy.

That ritual, he writes, bespoke its hatred of the outside world and its desire for a cloistered life. "Shut tight, Plassans said to itself: 'I am at home,' with the sanctimoniousness of the bourgeois confident that no one will crack his safe or interrupt his sleep."

Where money holds sway, secrets and caches abound. Bourgeois fearful of invasion live in terror of what may escape from within or below, which is to say that the wall around Plassans stands as a bulwark against instinct, primitiveness, nature. Rougon, who trades land for gold, not only buries his extramural past but nullifies it, and Macquart, haunting him, represents the return of the repressed. Zola announces this drama straightway, with the evocation of a cemetery purged of its tenants. "When one leaves Plassans through the Rome gate, situated south of the city, one notes, just beyond the first suburban houses on the right, a vacant area known thereabouts as the Saint-Mittre lot," is how *La Fortune des Rougon* begins.

It was once a cemetery named after a saint venerated in the region. Old folks . . . still remembered seeing the walls of the yard, which had remained closed for years. Gorged with corpses during a century or more, the earth exuded death, and a new site had to be found across town. The forsaken place had purified itself every spring by acquiring a cover of thick, dark vegetation. Its rich soil, which grave-diggers couldn't shovel without bringing up some human shred, proved remarkably fertile. Foliage billowed over the walls; inside was a dark green sea studded with flowers of unusual brilliance. One sensed the mold and sap underneath.

At length Plassans made real estate of the hallowed ground, harvesting the bones, and consigning them to oblivion: "Day after day the town saw a tumbril lumber back and forth transporting human debris as if it were so much rubbish. What's worse, it had to cross Plassans from one end to the other, and with each bump it littered fragments of bone and handfuls of loamy soil. No religious rite at all; a slow, brutal convoy. . . . People felt spooked for some years by the former grave-yard." Prefiguring gardens that reappear throughout *Les Rougon-Macquart*, this human field in which death nourishes life repels nouveaux riches, whose trees grow rootlessly. On the one hand we have a fertile graveyard where past generations "enrich" the soil, and on the other a barren, petrified, self-absorbed town where hoarders for whom the future is yet another hinterland fraught with danger breed nothing but gold. Town and country constantly reflect each other. As Plassans desecrated the cemetery of Saint-Mittre, so will Rougon loot his ancestral home. The minute he strikes it rich in Plassans, a gen-darme splatters Saint-Mittre with young Silvère's blood.

Money builds ramparts, but instinct breaches them, and events that occur beyond Plassans, in the *faubourg* or countryside, all proceed from the image of vegetation overflowing Saint-Mittre's enclosure. Townspeople cluck when Adélaïde and Macquart pierce the wall they share. Macquart fashions a door, which Silvère, in an unconscious reenactment of the family romance, reopens some fifty years later to admit Miette, who lives where Adélaïde once lived. "The little door . . . had stood forgotten in this obscure corner of the adjacent property. No one had even thought of condemning it, and, overgrown with moss, blackened by damp, locks and hinges rusty, it was indistinguish-able from its stone matrix." With no barrier between them, the lovers join as they shelter after dark under Miette's voluminous cloak. "In Provence, humble women—peasants and workers—still wear those

broad mantles of ancient design which are called pelisses in the region," writes Zola.

> Miette opened hers, which was embroidered with little lozenges and
> lined with blood-red calico, then threw one flap of this warm coat
> over Silvère's shoulders, enveloping him completely, pressing him
> against herself inside the same garment. Each put an arm around the
> other's waist in order to bind themselves together. When they were
> thus merged into a single being, no longer recognizably human inside
> the folds of the pelisse, they began to toddle toward the road.

While inhabitants of the walled city exist outside themselves, displaying false fronts or concealing a secret "other," these strays are centered
in love. For Félicité, beatitude is a place only money can buy—the tax
collector's palatial flat, which she enviously gazes at from her window
year after year; for the lovers, it is oneness inside a mantle that in its
style expresses continuity with the past and in its "blood-red" lining
emblemizes rebirth. Swaddled by nature, Miette and Silvère "toddle"
forth. Children of the land, they will turn their womb inside out and
wear red as a republican flag.

Merging, or fusing, reaches epic proportions in Zola's image of the
rebels marching at night, whom Silvère and Miette soon encounter.
"Nothing more awesomely grandiose than these several thousand men
shattering the dead and frozen peace of the horizon," he begins.

> The road was now a human torrent that swept forward irrepressibly;
> men came around the bend in dark waves and their hymns swelled
> louder and louder. . . . When the last battalions appeared, all let loose
> a deafening roar. *La Marseillaise* filled the sky, as if blared by mon-
> strous trumpets that made every corner of the valley ring. And the
> dormant countryside woke up; it shivered like a beaten drumskin; it
> resounded through and through and echoed the passionate notes of
> the national anthem. . . . Voices seemed to rise all around—from
> distant rocks, from plots of tilled earth, from meadows, from copses
> and scrub.

The slope between Plassans and the river Viorne is compared to "an
amphitheater crowded with invisible people hailing the insurgents."
Intramural order and extramural revolt thus constitute two essentially different modes of theater. One divides, the other unites. One
thrives on intrigue, the other on commotion. One features personae
for whom life means hoarding and coveting, feigning and spying, losing
and stealing; the other, like the festivals that had been staged during
the Revolution of 1789, has men embrace nature in an affirmation of
tribal identity. With Plassans as background, the pageant whose cele-

brants will sacrifice themselves en masse floods the mind, confuses the eye, abolishes the space between actor and spectator. "This endless parade of heads transformed by night and circumstance into masks unforgettably expressive of zeal and fanatical ecstasy produced the dizzying effect of a millrace," writes Zola. "At times [Miette] thought that they were no longer marching but being swept along by the . . . raucous hymn with its formidable dynamics. She couldn't make out individual words." The bacchanalia also confuses male and female, for Miette on the verge of womanhood strikes a martial pose as Liberty hoisting the republican flag over her ragtag army. Pubescent (the blood-red cloak, the torrent, the moon all suggest menstruation), she achieves virility. "Miette was becoming a boy. . . . As rifles and scythes marched past, her white teeth showed longer and sharper between her red lips, like the canines of a young wolf eager to bite."

La Fortune des Rougon was the second of many novels in which Zola created high drama around the opposition between individual and mass, between the separated tenants of chambered space and a throng driven by some instinctual force that obliterates boundaries, taboos, families.[1] In *Nana*, crazed thousands rise, row upon row, to cheer the sex goddess-cum-thoroughbred galloping past Longchamp's stadium. In *Au Bonheur des Dames*, where a department store swallows little shops, women become maenads of consumerism, engulfing the immense tiered gallery on sale day, and, flushed with excitement, ruining their husbands. In *La Débâcle*, armies slaughter each other on the hills that circle Sedan while shells blast the fortress town below. When order crumbles during a miners' strike in *Germinal*, an "underground sea" inundates the labyrinth of mineral corridors. Obsessed by *la bête humaine*, Zola invented over and over again a scenario that argued his deepest conflict. Devising intricate plots, following superstitious rituals, hoarding letters, systematizing notes, and pruning rosebushes, he yearned to unleash himself but felt anguish at the thought of what might befall him if he did. Sex rarely goes unpunished in *Les Rougon-Macquart*, and one can only conjecture that the death sentence Zola inflicts on pubescent females (Miette has various successors) is somehow bound up with a sense of his own masculinity being endangered. Is a boyish girl who bleeds as she marches against Louis Napoleon the inverted image of a rebellious boy who risks castration? Does her martyrdom disguise "the young wolf eager to bite" beneath a virtuous fleece? Zola may have answered this himself some years later in *Germinal*, where genital warfare becomes quite explicit, where another woman on the march hoists a pole, though attached to it is not a republican red flag but the bloody scrotum of a slain oppressor.

[1]The contrast is also between petrifaction and flux. Zola had already portrayed this vision in *Thérèse Raquin* with the Seine and the cubicles of a roofed arcade.

Miette affords a glimpse of two fantasies that Zola expressed through orgiastic or militant hordes. Impersonating the emasculated, she harbors the emasculator.

Had *La Fortune des Rougon* appeared in 1870, it would have benefited from the fact that revelations about Louis Napoleon's coup d'état were still politically germane. Several treatises on which Zola relied for information described rural skirmishing in December 1851; the uproar they caused grew very much louder midway through 1868, when *Le Figaro* and *La Tribune* assailed a prefect under whose authority men had been executed near Aix seventeen years earlier. But *la semaine sanglante* redefined the proportions of that massacre, and by 1871 it seemed a mere peccadillo. With Louis Napoleon in total eclipse, *La Fortune* was given scant notice or lumped among "retrospective" works, despite Zola's effort to have reviewers single it out. "We were hardly more than a handful of clairvoyants . . . raising our voices to greet a new star on the literary horizon," observed Edmond Lepelletier, Zola's future biographer. "Zola's admirers wrote for timorous papers. The silence of [the Commune's] terrible repression filled the land. Our premature bravos did not even excite catcalls." Lacroix found himself with many unsold copies, which in 1872 were flogged as a second edition.

High praise from distinguished men consoled Zola, however. Edmond de Goncourt recommended it to Victor Hugo's old comrade-in-arms, Théophile Gautier, and Gautier lost no time in declaring, with a romantic flair for the portentous: "He doesn't yet have his style down pat. It's bushy and full of creepers, but a Master is come among us, marked by his fateful Z, like Z. Marcas and Balzac himself."[2] Flaubert was equally enthusiastic. "I've just finished your torturous and beautiful book! I'm still stunned by it. It's powerful! Very powerful!" he wrote on December 1, 1871, some six weeks after Zola sent him a copy.

> My only quarrel is with the preface. I feel that it mars your work, which is so impartial and lofty. You give away your secret there, and in my poetics a novelist doesn't have the right to be so candid. But I am otherwise without reservations. What a bold talent and stout heart! Tell me when you're free so that I can come see you and chat at length about your book.

Although thrilled by this benediction, Zola knew full well that the quibble argued fundamental differences. Flaubert was, after all,

---

[2]Z. Marcas is the titular hero of a story by Balzac. Scholars have noted that *La Fortune* owes certain features to Balzac's *Pierrette*, as well as to Hugo's *L'Homme qui rit*.

pledged to a hermetic ideal in which authorial impersonality would triumph as "pure style," while Zola fancied himself a soldier, a teacher, a master builder scaffolding densely populated friezes on an armature of scientific law. Flaubert's dictum that "the author in his book must be like God in the universe, everywhere present and nowhere visible" did not square with Zola's militant agenda. Nor, indeed, did it favor his economic position. A man of independent means could afford the luxury of artistic self-effacement, but not so a resident of Grub Street whose signature was his livelihood. Flaubert fathered novels that entered the marketplace like dandies contemptuous of publicity-mongering. Zola begot wage earners, and had them shout for recognition.[3]

Good news from Aix-en-Provence also blunted Zola's disappointment. Shortly before *La Fortune des Rougon* appeared, the town he portrays so savagely in it chose to honor François Zola by affixing his patronymic to the monument he designed. The Canal du Verdon became the Canal Zola. "Through *Le Mémorial d'Aix* I've just learned of the tribute paid my father at your behest," Zola wrote on September 20, thanking a municipal councillor named Alphonse Aude. "I recall that your late father, when mayor of Aix, helped mine shepherd the canal project around bureaucratic pitfalls. It is poetic justice that the son should ultimately have vindicated the man whose father guided his first steps. I thank you, sir, with all my heart." Unlike Plassans, which was doomed to go from bad to worse, Aix could still redeem itself.

How did Zola look at age thirty-two? One acquaintance remembered "a robust fellow" with a cannonball head, a brush cut, a full beard, spectacles, a dimpled nose, an upper lip that tended to curl back in gentle mockery, a resonant, tenor voice that sometimes pealed very high, and the Midi written all over him. "His demeanor, which combined self-assurance and timidity, expressed quiet faith not only in the power of letters but in his own gift," observed Emile Bergerat, Théo-

---

[3]Edmond de Goncourt noted in his journal on February 19, 1877: "Flaubert attacks—though with tips of the hat to his genius—the prefaces, doctrines, the naturalist professions of faith . . . with which Zola helps his books sell. Zola says something like this in response: 'You inherited a small fortune which has allowed you to free yourself from many things. I, on the other hand, who have earned my livelihood with my pen, who have been obliged to do all sorts of dubious scribbling, to survive through journalism, I've retained a touch of the—how shall I put it?— of the mountebank. . . . Yes, it's true that I, like you, scorn this word *Naturalism*, and yet I drum it home, for unless things are baptized, the public won't believe them to be new.' " In his journal Goncourt felt quite free to play ventriloquist and have his own view of Zola come out of the latter's mouth.

phile Gautier's son-in-law. Life had transformed the young man of letters seen half-face amidst Japanese prints in Manet's 1868 portrait. As *Les Rougon-Macquart* bulked larger, so did Zola himself, and photographs taken after 1872 feature a paunchy, barrel-chested entrepreneur commanding his own imaginative landscape.[4] What such photographs can't reveal, of course, are the nerves that made him pay for success. His body continued to mimic angina, as a result of which he gave up coffee, and he still suffered attacks of colic, along with urinary problems. "Today," Goncourt noted on June 3, 1872, "Zola dines with me. He lifts a glass of Bordeaux with two hands and says, 'See how my fingers tremble!' And he tells me about incipient heart disease, a threat of kidney disease, a threat of rheumatism in his joints."

Colic or no, the life Zola led during this period would not have been possible without intestinal fortitude. *Les Rougon-Macquart* grew apace, but after *La Cloche* resumed publication, every hour spent on literature was time stolen from sleep. A legislative reporter by day, he commuted between Paris and Versailles, manning his post in the château's hot, overcrowded theater, where journalists occupied box seats, until parliament adjourned in late afternoon or early evening. "Versailles recovered its former animation, if not the elegance of yesteryear," wrote Henri Malo. "In the morning, trains discharged representatives from Paris, along with journalists. In the evening they'd ride back together and en route talk up a storm, continuing debates that had just roused the Assembly. . . . Momentous issues brought amateurs bitten by the political bug, who crowded the Gare Saint-Lazare and invaded Versailles's hotels." Even as he completed a second volume of *Les Rougon-Macquart*, Zola scribbled frenetically for *La Cloche* and *Le Sémaphore de Marseille*. By May 1872, when Louis Ulbach gave him a different beat, at his own request, he had written more than 260 articles, many running to 1,200 or 1,500 words, which form a chronicle of the Third Republic's turbulent infancy.

Observers who felt certain that the Commune would fatally besmirch the entire Left were soon proven wrong. By-elections held on July 2, 1871, saw republicans carry the day, foremost among them Léon Gambetta. After five months in limbo he had found his voice again, though civil war had meanwhile persuaded him that only a republic built along conservative lines stood some reasonable chance of surviving opposition from monarchist ranks. As soon became obvious, the fallen demagogue resolved to make common cause with the adroit strategist of conservative republicanism, Adolphe Thiers. These two

[4]How important food was in Zola's marriage may be inferred from a letter Emilie Zola, sojourning with relatives in the Midi, wrote to Alexandrine on May 6, 1872: "Go ahead, Gabrielle, go ahead and continue stuffing Mimi, make him even more gluttonous if that's possible, but I must warn you, out of friendship, not to acquire the same weakness."

formed a tenuous *mariage de convenance*. Gambetta minded himself during parliamentary debate but felt freer outside the Assembly, and on oratorical campaigns through provincial France he hoisted petards that could hardly fail to shake Thiers in Versailles. "Have we not seen laborers in the cities and fields win the vote?" he asked a sympathetic crowd at Grenoble. "Do the omens not suggest that our land, which has tried every other alternative, intends at last to risk a republic and call upon new social reserves [*nouvelles couches sociales*]? Yes! I descry, I feel, I proclaim the emergence of new social reserves." Thiers was later to complain that Gambetta never had the clear-cut ideas of a real statesman, that he always retreated into the role of tribune, which he played most naturally.

Lest "new social reserves" emerge straightway, the heterogeneous Right, which still greatly outnumbered the Left, sought to act in concert. At daggers drawn since 1830, Legitimists (supporting the Bourbon "pretender," Charles X's childless heir Henri, Comte de Chambord) and Orleanists (supporting Louis Philippe's grandson, the Comte de Paris) now agreed that Chambord should reign as a constitutional monarch and should be succeeded by the Comte de Paris.[5] What this simple arrangement did not consider was the obduracy of Chambord, who lived cut off from the world in a castle near Vienna, like a Pirandellian solipsist. For Chambord, either restoration would be a faithful restoration of the kingdom France had abolished in 1830 along with Charles X or it would enthrone someone other than himself. His absolute proviso was that the country raise the white lily-spangled flag, and rational heads could not prevail upon him to bend when he came home after four decades abroad. "[That flag] has always been for me inseparable from the absent fatherland; it flew over my cradle, I want it to shade my tomb," he declared in a statement published on July 6 by the royalist paper *Union*. "[Under that flag] the unification of the nation was achieved; with it your fathers, led by mine, conquered Alsace-Lorraine, whose fidelity will be the consolation of our misfortunes. . . . I have received it as a sacred trust from the old king, my grandfather, dying in exile. . . . In the glorious folds of this unblemished standard I shall bring you order and liberty! Frenchmen! Henri V cannot abandon the flag of Henri IV!" Eighty die-hard Legitimists in the parliament stood firm behind Chambord, but a majority of conservative deputies dissociated themselves from his manifesto. As patriotic gentlemen repelled by anachronism on the one hand and revolution on the other, they pledged allegiance to the tricolor flag while yearning for a polity that would be neither lily white nor true blue.

The schism involved not only monarchical absolutism but Catholic

---

[5]Chambord's grandfather, Charles X, was a brother of Louis XVI. Louis Philippe descended from Louis XIV's brother, Philippe II.

orthodoxy, and here the manifesto on either side of which parties aligned themselves was a papal bull. Seven years earlier, in his *Syllabus of Errors,* Pius IX had joined battle with secular Europe by denouncing the separation of church and state; claiming for his church control of all culture and science; rejecting liberty of faith, conscience, and worship; enumerating eighty such "errors" altogether; and declaring that the pontiff neither could nor should make any concession whatever to progress, liberalism, and modern civilization. The *Syllabus* marked France profoundly. Cultivated prelates like Bishop Dupanloup of Orléans and Archbishop Darboy of Paris resisted Rome, but the lower clergy embraced popish obscurantism with fervor, and in rural parishes, where miraculous visitations abounded, it was the lower clergy who were heard. "Of all the mysteries that fill Church history, I don't know any that equals or surpasses this swift and complete transformation of Catholic France into a farmyard annex of the Vatican's *anticamera,*" one liberal Catholic wrote shortly before the Vatican Council proclaimed the pope to be infallible and his episcopate universal on July 18, 1870. "I won't immolate justice and truth, reason and history in a sacrificial offering to the idol whom lay theologians have enthroned at the Vatican."

Far from halting the ultramontane movement, the Franco-Prussian War gave it further impetus, as Catholic churchmen used France's defeat to advance the view that God had thus punished a wayward child. The imperial saturnalia was over, repentance was in order, and devout souls, many of whom wore the insignia of the Sacred Heart, flocked to holy sites throughout France. In 1873 a national pilgrimage sponsored by the Assumptionists saw thousands descend upon Lourdes, La Salette, Pontmain, Mont-Saint-Michel, Chartres, and Paray-le-Monial for expiatory demonstrations that became political rallies. "Suspended in midair, equally incapable of adopting the republican format that promises terror and the monarchical format that demands obedience and respect, the French," declared Monsignor Pie at Chartres, "are a people [who] await a leader, who invoke a master." One hundred fifty deputies heard Pie preach this message and soon afterward went farther afield to hear Monsignor de Léseleuc bless them at Paray-le-Monial. "Since assembling in Versailles, you have often asked forgiveness of God for France's crimes," said the bishop. "You have often made honorable amends to the Sacred Heart of Jesus for the ingratitude shown him, especially during the last eighty years." It did not escape those present that eighty years earlier, in Year I by the Revolutionary calendar, Louis XVI had been guillotined.

Liberal Catholics as well set store by the belief that France would come undone if she did not harness herself to religious principles, and the quasi-official term for the government they exercised, *l'ordre moral,* bespoke their dour agenda. Staunchly patriarchal, men like Falloux and Albert de Broglie saw the Church as society's front-line defense against havoc wrought in the name of liberty, fraternity, and equality. Universal suffrage exasperated them. But disavowing the secular state or imagining the *ancien régime* to be a Holy Land that promised redemption from modern turmoil was something else again, and over this issue moderates often clashed with zealots. When, for example, construction began on the Basilica of the Sacré-Coeur in Montmartre, the Assembly, which licensed its founders to break ground, rebuffed a monarchist deputy who would have had legislators join priests in consecrating the cornerstone. Such behavior infuriated the Holy See. "I must tell France the truth," Pope Pius told French visitors in June 1871. "There is in your country an evil worse than the Revolution, worse than the Commune with its escapees from hell spreading fire through Paris. What I fear is the wretched politics of Catholic liberalism. That's the real scourge." Overt enemies he could suffer more easily, he said, than co-religionists who "propagate and sow revolution even as they pretend to reconcile Catholicism with freedom."

For lack of a suitable king, the conservative majority or coalition of centrist factions improvised government under the redoubtable Adolphe Thiers. Having caught his second wind at the age of seventy-four, Thiers energetically tackled the manifold problems that beset France. Repairing war damage, inventing an economy, negotiating new frontiers, building up the army, and calming restless cities, this plump, high-strung little man, who looked more like a ninepin than a pillar of state, manipulated the contentious legislature by flattering all hopes with bland courtesy. After three decades of writing history he enjoyed making it, and some observers wondered whether he did not, indeed, fancy himself the First Consul reborn. Certainly he had a Napoleonic zest for administration. But what kept him in power was a general belief that he alone could manage Otto von Bismarck, whose *Kulturkampf* against Catholics in Germany reinforced the Prussian disapproval of religio-monarchical stirrings in France. So long as German troops occupied French soil, which they would do until France paid Germany the five billion francs in full, Thiers was on safe ground. Availing himself of domestic turbulence to plead the case for a conservative republic, he exploited foreign relations to demand a title less nebulous than "chief executive" (*chef du pouvoir exécutif*).

Thiers triumphed nominally on August 31, 1871, when fellow deputies, in a masterpiece of ambiguous legislation called the Rivet Law, baptized him president of the French Republic while implying that France might yet become a monarchy:

Until the country's definitive institutions are established, our provisional institutions must, for the sake of labor, of commerce, of industry, assume in everyone's eyes, if not such stability as only time can vouchsafe them, stability enough to harmonize conflicting wills and end party strife. [Furthermore], a new title, a more precise appellation may, without working fundamental change, have the effect of demonstrating the Assembly's intention to abide by the pact concluded at Bordeaux. May an extension of the chief executive's period in office . . . stabilize the office without it being inferred that this compromises the sovereign rights of the Assembly.

As deputy, prime minister, and president all together, Thiers would have liked a free hand, but the majority, who feared his elusiveness even more than his tongue, controlled him through ministerial accountability.

For eighteen months these kindred opponents wrestled over everything from reform and trade policy to military law and administrative organization. When Thiers tried to make prefects his satraps and mayors his appointees, the conservative bloc, which held sway in rural France, championed decentralization. When he sought to impose tariff barriers, the Assembly rose in defense of free trade. When he insisted upon a small professional army—small enough to quiet Germany's fear that France might march east at the earliest opportunity—squires who had recently had him sue for peace advocated universal conscription. Important though they were, these skirmishes postponed the main battle, and on November 13, 1872, Thiers joined it. In a Report to the Nation, he declared,

It is the government of the country; to resolve anything else would mean a new revolution, and the one most to be feared. Let us not waste time in proclaiming it, but instead let us use time to stamp it with the character we desire and require. A committee selected by you [the Assembly] . . . gave it the title of Conservative Republic. Let us seize this title and watch that it be deserved. . . . The Republic will be conservative or it will not be.

Amplifying his message was *la voix du peuple*, which made itself heard in by-elections through 1872–73. Of thirty-eight legislative seats contested nationwide, republicans won thirty-one.

It was in fact one such contest that led to Adolphe Thiers's fall. On April 27, 1873, Charles de Rémusat, a moderate who held the foreign affairs portfolio under Thiers, ran against a republican known for his radical posture, and he lost decisively. Among right-wing conservatives, this event sharpened regrets of the kind Edmond de Goncourt had voiced in his journal almost two years earlier: "Society is dying of universal suffrage. Everyone admits that it is the fatal instrument of society's imminent ruin. Through it, the ignorance of the vile multitude governs. Through it, the army is robbed of obedience, discipline, duty. . . . Monsieur Thiers is . . . a very short-term savior. He fancies that he can save present-day France with dilatory tactics, temporization, finagling, political legerdemain: small means cut to the measure of his small frame."

Having outlived his position as the indispensable negotiator by raising five billion francs in short order and liberating French territory, Thiers could not rely on Bismarck to save him from the consequences of Rémusat's defeat. Conservative legislators blamed him for that defeat. They excoriated a government hospitable to "new barbarians [who] threaten society's very foundations" and, flouting national sentiment, demanded that the cabinet be reconstituted without any republican ministers. Thiers stood firm, but Duc Albert de Broglie, the conservative leader, drafted a resolution regretting that recent ministerial modifications had not given conservative interests the satisfaction that was their due. It carried by a narrow margin, whereupon Thiers felt compelled to resign. On May 21 the Assembly named General MacMahon president, and MacMahon, almost exactly two years after he had led Versailles's troops against the Commune, sounded the call for moral order. "With God's help and the devotion of our army, which will always be an army of the law, with the support of all loyal men, we shall together continue the work of liberating the country and reestablishing moral order in our land," he declared in his first presidential message. Broglie, the grandson of Madame de Staël and Benjamin Constant and the son of a Broglie who had sided with Louis Philippe in 1830, became prime minister of what was soon to be dubbed "the Republic of Dukes."

Zola had meanwhile grown increasingly dyspeptic. His "Lettres de Versailles" abound in scurrilous caricatures, which served to underscore his republicanism but also to detain readers whose attention might understandably have wandered from a neutral account of parliament worrying this bone or that one day after day. "M. de Gavardie, the man who goes unheard, mounted the podium with the single-minded intention of gaining applause at long last," he wrote when the Assembly debated newspaper censorship. "What a storm and, above all, what polemical skill! As far as that one is concerned, we journalists are potential brigands who hole up at night in the boulevard kiosks . . . Watching M. de Gavardie take his seat, I expected someone to fold him up carefully and put him under glass, like a wax Jesus." Another monarchist of small note fared no better. "Then came the interminable, the lackluster and sallow M. de Ventavon. Ah, what a dull chatterbox! I thought he'd tuck us in right then and there. His voice is a thin reed and he delivers speeches in the low monotone of a wet nurse lulling an infant to sleep." Invective used against the Salon five years earlier did double duty here, and Zola, as if challenging someone to sue him, was particularly vicious in his portrayal of the Comte de Chambord's entourage. "At bottom he may be a nice chap, this fat man who has been traveling since adolescence with a throne in his trunk," he noted on November 24, 1871:

> I believe that he issues from a jejune race and has, despite the admiration of his worshippers, all the blubber and divinely stupid ponderousness of an idol. Being fetishized must make him even more witless. People embark on pilgrimages to kneel at his feet. It's like kissing a bone. He lives in a tabernacle among crackpots who call him "sire," the better to convince themselves that they are prime ministers. A lunatic asylum where the monarchy is playing out the final act of its drama.
>
> Lately orthodox papers are full of letters sent by such pilgrims, in which the dominant note is lachrymose, elegiacal. How sweet is Chambord, how good, how tender, how precocious! One would think he was a five-year-old [rather than] a corpulent bloke of fifty. . . . Playing at dolls, these serious, grave men smile only when they visit their king. They drivel on about it, they tell old wives' tales about laborers and peasants coming to pay homage to the count.

Infantilism, senescence, and piety flock together in Zola's indictment, where monarchist deputies are often pictured as an aboriginal chorus howling at Thiers, who strives to allay fear or inculcate reason, like the *père noble* of old melodrama.

Reason dictated that the Assembly evacuate Versailles, but whenever the question arose, fear of Paris prevailed. To no other issue did Zola react so spontaneously, as no other issue epitomized so well everything he found loathsome about the Right. "The Right, on hearing M. Wolowski's firm speech, almost had an attack of apoplexy," he sneered. "Someone dared mention Paris to these gentlemen, bluntly, shamelessly. They all stood up with the wrathful air of a prude who had heard a swear word. M. de Marnier in his anguish couldn't help shouting: 'Would you have us risk invasion?' Not at all, sir! We just want to give you a less ridiculous place in history." For the refugee from Aix-en-Provence, this displacement became a personal affront. Leaving Paris every day was like entering a nightmare that reversed his triumphant itinerary and made him feel subject once again to the will of small-town oligarchs. Indeed, Versailles as he describes it in *La Cloche* is Plassans writ large. "What wicked foolishness, wanting to place France's heart on the right side, in this black hole, in this immense sepulchre!" he exclaimed on September 21, 1871, four months after *la semaine sanglante*, when the siege of Paris had not yet been officially lifted. "They'd have a prudent and pious bourgeois who snuffs out his candle at 8 p.m. . . . embody the French national genius. Imagine government seated in a town where dogs don't bark, where cats don't philander, where even gas lamps are weary of burning." Throughout the fall, when tribunals passed sentence on imprisoned Communards, condemning many to death or exile, funereal images crowded Zola's mind:

> Yesterday I spent two hours in Versailles. I'm still shivering from it. Never have I seen a town more dismal, more deserted, more gray, more unnerving. . . . Fallen leaves tinge the avenues yellow and crackle beneath the feet of rare pedestrians. . . . The long streets, the interminable *allées* plunge into the fog, sadly, with such mortal sadness that shuttered houses on either side look vaguely like tombs. . . . What a gigantic necropolis is this château!

In April 1872, having exhausted his patience, he wrote a sarcastic letter begging the Assembly to repatriate itself. "Return to Paris, for the sake of the press corps. I won't mention France, as I know you'd laugh. I mention only us journalists. And I tell you that you would be ill advised to push us too far. You're thin-skinned. A mere pen prick makes you bleed. Well then, don't drive us mad, or we shall wreak horrible vengeance!"

Bound up with the dichotomy between live Paris and sepulchral Versailles was a charge of cowardice that republicans leveled against monarchists after the Franco-Prussian War. Had the bourgeoisie who snuffed out their candles at 8 p.m. not sued for peace prematurely? In scorning Paris, had they not traduced the honor of France Militant bearing the torch of liberty through Europe and conquering at Valmy, at Jemappes, at Fleurus? By 1900, when Charles Maurras, a royalist, coined the phrase *La Revanche reine de France* (Revenge, queen of France), the Right would bellow as truculently as the Left, but in 1871–72, vengeance wore a Phrygian cap rather than a crown. Gambetta, over Mayor Kuss's tomb, enjoined republicans to "rally around the thought of a Revenge that marshals law and justice against force and infamy," and rally they did.

Zola, for one, found chauvinism therapeutic. "In France, certain things draw wild applause: military parades, government loans, whatever rings and shines," he wrote, hoping perhaps that the reader no longer remembered how contemptuous he had been of hoopla under Napoleon III. "Mock it though one might, such chauvinism does one good. It's a pleasure to abandon reason, to succumb to the illusions of national pride. Frenchmen will be very sick indeed the day they stop swaggering. Fanfare is in our blood. We will not really have recovered our balance until we once again believe ourselves the world's premier nation." Humiliated in battle, France mustered the huge sum needed to evict German troops more quickly than anyone thought possible, and Zola joined others in hailing this tour de force as proof of republican vigor. "Now that the Republic has brought off, overnight, the most colossal loan ever initiated, what will be its future triumphs? Tomorrow, gentlemen, unless [monarchist] pretenders seduce it like some poor, gullible maiden, it will save Europe from the Caesars of the North." Laced with expressions that qualify for Flaubert's *Dictionary of Received Ideas* ("Caesars of the North," "the French genius," etc.), the "Lettres de Versailles" preach a holy crusade. "Once a German has taunted us with our defeats, with our ignorance, he has exhausted his wit," Zola lashed out.

Yes, alas, we have been beaten. Yes, alas, we often imagine we know a host of things about which we know absolutely nothing. But I have many compatriots who wouldn't trade for all the learned and victorious heft of Germany that flash of lightheartedness, that vivacity of intelligence which is the French genius. When one possesses such weapons, one remains king of the civilized world, even in disastrous times.

Moreover, they don't know how to laugh. Call them clock thieves and they grind their teeth, contemplating a new invasion to shut us up for good. All the enormities they hurl at us are duds, and if by chance they found a single mot juste we would be the first to relish it. On the other hand, the least of our barbs hits home and avenges us for their accumulated fatuousness. . . . That is how we buy revenge. The pen must splatter ink over the colossus. Only after we have shaken it a little every day will our cannons be able to fell it.[6]

Dismissing art for art's sake as the fey gospel of "ingenious rhymesters, elegiac spirits, frock-coated Brahmins," he called for a poet with breath enough to rekindle *la furia francese*. "Where is the red flower of hatred, the flower that grew up in blood, beside some tumulus in Gravelotte?[7] It must blossom, the poet must issue forth, so that Germany won't

---

[6]Concerning "clock thieves," Flaubert, in a letter to George Sand written on March 11, 1871, referred as follows to the German troops occupying his corner of Normandy: "What barbarism! What regression! I'm angry at my contemporaries for having given me the feelings of a twelfth-century brute. *I'm choking on my bile.* These officers in white gloves who smash mirrors, who know Sanskrit and make a mad dash for the champagne, who steal your watch and then send you their visiting card . . . horrify me more than cannibals."
[7]Gravelotte is a village between Verdun and Metz where, on August 18, 1870, Germany hurled some 200,000 men, equipped with more than 700 artillery pieces, against the French.

say: 'They are so thoroughly rotten, those French, that one can leave a hundred thousand corpses on their soil without hearing a sublime rattle rise from the heap.' "

This histrionic style must have satisfied readers of *La Cloche*, or Louis Ulbach, who was often ruffled by Zola's expostulations, would certainly have let him go. As for Zola, meeting daily deadlines proved both onerous and beneficial. Working on the National Assembly reports "knock[s] me senseless," he told Paul Alexis. A note written to Flaubert nine months later conveys the same message: "I'm ashamed at not yet having paid you a visit. Journalism leaves me so stupefied that I don't have an hour free." In conversation with Edmond de Goncourt, however, he was more analytical about the conflict between journalism and literature. "It seems that men of letters have never been born stiller than in our age, yet never has work been so active, so incessant," Goncourt observed on June 3, 1872, soon after Zola had bidden farewell to the Assembly. "Though sickly and anxiety-ridden, Zola works every day from 9 to half past noon and from 3 to 8 p.m. That's what's required nowadays, if one has talent and almost a name, to earn one's livelihood: 'I must plug away,' he repeats, 'and don't think it's a matter of willpower, as I am by nature excessively weak and averse to discipline. In me, obsessiveness, or an idée fixe that would make me sick if I didn't obey it, replaces willpower.' " In the language of a canal builder or a man afflicted with urinary problems, Zola explained to Goncourt how journalism helped his creative work. "Previously he'd get so choked with ideas and phrases tumbling upon him that he'd sometimes let his pen drop. Now he produces a controlled gush, a stream less copious but flowing without impediment."

It would not always be thus. The impulse to say everything at once, to picture himself either demiurgic or impotent, to despair of ever achieving greatness remained very strong indeed, and three years later, when *Les Rougon-Macquart* bulked larger by three novels, he moaned: ". . . I've still accomplished nothing! I weep over this mountain of script, I can't bear the thought that . . . nature may be too broad for my short arms to encircle it. Seeing everything, knowing everything, saying everything: that's what drives me. I'd like to crowd humanity onto a blank page, all creatures, all things—to fashion Noah's Ark." The orphan whose father had been struck down in midcourse never experienced time as plentiful or benign. Time was always short. Time killed. But covering legislative sessions instilled the habit of scrawling through thick and thin. Almost every day Zola wrote enough to fill three printed pages and, unlike Flaubert, he seldom wrote more than one draft.

In a valedictory dated May 1, 1872, he swore that he would revisit Versailles only when conservatives heeded Gambetta's call to let

Frenchmen reelect the Assembly. "The day [the Assembly] is dissolved, I shall insist on seeing the bald pates above which I spent such awful afternoons turn pale and glisten with sweat. Meanwhile I shall prove myself wiser and cleverer than they by returning to Paris." *La Cloche* gave him a more congenial assignment, and on May 4, reprieved at last from exile, Zola feted his homecoming with the first of many "Lettres parisiennes." By then he had published *La Curée.*

Zeal, ego, genius, and necessity propelled Zola, but writing twenty novels in twenty-three years would not have been possible without the method he devised for building a plot. Each volume of *Les Rougon-Macquart* sprang from a file that records its gestation, and these "*dossiers préparatoires,*" which some disciples came to regard as canonical, all take after one another more or less. "First, there's what he calls 'the Sketch,' " wrote Paul Alexis, through whom Zola advertised his routine when it behooved him to confer a scientific modus operandi on naturalism.

> He has already chosen his Rougon or Macquart, he knows in which milieu he wants to situate him and has formulated the general idea or, better, the philosophical thought that must govern the novel. Then, with pen in hand, he speculates about his character while searching for minor figures determined by the milieu. He tries to tie together some primary facts. . . . But all that is still quite vague.

As the plot developed, Zola fleshed out these skeletons and gathered material to stuff their habitat:

> The "Sketch" enters one folder, whereupon he opens another for what he calls "the Characters," assembling those who showed up in the Sketch and preparing a civil register: history, age, health, physical appearance, temperament, character, habits, relationships, etc. In short, the facts of life. Then comes the milieu. He walks the neighborhood in which a story takes place and harvests observations. He also studies the trades his characters ply and inspects the decor that will furnish important scenes. This technical detail fills yet another folder. Documents culled from specialized works are likewise classified, along with information provided by friends and numerous letters solicited from acquaintances able to shed light on some particular point.

Although the above sequence varied, and sometimes cost Zola immense travail (he often discarded preliminary sketches), the result was always a dossier several hundred pages thick containing all he needed to draft a rough outline, episode by episode:

> First he combs the principal facts out of his "Sketch" and assigns each its chapter. He then does the same with his "Characters": here so-and-so's physical appearance, there a prominent trait, further along the personality change someone else exhibits under the pressure of events. . . . Gradually, every detail falls into place. Neighborhood, house, pivotal scenes [are] cadenced, balanced, distributed according to the dictates of the narrative.

Not until he had mapped the course of each chapter in a second, more detailed outline did Zola feel confident that his imagination was unlikely to founder on some hidden reef. Once the voyage began, his course was unswerving. He would sequester himself with his documentation and index cards near at hand, consult them every morning, resume his narrative where he had left off the previous day (often in mid-sentence), and advance a measured league. By the day's end he would usually have written about four pages with no margins on lined foolscap, in a firm, neat script. "M. Zola makes no drafts," Dr. Edouard Toulouse later observed. "What he writes is ready for the printer and his pages show few crossings-out, even though he doesn't wait for a sentence to have formed in his head before taking up his pen . . . He never goes back, never leaves a blank when the right expression doesn't present itself right away. Further, he needs his daily task. In this respect he has remained a sensible, well-behaved schoolboy." Other than his dossiers, Zola's only regular companions were a desk dictionary, a Noël et Chapsal grammar, and a handbook of verb forms.

The 469-page dossier from which *La Curée* emerged shows Zola at his most assiduous. He began this novel before he had finished *La Fortune des Rougon* and, spurred by the contractual agreement to produce two titles a year, wrote much of it between April and August 1870. It followed him south when war broke out, but his hectic peregrinations left little time for art. Completed during the summer or fall of 1871, it was published serially in *La Cloche* beginning on September 29.

With *La Curée (The Rush for the Spoils)*, *Les Rougon-Macquart* enters Second Empire Paris, where Aristide Rougon, after escaping the walled town that nurtured his appetites, runs riot in the wide-open space of a goldfield staked out by parvenus. "Aristide gets rich through expropriation, demolition, construction, speculation," Zola noted. "This fortune must reflect Paris itself: lightning-quick transformations, a rage for pleasure, a blindness of squandering, then a terrible crash. Like Monsieur Haussmann, Aristide conjures useless luxury out of empty pockets. Reckless, he embodies . . . the wealth displayed in Paris's new mansions, all façade." Façades, conjury, theater are what Zola set out to describe. Mindful of Balzac, he inspected ornate town houses built on the rubble of old neighborhoods and reconnoitered the Bois de Boulogne, through whose manicured groves *le tout Paris* ritually paraded their carriages. He read every society column and from *Le Figaro* clipped articles about the finery women wore to balls at the Tuileries or Saint-Cloud. He consulted *Les Travaux de Paris* for a surveyor's picture of the new capital taking shape around him. He studied the laws governing expropriation, the penetralia of government bureaucracy, the mechanism of credit banks, and above all the expedients by which a zealous prefect bent on reinventing Paris, even if it meant bankrupting France, had raised money without legislative approval. The preparatory file abounds in such information. But it also tells us that Zola reread the great seventeenth-century dramatist Jean Racine with a view to using his masterpiece as the backdrop for a drama in which ill-gotten gains breed and license monstrous fantasies. "What I'm about to write is decidedly a new *Phèdre,*" he reflected halfway through the Sketch.

With his wife, Angèle, and his young daughter, Clotilde, Aristide Rougon flies north several weeks after Louis Napoleon's coup d'état, "like a bird of prey drawn by the scent of the battlefield." Expecting Paris to yield him riches overnight, he chafes when his brother Eugène, now minister of the interior, offers him the job of "*commissaire voyer assistant,*" or assistant commissioner of roads, at City Hall. It soon dawns on him that Eugène has given him a strategic advantage in the treasure hunt rather than a job, for City Hall is where Baron Haussmann perches, and as road commissioner, Aristide (who changes his name from Rougon to Saccard) quickly uncovers plans detailing Paris's imminent metamorphosis. This knowledge sparks the realization that avenues not yet built will enrich men prompt enough to acquire doomed tenements, unscrupulous enough to jack up their value, and aggressive enough to bribe officials charged with the task of indemnifying expropriated landlords. "When he stood by the window and felt beneath him the gigantic labor of Paris, he was seized by a mad impulse to leap into the forge and knead the gold with his feverish hands, like soft wax."

Impecunious and family-bound, Aristide marks time until Angèle dies of consumption. Her corpse is still warm when the parvenu contacts his sister, Sidonie Rougon, whom Zola modeled after Balzac's louche go-betweens. Ferreting out dirty secrets, brokering marriages, procuring concubines for rich men and paramours for lovelorn ladies, selling both furniture and flesh in a world where everything is auctionable, Sidonie counts among her supplicants nineteen-year-old Renée Béraud du Châtel. Fresh from convent school, this daughter of a former magistrate who abhors Parisian licentiousness has been made pregnant by a married man. Someone is needed to impersonate the seducer and legitimize the unborn child. Sidonie recruits Aristide, who confers his name, or his pseudonym, on Renée in return for a dowry that will, through the magic of credit, generate millions.

The fetus dies, but no one mourns it on the whirligig of sexual intrigue and unbridled speculation where Saccard soon finds himself riding high, along with Renée and an adolescent son whom he had left behind in Plassans. That son, Maxime, looks every bit the androgyne. "At thirteen he was already terribly knowing. His was one of those frail and precocious natures in which the senses develop early. Vice appeared even before desire awakened. Twice he had almost been expelled from school. Renée, who had experience in detecting grace beneath frumpy, provincial garb, noticed that the little Napoleon, as she dubbed him, smiled, turned his neck, extended his arms with the mincing air of well-bred demoiselles." While Renée grooms him for the upper-class follies in which he will participate as a kind of depraved Chérubin, Saccard loots Paris tract by tract and after several years builds himself a town house overlooking the Parc Monceau, a monument to Second Empire hedonism that exhibits not only the success of his machinations but the vulgarity of his breed. Volutes of sculpted foliage wind around the windows. Gilt drips from wrought-iron balconies. Immense urns with tongues of flame surmount its roof. Sinuous nudes line the façade, dot the garden, and flank the grand staircase. Majolica, silk, marble, velvet are ubiquitous, and the floral counterpart to this glut of rich material is a jungle of tropical plants proliferating through a hothouse in whose midst, like *la bête humaine* triumphant, stands a black sphinx. "The hothouse, which resembled a church nave with slender iron columns soaring upward to support an arched glass roof, displayed its pulpy vegetation, its sheets of powerful leaves, its blooming sprays of verdure."

The residents of this soulless mansion have no center. Hectored by an insatiable appetite for change, they move incessantly, joining kindred itinerants at the Bourse, in the Bois de Boulogne, at the Tuileries, in one another's boudoirs or in gastronomic temples that double as houses of assignation. It matters little where they go provided the escapade yields some novel pleasure, and their sorties take them from imperial balls to obstreperous dance halls. "[They] loved the new Paris," Zola writes of Renée and Maxime. "They would often cruise through town in a carriage and make detours to see avenues they found particularly irresistible. From the swift brougham they'd follow the gray strips of wide pavement, endless, with their benches, their parti-colored columns, their slender trees." As movement induces eu-

phoria, stillness breeds despair, which means that there can be no rest
for the affluent gadabouts of La Curée, who live from day to day, vainly
seeking heaven in yet another liaison, in tomorrow's financial coup, in
ever more commotion. Thronged by acquisitive humanity, the Boulevard runs to an empty horizon.

Emptiness torments Renée, whose voyeuristic jaunts through Paris
evoke Emma Bovary's blind cab ride through Rouen. Like Emma, Renée feels trapped by life, but her fantasies of escape roost at home.
Where the village belle imagined herself reborn free in Paris, the Parisian locates transcendence in an underworld reserved for egregious
sinners. Where Flaubert's heroine spurned husband and daughter, Zola's commits incest with her stepson Maxime. "[She] grew accustomed
to her fault as to a new gown whose stiffness made her uncomfortable
at first. She followed fashions of the day, she dressed and undressed
in accordance with them and came to believe that hers was a world
exempt from common morality, where the senses achieved superior
refinement. . . . Evil became an ornament, a flower stuck in her hair
or a jewel hung on her brow." Renée dominates her effete stepson
and never visits her father. Between the Parc Monceau and the Ile
Saint-Louis, between the phantasmagoric realm whose preeminent
symbol is a hothouse ruled by a sphinx and the sober, seventeenth-
century mansion of a bourgeois patriarch, yawns an abyss.

That abyss swallows her in due course. The invertebrate Maxime
plays Renée's clandestine game until his father finds him a homely
young heiress to wed. Having learned about the incestuous liaison,
Saccard sees in it not grounds for divorce or murder but an opportunity for blackmail, and extorts from his wife what remains of her
dowry. Left with nothing, neither the fortune Béraud du Châtel had
provided her nor the dark secret that had become yet another trap,
Renée meets an end reminiscent of Emma's. She aggressively squanders borrowed money and then dies, though not before revisiting the
Ile Saint-Louis and mourning her lost innocence.

Prominent throughout Les Rougon-Macquart are scenes in which
Zola's mercurial characters gather for a banquet or ball that invariably
disintegrates into a melee, and one such scene marks the climax of La
Curée. A gala at Saccard's town house brings together ruttish dames
and unscrupulous profiteers, including a prefect with literary pretensions who has gotten the women to perform three tableaux vivants
based upon his poem Les Amours du beau Narcisse et de la nymphe
Echo. This meretricious allegory—which features costumes designed
for the event by Paris's reigning couturier, one Worms—mirrors the
larger plot. And it is also a spirited attack on the Englishman Charles
Frederick Worth, whose House of Worth at 7, rue de la Paix was a
sartorial mecca for rich women throughout the world. As Narcissus,

Maxime plays himself, while Renée as a lovelorn nymph seeks help first from Venus, then from Plutus, invoking the God of Wealth when the Goddess of Love fails to sway her self-infatuated tormentor. Zola's description makes it clear how utterly ridiculous he found the *féeries* or spectaculars that entranced Second Empire audiences:[8]

A new grotto appeared, but this one was not Venus's cool retreat bathed by wavelets dying on a pearl-strewn shore; it lay near the earth's molten core, in a fissure of hell, in the crevice of a mine Plutus called home. Silk made to simulate rock revealed wide, metallic seams. . . . Permitting himself a bold anachronism, M. Hupel de la Noue had carpeted the stage with twenty-franc coins—louis scattered everywhere and piled several feet high. Atop this gold mound sat Madame de Guende as Plutus, Plutus baring her bosom, Plutus robed in laminae of various metals and surrounded by the efflorescences . . . Madame Haffner, with a skirt episcopal in its stiffness and splendor, embodied Gold; Madame d'Espanet gleaming like a moonbeam was Silver; and Madame de Lauwerens, all fiery blue, was Sapphire. . . . Upstage, the drama sputtered on; Echo kept tempting Narcissus, Narcissus kept waving her off.

In death Narcissus grows green satin limbs. He emerges, that is, as yet another hothouse bloom, thanks to the virtuosity of Worms, who, like some primitive shaman, lords it over a make-believe world.

Where trollops sport aristocratic names, designing dresses is tantamount to creating selves, and Worms's mannequins, free at last from *Les Amours du beau Narcisse*, cavort around Saccard's villa much the way they cavort around Napoleon III's Paris. "The costume ball began," Zola writes.

It opened with a quadrille: "*Ah! il a des bottes, il a des bottes, Bastien!*," which was all the rage in low dance halls. . . . The billow of women dressed for every land and every period rose in a swarm, a

[8]As much can be said of high society's self-made entertainments. Zola undoubtedly remembered a revue staged in 1867 and described by Harold Kurtz in his biography of the Empress Eugénie: "The Empress had great faith in stylish entertainments as a kind of political tonic, and perhaps the Court's most notable contribution to the gaieties of 1867 was a repeat performance at the Théâtre des Variétés of *The Commentaries of Caesar*, a revue written and produced by Philippe de Massa at Compiègne in 1865 and performed by a group of distinguished amateurs, among whom Princess Metternich was the uncontested star. She was *commère*, she sang a little ditty as a *vivandière* of the Zouaves, another as a Parisian cabby and finally appeared, wearing a gorgeous dress of white satin trimmed with musical notes in black, as the embodiment of the *Chanson* of which the chorus went: "Dérider tous les fronts,/ C'était mon privilège/ Et les bouchons de Liège/ Sautaient jusqu'aux plafonds."

medley of bright fabric. After mixing colors and sweeping them away, the rhythmic pandemonium would suddenly, at a bow stroke, bring back the same pink satin tunic, the same blue velvet bodice, alongside the same black suit. Then another bow stroke or trumpet blast sent the couples round the ballroom single file, swinging like a balloon gondola torn from its moorings. On and on, uninterruptedly, for hours.

As *La Fortune des Rougon* culminates in a march of insurgents who "flood" the countryside, so *La Curée* leads to a cotillion of Offenbachian dervishes driven by greed and lust who trample history underfoot, discard patronymics, raze neighborhoods, muddle genres and genders, violate immemorial taboos. We have seen how obsessively Zola imagined *la bête humaine* ruining discrete space, and ruin it it does in this mad scene. Ballroom, bedroom, and dining room merge as frenzied dancers become promiscuous lovers and promiscuous lovers indistinguishable gluttons:

> When they opened the dining room, which had been rearranged buffet style with sideboards against the wall and a long food-laden table in the middle, everyone stampeded. . . . People threw themselves on the pâtisseries and the stuffed fowl, elbowing one another savagely. It was a sack. Myriad hands pawed cold cuts, and lackeys didn't know to whom they were answerable amidst this mob of gentlefolk whose outstretched arms expressed naked fear of arriving too late and finding platters empty.

That hollow men abhor a void is the principle informing *La Curée*. Shapeless, they wreak havoc. Empty, they must fill and fill and go on filling until Judgment Day.

Zola's own Judgment Day came on November 5, 1871, when, after publishing twenty-eight installments of *La Curée* in *La Cloche*, Louis Ulbach reluctantly cut it short. There had been a storm of protest from readers who found the novel morally repugnant, and certain right-wing papers hastened to characterize Zola as a Communard. "In literature, M. Zola belongs to the Vallès gang, who mistake smut for realism. Politically we know what this school, which is mother to the Commune, has nurtured," wrote one journalist.[9] Besieged by complaints,

---

[9]The journalist may have had in mind Vallès's novel *L'Argent*, whose main character was, like Saccard, modeled in part on the financier Mirès. Having founded a radical paper called *Le Cri du peuple* late in 1870, Vallès participated actively in the Commune, fled to England, and was condemned to death in absentia. Zola knew him from his Hachette days, but was never more than a sympathetic acquaintance.

the public prosecutor warned Zola during an otherwise cordial interview that he might take stern measures if *La Cloche* did not stop serializing *La Curée* forthwith.

Sooner than risk prosecution, Zola, in a letter-manifesto that appeared on page one, urged Ulbach to comply. "This debate isn't yours, and I daresay you are even hostile to my literary school," he declared. "You've attacked me in the past, you might do so again. But between us it would be a writers' quarrel. You would tell me what you've already told me and I would reiterate what I've already said. You would not impugn my motives as a novelist." Written with the intention of showing "how everything caves in when mores are rotten and family ties go slack," *La Curée* was not pornography but history: "Must I name names, tear off masks to prove that I am a historian . . . ? It would be useless, wouldn't it? Those names are on everybody's lips. You know my characters, and you yourself could whisper unrecountable facts to me." It exasperated him that France's ordeals had not made her more hospitable to reality, that in the matter of self-deception and censorship there was so little to choose between republic and empire:

> I still find it very odd that the person who warned me of the danger presented by this satire about imperial France is a republican prosecutor. We French don't know how to love freedom in a complete and virile way. We fancy ourselves the custodians of morality. We cannot accept the idea that shame, if it is genuine, polices itself without summoning gendarmes. What do you make, for example, of those who denounced my novel to the authorities? . . . Not one thought of burning the *feuilleton*. They all whine like little children gone astray and they call the watch. . . . As I told the public prosecutor just now, a people terrified of bogeys and in need of protection will never win true freedom.

Zola suggested, in conclusion, that pious Frenchmen settle accounts with the Lord by crossing themselves before bookstores displaying *La Curée*.

Despite this judicial charade, *La Curée* went virtually unnoticed when it appeared several months later between book covers. Young friends wrote encomiums, but older ones did not accord it the same warm reception they had given *La Fortune des Rougon*. Did Flaubert, for example, take a dim view of Emma travestied as Renée, and of marionettelike personae who can't quite make one ignore the strings that jerk them? Or was it that *La Curée* followed too quickly on the heels of *La Fortune*? Reading Zola threatened to become a full-time diversion, and with *La Tentation de Saint-Antoine* almost complete, Flaubert had much to occupy him.

Zola's book publisher proved distinctly unhelpful. Encumbered with debts that he had brought upon himself by investing in some speculative real estate venture, Albert Lacroix was struggling to stay afloat and, not long after *La Curée*'s appearance, went under. The irony of it all might have amused Zola, if another firm had stood ready to adopt *Les Rougon-Macquart*. But it soon became obvious that publishers did not want the controversial orphan. Difficult months would pass before Zola could begin to realize that this contretemps had been a blessing in disguise.

XI

CONFRONTING THE MORAL
ORDER

L A CLOCHE OCCUPIED cramped quarters on the mezzanine of a
dilapidated seventeenth-century tenement at 5, rue Coq-Héron,
halfway between the Palais-Royal gardens and Paris's central market. It was basically one large room, furnished with secondhand chairs
no two of which matched, and caricatures by Gill that had been hung
over discolored patches of wallpaper. Daylight filtered from an inner
courtyard through low, narrow windows, bathing the employees in a
crepuscular gloom that often suited their political outlook. Everything
spoke of impermanence and neglect. The boy responsible for tidying
up was always running errands, so the trouser seats of the editorial
staff served as dust mops. This squalor, the din from rotary presses
operated by Dubuisson and Company downstairs, and the large, be-
spectacled figure of Louis Ulbach, whose financial embarrassments
made him a sour man, discouraged camaraderie. Zola, for one, would
deliver his copy and hurry away. Even if he had relished it, he could
not have afforded much casual conversation with fellow journalists, to
judge from his output. Between May 4 and late December 1872, when
it folded, *La Cloche* published 110 "Lettres parisiennes" (versions of
which also appeared as "Lettres de Paris" in *Le Sémaphore de Marseille*). While writing his 1,200-word piece every second or third day,
Zola began work on yet another novel, *Le Ventre de Paris*.

It behooved him to respect the territory of various colleagues at *La
Cloche* (among them young Paul Alexis, whom Ulbach hired on Zola's
recommendation), but there was no interdiction against making occasional forays through literature and art. So, in a very early "Lettre

253

parisienne," he anathematized the operettas, the illusionist *féeries*, and the conventional dramas or "well-made plays" larded with worldly wisdom à la Alexandre Dumas *fils* that constituted the bulk of theatrical fare to be had on Paris's Boulevard. "[The theater] is dying for lack of blood," he announced on May 5.

> Since 1830, since Victor Hugo's innovations and triumphs, no one has dared to fight for something new on the stage. Comic verve has fizzled and familiar tragic themes have been worn thin. Nowadays, art is the business of lengthening strings, of knotting them differently, of winding up dolls and making them skip left if one's predecessors made them skip right. We have impotent playwrights skilled at humoring the public and minting money from crude ore. If anyone tried something new, you would hear a general hue and cry. Heaven forfend that the contract between theatergoers and their usual purveyors should be infringed upon. Gentle people would, with good reason, accuse you of blundering. Others, more ferocious, would call you dangerous and immoral. In France, he who seeks the truth offends decency and exposes society to grave peril.

This indictment of bourgeois taste resumed on May 12, when art became its object. The Salon having just opened after a two-year intermission, there was little to cheer the modernist at Paris's huge Palace of Industry, apart from several works by Boudin, Puvis de Chavannes, Jongkind, and Manet (*Le Combat du Kearsarge et de l'Alabama*). War had killed at least 150,000 Frenchmen since 1870, but Academic personae suffered no casualties. They had grown even more numerous, it seemed, and Zola deplored their fecundity.

> I meekly followed the crowd for three hours as it led me past all sorts of oddities, past nude women and well-dressed men who looked at me with a bewildered air, past Bretons and Provençaux and colors that made my head throb. . . . When I finally left, rain pelted me. Some ways off, I could blurrily see the ruined Tuileries, its windows wide open to a dirty-yellow sky. Two whole years! So very many shocks! Yet here, in these selfsame halls, are the same gingerbread gents and sugarcane ladies.

Ridiculing medals awarded by the jury as incestuous valentines, he declared official patronage to be the death of art. "Modern art will not flourish until government leaves it alone; . . . artists aren't prefects, which means that they need no minister to keep them in line."

Cultural politics went hand in hand with France's political imbroglio, and Versailles furnished grist for Zola's mill. No longer required to maintain some semblance of objectivity, he unleashed his satirical powers on the Catholic-royalist faction in one broadside after another. Deputies who supported the pretender, Chambord, became clowns, lunatics, and outright brigands. They troop through the "Lettres parisiennes" like revenants from a primitive world, subverting republicanism much the way heredity subverts reason in *Les Rougon-Macquart*. "At this moment, princes are rebelling," he observed. "When you hear gunshots, tell yourself that some prince has launched an insurrection. Barricades are now monarchical and responsibility for protecting legal order has devolved upon the common people." His picture of society being undermined not from below but from above, by anachronistic grandees rather than by uncouth plebeians, was drawn even more vividly in an article that featured the Bonaparte clan. "Strange family that won't die, that persists through its pale and moribund offspring. They have the ups and downs of adventurers—pockets empty today, coffers full tomorrow. They live in palaces, they die on rocks. They coin money with our blood and they are always there, at our throats or at the bottom of some ditch, waiting to ambush us." While Bonapartists, royalists, and Orleanists whited their various sepulchres, Zola etched irreverent graffiti thereon, lest Frenchmen idealize a past seemingly devoid of problems that beset the present.

Nothing pleased him more than Thiers's decision to close the Museum of Sovereigns, where Napoleonic bric-a-brac had been stored along with Capetian memorabilia. "Napoleon I's wardrobe was complete; the breeches, the waistcoats, the capes, even the linen. Oh, muse of history, your grave voice should sing these items—shirts in which the great man clothed his sacred person, hankies still moist with the sweat of Waterloo, socks warm from his last campaign! The aroma of the hero would penetrate you as you contemplated garments which a pious family had not allowed anyone to wash. . . . The crowd [also] caught this odor, and tears of regret filled all eyes." What justification could there be, he asked, for commemorating royal hose? "History suffices unto the glory or the shame of kings," he replied. "When some poor devil dies intestate, one auctions off his rags. So now kings have died, and the Republic is cleaning house."[1]

[1]This imagery foreshadows *L'Assommoir*, where the collapse of Gervaise Macquart, who had seemingly put the past behind her, or "cleaned house," when she opened a laundry, is heralded by her succumbing to the odor of dirty wash. Smell recurs throughout Zola's work as the sense that holds civilization hostage to a quadruped. Militantly progressivist, he nonetheless feared that mankind might follow its nose downward and would perhaps have found particularly congenial this passage from Freud's *Civilization and Its Discontents*: "[I conjecture] that with the assumption of an erect posture by man and with the depreciation of his sense of smell, it was not only his anal eroticism which threatened to fall victim to organic repression, but the whole of his sexuality; so that since this, the sexual

Political atavism was not only political, of course. To republicans, monarchy harbored the prospect of Catholic priests everywhere lording it over laymen, closing schools, and transforming France into an idiot child of Rome. "Royalists and Bonapartists feel that the danger lies there, in future generations who will know how to read and will no longer stoop before the Catholic police," wrote Zola. "Thus, lay schools, humble though they still are, frighten them, and they make a supreme effort to thwart a bloodless revolution more redoubtable for altar and throne than the guillotine of '93." To be sure, many Catholic theologians had been embarrassed by Pius IX's *Syllabus of Errors*, and liberal Catholics far outnumbered the so-called Intransigeants in the government at Versailles.[2] But Intransigeants spoke very loud indeed, and their organ, *L'Univers*, which regularly reported instances of divine intervention, was a God-given straight man for Zola to taunt. Reading about an incurable paralytic who recovered motor function after pledging himself to a novena, he suggested hilariously that the Jesuits, in whose chapel the miracle had taken place, operate on certain royalist deputies:

I know people who need you. You should, above all, open a branch at Versailles, where diseases of the spinal marrow abound. Other parts have gone soft as well and curing them would enhance your reputation. Besides, you owe it to your friends. M. Du Temple gets violent headaches, which make him feel that his skull is splitting and his brain flying among the stars. . . . M. de Belcastel has a single crack, but it requires immediate attention. Many gentlemen are unable, in their slumber, to digest the Republic: one fell ill when the Orleanist-Bourbon fusion didn't work [and] another, who exists on

---

function has been accompanied by a repugnance which cannot further be accounted for, and which prevents its complete satisfaction and forces it away from the sexual aim into sublimations and libidinal displacements. . . . All neurotics, and many others besides, take exception to the fact that *inter urinas et faeces nascimur*. The genitals, too, give rise to strong sensations of smell which many people cannot tolerate and which spoil sexual intercourse for them. Thus we should find that the deepest root of the sexual repression which advances along with civilization is the organic defense of the new form of life achieved with man's erect gait against his earlier animal existence."

[2]One may infer the embarrassment of Catholic theologians from the Dogmatic Constitution of Catholic Faith, in which the Vatican Council, attempting a compromise with secular knowledge, declared on April 24, 1870: "The Church neither ignores nor despises the benefits to human life which result from the arts and sciences, but confesses that, as they come from God, the Lord of all science, so, if they be rightly used, they lead to God by the help of his grace. Nor does the Church forbid that each of these sciences in its sphere should make use of its principles and its own method."

lily salads, has grown dangerously anemic. So you see, it's high time you administered novenas to this sick ward.

Zola's anticlericalism flared anew several weeks later, when *L'Univers* brought forth some peasant afflicted with a tumor that had made her stomach swell, to the utter bewilderment of every doctor who examined it. "[Only after science failed] did Heaven intervene," Zola wrote, tongue in cheek.

Françoise Roussel had already done several novenas at Notre-Dame-de-la-Salette. I cite this exquisite detail as it is intended to encourage the faithful. But Françoise was stubborn in her piety. She began yet another novena, drank a glass of miraculous water every day, applied to her stomach compresses soaked in that water, and, during the eighth night . . . well, here tact is required, and I shall quote *L'Univers* lest someone accuse me of immorality. "On the eighth day, between midnight and 2 a.m., she felt something like an invisible hand rubbing her stomach very gently. Under the influence of this friction, her disease seemed to melt, flow down her lower limbs, and disappear." Oh, invisible hand, gentle hand that roams over the bellies of young women, hand that cures swellings of the abdomen and drives them out the cellar door! If I had invented you—I, an immoral novelist— there would not be stones enough in clerical gardens to smash my head.

How strange, he went on to say, that the beneficiaries of such magic should invariably come from poor, devout, rural families. "Their God has a real predilection for cooks, farm girls, tenders of geese and turkeys. He doesn't traffic with chambermaids, and gentlewomen . . . can expect nothing from him, not even a cure for the common cold."

Erotic dreams masquerading as holy intercessions were all very well, but Zola wanted a real, live Tartuffe, and in September 1872, soon after newspapers reported that a Jesuit named Father Dufour had been caught fondling a female parishioner in a train compartment, he swooped on the culprit with talons bared.[3] "When the Jesuit Dufour was found holding Mme de Valmont on his lap, he uttered a dreadful phrase, a phrase only a priest could utter, and which would sound monstrous if it came from any other mouth," he began. "While the poor woman stammered out the sly, scared alibi of little children, 'We haven't done anything wrong,' Dufour calmly added—and his naiveté

[3]The figure of Tartuffe had preoccupied him for some time. Reviewing Victorien Sardou's *Séraphine* in the January 9, 1869, issue of *La Tribune*, he declared that there was a play to be written about the destruction brought upon the brain of certain women by a modern Tartuffe.

reveals the abyss yawning beneath this otherwise commonplace tale of a wayward priest: 'Besides, Madame is my sister.' " As Françoise Roussel's example lent credence to the idea that sexual fantasies beget mystical hallucinations, so Father Dufour's misdemeanor argued an intimate relationship between penitence and erotism. For Zola, who had written about people seeking love at fairground peep shows in one of his earliest stories, the confessional booth was antechamber to the bedroom:

> I see the Jesuit Dufour in his confessional on one of those warm summer afternoons when the church is cool, incense still lingers from the last mass and soft light filters through a stained-glass window, discreetly, casting blue shade over one corner. Beneath the vault there is no sound except the beadle's cough. Women who look faint as they sit on tilted-back chairs, their foreheads cupped in their hands, await the tender joy of confession. Now and then a low whisper, a sigh of gladness emanates from the confessional. A penitent has been penetrated by grace and ascends to heaven. The others, all impatient, quiver with desire. And each in turn, when summoned, approaches with mincing steps and fluttering heart, wearing the vague smile of a woman about to enter Jesus' alcove.

The threat of aristocrat hooligans wreaking political havoc had an analogue in the moral realm, where men vested with spiritual authority excited fantasies that were inimical to social order. Zola portrayed the Church as a playground ruled by an archaic brotherhood that sanctified the "lower" self and undermined lawful marriages while promoting forbidden liaisons. "[Confessor and penitent] have grown together as far as two beings can with a board between them. The moral marriage is consummated, and the dream of physical marriage throws them into each other's arms when they sleep. Theirs is a state of beatitude like no other; woman and eunuch bound by ties of carnal mysticism that make them monstrous kin; brother turns lover and joy turns incestuous." It was time, he concluded, for priests to come out of the closet and license the man inside the frock.

With his diatribe on Father Dufour (which announced a theme he later orchestrated to brilliant effect in *La Conquête de Plassans*) Zola went beyond the bounds of tolerable contumely. One right-wing paper, *Le Pays*, declared that he should be treated as a common criminal and locked up for indecent assault, or *attentat à la pudeur*. But conservatives were not alone in berating him. His own employer, who, it will be recalled, had once condemned *Thérèse Raquin* on moral grounds, took strong exception to the piece. "Zola's article on Father Dufour is quite simply *obscene* and *dangerous*," Ulbach notified *La*

Cloche's editor-in-chief, Théophile Guérin. "If we didn't have friends in high office, it would be curtains for us, and even so I'm not sure we're safe. . . . What we absolutely need is an editor to vet every word of copy and underline scabrous passages, repetitions, stylistic infelicities." Though proving again and again that he was indeed "dangerous" may have been half the reason for starting fights, this did not prevent Zola from pleading innocent when someone gave him his due. "Ah! my dear Ulbach, how the artist in me would, if I did not exercise restraint, blast that letter you wrote to Guérin!" he exclaimed. "Obscene! It's the word every Mr. Pompous uses nowadays, which makes me suspect that it doesn't belong to you at all but was planted on your person in some government office. . . . Oh, that word! If only you know how stupid I find it." As for having a censor vet his articles, "I think it's a very good idea," he went on cheerfully. "That way I shall no longer constitute a public menace. Your shareholders and friends will sleep the sleep of the chaste."

Of greater immediate consequence for both men than their spat was Ulbach's financial predicament. As early as November 1872, word spread that *La Cloche* might not see another year, and, indeed, the last issue appeared on December 21. By then Zola had entered negotiations with a paper called *Le Corsaire*, where his early novel *Les Mystères de Marseille* was being serialized anew under the title *Un Duel social* (and signed "Agrippa"). Honor-bound to stay aboard *La Cloche* until it sank but determined not to find himself marooned when it did, he proposed a Sunday causerie in which literary matters would overshadow questions of political moment. The publisher, Edouard Portalis, bought the idea, and so began a collaboration that ended in disaster.

Despite his promise to treat politics gingerly, Zola could not let 1872 go without dampening the artificial cheer of Christmastide. On December 22 he inveighed against social injustice in the sketch "Le Lendemain de la crise," which depicts an unemployed laborer frantically seeking work. As the laborer pursues his futile quest, four right-wing notables are seen gorging themselves:

Meanwhile there is a political dinner at Monsieur de Broglie's establishment. They've not yet gotten through the roast. Among friends, one speaks one's mind freely. They discuss petitions sent to M. Thiers by tradesmen and industrialists. M. de Lorgeril, whose mouth is stuffed with a very delicate pheasant breast, says, while wiping his lips, that Paris should count itself lucky for not having been razed. The host nods in agreement and speaks about the finger of God. Is poverty not divine punishment? M. d'Audriffret-Pasquier then flashes one of his wry smiles as he observes that if republicans are dying of hunger, it's the Republic's fault. This cheers M. Batbie, who is morose; he hasn't seen enough funeral corteges on the street, and urchins he's met in the populous quarters seem rather too robust.

Zola never relents. The worker finally trudges home empty-handed to his starving brood, while the deputies, overcome by their gastronomic exertions, fall asleep and dream of the ministerial portfolios they will acquire once the Republic has been toppled. "All that shows above their eiderdowns is the rosette they wear even at night."

No sooner did this acerbic little sketch appear in print than Portalis realized that it invited serious reprisals. He tried to atone for the piece by having Zola resign immediately, but half measures would not placate the enemy. Conservative organs demanded vengeance ("Bring Emile Zola to trial! Let him be judged and condemned!" cried *Le Pays*), while at Versailles right-wing deputies stampeded the rostrum. Thiers's ministers met in great haste. The majority, though not Thiers himself, felt that realpolitik justified a token sacrifice, and their callous view sat well with General Ladmirault, who wielded extraordinary power as governor of Paris. *Le Corsaire's* fate was sealed. Deaf to republican fulminations, Ladmirault abolished the paper for having published "articles that incite hatred and scorn among citizens and attack the rights and authority of the National Assembly."

This minor quake, which signaled a division that was to convulse France two decades later with the Dreyfus Affair, gave Zola deep satisfaction. What it cost him in income it earned him in kudos, and letters expressing admiration—some written by grateful workers— swelled his year-end mail. It also worked to the advantage of *Les Rougon-Macquart*, for which he had meanwhile found a new publisher, Georges Charpentier. "I'm sorry you haven't been here during these last few days," he wrote on December 25 to Marius Roux, who had lighted up Christmas at 14, rue de la Condamine with a gift of smoked eel from Normandy. "The blow dealt *Le Corsaire* has had enormous repercussions. Newspapers short of copy over the holidays have thrown themselves on my article. I've lost some money, but the formidable publicity compensates for it. Charpentier is having posters printed. I for my part am writing a pamphlet, a response or, rather, a defense. I shall wait until Monday or Tuesday before releasing it so as not to create the impression that I'm touting my custom. It's less a financial coup than a shot across the bow."

Charpentier was an imprint that had enjoyed wide recognition long before Georges Charpentier could read. His father, Gervais, had transformed the book business during Louis Philippe's regime, when, around 1838, he began publishing volumes in a format smaller than octavo (6 by 9 inches) and selling them cheap, at three and a half francs. This departure from tradition allowed people of modest means to buy serious literature even as it made it possible for serious writers to survive or enrich themselves. Bound between the wan yellow covers of La Bibliothèque Charpentier, which preceded the Everyman's Library by six decades, Musset entered households throughout France, alongside Théophile Gautier, Charles Nodier, Victor Hugo, Gérard de Nerval, Edgar Quinet, and Théodore de Banville. With some four hundred titles in stock, Gervais Charpentier drove a thriving trade until the 1860s. Then, as old age approached, everything collapsed around him. Rival publishers caught up, his marriage dissolved, his authors fled, and the emergence of realism killed his interest in belles lettres. A glorious shambles was what Georges Charpentier inherited in 1871, at the age of twenty-five.

Far from sharing his father's aversion to literary realism, Georges and his partner, Maurice Dreyfous, put Zola high on a list of authors they hoped to capture. Thrilled by his talent, both young men recognized in Les Rougon-Macquart the material with which to build a house of contemporary design, and fortune smiled upon them when Lacroix-Verboeckhoven suddenly went bankrupt in early 1872. "We didn't have [Zola's] address and knew nothing about him except that he covered legislative sessions for La Cloche," wrote Dreyfous, the son of prosperous Alsatian Jews, who, spurning a career in finance, had marched resolutely leftward under Napoleon III and in 1870 contributed articles to Ulbach's opposition journal. "I sought him out at the National Assembly. He seemed baffled by my words and treated me a bit gruffly . . . as he hurried toward the press gallery." Strange to say, Zola had not yet heard about Gervais Charpentier's death, which occurred soon after the Bloody Week of May 21–28. Laboring under the misapprehension that Dreyfous represented a firm even less likely to appreciate Les Rougon-Macquart than those which had rejected it since January (among them Michel Lévy, Flaubert's publisher), he found the overture inexplicable but agreed, out of desperation, to meet his suitors at their office on the quai du Louvre. "I can still see him seated on the tired little mahogany sofa covered in imitation leather whose least serious defect was that one slid forward every time one moved," Dreyfous recalled. "He was dressed modestly, his usual clothier being La Belle Jardinière, the department store where he outfitted himself throughout his life. Very shy yet full of the quiet and reasoned assurance by which truly strong men manifest their will and self-confidence, he seemed quite disoriented at first. Before long, however, the charm Charpentier exerted on everyone who came near him took hold."

Once Zola felt comfortable, he stated his desiderata, though not without coy protestations to the effect that they were the stuff of dreams:

Here, gentlemen, is what I would like. I would like a fixed monthly retainer so that I can work and not have to worry about putting bread on the table for my wife, my mother, and myself. It would take five hundred francs to cover my expenses, in return for which I would give you two novels a year. You would publish them wherever you like, in whatever form suits you, even as serials. I must warn you that in the last respect you will have a hard time of it, as newspapers eschew my novels. So you see, practically speaking, such pretensions can make no sense to businessmen like yourselves; they hardly make any to me.

For rebels who had only just emerged from bohemia, the impracticality of the venture was reason the more to undertake it, and within forty-eight hours they told Zola they would meet his terms. "That is how two very young men following the dictates of their heart and yielding to their enthusiasm committed a wonderful act of folly," wrote Drey-fous. "The adage that 'the heart has reasons which reason knows nothing of' applies. This time, exceptionally, the heart was lucky enough to conceive a profitable idea." On July 22, 1872, during one brief session, they drew up a contract that vouchsafed Zola a monthly retainer and guaranteed Charpentier publication rights over Zola's work for a period of ten years.

However sincere these contractual vows, neither publisher nor author could have felt safe in predicting that they would still be together in 1882. Experience did not argue for optimism. But their whirlwind courtship was, against all odds, to result in one of the nineteenth century's happiest and most durable alliances. Charpentier hid nothing from Zola, as we shall see, and when *Les Rougon-Macquart* became lucrative he willingly offered him the full measure of his success. Zola, in turn, gave Charpentier carte blanche, relying upon him to negotiate the sale of foreign rights, to arrange serials, to handle stage adaptations, to ferret out documents, to pay his bills. "For almost twenty-five years I have been the tender, staunch friend of my publisher, from whom, during that quarter-century, I never once demanded figures," he asserted on June 13, 1896, prompting Charpentier to echo him in a letter written a month later: "Never in twenty-five years has a cloud of any kind obscured our business dealings—and from those dealings was born an affection that will not end with my retirement; on the contrary."

The type plates and unsold copies of *La Fortune des Rougon* and *La Curée* cost very little. Charpentier paid Lacroix's liquidator eight hundred francs for them (anticipating the famous bargain Gaston Gallimard struck with Bernard Grasset for Proust's *Du côté de chez Swann*), and in due course he showed himself to be a keenly attentive steward. "My dear Monsieur Zola," he wrote at the beginning of September 1872. "Kindly correct as soon as possible the galley proofs of *La Curée* because we are going to print this first section right away. . . . I intend to make the book available early in October. We're better off stalling until then, as the moment is not yet propitious." *La Curée* reappeared on schedule and soon thereafter Charpentier turned his attention to *La Fortune:* "I'm pushing ahead with a new edition since what we have in stock will be gone today or tomorrow. How could we have known that sales of this book, which was never withdrawn from Lacroix's shelf, would be so brisk? We will, unavoidably, run short for a time, but that's no tragedy. *La Curée* is moving, which augurs well for *Le Ventre de Paris.*" To be sure, Charpentier may have indulged in some wishful thinking here. *La Fortune* and *La Curée* would not turn a significant profit until 1877, when, along with several other early novels in the *Rougon-Macquart* series, they rode the coattails of *L'Assommoir* to commercial success. But his faith helped Zola extricate himself from a quagmire and move forward. By December, *Le Ventre de Paris,* which had been six or seven months in the making, was ready for publication.

Among the many herculean labors Napoleon III assigned Baron Haussmann, none transformed Paris more spectacularly than the construction of a central market, Les Halles centrales. Built during the 1850s with connecting passageways, subterranean warehouses, reservoirs, cabins to house administrative personnel, and myriad gaslights, its ten iron-and-glass pavilions heralded a new age as they rose above weather-beaten tenements near the Church of Saint-Eustache like gigantic umbrellas. Occupying twenty-one acres of land once reserved for Paris's dead, the market constituted a world unto itself, a town that bustled while the metropolis round about lay asleep, and this nocturnal realm came, inevitably perhaps, to fascinate Zola. On August 18 he wrote in *La Cloche:*

> It is a colossal pantry that ingests food for the dormant city. When Paris wakes, its stomach will already be full. In the shivering rays of morning light, the crowd swarms around bloody quarters of meat piled high, around countless baskets of fish that glitter like silver, around mountains of vegetables coloring the darkness green and white. It's an avalanche of foodstuff, wagons emptied onto the sidewalk, cases ripped open and disgorging their contents, a rising tide of lettuce, eggs, fruit, fowl which threatens to spill into adjacent streets and flood the whole city.

Though he had reconnoitered Les Halles years earlier, not until *La Curée* was half written did it enter Zola's epic scheme. Can it be that one novel about imperial decadence begot another? Internal evidence suggests it, for the pavilions of *Le Ventre de Paris* appear to have sprung full-blown from the Saccard hothouse, with its glass canopy held aloft by iron ribs.[4] After lust comes gluttony, and gluttony, like lust, requires a stuffed, junglelike enclosure. "The stomach—Paris's stomach, Les Halles, where food pours in before flowing out to various neighborhoods" is how Zola envisioned the mise-en-scène in his preliminary notes. "Humanity's stomach and by extension the bourgeoisie munching, digesting, peacefully ruminating its joys and flaccid morals."

Fieldwork for *Le Ventre de Paris* began at the Courbevoie bridge west of Paris, where, every night, wagons laden with food and flowers crossed the Seine in long convoys. It was seven or eight miles from the customs gate to Les Halles, and on at least one occasion, when Dreyfous joined him, Zola hiked alongside the draft horses, noting as much as he could see by gaslight. This investigation continued at the market itself, which stood conveniently near the offices of *La Cloche*. "Many was the time, in 1872, that . . . he dragged me to Les Halles after we left 5, rue Coq-Héron," Paul Alexis recalled.

> Once, as we were walking away and had reached a certain point on the rue Montmartre, he suddenly said to me: "Now turn around and look!" It was extraordinary. Seen from that perspective, the roofs made a striking impression. Magnified by the dusk, they called to mind Babylonian palaces piled on top of one another. He noted this effect, which is described somewhere in the book. And thus did he study the market's picturesque physiognomy. Pencil in hand, he would visit it at all hours and in all weathers. . . . He even ingratiated himself with a chief custodian who took him underground through the cellars and high up through the rafters.

While exploring the terrain and closely observing the natives, Zola attempted to understand how Les Halles were administered. Here serious difficulties arose. Maxime Du Camp's *Paris, sa vie et ses organes* may have been useful as a general guide, but neither it nor any other treatise addressed the bureaucratic organization of wholesale commerce, and Zola needed precise details for the plot he had begun to weave. At police headquarters, where he found himself shunted from office to office, an amiable civil servant finally rewarded his persistence. "The man gave him invaluable information and let him take copies of all police ordinances bearing upon the subject," wrote Alexis.

[4]Similarly, the hothouse in *La Curée* descends from the glass arcade in *Thérèse Raquin*.

What came of his research was yet another voluminous dossier, this one thick with notes on the language, dress, background, and modus operandi of vendors, with exhaustive lists of the produce, maps of the neighborhood, diagrams of the market, descriptions of the storage facilities, blueprints of the underground network—with everything, in short, that promised to help the self-professed naturalist authenticate his representation of a "milieu" obsessed by food.

Le Ventre de Paris revolves around Florent. Of Provençal origin, Zola's unlucky hero loses his father in childhood. He struggles upward but takes another tumble in young manhood when his mother, who had meanwhile married someone named Quenu and lost this second mate as well, dies poverty-stricken, leaving a twelve-year-old son. Cast adrift, the half brothers cling to each other, occupying one room in the Latin Quarter, where, after abandoning law studies, Florent finds employment as a schoolteacher. "Florent, who had inherited his mother's capacity for devotion, treated Quenu like a big lazy girl. . . . He himself did all the shopping, cleaning, cooking." Though inseparable, they have nothing in common save the mother who bore them, and time magnifies their disparity. While rotund Quenu cannot absorb intellectual knowledge, gaunt Florent is immune to sensual pleasure. While Quenu delights in the aroma of food, Florent feeds upon utopian ideas that constitute the Otherworld of a would-be saint. "Accepting the woes of a poor, mediocre, ugly man was not easy. To exorcise malevolent feelings he made goodness his vocation, and sought refuge in absolute truth and justice. As desperate girls take the veil, so did Florent adopt the tricolor, but finding no republic tepid or meek enough to lull his demons, he created one of his own." An illuminé who at night preaches humanitarianism to political clubs, Florent remains by day an obscure schoolteacher, cut off from everyone except Quenu. Their alliance lasts until December 1851, when misfortune visits Florent once again. Seized during the riots that follow Louis Napoleon's coup d'état, he is held prisoner in Bicêtre, brought before a judge, falsely accused of having shed blood, and transported without further ado to the new penal colony on Devil's Island, off the coast of French Guiana.

Florent's fall marks his brother's rise. Thrust upon himself, Quenu, now twenty-two, appeals for help to an uncle named Gradelle, who sells charcuterie, or pork products, at Les Halles. Given room and board by this rich, tightfisted widower, he is soon transformed. Happily preparing sausage, the former ne'er-do-well discovers not only a métier that suits him but a woman equipped to make the most of his culinary gifts. Lisa, who tends shop for Gradelle, hails from Plassans, where she learned self-reliance as Antoine Macquart's eldest daughter. "Lisa believed that one must work to eat, that each individual is responsible for his own happiness, that encouraging sloth is wrong. . . . Though she condemned outright old Macquart's legendary binges, Macquart nonetheless spoke through her loud and clear. Having understood that one sleeps best in the nest one has feathered, the young woman was, with her craving for creature comforts, a disciplined, reasonable, logical Macquart. Material well-being occupied her every conscious thought." The minute Gradelle dies, logic tells her to marry Quenu, who will inherit the *charcuterie* along with gold hoarded in the cellar. And when Les Halles rise from the ruins of the old market, the Marché des Innocents, logic counsels her to start afresh. "The young woman dreamed about one of those well-lit modern shops as richly appointed as a salon, with windows gleaming on a wide street." Eventually the dream comes true. Gradelle's gold helps them furnish a pork palace in which Lisa, who "grasps the need for luxury introduced by modern commerce," holds sway. Unprofitable feelings never cloud her mind. Handsome but sexless, smiling but heartless, this fleshy petit bourgeois queen is all business, and in all her business displays the impersonal rectitude characteristic of what Zola scornfully calls *les honnêtes gens*. Content with a despotism that levies no income tax, M. and Mme Quenu prosper.

The world beyond Les Halles hardly impinges on their well-ordered ménage until one September day Florent reappears out of the blue. After escaping from Devil's Island and languishing for years in Dutch Guiana, he has sailed back to Europe, entered France incognito, and found Quenu. The latter greets him joyfully, but no sooner does Florent ensconce himself above the shop than Mme Quenu, for whom virtue is a balanced ledger, calculates his share of Gradelle's estate, hoping to make him go away. When he renounces it, she uses another ploy. If the outcast won't hide elsewhere, then let him feign legitimacy. An inspectorship falls vacant at Les Halles, and Lisa urges it upon him with such maternal persistence that Florent, though he would like to assassinate Napoleon III, succumbs. "He listened to her, dumbstruck," writes Zola. "She was right, no doubt. How could someone so robust, so serene, want evil? It was he, the skinny man with a dark, louche profile and unavowable fantasies, who must be wrong. He no longer knew why he had ever resisted the proposal."

Thus begins the second phase of Florent's martyrdom. An anorexic surrounded by food, he is a republic under siege, defending himself against odors and images that threaten to maim his will or emasculate the ideal in which he has vested his self-esteem. "Little by little a kind of dull anxiety reduced him to despair. He was unhappy, he found fault with himself without quite knowing why, he resisted as best he could the lethargy that seemed to have hollowed out his head and breast. Furthermore, whiffs of rotten fish made him nauseous . . .

Florent suffered from the food piled all around him." Though his past remains hidden, his physique declares that he doesn't belong, and the vulgar, big-bosomed costermongers who rule Les Halles consider a thin man inherently suspect. Hired to police this gynecocracy, Florent becomes the subject of its gossip and the object of its taunts. Every day brings humiliation. "Red faces stared him down. From the lewd inflection of voices, the jaunty angle of hips, the swollen necks, the swinging thighs, the obscene gestures, he guessed that they were slopping offal on him. Another man might have pinched their bottoms to clear a path, but not Florent, whom women still intimidated. He felt trapped in a nightmare crowd of prodigiously well-endowed females with husky voices and gladiatorial arms." The body of endomorphs festers around the stranger lodged in its midst. Just as he berates himself without knowing why, so Florent sets people against one another without meaning to sow discord. Rivalries erupt, families quarrel, rumors abound, and a malicious old maid named Mlle Saget, who half recalls his face from the distant past, relentlessly scavenges for information that will enable her to unmask him.

Tolerated at home and mocked at Les Halles, where the good he does is turned against him, Florent finds solace in the company of six or seven ill-assorted republicans, a woebegone group that meets regularly at a bistro whose proprietor seems well disposed toward them. Sworn to different ideologies, they fill a back room with idle chatter about revolution, enjoying the clandestinity of it all even as snoops record everything they say. Matters rest there until Florent concocts a preposterous scheme for bringing down Napoleon III. Mlle Saget tells Lisa about it, whereupon Lisa betrays her brother-in-law. We learn that she is not the first merchant to have fingered him, and when in due course police arrest Florent, the entire market, like some plague-stricken village, celebrates this casting-out of the demon intruder. "Gaiety returned to the huge, sonorous pavilions and engorged streets. Relieved of the weight on their collective stomach, people made an even louder racket than usual, as if saved from some disease." Fat expels thin, business thrives, despotism triumphs.

As a diatribe against the so-called *honnêtes gens*, *Le Ventre de Paris* turns upon Lisa, whose portrait is drawn nowhere more emblematically than in the scene that announces her marriage. Scouring the cellar for Gradelle's hidden treasure, she finds it at the bottom of a salting tub, gathers it in her apron, and waddles up five flights "with her thighs trammeled by the burden," then signals Quenu to follow her. "It was the first time she had ever invited him to enter her room," writes Zola.

She closed the door and, releasing the corners of the apron, . . . let gold and silver coins rain on the soft, downy mattress. Their joy was contained. They sat with the money between them, Lisa at the head of the bed, Quenu at the foot, and counted it right there, so as not to make any noise. There were 40,000 gold francs, 3,000 silver, and, in a tin can, banknotes worth 42,000 francs. Adding it up took several hours. Quenu's hands trembled a bit, so Lisa did most of the work. . . . Naturally they spoke about the future, about marriage, without ever having loved each other. This treasure seemed to loosen their tongues. Propped against a wall under white muslin curtains, they had sunk deeper into the bed . . . Digging through the pile as they chatted, their hands met and linked amid five-franc coins. Nightfall took them by surprise. Only then did Lisa blush at seeing herself next to this boy. The sheets were rumpled, and the gold, which lay on a pillow separating them, had made hollows, not unlike those made by heads aflame with desire.

Lisa will bear a child of flesh, but the child is as nothing compared to the mother lode she has discovered underground, toted upstairs in her improvised pouch, and delivered in her virginal bed. With a belly for hoarding gold and a brain for counting it, she foreshadows the mine lord in *Germinal* who provides his daughter with daintily furnished quarters over the pit from which worker-slaves extract mineral wealth. Both violate nature. Indeed, the magnificently ample but utterly dispassionate pork butcher violates it in her very person, having breasts that sit upon her like a prosthetic advertisement of womanhood. "Mirrors all around the shop reflected her from behind, from the front, from the side. . . . Lisa loomed everywhere, her shoulders broad, her arms solid, her round bosom so still and taut that it resembled a stomach, awakening no carnal thought." A "sacred cow" is how Zola describes Macquart's androgynous offspring. Smarter than her husband, Madame Quenu reckons while Monsieur Quenu cooks. It is she who penetrates secrets, who reads the future, who supplants Florent.

Money, excrement, and death accompany one another throughout *Le Ventre de Paris*. Lisa discovering Gradelle's treasure in the foul basement illustrates their collusion, but Zola makes it more explicit somewhat later, when Florent, to escape Les Halles, visits a market garden near Nanterre. "The peace and cleanliness of the earth made him profoundly happy. For almost a year he had seen vegetables bruised by their rough journey, uprooted the day before and still bleeding. He was delighted to find them at home, in the soil . . . Cabbages sported an air of prosperous well-being, carrots beamed, lettuce walked single-file, with the nonchalance of idlers. Les Halles . . . seemed in retrospect a vast ossuary, a landscape of corpses, a charnel house filled with the stench of putrefaction." Torn from nature, where all is pure, and stored beneath Les Halles in warehouses that constitute yet another penal settlement, fruits of the earth inevitably breed corruption.

At every turn rural virtue stands opposed to urban violence, and tours of the lower world argue this dichotomy. Lisa makes one such tour. Led through underground storerooms by a character named Marjolin, she witnesses animal hell:

> Gavard the poulterer had rented two compartments from which he had made a single chicken coop by removing the partition. On the ground, geese, turkeys, ducks squelched in the dung. Up above, on three rows of shelves, latticed crates held chickens and rabbits. Cobwebs covered the dusty iron gate like gray blinds, rabbit urine had eaten away the baseboards, chicken droppings made white splotches all over. Lest Marjolin take offense, Lisa did not betray her disgust. She stuck her fingers into the crates, lamenting the fate of these wretched hens so crowded together they couldn't stand. She caressed a duck hunched in a corner, its foot broken, while the young man told her it would be killed that same evening for fear that it might die during the night.

Marjolin is central to Zola's symbolic scheme. A foundling discovered one day beneath some produce and casually mothered by all the vendors, he knows nothing of the world beyond Les Halles. Like Paul and Virginie living in the bosom of provident nature, he and his female clone, Cadine, run wild on an island that feeds them, shelters them, entertains them. Children of Les Halles, whose stench has been their atmosphere since infancy, they emerge as brutal innocents, or grotesque perversions of the noble savage. Familiar with slaughter, they thirst for blood:

> Every day they'd visit the tripery. . . . What really gave them shivers were the large, bloody hampers full of sheep's heads, the fat horns, the black snouts with tufts of wool still clinging to live flesh. It conjured up for them the image of a guillotine decapitating endless flocks and hurling heads into these receptacles. They followed them as they glided downward on rails, their wheels screeching like saws. A spectacle of exquisite horror awaited them underground. They walked through dark, sticky puddles where, at times, purple eyes seemed to glow.

Such innocence will make them, too, accomplices in the manhunt. After his arrest, Florent, who "let himself be caught like a sheep," reflects "that Les Halles were of one mind, that he was surrendered by the entire neighborhood." All around him, Zola adds, "mud rose from the fat-soaked streets."

Le Ventre de Paris evokes not only the horror of an imperial regime whose unconscionable supporters fill their guts and purses, but also the anguish of neurotic conflict. Florent is a republican hounded by Napoleonic agents, but also a solitary undone by the lower self—the "beast"—he attempts to throttle. "His secret dream," writes Zola, "was to live forever with some young person who would never grow up, whom he would instruct devotedly, through whose innocence he would love mankind." Invading this utopian stronghold where he dispenses virtue, woman dethrones him. The priest-father for whom manhood means hunger, or absolute self-control, helplessly gives ground to the mother who derives her power from food. "[Lisa] gorged him like a little boy who had misbehaved. . . . Penetrated by kitchen odors, force-fed through his nose, he yielded despite himself to the spineless felicity of this milieu where people never stopped digesting. Fat grew upon him in a slow invasion of his whole being."

Le Ventre is another of Zola's novels in which an instinctual force engulfs a closed space or alters an identity. Florent fears that Lisa will "dissolve" him: "He avoided her for two or three days lest she melt his will on contact, like a solvent. These fits of puerile terror . . . always ended in tenderness, in a need for love, which, as it made him feel childishly ashamed, he dared not show." To let woman penetrate one is to become a woman oneself, with bones clothed in fat. But effeminization affects mind no less than body, emptying the one as it pads the other:

> After those seven years of hardship, he fell into a routine so monotonous that he felt barely alive. He gave way, his head a bit empty, continually surprised at finding himself each morning in the same armchair, the same office. This bare, cabinlike room pleased him. He found refuge there, far from the world, surrounded by the ever booming Halles, which he thought of as some immense sea that isolated him completely.

A monastic island surrounded by a high sea calls to mind the walled city of Plassans overwhelmed by a human torrent. Like Plassans, Florent cannot bear fecundity. Vegetable plots make him smile, but women are another matter, and in particular the ripe-bodied fishmonger Louise Méhudin. "To Florent she seemed colossal, very heavy, almost alarming with her gigantic bosom," Zola writes of this *"belle Normande."*

> [In her presence] he'd lower his head, he'd grow even thinner, discomfited by her pungent odor. When her underbodice gaped a little,

he thought he saw vapor rising from between her white mounds and covering her face, like a breath of life seasoned in the July heat with Les Halles' stench. . . . Moving amidst slimy seaweed, her huge body admirably pure and pale, she resembled the antique statue of some goddess rolled by the sea and brought to shore in the net of a sardine boat. Florent suffered.

Trapped between a marine goddess and a sacred cow, Florent emerges as a naysayer whose contempt for gold, though ostensibly more virtuous than Lisa's scrupulous arithmetic, denotes his fear of life. Sublimating desire in utopian reveries, the self-castrated hero is doomed to disappear, and, unlike Lisa, to leave behind no issue.

That Zola himself, during an interview held five years after its publication, should have given this novel highest marks, ranking it above *L'Assommoir,* may indicate how much of himself he poured into the war between fat people and thin. Spectacles of abundance excited him, and the Rabelaisian inventories that crop up on his pages reflect the eater whom Alexandrine strove to satisfy. Zola loved food for its own sake, particularly shellfish, but the lists also serve an aggressive purpose, which is to say that Zola used the cornucopia as a weapon against prudish taste, burying romanticism or spiritualism beneath odoriferous word matter. "His hands in his pockets and whistling, Claude descanted upon his great love for this tide of food that rose every morning right in the middle of Paris," he wrote, ventriloquizing here through the character of a painter destined to play a far more important role later on, in *L'Oeuvre.*

He described a meal some friend had offered him at Chez Baratte one splendid day, the oysters and fish and game. But Chez Baratte was no more. It had gone the way of the picturesque old Marché des Innocents, which now lay buried beneath this cast-iron colossus, this new and original city called Les Halles. Here stood the modern age, impervious to the attacks of imbeciles [and] Claude inveighed against romanticism. He put more stock in cabbages than in medieval tatters.

Later novels, notably *Au Bonheur des Dames,* where a modern department store rises on the ruins of old-fashioned boutiques, and *L'Argent,* where Saccard, defying the financial establishment, founds a credit bank that swallows nest eggs all over France, amplify this glorification of Les Halles. While sympathetic in his republican mode to little people, Zola was entranced by Leviathan and identified, as creator, with men of insatiable appetite. An article written for *Le Corsaire* says it very clearly. "I left my firedogs, opened the window, and gazed at my great, beloved Paris bustling in the ash gray of twilight," declared the naturalist-cum-glutton.

With its animated streets, its vistas flecked with signs and posters, its dreadful and tender houses where death neighbors love, it speaks to me of the new art. Its immense drama is what attaches me to the modern drama, to the existence of bourgeois and workers, to the milling crowd whose every joy and sorrow I would like to record . . . I feel it shaken by the terrific labor of this century. I see it pregnant with a world and if I entertained some one consummate ambition, it would be to throw the giant steaming hot into some gigantic work.

Aristide Rougon adopts a similar pose at the beginning of La Curée, when he surveys Paris from his apartment window with an eye for plunder.

Florent, too, contemplates Paris from a window—a top-floor window—and this obsessive scenario, which harks back to La Confession de Claude, would suggest that Zola was not all epic girth. A romantic starveling still haunted the naturalist omnivore. A voyeur still gazed hopelessly at the inaccessible. A young Aixois lost in a metropolis whose measure he couldn't take survived inside the Parisian demiurge. And no doubt Florent, who falls under the sway of enormous women after seven years abroad, was conceived in the image of a fatherless seven-year-old who came to regard his manhood as some provisional endowment that malignant spirits might confiscate overnight.[5]

Les Rougon-Macquart did not render Zola's "slender" self more voluminous, or so one gathers from contemporary accounts. "It's curious how this pudgy lad whines, and how his high spirits can instantly change into melancholia," Edmond de Goncourt observed rather waspishly in January 1875.

> He goes on about his work, about the litter of one hundred lines he forces himself to drop day in, day out, about his monasticism, about his stay-at-home life which offers no distractions in the evening save domino games with his wife and visits from fellow Aixois. Amidst all this he lets it slip that his greatest satisfaction lies in the influence he wields over Paris from his humble abode, and one hears in his voice the vengeful tone of a poor devil who stewed for years in the lower depths.

A more sympathetic portrait may be found in Notes d'un ami, where Paul Alexis quotes Zola as saying time and time again: "It seems to

---

[5]Deeply superstitious about numbers, which were talismans for controlling a world fraught with mortal danger, Zola told Dr. Edouard Toulouse, many years later, that at night, in bed, he would often blink seven straight times to prove that he wasn't going to die.

me that I am always the beginner. I forget the twenty volumes that lie behind me and tremble at the thought of what my next novel will be worth."

Charpentier arranged, not without difficulty, to have *Le Ventre de Paris* serialized in *La Cloche*'s new incarnation, *L'Etat*. The bound volume appeared on April 19, 1872, and was loudly assailed by reviewers. Voicing conservative opinion for *La Revue des Deux Mondes*, Paul Bourget declared that "one would be hard put to imagine a style more sensual and more depraved." Another novelist-critic, the flamboyant and dandified reactionary Barbey d'Aurevilly, with whom Zola had been crossing swords since 1865, went even further. "The import of his books is this: one makes art as one makes sausage," he wrote in *Le Constitutionnel.* "It's an idea that began to infiltrate painting and literature quite some time ago. People call it realism, and it springs from those two monsters that would squat on old French society until the breath goes out of it, i.e., Materialism and Democracy. . . . The human drama woven through *Le Ventre de Paris*, where, as in man's stomach, only physical things are to be found, is pitifully thin. I thought at first that it would deal with politics, that it would carry the torch of democratic passions . . . but not at all. The author uses his hero as a device. He has him dance around Les Halles in an endless waltz of description." Critics who gagged on Zola's lists might have learned something about the brevity of wit from Nietzsche characterizing Wagner as an overblown miniaturist. Those who found *Le Ventre* prolix were themselves inclined to natter on, while those who judged it immoral usually let cant argue the case for them.

But *Le Ventre* won Zola more readers than ever, and its first edition sold out in a month. It also won him the admiration of two young men, Guy de Maupassant and Joris-Karl Huysmans, who would enter the circle around him when, in due course, that circle formed. "I'm a bit like those Muslims intoxicated by hashish who can't talk rationally about their enthusiasms, and so I shall say straight out that *Le Ventre de Paris* made me jubilant," Huysmans, a Parisian of Dutch extraction, wrote in 1876. "Day dawning over Les Halles as vegetables rise and bistros flame behind fogged windows and crowds swarm is an absolutely incredible riot of color! There are still lifes that have the dash and wild palette of a Rubens! And how vividly Zola draws his characters, bringing them to life with some habitual gesture or idiosyncratic phrase. . . . In this volume the pit may be almost imperceptible, but the fruit tastes like nothing else."

XII

THE COMPANY OF FIVE

AT HOME, Zola, who sometimes fancied himself a gentleman farmer, relaxed after writing all day by cultivating the little plot of land that adjoined his quarters on the rue de la Condamine. There were rosebushes to prune, vegetables to water, hedges to trim, coops to build for the poultry Alexandrine raised, and in these rustic chores he took great pleasure. Bound up with memories of Provençal country houses, the garden was a quiet, fragrant refuge where, as had always been his wont, he often entertained compatriots from Aix. "On lovely summer evenings a table would be set up outside and the family would dine alfresco," Paul Alexis reminisced. "Then several intimate friends . . . would arrive and over hot tea, with elbows planted on the cleared table, we'd gab until midnight. If 'the gardener' had just finished a chapter of *La Curée, Le Ventre de Paris*, or *La Conquête de Plassans*, he might read it to us." This tight group included Alexis himself, Antony Valabrègue, Numa Coste, Philippe Solari, and Marius Roux, all of whom could depend on Zola to promote their work whenever the opportunity arose.

What made life at 14, rue de la Condamine feel even more marginal, perhaps, was the flight of painters from Les Batignolles. When, after 1871, the Guerbois became a rowdy brasserie, Manet deserted it for an establishment near the Place Pigalle called the Café de la Nouvelle-Athènes, on whose terrace he would match wits with Edgar Degas. These loyal antagonists performed almost every night for almost a decade, and young men like George Moore (who later wrote that the Nouvelle-Athènes had been his Oxford and Cambridge) flocked there to watch them spar until 1 or 2 a.m. Renoir often dropped by. But other alumni of the Guerbois were seldom present, many having left Paris in a diaspora that immortalized the countryside round about. Alfred Sisley found quarters in Voisins. Monet perched alongside the Seine at Argenteuil. Pissarro, who returned from England after the Franco-Prussian War to discover that German soldiers had wrecked his house at Louveciennes (together with many paintings in it), established himself at Pontoise. And several kilometers upstream from Pontoise, at Auvers-sur-Oise, which the Salon public knew through Charles Daubigny's exquisite landscapes, Cézanne settled with Hortense Fiquet.

Crawling out of his wartime burrow at L'Estaque, Cézanne headed for Paris in late 1871. Zola had not seen him for more than a year, but their reunion occasioned little fanfare, and Cézanne did not join the clan on the rue de la Condamine during his five-month sojourn in Paris. Nor, apparently, did he invite the clan to gather around him when Hortense bore him a son—also named Paul—in their dingy flat on the rue de Jussieu, opposite the wholesale wine market. "I've found him forsaken by everyone," wrote a friend from Aix, Achille Emperaire. "He hasn't got a single intelligent or affectionate friend. The Zolas, the Solaris, all the rest never see him now. He's the queerest duck imaginable." It being no secret that Alexandrine looked askance at Hortense, Cézanne might more readily have confronted her, or Zola, if he himself had been less ambivalent about his ménage. Just as the artist who flouted academic pieties sought recognition from the Academy, so the man who would not marry his son's mother craved legitimacy in the straitlaced world. Nothing, indeed, could induce him to reveal the existence of his mistress and bastard son to Louis-Auguste. By devious strategies, in which Emilie Cézanne reluctantly cooperated, he kept his father ignorant for years, thus avenging himself on the old banker while avoiding the danger of being stigmatized all over again through Paul junior.

No such danger threatened him in the neighborhood of Camille Pissarro, whose magnanimous spirit had room enough to shelter a motley brood of protégés as well as a numerous family. Cézanne wanted guidance and he found it at Pontoise, where, "like the good God," Pissarro taught him lessons that helped him accomplish his own inimitable vision. "Pissarro may have fathered us all; by 1865 he had already eliminated black, bitumen, raw siena, and the ochers," he declared many years later, adding on another occasion: "Until forty I lived as a bohemian and wasted my life. It was only when I kept company with Pissarro, who painted nonstop, that I learned discipline."[1]

---

[1] Though his unkempt beard made him look older, Cézanne was actually only thirty-three in 1872.

Their bond transcended the gospel of primary colors, which Cézanne worked into his brush by copying Pissarro's *View of Louveciennes*. Beyond Impressionist technique there was mutual affection and esteem. "We have high hopes for our Cézanne, and . . . I have in my house a painting of remarkable strength and vigor," Pissarro informed Antoine Guillemet. "Should he stay put at Auvers, as I hope he does, he will astonish many artists who have dismissed him rather too hastily." How many others would have ventured to tell Théodore Duret, the critic and collector, that "if it's five-legged sheep you fancy, Cézanne will satisfy you, for he's done some very odd studies, from an absolutely unique perspective"? Given constant encouragement by the man he regarded as his *père adoptif*, Cézanne, scouting the valley of the Oise like a bear with a straw hat, spent three years in this fertile pasture and left it only when summonses from Aix could no longer go unheeded. Forever susceptible to despair, he nonetheless felt more confident than ever. "I know that [Pissarro] thinks highly of me, as I do of myself," he wrote to his mother on September 26, 1874. "I've begun to consider myself more a painter than everyone around me, and you know that I don't make this assertion without believing that I have grounds for it. I must keep working hard, though not to perfect some high finish, which is what imbeciles admire most. Any skilled craftsman can do that, and the effect of it is always to make a painting inartistic and common. . . . Sooner or later [the truth seeker] achieves recognition and wins for himself admirers much more fervent, more staunch than those who are dazzled by empty shows."

Cézanne may have visited Zola at the rue de la Condamine. They may also have encountered each other at the Nouvelle-Athènes, where George Moore claimed to have seen Paul wax furious, or at Pontoise, where Zola spent a brief summer holiday with another painter, Edouard Béliard.[2] But there is no record of Cézanne and Zola together at this time, and when on December 25, 1872, Alexandrine prepared Christmas dinner for several friends, Cézanne was conspicuously absent from the table. Though a feeling of kinship survived between them, not until 1877 did it manifest itself again in word and deed. Estranged by circumstances as well as by temperament, Cézanne found society increasingly onerous, while Zola became more sociable, meeting *le tout Paris* through Marguerite Charpentier (who was mak-

[2]It seems likely that Zola occasionally visited Pissarro, who had attended his "Thursdays" before 1870. A note from the artist, dated September 21, 1872, speaks of mutual hospitality: "My wife begs Mme Zola to come fetch the pregnant rabbit we are holding for her and to do so quickly as she will soon give birth. We would be delighted to receive her at Pontoise. . . . I was supposed to drop by the rue de la Condamine today but must leave this morning so as not to miss Guillaumin, who is expected at our place. I beg you not to take this amiss."

ing her husband's imprimatur the emblem of a glamorous social circle)
and gravitating toward the lights of an older literary generation.

Zola had first endeared himself to Flaubert three years earlier with
a serious article on *L'Education sentimentale*. Since then the two had
greeted each other now and again by mail, but it was 1872 before Zola
visited the rue Murillo, where during his Paris season, which generally
lasted several months, Flaubert held court every Sunday afternoon in
a pied-à-terre overlooking the Parc Monceau. This initiation was significant indeed, as it marked the beginning of a ritual that bound Zola
in fraternity and enmity to Flaubert's other regulars: Edmond de Goncourt, Alphonse Daudet, and Ivan Turgenev. "I should like to describe
our dominical sessions, but to do so faithfully might offend, the language we sometimes used being rather coarse," he wrote after Flaubert's death.

> Flaubert, who in winter wore a clerical skullcap and overcoat, had
> designed for summertime a voluminous, red-and-white-striped culotte
> together with a tunic which made him look the caricature of a loung-
> ing Turk. He claimed it was for reasons of comfort but I'm inclined
> to believe that this attire descended from romantic fashions, for I
> also saw him sport checkered pants, frock coats pleated at the waist,
> and wide-brimmed fedoras cocked over one ear. . . . In Paris he would
> often open the door himself, embrace you if he had decided that you
> were kin, and usher you into his smoke-filled parlor. . . . Between
> three and six we'd cover many subjects at a gallop, always doubling
> back to literature, the latest book or play, general questions, the most
> risqué theories, but pressing beyond and scrutinizing individuals.
> Flaubert would thunder, Turgenev would tell exquisitely original and
> pungent tales, Goncourt formulated sharp judgments in an idiom all
> his own, Daudet brought to bear upon his anecdotes that charm
> which makes him one of the most adorable companions I know. As
> for myself, I seldom shone, for I am a very mediocre conversationalist.
> My candle comes out from beneath the bushel only when I get angry
> on behalf of some conviction.

Not to be confined by the cretonne-clad walls of Flaubert's flat or by
Sunday afternoon, the heterogeneous fivesome arranged in due course
to dine at regular intervals on the Boulevard.

Wherever they met, attention centered on Flaubert, who bid for it
incessantly. The sartorial eccentricities Zola called "romantic" went
hand in hand with the hyperbolic judgments and gratuitous paradoxes
that disconcerted his audience. Given to self-dramatization, he often
staged mad scenes, as if people might otherwise ignore him, and the
spectacle of this florid, mustachioed giant blustering against the *pro-*

fanum vulgus was a regular feature of matinees on the rue Murillo. "Flaubert had characteristic gestures and would, for instance, wave his big, thick arms at the ceiling, wildly, with fists closed," wrote Maurice Dreyfous, who received an invitation to the performance when Charpentier replaced Michel Lévy as Flaubert's publisher. "Midway through his pantomime, the apoplectic hue of his face and neck would turn even deeper red. It almost always ended in shouts loud enough to flay the gullet, in roars that made his knickknacks tremble. But they alone trembled. Intimates were accustomed to what Gautier dubbed 'Flaubert's spout.' " Even more enveloping, or imperious, was the hospitality he offered at his home in Croisset, near Rouen. When Jules and Edmond de Goncourt spent three days there in 1863, Flaubert displayed costumes acquired during his voyage through the Levant fifteen years earlier, trotted out the unpublished confessions of a homicidal pederast, and, lest the beautiful countryside distract them, read aloud his travel notes from early afternoon until midnight.[3] Friends who paid one visit seldom craved another.

Outside Croisset, where his widowed mother kept him company, he felt like Gulliver in Brobdingnag, which is to say that for all those travel notes Flaubert never left his childhood habitat. There were liaisons, of course, but none that ever reconciled the urge to let loose with the need to husband himself. Fantasizing about an ideal inamorata while making Salomes or Medusas of those near at hand, vaunting his cocksmanship while identifying with Saint Polycarp, he saw emasculation as the price exacted by carnal love and invited maternal support from women who embodied some essentially masculine virtue (he often called George Sand, among others, *"mon grand homme"*). Flaubert remained hostage to the family romance. "I sought to love you and love you still in a way that isn't that of lovers," he wrote in 1854 to his intermittent mistress, Louise Colet. "We would have put all sex, all propriety, all jealousy, all politeness . . . at our feet and on this pedestal stood above ourselves. The great passions—not the turbulent ones but the broad and lofty—are those *nothing can harm*." The Goncourts report him bellowing variations on this theme ten years later, over dinner at the restaurant Magny: "In a stentorian voice, his face enflamed and his eyes agog, Flaubert declared that beauty is not erotic, that beautiful women are not made to be tupped, that they are good for inspiring statues. . . . We tease him, whereupon he says that he has never really screwed a woman, that he is a virgin, that all the women he has had were mattresses for a dreamed-of absentee."

---

[3]Flaubert was apparently a collector of perverse erotica. The pederast in question, Chollet, killed his lover out of jealousy, and wrote detailed memoirs during his incarceration at Le Havre, where he was guillotined.

Dressed in a loose-fitting shirt, slippers, and a monkish robe, Flaubert wrote most uninhibitedly after dark, between midnight and dawn, when ordinary men lay asleep. He loved his work, he declared, as the ascetic loves the hair shirt that scratches his stomach.

The laborious chiseling and buffing of sentences for which he became famous exemplified this view of writing as an ascetic vocation. Eternally at odds with the raconteur who fleshed out stories was the lapidist who envisioned, Pygmalion-like, some perfect, self-referential form. "There are neither beautiful nor ugly subjects and . . . you could consider it almost axiomatic, from the point of view of pure Art, that there is no such thing as subject, since style itself is an absolute way of seeing things," he mused when in the throes of writing *Madame Bovary*. "What seems beautiful to me, what I would like to write is a book about nothing, a book without any external support, which would be held together only by the inner strength of its style, the way the earth hangs suspended in space, a book which would have almost no subject, or at least in which the subject would be almost invisible, if that is possible. The most beautiful works are those in which there is the least matter." In art as in love he proposed to stand above himself, self-sufficient, with a creed of authorial impersonality that protected him from humiliation and judgment. Having always felt dwarfed by his father and brother, both of them surgeons well known in Rouen, he devised his own Hippocratic oath, for creating skeletal masterpieces or hermetic bodies.

Vituperate though he did against society, Flaubert could never quite resist the impulse to measure his worth by the prizes it awarded, and after 1860 it awarded him many. *Madame Bovary* was so successful that he dared challenge Michel Lévy to buy *Salammbô* sight unseen for twenty-five thousand francs, declaring: "He must purchase my name and nothing else." Celebrity righted all wrongs. The novelist who had been prosecuted on moral grounds in 1857 found himself taken up in 1862 by Napoleon III's unconventional cousin the Princess Mathilde, at whose château in Saint-Gratien he regularly met men of power and influence. During his Paris season weeks were sometimes booked solid, invitations to attend court balls came from the Tuileries, and in due course the minister of public instruction made him a *chevalier* of the Legion of Honor. Hobnobbing with imperial demimondaines as well as with Napoleonic eminences, Flaubert sought intellectual company in the little restaurant on the rue Dauphine called Magny's, where Théophile Gautier, the Goncourts, George Sand, and Ivan Turgenev often gathered around Sainte-Beuve.

The critical abuse heaped on *L'Education sentimentale* shattered him, but even before he suffered this defeat Flaubert felt that his world had come undone. The Magny dinners ceased when Sainte-

Beuve died in 1869. In 1869 he also lost Louis Bouilhet, who had been his alter ego since *lycée*. One year later, after Napoleon III's fall, Princess Mathilde left Paris for Brussels. Then, in 1872, death claimed Madame Flaubert, leaving him utterly forlorn at Croisset. "My mother has bequeathed Croisset [to my niece] with the proviso that I keep my apartment here. So for the time being this is home," he told George Sand on April 16, 1872.

> Before I make any decisions about the future I must know what I'll have to live on; then we'll see. Will I have the inner strength to live in complete solitude? I doubt it. I'm getting old . . . I think I'll give up my Paris flat. Nothing calls me to the city any longer. All my friends are dead and the last of them, poor Théo [Gautier], is not long for this world, I fear. How hard it is to grow a new skin at fifty! I've come to realize during the past fortnight that my poor dear mother was the being I loved most. It's as if my guts had been torn out! I need to see you badly! So badly!

Beyond the graveyard only two figures seemed to offer some real hope of life-sustaining camaraderie. One was George Sand herself, and the other was Ivan Turgenev.

In a letter written the year before his mother died, Flaubert delivered himself of several lines that could serve as an epigraph to his friendship with Turgenev: "If we were to hunt about a bit, couldn't we perhaps put together a little group of émigrés, which would be pleasant? For we are all of us émigrés, left over from another age." The sense of being nowhere, of drifting anachronistically among "bourgeois," unmarriageable women, and confreres who had found refuge in aesthetic programs or political ideologies that struck them both as simplistic if not worse, is what they recognized to be their common predicament. By 1868, when they became intimate, it was no longer a question of young men imagining themselves shaping the future, but of two saddened giants leaning on each other as they entered late middle age with the conviction that they had no posterity —that they had, in fact, washed up on a desert island.

For Turgenev life had begun on an island of sorts, in 1818. The family estate, which he later called "my Patmos," encompassed twenty villages in Orel province, and the manor, Spasskoye, was itself a populous community equipped with barns, mills, stables, ateliers, an infirmary, and even a theater where serfs trained in music and dance gave performances whenever bidden to do so by Turgenev's mother, Varvara Petrovna. Until he entered Moscow University, Ivan had virtually never known schoolmates other than his brother. Like young princes, they received instruction from private tutors, who organized a curriculum that evinced their parents' ambition to raise them as European gentlemen. Though hermetically Russian in other respects, Sergei and Varvara Turgenev spurned Slavophile doctrine. At age four Ivan was taken abroad on a grand tour through Germany, Austria, Switzerland, and France, which ended with the family spending six months in Paris. Sergei, who had won citations for bravery during the war against Napoleon I, hewed to aristocratic tradition in speaking French at home, and Varvara, the rich commoner he married for her five thousand serfs, imitated him. It was her habit to call Ivan, her favorite son, "Jean."

Being Varvara Petrovna's favorite son entitled him to bear responsibility for the pain inflicted on her by unfaithful men, including her husband (who died young), and everything we know suggests that in the matter of sadistic strategies her imagination was as prompt as her will. At Spasskoye, where no civil or religious authority dared to overrule her, she invented a despotic queendom, giving her domestic staff not only ministerial titles but foreign surnames. Her whim was law, law was enforced by her private constabulary, and for any number of arcane transgressions a serf would be flogged or exiled overnight to some village far from his kinfolk. Addressing the mistress without having been granted that privilege constituted one such offense. But most peasants never saw their owner, except during her summer inspection tour, when, like *la maison du roi*, Spasskoye became a caravan progressing in state through one terror-stricken hamlet after another. Usually she governed from an office, which the few who could enter were invited to regard as her throne room. It contained a dais, and behind the dais a portrait of Varvara Petrovna herself.

This image may have been what Turgenev envisioned years later, before leaving France on a homeward journey the prospect of which filled him with dread. "Russia can wait—that immense and somber figure motionless and masked like the Sphinx of Oedipus," he told a friend. "Set your mind at ease, Sphinx. I shall return to you and you can devour me at your leisure, if I do not solve your riddle for yet a little while." Varvara had inspired in him a hatred of violence (which did not preclude fascination), a strong tendency to identify with victims of it, and an apprehension that yielding to desire must inevitably prove fatal. What made him the bachelor who engaged throughout his life in equivocal romances and the supreme ironist who mocked even that which commanded his deepest sympathy also made him the expatriate who preferred to contemplate his beloved country from afar.

In any event, to write or talk honestly about Russia involved great risk under a regime that stifled all discussion after the Decembrist plot against the tsar of 1825. Turgenev's critical intelligence did not awaken until the years 1839–41, which he spent as a student in Berlin reading

Hegel with Karl Werder, rooming with Michael Bakunin, and staying up late with members of the Russian intelligentsia whose passports had not yet been confiscated by Tsar Nicholas's secret police. Even more crucial for his development, perhaps, was a trip he took through Italy, where art offered him relief from those politico-philosophical systems furiously colliding to no immediate effect in boardinghouses up north.

Already a marvelous raconteur, whose anecdotes would enliven drawing rooms all over Europe, Turgenev did not seem cut out for solitary labor. Brilliant but weak-willed, with a high-pitched voice oddly unbefitting his majestic frame, he impressed people as incorrigibly dilettantish, and Turgenev himself concurred in that opinion. Without financial hardship to spur him on, he no sooner set himself goals than he lost sight of them and drifted off course. An academic career evaporated when, after passing the examination for a professorship in philosophy, he chose not to write his thesis. Then, on the strength of a paper titled "Some Remarks on the Russian Economy and the Russian Peasant," he was appointed to a post at the interior ministry. Before long, government service bored him, and a leave of absence for medical reasons turned out to be a final farewell.

That this waffling signaled not infirmity of purpose but a growing sense of his literary vocation became apparent the closer he drew to men connected with the review Pushkin had founded several years earlier. Turgenev wrote verse before he attempted fiction, and *Parasha*, a long narrative poem styled after *Eugene Onegin*, made Saint Petersburg sit up and take notice. Lauded by Belinsky—the critic who stood foremost in defending Pushkin, Lermontov, and Gogol against Russia's establishment—*Parasha* won Turgenev support even in Spasskoye, as Varvara Petrovna was pleased to learn that writing poetry, which she deemed unworthy of gentlemen, had not been for her son an altogether inconsequential exercise.

Varvara Petrovna could forgive him literature. Far more vexatious was a passion strong enough to pry him loose from her, which declared itself in 1843 when Turgenev met the renowned soprano Pauline García Viardot, who had come to sing Rossini at the Imperial Opera. Twenty-one years old, or half the age of her husband and impresario, Louis Viardot, this extraordinary woman cast spells on men with a narcissistic allure that more than compensated for her ugliness. "She is ugly but with a kind of ugliness which is noble, I should almost like to say beautiful," exclaimed Heine. "Indeed, the García recalls less the civilized beauty and tame gracefulness of our European homelands than she does the terrifying magnificence of some exotic and wild country." Maternal but wrapped up in her career, sensual and yet aloof, Pauline Viardot intimated pleasures quite irresistible to a man like Turgenev, whom one friend quoted as saying that the physical side of association with women had always mattered less to him than the spiritual, that orgasm was always less important than the emotions that preceded it.

For the rest of his life, Turgenev's movements were dictated as often by the desire to be near Pauline Viardot as by the need to wander alone, by tergiversations over Russia, or by force of circumstance. Perching "on the edge of another man's nest" sometimes induced vertigo, but it suited him better than having no nest at all. Ultimately the awkward ménage à trois he made with Pauline and Louis Viardot became a stable family in which he found contentment playing almost every part except that of lover.

It was unquestionably himself he described in observing that the Don Quixotes of his age kept pursuing Dulcinea though they knew her to be a hag. The ambivalence of his love life extended to the realm of ideas, where a deep-seated skepticism denied him the comfort that others found in dogma. "He who has faith has everything and can never suffer any loss, but he who doesn't have it has nothing, and I feel this all the more deeply since I belong to the company of those who have no faith," he wrote to his confidante, Countess Yelizaveta Lambert.[4] "Still, I do not lose hope." Forever self-divided, he would have liked to make a leap of faith but instead wrote novels that expose the element of sham in fanatical credos. His urbane demeanor concealed anguish from which he could not escape by embracing some god, and this *dégagement* mystified extremists, who, because they recognized no middle ground, invariably imputed to him sympathy for the enemy camp. How well psychological pithiness fared in Russia may be seen from the reception given *Fathers and Sons* when it appeared in 1862. Turgenev found himself damned as loudly by the Right as by the Left for having created in Bazarov, its nihilist hero, a character who either enhanced the prestige of revolution or furthered the cause of reaction.

Turgenev loathed Bazarov's radical materialism, but the clinical distance from self for which his character strives was an ideal he endorsed—to the extent of remaining awake when stomach surgery was performed on him in 1883 and watching it progress, much the way Bazarov observes himself die. "During the operation I was thinking about our dinners," he later told Edmond de Goncourt, "and I sought those words with which I could convey to you the exact impression of steel breaking my skin and entering my flesh . . . like a knife slicing a banana." Haunted by death from an early age, he came

[4]Yelizaveta Lambert was the daughter of Nicholas I's finance minister and the wife of General Count I. K. Lambert, aide-de-camp to Alexander II.

to regard his body as yet another provisional abode, and it is revealing that Turgenev already called himself an old man when he was only thirty-five. This same strategy begot novels whose most obvious character is their pervasive irony, the distant light they throw on human anguish. His search for the mot juste while on an operating table with his entrails laid open was what had made him the writer zealots could not tolerate. It exemplified his whole literary vocation.

And it promoted the spiritual kinship he felt with Flaubert, to whom he wrote on one occasion: "Oh, we have hard times to live through, those of us who are *born spectators*." Erudite, hypochondriacal, and equally sensitive to the clink of received opinion, the two men (who together weighed just under five hundred pounds, as George Sand mischievously observed) first met in 1863. A spark having leapt between them, they exchanged several letters, but mutual admiration did not become friendship until 1868. "Since the first time I saw you . . . I have felt a great liking for you—there are few men, particularly French men, with whom I feel so relaxed and at the same time so stimulated," Turgenev wrote in May 1868 from Baden. "It seems to me that I could talk to you for weeks on end, but then we are a pair of moles burrowing away in the same direction." *L'Education sentimentale* appeared soon thereafter, and Flaubert's novel about a feckless character drifting through time in the manner of Turgenev's own "superfluous men" consecrated their affinity.

Events conspired to deny them the nourishment of each other's minds. No sooner did war with Prussia break out in 1870 than Turgenev joined Pauline in London, where a formidable intelligentsia made him welcome. Even as Flaubert was inveighing against mankind, complaining that women robbed him of all his friends and angrily drilling a regiment that never left Rouen, the gregarious Turgenev took advantage of circumstance to converse with Ford Madox Brown, Algernon Swinburne, Thomas Carlyle, Benjamin Jowett, George Henry Lewes, and, above all, George Eliot. Most of 1871 had gone before the two reunited. Turgenev then moved back to Paris and into rooms on an upper floor of the Viardots' house near the rue Murillo. Every Sunday afternoon he visited Flaubert for several hours, unless immobilized by gout.

What came of this was a sequel to Sainte-Beuve's roundtable. Diverse in temperament but joined in contempt for the pieties upheld by conventional literati, Zola, Turgenev, Flaubert, Daudet, and Edmond de Goncourt—"les Cinq"—viewed themselves as a stigmatized mandarinate who could, *entre eux*, freely vent their souls while feasting once a month at the Café Riche on the Boulevard des Italiens and other great restaurants. Turgenev and Flaubert stood apart from Goncourt, Zola, and Daudet in their special closeness, however. By 1872 neither would see fifty again, and as the decades wore on, killing beloved witnesses, they felt increasingly antediluvian. Turgenev was yet to write *Virgin Soil,* but more often than not words failed him. "It's not that life is more difficult—it's that *undertaking* to do anything at all becomes more and more difficult," he confessed in November 1871. Flaubert had recently sent a similar distress signal: "Who is there to talk to now? Who is there in our wretched country who still 'cares about literature'? Perhaps one single man. Me! The wreckage of a lost world, an old fossil of romanticism! You will revive me, you'll do me good!" After *L'Education sentimentale,* which few people read, the savant in Flaubert gained the upper hand over the storyteller, and, with compulsive rage, he made his imaginative life serve his will to amass encyclopedic knowledge. Writing had always been hard labor for him. Now it became positively Sisyphean, as he walled himself up behind books and struggled first through *La Tentation de Saint-Antoine,* then through the misanthropic syllabi of *Bouvard et Pécuchet,* which he never finished.

Shocked at first to find that Flaubert in no way resembled the militant modernist he had expected to find, Zola was himself a source of irritation, with his penchant for pseudoscientific jargon derived from Hippolyte Taine. "[Flaubert] would declare in his booming voice that the modern doesn't exist, that there are no modern subjects, and when, taken aback by this statement, one asked him to elaborate, he'd simply add that Homer was just as modern as Balzac," Zola recalled. "Moreover, he denied evolution in literature. I discussed the subject with him time and again, but the examples I adduced to prove that writers don't sprout up like isolated phenomena . . . left him unconvinced. The rabid individualist swore at me: he didn't give a damn (or worse), what I showed didn't exist, every writer was independent, society had no part in making literature, one wrought beautiful sentences and nothing more." Neither ever conceded a point in this endless debate, but mutual admiration bred generosity. Zola, who could understand full well Flaubert's lifelong vendetta against bourgeois Rouen, came to love the older man for all that made him churlish or histrionic. And Flaubert, who once told Louise Colet, "One must know everything in order to write," marveled at the speed with which Zola dispatched novel after novel. As human beings rather than apostolic messengers, they leaned on each other staunchly, across a generation gap. Zola granted Flaubert his romanticism, while Flaubert, especially after he had read *La Conquête de Plassans,* forgave Zola his prefaces, his stylistic infelicities, his "isms," his scientific agenda.

La Conquête de Plassans tells a tale of provincial maleficence even more sinister than *La Fortune des Rougon.* Having written two successive novels set in the capital, Zola thought it wise to revisit the town from which his fictional clan sprang. "Given my general scheme, it's high time I returned to Plassans, where I shall not set foot again until the very end," he noted around February 1873. "This novel will portray provincial France under the Empire, and, once again, Pierre and Félicité Rougon's ascendancy. They must reappear and loom large, in the background." Thus do *Les Rougon-Macquart* proceed. Like a restless wanderer who cannot escape himself, the novels periodically call home from the various "milieux" they explore, their sequence being dictated as much by roots as by branches, as much by the concept of a hereditary *fatum* as by the imperative of social ramification. But here in *La Conquête* another consideration obtained. The villain of the piece is a priest who uses the mystico-erotic power he exerts over women to bolster Napoleon III, and Plassans seemed a better stage for such devilry than Paris.

Pierre Rougon's daughter Marthe and Ursule Macquart's older son, François Mouret, occupy the foreground. When *La Conquête* begins, this couple, half cousins who married, have spent twenty years together, most of them in Marseille, where they accumulated enough money to retire from the wholesale wine trade and settle in Plassans. At forty, Mouret won't give up business altogether and leisurely canvasses the hinterland. But more important to him is the neat, rational little world he has organized around family, house, garden. A nonbeliever whose watchwords are order and utility, the sharp-tongued merchant abides by the wisdom of *Candide*: "We must cultivate our garden." "He would prowl through the house, hold discussions with the children, spend his afternoons outside negotiating deals he never spoke about, eat and sleep as a man for whom existence had become a gentle slope, without bumps or surprises. Désirée [a retarded daughter] would play at his side. The two boys would always return from school at the same hour, in the same boisterous mood. And Rose, the cook, would lose her temper and scold everyone. Meanwhile the garden and dining room slept peacefully." Situated between the town hall, where a Napoleonic stooge holds sway, and the villa of a royalist magistrate named Rastoil, his three-story house overlooks gardens in which opposing factions periodically convene. From this box seat, Mouret, the hidden spectator, can watch his vegetables grow and his fruit trees blossom even as he derisively observes Plassans's beau monde playing out feverish scenarios on either side.

Life runs smoothly until avarice or boredom subverts common sense. With vacant rooms upstairs, Mouret agrees, after calculating how much additional income a tenant will provide, to lodge a priest en route from Besançon. His calculations go awry as soon as the priest materializes, for Ovide Faujas is not the meek curate Mouret may have had in mind but a large, powerful, hulking man accompanied by a troll-like mother who waits on him hand and foot. "Marthe noted his bare, rough-hewn head, his short hair graying near the temples . . . with a tonsure that looked like the scar of a battle wound. In late afternoon, when shadows enveloped him, his black figure stood out-lined against the ashen light of dusk." Nothing betrays their identity —neither their few personal effects, which they keep in a trunk, nor their words, which they hoard—and Mouret soon feels threatened by this occult phenomenon. He has his wife, children, and maid report clues of any kind. He ponders Faujas's comings and goings as if a mortal enemy were on the loose. He engages in espionage:

> Not a sound came from the third floor. Mouret stood on the staircase listening closely and even ventured up to the attic itself. Tiptoeing down the hallway, he thought he heard slippered feet behind the door, which made his heart thump. Still mystified, he descended to the garden and strolled through the arbor with eyes fixed on the windows, hoping to see something inside. But he couldn't detect any sign of the priest. Mme Faujas, who apparently owned no curtains, had stretched bedsheets over the panes.

Intrusion spells disaster. Overnight a safe, predictable enclosure be-comes a haunted house and Mouret, who had been utterly confident of the vantage point from which he judged the world around him, finds himself outside looking in. What was inalienably his is now some-one else's.

Before long we learn that Faujas has descended upon Plassans to implement the designs of Louis Napoleon, that his secret mission is to establish his moral authority and thereby promote Bonapartism among the monarchists leagued against the regime. Devoid of charm, he seems miscast in the role. Plassans's upper crust shrinks from a priest whose demeanor evokes the Church Militant or the Foreign Legion rather than the good old days, and his first sortie into polite society avails him nothing. "Walking through the salon, he caused a stir. One young woman, when she suddenly looked up, bristled on seeing this dark hulk in front of her. Opinion rose against him: his frame was too big, his shoulders were too square, his face was too hard, his hands were too rough. In the harsh light of the chandelier his cassock appeared so worn that the ladies felt embarrassed for him. They whispered behind their fans . . . while men exchanged knowing glances." Sentenced to pariahdom, Faujas is taught a fundamental les-son by the hostess, Félicité Rougon, who has received word of his mission from son Eugène. "The person in Paris counts on your suc-cess, and that's why you interest me," she confides. "Well, believe me, your fearsome manner will not do. Be amiable, please the women. Remember, please the women if you want to rule Plassans."

Unwittingly Mouret abets Faujas by suggesting that the priest and his mother sit near the hearth one cold winter evening. In due course this soirée becomes habitual, and while Mouret girds himself evening after evening for piquet, Faujas practices Félicité's advice upon Marthe. He doesn't proselytize her but instead stirs emotions that lead her to feel cheated of life, or to imagine an "elsewhere" more meaningful and felicitous than the orderly household in which she has hitherto known contentment. By degrees, priest supplants husband as her lord and master. More captivating than François Mouret's accounts of his mercantile success are Faujas's tales of penury.

> He often spoke about charity. Marthe was very tenderhearted, and other people's misfortune brought tears to her eyes. Seeing her shiver with pity seemed to please him. Every evening he told her some new sob story, he reduced her to a state of chronic compassion. . . . She would drop her knitting, clasp her hands, and regard him dolorously as he described wretches dying of hunger or paupers stealing for dear life. At such moments she was his thing, he could do with her whatever he wished.

What he would do is induce her to champion some cause that will gain the active support of every social matron in Plassans. No sooner has he proposed one—a shelter for certain pubescent waifs running wild through town—than she embraces the idea fervently. There are contributions to be solicited, blueprints to be drawn, workers to be goaded, feathers to be smoothed, and Marthe thinks about nothing else, least of all about her bewildered spouse, as she organizes "L'Oeuvre de la Vierge." When this monument stands complete, royalists join Bonapartists in hailing Faujas, who instantly eclipses rival clergymen. Three years later, a bishop fearful of the influence he wields appoints him rector.

His conquest of Plassans ends where it began, at François Mouret's residence. Marthe is herself a haunted house, part madwoman, part efficient bourgeoise, and Faujas, who knows it, sides with the Rougon ghost that inhabits her against the rational self propped up by marriage. Licensing her impulse to flee from reality, he offers her asylum in the Church. "The great, enveloping silence, the religious twilight of stained-glass windows induced sweet, vague reveries. She began to love the high vaults, the solemn bareness of walls, aproned altars, symmetrically arranged chairs." Estranged from her brood, Mouret's wife becomes Ovide Faujas's slave. She regards the frocked man as a kind of divinity endowed with magical powers who could, if he would, fill her, transport her, make her whole. That he remains aloof, and even takes sadistic pleasure in seeing her yearn to no purpose, enhances his prestige. Mouret watches helplessly as this nightmare unfolds before him. But so does Marthe watch helplessly. Although the spectacle of domestic chaos touches her, it touches her from afar, and when Faujas requests space upstairs for relatives named Olympe and Honoré Trouche, she overrules Mouret's objections.

What has declared itself is an internecine quarrel older than consciousness, and it drowns reason and affection in bad blood. "The old Rougon grudge revived in the presence of this Macquart, this man whom she accused of being the bane of her existence. . . . She would pounce on him for no good reason. Everything he did, his glances, his gestures, his rare words drove her mad. Arguments often broke out toward the end of dinner when Mouret . . . was folding his napkin and preparing to leave the table." Why can Mouret not struggle free? Because the paranoid logic that governs *La Conquête* admits of no escape. As Marthe talks louder, her husband grows meeker. As Faujas extends his dominion from the house to the garden, where notables from either camp now mingle at parties, Mouret, who has sent the children away, retreats to his small office. A supernumerary treated with contempt even by the maid, he is banished altogether when the unhinged Marthe starts flagellating herself. Word spreads that Mouret brutalizes her, no one doubts it, and Faujas prevails upon an obsequious doctor to have him carted off to a nearby lunatic asylum (the same asylum, in fact, that conceals the matriarch Adélaïde Fouque). Like Florent's arrest in *Le Ventre de Paris*, Mouret's internment occasions unrestrained gluttony. The nonconformist having been cast out, the swine who occupy his house exult.

Unlike Florent, Mouret laughs last. After his abduction Marthe recovers her senses enough to see Faujas for what he is and, griefstricken, visits the lunatic asylum. There another gruesome surprise awaits her. Bereft of everything else, Mouret has truly lost his mind. Imitating Marthe, as if imitating her were the only way of possessing her again, he rages uncontrollably. "Marthe stood spellbound. She recognized herself on the ground. Just so had she thrown herself to the bedroom floor, clawed her face, beaten herself. She could hear her own voice in his rattle. The poor devil was a creature of her own making." Mouret's fit is also witnessed by Antoine Macquart, his pariah uncle, who conspires, out of resentment toward Plassans society, to spring the madman loose. That same night, Mouret escapes, walks home in tatters, and introduces himself through the garden door. What he finds as he prowls about unseen infuriates him. His box trees have been cut down, his vegetables have been uprooted, his larder has been emptied, his orderly world has been pillaged, and the louts responsible for this desecration, Olympe and Honoré Trouche, lie asleep, drunk, in his bed. There they will die, for Mouret makes a funeral pyre of the

house he no longer recognizes. "When all was ready, he spent a moment admiring his handiwork," wrote Zola, whose description of the
uncanny moment owes much to Ulysse Trélat's *La Folie lucide,* among
other works on psychopathology.

> He went from one pile of kindling to another, circled each, made
> sure that they were all nice and square, and clapped his hands with
> satisfaction. Several pieces of charcoal had fallen down the stairs, so
> he fetched a broom and swept up the black dust. This inspection
> showed him to be still the tidy bourgeois intent on doing things as
> they should be done, in a deliberate way. But his joy frightened him
> a bit: he got down, began running on all fours, breathing hard and
> grunting. He then grabbed a brand to light the piles. Those on the
> terrace, under the windows, went up in flames. Then he bounded
> back inside and torched the salon, the dining room, the kitchen, the
> vestibule. He leapt from floor to floor, throwing embers into wood
> piled against the bedroom doors. A mounting fury shook him, the
> great blaze drove him completely mad.

When Madame Faujas tries to escape, somehow carrying her large,
semi-conscious son, Mouret hurls himself at them. All three are consumed in the fire.

Having found refuge under her mother's roof, Marthe escapes in-
cineration only to die soon afterward of grief. Eminent citizens mourn
the priest who made Plassans safe for Bonapartism, but not Pierre and
Félicité Rougon. Faujas had outlived his usefulness.

La Conquête de Plassans calls to mind Eric Bentley's thesis that
"melodrama is the naturalism of the dream life," for on one level this
otherwise fantastical work may be read as an entirely cogent dream
revolving around memories of the large house with a walled garden in
which Zola lived during his earliest years and from which he found
himself evicted when his father died. Mouret calls his fruitful plot of
land "paradise," but everything he does to render it impregnable (nail-
ing shut a door in the garden wall, for example) implies that paradise
will soon be wasted. Once he admits Faujas, death becomes his tenant.
Powerful yet chaste, the black specter—the devil/Christ who has no
offspring—establishes a mausoleum inside the close-knit household,
and Zola's description of Faujas's room clearly conveys this idea:

> The curtains over the windows were of such thick cotton that light
> filtering in gave the room a chalky pallor. This room was immense,
> high-ceilinged, with faded yellow wallpaper. Mouret made bold to
> enter, taking little steps on the mirror-clean tiled floor, which sent a
> chill right through the soles of his shoes. He examined everything
> furtively. Aside from an iron bed . . . whose sheets had been pulled

so tight that it looked like a white marble bench placed in one corner, there were only a commode lost at the far end of the room, a little table at the center, and two chairs. . . . Not one sheet of paper on the table, not one object on the commode, not one garment on the walls: bare wood, bare marble, bare plaster. This gray nudity would have been complete except for a large Christ hanging darkly over the commode.

The room resembled its strange occupant, writes Zola: "mute, cold, polished, impenetrable."

Inseparable from death is emasculation. Overnight a little potentate goes limp, and Zola, whose potentates often rule with their eyes, dramatizes the catastrophe in terms of sight. Seen only by the neighbor uphill ("people at the subprefecture can look over my wall"), Mouret has controlled his quasi-hermetic domain visually. For him it holds no secrets. The rational mind to which it bears witness pervades it, ordering its parts and clarifying its values. When religion introduces something opaque, some inwardness he cannot fathom, reason loses purchase and Mouret's futile espionage signals his fall. Suddenly baffled, he shrinks before eyes that burn, rape, expropriate. "One no longer feels at home," he complains early on, in the garden. "I can't raise my eyes now without noticing this cassock. . . . The bloke reminds me of crows, he has a round eye that seems always on the alert, waiting." Later, after Mouret has packed off his young daughter, Marthe and he will again meet in the garden under hostile eyes, this time to quarrel and grieve. "He raised his head, he examined the third-story windows," writes Zola. "Then, lowering his voice, he said: 'Don't cry like a ninny—they're looking at you. Don't you see that pair of eyes between the red curtains?' . . . Distressed and deeply moved . . . Marthe would have rushed into his arms. But they were afraid of being seen, they felt a kind of obstacle between them." His Adamic pride having deserted him, Mouret dares not embrace his wife. Unmanned by an image thrust upon him from above (or below), the stubborn nonconformist, the lord of his own creation, attempts to deceive the evil eye. But there is no hiding once self-consciousness, or knowledge of nakedness, breaches the wall that surrounds the garden. Paradise becomes hell.

As Faujas inhabits Mouret, so a fatherless son whose mother journeyed alongside him inhabited Zola the paterfamilias. Like Faujas, Emile was worshipped by two women after François Zola died, and perhaps that seven-year-old surrogate husband—chaste yet charismatic, immature yet powerful—survived as a phantom regularly infiltrating the walls of superstitious ritual that the adult writer raised against his guilty conscience. Identifying with marauder and gardener alike, Zola found himself threatened with destruction by each in turn.

One undermined the creative man, and the other exacted vengeance on the adulterous child. Both attacked at night, when Zola, fearfully blinking seven times to ward off death, felt most vulnerable. It is at night that Faujas's diabolic eyes burn brightest. And it is at night that Mouret burns his nemesis in what would appear to be the fatal self-confrontation of a *homo duplex.*

[Madame Faujas] hoisted Ovide on her shoulders like a child, and the sublime mother, devoted unto death, . . . did not stagger beneath the crushing weight of that large, limp body. She stamped out the embers with her bare feet and warded off the flames with her bare hands, clearing a path for her son. But just as she was about to descend, the madman, whom she had not seen, tore Faujas from her shoulders. . . . He beat the priest, scratched him, throttled him. "Marthe! Marthe!" he cried as he tumbled down the blazing stairs with the body.[5]

[5]Writing *L'Assommoir* several years later, Zola created in the character Goujet a virtuous paradigm of the chaste Hercules who lives with a widowed mother. Blond rather than dark, and impeccably gallant, he, too, lives by fire. Where Faujas's is the hellfire that consumes, Goujet's is the fire of the smithy, whom we see forging iron bolts while the woman he loves but cannot possess, Gervaise, watches admiringly. Here we have an act of sublimation in which Zola translated his own enterprise and predicament. The books he produced en masse argued his virility, but the ascetic discipline required to produce them exacerbated his sense of himself as deprived, monkish, impotent. He was not beyond seeing a novel as a sexual conquest or a child manqué.

As previously noted, one key to the rescue fantasy that informs this ubiquitous character type (Goujet asks only to rescue Gervaise, Faujas is summoned to rescue Plassans, Mouret having acquired herculean strength in madness would rescue Marthe, etc.) is suggested by Freud, who interprets it as an expression of what he calls the mother complex. It is worth quoting him at length: "The mother gave the child his life and it is not easy to replace this unique gift with anything of equal value. By a slight change of meaning, which is easily effected in the unconscious—comparable to the way in which shades of meaning merge into one another in conscious conceptions—rescuing the mother acquires the significance of giving her a child or making one for her—one like himself, of course. The departure from the original meaning of the idea of 'saving life' is not too great, the change in sense is no arbitrary one. The mother gave him his own life and he gives her back another life, that of a child as like himself as possible. The son shows his gratitude by wishing to have a son by his mother that shall be like himself; in the rescue fantasy, that is, he identifies himself completely with the father. All the instincts, the loving, the grateful, the sensual, the defiant, the self-assertive and independent—all are gratified in the wish to be *the father of himself.* Even the element of danger is not lost in the change of meaning; the experience of birth itself is the danger from which he was saved by the mother's efforts. Birth is in fact the first of all dangers to life, as well as the prototype of all the later ones we fear; and this experience has probably left its mark behind it on that expression of emotion which we call anxiety. Thus it was that Macduff of the Scottish legend, who was not born of his mother but 'ripp'd from her womb,' knew no fear."

On another level, Zola joined battle in *La Conquête* with proponents of "moral order," addressing himself to the custodial role, especially over woman, that French society vouchsafed the Catholic Church. No less a figure than Napoleon Bonaparte—whose maxims formed an army that survived Waterloo and held sway through every subsequent reformulation of the French polity—had made this abundantly clear when he said, "The weakness of woman's brain, the mobility of her ideas, the social role she was destined to perform, the necessity of constant and perpetual resignation along with a kind of easy, indulgent charity: all this demands religion, a charitable, soft religion." By and large, conservative opinion agreed that woman's "true" self was an invalid better spared pleasures and exertions of the mind, an organism whose fragile constitution would experience some fundamental derangement in absorbing "strong" material or in ruminating ideas other than those characterized as soft. If men proved their manhood by feats of retention, woman, on the contrary, suffered comparison to a leaky vessel that sailed through life discharging sentiment and alms, blood and progeny. Lacking the iron hull that made men men, she could safely transport only ethereal goods, baby flesh, and faith.

Woman's alleged invalidism had moral implications that justified her living as a legal minor under the government first of her father, then of her husband, and always of her Church—for in the "mobility of ideas" imputed to her by tradition, her protectors saw a generic inclination to stray or "err." "Of all the avenues that lead to happiness, the surest for a young girl just out of convent school is the one chosen by her provident father," wrote Sainte-Beuve, insinuating that when given her own way a woman would certainly leave the straight and narrow. "A young lady always knows too much," says Madame Vuillaume, the fanatical mother in a novel Zola wrote some years later, *Pot-Bouille*. "Modesty above all," she continues, by way of enunciating her pedagogical regime.

> No games in the staircase, the little girl always at home and in view, for little hoydens think about nothing but evil. The doors closed, the windows shut tight to keep out drafts, which bring nasty things in from the street. Outside, never release the child's hand, accustom her to keeping her eyes lowered, so as to avoid unseemly spectacles. Where religion is concerned, nothing in excess, but as much of it as is needed to enforce moral restraints.

A prenatal receptivity to whatever corrupts body and soul required that this porous being go forth, when forth she went, swathed in veils, imprisoned in trusses, and stuffed with precepts; that she live hermetically sealed, if not from the world outside, then from the secret intelligence given her by nature. It behooved young girls, who always knew too much, to unlearn what they knew and strive for innocent womanhood, just as it behooved fallen women to regret a childhood innocence not of this world. ("For a moment I built a whole future on your love, I longed for the country, I remembered my childhood—one always has a childhood to remember, whatever one may have become since then," declares the courtesan of *La Dame aux camélias* on her deathbed; similarly, Emma Bovary puts on a white confirmation dress before she dies.)

At convent school, where nuns taught the demoiselle skills that would serve the future wife in running a proper household, she spent some portion of the day, every day for five or six years, performing devotional exercises. Not until 1867 was there an alternative. And when in that year Victor Duruy had rectors throughout France organize secondary school courses for women, the otherwise divided Church closed ranks against what it considered to be a doomsday assault on *féminité*. From his pulpit in Orléans, where Duruy had struck the first blow, the relatively liberal Bishop Dupanloup insisted that young girls were reared "for private life in private life" and demanded that they not be led to the courses, examinations, diplomas, and award ceremonies that prepared men for public careers. "The secondary school education of young women has remained for the most part religious, and the family, nowadays shaken to its foundation, owes to this education what purity it still possesses. . . . I demand that the state not encumber the future with female freethinkers."

Whether to "secularize" womankind remained for years a political issue of signal importance. It provoked bitter skirmishes between republicans and antirepublicans, including one on April 10, 1870, at the Sorbonne, where Jules Ferry, who later became France's prime minister, declared that with "the *ancien régime* and its edifice of regrets, of beliefs, of antidemocratic institutions" arrayed in mortal combat against "the society engendered by the French Revolution," women could not occupy neutral ground. "Whoever commands woman's allegiance possesses everything, first because he possesses the child, second because he possesses the husband—not the young, tempestuous husband perhaps, but the husband worn down or disappointed by life. That is why the Church would keep woman faithful, and for that reason democracy must free her from its grasp." Nine years later a deputy named Camille Sée echoed his sentiments in the preface to a law that finally established public *lycées* for girls. "France is not a convent, nor was woman put on this earth to be a nun," he wrote. "She was born to be a wife, a mother. Called upon to live in emotional and intellectual communion with her husband and to raise her children, she is entitled to an education worthy of her, of the man whose life she shares, of the children who will receive their first lessons from her, and, finally, of the Republic that emerged from the Revolution of 1789."

From the perspective of this ongoing battle, *La Conquête de Plassans* may be said to present a schizophrenic portrait of woman before and after enlightenment. It is, among other things, an exemplary tale of regression. The wife, Marthe, having worked at Mouret's side, shared his beliefs, and raised three children without benefit of clergy, falls victim not only to her hereditary defect but to ecclesiastical hocus-pocus. She who had been her own mistress under the new dispensation becomes a slave under the *ancien régime* introduced by a misogynistic priest.

La Conquête was serialized, beginning February 17, 1874, in the moderate republican daily *Le Siècle*, whose prestige far exceeded its readership. When it appeared on bookshelves at the end of May it enjoyed less success than Zola's previous novels, and his friends were puzzled. "The mind of the public seems to me more and more degraded," Flaubert lamented to George Sand in September. "To what depths of stupidity shall we descend? Belot's last book [Belot wrote long potboilers] sold eight thousand copies in a fortnight, while *La Conquête de Plassans* has sold seventeen hundred in six months, and hasn't received a single review!" Though far more tautly constructed and powerful than *La Fortune des Rougon*, *La Curée*, and *Le Ventre de Paris*, the novel never quite took hold in France, even when the fame Zola later won redounded to the advantage of his early work. Better news came from abroad. Turgenev, who spent the summer of 1874 in Russia, wrote that a Saint Petersburg editor was enchanted with *La Conquête* and would soon propose to pay Zola handsome fees for his work.

Friends and acquaintances gave it a varied reception. Noting certain similarities between it and his own *Madame Gervaisais*, Edmond de Goncourt might have been flattered by evidence of Zola's respect but instead took umbrage. "Today, in literature, the essential thing is not to create characters whom the public greets like old friends, nor to express oneself in some original style; it is to invent a new lorgnette through which everything is seen as if for the first time," he reassured himself. "My brother and I invented that lorgnette; it is now the common property of all young authors, and I see them using it with the disarming candor of people who imagine they hold the patent." His jealousy, which was to become pathological, showed clearly when the book arrived: "I feel that it's a reproach when the mail brings me something published by a confrere. Today I threw Zola's *La Conquête de Plassans* into a corner, finding unbearable the sight of this pretty yellow volume with its brand-new cover and fresh print, which seemed to say to me: 'So what about you, are you all washed up?' "

Flaubert had no such misgivings, and his eagerness to tell everyone that *La Conquête* bowled him over could not have made life any easier for poor Goncourt. "This very day I've read Zola's latest novel straight through and I'm still completely dazed by it," he exclaimed in a letter to Turgenev. "It's strong stuff. It's better than *Le Ventre de Paris*. Toward the end there are two or three superb touches." From Croisset, he rained compliments on Zola:

> I read it, *La Conquête de Plassans*, read it straight through the way one quaffs a good glass of wine, then let it settle, and now, my dear friend, I can talk properly. I was afraid, after *Le Ventre de Paris*, that you'd get caught up in systems and dogma. Not at all! You're a fine fellow! and your most recent book is sheer pluck. It may lack a pre-eminent milieu or central stage (something one never finds in nature), and perhaps there is a bit too much dialogue in the sideshows. But those are the only nits I can pick. What power of observation! What depth! What firmness! The thing one really notices is its general tone, the passion seething beneath a calm surface. Well done, old man, well done.
>
> A fine figure of a bourgeois is Mouret with his curiosity, his avarice, his self-effacement and ultimate prostration. I find the curate sinister and great—a true father confessor! How well he manipulates *woman*, how adroitly he captures that particular one, snaring her with charity, then pummeling her! As for Marthe herself, you've brought her off to perfection, and I am at a loss for words to praise the art with which her character, or her illness, is developed. . . . But what overshadows everything else, what crowns the work is its ending. I can't think of a denouement more gripping than this one. . . . Mouret returning to his house and inspecting it! One is terror-stricken, as in reading a tale of the supernatural, and you achieve that effect with an exorbitance of reality, an intensification of the true-to-life . . . Sleep soundly, for you've done yeoman work. Also save all the stupidities [*bêtises*] it inspires. That sort of document interests me.

One author thrived on *la bête humaine*, the other on *la bêtise humaine*. For Flaubert, who told a friend that he would write *Bouvard et Pécuchet* to "exhale" his resentment, "vomit" his hatred, "expectorate" his venom, "ejaculate" his anger, and "cleanse" his indignation, *La Conquête de Plassans* undoubtedly served as a second-best purge.

Zola also received praise from a regular at Flaubert's Sunday gatherings, whose critical authority he had been invoking for many years. "As regards madness and growing delirium, you have no peer," wrote Hippolyte Taine. "The irresistible and painful onslaught of dream, and especially of this religious dream, is described with extraordinary power and lucidity. Your imagination and talent are equaled only by the wealth of your vocabulary and your rich, bold invention."

Enjoying a monthly retainer from Charpentier (whose faith in him was unshaken, despite one commercial fiasco and one very modest success) and a substantial income from journalism, Zola could now afford larger quarters for himself, Alexandrine, and Emilie. On April 1, 1874, the eve of his thirty-fourth birthday, he rented a narrow, three-story rubblestone house quite near the rue de la Condamine, at 21, rue Saint-Georges. With eight rooms plus a garden, it gave the family enough space to scatter when nerves got frayed, to accommodate a male servant, and to let Zola indulge his passion for scavenging in antique stores. There was space enough to furnish a nursery as well, but Alexandrine, who suffered various ailments including migraine headaches, did not conceive. Childless, they would remain on the rue Saint-Georges, subsequently renamed rue des Appenins, until their lease expired three years, or three novels, later.

XIII

THE LURE OF THE STAGE

IN FEBRUARY 1873, soon after Zola's diatribe against conservative potentates had led the government to silence *Le Corsaire*, its publisher, Edouard Portalis, bought another newspaper, *L'Avenir national*, and proposed that Zola serve as its theater critic. Although Zola distrusted Portalis, a genial rogue who flew the flags of republicanism one day and Caesarism the next, this proposal seduced him. He loved theater and loved to hate the theater available on Paris's Boulevard.

On the Boulevard little had changed since Zola had observed in 1869 that a regime ready to prosecute serious literature showed no disposition to quarrel with impresarios who exploited the public craze for spectacles of never-never land, feats of magic, displays of material wealth, glimpses of Babylon. Under Napoleon III dramatic art had gone into decline while illusionism flourished. Playwrights relied more often than not on technicians who devised special effects, and one such technician, Jean-Pierre Moynet, sensibly observed, "Special effects often save a play . . . when its literary elements are not sufficient to do so." Victor Séjour's *The Madonna of the Roses* owed its entire success to a fire simulated with Bengal lights, bellows, sparks, and lycopodium. For Adolphe Dennery's *The Battle of Marengo*, which played at the Châtelet, the manager requisitioned several four-inch artillery pieces from the war ministry and arranged to have their gun crews fire blank shells, without any assurance that the theater's glass roof would not shatter. A production of Meyerbeer's *The African Woman* took place on a stage transformed into an enormous ship that was made to rock back and forth by hands working machinery under-

298

neath it. *King Carrot*—a spectacular written by Victorien Sardou and Jacques Offenbach in which an old magician who is dismembered and burned piecemeal emerges from the fire a young man—inspired wizardly devices. "The machinist's art uses every resource in constructing gimmicks [*trucs*], some of which are veritable masterpieces," declared Moynet. "The machinist is at once a carpenter, a cabinetmaker, and a mechanic. The study of design and of dynamics is indispensable to him. Physics and even chemistry furnish him many effects. We will return to this when we develop more fully the subject of scientific progress applied to the modern stage."

While the Church was promoting Bernadette Soubirous's vision of the Virgin Mary at Lourdes in the hope of recovering its former authority, theater was discrediting occultism with *trucs* that enhanced the reputation of engineers. Frenchmen who did not fancy pilgrimages to Lourdes got all the magic they wanted on the Boulevard, where the supernatural became big business. Behind the backdrop and beneath the floorboards of several dozen stages, machinists and electricians, scene painters and upholsterers, locksmiths and blacksmiths, smoke-and-fire-makers, fountain keepers, and lighting masters did yeoman work in the cause of the entertainment industry, manufacturing fairy-tale scenes for the carriage trade.

Just as Aristotle's pieties, after serving neoclassical drama during the seventeenth century, came to tyrannize eighteenth-century imitations, so Victor Hugo's arguments for local color came to justify decorative tours de force. Like a frame that grows richer than the image it surrounds, romantic habitats built with great technical ingenuity made the romantic hero disappear, and this disappearance went beyond the stage. When Jules de Goncourt wrote, "Money is a very big thing that leaves men greatly diminished," he voiced an opinion held by many contemporaries that affluence had cost France her soul, that greatness had become the confection of newsmongers and paid auxiliaries, that the missing numeral between Napoleons I and III denoted a spiritual abyss in which the fallen soldiers of the Grande Armée had somehow fathered a nation of wee opportunists rising rank upon rank toward self-aggrandizement. Nothing was what it used to be, they mourned —not even opportunism. How could the writer create an Eugène de Rastignac when Rastignac's counterpart in modern France would have succumbed straightway to the devil without even making overtures to some loftier principle? How could he create a Vautrin when the devil, far from exerting animal magnetism, had acquired a respectable paunch? "Ah, it is very difficult indeed nowadays to find a man whose thought has some space in it, who ventilates you like those great swells of air one breathes at the seashore," sighs Norbert de Varenne, the poet in Maupassant's novel *Bel-Ami*, who sells his talent to a news-paper mogul. "I knew several such men. They're all dead."

Prominent among the hero's executioners was Eugène Scribe, who during the heyday of romanticism had created, in the *pièce bien faite* or "well-made play," an instrument wonderfully compatible with the values embraced by bourgeois eager to lord it over history. For him, historical drama was a means of demystifying the past, of trivializing exalted figures and exalting banality, of having great Shades undress before a bourgeois tribunal. In *Le Verre d'eau* his spokesman, Lord Bolingbroke, says:

> You shouldn't despise the little things; it's through them that one achieves the great things. You think perhaps, like everyone else, that political catastrophes, revolutions, the fall of empires, have deep, weighty, important causes. . . . What an illusion! Nations are subdued or governed by heroes, by great men; but these great men are them-selves led by their passions, their whims, their vanities; that is, by the most wretched and trivial things in the world. . . . The secret is not to try to compete with Providence and manufacture events, but to profit from events. The more trivial they appear, if you ask me, the more consequential they are.

This manifesto ends with Scribe's most famous line: "Great effects from small causes . . . that's my system."

Where the drama in Hugo's theater often moves toward some heroic assertion of identity, everything in Scribean theater argues a world governed by a nimble puppeteer. Hernani and Ruy Blas rise above imbroglios, prove their mettle, and die, while Scribe would have us admire an opportunist who rides an arbitrary contraption to a rational denouement, profiting from tricks of fate that coincide with those of the well-made play. The Hugo hero eclipses his role, but the Scribe tale conquers all—keeping its audience intrigued, then zipping itself up, leaving behind no residue of doubt, no hint of transcendence, no suggestion of mystery. Mystery was what Scribe meant to abolish, through plots that substitute their own devious logic for human com-plexity and simulate depth the better to expose it as a mirage con-cealing some all-important whim or key trifle. The large becomes commensurate with the small and greatness synonymous with puffery.

Foreigners who threaten domestic order, speculators who would get rich quick, young swains foolish enough to sacrifice comfort for love, vices that eat up patrimonies: this was the stuff of Scribe's nonhistor-ical work. Defending the tight little ship or *juste milieu* against im-providence, he had numerous followers, but none more successful than Alexandre Dumas *fils*. "You will use any weapon at your command to punish unfaithful wives" was how the Comte d'Haussonville welcomed Alexandre Dumas's bastard into the French Academy on February 11, 1875, twenty-three years after he had stormed the Boulevard with *La Dame aux camélias*. "Let them beware henceforth of those pretty jade-handled knives that lie on tabletops, of those pistols their husbands have been toting in their pockets and those shotguns forgotten in convenient corners." So constructed as to enforce the "social law" while taking turns that give the outlaw (courtesan, adulteress, rake, embezzler) a momentary but illusory advantage, the well-made play became, during the Second Empire, what d'Haussonville called "a formidable apparatus of moralization."

Seldom did Dumas send an audience home without the ashes of a foiled plot or the epitaph of an illicit passion. One might indeed conclude that he wrote plays to discredit theater, for his typical plot is a plot against bourgeois well-being, his villain an imposter who harbors a disreputable past, his denouement a trial scene in which the actor finds himself unmasked, and his hero Society as represented by a gentleman not unlike the sleuth of modern detective novels. Known as "the Reasoner," this stock character, whose celibacy argues his lucidity, straddled audience and stage. Dumas could titillate straitlaced clients in good conscience because his Reasoner was always present, at once actor and spectator, orienting the public's moral perception or distancing it from fantasy. A connoisseur of human turpitude, he never browbeats malefactors but stigmatizes them with bons mots. One journalist claimed that all over Paris people famous for their wit plagiarized Dumas *fils* every day. "No sooner does he strike an image, however banal and overwrought, than it becomes common coin," Zola observed.[1]

Dumas *fils* was in all his glory when Zola took him on, and a production of *L'Etrangère* at the Comédie-Française provided the occasion for this showdown. "Every great writer begets life and Dumas *fils*,

---

[1] The Reasoner himself became quasi-official, or so one infers from the brief against *Madame Bovary* delivered by France's imperial prosecutor in 1857. "Who in this book can condemn this woman?" he asked. "No one," he answered. "In this book there is not one character who can condemn her. If you find a single wise character, a single principle whereby adultery is stigmatized, then I am wrong. But if there is not a single character who can make her bow her head, not an idea or line in which adultery is scourged, then it is I who am right—the book is immoral." What he voiced was the fear that without some such figure relativism might triumph. And, indeed, time proved him right, for in time the formula Dumas wielded on behalf of a moral order was turned to the account of moral chaos by playwrights like Luigi Pirandello. In *Henry IV*, *Six Characters in Search of an Author*, and *It Is So (If You Think So)*, the Reasoner became the sleuth of an insoluble mystery, the advocate who indicts a criminal audience, proclaiming private delusions to be more real than the so-called real world.

at the outset of his career, invented that demimonde which has been the true source of his literary fortune," he wrote. "To give him his due, he fathered Marguerite Gautier and the Baronne d'Ange. Unfortunately he has not fathered anything else." Although Dumas *fils* knew his métier "better than anyone," his "lack of creative breath" sentenced him to mediocrity:

> Read his plays or see them: characters one more nondescript than the next parade across the stage like stilted arguments forgotten as soon as the book is closed or the curtain falls. . . . Whatever he touches becomes inert and forms a dissertation. Most of the time he gets lost in social problems instead of keeping his eye on humanity.

The all-purpose environment in which Dumas couched his fables was as vexatious as his didacticism. Zola, who believed that "character" could not be understood apart from "milieu," reprimanded Dumas for "shoving reality into a narrow, preestablished frame," even if it meant shattering it.

> When a character won't fit, he'll amputate, which produces grotesque results. His Frenchmen are no more French than his Russians are Russian. . . . The great wide world is a puppet gallery from which he selects Whites, Negroes, Redskins to furnish his whimsical plots.

To what, then, did Dumas *fils* owe his disproportionate stature? Above all, Zola thought, to a second sense that told him just how far one might safely push convention, a talent for offering spectators both the honor of virtue and the pleasure of vice. "His alleged audacities are calculated to draw a crowd without requiring the intervention of the constabulary," Zola explained. "In France, one need only announce something extraordinary and people imagine that they've gotten what they were promised. . . . [M. Dumas] has cultivated a legend that portrays him as someone who boldly delves into human guts. Curious readers investigate and are delighted to find nothing immoral. What passes for audacity are certain off-color expressions that leap out of his turgid prose."

Dumas's epigones fared no better than he. Traipsing from one inane production to another, Zola, who saw as many as four plays a week (often, on Monday evenings, with Alexandrine), handed out few valentines. "In the middle of the most loudly applauded, best-made plays, I have often found myself longing for someone to interrupt them with a sudden caper, for the lover to jump onto the mantelpiece, for the floorboards to collapse beneath the heroine, for a fit of madness to tangle the yarn. . . . Boredom, nausea. There are so many do-gooders around! We are served sugar at all our meals. One develops a ferocious thirst for bile." By madness Zola did not mean histrionics, and he chided actors who rode these merry-go-round horses like warriors spurring roans.

[Laurent Tailhade] was dandled on the knees of Shakespeare and Victor Hugo. Later the tragic authors took him in hand, but he never had a master to tell him about the modern world, the facts of life, everyday drama. That's why he affects the crisp gestures and cadenced voice of legendary heroes. He can't say hello, but he can brandish a dagger with the appropriate grimaces. Unfamiliar to him is the natural tone in which one addresses a young woman, but he can insult the gods or invoke the devil with perfectly modulated shouts. Few actors know the craft as well as he, and he's intelligent. All he lacks is the capacity to ring true.

Throughout his criticism, which angered many subscribers, he pleaded the cause of realism against a "quasi-hieratic" theater laced with compulsory formulae, liturgical dialogues, and prescribed situations. "May [the playwright] forswear the intricate contrivances of our hacks, may he dare write about the human drama—what I'd call modern tragedy—and delve deep to show how physiology works its way," he enjoined the young author of a play called *Un Lâche* (*A Coward*). "We must create men above all, in the theater as elsewhere. Once we have done that, situations will be nothing but the characters themselves, or the outgrowth of their personalities." Since true art shows people as they are rather than as they should be, the true artist is an observer whose categorical imperative transcends ideals upheld by society, left-wing, right-wing, or utopian. Zola sounded this article of faith in language that makes frequent reference to science. "Success will henceforth be reserved for intimate and real drama, for the analytic scenario that logically carries its investigation of a character or a fact to the very limit," he wrote on April 15. And on March 4, still discussing *Un Lâche:*

A *Coward,* the title struck me as audacious. It led me to imagine a physiological study of fear, a human drama with nerves jangling through it. Fear is complex, it chills the bravest among us, it is bred into our blood and bone. . . . So I thought that the work would beggar convention and explore what we call cowardice, which is only a particular kind of temperament. Here was a new subject, a very dramatic one in my view, offering scope to the analytic mind. At the very least one original hero would fill the stage. This livid, terror-stricken man would recoil from his own shadow while the author undressed him for us, explaining his womanish frailty as a doctor and a moralist.

A playwright like Dumas was thus to be supplanted by a Reasoner who argued for the human unreasonableness that bourgeois theater suppressed or denounced, and who did so from the high ground of scientific inquiry. Indeed, this paragon already figured in Zola's fictional master plan: Dr. Pascal Rougon, physician and naturalist, developed theories of heredity based upon observation of his hyphenated clan.

Unlike reviewers who dared not write for the stage lest their imaginative work impugn their critical authority, Zola the critic served Zola the dramatist. In a bottom drawer, among other unpublished manuscripts, lay a five-act play he had adapted from *Thérèse Raquin*, and out it came when he joined *L'Avenir national*. To be sure, his artistic conscience advised discretion. "It is always dangerous to extract a drama from a novel," he noted. "One of them is inevitably slighter than the other, and this will often diminish both. So incongruous are the laws that govern stage and book that an author must perform amputations on his own thought, must expose its gaps and its longueurs, must distort it to make it fit a new mold. Hacking away like Procrustes, he shapes monstrous forms." But artistic conscience was overruled by reformist zeal (along with fantasies of instant wealth, perhaps). Zola addressed himself to a feisty impresario named Hippolyte Hostein, and Hostein, who had helped Balzac achieve his one theatrical success, twenty-five years earlier, agreed to produce *Thérèse Raquin* at the handsome new Théâtre de la Renaissance.

It didn't work. A novel whose soul is the aqueous environment through which everything moves spectrally became a mere domestic melodrama. Lost in translation were all those images that show to such advantage Zola's genius for the macabre: coffinlike shops under the roof of a dank arcade, the morgue with stylish ladies taking ghoulish delight in the spectacle of bodies recovered from the Seine, a semi-invalid heaved overboard in mid-river, a guilt-ridden brute painting his victim's rotted face again and again, a mouth that bites posthumously. Thérèse, Camille, Laurent, Madame Raquin seem no less wooden than the cronies who gather every Thursday evening at eight sharp for a game of dominoes. Confined to one room, they mimic their fictional counterparts like fish out of water or characters in search of a medium. Zola may have had in mind "a purely human drama shorn of all extraneous detail, whose action would be the characters' internal strife," but what he wrote never comes alive. Worst of all is the climax. As a distant audience would not have seen the terrible eyes that Madame Raquin trains upon Thérèse and Laurent, Zola arranged to have her miraculously recover speech and deliver a ringing indictment of her son's assassins.

Premiered on July 11, 1873, when the only other show in town was the shah of Iran's state visit, *Thérèse Raquin* created a commotion during its brief early-summer run. Though many critics among the thirty or so who reviewed it allowed that Zola had talent, they out-hyperbolized one another in shaming him for his preoccupation with affairs of the groin. "The critical fraternity discussed my work passionately, even violently," Zola recalled a year later. "I'm not complaining and I thank them for it. It did me good to hear praise heaped on the novel from which the drama was extracted, the same novel journalists mistreated when it first appeared. Now the novel is fine and the drama worthless. Should I extract some work from the drama, perhaps it, in turn, will meet with their approval." His sarcasm belied the fact that blows suffered in the heat of battle had hurt, and none more than a savage review written by Louis Doré, who had succeeded Zola as theater critic at *L'Avenir national* on June 10, 1873. "I thank M. Louis Doré, whom I do not know, for the pan with which he favored *Thérèse Raquin,*" he huffed in a letter to Edouard Portalis. "I also thank you for having let it appear on a page still warm from my prose. I avail myself of this opportunity to request that you send, tomorrow at the latest, the nine thousand francs you owe me."[2]

As if to remind those critics who garrisoned the fortress of bourgeois convention that he had another siege gun at his command, Zola set about writing a comedy. "My explicit intention," he declared in his preface, "was to write a pastiche . . . to go back to the sources of our theater and resuscitate old Italian farce as practiced by our seventeenth-century authors. So that no one would misunderstand me, I lifted turns of phrase and pieces of scenario from Molière. . . . Only in the matter of dress and milieu did I permit myself any modern touches. Conflating old and new to picture a human reality that doesn't change with time is what interested me." Molière may show here and there, but the general idea for *Les Héritiers Rabourdin,* which Zola turned out very quickly, came from Ben Jonson's *Volpone.* It features a retired draper named Rabourdin whose parasitic relatives ply him with gifts and treat him with hysterical solicitude in hopes of inheriting a fortune they themselves have already been pilfering. Everything hinges on this nonexistent hoard—the marital prospects of an ingenue engaged to a venal suitor, the credit of a woman beholden

---

[2]Portalis owed him not only for his reviews in *L'Avenir national* but for his early novel *Les Mystères de Marseille,* which, as previously noted, had been serialized anew under the title *Un Duel social* in *Le Corsaire.* When Zola threatened litigation, Portalis ponied up twelve hundred francs.

to a loan shark, and the survival of Rabourdin, who teases his entourage like an auctioneer playing bidders against one another even as he
feigns poor health. Only Catherine, his goddaughter-cum-house-
keeper, knows how matters stand, and it is for her to lift the mask.
After learning that her own inheritance is gone, she choreographs a
mock death vigil during which the vultures are led to believe that one
last munificent gift will purchase them salvation. When finally the
truth emerges, they curse Rabourdin but realize straightway that they
must continue fawning over him, since social disgrace will be their lot
if word of his bankruptcy should become common knowledge. The
suitor will want no part of marriage, the usurer will extend no more
credit, the townspeople will gloat.

Directors whose clientele fancied light entertainment gave *Les Héritiers Rabourdin* a wide berth. Though he found it "true and poignant,"
Francis Plunkett declared that its asperity would upset patrons of the
Palais-Royal. This made it unsuitable for performance at the Gymnase
as well, according to Adolphe Lemoine-Montigny. "I've reread the play
carefully, I've reflected upon it, I'm quite sure it won't fly," he told
Zola. "Your work has lots of verve, spirit, keen observation. . . . But a
situation that doesn't change, the same stew simmering throughout,
. . . nothing to divert one from thoughts of death, sickness, last will
and testament, inheritance. One room, cold and gray, in which sunbeams never fall and party lights never shine. It's obvious that people
will conclude: talent galore, but wearisome."

Undaunted, Zola crossed over to the Left Bank and found hospitality at the Théâtre de Cluny, a former recital hall near the Boulevard
Saint-Michel, where Flaubert, after rebuffs of his own, had just placed
Le Sexe faible. "[Montigny] returned my manuscript in a charming
way, with assurances that he would like to stage something by me,"
he wrote to Georges Charpentier in July 1874, when his publisher was
vacationing on the Normandy coast. "As soon as I got the script back
I took it elsewhere. It's decidedly an illness, this need to be performed.
Having a theater of last resort, the Cluny, I knocked at Weinschenk's
door, and yesterday he accepted the play. It will open before Flaubert's, around mid-September, under heaven knows what conditions.
The company makes me shudder. What can I say? I felt compelled to
go ahead with this business for my peace of mind. I couldn't stand
the manuscript lying fallow in a desk drawer."

As it happened, *Les Héritiers* did not open until November 3, which
meant that Zola had all of October to reel between hope and despair
while observing, day after day, the ineptitude of a ragtag troupe. "I've
been silent because I didn't want to alarm you by unburdening myself
in the turmoil of first rehearsals, which were abominable," he warned
Flaubert. "Now things look somewhat better, except for one actor,

whom I must keep against my will. . . . I advise you to stand firm in the matter of casting for your comedy. If you let Weinschenk dictate, you'll have a hard time getting rid of the players he foists upon you. I'll tell you more when we meet. You can learn from my experience." Failure was writ so large that even Edmond de Goncourt, who attended one rehearsal at Zola's behest, felt moved to commiserate. "The Cluny is a theater that manages to look like a village playhouse smack in the middle of Paris," he noted without any of his usual Schadenfreude. "On the stage there is the forced gaiety of poor actors who don't eat every day. It's disheartening for a man of substance to be performed in such a place by such people. And the thought that Flaubert will suffer the same fate one month hence saddens me."

Friends thronged the Cluny on November 3, and Flaubert, banging his cane to signal his approbation, led the noisy claque like a demonic maestro. In the aftermath, several of them helped buoy Zola with letters of praise. "Ten years hence you'll probably devise more complicated, skillful things, which professional critics will laud," wrote Charles Duranty, "and we few will then miss the special flavor of this comedy which I liked very much for its candor, its naive devices, its violent imagery." Mallarmé, whose artistic credo marshaled the high and low of symbolism and illiteracy against rhetorical convention (or what he called *la langue de la tribu*), echoed this sentiment:

So what if *Les Héritiers Rabourdin* is (as reviewers have said) a popular illumination! Does the popular illumination not gratify people with refined taste? I myself—who admire an overdrawn and overcolored poster as much as a ceiling fresco or an apotheosis—consider all viewpoints in art equally legitimate and suit my pleasure to circumstance.

Had their mutual friend Edouard Manet painted for *Les Héritiers* a curtain or backcloth folksy enough to hang in a fairground stall, he surmised, then the press would have rhapsodized over the play.[3]

Zola needed moral support from friends, as foes handled him very roughly indeed. Montigny had predicted that his work would make a lugubrious impression, and so it did. "Do you like the atmosphere of sickrooms, the lard of yesterday's cutlets mingling with the stale aroma of poultices?" asked Auguste Vitu in *Le Figaro*. "Do you like talk about

[3]In *Une Saison en enfer*, which Mallarmé had certainly read when it appeared in 1873, Rimbaud declared that he loved "idiot paintings, . . . the canvases of traveling acrobats, shop signs, popular illuminations, outmoded literature, Church Latin, erotic books with misspelled words." Modernism argued the legitimation of naive or primitive forms and Mallarmé's reference to Manet was prescient. Some fifty years later Picasso painted a circus curtain for *Parade*, the Diaghilev ballet featuring a text by Cocteau and music by Satie.

catarrhs, coughs, gravel, cachexy, apepsia, dyspepsia, and lientery? Do you fancy moribund faces . . . and take some interest in the machinations of old women with grimy shopping baskets? If you answer yes, then head straight for the Théâtre de Cluny: M. Emile Zola is your man." Fair play was obviously not Vitu's forte, but in this respect he had strong competition. Determined to scuttle *Les Héritiers*, critics sang a chorus of opprobrium, with Francisque Sarcey, who held sway over Parisian theater from his rostrum at *Le Temps*, intoning the final judgment. "This humoristic comedy is quite simply a very boring comedy," he declared one week after the premiere performance.

Emile Zola wanted to make merry. But one does not make merriness. One is merry by nature or not at all. . . . There is no hint of that quality in his novels. To be sure, he could have spoken like Gringalet, who, when asked whether he can play the fiddle, answers: "Perhaps, I've never tried." Well, now the issue is settled. . . . It has often been observed that the most intense and open laughter is sparked by the saddest and most repugnant things—by sickness, death, and their retinue of woes. Gaiety thrives on contrast, but gaiety must be there to leaven these images or they remain what they are in fact—hideous and disheartening . . . This Rabourdin is insufferable with his eternal whining, his feigning mortal illness, his herbal infusions.

Lest Zola survive his drubbing, Sarcey delivered a last blow with: "The thing that especially displeases me in Emile Zola's manner is his pretensions. Each of his characters always seems to be saying to the public: 'See what an abyss of perversity I am!' "

On successive Sundays *Les Héritiers* filled the house with people from the neighborhood. Otherwise, theater buffs, who rarely ventured beyond the Boulevard unless Sarcey gave an off-Boulevard play his benediction, stayed away in such numbers that Zola had very soon to admit defeat. "I haven't forgotten you, my dear friend," he assured Flaubert on November 9.

Last Sunday the Théâtre de Cluny sold out, the play roused the audience, the evening was sustained laughter. But since then attendance has fallen off again. In short, we're not earning a sou . . . What's exasperating is that the play has a hundred performances in its gut: you can tell from how the audience welcomed it. As things stand, there won't be twenty. It will flop. The critics will triumph. That's my only regret . . . How right you were when you said at the premiere: "Tomorrow, you will be a great novelist." They all spoke about Balzac and sang my praises. It's odious.

Although Sarcey triumphed, Zola afterward found consolation in the knowledge that his fiasco spared Flaubert similar indignities. *Le Sexe faible,* a comedy as lame as *Les Héritiers,* was never staged by Weinschenk (or anyone else), for Flaubert decided not to risk humiliation and withdrew his play. "It's certain that I was riding for a colossal fall . . . with pitiful actors," he told a friend, concluding that theater was an art reserved for writers who wrote like cabbies, and resigning himself to the agonies of *Bouvard et Pécuchet.* Zola, on the other hand, wrote a preface-manifesto against Boulevard comedy, or comedy fraught with moral purpose. As he always wanted the last word, this gesture appeased him, no doubt, but his best response came years later when, salvaging *Les Héritiers* for fiction, he proved his critics right. The Volpone he couldn't animate on stage figures quite effectively as a minor character in the novel *Pot-Bouille.*

Zola sought and found sympathetic company on the rue Murillo, where everyone had a tale of blighted theatrical ambition to tell. Edmond de Goncourt still raged against the cabal that had driven *Henriette Maréchal* off the stage of the Comédie-Française in 1865. Daudet's *L'Arlésienne,* for which Bizet composed incidental music, earned him nothing during its brief run at the Vaudeville. Turgenev's *A Month in the Country,* written in 1849, reached the stage twenty-three years later only to die of exposure. Flaubert's *Le Candidat* won nobody's vote. Among these distinguished novelists, producing unsuccessful plays became a kind of initiatory ordeal, and so it was that they decided, in April 1874, to celebrate their brotherhood over food and drink at a *dîner des auteurs sifflés* or "dinner of booed authors." "Nothing more delightful than those dinner parties of friends, where one talks uninhibitedly, with minds alert and elbows on the tablecloth," Daudet reminisced in *Trente ans de Paris.*

We were all gourmands. There were as many different varieties of gluttony as there were temperaments; as many tastes as provinces represented. Flaubert wanted Normandy butter and Rouen ducks *à l'étouffade.* Edmond de Goncourt, with his delicate exotic appetite, relished sweetmeats flavored with ginger; Zola, shellfish; Turgenev, caviar. Ah! we were not easily fed, and the Parisian restaurants must remember us. We moved around a lot. At one point we dined at Adolphe and Pelé's, behind the Opera; at another on the Place de l'Opéra-Comique; then at Voisin's, where the cellar satisfied all our demands and reconciled our different palates. We'd sit down at seven o'clock, and at two we had not finished. Flaubert and Zola dined in their shirtsleeves, Turgenev reclined on the couch. The better to talk shop in private, we'd turn the waiters out of the room—an entirely useless precaution for Flaubert's roar could be heard from top to bottom of the house.

This feast, which brought them together almost every month, engendered another ritual. Because Flaubert felt lonely when his fellow gluttons scattered, Zola would walk him home through the dark streets, with frequent pauses for mutual enlightenment.

However unproductive any of the assembled may have been at their separate desks, language always gushed forth at the dinner table. Zola remembered Turgenev and himself arguing a six-hour brief against Chateaubriand. More than one epic battle was fought over Hippolyte Taine. And Flaubert lectured ad nauseam about the quiddities that kept him up all night. "Once I witnessed this very typical scene," wrote Zola. "Turgenev, who retained friendship and admiration for Mérimée, wanted Flaubert . . . to explain why he thought that the author of *Colomba* wrote badly. Flaubert read a page from it, and he stopped after every clause, blaming the 'whiches' and the 'thats' [*les 'qui' et les 'que'*], fuming over hackneyed expressions such as 'to take arms' or 'to lavish kisses.' The cacophony of certain syllabic sequences, the dryness of sentence endings, the illogical punctuation—everything received bad marks." Meanwhile, Turgenev, obviously perplexed by this withering *explication de texte*, sat wide-eyed. "He declared that no writer in any language had ever scrupled quite that way," Zola went on. "In his own country, there was nothing like it. Thereafter I'd see him smile whenever he heard us vilify 'whiches' and 'thats.'" No doubt the "dinner of booed authors" would have lost its raison d'être if they had subjected their own words to such scrutiny. But, although they criticized one another's work openly, the serious qualms were voiced out of earshot.

Frequently, literary talk led to bouts of collective self-revelation, or so said Edmond de Goncourt, who describes his confreres all trading confidences with the zeal, recklessness, and braggadocio of adolescents eager to win approval, to score points, or simply to talk dirty. One contest took place at a tavern behind the Opéra-Comique, over bouillabaisse, when the normally decorous Turgenev related a sexual adventure he had had during his *Wanderjahren*. "I was summoned back to Russia from Naples. I had only five hundred francs," Goncourt quotes him as saying.

There were no railroads then. The voyage involved many difficulties and left me no allowance for love. I found myself on a bridge at Lucerne watching ducks with almond-shaped spots on their heads. Next to me some woman stood against the parapet. It was a magnificent evening. We began to chat, then to stroll, and we strolled into the cemetery. Do you know that cemetery, Flaubert? I can't remember ever having felt more desirous, more excited, more aggressive. The woman lay down on a large tomb and lifted her dress and petticoats so that her buttocks touched the stone. Beside myself, I swooped on her and in my haste and awkwardness got my rod caught in gravelly tufts of grass, from which I had to extricate it. Never has coitus given me such keen pleasure.

Zola lacked Turgenev's anecdotal flair and store of exotic props. Unlike Flaubert, he knew little or nothing about Parisian brothels. For sheer lasciviousness he couldn't match Daudet, who claimed to have explored countless pudenda, often two at a time, with hand and tongue. But, if one may believe Goncourt's *Journal*, he spoke about himself as freely as they did on these occasions:

> Zola tells us that in his student days he would sometimes spend a whole week in bed with a woman, or anyway never get out of his nightshirt. The room *reeked of sperm*, as he put it. He declares that after these orgies his feet felt like cotton and in the street he'd grab shutter latches for support. Now he's very sensible, he says, and has intercourse with his wife every ten days. He confesses several curious idiosyncrasies of nervous origin having to do with coitus. Two or three years ago, when he began *Les Rougon-Macquart*, he wouldn't sit at his desk after a night of conjugal effusion, knowing beforehand that he couldn't construct a sentence, write a line. Now it's the opposite. After eight or ten days of mediocre work, coitus induces a slight fever that unblocks him.

Goncourt reports that at the start of Zola's career he would on occasion, when writing proved most difficult, have an ejaculation without erection after toiling over a sentence.

Another entry throws light on the prevalence in *Les Rougon-Macquart* of nubile girls, and it also suggests that the punishment François Zola meted out to his twelve-year-old Algerian houseboy years earlier had marked his son forever:

> We chat about how we feel after sexual satisfaction. Some experience sadness, others relief. Flaubert declares that he could dance in front of his mirror. "With me, it's curious," says Turgenev. "Afterward I feel back in touch with the things that surround me. Things reacquire the reality they hadn't had a moment before. I feel myself *me*, and the table becomes a table again. Yes, the bond between me and nature is restored." Zola with his wiry, straight hair cropped over his brow, his brutal Venetian head, his Tintoretto-cum-housepainter features, Zola, who had kept quiet until then, suddenly complains of being haunted by the desire to sleep with a young girl—not a child but a girl who is not yet a woman. "Yes, it scares me. I see myself hauled trembling before a jury."

Coming from a writer whose oeuvre dwells upon burial and immure-
ment, such indiscretions seem quite remarkable, the more so because
we know that Zola never conquered his fear of talking or reading in
public. (When in 1875 a fellow writer encouraged him to hold a public
reading, he demurred: "I'm too scared . . . I've done it once, I read
several pages to friends and I must confess that it didn't come off very
well. I splash about, I stammer, I sweat. The truth is, I'd make a poor
show.") Still, Zola himself might have recognized that his impulse to
cover up impelled him to strip, that inside the voyeur was an exhibitionist screaming to be let out. As naked as he stood among friends,
this shy man would lay himself barer still in middle age, when Dr.
Edouard Toulouse made him the subject of a thesis on the anatomy
of genius.

What knit the group together even more than meals shared or several confidences exchanged were services rendered, and in this area
Turgenev earned special credit, particularly with Flaubert. The latter
may have nicknamed him *grande poire molle* (big soft pear) but from
the moment they met, Turgenev found himself cast in the protective
role. It was for Flaubert to voice fears that he had lost his creative
power or his mind and for Turgenev to console him, praise him, hurry
him along, like an attentive father. "The time has come to brace yourself and to throw a masterpiece at the head of readers. Your Saint
Anthony could be that missile. Just don't linger over it. That's my
refrain." He offered much the same advice in 1874, when Flaubert
told him about his ambitious plans for *Bouvard et Pécuchet*: "The more
I think about it, the more I see it as a subject to deal with *presto* in
the manner of Swift or Voltaire. You know that has always been my
opinion." It exasperated him that his gifted friend should, in Henry
James's phrase, have "felt of his vocation almost nothing but the
difficulty."

Turgenev seldom visited Flaubert at Croisset. Whether house-ridden
with gout, detained abroad, or immersed in family affairs, he always
had some good excuse not to go there. Their correspondence tells a
story of broken appointments. And yet it also speaks of Turgenev's
loyal effort to disseminate Flaubert's work in Germany and Russia
(where the public for it proved as sparse as in France). No literary agent
could have been so assiduous. He dunned magazine editors, winkled
articles out of influential critics, recruited translators, and himself
translated two stories from *Trois Contes*, taking such pains over them
that Flaubert learned what it felt like to goad Flaubert.

Turgenev's beneficence profited Zola as well. Although the Rougon-
Macquart novels had become quite popular in Russia, unlike *La Ten-
tation de Saint-Antoine*, they generated no income at all until
Turgenev, who regularly migrated east, brokered an arrangement with

Mikhail Stasiulevich, editor of a Saint Petersburg journal called *Vestnik Evropy*, or *The European Herald*. This mediation took place in the summer of 1874, and Turgenev's report to the untraveled Zola began with a geography lesson. "If you have an atlas, find Russia and slide your finger from Moscow toward the Black Sea," he wrote on June 17.

> Just north of Orel you will find the town of Mtsensk. Well then, my village lies, as you see, ten kilometers from that unpronounceable place. It is a calm, green, sad, absolute solitude. If I can work here, I shall remain for some time; if not, I'll clear out and after a sojourn of six weeks in Carlsbad, I shall return to Paris.

Then he got down to business:

> At Petersburg I formed the conviction that given the present state of international laws, anyone who chooses to translate you can do so with perfect impunity, which is why I couldn't place *La Conquête de Plassans*. It hasn't been translated yet, but the editor I mentioned will not risk commissioning a translation that may be second to appear . . . As this editor is keen, however, to publish your works in his review, he proposes, through my mediation, to pay you thirty rubles (105 francs) per printed page for everything you send in manuscript or galleys. Since he must pay the translator a like amount, I consider it a reasonable fee and urge that you accept.

A historian imbued with positivism, Stasiulevich had resigned from Saint Petersburg University in 1861 to protest Tsar Alexander II's brutal suppression of the revolutionary student movement. Five years later, after writing works on ancient Greece and medieval Europe, he founded *The European Herald*, which soon established itself as the journal of choice for men like Turgenev who steered a liberal, Western-oriented course around Slavophilism, nihilism, populism, Marxism, and other militant creeds.[4] Given considerable latitude by the government censor, *The European Herald* reached beyond Saint Petersburg into the time warp of provincial Russia, where a thick monthly traveled almost as quickly as a thin daily or weekly, and found favor with squires inclined to ponder literary trends and political events at their leisure.

These tidings from Spasskoye were gold, frankincense, and myrrh

---

[4]Of reviews such as *Vestnik Evropy*, Ronald Hingley observes: "By the 1880s, about a dozen . . . were in being, with circulations rising to nine or ten thousand each. It was possible to finance a journal on a subscription list of only a few thousand, and these organs had influence out of all proportion to their readership, partly because the proportion of intellectuals in the population was so small."

all together, especially gold, and Charpentier, who had a ledger to balance though he sometimes pretended otherwise, shared his author's joy. "I thank you for the trouble you've taken on my behalf," Zola answered Turgenev. "Naturally I accept with enthusiasm the proposals you make in the name of the director of the review. Messrs. Charpentier, to whom I have communicated your letter, are delighted with your excellent mediation and instruct me to tell you that everything you do will sit well with him." Everything went as planned. Zola's newest book made its way to Saint Petersburg—no predictable journey via the Russian postal system—and appeared in *Vestnik Yevropy* just before it came out in France.

As soon as this transaction had been completed, Turgenev, who obviously fancied the part of benevolent go-between, made Stasiulevich another proposal. "Would you like to receive from Zola a regular Paris 'letter' (unsigned)?" he inquired, possibly at Zola's behest. "It would be intelligent and pertinent. I know that you already have a Parisian correspondent, but Zola could focus on literary, artistic, and social facts. Should this idea 'speak' to you, tell me what fee you could offer." Stasiulevich answered in the affirmative, whereupon Zola wrote a probationary piece demolishing Alexandre Dumas *fils* and sent it without delay to Turgenev. His covering letter well conveys both his anxiety for success and his journalistic readiness to adjust his copy to his editor's preference:

Here is my first article for the Russian review; be so good as to forward it *immediately*. I would be very happy if it came out in the March issue. It's a bit serious for openers, but explain that the tone of what I write hereafter will vary. Now then, ask your friend the following questions. What is the latest possible date for sending copy? Is this article too long? too short? Will he kindly put my manuscripts aside once he's had them translated and return them at his convenience? I'm counting on you—understand?—to dispatch it today.

Rising above the Oblomovian lethargy for which he was famous, Turgenev not only did as bidden but assured Stasiulevich that he himself considered the article "a masterpiece."[5] No further proof of Zola's

[5]To Zola, Turgenev wrote: "Thank you for your article on A. Dumas. It will put me even more decisively into his bad books, but I couldn't care less. I would like to take you and Flaubert out to dinner with Saltykov [a famous Russian satirist known by the pseudonym Shchedrin]. The bouillabaisse we had the other day made such a profound impression that I would not be averse to having it again at the same place. Does that suit you?"

In a letter to Stasiulevich dated March 13, Turgenev again promoted the collaboration: "I am very pleased that you liked the first of Zola's articles and do not doubt that your reaction to the second will be the same. I informed him of your brilliant suggestions and he has willingly agreed to them. You will find him an active contributor with whom both you and your readers will be highly satisfied."

essayistic talents was required. "If Zola accepts my terms," Stasiule-vich declared, "we shall collaborate beginning with the May issue, which means that he would send his manuscript on April 20. Fur-thermore, tell him that he need not stamp the envelope or worry about my postal expenses. He can write on any kind of paper. As for length, his thirty-three manuscript pages amounted to nineteen printed pages. Were his correspondence not anonymous but signed, he would receive fifteen francs per page, or 285 francs total. Let him know this. I thought of giving his future articles the general title 'Paris and Pari-sians.' What is your opinion? Will it suit them?" In Russia, where articles often went unsigned, it was not unusual to pay more for an eminent signature, and among "Westernists" the French name still carried greater cultural weight than any other.

From May 1875 through November 1880, Zola organized his pro-fessional life around two calendars, the Gregorian and the Julian, al-ways bearing in mind that Saint Petersburg lagged twelve days behind Paris. On the thirteenth of every month he would announce a topic, and one week later (or more quickly in December, when the drunk-enness that immobilized Russian typesetters during the Christmas sea-son became a consideration) he would dispatch an essay some thirty printed pages long. With equal promptitude, Stasiulevich would send him his remittance, at first via Turgenev, then directly. To be sure, any journalistic assignment that impeded the progress of *Les Rougon-Macquart* exasperated him, but the substantial sums he milked from Stasiulevich year after year purchased bourgeois comfort, and Zola augmented that income by recycling, or repatriating, his scripts.[6] Twenty-five of the sixty-four "Lettres de Paris" eventually made four volumes of criticism—*Le Roman expérimental, Le Naturalisme au thé-*

---

[6]Combined with his retainer from Charpentier and his income from *Le Sémaphore de Marseille*, for which he churned out several pieces a week, the Russian fees brought his yearly revenue to at least 15,000 francs and something more like 17,000 after July 1876. André Wallon, in *La Vie quotidienne dans les villes d'eaux de 1850 à 1914*, provides figures useful for determining where Zola stood on the salary scale of his contemporaries:

> The salaries of government functionaries, which varied from one ministry to another, . . . ranged between 1,200 and 25,000 francs. Doctors earned, on the average, between 6,000 and 15,000, though certain eminent ones made 50,000 or more. The chief executive officer of a large commercial or industrial enter-prise earned between 30,000 and 60,000 francs. Engineers with seniority had incomes of 10,000 to 20,000 a year. An army captain earned 3,400 francs. In most of these jobs and professions a household enjoyed revenue from dowries, which frequently doubled its income. Thus, many bourgeois families had a total income of 12,000 to 30,000 francs a year. . . . As for the salary of clerks and workers, it ranged from 1,100 to 1,500 francs.

The Zolas thus lived in quite comfortable circumstances and spent a smaller pro-portion of their income on rent than most Parisian bourgeois (it was customary to rent apartments rather than to buy them).

âtre, *Nos auteurs dramatiques,* and *Les Romanciers naturalistes* (all published in 1880–81). Others were excerpted for French newspapers.

This correspondence will be dealt with in due course. It suffices to say here that Zola promised Stasiulevich variety and did indeed serve up a remarkable potpourri. He evoked Paris in springtime. He reviewed the annual Salon. He wrote disquisitions on Flaubert, Goncourt, and Daudet. He surveyed the wasteland of Boulevard theater. When other commitments overwhelmed him, he scraped by with a passage from *L'Assommoir.* And when he couldn't bear literary reportage any longer, he gave free rein to his gift for social portraiture, often following Turgenev's cues. "I've just received a letter from Stasiulevich, who is lyrically enthusiastic about your installment on marriage in France," the latter informed him. "It's had thundering success in Russia. My nose did right to send you in that direction." Was it also at Turgenev's prompting that he described seaside resorts, various species of native clergy, modern youth, the French way of death and burial?

Along with his novels, these sociological essays won him fervent admirers, and Turgenev was pleased to bring him proof of it. "My dear Zola," he wrote on May 18, 1877. "I have an immediate request to make of you. Can you send me a photograph of yourself with the following inscription: 'To Madame Samarski-Bykhovetz. Paris. 1877. E. Zola.' She is a corpulent lady who lives in Saint Petersburg and adores you. You would make her blissfully happy and she would lavish her gratitude on me. She is an excellent person, quite deserving of this small sacrifice. Do it, I would appreciate it." By then the "Lettre de Paris" had become so much the talk of Saint Petersburg that Saltykov, who edited a radical left-wing review called *Otechestvennyye Zapiski,* or *Annals of the Fatherland,* engaged Stasiulevich in a bidding war from which Zola profited handsomely. To keep his star at *The European Herald,* Stasiulevich raised his fee schedule to twenty francs per page. "This means that my monthly contribution would fetch 650 francs instead of 500," Zola told Turgenev. "Under the circumstances, I felt obliged to accept, and am sure that you would have advised me to do so if I had consulted you. My relations with Stasiulevich have been excellent. I can't leave him when he offers me as much as the others. It's a matter of conscience."[7]

---

[7]Zola was also a favorite among expatriate Russians. In 1876, Turgenev, who organized a musical-literary matinee at Pauline Viardot's house to benefit poor Russian students living in Paris, requested Zola's collaboration. "Would you be up to reading a short excerpt (8 to 10 minutes long) from your work? . . . Your name on the bill (nothing public, mind you) would be to my countrymen as honey to flies." Zola agreed, despite his fear of public readings, and didn't sleep for three nights.

As early as 1868 Zola had envisaged a novel that would combine theology and physiology, or the doctrine of original sin and the idea of hereditary doom, in the story of a young priest torn between his instincts and his education. "I shall address . . . the great struggle between nature and religion," he wrote at the time. "The love-smitten priest has never, I believe, been studied humanly. There's a great dramatic subject there, especially if one gave hereditary influences full play." Novels about wayward priests abounded during this period, and Zola, who reviewed three of them, was not above exploiting a trendy theme. He was also mindful, no doubt, of the great eighteenth-century essays about human nature and would have liked to make a statement that evoked Rousseau's *Emile* and his second *Discours* or Diderot's *Supplément au voyage de Bougainville*. But his principal source of inspiration lay closer by, in his own psyche, where, as we have seen, fear held instinct captive. No one knew better than he how unfree a free-thinker could feel or how, against all reason, the militant positivist should harbor a bogeyman who constantly hobbled his movements with superstitious ritual.

"The story of a man neutered by his early education who recovers his manhood at twenty-five through the solicitations of nature but fatally sinks back into an impotent state": thus did Zola outline *La Faute de l'abbé Mouret*. Having begun the novel after *Le Ventre de Paris*, he had set aside his notes to write *La Conquête de Plassans* when it became apparent that the past that enmeshes his main character—the son of François and Marthe Mouret—needed elaboration. Work on *La Faute* recommenced one year later, in 1874. "This volume caused him more trouble than almost any other," Paul Alexis reported. "He had to collect a mountain of notes. For months his desk was encumbered with religious tomes. He got all his information about mysticism, in particular the cult of Mary, from Spanish Jesuits and borrowed liberally, almost word for word, from the *Imitation of Christ*. A defrocked priest recounted his experience as a seminarian." Stacked alongside the theological tomes were illustrated catalogues of ecclesiastical vestments and utensils. To understand the Eucharist he studied it through manuals written for clergymen, then observed it closely at a neighborhood church, Sainte-Marie des Batignolles. "Several mornings in succession the few pious women who attended early mass must have been edified by the presence of a man sitting apart from them and following the priest's every movement with rapt attention," Alexis went on to say. "Occasionally he'd hastily scribble two or three words in a prayer book. . . . I remember accompanying him one morning and watching the mysterious drama unfold." When the Catholic mass no longer mystified him, mysteries of a "physiological" order remained and in this connection his plot led him to various scientific or pseudoscientific treatises. Prosper Lucas's *Traité philosophique et physiologique de l'hérédité naturelle* still served, as did Morel's *Traité des dégénérescences physiques, intellectuelles et morales de l'espèce humaine*, but more to the point of *La Faute de l'abbé Mouret* was Dr. Jean-Ennemond Du-fieux's *Nature et virginité: considerations physiologiques sur le célibat religieux*. Nature is what Serge Mouret forswears, leaving a garden of earthly delights to crucify himself.

In *La Conquête de Plassans*, Zola had portrayed Serge as Marthe's boy. Whereas Octave, the older Mouret son, has a large appetite for pleasure and commerce, Serge exhibits none.[8] Goaded by his father to study law in Paris, he recoils from this and every other masculine challenge. "Indeed, he was of so nervous a temperament that the slightest frolic would send him to bed for two or three days with girlish indispositions. . . . Mouret had high hopes for him. Whenever the young man seemed robust enough, he'd schedule his departure. But no sooner were preparations made than he'd begin coughing again and the result would be one more postponement." A grave illness proves decisive. Teetering between life and death, Serge, like his mother, falls under Ovide Faujas's spell.[9] It is Faujas who nurses him back to health and who, after his perilous convalescence, delivers him to Christ. With maternal encouragement, Serge implores his father to let him take holy orders.

Tucked away at a seminary during the catastrophe that ends *La Conquête de Plassans*, Serge, whose mystical raptures distinguish him from fellow seminarians, would flee civilization altogether, and is granted his wish on being ordained. Outside Plassans, in the wild Provençal hill country, stands a church so dilapidated as to appear forsaken. Birds use it as a roost, weather has worn it bare, branches poke through broken windows. Here Father Mouret installs himself with his feebleminded twenty-two-year-old sister, Désirée, and while she delights in nurturing a barnyard menagerie, the young curate ministers to peasants untamed by Christianity. "He thought about this village of Les Artaud, which had grown there, among the stones, like one more species of gnarled vegetation," writes Zola, who shaped *La Faute de l'abbé Mouret* around a conflict between two modes of hermeticism—nature's mindless promiscuity and the priest's celibate vocation.

[8]These antithetical brothers call to mind the Greek myth that made such a strong impression on Zola and Cézanne in adolescence—the myth of Hercules at the crossroads wondering whether to take the path of pleasure or of duty. It's as if Zola resolved the hero's moral dilemma into two separate characters marked for one direction or the other by heredity.

[9]Zola's fascination with doubleness reveals itself in names. Faujas is linked to Ovid, and St. Sergius, Serge's namesake, is associated in the annals of Christian martyrology with Saint Bacchus.

All the inhabitants were related, all bore the same name, so that parents gave children nicknames in the cradle to distinguish them from one another. One ancestor, an Artaud, had come and settled in this region, like a pariah. His family had grown with the ferocious vitality of weeds sucking life from stone. It had become a tribe, a commune oblivious of its cousinships, which dated back centuries. People intermarried with brazen promiscuity. Not a single male Artaud in memory had sought a bride outside the village; only the girls, and even they on rare occasions, looked elsewhere. Rooted to this plot of earth, they sprang forth and died and multiplied on their dunghill, slowly, with the simplicity of trees dropping seeds, with no clear idea of the vast world beyond these yellow rocks.

Les Artaud's inhabitants constitute "a separate breed," "a race born of the soil," "a humanity of three hundred heads who lived at the beginning of time."

Hewn from the same coarse material as these benighted yokels is their schoolmaster, Frère Archangias, a large, brutal friar who hunts down truants in the bush. Although Mouret and Archangias both wear black, it soon becomes apparent that they represent different deities. Speaking for a wrathful patriarch, Archangias is fanatically misogynistic. Serge, on the other hand, ardently worships Mary the Mother of God, prostrating himself before her icons. "The abbé Mouret's devotion to the Virgin went back quite some ways. As a reclusive child who shrank from people, he would imagine a beautiful lady protecting him and two blue eyes, very soft, with a smile, following him everywhere. . . . From the age of seven he satisfied his need for affection by spending all his pocket money on holy images, which he'd hide jealously to enjoy in private. They were never Jesus carrying the lamb or Christ on the cross . . . but always tender images of Mary."

May is Mary's month, and the events of a day in May work a fateful change upon Mouret. After performing pastoral duties at Les Artaud, which he does with the cheerful self-satisfaction of an innocent thrust among Hottentots, the curate meets his uncle, Dr. Pascal Rougon, who has come to treat someone named Jeanbernat. The latter lives as caretaker on an immense seigneurial estate girded by a high stone wall. Built during the eighteenth century, Le Paradou (Provençal for paradise) is yet another ruin, and for Mouret it is a world apart. "[Its lord had] enjoyed it for one season, together with an adorably beautiful woman who died there, no doubt, as she was never seen to leave it. The following year their château burned down, the gates were nailed shut, dirt filled the wall's very loopholes, so that no eye had since penetrated the vast enclosure, which sat high in the scrubland, occupying one entire plateau." The geometrical landscape designed for a patrician rich enough to imitate Versailles had vanished. Where topiaries once spoke of man's will to groom nature or subjugate it to reason, vegetation had grown wild, and Mouret, magically removed from the arid countryside all around, glimpses Eden. "It was like some vision of a virgin forest, a huge grove looming thick in the rain of sunlight." Holed up in a lodge near the entrance, Jeanbernat, whom locals call "the philosopher," spends his days reading eighteenth-century works salvaged from the aristocrat's library. Although he finds the wilderness daunting, he is inspired by Rousseau to let his ward, a sixteen-year-old niece named Albine who has lived there since childhood, run about unsupervised. "You realize," Dr. Rougon tells Mouret, "that Le Paradou, with its pebbles, its thistles, could devour a dress a day. It ate the little girl's finery in three or four gulps, and she'd come home naked. Now she dresses like a savage. . . . You understand? Le Paradou is hers. She took possession of it right away. She lives in it, . . . camping heaven knows where, at the bottom of hidden culverts."

As if Le Paradou were not nature enough for one day, his sister Désirée prevails upon Mouret to tour the pens and hutches of her beloved menagerie. All this rutting, lusting life is more than he can endure, and after nightfall the priest, beset with anxiety, seeks refuge in his church. But that refuge, he discovers, has crumbled from within. Mary, before whose image he throws himself, does not offer protection, for he has transformed her into an erotic object. "He couldn't slip into the trance of prayer with his customary ease. However gloriously and purely it revealed itself in the curvaceous body of a mature woman with her naked child cradled under one arm, Mary's maternity perturbed him and seemed to open heaven's gates to the procreative surge he had witnessed all day long. His prayer lingered on his lips as he examined things he had never noticed before—the soft wave of chestnut hair, the slight swelling of a pink-daubed chin." Horror-struck by this sexualization of divinity, he reaches in vain for his lost innocence. Like those hereditary crazes that overwhelm rational selves throughout *Les Rougon-Macquart,* the biological brute breaches Serge Mouret's chaste stronghold and invades even the rhetoric of his baroque supplications. "Oh, death, death, venerable Virgin! Give me the death of everything! I shall love you in the death of my body, in the death of everything that lives and multiplies. . . . I shall rise to your lips like a subtle flame, I shall enter you through your half-open mouth, and the nuptials will take place whilst archangels shiver at the spectacle of our exhilaration."

That night Mouret succumbs to typhoid. When, days or weeks later, he awakens from delirious dreams of crawling through a dark, narrow, subterranean passage, he finds himself reborn in Le Paradou, where Pascal Rougon has arranged to lodge him under Jeanbernat's roof. Set aside for this convalescent, who doesn't remember that he was once a priest, is a sunlit room adorned with eighteenth-century frescoes of bare-bottomed cherubs. Over him hovers Albine.

Thus begins a prelapsarian idyll. Guided by Albine, Serge sets out every morning for some hitherto untrodden corner of Le Paradou. Together they lay claim to this extravagantly luxuriant Arcadia (in which "peace prevented the degeneration of species"), wading through its four limpid streams, dancing across meadows carpeted with wildflowers, exploring primeval groves, breathing the perfume of fruit and herbs and roses. "They possessed the forest . . . with all its trees, its shade, its avenues, its glades, its pockets of verdure unknown even to the birds; the forest which served as a giant tent for sheltering at noon the tenderness that had bloomed at dawn," writes Zola, whose vision amalgamates Eden, the island paradise of *Paul et Virginie*, and memories of a place called the Domaine de Gallice, which he, Cézanne, and Baille discovered during their expeditions high above Aix-en-Provence.

> They were masters of everything they beheld, they had conquered their domain, they walked amidst a benign nature . . . and they delighted, beyond that, in the sky, the wide blue patch spread overhead; it wasn't enclosed by the garden wall but belonged to their eyes.

Where heaven itself lies in the eyes of the beholder, there is no "outside" to limit Zola's inseparable playmates, no "other" to teach them nakedness, and no God to transcend a nature with which they enjoy perfect complicity. Living "at the beginning," Serge Mouret outgrows all signs of a former life as hair covers him and fills even the tonsured circle that emblemized his vow of servitude.

But the garden does not exist at the beginning. Haunted by its first inhabitants, it contains a legend that excites the imagination, a promise that subverts the newness of childhood, a "beyond" that fosters discontent. "What few people know is that [the lord and lady] discovered in their garden a place of perfect felicity where they ended up spending all their time," Albine tells Serge. "I am certain of it. . . . A fresh, shaded place, hidden behind impenetrable thickets, so magically beautiful that it makes one forget the whole world. The lady must have been buried there." This bower provides yet another opportunity for Zola to dramatize his obsession with the mortal danger of carnal knowledge. When Albine-Eve finally discovers it, she and Serge make love there, whereupon their idyll ends. Through a break in the wall, which Zola describes as a window upon the outside world, steps Frère Archangias, who, like Faujas before him, straightway introduces guilt. What nature has united, God the Father tears asunder, and the lords of Creation become unsightly creatures. "I see you, I know that you are naked," thunders this sanctimonious voyeur. "It is an abomination. Are you some beast that you prowl the wood with a female? She has led you a merry chase, admit it! She has dragged you through slime, and there you stand matted like a ram. Break off a branch and thrash her!" Albine watches disconsolately as her estranged lover, waking from a dream, follows the Christian schoolmaster into the extramural world of work and sin and death.

Serge Mouret dons clerical black again, but the blissful interlude has altered him. Tormented by consciousness of his sinful nature, he deserts Mary for Jesus, replacing pictures of the Virgin's Immaculate Conception with representations of death. And when Albine seeks him out, her appeal falls on deaf ears. She speaks of Eden; he descants upon Christ's Passion. She recalls their frolics; he escorts her, image by image, through the Stations of the Cross. "Jesus who died for us, tell her about our nothingness!" he exclaims. "Tell her that we are dust, offal, damnation!" The walled garden is now the crypt of his mind, and over it has risen a fortress-church.

Instinct proves to be a stubborn foe. Serge finds that Albine's image remains with him. Tugged by desire, he goes back to Le Paradou, where Albine keeps vigil by the ruined wall through which her lover was led away. Again they walk together, visiting their summertime haunts. But like some irrevocable *ancien régime*, perfect felicity turns out to have lasted only one brief moment. In a garden touched by autumn frost, Serge seems the ghost of his virile self, answering declarations of love with protestations of fear. "I have often thought about those saints of stone at the back of niches," he laments. "Showered with incense century after century, their entrails must be pickled in it. And so are mine. . . . I'm embalmed, which is what explains . . . the tranquillity of my flesh. . . . May nothing disturb me! I shall remain cold, rigid, smiling the eternal smile of granite lips. That's all I want." Albine, who is with child, plants a ferocious kiss upon his face, "as if to resuscitate the corpse," then tells him to leave.

Brokenhearted, the young woman harvests flowers from Le Paradou and makes a bower of her bedroom, then lies down and dies.[10] Jeanbernat wants to bury her in the garden, as aristocrats had done before the Revolution, but French law dictates otherwise. She is conveyed to

[10]Albine also succumbs to the erotic sleep of death, regarding which Bram Dijkstra writes in *Idols of Perversity*: "Zola's tale of Albine is a version of the familiar European legend of 'The Revenge of the Flowers,' itself the subject of numerous paintings. In this legend, to quote a commentator for *Famous Paintings of the World* (1897), a young girl, 'lying down to sleep surrounded by the many-hued plunder of the garden, is overcome by the influence of the air surcharged with their baneful odor, and passes from the slumber of perfect health to the endless sleep of death.' "

Les Artaud, where Père Mouret presides at her funeral, interring in the churchyard not only his *faute*, or lapse, but the unborn fruit of it. The words of the *De Profundis* are still echoing when his sister Désirée, overcome with joy, tells him that her cow had just calved. On this announcement, which foreshadows the last chapter of *Les Rougon-Macquart*, *La Faute de l'abbé Mouret* ends.

In *La Faute*, as in *La Curée*, incest is Zola's drama, and the Eden over which a wild woman holds sway descends straight from the hot-house ruled by a dark sphinx. Worshipping images of the Immaculate Mother in a church situated outside civilization, Mouret falls ill, or asleep, when Eros invades his hermitage. Transported to another, equally hermetic realm, he there deflowers the virgin under whose maternal care he was "reborn." But Zolaesque heroes can never with impunity possess what they desire. Nor do they ever arrive first, not even this would-be Adam, who finds paradise itself haunted. Beneath its chaotic vegetation lies the rational scheme designed by an eighteenth-century aristocrat given to reading *les philosophes*. And beneath that aristocrat lies François Mouret, whose well-tended garden ("an earthly paradise," as he called it) became the unkempt preserve of a frocked interloper. *La Conquête de Plassans* thus informs *La Faute* like some unconscious scenario for which new characters will be cast. Reborn amnesiac, Serge fulfills the patricidal wish hidden in Mariolatry and couples with a mother never penetrated by man. As Ovide Faujas made Marthe lovesick, so Serge fascinates the young mistress of Le Paradou, stirring in her the same demonic passion his father's nemesis excited in his mother. "In part three, [Albine] directs the action," Zola noted. "The woman awakens with untamed power. She wants Serge, he is hers. The ruthlessness of nature overcoming every obstacle in order to spawn. Absolute unconsciousness, Eve without any social sense, without any learned morality, the amorous *bête humaine*."

Out of *la bête humaine* Zola conjured up Les Artaud, a village whose inhabitants, all bearing the same patronymic and fornicating indiscriminately, live not in nineteenth-century France but in some primeval, pre-moral cocoon. "The peasants will be a gray, nameless background" is how the Sketch characterizes them, "a mass of stooped, toiling brutes against which I shall set in relief the human drama. My village will become a single being . . . a human herd that evokes mankind as it must have been during the first ages of the world." The oblivion that attends Serge Mouret's leap from this world into another—from generational time into a timeless enclosure where nature has overrun culture—is also the condition of life among his backward parishioners. Founded by some "pariah" centuries earlier, Les Artaud remains a "single being," a monster at once ancient and infantile, an endogamous collective walled off from the nation but without internal divisions or social taboos. Like Le Paradou, where "species don't degenerate" and time doesn't move, Les Artaud embodies the phantasmagoric underside of *Les Rougon-Macquart*. Shaping his historical saga around a family tree whose branches spread, year after year, throughout French society, Zola reserved this one episode for an anti-saga, a hermit family whose tree grows inward—as if to suggest that his imaginative travels, his scientific program, his very mind were always at the mercy of a primitive rooted in Provence. We know how strongly he identified with François Mouret pruning box shrubs and with Dr. Pascal Rougon analyzing kinship ties. But we also know that inside the taxonomist survived a fatherless son obsessed by the idea of internecine marriage. "I'm working feverishly," he wrote to Turgenev on June 29, 1874. "The novel about which I spoke to you is giving me a devil of a time. I believe that I want to pack it with too many things. Have you noticed the despair inflicted upon us by women we love too much and works we overfondle?"

Stasiulevich published a Russian translation of *La Faute* in the February and March 1875 issues of *The European Herald*. It came out in French soon afterward and, not surprisingly, caused pious reviewers to fulminate. "Here naturalism of a bestial kind is placed above noble Christian spirituality!" Barbey d'Aurevilly exclaimed in *Le Constitutionnel*. "I do not believe that in this low-minded age anyone has written anything baser in its general conception, its details, and its language than *La Faute de l'abbé Mouret*." *La Revue de France* declared it "the most immoral and most irreligious novel of the series," and *La Revue bleue* concurred: "No, [Mouret] is not really a descendant of the Rougons, nor a curate. He is a male animal let loose in the woods with a female animal." Mouret's self-flagellation did not hurt him enough for these propagators of moral order.

People quite prepared to judge Zola fairly expressed aesthetic qualms. "Isn't the abbé Mouret strange? But Le Paradou simply doesn't come off!" wrote Flaubert, who had trouble with every novel in which Zola created a sense of glut or explosive plenitude through lists. "No matter! The book contains passages of genius, especially the portrait of Archangias and the end, the return to Le Paradou." No less ambivalent was Ferdinand Brunetière, a critic destined to join the Académie Française: "There are charming things in the description of Serge Mouret's courtship, and the wild, virgin nature that frames it is depicted with unusual vigor. Unfortunately, M. Zola clings to materialism in his style and composition. Some sensual element alloys the hymns of love; and as for his tableaux, their design disappears beneath an impasto of colors."

But Hippolyte Taine found *La Faute* "intoxicating," and later, when they read it, Zola's younger confreres Huysmans and Maupassant heaped praise on this very personal, brilliantly conceived work. Moreover, the sound of controversy promoted brisk sales. "*La Faute de l'abbé Mouret* is doing *very well,*" Charpentier informed Zola a fortnight after publication. "At least five hundred copies of the second edition are already sold. I shall send you, in case you haven't seen it yet, a savage attack by M. Derome in *Le Journal de Paris*. It's dumb and not very funny. . . . Your book has caused a sensation. It has gripped everybody who's read it. A long article about you and your collective work will appear in a Copenhagen and Stockholm paper." He and Dreyfous hoped for a public trial at which Zola would demonstrate that passages deemed offensive to public morality had come almost verbatim from orthodox religious texts. MacMahon's minister of justice did not oblige them, however.

XIV

OCEANIC VISTAS

U NTIL FRANCE COLLAPSED before the Prussian juggernaut, Georges Charpentier gave no indication that he would someday acquire the capacity or desire to run a successful business. Handsome and raffish, he lounged at Tortoni's on the Boulevard des Italiens, where fellow playboys addressed him familiarly as "Zizi."[1] His wit, his wardrobe, his nonchalance, and his eye for art promised a life of rich bohemianism. But in fact there was more gilt than gold to this haut bourgeois. At war with his father, who, during the 1860s, allowed himself to be persuaded, by a malevolent woman under whose sway he had fallen, that his son was the product of an adulterous liaison, Georges became a vagabond, visiting his abandoned mother in Bourgival every weekend and camping with hospitable friends, Maurice Dreyfous among them. Father and son achieved some sort of reconcilation before the former's death, but in important ways warfare continued beyond the grave. Gervais Charpentier's shrew prevailed upon him to deny his family the lion's share of his estate, and nearly contrived to alienate the publishing house from Georges.

After his father died in 1871, Zizi reformed. No sooner had he taken command of the firm than he married a woman who suited him remarkably well. Like Charpentier, Marguerite Lemonnier knew how it felt to surrender upper-class expectations. Under Napoleon III, her

---

[1] "Zizi" derives from the French verb *zézayer*, meaning "to lisp." Like Zola, Charpentier had some slight trouble with *s*.

father, Gabriel, had been *joaillier de la couronne,* or jeweler to the crown. The title carried social weight, which meant that for Marguerite there were English and German nannies, holidays at a family château near Bretigny-sur-Orge, gowns from the House of Worth, birthday gifts from Isabella of Spain, musical soirées, teas with the titled, crinolined ladies who billowed through her parents' salon all year round. That salon looked out upon the Place Vendôme and Napoleon I stood overhead, protectively. Marguerite saw him every day. But she did not see him crash in May 1871, when Communards supervised by Gustave Courbet tore down the column glorifying his victorious campaigns. By then, Lemonnier had gone bankrupt.

As a hostess without a salon could no more happily resign herself to a life of obscure motherhood than an actress without a stage, Marguerite made the Bibliothèque Charpentier the vehicle for her boundless social energy. "In some considerable degree, our success was her doing," Dreyfous declared. "As early as 1872 she organized a series of receptions that showed to great advantage the charm of her person and the agreeableness of her intellectual culture, which she wore lightly. Delighted to find a meeting place where they could resume chats interrupted by the tragic events that had befallen France, the literary elite came in force. Little by little the salon on the quai du Louvre filled with an elegant crowd and the gatherings became fashionable. Unpublished plays by house authors were performed by famous actors, who found their reward in the sense of intellectual community they enjoyed with Charpentier's intimates." Assembling people unlikely to meet under any other roof, Mme Charpentier, in whose own character the ironical patrician mingled with the affectionate mother, displayed a genius for incongruity that rivaled Zola's. Her Friday-evening soirées, which juxtaposed writers, painters, actors, music-hall celebrities, industrialists, and political potentates, were her serial novel. Auguste Renoir evoked them charmingly for his son. "[My father] had come to know the family well, as he had painted Charpentier's mother in 1869," Jean Renoir wrote in *Renoir, My Father.* "He met him again as a result of an exhibition which he and Berthe Morisot and Sisley organized. Berthe Morisot was the sister-in-law of Manet, a great friend of M. Charpentier. The distinguished publisher came to the exhibition and bought Renoir's *Fishermen on a Riverbank* for 180 francs. As he was leaving with his picture, he invited my father to come to some of Mme Charpentier's receptions. Her salon was celebrated, and deservedly so, for she was indeed a great lady. . . . 'Madame Charpentier reminded me of my early loves, the women Fragonard painted,' he'd say." This small, plump, frizzy-haired Egeria, whom indeed Renoir immortalized in *Madame Charpentier and Her Children,* held court first on the quai du Louvre, then in a town house that had space enough for her crowd as well as her husband's business. Groomed by Napoleonic society, Marguerite created a republican salon where fuglemen of the left found themselves enveloped in an atmosphere of Parisian chic. At 11, rue de Grenelle, boundaries disappeared, and on any given Friday evening one might have seen Léon Gambetta greeting Sarah Bernhardt, Yvette Guilbert entertaining Georges Clemenceau, Aristide Bruant or the Duchesse d'Uzès chatting up Edouard Lockroy, minister of commerce and industry.

Life with a dynamo who bore four children while regaling *le tout Paris* was not always easy. Charpentier disliked pomp and ceremony, social agendas and party talk. But in his own insouciant way, he proved as willful as she. "Because he was witty, good-natured, playful and even mischievous, only we who worked beside him knew how sure his judgment was, with what intelligence he cut through problems," Dreyfous noted. "Boring people and onerous tasks repelled him. He adored everything vivacious, original, the best of its kind, and gave serious matters serious thought without assuming an air of gravity." Like the Impressionist paintings that filled his rooms, the literature he published argued an independent mind. It required immense self-confidence, or bravado, to wager heavily on Zola in 1872. And the notorious unsuccess of *L'Education sentimentale* did not prevent him from courting Flaubert when the latter broke relations with Michel Lévy. "Charpentier arrived yesterday at 11:30," Flaubert told his niece on June 21, 1873, noting that such deferential behavior was "unheard of" among publishers.

After lunch we got down to business and this is what we decided. He will reprint *Madame Bovary* with an appendix including the writ of summons, the prosecutor's brief, Sénard's defense and the judgment. Nothing else. Not a single snippet from reviews. I find that more dignified. I also sold him *Salammbô*, which will appear next winter. The aforementioned Charpentier never stopped petting Julio and Putzel. I believe that the view of Croisset, which was splendid yesterday, did not detract from his opinion of me and just now, on leaving, he thanked me effusively for my "hospitality."

Where Zola and Flaubert led, Goncourt and Daudet followed. Younger men then trooped behind. So effectively did Charpentier lure gifted writers that by 1890 it could have been said of him what Paris later said of another playboy turned publisher: *Hors Gallimard, point de littérature* ("Outside Gallimard, there is no literature"). Stamped on works by Maupassant, Huysmans, Mirbeau, Verlaine, Barrès, Rostand, and Maeterlinck, among others, his name figured as an emblem of literary distinction. "He had the audacity to collect us when doors were

Army regulars encamped on the Champs-Elysées, during the German siege of Paris in 1870.

The north wing of the Louvre in flames during *la semaine sanglante*. A distant barricade is visible on the rue de Rivoli.

"Federals" posing with the fallen statue of Emperor Napoleon I and the ruins of the Vendôme Column, which had supported it. They were demolished on May 16, 1871, in accordance with a decree issued by the Commune one month earlier.

The Hôtel de Ville, which had been the seat of government during the Commune, was set ablaze by Communards during the Bloody Week. The burnt-out shell is seen here from across the Pont d'Arcole.

Marshal MacMahon, a hero of the conquest of
Algeria, the Crimean War, and Napoleon III's
Italian campaign, who was wounded and taken
prisoner at Sedan. Under his command the
French army laid low the Paris Commune in
1871. Two years later he became president of
France and immediately announced the need to
restore "moral order."

Adolphe Thiers, photographed in his seventies,
when he was presiding over the infant Third
Republic.

Léon Gambetta, who, as a liberal deputy in
the Legislative Body, proclaimed the Republic
on September 4, 1870, and subsequently, as
minister of the interior, organized the last
desperate campaigns of the Franco-Prussian
War. A major force on the Left, famous for
his oratorical thunder, he became prime
minister in November 1881.

Edmond de Goncourt, in an undated
photograph, probably taken in the
1870s, after the death of Jules, which
left him so grief-stricken that satirists
often referred to him as "the widow."

Georges Charpentier, Zola's close
friend and publisher, as he might have
been attired during summers at
Royan. The photograph was taken by
Zola. Both of Charpentier's sons
predeceased him, the first dying in
childhood, the second at the age of
twenty. After the second tragedy,
Charpentier retired, and his firm
passed to Eugène Fasquelle.

A photograph of Flaubert, often attributed to Nadar, undated but perhaps taken in 1874, when Flaubert wrote to Turgenev: "I urge you to visit the lobby of Nadar the photographer . . . There you will see a life-size photograph of Alexandre Dumas, and next to it a terra-cotta bust of the same."

Ivan Turgenev, in a Nadar photograph taken in the last years of his life.

Zola at approximately thirty-five, a robust fellow with a
cannonball head, described by Emile Bergerat: "His demeanor,
which combined self-assurance and timidity, expressed quiet
faith not only in the power of letters but in his own gift."

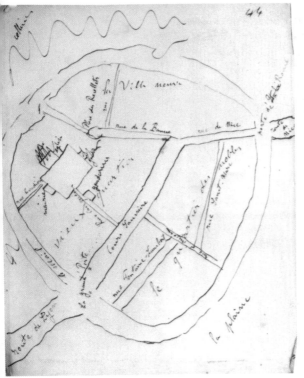

Zola's sketch of Plassans, birthplace of the Rougons and Macquarts, made while preparing the first novel in the twenty-volume saga, *La Fortune des Rougon*.

The caption reads: "The art of earning 3,000 pounds per annum by demoralizing one's fellow citizens." Coupling *L'Assommoir* and *La Fille Elisa*, *Le Grelot*, a left-wing periodical, followed the republican line in denouncing *la littérature putride*. Goncourt would not have been happy to see his novel linked with Zola's, and even less so to see himself mistakenly identified as A. de Goncourt.

Joris-Karl Huysmans. This photograph was taken a year after the publication of *Les Soirées de Médan*, in 1881, when Huysmans was thirty-three.

Paul Alexis. Seven years younger than Zola, he was one of the latter's most loyal friends and disciples. Alexis earned his living as a journalist and wrote several novels and plays.

Henry Céard, Zola's urbane and indisp factotum, who had a minor literary care and worked for some years at the Carnavalet Museum. Like Huysmans, he became a member of the Goncourt Academy.

closing all around," Zola observed. "Is it any wonder that I should find my favorite authors grouped together under the aegis of a publisher who took the trouble to recruit them one by one, staking his fortune on their questioned talent? They have to be somewhere, and they are there because there freedom and literary intelligence abound."

In Charpentier, "les Cinq" acquired not only a publisher who loved their work but a friend who valued their company. On Fridays he had them visit 11, rue de Grenelle. On Sundays they welcomed him *chez* Flaubert. Before long filaments became webs, as Georges and Marguerite spun around Paris, from author to author, dining at Goncourt's house in Auteuil, at Daudet's apartment in the Faubourg Saint-Germain, at Zola's residence in Les Batignolles. During two decades, hardly a month passed that some such occasion did not bring them together, and between private dinners there were public events. They gathered at book parties, at premieres, at the annual Salon, and—when Georges opened an art gallery near the Boulevard des Italiens—at vernissages. To consecrate this affinity the Charpentiers made Flaubert, Zola, and Goncourt godfathers to three of their four children.

The affection that bound Charpentier and Zola in particular may have been more the product of their different temperaments than of their kindred views. A truant determined to stay the course for once and a swotter haunted by dreams of leisure found fulfillment through each other. Zola relied upon Charpentier's savoir faire, while Charpentier, who would have bartered savoir faire for some creative fire, derived godfatherly satisfaction from the growth of *Les Rougon-Macquart*. Goncourt tried on several occasions to unyoke them, for example by telling Zola once a story about his nonappearance at a friend's wedding: "Charpentier remains the lovable June bug whom you know. . . . He donned formal attire, informed his employees that he had a wedding, then vanished into thin air. No one saw him at the town hall or the Protestant church or the lunch, and when I visited his flat, needing to discuss something that bears upon the illustration of *Marie-Antoinette*, I learned that he had left for the seashore. Charming fellow, our publisher, but not serious enough." No matter. Although Zola, too, complained about his editor's dilatoriness, he knew from the holidays they spent together that Charpentier positively enjoyed having him near.

By 1875 Zola needed a vacation badly. Four years had elapsed since he had last visited Bennecourt, the little village on the Seine, and the daily grind had taken its toll. Always subject to colic, which at times incapacitated him, he was now suffering cardiac disturbances as his heart went haywire, skipping beats and pulsing in his arm and thigh. He swore off tobacco, but this deprivation may have induced him to eat even more than usual, for he grew quite stout. What made matters worse was his wife's condition. Throughout the spring and early summer of 1875, Alexandrine, about whom it can be speculated that her childlessness preyed constantly upon her mind, languished with some mysterious ailment. She lay bedridden while Emilie and their manservant, Joseph, managed the household.

A physician having recommended ocean water, Zola assigned Paul Alexis (who was just then marooned in Brittany) the task of scouting villages near Saint-Malo but ultimately decided not to go quite so far afield and instead rented cheap accommodations at Saint-Aubin-sur-Mer, twenty kilometers from Caen.[2] There, on a flat, dreary stretch of Norman coastline (destined to become famous in 1944 during the Allied invasion as "Juno Beach"), he and Alexandrine spent two months. "Our house, which people joked about, suits us fine; it's more than modest, the doors don't shut tight and the furniture is rudimentary. But the view is superb," he wrote to Marius Roux on August 5, soon after his arrival. "The sea, always the sea! A gale drives waves to within several meters of our threshold. Nothing more magnificent, especially at night. It's quite different from the Mediterranean, both very ugly and very grand. . . . Otherwise, my head has not yet joined me. I'm hardly a traveling man. Any displacement capsizes me. It will be next week before I right myself." A week later, still mesmerized by the surf, he wrote to Alexis: "We have a superb variety of weather—storms, then, abruptly, brilliant sunlight, Neapolitan nights, phosphorescent seas. Never have I seen such rapid scene changes. Under a gray sky the sea looms immense. I've begun to grasp this region, which at first I found horribly repulsive. I'm noting every new aspect of the sea for some great descriptive episode, perhaps twenty pages long, which I'd dearly love to slip into one of my novels."

Planting the flag of *Les Rougon-Macquart* in the sands of an alien environment, Zola lost no time colonizing it with fellow southerners. Urgent invitations were dispatched to Numa Coste, to Marius Roux, and, above all, to his *fidus Achates*, Paul Alexis:

Here are a few figures, which I amicably submit in consideration of your purse. The round-trip voyage will cost 32 francs and change, or 37 including the Caen–Saint-Aubin omnibus. Why don't we say 50

[2]Alexis had recently survived a nightmarish imbroglio. In April, four years after *la semaine sanglante*, he was jailed, accused of having belonged to a Communard brigade known for its fierce resistance, and threatened with life imprisonment. Zola mobilized influential friends. After ten days the police came to realize that the "Alexis" they had winkled out of the Commune's captured files was a *journalier*, or laborer, rather than a *journaliste*, or journalist, and let him go. Alexis then traveled to Rennes, where an expected editorial position on the *Journal d'Ille-et-Vilaine* fell through.

to cover incidental expenses. Once you're here, your financial worries are over. Fifty francs in ten days is certainly what you'd spend in Paris, so nothing should hold you back. Come, drop a line and we'll make your bed. You can help me wait for Roux and his wife, whom I've given up expecting right away. If they surprise me, we'll be a full house. . . . The weather is splendid today. Excellent bathing, wonderful sea. This morning we caught some shrimp.

Sooner or later they all descended upon him, and the campers included Charpentier's mother, Aspasie, who felt so much at home among these exuberant Aixois that she ended up staying five weeks. Even on holiday, Zola abided by his motto of "no day without a line." Work progressed, he assured Charpentier. "I myself am astonished at how diligently I cleave to the desk I've improvised near a window. The boats distract me a bit. My pen falls from my hand as I follow the sails and realize after a minute that fifteen minutes have elapsed. But this does not prevent me from writing a daily piece for *Le Sémaphore de Marseille*, from composing a long study of the Goncourts for Russia, from scaffolding my next novel." The sea was irresistible, however. Together with Alexandrine, whose health improved, he splashed about every morning or afternoon in a ritual of semi-immersion. When August tides ran high, everyone went trawling for shrimp. And to escape the immediate neighborhood, where queer looks from "bourgeois" vacationers suggested that some may have recognized the lewd author of *La Faute de l'abbé Mouret*, they walked west, beyond Asnelles, along a shore lined with low, crumbling cliffs. "You can't imagine anything uglier [than Calvados around Saint-Aubin-sur-Mer]," Zola told Charpentier. "It's flatter than the sidewalk of a ruined city—and deserted and gray and immense! Leagues of prose, bourgeois platitude as far as the eye can see. In my depths there's still a romantic undertow, for I dream of rock walls that have steps cut into them, of reefs pounded by storms, of lightning-struck trees dipping their tresses in the sea. If I can take time off next year, I shall definitely go to Brittany."

The following summer Zola did go to Brittany, and with Charpentier. By then a year of work and a fiercely cold winter had undone the salubrious effects of the summer vacation in 1875. At Turgenev's behest he consulted a German physician, but the medicine prescribed only aggravated his palpitations, his spells of insomnia, his gasping for air, and his depression. Nothing helped except hydrotherapy, which, though it had gained acceptance in Paris through a zealous practitioner named Louis-Joseph Fleury, was still exotic enough to alarm concerned friends like Alexis. "Don't overindulge in hydrotherapy any more than in German medicine," the latter warned. "What I prescribe is *walking*. Walk to your heart's content. If, besides, you curb your particular vice, gluttony, you'll soon be as fit as that old cretin Father Hugo."[3]

In mid-July 1876, Zola and Charpentier set out for Brittany, intending to summon their families once they had found suitable quarters in some fishing village on the Guérande peninsula, near Saint-Nazaire. "Excellent trip, a splendid night, my beautiful Loulou," Zola wrote to Alexandrine.

> At first the train was stifling, but as soon as we threw open the windows and began to move, we felt quite comfortable. Turn over the bench cushions because on the underside they are stuffed with horsehair and smell fresher. There are two changes, one at Nantes at 6 o'clock and one at Savenay at 7:30. The Loire is superb at sunrise between Angers and Nantes, so sit on the left side. I'm writing from the Hôtel Couronné, where we've just emptied two pails of water washing away the soot that covered us. We've rented a coach which will cost 30 francs for two days, and now we're off to Le Pouliguen. Tomorrow we'll spend another night at this hotel and will meet you at the station on Wednesday morning with an omnibus. I haven't been cold at all and haven't missed my cardigan. Don't trouble yourself about getting it back. Just give notice and we'll collect it on our return.
>
> Take it easy. Make all necessary preparations. Hug Bertrand. And until Wednesday morning, my beautiful Loulou, I kiss you full on the mouth, again and again.

All went smoothly until the omnibus, laden with ten people and baggage enough to keep them well supplied for six weeks, left Saint-Nazaire. Eight kilometers from their destination, Piriac-sur-Mer, where a large house had been found, the omnibus keeled over, jamming passengers against one another and hurling twelve large trunks into a ditch. "Since I was near the door I climbed out through the window and began rescue work," Zola later recounted. "The accursed door wouldn't open, so I pulled everyone out through that same window— children and ladies, several of whom weighed a ton. When we were all out, safe and sound but stranded on the highway amidst scattered baggage, my wife fainted dead away. A coach eventually fetched us and a wagon brought our baggage some hours later." As deeply superstitious as her husband, Alexandrine would never thereafter board vehicles drawn by white horses.

This region, which Balzac had pictured in *Béatrix*, did not exactly

[3]Alexis had in mind Victor Hugo's sexual exploits, large and small. The seventy-five-year-old was as randy as ever and exacted favors from every female near enough to paw.

answer Zola's wider dreams. What he saw when he traveled several miles inland was a weird landscape of salt pans that made Calvados look hummocky in comparison. But there were also pine barrens and medieval fortifications and natives who had, mercifully, never heard of *Les Rougon-Macquart*. Paris, only twelve hours distant, belonged to some other world. "We're in a veritable desert here," he exulted. "There are only two or three families of bathers, and these bourgeois come from Nantes. We occupy a large house on the seashore, comfortable enough. The church and the cemetery lie close by, an adorable little cemetery overgrown with fennel where all the local cats convene to play hide-and-seek. I've described the geese and swine that bathe in the courtyard along with people. Nothing more primitive, more uncouth, more charming." Part of the charm it exercised was that of déjà vu, as fauna he knew from childhood kept popping up around him. "The really delightful thing is that this remote corner of Brittany bears an astonishing resemblance to Provence. Just think, I've found shoals of sea urchins, clams, *arapèdes*. You can imagine how I'm celebrating! I gorge myself day and night on shellfish. Along the paths there are butterflies and grasshoppers that transport me right back to the Hill of Paupers."[4] Even the sea at Piriac evoked Provence. Beyond a port where sardine fishermen discharged their catch every afternoon lay a blue immensity specked with islands and girded by the white cliffs of Le Morbihan.

The companions occasionally bestirred themselves to tour the peninsula, visiting Le Croisic, Batz, Kerkabelec, and Guérande, which Zola described as "a jewel, a feudal town one could display in the window of a curiosity shop." But for the most part they bathed, shrimped, talked, and, above all, ate. "Yesterday the Charpentiers showed me a Zola I had never quite seen," Goncourt gloated in his diary, "a glutton, an epicure, a Zola spending all his money on provender, haunting gourmet delicatessens and fancy greengrocers, . . . so excited when he had clams for lunch . . . that he couldn't eat them until his hands stopped trembling. And together with gluttony goes a knowledge of cuisine that enables the novelist to detect straightway the ingredient or spice missing from some dish or to tell how much longer it should have simmered. He will examine the aqueous chamber of a boiled egg and indicate professorially exactly when it was laid."

Although Zola made notes wherever he went (notes that yielded a short story for *The European Herald* entitled "Mr. Chabre's Shellfish"), he was, as he confessed to Edmond de Goncourt, nagged by the

---

[4]Flanking Mont Sainte-Victoire, the Hill of Paupers, or Collines des Pauvres, rises behind the dam designed by François Zola. *Arapèdes*, from the Provençal *arrapedo*, are a species of crustacean.

thought of other novelists progressing while he idled: "We spend our days on our backs. . . . A life of sloth, which would be perfect except for twinges of remorse. I've let everything drop and am not sure that this is how a true artist behaves. You, my friend, must be slaving away. Are you content? Is the material giving you trouble? Write me six lines so that I can rejoice in the script of someone hard at work." But these compunctions did not spoil his humor. A friendship with Charpentier was sealed during that Breton holiday. And if beforehand Alexandrine had felt apprehensive about living in intimate circumstances with upper-class sorts, the Charpentier children, whom she helped to mother, put her at her ease.[5]

Zola had no sooner finished La Faute de l'abbé Mouret than he began a novel about Félicité's oldest son, Eugène, the mastermind who flits omnisciently through La Fortune des Rougon, La Curée, and La Conquête de Plassans. Inspired by such examples of fiction steeped in political intrigue as Balzac's Scènes de la vie politique, Stendhal's Le Rouge et le Noir, and Flaubert's L'Education sentimentale, this installment of Les Rougon-Macquart had first taken shape in 1869, when Zola envisaged "a novel whose frame is officialdom and whose hero is . . . responsible for engineering Louis Napoleon's coup d'état. I can make him either a minister or a high functionary. [His] ambitions extend beyond those of his kin. Power interests him more than money, but he has no use for justice and is thus a worthy servant of the Empire." Five years later events combined to make his subject even more attractive. In 1874, the writer who exposed imperial skulduggery did not risk imprisonment. But neither would he have felt that he was belaboring an irrelevant issue, for in 1874 Bonapartism regained popularity throughout France. While the legislature, dominated by conservative factions, could neither crown a king nor embrace a republic and kept the country in limbo, many Frenchmen began to whiten the sepulchre of Louis Napoleon, who had died in England on January 9, 1873. He at least evoked la gloire.

How indeed had the National Assembly comported itself since

---

[5]Still, the sojourn did not dispel Alexandrine's feelings of social inferiority. In September 1877, when she interrupted a holiday at L'Estaque to attend her father's funeral in Paris, Zola wrote to her as follows: "I mention the Charpentiers although I know you'll be annoyed. If you don't contact them, it will seem very odd to them. The matter of wardrobe is not serious; you're in mourning and you can say that you left harum-scarum, which is true. Make an effort, my dear, if it doesn't cost you too much, and put in an appearance, saying that your family is waiting for you, that you have only ten minutes, that you're leaving in the evening. Anyway, if it bothers you too much, don't go."

Thier's fall from power in May 1873? Marshal MacMahon happily anticipated the prospect of being replaced by a king in the person of Henri de Bourbon, Comte de Chambord, when parliamentary royalists renewed their overtures to the pretender in August 1873. But almost no one outside Versailles wanted Chambord enthroned, least of all the right wing's own peasant constituents, who, though deeply Catholic, feared that a Bourbon monarch would restore the *ancien régime* under which their forefathers had groaned. "The return of Henri V is the greatest chimera that could possibly have entered the heads of intriguing politicians," the great chemist and future minister Marcellin Berthelot wrote to Ernest Renan from a lookout in the hinterland. "Anything is possible except that. The peasant will rise, note this well, in thirty or forty *départements*, because he really fears . . . that the common lands which he got in '93 will be taken away from him. . . . One must distinguish pilgrimages and popular superstitions—which represent art and ideality for all poor people—from acquiescence in the clergy's will to dominate. . . . People throng to pilgrimage sites, but not one in ten would countenance Henri V."

Blind to reality, Chambord's suitors returned from visiting the pretender in Austria with hopes that a new dispensation lay at hand. Chambord did not disabuse them until October 29, when he published an open letter vowing that he would never become the legitimate king of the revolution and "inaugurate a salutary regime with an act of weakness." Any a priori restraints upon his will—which would be imperative in a constitutional monarchy—were unacceptable. "My person is nothing, my principle is everything. . . . When God has resolved to save a people, he takes care that the scepter of justice be placed in hands strong enough to grasp it." On this sanctimonious note Chambord exited from French history, leaving royalist ranks broken.

The moderate Right regrouped straightway.[6] Its design was to prop up MacMahon for the long haul and to invest his office with such power that a republic, if formally instituted, would be a constitutional monarchy in disguise. Broglie, the prime minister, achieved one goal by getting MacMahon's term extended. "The executive power is entrusted for seven years to Marshal MacMahon, Duke of Magenta," stated a law promulgated on November 20, 1873. "His power will continue to be exercised with the title of president of the Republic . . . unless modified through some constitutional process." But this so-called Septennate did not console Legitimists, who had meanwhile agreed to blame the collapse of plans for a Bourbon restoration on the

[6]The extreme right of Legitimist deputies were given the nickname "Light Cavalry" because they often met among themselves on the impasse des Chevaux-Légers in Versailles.

Orleanist Broglie.[7] Thenceforth Broglie found himself regularly attacked by his quondam allies, as the "Light Cavalry" implemented a *politique du pire*. Eager to foul relations with Germany, they encouraged the Intransigeant Catholic newspaper *L'Univers* to publish a pastoral denunciation of Bismarck and his *Kulturkampf* against the Catholic Church in Germany. When France officially recognized the Kingdom of Italy, which did not honor the pope's temporal power, rallies were held to protest this impious gesture. Before long the extreme Right joined the extreme Left to expel Broglie from office with a vote of no confidence. Another Orleanist (whom Broglie would in fact control) replaced him.

The law that promulgated the Septennate called upon the National Assembly to organize a constitutional commission, which was duly elected, and throughout 1874 thirty truculent Frenchmen did nothing but quarrel. Even as *Le Siècle* declared that France could not continue to live in a tent, they wrangled over nomenclature, with right-wing deputies vetoing all formulae that incorporated the word "republic" or overtly legitimized republicanism. They might have wrangled another year had not an ex-royalist lawyer named Henri-Alexandre Wallon introduced some common sense. "All interest was concentrated on the affirmation or rejection of the word 'republic'; France had the thing, should she still be denied the name?" is how the historian D. W. Brogan put it. On January 30, 1875, when the commission was debating the law for the election of the president, Wallon proposed an amendment that said: "The president of the Republic is elected by the plurality of votes cast by the Senate and Chamber of Deputies united in a National Assembly." This simple formulation effectively ratified the Republic. "By providing for a regular succession to the Marshal," Brogan observed, "it ended the personal and temporary character given to the executive. It did not 'definitely' establish the Republic. What was definitive? But it ended the rule of the provisional."

Wallon's amendment passed by only one vote among 705 cast, a vote seeming to illustrate the Scribean dictum that great effects come from small causes. Liberating men frozen in mutual suspicion, it sparked a common purpose, and with every subsequent item the majority grew larger. After several months, France's Third Republic was crudely knocked together. Monarchical in design, it featured many of the safeguards against popular rule for which Broglie had lobbied, above all a bicameral legislature whose upper house or Senate could,

[7]Orleanists supported Louis Philippe's son, the Comte de Paris. Legitimists tended to recognize only the line that descended from Louis XVI to his brothers, Louis XVIII and Charles X, and to Charles's son, Chambord.

at the president's request, dissolve the lower house, or Chamber of Deputies. Although universal suffrage applied to the latter, election to the former was based on a system that gave disproportionate influence to rural, traditionally Catholic, sparsely populated boroughs; further, 75 of 300 senators would be elected for life by the Chamber, where, in 1875, the Right still outnumbered the Left.

The Left had had good reason to swallow its gorge and take up residence in this jerry-built structure, which violated almost every republican canon. Certainly Leftists recognized that if ever they should gain control of the entire legislature they could disarm a hostile executive or anyway fight him at equal odds.[8] But they also saw how chronic improvisation had been serving those who argued that another Napoleon was needed to restore order. With Bismarck forging a European alliance against France while France lay paralyzed by internecine conflict, Bonapartists exploited the public's thirst for revenge. Several had become deputies, and, to the chagrin of monarchists and republicans alike, Napoleon III's former equerry, the Baron de Bourgoing, won a by-election in March 1874. "Fear! That is their great political means. They engender it, they inoculate it, and, once they've frightened a certain class of citizens, they present themselves as saviors, the better to strip people of their freedoms, of their civic dignity, of their public rights," Gambetta declared at a public rally, inveighing against what he called "Caesarian democracy, this order obtained by force, this brutal power, this clerical connivance, this patronage accorded to representatives of old aristocratic clans." More than any other factor, the knowledge that "Caesarian democracy" had not lost ground in the countryside, in the army, in the administration, and in the magistrature impelled Gambetta to make his peace with the sober Orleanists. However hastily contrived, a body of law offered some protection against despotism, he thought. And so it did. It saved France then, and it would save her again thirteen years later, when General Georges Boulanger astride his black horse very nearly became Napoleon IV.

It was with this doctrinal and constitutional crisis simmering in the background that Zola wrote *Son Excellence Eugène Rougon*, a novel whose titular hero embodies, among other things, the arrogance, moral insensibility, and cronyism of political life in Napoleon III's heyday. "Exactly when during the Second Empire my novel unfolds is something I must decide," he noted early along, "but I can already pin down

[8]Between October 1873 and February 1875, Republicans won 16 seats, Bonapartists 6, and monarchists of either stripe only 1. As for the life senators, Gambetta foiled Orleanist or moderate conservative expectations by striking a bargain with the extreme Right, which once again voted Left. Fifty-five of the 75 senators elected in 1875 came from republican ranks.

certain details. My minister is absolutely opposed to the Liberal Empire; he understands only absolute power. . . . Once my Eugène has scrambled back after a fall, the reform movement halts, the Liberal Empire will have been postponed several years." This historical enterprise spawned yet another fat dossier. With pen in hand Zola read the three volumes of Ernest Hamel's *Histoire illustré du Second Empire*, the six volumes of Taxile Delord's *Histoire du Second Empire*, Vapereau's *Dictionnaire des contemporains*, Paul Dhormoys's *La Cours à Compiègne*, and relevant issues of the quasi-official *Moniteur universel*. In order to describe the legislative body as accurately as possible, he had its *questeur* or chief administrative officer guide him through the Palais-Bourbon. To visualize imperial receptions at Compiègne, he quizzed Flaubert, who had been a guest there, for details of atmosphere and decor. "Zola, on entering Flaubert's flat, sinks into an armchair and mutters in a desperate voice: 'What trouble Compiègne is giving me, what trouble!' " Goncourt observed on March 7, 1875.

> Zola then asked Flaubert how many chandeliers lit the dinner table, whether the table talk was noisy, what people discussed, what the emperor himself said. Yes, there he was, trying to capture through this third party *the physiognomy of a milieu,* when only eyes that had seen it could describe it. And the novelist who means to write history is going to portray a great historical figure after ten minutes with a confrere, and a confrere who hoards the meat of what he knows for his own future novel. . . . Meanwhile Flaubert, partly out of pity, partly for the gratification of informing two or three visitors that he spent a whole fortnight at Compiègne, plays a classic emperor. Dressed in his house robe, he shuffles around with one hand behind his stooped back, twirls his mustache, and improvises moronic pronouncements.

Available to Zola as well were mental pictures formed during his stretch at Versailles and, most particularly, an image of Napoleon III's "vice-emperor," Eugène Rouher, defending himself before a censorious Assembly. In May 1872, gentlemen and ladies *en grande toilette* had packed the gallery to honor this unreconstructed Bonapartist, whom many had last seen at Compiègne or in a ballroom of the Tuileries Palace.[9]

---

[9]"Stooped, crushed by public opprobrium, [Rouher] must have been reflecting bitterly upon the transience of glory as he left the hall with his tearful daughter beside him," Zola had written, little suspecting that within four months the fallen potentate would be elected to the Assembly from a district in—where else?— Corsica.

Son Excellence Eugène Rougon is the tale of one rogue pitted against fellow rogues in the jungle of Napoleonic government. A bully, for whom power is everything, Rougon first served the Republic, then helped Louis Napoleon crush it and reaped his reward under the Empire as president of the Council of State. He has temporarily fallen out of favor and been ousted, but after Orsini's bomb nearly kills Napoleon III, the emperor, in order to intimidate France, appoints him minister of the interior. Thus begins a reign of terror during which Rougon thrives. Venal toadies in his entourage are gratified and republicans are jailed as the minister, who has meanwhile concluded a *mariage de convenance*, becomes a law unto himself. No official is beyond his influence, no enemy beyond his purview. He secures a railroad concession for one sycophant, breaks a notarized will for another, waives civil-service requirements for a third, and has men of principle sent to Devil's Island. Omnipotent yet vulnerable, contemptuous of law yet open to attack by the lawless, he reigns supreme until his mercurial master removes him once again from office. Rougon haters gloat but gloat too soon, for after three years of silence he returns more eloquent than ever. Now a minister without portfolio representing Napoleon III in parliament, Rougon brings his oratory to bear upon the "Liberal Empire" and glorifies freedom of speech. "Strong states derive their strength from discussion held in broad daylight," he proclaims. "The tribune has been reestablished, this tribune distinguished by so many orators whose name history enshrines. A parliament that discusses is a parliament that works." On this note, which resounds through the Palais-Bourbon as through a theater, eliciting *bravissimi* from spectators disposed to mistake rhetoric for reality, *Son Excellence* ends.

Theater governs *Son Excellence*. It is, indeed, the very condition of Eugène Rougon — of the parvenu who feels alive only on stage, playing lead roles in a political tragicomedy improvised year after year by a mysterious, self-created demagogue. Obsessed with power, he can't acquire enough of it and his will crushes not only his political foes but his sexual impulses. However high he climbs, history catches up with him, as when two aristocrats, M. and Mme d'Escorailles, arrive from Plassans. "Their presence was an undreamed-of honor. Had the emperor himself knocked at his door, he would not have felt more flattered. These old people soliciting a favor were Plassans itself paying him homage — the cold, stiff, patrician Plassans that still seemed to him some inaccessible Olympus. And he satisfied at last an old ambition, which was to avenge snubs he had received as a grubby, clientless lawyer." Never will Rougon become Rougon under Napoleon III, for in this make-believe empire where everything rings false — trophies, titles, words, hearts — so does his identity. Awestruck by d'Escorailles, or by the "de" that bespeaks some inalienable substance, he is an actor who lives on credit.

Waxing and waning as chance dictates, Napoleon's satellite dreams of transcendence. "He pounded the void. . . . Would that he could enjoy some new incarnation, would that he could be resurrected as Almighty Jupiter, self-sufficient, ruling by the mere thunder of his voice." Without patents of nobility to legitimize him, Rougon has no fixed abode or definite shape. Now gigantic, now dwarfish, he finds refuge, when Napoleon evicts him, in the fantasy of a kingdom all his own—a kind of autocrat's Paradou. "He regularly imagined himself in Les Landes [a vast marshy expanse in Gascony] conquering a wilderness and peopling it with subjects," writes Zola.

> He secretly read technical works which helped him envision swamps being drained, rocks being cleared by immense earthmovers, dunes being arrested by plantations of pine, a miraculously fertile garden bestowed upon France. The pipe dream galvanized all his somnolent energy and unemployed strength. His clenched fists seemed already to be at work splitting recalcitrant stone; his arms turned the soil in a single thrust; his shoulders carried ready-made houses which he set wherever it pleased him on the bank of a river whose bed he himself had dug. . . . "Now there's an idea!" he'd say. "I'll give my name to the city. I, too, will found a little empire."

He, too, would be an eponymous hero, a progenitor, a Napoleon.

Inseparable from this grandiose dream is his sadomasochistic flirtation with Clorinde Balbi, a mysterious vamp modeled after Virginie de Castiglione, the "divine contessa" who descended upon Paris in 1855 as Cavour's secret agent and argued the cause of Italian statehood under Napoleon III's canopy. Spellbound, Rougon flails between lust and fear, between the urge to possess what everyone desires and the need to conquer himself. If he releases *la bête*, will it devour him? If he unsheathes his sword in passion, will he lose it? Therein lies the dilemma of a spymaster whose imperial vision has him dominating nature rather than enjoying it. Convinced that power or virility means absolute self-containment, he recoils from Clorinde as she, instead, penetrates him. "He cursed himself. At twenty he knew better. She had just made him confess, like a child, he who for two months had sought in vain to ferret out her secret. . . . She was gaining the upper hand." After several more skirmishes, during one of which Clorinde horsewhips him, Rougon retrieves his masculinity:

> He was afraid that the pain would sharpen his desire, that the welt on his cheek would keep him thinking about her. . . . He sat down

on the sofa, fists clenched. A servant entered to tell him that his dinner was getting cold, but he didn't budge. His tough face showed the strain of inner conflict, his bull neck swelled, his muscles tensed as if he were throttling some beast gnawing at his gut. The struggle lasted a good ten minutes. He could not remember ever having fought so hard.

In Clorinde, Rougon has met the embodiment of his most self-destructive fantasy—the huntress, the phallic virgin, the femme fatale who justifies the advice he urges upon others: "Beware of women!" As much as Rougon envies Napoleon III his omnipotence, Clorinde envies Rougon his gender. Seducing him is not an amorous enterprise but a war from which the victor will emerge virile and the loser unmanned.

Rougon vainly tries to control his "disciple" by having her marry a rich, amiable stooge named Delestang. Cloaked in matrimonial respectability, Clorinde continues to pursue her hostile design and helps Rougon rise again the better to lay him low. He gains strength in office; she gains ascendancy over Napoleon III in bed. And when Rougon exceeds himself, it is she who makes him suffer for his hubris, prevailing upon the emperor to appoint her inconsequential husband minister of the interior. "She exulted," writes Zola. "She made it clear [to Rougon] that anybody would have fit the bill, that she could have made a minister of his usher if she had so desired, . . . all of which went to demonstrate the omnipotence of women." Time proves her wrong, however. Three years later Rougon recoups his political fortune at her expense, and so the story concludes, inconclusively. Lashed to an infernal seesaw, the two will swing up and down until Judgment Day, with each enjoying momentary advantage in a war neither can win. Rougon will never become emperor (any more than Napoleon III will ever become Napoleon I), and Clorinde will always rule only through men.

Although Eugène Rougon inherited certain traits from Eugène Rouher, a more important model would appear to have been the underworld lord of Balzac's *Le Père Goriot*, Vautrin. Rough-hewn men, both fictional characters thrive on hugger-mugger, and Zola emphasizes this in a description of Rougon prowling around Paris the night Orsini attacks Napoleon III:

He found Paris enlarged, made to his measure, with air enough to fill him. The inky, gold-flecked Seine plashed softly, like some colossus breathing an accompaniment to his grandiose dream. When he reached the Palais de Justice, a clock chimed 9 p.m. He shuddered, turned around, pricked his ears. He seemed to hear panic overhead,

distant explosions, cries of alarm. All at once Paris became for him a
city stunned by some great crime. And he remembered the afternoon
of the Prince Imperial's baptism, when bells tolled in the hot June
sun and crowds thronged the quais and he felt crushed beneath the
weight of a triumphant emperor. This was his hour of revenge, a
moonless night, a city terror-stricken and mute, the quais deserted.
. . . He loved this cutthroat Paris in whose darkness he gathered
strength.

Like Vautrin, who has moles planted everywhere, Rougon is the om-
niscient voyeur. Like Vautrin, who proposes to conquer Paris through
an irresistibly handsome youth named Eugène de Rastignac, Rougon
vests his dream of conquest in a "disciple" whose beauty smites the
eye. And like Vautrin, who wages war against society under various
aliases, Rougon cannot endure being something other than All or
Nothing. Rougon's career illustrates Vautrin's dictum that "there are
no principles, there are only events; there are no laws, there are only
circumstances; and superior men wed events and circumstances the
better to direct them." Similarly, the fanciful empire that consoles
Rougon in defeat recalls his Balzacian predecessor's. "My idea is to
reign as patriarch over a great domain, say 100,000 acres, in the United
States, the South," Vautrin tells Rastignac. "I'll be a plantation owner,
with slaves, earning millions selling livestock, tobacco, lumber, living
like a sovereign, enforcing my will, doing what's inconceivable here,
where we crouch in a gypsum pit."

This paradigm goes beyond fiction, for it seems quite likely that
Rougon playing absolute monarch, and being castrated after every star
turn on the political stage, mirrors Zola himself emulating his literary
progenitor, Honoré de Balzac, and after every novel feeling defeated
again. Paul Alexis detected the resemblance and in *Emile Zola, notes
d'un ami* wrote: "I am persuaded that the novelist put himself in the
skin of his minister, Eugène Rougon: this chaste man who eludes
woman and loves power intellectually, less for the material advantages
it brings than as a manifestation of his own strength—is Emile Zola
as minister; he is the figuration of what Zola would have been had he
turned his ambition to politics." But did Alexis see that the "chaste
man who eludes woman" was driven by a patricidal fantasy? Rougon's
obsessive dream says it all: Whenever Napoleon III humbles him, he
imagines himself a civil engineer of Promethean stature designing a
whole city-state and, as if to secure forgiveness for his challenge, be-
stowing this "miraculously fertile" mini-empire upon the larger nation.
This fundamental dilemma plays itself out on every level throughout
Les Rougon-Macquart.

Unusual delays attended the publication of *Son Excellence Eugène
Rougon*, which Zola delivered to Philippe Jourde, editor-in-chief of *Le*

Siècle, on June 29, 1875. "[Jourde] told me that he couldn't respond before August," he told Charpentier. "I find that very long . . . Work on him. I got the impression that he holds your firm in high regard. The best strategy would be to send Dreyfous a week hence and have him explain that for certain commercial reasons you would like to launch my volume before December." But Jourde, to everyone's dismay, sat on the manuscript all summer long, like a broody hen. "Our mistake, my friend, is in dealing with my novels when they're finished; we should place them before they're begun," Zola advised Dreyfous in September. "We must see about finding someone likely to appreciate my next novel, which would avoid disastrous delays." Not until October did Jourde buy *Son Excellence* and by then Stasiulevich had arranged for a Russian translation. Three months later the novel began running in *The European Herald* and in *Le Siècle*, where it bore the very Balzacian subtitle of *Scènes de la vie politique sous le Second Empire*.

Those "scenes"—and particularly scenes in which Zola, with his genius for subverting gala events, portrays the Empire as Offenbachian kitsch or broad farce—made a great impression on his friends. To be sure, Flaubert, who had just buffed the thirty pages of *Saint-Julien l'Hospitalier* to an absolute fare-thee-well, was vexed by Zola's exuberant prose. "I don't share Turgenev's harsh view of *Jack* [a novel of Daudet's] or his immense admiration for *Rougon*," he confided to George Sand. "One has charm and the other power, but neither concerns itself *above all* with what is, for me, the goal of art: beauty. I remember having had palpitations, having felt violent pleasure when I gazed at a wall of the Acropolis, a perfectly bare wall (on one's left as one climbs toward the Propylaea). Well, I wonder if a book, apart from what it says, can produce the same effect. In the precise way parts join, in the rarity of its individual elements, in its polish and harmony, is there no inherent virtue, a kind of divine force, something eternal, like a principle?" This reflection made him feel lonely. "How difficult for minds to meet! Turgenev and Zola are two men whom I like very much and consider true artists. Yet they are no admirers of Chateaubriand's prose and even less of Gautier's. Sentences that ring for me clink for them."[10]

But others praised *Son Excellence* unreservedly and above all Stéphane Mallarmé, who never had to worry about dissociating himself from a realist or naturalist movement. "I read it straight through, then read it again piece by piece, over several days," he told Zola in March 1876.

---

[10]Sand responded: "You no longer look for anything but the well-turned sentence. That is something, but only something—it isn't all of art, it isn't even the half of it; it's a quarter at most, and when the other three quarters are admirable one overlooks the one that is not."

Son Excellence lends itself to both ways of savoring a work—the old way, which is how it was when novels unfolded like plays, and the new way, which reflects the intermittence of modern life. For beneath those pleats and tucks with which a narrator must nowadays embroider his idea lies, admirably concealed, something of profound interest.

A book whose special aesthetic weds form and function as this one does is a masterpiece, and that is why—though the poet in me (who's wrong) prefers *La Curée* and *La Faute* for their more tangible splendors—I consider this latest work the most accomplished expression of the viewpoint it will always be your honor to have understood and demonstrated, the viewpoint that governs modern art. All its elements cohere beautifully; not only the profound concept . . . of a powerful force split into two contradictory types, hostile yet riveted to each other . . . but its style—swift and transparent, light and impersonal, like the glance of a contemporary, of your reader.

The novel conquered new ground for its genre, Mallarmé asserted, by absorbing the flavor and perishable stuff of history. Future historians would be left with dry carcasses to pick.

Praise of a more supercilious kind came from the few newspaper critics who reviewed *Son Excellence*. Eager to cite Zola for good behavior but inclined to wonder whether the naughty boy might recidivate, they cautiously promoted him. "We could point out exaggerations here and there, apocryphal stories, faces that spring from the realm of pure, or rather impure, fantasy, deplorably cynical scenes," wrote one such critic, "but there are also some masterly bits." Another declared that "what Zola portrays here is less dull and trivial than the reality in which he has hitherto wallowed; we are not, thank God, overcome by the miasma of La Halle and the aroma of pork sausage." And in *Le Bien public*, Francisque Sarcey was reported to have praised the novel's "generally proper deportment" while "greeting with pleasure signs of a maturity that augurs well."

These congratulatory yawns worked against *Son Excellence*, but its critical reception did not explain its commercial unsuccess. Chance, or timing, played an important role, for soon after the bound volume finally appeared, *Le Bien public* began serializing Zola's next novel, and from the first, *L'Assommoir* created a sensation that made everyone forget Eugène Rougon. Eclipsed in fiction by Napoleon III, Rougon found himself shunted aside in the marketplace by a working-class cousin named Gervaise Macquart, who was to bring Zola fame and fortune.

XV

"IF THE GOOD DEMOCRATS
EXPECTED SYCOPHANTIC
DRIVEL . . ."

THE SOCIAL MYTHS or pieties against which Zola launched his novel about Paris's working class were not an outgrowth of the bloody civil war that still haunted everyone who survived it but the stuff of a creed that had been maturing for generations. It therefore behooves us to consider *L'Assommoir* in broad historical perspective.

Even before it enthroned itself in July 1830, the bourgeoisie that emerged from Revolutionary turmoil and Napoleonic despotism had made a ruling principle of thrift, of accumulation, of solidity. To be sure, it would never relinquish the belief that it had enlightenment to propagate and a spiritual mission to accomplish. But its fortune swelled rather more conspicuously than its heart during the 1830s and 1840s, when France entered the industrial age. Steam engines became commonplace, factories multiplied together with applications for commercial licenses, railroads appeared, and a revision of the Civil Code outlawed primogeniture. "Enrich yourselves by work and thrift," enjoined Louis Philippe's minister of public instruction. "Ascend," cried others, in language that distorted the traditional terms of Christian salvation. History was often portrayed as a dynastic saga, with bold men rather than meek inheriting the earth. "The father was a peasant, a factory worker, a merchant sailor," wrote Adolphe Thiers in *On Property*. "The son, assuming his father was diligent and frugal, will be a farmer, a manufacturer, a ship's captain. The grandson will be a banker, a notary, a doctor, a lawyer, a prime minister perhaps. Thus do the generations rise, one above the other."

In the matter of liberty, fraternity, and equality, a banker named

345

Jacques Lafitte formulated what the constitutional monarchy of 1830–48 might have used as its official agenda:

> I have always considered the material weal to be the least problematical, the least difficult to achieve, the least infiltrated by government; I have always thought that, when all other forms of well-being proved impossible, we had that one to fall back upon. A land cannot be given freedom: give it, instead, the fortune that will soon render it more enlightened, better, and free. Government will always accept the bait of wealth and will soon be surprised to discover that any development in man, whatever it may be, always leads to freedom.

Far from representing an inherent attribute of human nature, then, in this view liberty belonged to those who contrived to earn it. Though laws protected all men equally, under the *régime censitaire* (so called on account of a statute that bound up electoral privilege with the tax roll) only about 200,000 Frenchmen could influence legislation, and seldom did laws transcend their proprietary interests. Otherwise liberal bourgeois might speak of delivering Poland from the oppressive hand of Russia, of liberating Italy from papal tyranny, of supporting the little German states against a Lutheran Prussian squirearchy, but they ruled like Russia, Gregory XVI, and Prussia over France's disenfranchised poor. Not that they were baldly malevolent. On the contrary, they did what they did in good conscience, invoking Wealth or Production to justify a slave class much as Robespierre invoked the Supreme Being to legitimize "the despotism of liberty." In grade schools and at free public lectures organized for people who, because they paid no taxes, fell outside what Guizot called *le pays légal*, the state taught homilies rather than skills. "Workers are outside political society, outside the city: they are the barbarians of modern societies," proclaimed the arch-conservative *Journal des débats.*

Now teaching the prole to behave, now crushing him outright, bourgeois might have been neither so evangelical nor so callous, neither so supportive of charitable institutions nor so exploitative of labor, had they not believed their order to be threatened by an alien species, a primitive horde, a race innately different from themselves. "Drunk," "savage," "barbaric," "criminal," "nomadic": these figured prominently among the epithets often saddled on *le peuple*, and those who did the anathematizing consecrated their superiority by invoking crypto-racist mystiques such as phrenology. Where history had failed them in denying them aristocratic lineage, bumps would serve. What could prosperous bourgeois have in common with Celtic gnomes streaming into Paris from the Auvergne, or with wretches whose cranial structure exhibited, not the effects of lifelong hunger and ceaseless toil, but a natural propensity for destructiveness? How could nomads understand the concept of property or the sanctity of a hearth, and inebriates the life of reason?

Linked geographically and economically, the higher and lower orders regarded each other with terrified vigilance from either side of a palisade. Workers, wrote one social commentator, were as little duty-bound to their masters as the latter were to them; they considered them men of a different class, not only standing opposed but in violent opposition. "Extreme poverty brings about a regression to the savage state. . . . The indigent resemble those Saxon bands who escaped the Norman yoke by hiding out in the forests; they are outside society, outside the law, outlaws, and it is from their ranks that most criminals emerge." Similarly, Eugène Sue, a ship's doctor who gave up medicine and the sea to write novels about Paris's lower depths, presented himself in *Les Mystères de Paris* as an anthropologist recording the customs of a primitive society. "Everyone," he wrote, "has read those admirable pages in which James Fenimore Cooper . . . traces the ferocious customs of savages, their picturesque, poetic language, the thousand ruses by means of which they flee or pursue their enemies. . . . The barbarians of whom we speak are in our midst; we can rub elbows with them by venturing into lairs where they congregate to plot murder or theft, and to divvy up the spoils. These men have mores all their own, women different from others, a language incomprehensible to us; a mysterious language thick with baneful images, with metaphors dripping blood." Did one owe moral responsibility to creatures who spoke not French but a "mysterious" tongue, a language bereft of reason that voiced the instinctual life at its most brutal? The bourgeoisie felt compelled to defend themselves from this primitive "other" behind walls of politesse intricate enough to rival Louis XIV's Versailles. One manual argued that on a rainy day the "truly polite" person could shelter someone caught without his or her umbrella "provided age, sex, attire did not oppose the gesture, for it would be entirely inappropriate to address oneself to people of the lowest social class."

What is more, the bourgeoisie built a capital, a separate city that transformed such propriety into stone and marble and iron and glass. Under the constitutional monarchy during the 1840s, well-to-do Parisians deserted central Paris for new *quartiers* at the northern and western periphery, leaving behind what soon became an inner city whose labyrinthine streets and tenements swarmed with immigrants from rural France. It was, in part, to reverse these migrations that Napoleon III razed the old neighborhood. As a result of the upheaval wrought by Baron Haussmann, poor folk found themselves swept outward beyond the tollgates into a pariahdom that time and suffrage would dignify with a symbolic place name, "the red belt." "The circumstances that oblige workers to live at some distance from the center of Paris are generally noted to have had maleficent effects upon their conduct and morality," the prefect of police stated in 1855. "As a rule, they used to inhabit the uppermost stories of houses occupied down below by families of industrial entrepreneurs and the relatively well-off. A kind of solidarity would form among residents of such houses. . . . Workers would find succor and assistance when they fell ill or lost their jobs; in addition, human respect would inject an element of regularity into working-class habits. [Now] workers live where there are no bourgeois families and find themselves deprived of help and freed of the bridle that such proximity formerly imposed upon them." Matters had come to this sorry pass only one generation after *Les Trois Glorieuses*, the glory days of July 1830 when notables eulogized the "great populace" and the "saintly rabble" who had fought at the barricades. By turns sainted and damned, *le peuple* was, either way, an outsider.

Society expressed its values in play no less than in work. The honor bestowed upon an essentially antiquarian young dramatist like Casimir Delavigne, whose star easily outshone Hugo's or Musset's, is one measure of the extent to which academicism supported the bourgeoisie's racist mythology. As comforting as the liberal bromides strewn throughout *Les Vêpres siciliennes*, *L'Ecole des Vieillards*, *Marino Faliero*, and *Louis XI* was the emphatically regressive style in which Delavigne formulated them: periphrastic turns of phrase that curled backward to the old regime, for example, or embellishments that made his work seem venerable at birth. For commonsensical pleasure, people had recourse to other playwrights. What Delavigne gave those parvenus who eschewed Boulevard melodrama was a proprietary stake in the grand tradition, a deed to French culture. That one of their own could fabricate perfect alexandrines, that tragedy—the genre of genres—could emerge from within their own collective soul represented something tantamount to evidence of a generic distinction from the uncouth. Hugo might protest that "the French language is not fixed and never will be. A language cannot be fixed. The human mind is always on the march or, if you will, in movement, and languages move with it." No matter. Such words were anathema to a public of two minds about marches and movement, to arrivistes who attended the Comédie-Française to acquire a patina rather than to witness a drama. "If you dare," sneered one observer, "go sit once a week in the orchestra of the Salle Richelieu or the Odéon, amidst that group of amateurs whose starchy features and superdignified attitudes announce a pretension to judge far more than a desire to enjoy. . . . The theater is, in their eyes, a kind of academy where pompous orators come to declaim, methodically, long speeches."

Furthermore, Hugo called for a new dramatic style in which the verse line would, "like Proteus," he said, assume a thousand forms "without departing from character," its beauty or ugliness a mere consequence, not an end in itself. Here again his manifesto was calculated to fill ladies and gentlemen with consternation, for "Protean" was one of those epithets ritually convoked to denigrate the lower class: nomads who lacked a fixed place lacked a fixed shape. Without orthodoxies to distinguish high from low one could not predicate distinctions of breed, establish an essential hiatus between the orders, consecrate a structure of power and property. Everything would fuse, and anything would be possible. "If the effect of democracy is generally to question the authority of all literary rules and conventions, on the stage it abolishes them altogether, and puts in their place nothing but the whim of each author and of each public," wrote Alexis de Tocqueville in *Democracy in America.* "When the heroes and the manners of antiquity are frequently brought upon the stage, and dramatic authors faithfully observe the rules of antiquated precedent, that is enough to warrant a conclusion that the democratic classes have not yet got the upper hand in the theaters."

Even as romantics laid siege to the fortress of rhetorical Beauty, rolling out Shakespeare like a battering ram, the bourgeoisie took refuge behind its walls. When in 1833 the Comédie-Française had staged *Les Enfants d'Edouard,* a tragedy by Casimir Delavigne, critics who upheld *le bon ton* or *le bon goût* found it very much more to their taste than its model, Shakespeare's *Richard III.* One such critic praised the author for not leading his public, like Shakespeare, "on a three-hour jaunt through a labyrinth of crimes and horrors" and for sparing "delicate" nerves the obscenity of Buckingham's execution. "Never would a low word have the nerve to show itself," he wrote, defending Delavigne's work as if it were a private club and he its concierge. Indeed, monitors of Order drew upon the same fund of metaphors whether commenting on the stage in particular or on the city at large. Thus, "a labyrinth of crimes and horrors" might serve to describe either Elizabethan theater or infamous slums like "little Poland" on the Ile de la Cité.

Had the champions of Order been disposed to seek a perfect incarnation of their nightmares, they would have found it on the Boulevard du Temple, where, some few months after rebellious silk workers had been massacred by army troops in Lyon in 1834, the great actor Frédérick Lemaître created *Robert Macaire.* To say that this play won popular acclaim is an understatement. Its outlaw hero became proverbial among outcasts of every stripe—among *le petit peuple,* who recognized in him certain vestiges of the traditional bandit of popular literature; among aristocrats, who, with murderous irony, avenged themselves on history for having made sport of them; among intellectuals, who believed with Heine that "the thinking men who worked indefatigably throughout the eighteenth century to prepare the French Revolution would blush if they could see personal interest busily building its wretched huts on the site of the ruined palaces, and from these huts a new aristocracy emerging even more unpleasant than the old." A scarecrow amalgamating nobiliary particles, Revolutionary ideals, criminal slang, and poor men's rags, Macaire sprang from the bin into which industrial society dumped its waste.

Macaire, the stock villain of a melodrama written by three Boulevard hacks, *L'Auberge des Adrets*, would have disappeared along with the play itself after several dozen performances had it not been for Lemaître. Aiming to make his mark by a flamboyant departure from convention, he guyed the part. Instead of tiptoeing onstage with arms raised to hide his face, as villains ritually did, he strode forward like a father or a lover. Attired not in the uniform of evil but in a bizarre motley—patched trousers, bedroom slippers, a dirty white vest, a threadbare green coat, and a gray felt hat raffishly tilted to one side— he looked every inch the scavenger. *The Inn of Les Adrets* provoked gales of laughter, bringing its authors a "tearful success"—though neither the success nor the tears on which they had banked—and married its star to a role that shadowed him even beyond the grave. Some ten years later, Flaubert, who visited the original inn of Les Adrets during a trip through the Midi, wrote: "I looked at it with religious awe, thinking that it was here that the great Robert Macaire had taken wing for the future, here that the greatest symbol of the age, the epitome of our time, had originated. Types like Macaire are not created every day; indeed, I cannot think of a greater one since Don Juan."

In Macaire, who "quipped as he killed," black humor found its clarion. Parodying the moral scheme implicit in melodramatic formulae, he spoke to feelings of profound dissociation that beset his heterogeneous audience. Villains and heroes upheld the Just Society from opposite poles, but Macaire, who combined features of both, was a kind of con artist transcending ethical distinctions, an outsider pledged to no common ideal, a *homo duplex* killing gratuitously or assuming aliases for the fun of it. Heine exactly caught the reasons for Macaire's appeal. He wrote:

The people have so completely lost faith in the high ideals about which our political and literary Tartuffes prate that they see in them nothing but empty phrases—*blague*, as their saying goes. This comfortless outlook is illustrated by Robert Macaire; it is likewise illustrated by the popular dances, which may be regarded as the spirit of Macaire put into mime. Anyone acquainted with the latter will be able to form some idea of these indescribable dances, which are satires not only of sex and society but of everything that is good and beautiful, of all enthusiasm, patriotism, loyalty, faith, family feeling, heroism, and religion.

Transforming *L'Auberge des Adrets* into a vehicle for topical extemporizations, Lemaître-Macaire could pack the house by announcing as he did on one occasion: "Gentlemen, we regret that we are unable to murder a gendarme this evening, as the actor who plays that part is indisposed. But tomorrow we shall kill two."

How unbridgeable was the chasm separating haves and have-nots? In 1832, when cholera devastated Paris, word spread through working-class districts that the alleged disease was one more lie invented by authorities bent on poisoning poor people en masse. So firmly did this idea take hold that mobs lynched innocents unfortunate enough to have been caught leaning over wells or idling outside wineshops, and "To the lamppost with poisoners!" became a commonly heard cry.[1] Nomads in a land of property, drunks in a sober nation, and trash in a realm of avid collectors, the "little people" had some reason to believe that they could be expunged summarily. But men in high position were, on the whole, more inclined to marshal racist clichés than to admit the possibility of a social explanation for the rumor that had gained credence down below. "It is not the thought of civilized people, it is the cry of savages," said Prime Minister Casimir Périer, wrapping

---

[1]In April 1832 Heine sent to his Augsburg newspaper a horrifying report of lynch mobs in Paris:

> It was especially at street-corner taverns painted red that the groups gathered and deliberated. It was almost always there that men who looked suspicious were frisked and woe unto them if one found anything dubious in their pockets. The populace would set upon them like a wild animal. . . . No aspect of these events is more horrible than the blood lust of the angry populace setting upon unarmed victims. One sees a sea of men surging through the streets in black waves and, amongst them, like foam, white-shirted workers; all together, they roar and howl without a word of pity, like demons. . . . On the rue Saint-Denis I heard the famous cry: "To the lamppost!" And several voices trembling with rage informed me that a poisoner was being hanged. Some said that he was a supporter of the Bourbon monarchy, others that he was a priest and that such wretches were capable of anything. On the rue de Vaugirard, two men carrying a white powder were butchered. I saw one of these unfortunates when he was giving up the ghost; old women took off their wooden clogs and beat him over the head with them until he died. He was entirely naked and covered with blood and bruises. Not only had his garments been torn from him but his hair, his lips, and his nose as well. Then some disgusting man came along, tied a rope around the corpse's feet, and dragged it through the streets while shouting continually, "Here you have cholera morbus!" A woman, strikingly beautiful, her bosom exposed and her hands bloody, gave the corpse one last kick as it passed in front of her.

up the situation with a fine rhetorical flourish just before cholera silenced him.

Rich and poor were each other's plague. Although Casimir Périer scoffed at the notion of poisoned well water, lectures given year after year by spokesmen for the established order abound in images that equate rebellion with physical disease and foreigners with germs. (We have already noted Dumas *fils*'s preface to *La Dame aux camélias*, where the "local deterioration" of society's "organism" was blamed on "the invasion of foreign women, the daily cargo of exotic mores brought by railroad.") It was to "purge" society that General Cavaignac had more than ten thousand Parisian workers transported to Algeria after the insurrection of June 1848, when *Le National* declared: "The struggle these last few days . . . has been clearly and forcefully delineated. Yes, on one side there stood order, liberty, civilization, the decent republic, France; and on the other, barbarians, desperados emerging from their lairs for massacre and looting, and odious partisans of those wild doctrines that the family is only a word and property nothing but theft." And twenty-three years later, during *la semaine sanglante*, bourgeois virtue again employed the rhetoric of Armageddon. *Le Figaro* called for amputation, declaring that the civil war was a God-given opportunity to cure Paris of the moral gangrene that had long been consuming it:

> Today, clemency equals lunacy. . . . What is a republican? A savage beast. . . . We must track down those who are hiding, like wild animals. Without pity, without anger, simply with the steadfastness of an upright man doing his duty.

One historian observes that newspaper images were all racialist and animal. "The Communards, the whole Paris population even, were no longer regarded as human, and so the normal laws of civilization could be ignored."

The sanitary cordon that kept *le peuple* in its ghetto barred it from the canvas and the printed page. Yahoos were regarded as subjects unfit for artistic consideration until painters and writers who invoked the authority of "realism" began to challenge this quarantine during the 1850s, when the word "realism" first gained critical currency (though still often used in quotation marks). Courbet's good friend Jules-Antoine Castagnary issued a typical manifesto. "To show nature complete and being in all its forms, one must address society itself," he insisted. "One must depict men, women, children in the various conditions of their existence, . . . one must capture the essence of temperaments, note the imprint of passions, display both the poverty that degrades and the opulence that deforms." In 1864, when Jules and Edmond de Goncourt's novel *Germinie Lacerteux* was published, the preface, as previously noted, excited even more indignation than the story itself. "Living in the nineteenth century, in an age of universal suffrage, of democracy, of liberalism," they wrote, "we wondered why the so-called 'lower classes' should not be granted admission to the novel; why this world beneath a world, the populace, should endure the literary ban and disdain of authors who have until now shown no sign of recognizing that it might contain a heart and soul." (Hugo's *Les Misérables* had, in their view, conquered new ground for the self-exiled author but none for the outcasts it purported to represent. "Unjustified title," they note soon after its appearance. "No wretchedness [misère], no hospital, a prostitute barely touched. The lack of observation glares and vexes at every turn . . . Hugo built his book with verisimilitude rather than with truth.")

Germinie Lacerteux, which doesn't idealize its heroine, had impressed Zola greatly. No less obnoxious to him than the demonization of Paris's working poor by a callous Right was the sanctification of *le peuple* by a militant Left, and so, when the idea for what eventually became *L'Assommoir* first took shape in 1868, it expressed his desire to promote social justice without truckling to the pieties of an intransigent revolutionary such as Blanqui or even a nonrevolutionary liberal such as Louis Ulbach. He planned "a novel whose frame will be the workers' world," he wrote at that time.

Painting of a contemporary working-class household. The intimate and profound drama of a Parisian laborer destroyed by the milieu of the tollgates and of cabarets. This novel will make a strong impression only if its scenes are drawn with sincerity. Workers have hitherto been depicted as soldiers, in a completely false light. It would take courage to tell the truth and, by a straightforward account of how matters really stand, demand air, light, and education for the lower classes.

Zola did not depart from this general scheme, but his embryonic hero, after gestating for several years, became a heroine. "Worker novel— Situated in Les Batignolles," he noted around 1872. "A laundress; the atelier of ironers in Les Batignolles, in a shop, on the avenue; the washhouse, the washerwomen, etc. A celebratory feast at home (the laundress's shop). Little dishes in big ones—All their money spent on a dinner—Windows open, the joyful mingling of street and interior. Songs sung over dessert. Women fetching men at the cabaret. In short, women leading men." By then the motif of sexual warfare that recurs throughout *Les Rougon-Macquart*, connecting each "milieu" to every other, had already found expression in *La Fortune des Rougon* and *La Curée.*

Preparations for *L'Assommoir*—or *La Simple Vie de Gervaise Macquart*, as Zola originally titled it—began in earnest during his bourgeois-plagued holiday at Saint-Aubin. "[My next novel] lies dormant and will remain so no doubt until Paris," he told Alexis on September 17, 1875. "I have the main outline, I need Paris to flesh it out. It will be a very broad and simple canvas, extraordinary in its ordinariness, its portrayal of everyday life. I will be at some pains to find the appropriate style, but right now the howling of this banshee sea prevents me from thinking." Another letter, written to Georges Charpentier, reveals how confident he felt that something great lay in store, and excitement filled the long memoranda he addressed to himself. "It must be a miracle of exactitude. . . . Facts from first page to last, yielding *the entire life of the common people*," he noted grandiosely, influenced perhaps by his ocean view. "Don't flatter the worker and don't besmirch him. . . . Show how in Paris, drunkenness, the rout of the family, physical violence, acquiescence in every kind of shame and wretchedness arise from the conditions of slum life, from hard labor, from promiscuity, from slovenliness, etc. In short, a closely observed tableau of the worker's existence with its filth, its dissipation, its coarse language, etc. A frightful picture whose moral need not be spelled out." As defiant as ever, he was pleased to challenge those high-minded men of every political persuasion who anathematized what Ulbach once called *la littérature putride.*

Back in Paris, Zola plunged forward, working nine hours a day, past exhaustion. A slum behind the Gare du Nord on the eastern side of Montmartre was the neighborhood he chose for *L'Assommoir*, partly because it took no more than thirty minutes to walk there from the rue Saint-Georges. His dossier soon bulked large as he crammed it with hand-drawn maps, descriptions of the shops, tenements, interiors, hotels, restaurants, bistros, and street scenes sketched in telegraphic prose: "Bareheaded women running errands for dinner with baskets in hand, little girls carrying loaves of bread. Men talking in loud voices and walking quickly. . . . Drays, casks, flat-bottomed vehicles. . . . Paris's gaslights go on. The sky. Hands in pockets. A turncock with his trumpet. People alone, or in groups. Housepainters with their pots. Men hauling carts by means of shoulder straps. Red belts." Zola observed laundresses, roofers, bolt forgers, and chainsmiths, visiting their ateliers, noting their techniques, familiarizing himself with their tools. If he found inspiration in Degas's paintings of women ironing, as one contemporary claimed, it was undoubtedly after the fact, for his dossier, which predates the exhibition in which these paintings appeared (the second Impressionist exhibition of 1876), contains enough minutiae to reconstitute a nineteenth-century *blanchisserie*—starch bowls, "Polish" irons, coke-burning stoves, wallpaper, itemized rates, and all.

As usual, Zola read extensively, but he focused straightway on the subject of alcoholism, which ravaged working-class households throughout France despite measures taken by successive governments to arrest it. Paul Leroy-Beaulieu's *De l'état moral et intellectuel des ouvriers* assured him that "among workers of our day the saloon occupies a place formerly occupied by the Church," and in *L'Ouvrière*, where Jules Simon reported female textile workers doping their infant children with soporifics every Sunday so as to congregate at gin parlors, the future prime minister made it appallingly clear that this scourge did not respect gender. For bibliographical guidance Zola contacted a physician named Auguste-Alexandre Moret, who frankly acknowledged that what he wanted to know about the social history of alcoholism could not be located in the existing literature. Still, Zola was helped by one important lead:

> In its trimestrial bulletin the temperance society gathers and publishes examples of the ill effects of alcoholism, but that's anecdotal. Only forensic reports written by medical experts contain what you seek. I've written some myself and hope to publish them someday, but I repeat, the materials for a serious work of the kind I believe you have in mind are completely lacking. In the September and October issues of *La Gazette hebdomadaire de médecine et de chirurgie* . . . you will find a rather interesting article by Dr. Leudet of Rouen on alcoholism in the leisured classes. . . . Tardieu's forensic treatise on madness will also give you some pointers. I needn't discuss Magnan's book or Dr. Jolly's little homily on tobacco and absinthe; one is exclusively scientific, the other fraught with recriminations.

It turned out that Dr. Valentin Magnan's thirty-nine portraits of alcoholic devastation were eminently useful. Indeed, from Magnan's *De l'alcoolisme, des diverses formes du délire alcoolique et de leur traitement* Zola extracted the clinical particulars of delirium tremens for a scene as horrible as any he ever conceived.

De l'alcoolisme may have been useful, but a little-known treatise written before the war by a factory owner intent on regenerating the working class proved indispensable. In *Question sociale—le sublime ou le travailleur comme il est en 1870 et ce qu'il peut être*, this self-made man, Denis Poulet, strove not only to promote social reform and—as scientific positivism would have it—to classify laborers by various criteria, including the ideas they embraced, the language they used, the diligence or sloth they exhibited, the private lives they led. A "sublime," for example, was, in working-class parlance, a shiftless, drunken lout, and among "sublimes" Poulet distinguished the "simple sublime," the "withered and fallen sublime," the "true sublime," the "son of God," and the "sublime of sublimes." The simple sublime, he wrote (italicizing the slang),

works at most two hundred to two hundred twenty-five days a year, gets drunk at least once every fortnight and tipsy just as often. He pays his rent with difficulty but when he can move *à la cloche de bois* [on the sly], he does so. If he is a bachelor, he inhabits dismal boardinghouses because there nobody lectures him. "So one can't get a little high, *y faudrait pus que ça, que le pipelet de sa turne lui fasse un sermon parce qu'il est paf* [without the night porter giving me a sermon because I'm drunk]." If he's married, he pays his baker because there's no way around it; but his *mastroquet* [wine merchant], never. *Faire un pouf* [ducking a creditor] is for him a feather in his cap. *Couler son patron* [costing his boss money] is more than a habit, it's a duty. *Carotter* [cadging from] relatives and friends is the usual thing. For him all ateliers are *boîtes* [joints], tools are *clous* [nails], bosses are *exploiteurs* [exploiters], and foremen are *mufes* [from *mufles*, literally "muzzles"].

Here Zola found another of those "scientific" constructs that served to gird or validate his imaginative life. Just as Prosper Lucas's *Traité de l'hérédité naturelle* provided an underpinning for *Les Rougon-Macquart* in general, so Poulet's taxonomical differentiae helped him populate *L'Assommoir*. Out of *Le Sublime* trooped nameless, faceless mannequins wanting only a plot, and along with them numerous expressions from which Zola created argotic dialogue. One such expression was *L'Assommoir* itself. Deriving from the verb *assommer* ("to knock senseless"), it meant "saloon."[2]

L'Assommoir recounts the heroic but futile struggle of Gervaise Macquart to transcend heredity and milieu. The novel opens in a squalid hotel opposite Paris's toll wall where she, her two bastard sons, and their father, Auguste Lantier, have fetched up after emigrating from Plassans several weeks earlier. It immediately becomes apparent that Gervaise cannot rely upon Lantier, who answers Denis Poulet's description of the indolent, conceited, vaporous *fils de Dieu*. Provincial bonds, such as they were, have gone slack, and a spat is pretext enough

[2]During the 1850s a saloon in the working-class district of Belleville bore the name L'Assommoir, but the term was generic. "The true sublime is constantly between two eaux-de-vie; twenty centimes of *poivre d'assommoir* suffice to make him drunk," writes Poulet, noting that this "assommoir pepper" was vitriol.
Zola also used a *Dictionnaire de la langue verte*, by Alfred Delvau.

for Lantier to dump his cumbersome ménage. Moving in with another woman, he leaves Gervaise destitute. "The labors of the day made the very paving stones throw up a haze of heat over the city behind the toll wall. It was into this street, into this blazing heat that she was now thrown with her little ones, and she cast her eyes up and down the outer boulevards, stopping at each end with a dull terror as if life from now on was going to play itself out in this middle ground between a slaughterhouse and a hospital."

The laundry at which Gervaise finds employment helps her rise, with every cleansing gesture, not only above the moral and physical grime that pervades her neighborhood, but above the slum inside her. "She was like her mother," writes Zola, "a tireless worker who died in harness, having been a beast of burden to old Macquart for more than twenty years . . . Even her slight limp she got from the poor woman, whom old Macquart regularly thrashed. Her mother had told her a hundred times about nights when her father came home drunk and went in for such brutal lovemaking that her limbs were black and blue; and she must have been conceived on one of those nights, with her gimpy leg." Bliss, she says, would be "to work, to eat one's daily bread, to have one's own digs [*trou*], to bring up one's own children, and to die in one's own bed," but the prospect of fulfilling this modest dream, or of fulfilling it *à deux*, seems remote, until, soon after Lantier vanishes, she finds herself courted by a roofer named Coupeau, whose acrobatic métier keeps him sober. Fearful that conjugal life spells bondage, she nonetheless yields and marries him. At the wedding dinner Coupeau's sister, Madame Lorilleux, stigmatizes the lame Gervaise with a nickname that will dog her through life: "La Banban" (from *bancal*, meaning "lame").

The Coupeaus prosper. They work hard, save what they can, consort with like-minded workers, and produce a daughter, Anna, known affectionately as Nana. Gervaise splurges on only one purchase, but even this—her beautiful clock—speaks of order, of thrift, of ambition:

> The clock, in rosewood with twisted columns and a gilded brass pendulum, had to be paid for in a year by twenty-sou installments due every Monday. She got quite annoyed if Coupeau offered to wind it; no, she alone lifted the glass dome and wiped the columns religiously, as though the marble top of the chest had turned into a shrine. Under the dome behind the clock she concealed the bankbook, and often while daydreaming about [setting up a shop of her own] she would go off into a reverie in front of the dial.

Alas, disaster strikes before she can achieve her ambition. Coupeau breaks a leg in a terrible fall. Hard times return as Gervaise nurses him back to health and her dreams of independence evaporate along with her carefully husbanded resources. All seems lost when her next-door neighbor, a handsome young blacksmith named Goujet, lends her the money she needs. Gallant but shy, powerful but chaste, this paragon, whose companion is his widowed mother (his father having died of drink), figures as the lifeline Gervaise cannot bring herself to grasp.[3]

Up goes Gervaise's sign, *Blanchisseuse de Fin* ("Fine-Quality Laundress"), painted blue for the southern sky that haunts her, and from under it she beams upon her neighborhood with proprietary satisfaction. Where five windmills had stood only thirty years earlier, dominating the village of La Chapelle, nature is now the stuff of imagination. "She enjoyed putting her iron down for a minute and going out to the doorway," writes Zola.

> The rue de la Goutte d'Or belonged to her, and so did the streets nearby and all the neighborhood. Standing there in her white bodice, bare-armed and with her fair hair blowing loose from the flurry of work, she could crane her neck and take in, with a glance left and right to each end of the street, the whole scene, people, houses, road and sky. To the left the rue de la Goutte d'Or ran off, peaceful and empty, as it were into some quiet country town, with women chatting softly at their cottage doors, but only a few steps to the right there arose the din of traffic in the rue des Poissonniers, with its continuous tramp of people in a swirling stream, making that end of the street the hub of a working-class universe. Gervaise loved the street, she loved the jolting of the vans in the potholes between the cobbles, the milling crowds whose flow was broken at times when the narrow pavements turned into steep pebbly slopes; the three meters of gutter in front of her shop took on a profound significance for her, like a broad river which she loved to think of as a limpid, exotic, living stream on whose waters the dyeworks in her building bestowed the most delicate hues as it passed on its way through the black mud.

Gervaise drives a thriving trade. Customers flock in such numbers that she will hire two young women to help, thus acquiring the higher status of *patronne*.

Soon enough darkness gathers overhead. Coupeau, whose fall left him crippled even as it made Gervaise whole, becomes a malingerer, loafing in his wife's shop and pawing her apprentices or more often idling at the neighborhood saloon, L'Assommoir, where the most conspicuous object is a large still. Outside workaday Paris, the hopeless find refuge in a netherworld governed not by clocks but by a *machine infernale* that operates against time, that brews confusion, erodes barriers of every kind like some elemental force, and floods the mind:

---

[3]Goujet, the model of artisanal virtue who denies his flesh but labors in the heat of a forge (not unlike the writer) proudly shaping iron bolts, is also a blond paradigm of Faujas the priest. Both powerful, celibate, and riveted to Mother.

The still, with its weirdly shaped receptacles and endless coils of pip-
ing, looked dour and forbidding; no steam came out of it, but there
was a scarcely perceptible inner breathing or subterranean rumble. It
was like some black and midnight deed being done in broad daylight
by . . . a morose worker . . . The machine went noiselessly on, with
no flame, no cheerful highlights on its dull copper retort, sweating
alcohol like a slow but persistent spring which would ultimately spill
over into the room, spread to the outer boulevards and fill up the
vast hollow of Paris

Before long, Coupeau takes night for day.

Gervaise indulges him. Worse still, she indulges herself, and, as nature gains sway over will, the soiled linen that had been the stock-in-
trade of her regeneration becomes the agent of her fall:

She thrust her bare pink arms into chemises yellow with dirt, cloths
stiff with greasy dishwater, socks in holes and rotting with sweat. And
yet even as she was bending over the piles, the strong smell hitting
her in the face, a sort of drowsy contentment came over her. Perched
on the edge of a stool, bent double, reaching out to right and left
with slower and slower movements, she seemed to be intoxicated by
this human stench and smiled vaguely.

With *la bête humaine* ascendant, everything weighs her down. She
grows fat and self-neglectful. Her business declines. No one lends support save Goujet, whose virtue exacerbates her shame. Acquaintances
are distracted by calamities of their own or bent on spoiling an enterprise they resent. The umbrageous Madame Lorilleux whispers evil.
The gelded Coupeau turns mean. And when Gervaise's fate hangs in
the balance, her Nemesis, Auguste Lantier, contrives to reappear.

This apparition, which interrupts a birthday feast Gervaise has
staged for herself, leaves her aghast. But neither then nor later do
people spare her feelings, and everything unfolds as in a relentless,
paranoid dream. Coupeau is much taken with Lantier, who relies upon
his gift of gab to survive. They begin hobnobbing at local saloons,
where the fluent ne'er-do-well dazzles his audience with radical slogans. One day Coupeau brings him home and in due course offers
him room and board. "Coupeau and Lantier were having a grand time
together. The boon companions, chin deep in food and drink, were
guzzling away the shop and eating up the profit; they urged double
portions on each other and jocularly slapped their bellies over dessert."
Gervaise has meanwhile become weak, or indifferent, and her weakness begets total promiscuity. Unlaundered garments pile up, spilling
like bilgewater from the shop into the adjacent flat and polluting every
room. Encouraged by Coupeau himself, Lantier cuckolds his "bosom

friend" as little Nana looks on (the boys have long since departed). Weeks merge, oblivion infiltrates Gervaise's calendar of accounts, debts go unpaid, her clientele dwindles. Finally, even Goujet, who proposed in vain that they flee together, gives her up for lost.

Zola pictures hell as a huge, dark, labyrinthine tenement that beetles over the rue de la Goutte d'Or, and one room under the eaves of this seven-story maze is all the Coupeaus can afford after Gervaise's business fails. They still have enough purchase in society to celebrate Nana's communion, but when, lured by the fleshpots down below, Nana makes good her escape, society recedes. Bereft of religion, of kin, of regular employment, they live alone among other derelict souls.

> For the next two years they went steadily downhill. It was the winters especially that were so trying. . . . That villain December stole in under the door, bringing with him all the evils, the closing down of jobs, the frozen idleness of heavy frosts, the black misery of rainy days. During the first winter they did sometimes have a fire and huddled round the stove, preferring warmth to food, but the second winter the stove not only stood there rusting but chilled the room like a mournful cast-iron milepost.

Old at forty, Coupeau earns a pittance at odd jobs, between forced internments at a psychiatric hospital called Sainte-Anne, and spends everything on drink. But eau-de-vie has also become Gervaise's poison. Bloated and unkempt, with nothing left of the amour propre that helped her surmount every obstacle, the ex-laundress looks like a rag-picker limping about in wooden clogs. Unable to wash clothes, she stoops lower still and touches bottom when Virginie, a former employee who has acquired her shop, hires her to scrub the floors she proudly trod during her reign as *patronne*. Virginie's new lover, Auguste Lantier, supervises.

The little flame that somehow kept Coupeau alive finally dies in the wild crepitation of delirium tremens. Gervaise (like Marthe Mouret with her demented husband at the insane asylum in *La Conquête de Plassans*) visits Coupeau at Sainte-Anne and watches him incredulously; she then mimics his paroxysms for the neighbors (an inversion of Marthe seeing her husband imitate *her* hysterical fits). They, who have no theater or church—no access to comic relief or religious consolation—demand a repeat performance, as if wanting their fears exorcised. "Yes, yes, just a bit more, was the general clamor, and they all said it would be so nice of her if she would, because two neighbors just happened to be there who hadn't seen it yesterday, and they had come downstairs specially to see the show."

This *danse macabre*, which affords Gervaise one last moment of respectability, prefigures her own extinction. Destitute, she scavenges and begs and attempts, *malgré elle,* to sell a body no one wants. Her landlord is kinder than most. Evicting her from her room under the eaves, he lets her sleep, rent-free, in a crawl space under the stairs. There, like some poor animal on its straw pallet, she finally dies, forgotten by all.

> Death meant to take her little by little, bit by bit, dragging her to the end along the wretched path she had made for herself. It wasn't even quite clear what she died of. People mentioned the cold and the heat, but the truth was that she died of poverty, from the filth and exhaustion of her wasted life. As the Lorilleux put it, she died of slatternliness. One morning, as there was a foul odor in the hallways, people remembered that she hadn't been seen for two days, and she was discovered in her hole, turning green already.

The word *trou,* "hole" or "niche," recurs throughout *L'Assommoir,* together with the word *propre,* which can mean either "clean" or "one's own." Her laundry shop was the niche Gervaise yearned for; an early grave is the hole she gets.

These double entendres govern Zola's entire picture of slum life. Swarming with people who envy one another's *trous,* the rue de la Goutte d'Or is a frantic hive where survival requires the will to organize space, to defend boundaries, to keep clean. Madame Lorilleux, whose trade is making gold chain, compulsively sweeps her studio lest gold dust walk away under alien feet.[4] Of the Goujets, Zola writes: "The first time [Gervaise] went into their home she was amazed how clean it was. There was no denying it, you could blow anywhere and not raise a speck of dust. And the floor shone like a mirror." Gervaise herself stakes her proprietary claim by scouring a vacant shop. And when trouble looms during her birthday party, one portent is the obliteration of all that separates inside from out, or of "one's own" from the public domain. Named after a vineyard that once produced grapes for white wine there, the rue de la Goutte d'Or recaptures its past in an urban parody of the rustic bacchanalia:

> The aroma of goose spread joy and good cheer all along the street; the grocer's boys on the opposite pavement felt they were really eat-

---

[4] "It was quite a performance. The employers didn't allow for a single milligram of wastage. Lorilleux showed Gervaise the hare's foot he used for brushing particles stuck to his board, and the leather apron he had over his knees to collect them. They swept out the workshop thoroughly twice a week, kept all the sweepings, burned them, and sifted the ashes, in which they found up to 25 or 30 francs' worth of gold per month." Here, as with Lisa Macquart in *Le Ventre de Paris,* the proprietary act of cleaning argues an equation between excrement and gold. In fact Zola calls the Lorilleux' windowless atelier a "bowel."

ing it, the greengrocer and the tripe-shop woman constantly popped out in front of their shops to have a sniff and lick their chops. The whole street was really having an attack of indigestion. . . . Why should they make a secret of it? The party was now thoroughly excited and had lost all sense of shame at being seen at table—on the contrary, this gathering crowd, gaping with covetous greed, gave them a sense of superiority and carried them away: they would have liked to push down the shopfront and take the table right out into the street and have their dessert there, under people's noses in the busy traffic. There was nothing objectionable about the look of them, was there? Well, then, why shut themselves up like a lot of selfish pigs? Seeing the little watchmaker over the road positively watering at the mouth, Coupeau pointed at a bottle, and when the other man nodded yes, he brought over a bottle and a glass. The party and the street were now fraternally united. . . . The binge spread, caught on from one to another until the whole Goutte d'Or neighborhood was sniffing the food and holding its belly.

We have seen it often before in *Les Rougon-Macquart*. No sooner do walls fall down than the person whose being they compassed loses definition, spilling out or withering, merging with others or yielding to some invader. Anomie threatens every little niche, and anomie always manifests itself as a flood. There is the flood of booze that "will spread to the outer boulevards and fill up the vast hollow of Paris." There is the dirty wash that inundates Gervaise's apartment.[5] Above all, there is the proletarian army that swirls past the ghetto in "an endless stream of men, horses and carts cascading from the heights of Montmartre and La Chapelle." Gervaise witnesses this diurnal invasion from a hotel window the morning Lantier deserts her, and eighteen years later, when *L'Assommoir* comes full round, she witnesses it again, this time at nightfall and from its very midst, like flotsam carried out to sea by an ebb tide.

For the Goutte d'Or slum, an invader more to be feared than workers trooping downhill en masse is Paris demolishing every impediment as it pushes uphill under Baron Haussmann's command, and Zola introduces this imperial juggernaut at the very end of *L'Assommoir*. His conclusion would certainly have put readers in mind of the Commune overcome by MacMahon during the Bloody Week. To Gervaise,

[5]Psychological expropriation goes hand in hand with physical. The theory Zola learned from Michelet, according to which a woman is imprinted or "impregnated" once and for all by her first lover, explains Lantier's irresistibility and Gervaise's helplessness. When he reappears, her ego collapses. As for Coupeau, the complaisant husband hides an enraged Johnny-come-lately who in delirium boxes the ghost of his invincible predecessor.

wandering hunger-stricken, "night seemed as though it would never come," he writes.

So while waiting she strolled along the boulevards like a lady taking the air before going home to supper. This part of Paris made her feel quite cheap because it was becoming so grand, being opened up in all directions. The Boulevard Magenta, coming up from the heart of Paris, and the Boulevard Ornano, going off toward the country, had torn a gap in the old barrier—a huge demolition. These two great avenues, still white with plaster, had running out of them the rue du Faubourg Poissonnière and the rue des Poissonniers, the ends of which, jagged and mutilated, twisted away like dark, winding sewers. A long while ago the demolition of the customs wall had widened the outer boulevards, with footpaths at the sides and a central strip for pedestrians planted with four rows of young plane trees. So it was now a huge crossing extending to the far horizon along endless thoroughfares swarming with people on and on in the confusion of building operations. But mixed up with the lofty brand-new buildings there were still plenty of rickety old houses; between façades of carved masonry yawned black holes, gaping kennels exposing their wretched windows. Coming up through the rising tide of luxury the destitution of the slums thrust itself into view, befouling this new city being run up so hastily.

Lost in the crowds on the wide strip under the little plane trees, Gervaise felt alone and abandoned. These vistas along distant avenues only emphasized her emptiness.

Doomsday lies at hand. With its walls razed, the whole district—all the little niches in which people of small social consequence have struggled against enormous odds to survive, have helped and hindered one another, have bred and toiled and dreamed and drunk—the whole neighborhood faces extinction. Where a thousand Gervaises gained or lost a foothold, there will soon be one enormous *trou.*

On April 13, 1876, installments of *L'Assommoir* began to appear in *Le Bien public,* a republican daily that had moved quite far left since serving as Thiers's unofficial organ. The contract signed three weeks earlier, stipulating that Zola was to be paid at forty centimes a line and that the paper would advertise the novel widely by means of posters, eventually fetched Zola eight thousand francs. It was further understood that *Le Bien public* might alter some "rather vivid" words, but the enthusiasm with which his editor exercised this license caused Zola grief. "I have only one regret and that is to learn that you are reading *L'Assommoir* serially," he wrote to Ludovic Halévy, the author of libretti for Jacques Offenbach, who, despite Zola's diatribes against opera buffa, became a lifelong friend. "You wouldn't believe how ugly I find my novel in serial form. They steal all my thunder, they mutilate my prose by deleting sentences and opening up paragraphs. It makes me so sick at heart that I don't even review the galleys. If I dared, I'd insert an advertisement to the following effect: 'My literary friends are requested to wait until the bound volume appears before reading this work.' "

Le Bien public launched a vigorous campaign, with vendors hawking the paper at street corners and cabbies distributing it among passengers. By mid-June, however, it had halted serialization for political reasons, and in response to the outrage of liberal-minded subscribers. "If the good democrats [at *Le Bien public*] expected sycophantic drivel about the noble slums, or bait for catching republican subscribers, they soon discovered their mistake," wrote Paul Alexis. "As happened whenever a paper published one of Zola's novels, letters from scandalized, wrathful readers rained upon the editor; this time accusations of immorality were overlaid with a far more serious charge—that the novel slandered the populace, insulted the worker." Revulsion crossed party lines, but men of the Left outdid those of the Right in fulminating against Zola's use of slang. For them it was as if he had disenfranchised the working class, or denied it its birthright, or paraded captive barbarians through Paris especially to mock their gibberish. No one upheld the King's French more piously than straitlaced republicans, and Zola, who understood quite well how language legitimized power in France, later commented upon this obsession with formal matters. "Only its form has upset people," he wrote in a brief preface to the book edition of *L'Assommoir*. "They have taken exception to my words. My crime is that I have had the literary curiosity to collect the language of the people and pour it into a very carefully wrought mold. Form! Form is the great crime. Yet there exist dictionaries of this language, literary people study it and savor its vigor and its unexpected and forceful imagery." Some things hadn't changed very much since 1824, when Louis XVIII was king and liberals who had been brought up on Voltaire inveighed against the romantic "sect" for "desecrating good taste, insulting reason, stooping to the most offensive triviality" in order to achieve novel effects.

One month after *Le Bien public* dropped *L'Assommoir*, a literary journal called *La République des lettres* picked it up for one thousand francs. There it ran its course in twenty-six weekly installments, attracting attention from *Le Figaro*, with one of whose contributors, Albert Millaud, Zola engaged in an acrimonious debate that made the front page (much to Zola's delight). "There was reason to hope that M. Zola, although too realist, would secure his place and enjoy a good career in the difficult art of contemporary fiction," wrote Millaud. "Suddenly he stops short. At this moment he is publishing, in a little review, a novel entitled *L'Assommoir*, which gives us the distinct impression that it will be the downfall [*assommoir*] of his budding talent. It isn't realism, it is grubbiness; it isn't crudity, it is pornography." As soon as this salvo reached Zola at Piriac in Brittany, he fired off a brief rejoinder which *Le Figaro* printed on September 7, 1876. "*L'Assommoir* is the portrait of a specific working class . . . in which I sought to reconstitute the language of Parisian slums," it read in part. "The book's carefully wrought and researched style must therefore be considered a philological study, that's all. Furthermore, one cannot judge the moral scope of something still incomplete. I affirm that *L'Assommoir's* lesson will be dreadful, implacable, and that no novel has ever had more strictly honorable intentions." A longer statement followed one week later, after Millaud had characterized him as "democratic and socialist around the edges." The shoe, he declared, did not fit. "I mean to be a novelist plain and simple, without epithets. If you insist upon labeling me, I won't object if you call me a naturalist. My political opinions are not at issue." As for his description of the rue de la Goutte d'Or,

> it is as I wish it to be, without shadows or cosmetic touches. I say what I see, I simply articulate and leave the business of extracting lessons to moralists. I've exposed sores in the upper reaches of society, I shall certainly not hide those to be found in the lower. Mine is not a work of partisan politics and propaganda. It aims at the truth. I refrain from formulating conclusions because it is my view that the conclusion escapes the artist. If, however, you wish to know what lesson will emerge, of itself, from *L'Assommoir*, it goes something like this: educate the worker in order to elevate him morally; free him from the slums where air hangs thick and noxious; above all, curb drunkenness, which decimates the populace while ravaging its intelligence.

Although *L'Assommoir* was, in Millaud's view, heinous enough to warrant criminal prosecution, Zola contended that he had in fact spared delicate sensibilities the worst. "Rest assured, Sir and dear confrere, that I've filtered what's dirtiest out of the muck oozing through my hands, that—especially for *L'Assommoir*—I chose the least frightful truths."

This skirmish became a full-blown war when in January 1877 Charpentier published Zola's masterpiece without expurgations. Many more now joined the fray, and one new combatant was the government, which barred vendors from selling *L'Assommoir* at railroad stations. "The crude and relentless obscenity of details and terms aggravates the immorality of situations and characters," is how its official reporter described the work. "It is therefore our opinion that authorization should be denied this tableau of working-class mores, as authorization would be denied a work applying the same literary method to other social categories." A dozen conservative papers shouted assent, and the chorus of execration was amplified in brochures, pamphlets, caricatures. But again, radical republicans, led by those who wrote regular diatribes for Gambetta's *République française,* lambasted *L'Assommoir* even more ferociously than champions of moral order.

Beset on two fronts, Zola aimed his biggest gun at the Left. On February 13, an open letter appeared in *Le Bien public,* addressed to the editor-in-chief, Yves Guyot (who was himself not among Zola's detractors). "In politics as in letters, in letters as in all of contemporary thought, there are two distinct currents: the idealist and the naturalist," Zola declared.

> I call idealist that politics which talks in bombastic slogans, which speculates about men as if they were pure abstractions, which dreams utopias without studying the real world. I call naturalist that politics which takes its cue from experience, which is based on facts, which treats a nation according to its needs. . . . I myself am not a politician, and I voice here the ideas of an observer fascinated by human affairs. For several years, one thing has interested me most particularly—the spectacle of romanticism, complete with plumes and 1830-style apricot waistcoats, making itself at home in politics (like a washed-up matinee idol who's left the stage for some more profitable arena but taken along his outmoded props and repertory of gestures). . . . What results is a very strange politics indeed! . . . a politics that calls for rolling eyes and wild movements. Everything about it rings false, both the men who declaim and the things they say. It's a politics of gilded cardboard, a politics of theatrical pomp behind which yawns a void that will someday swallow everything. When the performance is over, when the populace has paid and acclaimed the actors, it will find itself on the sidewalk again, still shivering and as naked as before.

Linking utopianism to romantic hyperbole and radical republicans to the literary generation that had celebrated itself at the tumultuous premiere of Hugo's *Hernani* in 1830 (when Gautier wore a rose-colored doublet), Zola killed two birds, of the Left and of the Right, with one stone. Did *La République française* presume to scold him? Zola pictured his critics there as superannuated children ruled by a penchant for fairy tales or as acolytes of a senile king, the implication being that there was little to choose between men who courted Chambord in his Austrian castle and men who fawned upon Victor Hugo in his Paris flat.[6]

---

[6]Hugo disliked *L'Assommoir.* In 1880 a writer named Alfred Barbou reported him as having said: "The book is bad. It reveals, as if delightedly, the hideous sores of misery and the abjection to which the poor man finds himself reduced. . . . It's one of those tableaux one should not display. I won't countenance the argument

Others beside Zola defended the novel. Indeed, its partisans fought at equal strength with its detractors in what came to be known as *la bataille de l'Assommoir,* and they included not only eminent journalists but writers of promise or distinction. "*L'Assommoir* is certainly not likable, but it is a powerful book," Anatole France wrote in *Le Temps,* for example. "Life is rendered with immediacy and directness. . . . Its numerous characters speak the language of the slums. So does the author when he completes their thought or describes their state of mind. He has been criticized for this, but I praise him. One can faithfully translate a person's thoughts and sensations only in his native tongue." A week after publication, the future author of *Le Disciple,* Paul Bourget, sent Zola an extravagant valentine, assuring him, rather pompously for a twenty-five-year-old, that *L'Assommoir* was his best work:

> The very fury of attacks proves it. You've established your own, absolutely original ground. There's nothing in it of Flaubert, of Goncourt, of Balzac, or of Dickens. . . . Ah! what a formidable man you are. The young people whom I see, all of us, rank you very high, and if I write candidly what I think of the book [Bourget expressed some reservations about Zola's style], my candor testifies to my enthusiasm. In an argument last Sunday at Barbey d'Aurevilly's place, I defended you point by point.

Mallarmé, who, unlike Bourget, would support Zola through thick and thin—in literary wars as during the Dreyfus Affair—delivered his annual gift of finely wrought praise. "Here is a very great work, and worthy of an epoch in which truth has become the popular form of beauty!" he wrote on February 3, 1877. "Those who accuse you of not having written for the common people are mistaken, and no less so are those who uphold an ancient ideal; you've found a modern one, that's all. The book's somber conclusion and your admirable linguistic effort, thanks to which so many clumsy idioms forged by poor devils acquire the value of beautiful literary formulae, beautiful because they make us smile or cry—this moves me deeply." What he liked best were the simple descriptions of Coupeau roofing and Gervaise laundering. "You've endowed literature with something absolutely new in these tranquil pages that turn like the days of a life." Paris, he felt, had at last given Zola his due: "It fills me with joy . . . to see how, in many papers, the whipping boy of Criticism has become its darling. It was bound to happen, you yourself couldn't doubt it. Goodbye. Do you

---

that it's all true, that it's the way things are. I know, I've seen it with my own eyes, but I don't want a spectacle made of it. One doesn't have the right to undress poverty and unhappiness." Hugo had long been fascinated and horrified by slang, upon which he digressed in *Les Misérables.*

still receive on Thursdays? I should like to drop by and shake your hand warmly."

L'Assommoir produced mixed emotions in Flaubert. The lapidist for whom prose writing was a fundamentally aristocratic enterprise found Zola's language irksome, and it did not help that *Les Rougon-Macquart* had grown apace while *Bouvard et Pécuchet* lay stunted. "Like you, I've read bits of *L'Assommoir*," he told Turgenev (who had complained about "too much stirring of chamber pots in it"). "I didn't like it. Zola is falling victim to inverted preciosity . . . He is being carried away by his *system*. He has principles that constrict his brain." But letters written several months later show him rather more evenhanded. "Too many books like this one would not be desirable, but there are superb chapters, a narrative that goes full tilt, and incontrovertible truths. It stays too long in the same gamut, but Zola is a very powerful bloke and you'll see what success he'll have," he confided to one of his female correspondents. When his prediction was borne out, he exclaimed: "Zola's *L'Assommoir* is a huge success! It has sold *sixteen* thousand copies in one month. I'm weary of having people chatter about this book, and of hearing my own chatter, for I defend it when it's attacked. . . . What's certain is that the work is significant." Compared with *L'Assommoir*, Goncourt's *La Fille Elisa*, which Charpentier published soon afterward, seemed, as he put it, "anemic and summary."

The furor over *L'Assommoir* made Edmond de Goncourt insanely jealous. Eclipsed by his young brother-in-arms, he built a dubious case for plagiarism, bolstering himself with the thought that Zola had robbed him blind. "[From my manuscript of *La Fille Elisa*] I read Zola the description of Elisa tramping the pavement and, what do you know, I encounter it [in *L'Assommoir*], not plagiarized wholesale but most assuredly inspired by my reading," he noted. "The same chiaroscuro, the same lamentable shadow trailing her. It's all there, right down to *Monsieur, écoutez-moi donc!* ["Sir, please listen"]—a phrase used in the Quartier Saint-Honoré but not on the Chaussée Clignancourt." Even so, *L'Assommoir* was not, he decreed, an artistic success. While the best of Zola came from him, Edmond de Goncourt, the worst bespoke a vulgarian whom he professed to hold in contempt. "Zola triumphant resembles a parvenu who's unexpectedly struck it rich. . . . In his enormous, gigantic, unprecedented success I see a reflection of the public's aversion to style. For now that he has quite obviously renounced good writing, the book he's published is declared a masterpiece."[7]

[7]Zola did his best to cosset Goncourt's ego. In July 1876, when Paul Alexis sent him the manuscript of an article he had written on Goncourt, Zola proposed that he "delete your allusion to *L'Assommoir*, because I don't want you to draw parallels between Goncourt and me."

Goncourt's brief against Zola became increasingly dotty, and extended beyond

The adequate performance of Zola's previous novels had not prepared Charpentier for the immense commercial success of *L'Assommoir*. When the government forbade its sale at railroad-station bookstands, he would have counted himself lucky to sell the three thousand copies he had printed. Instead the novel became all the rage, making Rougon-Macquart a household name, boosting its six predecessors, and inspiring not only a stage adaptation but music-hall parodies and cabaret songs. "I am elated with the numbers [your cashier] has sent me during the past few months," Zola wrote to Marguerite Charpentier in August. "Do you know that in June we sold 2,580 volumes from the Rougon-Macquart series, 1,366 of them *Assommoir*; and in July, 3,167, including 1,800 *Assommoir*? What especially delights me is the brisk trade in my earlier novels. If we keep it up, it would be marvelous." Reality beggared his dreams. Before 1877 was out, more than fifty thousand copies had been sold, and that figure doubled within eight years. The first six installments of *Les Rougon-Macquart* followed suit. After 1877 they fared very well indeed, with sales exceeding 140,000 by 1885.

Zola must have felt a bit like Serge Mouret transported overnight from a bare rectory to paradise on earth. The combative but superstitious outsider who believed devoutly in *la guigne* (rotten luck) had become Fortune's favorite. Charpentier offered him a brand-new contract—he would now receive fifty centimes per copy rather than forty, and also divide equally with Charpentier all profits from translations; Nadar featured him in his "Pantheon"; at least one magazine made him the subject of a special issue; and people attended public lectures on *Les Rougon-Macquart*. In April 1877, Zola left the rue Saint-Georges for more substantial quarters near the Place de Clichy, at 23, rue de Boulogne (now rue Ballu), and set up Emilie Zola in a small apartment nearby. Several months later, during a brief sojourn in Aix-en-Provence, he arranged with a marble mason to renovate his father's grave, ordering a new headstone, a cordon of iron chain, and six granite stanchions. It was as if hard times had ended for everyone—for the dead, who might rise unless placated, as well as for the quick.

Zola: anybody's gain was his loss. "I know several people who made a pastime of following Goncourt as he went from bookstore to bookstore and glowered at the piles of some best-seller," wrote Maurice Dreyfous. "It was all he could do not to cry 'Thief!' whenever someone bought a copy. More than once I had occasion to meet him in these circumstances and I humbly confess that I'd invent stories of fabulous sales just to drive him up the wall. . . . Scorning everything that wasn't Goncourt, he made an exception for three or four confreres whom he treated with condescension, believing himself, at bottom, to be their superior."

XVI

LITERARY FATHERHOOD

ZOLA KNEW BETTER than to exult in Flaubert's company, or to solicit praise from his literary mentors, for even as he was achieving fame, they were feeling that life had passed them by. "Your letter reached me the moment I heaved myself with two crutches into a Moscow-bound carriage," Turgenev had written to Flaubert on July 12, 1874. "Another attack of gout—and this time in *both* feet—[has] kept me in bed for two weeks and has still not left me. To say that all this makes me look at life through rose-tinted spectacles . . . would be to tell a great lie. Illness, a cold, slow disgust, painful stirrings of useless memories are, my dear fellow, what await us once we're past the age of fifty." Flaubert echoed his sentiments. *"Things aren't going well,"* he lamented. "It seems to me at times that I'm empty. I'm experiencing what the mystics call a state of dryness. I have got no confidence. First sign of decrepitude. Ah! If only one could molt one's old skin as snakes do, renew one's self, be rejuvenated."[1]

---

[1]In *Trente ans de Paris*, Alphonse Daudet recalled the embarrassment of owning up to the success of *Fromont jeune et Risler aîné* in 1874: "Flaubert was tormented by the melancholy of past triumphs, triumphs drained to the very dregs, right down to the reproaches of the critics and the common herd who are forever throwing your first book in your face, and who held up *Madame Bovary* as a glorious obstacle to the success of *Salammbô* and *L'Education sentimentale*. Goncourt seemed fatigued, sick at heart, as the result of a great mental effort of which a whole new generation of novelists would reap the advantage, and which would, at all events he so believed, leave him, the originator, almost unknown. Suddenly I found myself the only one in the party who felt popularity coming his way to the tune of several thousand copies, and I was embarrassed, almost ashamed, in

In Flaubert the dream of self-renewal was overwhelmed by a nihil-istic rage that compelled him to labor year after year over a book about two retired clerks who feed their immense appetite for knowledge with heaps of scientific literature but end up regurgitating nonsense. "It's the story of two blokes who compile a kind of critical encyclopedia *en farce*," he told a correspondent in August 1872. "I'll have to study many things I don't know: chemistry, medicine, agriculture. I'm now deep into medicine. One must be mad and trebly frenetic to undertake such a project! Too bad, God save me." Rallying Flaubert the novelist against Flaubert the suicidal autodidact, Turgenev suggested that he toss it off as a Voltairean satire, but this advice fell on deaf ears. "On August 1, I at last start *Bouvard et Pécuchet!*" Flaubert announced two years after the previous letter.

I have taken a vow! There's no going back! But how frightened I am! I'm on tenterhooks! I feel that I'm setting off on a very long journey into unexplored territory, and that I won't come back. Despite the great respect I have for your critical judgment (for in you judgment and production match each other, which is saying a lot), I don't share your opinion as to how the subject should be handled. If it's done summarily, with a concise, light touch, it will be a more or less witty fantasy, but lacking force and verisimilitude, whereas if it's detailed and developed, it will give the impression that I believe in my story, and it can become a serious and even a frightening thing.

As *Bouvard et Pécuchet* progressed, Flaubert's reports made the se-quence of chapters sound like stations of the cross. "Niggerdom per-sonified" is how he described himself in one letter. "I'm working, hammering away, slaving. . . . What will be the result? Ah, there's the rub. At times I feel *crushed* by the mass of this work, which may well be a failure. . . . For the moment I'm dabbling in Celtic archaeology with B. and P.; what a laugh." Except for *Trois Contes*, there was no distraction from his self-inflicted martyrdom. "B. and P. are wearing me out," he complained to Turgenev on August 9, 1879, nine months before a cerebral hemorrhage spared him further research. "I have only four pages to go to finish the Philosophy chapter. After which I shall start the penultimate chapter. These last two will take me up to March or April. Then there'll be the second volume! In short I shall still be at it in a year's time. One needs to be a master of asceticism to inflict such labors on oneself! On certain days it seems to me that all the blood is drained from my limbs and that I'm on the verge of

the presence of authors of such talent. Every Sunday, when I arrived, they ques-tioned me: 'How about new editions? what's the number now?' "

croaking." Dumas *fils*'s observation that Flaubert was not unlike the giant who knocked down a forest to build a box rang all too true.

Material woes exacerbated the literary ones. Flaubert, whose income derived mainly from farmland near Deauville, used a seemingly competent young lumber merchant named Ernest Commanville, who had married his beloved niece Caroline, as his financial manager.[2] The arrangement had worked well enough for some years, but in 1874 unpaid bills began piling up and dividends stopped arriving. After much tergiversation, Commanville finally confessed that since the Franco-Prussian War, which had dealt his business a grievous blow, he had kept afloat by borrowing from one creditor to fend off others: bankruptcy was a very real prospect, and kinfolk—Flaubert included—might never recover the money they had given him for investment. This news left Flaubert shaken. "We're short a *mere* one million five hundred thousand francs!" he told one friend. "The worst of it is that I'll probably be obliged to leave Croisset, where I've lived for thirty years and have stored hallowed memories. . . . Since childhood I had sacrificed everything to peace of mind. It's destroyed forever, and nothing remains—nothing to which I can cling." To George Sand he despaired in even more hyperbolic terms:

> You know that I am not a poseur, so believe me when I say that I would like to croak as soon as possible, for I'm washed up, gutted, older in spirit than a centenarian. I should have to wax enthusiastic over some idea or over the subject for some book. But *Faith* isn't there any longer and all work has become impossible. So while I fear for my material future, the literary future seems obliterated. I'd be well advised to seek employment right away, a lucrative occupation, but what am I fit for? And note that at age fifty-four one doesn't change one's habits, one doesn't remake one's life.

Moving from Croisset would, he predicted, destroy him.

Caroline, who had inherited the house at Croisset with the proviso that Flaubert be allowed to live there undisturbed, might have sold it for her husband's sake, had her marriage contract not forbidden such altruistic gestures. Instead she urged Flaubert to sell *his* property, and this he did straightway, remembering how he had failed her twelve years earlier, when Madame Flaubert (among others) made her marry Commanville against her will. The farm near Deauville fetched two hundred thousand francs, which he threw into the sinkhole of a

---

[2]Caroline was only two months old when her mother, Flaubert's sister, died of puerperal fever. Soon afterward her father went mad. Brought up at Croisset, she became for Flaubert a pupil, an adopted daughter, and a confidante all in one.

doomed enterprise. It was sheer folly, but, driven by pride as well as by loneliness and guilt, Flaubert could neither reason with himself nor let friends break his fall. "I cannot tell you how deeply moved I was by what Raoul Duval told me—by what you and he propose," he assured Agénor Bardoux, a deputy eager to secure a government pension for him.

No one could have better friends than the two of you. That you should take the initiative in offering such help makes it doubly precious. But, my dear friend, I ask you to be the judge; were you in my place you would not accept it. The disaster that has overtaken me is of no concern to the public. It was up to me to manage my affairs better, and I don't think I should be fed from public funds. Remember, such a pension would be published, printed, and perhaps attacked in the press and in the Assembly. What could I—we—say in reply? Others enjoy this favor, it's true; but what is permitted to others is forbidden to me. . . . However, since my life is going to be restricted, if you can find me a post worth three or four thousand francs in a library, along with lodging (such as exists at the Mazarine or the Arsenal), I think that would suit me fine.

Even the idea of a sinecure troubled him. He regarded a paid position of any kind as a comedown, he told Commanville, soliciting advice from the author of his predicament like a child clinging to the illusion of a parent's superior wisdom. "But one must live, alas, and perhaps I shall later regret a missed opportunity. If Bardoux leaves the ministry with his boss after the legislative session resumes, I'll never find another patron like him. What should I do? I am most perplexed."

In Paris, where he had his leather armchair, his statue of Buddha, and several other cherished objects transported from the rue Murillo to a less expensive flat high above street level at the unfashionable end of the rue du Faubourg Saint-Honoré, the world weighed less heavily upon him. If anything, Sundays became more animated, as awestruck young writers, for whom Flaubert enjoyed playing Flaubert, flocked upstairs on the tails of Zola, Daudet, Goncourt, and Turgenev. Zola rejoiced over his recovery:

It was on the rue du Faubourg Saint-Honoré that I saw him spring back to life with his booming voice and large gestures, thumping all factions with a poet's disdain. Little by little he had grown accustomed to straitened circumstances. The *Trois Contes* entertained him greatly, along with the young men who began showing up. His circle had widened, and on Sundays we sometimes numbered twenty. When Flaubert reappears before our eyes, it's in the white-and-gold

salon, planting himself in front of us with a very characteristic movement of the heels—enormous, mute, blue-eyed—or brandishing his
fists at the ceiling while unleashing tremendous paradoxes.

Goncourt observed that Flaubert's fame, talent, and bonhomie did not
attract people to him, that he lacked *rayonnement,* or radiance. But
such was not the view of twenty-five-year-old Guy de Maupassant, an
aspiring poet employed at the naval ministry, who often joined Flaubert for lunch. Maupassant's deceased uncle, Alfred Le Poittevin, had
been Flaubert's closest friend. "[Flaubert] received his friends on Sunday between one and seven, in a very simple sixth-floor bachelor flat,"
he was later to recall in a famous memoir.

The walls were bare, the furniture modest, for he detested arty bric-
a-brac. When the doorbell announced the first visitor, he would throw
a thin swatch of red silk over his worktable, hiding the paper mess
and the tools of his trade, which were as sacred to him as liturgical
objects to a priest. Then, in the absence of his servant, who usually
had off on Sundays, he would open the door himself. First to arrive
was almost always Ivan Turgenev, whom he would hug like a brother.
Even bigger than Flaubert, the Russian novelist had profound affection for his French friend. . . . He'd slump into an armchair and speak
slowly in a somewhat weak, hesitant voice, the softness of which lent
great charm and interest to his observations. Flaubert would listen
with rapt attention, fixing his blue eyes upon the large white figure
of Turgenev, and trumpet his replies. . . . Their talk seldom . . .
strayed far from literary history. Turgenev often arrived with an arm-
ful of foreign books and fluently translated poems by Goethe, Pushkin, Swinburne. Gradually, others arrived. There was M. Taine, his
eyes hidden behind glasses and with a timid air, who would introduce
historical documents, obscure facts, a scent and taste of musty archives. . . . In due course, he would welcome Alphonse Daudet, who
embodied the animation and gaiety of Parisian life. With a few words
he'd draw hilarious profiles, sicking his lovely southern wit on everyone and everything. . . . Emile Zola then made his appearance,
out of breath for having climbed six flights and always followed by
Paul Alexis. He'd ensconce himself in an armchair and quickly glance
around to read on people's faces their state of mind and the tenor
of conversation. Seated at a slight angle, with one leg slung underneath him, holding his ankle and speaking little, he'd listen atten-
tively. Others arrived in turn. I see the publisher Charpentier, who
could pass himself off as an adolescent if not for the white strands
in his long, black hair . . . He laughs easily, with a young, skeptical
laugh, and promises everything asked of him by the writers who corner him. Almost always the last to arrive is a tall, slender man . . .

who wears the lineaments of nobility and haughtiness. He has the look of a gentleman, the refined and nervous air characteristic of the highly bred. This is Edmond de Goncourt.

The talk at 240, rue du Faubourg Saint-Honoré made an equally vivid impression on young Henry James, whom Turgenev introduced to Flaubert's *cénacle* in 1875. "What was discussed in that little smoke-clouded room was chiefly questions of taste, questions of art and form; and the speakers, for the most part, were, in esthetic matters, radicals of the deepest dye. It would have been late in the day to propose among them any discussion of the relation of art to morality, any question as to the degree in which a novel might or might not concern itself with the teaching of a lesson. They had settled these preliminaries long ago, and it would have been primitive and incongruous to recur to them."

Had James sought to revisit this scene two years later, he would, more likely than not, have climbed five flights in vain, for by 1877 Flaubert's Paris season was a thing of brief duration. *Bouvard et Pécuchet*, together with the penury from which he now suffered, held him hostage at Croisset, and fellow members of the Société des Cinq lamented his absence. "Well, my friend, what's what?" Zola inquired in January 1877. "You know we're all moaning, paging you, needing you. Sundays are deadly. You're spoiling my winter by coming to Paris so late. The worst of it is that we four don't see one another since you aren't here to unite us." Nine months later, in September, he repeated this complaint. Would they be compelled, he asked, to wander like lost souls fervently missing him?

Although Flaubert's protracted absence left Sundays vacant, Zola did not find himself bereft of company or of ritual. On Thursdays, friends would drop by after supper without special invitation. Fridays were generally spent at the Charpentier salon, where Zola polished his social skills. He, Turgenev, Goncourt, and Daudet met whenever circumstances allowed. And every month, often on Saturday or Tuesday evening, a group including the old boys from Aix-en-Provence (Marius Roux, Philippe Solari, Antony Valabrègue, Numa Coste, Paul Alexis) gathered at little restaurants near Les Halles for a meal that had come to be dubbed *le boeuf nature* ("plain-boiled beef"). Paul Cézanne, who participated in the third Impressionist exhibition of 1877, was never among them, although, as we shall see, he occasionally visited Zola and still felt free to call upon him for help, especially material help, during his family crises.

L'Assommoir enlarged this circle. It lured young writers wanting direction and, indeed, one of the first to arrive at Zola's doorstep, a former medical student named Henry Céard, presented himself as a disciple or a catechumen. Although he did not extend them a glad hand, Zola treated young writers courteously, remembering no doubt the letter he himself had written to Victor Hugo at the age of twenty—a letter that had gone unanswered.[3] "I entered the rue Saint-Georges and at number 21 . . . found a small private house," Céard reminisced many years later.

A greengrocer assured me in the sincerest way that this was where M. Emile Zola lived, so, with heart in mouth, I pulled the bell cord. A maid appeared to whom I gave my card, I was asked to wait, Zola appeared, and the introduction finally took place, though not without a comic hitch. Since my card gave my address as Bercy, the great wholesale wine market [where Céard's father was an assistant station-master], Zola assumed that some peddler had come around to offer free samples. . . . Once this misunderstanding was dispelled, I told him as best I could why I was there and how the strong admiration I and my friends felt for *Les Rougon-Macquart* had given me the courage to seek out the author of these masterpieces.

Céard returned in due course with Joris-Karl Huysmans, an even more enthusiastic admirer of *Les Rougon-Macquart*. Soon afterward, through Paul Alexis, Léon Hennique became another regular. "Following a public lecture he gave on *L'Assommoir*, a lecture that made the art-for-art's-sake crowd bristle," Alexis wrote, "I took him to the rue Saint-Georges."[4] Alexis and Huysmans were already friends, having encountered each other at a masked ball during carnival week in 1876, and soon the foursome of Céard, Hennique, Alexis, and Huysmans became five when Alexis introduced Guy de Maupassant, whom he knew from Sundays on the rue du Faubourg Saint-Honoré. It was as if five constituted, in Alexis's mind, the quorum of a literary generation. "Our little group thus stood complete," he wrote in 1882. "One fine Thursday evening, all five of us marched to Zola's place in a tight column. And since then we've returned every Thursday."

[3]"I am very busy and couldn't answer sooner," he apologized to one such writer on Christmas Day 1876. "It would be difficult for me to make an appointment to hear you read your *François Villon*, but if you leave me your manuscript, I shall quite willingly give you my opinion. I fear that it may be severe as I don't care much for period plays. Furthermore, I don't have much pull in the theater world and so even if your drama seduced me, I should despair of being very useful. I tell you this in order to dispel any illusions."
[4]Alexis played as fast and loose with chronological sequences as with shopgirls. There is reason to believe, for example, that Hennique had already visited the Zola household when he delivered this lecture on *L'Assommoir*.

If Zola found J.-K. Huysmans to be rather more exotic than the other four, there are respects in which this gaunt, blond-bearded, hollow-chested man pouncing on literary issues like a tomcat at play also came from a very familiar land. Long before Thomas Mann in *Tonio Kröger* and André Gide in *Si le grain ne meurt* portrayed the artist as a sport of nature or a hybrid of temperamental opposites, Huysmans declared that he was "the inexplicable amalgam of a refined Parisian and a Dutch painter." His mother, Malvina Badin, a schoolteacher, had married someone even more refined than herself in choosing Godfried Huysmans, a lithographer and miniaturist whose Catholic family had supplied Protestant Holland with competent painters since the sixteenth century. Their son, christened Charles-Georges, arrived in February 1848, on the eve of the bloody revolution that dethroned Louis Philippe. Growing up near Saint-Sulpice, visiting relatives in Holland, playing at the Jardin du Luxembourg, and keeping close to his father, who earned a livelihood illustrating missals, he was safe and secure until Godfried's health began to fail. Then, as the specter of economic ruin advanced upon the household, bitter quarrels ensued, and Georges found himself thrust aside. When Godfried Huysmans died in 1856, leaving his family destitute, the boy had already learned what it meant to fall from grace.

Another calamity soon followed. Seven months into widowhood, Malvina married a gentleman named, implausibly enough, Jules Og, who brought with him not only a modest fortune but two young daughters. Infuriated by her betrayal, Georges was promptly exiled to boarding school, where, like Charles Baudelaire damning the perfidious Madame Aupick (ex Baudelaire) from his cell at the Lycée Louis-le-Grand, he suffered agonies of loneliness. It was an icy childhood, and the slight thaw of Sunday dinners at home with his prosthetic family made internment at school feel even colder. This regime lasted nine years, during which he struggled to piece together a self worth saving from the shattered past. Mementos of his father, or of Holland, became identity papers for him. When in due course he embarked upon a literary career, he styled himself Joris-Karl (Georges-Charles). A regular museumgoer, he found solace in Dutch landscapes. And the talisman he retained throughout his life was a copy of Zurbarán's *Monk*, painted by his father.

The thin, gangly blond lad left the Lycée Saint-Louis—Zola's alma mater—equipped with classical baggage but with no destination or compass. As Monsieur Og had two dowries to nurture, Malvina resolved that her son should seek employment and work his way through law school. Thus Huysmans became, like his grandfather Badin before him, a government functionary, copying documents at the interior

ministry by day, studying torts when not otherwise occupied, and loitering at student cafés after dark.

> I haunted the Latin Quarter, and there I learned, among other things,
> to take some casual interest in students who regularly expectorated
> their political ideas over mugs of beer, and to sample the works of
> George Sand and Heine, of Edgar Quinet and Henry Murger. . . .
> This lasted a year. I matured gradually. The electoral battles of the
> late empire didn't touch me, for being neither a senator's son nor an
> outlaw's, I had only to follow, under any regime, the tradition of
> mediocrity and shabbiness in which my family was steeped.

Still sentimental enough to love Henry Murger, whose *Scènes de la vie
de Bohème* enjoyed a considerable vogue (it went on to enjoy a greater
vogue through Puccini's *La Bohème*), he set up house with a young
vaudeville actress, about whom it is known only that during their brief
time together she bore someone else's child. What eventually came of
this conjugal episode, which whet his appetite for self-degradation
even as it made him yearn for something else, was *Marthe*.

In 1867 Huysmans quit law school. Repudiating the professional
ambitions entailed upon him, he withdrew into the cocoon of France's
immense bureaucracy, where no one much cared whether he read *Les
Fleurs du mal*, haunted Left Bank brothels, or tried his hand at art
criticism. He led an altogether gray, punctual life until war broke out.
Mobilized, he spent more time in hospitals bedridden with dysentery
than at the front. Subsequently he endured the terrible siege of Paris.
What he didn't endure was civil war, for the provisional government
required functionaries to live at Versailles in May 1871, when French
troops invaded the capital.

Huysmans had felt less marginal in the famished fortress-city than
in the well-fed metropolis. Driven by an imagination that thrived on
hermetic ritual, on sadomasochistic grotesquery, on legends of depravity and martyrdom, on dreams of mankind losing all regard for law and
casting itself adrift, he began a novel about Paris under siege called *La
Faim* (*Hunger*). But he was unable to organize this ambitious work,
never progressing beyond a first chapter, and turned to fashioning
prose poems instead, as if the middle ground between epic and miniature offered no purchase. "A skillfully cut jewel from the hand of a
master goldsmith" is how one critic described *Le Drageoir aux épices*
when it was published (at its author's expense). Literary Paris gave
Huysmans scant notice, but the book recommended him to art magazines, for which he then wrote *transpositions d'art*, or descriptive exercises based on masterpieces in the Louvre. Like his father, he thus
became something of a copyist, and one has reason to suppose that

his mimetism did not end there. After reading *Manette Salomon,* a Goncourt novel whose artist hero is emasculated by a vulgar Jewish mistress, Huysmans produced *Marthe,* whose poet-hero is betrayed by a guttersnipe he rescued from the police.

Survival meant compartmentalization. The impeccable civil servant arranged to publish *Marthe* in Belgium lest it cost him his job under the conservative regime, and the fastidious author quarantined his "baser" self in a Belgium of the mind. For years Huysmans enjoyed physical intimacy with a dressmaker who had two illegitimate children. But Anna Meunier was always kept unofficial. Seeing her at prudent intervals on appointed days, he found more frequent companionship among young men who thumbed their noses at the aesthetic conventions, psychological stereotypes, and social pieties upheld by officialdom. However disingenuous this arrangement, there was no helping it, for he could not reconcile body and mind, or instinct and culture —not even after the death of his "refined" mother.

Malvina died just before *Marthe* appeared, and Huysmans's crucial encounter with Zola took place several months later. Huysmans, who craved solidarity as loners will, lost no time becoming Zola's most vociferous apostle. Already *plus catholique que le pape,* he trumpeted his literary faith in public and in private. "You said it—I am a realist of the school of Goncourt, Zola, and Flaubert, etc.," he told one friend. "In Paris there is a small group of us convinced that the novel can no longer be a story that is more or less true, more or less dressed up, coated in fish paste, like certain pills, to mask the taste. By realism we mean the patient study of reality, achieving an overall impression detail by detail, cruel ones if need be, trivial even, if that helps us to strike the right note. As you can see, we are far removed from the days of Alexandre Dumas's novels." A series of four articles written in March 1877 for a Belgian review and later republished as a brochure argues this position more extensively. Naturalists eschew the bohemian scribblers with whom Paris swarms, Huysmans declared. "A writer can be chaste yet treat scabrous subjects, [and] Zola proves it. May people who picture him in a slouch hat with a beard that reeks of absinthe and a vinous nose discard their illusions. . . . The bloodthirsty knave, the pornographer, is quite simply the most exquisite of men and the most benevolent of masters." Does naturalism thrive upon squalor? Does this creed, despite the virtue of its chief practitioner, have some special affinity to vice? Not at all, he wrote.

> Green pustules and pink flesh are all one to us; we depict both because both exist, because the criminal deserves to be studied as much as the most perfect of men, and because our towns throng with prostitutes who have the same *droit de cité* there as prudes. Society has

two faces; we show those two faces, we use every color on the palette, black as well as blue; we admire Ribera and Watteau without distinction because both . . . created living works! Whatever some may say, we don't prefer vice to virtue, corruption to modesty; we applaud both the coarse, spicy novel and the tender, sugary one—provided each is well founded, well written, and true to life.

Where Henry James reserved judgment "as to the degree in which a novel might or might not concern itself with the teaching of a lesson," Huysmans outdid everyone, including his exemplar, in professions of moral neutrality. "No, we are not sectarians but men who believe that writers, like painters, should be of their time. We are artists lusting for modernity, who would bury cloak-and-dagger romances and disencumber ourselves of hand-me-downs. . . . We go into the street, the living, swarming street, into hotel rooms as well as into palaces, into empty lots as well as proud forests. We wish to avoid doing what the romantics did, making puppets more beautiful than nature, which must be rewound every three or four pages, and enlarged by an optical illusion."

Still childless, Zola found satisfaction in the role conferred upon him by these younger men, and he was especially pleased to bolster or lecture Huysmans, whose depressions may have reminded him of Cézanne's "black spells." For his part, Huysmans, yearning for a surrogate father, discovered one at Les Batignolles. "What are you telling me? that Huysmans has abandoned his novel about women bookbinders?"[5] Zola asked Céard during the summer of 1877. "What is it? A mere fit of laziness do you think? Torpor brought on by the heat? He must persevere, and be sure to tell him so. He is our hope, he doesn't have the right to abandon his novel when the entire group needs works. And you, what are you about? I see you're publishing some old stuff, but that won't do. We must produce stories, dramas, comedies, novels. During the next few years we must crush the public under our bulk." Several weeks later, having meanwhile received a fretful letter from Huysmans himself, he again delivered his pep talk:

So you're working. Well, that's as it should be! How wrong you are to fret in advance! Press forward bravely, without wondering whether your book contains enough action, whether it will please, whether the censor will lock you up in Sainte-Pélagie! I've noticed one thing, that the novels that have given me the most trouble are those that have enjoyed the most success. I believe that one must rely upon

[5]Huysmans had inherited a bindery from his stepfather, Jules Og, and attended to this business in his spare time.

one's talent and take the straightest possible path. Now, of course, one wouldn't be an artist if one didn't tremble (and I, like you, have my days of terrible doubt).

Everyone in the group was counting on him, he concluded. "You're going to give us a work that will strengthen our cause."

Of a piece with his gruff encouragement was the criticism directed at Huysmans's mannered language. "If you want my frank opinion," wrote Zola, "I believe that plainer prose would have served [*Marthe*] well. Your style is naturally rich and with too much labor becomes precious. It seems to me that intensity derives from the value of words rather than the color. We all see things too dark and overcooked." But whatever his private reservations about Huysmans, or about his other protégés for that matter, he energetically recommended them to publishers, theater managers, newspaper editors, etc.—and expected as much in return. "Would that I were the person you've described" is how he thanked Huysmans for "Emile Zola et *L'Assommoir.*" "You've overdone the praise, and I accept your enthusiasm only because of the astonishment it must have caused in certain people. Then again, you've raised a banner, haven't you? Amongst ourselves, perfect candor must prevail, but before the world we shall be brazen-faced."

While this group went some way toward fulfilling Zola's dreams of paternity, it also revived memories of the brotherhood that had given him comfort and fortitude and joy throughout his adolescence. As sententious as he sometimes was in letters, in person he apparently behaved like an older chum rather than a mentor. To Alexis it seemed that "our relations with Zola, far from being those of student to master, differ in no way from the intimacy, the affectionate camaraderie we five enjoy amongst ourselves. If anything, each of us, I believe, feels less constrained with him than with the others, more disposed to confide certain things. He a monitor? Balderdash! A pontiff? Nonsense!" About "Thursdays" at Zola's apartment he wrote:

> His study on the rue de Boulogne where formal readings are never held, where one says whatever comes to mind, where opinions often clash, where one need not even have an opinion, where talk does not usually dwell upon a general theme—in short, this large study where we spend so many pleasurable evenings, often laughing like kids at everyone and everything and one another, is the very opposite of a chapel, despite its two stained-glass windows.

A more complete picture would have included house slippers, a samovar, the antics of Zola's little dog, Raton, and the hospitality of Alexandrine, who, when well enough, prepared meals that helped her

husband's bachelor friends survive their usual fare.[6] The five met almost every week, first at a chophouse in lower Montmartre which, for
gastronomic reasons, locals had nicknamed L'Assommoir, then at
a somewhat cleaner but equally rowdy establishment called Chez
Joseph.

Certain meals entered family lore, but one that took place on April
16, 1877, at Chez Trapp near the Saint-Lazare railroad station, made
Zola's group famous, and for this tour de force several people could
claim credit. Guy de Maupassant, who proposed the event to begin
with, set things in motion by having *La République des lettres* publish
a squib worded as follows:

> In a restaurant destined to become illustrious, namely Trapp's near
> the Gare Saint-Lazare, six young, enthusiastic naturalists also des-
> tined for celebrity—Messieurs Paul Alexis, Henry Céard, Léon Hen-
> nique, J.-K. Huysmans, Octave Mirbeau, and Guy de Valmont[7]—
> recently entertained their masters: Gustave Flaubert, Edmond de
> Goncourt, Emile Zola. One of the guests has told us the menu:
> "purée de Bovary" soup; salmon-pink trout "à la Fille Elisa"; truffled
> chicken "à la Saint-Antoine"; artichokes "au Coeur Simple"; parfait
> "naturaliste"; vin de Coupeau; liqueur "de l'Assommoir." M. Gustave
> Flaubert, who has other disciples, commented upon the absence of
> eels "à la Carthaginoise" and pigeons "à la Salammbô."

Soon afterward, diatribes ridiculing the bumptiousness of these young
men appeared in *Les Cloches de Paris* under the pseudonym "Tilsitt."
Tilsitt was none other than Paul Alexis, a practical joker whose hoax
achieved the desired effect of galvanizing satirists identified with
MacMahon's regime, the so-called Moral Order. "Alexis gave the stri-

---

[6]To Huysmans the atmosphere was very much more congenial than at Flaubert's.
"To tell you the whole truth, we have problems," he informed a Belgian friend
in April 1877, referring to the young Group of Five:
> Only Zola supports us unreservedly! Goncourt is an egoist who makes fun of
> us, and terrible as it is to admit it, Flaubert, acclaimed by Mendès and all the
> Parnassians, the man who wrote *Madame Bovary*, and who detests his own
> masterpiece and goes into ecstasy over his *Tentation de Saint-Antoine*, is more
> an enemy than a friend! We spent the day at his place on Sunday and Céard
> and I came away more distressed and dejected than I can say. . . . All these
> people hate one another: Flaubert runs down Goncourt, Goncourt knocks Flau-
> bert, both use Zola as a whipping boy behind his back. What blessings! It makes
> one want to bolt one's door and stay at home! Still, it looks as if that is the way
> it has always been, and that it is we who have been simpletons in believing
> great men to be incapable of baseness.

[7]Guy de Valmont was Maupassant's early nom de plume and presumably the one
by which he hoped to make his name. Octave Mirbeau's association with the
group ended when he accepted a political appointment in the provinces.

dent keynote for a polemics that has never let up," Céard wrote much later. "It's extraordinary to reread, after thirty years, the articles provoked by that innocent dinner on a mezzanine overlooking the rue Saint-Lazare! From afar one repeats the question posed in *Les Cloches de Paris*: 'How do six men of letters, totally unknown except for a modest binge at Trapp's, contrive to make such noise?' " Cartoons proliferated, and in many of them the six were portrayed as piglets being suckled by a sow that bears the motto *Omnes mecum porto* ("I carry them all with me"), or straddling their mother's curly tail, or walking single-file behind a porcine, snub-nosed Zola. They were also shown with brooms and chamber pots celebrating the apotheosis of naturalism.

The pact that had created a republic monarchical in structure did not appease dogged antidemocrats or weaken the resolve of their spokesmen to defend Church and army against subversion. MacMahon considered social order his sacred trust. Having succeeded Thiers reluctantly, this soldier famous for his exploits during the Crimean War occupied the Elysée Palace as if it were the Malakhov fortress, from whose mined rampart he had declared, twenty years earlier: "Here I am; here I stay."

By law MacMahon could stay put until 1880, but legislators were obliged to go home when the National Assembly that had governed France since 1871 dissolved itself on December 31, 1875, and in elections held soon afterward, conservatism suffered a heavy blow. Ignoring MacMahon's advice to reject all who might disturb the security of lawful interests or threaten it with the propagation of antisocial doctrines, voters returned republican candidates en masse. For every deputy seated right of center three sat left of it, and in the Chamber of Deputies Léon Gambetta's voice rang triumphant. Frenchmen had just given dazzling proof of their aversion to the clerical politics that informed every move made by those who formerly held sway in the Assembly, he exulted. It behooved France to break with ultramontanism—pro-Vaticanism—lest that attitude distort her foreign policy. But in no way would republicans "weaken," "diminish," or "modify" the powers of the president of the Republic.

Unable to focus on objects left of Left Center (especially voluminous objects like Gambetta) without seeing red, MacMahon appointed as prime minister one Jules Dufaure, a seventy-eight-year-old whose republicanism, like his frock coat and rhetorical style, evoked the fashion of 1830. No sooner had he taken office than troubles beset him. Damned by the Right for having dismissed conservative functionaries, Dufaure found himself damned by the Left for not having made the purge complete. Caught between Catholics, who insisted that his government deplore the omission of religious ceremony from funerals, and anticlericals, who held that the state must remain neutral, he proposed a compromise obnoxious to both. As D. W. Brogan has written: "The administrative favors and exceptions which had been enjoyed under the 'Moral Order' were now to be cut off, but there was a marked difference between what even sincere Catholics, like Dufaure and Marcère, thought were favors and what even a liberal bishop, like Dupanloup, thought were rights." The Chamber of Deputies and the Senate, ignoring Dufaure, clashed time and time again over religious matters. When the Chamber sought to disqualify priests from the juries that granted university degrees, the Senate, where conservatives enjoyed a bare majority, stood firm. It stood firm when the Chamber questioned the raison d'être of France's Vatican embassy. And when Gambetta persuaded the lower house to cut several items from the Public Worship budget, the upper house hastened to restore them.

Dufaure's diplomatic skill availed him even less in clashes provoked by left-wing deputies demanding exoneration for convicted insurgents. After all, Dufaure was the minister of justice who, under Thiers, had organized the machinery of prosecution that tried Communards, and this deed left him stranded between hostile allies and kindred foes. The leftist Chamber passed an amnesty bill over his protests; the rightist Senate then rejected it with a complicitous wink in his direction. "[Only] the union of the Centres, excluding both extreme Right and Left . . . could have saved Dufaure. For that union there was needed, on both sides, moderation and prudence. There was not enough of it on the Left; there was even less on the Right." Frustrated by the ambiguity of his position, he resigned on December 3, 1876, after nine months in office.

To succeed Dufaure, MacMahon appointed Jules Simon, a gifted intellectual whose occasional departures from leftist orthodoxy had earned him the reputation among conservatives of being the *merle blanc* or "white blackbird" with whom they could treat. "You know full well that I am both deeply republican and deeply conservative" is how he characterized himself in his inaugural address to parliament, and proofs were furnished straightway. "Simon showed considerable dexterity and tact," writes one historian. "In his own style, as an orator, he was Gambetta's peer. Mealy-mouthed he might be called, but he was infinitely persuasive. Not for him the thunderous summons to action, but honeyed reasoning." Simon might have stayed the course by tacking right and left had waves from abroad not capsized him. In January 1877, Pope Pius IX—he of the *Syllabus of Errors*—summoned good Catholics everywhere to condemn Italy's leftist regime, specifically the Clerical Abuses Law with which that regime had armed itself for use against subversive priests. The pope was echoed by the bishop of Nevers, and crowds marched throughout France in sympathy. Simon, while noting the restraint of the French episcopate, vowed to maintain order. But republicans wanted something more than order. They wanted ultramontane politics suppressed, brutally if need be, and most of them backed a resolution to that effect after hearing Gambetta exclaim in one of his most celebrated speeches: "Clericalism? There is the enemy!" A leader without followers, Simon the white blackbird now found himself shunned as a mutant by every political species. MacMahon accepted his resignation.

It would have taken supreme arrogance or desperation or both for MacMahon to flout the republican majority at this juncture, but flout it he did on May 16, 1877—a famous date in French political annals. He named Albert de Broglie prime minister, proclaiming himself responsible to "France" rather than to parliament, and had an envoy inform the Chamber that he would not suffer "radical modifications of all our great administrative, judicial, financial, and military institutions." Three hundred sixty-three republican deputies thereupon let it be known that France was not a mere figment of MacMahon's sovereign will, stating on May 17:

> The chamber, which deems it important, in light of the present crisis and the mandate it received from the nation, to recall that a preponderance of parliamentary power as exercised by ministers whom elected representatives may call to account is the basic condition of government by the people for the people . . . declares that the confidence of the majority will be bestowed only upon a cabinet free to act as it sees fit and resolved to govern in accordance with republican principles that alone guarantee order and prosperity at home and peace abroad.

This challenge was no sooner made public than MacMahon adjourned parliament. When it reconvened a month later (republican prefects and subprefects having meanwhile been sacked), the so-called "363" inveighed against Broglie's right-wing cabinet. "Considering that the government formed on May 17 by the president of the Republic . . . was summoned to power in violation of majority rule," they declared, "considering also that on its first day it contrived not to appear for questioning before representatives of the country, that it has meddled with the internal administration so as to influence voters in every possible way, that . . . it represents the coalition of parties hostile to the Republic—a coalition whose leaders fomented clerical riots . . . : considering all this, we say that this government does not enjoy the confidence of representatives of the nation." Had custom prevailed, a vote of no confidence would have brought down the government, but MacMahon, faced with yet another Hobson's choice, decided, shockingly, to dissolve the Chamber.

Elections were not scheduled until September, which meant that candidates had more than three months for haranguing, and slogans flew thick all summer long. "Paris is insufferable," the art critic Théodore Duret complained in a letter to Zola. "Thought is completely absorbed by the forthcoming elections and the crisis that will follow. All signs favor us, but after the return of the 363, what will happen?" Flaubert was equally exasperated. "Two things sustain me: love of Literature and hatred of the Bourgeois," he wrote on August 23, "the latter—my hatred of the Bourgeois—being resumed, condensed, nowadays, in what is called the Great Party of Order. I can work myself up just thinking about MacMahon, his minister of the interior Fourtou, and our perfect Lizot. After five minutes' reflection I have a paroxysm of rage, and that relieves me. I'm calmer afterward. Don't think I'm kidding. But why such indignation? I wonder. No doubt about it, the older I get the more easily I'm offended by fatuousness, and in all of history I know nothing as *inept* as the men of May 16. Their stupidity makes my head spin." More Frenchmen than not agreed with Flaubert, for the united left, though it lost several dozen seats, held its majority in September, and one year later it would win the Senate in an election that persuaded MacMahon to leave office before the expiration of his Septennate.[8]

Noise of the electoral campaign pervaded every hamlet, even L'Estaque, where Zola took Alexandrine in May 1877 for a long sojourn recommended by her doctor. This excitement bothered him. His loyalties remained republican, of course, but like Flaubert he was inclined to pronounce a pox on the Left as well as on the Right. More than ever, they monopolized public attention. "In a fit of anger, exasperated by the ridiculous ambitions and odious hullabaloo that surrounded me," he wrote not long afterward in an article entitled "The Hatred of Literature,"

I surmised that my generation would end up missing the great silence of the Second Empire. I dare confess now that I went too far. But do extenuating circumstances not plead in my favor? Is the clamorous, jolting world of alarums and bogeys in which politics have forced us to live for the past ten years not a world that stifles the mind? Consider our national history. Whenever there's been some

[8]By 1880 the seat of government had been moved back from Versailles to Paris, July 14 had become the Republic's official birthday, and *La Marseillaise* had been adopted as a national anthem.

convulsion—the League, the Fronde, the French Revolution—literature has suffered grievous injury and has needed some considerable time to recover. . . . No doubt social evolutions follow their own logic and necessity. One must yield. But when they last too long, disaster ensues.

One page from a great writer's work contains "more significance for humanity," he went on to say, than a year of politicians' "antlike scurryings."

The fear that politics would eclipse literature, that people would forget *Les Rougon-Macquart*, or that Gambetta might upstage him expressed Zola's doubts about a novel begun and largely written during his five months at L'Estaque. After capturing the attention of *le grand public* with *L'Assommoir*, could he hold it with *Une Page d'amour*? "Today the novelist in me is satisfied," he informed Huysmans on August 3. "I say today, for, like you, I have my days of terrible doubt. I've just finished the first part of my novel, which will have five parts in all. It's a bit dowdy, a bit stick-in-the-mud, but I believe it will go down smoothly. I want to astonish readers of *L'Assommoir* with a good-natured book. . . . I don't say that it will be entirely devoid of dark passages, but those will be the exception." Doubt hounded him all summer long, even as he gazed upon the Mediterranean from his sylvan perch and walked Raton around the neighborhood before sitting down to dinner. "There are days when I'm worried about this work, when it seems very flat and gray," he confided to Marguerite Charpentier a fortnight later. "On other days I find it good-natured—agreeable and easy to read. I've done about one quarter. I'm especially pleased with a great bird's-eye view of Paris in springtime. It's among the most virtuosic things I've ever written. Now I shall continue on a tender note. But it must be said that we won't repeat *L'Assommoir*'s success. *Une Page d'amour* (I've plumped for this title, which is the best I've found so far) is too sweet to excite the public. No sense deluding oneself there. Let's sell ten thousand and count ourselves lucky."[9] These sage observations apparently had little effect, for in September he wrote to Hennique that he was greatly perplexed about the value of what he was doing, that he thought he might be writing it in "the wrong key," and that it might make "no impression whatever."

[9]Ten thousand was modest only in light of the gaudy figures recorded for *L'Assommoir*. As Zola informed his Russian readers in an article on contemporary French novelists, selling out an edition of one thousand was considered *un joli succès*, and more than two printings was quite exceptional.

Although *Une Page d'amour*, which concerns well-heeled bourgeois who reside high up near the Trocadéro Palace, in the Paris district called Passy, has nothing of *L'Assommoir*'s squalor, "good-natured" hardly does justice to a novel about adulterous passion tormenting conscionable lovers. François Mouret's sister Hélène is the central character here, and the story opens eighteen months after the death of her husband, Grandjean, with whom she had come north from Marseille to start a new life. For Hélène, Paris remains terra incognita. "She didn't know a single street, she didn't even know what neighborhood she was in," writes Zola. "[She felt] quite alone, abandoned, lost, as on the far side of some wasteland." Saved by two transplanted southerners—a priest named Jouve and his rich merchant brother, Rambaud, who has given her elegant quarters rent-free—she contemplates Paris from afar while leading the sedate, eleemosynary life expected of widows with reputations to uphold. "She was very proud of her well-ordered existence," is how Zola describes this bourgeoise in purdah. "Dignity and absolute steadfastness had been the story of her thirty-odd years. Justice was her only passion. When she examined her past, she found no momentary lapses, she saw herself continuing straight. There would be no tripping over obstacles, she resolved, and her resolve made her a stern, wrathful judge of people led astray by the fata morgana of heroism." The oceanic metropolis that beckons outside her window, promising fulfillment but also threatening chaos, is as much a projection of dreams as it is a reality to be explored. "But by now Paris had almost emerged from morning haze and her heart suddenly went soft. To love, to love! Everything brought her back to the caress of that word, even the pride she took in her reputation." The novel's five segments each end with Paris seen, always from Hélène's window, in some new mood or light or season.

Wherever Hélène goes, there goes her daughter Jeanne, a frail twelve-year-old about whom we learn two things—that she will not suffer anyone else to enjoy her mother's affection and that she has not descended with impunity from the Rougon-Macquart progenitrix, Adélaïde Fouque—Tante Dide. Indeed, we learn the second truth right away, for Jeanne's cataleptic seizure sets in motion the plot of *Une Page d'amour*. Hélène runs outside in an aimless search for help and by chance fetches up at the doorstep of a physician named Henri Deberle, who accompanies her home. Love is born then and there, during Jeanne's "absence." In Hélène, Deberle finds not only a devoted woman to admire but a statuesque beauty, while Hélène responds to the power of a thaumaturge. Kind, rich, and scientifically distinguished, Deberle awakens the mother as well as the daughter from a deathlike trance. " 'Oh, sir!' she murmured. 'Don't leave me yet. Wait a few minutes. What if she has more seizures? . . . It is you who saved her.' " Again, the rescue theme.

Visiting her savior several days later, Hélène meets his wife, Juliette, an amiable flibbertigibbet who presides over garden parties where like-minded people traffic in the received ideas of upper-class society. Juliette invites her back, together with Jeanne; feelings for Deberle go unrequited until chance intervenes once again. They meet each other at the bedside of a neighborhood pauper known as Mère Fétu, whose garret then becomes a place for their chaste assignations. "Intimacy established itself between them. . . . There they were far removed from the world, sharing Mère Fétu's one chair, almost happy with the worn, ugly objects that brought them closer together."

Jouve, Hélène's moral counselor, advises her to take another husband lest some "painful and inadmissible" feeling occupy the "space" vacated by Grandjean, and he proposes his decent, gentle, unglamorous brother. Hélène demurs when little Jeanne objects hysterically, but the more important reason for her demurral lies elsewhere, hidden even from herself. She loves Henri Deberle, and, intent on believing that virtue rather than desire is what draws them to each other, nurtures adulterous fantasies under cover of Christian sentiment. "Every afternoon she'd descend upon the Deberle garden with Jeanne," writes Zola, who assigned this garden the same symbolic value he gave François Mouret's in *La Conquête de Plassans*. "Her place in it was marked, against the first elm on the right. A chair awaited her and the gravel would still be littered with bits of thread from the previous day's needlework. 'You're right at home,' Madame Deberle would repeat every evening . . . and Hélène was indeed at home. Little by little she grew accustomed to this patch of greenery, she'd fidget with childish impatience until the visiting hour arrived. What enchanted her above all was the tidiness of the lawn and shrubs. Not a stray blade of grass to spoil its symmetry."

Eventually nature defeats convention. By way of celebrating the advent of spring, Juliette Deberle organizes a costume ball for a hundred children. Parents come along, and what unfolds is something very like the bacchic finale of *La Curée* in miniature, with festivities that induce Hélène to ungirdle herself. A mischievous, fun-loving girl emerges from the decorous woman who had just cast off widow's weeds. "She became childlike," Zola observes of her reaction to a marionette show featuring Punchinello.

The resonant blows Punchinello dealt with his stick sent shivers through her and made her breast swell. "My God! how silly!" she'd say to Henri, eyes bright. "They really wallop one another, don't they!" "Oh, they have hard heads!" he'd answer, which was as much wit as his heart could muster. Both of them left adulthood behind, they yielded to Punchinello's unexemplary life. Then, at the climactic moment, when the devil appeared and an all-out donnybrook took place, Hélène threw herself back, crushing Henri's hand, which he had draped over the back of her armchair.

When everyone assembles on a dance floor for a "fairy-tale gala," Henri finally declares himself, and Hélène, no longer able to feign innocence, hides her shame behind a fan. "[The declaration] burned her from head to toe, like a red-hot gust. . . .. Swept up by the last quadrilles, children were stamping louder than ever. There were peals of silvery laughter, birdlike voices emitting cries of pleasure. A freshness rose from these little demons galloping round and round about." Like Renée Saccard, Hélène Grandjean attests to Zola's admiration for Racine's Phèdre, who also begins unraveling when a forbidden name is uttered or a sinful secret aired.[10]

Hélène cannot yield right away. She behaves as if nothing had ever been said, thus devising an expiatory ordeal in which high-mindedness thrives on sadomasochistic foreplay. "A feeling of joy, born of her very anguish, welled up from the deep. She cherished her pain and shuddered at the thought of Jouve curing her with his sound advice." Physical gratification is restricted to stolen kisses, lest Jeanne, who watches jealously, punish them by dying. Hélène's feigned innocence once whetted their desire; now her daughter's vigilance does the same. "Always in between, spying upon them, she forced them to hold back, to make a show of indifference that left them incredibly keyed up. As they felt that she was all ears, they kept their lips sealed for days on end." Stifled by this life, Hélène confides in the abbé Jouve and is told once again to marry Monsieur Rambaud.

A dinner party at which Juliette Deberle agrees to a tryst with an utterly insignificant popinjay named Malignon marks the beginning of the end of Une Page d'amour. Hélène overhears them, waxes furious, rushes home, lies awake pondering the assignation, then acts:

She had lost control of her will, she was undermined by unavowable thoughts that spoke to her like a sensual, wicked woman holding forth in a queenly voice, a voice she couldn't disobey. . . . Toward 2 a.m. she rose from bed with the stiffness and pale resolution of a somnambulist, she lit the lamp and wrote a letter, disguising her script. It was a vague denunciation, a three-line note begging Dr. Deberle to repair to a certain place that same day at a certain hour, without further explanation or signature.

[10]There are other indications of her Racinian cousinage. Writing Une Page d'amour in five parts (each with five chapters), Zola clearly intended to evoke the traditional structure of French classical tragedy.

Guilt gains the upper hand over rage just before the fatal hour strikes, and in a race against time Hélène scrambles through rain-swept streets to warn Juliette. The latter flees, whereupon Hélène receives Henri Deberle, who concludes that his inamorata has staged the mysterious encounter to gratify him at last. This she does. Helping him commit adultery in order to save his marriage, Hélène achieves both the honor of virtue and the pleasure of vice.

The imbroglio would be worthy of Boulevard farce if it did not kill Jeanne. Distraught at having been abandoned, Jeanne is looking out an open window during these events, gazing with incomprehension at the city that embodies and conceals her mother. "Paris remained for her that place to which children don't go—no one ever took her there," writes Zola.

> She would like to have known [where her mother was] but it seemed too vast for finding anyone. Her glances leapt across the plain. Was she perhaps in that clump of houses on a hill to the right? or nearby, beneath the large trees whose naked branches looked like faggots or dead wood? Would that she could have lifted the rooftops! What was that dark monument out yonder? And that street where something big was running? . . . She couldn't see anything very definite, but whatever it was, it moved and was ugly—little girls had no business looking. All manner of vague suppositions, which made her want to cry, disturbed her in her childish ignorance. Through the dank air came an odor of poverty, of filth and of crime that made her young head spin, as if, in leaning toward the imponderable city, . . . she had bent over a polluted well.

Tuberculosis erupts soon after this wet, cold vigil, and several weeks later the girl dies, unforgiveness written on her face. Accompanied by flower-decked maidens got up as for another spring masquerade, Jeanne is buried in the Passy graveyard overlooking Paris.

Grief-stricken, Hélène eventually resigns herself to the marriage of convenience Jouve had urged upon her, and she leaves Paris for Marseille with her middle-aged husband, Monsieur Rambaud. Juliette Deberle will bear another child, but not she. Revisiting Passy during a midwinter sojourn several years later, Hélène is confounded by memories of the passionate young woman she buried alongside Jeanne. As she beholds Paris from the Passy graveyard—from *d'outre tombe*, as it were—it, too, seems to lie somewhere far beyond her ken. "Tranquil and timeless under its coat of snow, Paris was much as she had left it, much as she had surveyed it every day for three years," Zola writes in conclusion. "Fraught with her past, with her loving and with Jeanne's dying, this regular companion maintained the impassivity of its giant

face. . . . Today she felt that she would never know what took place
behind it. . . . It unfolded, that's all; it was life."

The "sensual, wicked woman holding forth in a queenly voice" by
whom Hélène feels controlled resembles Phèdre, but this alien self
bears an even stronger resemblance to Emma Bovary, and Zola ad-
vertises the kinship. As Emma feeds her imagination on Sir Walter
Scott, so—despite herself—does Hélène Grandjean: ·

> Ivanhoe had bored her at first. Then something very peculiar hap-
> pened. It moved her, and, letting it slip from time to time as her eyes
> traveled from the book to the broad horizon, she finished it. . . . How
> these novels lied! She was quite right to eschew them. They were
> fables fit for numskulls with no clear sense of life. And yet it seduced
> her; she couldn't help musing about the knight Ivanhoe, so passion-
> ately loved by two women, Rebecca the beautiful Jewess and the
> noble Lady Rowena.

For both heroines, Paris looms larger than life. For both, the city,
which they see from afar, is inextricably bound up with the idea of
something limitless, with a dream of self-aggrandizement, with intimations of sexual rapture, with the ocean, with fear of death by drowning or falling. Of Emma Bovary, Flaubert wrote that "Paris, vaster than
the ocean, glittered before [her] eyes in a rosy light. The teeming life
of the tumultuous city was divided into parts, however, separated into
distinct scenes. She distinguished only two or three which overshadowed the others." And Zola followed suit in his description of Hélène
watching day break:

> On the Right Bank, the Tuileries district wore the pale pink of a
> flesh-colored garment, while toward Montmartre there appeared a
> glow of live embers, of crimson fired in gold. Very far away brick-red
> turned slate-gray over working-class neighborhoods. Like those sea
> bottoms which the eye can only divine, with their terrifying forests
> of long grass, their predatory swarms, their half-glimpsed monsters,
> the shivering and elusive city was not yet plainly visible. But it be-
> came so as the waters continued to recede. Soon they were nothing
> more than sheets of fine muslin; and one after another the sheets
> evaporated, Paris's image became clearer and emerged from dream.
> . . . Along the crest of hills, roofs by the score sprang into view. Many
> more billowed behind folds of terrain, invisible yet felt. It was the
> open sea in all its breadth and profundity.

Hélène is at first as attentive to her daughter as Emma is neglectful of hers, but then, on doomsday, Hélène forgets her maternal vocation, entering a narcissistic never-never world that effaces beloved images. The flat in which she couples with Henri derives, furniture and all, from the hotel room in which Emma offers herself to Léon. "[She and Henri] had both lost consciousness of time and place," writes Zola. "Round about them stretched a desert; not a sound, not a human voice, the impression of a dark, storm-swept sea. They were outside the world, a thousand leagues from landfall. And this obliviousness to all previous attachments was so extreme that they felt they had just been born and would die anon, in the throes of love." While Rougons and Macquarts who enjoy false reprieves from history are not uncommon, Hélène stands somewhat apart. Born possessed, like everyone else in the ghost-ridden saga, she is condemned to reenact, not an ancestral scenario, but, with variations, the misadventure of her literary antecedent.

As a "sensual, wicked woman" possesses Hélène, so Hélène possesses her daughter whose soul is preternaturally attuned to hers. Neither can keep secrets from the other, and when mother vibrates, daughter chimes. "As soon as Hélène and Henri drew close or looked at each other, Jeanne would begin to tremble," writes Zola. "Her tender flesh, her poor little innocent, sick being, had a nervous constitution of such sensitivity that she could guess they were smiling at each other behind her back." The daughter's effort to locate her mother in the view of Paris outside her window reinforces this mystical symbiosis. After stating that the city seemed too vast for finding anyone, Zola describes—vaguely, as in a dream—what may be construed as the fear and bewilderment of a child watching adults copulate. "She couldn't see anything very definite, but whatever it was, it moved and was ugly—little girls had no business looking. All manner of vague suppositions, which made her want to cry, which disturbed her in her childish ignorance." Does she see them, or does she not? Her eyes, which observe from without, may deceive, but the witness that speaks to her from within is infallible:

> At the window Jeanne coughed violently, but self-neglect was vengeance and she would have liked to catch cold. Her chest . . . hurt more and more. . . . She trembled with fear and dared no longer turn around, as the idea of looking once more at the [vacant] room made her blanch. When one is little, one has no strength. What then was this new malady, the onset of which brought shame and bitter sweetness? . . . Awaiting the shivers, her limbs stiffened in revolt. And from the bottom of her being, from her pubescent sex, came a sharp pain, as of a blow dealt by someone far away. She then uttered a

stifled cry: "Mama! Mama!," which might have been an appeal for maternal help or an accusation hurled at the woman responsible for inflicting mortal pain upon her.

The girl "vicariously" deflowered by the man who penetrates Hélène evokes the superfluous male or latecomer in those nightmarish triangles through which Zola dramatized the theory of "impregnation," and, indeed, Jeanne seems less a daughter entering womanhood than a travestied son fearing emasculation as he defends the mother he can't possess against the father she can't resist. Like Jacques Berthier —that ghost who, having imprinted himself forever upon Madeleine Férat, reclaims her from Guillaume de Viargue—Henri Deberle is, after all, a paternal figure. Where Jacques substitutes for Viargue *père*, Henri fills in for Grandjean. Where Jacques rises from the deep to thwart Guillaume, Henri brings Jeanne back from beyond only to kill her at puberty.[11]

The autobiographical details in which *Une Page d'amour* abounds— Grandjean dies as François Zola died, for example—confirms one's impression that this novel reveals more of Zola himself than any memoir could have done, that it throws light on a sensibility still haunted by childhood, that behind Jeanne and Hélène stand Emile and Emilie. From Zola's own life comes not only the girl's medical history but her emotional substance. "*Une Page d'amour,* which seems an adventitious work, is perhaps the writer's most personal novel," observes Colette Becker, "for besides containing personal memories . . . it is fraught with [Zola's] temperamental traits, his regrets, his secret desires." Did those regrets embrace conjugal life? Mindful of what the future held in store, Professor Becker notes a parallel between Zola leaving Paris for L'Estaque with the chronically unwell Alexandrine and Hélène departing for Marseille on the arms of a husband good as gold but unlikely ever to make her womb swell or her heart sing.

Between December 11, 1877, and April 4, 1878, the novel was serialized by *Le Bien public,* which in announcing publication had seen fit to promise subscribers that this book differed radically from *L'Assommoir,* that it would "address, above all, the sensibility of women readers" and do no harm when "left unguarded on the family table." Moreover, the editor-in-chief, Yves Guyot, asked Zola for a Rougon-Macquart family tree, as if to enhance the respectability of *Une Page*

---

[11]In *Zola et les mythes,* Jean Borie writes, apropos Jeanne's being raped when Dr. Deberle enters Hélène, that "the responsibility for incest is thus ingeniously fobbed off onto the parents."

d'amour, or magnify its scope, with roots and branches. Wrote Zola in a letter Guyot featured prominently,

> You argue that this tree will help guide readers through *Une Page d'amour.* . . . Until now I have hesitated for fear of taking the bloom off novels not yet written. But there are eight in print, I consider my enterprise far enough along, and I am impelled by other reasons to satisfy your request.

The family tree would prove that his Rougon-Macquart novels were not improvisations calculated to exploit some fad or create a stir:

> There are those who say that I hawk sensational stuff, that I profit from scandal, that I launch books at opportune moments. I have been accused of proceeding helter-skelter, of obeying nothing except the need for commotion, of completely lacking a general scheme. I've let people natter on, but the truth is that the enclosed plan was drafted ten years ago, before I had written a single line of *Les Rougon-Macquart,* and all who have read the first novel, *La Fortune des Rougon,* will regard what I say as self-evident. . . . Consider that within an exiguous time frame of eighteen years I resolved to crowd four generations.

Every novel written since 1868 had been foreseen, he declared (not altogether truthfully). "Since 1868 I have settled the territory to which I laid claim; the genealogical tree marks its general contours for me and prevents me from going off course. I must follow it strictly; it is at once my staff and my compass." External events did not dictate the form or personality of his hermetic offspring. "Each novel arrives at the preordained moment. The final conclusions are ready. I shall add that in my mind the attached chart was drawn up by Pascal Rougon, a physician, a family member, and that it will be incorporated into the last novel, where this physician occupies center stage; he will then elucidate it and complete it with learned commentary."

Zola thus girded himself against an attack that failed to materialize when bound-book copies of *Une Page d'amour* appeared in April 1878. Reviewers, cheered by the genteel decor, lavished praise upon it, and after fifteen months it was selling out its thirty-first printing.[12] "I assuredly do not like everything M. Zola writes: certain conceptions and partis pris unnerve me," Louis Boussès de Fourcaud declared in an article featured on the front page of *Le Gaulois,* where Rougon-Macquart novels had often been roughed up. "But everywhere mani-

---

[12]The interior ministry helped out by giving Hachette permission to sell the novel, along with *L'Assommoir,* in railroad station bookstores.

fest are the logic of his talent, the equilibrium of his design, the somewhat lofty stance of his personality. M. Zola is a very gentle poet wrestling with demons. . . . One feels the energy he has expended to portray us as we are in order that we may become what we should be." What was to become of the "flaccid, neurotic" society Zola described? he asked. "Whither France? Which barbarians will inject us with new blood?"

Among friends Zola received a variety of compliments. Mallarmé, who couldn't wait until the Thursday soirée on the rue de Bourgogne, wrote to say that he admired *Une Page d'amour* even more than the previous Rougon-Macquart novels. Zola, he thought, had succeeded in fabricating

> not just something magnificent—you've done that routinely—but a paradigm, as you yourself would define it, of the modern literary work: for some a long poem, for others a novel faithfully portraying life today. With what art you convey the impression that your milieu lies there before us, homogeneous and complete. . . . I admire very much your backgrounds, Paris and its sky, which alternate with the story, above all because . . . they prevent any inner wandering. Everything comes from you, horizons included, and when I the reader leave the page to muse, you, bold tyrant that you are, hang a drop curtain behind my reverie.

For Flaubert, who would have been puzzled by Mallarmé's comment, *Une Page d'amour* was not at all the kind of work that bullied readers into self-effacement. It aroused him, and made him envious. "*Mon bon,*" he wrote,

> I finished the volume on Monday evening. Rest assured that it doesn't mar the collection. I don't understand your doubts about its worth. But if I were a mother, I wouldn't recommend it to my daughter!!! Despite my advanced age, the novel disturbed and *excited* me. One desires Hélène excessively and understands your doctor very well. The double scene of the rendezvous is *sublime.* I insist upon that word. The little girl's character very true, very new. Her burial marvelous. The narrative carried me along, I read it all in one sitting.
>
> Now here are my reservations. Too many descriptions of Paris and Hélène's maid's country bumpkin boyfriend isn't very amusing. Among the secondary characters, Matignon [sic] is the best in my opinion. His chagrin when Juliette denigrates his pied-à-terre is delicious and unexpected.
>
> Mary's month, the children's ball, Jeanne's vigil all remain lodged in one's head. What else? I don't know. I'm going to reread it. I'd be astonished if it didn't make a *great hit with women.* Several times, while reading it, I stopped to envy you and reflect sadly on my own

novel—my pedantic novel! which will not entertain as yours does.
You're very much a male, but that's not news to me. Until Sunday.

Zola's heroine also appealed to Maupassant, who sent a note of congratulations on official stationery from his desk at the naval and colonial ministry. "I intended to go see you this evening with other members of the Half-Dozen," he explained, "but as that will be impossible, I don't wish to delay thanking you and voicing my admiration for *Une Page d'amour.*" It was, in his opinion, Zola's most stylistically felicitous novel, if not the most "colorful."

As for Edmond de Goncourt, who offered no praise, it had become obvious to him that unless something catastrophic befell Zola, every year another installment of *Les Rougon-Macquart* would interpose itself between him and glory, obscuring his own latest work like a dark cloud. The prospect made him ill. "I have never met anyone harder to please, less satisfied by the magnitude of his fortune than the chap named Zola," he noted in his journal on March 30, 1878.

> Charpentier told me that Zola had groused, whined, grumbled all through dinner after learning that *Une Page d'amour* would be published in an edition of 15,000. Meanwhile, Regamey's drawing of the Rougon genealogical tree arrived. The latter had been a formidable task, it seems, and Zola hadn't made it any easier. He complained about everything, about one branch being higher than another and repeatedly said, in an almost tearful voice, that no one ever did what he wanted.

Several weeks later, on April 23, when *Une Page d'amour* was quite clearly bound for greater success than Zola had anticipated, Goncourt consoled himself by declaring in his journal: "The critics may say whatever they like about Zola, they will never be able to prevent us, my brother and me, from being the two Saints John the Baptist of modern neurasthenia."

The great success of *L'Assommoir* enabled Zola to divorce himself from *Le Sémaphore de Marseille* in May 1877, after writing nearly seventeen hundred articles for Barlatier's paper. But his journalistic production did not otherwise slacken, not right away. Until 1880 he composed a long essay every month for *The European Herald* in spite of quarrels with Stasiulevich over censorship. And he wrote weekly theater reviews—first for *Le Bien public*, where Yves Guyot ran them on page one, then for its successor, *Le Voltaire*—the most important of which were published by Charpentier in a collection entitled *Le Naturalisme au théâtre.*

Throughout his *Revues dramatiques*, Zola went on heaving brickbats at the "well-made play," and he lost no opportunity to link it in derision to other sacrosanct institutions. "I remember my youth spent in a small town," he confided to his readers on October 22, 1877.

The theater gave three performances a week and I was smitten. I'd skip dinner so as to be first at the door, before the offices opened. There in that small auditorium the entire repertoire of the Gymnase and the Porte Saint-Martin paraded past me for five or six years. A deplorable education and even now I struggle with lessons it engraved upon my mind. Accursed little theater! I learned how a character must enter and exit. I learned about the symmetry of dramatic *coups*, the need for sympathetic and moral parts, the various ways of cheating truth with a gesture or a tirade. I mastered that intricate code, those strings and devices which have come to embody what our critical brotherhood calls, in absolutist language, "The Theater."

Hand in hand went theater and school, or a dramaturgy that led the spectator to mistake artifice for truth and a pedagogy that distinguished upper class from low by alienating the young from nature, by trussing their intellects, by having them speak foreign tongues: "I believe that a boy who has never stepped foot inside a playhouse stands closer to a masterpiece than one whose intelligence has received the stamp of many performances. This is how a theatrical convention establishes itself. It's another language, and we learn to speak it much the way small children in rich families learn to speak English or German from their nannies." Like the classical curriculum, the playhouse supported a regime that sought to mold perception. At issue for Zola was not just theater but selfhood, and in this context bourgeois stagecraft played the part of the seducer "imprinting" some virgin, or of the despotic father emasculating his son. Novelists unruffled by a blank page lost countenance on "the Boulevard," where clichés killed. "One of my good friends, who has more than ten novels to his credit and swaggers through plots," he wrote,

told me recently that the theater made him tremble. . . . The problem lies in his dramatic education, which hinders and harries him as soon as he embarks upon a play. He sees the familiar ploys, he hears the hackneyed retorts, he has his head so stuffed with this cardboard world that he doesn't dare attempt to abolish it and be himself. The public his imagination conjures up—all eyes riveted to the stage on opening night—scares him silly and he begins, despite himself, to slide down the slippery slope into applauded triteness. He would have to forget everything.

Might this schizoid writer have been Zola himself, pugnacious in print but subject to stage fright in public?

His campaign for naturalism, which did not endear him to the all-powerful theater critic Francisque Sarcey, glorified manliness. Against a "decadent" theater that made much too much of "skillful workmanship" and much too little of "rough-edged genius," Zola hurled epithets such as "puerile," "infantile," "small." On the Boulevard, grown men and women attended puppet plays. "Once I said that our theater was dying of moral indigestion," he observed.

> So it is. Our plays are diminutive because they would rather be respectable than human. Compare Shakespeare's philosophical scope and the catechism which our most illustrious dramatic authors pride themselves in teaching the public. How petty these conflicts over dubious points of honor, how ludicrous that they should ring above the clamor of suffering humanity. . . . Is that where our energies lie? Does the labor of our great century reside in these juvenile imbroglios? They are said to elucidate moral problems, but no, they merely reflect the dulling of our manhood and a willingness to waste precious time on marionette shows.

As for art's moral responsibility, there were, he continued, two views—one virile and the other craven, one progressive and the other anachronistic, one shaped by a commitment to the sovereign virtue of truth-telling and the other by a belief in the sanctity of convention:

> When we write a novel in which we strive to be precise analysts, the result is furious indignation as people declare that we have recruited monsters from the gutter, that we have indulged a predilection for the deformed and the freakish. Well, our monsters are just men, very ordinary men, the kind of men we meet everywhere in life without taking offense. . . . What is readily accepted in the street and under one's roof becomes unadulterated smut as soon as it's printed. If we muss a woman's hair, she's a tramp; if we take the liberty of removing a gentleman's frock coat, he's a knave. The lightheartedness of existence, the humdrum stuff, the sanctioned promiscuities, the tolerated licenses of language and feeling—all these assume, between two covers, the appearance of slander.

His optimistic forecast was that time would favor naturalism. "The great task of our century belongs to us. [Readers and spectators] will gradually take our side as it is borne home upon them that this convoluted literature with its ready-made formulae has no substance. They will realize that true grandeur does not lie in moral harangues but in the very action of life. When one may venture to portray what is, then dreaming about what could be seems child's play; and I repeat, there's nothing vulgar or shameful about the real, for the real has begotten this world."

Would time alone consecrate the new aesthetic order? No, for people in general were inclined by nature to stay put, sink, or fall backward. That mission devolved upon genius, and genius did not suffer crowds gladly. "The theory that ascribes ultimate authority to public taste is ludicrous," Zola sneered.

It leads straight to the condemnation of originality and everything idiosyncratic. Does it not happen, for example, that a silly song will delight a literate public? People find it all quite fatuous, but thrown together in a hall they guffaw and applaud. Individually the spectator is sometimes an intelligent person, but spectators en masse are a herd which genius must guide, whip in hand. Let it be understood that nothing is less literary than a crowd. A crowd is a malleable organism with which a powerful hand does what it pleases.

It is not the public that must impose its taste on authors, he insisted, but authors who are responsible for directing the public. "In literature there can be no other sovereignty than that of genius. Here popular rule is a dangerous and imbecile notion. Only genius marches forward, and genius molds the intelligence of generations like putty."[13]

Undaunted by this implicit challenge, Zola wished ardently to prove that he had in him the stuff of a playwright, that he could hold live audiences spellbound, and an opportunity presented itself in 1876, when Francis Plunkett, who had rejected *Les Héritiers Rabourdin*, commissioned something for the Palais-Royal theater. "Seeking new authors in that lean year and not knowing at which doors to knock, Plunkett showed up one day and requested a comedy," wrote Alexis. "Zola, who had, on the contrary, been revolving ideas for a full-blown drama, hesitated. The fact that the play was accepted beforehand finally won him over. He decided to compose a simple farce in accordance with his belief that no genre is inferior to any other and that a powerful dramatic imagination should be able to make theater of anything."

Plunkett must not have been hugely optimistic, but his expectations,

[13]One is reminded of the letter he wrote to Cézanne at age twenty, describing his adolescent struggle for self-esteem: "Derision! I heard [the crowd] around me murmur odious surnames. I saw it step back and point at me. I bowed my head and wondered what crime I had committed. But when I got to know the world better . . . I recognized myself as a giant among dwarfs. . . . Pride and scorn became my gods. I could have exonerated myself, but I chose not to stoop so low. Instead, I conceived another scheme, which was to crush them with my superiority."

such as they were, came to grief on *Le Bouton de rose* (*Rosebud*), an insipid play about men being cuckolded in a provincial establishment whose name, the Great Stag Hotel, conveys some idea of its humor. "Yesterday I received your manuscript," he wrote from Monaco in February 1877. "I read it straightway and reread it this morning. Let me give you my frank impression. The play possesses neither the bold form I anticipated nor the desired originality. It's cast in the mold of all our vaudevilles. With your name the public will expect and want something more. . . . When I return to Paris we must meet and talk seriously about *Le Bouton de rose*." Zola responded by explaining that *Le Bouton de rose* was designed to be conventional entertainment. Originality won no prizes on the Boulevard, theatergoers were repelled by anything strongly idiosyncratic, and he wanted a success, even if it tarnished his literary reputation, rather than another honorable fiasco:

> My name, my place, my reputation as a novelist are irrelevant. What I am is an apprentice who wishes to launch something with you, to observe the stage from close up and risk his all at some later date.

He would not, he vowed in the most cordial terms, put any pressure on Plunkett. "I just want this business settled quickly one way or another. I'm stubborn, as you know. If I must consign *Le Bouton de rose* to a bottom drawer, I'll start work the next day on a drama and employ the same strategy. The play would be modeled along conventional lines."

Gentlemanliness did not prevail, for by late May, when he set up at L'Estaque, Zola had bullied Plunkett into assigning roles and scheduling rehearsals. Then began a sequence of events rather more humorous than the comedy itself. The great sensation made by *L'Assommoir* induced Plunkett to court Zola assiduously, but as his reservations about *Le Bouton* diminished, Zola's doubts gathered strength. In a letter written on December 2 to Léon Dormeuil, who ran the Palais-Royal theater along with Plunkett, Zola directed against his own work, almost verbatim, Plunkett's critique of the previous winter. "Considered in light of my theater criticism, the play is rather commonplace, meek, devoid of that originality the public will demand, no doubt. We would be well advised to store it in a cardboard box until some more auspicious day dawns. I would like to work for you." Several weeks earlier, on October 12, he had confessed to Flaubert that he was disposed to keep *Le Bouton* under wraps, as "the thing just doesn't seem much good."

Vanity or wishful thinking overcame lucid judgment, and on May 6, 1878, when the farce opened at the Palais-Royal, Zola paid for his self-deception with yet another fiasco. Mallarmé assured him that a malicious claque had roused spectators against the play, but the public, which hooted Zola off the stage after the premiere performance, would appear to have needed no such urging. In *Le Temps*, Francisque Sarcey decreed that the play had fallen on the first night and that the fall was irremediable. It had left the audience unamused, he wrote, particularly where regimental officers were shown singing ribald songs. "He might have gotten away with such antics if there was anything funny about them, but no, it seems that they were more in the nature of a political statement or a dare. At this moment, one may broach things military on a theater stage only with extreme caution. Ascribing lewdness to the army goes against public sentiment."

A banquet for thirty at one of Paris's gastronomic temples, the Grand Véfour, which faces the Palais-Royal theater, turned out to be a wake rather than a celebratory occasion—or so one gathers from the unsympathetic Edmond de Goncourt, who joined Flaubert, Manet, Guillemet, the Daudets, the Charpentiers, Marius Roux, and Zola's protégés. "Disastrous, *Le Bouton de rose*," he noted in his journal on May 6.

> The public, which sat still during the first act, got mad during the second and hooted the third, barely managing to let the play finish. In truth, one can't blame people, for it's a poor specimen of Palais-Royal theater, without originality, without *humor*, without wit, even without the coarse jocularity of a farce. I really don't understand how a chap who aspires to be the leader of a literary school could have— and financial need did not prod him—aired something so ordinary, something indistinguishable from the commonest kind of vaudevillian fare. No, he doesn't really take pride in his handiwork, my friend Zola, and he doesn't understand that the part he wishes to play in letters requires an oeuvre every line of which speaks art.
>
> Nothing as lamentable as the fall of a friend whom you can't sincerely defend or support. I don't wish to give the impression of abandoning him, so I let him take me over to the Véfour. Completely distraught, the poor man relies upon his wife to order the meal. Absent, estranged from our chatter, his brow quite pale, bent over his plate, he holds a knife in his fist with the blade pointed upward and turns it mechanically. On occasion a phrase addressed to no one escapes his lips. He says: "No, it doesn't matter to me, but it does change my entire work schedule. . . . I shall be obliged to do *Nana*. . . . In the end it leaves one with a terrible taste, unsuccesses in the theater. . . . *La Curée* shall wait, I'm going to write fiction . . ." And he continues all the while to turn his knife. The wife, less disconsolate, eats, drinks, and betrays her irritation in joking remarks of a bitter kind made to her husband's acolytes, to poor Alexis for example, whom she calls her whipping boy even as she gives him playful taps.

Exaggerating or relishing the lugubriousness of it all, no doubt, he wrote that there had been long silences interrupted by halfhearted words of support, by the "squeals of Manet's cracked voice" and Alexandrine's expostulations about cuts Zola ought to have made. "At last we release the tired author, who says to Madame Charpentier descending the staircase in front of him with her gown trailing behind her: 'Ah! take care, I don't have strong legs this evening.' He adds: 'We, who are a nervous breed . . .' and never finishes his sentence."

Determined to set the record straight, or to coach posterity to interpret even his boners in the most favorable light, Zola portrayed *Le Bouton de rose*, when it closed after seven performances, as an irreverent imp thrashed by humorless chauvinists, a simple child martyred for not being ambitious enough, or an ingenue victimized by those who bore a grudge against its author. The play did not stir in him any "wildly paternal affection," he confessed in *Le Bien public*. He had hoped that audiences would understand *Le Bouton* to be a form of recreation, a game played between two important tasks. So why such abuse? he asked. Because his enemies seized this pretext to humble him, he answered, and any pretext would have served. "Not with impunity does one judge other people's plays for two years, saying what one thinks of the great and the small. The day one submits one's own work, reprisals will occur. I should think that insulted writers of vaudevilles and exasperated dramatists exclaimed: 'At last we have rope to hang him.' And the public undoubtedly shared their enthusiasm for a lynching party. . . . On May 6, I had to expiate the forty-two printings of *L'Assommoir* and the twenty of *Une Page d'amour*. A novelist messing in theater—a novelist, moreover, whose work sells so remarkably well—threatened the natural order of things."

But events of the day mollified this disappointment. In May, when tourists converged on France for a Universal Exposition that transformed western Paris into one large fairground, with exotic pavilions sprouting over both banks like mushrooms, Zola joined the crowd as a pleasure seeker and art critic.[14] Three months later he began work on *Nana*, a novel destined to bring him even greater notoriety than *L'Assommoir*. And that summer, which was the summer after Alexandrine's long convalescence at L'Estaque, he purchased a house some twenty miles downstream from Paris, just beyond the Seine's great loop around Saint-Germain-en-Laye, in the lovely riverine village of Médan.

[14]For the July 1878 issue of *The European Herald* he wrote a Paris letter about French paintings hung at the Exposition. After praising Courbet, Corot, and Daubigny for work that had survived them, he described the canvases of two prominent academicians, Cabanel and Gérôme, whose work had predeceased them. He then offered compliments to the Impressionist group, few of whom were represented.

XVII

❦

A VERDANT PARADISE AND
A BLOND HORIZONTAL

THE RUE DE BOULOGNE, where Zola and Alexandrine lived until 1889, bespoke their newfound prosperity. Angling up Montmartre from the rue Blanche, this street was an extension of the quiet, green neighborhood that had become known as "New Athens" after 1820, when famous artists and actors flocked to it. The great tragedian Talma, Mlle Mars of the Comédie-Française, Horace Vernet, and Napoleon's favorite portraitist, Jean-Baptiste Isabey, had all resided there. So, too, had the painter Ary Scheffer, whose villa on the rue Chaptal now accommodated Ernest Renan. Hector Berlioz had spent his last years nearby, on the rue de Calais. And two blocks north, in a town house owned by Louis and Pauline Viardot at 48, rue de Douai, Turgenev occupied a cluttered flat from which he regularly limped downstairs with bags packed for Russia or, on Thursday evenings, to enjoy musicales that attracted Gounod and Saint-Saëns, Jules Simon and George Sand.

Alexandrine may have nursed grievances against her husband, but an unwillingness to help her feather their nest was assuredly not one of them. Feathering the nest brought them closer together, and Zola's correspondence reveals as clearly as the Rougon-Macquart novels do his penchant for interior decoration. "Along with embroidery, see if you can find two central images for the valences: Gothic motifs against a gold background, which would complement the saints and have an elongated form—say, twenty-five centimeters by thirty-five," he instructed her from L'Estaque on September 13, 1877, in reference to a sixteenth-century-style canopied bed. "I know that they will be difficult to unearth. One might also put roundels of saints on all four sides of the baldachin, and since we already possess two, we shall need only two more. . . . I say this so that you may avoid a second shopping expedition. Don't run yourself ragged, however. If you can't find anything, why, we'll just search hard upon our return!" Search they did. The success of *Les Rougon-Macquart* profited curio shops up and down the rue de Rennes, and antique dealers, especially those catering to the bourgeois taste for medieval bric-a-brac, found an avid client in Zola, who opened accounts everywhere.

After the baldachin bed came altar frontals, ponderous oak credenzas, stained-glass windows, tapestries that featured hagiographical scenes. Bidding for ecclesiastical relics while anathematizing the Church, Zola valued his paraphernalia as other nineteenth-century bourgeois took pride in overstuffed museums and in the gallimaufry of Universal Expositions. For the self-made provincial whose ticket to Paris had been bought twenty years earlier with pawned furniture, collecting antiques was exorcising the specter of indigence. Paul Alexis knew this very well, and he observed it shrewdly:

> Balzac says somewhere that parvenus always re-create the salon they coveted when young and poor. Well, his rule applies here, for the romantic of yesteryear survives in the decor of our present-day naturalist. Although he argues that a luxurious modern household would cost more than he can afford, thrift serves as a pretext . . . In his flat on the rue de Boulogne . . . Zola has been able to fulfill old dreams. Wherever one turns, one's eye is greeted by stained-glass windows, by a Henri II bed, by Italian and Dutch furniture, by Aubusson antiques, dented pewter, 1830-style casseroles! When poor Flaubert paid a visit, these strange and sumptuous heirlooms sent his old romantic heart into raptures. One evening, in the bedroom, I heard him say admiringly: "I've always dreamt of sleeping under such a canopy . . . This is the bedchamber of Saint-Julien l'Hospitalier!"

In April 1878, for Zola's housewarming, his mentors, disciples, and publisher dined exquisitely on barded hazel hen. Only seven years had passed since Zola had written from Bordeaux urging Alexis to investigate refugees lodged at 14, rue de la Condamine and to save, if possible, his crockery and furniture.[1]

[1]The passion of the bourgeois for his household belongings—and his fear that the rabble might take them away—was the theme of a fascinating article written by the vicomte de Launey and published by *La Presse* on September 3, 1848, soon after the bloody revolution.

"Do you think, oh working class, that the proud bourgeois you hate so much has more than you?" asked the supercilious aristocrat. "He owns neither castle nor palace, neither woods nor pastures, but lives in a small, gloomy apartment

What Zola desired even more than a proper bourgeois flat, however, was a rural hideaway within easy reach of Paris—long railroad journeys to various coasts having become onerous—and the quest for one began in earnest soon after his six-month sojourn at L'Estaque. It led him northwest toward Verneuil, where he found himself bewitched by the landscape of cows grazing on loamy meadows, of poplar wind-breaks, of apple trees planted in quincunx, of enormous willows weeping into the Seine, of the Seine itself flowing around islets overgrown with vegetation. Except for the occasional chug of passenger trains and the muffled drone of propeller-driven barges, absolute calm enveloped this riverine district. A shaded main road ran cross-country, undulating between velvety-green slopes like a lane in some English park. "Paris seemed a hundred leagues away," declared Alexis. "Peasants were the sole inhabitants, and in the entire commune only one Parisian bourgeois had ever built a house." Soon there would be two.

A "For Sale" sign stopped Zola at Médan, whose few inhabitants nestled among walnut and aspen trees on the steep, thickly wooded left bank of the Seine south of Verneuil. It advertised a stone lodge hidden from the village by a nave of trees that swept downhill across a railroad bridge. Nondescript though it was, it looked out over a field of hay beyond which gleamed the Seine, and this prospect, including a slender island called the Ile du Platais, sufficed to banish his misgivings. "I've bought a house, a rabbit hutch, between Poissy and Triel, in a charming nook beside the Seine, for nine thousand francs," he told Flaubert. "I tell you the price so that you won't be too respectful. Literature has paid for this modest sanctuary, whose virtue is that it lies far from every railroad station and doesn't have a single bourgeois

---

in what is called a tenement, that is, a beehive made of bricks and mortar. In this he enjoys not one of the pleasures of a life of ease; he lacks space and light, a fine view, and fresh air, rest and privacy and silence. He lives cheek by jowl with people he doesn't know. . . . The bourgeois in Paris has one real treasure, his furniture, and it is to defend this that he courageously risks death. And is it you, of all people, who want to attack him and carry off these precious possessions? Are we not right in saying that this fight is ridiculous and at the same time painful? To die for furniture—and what furniture! A worthless conglomeration of pieces without shape or form in which the bad taste of every age is brought together; furniture without value, style, or art, ugly to behold and uncomfortable to use, furniture that would make painters and even daubers swoon with horror. But the bourgeois who admires it has given everything to buy it and having acquired it with patience and sacrifice, will defend it with his last breath. Demand his life—but not his appalling alabaster clock, flanked by two equally frightful alabaster vases with paper rosebuds in them. . . . Do you really want to murder him for that wardrobe with its distorting mirror? For that ghastly mahogany canopy that hangs over his bed like a real stone of Sisyphus?" Edmond de Goncourt, who was in the vanguard of aesthetes infatuated with Japanese art and craft, expressed a similar view.

in the immediate neighborhood. I'm alone, quite alone. I haven't seen a human face in a month. The only problem is, settling in has been a terrible ordeal, whence my negligence." Windows rattling from the trains that sped past at regular intervals did not upset him.

After the Zola family took up residence at Médan in July 1878, his typically succinct letters evoke, *en passant*, the pleasures, the discomforts, the seasons and rituals of his new estate. "We are lodged here in a verdant paradise, and I've gotten back to work but am still wobbly from the move," he wrote to Marius Roux. "Everything will be all right in several days. The welcome mat is out and I regret very much that you can't bring your wife and baby." There were excursions around the islets all summer long thanks to Guy de Maupassant, who, having bought Zola a wherry at Bézons, delivered the boat (which was promptly baptized *Nana*) on July 14. And when fall approached, it found the country squire well prepared with shotgun at the ready. "Change of program," he alerted Hennique on September 1, a week before the latter was scheduled to descend upon him for Sunday lunch, together with Céard, Huysmans, and Maupassant. "Hunting season opens on the 8th, and since I hope to scatter some local wrens, you'd find me tuckered out. Furthermore, my wife had agreed to do a heavy chore that day. So please tell our friends that I shall expect them Sunday the 15th instead, if they can make it."

Guests, of whom there were not yet many, would normally catch a Sunday-morning train at the Saint-Lazare terminus, descend at Triel, and double back for two or three kilometers, following a hedgerow that separated the railroad track from the river path. But by late autumn this delightful itinerary had become, more often than not, impractical. "Repeat to our friends that I await them next Sunday," Zola urged Céard on November 17. "But I don't want you to get stuck in mud coming via Triel. If the sky is the least bit threatening, get off at Poissy, and contact M. Salles, who rents vehicles opposite the station. He'll bring you here in two coaches or in a small omnibus. Seriously, it's not worth running risks on roads as bad as these." A month later the mud lay frozen beneath snowdrifts, which provided natural insulation for the writer happily toiling over *Nana*. "I doubt I shall be back in Paris much before January 5," he informed Céard on December 14. "The stage adaptation of *L'Assommoir* will probably not open until the 10th or 15th, and I shall avail myself of this delay to avoid New Year's Eve, remaining here buried in snow. You can't imagine how beautiful and silent the countryside is since frigid weather has gripped it."

Art and nature were not the only passions to detain him in Médan from July until January. No sooner had he signed a deed than he laid plans for the enlargement of the "rabbit hutch." Before long, building became inseparable from writing. The two activities kept pace with each other, and as Zola added volumes to his saga, masons added rooms to his house. "Nothing new, I don't see anybody," he wrote to Flaubert on September 26, 1878. "The Charpentiers are the exception. They recently visited us and seemed quite cheerful. I've been working hard. For distraction I shall have some annexes built. I want a vast study with beds everywhere and a terrace perched over the landscape. There are times when I wish never to return to Paris, so peaceful is it in my retreat. . . . *Nana* satisfies me." A fortnight later, in mid-October, Goncourt received a similar message. "I'd been intending to offer you our modest hospitality when I succumbed to a construction craze. Everything's topsy-turvy, which means that I'm waist-deep in plaster and can't possibly entertain anyone. Next year, however, the 'château' will be fit for company. I doubt I'll return to Paris before late December, as I'm supervising workers. The architect is yours truly. I shall have a vast study. Moreover, three months of winter don't scare me. I've never worked better." Cold weather arrested neither the growth of *Nana* nor the metamorphosis of a drab little cottage into a large ill-proportioned villa. "As you've gone through something of the sort, you will sympathize when I tell you that after acquiring a hut, I decided to add a wing bigger than the original structure," he wrote in December to Turgenev, who had built his dacha on the grounds of Pauline Viardot's country house at Bougival. "That's what's detained me, and now I'm holed up avoiding New Year's Eve, which I loathe." Among the first objects purchased for Médan, and installed in the baronial study overlooking the hills of Chanteloup, was a Renaissance fireplace on whose huge stone hood Zola had *Nulla dies sine linea* emblazoned in gold letters, a motto that suited the landlord as well as the novelist. Like Napoleon III, of whom one contemporary said that he had sentenced himself to hard labor for life, Zola could not stop building.

Journalism helped to defray the cost of this suburban Arcadia, and week after week Zola dutifully produced installments of his *Revue dramatique et littéraire*. Paris beckoned, but the reviews were designed to spare him from visiting the capital more than once a month. "Artists are crossing a dry patch," he had written on August 13 in *Le Voltaire* (which had replaced *Le Bien public* earlier that summer).

> These Exposition days do them no good whatever. The kermis now open in Paris engrosses Europe and there's no curiosity left over for things literary and artistic. . . . Except *Les Fourchambault*, a worthy and relatively new work, theaters feature plays exhausted from having toured the provinces and traveled abroad. It's truly remarkable that posters advertise not a single thing written and performed for the occasion. . . . Fiction has fared no better. . . . The truth is that the

Exposition will enrich hotelkeepers and restaurant owners. We writers are not invited guests. The best we can do is seek shelter until it
all blows over.

The next month he declared that, despite some signs of life in the
theater world,

> it's still the slack season. All of September will belong to provincials
> and foreigners. Predictions are that tourists in their thousands will
> crowd the Exposition on account of schools letting out and tribunals
> closing.

When normalcy returned, other expedients were required to legitimize
or conceal his absence, and the one that worked best involved Henry
Céard, who would often attend plays with a press card from *Le Voltaire*, then dispatch elaborate notes, which Zola, comfortably ensconced at Médan, used as material for reviews. In January 1880, Zola's
surrogate spared him the trouble of seeing *Le Beau Solignac* by Jules
Claretie and William Busnach. For example: "My dear Zola, the glum
Mirabeau [also by Claretie] is a masterpiece compared to *Le Beau Solignac*," wrote Céard.

> The audience remained glacial during the five acts and fourteen tab-
> leaux as silly gimmicks from hackneyed melodramas succeeded one
> another relentlessly. Everything mediocre finds its niche here. . . .
> What's sublime is the escape of a man held in a prison fortress. Hav-
> ing dug through the wall of an underground passage, he falls plop
> into a marquise's fancy-dress ball. . . . Even friends of the author
> dared not defend these platitudes, and the public sat there mourn-
> fully until some rascal shouted from the cheap seats: "We've had it
> up to here with your mug" [*nous en avons soupé, de ta fiole*], which
> apparently means, in military slang, that the far limits of implausi-
> bility have been exceeded.

Zola thereupon felt free to declare, magnanimously, that belaboring
the work's unsuccess did not please him. "There would be no point,
for either literature's sake or the public's, in analyzing a melodrama
that exhibits under glass the archaic gimmicks of old Boulevard theater. *Le Beau Solignac* is a radical mistake, and I commiserate with the
authors, who are otherwise intelligent, gifted men," is how his review
put it.

Money was not the only reason for preserving, by subterfuge if need
be, a column in one of France's better left-wing dailies. Only when
naturalism established itself on the Paris stage would he forswear the-

ater criticism, he told his readers. And *La Revue dramatique et littér-aire*, although often rather more tolerant than one might expect of Boulevard froth (operettas, *féeries*, year-end revues, etc.), did indeed remain his bully pulpit. He inveighed against squeamish audiences as well as vapid dramas, believing that the former were sometimes worse than the latter. "I should like to excoriate, not Henri Becque's *La Navette*, which is well observed and witty," he wrote in the November 26 issue, "but the stupefying prudishness of certain people. . . . It's always the same story. If one tainted spectator sits in an audience, rest assured that he will be the first to denounce bold portrayals. There's nothing like knaves for peddling virtue cheap. They've sold themselves twenty times over, they've plunged their hands wrist-deep in muck, they've accumulated dishonor along with gray hairs, but utter a mot juste in their presence or show them a truthful image of vice and they will cry 'Fie!' " Several weeks later he waxed wroth over the triviality of *La Princesse Borowska*, a play by one Pierre Newski (who had pre-viously written *Les Danicheff* with Alexandre Dumas *fils*), and once again denounced the Dumas style that so pervaded French theater. "I'm convinced that seeing M. Dumas too often has ruined M. Pierre Newski. The banter of his famous collaborator dazzled him, he re-solved to imitate him, to devise his own witticisms instead of writing good plain prose." For once, a Boulevard audience showed good sense. "Now he's flopped, and it serves him right. As I detest persiflage, I can't say I'm sorry it's brought him bad luck. . . . Wordplay leaves me quite cold. I prefer a clearly expressed observation, a human document formulated in registry-clerk French. Nothing rings as hollow as the wit that's ascribed to all characters alike, regardless of age, temperament, or sex!"

These tirades annoyed people, but when a full-blown controversy developed over Zola's criticism in late 1878, the article that sparked it off was one written for *The European Herald* rather than for *Le Vol-taire* and originally published in Russian. Entitled "Contemporary Nov-elists," it surveyed French fiction from the viewpoint of the naturalist in whose judgment "les Cinq" constituted a royal fraternity. Zola char-acterized novel writing as a great nineteenth-century growth industry. Novels, he began,

> multiply with terrifying fecundity. During the winter season, from September to May, not a day passes that two or three novels don't sprout like mushrooms on French soil. And Paris is by no means alone; the hinterland produces its own large crop. Booksellers tell me that their display windows could not contain them all. I have no idea what becomes of them. Many don't sell and repose on shelves un-derground. I understand that certain publishing houses specialize in

buying remaindered copies by the pound and shipping them to America, to the Far East, to the wild backcountry of colonies, where they fetch a handsome price.

This superabundance of production stemmed, in his view, from the greater area of human concern encompassed by the novel. It no longer served as a mere amusement or recreation.

Now it has monopolized all space, absorbed all genres. . . . It is whatever one wishes it to be—a poem, a treatise on pathology, . . . a political weapon, a moral essay. One understands why most authors have adopted this eminently seductive form. . . . I dislike classifications, as they always do violence to people and things, but I shall rig some up in the interest of clarity. All-inclusiveness is not, I repeat, my goal. I shall discuss only those novelists whose talent or bent strikes me as characteristic of some tendency.

Having elsewhere dealt with Flaubert, Goncourt, and Daudet at length, here he paid homage to lesser novelists of the realist school, notably Edmond Duranty. He also commented, in a passage reminiscent of his vituperations against political melodrama, on the relationship between journalism and literature. The glut of news made possible by modern technology had engendered information addicts who disdained literature. "Times have changed," he wrote.

Journalism has acquired formidable scope due to the speed with which information now travels—due, above all, to the public's feverish insistence upon knowing everything right away. Curiosity no longer draws readers to the "ground floor" [the bottom half of page one, where serial installments were published] but to the newspaper columns themselves. Moreover, the inventors of the genre, the original raconteurs, have grown old, and the new novelists, those redoubtable naturalists who wander off on ten-page descriptions and analysis, won't tailor their work to fit the serial frame.

Zola followed with a parade of the halt and lame and misbegotten, summarily consigning fellow novelists to oblivion, species by species. "He is very clearly the breed of novelist people call literary, meaning that his work has stylistic pretensions, unlike the serial novel, which runs roughshod over grammar," he wrote of Louis Ulbach, for example. "There's nothing odder than M. Ulbach's style; it's soft, it trails gossamer threads, and it tells you at every turn how poetic it is. Comparisons abound, the most farfetched images jostle one another, sentences float like painted muslin wanting a solid, logical frame to drape itself on." Others fared no better, especially not the immensely successful Octave Feuillet. "I admit that I am not excessively fond of M. Octave Feuillet, whose work is watered-down Musset," he declared. "Where his elder argued the cause of passion, Feuillet litigates for duty and morality. Wags have mischievously described him as the Musset of families, which is quite accurate, though, to be sure, he has lately shown that . . . he can write books that mothers dare not leave in their daughters' hands. I have a settled idea about the so-called morality of upper-class novelists; jesuitical arrangement that it is, it poisons hearts and minds by hanging scrims over the real world and letting passion fester inside the language of propriety." No one went scot-free, not even Jules Claretie, with whom Zola had enjoyed cordial relations. "Written correctly and with genuine literary fastidiousness, his novels reveal, at times, an observant eye," is how he sized up the future academician and director of the Comédie-Française. "But those novels have followed one another in monotonous succession. They're all alike, each no better and no worse than its predecessor. And as the pile grows, it releases an intolerable stench of mediocrity. M. Jules Claretie goes on making promises he never keeps." A succession of well-known figures, all forgotten today, received similar treatment. Moving aggressively from one extreme to another, from lapidaries who adored the well-wrought phrase to *feuilletonistes* who excreted prose, Zola gave no quarter.

Word of this article reached Paris via Switzerland, where a Lausanne review, *La Bibliothèque universelle*, published an abridgment in French translation. *Le Figaro* picked it up and denounced the author of *Les Rougon-Macquart* for going abroad to settle domestic scores. Taken unawares, Zola reacted furiously. "Would you do me the kindness of publishing in *Le Figaro* the article on contemporary novelists which . . . elicited remarks from one of your contributors, who prudently identified himself only as 'a novelist'?" he asked its director, Hippolyte de Villemessant. "I have never worn disguises, I have always spoken forthrightly. I have been sending monthly articles to *The European Herald* since 1875, and the French originals will appear in book form when it suits me. An exception must be made of 'Contemporary Novelists,' as certain people cannot, I gather, wait any longer." Always spoiling for a fight, especially during the Christmas season, Villemessant obliged him, with immediate results. Céard informed Zola on December 23 that his affair had caused an enormous flap: "Everyone's passing around *Le Figaro*, and your article. People are riled, some because they're named by you, others because they're not. . . . Letters are expected to deluge the editor. Charpentier is jubilant. . . . The portraits of Claretie and of Ulbach are remarked above all others. Many find in them a contempt they themselves lacked the courage to express. Bravo! I admire the serenity with which you exasperate people, and make no mistake, exasperation is what's going around."[2]

One week later, after Zola had had time to catalogue the slurs hurled at him in various newspapers, his rebuttal appeared in *Le Voltaire*. "Why this diabolical furor?" he asked. "It's true that I spoke my mind about several novelists, but if anyone has a right to candor, it is I, who have always been treated roughly. I believe I observed proper literary etiquette, unlike those who have called me a thug, or worse." A writer such as he, who rejected the "banalities, accommodations, ready-made formulae" without which most newspaper critics could not survive, might expect to be the object of willful incomprehension, he conceded, but:

> You'd think that during the dozen years I've been plying this trade they would have understood what I'm about and grown used to it. Not in the least. Every time it's the same startled indignation, the same dismay, the same fit of wounded vanity. It occurred first in 1866 apropos the Salon, when people were ready to slit my throat. Next they were provoked by my theater chronicles in *Le Bien public* and went after me like baying hounds. Now it's the piece on novelists.

His grievance was that the Zola they hanged in effigy did not resemble him at all. "I am portrayed as egregiously vain. When I tell people the truth, it's because I'm bursting with pride, they say. I wish to sit triumphantly upon the corpses of all my massacred confreres. Well, balderdash. . . . I would like nothing more than to be convinced that I am the man of the century, for I should think that anyone whose ego had achieved such hypertrophy would enjoy perfect peace. . . . It is my misfortune, alas, that I still weep tears of rage over my manuscripts, I call myself an idiot twenty times a morning, I never launch a book without believing it to be much inferior to its predecessors." Were he a skillful opportunist, as Claretie (among others) declared, would truth-telling be his stock-in-trade? "Do shrewd men ever risk their all in the daredevil exercise of candor? Look at those who win rewards and honors and you will understand that I have given up everything."

Zola may indeed have disqualified himself from government recognition, but not without wishing that he could at once speak his mind and still garner awards bestowed upon the tactful. Some months earlier, for example, Flaubert had urged the minister of public instruction,

---

[2]On December 23, Zola wrote to Charpentier, in jest: "Well, my good fellow, what will you give me for my 'commercial publicity,' as Claretie puts it? You didn't expect the pretty little bombshell that's just burst, any more than I did. No matter, I want 10,000 francs. That's what your rival publisher, Dentu, claims it's worth. And if you don't pay me, I'll enter his employ."

Agénor Bardoux, to name Zola a *chevalier* of the Legion of Honor. Bardoux agreed, whereupon newspapers rumored that the nomination would take place in August. Great was Zola's distress when in August his name did not figure on the list. "You know that your friend Bardoux has just played me a dirty trick," he protested to Flaubert. "After shouting for five months in every quarter that he planned to decorate me, he replaced me at the last minute with Ferdinand Fabre, so that here I stand, a perpetual candidate for a decoration I didn't solicit and which means as much to me as a rose to a donkey." Understandably enough, he hated having a decoration offered, bruited in the newspapers, then withdrawn at the last minute. "It should have been so easy to leave me alone in my corner and not cast me as a gent of questionable talent who sits around waiting in vain for a piece of red ribbon." But the matter did not end there, for Zola, most undonkey-like, wanted this special rose. Heeding Flaubert's advice, he arranged an interview with Bardoux and on September 19 informed Flaubert from Médan that the minister "was very nice. My absolute conviction remains, however, that he will never keep the promise he made to you. . . . I write to you out of a need to think things through. But if, when you see him again, he brings up this business, say that I was very happy with the way he received me, and pretend to count on all the promises he makes. A good lesson for my pride in all this."

Some weeks later, Flaubert assured Zola that Bardoux had slated him for New Year's honors, to which Zola responded by saying that "I love you but must, with your leave, disbelieve Bardoux until proven wrong." Zola's skepticism was more appropriate than Flaubert's credulity, as it turned out. Whether Bardoux never intended to honor him or, intending to, changed his mind when the article on contemporary novelists caused an uproar (among writers many of whom wore red ribbons in their lapels), Zola found himself passed over on New Year's Day 1879 and waited another nine years before receiving that half-coveted, half-despised knighthood. "Ah! if good old Parisians only knew how tranquil I am here, in the snow!" he wrote to Charpentier from Médan. "*Nana* is proceeding very well. *Nana* will avenge us."

The history of *Nana* goes back to 1869, when, in his original plan for the fictional saga that became known as *Les Rougon-Macquart*, Zola had envisaged

> a novel whose setting is the boudoir world and whose heroine is Louise Duval, the daughter of my working-class family. Just as the offspring of the Goiraud [Rougon], people mired in hedonistic pleasure, is a parasite, so the offspring of the Bergasse [Macquart], people gone rotten from the vices of poverty, is a creature noxious to society.

Besides hereditary effects, there is in both cases the fatal influence exercised by the contemporary milieu. Louise is a harlot extraordinaire. Draw the world in which these high-flyers live. Poignant drama about the appetite for luxury and facile pleasures ruining a woman's existence.

Courtesans who had regaled café society during the Second Empire lost nothing of their glitter after the disastrous French defeat at Sedan, and Zola devoted newspaper articles to them, linking the demimonde or *monde galant* with the official world, and Bonapartism with a penchant for erotic self-degradation. "Under the Empire, playboys obtained prefectures in the boudoirs of certain ladies, and a dance hall, the Bal Mabille, supplied ministerial bureaus with copy clerks," he wrote in *La Cloche* on July 14, 1872.

The shadiest characters got the most coveted appointments, but unless one had good looks, nice clothes, white flesh, pink lips, and a diploma from the school of vice, one didn't rate even a humble job. When a nation stands ankle-deep in slime, it decays. Disease eats away, rises inexorably, reaches the heart. . . . We must be sure not to let the good old days return and to sequester at Charenton the rakes of yesteryear. Senators who crawl on all fours playing doggy to some harlot[3] and septuagenarian magistrates who let their mistresses whip them don't have brains enough for the Republic.

The image of an aristocrat crawling before a harlot was squirreled away for future use. So, too, was the picture of titled gentlemen accompanied by titled ladies watching an English stallion defeat a French thoroughbred at Longchamp's racetrack and later slumming it at the Bal Mabille on the avenue des Veuves. "The ladies' grandstand is full," reported Zola, who in due course amalgamated the worship of equines and the idolization of trollops.

Aristocratic names, all that's beautiful and elegant in Paris are there. Squeamish women who swoon at the mere idea of seeing a chicken bleed come with the unavowable hope that an accident will occur, that a horse will break loose and stove in his jockey's rib cage. The sun burns white hands, the rain soaks flounced skirts. It's exquisite. The ladies smile divinely, survey the landscape through lorgnettes as if it were the stage set for a comic opera. Some even look at the horses. Meanwhile, carriages crush one another. The crowd flows down every path in the Bois de Boulogne, one hundred thousand curiosity seekers standing on tiptoe to see something and finally

[3]Like old Antonio in Thomas Otway's play *Venice Preserved*, which Zola knew of from a description in Taine. It's doubtful that he read it himself.

glimpsing, in a cloud of dust, four or five red, yellow, or blue splotches. These are the jockeys. The crowd understands nothing, but is nonetheless stirred.

After dark, pandemonium reigned at Mabille, he wrote, conjuring up the vision of a decadent empire, a late-Roman pornocracy. "Victors and vanquished celebrated this equine high holy day in the painted tinplate boudoirs of whoredom. At dinner, they wax patriotic—marquises, counts, plain millionaires unable to hold their liquor. They throw their horses at one another, shouting 'Long live France! Long live England!,' and engage in fisticuffs. It's the beginning of our revenge."[4]

By August 1877, when Zola promised Marguerite Charpentier that the licentious masterpiece he hadn't yet begun would, commercially speaking, atone for the sedate novel he hadn't yet finished ("My dream is of an extraordinary *Nana*," as he put it), there were marvelous scenes in his mind ready to be plotted. Not until 1878, however, did he open a fresh notebook and, in his obsessive way, embark upon an investigation of Paris's demimonde. Friends who had some acquaintance with the latter found themselves quizzed at length. During the few months that the gestation of *Nana* lasted, every conversation turned to women. "[Zola made us] summon forth memories," wrote Paul Alexis. "One of us gave him all the details he needed for his description of the famous lesbian restaurant on the rue des Martyrs where women customers greeted the proprietress by 'kissing her full on the mouth.' Another told him about the party of tipsy young gentlemen in formal attire, whom nobody knew, crashing a harlots' supper at 5 a.m. Yet another provided the anecdote about bottles of champagne being poured into the piano. Zola listened to everything, noted everything, digested everything. However shopworn, the image of a bee confecting its honey from the nectar of various flowers applies; what we brought him, and what he himself gathered on all sides, were indeed flowers of vice." Among Zola's younger friends, Huysmans never strayed beyond his familiar Latin Quarter brothels, but Henry Céard preferred upper-class venery and for Zola's sake recorded the antics of a histrionic courtesan named Lucy Lévy.[5] Even more helpful was

---

[4]From 1871 to 1914, "revenge," or *revanche*, meant only one thing, and here Zola alludes to it sardonically: revenge against Germany for the defeat inflicted upon France in 1870–71.

[5]Not to say that Céard—a man of many parts—disdained the *bas-fonds*. To help Zola portray the character named Satin, he wrote, on November 12, 1879:

In real life, many prostitutes of Satin's ilk, after growing weary of the sidewalk and finding a lover to finance them, open houses of assignation. This often happens on the rue Saint-Honoré, the rue du Château-d'Eau, and the passage Jarry, formerly passage Neveux, near the Strasbourg railway station. The women

Flaubert's industrialist friend Edmond Laporte, who knew every nook and cranny of the Boulevard. What Denis Poulet had done for *L'Assommoir*, Laporte did for *Nana*. The dossier shows that he plied Zola with minutiae about Second Empire "horizontals," describing their origins, their habits, their amusements, their typical day, their town houses, their views of men, their slang, their clientele. One page reads:

> She wants to ride horseback like Cora Pearl. Gets up at 10, 11 o'clock. Takes a bath in her room. The hairdresser arrives, cleans and knots her hair. She breakfasts (noon) with mother and a poverty-stricken old female friend. Spirited game of bezique until 2 o'clock. At her toilette from 2 to 3, slips on a dressing gown and receives from 4 to 6, or goes for a ride in the Bois de Boulogne. At 7 o'clock the hairdresser, afterward a grand sortie to the theater or restaurant. Returns with her lover, talks until 1 a.m. Goes to bed at around 2:30.
>
> Those who take riding lessons in the morning. Summers in the country, many parties.
>
> Some accumulate, others devour. Creditors queue up in the morning, fraught atmosphere. Interior decorators, horse merchants.

Elsewhere, Zola noted helter-skelter the salient features of certain women whom Laporte obviously took pleasure undressing for him:

> La Sancy very gay, a Paris bohemian, consumptive, dying year by year. Street urchin's mug, rather large physique, high-slung shoulders, graceful movement. Loves the cancan. Wicked joke about that, eating everything, anger. Marie Tournier a fleshy lymphatic, carefree, indolent, impassive when screwing. Stupid. Very much to the taste of Russians. Constance Violet living with her mother, who never leaves her. Makes her dresses. Luxurious coach. Perfect order, bookkeeping for her lovers. Town house. Doesn't miss financial opportunity. Saves money. Buys income-bearing real estate. Caroline Letessier ugly, old. Wit. Very mordant.
>
> The town houses well maintained, lackeys, butlers in powdered

---

they employ are not always registered prostitutes, carrying a government card. They're mostly workers who leave their families every morning with their little leather handbags on their arms, as if they were going to their ateliers. Instead they come there and share the proceeds with the mistress of the house, fifty-fifty. . . . To avoid police raids, the bawd will often (in certain places, notably the rue du Château-d'Eau) forbid her women to wear dressing gowns. They wear street clothes, sit on stools near the window looking very proper, and survey the scene as they knit. Should the vice squad come upstairs, they pass themselves off as seamstresses. These details have been furnished by a woman named Camille de Berlement . . . [who], like Satin, got to wallow through every gutter and to eat in every fancy restaurant.

wigs, grand staircases with enormous landings, divans, armchairs, flowers. Foulard nightshirts so that men don't rumple their clothing.

Masculine amour propre fared poorly in the demimonde, according to this informant. Women who caressed their client one moment, he observed, turned scornful the next, when they had lined up a replacement. "Abasement of the naked man, throwing everything to the winds for cunt. Everybody led by the tail, and the women indifferent. A pack of dogs in pursuit of a bitch who's not in heat."

Other anecdotes eventually woven into *Nana* were supplied by Offenbach's librettist Ludovic Halévy. For Zola, whom he admired greatly despite Zola's aversion to light opera, Halévy evoked the golden age of Offenbachian merriment as only an insider could, describing the international crowd that filled the Théâtre des Variétés for *La Belle Hélène* in 1864 and *La Grande Duchesse de Gérolstein* in 1867, but also the social comedies enacted backstage. As he reported in his notebook:

> The Prince of Wales in the dressing room of Offenbach's perennial star, Hortense Schneider. *La Grande Duchesse* was being performed. The prince goes backstage accompanied by Galliffet and Duvilliers [Napoleon III's son's tutor], both sloshed. The prince high. A birthday party for Hettman in progress. Someone attired in white satin with a grotesque royal headdress enters and offers champagne to the Englishman, who accepts. In the dressing room are Couder and other costumed actors. Strangeness of the scene. Schneider pretentiously maintaining her Grand Duchess airs: "Your Highness," etc. How the other actors behave, this parodic nobility confronted by the genuine article. Stage managers, comic actors, princes, tarts all jumbled together.

Halévy also served as guide when Zola set out to inspect the plant in which Offenbach manufactured sexy entertainment for Second Empire audiences. On February 15, 1878, they saw a three-act farce called *Niniche* at the Variétés and afterward wandered through the stagehouse, with Zola noting everything noteworthy about the arrangement of loges, staircases, backcloths, prop stores, and galleries. Here, he already knew, was where his voluptuous heroine would first cast a spell upon *le tout Paris*. Here was where Nana the tart would become Nana the goddess.

Certainly the final chapters of *L'Assommoir* had pointed to an uncommon fate for Gervaise's daughter. Brought up on the rue de la Goutte d'Or, where stray girls acquire precocious expertise in the bewitchment of grown men, blond and buxom Nana proves more skillful

A Verdant Paradise and a Blond Horizontal (419

than most. To save her from depravity, her aunt, who employs several dozen young women making artificial flowers, teaches her the trade, but handiwork does not instill virtue or throttle ambition. Exasperated by slum life, Nana keeps both eyes open and, at fifteen, flees when deliverance presents itself in the person of a fifty-year-old button manufacturer. "Tramping through the mud and splashed by passing vehicles, dazzled by the splendors of shopwindows, she had longings that twisted her stomach like hunger pangs, desires to be well dressed, to eat in restaurants, to go to the theater, to have her own room with lovely furniture," Zola wrote. "She would stand stock-still, quite pale with such desires, and feel a warmth rising from the Paris streets and creeping up her thighs, a fierce appetite for the enjoyments she felt bustling around her on the crowded sidewalk. And without fail, just when she was feeling like that, her old man would whisper his propositions into her ear."

No sooner has she given this protector satisfaction than she leaves him to embark upon a vagrant career, spending nights at dance halls, where her reckless performance of the cancan wins her local fame. The rue de la Goutte d'Or still offers this fugitive, half hooker, half waif, something like the comforts of home, but visits become rarer as her clientele becomes more genteel. " 'I've had some news,' " Gervaise tells Coupeau. " 'Your daughter has been seen. Yes, she's very chic and doesn't need you anymore. And happy as she can be she is, too! Oh, dear God, what would I give to be in her shoes!' "[6]

Had Gervaise lived another two years she would have lived to see the hoyden whom she couldn't keep from undressing adored for her nakedness on the Boulevard stage. *Nana* begins with this epiphany. An Offenbachian celebration of adulterous mischief called *La Blonde Vénus* has opened at the Variétés, and Parisians flock there to see music-hall artistes disport themselves as Olympian deities. It isn't theater that lures them but women, and in particular the debutante cast in the title role.

A street urchin came up whistling, planted himself before a playbill at the door, and cried out: "Hey, Nana!" in a tipsy voice before slouching away, dragging his old boots. This raised a laugh. Dapper gentlemen repeated: "Nana! Hey, Nana!" People were crushed together, a quarrel broke out at the box office, and there was a growing

---

[6]"When *L'Assommoir* appeared, Manet painted the Nana of that book, eighteen years old and a slut," wrote Félicien Champsaur, a friend of both Manet and Zola, speaking of Manet's 1877 painting entitled *Nana*. "She's essentially a Parisienne, an elegant, exciting woman of delicate build who has become plump from good living. . . . Nana has since grown. She's been transformed in the mind of her creator, M. Zola, into a lusty, opulent blond."

clamor caused by the hum of voices calling for Nana, demanding
Nana in one of those fits of haw-haw humor and crude sensuality
which take hold of crowds.

When it becomes obvious that Nana can't sing, move, or act, that she
has more brass than talent, an audience otherwise quick to sneer goes
wild. Among jejune Parisians who value low entertainment above high
art and delight in the spectacle of classical mythology profaned by
homegrown barbarians, her ineptitude serves her well, focusing attention on her physique:

> For certain rather spicy lines, she tilted her nose with pleasure and
> her pink nostrils quivered, while a bright flush colored her cheeks.
> She still swayed backwards and forwards, for that was all she knew
> how to do. And the audience no longer considered this repulsive; on
> the contrary, men aimed their opera glasses at her. At the end of the
> verse her voice failed her completely, and she realized that she would
> never finish the whole song. So, without getting flustered, she thrust
> out one hip, which was roundly outlined under a flimsy tunic, bent
> backwards so that her breasts showed to good advantage, and
> stretched out her arms. Applause burst forth on all sides. In the twin-
> kling of an eye she had turned around and gone upstage, revealing
> the nape of her neck to the audience, a neck on which her reddish
> hair looked like an animal's fleece. Then the applause became posi-
> tively frantic.

A charismatic animal, a *monstre sacré* born to devour men emerges
from this opera buffa. After several hours onstage, the eighteen-year-
old who at first squirmed under the gaze of high society has mastered
all eyes. "Every pair of opera glasses was fixed on Venus. Little by little
Nana had taken possession of the audience, and now every man sat
spellbound. A wave of lust was flowing from her as from a bitch in
heat, and it had spread further and further until it filled the whole
house. Now her slightest movements fanned the flame of desire, and
with a twitch of her little finger she could stir men's flesh. Backs arched
and quivered as if unseen violin bows had been drawn across their
muscles." Her sexual allure is "omnipotent."

The smart set loses no time courting Nana at her posh, half-
furnished flat. On one another's heels trip a rich, bushy-tailed Chérubin, a theater critic named FaucheIy for whom business serves pleasure, a lecherous Jewish banker, a numskull egregiously fond of his
aristocratic particle, a young count, Xavier de Vandeuvres, whose gambling debts are legion. These form her retinue, and when, soon after
the first night, she decides to congratulate herself by staging a mid-

night banquet, it is they who gather around her, arm in arm with sluttish showgirls. "Around the table the gentlemen in question looked irreproachable, with their white ties and evening coats and their pale features, the natural distinction of which was further refined by fatigue," writes Zola. "And as for the ladies, they were behaving very well. Some of them, such as Blanche, Léa, and Louise, had come in low dresses, but only Gaga was perhaps showing a bit too much, particularly in view of the fact that at her age she would have done better not to have showed anything at all." Nana's banquet on the Boulevard Haussmann seems a far cry from Gervaise's birthday feast on the rue de la Goutte d'Or, but as champagne flows, table scraps accumulate, and respectable personae wilt, the two occasions come to resemble each other. Both announce the crumbling of hierarchies, the miscegenation of high and low, of home and gutter. "The guests had stopped eating and were simply toying with their platefuls of *cèpes à l'italienne* and *croustades d'ananas Pompadour*," writes Zola. Nana's vulgar sisterhood exchange intimate details about famous men visiting Paris for the 1867 Exposition; the champagne

> was gradually beginning to fill the guests with a nervous intoxication. They ended up by behaving less decorously than before. The women began leaning on their elbows in the midst of all the plates and glasses, while the men, in order to breathe more easily, pushed their chairs back; dress coats mingled with light-colored bodices, and bare shoulders, half turned toward the table, took on a silky gleam. It was too hot. . . . The guests were telling jokes at the top of their voices, gesticulating wildly, asking questions which nobody answered, and calling to one another from one end of the room to the other.

Into every Zola celebration a revenant must burst. Like Lantier surfacing at the dinner held to affirm Gervaise's proprietary stake in life, memories of eviction spoil Nana's newfound prestige. "Ever since the beginning of the supper party she had had the impression of no longer being in her own home. All these people had overwhelmed and bewildered her, calling the waiters, talking at the top of their voices, and making themselves comfortable, just as if they were in a restaurant."

Among the patricians who fall for the ex-guttersnipe none falls harder than Count Muffat de Beuville, Empress Eugénie's chamberlain, and *Nana* is as much the story of his descent as of her rise. Muffat owes his office to the fact that Napoleon Bonaparte had conferred noble patents upon his father, General Muffat, who sired him late in life. Raised alone under the pious, autocratic regime of a mother infatuated with priests, he exudes lovelessness. "Muffat was . . . not very lighthearted but reputed to be absolutely honorable. He lived by an old-fashioned code of conduct, with so lofty an idea of his dignities, virtues, and duties at court that he carried his head like a holy sacrament."[7] Early along in his unhappy marriage with Sabine de Chouard, they generated enough warmth to produce a child, but since that birth, sexual congress has been rare, and after more than sixteen years together the unhappy couple present a picture of mutual deprivation. The Muffat mansion on the rue de Miromesnil—"lofty and dark and conventlike, with its great shutters nearly always closed"—is a place of muted light, drab color, and pervasive chill in which Sabine's soft red silk armchair looks sacrilegious.

Muffat would have shrunk from an operetta called *La Blonde Vénus* (even during the Universal Exposition, which excused a multitude of sins) if diplomacy had not compelled him to see it. When the Prince of Wales crosses the Channel for some French entertainment, Muffat serves as his cicerone. Together they visit the Variétés and between acts go backstage, where Nana, half naked, receives them in her dressing room. Queen Victoria's rakish son, who feels very much at home, converses with perfect aplomb. But exposure to the voluptuous tart unnerves Muffat. "He, who had never seen the Comtesse Muffat put on her garters, was witnessing the intimate details of a woman's toilet, in a chaotic disarray of jars and a cloud of sweet perfume," writes Zola. "His whole being rebelled: the way in which Nana had taken hold of him terrified him and brought to mind exemplary tales of diabolic possession which he had read as a child." Seen from backstage through a peephole in the backcloth, she fills Muffat's field of vision, looming over the audience like Salome triumphant or Liberty at the guillotine. Half real, half dreamed, this image transfixes him. "Beyond the dazzling arc formed by the footlights the dark auditorium looked as if it were full of a reddish smoke, and against this neutral background, to which the rows of faces lent a vague pallor, Nana stood out white and gigantic, blotting out all the boxes from the balcony to the flies. He saw her from behind, standing with body erect and arms outstretched, while on the floor, level with her feet, the prompter's head—an old man's head, with a humble, honest face—looked as if it had been severed from his body. At certain points in her opening number an undulating movement seemed to begin at her neck, descend to her waist, and die out in the trailing hem of her tunic. When she had sung her last note in the midst of a storm of applause, she bowed to the audience, the gauze floating about her and her hair reaching down below her waist. And seeing her like that, bent in two

---

[7]"He carried his head like a holy sacrament" is an expression Zola borrowed from Camille Desmoulins, who coined it during the Revolution to describe his fellow revolutionary Saint-Just.

with her hips broadened out, backing toward his peephole, the count straightened up, looking very pale." Effete societies, Zola implies, worship emasculating women.

To possess this illiterate siren becomes Muffat's idée fixe, and in due course Nana, who fancies titled Frenchmen, gratifies him. The sexual awakening that results is calamitous. Everything upon which Muffat built his life—honor, family, office, faith—loses meaning as he marks time between assignations or broods over suspected rivals. Spellbound, the patrician turns slave, laying before his indispensable mistress the shreds of his amour propre. His mistress thrives on his prostration, for female narcissism goes hand in hand with male self-hatred. A famous scene illustrates this conjunction:

> Nana was lost in ecstatic contemplation of herself. She bent her neck and gazed attentively in the mirror at a little brown mole just above her right hip. . . . Then she studied other parts of her body, amused by this examination, and filled once more with the depraved curiosity she had felt as a child. . . . Muffat sat looking at her. She frightened him. The newspaper had dropped from his hands. In that moment of clarity and truth, he despised himself. Yes, that was it: she had corrupted his life, and he already felt tainted to the core of his being by undreamt-of impurities. Now everything was going to rot within him, and for a moment he realized how this evil would develop.

Prescience does not avail him. Nor does prayer. Like "Venus fastened tooth and claw to her prey,"[8] the inextricable Nana engages in sadistic sport, canceling engagements, making him queue up for her favors, letting him know that Sabine has cuckolded him, and at last fleeing, as if to prove herself more independent than her keeper.

What follows is a period of obscurity that shows her torn between the desire for social elevation and *nostalgie de la boue*. Revolted by fine-feathered suitors, Nana suddenly loses her heart to a comedy actor named Fontan, whose ramlike face betrays his cruelty. Doting upon this monster, she feels young again. But only three weeks after they have set up house together, the first blow falls, and violence thereupon becomes habitual. "For the slightest thing Fontan slapped her face. She grew accustomed to it, and didn't resist. . . . The worst of it was that [he] would disappear for the whole day and never return home before midnight." Forsaken, Nana finds solace in the companionship of Satin, another young whore-cum-actress. When money runs out, they troll for clients side by side, with Satin, who is more experienced,

[8]*Vénus tout entière à sa proie attachée*: a verse from Racine's *Phèdre*. As we have seen, *Phèdre* was inspiration for *La Curée*, and Zola undoubtedly had it mind while writing *Nana*.

helping Nana surrender illusions to which she still clings. "Some wind-falls came their way now and then, from gentlemen who slipped their decorations into their pockets as they went upstairs with them," wrote Zola (who had just been denied his red ribbon).

> She felt a little nervous, for the most distinguished-looking men were the most obscene. The veneer cracked and the beast revealed itself, exacting in its monstrous tastes, subtle in its perversions. The result was that Satin showed a complete lack of respect, jeering at dignified gentlemen in carriages and assuring them that their coachmen were better than they, because they treated women right and didn't kill them with diabolic ideas. The way in which smart people wallowed in the cesspools of vice still astonished Nana, for she had a few prejudices left, though Satin was rapidly ridding her of them.

Nana is taught not only to see through masks that distinguish upper class from lower, but to violate taboos that forbid intimacy between members of the same sex. Initiated by Satin, who knows her way around lesbian Paris, she cherishes in this waif what she hasn't found in men. Sister outcasts inveighing against "the pigs," they nurture each other *tant bien que mal* until, one night, society drives them apart. During a raid on a hotel where the two women, evicted from their separate flats, have sought refuge, Nana watches horror-stricken as gendarmes arrest Satin. "She had always trembled before the law, before this unknown power, this vengeance of men who could suppress her without anybody in the world defending her," Zola observes. "Saint-Lazare prison was something she envisioned as a ditch, a black hole where one buried women alive after cutting off their hair."[9]

This incident moves her to leave Fontan and to end her sojourn underground. It also revives a dream of legitimacy which she can imagine fulfilling only through theatrical impersonation. Her mother, Gervaise, had achieved petit bourgeois status in real life as a shopkeeper, but Nana fancies herself winning social prominence on the stage, as the titular heroine of an operetta called *La Petite Duchesse*. Although the part is already assigned, Muffat, who has long since cast off all scruples, buys it for her, knowing that without a title—even this make-believe title—there will be no liaison.

When *La Petite Duchesse* flops, it ends one career but launches another, for with her designs upon *"le monde"* thwarted, Nana vows to

---

[9]The description of Nana's terror calls to mind a previously quoted entry in Goncourt's journal: "Zola . . . suddenly complains of being haunted by the desire to sleep with a young girl, not a child, but a girl on the verge of puberty: 'Yes, it frightens me . . . I envision assizes court and all the trembling.' "

become queen of the *"demi-monde."* If a whore cannot be a duchess, she can at least make duchesses envy whores. "I'll show your Paris something about great ladyship, I will," she vows (in a variation on the challenge that Balzac's Rastignac hurls at upper-class Paris), and so she does. "Nana became a woman of fashion, a beneficiary of male stupidity and lust, an aristocrat in the ranks of her calling," is how Zola introduces the paroxystic denouement.

Her success was sudden and decisive, a swift rise to fame in the garish light of lunatic extravagance and the wasteful follies of beauty. She at once became queen among the most expensive of her kind. Her photographs were displayed in shopwindows, and her remarks were quoted in the papers. When she drove along the boulevards in her carriage, people would turn around and tell one another who she was with all the emotion of a nation saluting its sovereign, while she lolled back in her flimsy dresses, smiling gaily under the rain of little golden curls which fell around the blue of her made-up eyes and the red of her painted lips. And the remarkable thing was that that buxom young woman, who was so awkward on the stage, so comical when she tried to play the respectable woman, was able to play the enchantress in town without the slightest effort. There she had the lithe grace of a serpent, a studied yet seemingly involuntary carelessness of dress which was exquisitely elegant, the nervous distinction of a pedigreed cat, an aristocratic refinement. . . . She set the fashion, and great ladies imitated her.

Fashion dictates that she live near the Parc Monceau, in a Renaissance-style mansion filled with precious knickknacks, Oriental tapestries, Gobelins, antique credenzas, period furniture. Managing this establishment, which includes horses and carriages worthy of the Tuileries, are five liveried servants, and subsidizing it is Muffat, who cannot, except at appointed hours, enter Nana's private apartment, where a huge quilted bed trimmed in Venetian lace occupies center stage. Money flows as if there were no end of it. Life, for Nana, becomes one continuous buying spree, with fortunes squandered every week on baubles, on costumes, on jewels, on decorative whims, on receptions attended by Napoleonic courtiers. Greed is not what drives her, however. She spends not for love of acquiring but rather to fill an unfillable void. "Nana was bored to tears," Zola explains. "Her life dragged on devoid of occupation, each day bringing back the same monotonous hours. The . . . certainty of being fed left her to stretch out in languid ease all day, lulled to sleep in conventual idleness and submission as if she were the prisoner of her profession." Bound up with languor is rage. She who mothers her own body delights in using it to render men servile, to exclude them, to bleed them dry, to abort their seed, to make them women. A killer inhabits the sumptuary creature, and when on one occasion she sends poor Muffat home crestfallen, there is "a sudden blossoming of her nature, with its need for domination . . . and its desire to possess everything in order to destroy everything."

Inevitably that destructive impulse suborns the will to live. Manipulated by a dead hand, Nana in all her glory turns against herself, auctioning every possession before disappearing once again. Rumors fly, but no one knows where she has gone until some months later she returns, penniless. Luck then abandons her completely. Summoned to the bed of her son Louis, who has caught smallpox, she catches it from him and decomposes overnight. Fellow actors and actresses, one of whom arranges for her to die in style at the Grand Hôtel, keep vigil outside her room, from which emanates an unbearable stench. And on the Boulevard below, crowds chant "A Berlin! A Berlin! A Berlin!" It is July 1870, which means that war impends. Tramping east with the same ecstatic zeal that saw them pack the Variétés in Chapter One, Frenchmen bring Nana full circle, from eros to thanatos. They will never have seen Venus's last face, these zealots. Nor will they have seen their own. "What lay on the pillow was a charnel house, a heap of pus and blood, a shovelful of putrid flesh. The pustules had invaded the whole face, so that one pock touched the next. Withered and sunken, they had taken on the grayish color of mud, and on that shapeless pulp, in which the features had ceased to be discernible, they already looked like mold from the grave." Rotting is suitable punishment for the child and agent of social degeneration.

The child and agent of social degeneration is how Nana appears from beginning to end. Zola has her friend Fauchery, the theater critic, picture her as a lethal insect. She is 'the Golden Fly.'

> With her, the scum that had been allowed to ferment among the lower classes was rising to the surface and rotting the aristocracy. She had become a force of nature, a ferment of destruction, unwittingly corrupting and disorganizing Paris between her snow-white thighs, and curdling it just as women every month curdle milk. It was at the end of the article that the comparison with a fly occurred, a fly the color of sunlight which had flown up out of the dung, a fly which had sucked death from roadside carrion and now—buzzing, dancing, and glittering like a precious stone—was entering palaces through the windows and poisoning the men inside, simply by settling on them.

What Nana mobilizes is not the procreative libido but an instinctual force that overwhelms men who despise themselves and their author- ity, casting them adrift in the wreckage of traditional values. Under her regime, everything is turned upside down. High culture becomes grist for low comedy. Noble patrimonies become capital for slumming and gambling. Princes of the blood honor stage royalty. Well-bred mar- quises follow where uncouth strumpets lead. Memory forgets itself as titled men who have lines to preserve sport with women who have pasts to bury. In short, gutter life enters officialdom through the front door, and we see it do so quite flagrantly at the marriage of Muffat's daughter, Estelle. Although Nana herself receives no invitation, she is there, triumphant, in the music. "People were already dancing," writes Zola. "The waltz, which happened to be the vulgar one from *La Blonde Vénus*, with its naughty, laughing lilt, came rippling into the old house to send a warm thrill along the walls. It was as if some wind of sensuality had come in from the street and were sweeping a whole vanished epoch out of the proud mansion, carrying away the Muffats' past, a century of honor and religious faith which had fallen asleep beneath the lofty ceilings."

For informants like Ludovic Halévy, who felt Second Empire Paris come to life again in Zola's fresco of rampant promiscuity, no historian could have written it better. At a time when restaurateurs were earning millions, even greater wealth had, indeed, accrued to those courtesans dubbed *lionnes* or *demi-mondaines*. Exempt from the punishment vis- ited on common whores and from the corset imposed on proper ma- trons, they held sway over the Boulevard. Zola got it right in portraying them as the delusion of an inflationary world. Linked with men whose titles gave them credit, they embodied a sexual magic inseparable from the appetite for patents of nobility, or from a dream of pleasure un- contaminated by mundane responsibilities. What led the parvenu fi- nancier to invest in some dubious venture that carried the Duc de Morny's endorsement also led him to stake a fortune on Morny's latest concubine. Gilding the idol of brass, he rewarded her not for her so- licitude nor even for her expertise, but for her narcissism. Did Cora Pearl, a working-class Londoner born Emma Crouch, who had her breasts reproduced in plaster, complain, when her jilted lover shot himself dead in her living room, that "the pig has ruined my beautiful carpet"? Did La Païva, an Eastern European Jewess born Theresa Lachmann who married a Portuguese marquis, dismiss her husband after their wedding night with the explanation that she was content to be a whore and had ceased to find him amusing? Such stories, far from compromising the *lionne*, won her fresh tribute, for they argued, along with her predatory instinct, a hard-heartedness reminiscent of the mineral world in which idols were expected to feel most at home.

If Les Frères Provençaux restaurant served an omelette garnished with diamonds, said the Duc de Gramont-Caderousse, Cora Pearl would eat omelettes there every night.

Certain men fancied the idea that nature had given this unmaternal species a born affinity for diamonds, silver, gold, pearls, crystal. And the *lionne* did not often disappoint them. In La Païva's establishment at 25, avenue des Champs-Elyséees, for example, they were shown a staircase made of pure onyx, a ceiling of naked nymphs, bathroom walls tiled with mirrors and agate, a tub of marble and silvered bronze into which water flowed from gem-encrusted faucets, a bed that cost one hundred thousand francs, and finally La Païva, who wore cheap garments as if to proclaim that the jewelry in which she habitually draped herself was clothing enough. "Marvelous thing, wealth! It pardons everything," wrote the Goncourts after dinner with her. "Nobody who comes here notices that there isn't a house in all of Paris more uncomfortable than hers. At table, drinking a glass of watery wine is quite impossible, as the bottles and carafes dreamed up by her are cathedrals of crystal it would take a water carrier to lift." Yet surely the Goncourts thought it self-evident that the Hôtel de Païva enshrined not only the body of a courtesan but the materialism of a godforsaken society, that the man was a fool who entered a temple expecting the comforts of home. Indeed, years earlier, during the Exposition of 1855, when people were queueing up to see the crown jewels, they had observed in their journal that "if it were possible to give [the people] Rembrandt's light or Hugo's poetry in material form, to make it visible and tactile, they would spurn it for a diamond like 'the Regent,' the diamond being the most concentrated essence of wealth."[10]

Like previous Rougon-Macquart novels, *Nana* owes as much to Zola's great gift for weaving his obsessive themes through the fabric of social circumstance as to history per se. "A corner of Creation reflected by a temperament" is how he defined the naturalist enterprise, and nowhere does this temperament operate more idiosyncratically than in a chapter about *le tout Paris* gathering at Longchamp to watch Thoroughbreds contest the annual Grand Prix. He pictures one hun-

---

[10]Fascination with "the most concentrated essence of wealth" was, as the Goncourts well knew, by no means peculiar to the *vulgus*. Among Parnassian poets such as Théophile Gautier (who frequented La Païva's), poetic practice became a lapidary art and the gem an object lesson. *Salammbô* and *Hérodias* demonstrate the lapidary in Flaubert, who liked to imagine scenes of orgiastic violence unfolding in the inertness of a mineral landscape or in palaces of precious stone. Even when Arthur Rimbaud broke free from the Parnassian school, the "alchemist" he fancied himself held him hostage to metal. And further ahead loomed the bejeweled sphinxes of art nouveau.

dred thousand spectators shouting themselves hoarse when a filly of no account named Nana challenges a famous English stallion named Spirit. Accompanied by this savage chorus, the race becomes a preview of war and a celebration of whoredom. "The main body of horses was now arriving like a flash of lightning," writes Zola.

> It was the brutal climax of a colossal game, with a hundred thousand spectators possessed by a single passion, burning with the same gambling fever, as they watched these animals on whose galloping hooves fortunes were riding. The crowd jostled and pushed, fists clenched and mouths gaped; every man for himself, and every man whipping on the horse of his choice with voice and gesture. And the cry of the multitude, the cry of a wild beast reincarnated in a frock coat, grew more and more distinct: "Here they come! Here they come! Here they come!"

As Nana the filly passes her male competitors down the stretch, Nana the woman, who watches from a gorgeous, silver-trimmed landau, comes to identify with her, as in some totemic ritual:

> On the seat, without realizing what she was doing, Nana had started swaying her thighs and hips as if she were running the race herself. She kept jerking her belly forward, imagining that this was a help to the filly. With each jerk she gave a sigh of fatigue, saying in a low, anguished voice: "Go . . . go . . . go."

Nana's repeated exhortation—"*Va donc . . . va donc . . . va donc*"— calls to mind the repeated plea for help of her mother, begging in snowy weather on the outer boulevards: "*Monsieur, écoutez donc . . . Monsieur, écoutez donc.*" Can this echo have been anything but deliberate? Where Gervaise finds herself penniless in front of the abattoir like a nag brought to slaughter, Nana queens it over purebreds. Where Gervaise goes unheard, Nana, avenging her, commands acclaim. Where Gervaise sinks meekly, Nana unleashes upon France—upon upper-class France—*la bête humaine.* "There came a sound like the roar of a rising tide: 'Nana! Nana! Nana!' " Zola continues:

> The cry rolled along, swelling with the violence of a storm, and gradually filling the horizon from the depths of the Bois to Mont Valérien and from the meadows of Longchamp to the plain of Boulogne. All over the public enclosure wild enthusiasm reigned, cries of "Long live Nana! Long live France! Down with England!" The women waved their parasols; men leapt and spun around, shouting and cheering, while others, with shouts of nervous laughter, threw their

hats in the air. And from the other side of the track the weighing-in paddock responded, as emotion swept through the stands, although nothing was really visible but a trembling of the air, like the invisible flame of a brazier, above the living mass of little disjointed figures with waving arms and black dots which were eyes and open mouths. Far from dying down, the noise swelled, beginning again at the end of the distant avenues among the common people camping under the trees, and spreading until it reached its climax in the emotion of the imperial stand, where the empress herself applauded. "Nana! Nana! Nana!" the cry rose in the glorious sunshine, whose golden rain beat down on the dizzy heads of the crowd.

Kindred images, of people filling an immense enclosure with passionate commotion as they throng together under a shaman's baton, recur throughout Les Rougon-Macquart (and one surmises that the prototype of these great sound chambers was the Infernets gorge filled with the din of water rushing over his father's dam). We have seen, for example, how insurrectionists led by Miette send up cries that reverberate through the amphitheater of the Viorne Valley. We shall see, in Au Bonheur des Dames, which appeared three years after Nana, how women whipped to a shopping frenzy by a retailer of genius invade his cavernous department store on sale day like drunken bacchantes. And here in Nana, Paris's hippodrome amplifies the roar of the multitude who have sought refuge from dull dailiness in the magic of gambling, in the savagery of war, in a world with totems but no taboos, in fantasies of carnal utopia. "Nana," writes Zola,

> could still hear her name, which the whole plain was echoing back to her. It was her people who were applauding her, while she towered above them, erect in the sunlight, with her golden hair and her white and sky-blue dress. . . . Nobody could tell whether it was the horse or the woman that stirred every heart.

Half human and half myth, Nana with her blond mane figures from the outset as femme fatale and apocalyptic Beast. "A delicate line, curving only slightly at the shoulder and thigh, ran from one of her elbows to her foot," is what Muffat observes early along. "Muffat's eyes followed this charming profile, noticing how the lines of the fair flesh vanished in golden gleams and how the rounded contours shone like silk in the candlelight. He thought of his former dread of Woman, of the Beast of the Scriptures, a lewd creature of the jungle. Nana's body was covered with fine hair, reddish down which turned her skin into velvet; while there was something of the Beast about her equine crupper and flanks, about the fleshy curves and hollows of her body, which veiled her sex in the suggestive mystery of their shadows."

Zola had written only a detailed sketch of the novel when he told Céard in August 1878 that it would "entertain and flabbergast." This conviction grew upon him during the following months, but nothing, not even *L'Assommoir*, quite prepared him for the huge success it was destined to enjoy.

Success began at the beginning, in contract negotiations with *Le Voltaire*, which expiated its predecessor's sins by outbidding ten other dailies for the right to serialize *Nana*. Where *L'Assommoir* had fetched eight thousand francs from *Le Bien public*, *Nana* earned Zola twenty thousand. Jules Laffitte, editor-in-chief, announced *Nana* on May 17, five months before delivery, hoping that by October multifarious rumors about its true nature would incite Parisians to pounce on the first installment. When October 8 rolled around he declared, as a way of saying that *Le Voltaire*, unlike *Le Bien public*, would never bow under pressure: "We recognize that to publish so audacious a writer, we, too, must demonstrate audacity, and that we may count upon intellectually valiant readers." Thus commenced a publicity campaign of unprecedented scope. "Enormous curiosity surrounds *Nana*," Céard informed Zola on the eve of publication, October 15. "The name is plastered over every wall in Paris. It's verging on obsession and nightmare. *Le Voltaire* distributes posters by the thousand. You can't imagine what walls look like, how cluttered they are."[11] Newspaper commentary amplified this tumult. *Le Gaulois*, which was read mainly by upper-class Parisians, ran a long article in which Paul Alexis chronicled the master's typical day at Médan with Boswellian attention to minutiae. One week later Albert Wolff, literary critic for *Le Figaro*, who exercised considerable influence, gave *Nana* his benediction by declaring Zola's frescoes of Paris to be the work of "a great artist."

Wolff's praise did not disarm hostile critics. *Le Voltaire* had no sooner published the first installment than they marshaled themselves against Zola, heaving brickbats of every kind. In *La Gazette de France*, Pontmartin characterized him as a *regardeur* (a euphemism for *voyeur*): "Given M. Zola's genre, given the subject he chose, his literary pro-

[11]An anecdote in Céard's letter provides one measure of the respect Zola now commanded among government officials: "Here's a good story which Huysmans will relate at length next Sunday. The bookstore commission of the interior ministry became indignant over a forbidden volume [*Marthe*] having been published in France, and members ordered a mass seizure. The matter was then taken under advisement by the minister himself, who rescinded their order on the grounds that Huysmans was your friend and that seizure might have grave consequences. He did not welcome the prospect of you attacking the ministry and its censorship."

On the other hand, the interior ministry avenged itself soon afterward with a law against the unauthorized posting of bills.

gram, the main sewer down which he leads us, the cloaca in which he has us wallow, the garbage dump to which he invites us, the smelling salts and cesspool boots he forces us to use—given all this, there is no excuse for his being even less faithful to reality than the disciples of Vicomte d'Arlincourt and M. de Marchangy." Other papers took up where *La Gazette* left off, and on October 24, in *L'Evénement*, Aurélien Scholl, who had been editor-in-chief of *Le Voltaire* until Laffitte replaced him, joined the crowd that damned *Nana* as "false." Zola's investigations backstage had been superficial, he observed, attacking the naturalist on his own ground. "Except for several coarse words which the public doesn't ordinarily encounter on a printed page, the latest novel by the author of *L'Assommoir* is, thus far, neither original nor true."

Although Zola expected such criticism, it upset him nonetheless. "What a dandy row!" he wrote to Laffitte on October 28. "I confess that it troubles me a bit, on account of the blood lust critics display. If *Nana* were finished, I'd be happy to attend your soirée. I am isolating myself, cloistering myself lest I lose my balance in this storm." Feigned indifference was not his strong suit, and after a fortnight of abuse he fought back in *Le Voltaire*, explaining how

> the thing that bothers me most is the aplomb of those gentlemen who demonstrate in four lines that my facts are wrong, predicating their contention on sheer fantasy. They learn that I spend several months of the year in the country and straightway make me out to be a yokel for whom Paris is unknown territory. They're told that I once visited a woman of ill repute working the Bois de Boulogne and conclude that this mythical interview must be the basis for *Nana*. Such are their sources.

The critics, he went on to say, construct a Zola worth demolishing from apocryphal odds and ends. "It's not foolishness, it's almost always bad faith, which is what the journalistic métier requires."

Undaunted, the new champions of truth in fiction continued to heckle him. "Nana is the whore at her rawest and most bestial, a fleshy streetwalker thrust by chance onto a stage and into a town house, then dragged down again by the law of gravitation," wrote Paul de Saint-Victor. "She is stupid and trivial, . . . yet Zola would have us accept this inferior wench as the only true, authentic representative of a world remarkable for its complexity and variety, where inimitable creatures abound!" Another journalist, Georges Ohnet, objected that a "goose like Nana, who can't pull herself together, would never retain lovers in this competitive age, when more intelligence is needed to succeed as an opulently kept mistress than as a legitimate businesswoman."

And then, with stern countenance, came old Louis Ulbach, who availed himself of the opportunity to avenge cruel slights. "The Marquis de Sade believed—so his contemporaries tell us—that what he had undertaken in his works was a moral endeavor," Zola's former employer fulminated in *Gil Blas* on February 24, 1880. "This mania resulted in his being locked up at Charenton. Zola's mania may not have such acute symptoms, and nowadays one often allows modesty to avenge itself unaided. But *Nana*, like *Justine*, falls within the province of pathology. . . . It betrays the incipient erethism of an ambitious, impotent brain driven mad by sensual visions."

Throughout the uproar Zola scribbled furiously, keeping one or two installments ahead of his readers, like a composer delivering music to an orchestra playing his unfinished score even as reviewers boo from the gallery. Friends in Paris were regularly called upon to send him needed information. "In high society, when there's a marriage, does one give a ball, and if so on which evening, the evening of the contract signing or of the church ceremony?" he quizzed Marguerite Charpentier (apropos of Estelle Muffat's marriage). "I would very much like to stage the ball in the Muffat salon, but if the ball is impossible, can I have them give a soirée? Also, if it's the evening of the contract signing, what would be the bride's attire? And if it's the evening of the church ceremony, should I have the newlyweds depart on their honeymoon trip after leaving the ball? I'm being so mercilessly harassed that I dare not get any details wrong. . . . Furnish me with as much precise material as possible; I'll tell no one that you collaborated on *Nana*." To Henry Céard, Zola assigned chores that required fieldwork—the description of a room in the Grand Hotel, for example, or of a corpse disfigured by smallpox— and this meticulous, nervy, learned former medical student never let him down. On December 16, when *Nana* stood nearly complete, Céard wrote:

I send you herewith the best I was able to glean about smallpox at Delahaye's bookstore. Pages 32, 37, 48, 59, 65, 66, 74, 75, 81, 111, 150 will furnish you, I believe, enough technical documentation. Note in particular the appalling picture of smallpox drawn at the end of the volume—a bit specialized, unfortunately. The Dupuytren Museum possesses no death masks of smallpox, so I went to Dr. Hardy's publisher, Hardy having compiled a marvelous atlas of skin diseases. Decorated gentlemen, all doctors, browsing at the back of the bookstore seemed astonished by my questions. . . . Should you find the technical jargon daunting, here's what I propose. From my medical school days I know staff at Lariboisière Hospital and I can contact them. With some luck there will be a smallpox-ravaged cadaver laid out in the amphitheater; they'll notify me, and I'll get the required information *de visu.*

Zola accepted his proposal by return post. "The book on smallpox came yesterday," he reported on December 18. "Obviously, it answers my needs. I shall *invent* a mask, by splicing together documents. I'm very tempted by black smallpox, which is more unusual in its ghastliness. But I admit that if you could inspect a corpse without inconveniencing yourself—strange request, eh?—it would please me. That way, I wouldn't invent anything, I'd have a true mask; and insist upon the state of the eyes, of the nose, of the mouth—a general and exact geography from which I shall of course extract only what I need." Being told of *Nana's* nativity before anyone else outside Médan was Céard's reward for loyal service. "Since *Nana* interests you, since you've given me such valuable information," Zola informed him on January 7, 1880, "here's the great news: I finished it this morning. What a sigh of relief I heaved! Never has a work agitated me as this one did. Now the novel is worth what it's worth, that's no longer any concern of mine. Give up the search for a death mask. I've written a description and am so satisfied with it that I wouldn't change a jot or tittle, even if it were proven inaccurate."

The appearance of *Nana* in book form on February 14, 1880, occasioned more salvos from the press. Cartoonists joined reviewers and bombarded Paris with "nanatomical" drawings so imaginative or malicious that Céard (whose curatorial instincts later benefited the Carnavalet Museum) was moved to collect as many as possible. Before long, rumors of imminent government action began circulating. In fact, Zola had been put on notice in December, when Laffitte insisted upon cuts lest Gambetta, president of the Chamber, punish *Le Voltaire.* After February 14 it was Charpentier's turn to fret. "*Nana* may be seized," Maupassant wrote in a letter to Flaubert. "My authority is Sir Charpentier himself, who, when the public prosecutor's office ordered him to disclose the name of his bookbinder, went slightly berserk and dashed all over town, alerting Zola, warning booksellers, hiding available copies in friends' houses. The corridors of the Comédie-Française were abuzz with speculation."

Speculation worked very much to Zola's pecuniary advantage. No one seized *Nana* except readers with three and a half francs to spend, and the demand was phenomenal. Fifty-five thousand copies sold overnight—and this in a time when a sale of four thousand was considered excellent for a novel. Charpentier thereupon had another eleven thousand printed. They, too, sold lickety-split, and soon orders for the other Rougon-Macquart novels began to multiply. The entire saga drove a thriving trade. Every month saw some new record set, and this boom was to continue month after month, then year after year. By 1885, 440,000 copies of Rougon-Macquart novels were circulating in France. *L'Assommoir* and *Nana* alone accounted for 249,000, which meant 125,000 francs in royalties, or quite enough to help Zola finance another large wing for his house at Médan.[12]

On April 1, 1880, when the now famous author turned forty, Zola's cup was running over. Not only had he achieved immense popular success, but he had done so without sacrificing those qualities that commanded the respect of writers whose judgment he valued. It is safe to say that one accolade from Croisset could make him forget any number of aspersions cast upon him in the press, and he received that accolade soon after *Nana* appeared. The letter is worth quoting in its entirety:

My dear Zola,

I spent all of yesterday until 11:30 in the evening reading *Nana*. I didn't sleep last night and "I remain stupefied by it." If I were to note everything rare and strong, I'd fill the margins of every page! The personalities are wonderfully accurate, *true-to-life* words abound; at the end Nana's death is *Michelangelesque!*

An enormous book, my good fellow!

Here are the pages I dog-eared (in the heat of my enthusiasm and on first reading): 82, 87, some longnesses? or slownesses? 205, Mignon! with his sons! ineffably beautiful! 33, 45, 46, 51, 52, 75, 105, 108, 126, 130, 134, 141, 146, 156, 173, 172 (adorable), 175 (*idem*). The vision of M. d'Anglars! 237, 256.

But what precedes: the night spent in the streets, is less personal; it would, moreover, have been impossible, given the scheme, to do otherwise, as it was essential to lead up to the "let's go to bed," which is excellent.

Everything that concerns Fontan, perfect.

295. All of chapter ten.

377! "So come! So come!"

N.B. 401, "Between Le Havre and Trouville." Geographically impossible! Substitute *Honfleur*.

415. Full of grandeur, epic, sublime!

427. The paternity of all these gentlemen, adorable. . . .

Nana becomes mythic, without ceasing to be real.

Dixi

And on that note, I embrace you.

[12]One hundred twenty-five thousand francs of that era are calculated to be worth approximately two million today, or four hundred thousand dollars. France did not levy income tax until 1916.

Your old chum . . .

Tell Charpentier to send me *a copy*, as I don't want to lend my own.
He must be content, young Charpentier? In *Nana* he's found a nice
little bonanza I should think?

To Charpentier, Flaubert wrote on the same day: "Millions must be
inundating you by way of *Nana!*[13] What a book! It's powerful stuff!
and that good man Zola is a genius; let us keep reminding one another
of it!!! This evening I begin *at last* the concluding chapter of *Bouvard
et Pécuchet* and do so in a blue funk. When will it be finished?"[14]

It embarrassed Zola that while preaching science in the public forum
he continued to observe superstitious rituals in the privacy of his home
or in the dark of his soul. A rational self scorned the believer who, like
those celebrants visited by ghosts in *Les Rougon-Macquart*, found himself assailed by presentiments of doom during his hours of greatest
success. But at times a jealous god did indeed seem to exact vengeance, and one such time was 1880. On May 9, while the battle over
Nana was still raging, news reached him that death had claimed Gustave Flaubert at fifty-nine. Five months later, Zola lost his beloved
mother.

Flaubert's self-inflicted martyrdom had never let up. Loyal to a book
that caused him infinite pain and to a niece who brought him financial
ruin, he had lived housebound in Croisset, now feigning death, now
loudly bemoaning his fate. "My silence must surprise you?" he asked
Turgenev in a letter written on December 22, 1878. "My excuse, alas,
is a valid one. I have had such *money worries*, such violent anxieties,

[13]The phrase used is *"par le canal de Nana,"* literally "by the canal of Nana," which
refers to Zola's father's canal as well as, of course, to Zola's heroine's genitalia.
[14]Flaubert's enthusiasm ran absolutely counter to the reaction of straitlaced liberal
bourgeois. How the latter considered *Nana* may be judged from a letter Zola
received from his childhood friend Jean-Baptistin Baille, who had married the
daughter of a rich manufacturer and gained distinction for his scientific work.
"Our friendship broke off, I no longer remember quite how or why, but of what
account are a few slights . . . when weighed against the life we shared for more
than twenty years?" he wrote in November 1880. "I have followed your swift and
well-anticipated ascent with joy and sometimes—I shan't deny it—with sadness.
I knew long before *L'Assommoir* that you have a very large talent, clear-cut and
powerful. But I also knew long before *Nana* that you had set yourself a course I
couldn't approve. Your portrait of humanity seems somewhat inexact and incomplete. Is the stomach with its various appendages king of this world? Are fine words
and sentiments usually window dressing for base instincts and needs? It's possible,
it's even probable, although these unpleasant truths need not be driven home so
often. But . . . don't you believe that the feeling of duty can, if not abolish, at
least modify the effects of these instincts?"

that I'm amazed I haven't gone completely mad. The hope of recovering my fortune is vanished." Three weeks later, he pleaded with Turgenev to visit him: "In [my last] letter, I told you I was counting on seeing you *here* at the beginning of January? Can you come now? Would it inconvenience you? It would be a *charitable act* to pay me a visit, for I really want or rather need to see you. . . . I foresee big problems . . . and if the typhoid fever currently raging in Rouen were to carry me off, it would be good riddance as far as I'm concerned." Bedridden with gout, Turgenev could not obey this desperate summons; and beset with inner conflict, Flaubert could not tear himself away from Croisset. Late in January, when there was some possibility of his wintering on the rue du Faubourg Saint-Honoré, he managed to break his leg. "Did you know," he informed Turgenev, "that I broke my leg five minutes after reading the letter in which you recommended walking for exercise?!! Funny, isn't it? It'll be six weeks or two months before I'm able to get around, and I shall limp for a long time. I am as well as can be expected, and I embrace you. Your old cripple, G. Flaubert."

That winter a struggle took place between Flaubert, who tenaciously resisted help, and his friends, who sought with equal tenacity to get him a sinecure in Paris. It began with Hippolyte Taine telling him that the directorship of the Mazarine Library, which was expected to fall vacant, would be his for the asking. "I cannot say how touched I am by your solicitude," he responded, but he had a dozen reasons to say no. Marguerite Charpentier then intervened. If Flaubert could bring himself to accept a post, she would do her utmost to extract one from Gambetta on favorable terms. Turgenev delivered this proposal in person and secured Flaubert's tentative agreement. Flaubert, like a reluctant groom, finally yielded when Turgenev, after consulting Mme Charpentier and Zola, gave him to understand that his salary would be six thousand francs, double the first offer. "Thank you for your telegram, my dear friend," wrote Flaubert. "I have just sent you one of my own, which you will receive before this note. I have put aside stupid pride, and I accept. For above all, one must avoid dying of hunger. . . . Now I would like to know what will come of it, and if I can *count* on the post. I fear that Jules Ferry [minister of public instruction and fine arts] may have his own protégés and that once it's out in the open, rivals will spoil my chance." The well-devised intrigue was in fact a woolly improvisation. With Flaubert now brought to his senses, no one knew what the next step should be. "Turgenev has just told me that he's leaving for Russia on Wednesday," Zola (who had meanwhile become deeply involved) warned Marguerite Charpentier. "He'd like to know if, before his departure, he should approach M. Baudry [Flaubert's friend and chief rival for the Mazarine post], M.

Ferry, or Gambetta himself. He's ready to do whatever you think best, but time is of the essence." Through influential lady friends Turgenev succeeded in putting Flaubert's case before the newly elected president of the Chamber, only to have it summarily dismissed. "You already know, from my telegram this morning, of the collapse of all our plans," he explained to Flaubert on February 13.

On my return to Paris, we had taken the following decisions: I was to try and speak to Gambetta, then to Ferry, and if necessary to Baudry. Thursday evening—first letter from Zola (enclosed)—and then a lull. I requested an interview of Mme Ed. Adam; no answer. Monday morning—a letter from Zola accompanying a note from Mme Charpentier (I enclose them as well). You can imagine my amazement. I took a carriage and went straight to the presidential palace to see Gambetta. . . . I was not received, but . . . the following day . . . I received a letter from Mme Edmond Adam, who they had said was in Cannes. I put on my suit, white tie—and there I was in her drawing room, where I found just about all of the political notables and from where France is governed and administered. . . . I explained the matter [to my hostess]. . . . "But Gambetta is here— he's having an after-dinner smoke—he shall know all directly." She came back two minutes later: "Impossible, my dear sir! Gambetta has already got people in mind!" The dictator arrived with measured step: ministers and senators were dancing around him as trained dogs around their master. He started to talk to one of them. Mme Ed. Adam took me by the hand and led me to him; but the great man declined the honor of making my acquaintance—and said, loud enough for me to hear: "I don't want it—it's been said—it's impossible." I made myself scarce and then returned home, *plunged*, as they say, in thoughts that I needn't spell out. And that's how much one can trust fine words and promises.

Turgenev added that he had just seen Zola, "who, through affection (this lad loves you very much, I know), regrets that I told you the whole truth; he didn't want you to give up all hope of it straightway." Zola may have felt inept, or even guilty. But except for *Le Figaro* making political hay by reporting Gambetta's boorishness in a gossip column, Flaubert himself was not disappointed by the outcome. He could now remain on his island and assure himself that he had made every effort to leave it. "I *mourn the loss*, with no difficulty, and deep down (here you'll recognize me, psychologist that you are), I'm *perhaps* not sorry. . . . As long as I can't get a real *sinecure* that provides around six thousand francs, I'm better off where I am. . . . So, my good old fellow, *an immediate end to all intrigue.*"

Intrigue did not end there. Others took up where Turgenev left off, but intrigued to better effect. On October 3, Jules Ferry came through for Flaubert, granting him a pension of three thousand francs per annum outright and honoring his request that it be kept secret. Five months later, on Easter Sunday 1880, in a belated celebration organized by Zola, "les Cinq" (less Turgenev), who hadn't dined together since 1878, gathered at Croisset. "Everyone feels cheerful," Goncourt wrote of their train trip north. "Zola rejoices like an auctioneer's clerk about to itemize an estate, Daudet like an escapee from some bourgeois household preparing to make whoopee, Charpentier like a student with visions of beer mugs, I like a man anxious to embrace his long-lost friend."[15] When they arrived, Flaubert, "wearing a broad-brimmed hat and short jacket, with his big behind in pleated trousers, and his kind, affectionate face," greeted them effusively. Croisset, Goncourt went on to write, was more beautiful than he remembered:

> The immensely broad Seine, with the masts of obscured vessels gliding past us against the backdrop in a theater, these beautiful tall trees that have been blown into tormented shapes by the sea winds; the garden and its espaliers, the long terrace-walk facing full south, a peripatetic's terrace: all these make it, after belonging in the eighteenth century to a community of Benedictines, the perfect abode for a man of letters, for Flaubert.
>
> The dinner is very good, but especially a wondrous turbot in cream sauce. We drink wines of all sorts and spend the evening telling ribald stories which make Flaubert burst into childlike laughter. He won't read from his novel, he's had it, he's "burned out." And we retire to chilly bedrooms populated by family busts. The next day we get up late and converse indoors, Flaubert declaring that walks are drudgery. We have lunch, then depart.

In high spirits, the group looked forward to May, when Flaubert planned on visiting Paris after completing the first volume of *Bouvard et Pécuchet*. No one—not even Zola with his premonitions—imagined that this agreeable sojourn had been the rehearsal for a wake.

On May 8, a massive stroke killed Flaubert. Maupassant spread the

---

[15]Zola's pollakiuria made even short voyages difficult—which Goncourt noted without sympathy: "Zola's happiness is troubled by a great preoccupation, that is, whether, traveling on this express train, he'll have time to piss at stations along the way: Paris, Mantes, Vernon. The number of times the author of *Nana* pisses, or at least tries to, is unimaginable."

dreadful news, and on May 11, Zola, who had just reestablished himself at Médan, headed for Rouen, where carriages awaited mourners coming by train. "No death could cause me greater distress than his," he averred in a long obituary.

During the two days before the funeral I had him vividly in mind; he haunted me, at night especially, and his image put a period to all my thoughts with bone-chilling definitiveness. . . . On Tuesday morning I left for Rouen, which meant tramping cross-country to catch a train at the station nearest Médan. A radiant morning it was, with long golden shafts of light piercing the foliage, birds chattering, mist rising from the Seine. Being all alone in this gladness and hearing the little crunch of pebbles underfoot made tears well up. I thought of him, I told myself it was all over, that he would never see the sun again. . . . At Rouen we recommenced the little trip that had been so cheerful six weeks earlier, but we didn't go as far as Croisset. No sooner had we turned off the Canteleu road than our driver stopped and parked his coach beside a hedgerow; approaching was the funeral cortege, still hidden from view by some trees at a bend. We got out, we bared our heads, and it was then that my grief really hit me. Our good, our great Flaubert seemed to be present, asleep in his coffin. I could still see him at Croisset, opening the front door and planting big, sonorous kisses on our cheeks. And now another meeting, the last. . . . When I beheld the hearse with its curtains drawn, its horses bearing down upon me in march step and its gentle, funereal sway, a chill went up my spine and I began to tremble. . . . Daudet and I stood on the roadside, silent and pale. The "old man" was passing by and into that expression, "old man," we poured all our tenderness, everything we owed the friend and master. . . . Goncourt and Charpentier joined us. We shook hands, looking at one another with the surprised and weary air that acknowledges great catastrophes. I glanced at the cortege. We numbered two hundred at most. Then I shuffled along, lost in the crowd.

Just as he had taxed Aix-en-Provence with ingratitude for not commemorating François Zola, so now he inveighed against Rouen for neglecting "one of its most illustrious sons." Few natives were seen to join the funeral cortege when it crossed the Seine and entered the city. "On the quais and along the avenue, a few knots of bourgeois gaped curiously," he wrote (evoking the famous scene from *Madame Bovary* in which Emma's coach circulates through Rouen with curtains drawn, "like a hearse," to the astonishment of pedestrians). "Many had no idea who the dead man was, not even after we told them, for the name Flaubert put them in mind of the great novelist's father and brother, eminent physicians quite well known locally. The best informed were newspaper readers who had come to see famous Parisian journalists."

A mishap at the cemetery seemed to indicate that Flaubert's chance of "fitting in" might be as poor on one side of the grave as on the other. Having dug too small a hole, laborers found it necessary to lower him at an angle, and the huge casket got stuck head down. They righted it with great difficulty, but by then Zola, Daudet and Goncourt had boarded a train for Paris. "We left without partaking of the evening feast and en route spoke reverently about the dead man," noted Goncourt.

Five months later it was borne in on Zola that another death could upset him far more than Flaubert's. At the beginning of October, Emilie Zola fell gravely ill while visiting her brother Gabriel near Verdun. Heart trouble with pulmonary complications made breathing almost impossible, but she would not die far from her son and traveled half-way across France to rejoin him at Médan. There, stertorous and bloated, the sixty-one-year-old woman lingered ten days in mortal agony. It was an excruciating time for everyone, not least of all for Alexandrine, who had been seriously at odds with her mother-in-law since 1877 or earlier. "Although good-natured, Alexandrine was sometimes quite bossy, and Mme François Zola had had too arduous a life to put up with quarrels in old age," one family member later revealed. "What provoked these quarrels? First there were the former creditors from Aix, who regularly showed up with IOUs. Then there were the poor Aubert relatives, who, once they had seen how Zola lived, felt free to borrow money, on permanent loan. Madame Emile Zola finally read the riot act, and this was not taken well. Wanting a life of her own, Mme François Zola rented a small flat down the street from her son." Resentments that had long smoldered in Emilie became a raging fire on her deathbed. Nursed day and night by Alexandrine, who may have wished to exculpate herself with this act of perfect devotion, she vituperated against her daughter-in-law, accusing her of putting vitriol in her medicine and copper in her broth. Zola sought refuge elsewhere, but he couldn't plug his ears or walk blindfolded, and a novel that appeared in 1884, *La Joie de vivre*, evokes something of the nightmare. "Mme Chanteau [a character based in part on Emilie] scolded Pauline for jostling her. The slightest movement took her breath away, and afterward she'd lie there sallow-faced and panting. Lazare withdrew behind the bed curtain lest he betray his despair. But he didn't leave when Pauline rubbed tincture of digitalis into the moribund woman's legs. Much as he feared the sight, his eyes were drawn to those monstrous legs, those inert blobs of pale flesh." Zola had always identified strongly with his mother, and under duress the compulsion to do so often overwhelmed him. So it was that his own cardiac disturbances now became incontrovertible harbingers of doom.[16]

Emilie Aubert Zola died on October 17, 1880. Friends gathered in Médan for the funeral service, a description of which was found, many years later, among Céard's notes. Setting ideology aside, Zola requested the Church to preside, and the Church answered his summons. "When we arrive," Céard wrote, referring to Zola's other protégés,

> the coffin is in the courtyard. We enter. Mme Zola in tears, Zola calmer than we thought he'd be. We are only ourselves, plus Roux. No announcement was made in the papers. Zola insisted that the public not be informed of the great blow he had suffered. As he explained it to me, he doesn't want private matters impinging on his literary battle. Quiet prevails in the dining room, which is flooded with the light of a beautiful autumn day. Zola begins to pace back and forth, silently, then halts, leans against a window and looks out. . . . In due course his servant tells him that everyone expected has arrived. "Let's go," he says, and we rise. Shaken by sobs, he takes Roux's arm for support. Around the coffin, candles blaze. . . . Priests stand in a circle and up above a few villagers in their Sunday best peer through the grille. Ten maladroit pallbearers have great difficulty shouldering the heavy casket, which lists with every step they take. The staircase looks insurmountable, but they somehow make it and we all proceed to the church.

Mourners entered the church single-file. Mme Zola, her face contorted with grief, leaned on a maid and manservant. Zola slumped onto the prie-dieu and remained there throughout the ceremony, prostrate amidst the singing of a countertenor who bungled words as well as notes "and the braying of a half dozen cantors."

Emilie's coffin was to be set beside her husband's in the vault built three years earlier with money from *L'Assommoir*, and so Zola immediately embarked upon the long voyage south. A crowd awaited him in Aix, where, as he wrote to Céard, he would once again suffer the "frightful pain" of a religious ceremony. "People tell me it's unavoidable. What consoles me is the fact that the vault is perfectly intact and that tomorrow everything will be over. My wife is so exhausted that we shall undoubtedly return in stages." They asked themselves whether, after all that had taken place during the previous fortnight,

[16]Of Lazare, a character into whom he poured himself, Zola wrote: "The fear that heart disease would claim him and his kin had haunted him. . . . To be afflicted in the heart, at the very source of life, was for him the most frightful, the most pitiless death. Thus would his mother die and thus he, too, would die."

they could endure the sight of Médan again, whether they could enter a house still inhabited by Emilie's anguished spirit. "At first we thought we'd flee Médan," Zola informed Marguerite Charpentier upon his return. "Then we changed our minds—fleeing our sorrow seemed cowardly. We'll therefore remain here another month, or until our house no longer seems cursed. . . . My wife has been quite ill. We're dazed right now. We'll be less so in time. It's a frightful thing to say, but time cures the deepest wounds. As for myself, I shall see if I can lose myself in work."

Sacred places—places where memory dwells—were supremely important to a writer whose saga of parvenus rising above the buried past opens in a graveyard from which bones have been removed. Zola built monuments, vaults, shrines. And this pious man enshrined his mother's memory at Médan. Her room there remained forever afterwards *her* room, with all the contents exactly as they had been before she died, including, on one wall, an old oil painting of herself and her infant son.

Yet another shrine was the superstitious conviction to which he clung thenceforth that the number seventeen, as in October 17, could only bring him misfortune.

XVIII

※

"THE FETISHISM OF MEDIOCRITY"

THE FRENCH REPUBLIC had meanwhile experienced many vicissitudes, and in that collective realm, too, a death proved to be of signal importance. On September 3, 1877, Adolphe Thiers expired. Born during Napoleon Bonaparte's victorious rampage across northern Italy in 1797, this astoundingly resilient little Provençal breathed politics until the last. Having won a parliamentary seat the year before, having joined the "363" who declared Broglie unacceptable as prime minister and found himself obliged to campaign all over again when MacMahon dissolved the Chamber of Deputies, he was, at eighty, buoyed by great expectations. If France returned a republican majority, he hoped, with Gambetta's assistance, to drive his nemesis from the presidential palace. He and Gambetta had indeed already effected a partnership that made the latter's agenda for social change less ominous to conservatives and the former's moderation less unpalatable to social reformers. "The old man was determined to have his revenge for his overthrow in 1873; and fortune gave him both his enemies as prey," observes one historian. "His revenge over Broglie and MacMahon would be complete; he would help to defeat the one and drive the other out of the presidency, where he proposed to replace the marshal." For Gambetta, Thiers was a valuable ally who through his influence over fence-sitters could thwart any attempt by MacMahon to counter Broglie's defeat with a Centrist coalition.

Thiers's dream of recovering executive power was dashed on September 3, but his vengeance survived him. From beyond the grave he posed an even more serious threat to MacMahon, for left-wing republicans who had shunned the live politician rallied around the dead statesman. Posthumously absolved of sins committed against the proletariat, Thiers (whose widow would not authorize a state funeral) received tribute from multitudes of workers as his flower-laden hearse clattered across eastern Paris to the cemetery where Communards had made their last stand during *la semaine sanglante.* This demonstration presaged a united republican front. "For me," Goncourt noted in his journal, "the idolatry that attended Thiers's funeral bears striking witness to France's monarchical temperament. In its president it will always want a monarch, a dominator, and not a servant of elected assemblies."

Republican deputies agreed, which may be why, after winning the national elections, they hastened to neuter the presidency. Dissolution was MacMahon's chief weapon against a recalcitrant Chamber, and this they made him surrender. "We must, in our national interest, resolve the present crisis once for all," he wrote in a dictated and grudgingly signed message that was to shape France's political course until 1939.

> The exercise of the right of dissolution is nothing more than recourse to a court from whose judgment there is no appeal: it cannot serve as a system of government. I felt that it was my duty to lodge this appeal and I shall respect the verdict. . . . A new era of prosperity will dawn and its development will be the common purpose of all public powers. Harmony between Senate and Chamber, with the latter now assured of completing its term, will bring to fruition the legislative programs demanded by the electorate. Then there is the Universal Exposition: commerce and industry will thrive as never before, and we shall offer the world fresh evidence of our national vitality.

With MacMahon stripped of effective power, the republican majority went about unseating seventy-two deputies in whose electoral campaigns priests and notables were alleged to have exerted "undue" influence. What became axiomatic thereafter was the principle that corrupt behavior manifested itself only in conservative ranks. No republican legislator would ever face expulsion because a Masonic lodge, an anticlerical schoolmaster, or a like-minded prefect had endorsed his candidacy.

The Universal Exposition imposed decorum upon the Chamber, but deputies of the republican Left, who greatly outnumbered the republican Center, had additional reasons to temper their reformist zeal. Too much zeal might alarm those cautiously progressive elements whom Gambetta described as *les nouvelles couches* ("the new layers") and whose support would be indispensable in forthcoming Senate elections. It behooved republicans, Gambetta declared, to table some reforms until they had been given a Senate majority. Until then, he warned, "no imprudence, no dissidence, no mistakes." On one occasion the fiery orator could not refrain from proclaiming that education must be laicized, that "wherever the Jesuit spirit finds a crack, clericals slip in and take over." Otherwise, he practiced what he preached. When, for example, Karl Marx's International Workingmen's Association was denied permission to convene in Paris, Gambetta raised no objections. And when police imprisoned thirty-four delegates who ignored the government ban, he did nothing to have their terms commuted.

This *entente cordiale* ended as soon as republicans gained control of both houses. Administrative, diplomatic, and judicial officers appointed by Broglie knew that the Senate victory would cost them their posts. The purge began straightway, on January 25, 1879, with ministers submitting long lists of candidates for dismissal. Poor, beleaguered MacMahon, who could not repel them, did not even fight, except to secure the reappointment of old army chums to high commands. On January 30, the seventy-one-year-old marshal tendered his resignation and walked into private life after congratulating his successor—a drab, cautious, tightfisted septuagenarian lawyer with impeccable republican credentials named Jules Grévy.

There were many who supported Grévy in order to keep the dangerous Léon Gambetta from occupying the Elysée Palace. Gambetta as chief executive would not do, they felt. He sucked up too much oxygen, he hogged center stage, he loomed too large, he schemed too fast.[1] But on January 31, the same legislators who begrudged him the presidency of the Republic elected him the president of the Chamber, and in that role, which he played until November 1881, the great tribune helped several prime ministers, notably Jules Ferry, steer a leftward course. Had he not already declared that unless the secondary school system was secularized, the Church would hold France hostage,

[1]"His attempts to live in a more decorous fashion, to abandon the Bohemian habits of his youth, did not convert his old enemies and angered his old friends," notes one historian. "He might be presentable enough for the prince of Wales, but not for M. Buffet, and, on the other hand, the man whose trousers at last met his waistcoat, who delighted in society, whose dinner-parties were smart as well as important, could hardly be a sound republican in the eyes of Camille Pelletan, whose own general grubbiness and rudeness were to be, for a generation, proof that he, at least, was immune from the seductions of the old order." While president of the Chamber, Gambetta kept open house at the Palais-Bourbon, spending the 80,000 francs of his salary on entertainment. His table was said to have been populated every day by petitioners and solicitants, as well as officers of the Chamber's military guard.

poisoning young minds against the Republic? This laicizing effort became almost the priority of government after MacMahon stepped down. When a reform bill met opposition from civil libertarians in the Senate, Jules Ferry, nothing daunted, issued decrees that required the Society of Jesus to quit France within three months and all other religious teaching orders to secure authorization to stay. "The decrees were duly executed; the Jesuits did not dissolve as ordered but waited to be expelled," writes D. W. Brogan.

> In Paris, the priests expelled by the deputy-turned-policeman, the Prefect Andrieux, left their houses on the arms of distinguished pupils. The spectacle of venerable men going into exile surrounded by the affectionate regret of a large number of gentlemen in frock-coats and top-hats was less moving than the simpler-minded Catholics imagined it would be, for the Paris crowds disliked the gentlemen for being friends of the Jesuits and the Jesuits for being friends of the gentlemen. Two hundred magistrates resigned their posts rather than take part in the expulsions, and their names were inscribed by the Catholics in a "Golden Book," but more important was the welcome opportunity thus given to Government to republicanize the legal system still further.

Protests were not confined to magistrates, but neither indignant Catholics nor republicans distressed at seeing their flag-bearers employ strong-arm tactics reminiscent of the imperial government, held Ferry back.

While taking charge of future generations by expelling, *manu militari*, teachers pledged to a hostile doctrine, the new regime took charge of its past in symbolic gestures that served to validate or glorify republican history. In July 1879 the seat of government was returned to Paris, after eight years at Versailles. It was decreed as well that *La Marseillaise* should thenceforth be France's national anthem. One year later, on July 6, 1880, the legislature made July 14 a national holiday, commemorating not only the fall of the Bastille but the Revolutionary festival called *"la fête de la réunion."* And just before Bastille Day 1880, Communards who had moldered in prison fortresses and penal colonies since 1871, or lived abroad in penurious exile, learned that they had been amnestied, thanks largely to Gambetta's relentless campaign on their behalf. "You must close the book of these last ten years," he enjoined the Chamber. "You must place the gravestone of oblivion over the crimes and vestiges of the Commune and say to all alike, to those whose absence one deplores as well as to those whose contradictions and discords one finds regrettable, that there is but one France and but one Republic."[2] Even as the black-robed soldiers of Jesus were bidding France farewell, the reds set foot on French soil again.

Although Zola welcomed this "Republic of republicans," it cannot be said that he did so with open arms. (Nor, as we shall see, did he endorse its attempt to inculcate a "civic" religion.) The abuse hurled at him since 1867 by gentlemen of the Left had made him bitter, and he relieved himself in a long article whose ostensible purpose was to examine the new, post-Moral Order era. Written for *The European Herald* but republished on April 20, 1879, in the literary supplement of *Le Figaro*, "La République et la littérature"—which opens with the assertion that its author wants nothing from the government, neither office nor recompense—is an extended discourse on the relationship between literature and politics in general, and between naturalist literature and the Republic in particular.

Today, although there is still noise aplenty, the Republic exists in fact. It functions, it can be judged on its acts. The time has therefore come to have the Republic and literature face each other, to find out what the latter must expect from the former, to see if we analysts, anatomists, collectors of human documents, savants who admit only the authority of fact, to see if we shall find friends or foes in republicans of the present day.

The very existence of the Republic, he stated portentously, hinged on its respect or contempt for a literature wedded to empirical observation. If it lived by anachronistic precepts, it would surely perish by them. "The Republic will live or the Republic will not live depending on whether it accepts or rejects our method. The Republic will be naturalist, or it will not be at all."

What followed was a diatribe in which Zola, sounding more like a born-again Comtean or a Saint-Simonian technocrat than like a stalwart republican, ridiculed all politics and politicians. "In every political

[2]During the great military review held on that July 14, Jules Grévy gave to army colonels the regimental flags surrendered ten years earlier at Metz in a military blunder for which Marshal Bazaine was sentenced to life imprisonment. The army could thus regard its soiled honor as having been cleansed. *Revanchisme* held sway on the Left no less than on the Right, and so, even when Gambetta swore that France had peaceful intentions, there were belligerent innuendos to his oath. "What makes our hearts beat fast," he declared in a speech to French naval forces at Cherbourg, "is not an ideal of bloody adventurism but the hope that France in its diminished state shall remain whole, that justice resides in the nature of things and that justice shall ring forth on its own appointed day and at the appointed hour." After hearing about this speech, Bismarck reportedly observed that "Gambetta in power would act upon the nerves of Europe like a man beating a drumroll in a sick ward."

problem there are two elements: the ideal design and the human agent. . . . If men were pure abstractions or toy soldiers or skittles, one could transform a monarchy into a republic overnight. But men muddle everything with their warring ideas, their wills, their ambitions, their follies." Are republican leaders less benighted than monarchists? he asked. No less benighted, only less coherent, for while invoking freedom in the social sphere they deny it in the realm of art and abolish institutions that disenfranchise citizens only to safeguard conventions that imprison writers. Just as the progressive men who emerged triumphant in July 1830 spurned Victor Hugo for Casimir Delavigne, so those who won in January 1879 spurned Emile Zola for Victor Hugo.

> In France, whenever political men have sought freedom for the nation, they have begun by sequestering writers in some antique formula, as in a dungeon. They smash government, but they regiment written thought. . . . The law seems constant. In 1830, liberals repudiated romanticism; today, republicans repudiate naturalism.

Illustrating the dictum that "power trembles before the written word," republicans—even republicans who trumpet their atheism—impose upon literature the pieties of an *ancien régime*. "How odd! Here are men who overturn dogmas and speak of killing God but in literature cannot do without a gimcrack Otherworld, without celestial paintings and superhuman abstractions. Where it bears upon social policy, religion is anathema to them, but dare secularize literature by not worshipping at the altar of the Beautiful, and they turn crimson."

Bolstered by his enormous recent successes, Zola enjoined politicians to recognize that what writers needed in order to achieve full development was laissez-faire rather than official patronage. With a combination of rage and entrepreneurial swagger, he declared, "Masters grow all by themselves in the national soil, and government, far from nurturing them, almost always disowns them. . . . At best a minister of state may be an enlightened Maecenas, if he has strength enough to disengage himself from routine and politics, to sweep away mediocrities and distribute his commissions, his pensions, his crosses among genuinely original talents." Now that the Republic was firmly established, would parliamentary exhibitionists who for years had been diverting attention from writers like himself at last yield center stage? "No one considers us writers and artists," he complained in one of those outbursts of self-pity that made Edmond de Goncourt seethe.

> It is apparently not recognized that our generation—men between thirty and forty—was drowned out first by the Empire's final con-

vulsions and then by the Republic's laborious birth. Does a writer
exist when political men occupy the limelight? Do people bother
about books when the newspapers are stuffed with accounts of parliamentary proceedings, of interminable and hollow debates? Politics,
always politics—politics in such massive doses that even women in
salons speak about nothing else. That's our predicament. Our share
in the century has been stolen, our best years have been wasted.

History was one thing, politics quite another. Zola could not gainsay
historical necessity, but it infuriated him to labor in the shadow of
dwarfs who had chosen public careers after bungling private ones. Any
dunderhead who mounted the podium, he found, attracted more attention than a writer delivering a masterpiece. "It's because there are
easy victories to be won in politics that it recruits so many washouts
and déclassés. And it's because of these victories, this magnification of
preposterous personalities . . . that we toilers who set store by genius
and patient study view politics with contempt."

Zola measuring *Les Rougon-Macquart* against the French Republic
(like Eugène Rougon measuring the mini-empire of his dreams against
imperial France) earned derision from friends as well as from foes.[3]
But derision only made him bolder. He challenged republican leaders
at every opportunity and surpassed himself with an article called
"Haine de la littérature" ("Hatred of Literature"), which Laffitte reluctantly published in August 1880. Politics was France's chronic disease, in his view. The prattle of a logorrheic nation filled newspapers
to overflowing. Politics left little room for literature or, indeed, for
anything else, and Zola pictured this state of affairs as deliberate.
There was inside almost every politician a writer manqué who had
chosen public life to avenge his lack of talent, if not to lord it over
those more richly endowed than they:

> If we set aside extraordinary political careers and consider only the
> swarm of journalists and agitators, the herd of electees—from mere
> municipal councillors right up to deputies—whom universal suffrage
> had benefited, we see failed artists or writers in all these secondhand
> statesmen. Nowadays literary bohemia supplies politics with recruits.

[3]"What do you make of Zola?" Maupassant asked Flaubert in a letter dated April
24, 1879. "I myself find him absolutely mad. Have you read his article on Hugo?
His article on contemporary poets and his pamphlet called 'La République et la
littérature'? Phrases such as 'The Republic will be naturalist, or it will not be at
all,' 'I am only a savant' (my, how modest) . . ." Maupassant had not yet published
any fiction or he might have felt some gratitude to Zola for condemning restrictive
practices maintained by republican leaders and especially the government seal of
approval required of books sold in railroad stations.

The aspersions cast at fellow novelists in "Nos romanciers contemporains" had been mild compared to the obloquy lavished on politicians here. "Take a scrofulous person, a cretin, a misshapen brain and you will find in all these the stuff of a political careerist," Zola frothed. "I know some whom I wouldn't want for domestics. . . . When one has flunked everything everywhere, when one has been a shyster lawyer, a hack journalist, a second-rater from top to toe, politics takes you and makes you a minister as good as any other." That newspaper editors should hang upon the words of such men sharpened his anger. "Is it not frightening, this pullulation of papers and this scorn for literature? There isn't one rag with a serious literary section. They all grind out the most discordant tunes on their political hurdy-gurdies." Together with a philistine government went a sycophantic press.

In his denunciation of these accomplices Zola never singled out *Le Voltaire* as a sterling exception to the rule. He could not reasonably have demanded more latitude or room than Jules Laffitte gave him— the paper featured his byline over a weekly theater review, over long essays written initially for *The European Herald* and republished in France, over art criticism, over installments of *Nana*. But because Laffitte had not been hospitable to his protégés and because he moved in high republican circles, Zola bore him ill will. When on one occasion Laffitte deleted from his copy a malevolent remark about Gambetta's newspaper, *La République française*, Zola declared him "an imbecile." On another occasion he portrayed him as *grinchu* or "crabbed." And in December 1879 they clashed over *Nana*, with Laffitte requesting that Zola mollify Gambetta by making several minor changes, and Zola threatening terrible reprisals. After eighteen months of friction, their alliance was mutually uncongenial. It ended the day Laffitte felt compelled to dissociate himself from statements made by his rambunctious contributor in "Haine de la littérature." More than once, he wrote in an editorial letter published on September 3,

M. Zola spoke about political men, about contemporary journalism and newspaper directors in a very personal way, and his high opinion of literature . . . led him to formulate paradoxes that generally lack impartiality. So, when he tells us that "a boy with talent enough to be a writer would never consent to splash about in the kitchen slops of politics," . . . one may characterize his remark as utter nonsense. . . . The solidarity existing among those who write for the same paper requires me to say clearly and categorically that the viewpoint of our eminent critic M. Zola is, especially on this occasion, his alone.

Zola had no sooner seen the above than he fired off a telegram to Laffitte: "Henceforth, you are dead for me." It took him another day to draft an open letter and, when *Le Voltaire* rejected it, to contact the conservative *Le Figaro*. "Your friends are not mine," he declared, suggesting that Laffitte was the puppet of certain republican bigwigs, notably Arthur Ranc, a militant radical with two novels to his credit, who had vehemently attacked *L'Assommoir* several years earlier.

> You have behind you that literary bohemia which is in the process of parceling up France. And I have no doubt that your friends dictated your article about me. There's one in particular whose only distinguished accomplishment is the fact that a court once sentenced him to death: a mediocre novelist whom no one reads, a mediocre deputy who never speaks, a mediocre policeman from whom the Republic still awaits real service. . . . You have thus chosen between your political friends and me, which is quite natural.[4]

Laffitte's directorial manners were, he continued, those of a bully and an oaf: "When a director takes issue with one of his editors, he sees him and has a chat before breaking relations. It's what well-bred people do. But you, instead, . . . loudly attack me in your newspaper and transform an internal administrative matter into a scandal. Obviously such deportment . . . betrays a complete lack of literary etiquette." Laffitte retorted four days later that these self-righteous grievances had no basis in fact. "You add, with an injured air: 'One chats . . .' How many times did I tell you that I found your theater criticism inadequate, inadequate because you seldom attended premieres and wrote about them, if you wrote about them at all, through hearsay. . . . You invoke tact, loyalty, candor. Ah, sir! You judge yourself very leniently indeed."[5]

A week after his departure from *Le Voltaire*, Zola signed up with Francis Magnard, director of *Le Figaro*, who, like a believer seeking to hook an important infidel, had been angling for him since December of the year before. Paris learned about it on September 16, when *Le Figaro* published a letter in which Zola explained what many of his

[4]The allusion in this letter is to Ranc, who had served in the Government of National Defense as "Directeur de la Sûreté Générale" (Chief of Secret Police), and who had been sentenced to death in absentia for having participated in the Commune.
[5]This debate provoked much commentary in the press. One of the most astute observations was made by Henry Fouquier, who wrote for the journal *Le XIXe Siècle*: "M. E. Zola . . . , while often voicing hostile feelings about the romantic school, has piously retained some of its prejudices. One of the most shocking is the idea that pure literature, the novel for example, is inherently superior to political discourse. M. E. Zola and his school affected disinterest in politics, counterfeiting the impassivity that held sway in Gautier's circle. This old-fashioned pose came down to the naturalists via Flaubert."

republican admirers regarded as treasonous behavior. "You wish to offer me space for waging a campaign in *Le Figaro,* my dear Magnard, and I accept," he wrote.

> I accept because it is becoming impossible in republican papers to judge the men and facts of our Republic freely. I accept because literature, which has been hunted down and banished from all pro-government sheets as cumbersome and dangerous, will soon have no refuge outside reactionary papers. It is a republican who now joins *Le Figaro* and who will ask that you accord him a great deal of personal independence there.

In return for independence, he promised to treat with consideration the "legitimate scruples" of Magnard's "large public."

Balanced against the obvious pitfalls were significant advantages. He would receive 1,500 francs per month for his weekly articles, or three times the fee paid him by Laffitte. He would also propagate the cause of *Les Rougon-Macquart* to an audience ten times larger (105,000 readers of *Le Figaro* versus 10,500 of *Le Voltaire*), and having at his disposal *le grand public,* which he characterized among friends as "imbecile," pleased him. Above all, he felt certain that missiles would alarm the new republican establishment more effectively if lobbed from without rather than from within. Not once but thrice did he "accept" Magnard's offer in the above-quoted letter, and this thrice-repeated "J'accepte" may be taken as a measure of his rage. It heralds, ironically, the oft-repeated "J'accuse" published years later on the front page of *L'Aurore.*

Zola launched his "campaign" from Médan with an attack upon Arthur Ranc in which he mercilessly insisted that the prestige Ranc enjoyed as a former Communard who had spent six years in exile exemplified "the fetishism of mediocrity." It hit home. "Your *Figaro* article has made a great splash," Céard informed him on September 22. "Even those who can't stand you . . . agree that you will do republicans damage by sustaining this tone of sharp-edged guilelessness. The Gambettist papers I sent you are confirmation." Céard thought it advisable that Zola answer straightway the accusation of treason, as everybody was expecting his rejoinder. "Many people plan now to buy *Le Figaro* on Monday morning."

Zola took Céard's advice and in an article entitled "Les Trente-six Républiques," or "The Umpteen Republics," he repulsed charges from the Left. "So, my brother republicans are not happy," it begins. "They call what I did plain treason, unleashing a flood of abuse, in bad French, which makes matters worse. . . . Here I stand, a perjurer and renegade. I've betrayed the Republic. The question is—which Republic?" With republicans themselves dispersed in hostile camps, each prepared to annihilate the others, how could his action be regarded as treasonous? Why was writing for the pro-MacMahon *Figaro* worse than writing for the virulently anti-Gambettist *Réveil?* "I am very perplexed," he declared.

> Could it be the republic of M. Gambetta that I've betrayed, this optimistic and satisfied republic, which savors victory and, amidst the daily shocks that have come little by little to exasperate our country, predicts a cloudless future? Or could it be the republic of M. Henri Rochefort, who declares the republic of M. Gambetta to be idiotic and who every morning [in *L'Intransigeant*] breakfasts upon a grilled slice of the dictator while assuring us that disaster lies straight ahead? Of course I could also have sold out the republic of M. Clemenceau, which joins that of M. Rochefort in devouring the republic of M. Gambetta even as it secretly fumes against the republic of M. Rochefort. I search myself, I explore nuances, I wonder whether I might not have sprung my evil coup against the republic of the semi-official M. Hébrard, a mixture of Protestantism and liberalism specially concocted for prudent bourgeois? or perhaps against the republic of M. About. . . .

As Céard suggested he do, Zola maintained a style that calls to mind the mock bewilderment of Persians touring France in Montesquieu's *Lettres persanes.* Good grief! he exclaims. "How shall I learn the error of my ways, in order to make public amends? It is true that I have a glimmer of suspicion about one thing: I may have betrayed all those republics. If so, I would regain some esteem for myself. Betraying the Republic after having loved it is one thing, and a heinous thing at that; but zounds, betraying the umpteen republics of an ambitious mob is a different thing altogether!"

With the tenacity of Cato the Elder urging Rome in season and out to destroy Carthage, Zola reminded readers of *Le Figaro* that France would not prosper until the Republic had transcended republican politics. What he wanted, he wrote, was a meritocracy, a Republic led by larger men with smaller egos. "After a tumultuous decade, I should like certain personages to let us breathe freely; I should like to enjoy our present-day Republic without being jostled every three months over issues that advance not the commonweal but personal status. In short, I should like the nation established upon a firm base of republican government, after its needs have been scientifically defined."

Political forms became indistinguishable from literary ones as he proceeded, week after week, to judge all human enterprise in light of the opposition between subjective and objective, between classical or romantic and naturalist, between bombast and science, between the rhetoric of yesteryear and the positivism of his day. Why, for example, did Gambetta exasperate him? Because the "great tribune" spurned modern art. "M. Gambetta is not a passionate lover of our modern world, and therein lies my brief against him," he wrote. "He's still a disguised Greek or Roman. He surely believes himself to be in classical antiquity; his republic is two thousand years old and when he entertains fantasies of reincarnation, he sees himself crowned with roses, a crimson cloak draped over his shoulder, drinking sweet wine in the company of Phryne and Aspasia. He will praise our sciences in a rhetorician's orotund language, but the spirit has not penetrated him. His mind cannot therefore get beyond the Latin conception of a dogmatic government, beyond the idea of some absolute beauty governed by an unconscious metaphysics." Much worse than Gambetta was Charles Floquet, a wealthy left-wing republican deputy who had rented the Théâtre de l'Ambigu for the sole purpose of denouncing Zola, in a public lecture, as a "slanderer of the common people" and execrating L'Assommoir as a work destructive of public morale. From his conservative emplacement, Zola hurled invective at this future prime minister. "Observe his head," he wrote on November 22, 1880. "It's as if Robespierre's death mask had been fused with some personification of the pompous and ignorant bourgeois. The brow slopes back, the chin juts forward with the insolence you would expect in someone who has never doubted himself. His whole face exudes an instinct for grabbing political territory, and his pallor says that his hunger has not yet been sated." Every party needs nonentities to plug gaps until substantial men materialize, he continued, and such an ersatz figure is Charles Floquet. Will he be a minister someday? he asked. "No doubt. . . . A journalist who made no mark, a lawyer and deputy who has neither grammar nor magnetism, a paragon of smug mediocrity, whom Paris ridiculed only yesterday, will, because he won't be deterred, and for no other reason, succeed one morning in becoming France's head of state."

Zola's articles were often about literature or mores or nervous diseases. Bourgeois adultery gave him grist for milling. So did divorce, Charcot's lectures on hysteria, Huguenot puritanism. Always the naturalist flag-bearer, he wrote in praise of Balzac, of Daudet, of Goncourt, of Littré. But his grudge against Gambetta et al. exceeded all other passions and burst forth with such regularity that he deemed it prudent, after one year at Le Figaro, to assert his republican bona fides. A piece entitled "Democracy" served this purpose. He began by quoting from Mémoires d'outre-tombe a passage in which its aristocratic author, Vicomte François-René de Chateaubriand, observed that Europe was hastening toward democracy, that symptoms of this social

transformation abounded, that masses would thenceforth hold sway.
"That is what the disabused paladin of a monarchy observed half a
century ago," wrote Zola.

> He draped himself in loyalty to his king and emitted this cry of black
> despair when he saw the new society rising like a flood tide. Today,
> the movement continues, stronger than ever, and sweeps away rem-
> nants of the old world. Well, there lies the whole century, in that
> social evolution! It is the advent of democracy which renews our
> politics, our literature, our mores, our ideas. I state a fact, nothing
> more. And I add that he who would impede it will himself be carried
> off.

It was not beyond his comprehension that the crumbling of the majestic old edifice called *vieille France* should fill "religious hearts" with
sorrow and wrath. Who could argue against nostalgia better than he,
himself an easy prey to its seductions? Still, he continued,

> why not have faith in life, in humanity? A secret process shakes and
> drives it, yes, a process that can only bring about an enlargement of
> being, a more complete mastery of the world. . . . I wish that every
> politician subscribed to this creed, above and beyond the abominable
> skulduggery of factional strife.

Here was a creed fit for the modern writer above all. Latter-day romantics waxing ecstatic over the Common People and world-weary
intellects "imbued with amiable erudition and malicious rhetoric"
would inevitably yield to "a stringent mind that relies on primary
source material and aims to supplant the literary amusements of another age with the clinical strategies of today's savant." So what if the
democratic era had fostered bad taste as well as scientific progress,
allowing France to be inundated by (for instance) pulp fiction and
sensational tabloids? Did not every virtue have its deficiency? "In every
phase of human evolution there are wretched and shameful concom-
itants," wrote Zola.

> Vulgar though it may be, the press accomplishes a useful task; it is
> the avant-garde of democracy, it makes reading commonplace and
> enlarges our public. I know that this enlarged public is precisely what
> vexes retired literati and young aesthetes. But why should we tremble
> before a clientele composed of the entire nation? Therein lies true
> literary democracy: speaking about everybody and to everybody,
> granting all social classes place in the realm of letters, and thus ad-

dressing all citizens. If our public becomes immense, it is for us to have voices powerful enough to reach it.

Far be it from him, with at least three best-sellers, to join the chorus of less successful confreres execrating commercialism in literature. "I have said it elsewhere—money gives us dignity because it makes us free. It's true, we are merchants; we no longer whimper like that booby Chatterton[6] when we have to sell our books—and since we've become the vendors of those books, we've also become the owners. We have conquered the right to say everything in them, while living by our labor, like all other productive entrepreneurs."

In November 1881, Zola and Francis Magnard agreed to part company. Although they respected each other, theirs had always been a marriage of convenience, nothing more, and after fourteen months it showed signs of wear. Zola's tirades against Gambetta did not altogether reconcile Magnard to the fact that *Le Figaro* had also become a platform for naturalist apologies. Zola, in turn, found self-censorship increasingly onerous. After skirting subjects about which Catholic, promonarchist readers might have "legitimate scruples," he concluded that fifty-eight articles were quite enough. With neither financial need nor lack of exposure to justify this distraction from *Les Rougon-Macquart*, he bowed out in a valedictory entitled "Adieux."

By this time, his correspondence with *The European Herald* had long since trailed into silence. Until December 1879, Zola had been punctuality itself, dispatching a thirty-page essay to Stasiulevich on the 20th of every month, six days after announcing the topic. For variety's sake he wrote as often about aspects of French society as about literature, theater, or art, and representative titles include "Contemporary French Youth" (April 1878), "The Opening of the Universal Exposition" (June 1878), "The Outskirts of Paris" (August 1878), "Types of Contemporary Women in France" (November 1878), "The Contemporary Theater Scene" (January 1879), "The Festival at Coqueville" (August 1879), "The Experimental Novel" (September 1879). It was in October 1879, when *Le Voltaire* began to serialize *Nana*, that problems arose. No sooner had the first installment appeared than Stasiulevich, who had been promised a chapter, found himself scooped by his rival Suvorin at *Novoe vremia* (*The New Times*). As there existed no copy-

---

[6]Thomas Chatterton, who at twelve composed the "Rowley Poems," claiming that they were copies of fifteenth-century manuscripts. He came to London in 1770, failed to sell his verse, and poisoned himself. Alfred de Vigny made him the titular hero of a play that enjoyed great success during the 1830s.

right law in Russia and no international copyright convention, anyone could translate anything with impunity. Russian papers exploited the chaotic situation, but Stasiulevich nevertheless felt betrayed and he unburdened himself to Turgenev, who also began to turn against Zola. "Our friend has become presumptuous and thinks that one can behave offhandedly with Muscovites," Turgenev observed. "You must absolutely teach him a lesson: he will see that one doesn't play us dirty and will henceforth be more careful. It's unlikely that he will continue to collaborate much longer." On October 24, Zola swore to Stasiulevich that he had not authorized *The New Times* to translate *Nana*. "It's simple theft, nothing more. I suppose that the minute an installment appears in Paris, someone translates it and sends it to Russia. I can't prevent that, as you well know. I can, on the other hand, see to it that future chapters reach you first." It did no good. Thereafter relations between them deteriorated. Laboring under enormous pressure, Zola twice offered excerpts from *Nana* in lieu of articles or essays, and Stasiulevich rebuffed him each time, perhaps because he found this proposed substitution demeaning, and took umbrage at not being offered material written especially for his paper.

What mattered more than editorial pride was disappointment in Zola's literary agenda. The pretensions to clinical neutrality, the impatience with idealists, or sentimentalists, or sentimental humanitarians, the campaign against a literature of social *engagement*—all set Stasiulevich's teeth on edge. Like many liberal Russian intellectuals, he revered Victor Hugo and estrangement became inevitable when Zola, in an article called "Victor Hugo and His *Légende des siècles*," predicted that

> Hugo, who has been followed through life by myriad believers, will not leave behind a single disciple to maintain the cult. As great as the noise made around the living writer will be the silence surrounding the dead one. Future generations will lose interest and judge harshly . . . because [unlike Balzac] the innovator with his baggage of personal phantasms never entered this century's mainstream, which moves toward exact analysis, toward naturalism. All the medieval bric-a-brac—imitation bric-a-brac at that—will go for knockdown prices.

Zola remained a regular contributor until late 1880. Then manuscripts stopped shuttling back and forth. "I appreciate the dispatch with which you returned 'Jacques Damour,'" he wrote on October 4, in regard to a short story published two months earlier. "I have been so ill for some time that I can't send anything this month." By March 1881, Stasiulevich had come to expect apologies every month, and when he didn't receive one, demanded an explanation. "I am indeed guilty, I was late in warning you once again not to count on me this month," wrote Zola. "My health is still not good, and I am so over-whelmed with work that I must neglect you. Since I foresee several months more of such neglect, wouldn't it be best if I notified you when I have an article ready?" Zola never sent another article, and Stasi-ulevich, although cordial in all his letters, was apparently not disap-pointed to see the collaboration lapse.

Having resigned first from *The European Herald* and then from *Le Figaro*, Zola gave up journalism. Beset with intimations of mortality, he decided at the age of forty-one to work full-time on his magnum opus. "I am seized by a violent distaste for my articles in *Le Figaro*," he confided to Céard on May 6, 1881. "I dream, when I've let all that go, of immersing myself in long works and disappearing for months at a stretch." This divorce was not painless, however. For all his animad-versions against the newspaper business, bylines and instantly pub-lished judgments and polemical jousts had always helped him endure the silence that attended novel writing. They had also compensated for the stage fright that kept him from speaking to live audiences.[7] "To any young writer who solicited my advice I would say: 'As you learn to swim by flinging yourself into water, so learn to write by fling-ing yourself into journalism,' " he declared in his farewell piece. "It is the only virile school we have; it is there that one measures oneself against other men, and there . . . that one forges one's style on the terrible anvil of daily deadlines." Had not "the best" among them sur-vived this ordeal? he asked. "We are all children of the press, we have all won our first stripes there. . . . I sheathe my sword, but I already miss the battle that so often reduced me to a state of exhaustion and disgust."

His journalistic travail had done more than temper him. It produced material sufficient for five volumes of criticism—*Le Roman expéri-mental, Le Naturalisme au théâtre, Nos auteurs dramatiques, Les Ro-manciers naturalistes, Documents littéraires*—which appeared, like a litter, in 1880–81, constituting all together the official formulation of naturalist doctrine.

One paper for which Zola would gladly have postponed his retirement from journalism was a weekly that J.-K. Huysmans almost succeeded in launching in late 1880. Eager to assemble the second-generation "Cinq" on the same masthead, Huysmans demanded their help when

[7]On May 6, 1882, in response to a correspondent whose identity is not known, Zola wrote: "I am very flattered by your offer but unfortunately I cannot accept it. I have already had to decline all similar offers because I have no talent for oratory and am of a nervous nature that makes me terribly awkward in public. This is a firm policy."

his French publisher, Léon-Victor Derveaux, offered him financial backing. Even with his obligations at the ministry of the interior, Huysmans found time to rent an office, to buy furniture, to organize a poster campaign, to place newspaper advertisements, to select type. "Can you send me the title of the short story you've promised me?" he asked Zola on October 1 and filled him in on all the plans.

> I shall design the posters myself, lest Sir Harelip[8] do something monstrous. The pact is still not completed. I've drafted fourteen slightly draconian articles and Derveaux seems intimidated. . . . Dr. Letourneau, a man well respected in philosophy, will cover scientific developments. This is good, I believe, as he can bring us the clientele that buys books at Germer-Baillière and Reinwald. . . . Alexis, who's at Trouville, has proposed a portrait of Laffitte. I vetoed the idea for fear that people might accuse me of wanting to reopen hostilities with that imbecile. Do you agree? . . . No short story from Maupassant, in Corsica. He doesn't answer my letters or Hennique's. Is it possible that he's been done in by banditti?

In short order, Huysmans also had enough copy for a first issue of *La Comédie humaine*, as he respectfully called it, including a "Letter-Manifesto" dictated in rough outline by Henry Céard and signed by Zola. This statement (which offered encouragement, but with "misgivings," because "truth is acquired at a steep price") was to precede some notes on Paris by Goncourt, an article by Huysmans on the "politics and nihilism" of Alexander Herzen, an essay by Céard on "the psychology of Jesuits," a portrait of Jules Ferry by Alexis, letters from abroad, and short fiction.

That first issue never appeared. Huysmans had already corrected proof when Derveaux, who intended to secure a loan on the basis of Zola's association with the enterprise, confessed that his pockets were empty. A publisher named Charles Marpon (of Marpon et Flammarion, which had published *L'Assommoir* in an illustrated edition) thereupon offered 30,000 francs, or less than one-third the amount needed for the stylish paper Huysmans envisioned. Zola suggested that they put out a four-page *canard* or rag, providing all the copy themselves and buying no advertisements. Huysmans agreed at first, then changed his mind. He told the Belgian art critic Camille Lemonnier:

> Céard, Alexis, and Hennique seconded him, while Maupassant and I argued loudly against. . . . It would exhaust its small editorial staff

[8]The harelip might not have been quite so repellent if Derveaux hadn't been Jewish. Like Goncourt, Huysmans was unabashedly anti-Semitic. When Derveaux later backed out of this venture, Huysmans called him in a letter to Zola a *terrible youtre*, "dreadful kike."

and leave us flat broke. It would spell total monotony. My arguments did not prevail. Under the circumstances I resigned as editor-in-chief, wishing neither to assume responsibility for a Latin Quarter broadsheet nor to reject copy submitted by friends whom I had pressed into service. So the paper will appear in January, but with me as a plain ordinary editor. It galls me that in this day and age, which demands the establishment of luxurious department stores on the avenue de l'Opéra, we are going to sell our wares from a pushcart.

Although Zola tried various means of salvaging the project, and this during the sorrowful aftermath of his mother's death, nothing availed. *La Comédie humaine* became an occasion for damage claims rather than for intellectual commentary, pitting Huysmans against Derveaux in the Tribunal de Commerce de la Seine.

Comédie humaine or no *Comédie humaine*, Zola continued, by favors asked and services rendered, to spin a web of militant fellowship around "les Cinq." Alexis remained the loyal pup he had been for a decade, eating from his master's hand when he wasn't snarling at his master's critics. How could Zola not love such unqualified devotion? But for any task that required savoir faire, erudition, or aplomb he turned more often than not to Henry Céard, who found satisfaction in the role of encyclopedic factotum. Having proved so helpful with *Nana*, Céard was called upon to gather information needed for another *Rougon-Macquart* novel, *Pot-Bouille*. "I appreciate the description of importer-exporters; it's very clear and full," Zola wrote on June 3, 1881.

Now, two more requests. I have an old, retired government clerk. I should like his pension to be about 2,000 francs. Please tell me what his job was, in which department (preferably interior ministry), at what age he left it, assuming that he entered at twenty. If a post with a a 2,000 franc pension would have been too lofty for him, tell me which jobs afford 1,200 francs, 1,500 francs, etc. My second question involves a stockbroker's clerk, a clerk whose father has apprenticed him there before buying him a share in the business. What would his duties be?

Once again Céard, who worked at the war department, answered in lavish detail. Even his futile searches were instructive. "As yet I have found nothing," he apologized, referring to a gynecological disorder Zola had visited on one of his characters.

Believe it or not, the library of the medical school has no catalogue! So it's impossible to find works on vaginismus. I'd need authors, names, and you haven't given me any. Same problem at Delahaye's. In my presence he rummaged through his bookstore for a quarter hour without finding even Dr. Lefort's thesis on genital deformities in women. I know that's not exactly your subject but there might have been footnotes directing us to the proper source. . . . That's not all. I wrote to one of my old buddies at Lariboisière Hospital. He himself couldn't enlighten me . . . but he offered to arrange a meeting with Dr. Regeard, who won the silver medal for interns this year, and who wrote a thesis on muscle tears caused by exertion. Unfortunately it contains no clinical data about women. There's one curious case noted in it: a man's abdominal muscles torn during the strain of his nuptial night. It would appear that Regeard, who heads the welfare bureau clinic, has among his patients a woman afflicted with the malady you desire, and that he will show her to me.

Imperturbable, he accepted every question thrown at him, either fielding them himself or—as when Zola wanted to describe the work of a diocesan architect—recruiting specialists. "Huysmans will handle the diocesan architect for you: he has a friend who holds that very position and can interview him. Gabriel, a lawyer, will tell you directly what he knows about court counselors."

Céard's usefulness extended beyond the domain of literature. During the winter of 1879–80—a severe winter marked by fuel shortages all over France—he arranged, through his father, to have ten thousand kilos of high-grade English coal transported from Dieppe to Médan. Not long afterward he visited some pauper who had begged Zola for help (such petitions multiplied with the publication of *L'Assommoir*), doling out money in his friend's name. There were, indeed, errands of every kind.[9] But literature, or literary politics, is what knit them together, and Céard, though eleven years younger than Zola, came to be valued as much for his shrewd advice as for his detective work. At the time of Zola's diatribe against contemporary novelists in 1878, he suggested that Zola reply to his critics promptly and publicly: "Would you like me to send along Hector Berlioz's *Correspondance?* He was in your position, the great musician at bay. Jeered, insulted, almost friendless, he fired salvos from the emplacement of a newspaper column. And with him as with you it was considered unforgivable that he should defend himself blow for blow. The comic-opera hacks who rose against him call to mind the confectioners and wigmakers of present-day fiction." The self-assurance with which he coached his

[9] "Could you do me a favor," Zola wrote on June 19, 1879. "Could you obtain, either at a stationer's or from Nadar himself, the large photograph of Dailly in the role of Mes-Bottes, holding his loaf of bread, and send it to my painter-glazier, M. Baboneau, 13, rue des Abbesses, Montmartre. I want Mes-Bottes reproduced in stained glass." Characters and motifs from *Les Rougon-Macquart* (Dailly, referred to here, appeared in a stage adaptation of *L'Assommoir*) filled the stained glass Zola commissioned for Médan. This pane was intended for the kitchen door.

elder is equally apparent in a letter written two years later, on September 28, 1880, soon after Zola joined *Le Figaro*:

> Will you allow me one small observation? In your article on Ranc and in "The Umpteen Republics" there is a pause at the beginning of Part Two. The initial movement does not continue. I miss a demi-crescendo and I'm not the only one to have noticed this break in rhythm. Reread "The Umpteen Republics." Your "I know them, those republican shops," etc., has the same same tonal value as your premises stated at the outset. . . . The form would have profited if you had affected a slightly more oratorical stance. Take the point for what it's worth. You've always listened to me with such benevolence that I dare communicate what I think and what I've heard said around me by well-wishers. Shall I send you the volume of Alexander Herzen entitled *De l'autre rive?* Published in 1850, it says exactly the same things that you say in 1880, the circumstances being the same.

When Céard had some book or political ploy or rhetorical strategy to recommend, Zola acted upon it, and so he did here. "Your good letter gave me the idea for a third political article which seemed to me necessary and which you will read tomorrow. Your observations are, furthermore, quite accurate; my second article contained two. I acquired Herzen's book, but fear that I've lost it. As I shall be in Paris next Monday, could you bring me a copy that evening at the rue de Boulogne?" It was Céard who acquainted him with the treatise by Dr. Claude Bernard entitled *Introduction à l'étude de la médecine expérimentale* from which he culled metaphors for his best-known and most radical manifesto, *The Experimental Novel*.

Zola gave as energetically as he received. Always hectoring his minions, he took great pains to guide them, to boost them, to find them newspaper assignments. Laffitte would not let "les Cinq" ride Zola's coattails at *Le Voltaire*, but for many publishers, especially foreign ones, a good word from Zola was a virtual guarantee of employment. "The newspaper director who wrote me from Italy and to whom I proposed your collaboration has just answered that he accepts," he informed Léon Hennique on September 10, 1878. "It's no big deal, as you see. The paper looks like a very small pamphlet. I believe that 100 francs a month is all you can ask. Still, I advise you to accept the offer, while waiting for something better. Contact posthaste: M. Angelo Sommuruga, editor-in-chief of the *Rivista Paglierina*, via Pontaccio, no. 1, Milan. Discuss literature, theater, Parisian events, and be frankly naturalist, as this little paper has raised the flag of our movement." Another such transaction involved Piotr Dmitrievich Boborykin, editor of a Saint Petersburg review called *Slovo* (*The Word*), who had met Zola through Turgenev. After hearing from Boborykin, Zola urged Huysmans and

Céard to contact him and gave advice on how to negotiate. Mindful of his flock, Zola kept after Boborykin. "The Russians are robbing you blind," he warned Céard several months later, on November 17, 1878.

From Boborykin's calculations I figure 280 francs per sheet of 16 pages. That's reasonable, or it would be reasonable if they weren't asking you to pay the 40% bank commission for currency conversion and to assume the cost of translation. I'll write Boborykin, but not until we've seen each other next Sunday. On that other score, my advice is that you nominate yourself rather than some friend for the job of political correspondent: let's occupy as much space as possible.

Boborykin had rejected an article by Huysmans, and Zola, voicing chagrin, suggested that he send it to *La Réforme*. "When I'm back in Paris, we shall see about opening some new markets for our work."

Since Maupassant, Huysmans, Alexis, Céard, and Hennique did not yet bulk large enough to help him achieve his imperial dream, or write prolifically enough to "occupy as much space as possible," their accomplishments needed inflating. "Very remarkable" was Zola's description of a modest piece by Céard. "You will without doubt be the critic I've long felt exists in you. Wait until you have the podium you deserve: sparks will fly." For *Le Figaro* he wrote laudatory essays first about Huysmans and Céard, then—much to the dismay of Francis Magnard—about Alexis and Maupassant. "My wish is obviously that you should enjoy complete freedom in matters of tone and taste," the editor-in-chief objected, "but let me say that a solemn piece about Messrs. Alexis and Maupassant appearing on *Le Figaro*'s front page soon after a piece about Messrs. Céard and Huysmans is quite excessive. Though the public may underestimate these gentlemen, the fact remains that it does not *yet* deem them important, and our readers would be justified in feeling mocked." His accolades, Zola responded, were meant to help the public exculpate innocent men. "Since I'm the culprit here, since they have borne the brunt of blows meant for me, it is my duty to show that they stand on their own ground, with feet firmly planted. People see disciples and a leader where there are six comrades one barely older than the others." He was, in short, merely *primus inter pares*.[10]

[10]To a critic who had roughed up Zola, Alexis wrote in 1880: "If you only knew all that I owe this man! What would I be today without him? I have no doubt that the little bit of notoriety I and a few others enjoy is a spark from the blaze this extraordinary man has created around himself! Reviled, misunderstood, ignored, he fought the good fight all alone and suffered the anguish of it . . . whilst we, like young men of means who will inherit a fortune they didn't earn, all we had to do was show up. Even before we've sowed, we've harvested!"

Primus inter pares perhaps, but this wish to nurture individuality among his younger comrades never obscured his vision of five men laboring as one for a cause synonymous with his own person and work. What profited him profited them, did it not? Collective effort spelled virtue, and Zola in the first person plural organized projects that Zola in the first person singular might have been disposed to consider vain, exploitative, or self-aggrandizing. There was, for example, the stage adaptation of *La Conquête de Plassans* (called *L'Abbé Faujas*), on which Henry Céard and Léon Hennique collaborated in 1879 at their master's behest. "I'm a bit rushed," Zola wrote on June 23. "I would like the play staged this November, or at least presented to some theater by early September. Would you, can you, send me your outlines— outlines with each scene clearly marked—toward the middle of next week? Then all [five] of you would come on Sunday, July 6. Discuss it with our friends, and tell me if they agree. *L'Abbé Faujas* can be magnificent." There were also those texts in which Paul Alexis, catering to a large public appetite for personal information about the author of *Nana*, let his hand be guided by Zola. "Do you authorize an article *Le Gaulois* has proposed I do on 'Zola at Médan'?" he asked. "If you have three minutes, jot down some facts or words of advice—what I should say or shouldn't." "Do it," Zola promptly responded from Médan. "I would suggest something shaped along the following lines: a brief description of Médan, a brief historical account of how he came to buy the little house and build the big one, the daily life of your hero as you've observed it, and, in conclusion, the man behind the legendary character ascribed to him." The better to propagate an image of himself as the country squire tending his well-ordered estate or the rustic paterfamilias conversing with his literary brood, Zola urged Alexis to write a biography. "Your articles on the critical reception of my work outside France wouldn't make a good pamphlet. . . . Save that for the biography, which should be growing apace. The time is ripe for it, and the occasion will not last."

The one work that may have done more than any other to consecrate this group as *le groupe de Médan* and thus to situate naturalism in Zola's backyard was an anthology entitled *Les Soirées de Médan*. Brought out by Charpentier in April 1880, soon after *Nana*, the book contained stories by each writer, all of them touching upon the Franco-Prussian War. Why the Franco-Prussian War? For no better reason, Alexis declared many years later, than that three of the group—Zola, Céard, Huysmans—had, unbeknownst to one another, already published war stories here and there. "Simply a coincidence, then, . . . and this coincidence was the 'pretext' rather than the cause of our collective volume. Had it not presented itself, I believe that the volume would have been scaffolded around a different, possibly less successful theme. At bottom, it sprang from our great literary friendship, that's all."

But in fact there was nothing fortuitous about the theme of *Les Soirées de Médan*. War obsessed Zola, and as he made his way through *Nana*, anticipating that final refrain, "A Berlin! A Berlin! A Berlin!," *revanchisme*, or the cant associated with it, became for him a prime example of the suicidal self-deception to which romanticism lent support. "Naturalist authors, those imbued with the century's scientific spirit, [must combat] the parade-ground heroism that wraps itself in flags, that recites odes and sings cantatas," he proclaimed in "Lettre à la Jeunesse," a long essay written for *Le Voltaire*.

> Can we ever get away from music? Like music, [patriotic] tirades conduce to heroic action by exciting the senses or jangling the nerves. They do not address the intelligence, the faculties of comprehension and application. Like a fife and drum corps that plays bravura tunes while soldiers die, they stimulate, they intoxicate, they make men scornful of danger. But this nervous excitation is short-lived.

Truly virtuous are those who dare to see the world as it is, not those who excite paroxysms of amour propre or conjure up images of old-fashioned gallantry. "We are the true patriots, we who want France well informed, purged of lyric folderol, larger for having embraced the culture of truth, confident that the scientific formula should be applied to every human endeavor—to politics as to literature, to social economy as to the art of war." France had been defeated in 1870–71 not from without but from within, not by some inherently superior Nemesis, but by its own obscurantism. "Dominion over the world will be exercised by that nation whose powers of observation and analysis are greatest," Zola prophesied. "Let French youth heed me, patriotism resides in [the prestige conferred upon science]. It is with science as its arm that another generation will one day recapture Alsace and Lorraine."

His "Lettre à la Jeunesse" was a centerpiece in Zola's campaign against Gambetta and Ranc in 1879, when their new regime immediately gave notice that they wanted the French public school system to serve as an instrument of moral regeneration, a seedbed of civic virtue, a propagator of militant patriotism. Except during the Terror almost a century before, *civisme* had never inspired such religious ardor, and never, not even during the Terror, had republicans showed such resolve in making its principles the substance of a new catechism. With one Moral Order overthrown, another, far more aggressive Moral Order established itself. "The new republican civism pervaded the entire curriculum, from elementary classes on up, and especially did it orient the teaching of history and the French language," notes one historian.

> Readings, recitations, dictation exercises, compositions, songs almost always betrayed some moralizing rationale; the point was not so much to develop a child's aesthetic taste or critical faculty as to inculcate the sense of certain very strictly defined duties. Among its promoters, this republican civism was inseparable from the teaching of a social ethics. Solidarity, discipline, work, providence, thrift were all exalted, along with the cult of fatherland or motherland, universal suffrage, and the principles of 1789. In this tangle of Jacobin politics and traditional bourgeois virtue, one element reigned supreme: patriotism, military patriotism. . . . Republicans did not enforce their Spartan model to the last detail, but preparation for military service remained, in their view, a crucial enterprise. The man who became minister of public instruction under Gambetta in November 1881, Paul Bert, created a "Commission of Military Education" and diligently went about organizing "schoolboy battalions" which would assemble every week to march, take target practice, study weapons.

Where Zola, in the "Lettre à la Jeunesse," extolled scientific reasoning, Paul Bert, a distinguished physiologist who succeeded Claude Bernard at the Collège de France before entering government service, reveled in images of passionate martyrdom. "Remain French!" he pleaded on May 1, 1880, to adolescents connected with a national youth association called the Union Française de la Jeunesse.

> Remain French, above all, in your cast of mind. . . . Do not let fogs and fuliginous mysticities—from wherever they come, from beyond the Alps or from beyond the Rhine—obscure your joyous, sunbathed minds. . . . Guard against cosmopolitanism, which is detestable, the red variety no less than the black. . . . Love our noble, our dear country with all the strength of your souls. Love it with an ardent, possessive, chauvinistic love, and if some sage with a well-balanced head should ever criticize you for being excessive, tell him that one doesn't discuss the merits of a mother, especially when she has lost children. And if this sage . . . was born on French soil, chase him away, banish him, call him traitor, for anyone is a traitor who loves his country in measured doses and speaks about it coldly, while its side still bleeds from . . . the wound it suffered over there, to the East.

Teachers echoed him all over France. Or so they were supposed to do, and those who needed help found it in such official periodicals as *L'Instruction primaire* (*Elementary School Instruction*), where, every week, the government dispensed pedagogical pointers, lesson plans, exercises. What, for example, might be the purpose of a schoolmistress teaching girls any kind of military education? "It behooves her, though she herself does not conduct exercises, to teach her students why their brothers drill," explained an editor of *L'Instruction primaire*. "The schoolmistress must know how to inspire in them, let us not say respect for strength—a base sentiment after all—but respect for dash or bravura. Ladies, you must teach our girls to appreciate courage, to scorn cowardice! We ask you to form, in the true sense of the word, citizens, Frenchwomen smitten with heroism . . . who will be ready, when the day of reckoning comes, to uphold the cult of flag and the religion of country." Or again, the journal outlined innumerable subjects for compositions, a typical one reading as follows: "A Good Frenchman. Composition—Sketch. At the Toulon hospital, a young sergeant wounded in Tonkin has his limb cut off. The wounded man wakes up after the operation, beholds himself and says: 'Better amputated than Prussian.' He comes from Metz [in Lorraine]." Like the Communards of March 1871, the republicans of 1880 could not accept the armistice.

Les Soirées de Médan burst upon this scene like an impenitent draft dodger. In its most famous story, Maupassant's "Boule de suif," rich refugees from Rouen—solid citizens—are held hostage by a Prussian lieutenant until the patriotic French prostitute traveling with them can be persuaded to gratify him. But all six stories eschew martial pageantry for sideshows of one kind or another. In Léon Hennique's "L'Affaire au grand 7," French troops invade a small-town brothel, whose inmates they slaughter. In Huysmans's "Sac au dos," which foreshadows Louis-Ferdinand Céline, war recedes from view as a soldier who contracts dysentery when he reaches Chalons-sur-Marne drifts among invalids behind the front line. No one dies on the battlefield except in Zola's "L'Attaque du moulin," and so it is that heroism dies on every page. As Maupassant explained to Flaubert on January 5, 1880:

We simply wanted to hit just the right note, to strip our war tales of chauvinism à la Déroulède,[11] of the false enthusiasm hitherto required in every narrative that features red trousers and a rifle. Instead of picturing generals as geniuses governed by the noblest sentiments and most generous impulses, we show beings who would be indistin-

---

[11]The name of Paul Déroulède, president of the Ligue des Patriotes and author of a collection of poems entitled *Chants du soldat*, was synonymous with love of army, *revanchisme*, etc.

guishable from the average man if they did not wear gold braid and have people killed for no good reason, out of sheer stupidity.

Their neutral stance in matters that excited such passionate interest would gall bourgeois far more than a frontal assault, he said. "It will not be antipatriotic, but simply true."

Zola liked the title *Soirées de Médan* better than the one originally proposed for their collection—*L'Invasion comique.* It added irony to stories already fraught with it by having the storytellers gather in an idyllic landscape. It challenged readers who considered him "pornographic" to imagine him entertaining friends *en famille.*[12] But above all, it gave him seigneurial status. As Voltaire had spoken from Ferney and Hugo from Guernsey, so he, Zola, would speak from Médan. Médan was a bastion, a refuge, an island for opposing, among other tyrannies, the reign of virtue thrust upon France by civic evangelists.

After the publication of *Nana,* Zola did not, as was his wont, sail straight into the next volume of *Les Rougon-Macquart.* Like a great galleon driven off course by adverse winds, he felt disoriented. There was some question, at first, of composing a novel about *la douleur,* or sorrow, which would have involved himself, Emilie, and Alexandrine. But Emilie's death made that subject unbearable. Before him loomed his master plan, with novels yet to be written about the peasantry, the art world, the scientific community, the military, railroad workers, department stores. But the extensive fieldwork all these required was more than a tired, grief-stricken man could manage. One year passed in distraction and false starts. Then, on February 28, 1881, *Le Figaro* published an article that contained the idea for what eventually became the tenth volume of *Les Rougon-Macquart.* "If, among working-class people, milieu and education drive girls into prostitution, among bourgeois, milieu and education drive them into adultery," Zola asserted. "Every level of society has some disease which an observer and moralist must study and expose. Along with the perversion that blooms in the dung of our poor neighborhoods, one must show the unwholesomeness that flowers in . . . the chlorotic stuffiness of bourgeois flats." To whom did the word "bourgeois" apply? "By bourgeoisie," he wrote, "I mean, above all, the vague and populous class ranging between

---

[12]Maupassant emphasized the bucolic in an article written for *Le Gaulois.* His apocryphal version of how *Les Soirées de Médan* came to be evokes Boccaccio's *Decameron.* "As nights were magnificent, fragrant with the odor of leaves, every evening we'd go strolling on the island opposite the house. I'd row everybody over in the *Nana.* Now on one moonlit night, the conversation revolved around Mérimée, of whom the ladies said: 'What a charming raconteur!' . . . etc."

workers at one end and the privileged of this world at the other. It includes salaried employees, shopkeepers, people with small private incomes, all who squirm in tight little niches and hustle furiously to achieve the bare satisfaction of their appetites." A portrait of this middle group made artistic sense, he felt. It would complete the triptych he had begun years earlier with his portrait of lost souls up above, on the Champs-Elysées, and had continued with his portrait of the damned down below, on the squalid rue de la Goutte d'Or.

For anecdotal material, Zola did not have to go far. Whenever the naturalist coterie gathered at Médan, tongues wagged incessantly. All four bachelors—Alexis, Huysmans, Maupassant, Céard—fancied themselves experts in the psychopathology of bourgeois marriage and no one more than Céard, whose notes on the subject came to fill Zola's dossier. Zola drew upon his own experience, of course, but it yielded nothing quite as piquant or arcane as the information furnished by his worldly friend. About the special character of adultery practiced among certain bourgeois women, for example, Céard observed:

They allow everything except coitus, and there the interdiction is categorical. Particularly among those brought up in convents. Such behavior points to a confessor's influence. It must be bound up with some casuistic argument derived from the Abbé Craisson's *De rebus venereis* [a manual on sexuality written for confessors].

Sometimes adultery is provoked by purely physiological situations. The husband's impotence, for example. Diseases of the womb bring about adulterous arrangements, which the women necessarily tolerate. Some very workable households. The man devoted, even loving his wife and keeping, in town, a mistress whom he visits by day. During the evening he stays at home, a good spouse and father. In this case the mistress is only an intimate piece of furniture who serves the ménage without ruining it. . . . She has been known to take an interest in the wife and ask after her.

There are districts in Paris, a bit out of the way but easily accessible, where, on the upper stories of apartment buildings or in shops selling haberdashery, one encounters women without profession, or socially indefinable, always well dressed. They are the mistresses of men with anemic or debilitated wives. In my building, for a very long time, there was a room on the 7th floor, furnished by the concierge and rented to a strange couple. They had been in love when young. They had gone separate ways but met up some years later, both unhappily married, she to a sick husband, he to a sick wife. . . .

As the entire coterie had urged Zola to show bourgeois couples leading lives of covert desperation, everyone felt honor-bound to assist him.

"Do you need notes on the Sunday family dinner right away or can you wait until I bring them to Médan?" asked Huysmans. "I think I'll have some free time soon, for spring is the slack season in the book-binding business. I'll give you all sorts of information about my ex-traordinary clan." Several months later, in June 1881, when Zola was fleshing out characters for *Pot-Bouille,* Huysmans helped with a de-scription of the second job to which many low-level government func-tionaries had recourse. "I send you a meager harvest of information today," he apologized.

> The employee I spoke to you about copies course notebooks for stu-dents at the Ecole Centrale who have to keep them up to date and present them on demand. He must therefore imitate each one's handwriting. The model used for making these copies is the notebook of a student who has diligently attended every lecture. They are made at night, perforce, so that the good student's notebook can be re-turned to him in the morning. I couldn't find out the price paid by students. When I broached this subject with the employee, he fell silent, fearing competition, no doubt.
>   Now another question arises: if you give this information, sketchy though it is, in a novel, you will open the eyes of professors at the Ecole Centrale, divulge the stratagem of students . . . and thus ruin the sideline of a poor devil who needs it to survive. These conse-quences, which I hadn't thought about when I first told you the story, should be weighed. . . . See if you can render it inoffensive, by not mentioning the school, etc.

Equally circumstantial were letters that helped Zola portray an archi-tect who colludes with a diocese. In one of them Huysmans explained at some length how ecclesiastical building projects made their way through the government department responsible for all matters of pub-lic worship, the Direction des Cultes.

Zola elaborated the stage set by himself. With forty characters, he went about populating an apartment house which readers were ex-pected to recognize as the bourgeois counterpart of that great, sinister hulk on the rue de la Goutte d'Or. "Just as he found, on the rue de la Goutte d'Or, a working-class tenement exuding poverty and vice, so now he scouted upper-class Paris for a brand-new residence," Alexis wrote in *Emile Zola, notes d'un ami.* "After he chose one, he had to study it from top to bottom, to make the stone walls transparent, to tear secrets out of the gilded wainscoting, to see everything that hap-pens behind the luxurious, hypocritical façades. And he straightway hit upon the title: *Pot-Bouille*—that is, the bourgeois stewpot, the household routine, the ordinary meal." His decision was that those forty tenants should live quasi-hermetic lives, or rather, that *Pot-Bouille*, like *La Fortune des Rougon* and *La Conquête de Plassans*, should unfold intramurally, for in this way the six-story Second Empire *immeuble*, like the wall around Plassans, would not be an objective container but an excrescence at once material and symbolic of the people it housed. As ants built formicaries and bees built hives, bourgeois built domiciles whose architecture consecrated a social order.

One principle upon which domestic architecture rested was that society might crumble if rank were not upheld floor by floor, with petit bourgeois having higher to climb than haut bourgeois. Another was that appearances counted for almost everything, and from the first page of *Pot-Bouille*, Zola made his building's façade a central issue. Where vice hid behind respectable insignia or impeccable nondescriptness, voyeurism served the cause of virtue. "The courtyard, clean and sad, with its even pavement, its fountain and bright copper tap," is what a new tenant observes from high up. "Not a living creature, not a sound; windows all alike in their white curtains and no birdcages or flowerpots adorning them. To hide the big bare wall of an adjacent building which squared off the courtyard, false windows were painted on it, windows with eternally closed shutters behind which the immured life of the flats next door seemed to continue." But what that new tenant also observes during his preliminary investigation of the milieu in whose claustral scenarios he will soon become embroiled— it is François Mouret's son Octave—is a central cavity, a shaft or well that catches kitchen odors and conveys gossip from flat to flat. "No sooner did one of the mistresses approach than all the chattering domestics would duck back into their kitchens; a silence as of the grave then filled the dark bowel, which stank as much from family secrets vented by rancorous help as from dirty sinks. It was the building's sewer, and while up front dignity held sway, with a grand staircase unfurling itself skyward . . . , here excreta streamed forth." Throughout *Pot-Bouille* this image serves to remind us that like its occupants, who behind closed doors profane everything they publicly hold sacred, the house itself is theater. A collective organism, it does what all bad bourgeois do—cultivating well-scrubbed looks while breeding rank corruption in its gut.

Bound up with its structural duplicity is its official imperviousness. Moral decay never originates here among ourselves but always out there among *les autres*—never in the bastion but always in the metropolis—and tenants from top to bottom share a xenophobic worldview. One such tenant, Madame Josserand, regularly scolds her husband for leaving the daily newspaper where their adolescent daughters can peruse it. "Every morning she'd implore him to take it away, not to let it lie about, as he had done the previous day when, unfortunately, it contained details of a lurid trial, which they might have read."[13] An even more enthusiastic champion of sequestration is Madame Vuillaume, whose pedagogical tenets, which we quoted earlier, result in her daughter's becoming an adulteress soon after becoming a bride.

Feared by everyone, the concierge, Monsieur Gourd, plays the part of Cerberus guarding bourgeois morals. A valet more priggish than his masters, he defends the house against external danger even as he monitors those resident aliens called maids, whose rooms on the uppermost story are a slave quarter or cellblock where young gentlemen and *pères de famille* alike furtively exact sexual favors. Vigilance is required to maintain propriety—to keep high and low apart—and Monsieur Gourd never sleeps. When the plot thickens, his nights grow very long indeed. "For some time, Monsieur Gourd had been prowling around with an air of mystery and consternation, noiselessly, his eyes wide open, his ears pricked. Up and down the two staircases he'd go, indefatigable, and tenants had even seen him at night. The moral weal of the apartment house preyed on his mind, no doubt about it; some shady business, he suspected, was disturbing the cold nudity of the courtyard, the sedateness of the lobby, the lovely domestic virtues of each floor." Not for nothing did Zola have him bear a name that means "numb" or "benumbed." For Monsieur Gourd, the best bourgeois apartment houses are but imperfect mausoleums.

After presenting greed, lust, pusillanimity, neurasthenia, and general heartlessness in acerbic, farcical scenes, *Pot-Bouille* concludes with the expulsion from this community of an innocent whose existence gives the lie to its façade. Zola never wrote anything more soul-searing. High above street level, in her cell, a much abused maid bears a child gotten on her by one or another of her roguish neighbors, possibly a Napoleonic jurist. Knowing that her mistress, who had attributed her swollen stomach to gluttony (while denying her food), would dismiss her instantly if the truth came out, this poor creature can tell no one. She gives birth alone, before dawn, and, when strong enough to walk, deposits the newborn on a doorstep several blocks away. Zola records the clandestine event as follows:

[13]Zola himself was not opposed to prudent custodianship in the matter of what children read. In 1879, when a Dutch girl, Marie van Casteel de Mollenstem, wrote to him complaining that her father had forbidden her to read the Rougon-Macquart novels, he answered as follows: "You must listen to your father. If he forbids you to read my books he must have reasons I don't wish to examine. Every family head has the strict obligation to direct as he sees fit the education of his children. Let me add that my books make very bitter reading for a person your age. When you're married, when you must live independently, read me. And I hope that my books, as cruel as they may seem to you, will foster in you the love of truth."

[Adèle managed to cut the umbilicus], then dozed off. Six o'clock tolled when consciousness of her predicament woke her again. Time was short. She rose painfully, did what had to be done without having planned it. A cold moon illuminated her chamber. After getting dressed, she wrapped the infant in old linen, then folded it between two newspapers. Though it didn't make a sound, its little heart was beating. As she had forgotten to see whether she had borne a girl or a boy, she unfolded the papers. A girl. One more luckless wretch! More meat for some coachman or valet, like that foundling Louise! The other maids had not yet stirred and she could leave, have M. Gourd, half asleep, pull the cord downstairs, place her package in the passage Choiseul, whose gates were just being opened, then quietly climb back up. She had met no one. Finally luck was with her, for once in her life.

She immediately tidied up the room. She rolled under her bed the oilcloth on which she had lain, dumped the placenta, sponged the floor. And absolutely exhausted, waxen-faced, with blood still flowing between her thighs and only a towel to stanch it, she lay down again. Thus did Madame Josserand find her when she came up at 9 o'clock to see why her maid had not yet begun work. Adèle having told her that she had been kept awake all night long by diarrhea, Madame exclaimed: "Naturally! You must have eaten too much again! All you think about is filling yourself up."[14]

Among other Rougon-Macquart novels that conclude with the sacrifice of a scapegoat, or an act of exorcism, *Pot-Bouille* most closely resembles *La Fortune des Rougon*. As Miette becomes fertile for nothing, dying at puberty, so Adèle must cast out the bastard she has delivered from her womb. And as Silvère is committed to a nameless grave after Louis Napoleon's soldiers kill him, so that bastard finds herself committed, nameless, to an inhospitable world. For the disinherited there is no room to live, or to die, except outside the walls.

Zola's feelings about *Pot-Bouille* as he composed it were ambivalent. On the one hand, it seemed to him (today one can hardly imagine why) excessively dispassionate. On the other hand, understatement was a naturalist virtue and the banality of everyday life a desirable

[14]Mme Josserand's reproach calls to mind the observations of a jurist named Marcel Cusenier. "In any event, the goal of masters is to differentiate servants from themselves, to establish between them a manifest inequality," he wrote, two years before World War I, in *Les Domestiques en France*. "They go even farther. They reduce domestics to a rank somewhere between men and things. No modesty in their presence. They endeavor to destroy their personalities, inside and out. They make mannequins of them. They imagine themselves to be in the presence of 'animated instruments,' admirable automata, and to achieve this result they exploit the absolute dependence of a class that must rent out its services. They regard domestics as human only to hold them in suspicion. They question their probity, their mores, their appetite."

effect. "My novel is a work of precision and clarity, nothing more," he wrote to Céard on August 24, 1881. "No bravura, no lyric self-indulgence. It doesn't warm the cockles of my heart; rather, it amuses me like some device whose mechanism requires careful calibration. I ask myself whether, being passionate, one is well advised to deny or contain one's feeling. If one of my books endures, it will surely be the most passionate. No matter, one must vary one's tune, and try everything. All this is woolgathering, for, I repeat, I am very pleased with *Pot-Bouille*, which I call my *Education sentimentale*." The parallel argued real self-satisfaction, for Flaubert's *Education sentimentale* was, in his view, a brilliant example of postromantic literature, a model to be imitated by artists who habitually drew figures larger than life. Compared with *L'Education*, he had declared several years earlier in *Le Voltaire*, most naturalist fiction seemed operatic, or egregiously poetical. "We would never have dared to break an analysis into fragments, to destroy the larger story by concentrating, obsessively, on brief episodes, to efface the book in the monochromatic atmosphere of thirty or so insipid characters, all going limp after every spurt of virile energy. For naturalists, that is unquestionably the prototype."

With its short chapters and interwoven dramas, *Pot-Bouille* may bear a certain formal resemblance to *L'Education sentimentale*, but in one obvious respect it is decidedly un-Flaubertian. Where Flaubert's protagonist, Frédéric Moreau, yearns for that which he cannot possess— always inviting bad luck, always lagging behind events or observing them from afar—Zola's young man, Octave Mouret, grabs every prize available. Where Moreau drifts through a life of missed connections, Mouret plunges ahead single-mindedly, and this difference announces itself in the two preludes. *L'Education* begins on a ferryboat slowly plying downriver from Paris to Rouen; *Pot-Bouille* opens with a coach entering the great city's commercial maelstrom.

Zola would have said that *Pot-Bouille* presented a literary equivalent of the invasive strategy by which "experimental" medicine brings to light what Dr. Claude Bernard called the *milieu vital*.[15] Like his creator, Octave Mouret spies, meddles, pokes. As Zola practiced vivisection upon the closed organism of bourgeois society, so Octave penetrates the arcana of a bourgeois residence. Lying in wait for fa-

[15]Zola's long essay *Le Roman expérimental* was a manifesto based upon the authority of Claude Bernard's treatise *Introduction à l'étude de la médecine expérimentale*. "Metaphysical man is dead," he declared toward the end of it. "Physiological man is the ground we explore. Unquestionably, Achilles' anger and Dido's love will always remain the magnificent portraits they are. But it is for us to analyze anger and love, to understand how these passions work within the human being." What his manifesto expresses most clearly—and Zola was by no means alone in this regard—is a malaise born of the conviction that unless he conferred the prestige of science upon his imaginative enterprise it would be subjective, "irrational," unmasculine.

vorable opportunities, sexual or mercantile, this parvenu means to succeed, and succeed he does. After several adulterous escapades, he marries his employer, Caroline Hédouin, the widowed proprietress of a dry-goods store called Au Bonheur des Dames, from which he will create—merchandising genius that he is—a huge, modern emporium.

Beginning January 23, 1882, the serialized version of *Pot-Bouille* appeared in Jules Simon's newspaper *Le Gaulois*. There was, as usual, organized fanfare, with cronies supplying much of it. Maupassant dashed off two articles for *Le Gaulois*, one on Zola himself, another on extramarital sex among bourgeois. And in February, Georges Charpentier brought out Paul Alexis's *Emile Zola, notes d'un ami*. But one week after the serialization of *Pot-Bouille* began, publicity came from an unexpected source when an appeals-court lawyer with the same name as the Napoleonic jurist who in the novel may have fathered Adèle's child—Duverdy—enjoined Zola to rename his character. Zola refused. After explaining in an open letter to the director of *Le Gaulois*, "It seems that the gentleman ran for the Chamber of Deputies from my rural district and suspects that I found his name on electoral posters," he dismissed this charge as fanciful:

> The truth is that I extract my names from an old Bottin directory: the names in *Pot-Bouille* were found there more than a year ago, or long before the elections. Anyway, I was at the seashore during that electoral campaign, in a remote corner of the Cotentin, and I am so repelled by politics that promotional literature doesn't get past my front door. I can therefore swear that I was utterly unaware of a lawyer named Duverdy.

Furthermore, the summons constituted an assault on creative freedom:

> Consider the awful predicament in which modern novelists find themselves. We don't live in the 17th century, in the age of abstract characters, and we cannot give our heroes names like Cyrus, Clélie, Aristée. Our characters are the people of flesh and blood against whom we brush in the street every day. They have our passions, they wear our clothing, and they must also bear our names. I defy any contemporary novelist not to consult the Bottin. It serves not only reprobates like myself but the elegant and discreet, the literati who write for convent-school boarders.

One could no more forbid contemporary novelists to rely on the postal directory for names, he concluded, than suppress the modern novel itself.

M. Duverdy then initiated legal proceedings. The battle was joined, and on they fought for almost a month, in court and in print, as people snapped up *Le Gaulois*, wanting to read not only installments of *Pot-Bouille* but accounts of the trial. A tribunal found against Zola, who announced, on page one:

Well, judgment has been passed! The honorable M. Duverdy will disappear from my novel and we shall replace him with M. Trois-Etoiles.[16] I believe this name is not commonplace, but if it should by chance grace some old family, I beg that family to make representations as soon as possible.

Given M. Duverdy's prominent position in high judicial circles, the verdict was not altogether unexpected. Nor could the letters Zola received soon afterward from three different Josserands and one Mouret have come as a surprise, all demanding that he honor their surnames. People wanted instant fame. But he stood firm in his resolve to ignore such petitioners and this time around he did so with impunity; no one sought legal redress.

In their reviews of *Pot-Bouille*, newspaper critics condemned everything *save* the names of characters, many indignantly. "Oh, bourgeois and bourgeoises, are you happy now, you who made M. Zola a best-selling author when he portrayed the working class and the world of prostitutes?" asked one critic. "Do you still believe in his so-called exactitude? Is it true that you are a bunch of imbeciles, sometimes monstrous, always ignoble, and grotesque even in your ignobility? Is this indeed your apartment house, this house in *Pot-Bouille*, which resembles the ward of Bicêtre psychiatric hospital, crowded with hysterical or deranged women, senile men, cretins, dodderers?" Detractors challenged him on his own ground and pilloried *Pot-Bouille* more for being inaccurate than for offending genteel sensibilities. Did Zola observe the world around him? Not at all, said Ferdinand Brunetière. "Facts do not impinge upon his scheme. He knows what he wanted to know. His future novels are already sketched and he has only to fill them in. . . . He did not 'study' the Parisian bourgeoisie for *Pot-Bouille*. Rather, he began with a certain image, which suffered no alteration. My view is that Zola is not an imaginative man but a logical man. He neither invents nor observes. He deduces." Yet another critic, Henry Fouquier, writing under the pseudonym "Nestor," listed thirty-one sociological blunders, which Zola refuted one by one in an open letter. "If you wish," he wrote, "my novel sometimes assumes the shrill tone

[16]Trois-Etoiles, or Three Stars, is a reference to the cloaking of identity by asterisks, as in Monsieur D***. Zola retained Trois-Etoiles in the serialized version of *Pot-Bouille* and substituted Duveyrier for Duverdy in the novel.

of satire; and I concede that the accumulation of facts within a single framework often gives it an intensity that the routine of daily life lacks. But as for the documents themselves, they are unimpeachable; you are old enough to have seen worse than I reported."

Zola missed a letter from Croisset. Nothing could quite make up for Flaubert's annual compliment, but this tenth volume of *Les Rougon-Macquart* had its champions, and not only inside the family circle.[17] "It increased the circulation of the paper happy or rich enough to pay Zola by the line," wrote a literary chronicler named Alfred Hamm. "Make no mistake, this is what irritates those charming little confreres who bark at him, as others barked at Hugo and Balzac. . . . The sale of his works enrages them, and their rage increases with each new edition." Even as French bookdealers were selling *Pot-Bouille* faster than Charpentier could reprint it, translations, pirated or authorized, appeared on either side of the Atlantic—in London, in Philadelphia, in Berlin, and in Vienna, where the newspaper serial alone fetched Zola 10,000 francs.

These were years that tried Zola's soul. An important part of him had died with Emilie Zola, and the grief continued unabated for a long time. "My heart goes out to you," he wrote on May 17, 1882, several days after Alphonse Daudet buried Mme Vincent Daudet. "Eighteen months ago I lost my mother, as now you have lost yours, and for me it is still, constantly, though I never talk about it, a poignant, stupefying absence." Photographs show him thirty pounds overweight, with sparse, close-cropped hair, bloated cheeks, eyes gazing mournfully from behind little ovoid lenses, and, all in all, the air of a man who no longer sees any reason to preen. Tormented by his stomach, by his heart, and above all by his bladder, which made him a slave to the chamber pot, he felt old at forty-two. If not for morphine there would have been more nights spent awake than asleep.

Despondency colored his view of *Les Rougon-Macquart* as well. Ten novels completed left ten novels unwritten, and the thought weighed ever more heavily upon him that death would catch him up before he had brought his enterprise to fruition. With Emilie gone, no one stood between him and the grave. Goncourt noted this on December 14, 1880:

Zola visits me today. He enters with that lugubrious, haggard air that marks his entrances. And truly, this man of forty creates a painful im-

---

[17]Huysmans and Céard greatly admired *Pot-Bouille* (the former for its *comique macabre*), but with certain reservations. Huysmans felt that Zola's language did not always do justice to the obliquity of bourgeois speech, while Céard missed an aroma that would evoke the bourgeoisie as persuasively as *L'Assommoir* had evoked the working class.

pression; he looks older than I. He slumps into an armchair, whining like a child about kidney pain, gravel, palpitations. Then he talks about his mother's death, about the void in their household, and intense compassion mingles with a touch of fear for himself. When it comes to literature, to works planned, he admits being afraid that time may run out. Ah, how skillfully the world was devised so that nobody alive should count himself happy. Here's a man whose name echoes through the world, whose books sell by the hundred thousand, who has made perhaps more noise during his lifetime than any other; well, thanks to this sickly state, to his hypochondriacal turn of mind, he is darker, more desolate than the most disinherited of withered fruit!

Where others rested upon their laurels, Zola toiled ceaselessly. Now denigrating his work as the product of his flawed nature, now extolling it as a monument wrought by some former, superior self, he found small comfort in the past. Never to be equaled or always to be atoned for, his oeuvre undermined him one way or the other. "Zola displays that agitated disquiet which is the special character of his nervousness," Goncourt wrote eighteen months later. "He is not satisfied with the novel in progress, *Au Bonheur des Dames.* 'There's too much said about linen and cotton. . . .' From afar, before starting it, he thought it would be more interesting. Then, too, the colossal success of yesterday spells disaster for his future career. He wishes it were otherwise, but it is so, and he confides, with deep sadness: 'I'll never again produce a novel that will stir people as much as *L'Assommoir* has, or one that will sell as well as *Nana!'* " What consoled him, he told Goncourt, was the fantasy of an interminable book that would save him from having ever again to prove himself, of a vast middle that would redeem him from new beginnings and endings. "Do you know a recurrent dream of mine? It would be, if I earned 500,000 francs during the next ten years, to hole up in a book I'd never finish, something like a history of French literature. Yes, for me it would be a way of breaking communications with the public, of tacitly retiring from literature. I would like to be peaceful. . . . Yes, I would like to be peaceful." Was this not the same fantasy that had once consoled an obscure twenty-year-old adrift in Paris? "If I didn't have my family," he had confided to Cézanne in 1860, "if I possessed a modest daily allowance, I would hole up in a Provençal cottage and lead a hermit's life."

Alexandrine's emotional balance being even more precarious than his own, Zola had to shore her up when he most wished to lean on her. In 1881, as in 1877, she suffered severe asthmatic attacks, and once again sea air was the recommended treatment. "Alas, my wife does not feel any better," Zola wrote to Céard from Grand-Camp-les-Bains, on the Normandy coast, in August. "Her nervous disorder persists and in the last few days has actually grown worse. It's very disagreeable. I am resolved, if her condition does not improve, to have her undergo some very rigorous treatment in Paris, as soon as we return. I should add, however, that I still count on our vacation producing a salutary effect, once we've settled down." The seaside resort did not immediately justify this optimism. "My wife struggles along, better one day, worse the next," he informed Céard on August 24. "I'd like to stick it out as long as possible, always hopeful—but if the cold snap continues, we may return to Médan in mid-September. . . . I have a stiff neck, which forces me to stand ramrod straight. You'd take me for a government prosecutor, and when I walk it hurts. Local bathers—there aren't many, thank goodness—exasperate us by peeping through our windows, to find out, no doubt, whether we roast little children on a spit."

One may suppose that Alexandrine's attacks were connected with the death of her mother-in-law, with a fear of abandonment, or with a sense of failure at not having become a mother herself; in one letter, Zola, who jealously guarded conjugal secrets, described her as subject to *idées noires*, or black moods. But all one knows for sure is that these attacks recurred year after year, at unpredictable intervals. Following the summer of 1881 there were apparently none again until November 1882, when Zola reported: "My wife feels worse than I: she experiences nervous suffocations that keep me up all night, filled with anxiety. Pessimism has gained the upper hand of my appetite for life." Another long reprieve led to another severe crisis, and twice, beginning in 1884, they vainly sought a cure for what ailed Alexandrine at the famous thermal springs of Mont-Dore-les-Bains, near Clermont-Ferrand.

Despite the constant hubbub occasioned by Zola—the polemics, the reviews, the first nights, the attentions of "les Cinq," the worldwide correspondence—visitors sometimes carried away from Médan an impression of profound loneliness, of emptiness. "Returning from Médan, I concluded that a couple can do without children in a Paris flat but not in a country house," Goncourt noted on July 6, 1882. "Nature calls for children." Zola would not have disagreed. That "nature calls for children" is what he himself implied several months later when it came to congratulating a gentleman from Atlanta, Georgia, who had named him his son's godfather. "I hope my godson enjoys a prosperous future. May he grow up and become a real man! The clamor that I, his godfather, make in the world is not worth a happy life. Wish him, for me, a good spouse and beautiful children and you will be wishing him something better than glory. I thank you all the same for your enthusiasm."[18]

---

[18]Zola's note was published a week apart in the Atlanta *Constitution* and *The New York Times*.

XIX

GATHERING SHADES

BY 1881, the original Médan cottage huddled insignificantly beside a large square tower built according to Zola's design. There, defended against the world outside, life followed predictable routines. Beginning around 9 a.m., Zola wrote all morning long. Lunch was a substantial meal eaten in a wood-paneled dining room where light filtered through stained glass. He then took a nap until 3 p.m., when the postman delivered five newspapers—later it would be seven—and mail that grew to be voluminous during the 1880s. As his own secretary and literary agent, Zola, who threw nothing out (neatly rolling up and filing even the string taken off parcels), sorted through letters from young novelists, lovelorn women, cranks, beggars, magazine editors requesting articles, foreign newspapers eager to serialize him, translators who had a stake in helping foil the worldwide pirating of Rougon-Macquart novels. This correspondence devoured many an afternoon, though Zola often walked his dog on the riverbank or spent some more time writing before Alexandrine called him to supper.[1] Once the supper table had been cleared, they conversed over tea and played games. When they retired at 10 p.m., Zola's day was not yet done. He read until 1 a.m. and only then fell asleep, unless he had somehow neglected to perform rituals that made sleep possible. "This

[1]"He never left the slightest litter of papers in his workroom," wrote Ernest Vizetelly. "Such documents as he might be using were set out tidily on various tables; the newspapers he read were always neatly folded directly he had finished perusing them. . . . He liked to have everything spick and span, and it was he himself who attended to virtually all the *ménage* of his Parisian and country workrooms."

evening, at Daudet's house, we discussed superstition," Goncourt noted in his journal. "On this score Zola is exceedingly strange. He speaks about such matters sotto voce, mysteriously, as if afraid of being overheard by some powerful, shadowy presence. He no longer believes in the virtue of the number three. For the nonce, seven is his talisman. And he gives us to understand that at Médan he shutters his windows after nightfall with certain *hermetic* combinations."[2] Hypochondria is what he called his terror of a murderous interloper stalking him at night. "You know I am a bit hypochondriacal; there are days when I need all my courage to continue the battle."

Commensurate with his epic enterprise was the room in which he accomplished it. "Everything is immense," declared Paul Alexis. "Its dimensions are those of a history painter's atelier: eighteen feet high, twenty-nine feet wide, thirty-three feet long. There's a colossal fireplace, big enough for roasting a whole sheep. At one end of it an alcove the size of one of our little Parisian rooms accommodates a divan that could sleep ten people comfortably. In the middle stands a very large table, opposite a wide bay window looking out beyond the Seine. I haven't mentioned a kind of gallery above the alcove to which one gains access by a spiral staircase: it houses his library." Another biographer who visited Zola was struck less by the gargantuan aspect of things than by the heterogeneous clutter. "There was indeed a huge couch with Turkish fabrics and Oriental cushions . . . which could be considered useful, as it served for the siesta, during painful digestions, or for a respite from work," wrote Edmond Lepelletier. "But of no possible use was the pretentious bric-a-brac littered all over—very ordinary old iron, ridiculous crockery, flea-market copperware, cheap ivory baubles, threadbare carnival finery, vulgar wooden sculptures, brightly painted Japanese curios of the kind sold at department stores. . . . Zola took great pride in all this romantic junk." Lepelletier's inventory should have included a Renaissance chest that supported a squatting Venus along with the Larousse dictionary.

Zola had always foreseen two towers for his house at Médan, but not until 1885, after the publication of *Germinal*, when his annual income regularly exceeded one hundred thousand francs, did he feel rich enough to build a second wing.[3] What this hexagonal structure

[2]It will be recalled that Zola was seven when his father died.

[3]In November 1885 a journalist named Lorédan Larchey canvassed several famous writers in order to demonstrate that the old proverb *A gens de lettres, honneur sans richesse* ("To men of letters, honor without wealth") did not always apply. He asked three questions and Zola answered them as follows:

Nana earned me the most, twenty thousand francs in the newspaper, and approximately seventy-five thousand from the book, not counting twenty thou-

afforded him was space for a living room that embodied his vision of squirearchical opulence. Twisted marble columns flanked the doorway, opposite which another huge fireplace had been installed. At the street end stood a billiard table. At the garden end, beyond a panoply of old instruments surmounting a harmonium on which he sometimes played chords, three windows pictured the lost paradise of *La Faute de l'abbé Mouret* in stained glass, with every detail stipulated by Zola himself. "Apropos of what we said yesterday," he warned his *peintre-verrier* when it was all still under construction, "I repeat that I insist absolutely upon everything being outlined in lead: animals, trees, foliage, flowers, even little birds and butterflies. That alone will give character to the scene. On the rectangular panes you can paint insects, flies, bees, and maidens as background, four or five per window. The central bay, a sketch of which you will provide, must feature a second peacock, but a peacock whose tail feathers stand erect and fanned. Don't shrink from enlarging the tail, from making it the principal motif. It can fill the whole window." On exposed beams that ran crosswise, some twenty feet above the mosaic floor, he arranged to inscribe coats of arms, including those of Emilie Zola's birthplace, Dourdan, and in this matter, as in research for novels, he drafted Henry Céard, who had meanwhile become assistant curator of the Carnavalet Museum. "My friend, would you perchance have near to hand, among your papers, the arms of Dourdan (Seine-et-Oise) and those of Médan: I mean escutcheons, with some indication of heraldic colors?" Zola asked. "I need them for my new billiard room. The arms of Médan would be those of the family that owned the château—the Médan de Beaulieu, I believe. Unfortunately, our village church can't help. . . . I am also looking for the arms of Corfu, one of the Ionian islands that belong to Greece. My paternal grandmother was born there." So much the worse if officialdom had found him ineligible for decorations. Excluded from the Legion of Honor, he displayed, at Médan, the paraphernalia of nobility (even a suit of medieval armor) and fortified himself inside allusions to his own work. His work was almost literally his castle.

Like the house, the homestead grew apace. What began as a small

---

sand from the illustrated edition. These are round figures. Annual revenue from my works has varied greatly. During my press campaigns it was very high, and it has decreased since I've withdrawn from the fray. Let's say that the novel I write each year brings in sixty thousand francs and previous novels bring in around twenty thousand (they have brought in as much as fifty thousand). Serializations earn a franc a line. . . . Add to this the approximately fifteen thousand francs in foreign rights. In short, some of us live very comfortably, without raking in the millions attributed to us.

One hundred thousand francs was roughly equivalent to three hundred and fifty thousand present-day dollars. Let us recall that low-level government functionaries of that period earned less than two thousand francs a year.

garden came to encompass four and one-half hectares, or ten acres. This development involved a war of attrition in which Zola mobilized against his neighbors the same iron resolve that produced four or five pages every day. Determined to enjoy forevermore an unobstructed view of the Seine Valley, he bought twenty-four separate parcels and by 1882 owned not only land sloping from the railroad tracks down to the river road but some considerable portion of the island beyond, the Ile du Platais. In due course outbuildings sprouted here and there. Among the first was a four-room guest cottage next to the square tower. Then came a lodge for the caretakers, whose province eventually included a vegetable garden, an enormous greenhouse that furnished cut flowers all year round, and a farm complete with horse, cow, chicken coops, rabbit hutches, dovecotes, watering trough, hayloft, beehive, and buttery. This rustic enclosure abutted the party wall. At another extreme limit of his domain, on the island itself, Zola built a retreat which acquired the name Le Paradou. "We lunch gaily and afterward go over to the island, where he's having a chalet built," Goncourt noted on June 20, 1881, after a Sunday excursion to Médan with the Daudets and Charpentiers. "It contains a large fir-paneled room with a monumental faience stove of great simplicity and in fine taste." Guests invited for lunch or tea at the chalet, which had a stone pier, were ferried over in the round-stemmed rowboat called *Nana* or in a skiff dubbed *Pot-Bouille*.

Always the faithful partisan, Alexandrine collaborated fully in the invention of this little world and despite her uncertain health presided with skill over the management of its various affairs. "My poor wife and I are quite worn out," Zola informed Céard on one occasion. "We've worked too hard, she at organizing, at overseeing this rascal of a house, I at tormenting sentences until 2 a.m. because they don't say what I want them to say." Nothing escaped her attention as she made her daily rounds or surveyed the scene, with needle and thread in hand, from a second-story linen room. "The efficient housekeeper she had always been fretted about hens incubating and the welfare of farm animals," a member of the family wrote many years later. "Everything had to be clean, had to shine, at the farm as in the master's house. Mme Zola loved luxury, but she loved order even more. . . . To the extent that she could, she protected him from material cares." A proud woman whose willfulness encouraged some and exasperated others, she ruled Médan, which is to say that not a tree was planted there, not a flower bed designed, not a path laid without her advice. When a new structure started going up, she monitored the operation alongside her husband. When account books needed keeping, she kept them. And when wages were paid out on Saturday evening, it was she, seated at the kitchen table consulting her ledger as workers filed past one by one, who performed this sometimes delicate task.

Fastidious though she may have been, Alexandrine never made order the supreme virtue. She had a capacity for *laisser-aller* and it showed to good advantage with Zola's protégés, who usually arrived from Paris in high spirits, as well as with the children of friends and relatives. "On Médan's patron saint's day, when it was Mme Zola's turn to provide bread for consecration, we'd accompany her to church," Céard reminisced.

> A redoubtable wind instrument called the "serpent," about eight feet long, which may have dated to the seventeenth century, . . . resounded furiously beneath the vaults. After nightfall there would be another kind of music, the sounds of a mechanical orchestra from a merry-go-round at the village fair. Under the glow of lampions we'd partner local demoiselles in polkas and quadrilles. . . . As Médan couldn't afford fireworks, starlight sufficed. On less hectic Sundays, we'd practice marksmanship in the Zola garden, with trains incessantly roaring past. What kind of freight did the rails and telegraph poles announce? Bets were laid as to whether the next train carried people or freight. Once it had disappeared, wreathed in fire and smoke, we'd resume taking potshots at improvised targets: pipes, lengths of string, etc. And the spent cartridges filled that wee patch of green with a smell of powder and warfare.

Recognizing that boys will be boys, she extended the benefit of her lenience to Emile, alias "Mimi," who often joined in the gunplay, myopically shooting at tufts of grass which he mistook for birds (so said Maupassant). She also indulged their habit of congregating around the huge divan upstairs after their host had awoken from his ritual siesta and, all more or less supine, gabbing nonstop until dinner or tea, which they'd take in the dining room under the mischievous eye of Manet's Punchinello. As laconic as he was in Paris, Céard noted, Zola became a tireless conversationalist in Médan, where he felt less embattled.[4]

Having won election to the village council in 1881, he sat on it until 1888, alongside farmers, a tile maker, a dairyman. Country life absorbed him, and interspersed among the many letters that touch upon

[4]"Stretched out for entire half days on that divan, inviting his interlocutors to do likewise, . . . he engages in conversations that touch on everything and from which, with characteristic sagacity, he always derives some profit, some piece of information," Céard reminisced. "He is the last person to talk for the sake of talking. He excels at drawing out of those around him some notion of a problem he had never studied, the confirmation of his hypotheses, the crux of matters they've investigated and know intimately well. And when the discussion wanders, when the clarifications get muddled, with what deftness he sets things right." Outside intimate circles, Zola maintained considerable reserve. An English biographer, Robert Sherard, who knew him personally, wrote that his manner, whether from diffidence or melancholy, was, even to old acquaintances, rather distant.

his magnum opus are others that show him taking care of humbler business. From Numa Coste he regularly ordered olive oil in eighty-eight-pound drums. Eager to transplant vegetation from Provence, he had Paul Alexis in Aix send him vine shoots and black currant seedlings via railroad. Whenever Alexandrine needed white eau-de-vie for the annual confection of fruit preserves he would have Théodore Duret, the art historian, whose assets included part ownership of a cognac company, ship one hundred liters. And with a domestic staff of four or five, there were servant problems to resolve. In September 1882 a charge of poaching brought against his valet, Henri Cavillier, required articulate intervention. He wrote (vainly, as it turned out) to the mayor of the village downriver from Médan:

> No one in Médan knew anything about the ordinance passed by the municipal council of your district. . . . I therefore plead our perfect good faith and ask that you issue a warning rather than a summons. A warning serves justice better. Should not landowners in adjacent districts have been notified through their mayors? That would have been the neighborly thing to do, especially as all of Vernouillet now hunts over here in Médan.

Cavillier and his wife, Zélie, who cooked most meals, lasted for many years.[5] But such was not the case with a succession of people hired to tend the garden and work the farm. "I have had only ignoramuses or drunks," he complained in 1885 to the proprietor of a horticultural establishment. "You would do me a very good turn if you sent me some appropriate couple. I'm prepared to offer, as beginning wages, fifteen hundred francs a year." Not until 1886, after yet another disappointment, did Zola find what he wanted. Sometime during that year a young couple named Octave and Léonie Lenôtre joined the household and remained part of it for two decades.

In the aftermath of Emilie's death, Zola, who first wondered whether he could ever endure Médan again, took to living there eight to ten months of the year, during which period a novel was generally begun and finished. "Paris tempts me very little, and I believe that I wouldn't set foot there except for the few friends I have left; work is my dominant passion," he wrote to Henry Céard on one occasion. Another time, writing from Médan after a prolonged absence, he expressed similar sentiments to his old painter friend Antoine Guillemet: "We reestablished ourselves here last week. I began my next novel right away. We aren't getting any younger, so the work in progress

---

[5] For an unexplained reason they were both fired at one point, then subsequently rehired.

needs urgent attention." What Zola needed, and what Alexandrine provided, was, as he put it in *L'Oeuvre*, "an affection standing guard over his tranquillity, an interior of tenderness where he could cloister himself in order to devote his entire life to the enormous work."

But for all his bearishness Zola very much relished the glamour of certain Parisian events. Every May 1, when the annual Salon opened, he and Alexandrine arranged to meet the Charpentiers, the Daudets, and Goncourt at a temple of gastronomy on the Champs-Elysée, Ledoyen, after touring the Palace of Industry. In 1882, when the Comédie-Française announced that it would revive Victor Hugo's *Le Roi s'amuse*, which had been performed only once fifty years earlier, he wheedled choice seats out of the director. And stage adaptations of five novels—*L'Assommoir, Nana, Pot-Bouille, Le Ventre de Paris, Germinal*—gave him purchase on the Boulevard, filling his calendar with dress rehearsals, premieres, hundredth performances, two hundredth performances, all-night dinners at Brébant to mark every such triumph, and costume balls at the Elysée-Montmartre.

That Zola achieved success at the theater where time and again he had failed was the result of his collaboration with one William Busnach, a stockbroker turned playwright known for light-opera libretti, vaudevilles, and *féeries*, which he produced by the score. Busnach admired *L'Assommoir*, and very early along, in 1876, he proposed the idea of a stage version. Though reluctant at first, Zola eventually realized that the partnership might afford him rich returns and cost him nothing of his artistic virtue, that by not signing the work himself, he could encourage his surrogate to use all the tried-and-true recipes of Boulevard theater without losing face.[6] Thus, when Busnach gave him a scenario for comment, Zola, safely hidden from view, rejected it as insufficiently melodramatic. "I know that making Virginie an assassin

---

[6]In adapting *L'Assommoir*, Busnach worked with a colleague named Octave Gastineau, who died before the play was staged.

Busnach, a nephew of the composer Fromental Halévy (remembered for his opera *La Juive*), described himself as a "neuropath" and in his letters to Zola complained about a variety of ailments, ranging from noises in his head and a "syphilitic throat" to gout and nervous fatigue. But this plump, irrepressible little bachelor eight years older than Zola had boundless energy for writing, drumming up business, touting his custom, partying, gambling. Zola was fond of him, unlike Goncourt and Huysmans, who disliked his Jewishness as much as his arrant vulgarity ("That foul Busnach, that despicable peddler of shoddy goods," Goncourt wrote). Relations cooled after January 1882, when Busnach confessed that he had lost at baccarat Zola's German royalty for *Nana* (the play), a total of almost nine thousand francs. Busnach made restitution in monthly installments and their partnership continued, but Zola never again trusted him unreservedly.

is going a bit far," he concurred, "but think of the originality of the mise-en-scène. It's very seductive, this scaffold with workers riding up and down and the woman in her sixth-floor flat plotting a murder. . . . Then, too, we're on the Boulevard, which means that Virginie must be a stock character, a traitor straight out of melodrama. . . . I'm keen on this dramatic effect." Naturalism, he continued, would be restricted to decor. "We need accurate decor, carefully arranged, custom-made, copied from nature, and really vast. . . . If we get that right, the play could be a great success, its dramatic poverty notwithstanding. All of Paris will want to see the laundry house, the forge, the bubbling still, etc. That's my opinion. *Now I'd like to know yours.*"

In articles written for *Le Voltaire,* Zola kept up the pretense of non-collaboration, reprimanding critics who dismissed his incognito and judged the play as if it were his own work. "The persistence with which certain critics ascribe to me the paternity of this drama is astonishing," he protested.

> My declaration should have sufficed. I repeat that I simply gave two talented playwrights, Messrs. Busnach and Gastineau, leave to extract a drama from my novel, imitating in this regard many illustrious predecessors. It therefore takes absolute bad faith to discuss the work as if it were mine, to see my ideas in it, to fight me with my own arguments against Boulevard theater. At issue here is an adaptation done by theater men, men of wit and skill who were, quite understandably, bent on commercial success and who, it seems to me, achieved their goal.

A young man might have tried to adapt his own novel, even a novel as fraught with danger as *L'Assommoir,* but three previous flops had taught him, he wrote somewhat disingenuously, that prudence was the better part of valor. "The day it pleases me to try my fortune a fourth time I shall choose my ground with greater care, in order to fight under the best possible conditions. And I admit that as a battleground *L'Assommoir* seems indefensible. I wondered why I should triple the difficulties any adaptation involves by taking characters, a milieu, a language that would demand brutal audacities if realism were one's guideline." Could he congratulate authors Busnach and Gastineau, who did not have his gods to placate? He could indeed. "It's undeniable that certain changes wrought upon the novel made the drama inferior. So be it. The drama was specially written for a Boulevard theater. We're at the Ambigu, not at the Odéon, which means that the authors felt obligated to reckon with the Ambigu's clientele, not the Odeon's. . . . *L'Assommoir* is not the manifesto of a new dramatic school, nor does it have any such pretensions. It is simply an adapta-

Zola's house at Médan, photographed from the river, with the railroad bridge on the left; the original cottage is squeezed between the octagonal wing and the square tower, where Zola had his study on the top floor. The smaller building on the right was the guest cottage.

Zola's chalet on an island in the Seine (from which vantage point Cézanne painted Médan), as photographed by Zola.

Zola in pajamas, working at his desk in Médan, amidst paraphernalia. The stained-glass window behind him faced the street; the balcony above, to which he gained access by a staircase not visible here, housed his library.

Zola at his desk in Paris, possibly on the rue de Boulogne, where Cézanne, after one visit, complained of feeling like a supplicant petitioning a "minister of state" enthroned behind a "carved wooden desk."

Zola in the cluttered splendor of his town house on the rue de Bruxelles.

Zola in his early forties photographed at the Nadar studio; he grew stout and suffered a prolonged period of depression following the deaths of his mother and Flaubert.

The first page of the manuscript of *Nana*, showing relatively few crossings-out (compared to a page of Balzac, for example). This manuscript was acquired by J. Pierpont Morgan. Manuscripts of all the other *Rougon-Macquart* novels are at the Bibliothèque Nationale.

The caption reads: "The Birth of Nana-Venus: a theme for Bouguereaus of the future." Alluded to are the operetta in which Nana achieves fame, *La Blonde Vénus*, and a famously plethoric representation of the birth of Venus by the academic painter William Bouguereau.

A poster advertising the illustrated edition of *Nana*.

Sheet music for a "Nana-Quadrille." *Nana* was a godsend to caricaturists, songwriters, and composers of dance music.

The caption, which bears the date July 14, 1880, reads: "The army swears to France loyalty to the young Republic." In 1880, July 14 was decreed the republican national holiday; and a law was passed mandating military exercises in the school system, with students required to handle regular infantry rifles.

The Champ-de-Mars in July 1888, with a half-built Eiffel Tower.

Pot-Bouille was serialized in the weekly *La Vie populaire*. The first installment appeared in this issue, May 7, 1882.

Zola with Jeanne Rozerot in 1893.

A flyer advertising the serialization of *La Bête humaine* in *La Vie populaire*.

Jeanne Rozerot, photographed by Zola, who often had her pose for him in elaborate fin-de-siècle millinery.

Zola's rather Monet-like photograph of Jeanne with a parasol walking on the Verneuil road, north of Médan.

Une Apothéose

The "apotheosis" of Zola after *Nana*, with a chamber pot hoisted on a pole and Nana herself holding the torch.

The caption of this caricature reads: "The brilliant triumph of naturalism received its official consecration today: an equestrian statue of Zola hovering at the summit of the Vendôme Column was solemnly inaugurated." In the lower right "idealists" led by Victor Hugo are shown staging a protest.

tion done by two talented men with much experience in theatrical matters."[7]

His ambivalence had no perceptible effect one way or the other on *L'Assommoir*, which enjoyed an immensely successful run, magnifying the renown of *L'Assommoir* the novel. Even with harsh winter weather upon them, people flocked from every quarter to the Ambigu, and none more determinedly than working-class Parisians. After ninety-nine performances, Zola suggested that the hundredth performance be a matinee given in their honor:

> We request that you give it gratis to the Parisian populace. *L'Assommoir* is an essentially lower-class drama. From the outset there have never been enough cheap seats. It is to the common people that we owe our sustained success. With admirable good sense, they understood that *L'Assommoir* is a lesson and not an insult, as some have sought to make them believe. We therefore feel that our success should profit the little purses, the people for whom this spectacle is often an unaffordable pleasure. You would be celebrating your first hundred-show run in fine style.

By November, when a three hundredth performance loomed, *L'Assommoir* had inspired all kinds of burlesque activity. André Gill, Stop, Alfred Le Petit, and other caricaturists dined off the play, filling satirical weeklies with drawings of Zola's characters. They were mimed by clowns at the Winter Circus in a parody that delighted overflow audiences. And at a dark little club on the rue Charras called Le Bal des Couapes or the Hooligans' Dance Hall, where attendance was by invitation only, aristocrats of high lineage dressed like characters from *L'Assommoir* to mingle, for the perverse thrill of it, with genuine specimens of Parisian lowlife—street toughs, panderers, whores, and so forth.

Success was not restricted to Paris or indeed to France. While a road company crisscrossed the provinces, packing theaters in Rouen, in Rennes, in Strasbourg, in Bordeaux, in Toulouse and Lyon and Marseille, *L'Assommoir* traveled abroad. It was staged in various European capitals, and nowhere with as much éclat as the English version, called *Drink*, which opened at the Princess's Theater in London on June 7,

---

[7]Like the Comédie-Française, the Odéon received a subsidy from the state, which enabled it to devote some portion of its repertoire to new works. The comedy of morals had become its stock-in-trade, with many plays by Labiche, Dumas *fils*, Sardou, Augier. As for the Ambigu, it was a theater traditionally associated with melodrama. During the 1840s and 1850s, its golden age, the repertoire included Alexandre Dumas's *Three Musketeers* and adaptations of *The Wandering Jew*, *Uncle Tom's Cabin*, and *The Hunchback of Notre Dame*.

1879, and remained there for almost a year, thanks mainly to the actor Charles Warner, whose virtuosic portrayal of Coupeau suffering delirium tremens thrilled everyone, including evangelical teetotalers. All this melodrama generated handsome sums for Zola. His share of gross receipts at the Ambigu alone amounted to some twenty-four thousand francs. As much, and perhaps much more, came from outside Paris.[8]

One year later, *Nana* yielded a successful play, and again theater directors all over Europe clamored for it. The ballyhoo did not move Zola to avow his co-authorship, however. Acutely embarrassed by these adaptations, he seconded Goncourt's judgment that *L'Assommoir* had been fabricated with the "strings, couplets, and sentimental refrains" of Boulevard melodrama and that the only naturalist thing about *Nana* was the water into which one character falls onstage. "I am mired in theater," he complained to Antoine Guillemet in August 1880, when his time was divided between the adaptation of *Nana* and a play commissioned by Sarah Bernhardt.[9] "*Nana* is just about done but my heart isn't in it. I shall finish the other play, then return to novel writing, where I feel more secure. Without leisure I cannot wage a serious battle in the cause of naturalist theater, as I should like to do."

Zola returned to *Les Rougon-Macquart*, true enough, but theater followed him there, shaping his vision of various social milieux. The apartment building in *Pot-Bouille* is a theatrical construct. And in *Au Bonheur des Dames*, which he wrote next, Zola envisaged a late-nineteenth-century Parisian department store with balconies strung around its cavernous main hall as a gigantic playhouse for the representation of Parisian women consuming linen, fabric, and finery.

It is symbolically apt that Zola should have outlined his original plan for a series of novels incorporated under one family name at almost

---

[8]*Drink* was done by the novelist Charles Reade. Zola's contract with the Ambigu stipulated that he receive 4 percent of gross receipts, which latter totaled six hundred thousand francs. Let us recall that the 1880 franc was calculated to have been worth about fifteen 1986 francs. Today that factor might be close to sixteen, producing a 1991 figure of three hundred eighty-four thousand.

L'Assommoir was revived at the Châtelet Theater in 1885 and by April 1886 had had its four hundredth Paris performance.

[9]According to Zola, Bernhardt took a great fancy to the incestuous heroine of *La Curée* and on various occasions implored him to construct a play around that character for her. At first he refused, believing that it would have been "radically impossible" to mention incest (unless the reference was classical) at the Comédie-Française, where Bernhardt then reigned. But a clever euphemism presented itself, and Zola, admittedly starstruck, set to work. By the time he finished *Renée*, Bernhardt had resigned from the Comédie-Française in anger and, preparing her grand tour of the United States, found the play to be an encumbrance. Six years passed before Zola placed it at another theater, the Vaudeville.

exactly the same time that Aristide Boucicaut, the owner of a burgeoning dry-goods establishment called Le Bon Marché, laid the foundation of an iron-ribbed building spacious enough to house under one
roof the stock of his several cluttered stores. Big business, like everything large-scale, enthralled Zola, and in 1868–69 he included among
his future heroes the *spéculateur sur le haut commerce,* or commercial
wheeler-dealer. The wheeler-dealer acquired a name three years later,
when Zola's master plan expanded. But that was all Octave Mouret
acquired for quite some time. This worthy son of François Mouret
waited backstage until 1880, maturing in the wings as Zola studied
Balzacian models (César Birotteau among them) and watched department stores more magnificent than any built during the Second
Empire proliferate throughout Paris. Mouret's turn came only after
Nana had made her apocalyptic exit. Launched upon a commercial
career in *Pot-Bouille,* where he marries the widowed proprietress of an
old-fashioned fabric store called Au Bonheur des Dames, he was born
to conquer Paris, to cultivate a genius for modern marketing, to exhibit
his infallible knowledge of the concupiscent shopper inside every
seemingly sober housewife. "I want *Au Bonheur des Dames* to be the
poem of modern-day activity," Zola wrote in his sketch. "Thus, a complete change of philosophy; away with pessimism, dwell not upon the
stupidity and melancholy of life, emphasize rather its continual labor,
the power and gaiety of its birth-giving. In short, go with the century,
express the century, which is a century of action and conquest, of
efforts in every direction. Then, as a consequence, show the joy of
action and the pleasure of existence." Were there not people whose
cups ran over with impunity? whose success did not, strange to say,
beget misfortune? Unless *Les Rougon-Macquart* embraced such blessed
specimens, he continued, the "truth" would have been slighted, "for
Pot-Bouille and other novels do sufficient justice to the mediocre and
the misbegotten." Unlike Huysmans and Céard, who found solace in
doctrinaire pessimism, he would not believe that only ill could befall
mankind.

Early in 1882, when Le Gaulois began serializing *Pot-Bouille,* Zola
opened a fresh notebook for *Au Bonheur des Dames.* His milieu was
the department store, or *magasin de nouveautés,* and he chose three
of them to study firsthand—Le Bon Marché, Le Louvre, and La Place
Clichy, where Alexandrine, who supplied him with Second Empire
mail-order catalogues, outfitted herself. No longer could he play God's
spy observing the world unobserved (especially not in female strong-
holds), but as compensation, fame guaranteed him the goodwill of
chief executive officers eager to have their firms immortalized. "Last
Monday we received a visit from M. Emile Zola," the secretary-general
of Le Bon Marché, Karcher, wrote on March 31 to his employer, Mme
Boucicaut. "The famous *naturalist* writer—that is what people call

him—wished to tour Le Bon Marché because he plans a novel in which a *magasin de nouveautés* will figure prominently. I showed him the whole establishment and he was wonderstruck. I hope, if he portrays a department store, that he will do so with some other pen than the one he used to write *Nana*—or *L'Assommoir!*" Karcher, whom Charpentier knew socially, escorted Zola through every phase of an item's career—from its arrival at the freight platforms down below, or its manufacture in sweatshops up above, to its departure on one of sixty horse-drawn delivery vans. He prepared a chronological table of Le Bon Marché's growth since 1861. He explained how individual transactions were recorded. He dilated upon the system of *guelte* or commission income that held sway at Le Bon Marché, motivating not only buyers, who operated their departments as semi-autonomous satrapies within the Boucicaut empire, but ordinary salesclerks. He gave Zola leave to inspect the library-lounge furnished with plush armchairs for a footsore clientele, two huge dining halls where male and female personnel ate separately, the kitchens, the lofts in which shirts were cut and rugs woven, the dormitory where young female employees fresh from the provinces, occupied minuscule bedrooms.

Zola's month of afternoons at Le Bon Marché and Le Louvre yielded a dossier that might have served quite well for helping someone administer department stores, or rob them. To comprehend the organism under study was to let no fact, however trivial, go unrecorded, and in almost one hundred closely written pages he describes its odor as well as its anatomy, its window displays as well as its security system and fiscal organization. "There are seventy-three tills," he noted in his file on Le Bon Marché.

Evenings, each cashier, after adding up the daily receipts, transmits them to the head cashier. The latter pools all these, does his own addition, then posts the total figure. . . . Three or four men accompanied by the chief cashier haul it upstairs, satchels full of bills and coins, every last sou. Imagine evenings when metal preponderates. At Le Bon Marché on ordinary good days, business exceeds three hundred thousand francs. On big sale days it reaches and tops one million. A hundred million francs' worth of business per year. So the money is brought up to the central treasury. . . . A large glass-paneled office, with desks and safes of majestic proportions. Green curtains, green carpets, an austere room. Next door is where bills are audited, twenty serious employees, arched double tables, green cardboard boxes lining the walls. In an identical room, somewhat larger but with the same tables, commissions are calculated by thirty employees, the youngest.

Le Bon Marché is seen not only by day but at night, when, with fire wardens taking turns patrolling it, the marketplace became a kind of well-stocked sepulchre. They made their rounds every half hour, he noted (several weeks earlier, on March 9, fire had gutted another department store, Au Printemps). Gas jets would be extinguished at 11 p.m., whereupon

oil lamps are hung from stanchions located a measured distance apart. Lugubrious spectacle. The wardens have punch boards for marking each round. Shop boys sleep wherever fancy dictates, on iron folding beds and, come morning, go upstairs to wash, in a gallery equipped with bathrooms. The rounds involve two or three men. There are, all told, six gas meters (protected by wooden grates), two very large, the others smaller. Forty-three hundred gas jets illuminate Le Bon Marché. In February it consumed forty-seven thousand cubic meters of gas.

This squirreling away of detail—a compulsion related to his gluttony, no doubt, or to the reassuring accumulation of fat—manifested itself as well in notes on the staff restaurant, which fed more than two thousand employees every day, and on the top-floor residence hall, which conjured up for him an image of capitalist phalansteries. He found Boucicaut's self-sufficient mini-empire fascinating:

The young women's rooms, in a curving corridor. Cells. The corridor with wooden floorboards, clean. Accommodations for about seventy-five women. Numbers on the doors. Rooms vary in size, some have two windows and others only one. Sloping walls from the mansard roof, low ceilings, a little iron bed, some with red quilts. Blue bedspreads. A walnut wardrobe. A washstand. Two chairs. Clothes behind a door. No trunks, which are forbidden. Wooden floors. A red bedside rug. In several, a branch of holy boxwood, or a crucifix over the bed. Some rooms have a skylight. It must be sweltering in the summer and freezing in the winter. A couple of big rooms with two beds.

A parlor in the middle of the corridor—oval, with a piano, a pedestal table in the middle, armchairs and sofas with slipcovers. Lit from above.

Two billiard tables for young men, only the youngest of whom, those who have no family in Paris, are lodged here.

There is a special concierge for the women, who are forbidden to visit their rooms during working hours. A barber has a salon upstairs, where employees can get a shave and a haircut between 8 a.m. and 1 p.m. at their own expense.

To three informants, two men and an efficient spinster named Mlle Dulit, who sold ready-to-wear apparel at another *magasin de nouveautés*, Zola addressed innumerable questions about the *calicots*, or salesclerks. They cooperated willingly, revealing the amatory habits of female workers, supplying him with anecdotes and trade slang, evoking the intramural competition for business that made every department store a monster red in tooth and claw, describing the ordeal of flogging goods all day long and the toll it took on ill-fed, corseted, button-booted young women, most of whom found a mate early or returned disconsolate to their provincial towns.

Borne in on Zola once again was the realization that here as elsewhere (in large factories, in the new Paris) society had come undone. Gone were those paternalistic scruples that bound employer to worker in family-owned businesses of another era. "At the Louvre department store," he wrote, "a salesgirl peremptorily dismissed because a woman client feels ill, accusing her of having eaten garlic sausage. In reality she had eaten bread. Sent packing without the opportunity to explain herself, to appeal. The other salesgirls lower their heads, don't even defend her. . . . For bosses who depend on custom, the customer is always right. They don't weigh services rendered, moral considerations or feeling. The steam engine: a worn cog gets replaced." Nor did scruples influence the average worker. "Clerks strip off their bosses like dirty linen. For another job, or for the capricious satisfaction of it, they'll make a beeline to the cashier: 'I quit, settle my wages.' The bonds of old-fashioned commerce no longer exist, the clerk sent to Paris, falling in with some particular firm and serving his entire apprenticeship there (Balzac). The struggle for survival is now all-consuming, everyone heeds his immediate self-interest." Where once people stayed married for better or worse, now they divorced one another unceremoniously. Self-interest had begotten a mobile culture, a population of vendors bouncing around like superheated atoms.

Although Zola gave class conflict full play, his larger intention was to portray not a ruthless machine but a "temple" in which woman figures as the sumptuary object of capitalist enterprise, or the profligate idol of a newly enriched bourgeoisie. "The book has its *poetic* side," he wrote in his sketch. "A huge business all about woman. Woman must be queen in the department store. When she enters it, she must feel that she is entering a temple built to please and glorify her, to celebrate her triumph. Woman's omnipotence, her scent dominates the whole place." Rigorously excluded from other capitalist shrines—the stock exchange, for example, where men speak a language all their own, communicating knowledge that spells feast or famine in the *lingua sacra* of high finance—here woman reigns supreme. Unable to earn great sums, she spends them instead, and Zola's hero, Octave Mouret, will exploit this sovereign consumer.

Among characters rewarded in *Les Rougon-Macquart* for twisting the arm of Providence, Octave Mouret ranks with those who owe their success more to courage and vision than to skulduggery. Having found employment at Au Bonheur des Dames, a prosperous, well-respected old dry-goods firm, he learns the business from Caroline Hédouin, daughter of its co-founder, and in due course becomes her indispensable factotum. Fiercely ambitious, he is neither daunted by local custom nor encumbered by neighborhood loyalties. Quite the contrary. Where Caroline Hédouin, who has a name to honor, sees boundaries, the cocksure provincial who has a name to make sees only room for expansion. Like Louis Napoleon leveling Paris in the service of his imperial design, Octave imagines Au Bonheur des Dames rising victorious over the rubble of antiquated commerce. "Once the house next door on the rue Neuve-Saint-Augustin had been bought and little merchants sent packing with their umbrellas and toys, they themselves could create huge departments in a much larger enterprise," is how he conjures up the future for Caroline. "He waxed enthusiastic; he heaped scorn on business conducted the old-fashioned way, in dark, dank shops lacking display windows; he evoked a new retail trade that built palaces of crystal for counters piled high with women's luxury goods, raking in millions during the day and blazing after dark, like a royal gala!" Although this fantasy excites the otherwise prudent Caroline, who is five years older than Octave, it does not bear fruit until her ailing husband dies. She and Octave then become bedfellows as well as business partners, uniting his boldness to her capital in a happy marriage of convenience.

The first risky step Caroline Hédouin had ever taken proves fatal. Before Au Bonheur des Dames opens, she dies in a fall at the construction site of her new store. Stunned by this loss, Octave nonetheless remains optimistic and indeed promises himself many more victims, having formulated a creed of commercial success in the language of sadistic eroticism. More important than any technical innovation, he tells Baron Hartmann, a financier whom he successfully courts, are strategies based on woman's psyche:

It was woman for whom the various department stores competed, woman whom they caught in the snare of bargain sales, after weakening her with displays. They kindled new desires in her, they presented a temptation to which she inevitably succumbed, starting with practical purchases, then, further down the slippery slope, indulging her vanity. Through vastly larger sales and a democratization of luxury, these stores had become a terrible drain on their clientele: they ravaged households, they lured them into the madness of keeping up with ever more expensive fashions. And if woman found herself treated like a queen there, worshipped and cosseted and flattered, she reigned as an amorous queen, . . . who pays for her every whim in blood.

The credit banker, the city builder, the master retailer all conspire against tradition. Neighborhood businesses which had passed from father to son (and we meet several such doomed merchants) fail one by one as hitherto loyal customers leave them for Au Bonheur des Dames. Each bankruptcy yields Octave another coveted parcel of land. But the great entrepreneur doesn't gloat over these obscure triumphs any more than Leviathan relishes the small fry it swallows while propelling itself forward. Rather, he rejoices in his volume, he jubilates in the full square block it was his manifest destiny to occupy. "On a Monday . . . Au Bonheur des Dames inaugurated its new wing with the grand exhibition of summer fashions," Zola writes toward the end.

> At 6 a.m., Mouret was already there in full command. Along the central axis, from end to end, ran a wide gallery flanked on either side by narrower ones, the Monsigny and the Michodière. Glass canopies had transformed the courtyards into palatial halls; and iron staircases led to bridges spanning both upper stories. The architect, . . . a young man enamored of his age, had used stone only for basements and corner piers; the skeleton was all metal and the inner partitions, including counter-arches that supported the floor, were brick. Space abounded, air and light entered freely, the public circulated without hindrance beneath the vaulting trusses. Here was the cathedral of modern commerce, solid and light, made for a population of female clients.

When, after five years, the "cathedral" stands complete, it looks out not upon the bustling urban village in which its humble predecessor, along with other family-owned shops, had thrived under Louis Philippe, but upon a broad new thoroughfare named for the election that first made Louis Napoleon a figure to be reckoned with, the "rue du Dix-Décembre" commemorating December 10, 1848, and his investiture as head of state.[10]

This consummation tells only half the story, however, for Zola's plot hinges on the paradox of a mercantile Don Juan who seduces women en masse being brought to his knees by a female subordinate. "The double movement," he wrote in his notes. "Octave making a fortune through woman, exploiting woman, speculating on her coquetry and,

[10]On December 10, 1848, Louis Napoleon, who had launched two preposterous invasions of France during his years in exile, was elected "Prince-President" of the Second Republic by a large majority. After 1870 the street was renamed rue du Quatre-Septembre and remains so to this day.

at the end, when he triumphs, finding himself conquered by a woman who did it without trying, who conquered him by the sheer power of her femininity. Create her: a superb specimen combining grace and uprightness." As *Pot-Bouille* begins with Octave Mouret entering Paris, so *Au Bonheur des Dames* begins with the arrival of Denise Baudu, a twenty-year-old woman from Valognes, near Cherbourg. Her father has died bankrupt, and, left to fend for herself and two brothers, she descends upon a paternal uncle who owns a dry-goods store called Le Vieil Elbeuf on the rue Neuve-Saint-Augustin. What she finds there are small shops being choked by Au Bonheur des Dames like an old forest stunted by a tree of gigantic proportions. Uncle Baudu anathematizes this monster, which threatens the traditional order, but Denise, sympathetic though she is, feels drawn to it. It offers employment and, for those who have more future than past, sex appeal. "Baudu's shop was filled with an old person's odor, a half-light in which the old-style commerce, simple and good-natured, seemed to mourn its abandonment. Through the front door Denise could see across the street the windows of Au Bonheur des Dames, which excited her. The sky remained overcast, a soft rain took the chill out of October, and on this milky-white day dusted with sunlight, a sale day, the department store came alive, producing in Denise the sensation of a machine running under high pressure. One felt that its impetus affected everything, even window displays. No longer inanimate spectacles, they warmed and vibrated to the store's inner agitation."

Despite the disapproval of old man Baudu, who regards her as one more faithless lemming, Denise gets a job at Au Bonheur des Dames and for her brothers' sake endures the rough-and-tumble of the huge marketplace. Veteran saleswomen jealous of their turf band against her. Her thick, stubborn tresses and provincial style of dress provoke laughter. Thirteen hours on the floor every day, after hours doing piecework in her tiny cell, leave her exhausted. A male supervisor makes sexual advances, which she rebuffs. And when the slack season commences, that supervisor avenges himself by dismissing her, along with forty-nine other employees.

Mouret has been aware of Denise from the first. If not for him, in fact, who straightway detected some special quality of "grace and tenderness" behind her awkward appearance, she would never have been hired to sell *confections*, or ready-to-wear. But only after she leaves Au Bonheur des Dames do the two engage each other as people. Meeting her by chance, Mouret offers to hire her back on advantageous terms. The flustered young woman demurs. Torn between past and future, between old-fashioned merchants for whom she feels profound compassion in their mortal struggle against capitalism and this bold entrepreneur, between the comforts of a known world and the "grandeur of new creations," between filial piety and romantic adventure, she waits until there is no choice, then accepts. "Gazing out the window, she has a sudden vision of Valognes, of the deserted street with mossy paving stones which she saw from her childhood room," writes Zola, who modeled Valognes after Aix and Denise's youthful conflict after his own. "She was seized by a need to go home, to take refuge in provincial peace and oblivion. Paris irritated her, she hated Au Bonheur des Dames, she no longer knew why she had agreed to return. She would certainly suffer there again, and indeed already felt some indefinable malaise."

Thus Mouret comes to desire above all other women the one he cannot seduce. Even as he surrounds her with jealous attentions, Denise tends shop and tends it very competently indeed, rising from drudge to department head. Malicious gossip, which portrays her aloofness as the strategy of a clever opportunist, misses the mark. Smitten though she is by Octave, she will not, as Gervaise Macquart did, forfeit entrepreneurial pride to lust, or self-respect to *la bête humaine*. In her the vertical proves stronger than the horizontal, and for once a happy ending results. When Denise, who can take only so much of fellow employees impugning her honor, decides to resign, Mouret sees that he will celebrate only hollow victories without her and proposes marriage. Their joyous betrothal occurs on the most profitable sale day ever held at Au Bonheur des Dames. Receipts surpass one million francs.

Did Zola do violence to his hero with this conventional denouement? So one might reasonably argue, for throughout *Pot-Bouille* and *Au Bonheur des Dames* it is made quite clear that monogamous love, if he were capable of it, would leave Octave Mouret unfulfilled. Mouret comes alive most convincingly not as a private man wooing Denise Baudu but in scenes of orgiastic commotion, when he surveys the bourgeois maenads whom he, Bacchus-like, has induced to desert their families, to enter his realm, to lose control. Sale days at Au Bonheur des Dames are wild, pagan festivals. "A compact wave of heads rolled beneath the galleries, widening in the middle of the hall, like a river overflowing its banks," is how Zola describes the crowd at a winter sale. "It was afternoon, the hour of frenzied dancing, when breathless female customers threw caution to the wind. Madness held sway, especially at the silk counter, where Paris-Bonheur caused such excitement that Hutin dared not take a step; and Henriette, dumbstruck, observed Mouret at the head of the stairs, exultant." He exults again at the sale of sales, a white sale that brings down the curtain on *Au Bonheur des Dames*. "Six o'clock approached and daylight filtering through the glass canopy had long since begun to wane," writes Zola.

> Mouret couldn't take his eyes off his horde of women. . . . Dark shadows stood out in bold relief against the pale background. Long

eddies swirled through the crowd, the fever of this sale day was subsiding like an attack of vertigo. . . . People began to leave, plundered fabrics lay strewn over counters, gold tinkled in the registers; and the clientele looked conscience-stricken, as if it had just slaked its passion in some louche establishment. It was he who possessed them this way, who held them spellbound with his endless piles of merchandise, his markdowns and rebates, his dalliance and advertising. He had conquered the mothers themselves, he reigned over them in the fashion of a brutal despot whose whim ruins households.

This strange encomium ends with the observation that Mouret had created a "new religion," that churches from which the holy spirit had fled were replaced, for stranded souls, by Mouret's bazaar. "In Au Bonheur des Dames women now spent the empty hours, the anxious and trembling hours they had formerly spent in chapels: a necessary burning of nervous energy, an ever resurgent battle of god against husband."

Although Zola wanted it understood that this love of commerce had been inherited from François Mouret, everything suggests that Octave's real spiritual predecessor was not his father but the priest who enthralled his mother. Just as Ovide Faujas conquered Plassans through its married women, offering them in church an eroticomystical consolation for the vacuousness of daily life, so Octave creates a "temple" to which matrons flock in their thousands. And just as Faujas eclipses the husbands, substituting for patriarchal authority the despotism of a charismatic brute, so Octave "frees" women only to enslave them, removing their social bonds the better to found a society of selfless, impulse-ridden hostages. In the outside world, laws and institutions hallow the space that makes individual existence possible; but where these two characters rule, individual space is anathema. Their power depends for its absoluteness on the outside world vanishing and on desire flooding minds, effacing boundaries, merging otherwise well-bred women into a single passionate body heedless of custom and taboo. The glass canopy through which daylight penetrates Au Bonheur des Dames evokes the greenhouse in La Curée, with its chaotic, superabundant flora.[11] Is not the nineteenth-century emporium a place in which reason comes to grief, and is Mouret himself not a savage child-king who has set his throne upon the grave of

[11]"Where Mouret revealed himself to be peerless was in the interior arrangement of the store. He set it down as axiomatic that no corner should remain empty: he required that noise, crowds, life should pervade every space; for life, he said, attracted life, begot life, and pullulated." The amphitheater of the Viorne River, Les Halles, the greenhouse, Le Paradou, the theater and hippodrome in Nana, the department store are all paradigms of an enclosure filled with appetite, desire, or rage.

family men? "Exasperated, the Baudu family had to forget about sleep," Zola writes, describing the enlargement of Au Bonheur des Dames, which was carried out at night. "They were shaken in their alcove, noises changed into nightmares as soon as fatigue overcame them. They'd then walk around barefoot to calm their fever, and if they parted a window curtain, they'd stand terror-stricken before the vision of Au Bonheur des Dames blazing through the shadows like a colossal forge shaping their ruin. . . . Whenever the big store opened new departments, several more neighborhood shopkeepers collapsed. One could hear the oldest establishments giving way." Indissolubly bound in Zola—we have seen it before, we shall see it again—are modernity and primitivism, the forward-looking and the radically archaic.

This novel, in which Zola indirectly celebrated his own authorial enterprise, with the construction of the great department store a metaphor for the construction of the multivolume saga, cost him more anguish than *Pot-Bouille*.[12] He had to struggle against his familiar demons, and these did not give ground as the book advanced. His dream, he said, was to accumulate a half million francs, then embark upon a "history of French literature" or some other "interminable" project that would effectively save him from public judgment. "At lunch he asks me to fill his glass of Bordeaux only halfway, so badly is his hand trembling," Goncourt noted on April 18, 1882. " 'I'm in for eight months of toil!' he continues with a kind of terrified air. 'Yes, eight months during which I must hoist an entire world. . . . And when that's done, not to know whether it's any good. . . . Five or six years must pass before one can feel certain that the volume deserves a place in one's collected works.' " Three months later, Goncourt, who, as previously noted, had gone to Médan with the Daudets and Charpentiers on a midsummer excursion, found Zola worn, and Zola's letters confirm this impression. "What a heavy thing is a pen!" he grieved to Céard in October, when he was bedridden with high fever. "It would take two or three years of vegetating for me to regain my strength.

---

[12]The metaphorical relationship between department store and saga touched upon Zola's most cherished fantasy and one of them informs the following passage: "Madame Marty . . . told herself that she was dead tired, but there was ecstasy in her fatigue, in the toll taken of her energies by the inexhaustible merchandise surrounding her. Mouret's stroke of genius captivated her, body and soul. As she made her way through the store, each department arrested her attention." Just so did Zola undoubtedly like to imagine women readers making their way through *Les Rougon-Macquart*, enthralled in novel after novel by the inexhaustible display of wares.

The unfinished novel terrifies me, I've become so pusillanimous." How many more naturalist "tours de force" could he pull off? he asked. "I shall end up loathing our complicated literature."

Zola finished this very long novel on January 25, 1883, after eight months of labor, and arranged, in often rather devious negotiations, to have official translators from England, Germany, Russia, and Italy receive installments before *Gil Blas* serialized them.[13] The *feuilleton* ran until March 1, 1883, whereupon Charpentier brought out a first edition of sixty thousand copies. For obvious reasons, *Au Bonheur des Dames* received much praise, happy though newspaper critics were to discount those great crowd scenes in which Octave Mouret plays the *magister ludi* orchestrating mass regression. They viewed the novel, despite its dark side, as a splendid romance, or as a success story embroidered with golden precepts. To be sure, they found Mouret's Darwinian justification of the wreckage left by Au Bonheur des Dames rather excessively crude, but his marriage to a woman bent upon making him humane assuaged them.[14] "Honesty" and "grace" were two of the compliments they paid.

As for Zola's friends, it appears that only Huysmans, who was about to cause some consternation with A *rebours*, the novel that signaled his eventual divorce from naturalism, sent a congratulatory letter. "I don't know how the devil you extract such variety from subjects that one wouldn't have thought had any," he wrote. "Portraying this ever ebullient store without repeating yourself took some doing. . . . It is, rest assured, a virtuoso performance—the crescendo of sale days to the final blaze of whiteness—that you alone could have completed safely." However, not even Huysmans seemed to appreciate the bril-

---

[13]To Hubert Welter, for example, who handled German rights and advised Zola to treat with one Gustav Grimm, a piratical publisher from Budapest, Zola wrote on December 14:

Since M. Grimm calls the tune, tell him that I accept his thousand francs. But try to get him to pay up front. It is understood that I shall transmit the manuscript to you in three stages, the first third right way, the second third on December 20, the last third on January 31. But he can begin publication only on December 16, after the first installment in *Gil Blas*. And all subsequent installments must lag behind *Gil Blas*.

[14]Zola's brief for free enterprise in literature may indicate how much of himself he poured into Octave Mouret. In 1880 he wrote:

Every powerful talent ends up manifesting and imposing itself. One does not help genius get born; it is its own midwife. . . . The state owes young writers nothing; writing several pages that no one will publish or stage hardly justifies pretensions to martyrdom; a cobbler who has made his first pair of boots doesn't force the government to place them for him. That's the worker's job. And if he's not equal to it, he is no one; he will remain unknown through his own fault and for good reason.

The story of the great man who falls in love with his employee is, moreover, one that Zola was to live out in his own life.

liance with which Zola shaped, in every detail of *Au Bonheur des Dames*—in window displays that startle spectators by juxtaposing cheap garments and luxury items, in the inexorable demolition of shops each occupying its traditional niche, in the thronging together of different classes on sale day—an image of universal promiscuity.

Creating a great emporium in which "life pervades every space" may also have served a magical purpose, for with Emilie Zola's bedchamber kept intact, it's as if death had installed itself at Médan, hollowing out existence. Forty-odd years weighed like sixty upon Zola (whose bald patch gave him the look of a fat, tonsured monk), and after 1880, when table talk was often about treatments or therapies, he came increasingly to fear that *Les Rougon-Macquart* would never be finished. "I've plunged into work with my usual shakes," he wrote Alphonse Daudet on May 20, 1883, "but I'm afraid I've forgotten everything, even how to spell. Maybe this time my head is really cracked." Presentiments of doom left little room for cheer as, one after another, old companions fell by the wayside. In 1882 his beloved dog Bertrand, who had followed him everywhere since 1867, departed this world, and a grief-stricken Zola buried him in a corner of the garden. Not many months later, death claimed Edouard Manet and Ivan Turgenev in swift succession.

Although during the 1870s Zola had not often visited Manet's studio at 4, rue de Saint-Petersbourg, where almost every late afternoon a crowd that included Georges Clemenceau, Emmanuel Chabrier, Méry Laurent, and Stéphane Mallarmé gathered over aperitifs, the two remained good friends. Dinner invitations were regularly exchanged, and so were kind favors. When Zola moved to the rue de Boulogne, several blocks away from him, Manet offered to have his portrait cleaned. When he learned that Zola planned a tower for Médan, he recommended an architect who lived nearby. Manet requested tickets to the stage adaptation of *L'Assommoir* and found nothing demeaning about Zola's request that he decorate a fan for him. "Impossible to do anything good on the fan you sent me," Manet apologized. "It's at once too beautiful and too ugly. I should have preferred a fan made of white wood—the cheap kind that has a sheet of white paper. I'd paint the handle and the paper. Combed the entire neighborhood this morning, in vain. Can your tradesman provide anything of this description? If so, I'll need two hours to do it." Instead of decorating Alexandrine's fan, Manet portrayed her (at Zola's request) in an exquisite pastel for which she sat during the spring or summer of 1879.

Zola continued to tout Manet's custom whenever the opportunity presented itself, despite qualms that became more insistent as time wore on. Reviewing the Salon of 1875 in *The European Herald* he singled out for praise *Argenteuil* a painting that would have looked entirely appropriate at the second Salon des Indépendants had Manet chosen to repudiate officialdom and exhibit alongside his Impressionist friends. Where one scornful critic saw "a marmalade of Argenteuil on a river of indigo," Zola admired Manet's "natural elegance," his "sense of the modern," the care he took to convey the "truth of a general impression." Lit by a brilliant sun, the scene commands attention with its vivid colors, he wrote.

> But that's a problem for some people: they find the water excessively blue, and jokes abound. I'm convinced that the painter saw this tone; his only fault was not to have diluted it. If he had made the water sky blue, everyone would have been thrilled. Meanwhile the figures, which leap off the canvas, went unnoticed: a woman in striped dress, a man in straw hat and fisherman's jersey. . . . Manet's work exhales the freshness of spring and youth. Fancy a green branch growing out of an old withered trunk, a little flower sprouting amidst the ruins of classical methods and romantic artifices, the crushing boredom, the opaque banality. Would one not take pleasure contemplating a green bud, saturated though it might be with bitter resin? . . . I'll be stoned for it, but I affirm anyway that in twenty-five years or so Cabanel's much decorated historical canvases will have died of anemia while Manet's will go on flowering with the eternal youth of original works.

Zola covered the Salon of 1876 as well, and he informed Russian readers, after describing his dismal itinerary through the Palace of Industry, that Manet had organized a one-man show on the rue de Saint-Petersbourg, with two paintings spurned by the Salon jury: *Laundry* and *The Artist: Portrait of Marcellin Desboutin*. "Manet has always been the apple of discord," he railed. Juries who had accepted his work ten years straight would have welcomed any pretext to reject it in the eleventh—to crush an "enemy," to punish a "bad character." And what made him bad? The fact that he depicted nature without reference to other people's images and views, Zola wrote (ignoring Manet's penchant for artistic quotations). This originality wrought havoc. How could the Salon exhibit something like *Laundry* for example, where a young woman is pictured in a garden with a tubful of wash and a small child beside her? "The scene unfolds out of doors; the colors acquire vivid radiance; the lines blur in plays of light. Never would certain peevish critics forgive Manet for having indicated so summarily that laundress's features. Her eyes are represented by two black dots; her nose and lips are reduced to simple pink lines." It was easy enough to understand the hostility Manet aroused, he concluded, but he, Zola, found such art "curious and original in the extreme."

Not until 1879, in a review of the annual Salon written, once again, for *The European Herald* did Zola allow himself openly to find fault with Manet, and his disgruntlement bore upon the artist's "capricious" technique. "His long struggle against the public's incomprehension may be understood in light of the difficulty he has executing, by which I mean that his hand does not equal his eye," Zola now wrote.

He has not been able to master a craft; he has remained the enthusiastic schoolboy who always sees quite distinctly what's happening outside himself but never knows for sure whether he has it in him to render his impressions completely and definitively. This is why, when he begins a painting, one never knows if, or how, he will carry it off. He does it by guesswork. When he succeeds, the result is magnificent: absolutely true and extraordinarily skillful. But he sometimes goes astray, and then his canvases are imperfect and unequal. In short, we have not seen during the past fifteen years a more subjective artist. If only his technical equipment matched the rightness of his perceptions, he would figure as the great painter of the second half of the nineteenth century. Moreover, all the Impressionists sin by technical inadequacy.

Zola's preference may always, at bottom, have been for more finish and detail than he ever found in Manet or Monet, for the meticulous brush of a Daubigny and for the anecdotal precision of a Courbet. Impressionist painting often seemed to him slapdash. "All those artists are too easily satisfied," he groused. "They disdain works born of slow meditation, and more's the pity. Because they make haste, it is predictable that they will clear the path for some great future artist instead of achieving greatness themselves." A common cause had formerly required absolute partisanship, but this changed after *L'Assommoir*. Success led Zola to identify with paragons of entrepreneurial vigor, to glorify struggle in Darwinian terms, to deprecate artists who enjoyed only the consolations of martyrdom. Could he thenceforth defend Manet against an unappreciative public without casting discredit upon himself, who wrote only best-sellers? Was it not (in part at least) for the sake of his own literary virtue that he attributed the Impressionists' unsuccess to technical "inadequacy" rather than visionary brilliance?

These cavils, like those that fill "Les Romanciers contemporains," came back from Russia to haunt him. They were republished in *La Revue politique et littéraire* with one erroneous substitution of Manet for Monet, and were soon afterward quoted by *Le Figaro* under the impudent title: "M. Zola has just broken with M. Manet." Zola hastened to reassure Manet, with half-truths, that *Le Figaro* had got it all wrong. "I am stupefied by the article in *Le Figaro* announcing that I've broken with you, and this note will serve as a hearty handshake," he wrote on July 27, 1879. "The translation of the quoted passage is not accurate; the meaning of the piece has, furthermore, been distorted. I spoke about you in Russia as I have spoken about you in France these past thirteen years, with staunch appreciation of your talent and liking for your person." These words did indeed reassure Manet, who had been shaken by the apparent betrayal. "Your letter gives me great pleasure," he responded, "and I hope you will find nothing wrong with my demanding that *Le Figaro* print it. I confess that I felt terribly disillusioned and hurt." Alexis, who hung around the studio on the rue de Saint-Petersbourg, thought that an outright lie would have been more effective, that Zola should have taxed the Russians with mistaking Manet for Monet. But Zola made amends after his own fashion. One year later, when he reviewed the Salon of 1880, which included *Portrait de M. Antonin Proust* and *Chez le Père Lathuile* he extolled Manet as the sovereign French artist in a "period of transition." Fourteen years earlier, wrote Zola, "I was one of the first to defend Manet against the imbecilic attacks of the public and press. Since that time he has worked hard, constantly fighting, impressing himself on men of intelligence with his rare artistic qualities and the sincerity of his efforts, and the originality, so apparent and distinctive, of his palette."

Having paintings accepted by juries almost every year never amounted to official consecration for Manet, or membership in the Club. Regarded as incorrigibly mischievous, he was given annual contracts, so to speak, but denied academic tenure. Not even *Le Bon Bock*—his Hals-like portrait of a rotund beer drinker, reproductions of which appeared all over France after it captivated spectators at the 1873 Salon—earned him deferential treatment from the powers that were. When in 1879 he proposed to decorate the new Hôtel de Ville with a large mural (tentatively called *Le Ventre de Paris*) showing various aspects of modern urban life, his proposal went unacknowledged. In 1881, however, fortune smiled upon him at last. By one vote, the Salon jury, to which several old friends had been elected (Guillemet among them), awarded Manet a medal. Being thus honored meant that he was *hors concours* or permitted thereafter to exhibit without going through the jury. It also meant that his most loyal supporter, Antonin Proust, who became minister of culture under Gambetta, could name him a *chevalier* of the Legion of Honor, and so he did. In December 1881, at forty-nine, Manet finally acquired the knighthood he had coveted all his life.

His luck was of brief duration. After 1880, when the first signs of

locomotor ataxia, or syphilis of the spinal cord, had manifested themselves, he who loved to stroll along the Boulevard des Italiens found
it increasingly difficult to negotiate the few blocks that separated his
flat from his studio. Hydrotherapy accomplished nothing. Nor did sojourns at Rueil, outside Paris, where, racked by pain, he spent days
painting in the garden of a rented villa. By October 1882 he could not
get around without Léon Leenhoff, his "secret son," and several
months later it was on Léon's arm that this consummate Parisian gentleman visited his studio for the last time. "I saw him the evening he
lay down never again to rise," Antonin Proust reminisced. "Spread
before him were sweets from an Easter egg sent by Méry Laurent. He
was calm, but slightly nervous about a consultation with Drs. Verneuil
and Tillot. The next day Léon Leenhoff told me that the consultation
had gone badly." His left leg being gangrenous, surgeons amputated
it. The tabes had progressed too far, however, and eleven days later,
on April 30, 1883, Manet died at the age of fifty-two.

Passy Cemetery was where his family buried him. Zola, whom Céard
had kept informed of Manet's swift deterioration, attended the funeral
and served as a pallbearer, along with Théodore Duret, Philippe Burty,
Alfred Stevens, Fantin-Latour, Claude Monet, and Antonin Proust. In
a letter thanking him for his "devoted assistance," Manet's younger
brother Eugène solicited one last review. "At Proust's request, J. Ferry
has set aside the Ecole des Beaux-Arts for an exhibition of Edouard's
work," he wrote to Zola on May 7. "This exhibition cannot take place
before October. . . . I beg you to join the organizing committee, along
with Proust, my brother Gustave, L. Leenhoff, Duret, the abbé Hurel;
I should also appreciate a brief biographical notice for the catalogue."
The exhibition opened at the Ecole des Beaux-Arts on January 5, 1884
(over protests by Kaempfen, director of the school), and Zola did as
requested, observing in his fine encomium that Manet's influence during the previous twenty years had extended even to *pompier* artists:

In 1863, the mob snarled at him at the Salon des Refusés, yet it was
he who became their leader. How often does one pause nowadays in
front of a bright canvas with pure colors and exclaim: "Goodness, a
Manet!" There is no painter more imitated, unavowedly, than he.
But direct imitations are not the most typical. What bears close scrutiny is the effect he has had on virtuosic hacks. Whilst his originality,
which was uncompromising, earned him derision, all sorts of opportunistic painters followed close behind, sweeping up what they could,
borrowing from his manner as much as the public could tolerate of
it, accommodating plein air to bourgeois sauces. I won't name names,
but I will say that many a fortune has been made on his back, many
a reputation built with his vital substance! . . . These thieves peddle

him in tidbits to ecstatic connoisseurs, who value counterfeit Manet above the genuine article.

Manet's genius, he concluded, was that of the precursor who changes our manner of perceiving things and of rendering them.

Zola had no sooner absorbed this loss than he received word of Ivan Turgenev's death. His informant was once again Henry Céard, and the sad news caught up with him in Bénodet, a Breton village near Quimper, where he and Alexandrine vacationed from mid-July until mid-September 1883. "The opportunity to eulogize him will no doubt present itself someday," he wrote, half contritely, to Céard, after asserting that a farewell in *Le Figaro* or *Gil Blas* might be interpreted as self-promotion.[15] "I shall say how much I liked Turgenev and how grateful I am for the kind of services he performed on my account in Russia. I believe that he regarded me affectionately. I've lost a friend, and the loss is great."

Zola had seen little of him since 1879. Although gout caused Turgenev enormous distress, it never kept him entirely housebound. Indeed, he spent more time in Saint Petersburg than in Paris during the years 1880–81. Disposed—until Tsar Alexander II's assassination—to underestimate or even justify terrorism, Turgenev found himself hailed by Russian university students as a great man, a would-be savior, a progressive mind capable of uniting left-wing elements, and he reveled in their adulation. But he also loved high society, which did not ostracize him for his romance with radical politics. "There were some grand, aristocratic dinners," writes the historian Leonard Schapiro. "One, in Princess Worontzoff's superb house, when there were violent diatribes against the depravity of the modern radical girl: 'High society understands *nothing* about what is happening below and around itself.' The second rather boring, at the Grand Duchess Catherine's, attended by the ambassador in Paris, Prince Orlov. Then there was a dinner at the house of Princess Paskevich; and, gastronomically the best (*cèpes* fried in cream and Tilsit cheese!), a banquet at Prince Worontzoff's mansion." After Saint Petersburg came Orel province, where pleasures of a different kind awaited him at Spasskoye. In his own private domain he dreamed, wrote stories about the supernatural, went hunting,

[15]Another incident shows how sensitive Zola was to imputations of opportunism. In 1890, after learning from John Singer Sargent that Manet's widow, who was in financial straits, planned to sell *Olympia* to an American collector, Claude Monet launched a subscription, raised almost twenty thousand francs (or one-fortieth the amount recently paid for Millet's *Angélus*), and offered it to the Louvre. Zola did not contribute, explaining in a rather convoluted letter that the French state should of its own accord honor Manet, that he, as an owner of Manet's work, might be accused of attempting to jack up the value of his possessions.

and inhaled snuff while dilating on the state of Russia. Friends came from afar to stay with him and they included Leo Tolstoy, whose genius he proclaimed at every opportunity but whose evangelism made him squirm.

However deeply he craved the homage of young intellectuals, the glitter of Saint Petersburg society, the ambiance of his native language, and the spectacle of childhood haunts, what made Russia absolutely irresistible to Turgenev was the prospect of rejuvenation. At sixty-one, this white-maned giant fell in love with a twenty-five-year-old actress named Maria Gavrilovna Savina, who reigned over the Saint Petersburg Alexandrine Theater. Having chosen A Month in the Country for the fall 1879 season, Savina won universal acclaim as Vera and, offstage, exercised her considerable charms upon a grateful dramatist. Not that she gave herself to Turgenev. It seems, indeed, that she did not. But then Turgenev, who by his own admission thrived more on platonic love than on carnal (or more on foreplay than on coitus), did not importune her. Unconsummated trysts proved agreeable enough, and many such trysts took place. They met in Saint Petersburg, in Moscow, in Paris. Turgenev had Savina visit Spasskoye and on one occasion, when she was traveling south, boarded her train at Mtsensk for the thirty-mile run to Orel. After that mobile assignation he wrote to her:

> Suddenly I notice that my lips whisper "what a night we could have spent together!" And immediately I realize that this will never happen, and that I will in the end depart for beyond without the memory of it. . . . You are wrong to reproach yourself, to call me your "sin." Alas! I will never be that. . . . My life is behind me, and that hour spent in the railway compartment, when I almost felt like a twenty-year-old youth, was the last burst of flame. It is even difficult for me to explain to myself what kind of feeling you have aroused in me. Am I in love with you? I don't know: it was different on past occasions. This insurmountable longing for fusion, for possession and for the surrender of oneself, when even sensation disappears in a kind of thin fire.

Almost liberated from one disastrous marriage but already committed to what would prove another, Savina found in this flirtation an escape from her conjugal entanglements. Meanwhile Turgenev, who had never wed Pauline Viardot nor ever unbound himself, enacted a mock version of adulterous love, tormenting his lifelong companion, when she confronted him, with denials that sounded like avowals.

In September 1881, when he returned to France, Turgenev seemed none the worse for his romantic ordeal. That was the impression of

English friends who saw him one month later shooting partridge and entertaining fellow literati at a London dinner party organized by his translator. To judge from Goncourt's journal, which describes "les Cinq"—the original five—reunited around Flaubert's empty chair, this confident mood buoyed him through several seasons. "What with some of us having emotional problems and others enduring physical pain, death occupies the center of conversation all evening long, until 11 p.m., despite efforts to push it aside," Goncourt wrote on March 6, 1882.

Daudet declares that it harrows him, poisons his life, that whenever he took a new flat, he'd automatically wonder where his coffin would stand. Zola in turn speaks about his mother, who died at Médan. As the staircase was too narrow, she had to be lowered from the window, and since then he cannot contemplate that window without wondering who will emerge from it first, he or his wife. "Yes, since that day, death has lurked at the bottom of our thoughts and often—we now keep a lamp lit all night long—very often, in the wee hours, I'll look at my wife, who can't fall asleep, knowing that she has it on her mind too. And yet neither of us talks, out of modesty. . . . There are nights when I'll leap out of bed and stand at the foot of it in stark terror. . . ."

Turgenev took a supercilious view of such hysteria. "Death is a familiar thought," Goncourt quotes him as saying, "but when it visits me, I give it the back of my hand. . . . For us Russians, the Slavic fog has its therapeutic uses. It helps us escape the logic of our ideas and the hot pursuit of deduction. . . . If you should ever be caught in a Russian blizzard, you would be told: 'Forget the cold or you'll die!' Well, thanks to that fog, a snowbound Slav forgets the cold—and so, by the same strategy, does the idea of death soon efface itself and disappear."

In due course, however, his optimism fled, for by mid-April he found himself afflicted with a "neuralgia" around the heart that made it painful in the extreme to walk any distance or climb stairs. Gout-induced angina was Charcot's diagnosis, and the eminent physician, who observed that "medical science is virtually helpless in the case of this disease," prescribed absolute immobility. Another eminence put him on a milk diet, which may have done more to comfort him than a German contraption for treating rheumatism called "Baunscheidts Lebenswecker." Doted upon at Bougival by members of the Viardot family, Turgenev regarded himself as the victim of some medical paradox. "Imagine a man who is perfectly well . . . but who can neither stand nor walk nor ride without a sharp pain, rather like toothache, attacking his left shoulder," he wrote to a woman friend in Russia.

> What would you have me do in these circumstances? To sit, to lie down, then to sit again and know that in such conditions it is impossible to move to Paris, let alone to Russia. . . . However, my state of mind is very peaceful. I have accepted the thought [that my condition will not get any better] and even find that it is not so bad . . . it is not too bad to be an oyster. After all, I could have gone blind. . . . Now I can even work. Of course, my *personal* life is at an end. But still—I will be sixty-four in a few days' time.

After six months he felt strong and in November, accompanied by Henry James, left Bougival for Paris, where he proceeded to lead a reasonable semblance of his former life, attending the opera, receiving innumerable Russians (among them the Grand Duke Constantine), having his portrait done, enjoying Pauline Viardot's musical soirées, ringing in the Russian New Year at the Russian Artists' Club, watching Parisians in their hundreds of thousands throng around Léon Gambetta's funeral cortege on January 3, 1883. It was through his loyal mediation that a satiric weekly called *Boudilnik* (*The Alarum*) brought out *Au Bonheur des Dames* in an illustrated supplement for subscribers, and it was he who made arrangements to have Maupassant's novel *Une Vie* translated. This schedule required spartan resolve, as the slightest movement often caused him agony. But his "Slavic fog," along with morphine, helped him endure. Neither then nor later did any of the distinguished physicians consulted suspect that he had cancer of the spinal marrow.

Except for delirious spells, when he demanded poison or fancied himself surrounded by poisoners, Turgenev bore his cross nobly until the end, which occurred on September 3, 1883. "The religious ceremony flushed out a small horde of men with gigantic frames, squashed features, patriarchal beards—a microcosmic Russia whose presence here in the capital one had not suspected," Goncourt observed four days later. "There were also many Russian women, German women, English women, pious and faithful readers paying homage to the great and delicate novelist." Hundreds mourned him at the Russian Church on the rue Daru, including a band of nihilists who laid a wreath from "The Russian Refugees," hoping to embarrass Tsar Nicholas. Hundreds more mourned him at the Gare du Nord, where a chapel was rigged up to accommodate his casket until authorization for the homeward voyage came from Saint Petersburg. And mourners filled railroad stations in Russia, awaiting the funeral train as it made its way through an obstacle course created by the imperial government, which feared that Turgenev would posthumously incite rebellion. "One would have thought," wrote Stasiulevich, "that the corpse belonged to Solovei the Robber rather than to a great writer." Still, Turgenev finally made it home and was laid to rest beside his dear friend Belinsky in the Volkova Cemetery at Saint Petersburg.

When he heard about this final voyage, Zola may have remembered a dinner given by Turgenev in January 1880, on the eve of a previous journey eastward. Dinner had begun cheerfully, according to Goncourt, but soon enough it turned somber. "Turgenev described how several nights earlier his heart had tightened at the vision of a large brown spot, which, in his half-somnolent, half-wakeful state, represented Death." Afflicted on that occasion with sciatica, Zola had felt entirely sympathetic and had "enumerated the morbid phenomena behind his fear that he would never finish the eleven volumes yet to be written," Goncourt noted. Since then, death had drawn much nearer, taking Flaubert, Emilie, Duranty, Manet, Turgenev himself. And this gathering of shades could only reinforce Zola's innermost conviction that he was destined one way or another to suffer his father's fate. Not that that conviction held him back. On the contrary, it goaded him relentlessly as he entered middle age. Instead of despairing he became even more prolific, and in the twelfth episode of *Les Rougon-Macquart* he bestowed his neurotic terrors upon a character who cannot complete anything.

La Joie de vivre evolved from an idea to which Zola gave vent in September 1880 at Médan, several months after Flaubert's funeral. "When he finished reading aloud his memoir on Flaubert, he complained of being old, and his conversation revolved around death," wrote Céard, who was present along with J.-K. Huysmans. "What is the point of all we do? And he told us he wanted to write a novel founded upon the ideas of grief [*douleur*] and nothingness. He didn't yet know how it would proceed. He wanted to avoid boredom, but there would be hardly any action. He thought that *L'Education sentimentale* could not be imitated. So what to do? He was full of doubts, of uncertainty, and always recurred to the idea of nothingness." Zola's original notes confirm Céard's report. He groped month after month for a handle to this doleful subject. There were three or four possible stories, none of which quite conveyed the grief he had in mind. And when at last he organized an acceptable plot, he couldn't flesh it out. "I put it aside," he later told Goncourt, "because I wanted to infuse it with myself and my kinfolk and lacked the courage to do so after my mother's death." Not until 1883—having meanwhile written *Pot-Bouille* and *Au Bonheur des Dames*—did he resume work on the project, but by then it was envisaged from a somewhat different perspective. He set out as much to preach against the poor of spirit as to lay himself bare, as much to deplore the infatuation with Schopenhauer or philosophical pessimism rampant among young French intellectuals (Céard and Huysmans included) as to exorcise his own nay-saying *Doppelgänger*.

La Joie de vivre takes place in a storm-swept village of thirty houses nestled precariously on a cliff that beetles over the Atlantic near Avranches, in Normandy. Bonneville is its name, and among its newer inhabitants are the Chanteau family. Having inherited a debt-ridden lumber business many years earlier, Monsieur Chanteau, who hails from Caen, lacked the spunk to make it fully profitable again. His father, a carpenter turned entrepreneur, had risen in the world, but Chanteau junior had done the opposite, and the physical sign of his moral invalidism is his gout. Disabled by recurrent attacks of the disease, he retired at fifty-four to the Cotentin with his wife, hoping that ocean air would cure him.

Madame Chanteau, née Eugénie de la Vignière, had not bargained for life on the margin of France when she got married. Born to Norman gentry who died young leaving her aristocratic lineage but little of material value, she had assumed that lumber money would help her establish herself socially. Marriage brought her wormwood instead. Twice betrayed—first by her frail father, then by her frail husband— this bitter, high-strung, domineering woman has invested her pride in her nineteen-year-old son, Lazare. The prefect or magistrate she expects him to become will restore to her her birthright.

That one more betrayal lies in store for her is what Lazare announces the moment he walks onstage. "He had left the *lycée* at Caen with his baccalauréat in August and during the next eight months hiked all over the cliffs, irresolutely pondering his future," writes Zola. "Music was the only thing he felt passionate about, which reduced his mother to despair." Intoxicated by oceanic sound, this philo-Wagnerian entertains grand designs:

> Lazare confided in his cousin Pauline. He could be a musician of genius, despite his mother, despite everybody. At the *lycée* he had a violin teacher who found his musical intelligence striking and predicted an illustrious career. Surreptitiously, he had taken lessons in composition; he was working on his own now and he already had a vague idea, which was a symphony about the earthly paradise. He had even composed a section of it—Adam and Eve expelled by the angels, a march written in solemn and mournful cadences.

It soon becomes apparent that Lazare's self-doubt matches his grandiosity, that he leaps, without any stable sense of himself, from enthu-

siasm to enthusiasm, like an ingenuous con artist. No sooner has he
embraced music than he abandons it for medicine. Good grades convince him that he is destined to be a "physician of genius," but after
one year medicine palls. He then finds himself captivated by the experiments of a famous chemist. "His letters [from Paris] spoke, at first
timidly, then buoyantly, about a project that involved the processing
of seaweed. It would earn millions thanks to . . . reagents discovered
by Herbelin." With financial help from home, Lazare builds a seaweed
plant near Bonneville. It proves unworkable, and the would-be entrepreneur, ruined, seeks consolation in German philosophy. Schopenhauer's *The World as Will and Idea* confers intellectual legitimacy upon
his despair.

Lazare's young cousin, Pauline Quenu, whom faithful readers of *Les
Rougon-Macquart* would have remembered from *Le Ventre de Paris*,
shores him up as best she can. A rich orphan, she had joined the
Chanteau household at age ten; *La Joie de vivre*, another of Zola novels
in which the drama hinges upon a drifter or wanderer or exile invading
a closed world, begins with her arrival. Thanks to her, light reaches
people enveloped in darkness, for Pauline possesses all the virtues they
lack. Her generosity is more than equal to their self-absorption, and
nothing about them daunts her—neither Monsieur Chanteau's excruciating gout nor Madame Chanteau's brittleness. She emerges as the
consummate yea-sayer, the born anti-Schopenhauerian, the natural
healer. "Her nature, which brimmed over with love of life, made her
what her aunt called 'the mother of God's little dappled things,'"
writes Zola.

> Everything that lived, everything that suffered filled her with active
> tenderness, with a need to shower attention and caresses upon the
> sufferer. She no longer thought about Paris. She felt that she had
> sprouted there, in that poor soil. . . . The unformed child was now a
> robust young woman with solid hips and an ample bosom. And the
> discomforts that attended this blossoming . . . had given way to joy,
> to the victorious sensation of growth and pubescence.

Akin to Désirée Mouret, the earth-girl in *La Faute de l'abbé Mouret*
whose naive sensualism clashes with her brother's abhorrence of life,
Pauline—part ardent positivist, part nurturing genius—also foreshadows Pascal Rougon, the titular hero of *Le Docteur Pascal*. It is, indeed,
at her urging that Lazare studies medicine, and it is she who reads his
medical textbooks when he casts them aside.[16]

[16]As for Lazare, his projected symphony about the earthly paradise underscores
his propinquity to Serge Mouret.

Virtue doesn't spread. If anything, Pauline's presence hastens the moral deterioration of the household by giving Madame Chanteau opportunities to betray her charge. She squanders the young woman's inheritance on Lazare: "One evening Lazare told his mother about a previously unavowed debt. . . . Mme Chanteau . . . straightway opened a drawer she had never before opened except in the presence of others, a drawer filled with negotiable securities, and took five thousand francs, promising herself to replace them after the first profitable transaction. A breach was thus made, and it widened." Where at first harmony prevailed there erupts a power struggle in which everything turns upside down, with guardian behaving like ward and ward like guardian. Subverted in her moral being by a fortune she embezzles, Madame Chanteau feels challenged in her sexual authority by an adolescent whose ripe physique threatens to captivate her son. Pauline finds herself portrayed as the hated outsider, the glass that reflects a vile image, the scapegoat responsible for "badness" in the Chanteau household. Had she not introduced money, Eugénie would not have become a thief. Had she not bolstered Lazare, whom she loves passionately, he would not have become a cripple hatching preposterous schemes.

Pauline grows in spiritual strength with every assault upon her pride. As much to humiliate her as to further her own social ambitions, Eugénie encourages a liaison between Lazare and the meek daughter of a Caen banker, Louise Thibaudier, who spends every summer under the Chanteau roof. Jealous, Pauline remains only for Monsieur Chanteau's sake. In time Eugénie contracts heart disease and on her deathbed accuses Pauline of poisoning her. Pauline nurses her devotedly nonetheless. When poor, feckless Lazare, whom Eugénie manipulates from beyond the grave, marries Louise, Pauline, grief-stricken though she is, gives them her blessing. And when Louise produces a blue baby, Pauline resuscitates it by breathing air into its lungs. Filled with spirit, this secular saint whose womb remains barren mothers all of Bonneville. "She was renunciation itself, love of others, goodness lavished upon wicked humanity," Zola writes at the end, where Pauline is seen rocking her surrogate child, named Paul. "The sun set in the immense sea, peace descended from the pale sky, a softness that comes with the waning of beautiful days pervaded the infinity of water and the infinity of air. There remained only one spark, a small white sail which extinguished itself on disappearing beneath the straight, simple line of the horizon."

That sea, to which Pauline has special affinities, makes itself felt throughout *La Joie de vivre*. As in *La Faute de l'abbé Mouret* a paradisial garden extends beyond the godforsaken village of Les Artaud, so in *La Joie de vivre* an oceanic immensity dwarfs Bonneville, whose wretched denizens live like brutes. A Great Outside, a vastness surrounding people trapped among themselves in the muck and mire of human veins, obsessed Zola (it had obsessed him since childhood, when he regularly fled Aix for the wild world up above), and this image of transcendence would appear again, notably in *La Terre*, where depraved kinfolk devour one another amidst wheat fields that stretch as far as the eye can reach.

Zola may have identified with Pauline viewing humanity from a compassionate, nonjudgmental remove, but he avowedly modeled Lazare Chanteau after himself, and this fact is nowhere more patent than in the description of fears that beset his protagonist after Eugénie's death. Determined to fail again and again lest he gratify a mother who would make him her spouse, the Oedipal victim cannot wrest himself free. "Underneath his feeling of being bereft was a terror of death," writes Zola.

> Aggravated by the fear of inherited susceptibility, this terror returned after the initial grief subsided. He would die as she had; he carried with him the certainty of imminent doom, and all day long, in such a state of nerves that he could hear his inner machinery work, he listened to himself live. . . . Louder than the noise of other organs was that of his heart, which resounded through every limb, right down to his fingertips. When he rested his elbow on a table, his heart beat in his elbow; when he leaned against the back of an armchair, his heart beat in the nape of his neck; when he sat or lay down, it beat in his thighs, in his flanks, in his stomach. . . . He thought that the whole thing might come apart at any moment.

Lazare's *manies* are in fact a catalogue of those ritualistic acts by which Zola himself sought to fend off the avenging angel. Unable to leave a room or close a book without thinking that he might never again enter the one or open the other, Zola felt compelled to bid the world around him continual farewells, to inspect his domain obsessively. And so it is with Lazare:

> Inseparable from this were ideas of symmetry. Three steps to the left and three to the right. Furniture on either side of a fireplace or a door touched an equal number of times, the idea being that five or seven times, for example, might help him avoid a definitive farewell. Despite his keen intelligence and his denial of the supernatural, he practiced this inane religion with brutish acquiescence, hiding it like some shameful disease. It was a revenge wrought upon . . . the positivist who had pledged himself to facts and experience. It made him bothersome. "Why are you pacing back and forth?" Pauline ex-

claimed. "That's three times now you've visited your armoire and touched the key. It's not going to fly away, you know." It took him forever to leave the dining room after supper what with his having to arrange the chairs in a particular order, to slam the door shut a specific number of times, to place his hands, first right hand, then left, on the buffet. . . . [Pauline tried to make light of it but] eventually stopped. One morning she came upon him as he was planting seven kisses on the wooden frame of his mother's deathbed. . . . When a newspaper article made him blanch by mentioning some date in the twentieth century, she'd look at him with compassion, and this caused him embarrassment. . . . How often had he denounced himself for such cowardice! How often had he sworn to take arms against his disease!

That every novel he wrote constituted a victory over Lazare—over impotence, over death, over guilt—was the message he would deliver some twelve years later in his preface to Dr. Edouard Toulouse's *Enquête médico-psychologique.* Just as elsewhere he defended his moral integrity against those who found *Les Rougon-Macquart* pornographic, so here he marched his neuroses against those who considered him an entrepreneur rather than an artist. Unless Lazare's demons were understood to inhabit him as well, then his writing—his completing whatever he began after a "pitched battle between will and doubt"—would lack the quality of heroism he claimed for it.

It is paradoxical that this most intimate novel often impresses one as Zola's most studied. He couldn't quite breathe life into the symbolic flesh of Pauline Quenu. But when Charpentier published *La Joie de vivre* midway through February 1884, critics who had always excoriated *Les Rougon-Macquart* treated it respectfully. "*La Joie de vivre* is *Candide* transported into the contemporary world and given a naturalist twist," Francisque Sarcey wrote in *Le XIXe Siècle.* "It pleased Zola to collect in a little corner of Normandy everything that narrowmindedness, everything that the various illnesses afflicting our poor species, everything that the throes of death . . . produce in the way of emotion and material distress. He has, as it were, poured upon this humble and frightful household all the black, bitter bile of Schopenhauer, and done it with a kind of ecstatic ferocity." Edouard Drumont, who would become Zola's most acrimonious opponent during the Dreyfus Affair, paid the book higher compliments. "This strange book, which offends all of one's sensibilities, is nonetheless singularly powerful," he allowed.

As literary subjects, the wan and the bleak are fashionable. One of Flaubert's *Trois Contes,* "Un Coeur simple," . . . is in some sense the germ of Zola's novel. Flaubert racked his brains for some way of portraying a void, of rendering visible that which has neither color nor relief. . . . But in this matter no one matches Zola. . . . With his usual candor, he has described modern world-weariness. He has given his contemporaries an exact image of themselves, and for that reason, *La Joie de vivre* will survive.

The anti-intellectualism that pervades *La Joie de vivre* agreed with militant, xenophobic nationalists like Drumont, in whose literature German philosophy, among other things foreign, was held responsible for nurturing a generation of deracinated Frenchmen. From this perspective, Lazare had, through Schopenhauer, forfeited his very Frenchness. Conversely, Pauline qualified as a true descendant of Jeanne d'Arc, the virgin saint behind whom reactionary France was to muster after the Dreyfus Affair, after World War I (when she was canonized), and during the Vichy regime.

As for Zola's friends, Maupassant, who found entirely congenial the story of life ravaging "a simple bourgeois family" even as the sea erodes Bonneville, praised it, and so did Huysmans, but with deep resentment. Already en route to a clamorous conversion, the author of *A rebours* could neither uphold naturalism nor yet embrace Catholicism, and Schopenhauer, whom Zola had, in his view, misrepresented, gave him purchase somewhere in between. "I know very well that you don't believe in pessimism and that Bourdeau's preface to Schopenhauer's *Pensées* states that this prodigious man was afraid of death," he objected in a letter, "but the theory transcends the man, who did not apply his ideas to himself. Given the fact that intelligent people cannot bring themselves to believe in Catholicism, these ideas are assuredly the most consoling, the most logical, the most evident imaginable. What it comes down to is this: if one is not a pessimist, the choice is to be a Christian or an anarchist."

Edmond de Goncourt, who, as we know, made Zola the scapegoat for his declining literary fortunes, lodged grievances of another kind. He could not help crying thief directly Zola finished a novel, and so it was in October 1883, when *Gil Blas* announced the forthcoming serialization of *La Joie de vivre*. "Do me a favor and tell Zola absolutely nothing about the part I read you," he entreated Henry Céard on October 6, referring to a manuscript entitled *Chérie*. "I see it announced in *Gil Blas* that his novel will feature 'a young woman who holds up valiantly in the struggle of life.' So we're both in the process of fabricating young women, and since he is wont to assimilate, unconsciously, what he hears with his own ears or through informants, I, whose work will appear after his, should not like to give the impression of having committed plagiarism." Three weeks later he inveighed against Zola in his journal, which was where he always built cases for posterity: "That Zola is a blasted assimilator and he does his filching with the slyness of an old peasant."

Zola appreciated the pathos of such behavior and usually let it go unchallenged, but when in December Daudet told him that Goncourt was once again ranting about plagiarism, his temper flared in a letter immediately dispatched to the latter:

> Tonight, after you left [the party thrown to celebrate the premiere of *Pot-Bouille*], I discussed with Daudet the similarity of our descriptions of puberty, and Daudet gave me to understand that you remember having read me your chapter before I wrote mine. I confess that this disturbed me profoundly. I protest as strongly as I can that you never read me that chapter . . . and that if you had I would have taken pains to obviate all possible comparison. That is what I wanted to tell you right away, and I hope that you refresh your memory. Remember, too, my friend, that during the past eighteen years I have been your staunch friend and defender. Affectionately . . .

Goncourt apologized without delay:

> Yes, I am somewhat annoyed that you chose this particular moment to portray a young girl. . . . Since you work much faster than I—I who began *Chérie* one year before you embarked upon *La Joie de vivre*—the public, which holds you much dearer than it does me, might conclude that my novel was inspired by yours. I'm just a bit vexed, that's all. As far as the chapter on menstrual flow is concerned, Daudet got it all wrong—I blame chance, and only chance, for the similarity between our descriptions. Be assured that this minor annoyance has neither impaired my friendship nor diminished my gratitude.

There matters rested until the next outburst of jealousy. Knowing that Goncourt would always begrudge him his success and mock him in his journal or in conversation, Zola resigned himself to a perfidious friendship.

In a letter written to Henry Céard from Brittany on July 27, 1883, Zola had described his isolation there as being complete. Separated from Bénodet by a wide cove, the house he inhabited through the late summer was indeed so difficult of access that extraordinary measures were required to ferry over visitors. "Take a coach from Brest to Quimper," he instructed Céard, "and when you arrive at Bénodet go to the Customs Office, where they keep a horn for alerting the guardian of this property I rent. Someone will blow the horn, I shall send over my boatman."

Still, Zola did not live absolutely alone. He made friends with people round about, and one such friendship, with Alfred Giard, a left-wing deputy and professor of natural science at Lille University, was to bear important fruit. In discussions held that summer, Giard, whose constituency embraced French Flanders, urged Zola to write a novel about mines. Zola pondered his advice and toward the end of February 1884, when strikes broke out at coalfields owned by Anzin, he met Giard at Valenciennes for a guided tour of *le pays noir*. Thus began the process that resulted, eleven months later, in his masterwork, *Germinal*.

XX

"MY RECURRENT DREAM
WAS OF BEING INSIDE THE EARTH,
VERY FAR AWAY"

ZOLA RECEIVED Giard's suggestion the more warmly for having decided years earlier, when he enlarged the master plan of *Les Rougon-Macquart*, that his saga should include two working-class novels, one about life in a Paris slum and the second about revolutionary politics prior to *la semaine sanglante*. He had not given this second project any deliberate thought since 1872, but as time wore on it underwent subliminal revision. After *L'Assommoir*, a fateful decade in French social history commenced. Between 1876 and 1881 labor organized itself against industry, with diminishing opposition from government. Hardly a month passed that papers did not carry news of some provincial or national congress, of strikes, of ideological warfare within proletarian ranks, of terrorist attacks, of trials, and by 1883 the Paris Commune seemed to Zola an inappropriate cadre for the drama he envisaged. "The populace always had a prominent place reserved for it in *Les Rougon-Macquart*," he later informed a journalist friend. "But not until I wrote *L'Assommoir* and found that it would not accommodate a study of the worker's political and social role did I decide upon a second novel. This one crystallized in due course, when I became fully aware of the great socialist movement that has been harrowing old Europe to such redoubtable effect. A strike naturally suggested itself as the most dramatic situation possible."[1] Where *L'Assommoir* portrayed a passive, besieged, self-destructive commu-

---

[1]His statement was not altogether accurate, since the idea for a second novel arose well before he wrote *L'Assommoir*.

nity, *Germinal* would show workers acting en masse, suffering martyrdom for a common cause, unleashing their anger upon the bourgeois
foe. "The most important matter of our age is the struggle between
capital and labor, the push that topples an unstable society," he wrote
on page one of his outline. "Evoke revolution through hunger."

Zola's memory was long enough to wrap itself around many of the
events that marked the history of this struggle between "capital" and
"labor." He might have remembered, for example, a protest called *Le
Manifeste des Soixante*, in which, soon after the 1863 legislative elections, workers representing various trades deplored the social and economic fetters placed on Frenchmen of their humble estate.
"Universal suffrage made us politically adult, but we have yet to eman-
cipate ourselves socially," it read in part.

> It has been repeated endlessly that there are no more classes, that
> since 1789 all are equal before the law. But we who have no property
> except our arms, we who endure, every day, the legitimate or arbi-
> trary conditions imposed by capital . . . we find it difficult to believe
> this assertion. We who have the right to vote for deputies but lack
> the means of learning how to read, we who are unable to organize
> professional instruction because we are forbidden to assemble
> freely—we cannot entertain this illusion. . . . We affirm that the
> equality written into the law does not exist in our mores. . . . Men
> deprived of instruction and capital who cannot, through freedom and
> solidarity, resist oppressive and selfish exigencies are doomed to suf-
> fer the domination of capital.

Such appeals had not gone unheeded by the emperor, who had published an essay proposing a quasi-socialist scheme for the abolition of
pauperism. To be sure, Napoleon III, through calculated largesse and
strict surveillance, had kept the proletariat quiet during the 1850s. All
workers, including domestic help, were required to carry a *livret*, or
employment record, in effect an internal passport; associations of more
than twenty men were forbidden; and provident societies created by
the government with mayors and curates as local sponsors received
state aid on condition that no money be squirreled away for strikes or
layoffs. But after 1860, when France joined England in a commercial
treaty, the emperor made bold to encourage the workers' movement,
if only to intimidate industrial aristocrats who opposed free trade.
Thus it was that in July 1862 a delegation of French workers traveling
without hindrance crossed the Channel, some two hundred strong, for
the London Exposition. They met representatives of English trade unions, compared notes on wages and hours, discussed the necessity of
preventing employers from hiring scabs, and laid initial plans for what

became, two years later, the International Workingmen's Association. Upon their return, French workers' cooperatives began to multiply, along with "societies of resistance." Imperial police relaxed their vigilance under the new dispensation, and in 1864, after miners' strikes had broken out all over France, the legislature passed an ambiguous law that recognized ad hoc coalitions while maintaining the seventy-three-year-old ban on guilds. Criminal penalties against "the concerted cessation of work" were abolished, but "infringements upon the free exercise of industry" remained punishable.

Napoleon III discovered that in the workplace, as in parliament, each concession justified a demand for more. It soon became obvious that the force he had unleashed would not suffer compromise. Even as his minister of commerce and public works was advising him to legitimize the "syndicalist chambers" prevalent in many trades, his interior minister was urging him to resist, with weapons if need be, an epidemic of strikes that paralyzed major industrial centers. In 1869 two bloody clashes took place, one at La Ricamarie near Saint-Etienne, where troops attacked by a mob killed thirteen coal miners, the other at Aubin near Villefranche-de-Rouergue, where a detachment fired upon striking ironworkers, leaving fourteen dead and twenty wounded. This violence won converts to the "collectivist" creed of the IWA, which had planted missionaries all over France. "As stated by the General Council of the IWA, 'the International did not throw workers into strikes; on the contrary, strikes threw workers into the International,' " notes one historian. "Agents traveled wherever labor unrest summoned them, to offer advice and establish sections of the IWA. Availing themselves thenceforth of press coverage given them in certain sympathetic quarters, they tried to explain what injustices were at issue. . . . For the first time, delegates of a central organization appeared on the spot, with expertise in framing demands." By 1870, when it recorded 116 strikes nationwide, Napoleon III's government had come to regard the IWA as a subversive government, or a "state within the state." The state prosecutor used that expression at a trial of nine members accused of staffing a society whose manifest purpose was "to undermine society, property, and capital" throughout the world. One such member, Eugène Varlin, later played an important role in the Commune and died for it during *la semaine sanglante.*

Bloody Week dealt the labor movement a serious blow. After May 1871, under the Moral Order, workers who dared challenge employers were often reviled as unpatriotic. Adolphe Thiers echoed public opinion when, alluding to a strike of miners near Lille, he told his prefect for the Pas-de-Calais region that "those who are now disturbing minds and threatening the credit of France are enemies of the liberation of the territory and must without delay be reduced by force and justice."

Republicans did, to be sure, shepherd beneficial laws through the Assembly. One law passed in 1874, for example, prohibited children younger than thirteen from being employed in factories and stipulated that at mines and quarries women could not work underground. But any attempt to organize labor inspired outcries of subversion, and this hostility raged as much against apolitical groups as against the International (even if it posed no serious threat during the postwar period, when Marxist collectivists were fighting Bakuninian anarchists). A legislature whose conservative parties believed civilization to be at peril banned the IWA in 1872. In that same year the Paris prefect of police dissolved a circle of nine unauthorized syndicalist chambers which forbade any religious or political affiliation in its statutes. It was preventive medicine, the prefect declared. Best to excise the benign tumor lest it turn malignant.

The desire for economic justice proved irrepressible. Syndicalism won strong support from radical republicans, and by 1876, when the Left gained control of parliament, a movement was afoot to stage a national workers' congress in Paris; its organizers decided that no politicians or theorists should actively participate. The great majority of the 360 delegates at this *ouvrièriste* congress, which opened on October 2, 1876, wanted reform rather than revolution. They called for the abolition of night work, the legislation of *syndicats* or unions, the passage of laws governing female and child labor, the institution of retirement funds. Certain traditional elements of the republican platform —public lay education, income tax, and so forth—were hailed, but by and large delegates remained politically discreet. And although the idea that one would not reap the full benefit of one's labor until one owned the means of production won unanimous assent, there was an inclination to condemn strikes, to defend the free market against statism or collectivism, to endorse worker cooperatives of the Proudhonian sort. "It seems monstrous that five years after the Commune men purporting to represent the proletariat would dare step forth and in its name make amends to the bourgeoisie, abjure the Revolution, deny the Commune," one well-known Communard railed from his place of exile. "Such men exist: they are syndicalists, and they've just held their congress." At another congress held fourteen months later in Lyon, two men proposing overtly Marxist resolutions were answered by a spokesman for the majority who declared that "the masters and disciples of collectivism" should seek tribunes other than "a national French congress."

Collectivism asserted itself willy-nilly, and the man most responsible for propagating it was Jules Guesde, a journalist whose vituperations against Thiers in 1871 had led the government to hound him out of France. Five years abroad converted a radical temperament into a doctrinaire Marxist. No sooner did he return from exile than he founded a paper called *L'Egalité*, which exerted enormous influence upon the working-class elite. "In it, Guesde addressed such matters as freedom, property, production, collectivism, the law of salaries. On March 18, 1878, he reexamined the Commune for the revolutionary lessons it offered; he then denounced the sterility of cooperatism, supported strike movements, published excerpts from Marx's work, sent fraternal greetings to members of the German social-democratic movement." Beset with lawsuits initiated by the government, *L'Egalité* disappeared after thirty-three issues, but its spirit lived on in *salles d'étude,* or study groups, of Guesdian inspiration where amnestied Communards found hospitality, where worker candidates for national office found support, and where ideologues bent on radicalizing union congresses were given a mandate to attend them.

In 1879, at the third such congress held since 1876—the *immortel Congrès de Marseille,* as it came to be known among socialists—the basis was laid for a workers' party. Left-wing deputies had been opposing, in the name of entrepreneurial freedom, certain reforms urged upon them by labor, and political self-effacement no longer seemed possible, or tolerable. Die-hard champions of independence through cooperatism fought at unequal odds against indignant Guesdists who preached the necessity of class warfare. In the end, twenty-seven votes were all that the moderates could muster against a motion that affirmed the goal of workers to be "the nationalization of capital, mines, railroads, etc., with workers in control, [and] the collectivization of the soil, subterranean property, instruments of labor, raw material." Before the congress disbanded to cries of "Long live the socialist and democratic Revolution! Long live the Republic! Long live the Amnesty!" it established a "class party" called the Fédération du Parti des Travailleurs Socialistes en France, appointed a directorate, and resolved that there be an annual congress, beginning in 1880 at Le Havre.

Enthusiasts who thought that men of goodwill would make common cause, and that the proletariat would march behind a serried vanguard, were soon proved wrong. Mindful of the 1881 legislative elections, Guesde visited Karl Marx in London to devise campaign policy for the party and came home with a manifesto that read, in part, as follows:

Considering that collective appropriation [of the means of production] requires revolutionary action by the productive class—or proletariat—organized as a distinct political party and that such organizing must be undertaken in any way available to the proletariat, even through universal suffrage, which will thus have been transformed from an instrument of dupery into an instrument of emancipation, French socialist workers . . . have decided . . . to enter the elections with the following minimal program:

—Abolition of all laws that apply to the press, to meetings and associations, and above all the law against the International Workingman's Association.

—Suppression of the *livret*, that mark branded on the working class, and of everything in the Code establishing the workingman's inferiority vis-à-vis his employer;

—Suppression of the budget for religious sects and alienation of goods held in mortmain, i.e., furniture and property belonging to religious corporations (decree issued by the Commune on April 2, 1871), including all the industrial and commercial annexes of such corporations.

—General arming of the populace.

—Communes given control over their own administration and police.

—A minimal wage determined each year by the local price of goods.

—Abolition of all indirect taxes and the transformation of all direct taxes into a progressive tax on annual incomes higher than 3,000 francs. Suppression of inheritances through a collateral branch and of inheritances, direct and collateral alike, greater than 20,000 francs.

—Responsibility of management in the matter of accidents.

Given full play in meeting rooms all over France, this document rallied not only the faithful but also an opposition that had seemed moribund after Marseille. At Le Havre, the latter sought to exclude delegates sent by study groups or associations with fewer than twenty members (Guesdists for the most part), and thereupon each faction held its own congress—moderates in the Salle Franklin, collectivists in the Salle de l'Union Lyrique. Never again would they come together. This schism did not fix battle lines in the labor movement, however. Far from it. Two years later, a congress of collectivists at Saint-Etienne fell apart when followers of one Paul Brousse, who acquired the name "possibilists" for demanding some accommodation with political reality, took exception to Guesde's intransigence. And anarchists wished a pox on everybody's house. Weary of talk, they began throwing bombs.

Meanwhile, workingmen, most of whom voted for the parliamentary Left, eschewing socialist candidates, survived as best they could. On March 21, 1884, they finally won the right to organize trade unions, but in other respects their lot had hardly improved since the Second Empire. There was still no insurance against crises and the workday was still often twelve hours long, or longer. Layoffs, sickness, and accidents still resulted in financial disaster and mutual-aid societies lacked the resources to tide people over. "In the provinces, the situation was often worse than in Paris," observes Jacques Chastenet. "In Lille, in Amiens, in Saint-Quentin, in Rouen, in Reims, working-class districts were veritable leper colonies, quarantined from bourgeois neighborhoods. Where boundary lines were less clearly drawn, as in

Toulouse, Lyon, and Bordeaux, industrialists' mansions often stood right next door to hovels occupied by their employees. Blocks of company houses sprang up around large factories and mine shafts, . . . but those that had amenities were the exception."

The speed with which France paid war reparations to Germany belied its troubled state. An economic depression that had begun two years after the war continued into the 1880s, crippling most major industries and at one point throwing more than one hundred thousand people out of work in Paris alone. Threatened with wage cuts or demands for increased productivity, the labor force rebelled. In 1880, 190 strikes erupted nationwide. By 1882 that number had risen to 271, and although strikes often became grim, tedious wars of waiting—the one Zola witnessed at Anzin in 1884 lasted fifty-six days—bloodshed was not uncommon. On May 1, 1892, for example, troops taunted by a crowd at Fourmies, near Belgium, where striking textile workers had been arrested, would kill nine people and wound ninety more. Republic or no Republic, proletarian wretchedness (*la question sociale* as socialists euphemistically called it) remained an explosive issue, inspiring, among other memorable remarks, Zola's prophecy that if France did not with all due haste mend its unjust ways, "the earth will open and nations will be swallowed in one of history's great cataclysms."

Research for *Germinal* was the usual cram course, and no complaining. In addition to technical works on the economics of the coal industry, Zola read *La Science économique* by his former boss at *Le Bien public*, Yves Guyot, who was later to become a minister of public works. For information about the workers' movement, he drew principally upon Paul Leroy-Beaulieu's *La Question ouvrière au XIXe siècle* (1872), Laveley's *Le Socialisme contemporain* (1883), and Oscar Testut's *L'Internationale: son origine, son but, son caractère* (1871). A medical treatise entitled *Traité des maladies, des accidents et des difformités des houilleurs* furnished all the pathological minutiae he would need to portray his cast of sacrificial victims, and other works helped him flesh out the subterranean landscape, notably Emile Dormoy's *Topographie souterraine du bassin houiller de Valenciennes*, Louis-Laurent Simonin's *La Vie souterraine ou les mines et les mineurs* (1867), Georges Stell's *Les Cahiers de doléances des mineurs français*, and Yves Guyot's fictionalized account of a mining family, *Scènes de l'enfer social: la famille Pichot*. Elaborate notes on this literature fill his preparatory file. Zola also had recourse to old newspapers, and much of what he learned about miners' strikes since 1869 was gleaned in the Bibliothèque Nationale. "You who are a walking encyclopedia of causes célèbres large and small, could you do me a favor?" he wrote on February 13, 1884, to Antoine Rocher, a former Communard who after years of exile had become a court reporter for *Gil Blas.* "Tell me, if you would, exactly when the trials occasioned by the following strikes began—Creuzot (70), La Ricamarie (69), Anzin (78), Aubin, Montchanin, Montdeau-les-Mines . . . As I must go through these trials in the relevant issues of *Le Droit* at the Bibliothèque Nationale, I want to spare myself unnecessary detective work." Rochet answered five days later, listing specific issues of *La Gazette des tribunaux* and informing Zola that the library would lend them out. "You are very kind, very kind indeed," Zola protested. "I am the more grateful because I now have everything I need; I shall ensconce myself in the periodical room, which is better equipped than my study for shifting bulky tomes."

Although he used to good effect his bibliographic gleanings (which included bits of other coal-mine novels written during this period), Zola could never have pictured hell as vividly as he did if he himself had not gone there, and the invitation to do so came on February 20, 1884, in a letter from Alfred Giard proposing that they tour *le pays noir,* or "soot country." Off he went three days later for one week of round-the-clock fieldwork outside Valenciennes, where twelve thousand miners had just struck Anzin. Arm in arm with Giard, who introduced him to all concerned as his private secretary (a very stout private secretary at two hundred and ten pounds, whose forty-five-inch waist must have been especially inconvenient underground), Zola reconnoitered company villages, inspected flats, had workers describe their daily habits, their diet, and their grievances, quizzed at great length a union leader named Emile Basly, and studied every aspect of the industrial operation, from machines overhead to veins down deep.

Zola's hundred or so pages of notes on Anzin show him, as always, licking up detail like an aardvark feasting in a termitarium. "Anzin, outside Valenciennes's fortifications," he noted.

> In the military zone, wooden houses, but the authorities tolerate bricks. Wide, straight roads, one-story houses interspersed among bourgeois buildings, also one-story hotels, but more ornate. Little by little roads linked towns and suburbs merged, which has resulted in one big industrial agglomeration. Numerous cabarets, a few dance halls, little shops. The road is paved; in summer, black dust; in winter, after the slightest rainfall, black, gluey mud, even on the pavement. On unpaved thoroughfares, wagons create deep sloughs, furrowed by the traffic.

There were common wells, and the company houses, each of which had a barrel in front to collect rainwater for washing clothes, looked like rectilinear barracks. "The downstairs room is entered at street level," he continued.

> The wall and ceiling painted a light color, very light. The floor neatly tiled: on Sundays it's washed and sprinkled with white sand (Creil) costing quite a lot (everyone uses it). Workers' furniture, a buffet of varnished pine, a table, chairs, elsewhere a large armoire, etc. A cuckoo clock. A high fireplace contains a coal grate in the middle, where the fire is lit. It burns badly. This coal, donated by the Company, amounts to slightly less than one ton per month (eight hectoliters, I believe). Bad quality, scraps collected in the tunnels. Each month the women have it delivered, many must buy more (three francs). During strikes, the Company cuts out this fringe benefit.

The men he met—most of them sporting bushy mustaches—were muscular but small and pale. Their day, for those who worked the day shift, began at 3 a.m., when they roused themselves in darkness.

> A fire always going. Wife and children remain abed. The worker drinks coffee (always coffee), sometimes eats a slice of bread with salt butter, cheese, or some meat. Then he leaves, taking along his lunch, slices of bread or meat, and a flask of coffee. At the mine pit, receives his lamp and descends. To lower five hundred workers takes an hour and a half; but they don't always wait, for they arrive one after the other, like shipments of merchandise. At the bottom, each one reaches his cut and begins work; they often have two kilometers to walk underground. Usually they have lunch from nine to ten, squatting beside pick and shovel (their usual posture: they squat at a corner of the company village to chat or smoke a pipe). . . . Women underground. In my strike, the cause of it will be the Company wanting to fire women who work down below. (At Anzin, women fired between 1840 and 1845).

Even if there was rapture in it, Zola needed all his courage to descend fifteen hundred feet in a cage that swayed and lurched as it passed older or disused galleries, then to enter the enormous labyrinth. Had nightmares of being buried alive not haunted him since childhood?[2] "We plunged into a gallery," he wrote afterward.

[2]It will be recalled that in 1874, while preparing *La Faute de l'abbé Mouret*, he wrote: "My recurrent dream was of being inside the earth, very far away, at the bottom of low, narrow underground corridors down which I had to crawl ceaselessly." Five years later he published in *The European Herald* a story about a man who is buried alive after suffering some sort of seizure, "La Mort d'Olivier Bécaille."

It was pitch black, the lamps we carried shed very little light (one gets used to it, however). In front of me, the engineer, who was bigger than I, cut a dark silhouette against the faintly luminous background. His lamp lit the ceiling more than the path ahead. First there were wooden trusses, a rather narrow gallery with only one lane not quite six feet high, steeply arched. These galleries very dry, no humidity; others very damp, it seems. In only one spot did I slog through mud puddles. The buttressing ends when the terrain becomes solid. . . . Between trusses one sees layers of shale that shine darkly, as if the surface were varnished. Sandstone, on the other hand, is dull. . . . We moved over to the haulage gallery, where all veins converge. . . . A distant rumble reaches my ears, announcing the arrival of a wagon train. If the gallery is straight, one sees the little glow of the lamp far away, a red star in a smoky night. The noise grows louder, one can, with difficulty, make out the white dray horse. A child seated on the first wagon is the conductor. Behind the train another child walks, or runs, . . . to guard against derailments. . . . The train recedes from view, the noise diminishes. When trains stop, one hears a snorting of impatient horses.

The spectacle of horses sentenced to lifelong labor underground, without reprieve, seemed even more grotesque than that of human beings clawing for coal ten hours a day.

The stable was situated on the left, just off a curve in the gallery. A room carved into the rock, sixty-five feet long, thirteen feet high, clad in brick, tiled, vaulted. The names and numbers of the horses behind them, stamped on boiler plate. Sixteen horses. A feeding trough the length of the wall. Well heated, a good odor of hay and living beasts. The horses are not brought up unless they're sick, dead, or too old. My horse will be blind, very intelligent, etc. A dead horse raised to the surface. They're dazzled by sunlight, these creatures.

Like these poor beasts, the whole community had been exiled from nature, and what Zola saw was a landscape made for Zolaesque portrayal—a dark, squalid village of prisoners surrounded by a vast, sunlit expanse of eastern Flanders. "I must capture, above all, the topographical configuration," he reminded himself. "The mine pit near the canal, in a trough, while the miners' village is built higher up, on a plateau at road level. All around stretches the immense plain— wheat, sugar beets, broadly undulating—transected only by the straight line of tall trees along the canal bank." It's as if, in entering Anzin country, he had left France behind and crossed a Stygian divide to live briefly among the damned.

Such is the atmosphere of *Germinal,* which begins with the hero, Etienne Lantier, drifting into *le pays noir* one windy March night, like a sailor blown off course, and wondering at the hellfire that spews from chimney stacks overhead. This is the same Etienne Lantier whom Zola introduced at the beginning of *L'Assommoir.* Cast adrift by his swinish father but raised dutifully by Gervaise, who apprenticed him to the blacksmith Goujet, he had left Paris for Lille at some unrecounted moment, finding employment in the railroad yards. There he worked well until his violent temper — a Macquart trait — got the better of his otherwise gentle, almost effeminate, nature. An assault upon a foreman made him persona non grata, and he fled south to Marchiennes, where in normal times forge owners would have hired him straightway. Times are not normal, however. Overexpansion has come home to haunt France during these last years of Napoleon III's reign, heavy industry is in disarray, layoffs are epidemic, hunger rages across the land. After one bootless week of job hunting, Etienne quit Marchiennes without a penny to his name, and it is at this juncture that *Germinal* opens, as the weary, famished exile approaches Montsou, a town very like Anzin, over which the Compagnie des Mines de Montsou holds feudal sway.

Montsou is not, he learns, immune to France's economic ills. Small manufacturers have failed, and the mining company, which employs ten thousand people in its nineteen pits, has been compelled to reduce production. But for once fortune smiles upon Etienne, albeit grimly. With the early-morning shift arrives news that an *hercheuse,* or haulage woman, died overnight. The crew chief, Maheu, three of whose children toil alongside him, hires this stranger on the spot, and Etienne receives a swift, brutal initiation. After descending eighteen hundred feet into the bowels of the earth, he walks almost two miles through ever narrower passages. "Strings of empty or loaded wagons kept passing and crossing one another, their rumblings carried off into the darkness by shadowy animals with ghostly steps," writes Zola.

Ventilation doors banged, closing slowly. And the farther they went, the narrower the tunnel, the lower and more uneven the roof, so that they were constantly forced to bend over. Etienne struck his head sharply. If he hadn't been wearing the leather cap, his skull would have been fractured. Yet he had been carefully following the least gesture of Maheu, whose dark outline ahead of him could be seen by the light of the lamps. Not one of the other workers bumped into anything — they seemed to know every little hump of the ground, every protruding knot of the timbers, every swelling of the rocks.

Etienne was also bothered by the slippery ground, which was becoming wetter and wetter. At times he passed through actual pools, discovered only as his feet sloshed through the muddy slop. But what astonished him most were the sudden changes in temperature. At the bottom of the shaft it had been very cold, and in the first haulage tunnel, through which the air for the mine passed, the narrow walls raised the strong icy blasts to storm level. But afterward, as they got into the other passageways, which had to compete for the available ventilation, the wind died and the heat increased—a suffocating, leaden heat.

When, after ten backbreaking hours, Etienne emerges from the pit (whose official name, Le Voreux, conjures up visions of some Moloch or Minotaur devouring human flesh), he decides, against all reason, to stay at Montsou. The androgynous charm of Maheu's fifteen-year-old daughter, Catherine, who befriended him down below, is one inducement. Another is the thought that he, a free man, can help these slaves who live in utter degradation, barely keeping body and soul together, voice their rage. Lodgings are found for this idealist at a local tavern—taverns outnumber all other businesses—called L'Avantage.

In due course Etienne grows accustomed to life underground, walking through the labyrinth with somnambulistic ease. Delicate in appearance but strong, he conscientiously performs every task assigned him and thus earns the respect of seasoned veterans like Maheu. Maheu, writes Zola, found it natural that Etienne, a railroad engineman, should be better educated than he, a miner. "But he *was* surprised by the boy's courage, by the boldness with which he had gotten into the swing of mining so as not to die of hunger. He was the first casual laborer ever to have caught on to things so readily. So, whenever there was a lot of work at the face and Maheu did not want to stop one of the cutters, he would have Etienne take care of the timbering, confident that the work would be done properly and securely." When in midsummer Etienne replaces one of Maheu's cutters, he will have needed only four months to ascend the infernal hierarchy from *hercheur* to *haveur*.

Aboveground, where several thousand households face slow starvation as a result of wage cuts imposed by the mining company, Etienne has long, ardent debates with two neighbors: the tavern owner, Rasseneur, an unofficial labor spokesman, whose pragmatic strategy for ameliorating the plight of workers anticipates Paul Brousse's "possibilism"; and Souvarine, a Russian medical student turned anarchist whose fanatical creed led him to plot an unsuccessful attempt upon Tsar Alexander's life. Each influences him in turn:

Etienne remained at the level of the fervent neophyte; his heart overflowed with noble indignation against the oppressors and strained toward the hope of the coming triumph of the oppressed. All his random reading had not yet led him to construct his own system; within him Rasseneur's practical demands were warring with Souvarine's demands for destructive violence, and when he left L'Avantage, where everyone met almost every day to rail against the company, he would walk about as though in a dream, seeing visions of the radical regeneration of nations brought about without so much as a broken window or a drop of blood.

But his real mentor is Pluchart, a foreman at the rail yard, with whom he corresponds. From Lille, Etienne receives scientific literature as well as ideological cues. Having joined the newly formed IWA, Pluchart urges Etienne to follow suit, which he does, enthusiastically.

Boarding at Maheu's house after the older Maheu son moves out, he gains purchase within the village. By September he has established a *caisse de prévoyance*, or contingency fund. What is more, he has become for fellow miners a scribe, a family counselor, an ombudsman, a priest all together and takes great satisfaction in seeing these simple folk respond to his utopian patter. That he who doesn't dare touch Catherine can seduce grown men and women intoxicates him. The would-be lover emerges as the revolutionary Pied Piper. "Etienne would begin to talk again," writes Zola, who intended *Germinal* to be among other things a *roman d'apprentissage*.

The old society was cracking; it couldn't last more than a few more months, he would affirm categorically. He was a bit vaguer about the ways and means, jumbling up all his reading and not hesitating, since he was dealing with uneducated people, to launch into explanations in which he himself lost the thread. All the various theories were thrown in, softened by his certainty of an easy victory and the universal embrace that would end this misunderstanding between the classes—though of course there would probably be some stubborn ones among the bosses and the bourgeois who might have to be forced to see reason. And the Maheus would seem to understand, approve, and accept these miraculous solutions with the blind faith of converts, like those Christians, in the first days of the Church, who expected the perfect society to be born on the dump heap of the ancient world. . . . Etienne's influence kept growing and he was gradually revolutionizing the village.

Not unlike Robespierre wearing young Werther's colors for the Festival of the Supreme Being, Etienne buys himself fine boots and a suit of broadcloth before leading his converts over the edge, into rebellion—a strike.

Rebellion, or the suffering that attends it, has a paradoxical consequence. On the one hand, it tears apart family life as hunger pangs
rout moral strictures. Wives go begging, children run wild in piratical
gangs, grandfathers snatch food from tykes, a lecherous grocer named
Maigrat offers bread for sexual favors. Everyone eyes the main chance
in an atmosphere that breeds secrecy. On the other hand, hunger leads
men and women to risk their all, exciting a fanatical communion. People with empty stomachs crave religious eloquence and they get it not
from Rasseneur, who preaches moderation, but from Etienne, who
evokes paradise on earth. The two men square off publicly at a clandestine meeting organized by Etienne to enroll worker delegates in the
IWA. Etienne wins that duel. And he prevails again some weeks later,
when three thousand starving workers assembled in the woods at night
hear him glorify their martyrdom. "The meeting was at the Plan-des-
Dames, a vast clearing [that] spread out in a gentle slope and was
surrounded by tall trees—superb beeches whose straight, regular
trunks encircled it with a white colonnade stained by green lichens,"
writes Zola as he sets the stage for yet another epiphany. From within
this natural amphitheater, Etienne the proletarian Jesus casts a spell
upon his audience by inviting them to picture "a return to the primitive commune," the end of patriarchal authority, the establishment
of an egalitarian family, the abolition of wage labor. "All this would
demand a total recasting of the old corrupt society; he attacked marriage and the rights of inheritance, he set limits to personal fortunes,
and he toppled the iniquitous monuments of dead centuries—all with
a repeated sweeping gesture of his arm, the gesture of a reaper mowing
down the harvest." In the way it stirs the multitude, collectivism re
sembles consumerism. What Octave Mouret accomplished with mountains of merchandise, Etienne accomplishes with images of virtuous
rapine, and, indeed, language used to describe sale day at Au Bonheur
des Dames—*la houle des têtes,* or "swelling sea of heads," for example—serves here to describe an insurrection. "From the depths of the
forest the acclamations rolled toward him," Zola continues.

By now the moon was bathing the whole glade in white light, throwing into sharp relief the swelling sea of heads that stretched all the
way out to the vague outlines of the underbrush between the great
gray tree trunks. And under the glacial sky there was a seething mass
of faces—burning eyes, open mouths, a whole people in heat, starving men, women, and children unleashed to justly pillage the ancient
inheritance of which they had been dispossessed. They no longer felt
the cold; Etienne's burning words had warmed them to the marrow.
A religious exaltation lifted them from the earth—like the feverish
hope of the first Christians awaiting the coming reign of justice.

Like Octave Mouret, Etienne exults in the spectacle of thousands—women above all—deliriously answering his call. To be sure, he wonders whether his crusade is not at bottom a pretext for demagogic self-aggrandizement, whether the issue is justice or, as Rasseneur suggests, virility. But his doubts are submerged by this emotional tide, and the strike, which grows even more acrimonious, spreads beyond Le Voreux.

Indeed, Etienne makes certain that it does. Marching from pit to pit with followers chanting *"Du pain! Du pain! Du pain!"* and singing the Revolutionary anthem, he is chief of a savage horde. "The women had appeared—nearly a thousand of them, their hair disheveled from racing across the countryside, their bare flesh showing through tattered clothes and exposing the nudity of females weary of bearing starvelings," writes Zola in a scene that gives the full measure of his genius for depicting collective paroxysms.

> Some of them had babies in their arms and were lifting them over their heads, waving them about like banners of mourning and vengeance. Others, younger, like full-bosomed Amazons, were brandishing sticks, while the old women, a terrifying sight, were shrieking so loudly that the cords of their emaciated throats seemed about to burst. Next came the men—two thousand madmen, a single compact, swarming mass of mine boys, cutters, and repairers, so tightly squeezed together that their faded trousers and their tattered woolen sweaters had merged into one uniform earth color. Their eyes were blazing, and all that could be seen were their gaping black mouths singing *La Marseillaise*, the stanzas of which were lost in a confused bellow accompanied by the clatter of wooden clogs on the hard ground. Above their heads, among the bristling iron bars, reared a vertical ax, and that single ax, the crowd's banner, was silhouetted against the clear sky like the blade of a guillotine.

A trail of wreckage snakes behind them. At one pit they break elevator cables to trap recalcitrant miners underground. At another they tear up wagon rails. At yet another they demolish the water pump and celebrate with gin pillaged from a company canteen. When bourgeois homes come into view, stones fly. But not until they reach Montsou does this mob, over which Etienne has lost all influence, avenge itself upon the oppressor in person. There, lecherous Maigrat tumbles to his death while fleeing over rooftops, and several women mutilate the corpse, making a trophy of his genitalia. It is a horrific scene, reminiscent of peasant *jacqueries*, or of marches during the Terror.

They pointed the bloody little lump out to one another as though it were some evil beast that had made each of them suffer, a beast they had finally crushed and now saw before them, inert and in their power. They spat on it, they thrust out their jaws, they repeated in a furious outburst of contempt: "He can't do it anymore! He can't do it anymore! . . . What's going to be shoved into the ground isn't even a man! . . . Go on and rot, that's about all you can do!" Then La Brûlé stuck the lump on the end of her stick, and lifting it high in the air, waving it like a banner, she started down the road, followed by the shrieking mob of women. Drops of blood were raining down and the pitiful flesh hung there like a scrap of waste in a butcher's stall.

In the symbolic nexus of Zola's novel, this castration becomes a fertility rite, it being understood that with the arrival of Germinal—the first month of spring in the French Revolutionary calendar—liberated humanity will push up from the soil on which enemy blood has spilled.[3]

Infantry are sent to patrol the coalfield and militant workers begin to receive their walking papers. Hunted by gendarmes, Etienne takes refuge underground, in an abandoned mine shaft where Jeanlin Maheu, Catherine's half-savage eleven-year-old brother, has a pirate's lair stocked with booty. Except for brief spells of candlelight, darkness envelops him, and in darkness he gravitates to the far reaches of his own character, swaying between guilt and grandiosity. There is the Etienne who set store by rebirth, by the hope that "day would dawn on the extermination of the old society." But there is also a conscience-stricken man in whom the revolt awakened personal demons—an Etienne unable to reconcile fantasies of classless harmony and archaic blood lust. "He was . . . overwhelmed by . . . remorse for the savage drunkenness that had resulted from guzzling in the bitter cold on an empty stomach," writes Zola. "When he had reached safety, here in this great calm of the bowels of the earth, he was so sated with violence that he had sunk for two days into the exhausted sleep of a glutted animal, and his despair persisted: he was crushed, there was a bitter taste in his mouth, his head ached as after some terrific binge." The thought that people may have suffered in vain grows upon him during nocturnal visits to the village. Destitute and bereft of moral support from the IWA, which has been crippled by ideological warfare, victims devour one another. Parent turns against child, neighbor against neighbor, lover against mistress. Were it not for the women who castrated

[3]The refrain of *La Marseillaise* includes the line: *Qu'un sang impur abreuve nos sillons* ("May impure blood water our furrows").

Maigrat, management would prevail straightway. Everyone loses heart except those furious matriarchs. It is they who keep industry idle, like spirits of the raped earth. It is they who wax indignant when scabs are brought over from Belgium. It is they who stand foremost when three thousand workers confront a regiment guarding Le Voreux. And it is they, among others, who fall when the terrified soldiers answer brickbats with fire. Fourteen men, women, and children die, including Etienne's friend Maheu.

Unable to escape hell, people whom Etienne had seduced with visions of utopia curse their would-be savior, and the crowd he once regarded as an extension of himself becomes a rogue elephant bent on trampling him. "Who was the guilty one?" he asks himself in despair.

> Was it really his fault, this tragedy from which he himself was bleeding, the wretchedness of some, the slaughter of others, these thin, starving women and children? He had had this same terrible vision one evening before all these catastrophes, but even then he was being carried away . . . and swept along. . . . [Now] he felt that his courage was gone; he was no longer at one with his comrades, he was afraid of them, of this enormous, blind, irresistible mass of people rushing onward like a natural force, sweeping everything before it, overriding rules and theories. A feeling of repugnance, due to the uneasiness of his more polished tastes and the slow growth of his whole being toward a superior class, had gradually detached him from them.

Having swung from the oceanic to the exorcistic, from the rapture of merging with an idealized proletariat to the bitterness of repudiating a violent mob, the collectivist learns to love an individual. Etienne embraces Catherine Maheu, who, after months of living in sexual bondage with someone named Chaval, is at last free for him.

Germinal comes full circle when the strike ends. As Catherine's charm had initially persuaded Etienne to remain at Montsou, so now it is her love that induces him to accept the humiliation of a company pardon. Down they go together in what will be their last descent, pushing aside Souvarine, who knows that disaster awaits them. He knows it because this champion of anarchistic renewal-through-terror has sabotaged Le Voreux. Panels that gird the pit against a "subterranean sea" have been pried loose, and no sooner do workers reach bottom than water comes gushing after them. Most save themselves via cable car, but twenty—including Catherine and Etienne—are trapped. They beat a desperate retreat in two separate groups, each seeking a way out of the labyrinth. All to no avail. Everyone dies except the lovers, who huddle for days in a steeply angled cul-de-sac. Then it is Catherine's turn. With rescuers only several meters away, she, too, dies, leaving Etienne the sole survivor. Aboveground he will gaze upon Souvarine's handiwork. Where an industrial power plant once stood, there lies a large lake. "Just as the engineers were cautiously moving forward, a final convulsion of the earth set them to flight," is how Zola described this apocalyptic event several pages earlier.

Subterranean explosions were detonating—a monstrous artillery shelling the abyss. On the surface the last buildings were toppling, crashing. First a sort of whirlpool sucked down the rubble of the screening shed and the landing room. Next the boiler house cracked and disappeared. Then the square tower housing the gasping drainage pump fell over on its face like a man cut down by a cannonball. . . . Only the tall, hundred-foot chimney remained standing, swaying like a ship's mast in a hurricane. They thought it was going to break up and crumble into dust, but suddenly it sank straight down in one piece, sucked into the ground, melted like an enormous candle; not an inch of it remained above the surface, not even the top of the lightning rod. It was all over; the evil beast squatting in its cavern, gorged with human flesh, was no longer drawing its heavy panting breath. Every bit of Le Voreux had just dropped into the abyss.

Etienne, who had risen white-haired from the grave, spends six weeks in a hospital before bidding Montsou farewell. A wayward boy entered *le pays noir* in darkness. A man with a mission leaves it in brilliant sunshine and marches toward Paris, where Pluchart has invited him to help organize the syndicalist movement. For all who survived, who still toil underground, nature burgeons anew. "Beneath his feet, the heavy, stubborn hammering of the picks continued," Zola concludes. "His comrades were all there—he could hear them follow his every stride. Wasn't that La Maheude under the beet field, her back breaking, her harsh breathing rising in time with the rumble of the ventilator? To the left, to the right, farther along, he thought he could recognize the others, under the wheat fields, the hedges, the young trees. Now the April sun was high in the sky, blazing gloriously, warming the teeming earth. . . . Buds were bursting into green leaves."

Throughout *Germinal*, Zola weaves the metaphor of an erotic underworld into his portrait of an industrial hellhole. The mine, that supremely invasive phenomenon, goes against nature. It blights the countryside, killing trees round about, even as it mechanizes workers, wasting their vital forces. Pleasure is humanness salvaged from Le Voreux, and in the symbol-rich landscape of *Germinal*, young people eager to make love do so amidst the ruins of an old, disused pit, Réquillart. "They would settle down, elbow to elbow, without paying any attention to their neighbors," writes Zola, "and it was as though all around this lifeless machine, next to this shaft weary of spewing forth coal, the powers of creation were taking their revenge—unbridled love, under the lash of instinct, planting babies in the bellies of girls scarcely more than children themselves." But where no avenue leads outward, pleasure itself ultimately benefits the industrial fiefdom, producing generation after generation of serf labor. Among free men, or upwardly mobile bourgeois, each birth opens a new perspective. Among miners, on the other hand, whose children will follow them downward ever deeper, birth is a grim redundancy.[4]

The escape that begets future prisoners was not ironical enough. Zola organized *Germinal* around a larger irony in picturing slaves as an object of envy to their master: imagining the repressor repressed, he created a general director tormented by the sexual license that prevails down below. For M. Hennebeau, who pulled himself up from poverty, attended the Ecole des Mines, and then married wealth, elevation has meant deprivation. His wife's infidelities make conjugal life a masochistic ordeal that his position forces him to endure. He endures it even after being cuckolded by his young nephew. Hennebeau, "always perfectly polite, dissimulated behind his cold-and-correct-administrator mask a ravaging desire for this creature [his wife], one of those violent, late-developing desires that increase with age," we learn. "He had never possessed her as a lover, and he was haunted by an inescapable vision—to have her, if only once, as she had given herself to another. Every morning he dreamed of conquering her that evening; then, when she looked at him with cold eyes, when he felt that everything in her rejected him, he avoided letting even so much as his hand brush against her. It was a pain without possible relief." To this inmate of a childless marriage whose walls are money, status, ambition, and self-contempt, the lower depths, where appearances don't count, are where men live free, and so it is that Hennebeau regards those over whom he lords it as more fortunate than he. "He would gladly have exchanged his high salary for their tough hides and their easy, casual lovemaking," Zola writes in a passage that calls to mind Freud's *Civilization and Its Discontents*. "If he could only seat them at his table and stuff them with his pheasant while he went off to fornicate behind the hedges, tumbling the girls and not giving a damn if anybody else had tumbled them first! He would have given

---

[4]Images of the excremental recur throughout, countering images of the erotic. Mines are "bowels" from which slaves extract dirty lumps to enrich their corporate master, and die in the process. As in *Le Ventre de Paris* (or, for that matter, *L'Assommoir*), so here the gullet becomes symbolically indistinguishable from the purse. Wealthy shareholders are seen gorging themselves on sweetmeats in one room as hungry miners plead their cause in the next.

everything." Unlike Maigrat, whose genitals are torn off by women of the lower class, Hennebeau finds himself emasculated from above, by an heiress.

As for Etienne Lantier, who *achieves* manhood, his achievement requires him to undergo not only a political initiation but a sexual one, and to challenge not only the Minotaur that devours human flesh but the brute sadistically holding sway over Catherine. Between him and Chaval—always called *le grand Chaval*—there is hatred at first sight. No sooner does Etienne join Maheu's crew underground than Chaval sets upon him verbally. "You little worm, you! My God, it hasn't got the strength of a girl! . . . Fill up that cart, will you! What're you doing, trying to save your energy?" This phallic warfare grows more intense, with the bashful stranger giving ground, and when, in due course, Chaval rapes Catherine at Réquillart, Etienne, who idles there amidst faceless couples, becomes a complicit spectator. "Etienne had listened without moving," writes Zola.

Another one taking the plunge! And now that he had seen the little comedy, he got up, disturbed by a feeling of uneasiness, a sort of jealous excitation mingled with anger. He no longer tried to be quiet—those two were much too busy to pay him any heed—and he strode over the beams. He was therefore surprised to see, after he had gone some distance down the road and had turned around, that they were already up and seemed, like himself, to be returning to the village. . . . Etienne felt a strong desire to see their faces, but, finding this idiotic, walked a little faster. No matter. His feet slowed down despite himself, and he hid in shadows at the first lamppost. The sight of Catherine and Chaval stunned him.

The strike, which transforms a lonely voyeur into a hypnotic exhibitionist, strengthens Etienne for his private feud. Pumped up by several thousand lungs, he uses his newfound stature to good effect when Chaval, after feigning solidarity, breaks ranks. Etienne humiliates him, and in a bloody fight at Rasseneur's saloon emerges the winner, with help from the demon that inhabits all Macquarts. "You goddam traitor, now you're going to get it!" he screams as Chaval writhes under his knee. "A hideous voice was deafening him, rising from his guts, beating hammer blows in his head—a sudden murderous madness, a need to taste blood. He had never before been so shaken by the fit— and yet he was not even drunk. And he fought against this hereditary evil with the same hopeless shuddering a maddened lover feels, struggling on the brink of rape. He was finally able to control himself." Etienne shrinks from murder, but it has already been announced that this quarrel will not end until someone dies, that there is not space in the world for both. "One would have to eat the other."

Nor, indeed, is there space for both beyond the grave. Zola surpassed even the dreamlike denouements of *Thérèse Raquin* and *La Conquête de Plassans* by having Etienne, Chaval, and Catherine all fetch up in the same cul-de-sac when water engulfs Le Voreux. Chaval paws Catherine (who has reached puberty since their separation), whereupon Etienne intervenes and this time gives free rein to the homicidal "other" in him:

> The old struggle was beginning yet again, here in the earth where they would soon be sleeping side by side forever, and they had so little room that they could not swing their fists without skinning them. . . . Etienne went mad. . . . A need to kill swept over him, an irresistible physical need.

Disencumbered of Chaval, whose corpse he throws into the flooded corridor below, Etienne finally possesses Catherine. Chaval returns, however—haunting Etienne as the drowned image of Camille haunts Laurent in *Thérèse Raquin*. "Chaval's body," writes Zola,

> which the flood had floated to the top of the inclined plane, was now pushing toward them. Etienne stretched out his hand and immediately felt the mustache and the smashed nose: a shudder of repugnance and fear went through him. Gripped by a terrible nausea, Catherine had spat out the water still in her mouth. She was sure that she had drunk blood, that all the deep water in front of her was now the blood of that man. "Wait," stammered Etienne, "I'll shove it away." He kicked out at the corpse and it floated off. But soon they could once more feel it bumping against their legs. "God damn it, get out of here!" And after the third attempt Etienne had to give up. Some current kept bringing it back. Chaval didn't want to leave, he wanted to be with them, against them. He was a gruesome companion, adding his pestiferous stench to the already foul air. For one whole day they drank nothing, struggled, preferred to die, and it was only on the next day that suffering made them relent; though they had to push the body away each time they drank, they drank nevertheless. It had hardly been worthwhile splitting his skull if in his stubborn jealousy he was again to come between them. Even dead he would be there to the very end, to keep them from coming together.

That this victory revives in Etienne the memory of seeing eleven-year-old Jeanlin kill a soldier makes its Oedipal content quite clear. And this victory, as Zola imagines it, is twofold, for not only does small

Etienne prove himself stronger than "big Chaval," but he abolishes Chaval's chronological priority. Chaval having cast his seed into an unripe womb, Catherine was not Catherine the woman until Etienne entered her.

Germinal, which Zola began on his forty-fourth birthday, took only nine months to write even with time out for Alexandrine's therapeutic sojourn at Mont-Dore; still, the latest birth always seemed the most difficult.[5] "The book pokes along," he informed Céard on June 14, 1884. "I'm working like a dog, working harder than I've ever worked on a novel, and without much hope of reward. It's one of those books one does for oneself, for reasons of conscience." Six months later he unburdened himself to a Dutch correspondent named Jacques van Santen Kolff: "*Germinal* will be serialized in *Gil Blas* until February 12 or thereabouts. I fear that this novel, which gave me no end of trouble, will be misunderstood." And he unburdened himself again to Edmond de Goncourt, from whom a rare compliment arrived after *Gil Blas* brought out the first serial installment. "Your note pleased me very much, my good friend, for I live here in utter solitude and with doubts about this accursed book, which has cost me so much difficulty," he wrote on December 1. "Would that it were done, but I'm in for another six weeks of hard labor. So much the better if the beginning pleases you; it proves that I'm not an imbecile, as I sometimes fear."[6] The tumult of the Anzin strike, which led to troops being arrayed against miners, to Giard interpellating his government, and to a parliamentary subcommittee convening outside Valenciennes, made Zola's task that much more difficult. Would he side with the strikers? asked an interviewer midway through June, when everyone was still

---

[5]Zola did not work well at the spa. "We are both exhausted for no good reason, disoriented by hotel life, trying, in bewilderment, to reestablish our habits," he wrote to Céard on August 12, 1884.

My poor wife gets up at 4 a.m., in order to be among the first at the steam rooms—a simple hygienic precaution. For now her treatment consists only of inhalations, footbaths, and two glasses of water. The serious stuff will follow in due course. Your young doctor seems reasonably intelligent. He is also very prudent and warned us against expecting immediate relief. . . . I appreciate this modesty. A friendship has developed, and he showed us slides of the tubercle bacillus: not a reassuring sight in these hotels, where it probably thrives. That's all that's new. I haven't touched my pen in a week.

[6]As we have often noted, loss of mind or of potency was a lifelong obsession. "The fear that I may empty myself before the series is complete and be compelled to finish it with mediocre books has pursued me since the very first volume," he wrote to a young friend named Louis Desprez. "Well, *Germinal* does not signal the beginning of decrepitude. That's all I need to be told. You speak for youth, I value your sympathy."

in high dudgeon. "Neither with them nor against them," he answered. "Naturalism does not make pronouncements. It undertakes examinations. It describes. It says: 'This is what is.' Let the public draw conclusions."

When Charpentier published *Germinal* in March 1885, one week after the *feuilleton* had run its course, Zola set aside his doubts and assumed a combative stance, defending or explaining himself. To Henry Duhamel of *Le Figaro*, who (among others) declared that the "gentle, calm, upright" coal miner had been slandered in this unrelievedly dark picture of Anzin, Zola replied that his colors were, if anything, not dark enough ("Go consult statistics. Go visit the place"). And to Jules Lemaître, who characterized him as brilliant at evoking the crowd driven by "blind instinct" but weak at analyzing the individual, Zola railed against bourgeois spiritualism. "You call *Germinal* 'a pessimistic epic of human animality,'" he wrote.

> So be it, I shall gladly accept your definition, provided you let me enlarge upon this word "animality". You situate man in the brain, I situate him in all his organs. You isolate him from nature, I have him occupy the earth from which he comes and to which he returns. You enclose the soul in a human being and I feel it to be there and everywhere else — in animals, in plants, in pebbles. . . . My characters think as much as they have to, as much as people think in daily life. Our whole quarrel revolves around the spiritualist importance you confer upon psychology, or the analysis of self-contained souls that you call psychology. Well, I have my own psychology, the one I chose to have, the one that puts the soul on this vast earthly stage and shows it manifesting itself in all the acts of matter.

It vexed him that his "philosophical" parti pris should be used to impugn his sensibility, that people should regard his dramatization of madness at work in human affairs as a symptom of innate vulgarity rather than a product of thought or even perhaps a sign of moral courage.

Zola let no cavil go unanswered, but his most interesting apologia was prompted by Henry Céard, who in a long article on *Germinal* astutely observed that Zola was apt to magnify naturalistic detail beyond the limits of verisimilitude, creating in almost every one of his novels a transcendent power or supernatural force. Since his greatness lay in that creation, wrote Céard, how much greater *Germinal* would have been if he had replaced detail with mass and all individual personae with collective movement. Launched upon a story that does not by its nature and scope accommodate psychology, why did he not give it a single gigantic character — namely, the crowd itself?

"I do not agree that my characters are abstract, with each one frozen in a particular attitude," Zola rejoined.

This novel is a large fresco. The narrative was so tightly constructed that nothing could enter it except in abridged form. Whence a constant simplification of the characters. Minor ones are indicated by a single stroke, as in my previous work. . . . But consider the major ones. Each follows his personal course: socialist ideas gradually percolating through Etienne's brain, the slow exasperation of hunger violently wrenching La Maheude from the fatalism that stamps her kind, Catherine rolling downhill into a slough of despond. Set against the indistinct mass, these broad developments would, I thought, suffice to express a thought. And speaking of mass, the idea that I should not have portrayed individuals at all but made do with a crowd escapes me. How could that be accomplished? My very subject was the interaction between individual and crowd.

Céard's comments about verisimilitude, far from eliciting a denial, led Zola to represent himself as a symbolist, or anyway to defend symbolic distortion in the name of truth-telling. "I wish you had explained how my eye works," he continued. "I enlarge, that's undeniable, but I don't enlarge the way Balzac does, any more than Balzac enlarges the way Hugo does. Everything hinges on that, the work resides in its style. We all lie more or less, but what is the mechanism and mentality of our lie? Well—perhaps I delude myself here—I still believe that my lies serve to advance the truth." Exact observation was a "springboard" for leaping skyward. "With a wingbeat, truth ascends and becomes symbol."

Ritual imprecations aside, the critical fraternity hailed *Germinal* as a masterpiece, and even those who had trouble with it couched their criticism in praise. "Of all the novels published by the author of *Les Rougon-Macquart*," wrote Victor Fournel in *Le Moniteur universel,* "*Germinal* is perhaps his most powerful, the one most fraught with vigorous scenes, the one most likely . . . to grip the reader's attention. Somber, pessimistic, frightful, it makes the kind of impact that few books do." Among other journalists, "epic grandeur" was a favorite formulation. "In their elephantine pace, their breadth of movement, in the tranquil accumulation of details and the storyteller's marvelous transparency of method, *Les Rougon-Macquart* resemble ancient epics," declared Jules Lemaître. "He doesn't hurry along any more than Homer does. He is (for different reasons) as interested in Gervaise's cooking as the bard is in Achilles' diet. He doesn't fear repetitions; the same sentences troop forth with the same words, and at regular intervals one hears the 'humming' of the department store in *Au Bonheur des Dames* or the 'heavy and long breathing' of the machine in *Germinal,* much as in the *Iliad* one hears the rumbling of the sea." Delivered from pariahdom, though never respectable enough for election to the Académie Française, Zola found his name being coupled with that of Delacroix, of Hugo, of Dante. The influential critic Jules Lemaître called him a great epic poet.

This state of grace held good even in left-wing political circles, where more than one ideologue who had reviled *L'Assommoir* joined the chorus of praise for *Germinal.* "There are books by M. Emile Zola that I haven't defended, but this one, *Germinal,* I shall defend here, elsewhere, everywhere," proclaimed Clovis Hugues, a militant deputy. "I shall defend it warmly because, unlike Hugo, who in *Les Misérables* proposes charity as an answer to the social question, in *Germinal* Zola proposes justice." Humbler folk agreed. *Germinal* became a proletarian gospel story, with little socialist organs all over France requesting permission to serialize it free of charge. "The editorial committee of my paper has instructed me to ask you whether we may publish gratis your magnificent novel *Germinal,*" wrote the editor-in-chief of a Marseille daily, *Le Réveil du peuple,* whose first issue had not yet appeared. "This work, really splendid, would help us overcome initial difficulties, as our paper, though there is money enough to keep it afloat until next year, has slender resources. We need your name, which is universally known." Socialists in central France wanted it for a weekly that was to aid striking metallurgists, and "Dear Citizen Zola" is how they began their semi-literate request. "We know no comparable work of propaganda at once socialist and naturalist that's why there's no other that could replace it. We're sure that if you find it possible you will give us this authorization to which we attach the greatest importance for we know how much it would help the workingman's organization of this region which makes huge strides every day." When, similarly, the Belgian Workers' Party launched *Le Peuple* in December 1885, its first issue featured an installment of *Germinal.*

All who asked received. Despite his aversion to doctrinaire or utopian socialism, Zola honored these entreaties with the statement that *Germinal* had been written for the poor and belonged to the poor. A "work of pity" is what he called it in a newspaper interview. "At the risk of being labeled a socialist, I must tell you that when I saw how miners lived, pity overwhelmed me," *Le Matin* quoted him as saying.

My book is a work of pity, nothing else, and if readers experience this feeling, I shall be happy, I shall have achieved the goal I set for myself. When, indeed, one wishes to see and understand, it becomes quite clear that 1789 did not help the worker: peasants got land while the worker lost ground, and royalists are right in saying that the old guilds protected him better than the present regime. There is a great social movement afoot, a desire for justice that must be taken seriously, or bourgeois society will be swept away. I don't think that the movement will begin in France, however—our race is too flaccid. That's why, in my novel, a Russian embodies violent socialism.

Had he done justice to the poor man's aspirations? he wondered. And had he made it clear that blame for the suffering of the working class should fall upon France collectively rather than bourgeois individually?

Germinal, which sold eighty-eight thousand copies during its first eight years, or far fewer than *Nana,* provoked no reaction from the Elysée Palace until Zola adapted it for the stage. William Busnach, seasoned veteran that he was, urged him to delete a scene in which policemen attack strikers, since the government, whatever its colors, would never tolerate so unvarnished a picture of civil war. But Zola ignored him and paid the price in October 1885, when the Théâtre du Châtelet sent two copies of the play to the censor's office, as required by law. Approval was denied. Busnach and Zola thereupon argued their case in a weeklong series of humiliating confrontations at the ministry of public instruction. The minister, René Goblet, would not compromise or accept compromise. Dead set against this play, he read excerpts at a meeting of the full cabinet, which was not disposed to bare its republican breast in the aftermath of legislative elections won by the Right. The cabinet endorsed Goblet, the Théâtre du Châtelet dropped *Germinal* (it would retrieve it several years later), and Zola, who had meanwhile conferred with Georges Clemenceau, leader of the parliamentary Radicals, spewed forth letters demanding an end to censorship. "It is the young whom we must question, those who bear within themselves a new art and who need the bracing air of freedom," he declared on November 7, 1885, in *Le Figaro.* "Summon those youths, and they will tell you that the theater is dead if you bar the truth, if you forbid the tears of the humble and satirical commentary on the powers that be, if you disqualify those political and social changes that will determine mankind's future course." He did not expect his campaign to succeed, but there was no backing off, he told Céard,

and when the Chamber will have voted to maintain censorship, you will see me separate myself from French literature. It's a scandal. And what makes me especially indignant is the fact that I stand almost alone. Except for brave Geffroy,[7] my good Alexis, two or three strays, not a word of support, no fraternity of talent and courage. . . . All this squalor makes me want to write masterpieces.

[7]Gustave Geffroy was a literary and art critic who became friendly with Zola in 1883. He wrote for Clemenceau's paper, *La Justice.*

Fifteen months later the Chamber voted to preserve theater censorship, and censorship remained in force throughout Zola's lifetime.

It was generally agreed that Zola had achieved new heights with *Germinal*. From his eminence, he surveyed all of Europe and in every capital recognized self-professed disciples. Naturalism, he told one of them, had blown over the continent "like a mistral," planting seeds in every field. Romanticism, he declared, was everywhere to be seen withering away.

But for at least one week in 1885 he found himself overshadowed by the greatest romantic of them all. Victor Hugo died on May 22, at the age of eighty-three. After a day of mourning, the National Assembly resolved that he should lie in state beneath the Arch of Triumph and then be borne to the Pantheon, which would serve once again as a mausoleum for national heroes. On May 31, Parisians thronged the Place de l'Etoile to keep vigil. "The scene had to be seen to be believed," wrote the novelist Maurice Barrès, "the coffin lifted in the black darkness, and the greenish glare of the streetlamps showing livid on the imperial gateway, and mirrored in the breastplates of the cavalrymen who, torch in hand, were restraining the crowd. People flowed en masse from as far away as the Place de la Concorde." Having lain all night long on a catafalque one hundred feet above street level, like some apotheosized king of old, Hugo was lowered at dawn and put in a pauper's hearse. Followed by two million people, the unadorned carriage proceeded down avenues lined overhead with shields that bore the titles of a lifetime: *Les Feuilles d'automne, Les Contemplations, Quatre-vingt-treize, Les Misérables*. All along its funereal route, gaslights were seen wavering inside veils of black crepe.

By Edmond de Goncourt's account, Zola witnessed this multitudinous spectacle dry-eyed and even triumphant, in the spirit of a dauphin who had begun to fear that the old monarch would outlive him. One can readily believe it. But if such were his feelings, they did not prevent him from offering dignified condolences to Hugo's sixteen-year-old grandson Georges. "One day you will perhaps learn, Sir, that I availed myself of a critic's rights even with Victor Hugo," he wrote on May 22, almost exactly twenty-five years after sending Hugo his seven-hundred-line poem "Paolo" for a verdict as to whether he should continue writing. "And that is why I insist upon telling you now, as you grieve, that all hearts have, like your own, been broken. Victor Hugo was my youth, I am fully cognizant of what I owe him. Today, discussion must cease. Hands must link, and French writers must rise to affirm, in honoring this Master, the absolute triumph of literary genius."

XXI

RIFTS AND BETRAYALS

IN CLEMENT WEATHER, Zola's guest cottage at Médan was seldom unoccupied. The Charpentiers often stayed there. So did a widowed cousin of Alexandrine, Amélie Laborde, whom Zola helped support and whose children, Elina and Albert, came to regard Médan as their second home. Paul Alexis always had a bed made for him, although impromptu visits may not have been quite so easy after 1886, when his future wife, Marie Monnier, bore him a child.[1] Henry Céard regularly arrived on Sundays, unattached. And at much wider intervals, Paul Cézanne invited himself over from Paris or Melun or Pontoise.

However divergent the paths they had taken through life, Zola and Cézanne remained loyal friends. At Médan the latter found his work prominently displayed in the entrance hall, alongside Monets, Manets, and Pissarros. And he sometimes found himself praised in newspapers to which Zola contributed art criticism. When, for example, the third Impressionist show opened on April 4, 1877, provoking widespread derision—much of it directed at Cézanne's seventeen paintings—Zola described Cézanne as a greater colorist than any of his fellow exhibitors. "In the show there are surpassingly beautiful Provençal landscapes. Bourgeois may laugh at such strong, deeply felt canvases, but they nonetheless contain elements of very great painting. The day Paul Cézanne comes into full possession of himself, he will give us works of the highest order." Three years later, Cézanne, who unavailingly

[1]Emile and Alexandrine were godparents many times over: to Alexis's daughter Paule Alexandrine, to Albert Laborde, to Paul Charpentier, to Emile Solari.

547

applied to the official Salon every year, earned another compliment from his friend—this one rather more ambivalent—in a piece entitled "Le Naturalisme au Salon," written for *Le Voltaire*. "I can't discuss every Impressionist painter of talent," Zola apologized.

> Some have hedged themselves off in specialties, like M. Degas. He, Degas, is above all a fastidious and original draftsman, who has produced some very remarkable series on laundresses, dancers, women bathing, whose movements he has rendered with truthfulness and great delicacy. Messieurs Pissarro, Sisley, Guillaumin have followed in the path of M. Claude Monet, whom I shall encounter presently at the official Salon, and they have taken as their subject the countryside round about Paris, evoking nature in true sunlight, without shrinking from the most unforeseen color effects. M. Paul Cézanne, whose temperament is that of a great painter floundering in his search for the right method, remains closer to Courbet and Delacroix.

At his friend's behest, Cézanne attended the Charpentier salon on one occasion, hoping no doubt to curry favor with the powers that were —how else could he impress his father?—or to have something good said about him in *La Vie moderne*. Nothing came of it, exept perhaps a renewed sense of being unassimilable.

Cézanne gained in artistic self-awareness with every passing day, but his private life revolved year after year around opaque idées fixes. Not under pain of death would he have acknowledged to old Louis-Auguste Cézanne the existence of his closet family, and when danger loomed, Zola was called upon, as his "good" father, to help him maintain the imposture. "My dear Emile," Cézanne wrote on March 23, 1878, "I shall soon be compelled to support myself, if I'm capable of it. Relations with my father are very strained, and my allowance may cease. A letter from Monsieur Chocquet in which mention is made of 'Madame Cézanne and little Paul' blew the gaff, for my suspicious father, having nothing more urgent to do in life, opened it, even though it was addressed: Mons. Paul Cézanne—artist painter. So I appeal to your benevolence and ask that you . . . use such influence as you have to place me somewhere. . . . There's been no break yet, but I couldn't tolerate another fortnight of suspense." Zola counseled restraint, whereupon Cézanne answered:

> I agree that I must not be too quick to repudiate the paternal dole. But judging from the snares laid for me, which I've eluded until now, I foresee that the great debate will touch upon money, and upon the use I must make of it. It is more than probable that my father will allow me only one hundred francs, though he promised me two hun-

dred when I was in Paris. I shall therefore have recourse to your kindness, especially as the little one has been sick for two weeks with a mucous fever. I take all necessary measures to prevent my father from obtaining certain proof.

Appalled as much by the thought of losing his secret life as of falling outside his father's domain, as much by the prospect of seeing his son repudiated as of being forced to get married, Cézanne often slept in Aix at the Jas de Bouffan and spent days in Marseille, where he kept Hortense hidden. "I beg you to send Hortense sixty francs at the following address: Mme Cézanne, rue de Rome 183, Marseille," was how the first of five or six such monthly pleas began.

Despite our treaty, I could obtain only one hundred francs from my father, and feared that he might give me nothing at all. Various people have told him that I have a child, and he tries by every possible means to catch me unawares. He wants to disencumber me, he says. I'll let that pass without comment. Explaining the gent to you would take too much time, but believe me, appearances are deceiving where he's concerned. A word from you, if you can find the time to write, would give me pleasure. I shall try to go to Marseille. I stole off Tuesday a week ago, to see the little one, who's feeling better, and walked all the way back as the train schedule was inaccurate and I had to be present at dinner—I arrived an hour late.

Zola, who also answered requests for money from the impecunious Claude Monet, faithfully sent Cézanne sixty francs every month and was treated in return to accounts of paternal espionage. "Before I left Paris [some four months ago], I left the key to my flat with a shoemaker named Guillaume," Cézanne complained on July 29 of the same year. "What must have happened is this: provincials in Paris for the Exposition descended upon him and he put them up in my place. The landlord, who took it amiss that no one had asked permission, sent me, along with a rent receipt, a stiff letter notifying me that my flat is occupied by strangers. My father read the letter and concluded that I'm hiding women in Paris. We're acting out a Clairville-like farce." No sooner had this interrogation ended than another began. "I'm in a calmer state of mind," he wrote on September 14 from L'Estaque,

and if I've crossed several rough patches without very much harm done, it's thanks to the good, solid plank you laid down for me. Here's the latest mess. Hortense's father addressed a letter to Mme Cézanne at the rue de l'Ouest in Paris. My landlord lost no time forwarding it to the Jas de Bouffan, where my father opened it. You can imagine the repercussions. I violently denied everything and asserted—as luck would have it, Hortense's name never appears in the letter—that it was meant for some other woman.

Cézanne often turned his rage against himself, as when he told Zola that "my good family, considerate of a woebegone painter who has never earned his keep, is a bit stingy perhaps: it's a minor fault, quite excusable here in the provinces." But self-reproach only anchored him in the conviction that nothing belonged to him for real, that everything he held dear might be snatched away at any moment by an all-powerful, all-seeing tyrant. When in 1882 he prepared his will—Louis-Auguste having just assigned him some considerable portion of his inheritance in order to spare him death duties—he sent Zola a duplicate lest the original disappear. "Safeguard it, if you don't mind, since there is no safe place in Aix." What did it matter that his father had just turned eighty-four? The old man was destined, he felt, to outlive him, to thwart him even beyond the grave, to pry forevermore, to have the very last word.[2]

A source of money and a guardian of documents, Zola also served as a receiver of clandestine mail. The latter role devolved upon him in 1885 when Paul—whose mother and sister Marie were demanding that he marry Hortense if only to legitimize his son—became infatuated with a woman of mysterious identity. Against strong family opposition, he kept the romance alive by correspondence. "I'd like you to do several favors, small for you, I believe, and huge for me," he entreated Zola on May 14, writing from Aix. "Would you receive several letters for me, then forward them to an address I shall give you later? Either I'm mad or very sensible. *Trahit sua quemque voluptas!* I need you and beg absolution. Happy are the wise!" Zola, who, far from feeling happy in his wisdom, may have envied Paul his agitation, did as bidden and sent mail downriver to La Roche-Guyon, where Cézanne spent a month with Renoir. It involved nothing more than that, for by summer's end the flame had apparently been snuffed out. "[I live] in the most complete isolation," Cézanne wrote on August 25, a week or two after his homecoming. "The brothel in town, or another, but nothing more. I pay; the word sounds dirty, but I need peace, and at a price I ought to get it. . . . I've begun to paint, because I'm more

[2]The Provençal patriarch was not a lenient species. Paul Alexis's illegitimate daughter reached the age of fifteen months before he could bring himself to disclose her existence to his father, a prosperous notary in Aix. He sent the elder Alexis a photograph of the child and immediately fled to Nevers, hoping that the anticipated explosion would be easier to bear in a bucolic setting.

or less free of annoyances. Every day I walk to Gardanne [about six miles distant], and return to Aix every evening. If only I had had an indifferent family, all would have been for the best."

After 1879, Cézanne visited Médan five or six times. The large, hirsute, disheveled man laden with paraphernalia was not always an entirely welcome sight, not when other guests were present at any rate, for his arrival could as well bode foul weather as fair. Cézanne still threw self-destructive temper tantrums and on one occasion, while painting Alexandrine in the garden, broke his brushes, tore the canvas, and stalked off. Quick to take offense, he gave no quarter and might depart without argument or farewell if some very Parisian type (like Busnach) made him feel cloddish.[3] A letter from Zola speaks, between the lines, of his tenuous sociability. "My old friend, I am terribly sorry," he wrote on July 2, 1885. "I'm going to have nine people to lodge, all my bedrooms will be occupied—besides which Goncourt and Daudet are threatening to descend upon me. I know how much you want to come right away, and I myself relished the prospect. But you'll have to wait until everybody has left, masters and valets. What consoles me is the thought that we'll be better off afterward, freer, more intimate."

Still, these sojourns, during which Cézanne arranged to paint Médan from the vantage point of Zola's island chalet or to transport himself elsewhere along the riverbank in Zola's skiff, were occasions for camaraderie. It was far more agreeable than visiting the Zola flat on the rue de Boulogne, where Paul felt like a supplicant petitioning a "minister of state" enthroned behind a "carved wooden desk."[4] At

[3]The American painter Mary Cassatt, who met Cézanne in November 1894, has left a vivid account of his social comportment. After dining at Giverny with Cézanne, Monet, Rodin, Clemenceau, Octave Mirbeau, and the critic Gustave Geffroy, she wrote:

> He resembles Daudet's description of a southerner. When I saw him for the first time, he impressed me as a kind of hoodlum whose large, red goggle eyes gave him a ferocious air. That air was accentuated by his almost completely gray goatee and by a manner of speech so violent that it literally made the glasses tremble. I later discovered that I had allowed appearances to deceive me, for, far from being ferocious, he has the most gentle temperament imaginable, like a child. . . . At first his manners surprised me. He scrapes his soup plate, then lifts it and pours the last few drops into his spoon; he even picks up his cutlet with his fingers, tearing the meat away from the bone. He eats with his knife and uses this instrument, which leaves his hand only when he finally leaves the table, to emphasize every gesture. But despite this utter disregard for table manners he behaved more politely toward us than any of the other men.

[4]Some years later, in conversations with the art dealer Ambroise Vollard, Cézanne reminisced sarcastically about the rue de Boulogne, where the maid, staring daggers, made sure that he scraped his shoes before entering the parlor. When Vollard asked him what Zola, Flaubert, Goncourt, Daudet, et al. discussed, he said:

Médan they talked with equal authority about their creative work and must, indeed, have talked about art and literature in general. But beyond that, each always rediscovered in the other the sovereign witness of his youth. How much did this count for Cézanne? More than he usually let on, to judge from a letter he sent Paul Alexis after reading *Emile Zola, notes d'un ami.* "I am very grateful to you for the good emotions you stirred up with your evocation of the past," he wrote on February 15, 1882. "What more shall I tell you? You already know that there's rich dough in the verse of this man who deigns to remain our friend [*Notes d'un ami* contained Zola's adolescent verse]. But you know how fond I am of him. Don't tell him. He'd only say that I'm being mawkish. It's between us, and spoken under our breath."

When Cézanne visited Médan in July 1885, four months after *Germinal* appeared, Zola had begun a novel about "the literary and artistic world," in which his own life was to be ransacked for material and characters. Little did the two men realize then, as they planned a September reunion at Aix-en-Provence, that their lifelong friendship would soon come to grief on this work, called *L'Oeuvre,* and that they would not see each other the following September at Aix, or ever again.

It is quite possible that Zola told Cézanne about *L'Oeuvre* (and even quizzed him for specific memories) without elaborating upon it. But Cézanne would have known something of the central theme from a passage he read in *Notes d'un ami* that summarizes future episodes of *Les Rougon-Macquart:*

> A work whose documentation shouldn't present great difficulties will be about art. Here the memory of what he's seen and experienced himself will suffice. The main character is all ready. He is Claude Lantier, the painter smitten with modernistic beauty who plays a bit part in *Le Ventre de Paris,* Claude Lantier whom Zola describes as follows in the Rougon-Macquart genealogical tree: "Born in 1842;— mixture, fusion;—spiritual and physical preponderance of the mother

---

Each one talked about the number of copies he had had printed of his last book, or how many he hoped to have printed of his next. Of course, they exaggerated a little. But you should have heard the women! Mme X would say proudly, casting a defiant look at Mme Z: "My husband and I have figured that the last novel, with the illustrated editions and the popular edition, has reached thirty-five thousand copies." "And *we,*" Madame Z would say, taking up the challenge. "*We* are promised by contract an edition of fifty thousand copies for our next book, not counting the deluxe edition."

Until their break, Zola sent Cézanne copies of all his works, and Cézanne read them.

(Gervaise, from *L'Assommoir*); an inherited nervous condition transforming itself into genius. Painter." . . . I know that he plans to study
in this character the frightful phenomenon of artistic impotence.
Around Claude, a sublime dreamer paralyzed by an inborn flaw, will
cluster other artists, painters, sculptors, musicians, men of letters, a
whole gang of ambitious young men equally determined to conquer
Paris: some flopping, others succeeding more or less, all exhibiting
. . . symptoms of the neurosis that paralyzes modern life. Naturally,
Zola . . . will have to press his friends into service, to collect their
most salient features.

Thus did Zola envisage the novel in 1881. By May 1885, when it acquired a dossier, he had come to see it more precisely as an obsessional
drama, built around the idea of a large work which the fixated hero—
gradually detaching himself from real life—can neither abandon nor
complete. "Toward the end of my novel, I'll say a word about today's
parlor painters and compare them to the poor, passionate artists of my
youth," he told a journalist from *Le Figaro* on June 6. "But that's just
one note. The drama lies elsewhere, in the struggle of an incomplete
genius with nature, in the struggle of a woman against art." It would
be more intimate than *Germinal*, he promised an agent involved in
peddling it for serialization abroad. "How a work of art grows, how it
succeeds or fails is what I wish to study. . . . I shall recount my entire
youth. I shall populate it with my friends, I shall include myself. Besides, you can affirm that the book will contain none of *Germinal*'s
crudities." He was not pleased with the title, which seemed to him
unexciting. But he liked it better than fifty others on his provisional
list.

Like so many other Zola novels, *L'Oeuvre* begins with the invasion
of a closed world. Returning home one rainy night, Claude Lantier,
who lives in Paris on the Ile Saint-Louis, finds huddled at his doorstep
a lost young woman who has just arrived from the provinces to work
as the companion of a rich old dame. Reluctantly Claude offers her
shelter, and fearfully Christine accepts. One enigma after another
greets this well-bred orphan fresh out of convent school. First there is
Claude's skylit studio high above Paris, which presents a spectacle of
absolute chaos. Then there are Claude's canvases, violent in color and
rough in execution, which resemble no art she has ever seen. And
finally there is Claude himself, a scrawny, bearded zealot who thwarts
his erotic fantasies in the deep-seated belief that letting some woman
enthrall him would ruin him for art, or that virility in bed would mean
impotence outside it. With the younger son of Gervaise, nothing hangs
together. Terrified of human nature, he nevertheless champions painting done in nature's midst, *en plein air*. Fearful of exposure, he scorns

confreres who prefer gaslight to sunlight. Obsessed by "nudities desired and never possessed," he worships the painted image of models he has driven from his studio. Even so, life would be tolerable if sensual deprivation yielded masterpieces. But poor Claude cannot consummate anything. What blocks the man blocks the artist, and this dilemma finds its most tormented expression in a large canvas the description of which strongly evokes several early Cézannes, notably *Venus and Cupid* of 1870–73 and *Modern Olympia* (where a darkly clad male figure whose back is turned to us contemplates a reclining nude). "It was fifteen feet wide, nine feet tall," writes Zola, who may also have had in mind *Le Déjeuner sur l'herbe*.

> Sketched at one sitting, it exhibited . . . an ardent play of color. Sunlight filled a forest glade immured by thick foliage. . . . There, on the grass, amidst early-summer vegetation, a nude woman lay with one arm folded under her head, inflating her bosom. She wore a smile, yet smiled at nothing in particular as her eyes were closed in the shower of gold that drenched her. Beyond her two more female nudes, one blond and the other brunet, . . . made adorable dabs of flesh against the green leaves. . . . And since the painter needed a dark opposition in the foreground, he accomplished it with a gentleman in a velvet jacket. This figure had his back turned; the only visible part of him was his left hand, on which he sat leaning in the grass.

The large, supine nude is his Nemesis. Still undefined, her face eyeless, this "dream flesh" or "yearned-for Eve" who "rises from the earth" eludes him. No sooner does he paint her than he paints her over, compulsively, murderously, like Don Juan rejecting every woman he seduces as a counterfeit of the Ideal. When she departs, Christine, whom Claude sketched during their brief encounter, leaves behind one such provisional image.

Christine's imagination also feeds upon that encounter, and after two months housebound with a blind old lady, she seeks out Claude. The sight of her face inserted in his big painting appalls her. "She rebelled, as if this naked body were hers, as if her virginity had been brutally exposed. What offended her above all was the painting's impetuous spirit; it whacked her, it bruised her flesh. She didn't understand it, she judged it to be execrable, she felt hatred for it, the instinctive hatred of an enemy." Two more months pass before she reappears, but her feelings have been stirred, and her visits become regular occurrences. Thanks to Christine, the atelier acquires a domestic air. She and Claude dispel each other's loneliness in affectionate banter and take walks along the Seine. Before long, Christine makes peace with an art she cannot quite accept. "She'd plant herself in front of the canvases, and no longer feared them. She didn't quite approve yet of such painting, but she began to parrot artists' talk, declaring it 'vigorous, very well composed, great for the light it captures.' He seemed so nice, she liked him so much that she ended up finding qualities in work she had formerly regarded as dreadful."

The good-natured young woman goes beyond talk when, on the eve of the annual Salon, Claude stands despondent before his incomplete oeuvre. Having painted Christine's face on another model's body, he can neither abide this schizoid nude nor ask Christine to help him make it whole. It is she who of her own accord offers up her modesty, stripping herself bare. Claude thereupon works like a man possessed. "He began to paint in the silence that enveloped them. He flung himself into work and for three long hours worked so potently as to complete a superb sketch at one go. Never had the flesh of woman intoxicated him in quite this way: his heart racing, he beheld her nakedness with religious awe." The adventure costs them their innocence, for during Claude's transport they have in some sense become lovers, and now find themselves overwhelmed by a kind of postcoital sadness. "They contemplated each other, hesitant, strangled by an emotion that prevented them from speaking. . . . Tears welled up in their eyes, as if they had spoiled their existence, or touched the bottom of human misery."

Carnal knowledge soon follows, on the day the Salon opens. Rejected by the jury, Claude's large work, called *Plein-Air*, is to be hung at an alternative exhibition, the newly created Salon des Refusés, and thither goes the painter arm in arm with fellow *plein-airistes*, walking into the cavernous Palace of Industry like a Christian bravely entering the Colosseum. He who bleeds at mere slights is subjected to the taunts of the multitude. "The word *plein-air* provoked shouts, hoots. . . . The crowd swelled, faces became congested in the heat, expressing . . . all the asininity that an original work can elicit from bourgeois ignoramuses." Worse still, Claude turns against himself, casting a critical eye upon his painting, from which, at first glance, he feels estranged. "His disappointment was so great that his heart stopped. . . . It was certainly not the same work he had seen in his studio. It had turned yellow in the cold light . . . ; it also seemed shrunken . . . ; and, whether on account of the paintings round about or of the new milieu, he instantly saw all its flaws." But bound up with self-hatred in Claude is self-righteousness, and the fractious *chef de mouvement* gains the upper hand over the doubter.

> In the disaster of his illusions, in the acute pain of his pride, he felt . . . cheered by all this brave painting gaily besieging old routine. . . .

It consoled and fortified him. . . . He felt . . . impelled to defy the public even more stubbornly. To be sure, there were many examples of clumsiness, many puerile efforts, but how lovely the general tone, how arresting the light—a silver-gray light filled with all the sparkle of the world outdoors! It was like a window suddenly opened in the old kitchen of bitumen.

When Claude returns to his studio, he finds Christine waiting for him, and only then does his militant persona collapse. Deeply humiliated by the scornful reception given *Plein-Air*, he weeps bitter tears before Christine, who consoles him. It is in the midst of this breakdown that the two make love.

Thus begins their common life. By June they have left Paris and set up house at Bennecourt. Avoiding the travails of art while he recuperates from the shock of public derision, Claude surrenders ecstatically to Christine. "Christine alone existed. She enveloped him in a breath of fire that dissolved his artistic mettle. . . . Thenceforth all his fondness for female flesh, all the desire he formerly satisfied in his works, made him lust after this supple, warm, living body, where he found well-being. He thought he had loved the silky bosoms he put on canvas, the beautiful pale amber of round hips, the downy bulge of pure stomachs. How misguided he had been! Now he triumphantly grasped a dream that had slipped through the painter's impotent fingers. . . . And she, happy at having killed her rival, prolonged the nuptials." Their fantasies, which bear fruit in little Jacques Lantier, have the effect of divorcing them from the outside world and blurring the past. Bennecourt is Le Paradou all over again, and it remains a closed paradise until Claude's "higher" self breaches the wall, like another Brother Archangias. Doubts then return en masse, along with the will to transcend nature through art.

He was haunted by the need to paint a figure clad in sunlight, and from that moment on, his woman became his victim. . . . He painted her twenty times over, clothed in white, clothed in red amidst the foliage, standing or walking, half prone on the grass, wearing a wide-brimmed country hat or bareheaded beneath a parasol whose cherry-colored silk bathed her face in pink light. He never felt completely satisfied, he'd scratch the paint off canvases after two or three sittings, stubbornly refusing to choose some other subject. A few incomplete studies, where his vigorous hand showed to good effect, were saved from the palette knife and hung on the dining-room wall.

Wandering afield with paints and easel, he captures light as never before. But the very act of painting undermines his aesthetic centeredness. Unable to produce images that equal Creation, he comes to feel, despite the love lavished upon him by Christine, that life is where he is not. The siren call of Paris reaches him again, and after four years he decamps with his woebegone family.

At first all goes well. The spectacle of friends who have prostituted their talent does not daunt Claude. Indeed, he experiences a reawakening and perceives that, with *plein-airisme* having during his absence infiltrated even academic art, the time has come to seize greatness. "How fine it would be if, from amidst the impotent dabblers unconsciously copying him and the slicksters taking fearful half measures, there stepped forth a master audacious enough to make his formula the truth of our fin de siècle!" This newfound belief in himself galvanizes Claude, who tramps around Paris for three years, painting the metropolis in all its seasons, all its lights, all its social guises. Intent upon vanquishing the Salon jury, he submits work to it every spring and year after year endures rebuffs. But far worse is his sense of an inner impasse. "Every rejected canvas seemed flawed, incomplete, not accomplishing what he envisioned. . . . At certain moments a wall rose in front of him, an obstacle he was not allowed to surmount." Does some physiological or hereditary defect explain his paralysis? he wonders. Sustained by the "mirage" of a masterwork that will disarm all critics, he reconnoiters Paris, seeking something enormous, something "decisive."

That enormous thing turns out to be the Ile de la Cité, which transfixes him one brilliant autumn day. Viewed from the Pont des Saints-Pères it presents an urban scene of compact variety, with barges docking down below and spires rising overhead, with the dark-green Seine flowing around its hull and the late-afternoon sun gilding its prow. "You see it every day, you pass in front of it without stopping, but it penetrates you and unbeknownst to you admiration grows until one fine day it becomes manifest," he tells Christine, who listens fearfully. "Nothing in the world is grander, it is Paris itself, glorious in the sun. . . . How stupid I was not to have thought of it!" Though he can ill afford the expense, Claude rents a hangar near Montmartre Cemetery and installs a canvas so large that scaffolding is needed to let him work on the upper reaches. "Living on his scaffold for days on end, wielding enormous brushes, expending energy enough to move mountains, he feverishly covered the entire canvas. Evenings he would fall asleep after dinner as if thunderstruck and be put to bed like a child. What emerged from this heroic ordeal was the sketch of a master, a sketch that argued genius, even with colors running riot." Once again his demons ruin his enterprise. The original sketch is replaced by others in a palimpsest of anguished improvisations as Claude, eternally unsure of himself, keeps visiting the Ile de la Cité for another look. Two years pass with no results.

Meanwhile, his family withers around him. Little Jacques, who radiated health at Bennecourt, acquires the grotesquely enlarged head of a child lapsing from potential genius into idiocy. And despair overcomes Christine when it is borne in on her that the man-child to whom she has bound herself will never be hers. After four years together they finally marry, but marriage consecrates their estrangement. "They clasped each other in vain—the passion was dead. Lying side by side, they understood that they would be strangers thereafter, with an obstacle between them, another body whose coldness had occasionally made them shiver even in their early, ardent days. Something irreparable had happened, something had broken, an emptiness had materialized." Of Claude, Zola might have said what Flaubert said of himself—that every woman on whom he had ever lain served as a mattress for the Ideal. Not only does Christine find herself spurned in bed; she agrees, as Claude's model, to help him conjure up in paint the image for which he spurns her.

That image emerges from the unfinished cityscape like a dream impinging upon the conscious mind. His Ile de la Cité remains, but in the foreground appears a nude of heroic proportions. This Woman, whom he wishes to embody "the very flesh of Paris, the naked, passionate city," will soon command all his energy. There is, indeed, no escaping Her once he moves his family into the hangar, where they live poverty-stricken. Over them, like Nana-Venus mesmerizing spectators, looms a figure that Claude paints and effaces obsessively. "Always at war with reality, but always vanquished, he spent blood and tears in the attempt to create flesh, to animate form. . . . Putting nature on canvas was an impossible task, and he endured interminable labor pains without bringing forth his genius." Nothing deters him, not even the death of Jacques, whom he has neglected completely. Able neither to consummate his artistic enterprise nor to nurture offspring, this "soldier of the uncreated" becomes reclusive, eschewing old friends and holding Christine in bondage. Years pass before the latter finally makes herself heard. When she finally denounces his work as monstrous, he realizes, as if awoken from a long sleep, that what he has wrought is not nature but its parody, not Venus or Ceres but a sterile, bedizened, fin de siècle harlot:

She stupefied him. Who then had painted this exotic idol? . . . Who had put her together with metals and precious stones, unfolding the mystic rose of her sex between the marble columns of her thighs? . . . Was it he who had unwittingly fabricated a symbol of insatiable desire? With mouth wide open he gazed upon it, trembling at this leap into the netherworld, and understanding full well that for him reality was no longer possible.

Christine begs him not to reject her (as Albine implored Serge Mouret not to leave the paradisial garden for the penitential church). But Claude, after a brief resurgence of conjugal passion, ties a rope around his neck and jumps from the scaffold on which he had toiled in vain, hanging himself opposite the divinity he could not possess.

Funeral arrangements are made by Claude's closest friend, Pierre Sandoz, a writer modeled after Zola himself. What began at the center of Paris concludes in a graveyard at its periphery, where the artist who set out to conquer Paris will for five years occupy a rented plot. En route—and this sorrowful coach ride across blighted suburbs to oblivion is easily the greatest scene in *L'Oeuvre*—Sandoz does some summing up. For all his talent, Claude was unequal to his vision, he tells a companion in mourning. "No, he couldn't accomplish the formula he introduced. I mean by this that he didn't quite have what it would have taken to plant it upright and impose it in a definitive work." Moreover, the romantics by whom he had been nurtured continued to hold sway over his sensibility, queering every major project. "Our generation immersed itself in romanticism, and we're still dripping wet." But Claude was undone above all by an age that had forfeited scientific optimism. "Pessimism twists people's guts, mysticism fogs their brains," Sandoz muses. "For the ghosts we routed with shafts of light have returned, the supernatural has armed itself again, the spirit of legends sees an opportunity for conquest in our weariness and anguish."

Like Serge Mouret and Lazare Chanteau, to whom he bears a strong resemblance, Claude Lantier inherited Zola's own hobgoblins. The thought weighed upon Zola more oppressively than ever during this period that he was damned if he did and damned if he didn't, that he would be struck dead or rendered impotent before finishing *Les Rougon-Macquart*, and that in finishing *Les Rougon-Macquart* he would have spent his life siring a fictional brood rather than children of flesh and blood. Had he not always identified with characters who drew mental pictures of a coveted object? who looked through windows at the metropolis they proposed to conquer or the goddess they couldn't possess? Did his dream of pantheistic union not spring from those very inhibitions that made him a bashful observer? One critic, Gustave Geffroy, noted the affinity between Zola and Claude in a review in *La Justice*. "It is not only through Sandoz that Zola has represented himself," he wrote. "We also see him in the artist who toils courageously without knowing for sure the outcome or significance of his effort. Do they not complement each other, Claude who seeks himself and Sandoz who explains himself? Passionately devoted to their tasks, furious in their desire to create, devastated by results, they are both *les damnés de l'art*—'art's damned souls.' Are Sandoz's laments not as painful as

Claude's miscarriages? Is Zola, who called himself, astonishingly, 'a perpetual beginner,' not as sad, as disillusioned as the suicide he portrays?" Geffroy argued that the novel was confessional.

Otherwise, Claude Lantier embodied Zola's well-known contention that modern art lacked the magisterial figure, the "necessary man," the "genius" to consecrate it. With bits of Monet, of Manet, of Cézanne, and of Jongkind he created a mongrel in whom the Impressionists saw themselves grotesquely caricatured. After reading *L'Oeuvre* halfway through, Pissarro declared it to be romantic moonshine. In May 1886 he sent his son a long report on the effect produced by Zola's novel:

> I went to dinner with the Impressionists. This time a great many came: Duret brought Burty, an influential critic, Moore, the English novelist, the poet Mallarmé, Huysmans, M. Deudon, and M. Bérard; it was a real gathering. Monet . . . arrived from The Hague at eight o'clock, just in time for dinner. — I had a long discussion with Huysmans, he is very conversant with the new art and is anxious to break a lance for us. We spoke of the novel *L'Oeuvre*. He is decidedly of my opinion. It seems that he had a quarrel with Zola. . . . Guillemet, who is furious about the book, also wrote Zola, but only to complain that the character named Fagerolles is too easily identifiable.[5]

Guillemet, upon whom Zola had relied for inside information about the Salon jury's modus operandi, was indeed exercised, and made his displeasure known in a letter dated April 4. "My compliments, Emile. It's a story invented out of whole cloth rather than a product of observation, is it not?" he asked sarcastically.

> All in all it grips the reader but casts him down. Everyone in it, those endowed with genius as well as those devoid of talent, thinks badly and works badly. . . . Happily, the real world is not so sad. Early in my career I had the honor and good fortune to know that splendid constellation of modern geniuses: Daumier, Millet, Courbet, Daubigny, and—purest and most human of them all—Corot. They all died at the height of their achievement and progressed throughout their lives. So have you progressed all your life, you whose friend I am proud to be. Have you not gone constantly forward? and is *Germinal*

[5]Like Zola, Sandoz has a circle of friends who gather around him for dinner every Thursday. This *bande* includes an artist named Fagerolles, who eventually betrays his principles for a fashionable career and who, when he becomes a jury member, avails himself of the "charity" choice allowed each judge to select Claude's macabre portrait of his dead son. As a model for Fagerolles Zola had in mind the painter Henri Gervex; but Guillemet, who was himself elected to the Salon jury and in 1882 made Cézanne his charity case, may well have felt implicated.

not one of the best things you've ever done? In your last book I see only sadness or impotence. . . .

God forbid that members of the little gang, as your mother used to called us, should recognize themselves in your characters. Mean-spirited, they are of little interest.

One day later Claude Monet wrote from Giverny to accuse Zola of having subverted the whole cause of modernism and, implicitly, of jeopardizing his livelihood. "You kindly sent me *L'Oeuvre,* for which I am most grateful," he began.

Your books always give me great pleasure and this one interested me all the more because it raises issues of art over which we've long been battling. I've just finished it and I confess that it has left me troubled, worried. Though you made certain that none of your characters should resemble any one of us, I am still afraid that our enemies in the press and in the public at large may seize this pretext to call Manet and the rest of us failures—which, I must believe, was not your intention.

He had read *L'Oeuvre* "with very great pleasure," encountering memories on every page, and retained his "fanatical admiration" for Zola's talent. But, he confessed, "I've been struggling for many years and I fear that now, even as success beckons, the foe may use your book to knock us down."

In Pissarro's opinion, Monet ascribed exorbitant power to Zola. "I don't believe it will do us any harm; it's just a novel in which the author of *L'Assommoir* and *Germinal* came up short, that's all," he told him. Renoir judged *L'Oeuvre* with similar aplomb. "What a beautiful book he could have written . . . if he had only taken the trouble to relate plainly the things he heard during our chats and saw at our studios. For there is no denying that he lived the life of his models." Not until reviews finally appeared, however, did Monet concede that potential clients were unlikely to shun him as one of Emile Zola's losers.

L'Oeuvre affected Cézanne more deeply than anyone else. To believe Joachim Gasquet, a young Aixois poet in whom he confided, Cézanne understood the composite nature of Claude Lantier and the "physiological" argument for his fall. But he could not read the fraternal aspersions that Sandoz casts upon Claude's work without feeling personally impugned. Whom else but him would Zola have had in mind when he wrote:

[Sandoz] recalled their efforts, their certainty of glory, the hunger pangs that made them talk of swallowing Paris whole. At this period how often had he imagined Claude the great man whose unbridled genius would race ahead, leaving mere talents in the dust! There were dreams of immense canvases, projects big enough to burst open the Louvre. . . . And what had come of it, after twenty passionate years? Nothing but this paltry item . . . ! So many hopes, so many tortures.

Another such page struck even closer to home. "[Sandoz] had been astonished at first to see Claude lose his footing . . . for he believed in his friend more than in himself and ever since their school days had put himself second. . . . Afterward, this collapse inspired dolorous empathy, bitter and bleeding pity for a man tormented by impotence. Did one ever know, in art, where the madman lurked?"

The wonder is that Paul and Emile's childhood bond still held them together after thirty-four years of growing apart. It had been frayed by unequal success, by boorishness, by spousal opposition, by faint praise—and had stood the test. But now, almost inaudibly, it snapped. When Zola sent Cézanne his copy of L'Oeuvre, Cézanne, who must already have read the feuilleton or heard about it in some detail, acknowledged receipt with a frosty note. "My dear Emile," he wrote on April 4, 1886. "I have just received L'Oeuvre, which you arranged to send me. I thank the author of Les Rougon-Macquart for this kind token of remembrance, and request that he allow me to clasp his hand as I think about bygone years. All yours, writing under the impetus of another time, Paul Cézanne."

Whether or not Cézanne regarded this as a valediction, a valediction it turned out to be. The two men never again exchanged letters or spoke. It was a third party who informed Zola, several weeks later, that Cézanne had finally knuckled under and married Hortense Fiquet at the Saint-Jean-Baptiste Church in Aix. And when on October 23 Louis-Auguste died at age eighty-eight, leaving a substantial fortune, Cézanne sent no announcement. It would seem that they resolved by some tacit accord to bury the friendship. But if so, various memoirs suggest that they buried it alive. Joachim Gasquet, for example, noted that Cézanne's reverence for Zola had never wavered, and that when he, Gasquet, saw Zola in Paris fifteen years after L'Oeuvre, the great novelist spoke of "his childhood friend" with great affection. "He still embraced Cézanne, in spite of the latter's surliness, with all the warmth of a great brotherly heart, 'and I am even beginning,' he told me, 'to have a better understanding of his work, which I always liked, but which eluded me for a long time, for I believed it mistakenly to be strained." By then Zola had written J'accuse, and Cézanne, whose need for a surrogate father led him to religion, had lined up on the other side as an anti-Dreyfusard.[6]

L'Oeuvre also provoked a new crisis in Zola's deteriorating relationship with Edmond de Goncourt.

Zola had seen Goncourt quite regularly during the previous year, for in 1885, at the urging of Daudet, who missed Flaubert's open house, Goncourt had founded a literary salon. Beginning in February, guests traveled to his suburban villa every Sunday and congregated in third-floor rooms which looked more like exhibition space for the Orientalia he collected than an agreeable environment for social discourse. The *Grenier*, as he called it—the garret—soon became famous. Its ceilings and walls had been painted Turkey red, its windows and doors trimmed in black. Turkish script, or something that resembled it, lay underfoot, woven into a large poppy-colored rug. Precious knick-knacks were everywhere to be seen, along with Japanese scrolls featuring peonies, wisteria, monkeys, and dogs. One such *kakemono* hung above a divan flanked by rows of eggshell plates. Others hung from a wide armoire, near eighteenth-century etchings in which the collector took special pride. And amidst all this art stood his library of nineteenth-century French literature. "Several low bookcases, about four and one-half feet high, . . . contain, apart from little pamphlets, original editions of Balzac's complete oeuvre," Goncourt wrote by way of memorializing the room in a fastidious catalogue. Other bookcases contained original editions of Hugo, Musset, Stendhal, Daudet, Zola. "There is Renan's volume *Souvenirs d'enfance*. There is *Madame Bovary*, with one page of painful script, full of crossings-out and marginal alterations, a page given me by Mme Commanville. . . . There is Barbey d'Aurevilly's *Diaboliques* illustrated with a page of his very mas-

---

[6]Ambroise Vollard, Cézanne's dealer, remembers him inveighing against *L'Oeuvre* not long after Zola's death, and though Vollard was given to invention, the account may be worth quoting:

"You can't ask a man to talk sensibly about the art of painting if he simply doesn't know anything about it. But by God!"—and here Cézanne began to tap on the table like a deaf man—"how can he dare to say that a painter is done for because he has painted one bad picture? When a picture isn't realized, you pitch it in the fire and start another one!" As he talked, Cézanne paced up and down the studio like a caged animal. Suddenly seizing a portrait of himself, he tried to tear it to pieces; but his palette knife had been mislaid, and his hands were trembling violently. So he rolled the canvas up, broke it across his knee, and flung it in the fireplace.

His anger subsided as soon as Vollard told him that Zola had spoken about him in affectionate terms:

Cézanne looked at me with sorrowful eyes. The destruction of his canvas had calmed him. His anger had given way to pain. "Listen, Monsieur Vollard, I must tell you. Although I stopped going to see Zola, I never got used to the idea that our friendship was a thing of the past."

culine handwriting in red ink. . . . And there is Michelet's *Ma jeunesse*."

Expansive gestures, which might result in the destruction of price-less curios, were discouraged. With a white silk handkerchief knotted around his neck to point up the blackness of his eyes, Goncourt sat ensconced in a thick, close-fitting jacket and offered each new arrival two limp fingers, never rising to greet anyone. There was no need to rise for women, as women did not intrude upon this narcissistic cer-emony until late afternoon, when they fetched their husbands. "Women go very well against the background," Goncourt observed, "and are completely in tune with the harmonies of the furniture. But the majority of my public demands that women should arrive late, late, late." In fact the majority of his "public" demanded that the afternoon elapse as quickly as possible, and even the presence of Daudet, a charming raconteur, didn't always help. So cheerless were these Sun-day receptions, which Céard dubbed "the Auteuil Vespers," that Gon-court himself succumbed to fits of yawning. "It wouldn't be so bad," Huysmans told one friend, "if one could hurry through one's devotions and then dash away. But it just isn't possible, and you have to stay there to the bitter end."

Why did people feel compelled to come or, having come, to stay? Because, Huysmans explained, habitués knew that anyone "insane" enough to leave early would, as soon as the door closed behind him, have his work "set upon, dismembered, disemboweled, devoured." So, "to avoid being eaten alive, you sit tight and stay on. And Goncourt, who is only interested in effects and never goes back to causes, is pleased to proclaim that his house is too small to hold so many friends!" Thus did Goncourt, for want of a masterpiece that might have vouchsafed him the reputation to which he felt entitled, exercise authority—with his money, with his private museum, with his slan-derous tongue. Some confreres refrained from speaking their minds lest he assassinate them in his journal. Some curried favor in hopes of becoming paid members of the Academy, for which he had made am-ple provision in his will. Others were led by their own self-doubt or vanity to credit his airs and looked upon him as a man of infallible taste—an *arbiter elegantiae*. "There are no discordant tones in the life of the elder Goncourt, or in his voice, or in his work—and no such discordances are to be found in his garret, where everything melds," wrote one of his admirers, Madame Alphonse Daudet. "A rare carpet, or some old tapestry brings to his eyes the glint of the connoisseur, and that's what gives him his redoubtable countenance."

When he was in Paris, Zola almost always visited the *Grenier*, but this demonstration of goodwill did not alter Goncourt's profound be-lief that the best of *Les Rougon-Macquart* had come from his own works. Zola was a thief, and *L'Oeuvre* gave Goncourt yet another chance to feel robbed. The fuss began even before the first serial installment appeared. On July 22, 1885, *Le Figaro* carried an article indicating that Goncourt's "followers" (though not Goncourt himself) were of the opinion that Zola might trespass on ground staked out in a Goncourt novel called *Manette Salomon*. Zola smelled trouble, and he wrote straightway to the reporter, Joseph Gayda, whom he had met more than once at the *Grenier*.

> You terrify me. Do you really think that Goncourt's friends, who are mine as well, I hope, await my book with such anxiety? Goncourt is quite right not to worry. *L'Oeuvre* won't be as advertised. It's not a succession of tableaux showing the world of painters, a group of etchings and watercolors lined up on the wall. Simply put, it's a study that probes into a mind and a deep-seated passion.

Le Figaro published this note (without asking Zola's permission), whereupon Goncourt took offense at the characterization of *Manette Salomon* as "a group of etchings and watercolors lined up on the wall" and wrathfully unburdened himself to Daudet, who demanded on Goncourt's behalf that Zola apologize. Zola stood firm, belching out a long, indignant rejoinder. "I am very distressed, my good Daudet, to see that my letter affected you so strongly," he answered.

> This letter was not meant for public consumption, but when I encountered it yesterday morning in *Le Figaro*, it didn't seem all that dreadful. I don't understand why you call it "unjust."
> I must confess, moreover, that Goncourt has begun to get on my nerves with his sickly and obsessive cries of thief. For quite some time now, he has let it be known everywhere he goes that I steal his ideas. *L'Assommoir* is *Germinie Lacerteux*, *La Faute de l'abbé Mouret* was lifted from *Madame Gervaisais*. Quite recently . . . he claimed that I wrote one whole section of *La Joie de vivre* after hearing him read a chapter of *Chérie*. . . . And now, even before *L'Oeuvre* has appeared, the tomfoolery starts again. No, no, my good friend. I'm a patient man, but enough's enough.

Although he knew that reporters often felt free to put "asininities" in the mouths of those they interviewed, the article could not have sprouted by itself.

> At the very least a conversation took place, meaning that the article would not have appeared if Goncourt had objected to it. . . . I myself have blocked twenty pieces of this kind. Gayda is a habitué of his Sundays, one always sees him conferring in corners. What would you

say if, in an article written by one of my crowd, you found words like "rupture" and "betrayal" bandied about in connection with your next book?

Under no circumstances would he placate the man.

You ask me to mend things with a conciliatory letter. First of all, I hope that nothing's been broken. And second, I don't have it in me. For what should I excuse myself? Instead of writing that letter, I'd rather you showed this one to Goncourt, for at least he'd learn the truth. Don't you think, frankly, that the one who should have written a letter the day after that wretched article appeared was Goncourt?

This letter never got beyond Médan. Visited by other thoughts and feelings, Zola saved it for posterity and sent Daudet a shorter, more innocuous version, preferring to swallow his gorge once again rather than to repudiate a literary father. It may well be said that with such friends as Goncourt and Daudet he needed no enemies. Zola himself may have thought so. But the ideal that accompanied him through life—an inseparable trio or an unbreakable family—was yet to be forsworn, however mortal its successive incarnations. He exchanged notes with Goncourt and went on feigning camaraderie until their next skirmish, which followed hard upon the completion of *La Terre* in August 1887.

La Terre does not figure in Zola's early master plans. One of the first indications that he envisaged a novel about peasant life was given by a journalist named Fernand Xau, who interviewed him shortly after *Nana* appeared. More references to such a novel followed in due course. Paul Alexis declared that his friend had been collecting material for it ever since he established himself at Médan. And on January 16, 1884, Goncourt wrote: "Zola visits me. He frets over the novel he must write next, *The Peasants*. It would necessitate a month on a farm in the Beauce . . . with the cooperation of some rich landowner willing to pass him off as a gentleman whose frail wife needs country air. 'You understand, what we need are two beds in a whitewashed room, plus the farmer's ordinary fare—otherwise I won't learn anything.' " Zola subsequently postponed *La Terre* in favor of *Germinal*, which seemed less daunting. Then came *L'Oeuvre*. But the ink had hardly dried on *L'Oeuvre* when preparations began for this fifteenth installment of *Les Rougon-Macquart*. From Médan he wrote in February 1886 to Céard, "I finished *L'Oeuvre* only this morning. I'm already hooked on my novel about peasants. It's obsessing me." Zola's remedy for depression was work. Céard having lamented that he saw the future unfolding before him as "an absolutely flat landscape, flat to the horizon," Zola answered: "Why don't you give yourself over to some project? I assure you that in the nothingness of everything, [writing] remains the most enthralling of all useless enterprises." Such admonitions had little effect. The spectacular example of Zola's industry was, if anything, oppressive.

In the usual way, Zola gathered information sufficient to his purpose, and friends did yeoman work as informants, research assistants, intermediaries. Céard was always ready to inconvenience himself. So, it seems, was a chum of Céard's named Gabriel Thyébaut, on whom Zola relied for his legal expertise, his grasp of the peasant mind, and his (apparent) knowledge of rural economics. Through *Le Cri du peuple*, where he worked, Paul Alexis found him articles by Karl Marx's son-in-law, Paul Lafargue. More importantly, he arranged a lunch with Jules Guesde, at which Guesde analyzed the agricultural crisis that had been in full swing since 1880, when competition from abroad, and particularly the importation of cheap wheat from the United States, began to drive prices down. While championing nationalization, Guesde, his eyes aflame, evoked the blessings of mechanized agriculture for tillers of the soil.

Zola's dossier includes "Thyébaut Notes" and "Guesde Notes." And it also includes notes taken during a weeklong sojourn in the wheat-growing region southwest of Paris—the Beauce—where Emilie Aubert Zola had been born. Accompanied by Alexandrine, Zola left the capital on May 3, having arranged beforehand to meet a deputy named Noël Parfait at Chartres. Parfait suggested that he investigate Châteaudun, several dozen kilometers farther south, and he lost no time doing so. "It's a little valley four leagues away, in the canton of Cloyes, between the Perche and the Beauce," he wrote to Céard on May 6. "I'll provide it with a little stream emptying into the Loir—which exists, moreover; it includes farms large and small, a very French village, a horizon like no other, a cheerful population, no patois. In short, just what I dreamed of." A brief tour, briefer even than the tour of the Anzin coalfields that preceded *Germinal*, had already been arranged. He made an appointment with a farmer whose operation gave him a clear picture of large-scale agriculture, attended a big cattle market, and on May 9 was back in Paris with a sheaf of jottings about the scenery, the market, farm equipment, animal husbandry, village life, peasant dress, the soil, the harvest. Writing three weeks later to his faithful Dutch correspondent, Jacques van Santen Kolff, who wanted a detailed description of *La Terre*, Zola declared that this request disconcerted him.

I'm still working on the plot outline. I won't begin to write until mid-June and the prospect is daunting because this novel, in its simplicity, will be more laden with material than most others I've written. I want to have it contain all our peasants, with their history, their mores, their role; in it I want to raise the social question of property; I want to show what the agricultural crisis that is weighing so heavily upon us means. Every time I tackle some subject nowadays I come up against socialism. With *La Terre* I would like to do with the peasant what I did for the worker with *Germinal*. Bear in mind that I intend to remain an artist, a writer, to make living poetry of the earth, the seasons, people, beasts, the whole countryside.[7]

By then the Paris daily *Le Matin* had published an excerpt from his preliminary sketch, and readers eager to help him understand rural France or to participate in the creation of a novel inundated him with letters. One such correspondent, a former city dweller who farmed land near Saint-Aubin, wrote some sixty pages on the Norman peasant, the mores of the Chartrain region, and the future of agriculture. These, too, entered Zola's dossier.[8]

Among other parallels linking *La Terre* to *Germinal*, the most obvious is a landscape that shows the human settlement couched in oceanic immensity. "To the west, a small copse made a rust-colored line against the sky. In the middle, a chalk-white road stretched from Châteaudun to Orléans, with telegraph poles marching down its entire length, at exact intervals. There was nothing else, nothing except three or four becalmed windmills. Villages looked like islands of stone. In the far distance a steeple whose church one couldn't see rose from a fold in the softly rolling terrain, soon to be covered with wheat." As in *Germinal* a canal flows straight across the northern plain, so here a road scores the Beauceron countryside. As in *Germinal*, people surrounded by unobstructed space live radically involuted lives, entering the labyrinth every day, so here villages are immutable "islands of stone." And in *La Terre* as in *Germinal* the story unfolds from the sojourn of a drifter among isolated, primitive people. Etienne Lantier's counterpart is Jean Macquart.

As the novel begins, we learn that Jean Macquart, who like Gervaise suffered at the hands of their brutish father, escaped from Plassans by joining the army for a seven-year tour which included action in Na-

---

[7]The agricultural crisis lasted for about fifteen years, from 1880 to 1895. The importation of cheap wheat from the United States had a particularly devastating effect upon the Beauce region.

[8]Something similar was to occur several years later, when Zola visited Alsace-Lorraine during preparations for a novel on the Franco-Prussian War. Local newspapers announced the project and surviving veterans sent him detailed memoirs of the battle of Sedan.

poleon III's Italian campaign. Afterward, he traveled north to the Beauce, where the father of an army chum offered him employment. No sooner had he settled down than his boss died, leaving him marooned at Rognes, a village near Cloyes. Sent there to repair a large farmhouse, he would have departed straightway had not the owner invited him to stay on as a *valet de ferme*, or resident jack-of-all-trades. He accepted with alacrity. Farm chores, however laborious, please him. Thoughtful and sensitive—sensitive especially to the majestic landscape round about—he is not the protagonist of *La Terre* but a witness to the commonplace events of village life and a bit player in the drama that overwhelms a family named Fouan.

As rooted in this province as the local vegetation, the Fouans had been Beauceron since the Middle Ages. Originally serfs, they gained their freedom centuries earlier but never moved, having bound themselves to the land they acquired, or to a collective mania for acquisition. "[With the acre or two bought from the lord] began a four-hundred-year-long struggle to defend and round out their parcel," writes Zola, who knew something about rounding out estates bit by bit. The Revolution, which consecrated Fouan ownership, also signaled, paradoxically, a decline in Fouan family fortunes, and since 1789 their saga of accumulation had become a nightmare of fragmentation. Three children—Marianne, Michel, Louis—had divided the property, but the arrangement proved disastrous, for Michel, or "Mouche," who got the poorest third, concluded that he was the victim of mischief rather than bad luck. As *La Terre* opens, in October 1860, this paranoid scenario is about to be repeated by another generation. Mouche's brother Louis has sired three children—Hyacinthe (called "Jesus Christ"), a lout who drinks himself sodden every night; Fanny, who has married a prosperous landowner; and Jules, known as "Buteau." Lest any bit of his acreage be sold for death duties, Louis divests himself of it, with his children drawing lots. Trouble follows when Buteau, drawing third, fails to win the patch he covets and, like Mouche before him, cries foul. "Buteau owed this nickname to his rebellious nature and a stubbornness in defending notions no one else shared. . . . For all his jocularity, cunning and violence showed through. He had his father's brutal, single-minded will to possess, and it was aggravated by his mother's penny-wise avarice." What galls him is division itself. Not unless he possessed everything would this youngest son consider himself adequately compensated for a lifetime of being last.

The invasion of a structured world by a blind appetite or instinctual force that effaces boundaries, abolishes compartments, levels hierarchies, and razes walls always constituted the stuff of drama for Zola. *La Curée* ends with upper-class Parisians milling wildly through Saccard's town house. When doomsday nears in *L'Assommoir*, dirty linen spreading from laundry room to living room announces it. Nana triumphs when musicians fill the air of a high-society wedding with her vulgar anthem, "La Blonde Vénus." The white sale orchestrated by Octave Mouret features the great entrepreneur jubilantly surveying a promiscuous mob. This motif recurs throughout *Les Rougon-Macquart*, and so it does in *La Terre*. Père Fouan having forfeited authority by dividing his land, moral chaos ensues. Devoid of scruples, but free now of external constraints as well, Buteau steers a course that will leave three people dead. The first to succumb is his mother, whom he knocks senseless while ransacking the parental house for hidden treasure. The second is nineteen-year-old Françoise Fouan, daughter of Mouche, whose older sister Lise—Buteau's wife as well as his cousin—comes to begrudge her her inheritance and lays her open with a scythe. The last is his father. Dependent upon the children, Père Fouan finds himself scorned by them all and flees from one ingrate to another, like some peasant Lear, ending up at Buteau's house in a storage room for vegetables. Humiliated, he makes silence his refuge. "Never, whatever the circumstance or necessity, did he address Buteau and Lise," writes Zola. "He slept there, ate there; he saw them, rubbed shoulders with them morning and evening, but never exchanged a word or glance. He behaved as if blind and dumb, shuffling about like a shade among the living." Loath to feed an accusatory presence who for all his infirmities suffers no loss of appetite—on the contrary, he eats noisily—Buteau and Lise resolve to commit murder. After robbing the old man they throttle him in his sleep, then set him afire. Everyone suspects the truth, but Rognes, which won't set aside money for a parish priest, is as tolerant of parricide as of incest.

What Rognes will not tolerate are outsiders, and that is the lesson Jean Macquart learns during his hallucinatory sojourn. Born a stranger, he remains a stranger throughout, known only by the sardonic nickname "Corporal." *La Terre*, which begins with Macquart gazing beyond Rognes as he broadcasts seed, ends with him encompassing the same vista as he watches Rognes bury Fouan. It is autumn again, and so the novel comes full circle, from *semence* to *semence*, from sowing season to sowing season, in an image of eternal renewal. "Fouan's coffin seemed so diminutive that everyone, including Jean, who tarried at the graveyard, was startled," writes Zola.

Ah! the poor duffer, reduced to skin and bone by old age and the hardships of life, at home in a toy box! He wouldn't take up much space, he wouldn't encumber this earth, the vast earth which he had loved with a passion that left him feeble. His corpse was brought to the grave, whereupon Jean glanced beyond it, beyond the cemetery wall, at the Beauce itself. And there, in that sweep of plowed fields, he saw sowers as far as the eye could reach ceaselessly rocking from side to side, like an animate wave washing seed into the open furrows.

Bereft yet hopeful, Jean leaves Rognes forever, on foot, heading east to rejoin his army corps and defend French soil against Prussian invaders. The year is 1870.

Zola fleshed out *La Terre* with marvelously vivid chapters on peasants bargaining and municipal councillors bickering, on market day at Cloyes, on planting and harvesting, on calving and shearing, on a village fair and a country wedding. But his larger purpose was to create another version of the aboriginal settlement first evoked in *La Faute de l'abbé Mouret*, to suggest that the Middle Ages lay only one hour from late-nineteenth-century Paris, that the traveler who left France's main roads would, like the civilized man plumbing his own depths, confront *la bête humaine*. Where people recognize only tribal justice, the priest summoned from Bazoches-le-Doyen for baptisms, marriages, and burials enjoys only ceremonial authority. Where people demonize machines, the "bourgeois" who introduces scientific agriculture is asking to have his farm burned down. And where people regard France as a feudal lord saddling them with onerous taxes and compelling them to bear arms, exogamy spells betrayal. No one thinks otherwise, not even Françoise Fouan, who dares to marry Jean Macquart. "[Jean] suffered above all from the feeling he had had ever since they moved into the ancestral house that his wife still regarded him as a stranger, someone bred elsewhere in a land beyond her ken, a man who didn't think like Rognes men; who seemed differently constituted and without any possible bond to herself, even though he had made her pregnant."

This insular village is, moreover, a flagrantly anal world. While eighty miles north Baron Haussmann has modernized Paris by building prodigious sewers, Rognes continues to wallow in muck and excrement. Excrement defines Zola's Beaucerons, pervading the air they breathe, fertilizing the soil they tread, informing the language they use, coloring the jokes they make, quickening the passions they feel. As much as earth itself it shapes their very culture, and almost every page of *La Terre* yields a scatological incident. There is, for example, "Jesus Christ" displaying his virtuosity at producing thunderous farts or on market day challenging an old peasant to swallow more coins than he. "Wide-eyed, the old man accepted and with some difficulty gulped his first coin," writes Zola, who had often before made much of the symbolic connection between feces and gold.

But Jesus Christ was bolting them down like prunes, loudly asserting meanwhile that there was no need to rush. When he reached five, a murmur ran through the café and a circle of people gathered round, spellbound with admiration: "Hell, some mouth he has to gobble them up that way!" The old man was just swallowing his fourth coin when he tumbled over backwards, purple in the face, choking and gasping; for a moment they thought he was dead. Jesus Christ stood up, quite unperturbed, with a sardonic look; he had stowed away ten five-franc coins in his own stomach, so at any rate he was thirty francs to the good.

There is the old woman who saves her own waste to fertilize the acre from which she extracts a livelihood for herself and her infirm husband:

> She worked like a slave, collecting the droppings on the road to ma-
> nure it, since they had no livestock, looking after her lettuces, her
> peas, her beans, and even watering her three plum trees and two
> apricots, and ending up with quite a sizable profit from this one acre,
> so much so that she went off to the market at Cloyes every Saturday
> bent double under the weight of two enormous baskets. . . . But she
> continually complained about a shortage of manure: neither the drop-
> pings which she collected from the road nor the sweepings from the
> few rabbits and chickens she reared gave her enough. So she had
> resorted to using what she and her husband themselves produced.
> . . . The fact became known and she was teased: people called her
> Mother Caca.

More follows. When natives dance at a village fair, the floor of beaten earth turns to mud. When Jean and Françoise discuss marriage, they stand on either side of a fence with *purin*, or liquid manure, flowing between their legs. When tempers flare, cowpats fly. And when Lise helps Buteau suffocate Père Fouan, she does it by sitting bare-assed on his face, "like a dropsical old cart horse." Symbolically and anatom-ically, the female rump acquires enormous proportions in *La Terre*.

At Rognes as at Montsou, the radical impossibility of ever scrubbing oneself clean comes to epitomize the predicament of folk for whom there exists no "outside"—no Paris, no fatherland, no afterlife, no transcendent law, no progress, no escape from matter. Where conser-vative voices—the Drumonts, the Barrès and Bourgets (who later took sides against Dreyfus)—glorified peasant rootedness, Zola described a fallen race. Prisoners of the earth rather than autochthons, his Beau-cerons argue their territorial claims ad infinitum. Indeed, they argue them beyond the grave, and *La Terre* ends in the Rognes cemetery, with two mourners quarreling over the disposition underground of their own future corpses as a priest vainly adjures the spirit to rise. "They stood jostling each other beside their plots," writes Zola,

> the few feet of earth where they would sleep forever. "But doesn't it mean anything to you, you wretched bugger, that your damned carcass will be next to mine, as if we were friends? It burns me. We've always hated each other's guts and now we're supposed to make our peace and lie side by side happily ever after. No, not for me, I'm never going to make it up with you." "I don't give a damn! You can lick my ass and go on licking it beside me as far as I'm concerned!"

Fouans would finally eat one another's bones, he concludes. "In this sunny graveyard, under the peacefully sprouting weeds, the dead old ancestors fought fiercely on with no quarter given, from coffin to coffin, as fiercely as the fight waged by their living descendants amidst the headstones."

Zola labored over this big, powerful book for almost fifteen months, and his progress reports were no more sanguine than usual. "I've gotten my book off to a so-so start," he informed Céard on June 16, 1886. "Chapter One is done: it promises something that will have breadth but none of the sublimity I keep dreaming about, despite myself." By late summer it was well underway, but doubts as to whether he could bring it off still nagged him. To Antoine Guillemet he wrote on August 22: "We haven't yet left Médan, and it is unlikely that we shall leave it this year, unless in the very near future we spend a week at Saint-Palais, near Royan, where the Charpentiers are vacationing. . . . My frightful novel has nailed me to the desk—a book that will cause me much difficulty and prevent me from returning to Paris before March or so. You know that I'm never satisfied when I work. All I ask is that my mind doesn't fail too quickly." The pleasure principle prevailed long enough to afford him ten days at Saint-Palais. Far from suffering untoward consequences he came home reinvigorated and throughout that fall worked productively.

Early in the new year, when he was taken up as much with a stage adaptation of *Le Ventre de Paris* as with his novel, the publicity campaign began. "You present *La Terre* in such flattering terms that I shall now be expected to produce a masterpiece," is how he thanked a *Figaro* columnist named Charles Chincholle (Alexandre Dumas's former secretary), who had read long excerpts. To Arsène Alexandre of *L'Evénement* he wrote: "You put my desultory notes to good account, for which I am grateful. It's clear from the broadside in *Le Gaulois* that I shall be accused of concocting an imaginary peasant. That's the way things are and I expect as much. Obviously a peasant who doesn't embody the chauvinistic and conservative spirit attributed to him by current opinion can't be real." These early salvos and the production of *Le Ventre de Paris* (which would enjoy a three-and-a-half-month run at the Théâtre de Paris) distracted him, but *La Terre* nonetheless grew apace. "It is only two-thirds written," he told van Santen Kolff on March 12. "This novel, which will be my longest so far, has given me lots of trouble. I'm satisfied with it, to the extent that my continual fever and eternal doubts let me feel satisfied. It will appear in *Gil Blas*, I'm not sure when, as the date hasn't yet been settled, perhaps around April 10, perhaps May 15." The last third kept him housebound most of the summer. *Gil Blas*, which began to serialize it on May 29, 1887, published a last installment on September 15. It appeared in book form two months later.

La Terre created an enormous furor, and many critics let fly their barbs even before the serial had run its course. "'This book is a deliberately assembled collection of sweepings, a compost heap, a monument to contemporary progress rivaling Eiffel's iron syringe," declared the conservative paper *La Gazette de France*.[9] "Any woman who will have soiled her mind with our maniac's latest picture of wallowing swine, any woman who will have endured, with no ill effects, the foul words he fished up from the cesspool in which he dips his pen, will be, by that very fact, shamed," Aurélien Scholl wrote in *Le Matin*. The most distinguished voice in this chorus of execration belonged to Anatole France, who had previously shown Zola great respect. The "Georgics of debauchery" is how he characterized *La Terre*. A misbegotten thing which should never have seen the light of day, it revealed Zola's disposition to exploit the public's appetite for obscene literature, he thought. Not only did he slander the peasant but, worse

---

[9]The piers of the Eiffel Tower had begun to rise in July 1887. Five months earlier, a letter signed by such academic eminences as Gérôme, Meissonier, and Bouguereau was sent to Alphand, minister of public works, denouncing the monstrosity. Conservatism joined battle with modernism in defense of a "stone" city, and those who had decried Haussmann's Paris as soullessly "cosmopolitan" now called Eiffel's tower the Tower of Babel:

Writers, painters, sculptors, architects, passionate lovers of the hitherto intact beauty of Paris, we come to protest with all our strength, with all our indignation, in the name of betrayed French taste, in the name of threatened French art and history, against the erection in the heart of our capital of the useless and monstrous Eiffel Tower, which the public has scornfully and rightly dubbed the Tower of Babel. Without being blind chauvinists, we have the right to proclaim publicly that Paris is without rival in the world. Along its streets and wide boulevards, beside its admirable riverbanks, amid its magnificent promenades, stand the most noble monuments to which human genius has ever given birth. The soul of France, the creator of masterpieces, shines from this august proliferation of stone. Italy, Germany, Flanders, so rightly proud of their artistic heritage, possess nothing comparable to ours, and Paris attracts curiosity and admiration from all corners of the Universe. Are we to let it be profaned?

still, he betrayed an inherently vulgar soul. "He has no taste," France proclaimed in *Le Temps* on August 28, "and I can't help wondering whether tastelessness isn't that mysterious sin of which Holy Writ speaks, the worst of sins, the only one that will not be pardoned."

Abroad the furor had more serious consequences. In England, *La Terre* was expurgated to make it minimally palatable but people took offense anyway, and a sanctimonious group that called itself the National Vigilance Association rose up against Zola's publisher, Henry Vizetelly, instigating legal action. Denounced in parliament by one Samuel Smith from Flintshire, who said of Zola's works that "the pen of man" had never written anything more "diabolical," Vizetelly found himself arraigned at Central Criminal Court by the Crown. The trial took place a year later, and although National Vigilants rejoiced when jurors returned a verdict of guilty, not until the court sentenced every novel of *Les Rougon-Macquart* to pariahdom would they judge their victory complete.[10] Vizetelly, who suffered bankruptcy, was fined on this occasion and seven months later, after a second trial, imprisoned for three months, at age seventy.

Of all the diatribes inspired by *La Terre*, the one that annoyed Zola most was an ad hominem attack on native ground that came to be known as the "Manifeste des Cinq," five young self-styled naturalists writing "at the behest of conscience," which *Le Figaro* published in all its unconscionable malice on August 18, 1887. Their disenchantment with Zola had begun ten years earlier, after the triumph of *L'Assommoir*, they averred.

> To the young it seemed that after leading the charge he backed away, like those revolutionary generals whose brains become the valets of their stomachs. We had hoped for something better than falling asleep on the battlefield; we awaited the sequel to that spirited thrust, we hoped that fiction and theater would be rejuvenated. . . . He, meanwhile, went on plowing his own furrow; he plowed ahead, tirelessly, and the young encouraged him with their bravos and their sympathy . . . ; he plowed ahead and the oldest and wisest among us closed their eyes, wanting to preserve their illusions, wanting not to see the Master bog down in muck. Certainly we reeled when he

[10]One of Vizetelly's sons, Ernest, noted: "The jury appeared to be of the usual petty-trading class. The prosecution was conducted by the Solicitor-General, then Sir Edward Clarke, who had already made a considerable reputation by certain cross-examinations, and who at a subsequent period defended the unhappy Oscar Wilde, when the latter was convicted of unnatural offences." Sir Edward asserted that *La Terre*, translated as *Soil*, was full of "bestial obscenity" and lacking "a spark of literary genius" or "the expression of an elevated thought." His mispronunciation of Zola's characters' names caused general hilarity among French newspaper correspondents covering the trial.

deserted us and emigrated to Médan, devoting such efforts as our organ of combat and solidarity would have required to satisfactions of an infinitely less aesthetic kind. No matter! Youth wanted to forgive the physical desertion of the man. But a far more serious desertion had already manifested itself: the writer's betrayal of his work.[11]

So said Paul Bonnetain, J.-H. Rosny, Lucien Descaves, Paul Margueritte, and Gustave Guiches. The five, who commanded little attention except at Goncourt's *Grenier*, where four of them regularly appeared, and at Daudet's house in Champrosay, proceeded to savage *Les Rougon-Macquart*. With every passing day Zola had done a little more to traduce his program.

Unbelievably lazy when it came to experimenting on *his own*, armed with trivial documentation gathered by third parties, full of Hugo-esque bombast which exasperated us all the more because he loudly preached simplicity, rehashing old material and tumbling into his personal clichés, he disconcerted even the most enthusiastic among his disciples. Acuteness of mind was not needed, furthermore, to recognize the fatuity of this so-called "histoire naturelle et sociale d'une famille sous le Second Empire," the tenuousness of the hereditary line, the childishness of the famous genealogical tree, the profound ignorance, both medical and scientific, of the Master. Still, we refused, even in private, to admit straightforwardly our mistaken judgment.

Their illusions, by whatever means they buttressed them, could not finally withstand evidence demonstrating that filth in *Les Rougon-Macquart* was an expression of Zola's appetite for lucre and of his personal psychopathology rather than the unavoidable consequence of a literary agenda.

It is quite true that Zola seems excessively preoccupied (and those of us who have heard him chat can vouch for it) with book sales. But it is also a matter of common knowledge that earlier in life he lived apart and practiced abstinence, at first out of necessity, then on principle. Penniless and shy during his youth, he did not lose his virginity at the appropriate age, whence the distorted vision of womankind that haunts him today. Then there is his renal disorder, which undoubtedly leads him to worry excessively about certain functions and to inflate their importance.

[11]The "organ of combat" is probably a reference to the short-lived *Comédie humaine,* founded by Huysmans in 1880.

Such misgivings as they entertained had been validated by *La Terre*, which they took to be a travesty of literary naturalism.

> We repudiate these creatures of Zolistic rhetoric, these huge, misshapen silhouettes devoid of complexity, which have been plopped down in milieux studied through the windows of a passing train. From this latest product of the great mind that gave us *L'Assommoir*, from this bastard *Terre*, we resolutely distance ourselves, not without sadness. It hurts us to rebuff the man whom we loved too well. . . . We would have waited longer still, . . . but we are convinced that Zola has touched bottom after a series of falls, that *La Terre* shows a chaste man becoming irremediably depraved.

It was Art that compelled them to denounce this imposture, not some personal animus. They would have kept quiet if it had only been a matter of Zola's talent decaying, they wrote in conclusion. "But that decadence compromises us, and some compromises are impossible. The naturalist label automatically attached to any book that draws upon reality can no longer suit us."

The indictment provided Paris with summer entertainment. Rumors flew thick and people in the know generally assumed that the "five" had hoped to ingratiate themselves with Goncourt and Daudet, at whose homes a favorite parlor game was ridiculing Zola. If so, they miscalculated, for by virtue of its ill will and pretentiousness, the article cast discredit upon their patrons as well as upon themselves. "What a singular adventure, singular even in the rough justice it has meted out," wrote Céard, who had urged Zola to keep quiet. "I've made inquiries, and your silence has produced bewilderment. They counted on you answering and also on your friends joining the fray. In the end, the whole thing has failed miserably, and those who hid behind the curtain have begun to squirm. They never suspected that the polemical center of attention might shift from the authors of the article to those who stand accused of having inspired it." As for who stood accused of having inspired it, different friends had different culprits. Huysmans leaned more toward Daudet, while Céard held Goncourt equally responsible.

Whatever Zola's own hunch may have been, he refrained, even in correspondence with Céard, from speaking plainly, as much perhaps to sharpen the point of an unspoken and therefore unanswerable accusation as to avoid a complete break. Not until October 13, almost two months after the Manifesto appeared, did he contact Goncourt, and on that occasion Goncourt found himself exonerated in the language of impeachment. "Only yesterday evening, mutual friends

(Alexis, Céard, Hennique) informed me of something quite astonishing," Zola wrote.

> It seems that you've accused me of identifying you as the one who deliberately inspired the imbecilic and scurrilous article published by *Le Figaro*. Do you think I'm stupid? The friendly thing would be to assume that I know how the article was written. I am convinced, I have repeated it everywhere, that if you had had foreknowledge of it, you would have prevented the publication, as much for your sake as for mine.

Expecting Goncourt to offer him some token of sympathy by way of apologizing for his disciples' "underhanded stunt," he had been reprimanded instead:

> If I've decided to write to you, it's because your situation is no longer clear and because dignity requires that we know how we stand as friends and confreres.

Called to account for the first time, Goncourt pleaded innocent and, furthermore, unburdened himself of a grudge he had nursed for two years, ever since Zola likened *Manette Salomon* to "a series of watercolors and etchings." Zola answered without delay, furnishing yet another scapegoat for yet another ceremony of reconciliation. He insisted that his letter of July 1885 in which the phrase appeared had not been meant for publication, and that it "implied nothing of the disdain you see in it." Did Goncourt feel that the phrase trivialized his "very large talent"? If so, Zola went on to say,

> the hundreds of pages I have written about you these past twenty years, pages that express unstinting devotion and admiration, should have weighed in your memory, and sufficed. . . . The problem with our friendship, my dear Goncourt, resides in an alleged rivalry which it pleases our enemies to excite. I have long hoped, I still hope, that they shall not succeed, for I know you to be a great gentleman with, at bottom, a tender heart.

In his journal, Goncourt derided this overture as pusillanimous, as "tortuously affectionate," as "the letter of a capon." But he felt disposed, for opportunistic reasons no doubt, to accept Zola's outstretched hand and on October 17 wrote: "I believe that we two must forget these little skirmishes and revive the brotherhood of times past." Some months later, in March 1888, a carefully choreographed rendezvous was arranged on neutral ground, over dinner at the Charpentiers'.

Zola also made peace with Alphonse Daudet, though ultimately to no avail. The "brotherhood of times past" had vanished forever, if it had ever truly existed. Between them—Zola on the one hand, Goncourt and Daudet on the other—lay an intellectual rift that became wider as the liberal or rational ideals by which Zola set store encountered mounting opposition, and nothing exposed it more ominously than their clash the year before over Edouard Drumont, the author of a long, vehemently anti-Semitic treatise entitled *La France juive*. Daudet reproached Zola for disparaging Drumont, whom he had befriended, encouraged, and recently seconded on the field of honor.[12] "Am I forbidden to judge freely a man who has, twenty times over, written about me without measure or dignity? Drumont is your friend, I know; but so am I, am I not?" Zola complained. "I don't remember having gone so far as to accuse him in your presence of 'working in latrines.' If I did, that's not the problem. The real problem is a growing misapprehension, an impossibility of speaking our minds candidly without wounding each other, a divergence of ideas that pulls us further and further apart."

La Terre quickly went through several dozen editions. It profited not only from the furor excited by the *Figaro* article but also from the turmoil of fin de siècle politics. Never had earth, French earth, been so saturated with religious feeling as at that moment. Zealous nationalists, many of whom regarded the economic plight of the peasant as one more manifestation of a Judeo-capitalist conspiracy against the Holy Land, spoke of crusades. For them, restoring France's sacred borders took precedence over everything, including the rule of law, and in 1887 they resolved, if the secular Republic could not be undone by other means, to march upon Paris.

[12]On April 24, 1886, Drumont fought a duel with the director of *Le Gaulois*, Arthur Meyer, whom he had besmirched in *La France juive*.

Several months later, Zola wrote to a distinguished lawyer from Odessa, Lev Kupernik: "You tell me that certain Russian papers claim that I collaborated with M. Drumont on *La France juive*, and you ask me if this is true. The statement is quite simply imbecilic. All my works bear witness against the possibility of my having contributed to a book whose form and philosophy, whose means and end are equally obnoxious to me."

XXII

ANOTHER DREAM

AFTER GENERAL MACMAHON'S resignation in 1879, the Gambettist republicans who took office had hastened to dismantle what architects of the Moral Order had built. They repealed, among much else, laws that maintained press censorship, that forbade public meetings without prior authorization, that restricted the activity of *colporteurs*, or book peddlers, that banned trade unions. No longer would police quarantine establishments in which subversion had been thought to breed, notably taverns and Masonic lodges. Nor would mayors find themselves peremptorily dismissed by antagonistic prefects. Between 1879 and 1887, almost every official measure helped to enlarge the sphere of democratic liberties, and this agenda, which profited Left rather more than Right, went hand in hand with the curbing of ecclesiastical influence. Hospitals were laicized. Crosses disappeared from courtrooms. Parliament passed a divorce law. Working on Sunday became legal again after sixty-five years. Cemeteries were thrown open to the dead of all denominations, and fraternal orders that sponsored nonreligious burial received support from the government. Above all, education was made compulsory, free, and secular. "When French youth will have . . . grown up under the aegis of compulsory, free, lay education," declared Jules Ferry, who would not rest until he had brought about a national community predicated upon positivist dogma, "there will be no need to fear incursions of the past, for we shall be defended by the spirit of these new generations, of these young, inexhaustible reserves of republican democracy, formed in the school of science and reason; they will halt obscurantism with the insurmountable barricade of free intelligences and liberated consciences." In March 1880, the Society of Jesus, at whose schools many conservative notables had studied, was ordered to dissolve itself within three months or be expelled by force. Two hundred magistrates resigned in protest, clearing the bench for men of anticlerical disposition.

Still, Ferry's brave new Republic remained a vulnerable creation. Arrayed against it were forces not quite strong enough to emerge victorious from battle, but strong enough to wreak havoc and even gather strength in defeat. One such defeat took place in 1882, with the crash of the Union Générale; another occurred eight years later, when General Georges Boulanger nearly attempted a coup d'état.

Chartered in 1875, the Union Générale was a commercial bank whose founders had made it known that they hoped to pool the financial resources of Catholics all over France and thus "constitute a power" rivaling Protestant and Jewish interests, which, they claimed, held the nation hostage. "The struggle against foes of their faith and their principles requires Catholics to oppose subversive doctrines that threaten Religion and Society," is how they advertised themselves. The enterprise received little notice until 1878, when new officers reorganized it, raised twenty-five million francs, opened a branch in Rome, and appointed an irrepressible gentleman named Eugène Bontoux chief executive officer. Bontoux had for some years shuttled between Lyon, where he wielded influence among Bourbon loyalists as well as important stockbrokers, and Vienna, where he directed a Rothschild-owned railroad—the Sudbahn, or South Austria–Lombardy Line. Although immensely rich by any other standard, this brilliant engineer measured wealth by the fortune of his employers, whom he came to resent bitterly. Three million francs (eight to ten million present-day dollars) did not satisfy Bontoux's imperial dreams. Part adventurer, part religious zealot, he saw in the moribund Austro-Hungarian Empire both a bulwark for European Catholics and an El Dorado for Western financiers. In 1861, soon after arriving in Vienna, he had declared that industrialization alone would save decrepit dynasties like the Hapsburg, that it behooved Austria to achieve the economic conquest of the Lower Danube and Black Sea basin. Since then he himself had shown the way, building a railway across northeastern Hungary, launching the Wiener Bankverein, forming a company to quarry slate, obtaining concessions to mine Styrian lignite. Larger projects—notably a railroad linking Vienna and Budapest with Salonika and Constantinople—waited upon further infusions of capital, and in this regard the Union Générale presented a golden opportunity. Bontoux was free to accept its directorship, having been dismissed by the Rothschilds in January 1878.

What the original founders of the Union Générale had envisioned three years earlier proved much easier to accomplish after Mac-Mahon's retirement. Thwarted politically, right-wing France sought from the stock exchange compensation for its losses at the ballot box, and disgruntled elements of the Church, the army, the magistrature, the would-be monarchy flocked around Bontoux. His visionary talk apparently won over the pretender himself, Henri, Comte de Chambord, whom he often visited in Frohsdorf, outside Vienna. "With the king, Bontoux discussed his financial plans at length, and showed him the enormous power of money," according to a police report. "Won over by his conviction and enthusiasm, the king offered him his support and that of his loyal entourage." Blessings may also have come from the Vatican, whose material well-being Bontoux promised to secure through portfolios called "The Treasure of Saint Peter" and "The Treasure of Catholic Charity." Among Union Générale stockholders, ecclesiastical potentates—including Cardinal Jacobini, secretary to Pope Leo XIII—outnumbered aristocrats. And where bishops led, priests followed. Indeed, news quickly spread all over eastern France, from parish to parish, that buying Union Générale was not only a miraculous investment but a pious act. "Gambling fever affected two social classes that one would not have thought vulnerable to such temptations," Le Temps declared on February 8, 1882. "On the one hand there were historical names, representatives of the ruling classes, a whole aristocracy swept up by expectations at once religious and pecuniary that hurled itself blindly into a financial adventure even more compromising than the unfortunate political move of May 16. On the other hand one saw normally cautious people seduced and reassured by these lofty examples: merchants, workers, employees, country priests, elderly maiden dames, widowed ladies of independent means, peasants." The combination of lucre and virtue induced many Catholic charities and boarding schools to entrust Bontoux with their liquid assets.

When Bontoux initiated this venture, France was emerging from a five-year slump. Industry had begun to make great strides, with colonies requiring goods, the internal transportation network expanding, and the republican government commissioning public works on a scale reminiscent of the Second Empire; and financial markets kept pace. Banks proliferated in 1878, the year of the Universal Exposition, but few enjoyed anything remotely like the success of the Union Générale as Bontoux announced one coup after another. At Vienna the Union Générale's subsidiary, the Landerbank, was accorded special favor by Count Taaffe, an archreactionary, anti-Semitic prime minister eager to divorce Austria from the Rothschild consortium. Taaffe had Bontoux's group float state loans and broker major state purchases. Bontoux's group also organized the syndicate that gained control of southern Austria's large coal reserves, merging eight metallurgical companies into one powerful firm, and then went on to orchestrate the development of similar enterprises in Hungary. With strong support from Taaffe, whose Balkan policy he served, Bontoux won a lucrative contract to build 365 kilometers of railroad across Serbia. This multifarious activity was more than French exchanges could handle. New securities engorged the market, producing a frenzy of speculation. Prices spiraled upward and by January 1882, just before the crash, Union Générale stock had risen sixfold in value.

The enterprise crumbled virtually overnight. Quoted at 3,005 on January 4, it fell 1,700 points in a fortnight, despite desperate and illegal measures to shore it up. One month later, the Union Générale was bankrupt and Bontoux was imprisoned. What had triggered the catastrophe? Bontoux himself bore a heavy responsibility, with his rampage of acquisitions, his financial legerdemain, his feverish salesmanship. Profit taking led to panic selling when several large banks decided to restrict credit. But Bontoux maintained that he had been the victim of a plot, that financiers, mainly Jewish, whom he had outfoxed in Central Europe, had brought down the Union Générale by conspiring to sell short. Many ruined shareholders, big and little, believed him. Still convinced of his evangelical mission, they joined him in his martyrdom, blaming the Jews, blaming Germany, blaming the Republic. "This enterprise was the creation of specific political and social groups," writes one historian. "Removed from high office, conservative muck-a-mucks were unable, five years after their electoral defeat, to avenge themselves on the battlefield of big business. The Union Générale's disintegration must be understood as an episode in the history of those who had held sway until May 1877—along with the flag imbroglio [i.e., white lilies versus tricolor], the Moral Order, Boulanger, the Dreyfus Affair. Hence the persistent rancor of those groups, the ongoing dispute over the crash, the cultic reverence accorded Bontoux right into the twentieth century."

No less repellent to Bontoux's constituency than the secularization that anchored republican government after 1880 was a foreign policy that scattered French soldiers hither and yon. In North Africa the French army invaded Tunisia, defeated Muslim fanatics at Sfax, and on May 12, 1881, compelled the bey to accept French dominion. In Southeast Asia, where France had made her presence felt since the eighteenth century, war against the combined forces of China and Annam led to the creation of a French protectorate over Cambodia, Cochin China, Annam, and Tonkin. In 1883 the stage was set for yet another occupation when French ships bombarded the port of Tamatave on Madagascar's east coast. And during the 1880s military thrusts along the upper Niger garnered territory eight times larger than the homeland. This global bullying found its most ardent supporter in Jules Ferry, who invoked France's civilizing mission even as he spoke about capitalist imperatives. "The Republican party has shown how well it understands that a political ideal like that of free Belgium and republican Switzerland would not suit France," he declared in parliament, "that France needs something else: that she cannot be only a free country, that she must also be a great country, wielding over the destinies of Europe all the influence that belongs to her, that she must spread this influence throughout the world and carry wherever she can her language, her customs, her flag, her arms, her genius."

But conservatives, whose patriotic pride did not extend much beyond Alsace-Lorraine, decried colonialism as an impious distraction from the crusade to recover France's eastern provinces, and radical republicans, with Clemenceau in the lead, echoed this protest. They let no one forget that in 1871 Communards had staunchly rejected the treaty by which those provinces had been surrendered. Now, they believed, Ferry et al. were not only playing Bismarck's game but wasting resources better spent at home, where, after the stock market crash, hard times prevailed: *revanchisme* went hand in hand with concern for the hundreds of thousands bereft of their livelihoods in a much diminished economy. All of Europe and England had been plunged into a depression after 1881, and to make matters worse in France, phylloxera ravaged her vineyards. "While you wander lost in your colonial dream," Clemenceau reproached Ferry, "at your feet sit supplicants, Frenchmen, who demand useful expenditures that will advance the development of French genius and will, by increasing cost-efficient production, open those touted markets you seal shut with your military expeditions." On March 30, 1885, a coalition of extremes brought down Ferry. In the election that followed, popular discontent threatened to give conservatives a majority until on the second ballot radical republicans, dissociating themselves from the Right, made common cause with other, more moderate republican parties. To repay this gesture, Charles de Freycinet, who became prime minister in January 1886, appointed as minister of war Clemenceau's nominee, General Georges Boulanger. It proved to be a fateful decision.

Army brass seldom hobnobbed with radical republicans, but then, Georges Boulanger was not typical of his kind. Four years older than Clemenceau, whom he had known since they were both students at a provincial *lycée*, Boulanger graduated from the Saint-Cyr military academy and under Napoleon III gained distinction for bravery on battlefields in Algeria, in Italy, in Cochin China. By 1870 he had collected five wounds and four promotions. A sixth wound, this one suffered in Paris during the Prussian siege, earned him a colonelcy. There matters stood throughout the 1870s. While serving as chief inspector of infantry, the handsome blond warrior, who was much addicted to riding about on stallions and chasing women, diligently cultivated notables of every political persuasion. Clemenceau befriended him, despite the fact that he had helped slaughter Communards in May 1871, but so did Louis Philippe's son Henri d'Orléans, the Duke d'Aumale. A born opportunist, Boulanger arranged to lean increasingly leftward as the Republic became increasingly republican, and promotions followed. Given command in 1884 of the expeditionary force that had overrun Tunisia, the general took advantage of the position to toot his horn, organizing gorgeous cavalcades across the desert, making public appearances with a spahi guard, delivering chauvinistic harangues, and working up the French military against Italian residents. Revered by conscripts (if not by fellow officers, many of whom found his bravura objectionable), Boulanger grew accustomed to hearing himself hailed as *not' brav' général.*

Clemenceau had had in mind a war minister capable of republicanizing the army, and the measures which Boulanger took, proposed, or endorsed during his fifteen-month tenure were designed to accomplish that end. He demanded that compulsory military service last three years rather than five but that three-year service be universal (until then student priests received automatic exemptions and fifteen hundred francs could buy anyone an abbreviated term). He stood foursquare behind a law forbidding members of former ruling families to enter the army or exercise any public function, and he expelled the very man whose sponsorship had helped him achieve high rank, General Henri d'Orléans. While officers imprudent enough to voice royalist sentiments suffered banishment, ordinary foot soldiers could thank Boulanger that they were sleeping on mattresses instead of straw pallets, eating off plates instead of mess tins, obtaining work furloughs during the harvest season, sporting beards with impunity, wearing more comfortable uniforms, and shooting better guns.

Although these substantive reforms endeared Boulanger to millions, what made him the popular idol he became was his gift for theater. A pivotal bit of self-display occurred on Bastille Day 1886. Boulanger had insisted that the traditional review include troops repatriated from Indochina, and at dawn Parisians began to swarm toward the Longchamp hippodrome. Every flag brought cheers as regiment after regiment marched past, but the crowd went positively berserk when Boulanger, riding a black roan, saluted President Jules Grévy with his sword. Escorted by three hundred cavalry officers and wearing his plumed two-cornered hat at a rakish angle, the bemedaled minister stole the show. *"Vive Boulanger!"* drowned out *"Vive la République!"* Several hours later, on the stage of the Alcazar, a popular musical-hall singer named Paulus glorified the occasion in lyrics that traveled all over France, *En revenant de la revue:*

> Gais et contents,
> Nous étions triomphants
> En allant à Longchamp,
> Le coeur à l'aise,
> Sans hésiter,
> Car nous allions fêter,
> Voir et complimenter
> L'armée française. . . .
> Moi j'faisais qu'admirer
> Not' brav' général Boulanger.[1]

Boulangism, as such hero worship came to be known, soon acquired other highly effective propagators. There was, for one, Henri Rochefort, now a rabid *revanchard*, who regularly lauded Boulanger at the expense of moderate republican legislators. There was, for another, Paul Déroulède, who led a militantly nationalistic organization called the Ligue des Patriotes, and who spent his breath vituperating against Germany in collections of verse, in speeches, and in his paper *Le Drapeau,* which reached more than two hundred thousand subscribers nationwide. Déroulède, whose talks with Boulanger would not have reassured supporters of parliamentary democracy, considered the general a providential figure.

Neither Paulus nor Rochefort nor Déroulède did more to consecrate Boulanger's reputation as France's avenging angel, however, than Otto von Bismarck. Mindful of warmongers who had made "the blue line of the Vosges" (that is, the mountainous profile of Alsace-Lorraine) the rallying cry for a crusade, the German chancellor wanted to put another seventy thousand men under arms. "In France there exist men who seek war against Germany and whose task is to fan the sacred flame of Revenge," he told a reluctant Reichstag on January 11, 1887. "Any day a French government may come to power with the express purpose of setting us ablaze. . . . Napoleon III launched the 1870 campaign to strengthen his domestic position, why would an empowered General Boulanger not do likewise?" Bismarck's additional troops were meant to match the seventy thousand reservists Boulanger had planned, for no good reason, to mobilize. When sober minds prevailed, canceling those plans by way of appeasing Bismarck, *revanchards* felt

---

[1]"Coming Home from the Review": "Gay and happy, we felt triumphant going to Longchamp, hearts at ease, without hesitation, for we were going to celebrate, to see and compliment the French army. . . . As for me, I was filled with admiration for our brave General Boulanger."

more certain than ever that the general was their man. Surrounded by opportunists, only he could restore French honor. Disarmed by cowards, only he intimidated the archenemy. Did they need further demonstrations of *cran*, or pluck? Boulanger gave them one in April 1887, when a commissioner of border police at Pagny-sur-Moselle found himself arrested after crossing into Lorraine. Had President Grévy heeded Boulanger, troops would have been mobilized overnight and ultimatums dispatched by wire. Instead, the cautious president, who wanted no casus belli, sent a legal brief complete with supporting documents, which persuaded Bismarck to dismiss charges against the alleged spy. Diplomacy proved more effective than saber rattling, but no matter. Boulangists ascribed this small victory to the general's derring-do. "His popularity was thenceforth based upon the absurd legend that he had made the chancellor retreat," observed Adrien Dansette. "For the first time since 1870 France enjoyed a foretaste of victory.... The previous year the war minister had swept away the pessimism of defeat like the sun bursting through clouds; now he satisfied national pride and promised a glorious future." In a popular song that included the lines

> D'un éclair de ton sabre, éveille l'aube blanche,
> A nos jeunes drapeaux, viens montrer le chemin
> Pour marcher vers le Rhin, pour marcher vers le Rhin.[2]

Boulanger was promoted from *not' brav' général* to *Général Revanche* —General Revenge.

Except for the Radical group, parties right and left looked upon Boulanger as a loose cannon on the deck, and even Clemenceau, who contemptuously nicknamed him "Boulboul," drew back from his former protégé. It was therefore decided in May 1887 to form a new cabinet with someone more manageable presiding over the war ministry. It was further decided to remove Boulanger from Paris, where the hero cult that had grown up around him propagated itself in almanacs, popular images, pamphlets, medals, songs. His successor, General Ferron, appointed him commander of the 13th Army Corps, headquartered at Clermont-Ferrand, and on July 8 he left amidst clamorous demonstrations, the Parisian populace having been rallied by Rochefort and Déroulède. A large crowd hailed Boulanger when he emerged from his hotel on the Place du Palais-Royal, opposite the Comédie-Française. A very much larger crowd awaited him in front of the Gare de Lyon and made it all but impossible for him to depart. Thousands sang *La Marseillaise*. Thousands more swarmed through

[2]"With a glint of your saber, awaken the white dawn to our young flags, come show us which way to march toward the Rhine, to march toward the Rhine."

the station, climbing lampposts, boarding his train, blocking the tracks, lying on the rails "like ecstatic Hindus," festooning the locomotive with posters that read: *Il reviendra*. Not until 10 p.m. did they finally disperse, in semi-darkness.

Although Boulanger lay low at first, a scandal of major proportions promoted the cause of Boulangism. In September police learned that official decorations—notably the Legion of Honor—were being sold for large sums by a ring that included a general, a senator, and, above all, President Jules Grévy's son-in-law, Daniel Wilson, who lived at the Elysée Palace. Under intense pressure from legislators, none of whom agreed to serve as prime minister when the government fell, Grévy resigned. It was hoped—on the liberal Left, at any rate—that this expiatory gesture would set matters right, but it did not. Everyone who wanted some pretext for besmirching the Republic found it here, and a wave of antiparliamentarianism swept across France. "The same brush that tarred deputy Wilson . . . tarred his fellow deputies, more or less without exception," writes one historian.

> Workers whose existences had become increasingly monotonous as a result of mass production, artisans reduced to wage earning, small merchants ruined by department stores, manufacturers unhappy with the importation of German products, landowners and farmers badly hurt by the decline in agricultural prices, . . . people wiped out in the crash of the Union Générale, disgruntled intellectuals, revolutionaries nostalgic for the barricades, patriots starved for national grandeur, Catholics unable to accept religion being banished from schools—in short, all who had seen their interests compromised or their ideals assailed made common cause against what they believed to be the rotten cause of everything that ailed them: Parliament.

These motley plaintiffs made it known as best they could that for them salvation wore a plumed, two-cornered hat. In a by-election held on May 22, 1887—even before the honors scandal erupted—thirty-nine thousand voters entered Boulanger's name, spurning the official list. When another by-election was held nine months later Boulanger received fifty-five thousand votes. Soon afterward, in February 1888, there appeared a self-proclaimed "Boulangist organ," *La Cocarde*, which summarized its demand for fundamental reform by a Constituent Assembly in the slogan "*Dissolution, Révision, Constituante.*"

Meanwhile, Boulanger himself entertained in secret political suitors bent on negotiating a marriage of convenience. No sooner had Clemenceau denounced him than monarchists sought him out, and first of all Armand Baron de Mackau, who represented the parliamentary "Union des Droites," or coalition of right-wing parties. What Mackau proposed was that if some future prime minister reappointed him war minister, Boulanger should effect a coup d'état, then have Frenchmen choose by plebiscite between an Orleanist monarchy and an "authoritarian Republic." Boulanger agreed, in exchange for promises of moral and financial support. Each felt that he could divorce the other when power had been won, but neither may have believed deep down that fate would call upon him to either honor or violate his troth. The conspiracy, which involved disguises and clandestine messengers, seemed more like opera than real life until something happened to make it very real indeed. On March 17, 1888, the government, distressed by the enthusiasm for Boulanger shown at the polls, forced him into early retirement, citing unauthorized absences from duty. It was hoped, no doubt, that his charisma would disappear along with his uniform.

The ex-general's political career began less than a fortnight later, triumphantly. As multiple candidacies were still legal, Boulanger ran for the Chamber of Deputies in two provincial by-elections and won them both by large margins. To many this brought joy, to many others consternation. "Exercised over politics and worried about the future, Paris wants only to forget itself at vaudevilles," complained Zola, who held Boulanger responsible for the failure of the stage adaptation of *Germinal.* "The point is, people needn't seek mayhem at the Châtelet Theater; it's all around them, on the street." Mayhem also reigned at the Palais-Bourbon during that summer of 1888, when Boulanger twice mounted the tribune to demand dissolution and constitutional reform. Upbraided by republican deputies—with one of whom, a sexagenarian lawyer named Charles Floquet, he fought and lost a duel—Boulanger returned blow for blow, deriding "negative programs," random majorities, jejune personnel, the moldering Chamber. To underscore his nationwide appeal through a plebiscitary maneuver, he resigned his seat and contested vacancies all over France, mostly with success. This campaign was financed by a "Comité Républicain de Protestation Nationale," or "Comité Boulangiste," which had received the fabulous sum of three million francs from the Duchesse d'Uzès.

Like Eugène Bontoux, Boulanger fell as quickly as he had risen, crushing the legions who had vested in him their hopes for a better day. It all began in January 1889. A seat from Paris was at stake, and with characteristic nerve Boulanger decided to join the fray. "One noticed early along that workers and clerks did not constitute an oppositional block, far from it," writes the historian Jacques Chastenet. "What prevailed in most of them were patriotic fervor, the desire to avenge themselves for the repression of the Commune, hatred of moderate republican deputies and the selfish bourgeoisie whose interests they protected. . . . At public meetings one saw elegant young men sporting red carnations à la Boulanger interspersed among workers wearing smocks and visored caps." On January 27, after a month of electoral hoopla, voters chose the general over the prosaic industrialist whom all Republican factions had endorsed. Paris went wild, with festive crowds invading the boulevards and gathering thick on the Place de la Madeleine, where Boulanger received news of his victory at Durand's restaurant. Had he marched upon the Elysée, as Déroulède advised him to do, hundreds of thousands would have marched behind him. Indeed, Republican leaders expected a coup d'état during the night, but Boulanger demurred, saying that there was no reason to conquer by illegal means what France would award him in six months. Had soldierly discipline spoken louder than ambition? Or had it been borne in on him at this decisive moment that he lacked the qualities needed to hold dictatorial sway over a great nation? "If you want my impression of the general, I shall tell you that he makes me doubt history," wrote Madame Arman de Caillavet, Anatole France's Egeria, who on one occasion had staged a dinner party in Boulanger's honor. "I wonder if all the great figures who seem so imposing from afar are not just feathers and faddishness." To Zola he was "un bicorne sur un pieu"—a two-cornered hat mounted on a stick.

While Boulanger reveled in the homage of aristocratic clans and the consideration of foreign dignitaries, the government launched a counteroffensive. First it trumped up charges against Paul Déroulède and other leaders of the Ligue des Patriotes. Then it spread the rumor that plans were afoot to try Boulanger for "endangering the security of the state." The government would not in fact have welcomed a public confrontation, but Boulanger spared it the embarrassment. Unstrung by the prospect of banishment to New Caledonia or sequestration in some prison fortress, he fled with his beloved mistress, Marguerite Bronzet, Viscountess de Bonnemains. Thereafter nothing could make him return—neither the entreaties of true believers, nor the mockery of foes, nor the trial at which he was convicted in absentia, nor a September election in which Paris's eighteenth arrondissement gave him more votes than the Republican candidate.

Except that Belgium declared him unwelcome because of political activity, his brave manifestos had little effect on the world stage. Coming from abroad, they rang increasingly hollow to Frenchmen, and by 1890 Boulangism was a lifeless movement. Boulanger himself did not long survive it. Uxoriously devoted to Madame de Bonnemains, who supported him during their exile, he was shattered when she died of tuberculosis. "I cry like a child and that's all. I can't do anything, I can't work, I can't think. I would never have believed it possible to live this way, with one's heart broken. Ah! if only there were a battle somewhere, a war, I would enlist straightway! And what terrifies me is that each day increases my pain, makes it worse, harder to overcome." Two and a half months later, on September 30, 1891, he sat down on her gravestone and put a bullet through his head.

His suicide, which many treated as a posthumous event, did not educate the passions that had invented Boulangism. If anything, disappointment made those passions blinder, and so France, whipped on by a jingoist press, entered the last decade of the century still spoiling for glory or redemption. What had led people to credit a false messiah named Boulanger would lead them anon to vilify a scapegoat named Alfred Dreyfus.

On April 16, 1889, a fortnight after Boulanger's sudden evaporation, Zola declared that freedom of the press was a mixed blessing inasmuch as journalists used it to sensationalize the banal and inflate the trivial, keeping people's nerves on edge. There were better plots between book covers than those fabricated every day in *Le Figaro* or *La Lanterne*. "If our parliaments are unpopular, it's because we are told too much about them, because there's too much noise made over too little substance. If tomorrow we embraced some dictator, an ardent desire to lie down, to blow out the candle and sleep without care would be the main impetus." Apart from this irascible observation, his correspondence—what remains of it—never alludes to Boulanger. It shows him, rather, cultivating his own garden, or expanding his own estate, materially and intellectually.

As the Zolas' collection of antique paraphernalia grew along with their income, cluttering the rue de Boulogne, more space became necessary. Disinclined to leave the immediate neighborhood, which was home for them during the winter, they found what they wanted two blocks away on the rue de Bruxelles and in mid-September 1889 began an evacuation that lasted two months. For six thousand francs a year, M. Dupont-Auberville, deputy director of the Angers stud farms, rented them half his double town house at number 21 bis.[3] They would occupy three floors, with servants' quarters under the eaves, a vestibule, kitchen, and laundry on ground level, and an ornate staircase leading to the equally ornate rooms of a spacious bourgeois apartment. Zola had Henri Baboneau design windows throughout and install some fourteenth-century stained glass. His study, where painted panels featured monks and saints, adjoined the salon.

Although, until the move to the rue de Bruxelles at least, Zola wrote

[3]At this point Zola's annual income from all sources is estimated to have been between eighty and one hundred thousand francs. By way of comparison, the president of the Anzin Coal Company earned forty thousand francs.

his novels largely at Médan rather than in Paris, adaptations of *Les Rougon-Macquart* gave him a stake in almost every theater season. In February 1886, the Bouffes du Nord and the Châtelet staged revivals of *Nana* and *L'Assommoir*. On February 18, 1887, a group of distinguished actors bound by a common desire to stage good old-fashioned drama—*drame populaire*, as they put it—launched *Le Ventre de Paris*. Before it finished a long, successful run, the Théâtre du Vaudeville began production of *Renée*, which Zola himself had adapted from *La Curée* at Sarah Bernhardt's request seven years earlier. Next came *Germinal*. When the government of René Goblet fell, Busnach lost no time pleading the case against censorship to a new minister of public instruction, and in April 1888, after some minor changes had been deemed sufficient to safeguard public order, the curtain at the Châtelet rose on the first of seventeen performances of *Germinal*. Despite his ambivalence about plays that relied on gimmicks or spectacular decor or technical wizardry, Zola took it all quite seriously. Did his compromising on these elaborate productions help him cultivate an audience for the serious theater? He thought it did. Did it not also bring substantial material rewards? *Le Ventre* earned him as much as twenty or thirty thousand francs. Cueing Busnach, sending tickets to the claque, attending rehearsals, hectoring slipshod directors, making his presence felt at premieres, and engaging in polemical fisticuffs with critics—notably Francisque Sarcey, who dismissed these adaptations as tripe—he defied his own misgivings.

Artistically, Zola's role in Paris theater would have remained nominal if not for the advent of an extraordinary young actor-director named André Antoine, who on March 30, 1887, produced without fanfare a one-act play inspired by the Zola novella *Jacques Damour*.

Antoine sprang from total obscurity. Born in 1858, he left school at the age of thirteen, to support his impoverished family in the aftermath of war, and since 1871 he had led a laborious life, with five years out for military service. Working first as an errand boy, then as a clerk at the publishing house of Firmin-Didot, and finally as a minor functionary at the Paris Gas Company, he foraged for intellectual nourishment whenever possible. There was much browsing through museums and at bookstalls along the Seine. There were evenings spent in the Bibliothèque Sainte-Geneviève and at public lectures, notably those given by Hippolyte Taine on the history of art. Most important for this zealous autodidact, who did not see Molière or Racine performed until late adolescence, there was the theater. Theater came to fascinate him. Not only did he haunt the Comédie-Française but, after taking lessons in elocution, he auditioned, unsuccessfully, for the Conservatoire des Arts Dramatiques. His enthusiasm survived the rebuff, which turned out to be providential, and found an outlet before long in one of the amateur dramatic societies that abounded in fin de siècle Paris. "A fellow office worker belonged to a group, the Cercle Gaulois, that gave little dramatic presentations every month for relatives and friends," he wrote years later. "Out of curiosity I attended one such modest presentation held in a little room in the passage de l'Elysée-des-Beaux-Arts, at the foot of a stairway from the rue des Abbesses." As soon as he joined, the director in him became manifest. Prevailing upon other members, whose taste was for fusty little dramas of the Eugène Scribe variety, to modernize their repertoire, he also maintained against lively opposition that the Cercle Gaulois would attract notice by offering hospitality to unpublished playwrights. In this matter, too, he prevailed, and once his plan was adopted, everyone became a talent scout. "But," he wrote,

> pent up all day long at the Gas Company, lacking connections, how could I reach these rare birds? The first was captured for me by a friend acquainted with my ambitious program. Arthur Byl sent me a one-act play which was rather formless and ingenuously violent but at all events unpublished and, above all, ours for the asking. Several days later, Byl brought along Jules Vidal, a man with a volume to his credit, who frequented the famous Goncourt garret at Auteuil, and who spoke of getting us together with Paul Alexis. . . . The mere prospect made me feverish. In due course I met Zola's friend, who offered me a one-act comedy by Duranty. Taken together with Byl's *Un Sous-Préfet* and Vidal's *La Cocarde*, I had enough for a full evening.

His head was sent spinning when Paul Alexis told him that Léon Hennique was inclined to give him a one-act play adapted from a story by Zola. The name Zola on his program, he realized, might attract the omnipotent critic Francisque Sarcey.

In fact, Sarcey did not witness the inauguration of what soon established itself, under the name Théâtre Libre, as France's foremost private repertory theater. But several prominent critics showed up, and sitting in the audience beside them were Zola, Alphonse Daudet, and Stéphane Mallarmé. "A singular place is Paris," wrote Henry Fouquier of *Le Figaro*, who praised Antoine, "a place fraught with surprises where, in the most obscure neighborhood, behind some half-opened door, you may discover one of those mysterious gleams, one of those lamps lit by a toiler or madman, that give rise to dawns or conflagrations. Last night I saw such a lamp."

In November 1887 the Théâtre Libre left Montmartre to perform one Friday a month at the twelve-hundred-seat Théâtre Montparnasse (which subscribers filled for Tolstoy's *Power of Darkness*) and in October 1888 it reappeared on the Right Bank, at 96, rue Blanche, very near the rue de Bruxelles. Wherever it went, a faithful clientele followed, applauding programs imbued with literary realism.[4] Among Antoine's several house gods, Zola unquestionably ranked highest. Not that Zola hogged the stage; the only original play of his ever performed at the Théâtre Libre, *Madeleine*, had been written decades earlier.[5] But Antoine came to depend upon him for friendship, for moral support, for sound advice; and, as the reverent young director's memoirs indicate, Zola responded generously. "I dined this evening with Paul Alexis at Zola's place on the rue Ballu [rue de Boulogne], a small flat the simplicity of which astonished me," he noted.

> The master complained about it, however, and wants to move. His pleasant, cordial wife served us an excellent meal: I was clearly among people who knew and appreciated fine food. After dinner we removed to the study, Zola opened a box of cigars with a key he carried on his person, then sat discoursing by the fireplace, legs crossed, while I followed the movements of his delicate, mobile, astonishingly expressive hands. In connection with *Madeleine*, an unpublished play he plans to give me, he related anecdotes from his years at Hachette. Then he showed us to the door, and as we donned hats and coats in the hallway, he said to his wife: "Very good. Success has not spoiled him, he has not changed his overcoat."

Antoine's eclectic tendencies were frowned upon by Henry Bauer, a drama critic who crusaded for naturalism in *L'Echo de Paris*, and Antoine compared this zealot with the equable "master," who did not expect him to toe an ideological line:

> In his column this morning, Henry Bauer, who otherwise wrote about us so warmly, finished by declaring: "If he wishes to continue to prosper, the Théâtre Libre will be naturalistic or it will not be at all." I disagree completely. I believe that too parochial a formula spells death, and that we should, on the contrary, welcome various creeds. . . . It's a ticklish situation. I must steer a middle course [between militant naturalism and poetic drama], between Bauer, who growls

[4]The Théâtre Libre was a subscription theater and therefore exempt from censorship, which was still quite strict.
[5]*Madeleine* had been gathering dust since 1865. Rejected by two theater managers, this three-act play was subsequently turned into the novel *Madeleine Férat*. "It would not be without interest for critics and the public to attend this exhumation of a work of youth, if only in order to measure the distance that separates the beginner from the mature artist," Zola reportedly told Antoine. "The one condition is that there be only one performance and that only the press and a few select *amateurs* be invited. Something like a literary experiment." Zola made a virtue of his inability to throw anything away.

when disregarded, and Catulle Mendès, who's more clever and devious but no less dangerous. Zola, who knows the enormous influence he could exercise on me, is always careful to avoid interfering,
and just now, though I'm surrounded by men and writers of stature,
he's the only one I feel to be great and clairvoyant.

Sound advice came on many occasions, in tête-à-têtes, at weeknight
gatherings of the inner circle, or at the Charpentiers' Friday soirées.
   Zola's inability to create great drama did not prevent him from recognizing dramatic genius in others, and when toward the end of May
1888 he urged upon Antoine an obscure Norwegian playwright named
Henrik Ibsen, his discovery atoned for the masterpiece he himself
could not furnish. "I have taken the liberty of giving your address to
M. Louis de Hessem, who is translating *Ghosts*, the Ibsen play we
discussed," he informed Antoine. "I believe that among literate spectators this play will excite quite as much interest as *The Power of
Darkness*, even if its effect is less resounding." Antoine heeded him.
In May 1890, the Théâtre Libre, after long delays for retranslation,
finally staged *Ghosts*, creating an enormous stir among those who
packed its new hall (the former Théâtre des Menus Plaisirs on the
Boulevard de Strasbourg). One year later, in April 1891, fashionable
Paris, which had not yet digested Ibsen's drama of tainted heredity,
reconvened on the Boulevard de Strasbourg to see *The Wild Duck*.
   What with mandatory appearances at the Théâtre Libre almost
every month, Zola's social life became rather more active than in previous years, but this activity did not impede *Les Rougon-Macquart*. It
seemed, on the contrary, to speed it along, for between 1887 and 1890
the saga grew longer by two installments, one entitled *Le Rêve* and
the other *La Bête humaine*.

Zola may have compelled individual characters to exemplify the dictum that heredity is destiny, but *Les Rougon-Macquart* as a whole was
shaped in part by his need to remain unpredictable, to take the reader
unawares. Twice before—with *Une Page d'amour* and *L'Oeuvre*—
quiet dramas followed loud, capacious, densely populated spectacles,
and thus it was with *Le Rêve* following *La Terre*. After the vastness of
the Beauce, which has no room for love, his imagination retreated to
a cloistered garden where love overflows, and dwelled upon the Rousseauian fairy tale that had become France's most widely read children's
story, *Paul et Virginie*. "I'd like to produce a book no one expects of
me," he wrote at the beginning of his Sketch.

   A fundamental condition is that it will be fit for everybody, even
   young girls. Hence, no violent passion, only an ideal. People say that

success awaits the author who remakes *Paul et Virginie*. So let's remake *Paul et Virginie*. On the other hand, people say that my work lacks psychology. So let the book contain psychology, or what passes for such, that is, the eternal struggle between passion and duty, or another conflict. . . . I would like the book to be informed with something of the beyond, of the dream world, . . . the unknown, the unknowable.

A year or so later, defending himself against accusations of opportunism, he told one correspondent that his intention had always been to write a novel about the *au-delà*, to give *La Faute de l'abbé Mouret* a spiritual companion in *Les Rougon-Macquart*. "Rest assured that nothing is unforeseen. *Le Rêve* arrived at its appointed hour, like the other episodes."

Scenes of hapless, destitute females teetering on the edge are among the most poignant Zola ever wrote, and *Le Rêve* begins with one. On Christmas Day 1860, in the episcopal town of Beaumont, where snow has fallen thick, a couple named Hubert and Hubertine awaken to discover an ill-clad little girl huddled on the porch of the cathedral opposite their house. They rescue her, then piece together her brief, sad story. Abandoned at birth, nine-year-old Angélique had been well treated by successive foster parents until the last, two besotted monsters from whom she fled after suffering cruel punishment. Her refuge under the arch of a tympanum that depicts the life of Saint Agnes is providential. Hubertine, who cannot conceive, yearns for a child, and in due course the couple adopt this waif. Angélique will never learn what Zola informs the reader, that her natural mother is Sidonie Rougon, a disreputable daughter of Félicité (previously encountered in *La Curée*).

In a house his forebears built four centuries ago, Hubert embroiders liturgical vestments, practicing a métier to which every generation of the family has been bred. For him as well as for Hubertine, twelfth-century Picardy seems more real than nineteenth-century France, and so will they have it be for Angélique. Determined to fend off not only the world outside Beaumont's walled medieval quarter but also the "vicious" or "tainted" self that lurks below, they become her beneficent warders. "It was like growing up far from the world, in a cloister. She left the house only on Sundays, for seven o'clock mass, Hubertine having arranged to teach her at home lest she go astray. This antique, cramped dwelling with its deathly quiet garden constituted her universe. She had been given a whitewashed room beneath the roof; she came downstairs each morning to eat in the kitchen, then climbed one flight to work in the atelier." Embroidering sacred images inspired by *The Golden Legend*, for which she spurns every other book, Angélique achieves great artistry. And when womanhood overtakes her, sexual desire, experienced as religious exaltation, bears her thoughts heavenward. There to point the way is her patron saint, Agnes, a thirteen-year-old virgin martyr who became Christ's bride after rejecting the son of a Roman prefect. Sculpted in stone, this exemplary tale unfolds *en permanence* outside her bedroom window.

Mysticism does not spoil Angélique for profane love. Romantic dreams are as much with her as thoughts of martyrdom, and those dreams revolve around a great patrician clan named d'Hautecoeur, whose line extends to the present bishop of Beaumont. What Hubertine tells her one day is that the bishop has had several former lives. First a courageous sea captain, then an idle rogue, he became enamored of, and married, a woman much younger than himself, Paule de Valençay, who died in childbirth, leaving him with a burden of grief that conduced to pious reclusion. Only after twenty years could he forgive or even acknowledge the heir delivered from her womb, and when father at last met son, he beheld an exact image of Paule. The story instantly captures Angélique's imagination. "Oh! What I would like, what I would really like is to marry a prince," she exclaims. "A prince I had never seen, who would appear at eventide, take me by the hand, and lead me to a palace. . . . I fancy him handsome and rich, oh! handsome and rich beyond compare! There would be horses neighing beneath my windows and jewels spilling from my hands." As Jesus miraculously redeems sinful mankind, so will the prince who belatedly discovered his own origins offer the foundling noble lineage. Angélique persists in this fantasy, much to the dismay of Hubertine, who believes that pride goeth before destruction and a haughty spirit before a fall.

Young d'Hautecoeur appears one night in the moonlit garden beneath her balcony, wooing her from afar. Before long they have nocturnal trysts face to face. He has presented himself as a *peintre-verrier* named Félicien, and the semi-incognito ("semi" because he is in fact a *peintre-verrier*) puts them at their ease. Between artistic souls heedless of social difference love flowers naturally. Then d'Hautecoeur's identity emerges, and this revelation, which is for Angélique a miraculous denouement, brings into play adult law, with all its nays. Opposed to their union are Hubertine, who preaches humility, and Monsignor d'Hautecoeur, who thwarts his son by way of exorcising his own passions. In Angélique the bishop sees Paule reincarnate. "Every evening, wearing a hair shirt and kneeling, he'd try to rout the ghost of his sorely missed wife. He invoked the dust she had become but instead raised her from her grave and pictured the fresh, blooming young thing with whom he, an already mature man, had fallen madly in love. It was no less painful now than it had been the day after her death. He wept for her, he desired her in the same spirit of revolt against God, who had taken her from him." Angélique's pleas fall on deaf ears. Separated from Félicien, she consumes herself in a struggle between the dictates of passion and of filial piety. When at last Félicien, whom the bishop would groom for a loveless marriage, proposes that they elope, she demurs, having made obedience her rule. Moribund, she prepares to die unwed, but on the verge of death, aided by divine grace, she causes Monsignor d'Hautecoeur to relent. His blessings sustain her through the marriage ceremony, which he himself performs amidst great pomp in the cathedral she first entered as a waif. And then, leaving this sacred world of dream for everyday life, Angélique expires:

> Angélique and Félicien walked slowly toward the door, between a double row of faithful. Now that the victory had been won, she emerged from her dream and prepared to enter reality. . . . But at the threshold, before descending steps that led to the square, she stumbled. Had she not gone to the limit of happiness? Was it not at this bourn that the joy of being ceased? With one last effort she raised herself and placed her mouth on Félicien's. Then she died.

Like Miette and Albine, she dies a virgin, having come under sentence of death at puberty. Here as in *La Fortune des Rougon* and in *La Faute de l'abbé Mouret*, sexual desire, which Zola equates with original sin or with *la faute héréditaire*, sets generation against generation, angering a father who will infantalize, castrate, kill.

What Rousseauianism was to *Paul et Virginie*, the spiritualism that pervaded art, music, and literature in fin de siècle Europe was to *Le Rêve*. Symbolist aesthetics, dream discourse, Pre-Raphaelite painting, Bayreuth, Russophilia all bespoke an enchantment with things mystical or supernatural or macabre—with the *au-delà*—and Zola, who often heard himself described as earth-bound, would have liked to persuade critics that he, too, could levitate when he so chose. Seeing his esteemed protégé Huysmans gradually move toward the literary fringe where occult creeds abounded undoubtedly preyed upon his mind. Zola began *Le Rêve* soon after Huysmans had begun *Là-bas*, a novel about the fifteenth-century child murderer and satanist Gilles de Rais.

But *Le Rêve* did not sway normally aloof critics. Many found it ponderous, and, indeed, the minute descriptions of this and that—of implements used in embroidering chasubles, for example—had as little to do with religiosity as the ecclesiastical oddments that filled Zola's flat. "I admit that M. Zola's purity seems extremely meritorious since it cost him all his talent," Anatole France chaffed in *Le Temps*. "By comparison with the impalpable heroine of this nebulous novel, La Mouquette [a good-natured slut in *Germinal*] comes off quite well. If forced to choose between the winged Zola and Zola the quadruped, I should choose the latter." More evenhanded was Jules Lemaître's review in *La Revue bleue*. "This fairy tale is, at bottom, a physiological story!" he wrote, acknowledging, to some extent at least, that *Le Rêve* had been woven from the cloth of Zola's familiar obsessions.

> The author will not let us forget that although Angélique comports herself virtuously, under different circumstances she might have been Nana. This lily has roots in Rougon muck, and Angélique's mysticism is but a fortuitous manifestation of the Macquart neurosis. . . . The story is, moreover, romantic in . . . demeanor, [by which I mean] that Angélique's symbiosis with the ancient cathedral calls to mind Quasimodo's with Notre-Dame.

In other novels, he concluded, form and matter are so congenial that Zola's method goes unnoticed, but in *Le Rêve* its bones poke through. "The grace of the naive little story disappears. Never has one seen so massive a fantasy. It's a fairy tale built with rusticated stone."

Zola did not brood over the critical disapprobation or pause to enjoy the commercial success of *Le Rêve*, which quickly sold out the first printing of forty-four thousand copies. Even before it appeared in book form on October 13, 1888, he had begun plotting another novel, one brutal enough to spoil the thesis propagated by certain ill-wishers that *Le Rêve* had been written with election to the French Academy in mind. Its title would give them proper notice: *La Bête humaine*.

Knit together in *La Bête humaine* are two historically discrete projects, one of which dated back to Zola's original master plan. There, the "murderer" figured as a promising subject for investigation, along with three other socially marginal types—the priest, the artist, the whore. Zola foresaw a novel whose framework would be "the judicial world" and whose hero would be Etienne Lantier, third child of a working-class family.

> [Jules] Michelet wrote: "The judge must be a doctor." Etienne is one of those strange criminals, born criminals, who, without being demented, are nonetheless driven by a bestial instinct and one day, in some morbid fit, commit murder. Just as his parents, whom poverty has made vicious, bequeath genius to his brother Claude, so they bequeath murder to him. There are recent examples of such phenomena. I should especially like to write an assizes court novel.

Murder appealed to him the more for being catnip to tabloid subscribers, but not until 1885 did he give the subject any sustained thought. In that year *Crime and Punishment* came out in French translation, and although premeditated, ideological violence of the kind Raskolnikov exemplifies fell outside his own domain, Zola read Dostoyevsky with great interest.

More to the point were criminological treatises published in 1886 and 1887, *La Criminalité comparée* by G. Tarde and *L'Homme criminel* (*L'uomo delinquente*) by the famous Italian psychiatrist Cesare Lombroso, who argued, with myriad statistics, that most criminals are born rather than made, that they are the products of atavism or degeneration, that they constitute a primitive subspecies remarkable for certain quirks and anatomical stigmata. Zola pondered Lombroso's work, which became gospel on the continent, even as he gathered evidence of his own from criminal anecdotes reported in Parisian newspapers.

Another novel gestating during this long interval was concerned with railroads. The seed may have been planted in 1878 when Zola established himself at Médan, where, just beyond the riverside boundary of his little estate, trains on the Western Line, the Ligne de l'Ouest, regularly sped between Paris and Mantes-la-Jolie or Le Havre. That year he had spoken to an Italian literary critic, Edmondo de Amicis, about a novel whose episodes would unfold along different routes and converge at one large station. By 1882 there was more detail. "What I already envision, amidst vast plains stripped and deserted like pine barrens, . . . is one of those tiny cottages on whose threshold one sometimes sees a woman holding a green flag to signal the passage of trains," Alexis quotes him as saying.

> And there, miles from anywhere yet two steps away from the humanity streaming over this trestle, I imagine a simple, profoundly human drama that ends in catastrophe, perhaps the collision of two trains brought about by someone with a score to settle. . . . What matters, what must come alive is the ceaseless transit of a great line between two colossal hubs. . . . And I want to animate the fauna peculiar to railroads: stationmasters, train crews, locomotive engineers, stokers, employees of the postal and telegraph carriage. . . . Everything will happen on my trains; people will eat there, sleep there, make love there, even give birth there, and, finally, die there.

From the outset death loomed large, and *La Bête humaine* may have originated in the need to dramatize a fear that had haunted Zola since adolescence, the fear of being buried alive. "One will hear, like musical accompaniment, the trepidation of this hurried life," noted Edmondo de Amicis, "and one will witness . . . an accident beneath a tunnel, the effort of the locomotive, the collision, the shock, the disaster, the flight, the dark, noisy, smoke-filled world that has long been preoccupying him." In this respect, the railroad novel, which he had put off at the beginning of 1884 to write about mines, anticipated *Germinal.* Indeed, the métier of *Germinal's* Etienne Lantier—*mécanicien* (locomotive engineer)—betrays their congeneric history.[6]

If the twenty-volume limit Zola imposed upon *Les Rougon-Macquart* dictated a merger between homicide and railroads, ready at hand to effect it was the paradox around which both ideas revolved: that breakneck progress begot catastrophic regression, or that inside nineteenth-century Europeans mastering nature with science, aboriginal man still wrought havoc. Could Rougon ever quite elude Macquart? Had atavism not presided, as a threat, over the birth of Zola's parvenu clan? "I shall study the ambitions and appetites of a family launched into the modern world, making superhuman efforts, prevented from reaching port because of its own nature and influences, nearing success only to founder, producing in the end moral monsters," he had written in his 1868 notes. "Intelligence exhausted by a mad dash toward the upper reaches of sensation and thought. Return to brutishness." The railroad line, with its employees, or *cheminots*, transporting people full steam "across the modern world" while inhabiting an archaically closed milieu, represented an ideal locus for this image of backward-forward movement. The opposition that perpetually captivated Zola was here, between "trains advancing civilization toward the twentieth century" and "wild beasts crouching underneath."

By late November 1888, Zola had sketched a plot and in the process replaced his original hero, Etienne Lantier, who could no longer serve after *Germinal*, with a newly invented brother, Jacques Lantier. For various reasons, he let the project languish until February 1889. Research then began in earnest, as his correspondence reveals. "You have requested permission of our company, through M. Pol Lefèvre, our assistant traffic manager, to visit a warehouse and to ride a locomotive round-trip between Paris and Mantes," wrote the director of the Compagnie de l'Ouest. "I freely grant you such permission and suggest that you contact M. Clérault, chief engineer of matériel and haulage, 44, rue de Rome, who will have been notified." In Lefèvre, Zola found a worthy successor to those cicerones who had guided him through coal mines, department stores, farms, and wholesale markets. Having

---

[6]Goncourt reports in his journal that Zola hadn't known which direction to take after writing *La Joie de vivre.* "*The Railroads*, his novel about the activity in a railroad station and a man whose livelihood depends on it, has not yet come into focus. He's more inclined to do something about a strike in coal-mining country; it would begin with a bourgeois having his throat slit. Then the judgment, certain men condemned to death, others sent to prison."

just published a book, on which Zola relied heavily for particulars about the infrastructure of railroad companies, Lefèvre took time out to reminisce, to walk Zola around the Gare Saint-Lazare (which had been rebuilt three years earlier), to explain in profuse detail how the long-distance express was prepared for its run, to locate architectural blueprints of various train stations, to describe workdays and careers at every level of employment. Their conversations extended through March, when Zola toured the Le Havre terminus, and into April, when he rode past Médan on a Western Line locomotive. The knowledge thus gained was indispensable, but none of it profited *La Bête humaine* quite as decisively as his few hours up front beside the engineer. "At first, great trepidation, fatigue in the legs and bewilderment produced by the jolts," he observed afterward.

> One's head seems to empty itself. The fields on either side don't disappear any faster than when seen from a passenger coach. It's just that there's more air, more space, the vast sky overhead. . . . Anyway, the engineer never looks right or left. The impression of long straight lines. Curves that hide the track, then a straight segment running to the horizon; and yonder a train approaching, very small, growing: one might think that it were traveling on the same track, that everything were about to crash. Then it passes with a roar. . . . And impressions at night, the lantern illuminating three hundred meters of track, a reflection on the distant bridges, on the trees, on the houses. White smoke caught in its beam appears to be burning. The blood-red light that flashes out when you open the firebox.

Notes on this dreamlike voyage joined his "Lefèvre Notes" in a file that served for the composition of two chapter-by-chapter outlines and then, after May 5, of the novel itself.

Zola solved the problem of never having mentioned Jacques Lantier in *L'Assommoir* by introducing him in *La Bête humaine* as the son Gervaise Macquart left behind when she and Auguste Lantier fled north. Thanks to his godmother, "Tante Phasie," who raised him competently, abandonment would seem to have been a blessing in disguise. After leaving Plassans, where he studied at the Ecole des Arts et Métiers, and working for the Orléans railroad, Jacques became an engineer first class with the Compagnie de l'Ouest. In physique and comportment there is little of Macquart about him. Handsome, well groomed, sober, industrious, he has, at twenty-six, made his way. But heredity will not be denied. Inside the model worker lurks a psychopath who asserts himself to savage effect as soon as women draw near. Jacques feels constantly threatened by this archaic self. "A nightmare procession of women had brushed against his sudden desire to kill them. . . . Since he didn't even know them, how could such fury be explained? . . . Each time it was a fit of blind rage, an irrepressible urge to avenge age-old offenses he could not clearly remember." Did it come from the remote past? asks Zola. Was it born of the "hurt" women had inflicted upon his race, or of rancor accumulating through male generations, since the first caveman suffered betrayal? Whatever its cause, safety for Jacques lies in the controlled environment of the railroad, aboard a locomotive that moves along iron tracks like a shackled colossus, reaching fixed points at scheduled hours. "He experienced peace and happiness only when detached from the world, on his engine. When . . . he clutched the regulator and was utterly absorbed in surveying the track or looking out for signals, he stopped thinking."

No sooner does his engine fall into disrepair than Jacques's mind runs riot, and these are the circumstances under which the reader first encounters him. Given several days' leave after a slight mishap, Jacques visits Tante Phasie, who some years earlier remarried, came north, and set up house at a remote crossing on the Western Line called Croix-de-Maufras, where her husband, Misard, works as gate-keeper. The sojourn passes without drama until Jacques meets Phasie's daughter Flore while strolling. Enamored of him since childhood, this robust seventeen-year-old blonde offers herself and risks more than she can imagine when Jacques becomes aroused. Reason somehow triumphs over madness, staying the killer's hand, but Jacques cannot fail to recognize how fragile is his civilized self, how tenaciously a primitive holds him hostage. Terror-stricken, he flees through the countryside, circling round about as conscience lashes out. And it is during this aimless ramble that the central event of *La Bête humaine* occurs. At a railroad tunnel near Croix-de-Maufras, Jacques witnesses a real murder. "He was standing still, beaten," writes Zola,

when the roar of a train emerging from the bowels of the earth, distant at first but increasing every second, rooted him to the spot. It was the Le Havre express, the 6:30 from Paris, which passed that spot at 9:25, a train he himself drove every other day. First Jacques saw the mouth of the tunnel light up, like the door of a furnace full of blazing wood. Then, bringing the din with it, the engine poured forth with its dazzling round eye, its headlamp blazing a gap through the landscape and lighting the rails far ahead with a double line of flame. But that was only a flash—the whole line of coaches followed, the little square windows, blindingly bright, making a procession of crowded compartments tear by at such speed that the eye was not sure whether it had really caught the fleeting vision. And in that precise quarter-second Jacques quite distinctly saw through the windows of a coupé [private compartment] a man holding another man down on the seat and plunging a knife into his throat, while a dark mass, probably a third person, possibly some luggage that had fallen from above, weighed down hard on the kicking legs of the man being murdered. Already the train had gone and was disappearing toward Croix-de-Maufras, showing no more of itself in the darkness than the three rear lamps, the red triangle.

An exsanguinated body found soon afterward by Misard tells Jacques that what he saw in one brief instant was not a figment of his guilt-ridden imagination. The victim is identified as M. Grandmorin, a rich, highly decorated, politically influential magistrate who owned the large house visible from Misard's cottage at Croix-de-Maufras.

Readers will be less shocked than Lantier, for *La Bête humaine* begins not with his imbroglio at Croix-de-Maufras but in Paris, with the incident that eventually dooms Grandmorin. There to spend several days are Roubaud, assistant stationmaster of the Le Havre terminus, and his wife, Séverine, a beautiful woman some fifteen years younger than he, who grew up at Croix-de-Maufras, first as the gardener's motherless daughter, then as the landlord's ward. Grandmorin had Séverine educated alongside his own daughter, dowered her, and after her marriage, through connections, placed Roubaud. What he also did was make Séverine his concubine, and when on this particular day she lets slip the secret, Roubaud—a man given to jealous rages—goes berserk:

> He could have clawed her heart out with his stiff, callused fingers. The questions went on and she told him everything, so obliterated by shame and fear that her voice was almost inaudible. The scenes she evoked drove him mad with jealousy, but he could not learn enough and compelled her to repeat the details, to be more graphic. With his ear pressed against the poor creature's lips, he kept his fist raised in a continual threat to hit her again if she stopped, even as he suffered agonies from this confession.

Convinced that life will be haunted unless Grandmorin dies, Roubaud instantly plots his murder. Using sex as bait, he forces Séverine to propose a tryst for that very night at Grandmorin's Norman hideaway (where, we soon learn, other nubile girls suffered abuse) and boards the one train headed north, the 6:30 Le Havre express. A private compartment, in which Grandmorin conceals himself en route to lecherous assignations, makes it easy to dispatch him in secret.

When word spreads that the foul deed had a witness (one more Zolian voyeur), Roubaud sinks still lower. To keep Jacques's memory blurred he urges Séverine to seduce the young man, and Séverine works sexual magic, arousing desire in him without, for some reason, exciting blood lust.[7] They fornicate passionately at either end of the Paris–Le Havre line. But, as Roubaud soon discovers, the thing that made him kill is the very thing that best protects him from arraignment. Clues that argue his guilt also expose his victim's turpitude; but the authorities, who have always known about Grandmorin's clandestine activity, must thwart the investigation, lest this pillar of Bonapartism, in suffering posthumous disgrace, compromise the regime itself. After talks with the ministry of justice, the examining magistrate dismisses all charges.

It hardly matters what justice does, for here as elsewhere in *Les Rougon-Macquart*, once the imp is loose, barbarism rages until nothing survives of the world that was. With dreamlike flagrancy, each chapter introduces some new wickedness. Misard poisons Phasie in order to search at leisure for money she kept hidden. Goaded by jealousy, Flore derails Jacques's locomotive, and then—seeing him emerge intact from the bloody wreckage—throws herself under another train. Séverine wants Jacques to murder Roubaud, who now loafs all day long, but instead revives his archaic grudge and dies by the same knife that slew Grandmorin. Finally Jacques himself dies when Pecqueux the stoker, whose girlfriend he stole, attacks him aboard a locomotive traveling at full steam. "With a final heave, Pecqueux pushed him over," writes Zola,

> and Jacques, feeling nothing behind him, frantically clung to Pecqueux's neck, and so tightly that he dragged the stoker along. Two terrible screams mingled and faded away. The two men, who for so long had lived together like brothers, fell together and were sucked under the wheels and hacked to pieces, locked in that frightful embrace. They were found headless and without feet, two bloody trunks still stifling each other.

In the end, the locomotive, that consummate symbol of mastery over nature, becomes a manifestation of nature unbridled. Once again, once for all, destructiveness weds libido, and to give their alliance col-

---

[7]From the beginning of *Les Rougon-Macquart*, burying the past—consigning old Adélaïde Fouque to the oblivion of an insane asylum, for example—is what unscrupulous people do, while remembering is pictured as a moral effort or an act of piety. At either extreme are the promiscuous denizens of Les Artaud in *La Faute de l'abbé Mouret*, who have no history, and Dr. Pascal Rougon, who, as we shall see in *Le Docteur Pascal*, analyzes the Rougon-Macquart, generation by generation, to understand the ways of heredity. Séverine arousing Jacques down below in order to cloud him up above as he searches his memory for details of the primal scene has kindred spirits in Zola's saga, notably Nana.

lective scope, Zola makes the runaway express a troop train bearing future victims toward the Eastern Front in 1870:

> They should have taken water at Rouen, and the station was transfixed with horror when this mad train rushed past in a whirlwind of smoke and flame, the engine without driver or stoker and cattle wagons full of troops yelling patriotic songs. They were off to war, and this was to get them sooner to the banks of the Rhine. Railwaymen gasped and waved their arms. Suddenly there was one general cry: that driverless train would never get clear through Sotteville station, which was always blocked by shunting operations and cluttered with vehicles and engines like all large depots. They rushed to send a warning by telegraph. A freight train standing on the line there could, as it happened, be backed into a shed just in time, for the roar of the escaping monster could already be heard in the distance. It had charged through the two tunnels on either side of Rouen and was approaching at a furious pace, like some prodigious, irresistible force that nothing could now stop. It scorched through the station at Sotteville, finding its way unscathed through the obstacles, and plunged into the night again, where its roar gradually died away.

All the horrors that converged at an obscure intersection called Croix-de-Maufras are now seen to have foreshadowed France's national bloodbath, as *la bête humaine*, liberated from timetables, runs out of control. "What mattered the victims that the machine destroyed on its way?" Zola concludes. "Wasn't it bound for the future, indifferent to spilt blood? With no human hand guiding it through the night, it roared on and on, a blind and defiant beast let loose amid death and destruction, laden with cannon fodder, these soldiers already dizzy with fatigue, drunk and singing."

Zola began *La Bête humaine* on May 5, 1889, and, propelled by a feeling of rejuvenation, made rapid progress. "I've worked like mad at my novel," he informed Charpentier on August 27. "I shall certainly finish by December 1. I believe that *La Vie populaire* will commence serial publication somewhere around October 20 and we shall hope to appear in bookstores toward the end of January. . . . Work has gone very smoothly for me. My health could not be more robust, and I am as I was at age twenty, when I wanted to swallow mountains whole." *La Vie populaire*, a literary supplement whose founder, Catulle Mendès, paid him the munificent sum of twenty thousand francs, planned to serialize it in twenty-six installments between November 14, 1889, and March 2, 1890. Charpentier brought out the volume on March 4.

Critics, even friendly ones, recoiled from what many characterized as a freak show. "Never has there been so much blood shed in a single volume," Charles Bigot protested in *La Revue bleue*. "Each one of the characters is implicated. . . . It's a manual, a complete repertoire of the human beast's techniques for slaughtering people. That they all kill without hesitation, without scruple, without remorse defies belief." Zola's apocalyptic vision of the world *ab origine*, of a humanity whose passions have obliterated its moral covenants was thought to be insufficiently naturalistic. "It's undeniable that the railroad does not constitute a necessary, fatal, indispensable frame for the drama, that the decor seems quite arbitrary," wrote Paul Ginisty, who did not let the fact that he was editor-in-chief of *La Vie populaire* hinder him from finding fault with *La Bête humaine* in the pages of *Gil Blas*. "There are some very beautiful pages, marvelous bits where M. Zola's talent, which always tends toward enormity, flourishes. But I must also say that I find the work strained, incoherent, crowded with exceptional beings—with monsters. I can express unreserved admiration only for the novelist's incomparable power of description."

But *La Bête humaine* also received high praise. A favorable review came, rather unexpectedly, from Anatole France, who was struck by the conjunction between modern technology and animism in passages describing Jacques's marriage to his machine. "When Zola speaks of 'the logic, the precision that constitutes the beauty of metal creatures,' do you find that he resembles Verne and Guillemin?" he asked. "No, not at all. This man is not a puerile vulgarizer of scientific conquests. He is a poet. His large, simple genius creates symbols. He begets new myths. The Greeks created the dryad, he has created La Lison, and both will live forever, on equal terms. He is the great lyrical voice of our age." No less enthusiastic was Jules Lemaître, who reviewed *La Bête humaine* at length in *Le Figaro*. "Here even more than in *L'Assommoir* or *Germinal*," he wrote on March 8,

> the characters are purely passive. They are absolutely subservient on the one hand to the intimate fatality of their temperaments and on the other hand to the pressure exerted by objects and external circumstances. Irresistible impulse is what makes them act. . . . One sees, in modern guise, the operation of elemental powers older than chaos. . . . Never have I read anything more horrific and mysterious about the eternal marriage between love and death. . . . I don't wish to discuss the novel's secondary merits. I seek only that which is truly great, and its greatness resides in its being a memento of our remote origins. There are among us innumerable brutes. We ourselves— Christian, civilized, well read, artistic—we experience upheavals of love or hatred, of concupiscence or anger that come from beyond us, so to speak; and we don't always know what we are obeying.

Zola was quick to thank Anatole France (who would never again attack *Les Rougon-Macquart*, however uncongenial he found the naturalist movement), but Lemaître's accolade gave him particular satisfaction. "I am most flattered, my dear confrere, and a little embarrassed by your piece, which contains praise enough to make blush even a man whom legend portrays as vainglorious," he wrote on March 9. "What delighted me above all was having my work so intelligently explained. I thought people might take it to be a sadistic fantasy, but now that you have hit just the right note, I need not fear—others will follow along."[8]

Even Edmond de Goncourt paid him homage, between clenched teeth. In his journal he consigned *La Bête humaine* to the scrap heap for being devoid of "true humanity" and scorned its characters as the "foul secretions of Zola's brain." But in a letter sent the next day he wrote:

> My dear Zola, . . . I can only repeat the compliments that everyone has paid you on the power of your creations, on the way your curious milieux weave through them, on the poetry you elicit from objects, on all the great and beautiful qualities of imagination that have made you the public's favorite author. It's obvious that we hew to different ideals. Where I have sought to render the novel as unnovelesque as possible, you go on working, felicitously, within the conditions of the genre. Who is right, you or I? Until now, incontestably you.

Skirting the aesthetic issue, which had to do with Goncourt's affection for very short, carefully wrought chapters, and his mannered idiom, or *écriture artistique*, Zola replied that there was no competition between them. "Why wonder which of us is right when you could quite simply say that we're both of us right?"

In Mallarmé's view—Mallarmé, who remained a devoted reader— Zola had transcended the "conditions of the genre." On October 5 he wrote that he had "long admired, and admired unreservedly, this art, yours, which lies between literature and something else, which is capable of satisfying the crowd while astonishing the literate commu-

---

[8]Encouragement of a different kind came several months later from Dr. Jules Héricourt, assistant director of the laboratory of physiology at the Paris School of Medicine. On June 7, *La Revue bleue* published his article "M. Zola's *Bête humaine* and Criminal Physiology," in which Héricourt, discussing Lantier, Séverine, Roubaud, and Flore, declared them to be clinically exquisite portraits of four criminal types. Soon afterward Zola sent him a letter of thanks, saying, among other things: "My method is invariably as follows. First I amass knowledge myself, through personal experience. Then I add to it by reading relevant documents, books, notes provided by friends. And finally imagination, or rather intuition, supervenes. With me the role of intuition is very important, greater than you allow, I believe. As Flaubert often said, taking notes is the correct thing to do; once they've been taken, one must be able to ignore them."

nity." Never, he continued, had life "streamed so torrentially as it does through this ravine dug by your drama between Paris and Le Havre."[9]

In 1888, ten years after Minister Agénor Bardoux's preposterous tergiversations over the Legion of Honor, Zola, by then the most famous novelist of his day, deigned to let the French government honor him. Behind this event was Edouard Lockroy, the Radical leader, whom Charles Floquet appointed minister of public instruction in April. Eager to redress a flagrant wrong but loath to suffer a rebuff from Zola, he asked their mutual friend Marguerite Charpentier to act as go-between, and Marguerite prevailed against Zola's fear of ridicule by arguing that the red ribbon, however trivialized (especially since the decorations scandal), would give his detractors pause and "rehabilitate him in the eyes of the vulgar." So it came to pass that on July 13, in the Charpentier drawing room, Lockroy made him a *chevalier*.[10] "Yes, my dear friend," Zola told Guy de Maupassant, who had also mediated for the minister.

> I accepted, after much reflection, which I may write about one day, for I believe that small fry in the world of letters would find it interesting, and this acceptance transcends the Legion, it includes all awards, even election to the Academy. If the Academy were offered, as this decoration was offered, if, that is, a group of academicians wanted to vote for me and asked me to submit my candidacy, I would oblige, simply, without campaigning. I think that's the right way and in any event it's the logical sequel to the step I've just taken. . . . I would be very happy if you shared my view.

[9]Mallarmé enlarged upon this five months later during an interview with Jules Huret, saying:
> To return to the subject of naturalism, it seems to me that the term designates the literature of Emile Zola and that it will perish when Zola has completed his work. I admire Zola greatly. Truth to tell, what he has done is not so much literature as evocatory art, and he has done it by using literary elements as little as possible. He has taken words, yes, but that's all; the rest flows from his marvelous organization and resounds immediately through the mind of the crowd. He has really powerful gifts; his unbelievable sense of life, his crowd scenes, Nana's skin, the grain of which we've all caressed—all that painted in prodigious wash tints.

[10]Goncourt claimed that Zola had trivialized his accomplishment by accepting the decoration, but it should be noted that thirteen years later, in 1901, 35,151 Frenchmen wore the cross of a knight, 5,998 the rosette of an officer, 1,059 the *cravate* of commander. These numbers were still rather modest and the honor still conferred prestige. By 1935 there would be 173,380 knights, 30,261 officers, 3,404 commanders.

Zola then elaborated upon this rationale in interviews, claiming for himself both the innocence of a glutton unable to leave anything un-eaten (or of an object propelled by inertial force) and the virtue of a leader who befriends his bêtes noires the better to legitimize his cause. "Once I've agreed to be something, I straightway wish to be every-thing," he explained grandly to a journalist from *La Presse*.

> I would certainly have cut an impeccable figure had I remained eter-nally immured in my scorn of official honors, but such conduct would not have done my work any good, and it was my work above all that I had in mind when I adopted this new policy. Do you imagine that romanticism would have flowered as it did if Hugo had been reclu-sive? Don't you think that the Academy, the Legion of Honor, even the peerage (for Hugo was a very skillful man of action) contributed significantly to romanticism taking root in our old classical soil? . . . It is quite natural that I should hope to witness, before my death, the definitive consecration of my work.

Ernest Blavet of *Le Figaro* reported similar observations. Tilting quix-otically with bourgeois institutions no longer satisfied Zola. Since the French were "deeply and irremediably committed to an establish-ment," he said, wisdom dictated that he arrange his life accordingly. "Why should I myself not accept the hierarchy when, above all, it would redound to the advantage of my person and my work?" he asked. He had no intention of prowling around the Academy until someone's seat fell vacant, "like a jackal sniffing carrion." But if one day he submitted his candidacy, his motive would be threefold: "prop-aganda for my work, proselytism for my ideas, the desire to put childish sulks behind me."[11]

[11]The official honor provoked yet another galling exchange with Edmond de Gon-court, who, eager to disparage Zola by any means, marshaled against him the undecorated great. On July 30, *Le Gaulois* published an article entitled "Zola Judged by Goncourt," in which Goncourt was quoted as saying: "I consider per-fectly ridiculous and out of touch an assembly that eliminated Balzac and Miche-let. It pains me to see M. Zola suddenly leave me and desert—I do not say renounce—his former convictions. Is the double consecration of the cross and the Academy indispensable to his talent and renown? He says it is; but I find that it diminishes him as a literary man. . . . M. Zola is at the height of his glory; he has entered the victorious period, he is in full possession of himself artistically, and it seems to me that he owed it to his position not to accept a distinction that trivi-alizes him, that discredits him in the eyes of those who loved him best. . . . My situation was very different from his. I was decorated in 1867 by the Princess Mathilde, who had not warned me. If she had, I would have promptly refused." Still burning from the "Manifeste des Cinq" and thoroughly unimpressed by Gon-court's aristocratic airs, Zola responded as follows: "It's not quite accurate to say that 'I've suddenly left you.' Jog your memory and get the facts straight. If bonds have slackened a little more each day, if today I walk alone, is it I who wanted it

With this palinode in mind, literary Paris could not have been very surprised to learn, fifteen months later, that the death of the play-wright-cum-academician Emile Augier had sent Zola on a round of official visits. "I'm no longer young, I work less and must give my life a more practical slant," is how one journalist quoted him. Fortified by glorious precedents (there was Hugo's successful candidacy but also, even more pertinently, Balzac's unsuccessful one), he decided to enter the lists after consulting his friend François Coppée. "I've just seen Halévy [also a member of the Academy], who still won't give me any definite advice," he wrote on November 8, 1889. "Remember my total inexperience and let me know when you think I should go forward." He submitted his name on December 2, a portentous anniversary, and, competing against twelve others, in seven ballots Zola never obtained more than four votes. That no one else obtained an absolute majority—neither the liberal historian Ernest Lavisse nor the conservative critic Ferdinand Brunetière—may have given him some satisfaction, but at all events the defeat ended his diplomatic imposture. As much to shame the Academy or make it define itself by his exclusion as to gain admittance, he reapplied one year later, when Octave Feuillet died, and applied yet again after the death of Admiral Jurien de la Gravière. During the next decade, which took a grim toll of Immortals, Zola suffered nineteen more rebuffs. Might this have been, as we have already suggested, an unconscious reenactment of his mother appealing year after year for restitution of the fortune stolen from her and her son? "The powerful writer was no more abundantly endowed with tact than with moderation," observed one student of the question. "Each of his candidacies had an aggressive air about it. He did not appear to solicit votes; rather, he demanded them as his due."

Along with the demand for official honors went a greater appetite for worldly pleasure, and after 1885 the pleasure-loving Zola spent three straight summer holidays at Royan on the Atlantic coast north of Bordeaux. What attracted him to this fashionable resort, where European high society disported itself, was not high society but the presence of Georges Charpentier, who built a villa across the bay from one of Royan's huge, ornate casinos and named it Le Paradou after the garden in *La Faute de l'abbé Mouret*. In September 1886, before Le Paradou was completed, they shared rented quarters for ten days.

---

so? Moreover, why blame me for having accepted the cross when I accepted it under the same conditions as you? I had my arm affectionately twisted by Lockroy as you had yours by the Princess Mathilde; and if you were set upon after *Germinie Lacerteux*, I was no less so after *La Terre*. Don't you remember how, one year ago, there was talk of drumming me out of literature and shutting me up in a hospital? Why should the cross, which consecrated you, not do as much for me?"

One year later Alexandrine and Emile returned with three servants in tow and rented a beachfront house of their own, despite Zola's fear of intruders enraged by *La Terre*. The six-week sojourn, during which Céard came down from Paris, proved so enjoyable that they braved the rigors of another cumbrous, bourgeois migration in August 1888.

Though housed under separate roofs, writer and publisher were hardly ever apart. "Life knit together the households of Zola, of Georges Charpentier, and of the engraver Fernand Desmoulin," wrote Albert Laborde, Alexandrine's young cousin, who vacationed at Royan in 1888.

Always together, and impeccably dressed in white flannel suits, the "three white men," as they were dubbed, stood at the center of meetings that amalgamated family and friends every day on the beach, at the neighborhood pastry shop, for excursions, at memorable lunches near oyster farms, where Théodore Duret, a native of that region, glorified and tasted with relish the local cognac.

Duret's family estate at Cognac was only seventy kilometers away, and in September 1887 the Zolas spent two days there being wined and dined before returning by boat up the Gironde from Bordeaux. More modest excursions took them past Saint-Palais-sur-Mer, where a broad, sandy beach lined with sea pines stretched north toward the ancient lighthouse of La Coubre. At Royan itself there were opera and theater, but the group usually fabricated its own entertainment in what Zola called *une fête perpétuelle*. Alexandrine and Amélie Laborde made willing impresarios. "With the complicity of Alexandrine and my mother," Albert Laborde recalled,

Zola's friends organized for him a surprise dinner featuring Antillean dishes. . . . Dressed in Roman togas and wearing lovely dark makeup, the twelve or fourteen guests bore crowns of roses, which each had to place upon the head of his neighbor when a signal was given during dessert. A professor of philosophy arriving that very evening was picked up at the train station, taken to the prop room of the Royan Theater, appropriately disguised, and brought to the meal; astounded, he kept repeating: "If my students could see me now! If my students could see me now!" . . . It lasted until after midnight. We needed fresh air, and on the empty road, walking past somnolent villas, a big group of black men, large and small, rang the bell of a nearby hotel to request glasses of "good white milk for poor little blackamoors."

Entertainment of a more dignified kind was occasioned by the betrothal of Charpentier's oldest daughter, Georgette, to a writer named
Abel Hermant. On September 9, 1888, *La Gazette des bains de mer de
Royan* listed the Zolas, the Desmoulins, Royan's mayor, the Italian art
collector Enrico Cernuschi, and Théodore Duret as celebrants at an
engagement party held in the garden of Le Paradou, with a group
called L'Harmonie de Royan providing background music.

In 1888 Zola looked dramatically younger than in 1887, for during
the previous November (when his forty-six-inch stomach caused him
great embarrassment in tight quarters), he had resolutely embarked
upon a diet. The trick was to drink nothing at meals, and it worked
so well for him that after three months he had lost thirty pounds,
or enough to contemplate without despair the prospect of squeezing past spectators at the theater. "His stomach has melted away,"
Goncourt noted on March 4. "His person has lengthened, as it were,
or stretched, and, what is particularly strange is that the fine modeling
of his past face has reemerged from the flesh in which it was lost,
buried; he has begun to resemble his Manet portrait, with just a hint
of nastiness in the physiognomy." While Alexandrine, who apparently
viewed the diet with skepticism and in any event doubted her husband's resolve, continued to suffer from a variety of ailments (water
on the knee, bronchitis, inflamed lungs, etc.), Zola thrived. Not that
his victory over fat was definitive. It required constant warfare and
more serious measures than food without drink.[12] But never again
would he balloon.

[12]Seven or eight years later, Dr. Edouard Toulouse noted that Zola regularly ate
a crust of dry bread for breakfast, abstained from starchy foods at lunch, had some
cakes with tea at 5, dined lightly, and drank two glasses of tea at 10 p.m. Though
wine was otherwise forbidden, he would allow himself a draft of white during
exercise, when he took up bicycle riding in great earnest. He sipped tea throughout
the day while at work, consuming as much as a liter. The Zolas also remained
great consumers of olive oil, which Numa Coste shipped up from Aix in forty-
kilogram consignments.

Zola's weight problem may have been aggravated in the first place by the decision to stop smoking. As regards tobacco, he wrote to a young doctor who in
1888 had quizzed him for a contest sponsored by the Society Against the Abuse
of Tobacco on the subject of "tobacco's effects on the health of men of letters
and its influence on French literature": "I have no clear-cut opinion on the matter
you raise. Personally, I stopped smoking ten or twelve years ago on the advice of
a doctor when I thought that I had heart disease. The idea that tobacco has had
an influence on French literature seems a bit outlandish. . . . I have seen great
writers smoke heavily without their intelligence suffering in the least. If genius is
a neurosis, why wish to cure it? Perfection is so dull that I often regret having
gotten over tobacco."

Zola apparently talked Alexandrine into embracing his dietary formula, but with
her it failed. She weighed 163 pounds in August 1888 and gained thirteen pounds
during the next nine months.

How closely connected were this physical metamorphosis and the sense of deprivation or of entitlement that crept over him as he approached the end of *Les Rougon-Macquart* becomes clearer when one examines his notebooks. No sooner had Zola undertaken to make himself more youthful than he began to sketch a story about a middle-aged man falling in love with a much younger woman. "A man of forty, hitherto engrossed in science, who, never having loved, now falls passionately in love with a child of sixteen," he wrote in November 1887. "She loves him in return, or thinks she does, so that his sensual awakening is complete. A young man then comes along, a relative of the scientist, whereupon youth conquers youth. The pain endured by the forty-year-old, who finally yields; he gives the young woman to the young man." From this character Zola soon derived d'Hautecoeur, the bishop of Beaumont in *Le Rêve*, who covets his son's inamorata as he covets his own lost youth. But more remarkable, biographically speaking, is a telegraphic notation that reveals Zola's own desire to vanquish middle age and enjoy, in love of a kind he had perhaps never experienced, the reward for his austere labors. "Me; work; literature, which has consumed my life; and the upheaval, the crisis, the need to be loved; I must study all that psychologically," he wrote *en passant*.[13] Was he himself not the desolate, lustful monsignor? Perhaps he also saw himself in Angélique, the gifted embroiderer of tales, being wooed from the garden beneath her balcony by a ghost that gradually—like some fictional character—becomes flesh.

Fiction prefigured reality, for during the month of May 1888 Zola's dream sprang to life in the person of a twenty-one-year-old chambermaid and seamstress hired by Alexandrine. Born on April 14, 1867, at Rouvres-sous-Meilly in Burgundy, Jeanne-Sophie-Adèle Rozerot was the second daughter of a miller, Philibert, who became a widower two or three years after her birth, and then sired a numerous family on his second wife. Jeanne received no fathering from Philibert Rozerot. Raised by her maternal grandparents, she began to support herself as soon as she was old enough to enter domestic service, for which she

---

[13]On January 22, 1889, Edmond de Goncourt noted the following in his journal: "At one point I was chatting with Zola about the way we had given our lives to letters, given them as lives had perhaps never been given in any previous age, and we admitted to each other that we had been true martyrs of literature and maybe even damned fools. Zola confessed that with age fifty approaching he has experienced a resurgence of life, of desire for material joys, and suddenly interrupted himself to say: 'As my wife isn't here I can tell you that I can't see a young woman like that one over there walk by without thinking: Isn't that worth more than a book?' "

had been trained at convent school. Nothing else is known, except that misfortune had not hardened her heart or spoiled her looks. With an abundance of blond hair, with stray locks curling over her delicate neck, with full lips and large, soft eyes, she cut a tall, lovely figure. "My mother hinted to her cousin Alexandrine," wrote Albert Laborde, "at the danger of admitting a young, pretty helper, worthy of notice and even of love—not suspecting that love had already blossomed. Heedless, Alexandrine only smiled. Feelings then took their course, inexorably." At Royan there was ample opportunity to dally. By year's end Zola had swept aside his compunctions and made love to a woman who may not yet have understood how large she loomed for him, or guessed that, in love as in literature, the great man considered himself an eternal tyro.

Jeanne did understand one thing full well, however. She understood that her forty-eight-year-old employer did not envision a casual affair when after the summer holiday he urged her to give notice and found her a flat conveniently near the rue de Boulogne, at 66, rue Saint-Lazare. Since the age of seven Zola had been the male attended by two women, one much older than the other, and now, entering upon a double life that was to afford him both ecstasy and guilt, to make him a father but a clandestine father, he restored his archetypal ménage à trois.

XXIII

"I'M ALWAYS DEVASTATED
BY THE LIMITED SCOPE OF
THE ACCOMPLISHMENT"

THE EROTIC GRATIFICATION of afternoons at 66, rue Saint-Lazare
had a paradoxical effect on Zola. It put the spring back in his step,
but it also drained him of creative energy and even distanced him
from the enterprise to which he had long been so exclusively wedded.
His pen felt like some foreign object. "I'm still lackadaisical," he told
Huysmans on March 6, 1889, after combining work and pleasure during a sojourn with Jeanne Rozerot at Le Havre in preparation for *La
Bête humaine*. "All my repressed laziness has burst forth. If I carried
things a bit further, I'd no longer touch a pen. What I am observing
in myself, from afar as it were, is a crisis of indifference, a feeling of
futility. I shall nevertheless resume work on my novel, without enthusiasm, I assure you, but because I must." Another near-confession
went to his Dutch chronicler, Jacques van Santen Kolff. "My dear
confrere, haven't I already told you not to worry when I don't answer?"
he groused. "I am either the laziest man in the world or the most
industrious. It is quite true that I am undergoing a crisis, the midlife
crisis no doubt. But I shall endeavor to turn it to the advantage and
honor of literature. So, forgive me my long silence. For weeks and
even months on end, my whole being is in a tumult of desire and
regret. Best to sleep under such circumstances." The dreamed-of reward for *Les Rougon-Macquart* did not come pain-free. At this juncture, his manhood, which he had always experienced as a prodigious
ability to sublimate—to sit alone each morning marshaling characters,
organizing plots, writing four pages day after day, producing long nov-

616

els year after year—was threatened by the very woman who made him feel young and virile.

When several months later Zola began the next episode of *Les Rougon-Macquart*, ambition gained the upper hand over lassitude. "It's been almost two months since I've accomplished any work," he wrote to Alphonse Daudet after removing to Médan early in May, "and now that I am far from human beings, in the grass and trees, I shall forge ahead. What about you? Have you kept your nose to the grindstone? This Exposition is making an insufferable racket." In truth, he did occasionally allow himself time off. One July evening, for example, the Zolas joined the Charpentiers at a Russian restaurant on the first platform of Eiffel's new tower and surveyed what Goncourt called "the Babylonian immensity of Paris" from 180 feet up. But his correspondence otherwise speaks of manic resolve and abounds in words like *furieusement* and *rageusement.* "There's nothing new here," Céard was told on May 31. "I returned and am working like mad. Alas, age has done little to calm me down. I hoped that accumulating years would bring greater wisdom, but it's clear that I can only act in passionate bursts. How peculiar! for, at bottom, I judge myself harshly and despise my very emotionalism." The end of his saga, which had come into full view, afforded him intimations of self-renewal. "I am seized with a furious desire to finish my *Rougon-Macquart* series as soon as possible," he told Charpentier. "I would like to be rid of it by January '92. That's possible, though it would mean constant swotting. . . . Here, as everywhere else, I believe, the weather is atrocious. Not that I suffer from it, cloistered as I am from morning 'til night. About the only people I've seen all summer are Alexis, Thyébaut, and Céard. . . . Ah, my friend, if I were thirty again, you'd see what I could do! I would astonish the world."

Neither Charpentier nor his associate Eugène Fasquelle found anything amiss. It may, indeed, be supposed that they were hard put to imagine what more their house demiurge expected of himself, and that their wonderment grew during the following year. As soon as *La Bête humaine* appeared in March 1890, Zola started gathering material for another large, densely populated novel, *L'Argent*, which would take him eight and a half months to write.

Like *La Bête humaine*, *L'Argent* evolved higgledy-piggledy from several unrelated ideas. The first bore upon politics and journalism. To complete *Son Excellence Eugène Rougon*, Zola had envisaged a story about the "authoritarian Empire" coming undone in reforms that unmuzzled the opposition press. This sequel received no further mention until Zola drew up new plans for *Les Rougon-Macquart* in 1882–83. In the revised agenda, "newspapers" were linked to an institution absent from every previous list—the Bourse, or stock exchange. It seems that he had decided to portray epidemic speculation as a prime symptom of imperial decadence. But the fillip was not one or another of the major financial collapses of Napoleon III's regime. What inspired Zola was the crash of the Union Générale, which had just ruined many French investors.[1] In the phenomenon of reactionary social interests embracing modern high finance, or of Catholic clashing with Jew, he saw great dramatic promise, and his conviction became stronger five years later, when Eugène Bontoux vented his anger against Rothschild in a book entitled L'Union Générale, sa vie, sa mort, son programme.

To understand Bontoux, Zola studied a book some thirty years old, but still relevant—La Bourse, ses abus et ses mystères by Eugène de Mirecourt (1858), where the arcana of market speculation, of puts and calls, selling short and buying long, are explained at length, and with commentary that invites the reader to see financial legerdemain as something akin to sexual dissoluteness. Also useful were Les Mémoires d'un coulissier by Ernest Feydeau, who had earned his livelihood trading unlisted equities over the counter (la coulisse) before achieving fame as a novelist. In this largely anecdotal narrative, Feydeau portrayed not only the lesser ruminants native to the Bourse but several members of its elephant herd, notably Isaac and Jacob Pereire, whose immense Crédit Mobilier had crashed in 1867, and James de Rothschild, after whom Zola modeled a character named Gundermann.

Among experts consulted, Eugène Fasquelle proved indispensable. Having worked for years at a large brokerage house, Charpentier's young associate plied Zola with information of every kind. He discoursed fluently on technical aspects of the Exchange, on financial argot, on the social life of brokers, on the chicanery of trade papers. And Zola took notes enough to flesh out L'Argent. "The broker arrives at the Bourse at 12:45," he wrote.

> The proxy, the assignee, the latter's assistant are together near the broker's loge, at a predetermined spot, so that clients can easily find them and communicate with the broker. . . . It is they who put the public in contact with the broker; they take orders, convey answers. . . . Bond and cash clerks are addressed by the name of their broker: Fasquelle was called Tavernier.

[1] The crash also provided grist to many writers of ephemeral fiction. During February and March 1882, Gil Blas serialized a novel by Louis de Chercusac entitled L'Amour de l'argent. A year later appeared Les Drames de l'argent by Raoul de Navery (which features a great Catholic bank called La Société Universelle) and in 1886 La Comtesse Shylock by G. d'Orcet.

Since easy money went hand in hand with facile pleasure, gambling did not end at the final bell. Fasquelle told Zola that the stock exchange crowd liked to enjoy itself, to eat well, to party, to play the horses. "Brokers pretend that . . . they lead impeccably conventional lives, . . . but . . . all connected with the Bourse are free at an early hour," he explained. "They're in evening dress by six and pride themselves in being dapper. Men-about-town, they frequent cafés, after-theater restaurants, theaters (for premieres). They have mistresses (stars at small theaters or bit players at large ones) whom they pay generously and exchange frequently." This preening was, at bottom, encouraged by the realization that noninitiates viewed the Bourse as a temple for magical rites and the broker himself as the thaumaturge of an affluent society. "The absolute mystery of it all, the fear and attraction of this imponderable gain, this strange turn of fortune's wheel," Zola noted to himself.

I must put that in the first chapter, the Bourse in the middle of Paris like a mysterious and gaping cavern where things take place that nobody outside can understand. It is known that millions are won there in an hour, that the kings of money are able, with a word, to affect the fortune of nation-states. But how? That is what eludes people. The unintelligible cries, the incomprehensible operations add terror to respect. Why shouldn't I, too, get rich quick? people ask. The desire, the rutting it stimulates.

No doubt Fasquelle or a broker enlisted by him stood at Zola's side when on April 17, 1890, he toured the Bourse with notebook in hand, observing first the interior or *parquet*, where listed stocks were traded, then the colonnaded porch where, all year round, over-the-counter traders, or *coulissiers*, conducted business in a furor of bids and offers audible blocks away on the Boulevard des Italiens.

As for the Union Générale, an economist familiar with its operations, Georges Lévy, led Zola, scene by scene, through the drama that had preceded its collapse, dismissing tales of a Jewish cabal. From this perspective, blame fell on Eugène Bontoux, but, much as he respected Lévy's analysis, Zola was inclined to view Bontoux leniently, or rather, to create a Bontoux-like hero in whom moral callousness served imaginative brilliance. In the person of Aristide Saccard, who had lain dormant since *La Curée*, the "poetry" of entrepreneurship would run up against the cold, merciless logic of the financial market. "A firm like the Union is but a pretext for jobbery and its sole raison d'être is to acquire large enterprises," wrote Zola. "Could the latter do without it? Given what I have in mind, the answer is no, because I consider speculation the necessary fertilizer, the unavoidable element of human

excess (no lust, no offspring). From such dung comes progress. . . . My
. . . Bontoux will be a superior example of [his] breed, . . . a big shot
at the Exchange, but a southerner, something of a poet in his ardent
passions, his capacity to get excited over some idea and coruscate."

After many financial vicissitudes, the most recent of which has left
him poorer than before yet none the wiser, Aristide Saccard at fifty is
poised to start afresh. A mutual acquaintance through whom he petitioned his brother Eugène Rougon for some high government post
makes it clear that Eugène, now the liberal prime minister under Napoleon III's antipapal regime, finds him superfluous. Eugène proposes
a colonial appointment, which enrages Saccard. Driven even more by
sibling rivalry than by love of lucre, he needs only this rebuff to dispel
his qualms about an enterprise he had been pondering—an enterprise
of gigantic proportions and commensurate risk. He promptly launches
a *maison de crédit*, or commercial bank, that will, he hopes, attract
Catholic money from all over France with ventures likely to profit the
Church, and he gives it a name eloquent of his own grandiosity: the
Banque Universelle. It is 1864.

Saccard's previous adventures had brought him into contact with a
devout young widow, the Princess d'Orviedo, who was spending her
colossal fortune on aid for indigent people. At first, Saccard fancied
himself as co-director of her philanthropies. "He would make those
millions fructify; he would double them, treble them, use them ingeniously. . . . His passionate nature enlarged everything; the thought of
distributing charity ad infinitum, of drowning a happy land in alms,
intoxicated him." But the princess did not want this eleemosynary
partnership, and Saccard's attentions soon fixed upon a neighbor, a
youngish engineer named Georges Hamelin, who lived with his thirty-
six-year-old sister Caroline.

In the Hamelins, Zola pictures a virtue exemplified by very few
Rougon-Macquart pairs: unshakable devotion. Brother and sister have
seldom lived apart. Orphaned in late adolescence, they came north to
Paris, he to study at the Ecole Polytechnique, she to support him as
a schoolteacher. After a disastrous marriage, Caroline rejoined her
brother, who had found employment abroad, on the Suez Canal project, and settled in Lebanon, where Hamelin helped build a road linking Beirut and Damascus. During these years Hamelin decided that
his mission in life was to awaken Asia Minor from its millennial sleep
by importing Western technology:

He had a portfolio stuffed with ideas and plans and decided that
revisiting France was an absolute necessity if ever he hoped to see
this great cluster of enterprises materialize, to form corporations, to
raise capital. So, after nine years in the East they came home via

Egypt, where the canal works inspired them; since they had last been there a city had sprung up on the sands of the Port Said beach, with people swarming through it like ants.

The portfolio includes plans for a syndicate of steamship companies serving every major Mediterranean port with modern vessels, a company to extract silver from Mount Carmel, a network of railroads crisscrossing the entire Near East and linking the Bosporus to the Red Sea. But what buoys Hamelin is not the prospect of personal gain, or not that alone. As naively pious as he is exuberantly technocratic, Hamelin sees himself rescuing the papacy from godless Europe. Hadn't Italian nationalists already encroached upon it? Wasn't France, under liberal rule, not likely to withdraw the garrison that protected its shrunken domain? Then why not, thought Hamelin, reestablish the *patrimonium Petri* in a newly prosperous, easily accessible Holy Land? This Catholic consummation leaves Caroline unmoved. Though tolerant and even envious of Georges's childlike vision, she, who has plumbed life far more deeply than he, no longer holds the faith inculcated by their father.

As soon as chance forges an alliance between engineer and financier, the former leaves Paris for Constantinople to obtain concessions from the grand vizier, Fuad Pasha, while the latter, with inimitable salesmanship, persuades several millionaires to form a syndicate that acquires four-fifths of the Banque Universelle's first stock issue. That it is illegal for a company to squirrel away its own shares in dummy accounts does not deter Saccard, nor does any other covenant. World conquest is what he has embarked upon, and this imperative matches Hamelin's apostolic dream. "In Napoleon's Egyptian expedition, Saccard saw something more than an attempt to give France commercial access to the Levant," Zola observes. "Behind it lay something vague and enigmatic, a colossally ambitious project. Achieving Alexander's goal, perhaps, and being crowned emperor of the East and the Indies at Constantinople? . . . The thought of succeeding where Bonaparte had failed . . . kindled Saccard's imagination. He would conquer the East, but he would do it methodically, with the two-edged sword of science and money. Since civilization had moved westward, why not move it back to humanity's first garden, to that Eden of the Hindustani peninsula . . . ?" In short order every obstacle falls, including the scruples expressed by Caroline, who detects Saccard's knavery. Reason warns her against him, but reason yields to the sheer élan of a man half charlatan, half prophet. She becomes his mistress.

Like Octave Mouret, Saccard feels most alive when holding sway over an empire mobbed with lustful, acquisitive subjects, and in dramatic structure the model for *L'Argent* was clearly *Au Bonheur des*

Dames. As the department store had sale days to celebrate its precipitous expansion, so the credit bank has successive offerings. A daily haul of a million francs was Mouret's apotheosis; a quotation of three thousand francs per share will make Saccard feel greater than Gundermann (i.e., Rothschild). And as aristocrats raced fishwives through Au Bonheur des Dames, so people of every class, all craving instant wealth, mill around the *magister ludi* in feverish promiscuity. Each plot is cadenced by physical enlargement: the department store came to fill an entire square block, and the credit bank occupies ever more ostentatious premises. Its first address is the d'Orviedo mansion, where a glass canopy, doubtless intended as an ironical offshoot of the greenhouse in *La Curée,* transforms the courtyard into a hall for tellers' windows. "Strikingly obvious at first glance . . . was its severe look, an atmosphere of old-fashioned integrity that filtered in from the dark, humid town house and made it feel rather like a sacristy." Three years later, in April 1867, when the Universal Exposition opens, Saccard inaugurates "monumental" offices on the rue de Londres. "There it was with its gingerbread face, a façade that combined the temple and the café concert," writes Zola. "Opulence continued inside, where millions from the cash registers trolleyed along the walls. A grand staircase led to the boardroom, which was operatically got up in red and gold. . . . In the basement, behind plate-glass partitions that allowed the public to see, . . . stood immense safes lined up like storybook casks containing the incalculable treasure of fairies."

For all of Saccard's conjury—the stock, which first sold at five hundred, increases sixfold in value—success is not based upon a total illusion. Shuttling between Paris and Constantinople, Georges Hamelin does do what he set out to do. Modern vessels owned by his conglomerate ply the Mediterranean. Quantities of silver have been extracted from Carmel. Authorization has been won to build a railroad spanning the Ottoman Empire from Bursa, near the Sea of Marmara, to Aleppo and Beirut.

Octave Mouret achieved stability in the end, but Saccard, who will be All or Nothing, can only rise or fall. Condemning Napoleon III's desertion of Pius IX on the one hand and on the other paying more than the emperor for one night with a fashionable courtesan, he uses every weapon against his brother Eugène, high holiness as well as phallic bravado. To the born runt, absolutes alone make sense, and Hamelin's prudent counsel is swept aside.

He got up and gestured heavenward in an attempt to stand taller on his little legs; and in truth he did stand taller, speaking as a poet of money whom bankruptcy and ruin had not sobered. Laying a whip to business and making it froth at full gallop was his instinctive method, the impulse of his entire being. He had forced success, had whetted covetous appetites with this thunderous march of the Universelle.

Sustained by magical thinking, the whole carnivalesque enterprise comes undone when Logic steps forward in the person of Gundermann the Jew. Gundermann, whose role is not sectarian but patriarchal, upholds financial order, challenging the reckless imp, and they joust for months as Saccard secretly buys Universelle stock dumped by Gundermann. One shores up what the other has driven down, until finally, like the Union Générale, the Banque Universelle expires in a crash that wrecks investors big and small. Through Eugène's intervention, Saccard is allowed to exile himself from France rather than serve the prison term to which he has been sentenced; at the novel's end he is organizing in Holland, with demonic resilience, another huge corporate venture.

The phenomenon of French anti-Semitism pervades *L'Argent*. Throughout, Saccard vituperates against the enemy race, ignoring Caroline when she meekly objects that "Jews are men like other men," who stand apart because they have been set apart. "Inextinguishable hatred for [Gundermann] flared up in him," Zola writes early on.

> Ah! the Jew! The Jew excited that age-old radical antagonism found especially in southerners and he felt it viscerally as the mere thought of rubbing against one filled him with a disgust over which reason had no sway. Oddly enough, he, the redoubtable wheeler-dealer, the financial executioner whose hands were dripping gore, lost all self-awareness when a Jew entered the picture; he'd speak about him with the asperity, the vengeful indignation of some upstanding hardworking citizen who had never engaged in usurious activity. . . . Has a Jew ever been seen using his hands? Are there Jewish peasants, Jewish artisans? No, work dishonors.

Without roots in France or any other country, Jews are, in Saccard's view, far from being "men like other men." They possess an "innate knowledge of numbers" that compels Saccard to admire them; and inseparable from "the natural ease with which they negotiate the most complicated operations" is their coldness. How can a southerner ruled by emotions win the financial game against dispassionate Jewry? "Gundermann was decidedly right: fever is worthless at the Bourse," Saccard laments after the crash. "Ah! the rogue, he's happy at no longer having blood or nerves, at no longer sleeping with a woman or drinking a bottle of Burgundy! . . . He epitomizes his whole race, this cold, obstinate conqueror." That Gundermann prizes family life as much as Saccard eschews it, letting small grandchildren climb all over him during business hours, doesn't alter this view. For Saccard, a man of real warmth—a man with fire in him—scatters his seed profligately.

Where Saccard ends and Zola begins is sometimes problematical. Unlike Goncourt, Daudet, Huysmans, and other literary confreres, Zola deplored anti-Semitism, but, as his notes indicate, certain elements of a xenophobic mythology were nonetheless woven into the fabric of L'Argent. Almost without exception, his informants assured him that Jewish heads differed from French heads, and this "otherness" went unquestioned. The Bourse was two-thirds foreigners—déclassés, Germans, and Levantines above all—constituting a "very motley" world, he wrote in his notes. "One can't enrich oneself there by playing honestly. Any honorable fellow who happens into it and finds escape impossible lives with disgust for his métier, a kind of shame. . . . Fasquelle, Busnach, and others give me the impression that French brains loathe the abstract side of finance. . . . It is a Jew's métier; a specially made brain is required, certain racial aptitudes." The capitalist wizard endowed at birth with special faculties for understanding and manipulating money was easy to picture as the foe of old-line aristocrats. Did it not make sense—novelistic sense at any rate—that nomads, fugitives, would bear an animus against quintessentially landed people? "I mustn't forget that at the bottom of my subject lies the Jewish question," Zola noted in his sketch, "for I can't discuss money without evoking the entire role of Jews then and now. I shall thus have the Jew triumph over the nobility; the once lowly and despised Jew finding himself raised on high and the once lofty nobleman laid low."

His observation chimed with the belief held by many Catholic rightwing ideologues that Jewry had had a decisive hand in every revolution since 1789. The abbé Augustin de Barruel first brought this occult influence to light during Napoleon Bonaparte's regime with his *Mémoire pour servir à l'histoire du Jacobinisme*, and eighty years later Edouard Drumont enlarged upon it in *La France juive*, a ranting compendium of anti-Semitic fables that sold as many as three or four hundred thousand copies in 1886–88. "Where was the Jew during the Revolution?" asked Drumont, whom Zola read.

On the roads. He sought a convenient corner, he entered through the breach, he took root in this society whose ranks had just been broken. . . .
From the outset, the Revolution, like today's Jewish Republic, had the character of an invasion. As in our day, the French element dis-

appeared before a pack of foreigners who seized all the important positions and terrorized the country. . . . Riding a foreign tide, the Jew came in unnoticed. . . .

The intellectual audacity and enormous impudence of which we have often spoken (for we encounter them at every turn, in financial enterprises as well as political) are based on an idea engraved in the Jew's brain for centuries. Religion, which teaches him that he is superior to other men, that he must annihilate everything that is not himself, that everything on earth belongs to him, is the powerful vehicle of those delirious conceptions.

The contest between two aristocracies, the monied and the blooded, pervades *L'Argent*. Upon Gundermann, whose bearish tactics ruin countless nobles previously induced to purchase Universelle stock, Zola confers royal or imperial titles. Lording it over the Bourse, that "foreign" enclave where "barbaric" shouts alarm Parisians outside, Gundermann speaks *ad urbis* and *ad orbis*. He is "the king of gold." He "makes bull and bear markets" as "God makes thunder." To his noisy, cluttered office Napoleon III's ministers come scraping. "There one witnessed the universal royalty of this man who had ambassadors in all the courts of the world, consuls in all the provinces, agencies in all the cities, vessels on all the seas." Yet he is no "speculator," no "conquistador" maneuvering other people's fortunes and dreaming, like Saccard, of heroic battles fought for colossal booty. "He was, as he himself put it good-naturedly, a simple merchant, the most skillful and zealous imaginable, who, in order to ground his power, had to dominate the Bourse."[2]

As with other novels, the writing of *L'Argent*, which Zola began on June 10, 1890, was accompanied by lamentations. He had been working on his novel rather cheerlessly, he confided to Céard on September 4. It was giving him terrific trouble, and he feared that his hardships would go unrecognized. "Money is decidedly a thankless subject, stock market business I mean." One week later he told Jacques van Santen Kolff the same thing: "Nothing, I believe, resists artistic shaping quite as much as . . . this financial matter, in which I find myself plunged neck-deep. You ask me if I am satisfied. I am never satisfied in the middle of a book, and tackling something so difficult to grasp leaves

[2]Gundermann's all-embracing consciousness—Zola describes him as an absolute master wanting to hear, see, and do everything alone—is a foil to the Unconscious that drives Saccard, and this dualism comes out in many different ways. Where Gundermann winkles out secrets, Saccard has a secret winkled out, the existence of a bastard son gotten on a shopgirl. "Victor," who has grown up in abysmal poverty and never learned civilized manners, is another Zolian example of the primitive lurking inside.

me, on certain days, exhausted." Still, his resolve saw him through with little time wasted. Serialized in *Gil Blas* after November 29, the book (published by Charpentier et Fasquelle) appeared on March 14, 1891, in a first printing of fifty-five thousand copies.

L'Argent fared better than expected. By 1891 the public considered the *Rougon-Macquart* saga a great nineteenth-century monument, and more than one otherwise unsympathetic or hostile critic saw fit to confess, grudgingly, that five years earlier he had not recognized in Zola's flaws the deficiencies of his virtue. Prophets must be forgiven breaches of measure and taste, Anatole France observed in *Le Temps*. "Taken as a whole, the picture seems true. *L'Argent* is vast, restless, vivid, full of life. One sees the strings being pulled, no doubt. One encounters again the long enumerations to which M. Zola has accustomed us and the set phrases that recur throughout like Wagnerian leitmotifs. Simpler than ever, the turgid style betrays neglect. All the same, an extraordinary power animates this heavy machine." Encomiums also appeared in *Le Figaro, Gil Blas, La Gazette de France, La République française, Le Rappel* (where Judith Gautier called attention to Zola's genius for making some "blind, unconscious, synthetic entity like the Bourse house a broad idea"). Even Edmond de Goncourt allowed *L'Argent* a compliment.

But the most ample, full-blooded treatment came from the Flemish poet Emile Verhaeren, who declared that Zola had moved increasingly toward abstraction in *Les Rougon-Macquart*. "As this writer has matured and broadened, he has attached himself to generalities, to laws, to ideas," he wrote in *La Nation*.

Yes, to ideas, with the particular case fading from his field of observation . . . , with the individual ceding to the group, with chiseled details making way for large features hammered out of the raw block. . . . Little by little his optic has become more abstract. It has transcended empirical evidence or life study. An a priori concept . . . has replaced reality, and this to such an extent that in *L'Argent*, where vice eclipses the vicious, speculation is portrayed as a kind of maleficent divinity hovering above human purpose, mastering men, guiding them, dooming them.

Far from disagreeing with Verhaeren, Zola might have found this review pertinent, and borne it in mind several years later when, as we shall see, circumstances obliged him to defend Auguste Rodin during a fierce argument over the sculptor's massively conceived, almost featureless statue of Balzac.

Fame had its allure, and the postman who made his rounds several times a day in Paris continued to bring requests of every kind to Zola's mailbox. There was the publisher wanting an interview-portrait of him for a new weekly. There was the journalist asking him how he felt about cremation (in connection with the installation at Père-Lachaise Cemetery of a crematorium, denounced by the archbishop of Paris). There was Guy de Maupassant urging him to speak at a ceremony inaugurating a statue of Flaubert in Rouen. There were obscure novelists soliciting prefaces or reviews. And there were young people needing advice their parents couldn't give them. In August 1890, for example, a letter came from an electric-company clerk named Louis de Robert. "I am nineteen years old [and] would like to write litera-ture," explained this frail young man, who eventually produced some thirty novels, including a very good one about his own life, *Le Roman du malade*. How, he wondered, should he prepare himself? "Unfortu-nately I have received a very skimpy education. . . . One of my friends, a lawyer, has offered to teach me Greek and Latin. It would mean eight hours of work a day for two years. I am inclined to undertake this program; and courage is not in short supply, for I am dead set on accomplishing something worthwhile and escaping an uncongenial mi-lieu. . . . But I wonder whether I would be better advised to spend my time making useful acquaintances." Confident that Robert had never read his diatribe against the cult of classics in French *lycées*, a rather more tolerant Zola brushed him off with high-minded advice worthy of Polonius. "What can I say," he replied, "except that at nineteen you are still a child, and that you must live and that you must work. Learn Greek, learn Latin, study anything at all, but study. You have five or six years in which to develop ideas and a style. . . . Above all, don't be impatient."[3]

Such formulae served as the novelist's indispensable concierge, turn-ing away petitioners without giving offense. But petitioners got through on occasion, and some actually became friends or collabora-tors or both. A case in point was Alfred Bruneau, who came recom-mended by the architect Frantz Jourdain. After studying musical composition with Jules Massenet at the Conservatoire, then living abroad on a Prix de Rome, Bruneau had made some few slight ripples in the Paris musical world. Lyric theater interested him more than symphonic composition, and the idea of extracting an opera from *La Faute de l'abbé Mouret* was what brought him to Zola in 1888. There he learned that rights for an opera had been reserved four years earlier

---

[3]Louis de Robert left the electric company soon afterward to work as a journalist. During the Dreyfus Affair, he made a good friend in Marcel Proust, with whom he often attended proceedings at the Palace of Justice.

by his ex-mentor. Massenet would not surrender those rights, so Zola offered Bruneau, whom he liked immediately, a consolation prize. "Don't despair," he told the thirty-one-year-old composer. "I am at work on a novel that will lend itself better than L'abbé Mouret to lyric adaptation, and where you will find an equal measure of mysticism. . . . We'll speak about this again in late September, but henceforth it is yours." Bruneau was ecstatic.

In October the composer joined forces with Louis Gallet, an older man who had produced numerous libretti for Bizet, Massenet, and Saint-Saëns while earning his livelihood as director of the huge Lariboisière Hospital. Gallet was quick to assure Zola that something artistically distinguished would come of his munificent gesture. "In asking me to collaborate," he wrote, "[Bruneau] guessed my mind, which was deeply impressed by the character of [your novel]. The result will surely be a musical tableau very modern in spirit, delicate and luminous in color, and you have given a young musician an undreamed-of opportunity to assert himself. Please tell me when and where I may chat with you. Like a young lover, Bruneau can hardly sit still."

Jeanne Rozerot and La Bête humaine kept Zola busy during the following year. He hesitated, moreover, to intrude upon an esoteric project. But Bruneau, who found him nonetheless musical for having little in the way of musical culture, invited his collaboration, and Zola eventually suggested numerous changes, which were incorporated with gratitude. "Several days ago," he told a Gil Blas reporter in January 1890, "I found myself at M. Bruneau's flat . . . hearing the second act of Le Rêve, which the composer had just finished. To say that I was asked for my opinion sounds pretentious, as I am . . . a layman, a complete layman. Common sense, or the tastes of a literary man shape my judgment, and what I heard of M. Bruneau's score made a very agreeable impression. It is very modern music." Other such readings had already taken place on the rue de Boulogne and at Médan.

Zola became more intensely collaborative when Le Rêve entered the practical world. Embraced at a huge, ornate new theater called the Eden after being cold-shouldered at the Opéra-Comique, Bruneau sought advice from his benefactor. "I didn't discourage [my music publisher] from [looking into the Eden for us], I admit, as it occurred to me that in a new theater, with a new director, we stood a better chance of having our work staged the way we conceived it than in an official monument where even supernumeraries pontificate." Zola found himself invited to opine on everything, props as well as singers, and he himself ended up designing the decor in eight cartoons.

The Eden went bankrupt after Saint-Saëns's Samson et Dalila opened there on October 15, and Le Rêve might have languished in obscurity had the Opéra-Comique not meanwhile come under the direction of a new man, Léon Carvalho, who signed it up without delay. Rehearsals lasted from March 1891 until June 18, when the opera began a very successful run. "Yesterday," Bruneau told Zola on July 1, "we had our largest take: 5,550 francs. Here, furthermore, are the last three takes: Saturday 5,300, Monday 5,200, Tuesday, 5,550. Yesterday we turned away 1,500 francs' worth at the door because of complimentary tickets." Such numbers were all the more notable because *Le Rêve* won public acclaim while flouting conventions that had immunized French opera against foreign influence since Meyerbeer's ascendancy in the 1830s and 1840s. French critics regarded everything Wagnerian as odious, so success could hardly have been predicted for a work in which continuous melody eliminated bravura passages and leitmotifs governed dramatic movement. "It received favorable reviews, despite the consternation Bruneau's music caused with its orchestral audacities," writes one scholar. "Frowned upon were certain 'cacophonous' harmonies and the absence of traditional duos, cavatinas and quartets . . . as well as the excessive 'realism' of scenes like the one involving Extreme Unction."

That autumn *Le Rêve* played to large, enthusiastic audiences abroad, first at London's Covent Garden, then at Brussels's Théâtre de la Monnaie (where the Zolas joined Bruneau for the premiere), and finally at the Hamburg Opera in a production directed by Gustav Mahler. "If, in the score of *Le Rêve*, I struck some deep chords, they come from the emotion with which the humanity of your entire work fills me and from my grateful affection for you," Bruneau wrote to Zola. "Right now I cannot imagine doing solitary work without feeling immense chagrin; I fear that discouragement would very quickly overtake me." As we shall see, this friendship outlived *Le Rêve*, made a librettist of Zola, and yielded half a dozen more works. By September 1891 plans were already afoot for an opera based on Zola's story "L'Attaque du moulin."

During the early 1890s, Zola's prodigious energies found another outlet in the Société des Gens de Lettres, a guild which had been chartered six decades earlier, under Louis Philippe, by novelists seeking to protect themselves against unauthorized serialization in French newspapers; it had since acquired as well the functions of a provident society for writers, helping the indigent and pensioning the old. "I have always loathed groups and societies," Zola told a reporter from *Le Temps* on February 11, 1891. "I didn't like regimentation. But in aging one revises one's opinions." Whatever qualms he may have had were dispelled by the enthusiasm with which fellow writers clasped him to their collective bosom. Elected unanimously on February 9, he became a member of the executive committee two months later, when *sociétaires* met in general assembly at the Hôtel Continental. On April 6, the committee made him president for 1891–92, and they reelected him president three times, almost as doggedly as the French Academy voted him down.

Except during sojourns in the country, Zola seldom missed weekly meetings of the executive committee, and his administration served membership very effectively indeed. Agreements governing the reproduction of literary works were negotiated with Parisian and provincial newspapers. Authors whose rights had been violated were given legal aid. And efforts that resulted in the passage of a copyright bill through the United States Congress were gratefully acknowledged. By turns ceremonial and magisterial, Zola wore several hats. He spoke at funerals and at the inauguration of busts, defying his stage fright. He traveled to London with four colleagues in September 1893, at the invitation of the English Institute of Journalists.

And on occasion he arbitrated disputes. When, for example, Arthur Meyer interrupted on moral grounds the serialization of a novel in *Le Gaulois*, he and the author, Edmond Tarbé, agreed to have their rival claims adjudicated by a committee that included Zola and Francisque Sarcey. "The novel, some thirty installments of which have already appeared, does not, we feel, . . . contain anything likely to offend the susceptibilities of *Le Gaulois*'s readership," Zola pronounced. "It is therefore quite natural that M. Tarbé should want publication resumed. On the other hand, certain as yet unpublished passages which may not have awakened the editor's scruples in manuscript caused alarm once they had been set in type. This is a very common phenomenon, and we in the trade are well acquainted with it. It is our impression that author and editor should be able, without difficulty, to agree upon certain passages for toning down and others for elimination." This tactful verdict bespoke a transformation that was evident as well in a memo chiding delinquent members for not heeding his call to discuss internal governance. The genial host who had perhaps always felt happiest when surrounded by fellow Aixois on Thursday evenings became a conscientious paterfamilias dedicated to the welfare of writers at large. "We announced a convocation for last January 31 and it could not be held, as those present did not constitute a quorum of members residing in Paris," he wrote on February 16, 1892. "Such lack of zeal is profoundly regrettable, the more so because we remain in suspense, as it were, until new statutes have been voted. . . . Our Society's good name requires that this time we assemble in strength."

Among his responsibilities, none afforded him greater satisfaction or cost him more grief than the dispensing of alms and pensions. It undoubtedly called up powerful childhood memories. "What [waggish confreres who joke about the Société des Gens de Lettres] would hear, [if they listened in on us,] is the ardent desire voiced at every meeting to increase the pension fund," he declared in an article published by *Le Figaro*.

> We discuss it all the time, we work at it the year round. Of our approximately six hundred fifty members, one hundred and forty are now pensioners. Whoever is eligible for a pension by virtue of age—sixty years—and length of membership—twenty-five years—gets one. But how wretchedly inadequate they have been until now! Five hundred francs, or barely enough to keep from starving. And we wouldn't be able to allow even that if we hadn't won the lottery ten years ago. So the committee racks its brains for ways of doubling the allowance, which would make it at least reasonable.

Although the Society never thrived, it became less impecunious during the 1890s, thanks in large part to Zola. He extracted funds from the government and the private sector, dunning the ministry of public works, the governor of the Land Bank, the Confederation of Railroad Companies. He also waged a successful campaign to have the guild recognized as an *établissement d'utilité publique*, which vouchsafed it important financial advantages.

What posterity mainly remembers of Zola's tenure as president is the statue of Balzac commissioned by the Society from Auguste Rodin in 1891. The project had been opened to public subscription six years earlier, and in 1888, with more than thirty thousand francs collected, the guild (over which Balzac himself had once presided) hired Henri Chapu, whose proficient busts were highly esteemed by fin de siècle Parisians. But Chapu died on April 15, 1891, leaving only a vague sketch from which nothing of the work he may have had in mind could be deduced. Confident that the Society would not invite legal action, Zola arranged to have a colleague question Rodin, who responded enthusiastically. "I most certainly would . . . do the Balzac statue in the event Chapu's sketch was not executed," he wrote at the end of June, "and not least among the satisfactions this gives me is having been chosen by you, dear M. Zola. . . . If nothing else comes of it, the honor will suffice, for I do not witness your victories as an indifferent spectator. . . . I belong to those who hail you." So smoothly did everything proceed that by July 1 Zola felt free to address details with the sculptor, using another go-between. "See him as soon as possible," he urged his architect friend Frantz Jourdain, who had recommended Rodin in the first place. "Persuade him that the statue must stand at least four meters tall, not counting the pedestal, and determine whether the whole can be executed and installed for thirty thousand francs. If so, he must write to me immediately, declaring that he would like to execute the statue for this sum. . . . He must agree in his letter to deliver the monument by May 1, 1893." One week later the executive committee, at Zola's instigation, chose Rodin over Marquet de Vasselot. "I found a Rodin full of joy, full of gratitude to you, and afire over his Balzac," a colleague informed Zola on July 10. "He'll take advantage of the holidays to visit Tours and soak up Balzacian atmosphere, see people, rummage through the museum; I believe that he will create a significant work and that the Society will not regret having chosen this enthusiast." Rodin would have further occasion for gratitude eight months later, when, after much badgering, Zola finally prevailed upon municipal and state authorities to let the statue occupy space on the Place du Palais-Royal.[4]

A statuesque presence in central Paris was, increasingly, what Zola wanted for himself. With late middle age upon him he began to see *Les Rougon-Macquart* as a pedestal for reaching beyond, into the political sphere he had always found subversive of literature. From the Palais de l'Institut, where the French Academy convened under Louis Le Vau's gorgeous seventeenth-century cupola, his eye wandered westward to the Palais-Bourbon, where deputies legislated, and uphill to the Palais du Luxembourg, which housed the Senate. "Right now I cannot consider politics," he told a reporter on June 23, 1891, after word had gotten out that a group of young people were urging him to run for office from the fifth arrondissement. "I must first finish *Les Rougon-Macquart* and I would find it quite impossible to fulfill both the duties of a deputy and my writing commitments. I don't want to do anything by halves. If I were a deputy I would work hard, and literature would be given short shrift. Five or six years hence it may not be disagreeable to join battle on another ground, and fight, with spoken words and through legislation, for literary property and workers' rights. Yes, at that point I believe I would accept a political mandate. But I'd prefer the Senate to the Chamber. In the Senate, deliberations are less hasty and therefore more thorough, more

[4]The sequel, however, was most unhappy. Rodin caused dismay by progressing slowly, and as time wore on, an opposition, shocked by his model of the Balzac, gathered strength. In 1898 this hostile group, which had become the majority, declared that "the committee of the Société des Gens de Lettres is regretfully obliged to protest against the plaster cast that M. Rodin has exhibited at the Salon, and in which it refuses to recognize the statue of Balzac." Zola remained loyal but by then he had the Dreyfus Affair to worry about. Although Rodin could have sued, he preferred instead to reimburse advances. His magnificent work was not cast in bronze until 1939, when the government granted it a few square feet at the intersection of boulevards Montparnasse and Raspail.

serious." Some two years later, when he had finished *Les Rougon-Macquart* and started another series of novels, he enlarged upon this postliterary dispensation in an interview with the *Figaro* journalist Jules Huret. "Would you be disposed to 'enter the Chamber,' Maître?" asked Huret. "Indeed I would!" Zola responded.

> Not now, but when I shall have finished the last three volumes I intend to write. And why not? For twenty years I have scrutinized crowds, I have studied society from top to bottom, I have put my finger on social sores, I have exposed iniquities, I have, in short, acquired a fund of beliefs that I am entitled and qualified to defend. . . . I have seen the unfortunate suffer. I know what they suffer from, and so why should I not use my remaining energy and strength to fight for them?

The problem, he continued, was that his ability to marshal ideas in neat formation deserted him before a live audience:

> I have one fault, a major fault, it's true, which is that I am, much to my regret, not an orator. I've tried to speak on various occasions, I've hurled myself into the water, at the Société des Gens de Lettres and elsewhere. It doesn't work. . . . I'm sure that a gift for the spoken word—and it is a *gift*—occupies some special compartment of the brain; there's the orator's compartment as there is the writer's compartment. Otherwise why would my ideas get muddled as soon as I want to speak in public yet flow of themselves, effortlessly, and in good order, when I have pen in hand? . . . Anyway, I shall try.

He would try because he imagined himself speaking for the poor, the convicted, the disenfranchised, the silenced. He would argue against censorship. He would demand abolition of the death penalty. He would support more lenient divorce laws. And, above all, he would join the campaign to bestow civil rights upon children born out of wedlock—*les enfants naturels.*

Had Zola run for office in 1893, the penultimate chapter of *Les Rougon-Macquart*—a novel called *La Débâcle*—would not have won him any votes from chauvinists intent on extolling the unclouded glory of "the Grand Army." Warfare was something Zola had always meant to give full play in *Les Rougon-Macquart,* and his 1868 scheme had provided for "a novel that will have the military world as its framework . . . ; an episode in [Napoleon III's] Italian campaign." But after the calamitous Franco-Prussian War, this installment acquired special significance. What had originally been envisaged as one tale among others came to be seen as the denouement of the entire saga, as the great

Niagara toward which Zola's multitudinous characters would move like flotsam bobbing on a wild torrent. "[There will be] a study of the army with Jean Macquart," Louis Desprez wrote in 1884. "M. Zola will candidly expose our prewar military situation. . . . The hurly-burly will end at Sedan."

When Charpentier published *L'Argent* on March 14, 1891, *La Débâcle* already had a bulging file. "I've started to assemble documents for my next novel, *La Débâcle*," Zola informed van Santen Kolff on March 6. "Next month I shall spend one week at Sedan, as I want especially to paint the formidable battle that took place there, an immense fresco—the worst of fates ever to have befallen a people." Documents there were in abundance. For an understanding of the confused prologue that saw thousands shamble to their doom, Zola studied *La Campagne de 1870* by Prince Georges Bibesco, an aide-de-camp on the general staff of the 7th Army Corps. With pen in hand he read *La Guerre de 1870: Bazeilles-Sedan* by General Lebrun of the 12th Army Corps, *L'Histoire militaire contemporaine: 1854–1871* by Colonel Frédéric Canonge, and *Froeschwiller, Châlons, Sedan* by Alfred Duquet, whom he often had occasion to interrogate in person. "I recall him more than once suddenly arriving at my office to get certain details straight and, above all, myself spending hours at his place on the rue de Bruxelles bent over maps as he fired questions about strategy and tactics," Duquet wrote several years later, after the Dreyfus Affair. "Well, I must admit that his sole guide seemed to be a desire to tell the truth about men and things, and I detected no hatred whatsoever of the army. He seized military concepts with surprising ease and always alighted on the appropriate solution." When Gaston Calmette of *Le Figaro* visited the rue de Bruxelles toward the end of March, he found Zola knee-deep in paper, plodding through four sets of general staff reports. Two months later he would have found him waist-deep, as answers to his many queries continued to arrive. People called upon for help almost always responded conscientiously, and with pride. One such diligent informant was a Monsieur Gougelet, domiciled at the Villa des Arts near Montmartre Cemetery, who furnished particulars about the organization of artillery regiments in the late 1860s. Another was Zola's lifelong friend Numa Coste, who until 1875 had been a professional soldier. "[You will . . . shortly receive] a package that contains the complete collection of army uniforms," Coste wrote on May 10. "It includes illustrated plates and synoptic tableaux describing each garment in detail. Although these plates correspond to the regulations of 1849, they will nonetheless serve, for the regulations of 1868 modified formal wear rather than campaign dress."

Zola decided almost immediately to recount in *La Débâcle* not only the virtual annihilation of half the Army of the Rhine but the bungled opportunities, political maneuvers, and missed cues that brought about this disaster. What ended at Sedan on September 1, 1870, had begun two weeks earlier at Châlons-sur-Marne, where four corps under Marshal MacMahon's general command regrouped after suffering terrible defeats to the east, at Froeschwiller and Wissembourg. The great question was whether to march east again and somehow unite with forces commanded by Marshal Bazaine, or to give up Alsace-Lorraine and fall back on Paris. Ever irresolute, Napoleon III ordered a retreat at the behest of staff, who thought that Bazaine might not escape his besieged position; then reversed himself at the behest of Empress Eugénie, who made it known through the minister of war, Palikao, that Paris would rise against the Empire unless he emerged victorious from battle. German cavalry sighted near Châlons forced the army to decamp for Reims, thirty miles northwest, but there 130,000 men stood paralyzed, like some ancient horde awaiting divine omens. MacMahon finally took matters in hand and reissued the retreat order, whereupon chance played him dirty. No sooner had the new order been drafted than a message arrived indicating that Bazaine expected to break free. This sanguine announcement altered everything. "Bazaine was not after all going to let himself be shut up in Metz," writes one historian. "It was no longer a question of marching to [Bazaine's] relief, but of joining him to give battle in the open field. MacMahon at once reversed his decision. The orders for the retreat on Paris were canceled." Ill-trained and ill-supplied columns lumbered across hill and dale toward phantom comrades, plundering the countryside en route. After three days their situation became desperate. While reports of an enemy presence abounded, nothing whatever was seen of Bazaine and his troops, who had in fact been sequestered at Metz. Harried by Saxon troops emerging from the Argonne Forest, MacMahon found himself cut off on three sides, and when he decided to flee north, the government forbade it. Palikao did not think that prudence was the better part of valor. "If you abandon Bazaine," he warned, "revolution will break out in Paris and you will yourself be attacked by the entire enemy forces. . . . You have at least thirty-six hours' march over the crown prince [Frederick William of Prussia], perhaps forty-eight; you have nothing in front of you but a feeble part of the forces blockading Metz. . . . Everyone here has felt the necessity of releasing Bazaine, and the anxiety with which we follow your movements is intense."

Political expediency dictated military strategy, and the result was self-immolation. As German horsemen watched from afar, MacMahon's soldiers marched forward, not knowing whither or why. A first disastrous engagement occurred on August 30 at Beaumont, near the river Meuse, where bivouacked French infantry were taken unawares. The next day the other units crossed the Meuse five miles downstream, within sight of a small fortress town called Sedan, which lay cradled between marshlands to the south and wooded slopes to the north. There, in what he viewed as an eminently defensible position, MacMahon declared that his men should rest. And there, in what the German general von Moltke viewed as a gigantic mousetrap, they died by the thousand when German cannon rained shellfire upon them from hilltop batteries. After twelve pulverizing hours of bombardment, Napoleon III, who had sought death all morning long, had the white flag hoisted.

It behooved Zola to retrace this tragic odyssey, and on April 17, he departed Courcelles (near Reims) with Alexandrine, in a large four-wheeled landau driven by a coachman who had fought at Sedan twenty-one years earlier. The itinerary of the 7th Army Corps, as Prince Bibesco described it, led across the Argonne plateau through minuscule villages that had become historical place names overnight. Pausing frequently, Zola took elaborate notes on the landscape, questioned witnesses, reconnoitered campsites, inspected Napoleon III's quarters. There was, for example, the notary's house in Le Chesne, where MacMahon and the emperor made the fatal decision to plunge ahead after receiving Palikao's message. "They more or less requisitioned the house," he wrote.

> The occupants had to sleep under the eaves. Mme Lefèvre, a woman of seventy who died soon afterward of stomach cancer, was loath to surrender her bedroom. . . . The occupants appear to have been indignant at all the crockery unloaded on them. Chefs cooked up a storm in the kitchen. . . . The emperor and Marshal MacMahon walked over to the town hall on the rue de Vouziers. For what purpose? There must have been police there. A few scattered cries of 'Vive l'empereur!' He tried to smile, but both men looked beaten. . . . Le Chesne was full of troops. One can't imagine what it's like, a whole army corps marching down a village street. For three or four days the artillery, the cavalry wheeled across the bridge nonstop.

His eye for detail remained sharp at Sedan, where Charles Philippoteaux, a prominent merchant and brother of Sedan's former mayor, guided him all around. Having divided the battlefield into seven parts, with notes on the position of French troops and Prussian batteries for each, Zola could visualize analytically the whole hellish pageant as he traveled hither and yon, from the Château de Belle Vue, where King Wilhelm and Bismarck had looked on, to a loop in the Meuse where thousands of French captives were penned like cattle, to the slope down which Colonel Galliffet had led desperate, suicidal cavalry charges. Witnesses were asked how matters had stood at every hour of the fatal day, where Napoleon III (who, like half the army, had contracted dysentery) paraded himself, over which rampart the white flag went up, what happened in Sedan during the aftermath:

> In the town, after the battle, the cleaning-up ordered by the Prussians, which cost six thousand francs. Garbage overflowed and threatened to spread disease through the countryside. Horse dung twenty centimeters high in the streets. Human excrement. Everything that a crowd of twenty-four thousand men can leave. Horses slaughtered for food; their carcasses—the heads and entrails—remained, rotting in the sun. . . . Soldiers everywhere, lying on doorsteps. Weak from fatigue and hunger, they would sooner have been crushed than moved.

When Zola left for Charleville on April 25, his file had grown thicker by 109 pages, entitled "Mon voyage à Sedan," most of which would enter the body of *La Débâcle* in descriptive passages and dramatic anecdotes.[5]

Almost as instructive as the expedition itself was the remarkable correspondence it generated. After describing his project in interviews published by *Le Figaro* and *Le Petit Ardennais,* Zola received innumerable letters, many of them pages long, from people who had played minor parts in the national tragedy. Soldiers and civilians alike relied upon him to set the historical record straight, but also to salvage by the written word some experience that had changed their lives forever. They came with burdens of grief or with grudges nursed since 1870, with tales of cowardice or of unchronicled heroism. Madame Ledant-Rivet wrote at length about the armies that ebbed and flowed through little Raucourt, hoping that Zola would commemorate the deeds of her husband, a doctor who cared selflessly for the wounded. On the other hand, Émile Lefèvre had seen little to praise among medical men who converted his country house outside Sedan into a field hospital. "On the lawn of my property two barracks had been constructed, each containing sixty mutilated casualties," this rich merchant informed Zola on April 29.

> Every kind of ailment. From five to ten deaths a day, corpses piled up in my bathroom, my living room, my dining room, bedrooms, all filled with the dead and dying. In my office, on the kitchen table, wounded men were cut open! Every bit of linen was buried along

---

[5]Charles Philippoteaux may not have felt properly rewarded for the inconvenience to which he put himself. The animation and charm Zola displayed during field trips vanished during meals at his host's home, where he was "taciturn, churlish, and rather disagreeable."

with the stench of wounds, some of them atrocious. I'd go from bed to bed, writing letters, distributing broth and tobacco. Whatever had been sent for the army and the sick—tins of meat, of broth, of fruit, etc.—ended up on the table of medical officers and orderlies, the most voracious rabble imaginable. Doctors were sick from gorging on good food and drink while the sick starved! Don't you believe what you heard about the valor of soldiers. . . . Oh, I beg of you, do not write quickly! Continue to reflect, and tell the truth.

There were, of course, as many truths as correspondents. Matthieu-Jeannin from Tulle recalled, among much else, the sight of intransigent Zouaves firing angrily on the white flag and of general officers sitting at a café in Sedan puffing cigarettes while recruits bled outside the walls. Frédéric Pérès from Bayonne wanted it known that late in the afternoon of September 1, when all was lost, four hundred men mustered by Commandant Lamy held their ground until nightfall. And a former sergeant major leapt to the defense of comrades in the 21st Infantry Regiment, declaring, at the conclusion of a long letter, that they had fought without respite and cooled their overheated rifles by pissing down the barrels.

To what extent Zola was seen as the great chronicler and redeemer of wrongs is best indicated by a letter from one P. Martine, a graduate of the elite Ecole Normale Supérieure and a *lycée* professor teaching history, who had participated actively in the Commune and spent years of exile in Russia. After reading several installments of *La Débâcle* in *La Vie populaire*, he wrote a letter expressing the hope that Zola would not end *La Débâcle* before absolving the Commune of sins imputed to it. "In the public's eyes, your judgment will be definitive. It is not possible to imagine the impartial painter of French society pronouncing, as others have done, a *Vae Victis!* over the tomb of so many obscure heroes whose modest sacrifices and proud ends I witnessed." In his view, Zola's work was more than a history. "It is a resurrection, a photograph, a living drama."

As nothing less than the total picture would satisfy him, Zola managed to encompass it all—the flight from Alsace, the *rassemblement* at Châlons, the ill-conceived advance eastward toward Montmédy, the debacle itself—in a narrative that constantly shifts between several dozen dramatis personae and the anonymous horde. On ground level, where individual stories unfold, men of every class and rank, each laden with his particular past, converse vividly. Bound together for the march are peasant and Parisian, intellectual and merchant, republican and emperor. Readers meet each in turn. But viewed through the eyes of the Prussian king, who sits enthroned on high like Thor, the individual shrinks to nothing, and this perspective has metaphysical import, for those who believe themselves to be endowed with free will are governed by a palpable fate. Strategies are suicidal delusions. "At seven o'clock the Prussian king had set out from Vendresse, where he had spent the night, and now he was up on Marfée Hill, safely out of harm's reach, with the whole Meuse Valley—the whole sprawling battle zone—spread out before him," Zola relates.[6]

> The huge relief map stretched from one side of the sky to the other while he looked on from the hill slope, as though from the seat of honor in a gigantic royal box. . . . At [his] feet the almost unbroken line of batteries between Remilly and Frenois were thundering away without respite, unloading shell after shell on La Moncelle and Daigny and firing clean over the top of Sedan so as to rake the plateaux to the north of the town. It was still only a little after eight o'clock and already he was awaiting the inevitable outcome of the battle, eyes trained on the giant chessboard, mind engrossed in the task of steering this human dust, of controlling this handful of black dots as they scurried about amid nature's cheerful and everlasting presence.

Chapters later, at the end of a battle whose frantic, bloody episodes have been recounted charge by charge, Zola's eye returns once again to that height from which the human enterprise appears theatrical, abstract:

> In the wavering light, the slow winding Meuse gleamed like a river of pure gold. And beneath the sun's last rays, the monstrous, blood-soaked battle, seen from above, was like delicate painting; dead horsemen and disemboweled horses strewed the plain of Floing with patches of bright color; on the right, toward Givonne, the fleeing men, in a final stampede, were no more than whirling black specks. . . . This was victory unlooked for, overwhelming victory; and the king looked down upon it without any feeling of remorse.

Fate weighed upon Sedan, Zola had noted at the beginning of his sketch. "Destiny swooping down on a nation. But there were causes, and it is precisely these causes I wish to study."

The only promise of redemption in *La Débâcle* is the fraternal bond that unites two soldiers who except for war would never have become acquainted. Immediately he joins his unit, Jean Macquart, the corporal

---

[6]Although Zola doesn't mention it in *La Débâcle*, among the spectators invited to watch the battle from Wilhelm's "royal box" was General Philip Henry Sheridan, the Union cavalry leader who five years earlier had cut off Lee's retreat at Appomattox Courthouse, forcing his surrender.

turned peasant last seen leaving the Beauce (in *La Terre*), meets Maurice Levasseur, a man so unlike him as to defy comprehension. While Jean has always shouldered burdens, Maurice has always caused grief. Jean exemplifies steadfastness; Maurice reels from mood to mood. Jean the yeoman transcends a flawed heredity; Maurice the degenerate cannot equal a heroic past. His grandfather was one of the heroes of the Grande Armée, but his father "had sunk to the lowly and ill-paid status of tax collector," writes Zola.

> His peasant mother had died giving birth to him and his twin sister. . . . His presence here as a volunteer was the aftermath of years of general dissipation and wrongdoing, resulting from a weak, impetuous nature. Ah, the money he had thrown away on gambling and on women and on all the wild pleasures of Paris, that predatory city where he had been sent to complete his law studies at the expense of a family who had pinched and scraped in their efforts to make a gentleman of him. His behavior had brought about the death of his father.

Fascinated by this high-strung, boyish, mercurial creature, Jean takes him under his wing, and Maurice responds in kind. They stick together on the road and on the battlefield, comfort each other and keep each other fed. When German fire hits Jean in a culvert north of Sedan, Maurice, after bearing the much larger man to safety, dresses his wound. And when Maurice goes limp with hunger trekking across the Argonne plateau, Jean carries him forward. "Here, surely, was the spirit of brotherhood which had existed in the early days of the world. . . . Maurice could hear his own humanity in the sound of Jean's heartbeats." Captured, they help each other survive nine days in a German concentration camp outside Sedan, at Iges, to the description of which Zola brings his incomparable talent for evoking human hellholes. They make good their escape with ruses that need one man's aplomb and the other's bravado. Then they part: Jean, wounded again and in the care of a peasant uncle, encourages his friend to regain Paris via Belgium.

But *La Débâcle* cannot end until the bond that promises redemption becomes the ultimate plaything of man's inhumanity toward man. After Maurice embraces the Commune and Jean, recuperated, joins the army that invades Paris, the two friends are led by malign fate to either side of the same Left Bank barricade. Maurice's frustrated dream of universal brotherhood has transmuted itself into fantasies of homicidal apocalypse, of a purifying conflagration, while the sight of Paris in flames has outraged Jean Macquart to the pious quick of his soul. "Burning down houses, burning down palaces because one didn't have the upper hand—intolerable! Only bandits were capable of such mischief. He whose heart had been wrung by summary executions the previous day was now beside himself, ferocious, eyes starting from his head, thumping, yelling." Ideology pitted against ideology, the Communard blindly shooting from behind sandbags and the army regular blindly rushing forward with fixed bayonet recognize each other as men only after Jean has impaled Maurice. For them civil war ends in a posthumous embrace:

> Thunderstruck, brought back to his senses, Jean gazed down at him. They were alone, the rest of the soldiers had hurried off in pursuit of fugitives. All around, the fires burned higher, and huge tongues of flame shot out of windows while inside ceilings collapsed with a roar. Jean flung himself down beside his friend, sobbing, stroking his face, trying to lift him up in the hope that he might yet be saved. "Oh, my boy, my poor dear boy!"

Zola began *La Débâcle* on July 12, 1891, two days before the annual military review at Longchamp, which he made a special point of attending. By February 1892 almost two-thirds had been written, despite a monthlong voyage through the Pyrenees with Alexandrine. As always, disappointment harried him. "You want to know if I am satisfied," he wrote to van Santen Kolff on January 26, 1892. "Haven't I already told you that I've never felt satisfied with a book while writing it? I want to get everything into it, I'm always devastated by the limited scope of the accomplishment. Giving birth to a book is always an abominable torture for me, because it cannot answer my imperious need for universality and totality. This one has made me suffer more than the others, because it is more complex and dense. It will be the longest of my novels, with a thousand manuscript pages, or six hundred printed pages." He wrote again on June 8: "I penned the last word of *La Débâcle* on May 12. . . . I've caught my breath during the past three days, after many exhausting months, for you cannot imagine what relentless labor my last book required." Serialized in *La Vie populaire*, it was published by Charpentier et Fasquelle on June 21 and soon became Zola's greatest commercial success. One hundred thousand copies had been sold after four weeks, and after four months, half again as many.[7] *Feuilletons* appeared simultaneously in various

---

[7]On July 19, Charpentier notified Zola: "Yesterday I sent you a copy from the printing that brings circulation up to one hundred thousand. We have, I hope, a very good thing going! And it won't stop here. Sales are not slowing down and we have every reason to hope for a total of one hundred fifty thousand by year's end. My own feeling is that we'll exceed that figure. It's on everybody's lips. At Etretat, from which I returned yesterday, the whole town is reading it."

European capitals, including Rome and London. "I hope that people will recognize my impartiality," Zola fretted. "While sweeping nothing under the rug, I sought to 'explain' our disasters. This seemed the wisest and most dignified attitude, commercial success aside. . . . I would be quite happy if, in France and in Germany, I got proper credit for my effort at truth-telling."

Proper credit was not something he could reasonably expect from Bonapartists, monarchists, and right-wing nationalists pledged to Church and army. These elements—the same who would soon fill anti-Dreyfusard ranks—lost no time wheeling their artillery against *La Débâcle*. The first important salvo, a moderate one, was fired by a prominent academician best known for his book on the Russian novel, Eugène-Melchior, Vicomte de Vogüé. The viscount had fought at Sedan, and he rose to the army's defense in a long article published on July 15. "Was everybody, except for several impotent colonels, ignorant, frivolous, corrupt, boastful, or brutish? All Rougons! All Macquarts! The novelist's verdict is too general even for that poor army of Sedan, that random, uncohesive agglomeration battered from the Rhine to the Meuse by panic." If, as Zola suggested, France's vitality had been sapped by despotism, it would have been impossible, for six months, to put up a fight "unique in the annals of recent warfare." "*La Débâcle* did not for a moment reflect the true face of this resistance," Vogüé insisted, "a resistance insanely led, no doubt, and denounced at the time by myopic people, but infinitely wise in its principle and eternally blessed, for all that we are in the world today we owe . . . to that initial proof of strength."

Zola defended himself tenaciously against the imputation that he lacked patriotic feeling. Was it unpatriotic to offer reasons for a defeat? to suggest that France lost because it had been incompetently led and had conceived a false idea of its might on the battlefields of North Africa? to show that war elicited savage blood lust as well as *grandeur d'âme?* "I've just read the article you were good enough to devote to *La Débâcle*, and it contains such glowing literary compliments that I must express my profound gratitude for them," he answered Vogüé. "Still, I cannot let it go unsaid that your essay made me profoundly sad. I thought about the insuperable wall that separates two men when other beliefs stand between them. . . . You draw from the work a conclusion diametrically opposed to that which I intended." In an interview published several days later by *Le Gaulois*, Zola said he was sure that *La Débâcle* was a book from which French soldiers could take heart, a book about "pluck," a book maintaining "the necessity of revenge." He made this assertion, he said, not only as a Frenchman who wanted France strong militarily but as a Darwinian for whom the necessity of conflict transcended the particular circumstances of *re-*

vanchisme. "War is inevitable," he had written in *Le Figaro* on the twenty-first anniversary of the battle of Sedan. "Tender souls who dream of its abolition, who organize congresses to decree universal peace, thus indulge in generous utopianism. . . . Nothing exists in nature, nothing is born, nothing grows, nothing multiplies except through conflict. One must eat and be devoured for the world to survive. Only warrior nations have prospered, for a nation dies as soon as it disarms. War is the school of discipline, of sacrifice, of courage."[8]

Despite Zola's martial bombast, right-wing France hewed to the belief that anything he wrote subverted institutions it held dear, and red joined black in condemning *La Débâcle*. Pamphlets with titles like "A refaire *La Débâcle!*" and "Gloria Victis. L'armée française devant l'invasion et les erreurs de *La Débâcle*" circulated among the same people who hailed Father Théodore Delmont's characterization of the novel as "a nightmare, a hideous nightmare, heinous in its unpatriotism." *Le Figaro* published attacks by various French generals—Barail, Jung, Morel—and Catholic reviews carried denunciations by various Jesuit priests. But the most sensational indictment came from beyond the Rhine, in a lengthy letter written by a former German aide-de-camp, Karl Tanera, who had produced volumes of history about the Franco-Prussian War. "What I saw as a combatant, what I learned during my long sojourn in France, what I was obliged to study for my works of military history all tell me that M. Zola is wrong, wrong not only in his account of the events of August and September 1870 but in everything that touches on military affairs," this Bavarian assured the editor-in-chief of *Le Figaro*. German readers, he went on to say, frowned at Zola's ingratitude, at

> his lack of pity for MacMahon's poor army. . . . From general down to foot soldier, it gave proof of courage and went down to defeat . . . convinced that it had shed its blood to repair . . . what the French people had done in a moment of senseless pride and insane scorn for her neighbors.

La Débâcle covered with "mud and ridicule" the "ill-prepared" army that had "hurled itself heroically" against a superior foe. "To see Zola describe generals so revoltingly stupid that even schoolchildren would appreciate the humor of it fills one with repugnance. . . . Preposterous, the idea that a general ten kilometers from Beaumont should never have heard of Beaumont! Or that another general, having reached

---

[8]It will be recalled that Zola began to sound this harsh note after the success of *L'Assommoir*, in an article praising the rough-and-tumble of school days at the Collège Bourbon.

Carignan, should not know how close it lay to Belgium!" Tanera's allegiance to professional officers was genuine. Otherwise one might suspect him of collaborating as straight man in Zola's dramatization of the blunders of the French general staff. Zola had done his homework thoroughly and defended himself point by point in a response published first in Le Figaro, then in pamphlet form, noting that Tanera's real objection may have been to his account of Bavarian troops pillaging and massacring French villages.

The person to strike a sane note in this contest of martial oaths was Henry Céard, who held that La Débâcle, which he admired enormously, made a poor case for Zola's idea of regeneration through fire. "You can excuse and legitimize war all you like—your entire book condemns your theories and gives the lie to your paradoxes," he pointed out in a letter written one week after the book appeared. "It assuredly doesn't encourage a taste for battle. On the contrary, it inspires horror of it, not even so much because of the blood that gushes and the corpses that pile up as because of the immense stupidity that envelops everyone, including the victors. . . . Does it therefore serve any purpose, practical or philosophical, to desire a second round of such uncertainties? Making France anew sounds nice, but don't you think that her renewal will better come from intelligence exalted by peace rather than brutality exasperated by war?"

On the whole, literary critics lavished praise on La Débâcle. In Le Temps, Anatole France declared that Zola had surpassed himself by portraying all the woes of human flesh with "virile pity." In Le Journal des débats, Gaston Deschamps assured his conservative readership that "after one has closed this massive, tufted book where life overflows, where crowds swarm, where Napoleon's moribund empire crawls and groans and bleeds, one is haunted by the anguish of a frightful, ineffaceable drama; one has seen a dynasty, a society, a nation crumble." And in La Revue politique et littéraire, Emile Faguet, who became famous for a history of French literature, pronounced La Débâcle Zola's greatest work. Nothing could have been more awkward, he wrote, than composing a story about deliriously incoherent marches and countermarches, orders and counterorders. "The nightmare needed organizing and the author's excellent idea was to have the man who presided over chaos serve as the thread that unifies events . . . , to have him symbolize disorder because he creates it with his equivocations, to make him the passive and unconscious God of these immense ebbs and flows." In sum, Faguet concluded, Zola's supreme talent for bringing alive and moving large masses emerged more vividly than ever.

Zola was particularly delighted with an accolade from his former bête noire, Francisque Sarcey. But he never read the grandest review of all, which appeared eleven years later, or one year after his death, in an essay on *Les Rougon-Macquart* published in *The Atlantic Monthly.* "As for *La Débâcle,* finally, it takes its place with Tolstoy's very much more universal but very much less composed and condensed epic as an incomparably human picture of war," wrote Henry James.

I have been rereading it, I confess, with a certain timidity, the dread of perhaps impairing the deep impression received at the time of its appearance. I recall the effect it then produced on me as a really luxurious act of submission. It was early in the summer; I was in an old Italian town; the heat was oppressive, and one could but recline, in the lightest garments, in a great dim room and give one's self up. I like to think of the conditions and the emotion, which melt for me together into the memory I fear to imperil. I remember that in the glow of my admiration there was not a reserve I had ever made that I was not ready to take back. As an application of the author's system and his supreme faculty, as a triumph of what these things could do for him, how could such a performance be surpassed? The long, complex, horrific, pathetic battle, embraced, mastered, with every crash of its squadrons, every pulse of its thunder and blood resolved for us, by reflection, by communication from two of the humblest and obscurest of the military units, into immediate vision and contact, into deep human thrills of terror and pity—this bristling center of the book was such a piece of "doing" . . . as could only shut our mouths.

XXIV

A CELEBRATION AT
THE CHALET DES ILES

AN OBSERVATION Zola made at twenty-six about Jules Michelet—
that youth caught him up late in life—could have been made of
himself as well. The years surrounding his own fiftieth birthday
proved to be greener than any he had ever known, for even as he was
with great fanfare adding three chapters to the Rougon-Macquart saga,
he was anonymously creating a whole new generation of Zolas.

The first hint of this development appears in a letter addressed to
a gynecologist named Henri Delineau. "Many thanks, my dear doctor,
for the good news you impart," he guardedly wrote from Médan on
May 31, 1889, when Jeanne Rozerot was five months pregnant. "Take
good care of my special friend ["*mon petit ami*," in the masculine],
and if everything turns out right I shall be deeply indebted. I have told
you how much joy a successful result would give me." From Médan
he wrote again on September 4, to arrange a rendezvous in Paris.
"Dear Doctor, I shall remain at my friend's apartment until 4:30 and
would be most happy to see you there, if you can make it. Although
there is no danger, I should like you to dispel any lingering doubts."
Attended by Delineau, Jeanne gave birth seventeen days later, whereupon Zola, who had reestablished himself at 23, rue de Boulogne with
Alexandrine (in anticipation of their move that fall), made all necessary
arrangements to have the birth recorded at the ninth arrondissement
town hall, enlisting Henry Céard as a second witness. Delineau
brought along the infant, and on September 23, Denise Emilie Henriette, "daughter of Jeanne Sophie Adèle Rozerot, age twenty-two, no
occupation," had her name inscribed in the civil register. On Decem-

646

ber 27, Jeanne herself, with Zola and Céard present, signed a document officially recognizing Denise to be her child.

That Alexandrine could remain so ignorant of her husband's secret life was especially remarkable because Zola, whose face was much photographed, did not always take great precautions to conceal the liaison. As previously noted, he traveled with Jeanne to Le Havre in March 1889, when gathering material for *La Bête humaine*. In Paris he visited her almost every afternoon, often carrying a bouquet purchased from flower vendors at the Gare Saint-Lazare. And in Cheverchemont, a village quite near Médan on the opposite side of the Seine where Jeanne spent summers between 1889 and 1895, he was, no doubt, occasionally observed by locals. Then, too, friends were not all as discreet as Henry Céard, least of all Paul Alexis, whose wife, Marie, had been made Denise's godmother. Alexis tattled to Goncourt, and Goncourt spilled it in his journal. "Today, Paul Alexis . . . confirmed the rumor that Zola has a closet family [*petit ménage*]," he wrote on November 21, 1891.

> He apparently confessed to him that there is no better housekeeper than his wife, but that she has many "refrigerating" characteristics, which drove him to seek some "warmth" elsewhere. And he, Alexis, talks about Zola's "late blush" of youth, about a rage for pleasures of every kind, about the desire in this old man of letters to satisfy various worldly whims. Zola recently asked Céard whether, after twelve lessons, he could ride a horse well enough to negotiate the bridle paths of the Bois de Boulogne. Ah! an equestrian Zola! I just don't see it.

What Goncourt knew was already whispered in many households, including of course the Daudets' and the Charpentiers'.

Alexandrine may have first consciously suspected that something was amiss during the summer of 1891 when, without encouragement from her and disregarding his own aversion to travel, Zola organized a two-week trip through the Pyrenees. "I must tell you that the famous voyage will definitely take place!" she confided to her cousin Amélie Laborde on September 5. "Where am I going? Why, naturally, as you must have guessed, where I desire least to go. The Pyrenees, and ending up at Royan. I can just see you leaping up, but, dear friend, it's the story of my life, never having what I want, or getting it when I no longer desire it. Anyway, here I am surrounded by valises and packing dutifully." Did Alexandrine tell herself, or allow herself to be convinced, that the effort spent on preparations for *La Débâcle* required this anomalous tour? Certainly Zola had been suffering from what he described in one letter as "nervous malaises." But those malaises were bound up with his secret life, not with his creative endeavor. For by September, Jeanne Rozerot had almost completed another pregnancy; she would, if all went well, give birth during his absence. This journey southward was thus something in the nature of an evasion rather than a vacation. Torn between guilt and pride, between fear of exposure and the shame of concealment, between conjugal vows and paternal responsibilities, Zola fled, having prevailed upon Céard to act as his surrogate. "My old friend, I would . . . have very much liked to see you, for I had certain favors to ask," he wrote on September 8, the eve of his departure.

> After the 20th of this month, when you return, please go see my poor J. some afternoon. She will probably not need anything, but I shall rest easier knowing that she has nearby, at her beck and call, a heart as solid and discreet as yours.
>
> I'm sending your address to the doctor in order that he notify you as soon as the birth has taken place. You will kindly join him in registering the child: Jacques Emile Jean if it's a boy, Germaine Emilie Jeanne if it's a girl. And for the second witness you will take Alexis or whomever J. designates. If anything were to go wrong, you would act in my place and try to notify me as soon as possible. I shall come up with some means of communication.
>
> We leave tomorrow morning for Bordeaux and the Pyrenees. And I thank you with all my heart, dear old friend. Everything you do will be a good deed, for I am not happy.[1]

Twelve days later, on September 20, Zola in San Sebastián sent Céard two missives, an official greeting and a clandestine note. "My old friend," ran the former. "Here we are in Spain for two days and naturally we have been welcomed by a driving rain. . . . I shall reserve our impressions of what we've seen for the return. Suffice it to say that we are satisfied: beautiful landscape and not too many annoyances. I forgot to tell you that we visited Lourdes, which captivated me. Ah, what a marvelous book remains to be written about this extraordinary town! It haunts me, I stayed up one night constructing a plot." Under separate cover, he made the following arrangements:

> If you have something special to tell me, write to me at M.A.B. 70, Biarritz, poste restante. I shall remain there until the 25th. In addition, I beg of you, when J. has been delivered, and the doctor has

---

[1] At the same time, he wrote as follows to Dr. Delineau: "After the 15th, drop by the flat on the rue Saint-Lazare. The child has had a heavy cold and the mother is nearing term. . . . I confide both of them to you, and do so all the more insistently because I cannot be there."

Zola taking late-afternoon tea with Jeanne, Denise, and Jacques in the garden of the house he rented for them in Verneuil after 1895.

In the garden at Médan: Zola, Alexandrine (holding a mandolin), the Charpentiers, and, seated, the engraver Fernand Desmoulin, with whom Zola formed a close friendship.

Zola on his bicycle in 1897.

Zola looking at developer in a measuring glass.

Zola photographed by Alexandrine in 1895, on a haystack at Médan, with his wife's hat in front of him.

After the publication of *Lourdes*, Zola is pictured in an anguished quandary, seated on the ground between the saddles of faith and science.

Zola and Alexandrine in England in 1893, for the congress of the English Institute of Journalists, surrounded by several dozen top-hatted confreres, in front of the Savoy Hotel.

LE TRAITRE
Dégradation d'Alfred Dreyfus

The degradation of Dreyfus. The republican guardsman, after stripping away Dreyfus's gold braid, drew Dreyfus's saber from his scabbard, broke it in two, and flung the two pieces, with insignia, on the ground.

A violent anti-Dreyfusard broadsheet distributed in 1897, when evidence was beginning to implicate Esterhazy. The headlines tell the story: "Crushing Proof of Treason. Call to All Frenchmen. Death to the Traitors. The Honor of the Army. The Indignation of Our Soldiers. The Dreyfus Syndicate. Down with the Jews! Where the Money Comes From."

The front page of *L'Aurore*, January 13, 1898.

In hostile caricatures, the image of Zola as a jester and publicity hound beating the drums for himself was commonplace.

Zola pictured in the February 12, 1898, issue of *Le Grand Guignol* as a circus strong man and jester, tattooed with pigs and a Star of David. Unsavory sheets such as this one abounded; *Le Grand Guignol* lasted longer than most, surviving on secret funds and blackmail.

J'accuse inspired anti-Semitic denunciations of every kind. This *"chanson-scie,"* or catch tune, is a musical specimen.

A broad-beamed peasant woman, presumably expressing the sentiments of *la France profonde*, barring Zola's entrance to the Institute, which houses the French Academy.

Alfred Dreyfus facing his seven judges at the Rennes court-martial.

During the Rennes trial Dreyfus was escorted every day from the military prison and marched between soldiers with their backs turned to him, who formed a guard of dishonor.

Alexandrine in her late fifties.

Zola photographed in the morning at Médan wearing his favorite beret, and a silk cord around his neck.

A jaunty Zola, carrying his portable camera, with Alexandrine at the Universal Exposition of 1900.

Zola at the time of the Dreyfus Affair. A photograph by Nadar.

Zola's coffin being removed from 21 bis, rue de Bruxelles for the procession to his grave in Montmartre Cemetery. A company of the 28th Regiment of the Line stands at attention. The pallbearers were Abel Hermant (president of the Société des Gens de Lettres), Ludovic Halévy (president of the Société des Auteurs Dramatiques), Georges Charpentier, Alfred Bruneau, Eugène Fasquelle, Octave Mirbeau, Théodore Duret, and M. Briat, secretary of the Labor Exchange.

A musical tribute to Zola, written by Gaston Montéhus, who describes himself here as "the songwriter of the people."

Zola's interment in the Pantheon on June 4, 1908.

given you the news, to put in the personal correspondence column of *Figaro* a note which you will sign Duval and in which you will inform me by code. Make it pheasant [*faisan*] for a boy, hen-pheasant [*faisane*] for a girl, as if talking about an aviary.

Céard did as bidden, accompanying Delineau and Paul Alexis to the same town hall at which, almost exactly two years earlier, Denise had been registered, then notifying M.A.B. 70 in the September 27 edition of *Le Figaro* that the *faisan* had arrived. "Thank you, my old friend," Zola answered from Biarritz. "It was through your little note that I learned of the event, and despite the terrible distress this adventure has caused me, I've also been touched to the core of my being. At fifty such things go deep." Had Alexandrine finally begun to suspect something? Or is it that his secret family, larger now by one more child, burst beyond the emotional space in which he had until then confined it, invading other quarters of his mind?

Before long it burst beyond its confines outside his mind as well. The Zolas had been back in Paris one month when Alexandrine received an anonymous letter telling her about the ménage on the rue Saint-Lazare. This revelation infuriated her, and Zola, panic-stricken, begged Céard to help him avert tragic consequences. "Old friend," he wrote on November 10 in an urgent dispatch, "my wife is going absolutely mad. I'm afraid that a calamity will result. So please, tomorrow morning, visit the rue Saint-Lazare and do what must be done. Forgive me." The next day, or several days later, Alexandrine somehow arranged to enter the flat on the rue Saint-Lazare. As Jeanne had already been evacuated, she vented her rage upon the furniture, breaking open a secretary and confiscating Zola's letters to his mistress. This appropriation of evidence did not placate her, but if anything humiliated her the more. By one account her fits became so uncontrollable that Zola ended up having their bedroom padded lest the terrorized servants flee. "I did everything to stop her from going to your flat," he apologized to Jeanne. "I am very unhappy. Do not despair."

The Zolas soon effected a conjugal truce. To all appearances their rift healed, as they went on doing what they had always done—entertaining old friends at Médan, dining at the Charpentiers', attending the theater, ministering to each other's illnesses. But anger lay just beneath the surface, and periodic eruptions of it destroyed any illusion of harmony. "Tomorrow you will find life a bit less stormy at Médan," Céard, who often played mediator, assured Amélie Laborde on August 2, 1892.

I went there yesterday, Monday, and tried to calm things down. I don't doubt that it's only a lull and that sooner or later a more durable solution will have to be found. . . . But what must we expect? Our poor friend talks of leaving, being alone, even earning her own livelihood. . . . It's quite clear that life in common is a daily combat tearing her apart and I fear that any attempt to attune hearts so profoundly discordant will prove futile. . . . We shall . . . gain one week of détente perhaps. Ah, the aftermaths of glory!

When this crisis subsided, the unhappy couple, whose friends were very much alarmed, set out on a long journey, hoping perhaps that the distractions of travel, the relentless intimacy of life in hotel rooms, and Jeanne's absence would teach them to accept each other again. They spent a fortnight in Lourdes (where Zola gathered more material for his future novel), then journeyed east via Toulouse, Carcassonne, Nîmes, Arles, and Aix-en-Provence. After one week at the Hôtel Nègre-Coste in Aix, during which Zola visited his parents' graves as well as his childhood pension and took long walks through the countryside with Numa Coste, who must have given him an account of Cézanne's increasingly reclusive behavior, they looped south along the Mediterranean coast, pausing at Monte-Carlo before entering Italy.[2] In Genoa, a very private trip became unexpectedly public when, as part of festivities celebrating the four hundredth anniversary of Columbus's voyage, an enormous crowd, mindful no doubt of his Italian origins, greeted him with hurrahs. "The enthusiasm was indescribable; a young man came toward me and tried to kiss my hands," he later told a French journalist. "Never have I been the object of such adulation." Toasted between every course at banquets held on successive days, Zola and Alexandrine recovered from the rigors of Italian hospitality during a second, longer sojourn in Monte-Carlo.

Zola and Alexandrine's seven-week peregrination served some useful purpose, but they could not wander indefinitely and almost as soon as Paris reappeared, the goodwill they had stored up began to seep away.

[2]There is melancholy in a letter Alexandrine wrote from Monte-Carlo to Amélie Laborde's seventeen-year-old daughter, Elina:
My dear little Linette, you do well to write me sweet letters. It gives me great pleasure reading you, I enjoy the anecdotes you relate; furthermore, your affection comes through. You see, my dear, at my age one needs to be surrounded by much friendship. From Marseille on, the so-called wintering cities have all been absolutely empty and locked up. This produces an overwhelming impression of sadness. Even the gardens, which I imagined very beautiful, bursting with flowers, are abandoned. . . . Each of us was supposed to wager twenty francs at the gaming tables this evening, but yesterday, after a reconnaissance expedition through the Casino, we left, your uncle and I, disturbed by the fact that people can give themselves over passionately to something that struck us as idiotic. . . . The people there looked jaded, laid down money and collected it as impassively as possible. Only the nonplayers . . . manifested interest in your uncle's presence. No sooner did we enter than the whisperings began.

By the following spring they were once again souls in torment. Alexandrine spoke of separating once and for all, and friends, especially Céard and Amélie Laborde, tried to help the couple find a solution.

Zola rejected the obvious way out. Answering a letter from Charpentier's daughter Georgette, he wrote: "Rest assured . . . that I shall never be a cad. My wife will not leave me, unless of course she should decide that leaving me would make her happy, which is not now the case." To abandon Alexandrine, he told Jeanne, would be to poison their "tenderness" with "remorse." But neither could he abandon Jeanne, and this dilemma resulted in alibis, in surreptitious expedients, in constant mea culpas. "Tell my little Denise," he wrote from Lourdes on August 30, 1892, "that if her papa does not come see her, it's because he's occupied elsewhere and that he loves her very much nonetheless. He thinks of her and of you two every evening and every morning. You are my entire prayer." At Médan the surveillance was such that Zola often found it easier to meet Jeanne in Paris than to visit Cheverchemont, and when Paris, too, proved inconvenient, he consoled himself by observing her through a spyglass from the balcony outside his study window.[3] Did it strike him perhaps as condign punishment to be the prisoner of his troth and the voyeur of his desire? "I would like to have made your youth pleasurable and not forced you to live like a recluse," he lamented in late July 1893, after Jeanne and the children had gone north for a holiday at Saint-Aubin on the Normandy coast.

> Happiness would have been to be young with you, to have your youth rejuvenate me. Instead it is I who am aging you, I who am enveloping you in sadness. . . . Nothing pains me more about our separation than the fact that I cannot play the good daddy with my dear children. I would have been so happy to dandle little Denise and splash with her in the cool water! And with Jacques I would have built castles in the sand.

Alexandrine gradually accepted the existence of Zola's offspring, but a letter to Jeanne written a year later, on July 13, 1894, shows the father as tormented as ever by his separation from them. "I am not happy. This division, this double life I am obliged to live fills me with despair. So I implore you, be good and forgive me when things don't go the way I'd like. My dream was to make everyone around me happy, but I see now that that's impossible, and I am the first to suffer."

[3]In July 1893, Zola wrote to Jeanne: "I must have a portrait of the three of you at that distant window where I'd so often train my eyes." The spyglass must have been quite powerful, as Cheverchemont is several kilometers from Médan.

Everything spoke of division—even, by inference, the ring Zola had given Jeanne Rozerot. It was a copy of Marguerite Charpentier's, and it bore the motto that Saint Louis, Louis IX, had had engraved on Queen Marguerite's wedding band in the thirteenth century: *Hors cet annel, point n'est d'amour* ("Outside this ring, there is no love").

Had Zola screamed this pledge from the rooftops after slipping it around Jeanne's finger, the effect on Alexandrine would not have been more hurtful than the publication of the last installment of *Les Rougon-Macquart*. *Le Docteur Pascal*, for which he began to assemble material in May 1892, almost brought about a divorce.

Rougon though he is, Pascal is nonetheless *sui generis*. The only "good" Rougon, he exemplifies a phenomenon called "innateness," by which Dr. Prosper Lucas had explained the appearance of offspring seemingly exempt from the iron law of heredity. "The common people with their unconscious intuition understood so well how radically he differed from the other Rougons," Zola had written in *La Fortune des Rougon*, "that they called him M. Pascal, never uttering his family name." *La Fortune des Rougon* also tells us that this mutant, whose scientific reputation outside Plassans has never impinged upon the consciousness of fellow townspeople, used his own family as material for research. But not until the mid-1880s did it become quite clear that Zola intended through Pascal to encompass all of *Les Rougon-Macquart* retrospectively. The novel would, Goncourt quotes him as saying, bring the whole twenty-volume saga full round and have it coil back upon itself, like a serpent biting its own tail. "I always wanted to finish with a kind of résumé spelling out the scientific and philosophical import of the whole," he informed van Santen Kolff on January 25, 1893. "Moreover, I always meant Pascal to figure as hero. . . . As for its title, *Le Docteur Pascal*, I didn't seek it. It was thrust upon me by friends, by newspapers, by everybody." Representing Zola himself, Dr. Pascal Rougon, like the Reasoner in one of Dumas *fils*'s plays, was to place the appropriate philosophical construction on *Les Rougon-Macquart*. Like the Reasoner, he was to live onstage yet view the drama from afar. And like the Reasoner, he was to have the last word. "I have loved life [and] its ceaseless effort . . . despite the ill and heartache it breeds. My conclusion should reflect this. . . . Dr. Pascal must be clearsighted. . . . No consoling illusion; man as he is, man as his milieu has made him. Yet the doctor loves everything alive. . . . He knows what's what, and . . . loves anyway."

In order to create a learned geneticist, Zola plodded once again through the medical literature. After revisiting Prosper Lucas's *Traité de l'hérédité naturelle*, he acquainted himself with every major hypothesis propounded since 1868 and received invaluable guidance from Maurice de Fleury, a young neurologist who wrote about medicine for *Le Figaro*. Fleury lent him August Weismann's *Essais sur l' hérédité et la sélection naturelle*; the book's exposition of germ-plasm theory proved useful for Chapter Two of *Le Docteur Pascal*. To achieve a clearer understanding of Weismann, Zola talked with Professor Jules Déjerine, author of *L'Hérédité dans les maladies du système nerveux*, who also helped him assimilate Darwin, Spencer, Galton, Haeckel, and Virchow. Otherwise his most useful informant may have been Georges Pouchet, professor of comparative anatomy at the Museum of Natural History, from whom he elicited long memoranda on such questions as innateness and atavism.

With *Le Docteur Pascal*, Zola's cycle ends where it began—in Plassans. The year is 1872, and the Rougons, who had risen from obscurity after Louis Napoleon's coup d'état twenty-one years earlier, have weathered political change more successfully than their emperor. To be sure, Pierre dropped dead on receiving news of the defeat at Sedan. But his two sons still figure in the public eye. Eugène, staunch Bonapartist, was elected to the legislature and upholds the faith at Versailles while Aristide, absolved of his prewar sins by the postwar government, has emerged, chameleonlike, as director of an important Republican newspaper, *L'Epoque*. Back home their eighty-year-old mother, Félicité, plays the grande dame. Enormously rich and obsessed with social status, she devotes herself to building the whited sepulchre on which the name Rougon shall be inscribed. Not until family skeletons have been purged from memory will she rest easy, and her revisionist enterprise brings her up against her middle son, Pascal.

Pascal, a fifty-nine-year-old bachelor, has never repudiated the clan, nor ever quite belonged to it. Decades ago he infuriated Félicité by spurning a rich practice and treating poor people, often free of charge. Now he infuriates her by digging up what she would bury and assembling evidence of Rougon pathology for scientific consideration. He lives in his dilapidated villa just outside town, La Souleiade, with two devoted women. Martine has been his only domestic for almost thirty years, or half her life. Clotilde, his twenty-five-year-old niece, has been his ward since the age of seven, when her widowed father, Saccard, sent her away so that he could live disencumbered with his new wife. While Martine, a nunlike spinster, runs the household, Clotilde, a tall, supple, blue-eyed blonde, does the paperwork. She knows enough about his research to organize his manuscripts, and prepares fastidious drawings and watercolors to illustrate his articles.

One discordant note resounds inside the otherwise harmonious ménage à trois. Having always tolerated Martine's piety and never protested against her catechizing young Clotilde, Pascal finds his tolerance repaid with admonitions. While Martine implores him to secure his well-earned place in heaven, Clotilde reminds him that there truly exists what "eyes of flesh" cannot perceive. To be sure, he himself taught Clotilde formative lessons, and she calls him "master." But, improbable combination that she is of *femme savante*, country girl, and mystic, she will not be moved from her commitment to the "unknown," defending her ground with determination, as if it were there that she enjoys independence of mind or cognitive superiority. When Pascal declares (sounding like Ernest Renan in the recently published *Avenir de la science*):

> I believe that the future of humanity lies in the progress of reason through science. I believe that the pursuit of truth through science is the divine ideal by which man must abide. I believe that all is illusion and vanity save the treasure of truths slowly acquired, and acquired never to be lost. I believe that the sum of these ever mounting truths will, in the end, give mankind incalculable power, and serenity, if not happiness. . . . Open your eyes, look!

she answers:

> I open them, and still I don't see everything. . . . Out there is an unknown realm which you will never enter. Ah, I know! You are too intelligent not to realize that it exists. It's just that you won't take it into account. . . . It's useless telling me to ignore the mystery. . . . I can't! The mystery claims me straightway, and perturbs me.

This rift makes room for mischief, and old Félicité urges Clotilde to help her confiscate Pascal's family dossiers, arguing that anyone who seeks forbidden knowledge invites vengeance from above.

Sermons against the illusions of science eloquently delivered at Saint-Saturnin by a new priest aggravate the quarrel. Increasingly, Pascal's dictum that happiness may be found only in ceaseless effort falls on deaf ears. The naturalist continues to set store by the truths revealed in science's slow progress, but Clotilde demands, now more than ever, the instant and total certitude of mystical Revelation. She wants something else besides. Religion translates into virtuous terms a desire for union with her uncle-mentor. "Our affection lacks something," is how she declares herself. "Until now it has been empty and useless, and I feel an irresistible need to fill it, yes, to fill it with all that is divine and eternal!" Between them stand the children of his mind—the books, articles, notes, dossiers engendered behind closed doors—and Clotilde means to preside over an auto-da-fé. Destroying the family chronicle would not only fortify Félicité's social pretensions but legitimize Clotilde's amorous fantasies. To abolish genealogy is to abolish consanguinity, generations, time itself. "You must change your life and repent," she cries. "You must burn everything of your past errors, and yes, your books, your files, your manuscripts! Make this sacrifice, master, I beg of you on my knees. And you will see what a delicious existence we shall lead together."

Horrified, Pascal combats this fanatic prescription for transcendent rebirth with the argument that man can possess himself only when he understands how his physiological being holds him hostage to the past. Accordingly he analyzes for Clotilde the operations of heredity in every Rougon-Macquart born since 1769, dozens all told, hoping that this exhaustive survey will convert her. Instead it leaves her bewildered. In her confused state she pointedly eschews all talk of religion, and Pascal, sensing that the enemy has gone underground, is overcome by paranoid delusions. Afraid that his work will be seized, he stays awake at night, laying traps or wandering through rooms. Like François Mouret eclipsed by the abbé Faujas, he feels himself to be a stranger in his own house. "And what made it more painful was the growing, persistent idea that his wound had been inflicted upon him by the only creature whom he truly loved, his cherished Clotilde." Madness looms.

It becomes apparent during this tormented interlude that Pascal Rougon's most redoubtable enemy is himself, that vengeance has been wreaked not from above but from within, where a shy, lovelorn prisoner serving a life sentence of hard labor dares at last to vent his rage. "Ah, if only he had lived!" Zola writes.

> Certain nights he'd curse science for having consumed the better part of his virility. He had let work eat his brain, his heart, his muscles. The only thing that had come of this solitary passion was books . . . whose cold leaves chilled his hands when he opened them. No woman's bosom to press against his own, no child's warm hair to kiss! He had slept alone all his life in the ice-cold bed of an egotistical savant, and alone he would die there. Was it truly going to happen that way? Would he never taste the happiness of the ordinary carters and porters whom he heard every day cracking their whips on the road?

Everything in Pascal now focuses on Clotilde, whose image comes to obsess him. He invokes biblical precedent and fancies himself another David warmed in old age by another fair young Shunammite. But once again desire bows before reason, or propriety, or something more fearsome. When a plausible suitor requests Clotilde's hand, Pascal urges him upon her.

Clotilde rejects the suitor in favor of Pascal, to whom she offers herself with the declaration that she is his "servant" and "handiwork" and "possession." Thus begins an affair which they conceal neither from Félicité, who excoriates them for compromising her socially, nor from Martine, who, finding herself *de trop* under this new regime, swallows her pride and intensifies her piety. After one month of seclusion the couple celebrates spring in walks that take them past Le Paradou. Pascal, yearning to obliterate his critical faculty, speaks of rapturous self-annihilation. "He anathematized cities. One could be physically well and know happiness only on vast plains, in broad daylight, assuming one had renounced money, ambition, even the vainglorious excesses of intellectual work." Experiments through which the savant had hoped to strengthen defective constitutions now strike him as hubristic. "Is it a laudable task, correcting nature, intervening, modifying it and deflecting it from its goal?" he asks. "Doubt has seized me, I tremble at the thought of my futuristic alchemy, I conclude that the greater, saner course is to let evolution accomplish itself."

Darwinizing an earlier idyll, *Le Docteur Pascal* echoes *La Faute de l'abbé Mouret*, but bound up with this apotheosis of nature is a fin de siècle penchant for erotic artifice that harks back to *L'Oeuvre*. On the one hand Pascal extols fertility. On the other hand he makes Clotilde the image of a sterile, Klimtean queen and ruins himself to deck her out in jewels. "She was like an idol, seated against the pillow, . . . a gold band in her hair, gold on her naked arms, gold on her bare breast, naked and divine, dripping with gold and precious gems." Knowing that such prodigal behavior will appall his mother, whose greatest passion has always been for wealth, heightens the pleasure of extravagance. Pascal spends until nothing remains, consummating the virile extravaganza with an impotent swoon.

Impotent is how he comes to regard himself, for he does not impregnate Clotilde, and when he seeks refuge in work, writing proves impossible. Biologically, and now intellectually as well, fatherhood eludes him. "Was it due to his senility, the fact that he couldn't write a page any more than he could beget a child? The fear of impotence had always tormented him. Slumped over his desk, worn out by troubles, he dreamed that he was thirty again, that every night Clotilde invigorated him for the next day's task." Meanwhile, Félicité, like some nasty bacillus, thrives. At her behest, Pascal, in a final act of self-abnegation, frees Clotilde, prevailing upon her to leave Plassans for Paris. No sooner do they part than fateful events occur. Pascal discovers that his days are numbered, that nature has not exempted him from the degenerate organization of the Rougon family. Clotilde, in turn, discovers that she is pregnant with his child.

Just before suffering a fatal heart attack, Pascal, ever the naturalist, revises the genealogical tree over which he has pored year after year to show his imminent demise and his child's future birth. This chart will survive him, but the dossiers that constitute his scientific estate will not. The thing he had always feared happens when Félicité breaks open an armoire, seizes those files, and jubilantly sets them afire. Intellectual murder thus follows hard on physical death, devastating Clotilde. She resolves to inhabit La Souleiade, and there, seven months later, in yet another example of life springing from death, bears Pascal a robust son.

With this conclusion to the last volume of *Les Rougon-Macquart*, Zola, for whom memory and oblivion had always been central preoccupations, invited readers to recall the opening scene of Volume One, written almost twenty-five years earlier. What began outside Plassans, in a graveyard emptied of bones whose fertile soil nourished thick vegetation, ends outside Plassans, in a house despoiled of family skeletons, where Pascal fructifies after death. Zola evokes in passing other scenes from the saga. Indeed, *Le Docteur Pascal* commemorates every preceding novel. But the work it brings most forcibly to mind is *La Conquête de Plassans*, and not only by virtue of the kindred ordeals inflicted upon two freethinkers. Pascal Rougon resembles Ovide Faujas as well as François Mouret, with everything sinister about the priest being turned to positive account in the scientist. Worshipped by his flock, who consider him a "messiah" or a "savior," Pascal endeavors to heal the poor rather than to mesmerize the genteel. Celibate, he defends his intellectual virility against a powerful mother instead of living with her. Secluded in a bedroom as unenterable as Faujas's, he, unlike Faujas, finally yields to nature, admitting his inamorata. And fire strengthens this antithetical bond. Where Faujas vanishes altogether in the conflagration produced by François Mouret, Pascal Rougon will survive Félicité's book-burning through the child he has fathered on Clotilde.

On February 22, 1893, not quite three months after he had begun the novel, Zola informed van Santen Kolff that it was half written. A first serial installment appeared in *La Revue hebdomadaire* on March 18, 1893, and by late April interviewers had worn a path to his door. "I shall discuss the anxieties that beset this fin de siècle, provoking flights into the past, calling for a resurrection of ancient religious and philosophical doctrines," he told one such journalist. "My young comrades will be shown the dangers of illusion and mysticism. . . . I have faith in science, and . . . history offers no example of a moribund religion suddenly recovering its lost power and vitality. It is nevertheless true that this spiritual disquiet must be taken seriously, lest it have baleful consequences and lead to discouragement." On May 14 he wrote the last word of *Le Docteur Pascal* and, with *Les Rougon-*

Macquart now complete, immediately announced this signal event to Georges Charpentier. "I finished *Le Docteur Pascal* yesterday, Sunday, in a joyful state." Charpentier, who had offered him new terms the previous November, raising his royalty from sixty to seventy-five centimes, published it on June 19. It would not match the colossal success of *La Débâcle*, but, despite its preachiness, it sold eighty-eight thousand copies in 1893 alone, or enough to exasperate Edmond de Goncourt, whose *La Fille Elisa* had not sold half that many since 1877. Commercially speaking, Zola's name made up for his creative lapses.

Such scattered applause as he received came from critics who admired *Le Docteur Pascal* especially for two gruesome scenes, one involving the death of an old drunkard and the other describing the fatal nosebleed suffered by a young hemophiliac. "Even if this volume, which is the epitome and scientific conclusion of Zola's work, should not impose itself upon the public esteem as the crowning achievement of a splendid life's work," wrote A. Badin in *La Nouvelle Revue*, "its emotional power, its imaginative wealth and a tender note unusual for the master writer would still command admiration. What wonderful pages are those in which he recounts the death by spontaneous combustion of the drunken old uncle, Dr. Pascal's discovery that an attempt has been made to steal his files, Clotilde's capitulation to her love." Fraught though it was with imperfections, according to E. Ledrain in the daily *L'Eclair*, Zola's "prodigious genius" showed through. "The death of Charles, Maxime's son, bleeding to death from his nose in the presence of the hundred-year-old Tante Dide, who sits there tragically paralyzed, is one of the most admirable things in French literature. I've never read anything so strangely beautiful. . . . Had he written only those three pages, M. Zola would still deserve a place among the four or five whom France counts as its greatest in this second half of the nineteenth century."

The reception accorded *Le Docteur Pascal* was otherwise less than enthusiastic. Where Zola saw an elegant summation, most critics— and it would require unusual partisanship to gainsay them—saw a clumsy appendage. "*Le Docteur Pascal* is a kind of index to *Les Rougon-Macquart* in the inappropriate form of a novel," one reviewer observed. "What bothers one constantly about it and what makes it so difficult to read is the problem the author keeps trying to solve: how does one dramatize a table of contents? how does one transform the genealogical tree of the Rougon-Macquart into a thing of fire and poetry?" In a long article written for *La Revue encyclopédique*, Georges Pellissier noted contradictions of a philosophical order. "The consistent pessimism of *Les Rougon-Macquart* appears to have been supplanted by a fatalistic optimism based upon invincible faith in the triumph of life. Here again certain things don't square. Pascal proposes at first to establish the laws of heredity . . . the better to remake the human species and ends up, on the contrary, believing that one must let evolution take its course."

Zola might have been forgiven his philosophical awkwardness and pseudoscientific bromides if he had steered clear of incest. To cause ennui was more acceptable than to glorify a "monstrous" fantasy. "Through education, by imparting something of his soul to her, the doctor makes his adopted daughter his real daughter," wrote Ledrain. "What is worse, and more unlikely, than the father loving his daughter is the daughter falling deliriously in love with her father. . . . I know nothing, in any literature, more monstrous, and at the same time more improbable, than this incest." Pellissier seconded him. "Not only is this love improbable; there is something indecent about it," he argued. "The idylls of biblical patriarchs and kings will be invoked, and M. Zola takes good care not to omit them. . . . If such memories from the Old Testament are highly decorative, they are not enough to sanctify Clotilde's fling with Pascal, nor to diminish the repugnance it inspires in us. Lacking here is distance, perspective, hallowed antiquity, angel wings brushing Boaz's forehead during the night."

Alexandrine let others defend her husband against these reproaches. But everything in *Le Docteur Pascal* must have galled her, not least of all the parallel implicitly drawn between her and Félicité. After all, she had, like Félicité, seized documents that humiliated her, destroying evidence of her husband's adulterous passion as Félicité burns evidence of her son's intellectual infidelity. And like Félicité, she was much concerned—some thought overly concerned—with matters of social status. Zola dedicated *Le Docteur Pascal* to "the memory of Mother" and to "my dear wife." But one wonders whether this official gesture placated his dear wife. Even if Alexandrine did not know that Clotilde's namesake, Queen Clotilde, hailed from the same province as Jeanne Rozerot, she knew full well for whom the novel had been written. Indeed, the day after its publication Zola gave Jeanne a copy dedicated to "my Clotilde, who has offered me the royal feast of her youth and rejuvenated me by making me a gift of Denise and Jacques, the two dear children for whom I wrote this book so that they might know, on reading it someday, how much I adored their mother, and how tenderly they should repay her the happiness with which she consoled me in the midst of my great sorrows."

By way of celebrating the completion of *Les Rougon-Macquart*, Charpentier and Fasquelle invited as many people as would fit to the Chalet des Iles, an elegant restaurant on an island in the Bois de Boulogne's "lower lake." Present on June 21, 1893, were Zola's oldest friend, Marius Roux, and his faithful Achates, Paul Alexis. Also present were Octave Mirbeau, the playwright Georges Courteline, the poet Catulle Mendès. Publishers and literary journalists abounded, along with stars from the world of popular entertainment, notably the singer Yvette Guilbert. Officialdom was represented by Raymond Poincaré, a brilliant young minister of public instruction and fine arts, who was destined for great fame as a prime minister. All told, some two hundred celebrants disembarked on that warm, sunny June day. They disposed themselves under a large tent, ate copiously, then, after dessert, heard the publisher exchange toasts with his author.[4] "This is not a banquet," Charpentier declared.

> We thought that it would perhaps be pleasant and joyous to fete—glass in hand, at waterside, in the shade of large trees, under a beaming sun, among friends—the completion of these *Rougon-Macquart*, which have caused, and still cause, such a stir in the world, and to honor twenty-five years of tireless labor and unfailing literary probity. . . . My dear Zola, allow me to tell you that this celebration for the *Rougon-Macquart* is all the dearer to my heart because it celebrates our friendship, a friendship which in fact began with the first volumes of this saga almost—alas!—a quarter-century ago, and whose luminous nature has never been clouded. . . . With your leave, I should also like to toast you, my dear Madame Zola, you, the devoted and courageous companion of bygone days, days of poverty and dismay, which are now, thank goodness, remote indeed.
>
> So I drink to all our guests, I drink to Madame Zola, I drink to my friend Emile Zola.

Tears had filled Alexandrine's eyes when Zola stood up, affectionately placed a tremulous hand on Charpentier's shoulder, and said: "We celebrate our silver anniversary today. No, you are not a publisher for me; you are indeed a friend—sincere, firm, devoted. Do we have a contract? I'm not sure, but I do know that we can get along without one. There was a contract at the beginning of our relationship—yes, I remember how you tore it up. I asked nothing of you, it was you who volunteered everything. Let us hope that twenty-five years hence we shall meet again . . . to celebrate our golden anniversary." After thanking previously hostile newspaper critics for their bracing oppo-

---

[4]Charpentier did not imitate the celebratory dinner given at Trapp's sixteen years earlier and name items on the menu after titles of novels. The meal began with melon and continued with *truite saumonée sauce verte*. The entrées included *filet de boeuf Richelieu, noix de veaux aux pointes d'asperge, rôti, dindonneau nouveau, salade de légumes,* and *galantine truffée de perdreaux*. These were followed by a *bombe panachée,* cheese, and fruit.

sition, he toasted the activity that had always carried him through—hard work. This last gesture excited applause and shouts of bravo.

One toast followed another. Catulle Mendès praised with great orotundity the "colossal" monument which, he said, would thrill posterity. A Swiss writer named Edouard Rod hailed Zola on behalf of foreign writers whose creative lives he had helped to shape, and one Adolphe Tabarant, invoking *Germinal*, expressed the gratitude of young socialist literati. At the end, General Théodore Jung, the author of numerous historical works, whom Zola knew from the Société des Gens de Lettres, felt honor-bound to introduce a patriotic note. "My dear and illustrious friend," he bugled over the roar of conversation, "You have made *La Débâcle*; I hope that someday you will fashion for us *La Victoire!*"

No sooner had the speeches concluded than a piano was brought outside, to everyone's relief no doubt, and Yvette Guilbert and others improvised a concert of music-hall songs. Jules Huret described the scene in *Le Figaro*: "Sunshine filtering through the leaves dappled the lawn, played on women's light-colored apparel, enhanced jovial faces," he wrote. "The water round about was flecked with gold and these delicate hues, these popular songs, these bursts of laughter, this lovely occasion celebrating the most massive . . . intellectual accomplishment of our time will long remain engraved in my memory."

For Zola, jubilation went hand in hand with mourning, and those two hundred guests may not have been numerous enough to crowd out the painful awareness of certain empty seats. His surviving *compagnons de route*, Alphonse Daudet and Edmond de Goncourt, had both declined Charpentier's invitation. Racked with pain from tabes dorsalis, or syphilis of the spinal cord, which would eventually kill him, Daudet could neither walk any distance unaided nor sit erect for long, and every day drugged himself on laudanum. But Goncourt, more spiteful than ever, had no such excuse. Boycotting the celebration, he preferred a parodic account of it given one week later by Yvette Guilbert over dinner at a mutual friend's apartment. "There is, in this woman, a highly amusing vivacity of language that matches the feverish animation of her body," he wrote on June 28. "She enters and right away describes the famous *Rougon-Macquart* dinner in the Bois de Boulogne, evoking the various categories of 'stunning' women who appeared there, the caricatural silhouettes of those who delivered orations, Zola sputtering with emotion: a very droll report."

Absent as well were almost all the younger men who had once gathered around Zola and contributed to *Les Soirées de Médan*.

Guy de Maupassant, his mind beset with delusions induced by syphilis, had attempted suicide on New Year's Day 1892, soon after notifying a friend: "*I am absolutely lost, I am even dying. I suffer from a* softening of the brain caused by the salt water with which I washed out my nasal passages. Cerebral fermentation has resulted and every night my brain leaks out of my nose and mouth in a gluey paste. . . . *Death is imminent and I am mad.* My head is reeling every which way. *Farewell, friend, you shall not see me again.*" Transported to Dr. Jacques Blanche's sanatorium in Passy, the powerful, athletic Maupassant wasted away there and became uncontrollably spastic as the disease galloped through its tertiary phase. He would die on July 6, 1893, at the age of forty-three.

In his own way, Joris-Karl Huysmans, whose works had long since earned great notoriety at home and abroad (Oscar Wilde tipped his hat to *A rebours* in *The Picture of Dorian Gray*), also left the world. Having abjured Zola's ideal of rational or scientific inquiry, he had moved toward the literary fringe, where naturalism had no purchase whatever, and then beyond the fringe altogether into a shadowy realm of people who practiced black magic. After several desperate years this search for some spiritual home, or for another paternal authority, led him to Father Arthur Mugnier at the Church of Saint Thomas Aquinas, near the rue du Bac. "Two weeks ago on Thursday, you saw me quite dumbfounded," he wrote to Mugnier in June 1892. "I was trembling, in fact, at the idea of going and knocking on God's door, going myself to his house. Even now I am not very confident, but still, I am hoping. You who have always had Faith, if only you knew what it is like to get it back! In fact I am so weary, so truly disgusted with my life, that it is impossible for him not to have mercy!" Mugnier urged him to undertake a retreat among Trappists, and at a Cistercian monastery outside Reims he brought himself to make confession. In 1893 he would return for five days, after months of anguish occasioned by the mental unraveling of his former mistress. Only there, he lamented, could one feel keenly the separation between body and soul, and experience the infinite joys that attended withdrawal from the world. While Zola made of fecundity a *summum bonum* and of procreation a categorical imperative that argued louder than marriage, Huysmans became the apostle of a cenobitic ideal.

As for Henry Céard, above all Henry Céard, it would appear that playing surrogate in Zola's private drama had come, little by little, to roil him. His complicity weighed upon his conscience, and after the birth of Jacques, or the exposure of the secret family, he avoided Jeanne Rozerot altogether. "Was it not natural that Alexandrine should have accused him, too, of having betrayed her by seeing us?" observed Denise, whose godfather Céard was. "He left one fine day and no one among us ever saw him again. Throughout her life, my mother kept a box from my brother's baptism for him. 'It's unimaginable that I shall never see him again,' she would say. But he never returned." This break, which left Jeanne even more isolated, did not free Céard from internal conflict. Mediating as best he could between husband and wife, both of whom confided in him, Céard, guiltily no doubt, sympathized with Alexandrine rather than with Zola, and made his feelings known to Alexandrine's beloved cousin, Amélie Laborde. "I don't want you to misconstrue the reasons for my absence from the recent gathering," he wrote on June 23, 1893, two days after the *Rougon-Macquart* banquet.

> Consider the dangers my presence would have introduced. Had I, as a long-standing intimate of the household, not offered a toast, my silence would have raised eyebrows. What I would have said, however tactfully I said it, might have provoked a serious incident. I would have acknowledged the poor woman's large contribution to this success, but even my compliments would have given her grief. . . . I had some vague notion that a scandal loomed and that I myself, with the best intentions in the world, could provoke it. I thus resolved to stay at home. If literature did not receive the homage I should have liked to pay it, at least I didn't provide grist for the mill of public malevolence.

He hoped that Amélie would not join those who, not knowing what had gone on, were ready to find fault with him.

Did this tortured argument conceal some unavowable grievance? Can it be that Céard begrudged Zola his extramarital happiness? that he wanted a pretext to divorce a *chef de mouvement* with whose thought he was no longer in sympathy? or that after seventeen years of consideration for his protector, the exemplary factotum had had quite enough of running errands?[5] Certainly no quarrel took place between them. Later in the summer they exchanged letters that give no hint of estrangement. But from 1893 until his death, Zola may have met Céard only once or twice, at funerals. And during the Dreyfus Affair he was to find himself publicly admonished by a patriotic Céard to see the error of his ways.

Three weeks after the *Rougon-Macquart* party, on the eve of Bastille Day, Raymond Poincaré promoted Zola to the rank of officer in the Legion of Honor. Some months later, as a candidate for two vacated seats in the French Academy, Hippolyte Taine's being one, he was rejected unanimously.

---

[5]The last such errand was run in May, when Céard arranged to buy Zola a horse and have it transported by railway to Triel. A letter dated May 23 contains typically exact instructions from Céard concerning the horse's transportation, diet, habits, etc.

XXV

A DOUBLE LIFE
AND A TRILOGY

EVER SINCE THE TRIAL that ruined his London publisher, Henry Vizetelly, Zola had been disposed to regard England as invincibly hostile, and when in July 1893 a letter arrived from the English Institute of Journalists inviting him to represent the Société des Gens de Lettres at its annual congress, he feared a hoax or an ambush. Still, he was tempted, the more so because Alexandrine's poor health had sabotaged plans for a Breton holiday with the Charpentiers, and asked Ernest Vizetelly to verify it. Vizetelly's inquiry determined that the invitation was genuine, but Zola's anxiety did not subside. On the contrary, presentiments of stage fright gripped him. "I rely upon you as well to let me know as soon as possible to what toast I shall have to respond," he instructed Vizetelly. "I believe I shall also be asked to address the subject of anonymity in journalism. It's an important question for the English, is it not? Kindly give me your opinion in the matter and tell me what the majority of English journalists think. I want to acquaint myself with the terrain in advance."

Together with a dozen well-known French journalists, the Zolas left the Gare Saint-Lazare at 11:30 a.m., on September 20, and at 7 p.m. entered Victoria Station, where Sir Edward Lawson, principal owner of *The Daily Telegraph*, welcomed them in French, declaring that "the feeling of respect and admiration which [Zola's] marvelous fecundity inspires" would grow as "the author of *La Débâcle* pursued his triumphant career." This gesture, which a sizable crowd applauded, touched Zola. "I thought about our dear Paris," he noted. "Which director of a major paper would have taken the trouble to greet in English a mere novelist disembarking from London?" Equally unexpected was a large floral bouquet sent to their hotel room by Oscar Wilde. Later that evening, after an hour or so of sitting through a play called *Chicago* at the Alhambra Theater, Zola conversed briefly with the flamboyant Irishman, whom he found to be "charming and remarkable."

The inaugural session of the congress began with Sir Charles Russell, Gladstone's attorney general, welcoming everyone present and Emile Zola in particular. "We march from ovation to ovation, through what seems to us a dream," Zola told Eugène Fasquelle. The ovations grew louder; it soon became apparent that the national press wished to apologize for its cowardice during the battle over *Soil* and that the congress had been organized as a glorification of the author whose work spoke so forcefully against Victorian cant. On September 22, Zola addressed the subject of journalistic anonymity in a paper that excited lively comment among those who heard it at Lincoln's Inn Hall and afterward, when newspapers published the text, throughout England.[1] That evening a reception held at the Guildhall left him wonderstruck, as the pariah previously vilified by the National Vigilant Association found himself transformed with great pageantry into a lion of London society. "This celebration at the Guildhall was splendid," reported a correspondent for *Le Temps*.

---

[1] Some idea of his speech may be gained from the following excerpt, which was distributed to spectators in English translation:

It is very certain that the British press owes to anonymity its power, its unquestionable authority. For the moment, I will confine myself to the political articles, the portion of the journal embodying its policy. Thus viewed, a political newspaper, in which the individual disappears, is nothing more than the expression of a party, the daily bread of a crowd. It gains in power what it loses in personality, for it has no object but to satisfy an opinion, to be the exact representation of that opinion. It follows that, for such a newspaper to meet a social want, it must have behind it a devoted public, reading it alone, and perfectly contented so long as it sees reproduced in print every morning its own ideas, the ideas which it expected to see. Observe that it is just this public which, in your country, has made the Press what it is—a public that has not been fragmented by revolutions, . . . a public that has no feverish desire when it gets up in the morning to go through ten or a dozen newspapers, but of which every reader sticks to his own, which he reads from beginning to end, asking nothing more than that it shall think as he himself thinks. Under such conditions, anonymity is necessary. . . . At the same time, I confess that if I recognize the necessity for anonymity in political matters, I am nonetheless surprised that it can exist in literary matters. Here I entirely fail to grasp the situation. I refer especially to articles of criticism, judgments pronounced upon the play, the book, the work of art. Can there be such a thing as the literature, the art of a party?

There are not many courts in Europe as gorgeous as the old Gothic palace. . . . Beneath its curved ogival vault, supported by twelve columns decked with shining coats of arms painted with golden flames on a lapus lazuli ground, the lord mayor's throne had been erected. He presided in a red cassock, his insignia suspended from his neck on a heavy gold chain. . . .

The journalists entered and trumpets hidden behind the pillars sounded. The lord mayor offered his arm to Madame Zola. . . . Invited guests thronged the dance floor and our appearance provoked thunderous applause with shouts of "Zola! Zola! Hurrah!" The young Englishwomen who had been dancing now stood in the first row, and their eyes—large, naive, pure eyes that had never read the things written by the honored gentleman—fixed upon him intently, devoured him.

Delighting in this female attention, Zola was led between a double hedge of lustrous, milky-white idolizers. The evening ended just as pleasantly. "Many introductions. At last we could escape. . . . There were four or five thousand people present. We went and ate oysters at the Café Royal before retiring," wrote Zola.

On Saturday, September 23, the celebration continued. Zola lunched at the Athenaeum with Francis Magnard, director of *Le Figaro*. When evening came he found himself seated once again beside the lord mayor (with whom conversation was impossible, as neither spoke the other's language), this time at a banquet in the Crystal Palace, where thousands heard him decry literary factionalism and extol the universal fraternity of labor—or procreation. "Yes, I demand that once the battle concludes, there no longer be realists, idealists, positivists, symbolists, and that only two things remain—the labor that plants seed and the genius that begets life," he declared in a carefully prepared toast whose double entendre could not have failed to make Alexandrine wince.

So long as the work exists and adds to the glory of the nation, of what importance are the soil from which it sprang and the meaning in which it grew? It would be unnatural indeed for a people to banish glorious books from its literary history on the pretext that they belong to such and such a school. In our homeland, does Rabelais crowd Racine? Does Lamartine stand in Balzac's way? No free production of the race should be condemned when it offers proof of its virility. A literary history is nothing other than a national history relating the evolution of a people, with its passions, struggles, defeats, victories. So that the richest, the most original is the one that reflects life most broadly, in its infinite variety.

His peroration was a salute to "the common fatherland," to "immortal literature," to "all talents," to "geniuses whether for reality or for dream," and, finally, "to human intelligence, sovereign of the world."

Had he waxed too literary for English journalists? he wondered. Prolonged applause should have reassured him that he had not, and what followed went beyond mere applause. With the imperial panache of men who felt, perhaps, that it was theirs to consecrate greatness, his hosts staged a fireworks display in which Zola saw his portrait emblazoned against the night sky. Witnessing this extraordinary spectacle, which gave the measure of a city whose scale astonished him, he thought about death, immortality, the name he bore, the children he had fathered incognito. "I've described [the banquet] for you, my wonderful Jeanne, because at that moment I thought of you three," he wrote soon afterward. "Yes, in a little corner of France there were three beings who are dear to me, and though they stood in darkness, they nonetheless shared my glory. That you and my two darlings should have their share is what I want. Someday they will become my children officially, and when that's the case all that is happening here will redound to your honor as well. I want them to share their father's entire name!"

Zola left England one week later, but not before viewing the Thames upriver at Taplow, visiting Greenwich, admiring Turners at the National Gallery, touring slums around Whitechapel, inspecting the new Underground and, above all, attending a dinner at the Authors' Club, where some eighty members—among them Walter Besant, George Moore, Frank Harris, Arthur Conan Doyle, and Oscar Wilde—paid homage to him. Portrayed by Oswald Crawfurd as an *"imperator litterarum,"* he replied:

Amidst all the plaudits, I well understand that the opinion of your critics has not changed in regard to my works. Only, you have now seen their author, and have found him less black than report painted him. Then, too, you have reflected: "Here is a man who has fought hard and toiled ceaselessly." And belonging as you do to a great nation of workers, you have honored work in me. Lastly it has occurred to you that a man cannot have conquered the world—to use the facetious expression of two of your number—without being worthy of some praise. Works of a different order in art to your own may have affronted you, but you . . . came to realize how much effort and sincerity they embody. I am departing London not, indeed, as one who has triumphed, but as a man who is happy at leaving some sympathetic feelings behind him. My heart overflows with gratitude for the hospitality, so extensive and refined, that you have accorded me.

It behooved him to propose a toast of his own and so he toasted "the good-fellowship of all authors in one universal republic of letters."[2]

Did Zola, at Victoria Station for the return trip, wonder briefly whether those Englishmen from whom he had expected "ambushes" were after all taking a broader view of his work, or ignoring it altogether? The clamor of adulation had not yet died down when, in Ernest Vizetelly's phrase, "the fanatics once more raised their heads." During a Church Congress at Birmingham, Dr. Perowne, bishop of Worcester, exclaimed that "Zola had spent his life in corrupting the minds and souls not only of thousands of his fellow countrymen and especially of the young but also, by the translation of his works, thousands and hundreds of thousands of young souls elsewhere." On that same occasion, J. E. C. Welldon, headmaster of Harrow and future bishop of Bombay, called Zola "infamous" as he urged all churchmen to support the National Vigilant Association.

Evoking universal fraternity in England could not save Zola from returning to a quarrelsome ménage in France. Before the sojourn abroad, relations between Alexandrine and him had apparently deteriorated once again. "As Zola spoke," Goncourt noted on August 4, when everyone convened at the Daudets' summer house outside Paris,

> Madame Zola—aged, wrinkled, sick with flu, and . . . looking like an old doll from the display case of a bankrupt store—sat in a corner telling Mme Daudet about her sad life at Médan. "I see him only during lunch," she said of her husband. "Afterward he takes several turns around the garden, waiting for the newspapers to arrive at two o'clock, and throwing terse comments my way. . . . He urges me to take care of the cow, but I know nothing about cows—that's the gardener's business. . . . Then he goes upstairs with the papers and naps. . . . Normally I'd have my cousin for company; this year, alas, she's at the seashore."

[2]Zola also conversed with Henry James during this visit to England, and James remembered their conversation as follows: "I happened to ask him what opportunity to travel (if any) his immense application had ever left him, and whether in particular he had been able to see Italy, a country from which I had either just returned or which I was luckily—not having the Natural History of a Family on my hands—about to revisit. 'All I've done, alas,' he replied, 'was, the other year, in the course of a little journey to the south, . . . to make a little dash as far as Genoa, a matter of only a few days.' *Le Docteur Pascal*, the conclusion of *Les Rougon-Macquart*, had appeared shortly before, and it further befell that I asked him what plans he had for the future, now that, still *dans la force de l'âge*, he had so cleared the ground. I shall never forget the fine promptitude of his answer— 'Ah, I shall begin at once [a trilogy called] *Les Trois Villes*.' 'And which cities are they to be?' The reply was finer still—'Lourdes, Paris, Rome.' "

Hints dropped every so often suggest that after the trip to England relations grew still worse. To Jacques van Santen Kolff, Zola wrote on March 9, 1894, that he had just traversed "a long crisis of moral and physical suffering." And four months later he lamented, as quoted previously, that the "double life" he led reduced him to despair. Under constant surveillance, he found himself regularly convicted of smuggling contraband affection across the river at Médan or down the hill in Paris. Love bestowed on one household was felt to have been stolen from the other.

With Jeanne and his children, at any rate, a little contraband went a very long way. "I never perceived anything of the melancholy that imbued this period, being much too young," Denise LeBlond-Zola, the main and almost exclusive source of information about Zola's secret life, recalled in 1930. "When I stretch my memory as far back as it will go, I see my father walking across the sunlit slope of Cheverchemont, carrying a large gray parasol lined with green material. And I daresay that what fixed my attention mostly was that beautiful alpaca parasol!" To make amends for his intermittence, Zola seldom appeared without offerings:

> An indulgent father, he never punished us. How many treats there were! One's least desire was his command! At Christmas, on New Year's Day and all birthdays, little gifts spilled out of his pockets. Zola wanted to brighten up the household, so he'd bring armfuls of flowers all year round, stopping in the neighborhood of the Gare Saint-Lazare, where street vendors watched for him. Sometimes he'd buy their entire stock, leaving them dumbfounded and ecstatic. On January 1 he always sent us sweets stashed away in various receptacles: in a miniature Chinese chest, in an enormous perfume brazier, in a copper bucket, in some bauble for my mother. . . . I believe that my dear father derived great joy from seeing our faces light up. . . . Life seemed lovely to us, embellished by the attentions of a man whom others [a reference to Goncourt no doubt] portrayed as vainglorious and brutal.

For Jeanne Rozerot, who accepted her reclusive life and taught the children to revere Zola, there were many gifts, though none more cherished than a necklace with seven pearls which she wore every day of her life.

When, by 1895 or so, it had become obvious to Alexandrine that the past could not be undone, and that there was little profit in continuing to exploit her husband's sense of guilt, yet that divorce was a humiliation she would not endure, she accommodated herself as far as possible to reality. At Edmond de Goncourt's funeral on July 20, 1896,

Henry Céard asked her whether she still suffered deeply, and one week later she responded:

> It has pained me all week that I did not answer your friendly question straightway, and I beg your forgiveness. . . . I would say this, my dear Céard. Ever since I came fully to understand the futility of my efforts and the irremediable character of the break, I promised myself to keep calm, to discuss nothing, to resign myself to the sad life I had been awarded in recompense for the hard times of years past. . . . Do you find me reasonable enough?

As a result, Zola felt fewer compunctions about visiting his brood, whom he moved from the rue Saint-Lazare to larger quarters at 8, rue Taitbout. "I believe that my father at last pleaded so eloquently with his wife that he won the freedom to come see us every day," wrote Denise. "I have a vivid memory of his afternoon visits, of the tea that united us, of the cakes we'd sometimes select together, of the newspapers, *Le Petit Temps*, which the maidservant would go downstairs to purchase at a stand on the Boulevard des Italiens. There was a large blue armchair my father especially liked. He'd sit in it reading the evening papers and he'd often prop us children on his knees and tell us stories." In the course of time, this shuttling between his two lives had made the boundary that separated them indistinct enough for Alexandrine herself to cross over. Not only did she concede that Zola had paternal responsibilities, but she had begun accompanying him every week on strolls with Denise and Jacques around the Palais-Royal gardens and the Tuileries, down the Champs-Elysées, or through the Bois de Boulogne. What feelings this stirred in all concerned one can easily imagine. Again we owe a description of the event to Denise, who for several years remained ignorant of Alexandrine's identity:

> We were a bit intimidated by "the lady," as we called her, who watched us play with a benevolent smile, who laughed at our childish prattle, but our father was there, which reassured us. An air of mystery hovered over the scene, since our mother was absent; there was no mention of her and we received no advance notice of these walks. We'd never return from them empty-handed: "the lady" always had gifts for us. . . . I was around ten when Alexis's older daughter spoke to me one day, by chance, about her godmother, Mme Emile Zola, whom she seldom saw. This revelation did not astonish me, or trouble my serene childhood; we were happy, we loved one another dearly, parents and children, nothing seemed capable of diminishing this happiness.

Alexandrine eschewed Jeanne Rozerot, but she embraced her husband's offspring and during prolonged absences from Paris inquired after them with grandmotherly solicitude. "Poor Denise is very taken up by school, and we must find some other time than Tuesday afternoon to have our outings with her and Jacques because she's spoken for on that day," Zola explained in November 1895, soon after he had personally enrolled his six-year-old daughter at a private establishment. "I think that I shall choose Wednesday, if you have no objection. We'll talk about it." On another occasion he helped Denise with her homework and immediately reported this to Alexandrine, who was then in Rome. "I had her go over her Bible history. You should have seen her describe Isaac's marriage and Joseph sold by his brothers, with gestures and in a voice of absolute conviction. From hearing her recite the same lessons, Jacques, too, has learned them, and it's comical hearing him pronounce words like Canaan and Mesopotamia, which fill his whole mouth. They are well, and today they finished the candied fruit [you sent from Italy], which they both adored."

Days in the country unfolded much as they always had, except for Zola's habit of quietly disappearing every afternoon at teatime to spend several hours with Jeanne, Denise, and Jacques in Cheverchemont or, later on, Verneuil. He ate breakfast between eight and nine, sorted through the morning mail, trudged upstairs in slippered feet to his study—accompanied by a fiercely possessive little pooch named Pinpin—and wrote undisturbed until one o'clock, when two bells announced lunch. Céard's jovial presence was missed, no doubt, but the Zolas often had beloved guests at table, and their regulars during this period included the Charpentiers, the Fasquelle family, who summered nearby at Saint-Germain-en-Laye or Maisons-Laffitte, the Bruneaus, Amélie Laborde and her children Elina and Albert, the engraver Fernand Desmoulin and a cousin of Desmoulin, Dr. Jules Larat. Postprandial liqueurs were served in the "billiard room," where talk revolved around the subject of afternoon entertainment. Before napping, Zola played bowls or croquet or led his company on jaunts through the Verneuil wood. "We'd take little walks along the Seine toward Villennes or Triel," recalled Albert Laborde, who turned seventeen in 1895. "Visiting Saint-Germain meant a carriage ride, and Zola sometimes treated us to lunch there at the pavillon Henri IV. . . . By 1893–95 no one went swimming any longer; it was I who used the rowboat Nana and the skiff Pot-Bouille. . . . Maupassant had no successor." Laborde also recalled evening strolls around the garden, where linden trees formed a pleasant allée. At nightfall, everyone gathered once again in the octagonal tower, some to play billiards, others to socialize around a large table. Alexandrine sewed and chatted while Zola, stretched on a divan, perused the latest arrivals from Charpentier et Fasquelle. By eleven o'clock, candles were being lit for the walk upstairs.

Villagers grew accustomed to seeing their famous neighbor mounted on what may have been the first bicycle in Médan. Zola acquired it after various models had been carefully studied, and rode with youthful gusto. "The weather is terrible," he complained on August 8, 1895, to Fernand Desmoulin, a recent widower, who found distraction from his grief in cycling. "With me as with you, cycling takes my mind off things. I've done a great deal of it, under all conditions, even in pouring rain, which means that I've come home drenched, mud-splattered. No matter, it does me good. Help me train. I'd like to attempt a long jaunt with you." In short order, Desmoulin became a steady partner on excursions that attest to Zola's physical stamina. Built for marathons rather than sprints, the author of *Les Rougon-Macquart* was not intimidated by the thirty-four kilometers separating Médan from his apartment on the rue de Bruxelles or by the prospect of a two-hour spin around the Bois de Boulogne. After one such, he wrote Alexandrine, when she was away for an asthmatic cure, "Splendid weather, a real summer day, sunny and cloudless—if anything, too warm. The paths were still muddy from the recent rains, however. . . . [Desmoulin and I] had lunch at the Chalet du Cycle. . . . Alone, on my way home, I found carriages jam-packed along the Boulevard des Batignolles. But I broke free and returned triumphantly to the rue de Bruxelles." On occasion Desmoulin and Zola persuaded Eugène Fasquelle to accompany them. But for Zola, who joined the Touring-Club de France, the bicycle was not exclusively a means of flight or a vehicle of masculine camaraderie. He bicycled with Jeanne and would have bicycled with Alexandrine had she learned to keep her balance. When *promenades à bicyclette* were organized at Médan, Madame Zola followed her husband and her Laborde cousins as best she could, on a three-wheeler.[3]

Zola developed yet another, even more intense, enthusiasm in middle age, and it, too, made its mark on those around him. The first signs occurred during the summer of 1887, when Victor Billaud, a minor poet and publisher of *La Gazette des bains de mer de Royan*, taught him how to take photographs. "A photographic craze has seized Charpentier and Billaud," he told Céard, implying that he himself, though curious, had not yet succumbed. "We'll show you some inter-

[3]If, as Goncourt claims, Zola expressed a desire to take horseback-riding lessons, perhaps the bicycle was the horse he never rode. Letters sent to Jeanne Rozerot several years later from England show him appreciating the equestrian posture of female bicycle riders. As for the tricycle, Alexandrine made the best of a lesser vehicle and learned to travel considerable distances on it. "I went into the Verneuil woods," she informed Albert Laborde in July 1896. "On the return trip, I covered 7 kilometers in 35 minutes. I'm very proud of my progress."

esting prints." Technological innovations—notably film coated with gelatine-bromide emulsion—were only just making photography accessible to amateurs, but many professional studios had already started doing a brisker business in equipment, service, and supplies than in portrait work, as portable cameras entered the market. George Eastman established himself all over Europe with the most famous of these, the Kodak, which appeared in 1888 and soon became what it has never ceased to be—an indispensable chronicler of bourgeois life. "At the end of the century the social class that under the Second Empire had had their portraits done in 'temples of photography' were buying portable instruments," writes one historian. "Nadar himself, the great Nadar [who had retired from business], asked his son Paul to send him a Kodak. Mailing the camera to Paris for development of the film, he couldn't wait to see the little images. 'The Kodak has departed. Quickly send us the prints, about which we are very worried. The last two are of our house at low tide.' " Painters followed suit, or several very gifted ones did, and for Degas photography assumed considerable importance. While sojourning at Mont-Dore in 1895 he ordered a camera, enlargements, and dozens of plates from his Parisian furnishers, Tasset et Lhote. "In the evening I digest my dinner and practice photography by twilight," he wrote.

By 1895, Zola had succumbed. Unlike Degas, he did not restrict his picture taking to the late afternoon. Nor did he limit himself merely to taking pictures. He mastered the technique of developing them as well and ultimately installed darkrooms in all his residences—the apartment on the rue de Bruxelles, the house in Médan, Jeanne's house in Verneuil. Alexandrine informed Elina Laborde on August 9, 1897:

> Yesterday your uncle tried to develop twenty-four snapshots. It had been raining buckets since the morning and though he wanted my help, which I would gladly have given him in nice dry weather, I let him shut himself up in this humid little laboratory while calling his attention to the fact that it was most unhygienic, especially after lunch. He persisted nonetheless, and remained in the dark for two and a half hours, railing and muttering nonsense because he had mishandled some plates. The result, in short, is that he took sick after this protracted period of immobility.

Might Alexandrine have remembered that when she first met him thirty-three years earlier, this man preoccupied with images on glass plates had been using an optical figure to describe different literary schools? "Every work of art is like a window opened on creation," he wrote to Antony Valabrègue on August 18, 1864. "Framed in its embrasure is a kind of transparent Screen through which one sees objects more or less deformed, with their lines and colors suffering more or less noticeable changes. These changes depend upon the nature of the Screen. One no longer has exact and real creation, but creation modified by the milieu through which its image filters."

As it did with so many other tourists, the folding camera accompanied Zola outside France during these peripatetic last years of the century, helping him "collect" everything in sight. From Italy, where he gathered material for his novel *Rome*, he brought back, among much else, images of excavations at the Forum. And later his self-imposed exile in the aftermath of *J'accuse* produced a London album, with wonderfully vivid photographs of street sweepers and art vendors, of funeral coaches and market wagons, of families wearing their Sunday best and women shopping, of private greenhouses and the Crystal Palace looming over blocks of row houses.

Zola also lavished attention on Paris, especially in 1900, when the gingerbread palaces and exotic pavilions built for the Exposition provided shutterbugs like himself with a regular feast. But his favorite subjects were his two households, and hundreds of photographs attest to it. After photographing Alexandrine and guests at Médan, he often photographed Jeanne and the children at Verneuil, as if to unify his divided life with portable images, or to bestow upon each half an illusion of wholeness through self-commemorative theater. Jeanne, who seldom spent evenings out and by the age of thirty already looked matronly, posed for many portraits wearing fashionable costumes from which the unwitting observer might infer that she otherwise had occasion to wear them at the Opera, at the Café Riche, at soirées, at spas—as Zola's young wife. They were, indeed, costumes rather than clothes.[4]

The first strong indication that *Le Docteur Pascal* was not to mark the end of Zola's creative life appeared on March 31, 1891, in an interview with Jules Huret. It was understandable, Zola told Huret, that impatient, self-doubting youth should assail science for not having dispelled every mystery or captured the bluebird of happiness. Young people scorned the "immense positivist labor" of the previous half-century and derived solace from the pseudomystical revelations of literary symbolism. "To conclude the brilliant last decade of our enormous century, to formulate . . . the turmoil of minds that crave certitude, here is some meager verse written by poetasters who make their home at

---

[4]Zola also liked to photograph her from the back, *profil perdu*, in a lacy bodice, with bare shoulders and hair hanging down to her buttocks, which puts one in mind of Count Muffat peeking at Nana through a hole in the backcloth.

Parisian brasseries." But this flight from reality would not prevail. "The future," he declared, "will belong to . . . those men who will have grasped the soul of modern society, who, disengaging themselves from excessively rigorous theories, will yield to a more logical, more compassionate understanding of life. I believe in a broader, more complex portrayal of human truth, in a larger view of humanity." If time remained, he, Zola, would provide that "more compassionate understanding" and thereby restyle the novelistic genre for the next generation. As Jeanne Rozerot had made him feel young again, so would another saga.

A subject presented itself six months later, during his voyage through the Pyrenees with Alexandrine. On the way from Cauterets to Tarbes, Zola visited Lourdes and felt impelled by what he saw to stay awake all night scribbling down impressions of the pilgrimage scene. "A novel about Lourdes," he began. "At this moment of mysticity [*mysticité*], of revolt against science, here is an admirable subject: show how persistent is mankind's dependence upon the supernatural, with this extraordinary story of Bernadette Soubirous, the twelve-year-old peasant girl having visions of the Virgin in the grotto and provoking this enormous movement of humanity . . . the multitude that converges here, one hundred fifty thousand people per year, I believe. Study and dramatize the endless duel between science and the longing for supernatural intervention." Young literati rejected the scientific precepts by which he himself set store in favor of symbolism, and likewise, ordinary people for whose ills medicine offered no cure embraced religious magic. "This movement astonishes us all the more for having arisen in a skeptical, irreverent century. . . . Some doctors deny the miracles, others affirm them; cures are recorded, in good faith (?), by the thousands." What fascinated him as much as the survival of primitive Catholicism was the economic exploitation of credulous supplicants and the promiscuity that attended this mingling in close quarters. "The whole town swells, thrives, fattens on pilgrims," he continued.

> The traffic through hotels, the commerce in holy objects, the refreshment bars, the food stands, the innumerable church masses, the candles, the profits of the clergy. Huge amounts of money change hands. . . . Convents have sprung up in the vicinity of the grotto, many serving at hostelries for the pilgrims. Strange phenomena to be uncovered there, no doubt. . . . Pilgrims sleep just about anywhere in town, eating, guzzling. People claim that all manner of deplorable things go on. It would mean my digging deep, winkling out the truth. Similarly, the truth as to how this enterprise was devised, launched, and how it's managed. In short, all the hidden stuff.

What also fascinated him in Lourdes was the apocalyptic commotion. To his repertoire of human throngs he welcomed the prospect of adding a doomsday crowd limping toward salvation. "How many interesting tableaux there are to be drawn: packed trains arriving from afar, . . . great crowds, twenty thousand people invading the town all at once, processions leading down to the grotto, invalids parading by the score, dragged in armchairs by priests and laymen, . . . their heart-rending ugliness, every abominable sort of suffering, which hope sometimes transfigures."

With *La Débâcle* still unfinished, Zola gave this future project little thought until the following July, when journalists, who welcomed copy from the ever controversial novelist and stalked him everywhere, caught wind of his intention to spend some time at Lourdes gathering material for a novel in which the "sublime" would neighbor the "grotesque." Miracles occur at Lourdes, he told reporters from *Le Figaro* and *Gil Blas.*

> Lourdes does wonders for people with nervous afflictions, but for poor consumptives who are immersed in pools there it spells certain, often instant, death. It seems that religious faith has staked out this place as a fortified refuge, and one can readily imagine why bishops . . . , who have had it closed on several occasions, finally made their peace with a feeling stronger than any other. . . . What we encounter is a remnant of the old world, a world that takes us back ten centuries.

Catholics "who believe in Lourdes" had nothing to fret about. The book was to be written "without any malevolent intention."

For attracting notice and witnessing mysticism at its most frenetic, Zola could not have chosen a more propitious moment than 1892. Pope Leo XIII had awarded repentant Christians a period of plenary indulgence for their sins by way of celebrating the new holiday of the Appearance of the Immaculate Virgin at Lourdes. This so-called extraordinary jubilee was to coincide with the annual "national pilgrimage" and, indeed, beginning on August 18, trains from all over France converged on Lourdes. During the afternoon of that day fifteen trains departed Paris alone, including the so-called *train blanc*, which carried people with terminal illnesses. The little sisters of the Assumption, called 'La Croix,' installed the moribund on makeshift beds in third-class carriages, and praying, which began right away, lasted throughout the twenty-two-hour voyage. "The remarkable fact is that many invalids selected for Lourdes die just before their departure," noted an obdurate unbeliever. Had Zola boarded one such train (instead of taking the Pyrenees Express in comfort) he would have spent an entire day at Poitiers, where round-the-clock prayer sessions were held before the tomb of the sixth-century Frankish queen Saint Radegunda.

Zola's sojourn at Lourdes, which lasted almost two weeks, from August 19 until September 1, yielded 242 pages of notes. After visiting the train station to observe pilgrims as they poured out in a confusion of luggage, mattresses, pillows, wicker baskets, wheelchairs, stretchers, and floral bouquets for the Virgin, he observed them again at the grotto in which, thirty-four years earlier, a young country girl, Bernadette Soubirous, had had repeated visions of the Virgin Mary. "Expressions on their faces," he wrote.

> Some lie prone on stretchers while others are in a sitting position; intermingled. Children, priests. The woman whose face is eaten away, with two red eyes, two bloody holes for nostrils, weeping. A young woman gets up holding her crutches in her hand, walks forward to thank the Virgin, then ha. this miraculous cure certified by the Medical Verification Bureau ["Bureau de Constatation"]. Another, paralyzed, stood up violently, walked, then prayed for a long time. Rumors of miracles fly through the crowd. Attempts to make miracles happen: the priest who exhorts a paralyzed man with "Walk! Walk!" And the paralyzed man, trying to do so without crutches, falls down. . . . Many kiss the rock at the feet of the Virgin. One hears the *Magnificat*, the *Laudate*, the *Ave Maria* being sung. "Another miracle!" someone shouts and a crutch is seen above the crowd, moving toward the grotto.

Holiness allowed no respite. By 4 p.m. the dirty, sweating, ill-clad mob, a mass of common faces, had formed up behind richly attired priests to march in a Procession of the Holy Sacrament, and as soon as night fell they returned to march some more in a candlelight parade that wound its way around the enormous Basilique du Rosaire, like a luminous serpent. There were twelve to fifteen thousand candle-bearers, Zola noted. "Men, women, children. The main square fills little by little, a lake of fire. All voices unite in the Credo." After several days and nights, the same songs sung "obsessively" could not but induce a "state of nervous exaltation" that prepared the mind for apparently supernatural phenomena.

The ecclesiastical orders that held sway at Lourdes, administering holy sites and organizing the national pilgrimage, did not rebuff Zola when, with guidance from a well-disposed Catholic journalist, he sought out their most influential members. They seemed, on the contrary, flattered by his project, which had already been bruited about in the press, and opened doors normally closed to outsiders. Thus was he able to see dying women packed together in the Hôpital des Dou-

leurs, to inspect every corner of the grotto, to visit the Medical Veri-
fication Bureau, where Dr. Boissarie produced three beneficiaries of
miraculous intercession, to visit the storeroom in which candles, a
highly profitable item, lay stacked ten feet high and the factory for
bottling holy water, to observe the scrofulous being bathed in polluted
pools. "No medical precaution is taken," he wrote,

and why indeed should any be taken, since here one is in the domain
of the miraculous? Our Lady of Lourdes can do no harm to those
who beseech her help. The moment one places oneself outside all
natural phenomena, everything goes. One bathes menstruating
women and baths are given right after meals, even to consumptives,
unless the doctor categorically disapproves, which he can't always do
as the sick are often led straight to the grotto and pools upon getting
off the train. . . . On average sixty are immersed in the same water.
. . . One of them told me that he saw blood from an ulcer, and there
is more—bits of skin, scabs, pieces of bandage—a real microbial
broth. . . . In front of the pools, priests and monks and capuchins
pray and call for cures, sending up shouts which the kneeling pilgrims
repeat as they cross their arms over their breasts and often kiss the
ground. It's a scene of intoxication, of rapture, of frightful tumult.
"Mary, conceived without sin, pray for us!" "Lord, we adore you!"
"Mary, cure our sick!"

The warm welcome given a notoriously atheistic author would appear
to have been bound up with the credulity that pervaded Lourdes. How
could anyone, even Zola, resist the evidence of miracles? "[Believers]
speak about cures, miracles, with mind-boggling glibness," was how he
put it himself. "The most astonishing facts leave them unperturbed
. . . without common sense registering the slightest protest. . . . And
I'm not talking only about cretins or illiterates. . . . It often made me
uneasy, and beneath the uneasiness smoldered feelings of anger that
might finally have burst forth. My wits struggled. I imagine that people
who end up converting must experience this state before reason
succumbs."

Zola assembled biographical information about Bernadette Soubirous, whose life, told choruslike by other characters, would occupy a
central place in this novel. The Catholic writer Henri Lasserre de Mon-
zie, who had met Bernadette and written books about her after being
cured at Lourdes of some ophthalmological disorder, reminisced freely
to him. So did the author of a *Guide de Lourdes*, Jean Barbet, who
many years earlier had taught school at nearby Bartrès, where Bernadette tended lambs for her foster mother. This inquiry resulted in
conversations with Bernadette's brother, with an aunt, with a child-

hood friend, with a foster brother. Zola retraced her steps back to the room she inhabited at the time of her visions, and nothing moved him more than the sight of this wretchedly poor little nook, from which a gigantic movement had emerged. "I do not deny the unknown," he reassured Lasserre.

> If this child brought such a world into being, it's because she addressed an inherently human need for the unknown. You organize the unknown with dogma and you make a revealed religion out of it. One need not believe in a religion to explain the phenomena brought about by the visions of an emotionally distraught girl. If the latter reared a city from the ground, made money flow in torrents, brought people in droves, it's because they answered our immense, devouring hunger for the miraculous. Our demand is to be deceived and consoled. She opened the unknown at a historically favorable moment no doubt, and everyone rushed forward.

Therein lay the philosophical point of his book, he wrote. As human as the material factors that determine man's condition is a childlike impulse to worship an intercessor who transcends nature.

When, soon afterward, he began plotting *Lourdes*, his story jelled around the idea of several afflicted souls seeking miraculous relief during a national pilgrimage. Months later, in July 1893, he decided that this novel, from whose dominant theme the reader was not to be distracted by too much detail, must have a protagonist. "What's needed is a man who represents free thought, undogmatic examination, faith only in progress through science, who opposes superstition, . . . who has concluded that Christianity's day is done, . . . that it will founder and be replaced, though he does not know what form the replacement will take," he noted.

> He'll visit Lourdes to look around, to inform himself. . . . The hocus-pocus will make him indignant, but in order to portray him as evolving, it is important that the whole scene move him deeply at first, and that toward the end he come to feel a need for something else. This character could serve me later (in sequels). . . . I'd rather he weren't a doctor, because of Dr. Pascal. I'm tempted to make him a priest, but that would be hard. A priest has certain indelible marks, which would hamper me considerably.

Zola's rumination produced a *homo duplex*—a man born to an illustrious freethinking scientist and a pious bourgeoise, who harbors grave doubts under his cassock. Reason having gained the upper hand over faith—or his dead father having posthumously countered the influence of his mother—he visits Lourdes but cannot escape from his internecine quarrel. There, on the contrary, it rages stronger than ever, as he hesitates to oppose beliefs that lighten the terrible burden of simple folk while finding it painful to propagate or acquiesce in superstition. Zola named this character, who obviously spoke on his behalf, Pierre Froment.

Research for *Lourdes* concluded a year after the national pilgrimage of 1892. In August 1893, Zola witnessed once again the departure of the "white train" from the Gare d'Orléans (now the Musée d'Orsay) and entered carriages to question personnel accompanying the sick. Not without repugnance he studied works by Henri Lasserre, particularly *Episodes miraculeux de Lourdes*, but to fortify himself against this hagiographical literature, which of course did not recognize that certain physical disabilities might have emotional causes, he interviewed the famous neurologist Gilles de la Tourette, Charcot's former right-hand man at Salpêtrière Hospital, who was writing a three-volume work on hysteria entitled *Traité clinique et thérapeutique de l'hystérie.*

Zola set down the first words of *Lourdes* on October 5, in the aftermath of his triumphant voyage to London. By March he had gotten more than halfway through it, notwithstanding domestic crises. "I am very far behind, my health has been so bad that *Gil Blas* will not begin serialization until April 15," he informed van Santen Kolff on March 9.

> The book is divided into [the] five days . . . that the national pilgrimage consecrates each year to Lourdes. My novel is quite simply an account of this pilgrimage, with Lourdes described from every viewpoint. . . . As for the romantic conflict, it's as weak as in *La Débâcle*, even weaker. You must already know that I start with the premise that this blind plunge into faith is symptomatic of our contemporary *taedium vitae*. . . . Imagine wretched invalids whom doctors have abandoned: they do not resign themselves but invoke a divine power and beg him to cure them, against the very laws of nature. . . . Making this situation symbolic of our age, I portray humanity at large as a sick man whom science apparently dooms and who, to console himself, grasps for miracles. . . . I can't convey a clear idea of *Lourdes* in several sentences. It's one of my most complex and involved works.

Among other elements the résumé omits is Pierre Froment's unconsummated love for Marie de Guersaint, a childhood friend paralyzed since the onset of puberty ten years earlier, who has him escort her to Lourdes, where her affliction, diagnosed as organic by various doctors, "miraculously" disappears.[5] With Marie burying womanhood at thirteen (she travels in a coffinlike vehicle) only to recover it from beyond the grave at twenty-three, and Pierre taking vows of chastity at eighteen only at thirty to find his inamorata available, this scenario relates once again Zola's story of the dark, violent passage through adolescence. But here it is more a contrivance than a drama, a skeleton for supporting descriptions of the horrifying kermis to which Bernadette's visionary trance state had given rise. Mass delirium was what interested Zola most, and from his notebook he transcribed crowd scenes verbatim, writing *Lourdes* in eight and a half months. *Gil Blas* serialized it between April 14 and August 14, 1894. Charpentier published it on July 25.

Journalists who had been hounding Zola for interviews ever since his sojourn at Lourdes went on doing so. The project aroused enormous interest—as much as any he had previously undertaken—and this was early along turned to financial advantage in negotiations with book and newspaper publishers. Offers came from all over Europe: Italy, Hungary, Scandinavia. Andrew Chatto bought Vizetelly's English translation sight unseen for four thousand francs. After April 15 another English translation ran in the *New York Herald,* James Gordon Bennett having bid twenty thousand francs. At home, where stakes were higher, *Gil Blas* paid fifty thousand francs and, by way of clinching the deal, hired Alfred Bruneau as its music critic at Zola's behest. On April 27, four thousand Parisians crowded the Trocadéro Palace to hear Zola read from *Lourdes*. Most of them purchased it in due course, apparently, for by 1896–97 it had sold about 140,000 copies, or more than any Zola novel except *Nana* and *La Débâcle*.

The critical reception given *Lourdes* was ambivalent at best, however. While admiring Zola's genius for "transforming crowds into colossi who have an existence unto themselves, who astonish and confound us with their enormous life," Francisque Sarcey found the principal characters so tiresome—Pierre in his tergiversations, Marie in her sublimity—as to make him skim whole pages. Adolphe Brisson agreed. "When one closes the volume," he wrote in *Les Annales politiques et littéraires,* "there remains the vision of an admirable nocturnal procession, an immense and prodigious scene of exaltation and devotion. . . . I cannot think of a more spectacular episode than the one in which pilgrims follow Father Judaine as he carries the Holy

---

[5]In December 1892, *La Revue hebdomadaire* published an article by Charcot on illness and religion that was very widely discussed. In *Lourdes,* a doctor named Beauclair voices Charcot's observation that paralyses of hysterical origin had frequently responded to faith healing. Faith healing was, Charcot had written, a "natural phenomenon" which had worked "in all ages, in all climes, among pagans, Christians, Muslims alike."

Sacrament up the side of the mountain. Over this scene passes a breath of mystery that increases its grandeur." Otherwise, he continued, Zola had produced stuff and nonsense. "M. Zola is not at ease here. . . . He does not recognize miracles, . . . and is nonetheless moved, or pretends to be, by this explosion of fervor, this collective genuflection, . . . calling it sublime." In *Le Figaro*, Maurice Barrès examined the novel from a different angle. Unlike "German socialists" entranced with "economic forces," Zola, he declared, understood that human affairs were ultimately shaped by "the Word" and that Lourdes, which had sprung from the "spontaneous discourse" of a young girl, illustrated this truth. But the picture of a fin de siècle generation making Pascalian wagers en masse after losing faith in science was highly distorted. "One exaggerates our scientific knowledge and the weariness it causes us. . . . As we are for the most part ignoramuses, it would take considerable audacity to declare ourselves disillusioned with the results of science; we don't even know what those results are." For Barrès, whose own fiction argued the proto-fascist creed that France would not achieve salvation until she recovered her roots in the ancestor-worshipping collective unconscious of the Folk, Zola was an "orator" rather than a "thinker."

What Henry James said about another late Zola novel conveys, in brief, the sense of what most reviewers thought about *Lourdes* (apart from its crowd scenes), that "we really rub our eyes . . . to see so great an intellectual adventure as *Les Rougon-Macquart* come to its end in deep desert sand." They did not appreciate its morbid promiscuity. But Catholics hated it for quite different reasons, all of which bore upon Bernadette Soubirous. The final chapters of *Lourdes* had not yet appeared in *Gil Blas* when Monsignor Antoine Ricard, vicar-general of the archdiocese of Aix-en-Provence, published a book entitled *La Vraie Bernadette de Lourdes, Lettres à M. Zola.* Rejecting Zola's argument that Bernadette had been a lonely, emotionally unstable girl afflicted with hallucinations, he marshaled the testimony of physicians, among them Dr. Vergez, professor at Montpellier, who had examined all the "occurrences" and declared eight of them to be unquestionably "supernatural." *Lourdes* abounded in errors, he wrote, and the municipal councillors of Bartrès (behind whom stood rich local clergy) agreed. "You [Monsieur Zola] repre· nt our humble church as a place that may have excited the devout child's imagination and to prove your point you furnish it with a sumptuous, gilded altar—a blue-eyed, crimson-lipped Virgin," they charged in a letter quoted by Monsignor Ricard.

> That's all false, as you well know. . . . Bernadette's foster father never read aloud to his family the texts of which you speak; his own son has sworn it. . . . You affirm that throughout one winter fireside

gatherings took place in our church with the authorization of Father Ader. We deny this categorically.

Letters and pamphlets reviling *Lourdes* flew fast and thick. The year 1894 was a banner one for hagiographical works produced by churchmen eager to counter the evildoer's influence. The commotion continued all summer long and may have bothered Zola even at Houlgate in Normandy, where he and Alexandrine spent late August with the Fasquelles. Then, on September 21, a dispatch from Rome announced that *Lourdes* had been placed on the Index. Papal formalities usually took longer, Zola told a reporter interviewing him at Médan for *Le Matin.*

For some time now the whole religious world has been swept by a wave of anger which I find somewhat surprising. At first there was sympathy as people appreciated my moderation. . . . But those people believe they possess the truth and admit neither contestation nor contradiction. I have received slanderous letters and religious papers have called me a priest-eater and a scoundrel. I have a whole collection of curious articles. It's all absurd.

Did these adversaries regard Pierre Froment, a priest who keeps his ministry even after losing his faith, as a malicious figment of Zola's anticlerical imagination? France, he protested, was filled with Pierre Froments, some of whom had confided in him long before he wrote *Lourdes.* Did they find Bernadette Soubirous scandalously besmirched? He had, on the contrary, idealized her, for the facts of her life left little doubt that she was not only a "hysteric" but an "idiot." Did they want him to recognize the cures effected at Lourdes? He had always recognized them and had, furthermore, consulted physicians well acquainted with the power of mind over body, notably Jean-Martin Charcot. Did they nurse some other grievance against him? Yes, he concluded. "It's neither my novel as a whole nor my incredulity that vexed the religious world so sorely. What they can't forgive is my laying bare all the secret dramas of Lourdes . . . all the little mysteries of Lourdes unveiled: that's the real explanation for all this anger."[6]

[6]Zola's informants had told him that the abbé Peyramale, curate of Lourdes at the time of Bernadette's visions, had been the victim of a power grab by the Fathers of the Immaculate Conception, later known as "Fathers of the Grotto." He had raised enough money to begin building a new parish church where pilgrims would assemble before proceeding to the grotto, but after the Fathers arrived, all contributions were diverted to the construction of their basilica; the parish church remained half built, and Peyramale, a broken man, carried his huge burden of debt to the grave.

As Zola had conceived it, *Lourdes* was not to stand alone. It was to inaugurate a trilogy called *Les Trois Villes*, with the middle volume set in Rome under Leo XIII's very nose, and the papal ban only spurred him on.[7] His notes indicate that the idea for this cycle had first arisen two years earlier, in September 1892, when he wrote:

> Make two volumes. The first would be called *Lourdes*, the other *Rome*. . . . In the first put the naive awakening of old Catholicism, . . . the need for faith and illusion, and in the second all the neo-Catholicism or rather neo-Christianity of this fin de siècle. Vogüé and the others, the high clergy, the pope . . . Rome trying to accommodate modern ideas. . . . If I did *Rome*, I'd keep one or several characters, the bishop and others, to create continuity between the two volumes. . . . My fear is of not finding a congenial subject, a frame in which I'd feel at home, with crowds, large masses to move around, grand effects. . . . I shall have to search, to see what *Rome* may be.

Soon afterward, in a newspaper interview, he mentioned a third novel, *Paris*, envisaging therein the climactic drama of Catholicism struggling with socialism—"a door open upon the twentieth century." In another ten months he was able to formulate precise plans for this trilogy. "The outline of *Lourdes* is more or less complete," he told van Santen Kolff on July 20, 1893. "All I have to do now is write it. What held me up a bit was my reluctance to take the plunge before knowing about *Rome* and *Paris*. I couldn't seriously tackle the first until I had found the main lines of all three. It's clear now, and I'm satisfied. I have a big new hunk on my plate, which means four interesting years of work."

Contemporaries would have understood without further explanation that the "neo-Catholicism" to which Zola addressed himself in *Rome* described Pope Leo XIII's program for wresting the Church free from the systematic obscurantism, the backward social thought, and reactionary politics of his predecessor, Pius IX. Much concerned with France, Leo concluded that the cause of the Most Christian King had no life left in it, and that for French Catholics to uphold monarchy was to make a virtue of impotence. Monsignor Mourey, French auditor of the Sacred Roman Rota, confirmed this view, assuring the pope a year before the 1895 elections in France that the country "is steadily moving toward the Republic. . . . What is to be done? Two things: first of all publish a doctrinal declaration on the adaptability of the Church to different kinds of political institutions and apply the traditional prin-

---

[7] We have seen how, for Zola, things often came in threes—first of all his own original family, then the three "inseparables." The "Three Cities" call to mind the social division into three discrete towns of Aix-en-Provence.

ciples to the present condition of France; then tell our bishops to prefer a republican candidate if he gives adequate guarantees on religious matters." It did not escape Mourey that Leo's conciliatory gambit also served the Church's temporal ambitions. If some internal crisis undermined the Italian state, which hung together tenuously, might France assist the Holy See in regaining extensive territories lost in 1870? Certainly, relations between Paris and Rome were poor. Incensed by the French occupation of Tunis, Italy had allied herself with Germany and Austria-Hungary in 1881, creating a diplomatic axis that was to last until World War I.

Through various spokesmen, particularly the renowned cardinal Charles Lavigerie, Leo campaigned for Catholic accommodation to the Republic, or *Ralliement*, and in short order opinion was swayed. The ultra-orthodox journal *L'Univers* came around. So did the large-circulation tabloid called *La Croix*, which exuberantly lambasted royalism. Count Albert de Mun envisioned a Catholic party compatible with republican government that would devise legislative programs for protecting the working class against abuses of power. But many monarchists stood firm, even after the Boulanger disaster. Opprobrium was heaped upon Lavigerie, who received virtually no support from episcopal brethren. To thwart him, Cardinal Richard, archbishop of Paris, organized a Union of Christian France, in which aristocrats and high clergy huddled together as they had ten years earlier under Bontoux's fragile umbrella. Freppel, bishop of Angers, repeatedly condemned the *Ralliement*; Lavigerie's policy, he argued, was based on the mistaken belief that "the Republic, *in France*, is simply a form of government as in Switzerland or in the United States, and not a doctrine, a doctrine fundamentally and radically contrary to Christian doctrine." The Count d'Haussonville, who represented the pretender Louis d'Orléans, declared the necessity of safeguarding "an inviolable and sacred domain," "the domain of honor."

At the beginning of 1892 Leo decided that his whipping boy Lavigerie had absorbed quite enough punishment, and on February 20 he spoke ex cathedra in an encyclical entitled *Amidst Numerous Anxieties*. Time brings about changes in political institutions, the pope observed. Violent crises produce anarchical disorder, whereupon social necessity requires that new governments be created. "All that is new is the political form of civil powers or their mode of transmission; not at all affected is power in and of itself (which always derives from God)." Governments thus constituted must be accepted, for the commonweal. "Hence," he continued, "the wisdom of the Church in maintaining equable relations with the many governments that have successively held sway over France during this past century. Such an attitude is the surest and most salutary line of conduct for all French people in their civil relations with the Republic, which represents the current government of their nation." A distinction was to be made between constituted powers and legislation. Given that even a good regime could pass execrable laws, it behooved men of probity to fight legislative abuses by legal means.

Amidst Numerous Anxieties electrified Catholic France. Lower clergy generally submitted to papal authority, but the episcopate broke ranks. While some twenty or more bishops welcomed Leo's intervention, a majority remained silent, either for reasons of conscience or for fear of alienating rich benefactors. "Do you think perchance that my diocese consists of parishes?" one such prelate is reported by a Catholic journalist to have said in private.

> You're wrong; it consists of one hundred fifty châteaux, which subsidize charitable works. The rest is a charge, nothing more. In twenty-five châteaux I find the portrait of Prince Victor, and I bow once. In twenty-five others I see the photograph of the imperial prince and the Count of Paris together in a single frame: I bow twice. In the other hundred, the Orléans family reigns alone: I bow three times. But at all of them I find financial aid for my schools and my paupers. Only these three milieux afford me this happiness. How can you expect me to [join the *Ralliement*]?

Prominent Catholic laymen were even more torn between throne and altar than prominent ecclesiastics. Magistrates, functionaries and professors with compromised or blighted careers could neither accept the anticlerical Republic they had fought tirelessly since 1880 nor disobey the pope. Like Pierre Chesnelong, a right-wing deputy of note who exclaimed that "to deny one's past is to dishonor oneself," many decided, at Leo XIII's behest, to retire from the fray. "As Chesnelong put it, the new policy needed new men," writes one historian. "That would have been true even if he had thought the Pope right, but he thought the Pope wrong and the Pope insisted on a formal acceptance of the policy of the *Ralliement*. Chesnelong submitted and, after reading without comment the papal message to the Catholic Congress that had met while still hoping to evade the issue, he left the hall, saying tearfully, 'Twice disowned; by the King and by the Pope.' "[8] The Union of Christian France, which had been born decrepit, quickly fell apart, and the Comte de Paris's barbed allusions to Pope Gregory VII

---

[8]Chesnelong was one of two deputies chosen by the promonarchist contingent in 1873 to visit Frohsdorf and present the Comte de Chambord with plans for a Restoration. The report he gave on returning made no mention of the pretender's unwillingness to accept the tricolor flag, which prompted Chambord to withdraw.

subjugating the Holy Roman Emperor at Canossa carried wide of the mark.

Republicans who stood on the extreme Left had much preferred a world of hostile political ideologies in which the enemy was forever and dependably trying to repeal 1789. They feared that the *Ralliement* served as a Trojan horse from which soldiers of the crown and the cross would someday pour into the National Assembly. But moderate republicans, for whom greater dangers loomed than a royalist coup d'état, welcomed this New Order. As Leo XIII sought by renouncing dynastic allegiances to save the Church from further molestation and give it purchase in twentieth-century France, so moderates hoped by assimilating men of conservative temper to buttress the state against revolution. Since 1890 hundreds of strikes had broken out all over the country, some with fatal consequences. On May 1, 1891, the Marxist-oriented Parti Ouvrier Guesdiste organized a nationwide demonstration in support of an eight-hour workday. Anger over proletarian misery grew ever more violent, provoking the pope himself to state, in his encyclical *De Rerum Novarum* (May 15, 1891), that if neither employers nor unions nor cooperatives afforded workers a decent standard of living, governments were duty-bound to intervene.

Socialism, which had several outstandingly eloquent spokesmen at the Palais-Bourbon, cast a dark shadow upon bourgeois assemblies, and darker still was that cast by anarchism. During the 1880s the latter came to espouse a doctrine of *propagande par le fait*—"propaganda through deeds"—as young working-class sociopaths intent on wreaking havoc joined the idealistic utopians who cogitated Proudhon or staffed *La Révolte*. In 1892 between February 29 and March 27, several such desperate men sowed terror with bombs that rocked the capital, damaging an aristocrat's town house on the rue Saint-Dominique, the barracks of a National Guard regiment near City Hall, and, on the rue de Clichy, not far from Zola's residence, the apartment of the deputy public prosecutor. More attacks followed, to even greater effect. In December 1893 a thirty-two-year-old worker named Auguste Vaillant hurled a nail bomb from the spectators' gallery of the Chamber of Deputies. And six months later, shortly before Captain Alfred Dreyfus was arrested on espionage charges, an Italian anarchist named Caserio assassinated Sadi Carnot, president of the French Republic, in Lyon. "Bloody repression is necessary, inevitable," Zola told a reporter from *Le Journal des débats*. "But it . . . only fortifies the doctrine one wishes to combat, or rather the religion one wishes to destroy. Yes, I say religion, for anarchists so consider their doctrine, and when they mount the scaffold, they proclaim themselves martyrs."

Zola's *Rome* was a product of the *Ralliement*, or, rather, of the commentary excited by Leo XIII's ambiguous observations in *De Re-*

rum Novarum. Although the pope dissociated himself from socialism per se, declaring that collective property violated "natural justice," several important Catholic writers concluded, approvingly, that he had entered modern times as a champion of the poor and the weak. *De Rerum*, they noted, voiced his sympathy for Albert de Mun's Christian Socialist movement, which proposed to have workers and employers combat the evils of liberal economics through Christian guilds, with disagreements adjudicated at the Vatican. Others interpreted *De Rerum* in a different light, notably Anatole Leroy-Beaulieu, who assured readers of *La Revue des Deux Mondes* that the Church under Leo XIII would continue to stand guard against "cupidities and appetites lurking down below." Where Georges Goyau in *Le Pape, les catholiques et la question sociale* argued that the encyclical was imbued with the ideal of social justice, Father Hyacinthe Loyson, a former superior of the Carmelite Friars who had preached barefoot in Notre-Dame Cathedral before breaking with the Church of Rome, wrote in *Le Figaro* that Leo XIII "rather clumsily" disguised his dreams of temporal power under "the mask of Christian socialism." Zola absorbed all this controversy and in August 1894 studied a book by a young Italian named Francesco Nitti, *Le Socialisme catholique*. Nitti's pseudohistorical survey of Judeo-Christian institutions, in which Jesus is portrayed as an 1848-style utopian restoring the collectivist ideal that originally bound together God's Chosen only to be betrayed by the medieval Church with its immense property, its tithes, and its reliance upon the rich, helped Zola to structure his fictional argument. He took seventy-six pages of notes, then reduced them to a nine-page synopsis.

Sometime after September 21, when he began plotting *Rome*, Zola decided to revive the woebegone Pierre Froment for a second voyage of disillusionment across Catholic Europe. *Lourdes* having alienated him from "dogmas, mysteries, and miracles," he now embraces Catholic socialism and not only practices it as vicar of a poor congregation outside Paris but preaches it in a book that riles his superiors by arguing that the loss of temporal power has given the papacy greater spiritual stature. Threatened with being listed on the Index, Pierre visits Rome to defend himself, and there his suit leads him through the penetralia of a hermetic bureaucracy. He discovers two unrelated cities. "I am told that as soon as one walks beyond the bronze portal [of the Vatican], one enters the fifteenth century," wrote Zola in his notes.

> Completely frozen in the past. On the other hand, the atmosphere remains pagan. The identity of women kept by cardinals is an open secret. And above all, great indifference in religious matters. What excites passions here leaves them cold there. The political conflict

has relegated the pope to his corner. He counts much less in Italy than in other countries. There everything is diplomacy. This is the singular situation that must be studied and elucidated. The two present-day Romes.

Had the struggle with Protestantism not kept Catholicism vigorous in Germany, England, America? For that very reason it was in the closed world of Rome a moribund faith. Pierre—an evangelical dreamer modeled after the great nineteenth-century revolutionary priest Lamennais—loses hope in this petrified milieu, but meanwhile weeks will have been spent loitering through the ruins of Latin antiquity, inhaling the must of papal inner sanctums, conversing with a cardinal who would sooner see the Church perish in the full regalia of its glory days than survive in modern dress, undergoing examinations, and awaiting judgment by the Congregation of the Index, which finally condemns his book. "Rome must destroy present-day Catholicism in Pierre's mind," wrote Zola.

Bearing in mind other French books about Italy—Bourget's *Cosmopolis,* the Goncourts' *Madame Gervaisais,* Taine's *Voyage en Italie* —Zola made preparations in October 1894 to visit Rome. These included an impromptu conference with Edmond de Goncourt, whose cousin, Edouard Lefebvre de Béhaine, had been France's ambassador to the Holy See since 1882. "With some astonishment I heard Zola's voice coming up from the entrance hall," Goncourt noted on October 24. "He wants a letter of recommendation for de Béhaine. He tells me that he'd like his advice whether or not to request an audience with the pope." The ceremony of an audience would be a nuisance, he confessed to Goncourt, but, having made public commitments, he couldn't not go forward with it. "Then, with the verbal mutability so characteristic of him, he admits how curious he is to see the face of the Holy Father and the enfilade of papal chambers."

As much as *Lourdes* had done, *Rome* provided grist for the newspaper mill. What Zola wrote could change Franco-Italian relations, which were hostile, and journalists welcomed the assignment of chronicling his bold, or some said arrogant, venture. *Le Matin* instructed its Rome correspondent, Henry Darcours, to tail him closely. Count Edoardo Bertolelli, administrator of *La Tribuna,* where several *Rougon-Macquart* novels had been serialized, offered Zola and Alexandrine sumptuous accommodations in the hope that this gesture would elicit an image of Italy consonant with his politics. On the rue de Bruxelles, hardly a day went by that Zola did not grant an interview, always arousing curiosity without fully satisfying it, and implying that *Rome* would neither offend the faithful nor disappoint the impious. "I know for a fact that M. E. Zola will not go beyond the bounds of propriety," Henry Fouquier declared in Le Gaulois on October 14. "It is possible and even probable that he will not come home a convert, but he will maintain respect." Zola's honor would not, Fouquier felt certain, let him sacrifice truth to ambition, meaning that he would not write Rome with the French Academy in mind.

The Zolas reached Rome early in the morning of October 31. A reception committee accompanied them to the Grand Hotel, where journalists recorded the distinguished visitor's every word. Thereafter solitude was often hard to come by as fellow novelists, friends of friends, and well-wishers vying with one another for the privilege of helping him research his novel passed through in a constant stream. "I must thank Count Joseph Primoli for his kindness in referring you and I shall gladly receive you if you come here on any evening at six o'clock," Zola wrote on November 4 to Ugo Ojetti, for example, a newspaperman who served as interpreter when the novelist Luigi Capuana visited several days later. On November 7 a similar invitation went out to William J. Stillman, correspondent for the London Times, who had requested a meeting and promised, "I am neither an interviewer nor an interviewist, but as a veteran of Rome, . . . I could tell you some (perhaps) curious things." The Press Association organized a banquet at the Hôtel de Rome, to which were invited, among other eminences, Ruggiero Bonghi, former minister of education, who had enraged the Vatican by preventing the establishment of a Catholic university in the capital, and who now found himself banned from King Humbert's court for promoting friendship with France against the Triple Alliance. Bonghi praised Zola as a great champion of free thought.

With a well-thumbed Baedeker in one hand and a notebook in the other, Zola began as soon as possible to tour the city whose classical past had been the bane of his schoolboy existence. The Forum, upon which he gazed from the Capitoline after riding down the Corso, seemed "small and gray," but a view of Rome from gardens high up on the Right Bank compensated for it. "Ten a.m., on the Janiculum, in the gardens of the Villa Corsini, in front of the Spanish Royal Academy," he wrote in his journal, which would, after six weeks, fill four hundred pages.

> A light blue sky of admirable purity. A breeze from the north, Mount Testaccio on the right, dark violet against the bluish remoteness of the hinterland. The Aventine with three somber churches behind which, forming a light background, rise the Alban Hills, very pale and vaporous. Similarly the Palatine, square, with its cypresses. The Capitoline barely discernible, blurred.

At the foot of the Janiculum he surveyed newly built neighborhoods, with wash hanging from the windows of large apartment blocks. Off to the left, however, rose glorious domes, above all the great cupola of Saint Peter's, which, shooting out of a fold in the terrain, looked to him "like some excrescence of the foliage."

Zola then visited Saint Peter's itself and gazed awestruck at a space that reduced the many hundreds who had come for All Saints' Day to the proportions of an ant colony.

> The huge nave, the branches of the transept and the apse as big as one of our ordinary churches. . . . Not a chair around, the immensity of marble pavement is empty, deserted as far as one can see. Museum flooring, palace flooring. No nook for meditation, not a shadowy corner in which to kneel. . . . Crude light, illumination everywhere. The soul with its mysteries is absent. Atavism, faith designing this pagan colossus. The bronze statue of Saint Peter: some wipe the thumb, kiss it, press their foreheads against it, kiss it again, and wipe it. Others kiss it without wiping it.

What would Pierre Froment's feelings be in this vast "opera house" traversed by brilliant rays of sunlight? he asked himself. "Pierre, who arrives there with the memory of our Romanesque or Gothic cathedrals, with the emaciated statuary of the Middle Ages, all soul, in this majesty, this empty pomp, which is all body. It took the whole extent of papal magnificence to fill it."

How Pierre might feel about such a visit was the question that accompanied him everywhere, as, like a photographer oriented by his camera, Zola moved hither and yon relentlessly, driven by his plot. After reconnoitering the *vicoli*, or alleyways, that run between the Tiber and the Via Giulia, he wrote:

> For my Pierre, the day of his arrival. He jumps into an open coach at 7 a.m. And the coachman throws the names of monuments at him as they descend the Via Nazionale. The Thermae . . . The Quirinale on the right, above a green garden, palm trees, etc. . . . The Trajan Column seen down below in brilliant, white sunlight, . . . and the sudden chill one feels when passing in front of the Venetian Palace, then in front of the Gesù.

A "symbol for the entire book," as he put it, was the contrast between old streets sunk in the shadows of antiquity and the sunlit thoroughfares of modern Rome.

As arrivals in cities always quickened Zola's imagination, so did descents underground, and a walk through the catacombs of Saint Calixtus again brought Pierre to mind. "My Pierre, after seeing tombs along the Appian Way, those mementos of pride in broad daylight, must descend and see the first Christians, humble and hiding their bodies, with modest inscriptions, the childish frescoes, the rough-hewn sculptures," he wrote. The point was to be borne home that these primitive tunnels housed the true faith, that later, during the Renaissance, paganism had triumphed again, this time inside established Christianity:

> On November 22, Saint Cecilia's day, a mass is held in the grotto called Saint Cecilia's Chapel and the catacombs are lit up. . . . I believe that I prefer leading my Pierre into the catacombs and leaving him there alone for a moment, abandoned by his guide.

For the sake of his Catholic socialist priest, who has suffered alongside the Parisian poor, Zola also inspected the narrow streets of Trastevere, remarking—as Pierre would do—the dirt, the half-rotten carcasses outside butcher stalls, the stench emanating from wineshops. Recapitulated in these hectic sallies through Rome was the longer journey which had led from worship of classical monuments to naturalist fiction, or from the high-flown orations exacted from him at school to his mature portrayal of urban *bas-fonds*.

Zola never saw the bronze door of the Vatican swing open for him. On November 1 he asked Count Lefebvre de Béhaine to transmit to the papal secretariat his request for a private audience:

> The Congregation of the Index has condemned one of my books, but I do not intend to protest a decision it reached in the fullness of its rights and duties. If, unhappily, I cannot yet offer His Holiness the retraction of a believer, I wish to show him the profound deference of a man who has suffered much, worked hard, and who has concerned himself only with the truth. It is to the goodness of the Father that I address myself, a goodness open to all children of the Catholic community, to little men and great ones alike, to rebels as well as to the faithful.

But Leo XIII rebuffed him and rebuffed him again one week later, when a second request was made. Nothing daunted, Zola proceeded to find out all he needed for *Rome* by quizzing informants who had been where he could not go, by prowling round about the palace, by looking out at it from Raphael's Loggia or gazing down on it from atop Saint Peter's. On November 9, after a conversation with François Carry, former editor of the official Catholic paper *Moniteur de Rome*, he recorded the events of an average date in the pope's calendar:

He rises at 6, says his mass in his chapel, breakfasts at 7, always alone. That's the ceremonial. This man who since the age of eighteen has eaten alone. Chocolate. Clear broth. At 8 o'clock church business with prelates and the cardinals of congregations. At noon, the public and collective audiences. The meeting room changes. He then rests a bit and lunches at 2. A nap or a walk in the gardens until 4 or 5. Private audiences from 6 to 7. He returns to his private apartment, dines at 8:30 or 9. Sometimes he says the Rosary with his attendants, then retires at 10. His secretary is a Monsignor Angeli, the *"santissima tavolina."* Moreover, he sleeps little: nervous insomnia, sometimes calls a secretary to take dictation, an intelligence constantly at work. That's his life. . . . A waxen face, of diaphanous whiteness, an alabaster lamp lit from within. A large nose that accentuates the physiognomy. Very black eyes, two black carbuncles that animate everything. The flaming eyes of a twenty-year-old. A singular youthfulness in his look. An intellectual, not a sentimentalist.

Felix Ziegler, who wrote for *Le Figaro*, furnished detailed information about the pontifical garden, which intrigued Zola as much as anything else. It was situated almost two kilometers from the pope's apartment, he learned, and valets carried Leo down labyrinthine corridors on an armchair designed to fit through the narrow little doors and stairways en route. "In the garden," wrote Zola,

he perambulates by carriage, but sometimes walks. I must acquaint myself with this garden, well enough to stage a scene in it. The pope's confidants chat with him; it's there that he has talk of the town related to him, and informants (the prelates who approach him more than the cardinals) thus exercise influence. He chats with gardeners, takes an interest in their work; he asked, for example, how many oranges the orange trees produced. About twenty thousand.

While visiting the Gregorian-Profane Museum three days later, he glimpsed this garden, which straightway became for him, in its juxtaposition with classical statuary, an avatar of the walled paradise in *La Faute de l'abbé Mouret*:

What strikes me is all this antiquity . . . surrounding the papacy. . . . One sees Venus in all her glory, and Pan, and omnipotent Jupiter. Here nudity trumpets the supremacy of nature, eternal matter. And this pope who, every other day, walks amidst these Venuses, these Apollos, . . . all this naked flesh; the pope in a garden redolent of boxwood, of pine and eucalyptus, after hot summer days, inhaling the strong perfume of orange trees beneath a beautiful sky. How far we are from poor, ignorant, soulful Christianity, the Christianity that scorns flesh and anathematizes nature.

Under the circumstances, reclusion did not signify asceticism or impotence. The pope, as Zola imagined him, cast upon the world outside an imperial eye. "A prisoner yes, but the immense expanse [seen from his window]: the whole city and the Roman countryside and the Alban Hills opposite. . . . And just beyond all that a hint of sea. He can dream about freedom. . . . What the modern world brings him, Rome illuminated by electricity at night. . . . He can know everything about the Rome stolen from him and rebuilt beneath his very eyes."

On November 23, Zola took Alexandrine south to Naples, where, between their excursions, two hundred people honored him with a banquet. After another week in Rome, toward the end of which Queen Margherita granted them an audience, they set out for parts north, spending three or four days each in Tuscany, Venetia, and Lombardy. Warmly welcomed at Venice (though not by the bishop, who ordered defensive prayers to be recited during his stay), Zola took an unsentimental view of the city François Zola had left seventy-three years earlier. "It's a curio city which should be put under glass," he wrote. "It anticipates its own doom and rejects modernization, sensing that this would kill it all the more quickly. The owners of palaces repair nothing and shriek when others propose to replace stones that have fallen: it would ruin the patina. . . . The Piazza San Marco is marvelous . . . but one feels stifled." Milan, which reminded him of Paris, was more to his taste, and there the dramatist Giuseppe Giacosa organized a banquet attended by several dozen artists, among them Leoncavallo and Puccini.

Having long since arranged for the transportation of bas-reliefs, two immense sarcophagi, and antique marble busts purchased in Rome, Zola left Italy on December 15, satisfied with his loot.[9] But not until April 2, 1895—his fifty-fifth birthday—did he begin *Rome*. The plot needed further development. And several books relevant to his project had meanwhile appeared, especially *Le Vatican, les papes et la civilisation: le gouvernement central de l'Eglise*, a ponderous tome that yielded seventy pages of notes.

Lest readers taxed by the religious arguments desert Pierre before

---

[9]One sarcophagus was placed in front of the guest cottage at Médan, the other on the porch in Paris. As might have been expected, Edmond de Goncourt did not think much of Zola's acquisitions. Invited for dinner on March 22, 1895, along with his cousin Lefebvre de Béhaine, he wrote in his journal: "Zola gave us a very good dinner yesterday, but as a result of all the doors being open for the exhibition *a giorno* of the frightful statues and bas-reliefs, his living room was ice-cold and I fear I am down with influenza again." Both sarcophagi now belong to the Louvre.

his final confrontation with Leo XIII, Zola, giving fantasy free rein, invented a romantic subplot in which the young priest figures peripherally. It involves Cardinal Boccanera, a Roman patrician with enemies, whose deteriorating mansion on the Via Giulia reflects his stubborn, passionate allegiance to a dying social order. Under his roof live two relatives—a niece by one sibling, Benedetta, and a nephew by another, Dario. Married against her will to an unscrupulous arriviste, Benedetta denied her husband carnal relations and has separated herself from him while awaiting an annulment. Her love is all for her cousin Dario, the last male representative of the Boccanera line. For him, whom she would wed despite his notoriously rakish life, this romantic keeps herself "pure." But disaster strikes, in more senses than one, and a plausible study of manners portraying the inversion of Roman high society becomes a melodrama in the style of Gabriele D'Annunzio, or worse. It begins with poisoned figs, a gift made to Cardinal Boccanera by a country priest who takes orders from another cardinal. Dario eats them instead and falls mortally ill. Distraught, Benedetta strips herself naked at his deathbed in the presence of Pierre and Cardinal Boccanera, then, cursing her virginity, attempts to make love:

> As if floored by some apparition, the glorious effulgence of a holy vision, Pierre and her maidservant Victorine looked at her dazzled. The terrified respect one feels for the follies of passion and faith prevented Victorine from attempting to hold her back. And Pierre, paralyzed, . . . could only shiver with boundless admiration. Nothing impure crossed his mind from seeing this snow- and lily-white nudity, this frank and noble virgin, whose body seemed to shine of its own light.

With Dario past being able to beget an heir, Benedetta clasps him unto death and dies in his arms. Inseparable, they are buried in a single coffin.

Rome, which sprawls over 751 pages, consumed Zola for eleven months, presenting far greater problems for him than *Lourdes* had. "I resolved as usual to put everything in it—past, present, future—and with Rome you can imagine where that led me," he wrote to van Santen Kolff on October 12, when somewhat more than half the novel had been written. "Never have I been overwhelmed by so many documents, so many notes, so many personal impressions. . . . It's the Ocean, this time, and although I'm satisfied with my progress, I shall remain terribly distressed until it's finished." Five weeks later he complained to Alexandrine, who had returned to Rome unaccompanied, that his eleventh chapter was not progressing very well, and his "poor

old head" was "sometimes very weary." Still, in his weariness Zola set
a pace that would have left young men panting. Thus, on December
1, 1895, before *Rome* was finished, he published in *Le Figaro* the first
of seventeen longish articles, commenting upon such diverse subjects
as Leo XIII's opportunism, his own affection for animals, France's
demographic problems, and the rising tide of anti-Semitism.

Charpentier et Fasquelle published *Rome* on May 8, 1896, after its
serial run in *Le Journal*. As expected, it was widely reviewed, and for
the most part praised or decried depending on the ideological slant of
this or that newspaper. In *Paris, Le XIXe Siècle,* and *La Presse,* critics
admired it greatly. With his "often surprising intuitions," wrote one,
Zola had seen, better than politicians, the pope's stubbornness, his
ignorance of the modern world, and his fear of science. "The pope is
the eternal prisoner, enclosed behind a thick wall eighteen centuries
in the making." Never had Zola addressed a larger subject, wrote another (who praised the deathbed scene as "Shakespearian"), "and
never has he emerged more triumphant." But in *L'Illustration, Le
Monde* (a Catholic organ), and *Le Temps,* the work received harsh treatment. "He has never been realistic and in *Rome* he is less so than
ever," declared Augustin Filon. "Is it a realist who imagines the marble
gods of the Vatican 'looking at Leo XIII with all their naked flesh'? Is
it a realist . . . who confected this monstrous and delirious scene where
a young woman climbs naked into a deathbed, before two witnesses,
one of them a young priest . . . ? . . . The task that faces the young
generation is not to restore some vague, fruitless idealism, but to save
realism from the hands of M. Zola and his school." René Doumic
echoed these sentiments in *La Revue des Deux Mondes.* "A novel is
essentially a work of imagination," he remarked.

> Claiming that M. Zola lacks imagination is doing him an injustice;
> he possesses imagination in abundance and of the most extravagant
> kind, . . . a taste for the extraordinary, a passion for the implausible.
> . . . Until M. Zola, informed by good sources, opened our eyes, we
> didn't know anything about the role that poison plays in pontifical
> elections. How many cardinals have died young, whose deaths were
> not natural. . . . You're all poisoned, Your Eminences.

This new novel was not much inferior to its predecessors, he continued snidely. "It's more boring only because it's longer." And in *Le
Temps,* Gaston Deschamps, who took Zola to task for plundering *Le
Vatican, les papes et la civilisation* without restraint, called *Rome* a
"bungled compilation" where "picturesque details illuminate a dark
swamp of facts and figures." No one—neither Filon nor Doumic nor
Deschamps—saw fit to comment upon the relationship between

Pierre's encyclopedic walks and the waning of his reformist energies, or to note the influence exerted by Stendhal, who once said of Rome: "Everything is decadence here, everything is memory, everything is dead. . . . This sojourn tends to weaken the soul, to plunge it into stupor."

If *Rome* had been written with academic consecration in mind, and one imagines that it was more than a passing thought, it failed of its purpose. On May 20, Zola went up against yet another bevy of minor figures in an election held to replace Dumas *fils*. His staunch supporter, François Coppée, argued that by electing Zola the Academy could partly make amends for having rejected Balzac. But to no avail. After numerous ballots, during which Zola received as many as fourteen votes, one André Theuriet emerged victorious. "Judging from the latest tips, I foresaw the result," wrote Charpentier, "but I still hoped that the last few necessary votes, whose obstinacy defies belief, would be won over. It was a great effort, . . . and yet it must be expected that those holdouts will not relent. They'll come up with some nasty maneuver the next time. It shouldn't disturb your sleep or diminish the pleasure of bicycle riding."

Italy had made a deeper impression on Alexandrine than on Zola. While he never again visited his fatherland, she returned every August, September, or October, always traveling alone in what became, until the Dreyfus Affair interrupted it, an annual migration. The saline waters of Salsomaggiore, a spa situated near Parma, at the foot of the Apennines, apparently did her good. Certain letters suggest, furthermore, that without Zola crowding her, pencil in hand, her sensibility found room for play. "I can't accomplish as quickly as I should like all the excursions I promised myself," she wrote to Elina Laborde from Naples on August 15, 1896. "It is even likely that I shall have to give some up. Still, how interesting I find everything I see. So many things one knows in the abstract but which really spring to life when one strolls through these historic precincts. . . . I see things which give me the shivers, and that sensation is still more intense when, afterward, I reflect upon what I've seen." More important than antiquities and thermal springs, however, was the relief Italy offered from a domestic arrangement to which she could never happily reconcile herself.

Relief did not come right away, and Zola's guilty, oversolicitous voice followed her south, causing some irritation at first.[10] "Dear wife," he wrote on November 12, 1895.

---

[10]The letters she wrote to Zola during her Italian sojourn have not been made available.

I've now received your letters in the morning and your first letter from Rome, today, gave me much pleasure, for I see that you are getting around and I am eager that you distract yourself. Amidst all these people whom you know and who will entertain you, your dark thoughts will vanish. . . . I sent you a dispatch this afternoon, after I read your letter, telling you to accept all invitations. . . . I was annoyed that . . . you had already refused everyone, but annoyed for your sake alone, as the idea behind my telling you to accept was to make you put yourself in the way of having pleasurable evenings. I had nothing to gain from it, so don't regret anything. . . . But again, it's of small importance, so long as you have a good time, one way or another. . . . Get as much rest as you need, write me letters like the one I received this morning, in which you vividly describe your life, and I shall be very happy, for knowing that—despite everything that has happened—you aren't too unhappy will always be a great consolation to me.

The same tone informs a letter written five days later:

You know that I purposely say nothing that may lead you to lengthen or shorten your trip. But really, you could, if you had any wish to do so, remain in Rome until the 25th . . . a month in all. I say this to put you at your ease, leaving you absolutely free to choose your own dates. About the Consistory . . . Perhaps you could get yourself admitted, through de Béhaine or someone else. It would be funny if you, rather than I, ended up seeing the pope. Do whatever pleases you.

And even the announcement that he would meet her at the train station was couched in protestations of concern:

I absolutely insist upon fetching you at the station on Monday morning. . . . I don't want you to be all alone in a coach, bumping along a muddy pavement and entertaining sad thoughts. I want you to return with joy and hope. So let me do it, don't pity me for having to rise very early, since it will give me great pleasure. . . . Eugénie has received the menus for Monday. You will eat the thighs of the Médan goose, which she saved.[11]

[11]Zola's letters were filled with domestic news. On November 13, for example, he wrote: "This week Octave wrote to me that everything is in order at Médan. The animals are all in good health. La Mouquette [the cow, named after a good-natured slut in *Germinal*] calved yesterday morning. René [Lenôtre] sprained his ankle and was immobile for several days. The last goose caught its neck in one of the little doors to the duck coop, and wasn't mending, so Léonie decided to kill it and send it to me. My Lord! what a bellyful for me alone! . . . You must know that Albert

But after 1895 this Italian interlude ceased to fluster either one. It established itself as a salutary ritual, with Alexandrine acquiring in Rome a life of her own. Befriended by the many people she had met during her sojourn with Zola, and particularly by Count Bertolelli, who visited her almost every day, she never wanted for company. There were day trips to Frascati, fox hunts, evenings at the theater, dinners in private homes, and receptions, endless receptions, where her presence excited interest. "Thus shall I rest for an entire month," she wrote Elina Laborde on September 9, 1897, "and I shall preserve your aunt's old carcass as best I can in order, next winter, to describe all my sensations and instill in you all my enthusiasm for this Italy, which delights me more with each successive voyage."

.

[Laborde] was only half successful in his entrance examination [for engineering school], that is, he passed the written part, but failed the orals. Amélie must be disappointed."

XXVI

AND THEN THERE WAS ONE

A LFRED BRUNEAU, who had been born the year Zola came to Paris, was nurtured by devoutly musical parents. After taking first prize in violoncello at the Paris Conservatory, he played under the baton of Jules Pasdeloup, a conductor famous for promoting new music, and witnessed from the orchestra pit the tumultuous reception accorded Richard Wagner's works, notably the *Götterdämmerung*, which helped shape his own musical personality. Indeed, being Wagnerian argued against him when, as Jules Massenet's pupil, he wrote a cantata for the Prix de Rome competition. Irked by what they perceived to be "advanced" tendencies in this otherwise praiseworthy piece, the jury ranked him highest but awarded him only second prize—its most influential member, Charles Gounod, having concluded that the unruly pup needed obedience training. Bruneau turned away from the musical establishment. Prepared neither to betray his convictions nor to seek another, easier livelihood, he labored on. In 1884 Pasdeloup performed his *Ouverture héroïque* and a choral symphony. Two more choral symphonies followed in due course, then song groups, some chamber music, and a requiem, as well as a lyric drama called *Kerim*, which lasted only one evening at the Théâtre Lyrique. Not until 1891, however, did Bruneau emerge from respectable semi-obscurity. His opera *Le Rêve* changed everything. It made him famous, and it persuaded him that his creative powers would thenceforth best be employed in the service of Emile Zola's oeuvre. Let us recall what he wrote on that occasion: "If, in the score of *Le Rêve*, I struck some deep chords, they come from the emotion with which the humanity of your entire work fills me and from my grateful affection for you. Right now I cannot imagine doing solitary work without feeling immense chagrin; I fear that discouragement would very quickly overtake me."

Increasingly alone (though constantly dunned for interviews), Zola found such loyalty irresistible, the more so perhaps because this artistic son provided him, through musical orchestration, with a range or amplitude he may no longer have felt his solo voice to possess. After their collaboration on the opera *L'Attaque du moulin*, which also enjoyed some success, Zola boosted Bruneau at every opportunity. As previously noted, Zola sold *Lourdes* to *Gil Blas* for serialization on condition that it name Bruneau its music critic, above thirty-one other candidates. When his benefactor joined *Le Figaro*, Bruneau followed him there, and to secure him a knighthood in the Legion of Honor, Zola pestered the minister of public instruction, Georges Leygues. This bond extended to the two men's wives, and the childless Zolas undoubtedly found strength as a couple in the affection they lavished on Alfred and Philippine Bruneau. All four spent much time together—at Médan, at vacation homes, at concerts in Paris, over dinner on the rue de Bruxelles, at Lugné-Poë's Théâtre de l'Oeuvre (where they would have seen stage sets designed by Bonnard and Vuillard for plays by Ibsen and Maeterlinck).

Although Zola had lent Louis Gallet a hand in writing the libretto of *L'Attaque du moulin*, he came to feel that a more intimate collaboration with Bruneau might be possible. "Late in the day, I have gotten interested in music, thanks to Alfred Bruneau, a man of exceptional intelligence, gentleness, and penetration, whose happy acquaintance I made not long ago," he wrote in *Le Journal* on November 24, 1893.

And apropos of this highly interesting matter of music in theater, I am struck more and more by the paramount, decisive importance for the musician of what is called a good "poem." Reading articles about Gounod's work last month, when he died, I noted that his many unsuccesses in theater were all attributed to misbegotten texts. . . . The librettist was accused of having paralyzed the musician. And yet, that was an era in which the libretto was merely a pretext for music. Did Rossini not offer to use the classified section of the daily newspaper as material for an entrancing score? What he surely meant was that music had its own intrinsic interest, that it was self-sufficient, that the action and characters mattered little so long as the musician sang. . . . Now that the new concept of lyric drama has prevailed, . . . a lyric drama must have a clearly defined milieu and living characters, or, in other words, a human action, and the musician's only role is to comment upon and develop it.

Zola's first effort at writing libretti produced neither living characters nor a clearly defined milieu but a stilted one-act drama called *Lazare*, in which Christ raises Lazarus from the dead at his family's urging only to hear him bemoan the loss of eternal peace. Bruneau, who felt certain that Catholics would take umbrage, expressed reservations, whereupon Zola devised another, very different plot and called it *Messidor*, after the harvest month in the Revolutionary calendar. This one worked well.

More a parable or a fairy tale than a realistic drama, *Messidor* makes its point in images that oppose sterility to fertility, mineral wealth to grain, men who excavate to men who till. Formerly rich peasants, through whose mountain village ran a torrent carrying gold, now live as best they can off the parched earth. Misfortune befell them when one of their number, Gaspard, diverted the stream with modern machinery for his own enrichment. This capitalist *coup de main* insulted nature not only by rearranging the watercourse but by disrupting affairs of the heart. Torn asunder were Gaspard's daughter, Hélène, and her childhood sweetheart, Guillaume, who believes that his father was murdered by Gaspard five years earlier. As *Messidor* begins, trouble is brewing. At the instigation of a malevolent cousin named Mathias who has come home after a five-year absence, Guillaume leads his fellow sufferers against Gaspard. No sooner do they confront one another than Guillaume's mother, Véronique, descends from the mountain, proclaiming that on high she has found the cavern where, according to local legend, the infant Jesus transmutes sand into gold by divine alchemy. "All of you poor people, my brothers, listen!" she shouts.

> In the storm, amidst the chasms, I found it at last, the cathedral of gold, where no living being had ever entered. Ah, what unimaginable splendor! The divine child, on his mother's lap, let flow from his little hands a river of gold, in limitless quantity. And suddenly, when they saw me, everything collapsed, with a great thunderclap. All at once night fell, black and chill! I was there, beneath the snow, and there was no more gold!

A huge avalanche crashes down upon the scene, destroying Gaspard's machinery and driving the river underground. Thanks to this providential catastrophe (so like the destruction of Le Voreux in *Germinal*), barren earth will, by springtime, have become fertile. Where gold had been everything, water reigns supreme. Where nothing grew, fields of wheat gladden the eye. Where one man enriched himself at the expense of others, all together sow and reap. *Messidor* ends during the days of solemn supplication called Rogations, with the community marching behind a priest as Guillaume and Hélène exchange eternal vows. A murder no longer stands between them, it having been discovered that Mathias rather than Gaspard killed Guillaume's father. They will therefore marry and themselves bear fruit. "The wheat will ripen, the laughter of beautiful children will fill the household," Zola's tenor prophesies.

With *Messidor*, which obviously celebrates paternity in himself as well as in his father, who made arid soil bloom, Zola liked to think that he and Bruneau were shoring up French lyric drama against the Wagnerian juggernaut. "When a despotic, all-powerful genius like Wagner bursts forth, he's sure to weigh heavily on the following generations," he had written several years earlier.

> The logic, the fullness, the totality of the Wagnerian system have afforded it such sovereign prestige that people doubt whether anything excellent and new can be created outside it. . . . That is why this concerns me. . . . Instead of standing still with Wagner, whom it would be childish to neglect, one might use him as a point of departure. . . . I see drama emanating from the reality of our humble miseries and joys rather than from the vagueness of Nordic mythology. I don't mean that opera should dress in overalls and smock coats. . . . Let it wear velvet, provided the velvet contains human beings."

But Zola may have had Wagner to thank for the alacrity with which the Paris Opera accepted *Messidor* in September 1896. Wagnerianism was indeed, as he noted, all the rage. Since May 1893, when *Die Walküre* overwhelmed audiences, "continuous melody" had become a kind of shibboleth, and young French composers who set store by it, or who imitated the German master in other ways, found doors opening for them. Thus did a most important door open for Bruneau at the Garnier opera house. As early as January 1894, its directors, Bertrand and Gailhard, had begun prodding him to collaborate with Zola.

Rehearsals, which began on December 7, 1896, after mock-ups of the decor had been approved, progressed smoothly, except for a disagreement over whether or not to have dancers wear conventional tutus in a ballet depicting the supernatural cavern. Zola often showed up and made numerous comments, as in a letter to Bruneau dated January 22, 1897: "It seems to me on reflection that in the last act, four or five measures of music are needed to lower the curtain with appropriate solemnity. How would you feel about a resounding orchestral fanfare, a bit longer than the present one?" The slight injury he sustained on February 19 when a cab knocked him down did not prevent him from attending the premiere of *Messidor* several hours later. "Our father visited us in our box at the Opera to reassure us," Denise recalled in her biography of Zola. "It was the first time my brother and

I had ever entered an opera house and we were amazed at seeing our father's work manifest itself in such palpable form. Small though we were, we already knew the titles of several of his novels, which had been pointed out to us in a glass-enclosed bookcase. That evening, . . . amidst the applause of the beautiful, elegant hall, I must also have understood for the first time what the word 'glory' signified." High society surrounded them, and the notabilities present included Félix Faure, president of the French Republic.

Although *Messidor* remained at the Opera for three full months, critics, most of whom lauded Bruneau's score, were virtually unanimous in deriding Zola's libretto. Some objected to its ponderous prose and slow movement, others to its shallow personae and the high-flown language spoken by putative peasants. "In theory, it doesn't matter whether a text destined to be sung is verse or prose," Louis de Fourcaud declared in a long review written for *Le Gaulois*. "But the prose must at least be cadenced, terse, capable of striking sparks with clever turns of phrase or witticisms or *mots de théâtre*. The author of *Messidor* couldn't care less about this indispensable concision. He indulges his taste for the elaborate sentence, never heeding the requirements of musical drama." Zola answered straightway, with an open letter that invited Fourcaud—and, inferentially, every other unsympathetic critic—to admit that quibbles about concision or class-appropriate speech disguised a more fundamental animus. Hurt by Fourcaud's trenchant criticism, he abandoned musical ground for the pulpit and presented himself as a life lover martyred by fashionable necrophiles, or a modern man beleaguered by regressive mystics:

> If my libretto displeases you, it's because you sense that it's the very negation of Wagner's plots. I'm not talking here about literature, I'm talking about social and philosophical tendencies. Wagnerian mysticism is what it's all about! The indispensable legend, the gods of one Olympus or another, salvation via the Beyond, in the transcending of humble nature! Nothing but fatal perversions, love leading to death, the sexual parts themselves useless and infertile, the religion made of self-denial. . . . And you are right not to admit me into your scheme, for I find this mysticism horrifying. . . . I side with the love that begets, with the mother and not the virgin. . . . I have vested my hope only in our human labor. . . . How could you not have seen that, in *Messidor*'s central symbol, the only true believer, Véronique, comes forth to announce the death of the old legend?

Fourcaud responded by saying that if Zola acquainted himself more thoroughly with Wagner's work, he would realize that "mysticism did not absorb the whole of his thought." But Zola continued to regard

adverse criticism as "sectarian" and furthermore predicted the imminent crumbling of Wagnerian mysticism "before a rebirth of human
reason and health." Did he also have in mind perhaps the sphinxes,
the snake-queens, the homicidal bacchantes, the drowned Ophelias,
the androgynes and Circes who swarmed through late-nineteenth-
century painting? Not for him certainly were these offspring of art
nouveau and of symbolist aesthetics.

Not for him either was little Jesus' miraculous stream of gold. *Messidor* proposes that people embrace their humanity by cultivating a
fertile garden, and this Voltairean message also informs the last novel
of *Les Trois Villes, Paris,* which he began to write during rehearsals of
the opera. It takes up Pierre Froment's story three years after his return from Rome. Domiciled in the family house at Neuilly, where
mother and father Froment never reconciled their differences, he leads
a life of quiet desperation. Wearing the uniform of a faith he has
definitively lost would be insufferable if not for the alms and solace it
has enabled him to bestow upon famished, unemployed workers, but
as *Paris* opens, a death from starvation convinces him that the Church
is useless, that Christian charity—the miraculous stream of gold—cannot make amends for social injustice. "Catholicism, Christianity itself,
would be swept away, since the Gospel, aside from a few moral maxims, was no longer a viable social code," writes Zola. "How could
[Pierre], who had leaned on it, continue to stand upright?" Here Zola
introduces a deus ex machina in the person of Pierre's older brother,
Guillaume, from whom he has long been estranged. Brought together
by chance, the brothers embrace. Pierre unburdens himself to Guillaume, a distinguished chemist with utopian schemes, whereupon
Guillaume urges him to visit the large atelier high above Paris in which
he and his three grown sons—an artist, a student of science at the
Ecole Normale, and a mechanic-inventor—often congregate, each absorbed in his own task. Pierre hesitates, even though he felt, "confusedly," that "affection, truth, and life" awaited him.

> Each time an invincible malaise, . . . composed of shame and fear,
> held him back. Would those beings who were all redolent of nature,
> freedom, and health not inflict wounds and suffering upon him—the
> priest, the gelding, the creature cast away from the world of love and
> common endeavors?

But eventually he wrests himself free from this fear and finds salvation
in work, assisting Thomas Froment, the inventor. He also finds it in
the orphan rescued by Guillaume some years earlier, Marie Couturier.
Love blossoms between these two, and Guillaume, jealous though he
is, encourages a union. Unfrocked, Pierre, like Dr. Pascal, achieves

himself through fatherhood, siring on Marie a son named Jean. "Life had begotten life, the truth had burst forth, as triumphantly as the sun," Zola concludes. "After two abortive experiments at Lourdes and at Rome, happiness came at last. First the law of work had revealed itself to Pierre and he imposed upon himself a task . . . to be performed every day without fail, which would vouchsafe him the serenity of the accepted role. . . . Then he had loved, and the instruments of his salvation were the woman and child. Ah, what a roundabout path he had taken to arrive at so simple, so natural a denouement!" From Pierre's private solution, Zola, who elsewhere gave utopian theories short shrift, extrapolated a social program reminiscent of Fourier. The Froments' large atelier is, indeed, the ideal phalanstery. "Allow the religion of science time enough . . . and you will see Fourier's admirable ideas form a new gospel, where desire is glorified as a lever capable of lifting the world, where work is honored by all alike, . . . where the passionate energies of mankind are mobilized, satisfied, exploited for human happiness!"

Mercifully, there is more to *Paris* than this sententious plot. Woven through it are scenes from the beau monde over which Montmartre rises—the world of venal politics, of financial chicane, of social opportunism, of high harlotry—and here, down below, Zola's novelistic genius found the oxygen it lacked up above. Even as Marie Froment suckles little Jean, moral rot undermines *le tout Paris*, with Titanias swooning over Bottoms in a kind of decadent phantasmagoria. Promiscuity is rampant. On the bohemian fringe of the upper class, Princess de Harth, who exemplifies what came to be known seventy years later as radical chic, entertains anarchist bombers. The colossally rich Baron Duvillard spends millions on a beautiful young strumpet and finally, leaving no palm ungreased, helps her satisfy her perverse ambition to star at the Comédie-Française in the role of Corneille's Christian heroine, Pauline. His wife, Eve, née Steinberger, clings tenaciously to a young aristocratic lover whom her own daughter will marry in the end. His son Hyacinthe scorns everything bourgeois, professing an aversion to women, imitating effete English dandies, and, for the masochistic thrill of it, frequenting the very dark cabaret where Montmartre's reigning chansonnier maligns rich people in foul slang.[1]

---

[1] Among aristocrats who set fashion and bourgeois who followed them, to be "primitive," or loudly to declare a love of whatever went by that name, was to establish one's class credentials. Like eighteenth-century nobles who relished the vulgar "fishmonger" style in theater—the *genre poissard*—dandies of the 1890s would affect *le parler rosse*, "tough talk," which required them to slur their speech and punctuate their conversation with underworld argot or expressions borrowed from Aristide Bruant (*bruandailles*). "Snobbism has it that one must talk tough if one wants the reputation of being in the swim," declared a social chronicler reviewing Talmeyr's play *Entre Mufles* (*Among Low Breeds*).

With its various idées fixes, this crowd gives anecdotal body to a political drama that unfolds throughout *Paris*. Mindful of the recent Panama Scandal—which exposed newspaper publishers and politicians who had accepted bribes to cover up the engineering disaster perpetrated by de Lesseps or to keep his ill-fated canal company afloat with a government-authorized bond lottery—Zola imagined Baron Duvillard buying official support for an African Railroad Company. Just as Panama fortified the anti-Semitic and antirepublican press, which made much of the fact that de Lesseps's chief dispenser of graft was a Jewish financier named Baron Jacques de Reinach (who died—apparently by suicide—before standing trial), so the African Railroad exposé redounds to the advantage of *La Voix du peuple*, a Jew-baiting paper clearly modeled after Drumont's *Libre Parole*. In the fictional plot as in the historical event, suspicion falls on two ministers, one of whom confesses. And in *Paris* as in reality, other probable culprits emerge from a commission of inquiry with all saved except honor. "Wasn't he, Duvillard, the sole victor, he who bought his daughter a son of the aristocracy for five million francs, who embodied the now sovereign bourgeoisie reigning like an absolute monarch, master of the public wealth and resolved not to yield one little bit of it, even under the threat of [anarchist] bombs?" Zola asked rhetorically. The Third Republic of *Paris* differs little from the Second Empire of *La Curée* and of *Son Excellence Eugène Rougon*.

Zola finished *Paris* on August 31, 1897, after only eight months of labor. Under normal circumstances, it would have run a tranquil course in *Le Journal*, where serialization commenced on October 23, but circumstances proved other than normal. The last installments of *Paris* appeared during the furor caused by *J'accuse*, and inevitably the novel began life as an epiphenomenon of the celebrated philippic. Locked in mortal combat, Dreyfusards and anti-Dreyfusards made more and less of *Paris* than it deserved. Even so, some commentators attempted to rise above this particular fray when Fasquelle brought out the volume on March 1, 1898. In a review written for *La Revue des Deux Mondes*, Ferdinand Brunetière allowed that the various subplots were skillfully interwoven. He also found "the progress of love" in Pierre Froment compelling, despite a prose style fraught with hyperbole. But *Paris*, which is virtually unread today, bespoke Zola's arrested development, he thought. "While everything around us was changing during the past quarter-century—men and things, ideas and mores, doctrines and interests, questions asked and science itself— M. Zola was remaining obstinately faithful to the world as he had known it [at twenty-eight]." How could the "delicate" issues raised in *Les Trois Villes* be probed with the old-fashioned instruments of *Les Rougon-Macquart*? Jean Jaurès, a prominent socialist who upheld all that Brunetière anathematized, did not disagree with him here. Although *Paris* seemed to him "a beautiful book, . . . a bold protest against all the powers that enslave and lie," he found Zola's picture of socialists apparently oblivious of *Das Kapital* quarreling over Proudhon, Fourier, and Auguste Comte terribly dated. "It is hard to recognize in this brief study the vast movement that has developed throughout the country during the past fifteen years. . . . The socialist party has principles, . . . but principles roomy enough to accommodate within the socialist framework any problem, any form of human action, any thought, however daring." In *La Revue blanche,* young Léon Blum agreed that a just society could not be fathered by science alone, as Zola argued, but *Paris* was, he felt, more humane than its author's technocratic premise. "Never has M. Zola developed so forcefully and lucidly his hopeful vision of mankind marching forward, this naturalistic pantheism which is also Darwin's, Fourier's, the Stoics', Goethe's."

One critic unable to cast aspersions upon *Paris,* or to lament the fact that it, too, enjoyed far greater commercial success than most novels, was Edmond de Goncourt, who had died almost two years earlier, on July 14, 1896, while visiting Daudet at Champrosay. Goncourt never forgave Zola his magnanimity, his ambition, his genius, his great fame. Scurrilous tittle-tattle appears throughout his well-known journal.[2] But on July 20, Zola was asked to serve as a pallbearer in the funeral service at Goncourt's village church in Auteuil. And later that day, when Edmond joined his brother Jules for all time in Montmartre Cemetery, Zola delivered a graveside eulogy, at Daudet's request. "In the name of literary friends, of the family that sprang from him and grew up around him, I hereby bid Edmond de Goncourt the supreme farewell," he began (with Léon Hennique standing at his side to read the speech should emotion overcome him).

> It has already been sixteen years since Gustave Flaubert passed away in full glory, and of the literary brotherhood we formed, only Alphonse Daudet and I remain. . . . And if I speak, it is in Daudet's name as well as my own, for grief has made our two hearts one.

[2]Zola might not have described the journal as "a misunderstood document of poignant interest" if he had read it unexpurgated. On March 19, 1896, for example, Goncourt wrote: "For years I have had the conviction, and proof to support it, that despite his warm handshakes and his greetings of 'My good friend,' Zola, perfidious Italian that he is, has been endeavoring to sabotage my work, which he regards as a threat for the future." And on May 18, referring to articles by Zola on politics and anti-Semitism, he called Zola the "greatest turncoat" in the whole history of letters. "A week ago this ex-debunker of politicians glorified every minister who is or ever was. Now he's singing the praises of Jews, all to secure Ludovic Halévy's vote [for the French Academy]."

If I speak, it is also because the thirty years of affection and admiration I have shown the Goncourt brothers and their works give me seniority among all their literary friends. Thirty years ago I wrote my first enthusiastic article about *Germinie Lacerteux*, that absolute masterwork of truth, emotion, and justice, to which the public, in its imbecility, now pays scant attention. And since then I have never ceased to love them, and fight for them. It is with joy that I recall today my unwavering loyalty, the love and respect of my youth . . . and place them upon this tomb like beautiful, rare flowers—rare in our age of fratricidal polemics.

After us came other young writers. They, too, loved the old master, who had been shattered by his brother's death, and they too fought for his works, the magnificent fate of which has been to endure constant attack. It behooves us to note how, . . . by helping him stand firm and erect against the horde, they took the edge off his bitterness. . . . But is it not so that an elder can best recognize what we all owe the brothers Goncourt? . . . Along with Stendhal, Balzac, and Flaubert, they created the modern novel.

However future generations might judge the forty-odd volumes Edmond de Goncourt had left behind, he and his brother would remain masters, Zola continued, for their "posterity" was everywhere.

Oh, the intellectual bravura [Edmond] showed, saying what he believed to be the truth, though it might cost him peace and quiet, suffering no compromise for the sake of propriety. Nothing is rarer, nobler, more splendid. Such was his commitment that he experienced joy and pain only through literature, sacrificing his all to it. . . . Dear and close friend, "our own" old Goncourt, it is the young man, the novice of 1865, who now bids you farewell; it is also the novelist whose development you observed and who remained your pupil while becoming your rival; it is also at this moment the graybeard who, following your example, has sought consolation in work. Today, at last, you . . . come to sleep at your brother's side.

Mourners considered it a fine speech, especially Céard, no doubt, who knew better than most with what lenience Zola, for reasons he chose not to plumb or divulge, had always treated his hostile friend. All was forgiven: the "Manifeste des Cinq," the invidious asides, the endless accusations of plagiarism.

Daudet himself survived Goncourt by only seventeen months. Since 1890 things had gone badly for him. He produced, among much else, three didactic novels in praise of family, one worse than the next. But with syphilis ravaging his nervous system, it is extraordinary that he produced anything at all. Drugs alone made consciousness bearable. There was no regular distraction to be found in the world outside, where every step cost him enormous pain (he would jerk forward spastically, like a marionette on wires). And when the strength for gripping a pen deserted him, he began dictating his works. After a summer in Champrosay, he and his wife left their sixth-floor residence at 31, rue de Bellechasse for another apartment nearer street level. There he died on December 16, 1897. "I arrived a bit late for dinner," recalled his son Léon, who, like Zola, had been a pallbearer at Goncourt's funeral. "I found our little world gathered as usual in the study. I helped him to the dining room and sat him down in his large armchair. While eating soup he began to chat. Nothing about his movements or general demeanor announced the catastrophe. But suddenly, during a brief, terrible silence, I heard that noise one never forgets—a muted rattle." Four days later, mourners packed the courtyard of 41, rue de l'Université, which had been covered with black, silver-spangled crepe, then followed Daudet's hearse to Sainte-Clotilde. Once again Zola served as a pallbearer, walking—in ironical juxtaposition—alongside Edouard Drumont, the anti-Semitic author of *La France juive*, with whom he had already locked horns.[3] And once again he delivered a eulogy, this time at Père-Lachaise Cemetery, before a huge throng that included ministers of state, prefects, the entire Goncourt Academy, Sarah Bernhardt, Maurice Barrès, Robert de Montesquiou, Stéphane Mallarmé, Rodin, Monet, Renoir, Carolus Duran, and Jules Massenet. "If I have been chosen to pay Daudet homage—would that I could make such homage absolute, definitive, expressive of my entire being—it's only because our friendship, our companionship, goes back so many years," he said.

It's above all because I'm a witness, the last surviving witness, the one who can say what we whose works grew along with his thought of him. Rivals, ah yes!, for we didn't all share the same ideas, we didn't march in lockstep. But good comrades nonetheless, clearsighted, and each allowing the others their legitimate portions of

[3]A reporter for *Le Figaro* noted this coincidence, and used it to good account in an elaborately sentimental piece:

Polemicists of very different temperament, both delight in battle. More than once they have clashed; on almost nothing do they see eye to eye. Neither their ideas nor their hearts are in sympathy. Yet these two men, on this occasion of deep mourning, walked together toward the cemetery, separated only by the flower-decked coffin, by the cold, inert body of the man who was their friend. . . . If, on returning from the burial, each recorded his thoughts, the latter would perhaps be identical, for once. . . . Tombs are the supreme meeting ground and death the great pacifier.

Had they lived, Goncourt and Daudet—both of them exuberant anti-Semites—would certainly have sided against Dreyfus. Daudet's elder son, Léon, was to carry the torch of nationalist xenophobia as an extreme-right-wing militant directing and writing for *L'Action française*.

glory. For us Daudet was always the freest spirit, the one least bound to formulas, the one who treated facts most honestly. I have already said it elsewhere, that he was the realist respectful of life in its ordinariness, . . . whereas we others, who gave vent to lyrical effusions, were the more or less disguised offspring of romanticism. His compassionate love of humble folk, his triumphant laughter pursuing knaves and fools, the abundant goodness and righteous satire that make each of his works vibrate with humanity: these are the virtues for which he will be honored.

That Daudet had always willingly lent an ear to Goncourt's jealous vituperations could not have escaped Zola. When, for example, Robert de Flers of *Le Journal* solicited from Daudet an article about *Les Rougon-Macquart,* he responded that "with the genealogical tree of *Les Rougon-Macquart* now complete," he would advise Zola "to hang himself from the highest branch." But at Daudet's funeral, as during Daudet's lifetime, Zola expounded a myth of heroic solidarity, of kindred spirits leagued against a hostile world, and even wept in the telling. "We were four brothers; three have already departed, and I remain alone," he concluded. "France has lost one of her glories. May he thus, at last, sleep the undisturbed sleep of immortality."

Did Zola decide, with everyone falling sick or dying around him, that the time had come to protect his own image against posthumous abuse? Intimations of mortality may indeed explain the warm welcome he gave Dr. Edouard Toulouse in 1895 when this psychiatrist, who at thirty had already attracted notice, proposed to make him the first subject of a "medico-psychological" inquiry into the relationship between "intellectual superiority" and "neuropathy." Good positivist that he was, Toulouse mobilized a battalion of auxiliaries—medical specialists, alienists, anthropologists, psychologists, graphologists—to accumulate as much data as possible, and Zola cooperated fully in examinations that lasted almost a year, letting himself be weighed, measured, tested, poked.[4] *Enquête médico-psychologique* appeared in

---

[4]During his sojourns at Médan, Zola sometimes found it more convenient to answer written questionnaires prepared by Toulouse. Thus, on June 1, 1896, he wrote as follows:

> I told you that I couldn't vouch unreservedly for the luminous sensations that I've sometimes thought I had during the night, for they've never occurred except in places with which I am altogether familiar. I have them in both eyes, and perhaps it's only an evocation or the very intense memory of objects I know to be there. . . . The ringing noises about which I spoke to you occur in both ears. Just yesterday I heard a very loud one, which lasted all day, in the left ear—my better ear, I feel. . . . When I inhale deeply, my chest measures 98 centimeters around the nipples [38.5 inches]. Measured at the navel, my stomach is 1 meter around [39 inches]. Cordially.

October 1896, with a prefatory benediction by Toulouse's subject. "I have never hidden anything, or had anything to hide," Zola declared, sounding very like Jean-Jacques Rousseau in *The Confessions*. "I've lived openly, I've said out loud what I considered it good and useful to say. Among the thousands of pages I've produced, I need not repudiate a single one. . . . My brain is ensconced in a glass skull as it were, for all the world to see, . . . and I fear no one." The book would, he wrote, dispel the myth that he had a coarse, insensitive nature:

> You cannot be unaware of the fact that for thirty years I have been portrayed as a lout, an ox with thick hide and dull senses, whose ignoble appetite for money is all that keeps him plowing ahead. Good Lord! I who scorn money, who have never strayed from the ideals of my youth! Ah, poor flayed man that I am, painfully sensitive to every breeze, never embarking upon his daily task except in anguish, and accomplishing it only after will has vanquished self-doubt! How it has made me laugh, and also weep at times—this notorious ox!

Toulouse had done him "a good turn" in studying his "tattered person." If he wasn't perfect, he was at least a man who had "given his life to work and poured into that work all his physical, intellectual, and moral resources."

Toulouse himself concluded that for all his nervous problems, Zola did not belong to the category of "superior degenerates." He had never seen an "obsessional or impulsive type" as "well balanced" as this writer. "And I have seldom seen even people free of all psychic tares exhibit such fine mental stability," he wrote.

Had Edmond de Goncourt lived long enough to read the *Enquête*, he would have mocked Zola's assertion that his life had been guided by reverence for truth rather than the acquisition of lucre. But incredulous ears were certainly not lacking, even after January 1898 when, with *J'accuse*, Zola made a moral commitment that forced him in due course to flee his country and pushed him to the edge of financial embarrassment. "Besides himself, Zola worships only one thing: money," a journalist stated in *La Dépêche* on January 23, 1898. "He sees the Dreyfus Affair as an immense and colossal opportunity for self-advertisement. He could not in fact care less for Dreyfus; what interests him is himself, Zola."

XXVII

※

J'ACCUSE

HEN ON NOVEMBER 1, 1894, Drumont's *Libre Parole* announced in bold headlines that charges of espionage were to be brought against "a Jewish officer" named "A. Dreyfus," Zola was abroad busily gathering material for *Rome*. And when on December 22, after four days of secret deliberations inside the Cherche-Midi prison, seven military judges found the obscure artillery captain guilty, Zola was distracted by his own impending trial.[1] Not until November 1897, at the behest of men who had spent three years gathering evidence of an elaborate frame-up, did he seriously consider Alfred Dreyfus. On the 13th of that month, the facts of the case were made known to him over lunch in the home of Auguste Scheurer-Kestner, vice-president of the Senate.

It had all begun with the discovery of a secret memorandum addressed to Maximilian von Schwartzkoppen, military attaché at the German embassy on the rue de Lille. This so-called bordereau, which reached French spymasters in September 1894 after being fished from Schwartzkoppen's wastepaper basket by a charwoman in the employ of the French intelligence service, read as follows:

[1]In *Lourdes*, Zola accused contractors of having robbed the priest who hired them to build Notre-Dame de Lourdes. One such contractor, Henri Bourgeois, sued Zola for defamation of character. The case went to trial in February 1895 and Zola was acquitted. He was represented on this occasion by René Waldeck-Rousseau, who later became prime minister and exercised a strong hand over France in the turbulent aftermath of Dreyfus's pardon.

I have received no word as to whether you wish to see me, but I nonetheless send you, Sir, some interesting information, viz:
1. A note about the hydraulic brake of the 120 and the manner in which this part has performed. [The reference was to the hydro-pneumatic brake of the gun called "120 court." It was a heavy field-piece, recently brought into use; the mechanism of the brake which overcame the recoil of the gun was a profound secret.]
2. A note on covering troops (some modifications will be carried out, according to the new plan). [These troops were those to be called to the frontier at the beginning of mobilization. They were slated to "cover" the concentration of the rest of the army; hence their name.]
3. A note concerning a modification in the formations of artillery.
4. A note about Madagascar. [The ministry of war was preparing an expedition to conquer that island.]
5. An outline of the proposed firing manual for field artillery (March 14, 1894). This document is exceedingly difficult to obtain, and I can only have it at my disposal for a very few days. The minister of war has distributed a certain number of copies among the troops, and the corps are held responsible for them. Each officer with a copy is re-quired to return it after the maneuvers. So, I shall arrange to lay hold of it and you will return it straightway, after gleaning from it what-ever interests you. Unless you prefer that I have it copied in extenso and send you the copy.
I now go on maneuvers.

Colonel Jean Sandherr, director of intelligence, took it for granted, despite evidence pointing elsewhere, that Schwartzkoppen's informant was a general staff officer trained in artillery. General Mercier, the minister of war, concurred. But among those to whom photographic copies of the bordereau were shown, no one recognized the hand-writing—neither the heads of general staff bureaus nor the heads of artillery. Sandherr's investigation might have died there had not a col-league, Lieutenant Colonel d'Abboville, revived it. Only someone ac-quainted with four different bureaus of the ministry could have secured the intelligence offered to Schwartzkoppen, declared d'Abbo-ville, and such widespread exposure suggested that the culprit might be a *stagiaire*, a newly commissioned staff officer serving probationary internships or *stages* in all four bureaus. This conjecture became cer-tainty when Colonel Pierre Fabre of the fourth bureau alighted on the name of Alfred Dreyfus, who had graduated from the Ecole Polytech-nique as a student artillery officer, had won captain's rank, then had attended the War College. It hardly mattered that interns never went on maneuvers. To Sandherr, Fabre, d'Abboville, et al., everything in-stantly argued Dreyfus's guilt, above all his "racial" origin, and a handwriting analysis prepared by yet another staff officer, Commandant du Paty de Clam, who dabbled in graphology, furnished them with absolute proof that the Jew had written the bordereau.

Like a carefully cultivated aerophyte, the case against Dreyfus did not at first thrive outside the hothouse atmosphere of Mercier's ministry. It left President Jean Casimir-Périer unimpressed. It won no support from General Félix Saussier, military governor of Paris and de facto commander-in-chief of French armed forces (whose mistress had a Jewish husband). And it led Gabriel Hanotaux, minister of foreign affairs, to state categorically that an investigation or trial based upon one fragile document defied common sense. Mercier persisted, however. Belabored by the right-wing press, which held him responsible for, among other sins, harboring unpatriotic elements (i.e., Jews) in the officer corps, this taciturn, austere graduate of the Polytechnique, who had embraced republicanism rather more vigorously than most generals, was receptive to a cause célèbre that might placate his detractors. "[Mercier] told [Hanotaux] that the law compelled him to prosecute so manifest a crime and that, moreover, disclosure would be inevitable if the traitor was not arraigned since several officers and experts already knew about it. The inverse scandal might then arise. 'I should not like to be accused of having compromised with treason!' " he protested.

Instead, Mercier betrayed his honor by fostering the nascent conspiracy. When an expert graphologist from the Bank of France named Alfred Gobert concluded after close examination of the bordereau that "someone other than the suspect" could have written it, Mercier recruited other experts, notably Alphonse Bertillon, who ran the police prefecture's service of judiciary identity. Bertillon knew what was wanted of him and, being a vocal anti-Semite, complied. To explain the obvious dissimilarity between Dreyfus's script and that of the bordereau, he showed, in great detail, how the traitor had forged his own handwriting with calculated discrepancies. The proof was irrefutable, he wrote. "From the very first day, you knew my opinion. It is now absolute, complete, and admitting of no reservation." The general staff hailed Bertillon's lunatic argument as a scientific tour de force.

To Alfred Dreyfus, in whom religious feeling was bound up with love of country, no insult could have been more heinous than the charge of treason pressed upon him by du Paty de Clam on October 15 at the war ministry. An Alsatian whose family had chosen French citizenship after 1871, when they left Mulhouse (all except one member, who managed the Dreyfus cotton mill), Alfred vividly remembered that catastrophic evacuation. Seeing French infantry trudge westward in "despair and humiliation" determined his future career, he later avowed. But if fervent patriotism made him a soldier, so did his profound need for the clear-cut orthodoxies of army life, and it is supremely ironical that that tidy, disciplined, hierarchical world should all at once have become a Kafkaesque enigma. Torn away from wife, from children, from fatherland, this Jew who gave Judaism short shrift found himself shut up in the Cherche-Midi military prison, without explanation. "They put me in the strictest solitary confinement and all communication with my kin was forbidden me," he wrote in a memoir some years later.

> I had at my disposal neither paper, pen and ink, nor pencil. . . . In that gloomy cell, still under the appalling influence of the scene I had just endured and of the monstrous accusation brought against me, when I thought of all those whom I had left at home only a few hours before in the fullness of happiness, I fell into a state of fearful excitement and raved from grief. I walked back and forth in the narrow space, knocking my head against the walls. Commandant Forzinetti, director of the prison, came to see me, accompanied by the chief guard, and calmed me for a little while.

A fortnight passed before he was shown a photograph of the bordereau. Meanwhile du Paty de Clam had searched his apartment on the avenue du Trocadéro and warned Lucie Dreyfus that any attempt to publicize the arrest would spell the downfall of her husband. "One word could mean war."

Discretion became irrelevant after October 29, when *La Libre Parole* asked, in its first article on the case, whether an extremely important arrest had not taken place by military order. "The individual arrested has reportedly been accused of espionage. If this item is true, why have military authorities maintained absolute silence?" Other right-wing papers—*L'Eclair, La Patrie*—thereupon bayed in chorus, like hounds getting wind of prey, and the general staff, which had hoped that Dreyfus would confess his guilt or commit suicide, was obliged to go forward. Needing some motive for treason, Major Bexon d'Ormescheville, judge advocate of what was to be the first court-martial, in whose hands the judicial investigation had been placed, sought evidence with which to portray Dreyfus as a debt-ridden gambler, a whoring libertine, or an inquisitive rogue. Classmates from the War College testified that wherever he passed, documents disappeared, and d'Ormescheville concluded as follows:

> Along with his extensive knowledge, Captain Dreyfus possesses a remarkable memory; he speaks several languages, including German, which he knows thoroughly, and Italian, of which he claims to have only a vague notion. He is, moreover, of a rather supple—even obsequious—character, quite suited for relations of espionage with

foreign agents. He was thus the perfect choice for the miserable and shameful mission that he either inspired or accepted and to which — quite luckily for France, perhaps — the discovery of his intrigues has put an end.

Of such vaporous stuff was his entire report made. Nothing in it promised to nail the captain, and with newspapers predicting that Mercier would fall if Dreyfus went free, consternation grew at the war ministry. "The Dreyfus Affair sticks to General Mercier's back as the centaur's tunic stuck to the shoulders of Hercules," is how one journalist put it. "If Dreyfus is acquitted, the minister departs; that much is certain, since he would be crushed beneath the awful responsibility of having frivolously brought about a very grave predicament. But if Dreyfus is convicted . . . Mercier gains stature and, profiting from the trial, becomes his country's savior." Exasperated by the lack of hard evidence against a man in whose guilt they ardently believed, Sandherr and his assistant, Commandant Joseph Henry, set out to fabricate some — with Mercier's knowledge no doubt. Rewriting two memoranda dated March 1894, which contained information furnished by a Spanish military attaché, they inserted several quotes, notably this one: "Someone in the ministry of war, almost certainly an attaché, has tipped off the German military attaché. . . . That is further proof that you have one or several wolves in your sheepfold. . . . Find out, I can't tell you often enough, because I am certain of it." The forged papers joined other dubious material in a file to which du Paty de Clam contributed explanatory notes. Dreyfus's lawyer, Edgar Demange, never saw it. It emerged from the war ministry under the seal of secrecy on December 22, when jury deliberations had already begun. Du Paty de Clam handed it to Colonel Maurel, president of the court-martial, which was being held behind closed doors, and declared on behalf of General Mercier that "the most urgent moral imperative possible" argued for showing the jury its contents. In fact, neither Maurel nor his fellow judges needed surreptitious guidance. Swayed by testimony that Henry had given two days earlier, they would have convicted Dreyfus anyway.[2] But all seven officers followed orders. "Not a single judge

[2]Henry's was a bravura performance. After declaring that an "honorable person" had twice advised him to watch out for a traitor in the intelligence service, he pointed at Dreyfus and shouted: "This man is the traitor." Demange inveighed against anonymous denunciations and challenged Henry to reveal the informant's name, whereupon Henry, slapping his kepi, rejoined that "there are some secrets in an officer's head that his cap does well to ignore." Colonel Maurel asked him solemnly whether he would affirm on his honor that the treasonous officer was Captain Dreyfus, and Henry swore to it while lifting his hand toward a painting of Christ.

appears to have suspected that such a communication, hidden from the defense, was in violation of the law, the military code, or common equity."

The trial served an exorcistic purpose rather than a juridicial one. Having cast out the alien, France celebrated her salvation. Everyone rejoiced, socialists arm in arm with monarchists, and indeed, men of the Left proved even more vindictive than men of the Right, as they had during the Franco-Prussian War. "He has no relative, no wife, no child, no love of anything, no human—or even animal—ties, nothing but an obscene soul and an abject heart," railed Clemenceau (who later led the fight for retrial, or "revision"). In turn, Jean Jaurès, the redoubtable Socialist orator, maintained, during a parliamentary debate on the question of restoring capital punishment for high treason, that Dreyfus should have been sentenced to death. "The country sees that simple soldiers are shot without pardon or pity for a momentary lapse or act of violence. . . . We must ask ourselves whether the nation's justice should remain unarmed in the event that abominable acts analogous to that committed by Captain Dreyfus were to recur."[3]

Germany, which looked on fretfully, denied that it had ever had any traffic, direct or indirect, with Alfred Dreyfus, but the denial only confirmed his guilt, the French thought. In these circumstances, where did one seek justice? A petition for appeal fell on deaf ears, and five days later Dreyfus, who had hardly eaten or slept since his condemnation, was publicly degraded in the main courtyard of the Ecole Militaire. Despite frigid weather, thousands had gathered outside, on the Place de Fontenoy. Pressing against the iron gate, they sent up shouts of *Mort aux juifs! A mort le traître! A mort Judas!* ("Death to the Jews! Death to the traitor! Death to Judas!") as a burly republican guardsman surrounded by silent troops tore all insignia of rank from Dreyfus's uniform—epaulets, braid, buttons—and finally broke Dreyfus's sword over his knee.

On January 17, 1895, army officials packed Dreyfus off to the Atlantic port of La Rochelle in a convict train. There, too, people gathered, but this mob rained blows upon the "Jew's" head before his escort could intervene. A launch then transported Dreyfus to the Ile de Ré, where he spent more than a month under constant surveillance. Lucie, who visited him twice a week, saw him last on February 21. The following day Dreyfus found himself aboard the ship *La Ville de Saint-Nazaire*, sailing—though he knew nothing yet of his destination—for French Guiana. The transatlantic voyage took more than

---

[3]Like Clemenceau, Jaurès later became a staunch Dreyfusard, but most socialists were slow to follow him. For them, anti-Semitic and often jingoist, the sin of being a Jew whose family had enriched itself in industry made Dreyfus inherently detestable.

a fortnight, and on March 12 *La Ville de Saint-Nazaire* dropped anchor off the Iles du Salut. Devil's Island, a nearly treeless volcanic rock baked by the equatorial sun and plagued with malaria, from which deportees seldom returned alive, was to be his home, or his hell, for more than four years. The local commandant jailed him in a stone cabin twelve feet square.

Stunned by this random blow, Dreyfus's family drew close together. The task of rescuing him devolved upon an older brother, Mathieu, who made it his sacred mission. But with nothing to help him argue the case for a judicial error—nothing except the marginalia Dreyfus himself had scrawled on Major d'Ormescheville's indictment—where could he begin? While police agents dogged his steps, he visited politician after politician, all in vain. Only Dreyfus's former wardens showed any real compassion, and one of them offered advice from which Mathieu profited greatly. "Your brother's cause must be defended before public opinion," declared Patin of La Santé prison, suggesting that the collaboration of a militant journalist might prove invaluable. The name Bernard Lazare came to mind.

Bernard Lazare must have seemed an improbable ally. Known for his spirited defense of anarchists and Marxist union organizers, he was unlikely to sympathize with the problems experienced by some rich Jew. Though Jewish himself, this left-wing idealist had, in a long essay entitled "L'Antisémitisme, son histoire et ses causes," blamed anti-Semitism on its victims and held the "religious impulse" responsible for impeding revolutionary development; he found Dreyfus's Jewishness no less obnoxious than his wealth. How remarkable, then, that one or two conversations should have converted him to the cause. "Lazare lost no time," recounts one historian. "In the spring of 1895 he was already at work on the first draft of his essay. With very few documents at his disposal, he made numerous errors. But his intelligence, exactitude and even his prescience were astonishing. A simple and rigorous style shorn of all bombast gave force to the argument."

Lazare would have circulated the essay straightway had not Dreyfus's lawyer, Demange, urged that it be held for some more auspicious occasion. Reluctantly, he heeded this advice and let off steam in bitter exchanges with Edouard Drumont of *La Libre Parole*, declaring that the "ancestral tradition of humility" under which his co-religionists labored did not bend every Jewish back. "I know some who . . . have had enough of anti-Semitism," he wrote in *Le Voltaire*. "They are tired of the insults, the slander, the lies, the dissertations on Cornelius Herz and the prosopopoeias on Baron de Reinach.[4] And tomorrow they will be legion, and if they thought as I do they would mobilize openly,

[4]Both were Jewish bankers, and both had been deeply involved in the Panama Scandal.

courageously, against you, against your doctrines, and no longer satisfied with defending themselves, they would attack you; and you are not invulnerable, neither you nor your friends." On June 18, 1896, the exchange of invective brought about an exchange of bullets, which, however, harmed neither duelist. By then, Lazare had come to view himself as "the spokesman of a Jewish resistance too long deferred."

After eighteen months of largely futile supplication, Mathieu concluded that drastic measures were needed to break the silence enveloping his brother's case. Galvanized by horrible news from Devil's Island (where, according to one published report, Alfred Dreyfus had become "ageless, his body stooped over, his hair white, his face sallow and hollowed, his beard gray, weary and slow of pace"), he hired an English agent to spread the rumor through London newspapers that Captain Dreyfus had disappeared. His strategy worked. The French government immediately set matters straight, but the French press erupted in gossip, second thoughts, and calumny. La Libre Parole denounced a vastly rich Jewish syndicate for plotting Dreyfus's escape. L'Autorité, which did not ordinarily sympathize with Jews, dared to wonder whether Dreyfus had perhaps been the victim of a judicial error.

Most important were articles published by the anti-Semitic Eclair, whose best-known writer, Ernest Judet, cultivated General Mercier. Eager to banish all doubts about Dreyfus, it naively evoked a "secret file" containing, in one decoded letter, irrefutable proof of his guilt. "It may be imagined that [the code] was much too useful for public dissemination," L'Eclair explained.

> Later on, it will be seen that for this same reason the letter in question was not included in the official dossier and that it was only in secret, in the deliberation room, out of the presence even of the accused, that it was transmitted to the judges of the court-martial. About September 20, Colonel Sandherr, head of the section of statistics, communicated to General Mercier the letter, which had been deciphered.[5] It concerned the espionage service in Paris and contained the sentence: "Decidedly, that animal Dreyfus has become too demanding."

This disclosure stunned Mathieu, and when the government made no effort to refute it, Lucie Dreyfus, armed at last with specific evidence of malfeasance, sent the president of the Chamber of Deputies a petition, which was carried by various newspapers, including Le Figaro. "I could not believe [what L'Eclair reported] and expected the denial that the semi-official Agence Havas supplies in the case of all errone-

[5]"Section of statistics" was used as a disguise for the intelligence bureau.

ous news," she wrote, at the dictation of Edgar Demange. "The denial did not come. It is thus true that after debates shrouded in the deepest mystery, because of a closed session, a French officer has been convicted by a court-martial on the basis of an accusation that the prosecution has produced without his being informed and without his lawyer being able to counsel him. This is a denial of all justice. . . . I have kept silent, despite all the odious and absurd slander propagated amidst the public and in the press. Today it is my duty to break that silence."

Soon afterward, on November 7 and 8, members of parliament and influential journalists received copies of Bernard Lazare's pamphlet *Une Erreur judiciaire: la vérité sur l'Affaire Dreyfus*, which had been secretly printed abroad. Then, two days later, yet another crucial disclosure strengthened the cause of Dreyfusism. After obtaining a facsimile of the bordereau from one of the graphologists consulted three years earlier, *Le Matin* published it on November 10. For Mathieu, no reasonable person could deny any longer that Alfred Dreyfus was innocent, and to drive home this message he had the notorious document, framed by samples of his brother's handwriting, reproduced as a poster. "Our circle of action was growing, expanding from day to day," he later recalled.

Meanwhile, unbeknownst to Mathieu, a lone truth seeker had been at work inside the general staff itself. On July 1, 1895, Commandant Georges Picquart, who had witnessed Dreyfus's court-martial and applauded the verdict, replaced Colonel Sandherr as chief intelligence officer. A highly decorated veteran of campaigns in Africa and Tonkin, he did not relish espionage but nonetheless applied himself to it with characteristic thoroughness. Months passed more or less routinely until in March 1896 something deeply disturbing occurred. Schwartzkoppen's fecund wastepaper basket yielded an unsent letter-telegram, or *petit-bleu*, from which intelligence deduced that the addressee, Major Walsin-Esterhazy of the 74th Infantry Regiment, had been passing along military secrets. Was another Dreyfus on the loose? So it seemed to Picquart. Information gathered by the police convinced him that the forty-nine-year-old major, who descended from the powerful Austro-Hungarian Esterhazy clan through a bastard, expatriate line, might well do anything for money. "[He] had serious financial problems. He was keeping a mistress . . . whom he visited every evening before returning to his conjugal home at night. He was renting an apartment for her at 49, rue de Douai, and gave her a monthly allowance.[6] He was saddled with creditors and could not pay his bills on time."

---

[6] Zola could conceivably have brushed against him on any given day. This was almost next door to the Zolas.

Not every adulterous, debt-ridden officer made a traitor, but Esterhazy had taken unusual measures to familiarize himself with the latest technological developments in artillery. He had, moreover, been spotted on several occasions entering the German embassy. By June, Picquart lacked only some document in the suspect's own hand, and that lacuna was filled during the summer, when Esterhazy persistently requested a desk job at the war ministry. Toward the end of August, two letters of ardent solicitation were forwarded to intelligence (with approval from the minister of war). Picquart could not have been more stunned had he been struck by lightning, for what he thought he saw in reading them was the script of the infamous bordereau. A close comparison bore out their identity and left him to draw the painful conclusion that an innocent man had by then served one and a half years on Devil's Island.

After examining the "secret file," which contained no definitive proof against Dreyfus of the kind he had expected to find there, Picquart reported his discovery to General Raoul de Boisdeffre, chief of the general staff. That the file was still intact shocked Boisdeffre, but neither he nor his deputy, General Gonse, betrayed any chagrin over the apparent miscarriage of justice. On the contrary, they urged him to "keep the two cases separate." How could they be kept separate? Picquart wondered. The stubborn young intelligence chief, whose respect for truth proved stronger than his own prejudice against Jews, questioned this cynical recommendation, citing the recent disclosure of the secret file in *L'Eclair* as all the more reason to investigate. "In my opinion it is imperative to act without delay," he advised Gonse. "If we wait any longer, we will be overwhelmed, locked into an inextricable position, and we will no longer have the means either of defending ourselves or of ascertaining the real truth." His argument went unheeded. Picquart thereupon secured an interview with General Jean-Baptiste Billot, the new minister of war, who had not been compromised by the Dreyfus trial, but he, too, wrapped himself in silence. It became quite clear that the general staff had decided to make common cause against any threat of exposure. "What do you care that that Jew is on Devil's Island?" Gonse asked Picquart on September 15, after an acerbic discussion. "His possible innocence is irrelevant. Such matters ought not enter into consideration." Picquart was appalled. "What you've said is abominable," he rejoined. "I do not know what I will do. But in any event, I will not take this secret to the grave with me."

Rather than dismiss Picquart outright, the conspirators decided to remove him from Paris on some pretext. He was told that the intelligence service affiliated with military groups stationed along France's eastern border needed reorganization, and on November 14 Billot ordered him there immediately. Six weeks later another order dispatched him to Tunisia, where, though still nominally head of intelligence, he found himself attached to the 4th Regiment of sharpshooters in garrison at Sousse. "The minister has just told me that he is expanding the range of your mission and charging you with the organization of the intelligence service in Algeria and in Tunisia," Gonse informed him on December 24. Did his superiors hope that an early grave could more easily be arranged abroad? Apparently so, for in due course Boisdeffre instructed General Leclerc, who commanded the army of occupation, to have Picquart verify at first hand reports of local tribes gathering beyond Gabès, near Tripoli—a notoriously dangerous region. Picquart had long since taken the trouble to record everything he knew in a codicil to his will.

It was a matter not only of exiling Picquart but of incriminating him, and as early as November the general staff embarked upon a frenzied program of deception that ultimately saw Boisdeffre, Gonse, Henry, du Paty de Clam, and several lesser figures collude with none other than Esterhazy himself. For mischief, Picquart's de facto replacement, Commandant Joseph Henry, had no peer. To bolster the case against Dreyfus, this shrewd, rough-hewn bully decided to prepare yet another false document. Borrowing the salutation and signature from a letter written to Schwartzkoppen by his Italian counterpart, Alessandro Panizzardi (and of course retrieved by the charwoman, Madame Bastian), Henry inserted between them the brief message: "I have read that an elected deputy is to pursue questioning about Dreyfus. If Rome is asked for new explanations, I will say that I never had any relations with the Jew. If they ask you, say the same, for no one must ever know what happened with him."

Here indeed was "conclusive proof," and into the Dreyfus file it went as soon as Boisdeffre advised the war minister, Billot, of its existence. Henry then turned his wits upon Picquart. On November 27, the latter's mail, which had been routinely opened since October, produced a note from a friend describing certain mutual acquaintances by nickname. This private language inspired Henry, who right away used it in a letter made up to suggest that a syndicate of powerful Jews with whom Picquart had clandestine relations frowned upon his reassignment. Signed "Speranza," the bogus communication, which intelligence "intercepted" on December 15, read as follows:

Paris, Midnight 35 — I am leaving the house, our friends are in a state of consternation; your unfortunate departure has upset everything. Hasten your return here; come quickly, quickly! The holiday season being quite auspicious for the cause, we count on you for the 20th. She is ready, but cannot and will not act until she has spoken to you. Once the demigod speaks, we will act.

Lest Picquart awaken before the web had been spun, rumors of his disgrace or dismissal were floated so as categorically to deny them. At year's end, Henry and Gonse sent the lieutenant colonel expressions of affectionate camaraderie, wishing him "good health" on his "splendid trip" in North Africa.

By mid-year 1897 the conspirators felt certain enough of victory to declare war. In May, when Picquart demanded that the general staff clarify his status, Henry sent him a list of charges arising from an investigation of his conduct as intelligence chief. The grotesque truth now dawned on Picquart, who hurriedly arranged to visit a lawyer and close friend in Paris, Louis Leblois. During the last week of June, anguished discussions took place, with Leblois (wrote Joseph Reinach in his monumental history of the Dreyfus Affair) "more insistent as the hours passed, more curious for details, more impassioned by the great cause it was his ambition to make his own," and with Picquart "perplexed, racked by doubt, utterly disoriented." Torn between his military oath and his personal honor, Picquart told Leblois as much about Esterhazy as conscience allowed (conscience did not let him mention the *petit-bleu*, for example). He also gave him power of attorney to inform the government, if need be. Under no circumstances, however, was Leblois to contact Dreyfus's brother or lawyer.

A fortnight after Picquart's departure from Paris, Leblois sought out Auguste Scheurer-Kestner, vice president of the Senate, and unburdened himself freely. This choice of confidant made perfect sense. Scheurer-Kestner, who had led the protest against Germany's annexation of Alsace-Lorraine in the National Assembly of 1871, where he represented Mulhouse, enjoyed an unparalleled reputation for probity and patriotism. As former political editor of Gambetta's paper, *La République française*, he presided over a Gambettist fraternity that counted among its members General Jean-Baptiste Billot, the minister of war. And finally, he was one of very few politicians known to entertain serious doubts about the Dreyfus verdict. Leblois convinced him that general staff officers had framed Dreyfus. Scheurer-Kestner, in turn, called upon Prime Minister Jules Méline, President Félix Faure, and General Billot, begging the government to initiate a judicial appeal while reluctantly honoring the pledge of discretion exacted by Picquart. Rebuffed at every turn, he suffered abuse from anti-Dreyfusard newspapers that had been given inside information about his high-level rendezvous:

Le Matin, La Patrie, La Libre Parole, and L'Intransigeant showered Scheurer-Kestner with insults: "the gray eminence of treason," "lipomatose gorilla," "slime that had to be washed into the sewer." "A vague jingling of large coins could be heard." He was a "Kraut," a

"Prussian," the "valet of the Germans." "If he is not a scoundrel, he is a madman, and an asylum is called for." Scheurer-Kestner, the old voice of protest from French Alsace, a man whose very reason for living was patriotism, was deeply affected. He nevertheless pursued his initiatives without flinching.

In one quarter, enormous gratitude was felt. To Mathieu Dreyfus, the scurrilous outcry against Scheurer-Kestner had a reassuring ring, for it meant that his brother's case had been disinterred and awakened.

Fortune then began to smile on Dreyfus's supporters. Early in November 1897, Mathieu received a visit from a stockbroker named de Castro, who, having chanced upon the facsimile of the bordereau distributed a year earlier, recognized his client Walsin-Esterhazy's handwriting. De Castro brought along several letters, and Mathieu, after inspecting them closely, made this remarkable development known to Scheurer-Kestner. With Picquart's stipulation thus circumvented, Leblois, Scheurer-Kestner, Mathieu, and Edgar Demange could now work in concert. On November 12 all four held a strategy meeting at which they were joined by Emmanuel Arène, editor of Le Figaro. And on November 15, Mathieu published there a letter sent to General Billot:

> The sole basis of the accusation brought in 1894 against my unfortunate brother is an unsigned, undated letter establishing that confidential military documents were delivered to an agent of a foreign military power. I have the honor of informing you that the author of that document is M. le Comte Walsin-Esterhazy, an infantry commandant, withdrawn from active duty last spring because of temporary infirmities. Commandant Esterhazy's handwriting is identical to that of the document in question. It will be quite easy for you to procure a specimen of the handwriting of the officer. I am prepared, moreover, to indicate to you where you may find letters of his, the authenticity of which is incontestable and which date from before my brother's arrest.

He did not doubt, he wrote in conclusion, that the minister of war would act swiftly to see justice done.

A lunch organized at Scheurer-Kestner's residence on the day after the strategy meeting marked the beginning of Zola's involvement in the Dreyfus Affair. Recruited for the valuable advice he could give as a writer who knew more than most about influencing mass audiences, he found himself captivated by Leblois's account of events. There was no need to tell those present—Leblois, Scheurer-Kestner, an appeals court judge named Louis Sarrut, the novelist Marcel Prévost—that anti-Semitism disgusted Zola. Eighteen months earlier, on May 16, 1896, *Le Figaro* had published an article entitled "For the Jews," in which he declared:

> For several years I have followed, with growing surprise and revulsion, the campaign against Jews in France. I see it as a monstrosity, by which I mean something outside the pale of common sense, of truth and justice, a blind, fatuous thing that would push us back centuries, a thing that would lead to the worst of abominations, religious persecution, with blood shed over all countries.

It "stupefied" him that such fanaticism should have erupted

> in our age of democracy, of universal tolerance, when the movement everywhere is toward equality, fraternity, and justice. We are at the point of effacing boundaries, of dreaming the community of all peoples, of holding religious congresses where priests of every persuasion embrace, of feeling that common hardship unites us in brotherhood. . . . And a bunch of madmen, imbeciles or knaves has chosen this moment to shout at us: "Let's kill the Jews, let's devour them, let's massacre, let's exterminate, let's bring back stakes and *dragonnades!*"

But the Dreyfus drama spoke to him in other ways as well. His imagination had, after all, always dwelled upon the victim, the alien, the outcast. Characters expunged from a closed, hostile world figure prominently throughout *Les Rougon-Macquart*, shaming bourgeois hypocrisy or political despotism, and the story of François Mouret, for example, may be said to have anticipated the defense of Alfred Dreyfus. Two Zolas appeared at Scheurer-Kestner's on that fateful November 13. Bound up with a man haunted since childhood by rigged trials was a novelist enthralled by persecutional schemes. Did the Affair present itself as, among much else, an elixir for the played-out creator? No doubt. "Our factual accounts became poetry for Zola," Scheurer-Kestner recalled. " 'It's gripping!' he'd say from time to time. One felt that his little body was clambering up the curtains the better to hear and see. And he exclaimed: 'It's thrilling! It's horrible! It's a frightful drama! But it's also drama on the grand scale!' " The warden of La Santé had once urged Mathieu Dreyfus to defend his brother before France at large, and now, three years later, Zola argued that legal ploys would not suffice. A campaign was necessary, he said, with brief, trenchant articles challenging the enemy and stirring public indignation.

Zola's article on Scheurer-Kestner launched that campaign. Published on November 25 by *Le Figaro*, it celebrates the old man's perseverance and makes an assertion that was to become the *cri de guerre* of Dreyfusards: *La vérité est en marche, et rien ne l'arrêtera* ("Truth is on the march, and nothing will stop it"). One week later, on December 1, Zola published another article in *Le Figaro*, this one directed against the myth of a Jewish "syndicate," against the press that propagated it and the government agencies that fostered it. "Captain Dreyfus was condemned by a court-martial for treason," it begins.

Since then he has become the traitor—no longer a man but an abstraction embodying the idea of the fatherland bled dry and handed over to the conqueror. He represents not only treason present and future, but also treason past, for people blame our old defeat on him, in the stubborn belief that only treason can explain it.

There he is with his black soul and hideous face—the shame of the army, the thug who sold his brethren as Judas sold his God. But since he's Jewish, it's clear what will happen. Rich and powerful as they are—and, moreover, without national allegiances—Jews will work clandestinely, using their millions to bail him out. They will buy consciences, they will envelop France in a damnable plot, they will substitute an innocent man for the evildoer.

Thanks to twenty or so newspapers whose stock-in-trade was xenophobia, the idea of a subversive brotherhood invested with diabolical powers had taken root in the public mind. "How many simple folk," he continued, "have accosted me during the past week to say: 'What? Isn't M. Scheurer-Kestner a knave? How can you consort with the likes of him? Don't you know that they've sold out France?' Such talk makes my heart clench, for I know very well that misdeeds will thus be conjured away."

But if newspapers perverted public opinion, behind them lurked the ministry of war. "Who doesn't sense that we stand before the most impervious of ill wills? There are those who won't admit that errors— I was about to say transgressions—have been committed. They persist in shielding the compromised parties. They will stop at nothing to avoid the purge that looms." The fact was, Zola declared, that France, bereft of her reason,

turned against a poor wretch who for three years has been expiating in atrocious conditions a crime he didn't commit. Yes, there exists over there, on a godforsaken rock under the harsh sun, a being cut off from everyone else. He is isolated not only by the ocean but by eleven guards who surround him night and day, like a human wall.

... The eternal silence, and the slow, protracted death suffered beneath the weight of a whole nation's execration!

Deriding the Jewish syndicate as obfuscatory nonsense, Zola called for the creation of a virtuous syndicate, "a syndicate to shape opinion and cure it of the madness fostered by the gutter press. . . . A syndicate to repeat each morning . . . that the honor of the army is not threatened, that only individual parties can be compromised. . . . A syndicate to campaign until the truth has been established, until justice has been restored, however great the obstacles, however long the struggle." To this syndicate he, Zola, belonged, and to it, he hoped, "all the decent people of France" would flock in their thousands.

Threatened then with mass desertion by its conservative readership, *Le Figaro* reluctantly allowed Zola to fire one last salvo, and the campaigner held nothing back, lamenting in his most pugnacious style the spectacle of virtue jeered and vice acclaimed. "We have witnessed a base exploitation of patriotism, the bogeyman 'foreigner' trotted forth in an affair of honor that concerns only our French family," he wrote in a piece entitled "Court Minutes."

> The worst revolutionaries make all kinds of noise about the army and its leaders being insulted when the effort has been, on the contrary, to place them very high, above reproach. And the rabble-rousers, the several papers that stir up opinion, maintain a reign of terror. Not one man in our assemblies has had the decency to stand up and protest, . . . as they cast a nervous eye on the coming elections. Among those who guard our civil liberties—moderates, radicals, socialists—not one has yet let his conscience speak. How shall the country find its way through the storm if those very men who call themselves its guides keep quiet in the service of narrow-minded political strategy or for fear of compromising their personal situations?

The curtain had fallen on the first act of a frightening drama, he concluded. "Let us hope that tomorrow's action will restore us our courage and console us."

Zola could not yet have known how labyrinthine the drama really was, or how far the conspirators had already gone to shore up their case against Dreyfus. Alarmed by reports of Scheurer-Kestner visiting high officials and conferring with Picquart's lawyer, they decided that the secret file needed more bulk. Accordingly, Gonse and Henry prevailed upon Captain Lebrun-Renault, the officer who had been responsible for guarding Dreyfus at the Ecole Militaire on January 5, 1895, to swear that his prisoner had made a clean breast of things just before the public degradation. Further, Henry, who could still draw upon Schwartzkoppen's wastepaper basket for raw material, produced a whole slew of forged or falsified documents, with encouragement from above. "Set your mind at rest," he assured Maurice Paléologue of the ministry of foreign affairs on November 3. "Dreyfus was rightly condemned. While he was shark fishing on his island, we were uncovering proofs that damn him outright. I have a closetful."

Before long, perjured testimony and forged documents led them all down the slippery slope to active collusion with the traitor himself. It had begun on October 16, when Generals de Boisdeffre and Gonse discussed the danger of Esterhazy's exposing himself in some flagrant way. Could they afford this risk? If their elaborate construction fell apart, would they not perish in the ruins? Increasingly divorced from reality, Dreyfus's guilt had become a dogma to be preserved by any means, and so it happened that on the evening of October 22 Henry and du Paty de Clam — the latter wearing a fake beard — met Esterhazy at the Vanne reservoir, near the Parc Montsouris. There they told him that he had resolute and indefatigable champions. "But he would have to obey the instructions that he would be given and do nothing without consulting his defenders," writes the historian and legal scholar Jean-Denis Bredin.

Esterhazy was reassured. They separated, with the promise of maintaining daily contact. Esterhazy returned to the German embassy to take leave of Schwartzkoppen, whom he would not see again. He was quite cheerful, even wearing a rose in his lapel. He told of his meeting, which had been extremely reassuring, with "two representatives of the ministry of war," who vouchsafed him the "government's assistance." Schwartzkoppen was delighted that things had worked out so well.

Daily contact did indeed occur as they all set about persuading high government officials that Lieutenant Colonel Picquart was the agent or pawn of a Jewish syndicate determined to substitute innocent Esterhazy for guilty Dreyfus. In letters dictated by Henry and addressed to President Faure, Esterhazy claimed that he had been informed by an anonymous benefactress — a "veiled lady" — of the plot woven against him and had been given evidence, stolen from some "foreign legation," of Dreyfus's "baseness." Now pathetic, now insolent, he implored Faure to rescue him and threatened, if he were not rescued, to publish a document that might provoke war. The accuser should have been jailed without delay, but instead the accused down in Tunisia was questioned at length. Feeling quite invulnerable, Esterhazy carried his offensive farther still. He bearded Picquart directly, in a letter written on November 6 or 7:

I have received these last days a letter in which you are formally accused of having fomented against me the most abominable machination to substitute me for Dreyfus. In that letter it is said, among other things, that you have bribed noncommissioned officers in order to have specimens of my handwriting, a fact which is true, since I have verified it. It is also said that you have diverted from the ministry of war documents entrusted to your honor in order to compose a clandestine file that you have delivered to friends of the traitor. The matter of the clandestine file is precise, since I have in my possession today items that were taken from that file.

In the face of such a monstrous accusation and in spite of the proof that has been given me, I hesitate to believe that a superior officer of the French army could have been trading in the secrets of his service in order to attempt to substitute one of his comrades for the wretch the proof of whose crime he has evidence of. It is unthinkable that you evade a clear and frank explanation.

Meanwhile, Henry sent Picquart several bogus telegrams signed "Speranza" and "Blanche," one of which suggested quite pointedly that Picquart himself had fabricated the *petit-bleu*. Intercepted by the post office at Henry's behest, and photographed before leaving Paris, they were thrust, with feigned outrage, upon Minister Billot.

Henry and Esterhazy might have gone on devising evidence unperturbed had not two events combined to open their secret world a crack. On November 15, as we have seen, Mathieu Dreyfus made public his denunciation of Esterhazy. On that same day Picquart, in high dudgeon, filed an official military complaint against Esterhazy, "who, having been informed, I know not by whom, of the probe I conducted in the exercise of my office, has attacked me slanderously, first in a private letter, then in telegrams." The battle was joined at last, though not on level ground. Confronted with Mathieu Dreyfus's charge, Billot ordered General Georges de Pellieux, commandant of the Department of the Seine, to conduct an investigation. After only three days, Pellieux, to whom Boisdeffre showed the "coded" telegrams from "Speranza," declared Picquart more suspect than Esterhazy. Billot's fellow ministers then recommended another, fuller investigation, which lasted two weeks. Led by the same general, who had grown quite fond of Esterhazy, it produced the same verdict, with independent-minded witnesses never having been questioned and the conspirators' crudely forged evidence never having been subjected to graphological analysis. Pellieux's report described Esterhazy as an innocent victim, Picquart as the "unwitting agent" of someone who had almost brought dishonor upon him, and the *petit-bleu* as a document "without authenticity or plausibility."

But even then the matter was not yet resolved once for all. Would Pellieux's report, if accepted, not compel the military men to press charges against Mathieu Dreyfus in criminal court, before a jury beyond their control and a judge invoking hallowed rules of evidence? Lest the Dreyfus trial take place all over again, this time out in the open, Generals Billot, Boisdeffre, Saussier, and Pellieux agreed that Esterhazy should beseech them to reject the report and give him the opportunity to exonerate himself at a court-martial. Fearfully, Esterhazy played along. "I believe that you have in your hands all the evidence of the infamous plot that was fomented in order to ruin me," he wrote on December 1 to Pellieux (who corrected the letter in draft). "Only a decision reached [in a court-martial] will be able to blast—by acquitting me before public opinion, which they dared to address—the most cowardly of slanderers." The press, which had accompanied Pellieux's investigation with xenophobic choruses, hailed Esterhazy as admirably brave.

No more rational than the press was the National Assembly, where, following Pellieux's report, deputies rallied round the flag in a tumultuous display of anti-Semitism orchestrated by Count Albert de Mun, who vilified the "Jewish syndicate." "We must know whether it is true that there is in this country a mysterious and hidden power strong enough to be able to cast suspicion at will on those who command our army, those who, on the day when great duties befall it, will have the mission of taking our army to the enemy and conducting a war," he exclaimed on December 4. "We must know whether such a hidden power is strong enough to overwhelm the entire country, as it has done for more than a fortnight, introducing doubt." These sowers of doubt were all foreigners, even if nominally French, whereas the elected representatives were, with some few exceptions,

> Frenchmen concerned to preserve intact what is most precious, what remains, in the midst of our partisan discord and struggles, the common domain of our invincible hopes: the honor of the army.

Not daring to utter a word or lift a finger amidst the furor that de Mun's speech excited, Joseph Reinach, who sat as a deputy from Digne, could feel "the hatred of three hundred hypnotized individuals" surge over his head. In this revivalist commotion left-wingers participated as stridently as those of the right. The Socialist leader Alexandre Millerand lambasted the government for even allowing an inquiry. Why didn't Reinach do something about rehabilitating his own tainted family (i.e., his uncle Baron Jacques de Reinach, of Panama fame) instead of trumping up a new Calas Affair?[7] he wondered—to the general acclaim of fellow legislators. Hadn't Jewish financiers enriched themselves in one scheme or conspiracy after another, always at France's expense?

By a very large majority, the Chamber of Deputies declared itself "respectful" of Pellieux's verdict. It endorsed General Billot's "homage to the army." It denounced "leaders of the odious campaign undertaken to trouble the public conscience." It buried the Dreyfus Affair.

Undaunted, Zola immediately dashed off "Court Minutes," then continued his personal campaign with a pamphlet scolding students who had demonstrated against Dreyfus in raucous marches through the Latin Quarter. "So there exists such a thing as anti-Semitic youth?" he wrote in mock amazement.

> So there exist fresh young brains and souls that this idiotic poison has already deranged? How very sad, and how ominous for the coming twentieth century! A hundred years after the Declaration of the Rights of Man, a hundred years after that supreme act of tolerance and emancipation, we return to the age of religious strife. . . . Oh, youth, youth! Be humane, be generous. Even if it turns out that we were mistaken, stand beside us when we say that an innocent man is suffering horrendously and that our anguished heart protests. Admit for only a moment the possibility of error and such disproportionate punishment will make tears flow. . . . Who if not you will join the lists, will stand fast against overwhelming odds, will break a lance for justice? Are you not ashamed that we old men are the ones who have become impassioned? that the generous madness of youth has inspired not you but your elders?

Three weeks later he addressed the whole nation in a pamphlet entitled *Lettre à la France*, which Fasquelle brought out on January 6, 1898, just before Esterhazy's court-martial. Here Zola sounded a graver note, warning his compatriots against their weakness for military rule and declaring them to be infected still with the virus of Boulangism:

> Republican blood does not yet run through your veins. Plumed helmets are what make your heart beat faster, and a king can't come to town without your falling in love with him. As for your army, you hardly think about it. It's a general you want in your bed. How remote is the Dreyfus Affair! When General Billot was being hailed by

---

[7]In 1765, a Huguenot from Toulouse named Jean Calas was falsely accused of killing his son to prevent him from converting to Catholicism. He was tortured and put to death. Voltaire rehabilitated him with his famous *Treatise on Tolerance*.

the Chamber of Deputies, I saw the shadow of a sword lengthening on the wall. Beware, France, lest you end up with a dictatorship!

Right behind the scepter marched the cross. To bargain for one was to bargain for the other and thus revive a past of intolerance and theocracy.

Today the tactic of anti-Semitism is quite simple. Catholicism tried in vain to gain sway over the populace by creating workers' circles and multiplying pilgrimages. . . . Churches remained deserted, the people no longer believed in God. But here an opportunity presents itself to stir up those common people, to poison them with this species of fanaticism, to have them march through the streets shouting: "Down with the Jews!" "Death to the Jews!" What a victory it would be if a religious war could be unleashed! . . . When Frenchmen will have been turned into fanatics and executioners, when their love for the rights of man has been torn from their hearts, . . . God will undoubtedly do the rest.

Zola implored France to come to her senses, calling the liberal bourgeoisie and emancipated working class "dupes" who would not have sided against Dreyfus, he felt quite sure, had they recognized the machinations of the army and the Church.

Duped himself, Zola interpreted the decision to prosecute Esterhazy as a sign of truth gaining the upper hand over villainy.[8] It soon became clear, however, that Esterhazy's court-martial, which lasted only two days, January 11 and 12, was ritual theater. Everything had been arranged beforehand. Not Esterhazy but Picquart emerged as the real defendant, and while the former answered questions in a public session, playing the part of slandered warrior to applause from fellow officers, Picquart suffered rude treatment in a session held behind closed doors on the grounds that information aired during it might compromise national defense. No sooner had he mentioned Billot, Boisdeffre, and Mercier than General de Pellieux, flouting legal procedure, forbade him to "implicate such glorious names." The presiding magistrate, General de Luxer, would not let Picquart utter complete sentences until another judge, Commandant Rivals, who apparently had not attended rehearsals, asked that he be "permitted to furnish explanations necessary to his defense." And the general staff—Gonse, Henry, et al.—bore witness against him, with tales of files rifled or of

[8]In *Lettre à la France,* Zola mocked reports that the court-martial had been arranged to placate Esterhazy, as a kind of "judicial apotheosis." He found this idea "perfectly stupid." But he changed his mind well in advance of the trial, for the first drafts of *J'accuse* had already been written when the verdict came down.

collusion overheard. It all worked out as planned. Esterhazy's lawyer, though he knew exactly what outcome to expect, delivered a five-hour plea. The judges then acquitted the defendant after a three-minute conference. Inside Cherche-Midi prison, where Picquart and Mathieu Dreyfus found themselves insulted and threatened, this verdict provoked shouts of "Long live the army!" "Long live France!" "Death to the Jews!" "Death to the syndicate!" Outside, some fifteen hundred people cheered Esterhazy, with one stentorian voice proclaiming: "Hats off to the martyr of the Jews!"

Seven weeks earlier, at the beginning of his article on Scheurer-Kestner, Zola had declared that his intention was not yet to discuss the Affair in detail. "If circumstances have permitted me to study it and to reach a settled opinion," he wrote, "I am mindful of the fact that an inquest has been launched, that judicial procedures have begun, that common decency requires me to wait." But now the self-imposed stricture no longer applied. Justice had miscarried once again, uniformed magistrates had convicted Alfred Dreyfus for the second time, and Zola made up his mind to lay bare the dastardly plot. What came of this resolve was a *Lettre à M. Félix Faure, Président de la République*, better known as *J'accuse*. Published on the front page of a new daily paper, *L'Aurore*, it owed its more famous title to *L'Aurore's* co-director, Georges Clemenceau, who extracted it from the litany of indictments with which Zola's philippic concludes:[9]

I accuse Lieutenant Colonel du Paty de Clam of having been the diabolic agent of the judicial error . . . and of having for three years bolstered his dastardly deed with the strangest, most culpable machinations.

I accuse General Mercier of having become an accomplice, at the very least out of weakness, in one of the century's most iniquitous plots.

I accuse General Billot of having held in his hands the proof of Dreyfus's innocence and suppressing it, of having rendered himself guilty of this crime against justice and humanity for political reasons, to save the compromised general staff.

I accuse Generals de Boisdeffre and Gonse of having helped commit this same crime, the one out of Catholic fervor, no doubt, the other in a spirit of solidarity that portrays the war ministry as the unassailable holy of holies.

I accuse General de Pellieux and Commandant Ravary of having

---

[9]Ironically, Zola was concerned that Clemenceau might write a denunciation before he had finished his and rob him of the glory. There can be no doubt that he saw this as his opportunity to play a historic role.

led a vile—that is, a monstrously biased—investigation, the report of which constitutes an imperishable monument of naive audacity.

I accuse the three expert graphologists—Messrs. Belhomme, Varinard, and Couard—of having prepared fraudulent and deceitful analyses, unless a medical examination should prove them to be afflicted with impaired vision and judgment.

I accuse the war ministry of having used the press—particularly L'Eclair and L'Echo de Paris—to lead opinion astray and cover up its mischief.

Finally, I accuse the first court-martial of having flouted the law by convicting the defendant with a document introduced secretly, and I accuse the second court-martial of having papered over this illegal act by . . . deliberately acquitting a guilty man, on orders from above.

I am aware that these accusations expose me to prosecution under Articles 30 and 31 of the press law of July 29, 1881, which deal with slander. And I run the risk willingly.

As for the people I accuse, I do not know them, I have never seen them, I entertain neither rancor nor hatred. For me they are mere entities, spirits of social maleficence. And the act I accomplish here is but a revolutionary means of hastening the explosion of truth and justice.

I have only one passion, a passion for the knowledge that will alleviate human woe and bring mankind the happiness to which it is entitled. My burning protest comes from deep down. Let those who would dare do so try me at assize court and let the inquest take place openly, in broad daylight.

I shall wait.

Exaggerating the better to impress and relying upon his intuitive power where he lacked certain knowledge, Zola captured in these incantatory phrases the essence of what had transpired behind closed doors. On January 13, 1898, several hundred news criers recruited for the day by L'Aurore fanned out over Paris to hawk a special edition of the paper. Three hundred thousand copies had been printed, with the front page entirely taken up by J'accuse; few went unsold.

J'accuse electrified France. Around this manifesto gathered the disparate energies that became a coherent Dreyfusist movement, and almost instantly Zola acquired the political role urged upon him five years earlier, when he was finishing Les Rougon-Macquart. "The party of justice had been born," declared Joseph Reinach. "Dreyfusism was reinvigorated. . . . We could feel the confidence boil and rise within us," wrote Léon Blum, who called J'accuse a polemical text of "imperishable beauty." High-minded youths—students at the Ecole Normale Supérieure, young writers associated with the avant-garde literary magazine La Revue blanche, young socialists alienated by official party doctrine—sprang forward as if awaiting some such clarion call and marshaled signatures (among them Anatole France's) for a "Protest." During the following weeks their numbers multiplied, along with the protests. "We the undersigned," read one, which appeared in L'Aurore on January 16,

> struck by the irregularities in the Dreyfus trial of 1894 and by the mystery surrounding Commandant Esterhazy's trial, persuaded furthermore that the whole nation is concerned with the maintenance of legal guarantees, which are the citizen's sole protection in a free country, astonished by the searches of Lieutenant Colonel Picquart's residence and by other, no less illegal searches visited upon that officer, . . . demand that the Chamber uphold the legal guarantees of citizens against all arbitrary conduct.

After that, readers of L'Aurore seldom opened the paper without encountering statements of this kind or collective tributes. On February 2 a group of writers, artists, and scientists lauded Zola's "noble, militant attitude" even as they promised support "in the name of justice and truth." On February 6 support came from attorneys who offered him heartfelt thanks "for service rendered to the cause of Law, which touches all civilized nations." Every day brought more encouragement, and on his editorial rostrum Clemenceau described the pledgers of allegiance as a vanguard of "intellectuals," giving that nineteenth-century term its full, modern sense for the first time. "The syndicate grows apace," he exclaimed. "It redounds to the honor of thinking men that they have bestirred themselves before everyone else. Not a negligible thing. In the great movements of public opinion, one doesn't often see men of pure intellectual labor occupy the front rank." There could be no ambivalence where human right was concerned, he insisted. "One is either pro or con. And if the 'syndicate' grows more numerous, that is because France, after so many ordeals, has started to make common cause."[10]

On the side of justice for Captain Dreyfus, intellectuals were not alone in marching behind Zola. To many ordinary people the great novelist, whom they may or may not have read, became a culture hero. J'accuse traveled with remarkable speed, and at 21 bis, rue de Bruxelles, where life had been turned upside down, fan letters arrived by the pouchful from every corner of Europe. A French restaurant waiter, saluting the "defender of humanity," enjoined Zola not to let "those ciphers of the general staff" intimidate him. "You have with you, cit-

---

[10]The sarcastic use of "syndicate" takes up where Zola left off in his Figaro article of December 1, 1897.

izen, the proletarian mass; it admires you in this work of moral cleansing and I am certain it is glad to see your colossal genius placed at the service of the oppressed." In Smyrna a woman named Helen Wood wrote: "May my admiration and enthusiasm leap into your home. My heart is profoundly moved by the grandeur of yours." More admiration came from Rose Heller in Moravia, who had read his letter to Faure in the *Neue Freie Presse*. "Please allow a young woman who has long admired the great novelist to thank you a thousand times over for your ardent and free language, in the name of truth and also in the name of the unfortunate Dreyfus family, which enjoys the sympathy of all just men." Austria-Hungary also produced this anonymous encomium, from "one voice for the thousands in Austria":

Your free words and Your divine anger have won You a hero's wreath in universal history. Whatever the outcome of the tragic drama unfolding in France, of the anarchy in mores and opinions that now prevails there—whether You emerge as a martyr or a conqueror, You will have done everything a brave, noble man can do for his country, and the whole world approves You with enthusiasm. In Paris, they shout in the streets: "Down with Zola!" Here we shout: "Long live Zola, the modern *chevalier sans peur et sans reproche*."

England, Norway, Russia, Italy, Germany were all represented, and by correspondents of every age. "Yesterday evening, my father gave me the *National Zeitung* and told me to read your letter . . . about the Dreyfus Affair," Kathy Harkfeldt wrote from Berlin on January 15. "I was very curious, especially as I had never read anything by you, my mother having warned me that your books are not fit for seventeen-year-old girls. But now I shall read *Le Rêve*, and as soon as I'm older, I'll read all the other books. I write with the full consent of my parents, who hold in high esteem the author who has heroically come forward to defend an innocent man."

But in the civil war that had already divided friends all over France, *J'accuse* excited as much wrath as adulation, and for every valentine there were piles of hate mail. To nationalists who opposed review or "revision" of Dreyfus's sentence, *J'accuse* was a pernicious document undermining institutions that mattered more than the guilt or innocence of one man. How light, after all, was Alfred Dreyfus when weighed against *la grande armée!* If the latter, to prosper, required the former to serve out his life on Devil's Island, so be it, declared anti-revisionists like Maurice Barrès, novelist and deputy, who may be said to have anticipated the totalitarian concept of an "objective crime." If France, to survive in its "organic" wholeness, required the French to sacrifice an exemplary alien, why suffer misgivings? "At the end of the nineteenth century, in one sector of public opinion, a fortress-France nationalism asserted itself whose mission was to defend the cohesive social organism against modernity," writes the historian Michel Winock. This nationalism, for which Germany was a convenient enemy, an enemy that fostered intellectual and moral reform by threatening invasion at the border, thus went far beyond *revanchisme*.

> It oriented itself toward the interior, toward the past. . . . It directed its antagonism first and foremost against the democratic and liberal regime, the "Jewish, Masonic Republic." But beneath the political agenda one observed a spiritual reaction against decadence by people who understood the defense of French interests to be that of a completed civilization at war with the new mobility of things and beings. . . . Anti-Dreyfusards banked on two institutions: the Church and the army. Organized in accordance with principles of unity and hierarchy, these served, by their very nature, to strengthen the social fabric.

From this vantage point, Zola had already committed more sins than one man could ever expiate. After *La Conquête de Plassans* and *La Débâcle* and *Lourdes, J'accuse* did not surprise anti-Dreyfusards. It was, rather, the polemical epilogue to novels listed high on their Index, the final flourish of a subversive career, the work of a foreigner. "Just who is this Monsieur Zola?" asked Maurice Barrès, who in 1897 had regularly dined with Monsieur Zola at Durand's. "The man is not French. . . . Emile Zola thinks quite naturally with the thoughts of an uprooted Venetian."

Zola had invited prosecution, and in the National Assembly, where the great majority of the legislators shouted hurrahs when Albert de Mun called *J'accuse* "a bloody outrage," radicals as well as conservatives saw to it that his challenge was met. Under intense pressure, the cabinet drafted a complaint on January 18. Making no mention of the Dreyfus case lest grounds be given for revision, it retained only the phrase in which Zola accused the second court-martial of having "deliberately" acquitted a guilty man "on orders from above." Although Esterhazy, among others, felt quite certain that testimony would spill beyond this grievance, Prime Minister Jules Méline, with his government's honor at stake, could hardly avoid litigation. To fortify itself, the general staff, seeking to discredit the principal witness for the defense, had an investigatory board recommend on February 1 that Billot retire Picquart because of "grave misdeeds committed while in service."

Zola's trial opened at assizes court on February 7 and lasted more than two weeks, affording those who thronged the Palais de Justice—Marcel Proust among them—a spectacle fraught with dramatic incident. Led by Fernand Labori, behind whom Zola effaced himself, the defense team summoned nearly two hundred witnesses, from Mercier to Esterhazy, from chiefs of the general staff to members of the intelligence service, from the graphologists consulted during Dreyfus's trial to the judges who presided over Esterhazy's court-martial. At first all went better than expected as Labori obstinately challenged the absurd order that Dreyfus's trial was to be considered a *res judicata*, or a closed case—that jurors might hear testimony arguing against Esterhazy's innocence but not evidence casting doubt upon Dreyfus's guilt. Transgression by transgression, the great lawyer built a case for revision, and one by one the men who had convicted Dreyfus helped exculpate him despite themselves. The pseudoscientific nonsense of Alphonse Bertillon's handwriting analysis provoked laughter even among the generals. Henry (now a lieutenant colonel) remained mute on the witness stand, claiming to be in a stupor induced by insomnia and illness. Commandant du Paty de Clam, whom Maurice Paléologue of the foreign affairs ministry described as a "bizarre mixture of fanaticism, extravagance, and foolishness," played du Paty de Clam. Jean-Denis Bredin writes:

> Buttoned tight at the waist in his finest uniform, a monocle riveted to his eye, he crossed the courtroom with the cadenced step of a Prussian military parade, stopped like a robot two feet from the stand, heels together, knees braced, back arched, saluted the Court and the jury in military fashion, and waited, stiffly, as would a soldier before his superior officers. Once the oath had been taken, he refused to answer most of the questions. He then saluted the Court and the jury, pivoted, and left the room, resuming his earlier formality amid laughter and sarcasm.

Beside these preposterous figures, Picquart in his sky-blue, gold-braided jacket must have looked like Apollo. Normally controlled, the tall, thin colonel delivered a passionate tirade against those who had sought to dishonor him—"artisans of the other affair," as he called them—and undoubtedly swayed the jury, even with a dishonorable discharge pending. By February 16, Zola's prosecutors felt deep concern. "Yesterday evening the war ministry received police reports indicating that jurors at the assizes court are weary of interminable squabbles [among graphologists pro and con], that they feel uncertain of where the truth lies and are inclined to acquit Zola," noted Paléologue.

At this juncture, General de Pellieux, a "superb swordsman deploying in the service of his conviction the ardor, eloquence, and fearlessness of a true believer," joined the fray, to decisive effect. First he stated that Esterhazy could not have obtained the documents listed in the bordereau; then, with rhetorical bravado, he pronounced the whole issue of handwriting irrelevant and asked the jury:

> What do you want this army to become on the day of danger, which may be closer than you think? What do you want the poor soldiers to do, who will be led into battle by leaders discredited in their eyes? It is to the slaughterhouse that your sons would be led, gentlemen of the jury! But Zola would have won a new battle; he would write a new *Débâcle*; he would carry the French language everywhere in a Europe from which France would have been expunged.

A transfixed courtroom heard him conclude that revision mattered not at all to him.

> We would have been happy had the court-martial of 1894 acquitted Dreyfus; it would have proven that there was not a traitor in the army, and we are still in mourning over that fact. But what the court-martial of 1898 would not countenance, the abysmal deed it would not commit, is this: it would not put an innocent man in the place of Dreyfus, be he guilty or not. I have finished.

It was altogether a virtuosic performance, but Pellieux outdid himself one day later, on February 17, after Picquart had explained at length how Esterhazy could easily have obtained documents listed in the bordereau. Because Labori had broken the "pact of silence" about Dreyfus's court-martial, Pellieux now took the witness stand again and declared:

> I will repeat the very characteristic words of Colonel Henry. You want the truth? Well, here it is!
> [In November 1896] there occurred an event that I would like to bring to your attention. We had at the ministry of war—and note that I am not speaking of the Dreyfus Affair—absolute proof of Dreyfus's guilt! And that proof I saw. At that time the ministry received a paper whose origin cannot be contested and which says—I will tell you what it contains: "There is going to be an interpellation concerning the Dreyfus Affair. Never disclose the relations we had with the Jew." . . . That is what I have been anxious to say!

No sooner had Labori requested that Pellieux produce this document than Gonse, who knew it to be Henry's crude forgery, intervened, claiming that national security or *raison d'état* superseded rules of evidence. In a final bit of theater, Pellieux then ordered an aide-de-camp to fetch General de Boisdeffre. Was not Raoul Le Mouton de Boisdeffre's word better than any document? Was it not as good as gospel? So he implied, without contradiction from the presiding magistrate. And on February 18 Boisdeffre played his part impeccably.[11] "I will be brief," he testified. "I confirm on all points General Pellieux's deposition as being exact and authentic. I have not a single word more to say; I don't have the right to; I repeat, gentlemen, I don't have the right to." Answerable to a higher authority than assizes court, this custodian of sacred intelligence warned the nation against itself. "You are the jury, you are the nation. If the nation does not have confidence in the leaders of its army, in those who bear the responsibility for national defense, they are ready to surrender that onerous task to others. You have only to speak. I will not say a single word more."

The verdict could have been returned then and there. Three days later, Zola made his own direct plea to the jury, in a tremulous voice often drowned out by hoots and insults.[12] "Dreyfus is innocent, I swear it," he exclaimed.

I pledge my life that that is so, I pledge my honor. At this solemn hour, before this tribunal, which represents human justice, before you, gentlemen of the jury, who emanate from the nation, before all of France, before the entire world, I swear that Dreyfus is innocent. And by my forty years of work, by such authority as this labor may have given me, I swear that Dreyfus is innocent. And by all that I have conquered, by the name I have made for myself, by my works, which have advanced the cause of French letters abroad, I swear that Dreyfus is innocent. May it all crumble, may my works perish if Dreyfus is not innocent! He *is* innocent.

But neither this prepared speech nor Labori's exhaustive summary succeeded in working the jurors free from Boisdeffre's appeal. On February 23 it took them only thirty-five minutes to find Zola guilty and to recommend the maximum punishment of one year in prison.

For Zola it had been a fortnight even more obstreperous and dis-

---

[11]In *Jean Santeuil*, Proust describes him as follows: "He seemed quite calm, quite slow, although clearly rather preoccupied. . . . As he passed, hats were removed and he saluted with great politeness . . . blinking at times, stretching out his stiff leg, stopping, drawing out his mustache, passing his hand over his reddened cheek as if he were an old warhorse he had tired out."

[12]"M. Zola speaks, or, rather, reads, in a toneless, jerky voice, raising his conceited head after each sentence," noted an anti-Dreyfusard journalist. The prepared text would have mitigated Zola's stage fright, but just as important in this regard was the fact that he had always found courage, or presence, in combative situations, fighting for some victim of unjust authority. It seems quite possible that he faced a hostile audience with less trepidation than a sympathetic one.

heartening outside the courtroom than in. Shouts of "Down with Zola!" "Death to the Jews!" "Death to the traitors!" "Drown the kikes!" echoed through streets near the Palais de Justice, where mobs gathered every morning and late afternoon. On February 8, after the second session, policemen found themselves overwhelmed by five or six hundred hostile demonstrators, many armed with leaded canes, when Zola, Labori, and Clemenceau emerged at 5 p.m. Fists lashed out as these three ran the frightening gantlet across the Boulevard du Palais to Zola's coach on the rue de Lutèce, and some pursued them south toward the bridge, shouting obscenities.

Thenceforth, security improved. Zola's arrivals and departures took place through a side door on the quai des Orfèvres. His itinerary between home and court was revised from day to day lest anti-Semitic thugs—the same, no doubt, who smashed the windows of Jewish-owned shops—set upon him en route.[13] And police guarded him during lunch. "Every morning, very early, Desmoulin and I [who acted as bodyguards] told the police . . . where we planned to have lunch," wrote Alfred Bruneau. "Two carriages would wait in front of the restaurant: one for Zola and us, the other for detectives instructed to keep the crowd at bay near the Palais de Justice and thwart any aggressive maneuvers."

Nonetheless, danger was palpable, with death threats coming in the mail and hooligans on the rue de Bruxelles yelling "Down with Zola!" after dark. It made itself felt more than ever when the guilty verdict was announced. People went berserk. Their jubilation reverberated through the Palais de Justice, where military officers (who looked like "cannibals" to Zola) embraced one another and upper-class ladies had themselves hoisted onto banquettes. The same ugly slogans heard over and over since February 7 were chanted ferociously. One witness, a writer named Séverine, recalled feeling that if, by some miracle, the jury acquitted Zola, "this handful of maniacs" would hurl themselves at the accused. "I told companions, and we closed ranks," she wrote.

---

[13]Anti-Semitic violence was by no means limited to Paris. *J'accuse* provoked demonstrations all over France. "On January 17 in Nantes, three thousand youths paraded through the streets shouting cries of death. Windows of Jewish storefronts were shattered, and an attempt was made to force open the synagogue door. That evening in Nancy, Jewish-owned shops were invaded and the synagogue besieged. At Rennes, a mixed crowd of two thousand peasants and city dwellers attacked the homes of the Jewish professor Victor Basch, and of Professor Andrade, who had sent a letter, which had been published, to General Mercier. In Bordeaux, violent demonstrations erupted to cries of 'Death to the Jews!' 'Death to Zola!' . . . The police were barely able to prevent the destruction of Jewish shops." Similar scenes, often accompanied by burnings in effigy of Zola and Dreyfus, occurred in Poitiers, Tours, Toulouse, Montpellier, Saint-Malo. Nowhere, however, did anti-Semitism explode more violently than in Algiers. There 158 Jewish-owned shops were pillaged and several owners killed.

"Labori's exquisite wife, very young and pretty, had brought her two little boys along, saying, with a brave little smile: 'This way, we'll all be together.' Madame Zola, friends, relatives, allies formed a compact group in the middle of the courtroom." Clemenceau agreed that the guilty verdict may have saved them from grievous injury, even that "not one of us would have come out alive had Zola been acquitted."

Again, letters, telegrams, newspaper articles, bouquets, and gifts flooded 21 bis, rue de Bruxelles. All over Europe people wanted to ally themselves with the intellectual hero. A message from Switzerland, for example, declared that citizens of Saint-Gall would honor Zola by proceeding up the mountains round about and lighting candles in his name. *The Times* of London stated that "Zola's true crime has been in daring to rise to defend the truth and civil liberty. . . . For that courageous defense of the primordial rights of the citizen, he will be honored wherever men have souls that are free." Closer to home, poets, novelists, and painters—mostly of the unconsecrated kind—expressed their admiration, among them Monet, Proust, Pissarro, Henri Barbusse, and the ever faithful Mallarmé. "Awed by the sublimity [of your deed], I didn't think I could distract you with applause, or break a silence that grows more and more poignant," wrote Mallarmé. "The spectacle has just been enacted, once for all time, of a genius's limpid intuition pitted against the powers that be. I venerate this courage and admire a man who, after a lifetime of glorious labor, . . . still appears fresh, whole, and so heroic!"

But the Affair also widened rifts. On February 18, *L'Evénement* published an open letter in which Henry Céard attributed Zola's deed to his endearing gullibility and conjectured that skillful manipulators had laid a trap for him. One week later *Le Gaulois* published another "loyal" remonstrance. "M. Zola having been convicted, as well he should have been, for attacks against the nation," wrote Céard, "we still don't know by what fatal flaw of temperament he was led to commit those excesses that the assizes court rightly punished. . . . M. Zola treats nothing with indifference. For him passion is an almost divine faculty. . . . We can't imagine how this softhearted man, whom we knew to be so affectionate, could have written sentences capable of provoking catastrophe and of stirring up wretched humanity, all to evil effect."[14] Such articles hit the mark. Indeed, Zola would later confess

[14]As vindictive as his open letter to Zola was a private letter, written several months later, to Alexandrine, offering her sympathy, or moral support, for the ordeal provoked by *J'accuse*. Only her answer survives: "Arriving in the midst of this tempest, your letter astounds me. . . . You say that whenever you open a newspaper you think about my daily bitterness. Then how come you didn't bear in mind the pain I had to feel on reading your articles. Thank you for your kind impulse, my poor Céard. You who care so much for my tears have often made me shed them."

that nothing had pained him more than the desertion of certain writers. Among the surviving contributors to *Les Soirées de Médan*, only Alexis kept faith with him. While Huysmans (who was even more flamboyantly anti-Semitic than Edmond de Goncourt) entered the Benedictine order as an oblate, Céard joined the ultranationalist Ligue de la Patrie française.

During the trial Zola maintained as best he could the habits of ordinary civilized life, ignoring the jungle sounds outside his window, and after the verdict, which Labori immediately appealed, he continued to put on a brave face. Close friends convened on Thursday evenings, in the usual way. Servants presented themselves every morning for their usual *ordre du jour*. Denise, Jacques, and Jeanne were visited whenever possible, and Zola gave his children little watches on which February 23, 1898, the date of his conviction, had been engraved.[15] Some attempt was made to answer letters, to acknowledge the receipt of books, to accommodate people who wanted his photograph, to calm a little dog unnerved by its master's change of schedule.[16] But in correspondence, anxiety occasionally crept out from behind the mask. "Why assume that incarceration at Sainte-Pélagie awaits me when the Court of Appeals has not yet spoken?" he chided. "The impossible may happen, and it would be ridiculous to have embraced me on the threshold of a prison I'm not entering." To Georges Charpentier he wrote at the beginning of March:

> Nothing new here, things continue and will eventually become somewhat more peaceful, unless a new catastrophe befalls us. I believe that I'll enter Sainte-Pélagie in early April, and that will be for the best as I can't get back to work here at home amidst this mayhem. Furthermore, I must do prison time so that the abomination will be complete. I am otherwise well and quite calm. My wife is a bit weary, but valiant.

Not only would prison allow him to write another novel: it would itself be an appropriate last chapter, a well-conceived denouement. This,

[15]Denise later recalled the long conversations Zola had with Paul Alexis at the flat on the rue du Havre, the offensive songs sung on the street by young anti-Dreyfusards, and her mother's anxiety. "My mother feared for his life. One day she seemed more anxious than usual, I'm not sure why, and as soon as my father had left, at around 6:30, she had us quickly put on our hats, go downstairs with her, and follow him from afar through the crowd which filled the Place du Havre, the rue d'Amsterdam, the rue d'Athènes, and the rue de Clichy. She didn't breathe freely until the door of Zola's building had closed behind him."
[16]That little dog died during Zola's exile in England, leaving him absolutely grief-stricken.

and the knowledge that his ordeal had mobilized numbers of previously uninvolved intellectuals even as it made the Affair a national issue, helped him muddle through. He must also have taken comfort in an article by Léon Blum listing the advantages gained for Dreyfus during the trial. Blum later asserted that Zola's trial had been decisive.

On April 2, the Court of Appeals, following a session in which the eighty-year-old public prosecutor, Manau, denounced anti-Semitism and proclaimed that revisionists were "the honor of the country" rather than "traitors" or "sellouts," quashed Zola's conviction on technical grounds.[17] But rejoicing was brief. Despite advice to the contrary from Prime Minister Méline, the military judges who had found Esterhazy innocent filed a slander suit against Zola based upon one sentence in J'accuse: "A court-martial has just dared to acquit Esterhazy by order, a supreme offense to all truth and all justice . . ." Eschewing Paris as the venue of this second trial, the government chose Versailles, which swarmed with military personnel all year round. Further, it scheduled hearings for May 23—that is, after legislative elections. "Since nothing surprises me anymore," Zola wrote to Alfred Bruneau on April 10 (hours before being pelted with stones by a group of nine soldiers near Médan), "the new lawsuit has left us rather calm and we shall quietly remain here [in Médan] until the 18th. I'm glad . . . that the trial date is in late May. We'll be able to breathe a little, barring the unforeseen." A day earlier, he had pictured the situation in darker hues to the famous Norwegian novelist Björnstjerne Björnson: "Your letter is admirable—it expresses magisterially what has tormented me for weeks, and it reaches me at a tragic moment, the day after new charges have been pressed against me, the day after the frightful battle against truth and justice has recommenced."

Nationalist zealots who spent the next six weeks sharpening their knives for a bloody showdown experienced bitter disappointment. Many gathered at the Versailles train station early on May 23 but never saw Zola, the Clemenceau brothers, or Labori. To everybody's utter amazement, these gentlemen (along with Alfred Bruneau) entered town in an automobile driven from Saint-Cloud by the art dealers Gaston and Josse Bernheim.[18] Then came another unpleasant surprise. No sooner had order been called than Labori questioned the competence of the Seine-et-Oise court to deliberate on misdemeanors that had

[17] The complaint that resulted in his trial had been lodged by the minister of war instead of the judges at Esterhazy's court-martial.
[18] To avoid reporters, Zola had spent the night at a house in Saint-Cloud, where the others joined him for breakfast. "At the entrance to the sumptuous villa, Zola and Desmoulin smiled at us," wrote Bruneau. "The establishment belonged to a woman friend of Desmoulin and she had discreetly left the previous day, though not before decking it with flowers from top to bottom. Charpentier and Fasquelle soon joined us and we had a prodigiously cheerful breakfast."

taken place outside its jurisdiction. The presiding magistrate, Périvier, who had made no effort to conceal his bias against Zola, rejected this point out of hand, whereupon Labori filed an appeal. Périvier was compelled to suspend proceedings, which he did with the irate observation that "nothing is above the law, nothing, nothing, not even M. Zola," and after only one and a quarter hours, Zola departed Versailles the way he had come. "We were mindful of the peril that attended our departure," Bruneau recalled. "Versailles's police commissioner had whispered to us mysteriously, 'Fear not, I am your man,' but we could hear the hostile roar of the crowd massed outside. We climbed back into the automobile, which the Bernheims drove full speed ahead as soon as the main gate swung open, and we cut through tight groups of demonstrators, executing a prodigious turn. Pelted with stones, chased by a screaming mob, we finally reached the outskirts of town and the route home."

About his lawyers' strategy, Zola himself had mixed feelings. He told a reporter from Le Temps that the suburban venue could not be justified, that so important a debate deserved Paris. But eluding the consequences of J'accuse also made him feel pusillanimous, and this feeling had haunted him since February 23. Were others not paying more dearly than he? On February 26 the minister of war had discharged Picquart for having committed "grave misdeeds while in service" and had annulled his pension. A scientist who had testified as an expert witness for the defense lost his chair at the Ecole Polytechnique soon afterward. On March 22 the Paris bar had accused Louis Leblois, Picquart's lawyer, of "betraying to Scheurer-Kestner the confidence of his client" and suspended him for six months. In the legislative elections of May, two men who had vigorously supported Dreyfus, Joseph Reinach and Jean Jaurès, found themselves deserted by their constituents. Why then shouldn't Zola endure incarceration? That he had never gone to prison detracted from his heroism, he thought. Would he not, furthermore, have gotten more work done behind locked doors, under state supervision? "I would have bicycled every morning for an hour in the prison courtyard," he lamented to Reinach, "and I would have written the rest of the time."

The abuse Zola dodged at Versailles awaited him at home. On reaching the rue de Bruxelles he found a copy of the mass-circulation Petit Journal, with half its front page given over to an article entitled "Zola Father and Son" by the editor-in-chief, Ernest Judet. In this scurrilous parody, Judet, who worshipped the army, turned Zola's penchant for genetic explanations against Zola himself. It did not suffice to observe that Zola had always been "a fool, a peacock, a vice monger, a smut fancier," he wrote. The "phenomenon" would be incomprehensible if not for some "deeper cause, some sinister blemish, some unheard-of mystery, some hitherto undetected flaw, some corrupting shame that holds implacable sway over Zola's impure work and infamous life." The "deeper cause" was a crime committed by François Zola sixty-six years earlier in Algeria, and Judet elaborated upon it with help from Lieutenant Colonel Henry, who had not only exhumed François Zola's military record but had forged documents that gave greater dimension to the petty theft of 1832. "It stands to reason, it was inevitable that Zola should have immediately seen Dreyfus as the model officer in this army which he detests," Judet concluded. "He could not but make a beeline for treason, the way stercoraceous animals make straight for dung and wallow in rot. A captain in the pay of the Triple Alliance is the paragon he would have us obey."

A well-aimed blow could still floor Zola, and when François Zola, in whose exploits he had vested so much pride, was subjected to base calumny, he lost control. "I was there, I saw him cry," Clemenceau recalled. "No complaint left his lips. I remember the only words he uttered. He said: 'I shall continue.'" Five days later a rejoinder appeared in L'Aurore. "How could Louis Philippe have authorized the construction of the canal if its architect were a dishonored soldier?" Zola asked indignantly, after describing at some length his father's distinguished career. "How could my father have made illustrious friendships? How is it that voices joined in a concert of gratitude and admiration?" Ambushed without historical particulars at his command, he was unable to answer blow for blow:

> The alleged misdemeanor, which is news to me, dates back sixty-six years. I repeat what I've already said: there's no way of verifying it and, above all, no way of discussing it. So here I am at the mercy of this outrage, unable to defend myself except with a recitation of all that I know to be good and great about my father—the fact that all of Provence knew and loved him, the fact that a canal bears his name, and a boulevard as well, and the hearts of people old enough to remember.

But even if the insult were true, what had become of France, he asked, that Frenchmen could "foul the memory" of a man who distinguished himself "by his work and intelligence," simply in order to smite his son for political reasons?

> Our great country has descended to such ignominious depths. . . . Our soul is so profoundly poisoned, so shamefully crushed by fear, that even decent people no longer dare to express their revulsion. It is of this vile disease that we shall soon die unless those who govern us, those who know, finally take pity on us and restore truth and

justice to the nation. . . . As for me, my quarrel is my own responsibility, and my resources will suffice to pursue it. Since I have a pen,
since forty years of work have given me the power to address the
world and be heard by it, since the future is mine, rest easy in your
tomb, Father. . . . Your son stands vigil.

Life had, by strange indirections, come full circle for Zola. In adolescence there had been the long, futile attempt to retrieve his father's
material estate from swindlers, and now it behooved him to retrieve
his father's name from political ghouls. On May 28, Zola served Judet
a writ charging defamation of character, whereupon Judet, confident
that Henry and Gonse would supply him with abundant evidence,
engaged in further defamation. "Backed up against the wall," he
wrote, "Zola maintains that a crime whose author bears the name Zola
warrants automatic absolution; he imagines that by making his father
a fictional character, he can construct him anew, with a reputation
and a conscience. But even a six-hundred-page novel can't cure certain
wounds. Once again, the swollen-headed littérateur has vainly endeav-
ored to persuade himself that his pen confers brevets of virtue."[19]
At this juncture in the Dreyfus Affair, xenophobia still held the
upper hand, and when, on July 7, the new minister of war, Godefroy
Cavaignac, who had been shown Henry's forged letters, quoted them
in a speech denouncing Dreyfus—a speech loudly applauded by the
Chamber, then posted in France's thirty-six thousand town halls—
anti-Dreyfusards may never have felt more confident.[20] But two days
later the edifice of lies constructed since 1894 developed another serious crack. On July 9, Paul Bertulus, a magistrate investigating Picquart's charge that the "Speranza" and "Blanche" telegrams were
fraudulent, received dramatic testimony after months of largely futile
research. It came from Esterhazy's young cousin Christian, who had
often borne secret messages between Esterhazy and du Paty de Clam.
Upon discovering that the major had robbed him blind, Christian had
sought out Fernand Labori and given him not only his remarkable
story but documents to prove it. Labori notified Bertulus through an
intermediary, and on July 12 Walsin-Esterhazy was incarcerated at La
Santé. This turn of events infuriated Cavaignac, who avenged himself
by having Picquart locked up—also at La Santé—on a charge of criminal indiscretion.[21] At the general staff shock waves were felt. Boisdeffre and Gonse fell ill. Henry, his nerves frayed, sank into despair. "Save

[19]The legal wrangle continued for several years, and ended with a victory for Zola.
[20]After the elections of May 1898, Henri Brisson replaced the more conservative
Jules Méline as prime minister and appointed Cavaignac his minister of war.
[21]Three general staff officers alleged that he had shown classified material to his
lawyer, Leblois.

us; save us . . . you must save the army's honor!" he begged Bertulus during a tearful interview that took place on July 18.

What also took place on that very hot July 18 was Zola's second trial in assizes court at Versailles. It lasted somewhat longer than the first, although Zola, who spruced himself up for it and looked upon the agitated scene with a tranquil, even indifferent air, knew that it would not last two afternoons. As soon as proceedings began, Labori argued that members of a court-martial could not sue his client since they enjoyed no "civil personality." Judge Périvier gruffly ruled against him, whereupon Labori stated that he could represent Zola properly only if debate were allowed to extend beyond the one sentence cited in the writ. Once more Périvier ruled against him, which prompted the attorney general to accuse Zola of seeking refuge in "the brambles of legal procedure." Labori then lodged an appeal, and when Périvier declared that the trial would continue nonetheless, Labori walked out, with Zola in tow. As Dreyfusards battled anti-Dreyfusards outside, Zola—who heard shouts of "Back to Venice!" "Go back to the Jews!" "Coward!"—was escorted through the crowd by dragoons.

This exit had been planned well in advance, but, strange to say, the next move was apparently decided upon only during the coach ride home. Labori, arguing that the government wanted to stifle Zola's voice by casting him into prison, urged him to flee France rather than accept a default judgment in person. If the judgment were accepted, he explained, it became definitive; if not, Zola would retain the right to demand a new trial at his own convenience and thus keep the whole Dreyfus Affair open for whatever light the future might shed. Did Labori calculate that the element of surprise would strengthen his plea? that given time for reflection, Zola would sooner have avoided the appearance of cowardice than yielded to a legal strategy? or that other respected voices might, if asked, condemn flight as detrimental to the cause? Whether designed or improvised, his argument prevailed. At the Charpentiers' residence, where Labori and the Clemenceaus held a council of war, all agreed that Zola should leave for London that same evening, before border police had been alerted. Fernand Desmoulin immediately fetched Alexandrine, who, not daring to pack a valise with the rue de Bruxelles under constant surveillance, brought only a nightshirt folded inside a newspaper. Several days later, Zola, still bewildered, wrote in his diary:

This was the sum total of luggage we took, she and I, in a hackney cab, to the Gare du Nord. The suddenness of the event bowled us over. I had grasped her hand, my heart went out to her, we exchanged only a few choked words. Charpentier, who was following us in another carriage, bought my ticket. Both accompanied me to the train and stayed a quarter hour, disguising the interior of the compartment until departure time. . . . What an abrupt separation! My dear wife, her eyes clouded, her trembling hands joined, watched me leave.

He had not had time to bid Jeanne farewell. The following day Desmoulin visited her at Verneuil, where she seldom strayed beyond her walled garden for fear of being hounded by journalists, and gave her a note. "Dear wife," Zola had written in great haste. "Events compel me to leave this evening for England. Don't worry, quietly await news from me. As soon as I've made a decision, I'll notify you. I shall try to find quarters where you and the children can join me."

Alone in his compartment, Zola felt overwhelmed by the fear, sorrow, and rage he had kept at bay all day long. The train reached Amiens before he calmed down enough to realize that he hadn't eaten since breakfast. Amiens was followed by Abbeville, then Boulogne, and finally Calais, where he boarded a Channel steamer. "It was done, I was no longer in France," he later wrote. "My watch read 1:30 a.m. With no moon overhead, deep darkness enveloped us. The boat had some thirty passengers, all English. And I remained on the deck, watching Calais's lights disappear. I confess that tears welled up and that my poor being had never yet experienced such distress. Of course, I didn't think I was leaving this land forever, I knew that I would return in several months, that procedural tactics had dictated the separation, but still and all, what an abominable thing." Daybreak found him on deck again, within sight of Dover and about to enter incognito the country that had hailed him so grandly not long before. "I don't know a word of English, I had fallen into a remote world, as if cut off from men," he continued.

> I who detest travel, who am sedentary to an almost maniacal degree, who feel at ease only in my old habits, I lack the faculty for enjoying myself abroad, I feel horribly disoriented and am prey to the malaise induced by all this newness. . . . Worst of all are the first hours I spend in a foreign land. I rebel at not grasping what people say and feel terribly distressed. Some compatriots, to insult me, have called me "the foreigner." Good Lord, . . . how little they know me.

The situation was, of course, altogether different from that of 1870, when, with Prussian troops swiftly advancing upon Paris, he and Alexandrine had fled south. Even so, this second flight surely reawakened feelings he had had twenty-seven years earlier. His description of it as a sympathetic martyrdom rather than as a mere flight, as a self-punitive gesture inspired by Dreyfus himself, seems intended to leave no doubt

that the expatriation was spontaneous, even reckless, rather than calculated. "Zola told me long afterward that he thought he heard Dreyfus on his rock asking him to make this supreme sacrifice," recalled
Joseph Reinach. "He finally acquiesced because it occurred to him that
whichever cost him the most pain, exile or prison, was where duty lay,
he said. 'I disappeared and on that day felt that all the blood had
drained out of me.'"

But doing what "cost the most pain" may also have been Zola's way
of settling moral accounts with himself. Did he hope to atone by his
political heroism for the pain he had inflicted, by his double life, upon
those whom he loved most? Did he see exile as a quasi-religious withdrawal, for which the reward would be, if not a fresh start, a renewed
sense of virtue?

At 5:40 a.m. passengers flitted through Victoria Station like errant
ghosts. Clemenceau had recommended the Grosvenor Hotel without
indicating that it adjoined the terminus, so Zola hired a perplexed
cabbie to drive him the hundred yards down Buckingham Palace Road.
There he registered under the name "M. Pascal" and was given a
dreary sixth-floor room which looked out on the back of an ornamental
cornice. Though it put him in mind of "cellar vents, portholes, garret
transoms," he felt relieved by the profound quiet. "Except for a few
close, loyal friends . . . no one knew my whereabouts. It was a far cry
from Paris and five months of being recognized and insulted at every
turn." After lunch he purchased clean linen, making his needs understood in pantomime, and then, with the rosette of the Legion of Honor
prominently displayed as if his pride clung to this one last token of
eminence, wandered around Belgravia. That night Ernest Vizetelly,
who was to be his principal cicerone during the next eleven months,
received a note summoning him for an 11 a.m. rendezvous. "You will
page M. Pascal. And above all, absolute silence. The most serious interests are at stake."

When Vizetelly arrived the next day, July 20, he found Zola with
Bernard Lazare, who would return to France immediately (after having
Zola sign certain legal documents), and Fernand Desmoulin, who
would keep Zola company for several more days. The urgent question,
as he soon learned, was whether French justice reached beyond France
for nonextraditable crimes. Vizetelly promptly consulted a solicitor
named F. W. Wareham, who did not think that notice of the verdict
could be served on Zola via diplomatic channels or by an English bail-
iff. But might notice be served in other ways? Labori counseled extreme wariness. "I believe that you must, at all costs, eschew legal
writ," he warned on July 20 or 21. "You must not sign for registered

mail. You must refuse delivery of all printed paper, parcels, documents. You should conceal yourself. I believe that silence is now in order." This missive charted Zola's course. He resolved to achieve total obscurity and, heeding the advice of his English friends, left London, which did not favor the clandestine life. "He was . . . so conspicuous, so characteristic a figure that, looking backward and remembering how repeatedly the illustrated papers had portrayed him and how many photographs of him were to be seen in shop windows," wrote Vizetelly, "I often wonder how it happened that he was not recognized a hundred times during those few days spent in London."

Thus began Zola's suburban peregrinations. At Wimbledon, where Wareham put him up overnight, he took a fancy to the Broadway with its greengrocers, drapers, carriage builders, and hairdressers. It seemed far more stylish than any French town of comparable size. For several reasons, however—among them the fact that Wimbledon abounded in newspapermen and literati—there could be no question of settling there. A private house screened from observation was needed, and the search led twenty miles southwest to Weybridge. Guided by Vizetelly, who presented them as French artists enamored of Surrey's interminable holly hedges and stately elms, Zola and Desmoulin found accommodations at Oaklands Park Hotel. This pile, which incorporated vestiges of a ducal mansion, would serve as a base for surveying local real estate. Meanwhile the park round about it would provide an object lesson in patrician dottiness: situated near the cemetery containing several dozen of the late Duchess of York's beloved dogs and monkeys was an artificial grotto designed by the Duke of Newcastle, where in shell-encrusted passages classical statuary mingled with stuffed alligators.

The limp-wristed reception given him at Oatlands Park Hotel convinced Zola not to temporize. After a day of house hunting he fixed upon a villa in Walton called Penn, which was available for one month, beginning August 1. On July 27, the fugitive, who now passed himself off as Jacques Beauchamp, signed a lease, and five days later he packed his newly acquired Gladstone bag. "My wife hastily procured servants for the new establishment," Vizetelly recalled.

These servants, however, did not speak French, and I settled with M. Zola that my eldest daughter, Violette, should stay with him to act in some measure as his housekeeper and interpreter. . . . As she was then at home for the summer holidays she was sent down to M. Zola's without more ado. . . . A Parisienne by birth and speaking French from her infancy, it was easy for her to understand and explain the master's requirements.

Violette followed Zola when on August 27 he moved to a larger furnished villa called Summerfield in Addlestone, several miles upriver
from Walton. Surrounded by a large tousled garden ideal for the games
Jacques and Denise played during their sojourn there, it would be
home to Zola until mid-October.

Zola's emotions shifted as rapidly as his person. Forlorn and buoy-
ant, self-absorbed and alert to every detail of English life, humbled by
the language he couldn't speak and grateful for its protection, he felt
terribly homesick but wanted nonetheless to distance himself from
civil war, from all strife. The journal he kept is that of a man sated
with news of the Dreyfus Affair. "A very tranquil day," he noted on
July 25 in his *Pages d'exil.* "The silence cure. Being alone has an infinitely calming effect on me. . . . [I] spent the afternoon in the park
reading *La Chartreuse de Parme.* I knew I couldn't receive any news
and that was balm to my soul. I couldn't talk to anyone." Three days
later, not having been informed yet that the Council of the Order of
the Legion of Honor had suspended him, he wrote again about the
pleasures of oblivion.

> A day of great calm. No one came. Still no newspapers. I don't know
> what's going on and am delighted by this. . . . I remained in my room,
> I took short walks in the park. During the afternoon I was caught in
> a torrential downpour, sought shelter in a log cabin and spent a joyful
> hour there, in the most profound solitude, with *La Chartreuse de
> Parme.* It's an extraordinary book, which I feel I'm reading for the
> first time. . . . This morning a dispatch from Wareham informing me
> that he had received funds on which I've been counting pleased me,
> for I realize that being penniless and at the mercy of events contrib-
> uted greatly to my malaise.[22]

The impulse to cut himself off from news was above all bound up with
the need to resume work, after his polemical campaign, on a tetralogy
he entitled *Les Quatre Evangiles* (*The Four Gospels*), about which more
will be said anon. The orderly life of the novelist producing four or
five pages every day had always been a panacea for grief, and so it
would be now. As important as the funds deposited by Wareham were
the dossiers, stationery, and heavy ivory-handled pen brought over
from France by Desmoulin. "I unpacked my manuscripts, I organized

[22]Vizetelly calculated that in 1898 Zola earned only a third of what he had earned
the year before, or not nearly enough to cover the expenses of his various households and his exile. How broadly anti-Dreyfusard the reading public was may be
judged from the fact that *Rome* had sold 100,000 copies in 1896–97 but only 6,000
more between 1898 and 1902, the year of Zola's death.

my worktable in a small room with a garden view," he noted on August 2, at Penn.

These preparations were exhilarating. Then anguish returned and I wondered whether I would have the strength to write. The torrent that surged through a formerly calm, well-ordered existence has left me bewildered, with ideas scattered hither and yon. . . . Fortunately the outline is more or less complete.

Forty-eight hours later the new novel was five pages long and England felt less foreign. "Today, at 10 o'clock, I began *Fécondité*," he wrote on August 4.

I worked until 1 p.m., writing my regular quota. This accomplishment makes me very happy. . . . It's been eight months since I finished my last novel, *Paris*. Almost one year already that the monstrous Affair has taken its toll of my life and work. I don't regret anything, I shall resume my struggle on behalf of truth and justice. Still, what an extraordinary adventure for a methodical, sedentary sort like myself, in the last lap of an existence devoted to writing!

In that countryside, where rain kept everything lush, it was as if a great green curtain had been drawn over the outside world. *Fécondité* answered Zola's need for a sense of work in progress, of daily accumulation, and Penn restored him to something like the peace he enjoyed at Médan. After work he would eat lunch, nap, then entertain himself as best he could by reading or inspecting the vegetable garden or, when weather permitted, pedaling down Surrey's tree-shaded lanes, with an eye to female cyclists. The roads were a bit muddy, but wonderful nonetheless, he wrote on August 8, noting that they run absolutely level between parks planted with beautiful trees and enclosed by holly hedges so thick that even a scrawny cat couldn't squeeze through. "What struck me was the number of women. They certainly outnumber men. . . . And I must confess that I, who have scorned skirts, who have fought for the culotte and declared it alone to be appropriate and comfortable, I am shaken in my beliefs by the daily spectacle of hundreds of women gliding past my window. English women are elegant cyclists—they sit erect on the seat and their skirts fall in long folds." Hundreds of women gliding past his window no doubt evoked Jeanne Rozerot, to whom he reported this obliquely erotic observation.

No longer taken up with the minutiae of flight and resettlement, Zola was able to think more intently about having his two households visit him, each in turn, and to consider the diplomatic questions raised by this prospect. Common sense said that Jeanne should come first, during the children's summer vacation, but protocol favored Alexandrine (who had meanwhile endured much abuse from anti-Dreyfusards). It was her right to come first; it was therefore her prerogative to exercise that right or to surrender it. "Day after day I've discussed with dear Desmoulin what the best arrangement would be," he informed her early in August. "I've persuaded him to convey my doubts to you and my desire that you handle the situation exactly as you please. He will set forth all possible hypotheses. You will discuss them. But in the name of our old relationship, our thirty years together, I beg you to act as if the only issue were your happiness, as if I myself did not exist.... My well-being hinges on yours." Alexandrine did the generous thing, though not without asperity, answering Zola's letter as follows:

> I understand very well all of your internal debates. I prefer to believe that you will understand me, in turn. I feel just as impelled as you to do extravagant things—to make a long, circuitous journey losing my tracks, for example. But when I listen to my reason rather than my heart, I see our situation differently. Right now I believe that if I came and agreed to stay until your return, my presence would soon begin to pall on you. You would feel sad, perhaps remorseful, at being deprived of more cheerful and consoling affections.

Happiness, she continued, was irrelevant:

> You say that you would like to see me happy. Alas, my poor dear friend, you who know me better than anyone do not know me very well at all if you can still preserve the hope of seeing me happy, with all the sadness and bitterness I have had to absorb during the past ten years. I told you two years after [you took up with another woman] that it was all over for me, that the only thing left for me to do was to use my poor existence to help those I loved in whatever way I could. I endeavor to do just that, and I shall continue as long as I can.

With a heavy heart, Zola summoned Jeanne, instructing her through Desmoulin to leave Verneuil under false pretenses lest the servants, neither of whom could be trusted, sniff out her design.[23] She was to

---

[23]Zola wrote to Desmoulin on August 6: "I am going to have my children, but you wouldn't believe the anguish that thinking about my poor wife causes me. ... It's all very distressing, and my bed has become a bed of thorns on which I toss and turn all night long." Professor Colin Burns has suggested quite plausibly that the Dreyfus Affair may have, as noted above, given Zola the opportunity to absolve himself of guilt—to make amends in an act of great public courage for the moral shortcomings of his private life. But guilt, a faithful companion, followed him into exile.

pack warm clothes, his cycling outfit, piano music (Denise had been taking lessons), and food for the entire voyage. She was to sit between decks if the ship rolled through heavy seas and to remain in the cabin if the children got sick. She was urged, finally, to bring no camera, as he had acquired one, and, above all, to leave behind her culottes. "I believe that luggage is not inspected by customs before London," he concluded. "Have the keys ready. At Dover the train is near the boat. So as not to go astray, show an employee your tickets, repeat the word 'Victoria,' and go where he directs you. Then, stay aboard until the last stop, London."

Jeanne and the children disembarked at Victoria Station on August 11 and were met by Ernest Vizetelly, who transported them to Penn. What happened then cannot be learned from *Pages d'exil*, where, for Alexandrine's sake, Zola made no mention of his extramarital family, implying always that his only pleasures were literary ones.[24] But correspondence with friends, in which he disguised Jeanne as "Jean," offers a more sentimental picture. "Jean arrived with the children yesterday evening," he told Desmoulin. "They were put to bed, slept soundly, and here they are this morning as gay as larks. They will be a great comfort to me in my solitude." And his daughter Denise, who had been told on leaving Verneuil that their destination was Russia, would later, with great tact, sketch in the blank spaces ordained by conjugal piety. "I can still see Penn, and the door of the white house opening, and my father stretching his arms toward us while Violette Vizetelly stood there smiling," she wrote.

Zola had never enjoyed so much consecutive time with his children. Nor would he ever again. And although thoughts of Alexandrine alone at Médan suffering terrible indignities on his behalf threatened the pleasure of Jeanne's company, he absolved himself by sending her two long letters every week.[25] Life was, for the most part, serene. Mornings,

---

[24]On the day of Jeanne's arrival, Zola wrote in his diary: "I don't go out and I see no one, whence the emptiness of these notes. Mornings I rise at 8, I drink café au lait at 9 and work until 1. Then, after lunch, I try to kill the afternoon as best I can. In the evening I read, then retire at 9. The next day it begins again. No facts, no events. . . . This morning I began my second chapter. I achieve peace of mind, I live happily only when I'm at work."

[25]On July 23, Alexandrine wrote to Mme Bruneau:

I needn't tell you anything about the situation, I believe; you read the papers and they keep you informed. Moreover, I cannot be prodigal of explanations since I'm sure that my letters will be opened; I can assume it, given what's going on here and in Paris. Secret police agents stand in front of our door; there are some as well in the town house opposite us on the rue de Bruxelles. Reporters for the gutter press also snoop. I can't blow my nose or cough without news of it being published the next day. It is known at what time the domestics retire, at what time I do the same. Scurrilous things are written on the walls of

Jeanne read or knit and made it her business to shoo the children away from under their father's window. After lunch she accompanied him on bicycle rides around Walton and Addlestone, unless the heat, which was almost tropical that summer, immobilized them. When Zola's appetite for news returned, he often spent hours on a wicker chaise longue deciphering *The Standard* or *The Daily Telegraph* with the aid of a grammar, but in those linguistic exertions no one joined him. The family lived unto itself, virtually incommunicado. They celebrated Denise's and Jacques's birthdays. They marveled every day at the fiascoes of their native cook. They discovered one another in small talk. They remained vigilant. Only once did they dare venture forth as ordinary tourists, and then it took a visit from Georges Charpentier to winkle them out of the immediate neighborhood. "Charpentier's presence was an excuse for visiting Windsor in a rented landau," Denise recalled.

I have never seen deer in such number and of such elegance. I remember baskets full of marvelous flowers simulating the English crown in gardens at the foot of that impressive fortress. We all wanted to sit in the queen's armchair!

In the restaurant, we ate an extraordinary turtle soup. My father and his friend, being in a cheerful mood, teased my brother and me with fanciful details about the method of preparation.[26]

---

the property, I receive letters that threaten to blow up the house with me and the servants inside. Well, my dear, I'm stiff as a ramrod, you'd never guess I'm being assailed in this way. I go to Paris when summoned, and this Sunday, the local feast day, I shall offer the consecrated bread and, as I do every year, attend the awarding of prizes.

Another kind of humiliation was to occur in August when an appeals court, concurring that Zola had slandered the three graphologists who had brought suit against him, awarded them ten thousand francs each and ordered that Zola's furniture be auctioned to pay the fine. On October 10, Zola suffered Nana's fate. Like vultures, souvenir hunters gathered at 21 bis, rue de Bruxelles, but they were thwarted by Fasquelle, who, with money that Joseph Reinach had donated to the cause, bid thirty-two thousand francs for the first item offered, a Louis XIII table, thus cutting short the sale.

[26]Lest the press catch wind of the fact that Zola was living with his extraconjugal ménage and thus aid and abet anti-Dreyfusards, Alexandrine urged Zola to conceal himself. Her fears were not groundless. On April 19, 1898, a police spy submitted the following report to the prefect: "Since the Zola affair is back in the news, it may be worthwhile noting that the naturalist novelist is no better a husband than he is a patriot. It is rumored that he terrorizes his wife and kisses the chambermaid in her presence. . . . It is also rumored that he makes overtures to a niece that go beyond the familial. Finally, gossips claim that he has a mistress named Rozerot. She is thirty, lives at 3, rue du Havre, and pays an annual rent of 4,000 francs. She is a tall blonde, very elegant, living on the grand scale."

Otherwise, Zola never even visited Claremont House near Walton, where exactly half a century earlier King Louis Philippe had settled after fleeing France, or the Catholic chapel in Weybridge, where the monarch's remains were interred. Since a numerous body of anti-Semitic, anti-Dreyfusard monarchists led by Jules Guérin received financial support from the latest Orleanist pretender, Duke Philippe, he may have been little inclined to reflect at either place upon the transitoriness of glory.[27]

As August wore on, startling developments in the Dreyfus Affair raised Zola's hopes of being able to return to Paris before November. This new chapter began with a decision of the war minister, Cavaignac, to have documents in the so-called secret file closely examined. A man stubborn for good and ill, he determined that rumors about forgery, which were growing louder every day, should be disproved without further delay. Quite the opposite happened. On August 13, a staff officer assigned to the investigation, Captain Louis Cuignet, discovered under lamplight that the famous Panizzardi letter quoted by Cavaignac himself before the Chamber and posted in town halls all over France had been spliced together from two different kinds of ruled paper. Once informed of this, Cavaignac did not approach the general staff right away. What he did instead was appoint a board to question Major Esterhazy, for whom he had as little use as for Captain Dreyfus. Panic-stricken, Esterhazy turned against his former protectors and, after claiming that the Jewish syndicate would have given him 600,000 francs to declare himself the author of the bordereau, swore, with evidence in hand, that du Paty de Clam had dictated his every move. Du Paty de Clam hemmed and hawed, whereupon the investigatory board judged Esterhazy to have violated neither honor nor discipline. Cavaignac discharged him anyway and went after Hubert Henry, like a hunter crushing a slug underfoot while stalking his real prey.

On August 30, Cavaignac himself interrogated Henry in the presence of Generals de Boisdeffre and Gonse, who remained silent throughout. The minister gave the by now unhinged colonel no quarter. Henry's indignant denials became weak equivocations as Cavaignac challenged him relentlessly. Point by point the truth was wrung forth and when at length Cavaignac asked, "In 1896, you received an envelope with a letter inside, an insignificant letter; you suppressed the letter and fabricated another one?" Henry surrendered. Arrangements were immediately made to have him placed under fortress arrest

---

[27]Zola did visit Weybridge, however, and take photographs of the banks of the river Wey and of the Thames.

just outside Paris, at Mont-Valérien, where he spent the night in a room occupied seven months earlier by Georges Picquart. On August 31, he drank much rum, assured his wife in a farewell note that the forged letter "merely confirmed" information imparted to him orally, and having told one last lie, slit his throat with a razor.

Henry's imprisonment caused greater astonishment than any previous development in the Affair, but did it portend revision? Even conservative journals thought that Dreyfus would now leave Devil's Island, and Dreyfusards everywhere warmed to the prospect, not least of all Alexandrine Zola, who on August 30 wrote to Elina Laborde:

> Ah, my dear, how happy I was this morning to have remained here, with the news that you, too, must have read. Had I gone off [to Italy for the waters], I would have joyfully turned around in mid-journey. Yes, yes, I believe that the truth is advancing, at a snail's pace to be sure, but advancing nevertheless. What exasperates me is that I haven't been able to write this good news to the interested party, and I'm jealous of whoever will inform him. . . . [As for anti-Dreyfusards of my acquaintance], I've had my fill of them, to put it politely. Next winter they'll come around scraping and bowing, if things continue fair, which I'm sure they will. I'll thank them vigorously by having the servants boot them out the door. To some few I'll speak my piece. I've already done so to Céard and I've just done so to [Marius] Roux.[28]

Over in England, a cryptic telegram of four words, "Tell immediately Beauchamp victory," prepared Zola for the exposé, which came soon afterward via English journalists. As soon as *The Daily Telegraph* published it, Vizetelly triumphantly hurried off to Summerfield, and found Zola expecting him:

> As was natural, [he] was quite excited. First, the document which Henry confessed to having forged was the very one that General de Pellieux had imported into the Zola trial in Paris as convincing proof of Dreyfus's guilt. At that time already its effect had been very great; it had destroyed all chance of M. Zola's acquittal. Then, too, it had been solemnly brought forward in the Chamber of Deputies by War Minister Cavaignac, who had vouched for its authenticity. And now, as previously alleged by Colonel Picquart, it was shown to be a forgery of the clumsiest kind. Here at last was "a new fact" warranting the revision of the whole Dreyfus case.

[28]Roux had worked for years at *Le Petit Journal* and did not resign when the director, Ernest Judet, began a campaign of defamation against Zola's father.

Zola and Vizetelly would have been even more amazed, no doubt, had they known that another protagonist of major importance was just then preparing to exile himself. On September 1, when Henry's blood-soaked bed commanded universal attention, ex-Major Esterhazy boarded a train at Maubeuge, descended at the Belgian frontier, shaved his mustache, and sneaked out of France. After a brief residence in Brussels he crossed over to London and lived there under the alias of Count Jean de Voilemont.

But those who believed that a triumphant denouement lay at hand did not reckon seriously enough with anti-Dreyfusism. Reason was not what had sent Alfred Dreyfus to Devil's Island in 1895, and the ideological fortifications that kept him there proved stronger than the barrage of evidence arguing his innocence. Colonel Henry had no sooner been buried in unconsecrated ground than zealous nationalists made him a whited sepulchre. The counterfeit documents for which Cavaignac had imprisoned him were said to be "patriotic" forgeries, lies that told the truth. "Colonel, there is not a drop of your precious blood which does not run warm where the heart of the nation beats," Charles Maurras wrote in the royalist paper *La Gazette de France* on September 6.

> We were not able to give you the great funeral that your martyrdom deserved. We should have waved your bloody tunic and the sullied blades down the boulevards; marched the coffin, hoisted the mortuary banner like a black flag. . . . But the national sentiment will awaken to triumph and avenge you. From the country's soil . . . there will soon arise monuments to expiate our cowardice. . . . In life as in death, you marched forward. Your unhappy forgery will be counted among your best martial deeds.

Maurras was echoed by *La Libre Parole*, by *Le Petit Journal*, by *L'Eclair*, by *La Croix* (where, moreover, members of the Assumptionist religious order, which published that large-circulation daily, accused unnamed Jews of having murdered Henry). And among high military officials, this exculpatory parti pris found full expression in the argument that Henry acted as he did to thwart Picquart, that his "patriotic forgery" foiled a treasonous plot. On September 5, Cavaignac had resigned from the war ministry rather than accept Prime Minister Brisson's argument that revision was inevitable. Twelve days later his successor, General Emile Zurlinden, followed suit when Brisson refused to let him initiate legal proceedings against Picquart. A third war minister, General Charles Chanoine, then appointed Zurlinden military governor of Paris, and in that capacity the implacable Alsatian ordered Picquart court-martialed on charges of having forged the *petit bleu.* Just three weeks after Henry killed himself, guards escorted Picquart from La Santé, an ordinary prison, to the Cherche-Midi military compound.

Outfoxed, Brisson, a politician whose cautious disposition infuriated Clemenceau, at last took matters in hand. Since July his government had sat upon a plea for revision submitted by Lucie Dreyfus. Not until September 21 did a "revision commission" convene, and after two days of fruitless debate it adjourned without proposing any course of action. Brisson immediately resolved that the High Court of Appeals —the Cour de Cassation—should adjudicate the issue. In a vote held on September 26 his cabinet supported him 6-4, although shaken by the mass demonstrations raging outside and by the prospect of Dreyfus being "torn to pieces" (as one zealous chauvinist put it) if ever he returned from Devil's Island. "The same day, the minister of justice, constrained by the government, contacted the High Court of Appeals," writes Bredin. "[Initiating the revision process] was . . . a major step toward truth, and it brought about a decisive change in the composition of forces arrayed against each other, for the Affair no longer concerned only the executive and the military. These two would thereafter have to reckon with the judiciary."

Like Alexandrine, Zola had, since August, rolled through emotional highs and lows. The joy he felt on learning of Henry's imprisonment gave way to despair as the clear path toward revision became yet another obstacle course. Where scoundrels wore crowns of thorn, could reason ever prevail? The conviction settled upon him that France had had her day, and although Brisson's successful maneuver raised his spirits, he continued to expect some fatal ambush or unanswerable ploy. On October 4 he wrote to Alexandrine:

Never have I seen an autumn more clement or luminous. Living would be a delight were it not for this anguish which, despite everything, continues to stifle me. . . . For peace of mind, I should very much like to recover my lost faith. You will remember the equanimity with which, even during the darkest days of my trial, I predicted that truth would somehow triumph. I'm no longer so sure, for what we're witnessing has ruined my fundamental belief in the reason and decency of men. I can imagine nothing more frightful. When Picquart remains behind bars, when the idea that Dreyfus is innocent does not bring Paris to its feet, when France continues to collude in so many crimes—anything is possible. . . . Never has a country passed through such terrible straits, and I venture to say that even if Dreyfus goes free, we shall still be treated as sellouts and traitors. It surprises me that you should think I'm still in danger of being sought and found. First, they can't do anything against me. Second, their most earnest prayer, I assure you, is that I not reappear during the struggle over revision.

With every new turn of events, hiding out seemed less honorable. "The nervous, passionate man I am is not made for exile, for resignation and silence," he confided to Octave Mirbeau's wife. "You guessed right that being sheltered here, in too much peace and security, while the others fight, torments me." But worse than self-censorship was the realization that allies as well as foes wanted him out of the picture. A quiet, diligent, pragmatic strategy was Reinach's plan. "Zola must remain over there," he advised the like-minded Scheurer-Kestner on September 7. "His presence would rekindle bad feelings and possibly ruin everything. I shall tell him that he must wait because later . . . he will be received like Hugo the Second. . . . Showing people their best profile is how you win their consent."[29] Fernand Labori also counseled patience, it seems, for sometime after September 26, Zola wrote him a long letter in which exasperation simmers just beneath the surface. "If my friends judge my return to be impossible, let them at least explain their anxiety with reasons I can fathom. Surely they are not afraid of battle. Why then are they so squeamish where I'm concerned? I shall stay put only if they demonstrate that by returning I would compromise the cause." He never sent the letter.

Midway through October, when Jeanne, Denise, and Jacques went back to France, Zola concluded that he could not do without the bustle of city streets. Devoted as ever, Wareham and Vizetelly obliged by finding him accommodations at the residential Queen's Hotel in Upper Norwood, near Dulwich. There, some eight miles from central London, he registered as "M. Richard" even though he was no longer persuaded of the need for secrecy, and established himself in a flat that was to be home until the following spring.[30] "I can still see before me the sitting-room on the second floor . . . in which M. Zola spent so much of his time and wrote so many pages of *Fécondité* during the last six months or so of his exile," Vizetelly recalled. This spacious salon had three windows overlooking the street and abounded in tables.

On a folding card-table in one corner M. Zola's stock of letter and "copy" paper, his weighing scales for letters, his envelopes, pens, and

---

[29]In his history of the Affair, where he did an about-face, concluding that Zola's exile did not after all serve Dreyfus, Reinach asserted that Zola's stature would have increased if he had gone to prison. Knowing this to be the case and exiling himself all the same gave the measure of Zola's "moral nobility," he wrote.
[30]By the same token, Alexandrine signed her letters with her mother's name, Caroline Wadoux.

pencils were duly set out. Then in front of the central window was the table at which he worked every morning. It was of mahogany. . . . On a similar table at another of the windows he usually kept such books and reviews as reached him from France. In the center of the room . . . stood the table at which one lunched and dined. It was round and would just accommodate four persons. Finally, beside M. Zola's favourite arm-chair, near the fireplace, was a little gipsy table, on which he usually kept the day's newspapers, and perchance the volume he was reading at the time.

As always, mornings were reserved for work, but after lunch (served him in his quarters) he took to reconnoitering Upper Norwood until teatime. Built on high ground, the hotel stood quite near the Crystal Palace, which, with its huge barrel vaults, loomed over the brick row houses round about like a Romanesque greenhouse. Zola's walks led him around this glass behemoth or, the other way, past Beulah Spa toward Streatham Common.

How exile affected Zola is most intimately described by Alexandrine, who arrived at Upper Norwood late in October and remained until early December. Her letters from England, where she found little to praise, often speak of physical pain and emotional distress. "Loulou's English is more than adequate for reading local papers, which give us the morning news rather quickly. . . . Let me jog your memory about the subscriptions to Le Temps, La Petite République, Le Figaro," she wrote to Dr. Jules Larat on November 2, after the High Court of Appeals had agreed to consider Lucie Dreyfus's petition.

> My keenest desire is that my comrade calm down, but he's not likely to master his nerves under the present circumstances, and it's not certain he will do so ever. . . . I've been working on him for years, in vain, to consult you, but right now he says he will heed me because his stomach is under attack, with nervous seizures so acute that when he begins reading or writing, he must often stop; also, when the papers arrive and he tears open the sleeve that contains them, his whole being convulses.[31]

During the next few weeks, Zola responded to Alexandrine's ministrations, but English weather and English cuisine proved almost as daunting as the skulduggery of the French general staff. "For two whole days we haven't had any fog," she reported to Amélie on November 20.

[31]Larat was a specialist in electric-shock treatment and in 1890 had written a textbook entitled Précis d'électrothérapie.

The problem is, it's turned much colder, seven degrees C. today, so my companion caught cold and has again been suffering bouts of neuralgia in the mouth. Everything appears calmer today. No wonder, Sunday has come, and we don't go out on that day. Sunday is really charming here! People eat only stale bread. Fortunately we were served exquisite pâté at lunch; it's a cold dish, prepared in advance to avoid work [on the Sabbath]. I believe that if they could get away with it they wouldn't feed the guests at all. Whenever a meal arrives, the boss [Zola] feels nauseous. Boiled potatoes are the only thing they do well. . . . I think I'll be able to return as originally planned, without any hitches. The cure I sought to effect by coming over has worked, which gives me no little satisfaction. . . . Another trip over here seems likely.

Soon afterward the rains came, along with news that Picquart's court-martial had been scheduled for December 12. "Despite the sadness of the situation," wrote Alexandrine, "I would liken [the enemy] to someone who leans too far out the window and falls when the sill gives way. I'm convinced that in time the sill will give way and that the whole wretched lot of them will tumble, once and for all. It will be their last croak, and they themselves must sense that the day of reckoning lies at hand, or they would show more conciliatory manners. We're anxious, because Europe can't go on frothing over this situation without consequences."[32] The wind was blowing through their flat as through a deserted barracks, she complained. It froze them on one side while the fire cooked them on the other.

Alexandrine left England on December 3, only to return on December 23 for what proved to be a longer, more arduous sojourn. Cold winds blew down from the northeast, and four days after setting foot in Upper Norwood, she fell ill with bronchitis. Now it was Zola's turn to play nurse. "As for myself, my poor dear, start getting used to my absence, for you know that I can't have much life left, sick as I am," Alexandrine warned Amélie. "The least little cold may carry me off, and for some time I've felt so shaken that the great quietus would, I often think, come as a relief. I'm taking good care of myself anyway, lest death catch me up here; my bronchi are ravaged and the emphysema has gotten worse rather than better." Her health improved during the first weeks of January. With energy available for political passion, she fulminated against wafflers more or less anti-Dreyfusard

---

[32]Picquart's court-martial provoked a general outcry. Lists circulated, and such eminent figures as Anatole France, Jean Jaurès, and Georges Clemenceau spoke out against it. In the Chamber of Deputies, Alexandre Millerand, another Socialist who had embraced Dreyfusism late in the day, argued eloquently but to no avail that parliament should halt the court-martial proceedings.

who had founded a Ligue de la Patrie Française to rally conservative intellectuals. But another bout of bronchitis kept her hotel-bound until her departure in late February. "I hope with all my heart," she wrote to Elina Laborde on February 16, "that I'm well enough to be able to leave on the scheduled date." Her fervent desire to escape from the Queen's Hotel was fraught with guilt, especially as the prospect of Zola following her home before Easter had been made more remote by new setbacks in the fight for revision. "Over here," she continued,

amazement is general, and the papers fire terrifying volleys of insults at poor, martyred France. How can one answer them? Only by saying that we deserve the wounds inflicted upon us. . . . If matters don't improve, expatriation will become unavoidable. . . . A Guérin, the scum of society, his acolytes, recidivists every last one, a Quesnay de Beaurepaire, the slanderer using false papers—these swine don't worry at all.[33] How can one live in such a country? We're absolutely sunk in discouragement, not a spark of hope. It's so bad that despite my desire to quit this gruesome place, I'm distressed at leaving my poor husband alone. He will beat his head against the wall with remorse over the foolish decision that compelled him to exile himself.

On February 27, she left England all the same.[34]

Alexandrine regained French soil during the aftermath of yet another violent confrontation between Dreyfusards and anti-Dreyfusards. On February 16, President Faure had died of a stroke after entertaining his young mistress in the Elysée Palace. This bolt from the blue augured well for revisionists, who straightway nominated one of their own to be Faure's successor—Emile Loubet, president of the Senate. Elected on February 18 by the bicameral legislature meeting in plenary session at Versailles, Loubet boarded a train for Paris, where crowds shouting *L'élu de la synagogue!* ("The synagogue's candidate!") and *Victoire de la trahison juive!* ("Victory of Jewish treason!") filled the Gare Saint-Lazare. The Ligue Antisémite had recruited a great many demonstrators from among the capital's vagrant population, and these ran riot through the streets as Loubet proceeded to the Elysée, then to the ministry of foreign affairs. "All along his route, he was pursued by the whistles, hoots, vociferations of the patriotic and anti-Semitic leagues," Maurice Paléologue observed. "When at last the cor-

[33]Jules Guérin was the founder and leader of the Ligue Antisémite. Quesnay de Beaurepaire was a judge on the High Court of Appeals who resigned over Lucie Dreyfus's petition, declaring that there was collusion between his colleagues and the Dreyfus camp, and then launched a violent campaign against Dreyfusism.
[34]In March, Jeanne returned with the children and stayed with Zola until April 12, through Easter.

tege halted in front of the ministry on the quai d'Orsay, the din was so formidable that I and my colleagues couldn't hear a single note of *La Marseillaise,* which a military band was playing twenty steps away." Another mob swarmed up the rue de Rivoli to the Place des Pyramides, where, leaning against the statue of Jeanne d'Arc, a noted ultramilitarist named Paul Déroulède declared: "Today's election is an insult. . . . It is up to the people to choose the president of the Republic. . . . Let us not do anything right now, for in the Elysée lies a man whom I loved. . . . Come Thursday, I shall do my duty."

Five days later, during the state funeral for Faure, Déroulède made good his threat. Joined by fellow members of the Ligue des Patriotes at the Place de la Nation, he intercepted an infantry brigade returning from Père-Lachaise Cemetery and, resplendent in his deputy's sash, twice exhorted the brigade commander, Gaudérique Roget, to lead a coup d'état with the words: "Save France and the Republic! To the Elysée, General!" Roget placed him under arrest instead, and Déroulède was then subjected to one more indignity: afraid of provoking truly competent attempts at insurrection, the government treated the aborted coup as the act of a quixotic simpleton, a benign offense, and tried Déroulède accordingly.[35]

Thereafter, events favored the revisionist cause, and eloquent men —Jean Jaurès, René Waldeck-Rousseau, Anatole France—spoke tirelessly on its behalf, swaying public opinion. First, in March, the High Court of Appeals ruled that for technical reasons the charges preferred against Georges Piquart by General Zurlinden fell under common law rather than military jurisdiction; Picquart thus escaped a court-martial, much to the dismay of anti-Dreyfusards, who screamed in *La Libre Parole* that the Jewish syndicate had obviously bought out key magistrates. Then, in May, the High Court ended its seven-month inquiry with a decision—rendered in solemn conclave on June 3, 1899—to annul the verdict of 1894 and summon Alfred Dreyfus before another court-martial. Attorney General Manau reported:

The Court admits the new facts and new documents, etc., of a nature to establish the innocence of Dreyfus,
Declares as admissible and legally justifiable the demand for a revision of the judgment of the court-martial of December 22, 1894;
SETS ASIDE and ANNULS the said judgment and dismisses the

---

[35]In fact, it was by no means benign. The brigade was supposed to have been led by the passionately anti-Dreyfusard General de Pellieux, with whom Déroulède had conducted negotiations during the previous week. Pellieux made encouraging noises but apparently took fright at the last minute and handed his command over to Roget.

case and orders that Dreyfus remain as the accused before another court-martial that it will be pleased to designate.

On that same day, *Le Matin* published an interview with Esterhazy in which the psychopathic ex-major, while portraying himself as a mere pawn, admitted having written the bordereau. "This unexpected declaration left me flabbergasted," the interviewer confessed. "I cried out: 'What, it was you!' He said: 'Yes, I wrote the bordereau in the year 1894 at the order of Colonel Sandherr, my immediate superior officer. There was on the general staff an officer who committed treason. That officer was named Dreyfus. He had to be caught. And that is why I wrote the bordereau. As for the real reasons, I shall reveal them later.'"

Zola, who had decided he would terminate his exile when the High Court of Appeals announced its judgment, even if the judgment was altogether unfavorable, could now return more victorious than not. On Sunday, June 4, the Fasquelles called at the Queen's Hotel and accompanied him to London, where Vizetelly and Wareham joined them for a hastily improvised farewell dinner. Then, at Victoria Station, which he had not seen since July 1898, Zola boarded the 9 p.m. boat train with his new manuscript in hand and his publisher close beside him. For half a minute he stood at the carriage window waving goodbye. "The responsibility which had so long rested on Wareham and myself was ended," recalled Vizetelly. "Emile Zola's exile was virtually over: shortly after five o'clock on the following morning he would once more be in Paris, ready to take his part in the final, crowning act of one of the greatest dramas that the world has ever witnessed. Truth was still marching on, and assuredly nothing would be able to stop it."

Zola had already sent Ernest Vaughan of *L'Aurore* an article explaining in detail the rationale for his protracted exile. Entitled "Justice," it appeared on June 5—just as Captain Dreyfus was being released from military prison—and with characteristic bravado informed the attorney general that its author would thenceforth be home to receive notice of the default judgment pronounced against him one year earlier by the assizes court at Versailles.

XXVIII

✦

THE FIFTH ACT

OVERWHELMED BY EVENTS, the government did not want trouble from Zola. It postponed further consideration of his case until November 23, leaving him free to reorient himself and to witness the repercussions in Paris of the High Court's momentous decision. On June 10, former Minister of Justice Ludovic Trarieux hosted a large, celebratory dinner for Georges Picquart, against whom all charges were soon to be dismissed. On Sunday, June 11, a week after a young nobleman named Fernand Chevreau de Christiani had attacked President Loubet with his cane at the racetrack, tens of thousands of republicans marched toward Longchamp singing *La Marseillaise*. On June 12, the Chamber, which passed a motion in which it resolved "to support only governments bent on vigorously defending the Republic's institutions," ousted Prime Minister Charles Dupuy, who had been more than tolerant of nationalist hooliganism. And ten days later, René Waldeck-Rousseau, president of the Senate, formed a new government with ministers known mainly for their devotion to him and their sympathy for Dreyfus. "Waldeck, lawyer to Eiffel and Dreyfus, is presiding over the Witches' Sabbath, just to save an ignoble Jew," hissed *L'Intransigeant*. In *Le Gaulois*, François Coppée (once Zola's staunch supporter for election to the French Academy but now an anti-Dreyfusard) wondered when "the Terror" would begin.

Taken aboard a cruiser that proceeded slowly across the Atlantic, Captain Dreyfus, feverish and bruised from clambering down ship ladders, set foot on French soil at Port-Haliguen during the early hours of July 1. No one spoke. By lantern light a carriage drove the pariah

768

between rows of soldiers to Quiberon, where gendarmes put him on a special train bound for the city in which his second court-martial would unfold: Rennes. At 6 a.m., Dreyfus entered yet another military prison. Finding himself ostracized shocked him. "The succession of emotions to which I was prey may be imagined," he wrote,

> Bewilderment, surprise, sadness, bitter pain at that kind of a return to my country. Where I had expected to find men united in common love of truth and justice, desirous to make amends for a frightful judicial error, I found only anxious faces, petty precautions, a wild disembarkation on a stormy sea in the middle of the night, with physical sufferings added to the trouble of my mind. Happily, during the long, sad months of my captivity I had been able to steel my will and nerves and body to an infinite capacity for resistance.

On the heels of Lucie and the children came Edgar Demange and Fernand Labori, who gave him a detailed chronological account of what had happened since 1895. At that point, few people knew less about the Dreyfus Affair than Alfred Dreyfus, but trial transcripts and investigatory reports supplied by his two lawyers helped him catch up. He studied them with horrified fascination, especially the Zola trial, which kept him up all night. "I saw how Zola had been condemned for having upheld the truth, I read of General de Boisdeffre's swearing to the authenticity of the letter forged by Henry. But as my sadness increased on reading of all these crimes and realizing how men are led astray by their passion, a deep feeling of gratitude and admiration arose in my heart for all the courageous men . . . who had cast themselves valiantly into the struggle." When word got out that Dreyfus had landed in Brittany, people from all over France, Europe, and beyond extended fraternal greetings, Zola among them. Letters by the thousand were delivered to his prison cell.

Even before Dreyfus's second court-martial began, there was drama aplenty to occupy the newspaper correspondents who gathered in Rennes.[1] On Dreyfus's side, Demange and Labori clashed over legal

---

[1] It has been said that no event in the history of journalism had ever been so thoroughly reported. There were something like three hundred newspapermen present, from every part of the world. Six telegraph lines had been strung up between Rennes and Paris, over which, on the first day alone, more than six hundred and fifty thousand words were transmitted. The civil authorities were extremely hospitable. "[They] provided . . . a great hall with a special telegraph office, for the use of visiting correspondents," wrote H. R. Chamberlain, correspondent of the New York *Sun*. "The Bourse du Commerce was transformed into a vast editorial room. One hundred and fifty writing tables, nailed to the floor to prevent noise and confusion, comfortable chairs, pens, ink, and paper, and courteous attendants were all at the disposal of French and foreign writers during the five weeks."

strategy, with Labori wanting unconditional warfare and Demange favoring the government's proposal that Dreyfus accept a minority acquittal in exchange for a polite defense.[2] On the other side, notable anti-Dreyfusards promised marvels and horrors, like showmen outside a carnival booth. General Mercier let it be known that the original bordereau, of which he possessed a photographic copy, had marginal notes in Emperor Wilhelm's own hand. Quesnay de Beaurepaire, the High Court of Appeals magistrate turned hatemonger, announced that the prosecution would conjure up a witness with categorical proof of Dreyfus's guilt. François Coppée declared that if war resulted from the publication of new documents exposing Dreyfus's servitude to Germany, then so be it: war might engender France's "rebirth and salvation." And for Maurice Barrès, who was interested less in justice than in the mythic underpinnings of a national identity, the trial at Rennes loomed as the battle at Armageddon. "The choice is clear," he wrote in Le Journal. "Dreyfus or our principal leaders. . . . [Dreyfusards] insult everything dear to us, the nation, the army. . . . Their plot is dividing and disarming France, and they are delighted at the prospect." On this ultimate field of honor, "Aryans" pledged to save France from Mammon would confront the faithless, cosmopolitan Jew.

Dreyfus was brought before his seven judges early in the morning of August 7, with spectators jamming an improvised courtroom at the Rennes lycée. Fortified by stimulants, he walked quickly to the witness box, as if wound up for the occasion. "There was in everybody's eyes an amazement that reflected the difficulty they had in believing that this was really Dreyfus," Paléologue observed.

> From afar, from the mystery of his infernal island, this man, around whose head so much hatred and pity have accumulated in the past five years, seemed, indeed, a symbol, an abstraction. For some he was a traitor, Judas, the personification of disloyalty; for others he was the personification of innocence immolated in the interests of a caste, the victim of a new Calvary, of the most monstrous crime ever committed against justice and truth. Now here he was, in flesh and blood, wearing a uniform, with gold braid on his sleeves, booted and spurred. . . . But how worn and emaciated he was, what a wreck of a human being he had been reduced to! His arms were withered, his knees so thin that they seemed to pierce the cloth of his trousers.

Even Maurice Barrès felt twinges of compassion, but compassion did not visit the presiding judge, Colonel Albert Jouaust, who drove the

---

[2]In court-martials, three votes out of seven were enough to secure acquittal and the government believed it could garner three, if not more.

white-haired, cadaverous defendant through a gantlet. The questioning was harsh in tone. Rebuked when he sought to explain himself, Dreyfus, always the self-disciplined soldier, most often gave terse replies—"No, my colonel," "Never, my colonel"—and left the impression with many sympathizers that he hadn't risen to the challenge, or that he lacked the stature of his predicament. One such sympathizer was Paléologue, for whom Dreyfus's protestations of innocence somehow didn't ring true. "I recognized these pathetic phrases, having heard them on the sinister morning of the degradation," he wrote. "Then they had given me the inner certainty that Dreyfus was lying. Why, now that I *knew* that they were true, did they still sound so false to my ear? Why is this man incapable of putting any warmth into his words? Why in his most vigorous protestations can nothing of his soul emerge through his strangled throat? There is something incomprehensible and doomed about him." Joseph Reinach put it another way: "The trial called for an actor, and he was a soldier."

When General Mercier mounted the witness stand in closed session several days later, it became clear that soldiers could in fact make very accomplished actors. Although no remarkable new evidence was adduced, he spoke for four and a half hours with perfect composure, recalling a mass of precise detail the better to validate dubious insinuations. Throughout this well-rehearsed speech he ignored Dreyfus, who sat nearby, and deigned to look at him only during his peroration, which began:

> I have not reached my age without having discovered by sad experience that everything human is fallible. Consequently I have followed with keen anxiety all the arguments of the revisionist campaign. If the slightest doubt had crossed my mind, gentlemen, I should be the first to tell you so, for I am an honest man, and the son of an honest man. I should come before you to say to Captain Dreyfus: "I erred in good faith."

The last phrase sparked a moment of high drama, for no sooner had it been uttered than Dreyfus leapt to his feet like a galvanized corpse shouting: "That is just what you should do! . . . It is your duty!" Momentarily taken aback, Mercier waited until the courtroom officer sat Dreyfus down, then said in conclusion: "But no! The certainty I have felt since 1894 has not undergone the slightest change; it has, on the contrary, been deepened by a more complete study of the case; and finally it has been strengthened by the futility of the efforts made to prove the innocence of the convict, despite the enormous sums squandered to that end!"

After a week, observers of every persuasion concurred that Dreyfusards enjoyed the advantage, Dreyfus notwithstanding. There were several reasons for this. Mercier's empty boast about conclusive proof had detracted from his otherwise splendid performance. The very day he gave testimony, fifteen nationalists, Guérin and Déroulède among them, were arrested in Paris for plotting to overthrow the Republic. And on August 14, Rennes was shaken by the announcement that an attempt had been made upon Fernand Labori's life: someone (whom the police never identified) had shot him in the back as he made his way to court early that morning with Georges Picquart. Labori, who found the prospect of surrendering center stage more painful than his wound (the bullet had lodged near his spine), immediately declared that one week would suffice for convalescence. Sentiment went against nationalist fanaticism, and the great lawyer received messages of encouragement from every quarter. "Ah! my dear, my great and valiant friend," Zola wrote on August 16. "What joy when we learned this morning that you are out of danger. . . . We sat on pins and needles, . . . fearing for your dear life but also for the cause of truth and justice, whose indispensable soldier you are. With you absent, all our worst premonitions sprang up again. . . . We have counted on you to pillory the culprits."

Those premonitions were richly justified. When Dreyfus's court-martial resumed in Labori's absence, Dreyfus himself became a kind of supernumerary. The big lie gained credence, as general after general and minister after minister stepped forward, like undying spirits of vengeance, to reaffirm their belief that justice had been served five years earlier. Cavaignac lorded it over the courtroom. Wraithlike, with greenish skin and eyes glistening inside deep sockets, he presented a brilliant summary of the general staff's case. "His imperious mask, his dogmatic self-assurance, the severity of his demeanor, gave him the air of an inquisitor addressing the Holy Office *de pravitate judaica*," Paléologue noted. "The members of the court listened in fascination; I could feel his indictment biting into their minds like acid eating into a copper plate." Equally effective was Cavaignac's former principal private secretary, General Gaudérique Roget, who argued that Dreyfus and Esterhazy had in all likelihood been collaborators. "With his very first words he established an ascendancy over members of the court," wrote Paléologue. "His martial figure, his crisp phrases, his loud voice, quickly put them all under his thumb; he might have been ordering them to carry out a maneuver."

On August 17 and 18, Georges Picquart spoke at length, but his elaborate testimony hit the mark only a glancing blow, and his appearance in civilian dress seemed to rob him of authority. Lesser military figures then paraded through the witness box with stories orchestrated by General Mercier, whose quarters in Rennes had become an anti-Dreyfusard salon. Where the Dreyfus camp featured quarreling coteries, anti-Dreyfusards marched as one and their monolithic organization trampled evidence underfoot. The return of Fernand Labori did not help. If one may believe Paléologue, who disliked him, his blustery, histrionic style of litigation made potential witnesses run for cover, even as it estranged the jury.

By August 24 or so, Dreyfus's counselors were agreed that the verdict would go against him unless Germany could somehow be induced to betray Esterhazy and surrender the handwritten notes that had accompanied his bordereau. Soon thereafter, Waldeck-Rousseau himself solicited this material, but the effort failed. Fürst von Bülow, German secretary of state for foreign affairs, explained that although "the present French government" was obviously "motivated by the proper point of view," German foreign policy had to consider the mutually hostile forces tearing France asunder. "Concerning such public opinion," he wrote, "Germany and specifically the person of the monarch . . . have been discussed in a manner that compels the imperial government to avoid, insofar as possible, any further involvement of Germany and her emperor in [the Dreyfus Affair]. After all that has happened, we cannot expect that any fact or person thrown into the debate by Germany will be evaluated objectively."

On September 9, Edgar Demange delivered a poignant, well-wrought summation in which, after five hours of analysis, the judges were implored to base their verdict on reasonable doubt.[3] By way of rebuttal, prosecutor Carrière urged them to heed their inner conviction, even if available evidence did not fully support it, saying: "The law does not ask jurors to account for the ways in which they have reached their beliefs. It does not prescribe rules to which they are obliged to submit their sense of the sufficiency of evidence. It asks them only one question, which comprises the full measure of their duty: are you deeply convinced?" In a final statement, Dreyfus protested his innocence once again, whereupon the judges' deliberations began. They lasted one and a half hours, until late afternoon. At 4:45 p.m., with gendarmes having cordoned off the podium, Colonel Jouaust announced that a majority of five (which did not, surprisingly, include himself) found the accused guilty, that it recognized "extenuating circumstances," and that the court-martial sentenced him to ten years in prison. Demange wept while Dreyfus tried, as always, to

---

[3]Because Labori exuded truculence, Mathieu Dreyfus was of two minds about letting him deliver a summation. Labori took offense and, even after Mathieu begged him to argue, spoke not another word on Alfred Dreyfus's behalf. They never reconciled their differences. When the Dreyfus family accepted a pardon, Labori, *plus dreyfusiste que Dreyfus*, made it known that he considered them to be unworthy of the cause they embodied.

show no emotion. Instantly, telegraph lines all over Europe and America were abuzz with news of the unspeakable outrage.

Two days after the sentence had been read, Joseph Reinach proposed in *Le Siècle* that the government grant Dreyfus an immediate pardon, "shredding a military judgment even before the ink has dried." A pardon, as he saw it, would be a transitional move or a first step toward full exoneration, and the idea took hold. With Mathieu Dreyfus's encouragement, Reinach approached Waldeck-Rousseau, who lost no time gathering support from his heterogeneous circle. It was difficult work, for at first conservative allies found the idea as objectionable as extreme Leftists. General de Galliffet, who knew all about civil war, feared the predictable wrath of army brass and Catholic bourgeois, while Clemenceau, noting that Dreyfus could be pardoned only if he withdrew his appeal, gagged over an implicit admission of guilt. But compassion prevailed, and on September 12 Mathieu carried the following text, which had been composed by Jean Jaurès, to his brother in the Rennes military prison:

> The government of the Republic grants me my freedom. It means nothing to me without my honor. Beginning today, I shall persist in working toward a reparation of the frightful judicial error whose victim I continue to be. I want all of France to know through a definitive judgment that I am innocent. My heart will be at rest only when there is not a single Frenchman who imputes to me the crime committed by another.

Everything—everything save the adamantine pride that had borne him through hell on earth—told Dreyfus to sign this defiant letter of submission: his broken health, his horror of a second ritual degradation, his yearning for family and freedom. So he signed it that day, with anguished reluctance. It was made public one week later, after President Emile Loubet officially pardoned him at Galliffet's request.

Zola had been under great stress since his return from England. Not only living amidst danger, but contending every day with his two families took some getting used to. He periodically suffered what Alexandrine called "nervous fits," and the court-martial, which he followed closely, made matters worse. As Dreyfus's case deteriorated, gloom settled over Médan. "My good friend," he wrote to Desmoulin on August 26, in the aftermath of a strange seizure that temporarily paralyzed his chest and right side, "I . . . thank you with all my heart for the information you've sent [from Rennes] and the pains you've taken. . . . I know nothing, I do nothing, I am filled with rage and sorrow at being powerless to help fend off the terrible misfortune that threatens our poor country and, I daresay, the whole civilized world. Our collective honor would come crumbling down." Other witnesses gave optimistic reports, particularly Eugène Fasquelle, who at dinner on September 1 declared acquittal to be a virtual certainty. But Zola was dubious, and when news of the verdict arrived, it found him already mulling over an appropriate response. "That business about extenuating circumstances left us flabbergasted," Alexandrine told Elina Laborde. "Again and again we puzzled over it. Fortunately, . . . we hadn't rejoiced prematurely, so the new condemnation didn't take us by surprise. . . . Ah! the scoundrels. . . . In one or two months there will probably be a *pardon*, then, in due course, a general amnesty freeing the forger and the whole vile gang to resume their mischief, at the expense of other poor souls. . . . After dinner [Emile] began his article."[4] Zola wrote with passionate intensity. By Sunday evening, despite visits from friends, he had completed a long piece entitled "The Fifth Act," which Alexandrine brought to *L'Aurore* on Monday morning for immediate publication. It opens with a splendid salvo:

> I am in mortal fear. It is no longer anger, vengeful indignation, the need to proclaim the crime and demand its punishment in the name of truth and justice that I feel now; it is terror, the holy terror of the man who sees the impossible being realized, rivers flowing back to their sources, the earth tumbling under the sun. And what I fear is the distress of our generous and noble France. I dread the abyss into which she is falling.

Before August 7 he had imagined that the "fifth act" of a terrible tragedy was beginning in which innocence would finally triumph and harmony be restored in a classic denouement. Instead, the Rennes court-martial proved to be only a fourth act, with nothing yet resolved.

> Ah! that fourth act! that trial at Rennes! . . . Events have taken an inexorable course, with wickedness following wickedness, and the Rennes trial tops it all, like a grotesque flower blooming on a dunghill. We have seen truth and justice molested in the most brutal ways. A gang of witnesses decided how testimony should proceed; plotting

---

[4]Dreyfus, too, was flabbergasted. "Since when have there been extenuating circumstances for the crime of treason?" he asked. In the matter of strategies for assuaging guilt, the judges went further still. At a meeting held on September 10, the day after sentence had been passed, they unanimously decided to request that the president of the Republic spare Dreyfus a ceremony of degradation. "It was a strange initiative on the part of judges who were thus expressing their wish that their sentence not be carried out," writes Bredin.

every evening the next day's cowardly ambush; pressing the charge, in place of the public prosecutor, with arrant lies; terrorizing and insulting those who dared to contradict them; using stripes and plumes to force acquiescence. A tribunal vulnerable to such pressure, visibly pained at seeing senior officers in criminal posture, obeying a special mentality which must be dissected layer by layer so that we can judge the judges. A public prosecution that gives new meaning to the word stupidity and leaves future historians an indictment whose imbecilic, lethal emptiness will strike them with wonder—an indictment so senile and obstinate in its cruelty that it would appear to have issued unthinkingly from some hitherto unclassified human animal. A defense that was literally wounded and muzzled whenever it became troublesome and denied permission to introduce witnesses who could have furnished decisive proof.

For one month an innocent victim, whose emaciated figure wrung tears from strong men, sat straight, as former superiors came and "flogged him with their gold braid" the better to escape punishment themselves. The court record of the Rennes trial would, he predicted, constitute

> an execrable monument to human infamy. . . . Ignorance, foolishness, cruelty, madness, charlatanism display themselves with such impudence that future generations will shudder. Therein lie examples of human baseness that will make all of humanity blush for shame.

And the fifth act? The fifth act would unfold when an obstinate government prevailed upon Germany to release Esterhazy's memoranda, or when, at his, Zola's, own trial in November (which never took place), Labori, by sheer eloquence, made the truth finally irresistible.[5]

Waldeck-Rousseau wanted a different fifth act, however. Eager to whitewash everyone tarred by the Affair, he kept deferring Zola's second trial. The denouement he had in mind was, as Zola predicted, a general amnesty, and throughout 1900 he bent his energies toward that end. Legislative debate began in March amidst cries of shame and perfidy from committed Dreyfusards—Clemenceau, Labori, Picquart, etc.—who spurned Waldeck-Rousseau's contention that "there are punishments more severe than some meted out by law and there is justice other than the justice of courtrooms—there is that which is born of public awareness, which survives in the teaching of successive generations, and which has already entered history." Debate ended at

[5]On August 31, Zola was summoned to appear on November 23 at Versailles, for his second trial (it will be recalled that the first verdict had been quashed on a technicality). In November, the government postponed it indefinitely.

Christmastime, when, with President Loubet's signature, the amnesty proposal became law. "The view that one can save a people from the disease that gnaws it by decreeing that the disease no longer exists is myopic indeed," Zola mourned in a public letter to President Loubet published by *L'Aurore* on December 22.

> The amnesty is a fait accompli, the trials will not take place, one will no longer be able to pursue the guilty. But the fact remains that an innocent Dreyfus was twice condemned, and that this iniquity, until it is dealt with, will continue to give France horrible nightmares. You bury the truth in vain; germinating underground, it will one day spring forth in flowers of vengeance. And still worse, you subvert the education of our youth by clouding their notion of right and wrong. Where no one is punished, no one is guilty. How can you expect the young to acquire moral discernment when they have been fed corrupting lies? They needed light, and you have given them darkness.

Politicians desperate for peace had bought themselves a momentary reprieve, nothing more, he warned. "The truth will awaken, will clamor, will unleash storms. . . . When, someday, after learning what happened, the country demands justice, will its wrath not fall first of all upon those who could have enlightened it, but didn't?"

With the mission he had undertaken now accomplished, he himself would return to his books. "I played my role as staunchly as I could, and henceforth I shall speak no more."

The books Zola referred to were his tetralogy *Les Quatre Evangiles*. His original idea for it had been sketched toward the end of 1897, when the Dreyfus Affair was beginning to absorb him. Successive novels—at that point there were still only three—would illustrate the fundamental values of a social religion and celebrate, by turns, fertility in a numerous family, productive labor in a Fourier-like city of the future, and universal peace in a supra-racial congress of nations. All three, as he first envisaged it, would have one narrator—Pierre Froment's son, Jean. But soon afterward the biblical paradigm imposed itself, suggesting a fourth novel and four distinct heroes. "I think I shall compose four gospels rather than three, to parallel [the New Testament]," he wrote.

> I shall then have *Fécondité, Travail, Vérité* (or perhaps *Humanité?*), *Justice*—but above all I shall jettison the idea—which hampers me and even seems illogical—of having only one hero, as in *Les Trois Villes*. I shall give Pierre four sons: Jean, Luc, Marc, Mathieu—four

brothers who will be the heroes of separate episodes. The great advantage this presents is that in each novel I can portray, if I wish,
the skein of a man's eighty or ninety years, the next century in its
entirety, without chopping things up. Each brother represents what
the title of his volume signifies. . . . The fertility of a century, the
pullulation of the family around one man, a great oak: this enlarges
my frame dramatically and allows the family to be developed in the
most complete way. Likewise for work—I can picture the development of the future city. Likewise for truth, with science ever more
triumphant and error retreating.

After portraying reality at epic length, he was now disposed to "indulge" his "lyricism" with a leap off the deep end of "dream" and
"hope." All effusions were thenceforth licensed, he wrote. "I want
sunbursts of optimism."

As the author of Les Rougon-Macquart, Zola had operated inside a
fictional universe circumscribed by disaster. The family proliferates
even as the world round about moves inexorably toward a hecatomb,
and this paradox haunts countless episodes en route. Wherever passion
fills a closed space, death waits nearby. Miette leading a revolutionary
horde through the Viorne Valley will be slain at the threshold of womanhood. Albine's wildly luxuriant garden in La Faute de l'abbé Mouret
becomes her walled graveyard. The ecstatic hosannas that rise from
the hippodrome in Nana celebrate a putrescent Venus. Catherine Maheude's nuptials take place underground. The glut of material goods
that embodies Octave Mouret's imperial genius transforms women
into consuming, self-devouring maenads. But Les Quatre Evangiles—
and Fécondité in particular—were designed to free him from the conjunction of eros and thanatos. No longer death-bound, or confined
within a historical crypt, Zola would sally into the vacant, guiltless
expanse of twentieth-century France and, he told himself, people it
jubilantly—as a Creator taking full possession of his own imaginative
realm. He would "create the Family," he noted. He would "create the
City." He would "create a humanity that transcends frontiers."[6] Had
heredity and milieu shaped character in Les Rougon-Macquart? In Les
Quatre Evangiles heroes would reinvent the world. Had everything in
his hyphenated saga bespoken internal division? Here everything
would herald Oneness. Among other precedents Les Quatre Evangiles
brings to mind is the rational, Saint-Simonian empire that Eugène

---

[6]The post-Rougon-Macquart epic has an old, familiar ring, however. These notes
call to mind the positivist trilogy entitled Les Héroïsmes that Zola had proposed
to write after leaving Hachette thirty years earlier, in 1866. He had envisaged
volumes devoted to "heroes of the family," "heroes of the nation," and "heroes
of humanity."

Rougon, Napoleon III's perpetual second-in-command, dreams of fathering after his fall from political grace.

Zola gave this private argument greater scope and pertinence by tying it to an increasingly urgent debate over the decline in the national birth rate. During the nineteenth century, France, which had previously been more populous than any other European state, lost its demographic edge. Whatever the reasons for this phenomenon, and theories still abound, the numbers were indeed alarming, especially to *revanchistes*, who saw every spilt seed or aborted fetus as one less rifle pointed at the Rhine. Although France's population had risen from twenty-four to thirty-seven million since 1800, over that same span of time Germany's had increased by thirty-two million, Great Britain's by twenty-six million (or threefold), European Russia's by seventy million. In 1868, when the distinguished statesman Lucien Prévost-Paradol had called for government measures and predicted that France "would either be a shameful nonentity living in sporadic and impotent turmoil on a globe ruled by her rivals' posterity . . . or else would boast eighty to a hundred million souls planted on either shore of the Mediterranean . . . maintaining the name, language, and legitimate stature of their fatherland," thirty-seven prefectural subdivisions across the country showed net reproduction rates below the level of replenishment. Twenty-two years later, in 1890, that number was forty-nine (of a total eighty-seven), despite loud, nationalist propaganda.[7] Deserted villages had become commonplace.

Zola, who had obvious reasons for preaching that childbirth was its own justification, first joined the chorus of pro-natalists with an article entitled "Depopulation," which *Le Figaro* published on May 23, 1896. "For about ten years I have been haunted by the idea of a novel whose first page I shall doubtless never write," he began, harking back to a period in which the specter of degeneracy presided over his work (*Pot-Bouille, La Joie de vivre, L'Oeuvre*).

> My novel would have been called *Le Déchet* [*Trash*], and I imagined a huge fresco of Paris wasting seed, devouring unborn beings, committing abortions, yet remaining an eternally ardent source of new life. People don't know about these natal tragedies, about . . . the dark underground lake flowing into nothingness. What could be greater, vaster, more honest than a work in which I would have argued for the right to life, with all the passion I can muster?

[7]One vehicle for such propaganda was the illustrated postcard. They circulated through France in great numbers, urging newlyweds to do their patriotic duty and showing, for example, five Germans bayoneting two Frenchmen or large German babies looking down on their puny French counterparts.

Widespread concern over the diminishing birth rate had revived memories of his unrealized project, and a newly founded association, the National Alliance for Raising the French Population, encouraged him to believe that France might at last mobilize herself against doomsday. Even if no useful work had been accomplished during its first meeting, at which people seemed content to enumerate the generally accepted causes of population decline (alcoholism, the flight from the countryside, the high cost of living, birth control practiced by upwardly mobile families),

> the meeting may stir commotion, and since the fundamental problem here is one of mores, I believe that change fostering large families can be wrought only through the spoken word, through newspapers, through books.

Although fashions in literature, music, and philosophy did not influence the bourgeoisie as dramatically as *la mode*, which was bent on promoting a sleek, uneugenic image of feminine beauty, they too crippled society's will to multiply. Schopenhauer and Wagner had begotten a host of disciples enamored of virginity, who identified the sublime with "the immaculate and the barren." Could one deny that sterile love reigned supreme? that in art as in life, abundance was made to appear uncouth? "If we descend a step from our novels of sophisticated psychology, where great talent occasionally emerges, and inspect the most recent blooms of what has been called the decadent school and the symbolist school," he continued,

> we find only war being waged against love, against the healthy, loyal love that procreates and boasts of doing so. There one encounters a spate of indeterminate women, thin as sticks, without those organs that make it possible to bear and nurse children. Nebulous virgins float through twilight zones. And on the male side, pale ephebes who might be, and indeed are, mistaken for girls, preponderate. Children are considered coarse, unseemly, shameful—an assault upon the intellectuality of lovers. . . . In love everything is countenanced, save the natural act for which it was intended. Death to life, and may human seed be cast to the winds, so that the winds may disperse it, as something useless and scorned.[8]

[8] In the eighteenth century the idea that France's population had fallen (it hadn't) had been used by *philosophes* to indict an unworthy monarch, abundance being one measure of royal virtue. In the nineteenth century, population decline, as pronatalists saw it, spoke against a degenerate race, or a decadent upper class.

The article concluded with a broadside that could have come unedited from certain of those nationalist zealots with whom Zola was soon to find himself at daggers drawn. "Where once there were fields of wheat offering nourishment there are now fields of lilies that poison humanity. . . . [The avant-garde] are out to ruin our robust Gallic health, our good nature and fruitfulness, all for the pleasure of being intellectual nincompoops, hairsplitters, analysts of shadows cast by the invisible."[9]

Research for *Fécondité* began toward the end of 1897 in the usual way, with Zola assembling specialized works and taking extensive notes. Particularly useful was René Gonnard's *La Dépopulation en France*, a well-documented study that follows Herbert Spencer's *Biology* in characterizing low birth rates as the price paid everywhere for democratic civilization and ascribes them above all to the voluntary restriction dictated by upward mobility or "social capillarity." This predicament admitted of no obvious solution, but in France custom aggravated it, and Gonnard set forth a program of social reform that included measures against contraception, the reduction of military service, the vigorous development of colonies, the abolition of dowries and of a Revolutionary law against primogeniture. To bolster his creed, Zola then read *La Population et le système social* by Francesco Nitti, the same Nitti whose *Le Socialisme catholique* had helped him prepare *Rome*. Charging capitalism with society's demographic ills, Nitti examined Darwin, Spencer, Marx, and Nietzsche, but dwelled at greatest length on Thomas Malthus, in whom he saw the ideologue of a class that placed individual profit above collective well-being.[10]

Zola digested all this theory as best he could and proceeded to comb through medical literature with an eye for gruesome detail or the seamier aspects of birth control. From Dr. L. Bergeret's *Des fraudes dans l'accomplissement des fonctions génétrices* (*On Expedients Used to Defraud the Reproductive Functions*), which had been around since 1868 conferring scientific legitimacy on the biblical injunction to be fruitful and multiply, Zola derived a catalogue of disorders associated with contraception. The fruit of pleasure alone justified coitus, "maneuvers" that thwarted "nature's wish" fostered degeneracy, and Dr. Bergeret had innumerable case histories to prove it. A recent book about

[9]Interestingly, many of the symbolists and so-called decadents whom Zola may have had in mind arrayed themselves against Dreyfus: J.-K. Huysmans, the young Paul Valéry, and others.

[10]In fact, Nitti concerned himself not with population dearth but with population imbalance, arguing that an unequal distribution of wealth explained the low birth rate high up in the social order and the high birth rate low down. Although Zola's *parti pris* for unrestricted increase did not chime with Nitti's ideas, he was sympathetic to any argument that discredited Malthus.

hysterectomy complemented this baleful demonstration. In *La Castration chez la femme*, which Zola read carefully, Dr. Etienne Canu inveighed against the licensed Jack the Rippers of French medicine, who
had won fame and fortune eviscerating women. Hysterectomy more
than any other factor was responsible for France's low birth rate, he
claimed. During the previous fifteen years thirty to forty thousand
fertile women had been operated upon in Paris alone, and most
emerged from "castration academies" like the Broca Hospital not only
barren but deranged. They had undergone personality changes. They
had suffered "nervous problems," stomach pains, headaches, loss of
sight. They had lost their sexual appetite altogether or experienced
flushes of insatiable desire. They had aged prematurely. "[They] are
on the road that leads to the insane asylum," noted Zola.

When, in exile, Zola unpacked the trunk Fernand Desmoulin had
brought over from France on July 29, 1898, he found his dossiers and
these books, along with two more that addressed the grave problem of
abandoned children: *La Vérité sur les enfants trouvés*, by Dr. André-
Théodore Brochard, and *L'Enfance malheureuse*, by Paul Strauss.

Fécondité, which presents relentlessly schematic contrasts between
the blessed and the damned, is cut from the same cloth as *Paris*. In
Paris, corruption breeds down below while up above Guillaume Froment presides over a household that awakens his brother Pierre to the
possibility of paradise on earth. In *Fécondité*, Pierre's son Mathieu pro-
creates joyfully while all around him people use one expedient or
another to thwart conception. Mathieu, who designs agricultural
equipment for a Parisian manufacturer named Alexandre Beauchêne,
commuting every day from Jonville near Chartres, purchases some rich
Beauceron acreage and establishes himself on it. The farm—
Chantebled—will thereafter stand in opposition to the factory. While
everything at Chantebled multiplies, tainted blood and niggardliness
and lust and the desire for social advancement make the factory a
perfect wasteland. At Chantebled, Marianne Froment delivers healthy,
happy babes, often a new one on every second page, even as corpses
keep piling up at the tool plant. Eventually Alexandre Beauchêne dies
intestate, but Mathieu's numerous progeny spread out beyond Chantebled with imperial exhuberance, acquiring everything lost by those
who revered sparseness. This conquest is amplified toward the end,
when four generations of Froments—one hundred fifty-eight people
all told—gather at Chantebled to celebrate Mathieu and Marianne's
seventieth wedding anniversary. Attention focuses on a hitherto unknown grandson born in Africa, Dominique, who harangues his newfound kin about colonialism, glorifying the impulse to fill and fructify
desolate quarters of Creation. "We open the road, we set the example," he exclaims.

In the midst of wilderness we have cleared a limitless field, which will someday join the motherland as a province. . . . Sterile though it appears to have become on its ancient soil, overseas the French race is unrivaled in its fecundity. And we shall swarm, and we shall fill the world! . . . Come then, come then, all of you, since you live piled too closely together. . . . Over there, there is space for everyone.

The youngest son of the family heeds this call, whereupon Mathieu and Marianne, their own nest empty at last, feel ecstatically connected with the world they helped to populate. "They now had nothing for themselves, nothing but the happiness of having given all to life," Zola concludes. "The nevermore of separation was becoming the evermore of increased life, spilling beyond a boundless horizon."[11]

This sprawling novel, which combines the most unfortunate features of a *roman à thèse* and of a Gothic potboiler, was published serially by Ernest Vaughan in 136 installments between May 15 and October 4, 1899. One week after it completed its run in *L'Aurore*, Fasquelle had the volume delivered to bookstores.

Denise LeBlond-Zola would later contend that *Fécondité* fared poorly for being ignored by the nationalist press (though it could not have found Zola insufficiently patriotic) and eclipsed by reports from South Africa, where the Boer War had broken out. In fact, the novel excited considerable controversy, with Catholics, socialists, symbolists, naturists, demographers, Dreyfusards, anti-Dreyfusards, and a few others commenting upon it at length. The poet Gustave Kahn in *La Revue blanche* and Lucien Victor-Meunier in *Le Rappel* declared *Fécondité* worthy of Hugo. In *Le Mercure de France*, Rachilde, a fashionable woman of letters, who took umbrage at Zola's assault on symbolism, railed against it savagely. To Laurent Tailhade the novel had mythological grandeur. "[It] seems less a novel than a poem," he wrote. "Despite their intense personality, their here-and-nowness, the characters embody the august generality of eternal symbols. . . . The calm displayed by [Mathieu and Marianne], their ardor, and the pride they take in their sacred task call to mind the divine couple Isis and Osiris, creators before birth and creators after death. One is put in mind as well of Virgil's sweet hymn acclaiming the gods who make the harvest joyous, of Lucretius' immortal poem invoking Venus Victori-

[11]It is well to recall the lifelong relationship in Zola's work between warding off death and filling empty spaces. For the fatherless boy afraid of falling out of the world, what could have been more comforting than the fantasy of universal consanguinity, or total connectedness? "Life pervades every space," he wrote of the department store in *Au Bonheur des Dames*.

ous." A Catholic critic named Jean Lionnet regretted that the prolific couple send their fifteen children forth to conquer the world rather than eternal life, and Charles Péguy expressed profound disappointment in a hero who embodies the spirit of capitalist imperialism rather than working-class solidarity. "Far from being about humanitarianism and solidarity, *Fécondité* is about the conquest of humanity by the Froments," he observed. "In a way it's *Les Rougon-Macquart* all over again but more dangerous than Zola's previous stories because of its ostensible morality. What we have here constitutes a *Fortune des Froment*, disguised beneath lyric ornamentation." If Mathieu Froment spent as much energy rescuing society's economic victims as he does founding his own race, he might have some claim to virtue, Péguy continued. "This gospel is no more concerned with the wage slave than Jesus' Gospel was concerned with slavery itself. It is a conservative book."

Zola's own opinion of *Fécondité* (which sold ninety-nine thousand copies during its first four years) emerges from a letter to Octave Mirbeau thanking him for a favorable review. "I know what my book's flaws are, the implausible bits, the strained symmetries, the banal truths of morality in action," he wrote on November 29, 1899. "And my only excuse is the one that you yourself furnish: the particular construction that the subject imposed upon me. . . . I also believe that I shall be better understood when the three following novels have completed my thought. All *Fécondité* does is stock more humanity for the tasks that lie ahead. But it may suggest that the final victory celebrates strength alone, and that impression will be corrected by the social organization of work, by the advent of truth and justice. This is utopian indeed, but what do you want? I've been dissecting for forty years. Let me dream a little in my waning days."

After Zola's return from England, petitioners wanting interviews, magazine articles, references, prefaces, and speeches seldom received satisfaction. His sixtieth birthday loomed large, a world rife with ideological hatred spelled danger, and for both reasons Zola was more inclined than ever to seek refuge inside the tightly drawn circle of his intimate friends. Alfred Bruneau, who had meanwhile composed yet another opera based upon a Zola libretto, *L'Ouragan*, accepted and extended many dinner invitations. Eugène Fasquelle stood by for every practical need. Fernand Desmoulin often visited on Sundays in the country or on Thursday evenings at 21 bis, rue de Bruxelles. Octave Mirbeau remained close. And the Labordes, who celebrated Elina's marriage to a young writer named Georges Loiseau, kept constantly in touch. It would be some time, however, before the Charpentiers sojourned again at Médan, Marguerite Charpentier and Alexandrine having quarreled bitterly during Zola's absence.[12]

As for wife and mistress, Zola took up where he had left off, commuting between one and the other. Alexandrine wore a brave face, but his absences, which became more frequent, were always to cause her profound distress, and confidantes sometimes received hints of it. "I'm terribly sorry that my remarks made you feel remorseful, and I assure you that I did not accuse you of neglecting me," she apologized to Elina Laborde on November 19, 1899, after Albert Laborde's departure for military service. "I understood all too well what was happening with you. . . . I can imagine how empty you must find the house, for men occupy an important place in our houses, especially when they are loved. You appreciate that I know whereof I speak since that was what I had to endure last year, . . . and now your uncle's existence takes him away from me almost all the time: being near each other, we yet live so little together." She was often alone, she told Amélie Laborde, and obliged "to struggle with dark thoughts in my continual solitude." In June 1900, a brief sojourn with Amélie produced a plaintive expression of gratitude for "five days that marked a happy truce in my otherwise sad life." Six weeks later, on Bastille Day, writing from Paris, where the Universal Exposition was in full swing, she confessed to Elina: "I envy you your calm and repose. I wish that I could enjoy those things at Médan, but if I change addresses, it's hardly repose I expect to find." One way or another, she lamented, "life is ceaseless pain."

Italy offered Alexandrine a brief reprieve from melancholy as well as from the asthmatic disorders that plagued her all year round. After 1899 she began visiting Salsomaggiore regularly each October, and Zola's children looked forward to her annual migration. "We children waited impatiently for those October days, when we had our father more to ourselves than usual," Denise recalled.

[12]The quarrel occurred on October 6, 1898, when Marguerite Charpentier informed Alexandrine that Georges Charpentier had crossed the Channel to spend several days with Zola, apparently at Zola's urging. What infuriated Alexandrine was the fact that Charpentier would be visiting not only Zola but his mistress and children (it will be recalled that Jeanne remained in England until October 15). On October 9 she wrote to Zola: "[When Marguerite told me that Georges planned to visit you], I [answered] that it wasn't possible, that you were absolutely refusing to receive anyone, that he should wait a few days. She declared that G. had in fact already left. I do not have words to describe my despair. I was thunderstruck. Then, to complete her mischief, she added that you . . . had been extremely ill and . . . since I didn't want to go see you, affection and duty compelled her to do something about your woebegone state." That Zola had invited their old friend Charpentier into his extramarital life mortified Alexandrine, and she made this known to him four days later. But it was apparently easier to scapegoat Marguerite Charpentier than to remain angry at her husband.

The whole afternoon, dinner, evening were set aside for us—my mother, Jacques, and myself. Zola resolved to acquaint us with Paris. He had us stand before Carpeaux's *La Danse*, Rude's *La Marseillaise*, Jean Goujon's *La Fontaine des Innocents*. Listening to him discourse was marvelous as he would get carried away by his own enthusiasm. The affection he showed my mother made me a little jealous: I kept wanting to clutch his arm, I breathed the atmosphere of glory that palpably surrounded him. Never did my mother get angry; on the contrary, she would smile at my imperious affection and let me savor the infinite sweetness of leaning against him. I haven't forgotten it. Sometimes, all four of us would go dine in some luxurious Parisian restaurant. In October 1900, after dinner at the Eiffel Tower, we attended the electric light show and saw the illuminated fountains of the Château d'Eau, which were at the time a new curiosity.

In 1900 Zola was reluctant to display his fatherhood publicly, even during Alexandrine's sojourn abroad. "No, my friend," he informed Bruneau on October 12. "I shall not go to the Opéra-Comique to-morrow evening, for I do not wish to show myself in the theater at the same time as my children." But two years later such compunctions no longer hindered him. In 1902, he took Denise and Jacques to hear Sarah Bernhardt in Edmond Rostand's play about Napoleon Bonaparte's ill-fated son, *L'Aiglon*. "He thought it important that we hear her because she had aged and might not, in his view, act much longer," Denise recalled. On another evening, he sat with them in a loge at the Opéra-Comique, where Gustave Charpentier's *Louise* was being performed; he wanted them to hear what he regarded as a musical masterpiece that chimed with his own ideas.

If the father delighted in teaching his children, it may also be that he gave so generously of himself after 1900 by way of helping them to accept the loss of Marie and Paul Alexis. Alexis had from the outset occupied a more prominent place in their semi-cloistered lives than any other Zola intimate except, briefly, Henry Céard. Every summer the Alexis family, which included two young daughters, Paule and Marthe, vacationed at Verneuil and during those weeks spent as much time in the garden of Jeanne Rozerot's house on the rue d'Agincourt as in their rented rooms. When Zola dropped by for late-afternoon tea or a bicycle ride, Alexis (who, like Alexandrine, needed three wheels) was often there to greet him. And in Zola's absence he played the part of surrogate father. "An inveterate noctambulist, Alexis would hike all over the fields and woods after dinner, enjoying beautiful nights and stretching out on our hammock," wrote Denise.

Going upstairs to bed one evening, I noted with astonishment a little lamp burning in the staircase niche. . . . I asked why and learned that it was for when my godfather returned from his walk. This nocturnal vagabondage struck me as rather odd, wandering around when everyone else was sleeping, but I loved the short walks I'd sometimes take after dinner in the company of my good friend. We'd follow him, my brother and I, together with his daughters. I believe it was he who taught us the constellations.

Tragedy came out of the blue on May 31, 1900, when Marie Alexis, who had been nursing fourteen-year-old Paule through typhoid fever, herself succumbed to the disease. Alexis notified Zola in a telegram that read: "My beloved wife dead—this evening, Thursday, at midnight. What am I going to do now, bereft of her, with two daughters, one of whom is still sick? Next October would have been the sixteenth anniversary of our love affair. Your old friend." Zola urged him to persevere for his children's sake. But despair overwhelmed Alexis, and women friends took in Paule and Marthe. Always a fancier of seedy, working-class bar life, he often stayed up all night drinking in the low dives near his house outside Paris, at Levallois-Peret. On July 28, 1901, the staunchest ally Zola ever had died of an aneurysm, with no one around to comfort him but the housemaid. Three days later he was buried next to his wife in a little graveyard not far from Verneuil. Zola, who had recently heard about the death of another Aixois friend, Antony Valabrègue, delivered a brief eulogy:

> I am not giving a speech, I am addressing a sorrowful farewell to the departed friend. For more than thirty years his life was bound up with my own and I cannot put a price on his collaboration. . . . In Alexis one of the last survivors of the soirées de Médan has disappeared. Flaubert had gone! Goncourt, Maupassant, and Daudet had died! It was your turn, Alexis!
>   A writer to whom words came slowly because he was conscientious, Paul Alexis produced little, but his taste was sure. He had talent. Above all, he had a noble character. His memory will not soon be effaced from my heart. I shall bestow upon his two girls the affection I devoted to him. Goodbye, my friend. I say goodbye with all my heart.

Zola's idea was to have Frantz Jourdain design a funerary monument, and sponsors eventually raised enough money for one, but the unveiling did not take place until June 4, 1905, when Zola could not attend. Denise, who did attend, promised herself on that occasion that someday she would, after her fashion, "perpetuate the memory" of both men—her father and her avuncular friend.

Certainly the strength to persevere never deserted Zola himself. Nor did the rescue fantasy which had been with him since adolescence and which now expressed itself through his four evangelists. As soon as Mathieu the Progenitor bowed out, Luc the City Builder stepped forward. "It is not true that [work] has been imposed on man as a punishment from above," he wrote in his early preparations for *Travail*.

> It is on the contrary an honor, a title of nobility, the most precious possession, joy, health, strength, the very soul of the world, which is always in labor, creating the future. It is through labor that children enter the world, through labor that people live life normally, without imbecilic perversions. . . . And indigence, that abominable social crime, will disappear in this glorification of work, this parceling up of the universal task among all alike, with each individual accepting his legitimate portion of rights and duties.

Under the new dispensation, Catholicism, from whose "nightmarish" yoke humanity had more than once in recent years tried to free itself, would be replaced by a secular faith "sanctifying" life.

After taking prolific notes at the Unieux steel plant in the Loire Valley, consulting savants familiar with the industrial applications of electricity, inspecting the "Galerie des Machines" at the Universal Exposition, and above all studying the theory and practice of Fourierist social organization, Zola composed a three-act plot for Luc Froment's heroic development. In the first act, which stirs memories of *Germinal*, Luc, an engineer, reconnoiters a factory town called Beauclair, where steelworkers at a plant known as L'Abîme have gone on strike. Invited there by Jordan, an old friend who finds himself torn between his research and his family enterprise—a blast furnace just outside Beauclair, at La Crêcherie—Luc comes to rebel against the wretchedness that deforms life in industrial civilization and decides to establish around Jordan's furnace a collectively operated plant. This he does in Act Two, encountering strong opposition from L'Abîme, which sees its doom writ large in the phalansterian community that materializes at La Crêcherie. "During the first four years of La Crêcherie's existence, Beauclair hated Luc more and more furiously," writes Zola. "At first there was only hostile astonishment. . . . But when business suffered, anger flared and with it the need to repulse a public enemy at all costs." In Act Three, L'Abîme withers away as La Crêcherie blooms. Shareholders of the former become cooperative members of the latter. Electrical power banishes smoky air. Rails and steel beams replace cannon and shells. Couples at war learn mutual respect. The "religion of humanity" takes permanent root, consecrating urges that neither Catholicism nor capitalism will tolerate, and Luc, who has engineered the new dispensation, dies happy at a great age.

Zola completed this long work in February 1901, after eleven months of steady labor. No one rejoiced more wholeheartedly over the novel than advocates of the cooperative or "association" movement, which derived from Fourier. A banquet was held on June 9, 1901, to celebrate *Travail*, and a prominent Fourierist, J. Noirot, described Zola's novel as giving their beneficent idea "a powerful boost." Jean Jaurès also praised it, but with reservations that might have been greater had *Travail* been written by someone other than the author of *J'accuse*. "Zola, who would achieve communism through calm, cooperative evolution, is careful not to squeeze the vast movement of history into some tight formula," he declared, noting that at the end Luc recognizes avenues to the future other than his own: revolutionary action, collectivism, anarchism.

> This great work cannot be taxed with timidity or parochialism. Zola's only fault, perhaps, has to do with his yielding, unconsciously, to an artistic perspective that led him to isolate the spontaneous and evolutive [sic] action of communist cooperation from the general picture of revolutionary and political movement.

Otherwise, *Travail* displeased most critics. In *La Nouvelle Revue*, for example, Gustave Kahn observed that the novelist who "once shook crowds with his striking visions of vice and social rot" had relaxed his grip. More than a novel, *Travail* was, Kahn wrote, a social tract.

Even when it hit home, adverse criticism never deflected Zola from his goal. Like Leo Tolstoy, he had come to fancy himself a teacher or spiritual leader and thus preserved in late middle age some version of the image drawn forty years earlier of François Zola as Moses. "I am writing these books with a certain purpose before me, a purpose in which the question of form is of secondary importance," he reminded his English translator, Ernest Vizetelly, after the publication of *Travail*.

> I have no intention of trying to amuse people or thrill them with excitement. I am merely placing certain problems before them, and suggesting in some respects certain solutions, showing what I hold to be wrong and what I think would be right. When I have finished these *Evangiles*, when *Vérité* and *Justice* are written, it is quite possible that I shall write shorter and livelier books. Personally I should have everything to gain by doing so, but for the present I am fulfilling a duty which the state of my country imposes on me.

By August 1901, he was already at work on *Vérité*, which occupied him for more than a year. Relating the Dreyfus Affair in the guise of a small-town scandal, he set out to vilify the Church and dramatize the evil it had wrought even while its gospel beatified "the poor of spirit," to celebrate secular education and the Republic's "holy battalion of elementary school teachers."

In private, Zola sometimes voiced deeply pessimistic sentiments that contradicted the utopian spirit of *Les Quatre Evangiles*. Nevertheless, a Dreyfusard—and particularly an anticlerical Dreyfusard—would, after the Rennes trial, have observed political life with vindictive pleasure rather than dread. On January 24, 1900, at Prime Minister Waldeck-Rousseau's behest, a tribunal dissolved the order of the Assumptionists, which in its influential paper *La Croix* had consistently represented the Dreyfus Affair as a religious war pitting Catholics against Jews and Freemasons. Six bishops who expressed outrage lost their government stipends straightway. Then, in January 1901, the prime minister introduced legislation that reinvigorated Jules Ferry's decrees of 1880.[13] Designed to prevent the several hundred monastic orders, known as "congregations," from preaching or teaching without official authorization, it inspired fierce debate all year long. Catholic deputies fought hard, but the bill emerged from parliament more radical for its turbulent gestation. Thereafter, no religious order could constitute itself unless both chambers of the legislature had authorized its existence by majority vote, and no member of an unauthorized congregation could teach at any level.[14]

Waldeck-Rousseau applied the law diplomatically. Not so Emile Combes, a theologian manqué who became prime minister on June 15, 1902, after elections that favored radical Leftist groups. Determined to destroy the congregations, Combes immediately closed more than three thousand schools in what some described as a Revocation of the Edict of Nantes turned against Catholics. Bishops protested. The papal nuncio complained. The League of French Women petitioned President Loubet's wife. Breton peasants, who had hardly changed since the Vendée rebellion against Jacobin government in 1793, raised barricades. All for naught. Combes avenged himself by threatening to deny Breton priests their stipends if they ever used the Breton language. "How do you like the dismissal of members of congregations?" Alexandrine asked Philippine Bruneau in a letter dated

[13]These had required the Jesuits to disband within three months, and other unauthorized orders or congregations to apply for authorization or suffer the same fate. The second decree, known as Article Seven, was never implemented. Sooner than declare unconditional war against Catholicism, the government entered upon secret negotiations with the papal nuncio and agreed that congregations other than the Society of Jesus should be left alone, provided they "respected the institutions of the country" and eschewed political affiliation.

[14]"[This] prohibition," writes one historian, "created a new class of Frenchmen with fewer rights than any other, a departure from the common law . . . justified on the ground that it forbade teaching by propagandists for the 'Counter-Revolution.'"

August 19. "It's certainly not being done with tact. I don't understand why these rabid cretins weren't brought to heel long ago. Anyway, it's done at last."

The summer of 1902 passed quietly at Médan. Every morning Zola labored over *Vérité*, and when his labors ended on August 7, he celebrated the event by eating a lobster that Georges Loiseau had dispatched from the coast. On August 11 the Charpentiers arrived for their annual sojourn, and Zola recorded it in photographic portraits. Otherwise, visitors were few. Gray weather prevailed that summer, much to the dismay of Alexandrine, who often felt unwell. "You're all very lucky indeed to have blue overhead," she reminded Georges Loiseau on August 6. "Here . . . the clouds weigh upon us like mountains, the air never moves. Every day I pray for rain, hoping that a good downpour will save us from this stifling closeness. . . . No, my friend, I've not caught a new cold. The old one finds its pleasure in never quite deserting me. And the same goes for my pains. . . . Fortunately I am compelled by nature to keep active, which works better than any other remedy." When the sun did break through, it shone more brightly on Verneuil than on Médan. Denise would later recall how Zola rowed his whole family upriver from Triel to the island chalet one fine September day in a newly acquired boat. She would also recall how, at summer's end, on September 27, he bade them all farewell. "I no longer know why we didn't accompany him, as we always did, up to about one hundred meters from his house, through those village streets where, so often during the Affair, people would heave kitchen slops on our wheels as we bicycled past. We had remained in front of our entrance, looking at him walk away and turn his head toward us one last time before disappearing around the corner." During the previous week he had been harrowed by a toothache, which required urgent treatment in Paris.

His family would never again see him alive. September 28 dawned wet and chilly, and soon after the Zolas reached the rue de Bruxelles they had their valet, Jules Delahalle, light a fire in the bedroom grate. Although the flue was not drawing properly, they suspected nothing, because the fire had been made with smokeless coal briquettes. At 3 a.m. Alexandrine, feeling nauseous, got up and visited the bathroom. Zola, who had also awoken in a nauseous state, discouraged her from rousing the servants for what he imagined to be mere indigestion. Alexandrine then lay down again and in due course found herself overcome by a sensation of lethargy so profound that when Zola fell to the floor she could offer no assistance. Nine o'clock struck before Jules Delahalle realized that something must be amiss. Zola having bolted the bedroom door from the inside (as previously noted, he had always feared nocturnal interlopers), force was needed to open it. Alexandrine lay on her bed unconscious. Zola lay on the floor lifeless, with his head propped against the bed's wooden dais. By 10 a.m. or so doctors had been summoned and for at least twenty minutes administered artificial respiration, but in vain.

Jeanne Rozerot learned the terrible news four hours later, when Alexandrine was recovering in the Neuilly clinic to which she had been rushed. "We were about to leave the apartment on a shopping expedition for home-from-vacation and back-to-school necessities and were in something of a rush because my father was expected at 4 o'clock," Denise recalled. "The doorbell startled us. Eugène Fasquelle and Fernand Desmoulin stepped forward. They had been sent by Mme Emile Zola, who, even in her terrible distress, had not forgotten us. . . . My mother understood everything before they uttered a word, though she imagined that someone had killed Zola. Oh, how she shrieked! and folded her arms around us protectively! Oh, her grief, and ours! I don't know how we survived until the funeral on October 5, but thinking about it still makes me weep; my tears spring from the realization that the death of our wonderfully kind, fair-minded, affectionate father was for us an immense, irreparable loss."

Spectroscopic analysis of Zola's blood determined that he had died of carbon monoxide poisoning, and an autopsy confirmed this determination. Amidst widespread rumors that fanatical right-wing nationalists had assassinated him, or that he had committed suicide for any number of reasons, an inquest was launched. Two chemists retained by the coroner to conduct toxicological tests at 21 bis, rue de Bruxelles lit coal fires on October 8 and 11, reconstituting the original circumstance as best they could ten days after the event. Not only did air samples show only minuscule concentrations of carbon monoxide, but guinea pigs locked up overnight suffered no ill effects. On October 14, two architects dismantled the flue, which angled across Zola's roof and ran up the wall of number 19, next door. Here again nothing conclusive emerged, for although much soot was found in an elbow joint, not enough had accumulated to block the flow of air. Might Zola have met with foul play? The coroner, M. Boursouillou, apparently staved off any suggestion of it lest civil war recommence. The experts' reports warranted an open verdict, but Boursouillou kept them under lock and key and in his own report categorically attributed death to accidental causes.

There matters rested for more than half a century, until in 1953 the newspaper *Libération* received from one of its elderly subscribers named M. Hacquin a letter stating that he knew Zola to have been murdered. The malefactor had been a friend of his, a stove fitter by trade and an anti-Dreyfusard by persuasion, who in 1927 made the following deathbed confession:

> Hacquin, I'll tell you how Zola died. I trust you and anyway, the statute of limitations will soon obtain. Zola was deliberately suffocated. I and my men blocked his chimney while doing repairs on the roof next door. There was a lot of coming and going and we took advantage of the hubbub to locate Zola's chimney and stop it. We unstopped it the next day, very early. No one noticed us.

Although the story leaves questions unanswered, it is noteworthy that M. Hacquin did not know about the experts' reports casting doubt on Boursouillou's verdict, because this information came to light only later and as a direct consequence of *Libération*'s exposé. It is also noteworthy that between 1898 and 1902 Zola had received scores of death threats. Not for nothing did Jeanne Rozerot assume, on seeing the dark messengers at her doorstep, that Zola had been killed. In 1953, when the Hacquin story broke, Zola's son, Dr. Jacques Emile-Zola, echoed her conviction. Still, the mystery remains a mystery, and, as Professor F. W. J. Hemmings put it, "it seems prudent to conclude that Zola might have had to pay with his life for his audacity in publishing *J'accuse*; but we shall probably never be able to say with certainty that he did die a political martyr."

In order that Alexandrine might embrace Zola one last time, his body was taken downstairs, embalmed, and afterward brought up to the study, where, surrounded by flowers, it lay all week in an open coffin looking like an effigy from the Musée Grevin waxworks. Fernand Desmoulin and Alfred Bruneau, who four years earlier had accompanied Zola to the Palais de Justice every day, now organized a round-the-clock vigil, recruiting—among others—Georges Charpentier, Eugène Fasquelle, Octave Mirbeau, Frantz Jourdain, Théodore Duret, Denise's future husband (Maurice LeBlond), Alfred Dreyfus, and Georges Picquart. Since the prefecture of police had forbidden the house to be heated during its investigation, these sentinels sat huddled under blankets with their feet on stone foot warmers. Meanwhile, strangers respectfully gathered on the sidewalk, close friends wandered around as if searching for a lost compass, and Zola's children, led by Jeanne, at last crossed the threshold of their father's other life. On Thursday, October 2, doctors released Alexandrine, who came home in the company of Amélie Laborde. "Her face enveloped in a long crepe veil, Mme Zola descended with difficulty from the coach," observed *Figaro*'s reporter.

She then entered the house . . . made straight for the little room on the first floor where Emile Zola's body lay. The poor woman, shaken by sobs, fell to her knees and embraced her husband; and for almost an hour she remained there, kneeling and sobbing. Only Mme Laborde remained at her side. Her friends had withdrawn. She finally rejoined them in the adjacent salon and embraced them while weeping, already calmer and more controlled.

A notary read Zola's will, whereupon Alexandrine turned her attention to details of the funeral, which was scheduled for Sunday, October 5. It was important, she felt, that Zola be eulogized as a literary man rather than a political activist. "Several political associations have . . . sent Mme Zola condolences and funeral wreaths," wrote the *Figaro* reporter. "But however much she and her friends value these tokens of sympathy, we understand that the widow of the great novelist would very much like Sunday's ceremony to preserve the character of a literary tribute. One hopes that this very sagacious wish will be borne in mind and Zola's admirers would serve his memory ill if they flouted it."

After mooting the question of whether Zola, who had been suspended but not expelled from the Legion of Honor, should depart this world with military honors, the government assigned a company of the 28th Regiment of the Line to the funeral.[15] Some fifty thousand people accompanied his casket to Montmartre Cemetery, and the crowd included people of every walk: a delegation of miners, representatives of various leagues, Prince Albert of Monaco, Alfred Dreyfus (whom Reinach could not dissuade from attending), government officials, ordinary residents of Les Batignolles. En route, police saluted and soldiers presented arms. Despite well-founded apprehensions, there was no donnybrook. At Montmartre Cemetery, where a sepulchre had yet to be built, Zola's hearse stopped before a temporary vault as hundreds of shiny felt top hats clustered around. The minister of education spoke. Abel Hermant, president of the Société des Gens de Lettres, followed him.[16] But most mourners remembered only the third eulogist, Anatole France, whose courage during the Dreyfus Affair had rivaled even Zola's. France made up for old slights with an oration worthy of his subject, and after glorifying the literary genius he paid

[15]The company was commanded by one Captain Ollivier. When he returned to his barracks after the ceremony, a fellow officer slapped him. A duel ensued in which Ollivier was wounded.
[16]Hermant was also a pallbearer, along with Ludovic Halévy, Alfred Bruneau, Georges Charpentier, Eugène Fasquelle, Octave Mirbeau, Théodore Duret, and M. Briat, secretary of the Bourse du Travail, or Labor Exchange.

homage to the political hero. "Still young, Zola had conquered glory," he declared.

> At ease and famous, he was enjoying the fruit of his labor when suddenly he sacrificed it all: his repose, the work he loved, the quiet pleasures of his life. Over a coffin it behooves one to pronounce only grave and serene words and to admit only signs of calm and harmony. But you know, gentlemen, that there is calm only in justice, repose only in truth. . . . I shall not hide the truth in craven silence. And why indeed should we hold our tongues? Do his slanderers hold theirs? . . . If I concealed their lies, I would be concealing his heroic rectitude. If I concealed their crimes, I would be concealing his virtue. If I concealed the outrages and calumnies with which they hounded him, I would be concealing his recompense and his honors. If I concealed their shame, I would be concealing his glory. No! I shall speak out.

In defiance of what *Le Figaro* called Alexandrine's "sagacious wish,"[17] France extolled *J'accuse*.

> With the calm and firmness that the spectacle of death inspires, I shall recall the dark days, when egoism and fear held sway in the highest councils of government. The iniquity was just coming to light but one sensed that it had the endorsement of public and secret forces so powerful that the staunchest hesitated. Those who should have spoken kept quiet. The best among us, who feared not for themselves, were afraid to embroil their party in a frightfully dangerous situation. Led astray by monstrous lies, stirred up by odious harangues, the populace, imagining itself betrayed, lost all patience. Opinion makers too often embraced the error, since they felt unable to correct it. Shadows gathered thicker. A sinister silence prevailed. Then it was that Zola wrote to the president of the Republic his measured and formidable letter denouncing the forgery and the abuse of power.

The consequences of his act were incalculable, he declared.

> It inspired a movement of social equity that will not halt. From it has emerged a new order of things based on sounder justice and on

[17]Alexandrine had sent France a telegram saying: "I rely on your tact and leave you free to do as you wish. I know I can depend on you." France, who interpreted this as a polite gesture of censorship, answered: "In the circumstances, it will be impossible for me to speak at Zola's funeral." On Dreyfus's advice, she then invited France to speak his mind freely.

a deeper knowledge of everyone's rights. . . . Zola deserves well of his country for not having lost faith in its ability to rule by law.

Let us not pity the man who endured and suffered. Let us envy him. Enthroned atop the most prodigious collection of outrages that folly, ignorance, and wickedness have ever heaped up, his glory attains an inaccessible height.

Let us envy him: he has honored his country and the world with an immense body of work and a great act.

Let us envy him, France said in conclusion, "for his destiny and his heart have earned him the highest distinction of all: he was a moment in the history of human conscience."

Friends, family, and officials dispersed, but other mourners filed through hour after hour. There were the three men sent by the town of Denain—a miner, a blacksmith, and a peasant, each attired in the garments of his trade. There were young people in their thousands. There were Freemasons wearing their insignia. There were deputations crying "Glory to Zola! Honor to the apostle of justice!" or "Germinal! Germinal!" There was the multitude streaming down from upper Montmartre. By nightfall Zola's coffin could hardly be seen for all the wreaths, silver palms, and flowers heaped upon it.

EPILOGUE

O N MAY 27, 1906, a bust of Zola sculpted by Philippe Solari, who had finished it shortly before his own death, was installed at the Méjane Library in Aix-en-Provence. Alexandrine attended the ceremony and sat beside members of the municipal council. The mayor, M. Cagassol, reminded his constituents that Aix had attained literary immortality in *Les Rougon-Macquart*. Numa Coste then spoke at length, his voice shaking with emotion as he evoked Zola's youth. "We were at the dawn of life, swollen with vast hopes, desirous of rising above the social swamp in which impotent jealousies, spurious reputations, and unhealthy ambitions stagnate," he recalled.

> We dreamed of conquering Paris, of occupying the world's intellectual home, and out of doors, amidst lonely and arid spaces, by the shaded torrent or the summit of rocky escarpments, we forged armor for the titanic struggle. . . . When Zola preceded the group to Paris, he sent his first literary efforts to his old friend, Paul Cézanne, at the same time letting all of us share his hopes. We read those letters in the hills, under evergreen oaks, as one reads the communiqués of a first campaign.

Many people wept, but no one more copiously than Paul Cézanne and the tears turned bitter when Coste continued: "As [Zola] often said, one thinks one has revolutionized the world, and then one discovers at the end of the journey that one has revolutionized nothing at all. . . . Men remain the ephemeral creatures they have been since they first appeared on earth." Mindful that six months after Zola's death Alexandrine had sold at auction nine of his early works, along with one Monet and two Pissarros (the ever acerbic journalist Henri Rochefort was moved by this collection to expatiate upon "the love of ugliness"), Cezanne may not have been inclined to approach her. Soon, he, too, would be dead. In the autumn, overtaken by a storm while painting near his studio high above Aix, on the Chemin des Lauves, he was brought down in a laundry cart, chilled to the bone, and, already seriously ill with diabetes, expired on October 22.

Two months after the ceremony in Aix, several deputies laid before the Chamber a bill that provided for the transfer of Zola's remains from Montmartre to the Pantheon. It carried by a substantial majority and went on to the Senate, where the new prime minister, Georges Clemenceau, spoke in its favor. The bill carried there, too, and in a subsequent vote, which saw Jaurès argue down Maurice Barrès, thirty-five thousand francs were appropriated to cover the cost of the ceremony. This public consecration devastated Alexandrine, who felt robbed of her husband all over again. "I can't get over this most recent separation from the dear remains of my beloved husband," she wrote from the spa on Mont-Dore on July 30.

> It's all I have of him, and it's cruel to have it taken away. They could bestow honors upon him without my being reduced to this painful sacrifice. I shall make it, believe me, more for the children's sake than for my own; otherwise they may accuse me later on of not having wished to separate myself from their poor papa. Over the years I made many sacrifices for him, and I understand that now I must make more in the service of his dear memory. I yield with immense resignation.

Despite his "departure for so-called glory," she vowed to maintain the tomb at Montmartre Cemetery. "As it remains sacred to me, I shall not remove from my will the clause stating that sufficient money be set aside to produce five hundred francs per annum for its upkeep."

The posthumous *déménagement* occurred almost two years later and revived the undying hatred Zola had unleashed upon himself with *J'accuse.* On June 3, 1908, in the early evening, a hearse entered Montmartre Cemetery to transport his coffin across Paris. After witnessing the exhumation, which took place quietly, Alexandrine together with Denise and Jacques left for the Pantheon, where a very different scene awaited them. Some five thousand raucous nationalists had spilled from streets round about onto the Place du Panthéon. Assembled in front of the huge edifice, they made it known that nothing would get past them except by force. Force was applied. A squadron of horse guard, a company of foot soldiers, and gendarmes drove them back toward the Place Médicis (now Place Edmond-Rostand). But when Zola's hearse appeared, anger swelled. "The line needed reinforcement," wrote one reporter. "A skirmish ensued, punches were exchanged and forty arrests were made."

Not until 8:15 did Zola enter the Pantheon. Four undertakers carried him past Rodin's crepe-veiled *Thinker,* where Alexandrine waited with the children, Bruneau, Fasquelle, and Desmoulin. Alfred Dreyfus was also there, now Commandant Dreyfus, for he had been completely exonerated three years earlier, on July 12, 1906.[1] This group accompanied the coffin to a catafalque almost forty feet high that stood at the center of the cavernous ex-church. Alexandrine then sat vigil, alone, while outside, under lamplight, gendarmes patrolled the rue Soufflot.

Worse lay in store. The official ceremony of reburial began the next day at 9:30 a.m., when the orchestra of the conservatory greeted Armand Fallières, president of the Republic, with a rendition of *La Marseillaise.* It went on to play the funeral march from Beethoven's Third Symphony as ministers, generals, diplomats, magistrates, Alexandrine, Jeanne, Denise, Jacques, and various friends, including the whole Dreyfus clan, took seats around the catafalque. A single encomium was delivered, and in it Gaston Doumergue, minister of public instruction and fine arts, praised Zola for the extraordinary courage he had displayed during the Dreyfus Affair. "All at once this shy, solitary man left his ivory tower . . . and joined the political fray," he observed,

not to flatter the crowd, which he regarded with instinctive apprehension, nor to serve its passions and follow its movements, but to confront it head-on, to resist it, to absorb its insults and blows. There he was in the rough-and-tumble, heroically braving courtroom assaults and the frenzy of popular protest. How came he suddenly to choose this path when neither his ambition nor his responsibility nor his friends were involved? Only those who didn't understand the true character of his work and the lifelong passion from which his work sprang could ask themselves this question. His act, which seems even now to astonish certain people, was neither impulsive nor exceptional and unexpected.

[1]In 1903 Jaurès demanded before the National Assembly, to which he had recently been reelected, that the Dreyfus case be reopened on the basis of new or concealed evidence. The minister of war, General Louis André, offered to initiate an investigation. His report and a separate petition from Dreyfus led the government to activate the revision commission. Eventually the Court of Appeals considered the case and annulled the Rennes conviction.

Just after Doumergue finished pronouncing Zola a hero, President Fallières walked out to review a procession of republican guard. At that moment two shots rang out from within the group still seated, and panic-stricken witnesses realized that Alfred Dreyfus had been hit. "[The president and official cortege] had just reached the entrance when I heard a muffled detonation," Albert Clemenceau, George's brother, told *Le Figaro.*

> It seemed to originate from the foot of the catafalque. Neither my neighbors nor I understood the cause at first. Out of curiosity I got up and looked. Then there was another detonation. I noticed smoke and saw Mathieu Dreyfus wrestling with one of the guests seated near him. I stepped over the bench that separated me from Mathieu Dreyfus and his neighbor. . . . Mathieu Dreyfus was holding the right hand of the man with a pistol, who had dropped his weapon but who continued to fight furiously. I, in turn, seized his left arm. Several indignant people rained blows on our prisoner, while Mathieu Dreyfus, still holding him, shouted: "Don't strike him! Don't strike him!"

Gendarmes immediately arrested the would-be assassin, a shady character named Louis Grégori who wrote on military affairs for *Le Gaulois.* Unnoticed by the crowd, which had heard nothing but band music, they led him to the nearby police station. Meanwhile, Dreyfus was found to have suffered a flesh wound, with one bullet embedded in his forearm. A well-known physician dressed it at the Dreyfus home, where throughout the afternoon friends and high government officials paid their respects. The minister of war arrived first, in the person of Georges Picquart, whom Clemenceau had promoted to general in 1906.

After the ceremony, Alexandrine, Jeanne, and the two children descended into the Pantheon's crypt. There, so near the rooms of his impoverished adolescence, Zola was laid beside Victor Hugo.

Zola had always spent what he earned and had also incurred extraordinary expenses during the Dreyfus Affair. Thus Alexandrine, who inherited the entire estate, was forced, with no new Zola novels in progress, to live less grandly. In March 1903 an auction at the Hôtel Drouot of books, paintings, furniture, stained glass, musical instruments and other paraphernalia netted 152,412 francs.[2] Vacating 21 bis, rue de Bruxelles, she rented smaller quarters not far away at 62, rue

---

[2]Prices for the nine early Cézannes, which included *L'Enlèvement,* ranged from 600 to 4,200 francs. A Monet was sold for 2,805 francs and two Pissarros for 500 and 920.

de Rome and unburdened herself of the country house at Médan. In 1905 that celebrated house was given to Assistance Publique (Public Welfare), which made it into a nursery for convalescent children operated by Paris's Necker-Enfants Malades Hospital. Alexandrine eventually sold the land Zola had acquired beyond the railroad tracks and their portion of the island as well. The chalet on the island remained standing until 1935, when developers built a large bathing establishment over it.

Alexandrine's strong maternal instinct found an outlet in the nurturing of her husband's illegitimate children. Although Jeanne apparently enjoyed some income from an insurance policy that Zola had purchased, she relied upon Alexandrine for financial support, and Alexandrine behaved generously, giving her six thousand francs a year, assuming medical expenses (which were considerable), paying tuition, buying clothes. What she got in turn was the opportunity to help Jeanne raise her son and daughter. Strictly quarantined from each other during Zola's lifetime, the two women formed, after his death, a pious sisterhood, cherishing in Denise and Jacques the man they had divided between themselves. When, for example, several young writers conceived the idea of an annual commemoration at Médan—a *pèlerinage*, or pilgrimage—Alexandrine suggested that they all go as a group to the inaugural event on September 29, 1903. "I shall arrange a lunch for the four of us," she told Jeanne in a letter the logistical fastidiousness of which calls to mind many composed by Zola. Jeanne was at Berck on the Channel coast nursing twelve-year-old Jacques through treatment for a tubercular arm.

> We could go together or, if my train departs too early for you, you could catch the following one. There is now an express that leaves Paris at 11:30 and reaches Villennes at 12:06. There you'd find the carriage waiting. I said nothing about this in my recent letters for fear of intruding upon our dear one's treatment. . . . Don't upset anything, but you understand that . . . the presence of the children would mean a lot to me. I couldn't endure the idea of their not joining in this pilgrimage to venerate their dear papa. You will keep me informed, won't you.

One year later, after the second pilgrimage, which Jeanne, who was still at Berck, had not attended, Alexandrine wrote as follows:

> The demonstrations of homage to our dear great hero were truly superb. . . . People are waking up and beginning to realize what he was. The future bodes well for the father of our dear children and you, you will be around to see it. As for them, they are not old

enough yet to appreciate his stature. When, in time, they wish to know about him, to be initiated into that life of labor snuffed out so early . . . they shall, I hope, understand that the name Zola, which was raised to such heights by those who bore it—their father and grandfather—requires that they comport themselves appropriately. You will be there to direct them and teach them many things. Unfortunately, you didn't know him as well as I, who for thirty-eight years lived near him and who, during twenty-four of those thirty-eight years, never spent an hour away from him.

In this violent disappearance which has smitten both of us so cruelly, the affection I receive from his dear children has given me keen pleasure. It's as if this affection were coming from him, which makes me cherish them even more than I would have thought possible.

Alexandrine concerned herself with Denise's education and with Jacques's health, seeking out good teachers for the one and consulting distinguished physicians for the other, much as Zola himself might have done. She cosseted them, advised them, scolded them—all with full encouragement from Jeanne, who, though perhaps vexed at times by Alexandrine's imperious tone, accorded her the respect she considered due to an older, more worldly woman and a social superior. Every Thursday the two children, who came to regard Alexandrine as their second mother, lunched at 62, rue de Rome. And on Sundays, the day Alexandrine received, it was often Denise who poured tea.

In November 1906, Alexandrine set in motion the complicated legal procedure for entitling Denise and Jacques to bear the hyphenated surname Emile-Zola and to inherit her estate. "If I die before I can see this through," she advised Jeanne, "it will be for you to do so with our friends on the Family Council." She saw it through, and on October 14, 1908, when Denise married Maurice LeBlond, a young critic who had given Zola moral support during the Dreyfus Affair, it was as Denise Emile-Zola that she plighted her troth.[3]

Jacques recovered from tuberculosis after years of painful treatment which left him with one arm slightly shorter than the other, and became a physician himself, living out his father's fantasy.

Motherhood absorbed Jeanne Rozerot until the end. Tender and self-effacing, she welcomed Alexandrine's friendship, but always felt uncomfortable at official functions and in high society. An invitation

[3]Maurice LeBlond, whose name was associated with the "naturist" movement, had written literary criticism for La Plume and a regular chronicle for L'Aurore. In 1906, when Clemenceau became prime minister, LeBlond became his private secretary. Two years later Clemenceau appointed him subprefect at Clamecy in Burgundy. It was LeBlond who, between 1927 and 1929, brought out the first edition of Zola's collected works, in fifty volumes.

from the Fasquelles, for example, caused her agonies of doubt. "The Fasquelles are having a soirée to celebrate the engagements of their two daughters," she wrote to her daughter in May 1909. "You've already heard, no doubt. But what you don't know is that I'm invited and thought that instead of going I'd send Coco [Jacques] with B.A. ["Bonne Amie," signifying Alexandrine], and here B.A. told Coco just now over lunch that I should accept. I no longer know what I should do. The Fasquelles are terribly nice but they would have been well advised to forget me. Don't you agree?" Like Alexandrine, Jeanne never left Les Batignolles, keeping faith with Zola's old neighborhood. She died an avoidable death in 1914, while being operated on for some normally benign gynecological disorder.

Alexandrine survived her by eleven years, despite the respiratory problems for which she continued to seek relief at Mont-Dore in the Auvergne. Always attentive to Zola's reputation, she died in 1925, at the age of eighty-six.

NOTES, BIBLIOGRAPHY, AND INDEX

NOTES

ABBREVIATIONS

B.N., n.a.f.—Bibliothèque Nationale, nouvelles acquisitions françaises
CE—*Carnets d'enquête* (Plon)
CN—*Contes et nouvelles* (Pléiade)
CORR.—*Correspondance d'Emile Zola* (Université de Montréal/CNRS)
O.C.—*Oeuvres complètes* (Cercle du Livre Précieux)
RM—*Les Rougon-Macquart* (Pléiade)

I. A BIRTH AND A DEATH

4 "He fell on arriving": *Le Mémorial d'Aix*, April 4, 1847
4 "more splendid" monument: *La Provence*, April 8, 1847
5 "About one year ago": René Ternois, "Les Zola. Histoire d'une famille véni-tienne," *Les Cahiers naturalistes*, no. 18, 1961, p. 56
7 "it was really like passing": Nathaniel Hawthorne, *The French and Italian Notebooks*, Boston, James Osgood, 1873, pp. 249–50
8 "Zola was not on board": O.C., XIV, p. 1019
8 "although Marseille be situated": André Bouyala d'Arnaud, *Evocation du vieux Marseille*, Paris, Editions du Minuit, 1959, p. 39
9 "It is astonishing": B.N., Vp. 2630
10 "M. Zola, engineer-architect-topographer": Ternois, "Les Zola," p. 58
10 "to accord us the tutelary protection": B.N., Vp. 2630
10 "Councillor Francesconi": Ternois, "Les Zola," p. 60
11 "I have spent three years": Ibid., p. 61
11 "He first noticed her": "In the Days of My Youth," *The Bookman*, vol. XIV, December 1901, p. 344
12 "At last I've read you": Ternois, "Les Zola," p. 62

12 "you must curb your fantasy": Ibid.
13 "It really seems": Archives Municipales d'Aix-en-Provence
14 "As you see": MS, Archives Programme Zola
14 "Our mayor promised": Ibid.
14 "My father had lived": "In the Days of My Youth," p. 344
15 "Yesterday . . . Monsieur Thiers": O.C., XIV, p. 1008
15 "My father passes like a shadow": Ibid., p. 1005
15 "a continual exercise": Zola in preface to *Enquête médico-psychologique sur les origines de la supériorité intellectuelle,* Edouard Toulouse, Paris, Flammarion, 1896, p. vii

II. UNDER THE MOUNTAIN

16 "very lively, very gay": Paul Alexis, *Emile Zola, notes d'un ami,* Paris, Charpentier, 1882, p. 15
16 "When circumstances demanded": Ibid., p. 16
18 "The prefect of Marseille": CORR., I, 291
19 "It is not love of work": Maurice Gontard in *Histoire d'Aix-en-Provence,* Aix-en-Provence, Edisud, 1977, p. 276
19 "It is a curious experience": Ibid., p. 290
20 "The mayor read a request": Colette Becker, "Quelques documents sur la jeunesse d'Emile Zola à Aix-en-Provence," *Les Cahiers naturalistes,* no. 55, 1981, p. 171
20 "in the provinces": RM, I, 115
20 "In early childhood": Alexis, *Emile Zola,* pp. 26–27
21 "Ah, what cuisine!": O.C., XIV, p. 242
21 "a paternalistic discipline": Alexis, *Emile Zola,* p. 23
21 "they would graduate directly": O.C., XIV, p. 239
22 "Almost all of them": Ibid., p. 240
22 "My mother and grandmother": Emile Zola, "In the Days of My Youth," p. 345
23 "Nothing can replace": O.C., XIV, p. 242
23 "the regrettable facility": Archives Nationales, F17 6775
23 "Let us remember": O.C., IX, p. 929
23 "I had a perverted youth": Edmond and Jules de Goncourt, *Journal,* Paris, Fasquelle and Flammarion, 1956, vol. II, p. 1134 (May 5, 1876)
23 "We conducted": *Mercure de France,* March 1, 1929
24 "My years in *collège*": O.C., I, p. 55
24 "Opposed by nature": Ibid., V, p. 455
25 "Marthe loved her husband": Ibid., II, p. 888
26 "A quiet and docile student": Jack Lindsay, *Cézanne,* New York, New York Graphic Society, 1969, p. 9
26 "Cézanne has many spells": CORR., I, p. 300 (June–July 1861)
26 "[Masters] taught four hours": O.C., XIV, p. 244
27 "In the provinces": Ibid., p. 245
27 "like horses at a riding academy": Ibid., p. 246
28 "The ruling classes": Antoine Prost, *Histoire de l'enseignement en France. 1800–1967,* Paris, Armand Colin, 1969, p. 332
28 "In Latin . . . they have conversed": Ibid., p. 65

28 "sins on the experimental side": Colette Becker, "Quelques documents sur la jeunesse d'Emile Zola," p. 171
28 "To write an oration": Prost, *Histoire de l'enseignement,* p. 52
29 "The city of Aix": *Le Mémorial d'Aix,* October 3, 1852
30 "If one wished to depict": Ibid., February 3, 1856, quoted by Colette Becker in "Quelques documents sur la jeunesse d'Emile Zola," p. 173
30 "mossy path": Octave Gréard, *Prévost-Paradol,* Paris, Hachette, 1894, p. 252
30 "Nowhere outside Mazas": Ibid., p. 265
31 "The children come forward": O.C., XIV, p. 252
32 "a lame Catholicism": Ibid., IX, p. 411
32 "Of course one finds": Ibid., XIV, p. 312
32 "I saw ravishingly beautiful creatures": Ibid., IX, p. 433
33 "We'd follow them on the wide white roads": CN, p. 506
33 "These were flights": RM, IV, p. 38
34 "With every return": Ibid., p. 39
34 "When he says something hurtful": CORR., I, p. 165 (May 14, 1860)
34 "Timid and maladroit": RM, IV, pp. 40–41
35 "We didn't amble alone": O.C., XII, p. 328
36 "We were born": Ibid., p. 329
36 "Brewing in our confused minds": Ibid., p. 330
37 "We adored medieval decor": Ibid., p. 329
37 "I have often spoken": Alexis, *Emile Zola,* p. 23
38 "You will receive a letter": MS, Archives Programme Zola
39 "For the first time": R. D. Anderson, *Education in France: 1848–1870,* Oxford, Clarendon Press, 1975, p. 68
40 "[Scientific education] is the seed": O.C., XIV, p. 248
40 "I want to do law": CORR., I, p. 105 (January 23, 1859)

III. "THEIR CIRCLES WERE PERFECTLY ROUND"

42 "What a journey!": Alphonse Daudet, *Trente ans de Paris,* Paris, Flammarion, n.d., pp. 1–3
43 "I want to be a second Augustus": Jean des Cars, *Haussmann,* Paris, Librairie Académique Perrin, 1978, p. 204
43 "I am a stranger": Goncourt, *Journal,* I, p. 835
43 "Haussmann's new, monotonous": Georges Duveau, *La Vie ouvrière en France sous le second Empire,* Paris, Gallimard, 1946, p. 206
44 "You must understand": Colette Becker, "La Correspondance de Zola, 1858–1870: trente lettres nouvelles," *Les Cahiers naturalistes,* no. 57, 1983, p. 148
45 "Our legal business": Ibid., p. 149
46 "At first I was amazed": "L'Ecole et la vie scolaire en France," O.C., XIV, p. 252
47 "Out of sixty children": Ibid., p. 255
47 "The professor forgot us": Ibid.
47 "Being twentieth of sixty": Ibid., p. 252
48 "Do you swim?": CORR., I, p. 97
48 "I see so much intellectual pretension": Ibid., p. 96
48 "Wait and I shall vent": Ibid., p. 98
49 "Since you've left Aix": Paul Cézanne, *Correspondance,* ed. John Rewald, Paris, Grasset, 1978, p. 18

49 "Je frémis": Ibid., p. 34
50 "Out of fear!": John Rewald, *Cézanne et Zola*, Paris, Editions A. Sedrowski, 1936, p. 100
50 "For through the mighty swipe": Cézanne, *Correspondance*, p. 37
50 "After starting this letter": Ibid., p. 31
51 "Hang it all": Ibid., p. 25
51 "Everything you have": Ibid., p. 20
52 "He had a celibate's passion": in *L'Oeuvre*, RM, IV, p. 50
52 "I shall let my beard": Cézanne, *Correspondance*, p. 35
53 "Oh, my guardian angel": Becker, "La Correspondance de Zola, 1858–1870," p. 151
54 "My dear friend, I have delightful news": CORR., I, p. 96
54 "Trammeled from an early age": Toulouse, *Enquête*, pp. 178–79
55 "Time and again I dreamed": CN, p. 294
56 "Things are going beautifully": CORR., I, p. 107
57 " 'Life is a struggle' ": Ibid.
57 "One lovely morning": Ibid., p. 112
58 "If I weren't afraid": Ibid., p. 109
59 "Boarders . . . had day students": O.C., XIV, p. 253
60 "France has drawn the sword": Harold Kurtz, *The Empress Eugénie*, Boston, Houghton Mifflin, 1964, p. 128
60 "Shall we talk about the war?": CORR., I, p. 112
60 "To the Empress Eugénie": O.C., XV, p. 867
61 "Baille told me that your confreres": Cézanne, *Correspondance*, p. 52
62 "In the brief time allotted him": O.C., XIV, p. 255

IV. Closed Doors and Fearful Mysteries

63 "Government exists in order to help": Louis Napoleon Bonaparte, *Des idées napoléoniennes*, Paris, Plon, 1860, pp. 16–17
63 "Government loans of the old regime": J. M. Thompson, *Louis Napoleon and the Second Empire*, Oxford, Basil Blackwell, 1954, p. 233
64 "France is like Molière's miser": Goncourt, *Journal*, I, p. 371 (June 15, 1857)
65 "Fould counts on the market's decline": S. C. Burchell, *Imperial Masquerade*, New York, Atheneum, 1971, p. 174
65 "The steps and colonnade": RM, V, p. 23
66 "there is no longer a race": Adeline Daumard, *Les Bourgeois de Paris au XIXe siècle*, Paris, Flammarion, 1970, p. 120
66 "The Second Empire was for French cuisine": Jean-Paul Aron, *Le Mangeur au XIXe siècle*, Paris, Laffont, 1974, pp. 80ff.
66 "[Our maid] tells me": Goncourt, *Journal*, I, p. 588 (February 17, 1859)
67 "[I shall enjoy] the highest vantage point": CORR., I, p. 176 (June 13, 1860)
67 "You must know that I am not exactly": Ibid., p. 126 (January 5, 1860)
68 "I haven't finished my studies": Ibid., p. 133 (February 9, 1860)
68 "All I want is a cave": Ibid., p. 159 (May 5, 1860)
68 "The world is not my stock-in-trade": Ibid., p. 134 (February 9, 1860)
68 "literary ablution": CN, p. 200
68 "Want, real want": *Le Siècle*, February 14, 1859
69 "Ministerial offices have their own peculiar odor": Gaboriau in *Les Gens de*

bureau, as quoted by Pierre Guiral, *La Vie quotidienne en France à l'âge d'or du capitalisme, 1852–1879,* Paris, Hachette, 1976, p. 148

69 "My life is still monotonous": CORR., I, p. 151 (April 26, 1860)
69 "At the Docks, May 14": Ibid., p. 165
70 "the wound of our century": Ibid., p. 191 (June 25, 1860)
70 "My entire excuse": Ibid., p. 169 (June 2, 1860)
70 "Derision!": Ibid., p. 192 (June 25, 1860)
70 "Your guiding principle": Ibid., p. 211
70–71 "For almost a fortnight": Ibid., p. 176
71 "Un soir, je l'aperçus": O.C., XV, p. 892
72 "Should you see Aeriel": CORR., I, p. 117 (December 29, 1859)
72 "I wanted to ask you": Ibid., p. 217 (August 1, 1860)
72 "I should have done my utmost": Ibid., p. 188 (June 24, 1860)
72 "Allow me to declare myself": Ibid., p. 228 (August 10, 1860)
73 "In this materialist age": Ibid., p. 223
73 "Would not the high school boy": Ibid., p. 129 (January 14, 1860)
73 "How beautiful it would be": Ibid., p. 182 (June 15, 1860)
74 "The wise and charming woman": Jules Michelet, *La Femme,* Paris, Flammarion, 1981, p. 345
74 "You must make a person of her": Ibid., p. 244
74 "You are [your wife's] father": Ibid., p. 232
74 "It is for the husband alone": Ibid., p. 239
74 "All is secure": Ibid., p. 195
75 "Such is the strength": Jules Michelet, *L'Amour,* Paris, Hachette, 1859, p. 44
75 "a woman's glance, a mere trifle": CORR., I, p. 203 (July 25, 1860)
75 "putrid stable": Ibid., p. 160 (May 5, 1860)
75 "You ask me for details": Ibid., p. 213
76 "I know perfectly well": Ibid., p. 253 (October 31, 1860)
76 "The other day, on a beautiful morning": Ibid., p. 174
76 "Sunday is . . . the day when": Thomas Forester, *Paris and Its Environs,* London, Henry G. Bohn, 1859, p. 374
77 "Last Sunday, Chaillan": CORR., I, pp. 150–51
77 "He showed me a copy": Ibid., p. 166 (May 16, 1860)
77 "We've begun the painting": Ibid., pp. 213–14
78 "[He said that] he had never": Goncourt, *Journal,* III, p. 552 (March 27, 1886)
78 "I know very well that I am still floundering": CORR., I, pp. 216ff.
78 "Banish the clergy": Ibid., p. 226 (August 10, 1860)
79 "Sir, It is often said": Ibid., pp. 235–36
80 "I am nothing, . . . but the situation today": Ibid., p. 237
80 "Ah! sois ma Béatrix": O.C., XV, p. 901
81 "My verse was very weak": Ibid., p. 855
81 "Depuis deux ans": Ibid., p. 903
81 "Rodolpho s'accouda": Ibid., p. 887
82 "Toujours, toujours": Ibid., p. 924
82 "The ground is covered with mud": CORR., I, p. 131
82 "Something like a veil": Ibid., pp. 276, 305 (March 17, 1861, and July 18, 1861)
82 "The word civilization": Ibid., p. 305 (July 18, 1861)
83 "Aussi viendra": O.C., XV, p. 902
83 "It is true": CORR., I, pp. 153–54 (May 2, 1860)
84 "Le Seigneur, entendant": O.C., XV, p. 902

84 "They saw the child halt": CN, p. 91
85 "Their lips united, their souls flew": Ibid., p. 19
85 "He began his studies in Aix": O.C., I, p. 119
85 "If I did not find food": "In the Days of My Youth," *The Bookman*, p. 346
86 "What harm is there in Paris": CORR., I, p. 210 (July 25, 1860)
86 "We do with the spoken word": Emile Deschanel, *Les Conférences à Paris et en France*, Paris, Pagnerre, 1870, p. 7
86 "spread knowledge, stir ideas": Ibid., p. 10
87 "What one seeks in a piece of writing": Emile Deschanel, *La Physiologie des écrivains et des artistes*, Paris, 1864, p. 196
87 "one recognizes the true greatness of a people": From a review in *La Jeune France*, March 17, 1861
87 "Let the muse take off": Léon Laurent-Pichat, *Les Poètes du combat*, Paris, Hetzel, 1862, p. 9
87 "If I see a dreamer": Ibid., p. 4
88 "A work of art": "Proudhon et Courbet," O.C., X, p. 38
88 "A work is simply": "Germinie Lacerteux," ibid., p. 62
88 "a poet in every sense of the word": CORR., I, p. 140 (March 24, 1860)
88 "Yes, one must drop the gutter muse": Ibid., p. 284 (April 22, 1861)
88 "Man partakes of the brute": Ibid., p. 283
88 "study his contemporaries": Ibid., p. 304 (July 18, 1861)
89 "I really don't know": Ibid., p. 258 (February 5, 1861)
89 "by way of reconciling": Ibid., p. 244 (October 2, 1860)
89 "My stomach and the future": Ibid., p. 292 (June 10, 1861)
90 "In the past several days": Ibid.
90 "Determined to earn my livelihood": Ibid.
90 "I enter, I find a gentleman": Ibid., pp. 287–88 (June 1, 1861)
91 "There is a delicate matter": Ibid., p. 270 (February 20, 1861)
91 "I've known you for seven years": Ibid., p. 204 (July 25, 1861)
91 "Tell yourself, tell yourself every day": Ibid., p. 316 (January 20, 1862)
91 "August . . . is far off": Ibid., p. 290
92 "I've tied up with an economist": Ibid., p. 309 (July 18, 1861)
92 "Real love has been a school": Ibid., p. 259
92 "I can speak knowledgeably": Ibid., pp. 263–64 (February 10, 1861)
93 "We display prostitution": Ibid., p. 266
93 "The widow is not the ideal": Ibid., p. 265
93 "The impulse to 'rescue' the beloved": Sigmund Freud, *Sexuality and the Psychology of Love*, New York, Collier Books, 1963, p. 56
94 "When dirty words": O.C., I, p. 28
94 "I accuse the heavens": CORR., I, p. 274
95 "The more vile and soiled": O.C., I, p. 59
95 "[waiting] for some external force": Colette Becker, "Un Ami de jeunesse d'Emile Zola: Georges Pajot. Lettres inédites," *Les Cahiers naturalistes*, no. 53, 1979, p. 118
95 "Her eyes followed me calmly": O.C., I, p. 58
95 "As for the future": CORR., I, p. 232 (late August or early September 1860)
96 "You must placate your father": Ibid., p. 141 (March 25, 1860)
96 "Be firm": Ibid., p. 152 (April 26, 1860)
96 "Is painting nothing for you": Ibid., pp. 212–13 (July 1860)
97 "The news charmed me": Ibid., p. 259

97 "Chaillan claims that here": Ibid., p. 249 (October 24, 1860)
97 "I've seen Paul": Ibid., pp. 284-85 (April 22, 1861)
98 "Sundays we shall take flight": Ibid., p. 272 (March 3, 1861)
98 "Paul is still the excellent": Ibid., p. 294 (June 10, 1861)
99 "I must then make long speeches": Ibid., p. 300 (June-July 1861)
99 "Paul may have": Ibid.
99 "It's been a long time": Ibid., p. 316 (January 20, 1862)

V. Someone to Reckon With

101 "Twenty journals are produced there": Colette Becker, "Zola à la librairie Hachette," *University of Ottawa Quarterly*, October-December 1978, p. 299
102 "religion, monarchy": Jean Mistler, *La Librairie Hachette de 1826 à nos jours*, Paris, Hachette, 1964, p. 21
102 "I have found another way": Ibid., p. 35
102 "It behooves us": Colette Becker, "Zola à la librairie Hachette," p. 303
103 "You ask me if I could send you": CORR., I, p. 334 (October 31, 1863)
104 "I can tell you . . . that every young man": Ibid., pp. 318-19 (May 20, 1862)
104 "arrange man's return": Ibid., p. 129
104 "Let a publisher stand up then": Ibid., I, p. 318
105 "How often, even now": Alexis, *Emile Zola*, p. 58
105 "I shall write to you anon": CORR., I, p. 348 (January 8, 1864)
105 "You propose to run a list ad": Ibid., p. 392 (December 14, 1864)
106 "My mother must have acquainted you": Ibid., p. 338 (December 2, 1863)
106 "I am ashamed": Ibid., pp. 361-62 (May 18, 1864)
107 "Someday . . . , in a year perhaps": Ibid., p. 321 (September 18, 1862)
107 "Where are those evenings": Ibid., p. 406 (February 6, 1865)
107 "Today I must walk quickly": Ibid., p. 380 (August 18, 1864)
107 "Outside prose, no salvation": Ibid., p. 381
108 "Poetry no longer suits": Halina Suława, *Naissance d'une doctrine. Formation des idées littéraires et esthétiques d'Emile Zola*, Warsaw, 1976, p. 93
108 "a great amphitheater": Ibid., p. 104
108 "If I pride myself in one thing": Alexis, *Emile Zola*, p. 232
109 "We must violently separate ourselves": O.C., X, pp. 313-14
109 "depopulated heavens": Ibid., p. 325
110 "Everyone can and wants to be": Ibid., p. 147
110 "An idealistic representation": Ibid., p. 37
110 "I state it as fundamental": Ibid., p. 38
110 "a negation of society": Ibid., p. 46
110 "I love . . . the free play": Ibid., p. 40
111 "A work of art is a corner": Ibid., p. 38
111 "corner of earth left intact" . . . "unfinished sketch": Ibid., XV, p. 861
111 "A work is simply the free": Ibid., X, pp. 62-63
111 "Schools have never produced": CORR., I, p. 377
111 "I would rather not retrace": Ibid., p. 232 (August-September 1860)
111 "Anarchy reigns and for me": O.C., X, p. 147
112 "Panting with anxiety": Ibid., p. 27
112 "Do you believe": Jules Vallès, *Littérature et Révolution*, Paris, 1970, pp. 393-94

112 "bestial and filthy rump": Quoted by Victor Giraud in *Hippolyte Taine*, Paris, J. Vrin, 1928, p. 101
112 "One feels that the author": O.C., X, p. 140
112 "Out in the open countryside": Hippolyte Taine, *Nouveaux essais de critique et d'histoire*, Paris, Hachette, 1866, p. 152
113 "The first canto . . . will relate": CORR., I, p. 182 (June 15, 1860)
113 "Everything alive": O.C., X, p. 144
113 "The doctor finds": Ibid.
113 "Every great artist gathers": Ibid., 147
113 "[Every great artist] draws": Ibid.
113 "spiritual dictators": Ibid.
114 "I should be very much in your debt": CORR., I, p. 400 (January 10, 1865)
114 "I wish to improve": Ibid., pp. 408–9 (April 11, 1865)
114 "You understand that I'm not writing": Ibid., p. 405 (February 6, 1865)
114 "If only you knew": Ibid., p. 414 (September 24, 1865)
114 "I have often let you know": Ibid., p. 444 (February 1866)
115 "We have a big apartment here": Ibid., p. 453 (July 26, 1866)
115 "Belonging to a band of friends": L'Oeuvre, RM, IV, p. 82
115 "[Sandoz] envisioned": Ibid., p. 193
116 "I wholeheartedly approve": CORR., I, p. 324 (September 29, 1862)
116 "Didn't I judge rightly": Camille Pissarro, *Correspondance*, Paris, Valhermeil, 1986, IV, p. 128
117 "Cézanne has cut his beard": Ibid., I, p. 360 (April 21, 1864)
117 "[I often see Paul in the afternoon]": Henri Perruchot, *La Vie de Cézanne*, Paris, Hachette, 1956, p. 127
117 "Every work of art is a window": CORR., I, p. 375 (August 18, 1864)
118 "I fully accept its procedure": Ibid., p. 380
118 "At first glance I took her for a saint": CN, p. 39
118 "Opposite me, behind a little pane": Ibid., p. 45
118 "I've won my first victory": CORR., I, p. 368
118 "My volume of stories": Ibid., p. 365
119 "Don't trouble to get one of the stories": Ibid., p. 384 (October 4, 1864)
119 "I hasten to send you": Ibid., p. 387 (November 24, 1864)
119 "The author, M. Emile Zola": Ibid., p. 388
120 "All in all the press has been benevolent": Ibid., p. 406 (February 6, 1865)
120 "Here are my stories": CN, p. 10
121 "The peaceful sleep of vice": O.C., I, p. 19
121 "I was ashamed for the young woman": Ibid.
121 "My suspicions became flesh": Ibid., p. 83
121 "I thought I was mature enough": Ibid., p. 110
122 "I looked at the three of them together": Ibid., p. 63
122 "M. Emile Zola, whose maiden work": Ibid., p. 118
122 "find his way": CORR., I, p. 415 (November 14, 1865)
122 "It is understood that I prefer": Ibid., 420 (November 14, 1865)
123 "It will please their families": Ibid.
123 "The psychological side of this study": Ibid., p. 446
123 "It's hard for me to answer": Ibid., 434 (January 8, 1866)
124 "To be sure it inspires reservations": O.C., I, pp. 118–19
124 "Today I am known": Ibid., p. 434 (January 8, 1866)
124 "I am a great ignoramus": Ibid., p. 444 (February 1866)

VI. A Hearth, a Café, a Cause

126 "Tall, olive-skinned": Pierre Cogny, Le "Huysmans intime" de Henry Céard et Jean de Caldain, Paris, Nizet, 1957, p. 127

128 "[Le Figaro figured as]": from the entry on Villemessant in the Encyclopédie Larousse (nineteenth century)

128 "No longer will I force myself": O.C., X, p. 363

129 "I beg readers to observe": Ibid., p. 422

129 "It seems that telling the truth": Ibid.

129 "I am sympathetic to these violent stories": Ibid., p. 379

130 "I like historical indiscretions": Ibid., p. 390

130 "I'm not a disciple of art for art's sake": Ibid., p. 430

130 "Personally, I prefer": Ibid., pp. 400–1

130 "Myself, I'm a rebel": Ibid., p. 450

131 "the future of painting is being realized": Elisabeth Gilmore Holt, The Triumph of Art for the Public, New York, Doubleday Anchor, 1979, p. 378

132 "I have wanted quite simply to draw": Courbet raconté par lui-même et par ses amis, Geneva, Pierre Cailler, 1950, II, p. 60

132 "I have lately had the honor": Rewald, Cézanne et Zola, p. 50

133 "I wanted to see where the unhappy man": O.C., XII, pp. 1054–55

133 "Nowadays a Salon is not the work": Ibid., pp. 789–80

133 "They mock truth and justice": Ibid., p. 791

133–34 "If the future treats me generously": Guy Robert, "Des Inédits d'Emile Zola. Une polémique entre Zola et Le Mémorial d'Aix en 1868," Arts et Livres, no. 6, 1946, p. 18

134 "a dike . . . so many individualities": R. H. Wilenski, Modern French Painters, New York, Vintage, 1960, I, p. 23

134 "I hold that a work of art": O.C., XII, p. 796

134 "Do you fear your own language": Ibid., p. 797

135 "I liked him right away": Ibid., p. 803

135 "What certain confreres pass off": Ibid., p. 804

135 "You know what effect Monsieur Manet's canvases": Ibid., pp. 805–6

135 "Monsieur Manet has a no-nonsense temperament": Ibid.

135 "The waggish scapegrace": Ibid., p. 803

135 "Now there's a temperament": Ibid., p. 808

136 "I have tried to restore to M. Manet": Ibid., p. 806

136 "Lunatics tore up the paper": Alexis, Emile Zola, p. 68

136 "I don't give a hoot": O.C., XII, pp. 817–18

136 "Dear Monsieur Zola, I don't know where to find you": Manet, 1832–1883, exhibition catalogue, Paris, Editions de la Réunion des Musées Nationaux, 1983, p. 520

137 "One evening . . . I was walking down": Ibid., p. 13

137 "Art is a circle": Ibid., p. 15

137 "as if he had never painted before": Ibid., p. 14

137 "Anything that distinguishes one": Ibid., p. 17

138 "[Manet] has admitted to me": O.C., XII, p. 827

138 "It's criminal to live far from Paris": CORR., I, p. 451 (June 14, 1866)

139 "Nothing could have been more interesting": Roy McMullen, Degas, Boston, Houghton Mifflin, 1984, p. 155 (from interview with Monet by François Thiébault-Sisson, Le Temps, November 26, 1900)

139 "I won't offer you my hand": Rewald, *Cézanne et Zola*, p. 58
139 "They're a lot of bastards": Lindsay, *Cézanne*, p. 102
139 "Last winter's ashes": O.C., V, p. 444
140 "I don't need a woman of my own": Rewald, *Cézanne et Zola*, pp. 58–59, from Zola's notes for the novel *L'Oeuvre* (B.N., n.a.f., 10,328)
140 "Happy those with memories!": O.C., XII, p. 785
141 "I am surrounded by painters": CORR., I, p. 473 (February 19, 1867)
141 "I feel like an atom in the bosom": *Le Capitaine Burle*, O.C., IX, p. 625
141 "He is as ambitious and domineering": Alexis, *Emile Zola*, p. 200
142 "I am impatient": CORR., I, p. 454 (July 26, 1866)
142 "After one week, he'd fall sick": Alexis, *Emile Zola*, p. 201
143 "Right now there's warfare": John Lough, *Writer and Public in France*, Oxford, Clarendon Press, 1978, p. 333
143 "He sacrificed everything": O.C., I, p. 163
144 "Why this grief": Goncourt, *Journal*, III, p. 70 (April 22, 1880)
144 "I will always be on the side": O.C., XII, 817–18
144 "A New Manner": "Une Nouvelle Manière en peinture. Edouard Manet," *La Revue du XIXe siècle*, January 1, 1867
144 "[Manet] paints neither history nor the soul": O.C., XII, pp. 832–33
145 "Originality, there's the great bugaboo": Ibid., pp. 842–43
145 "In France, in this land of pluck": Ibid., p. 841
145 "You've made me a dandy New Year's gift": *Manet*, exhibition catalogue, p. 520
146 "The novel. Definition": CORR., I, p. 465
146 "I can't explain at length": Ibid., p. 462
146 "When heaven came down to earth": O.C., X, p. 280
146 "Fabulation is less complicated": Ibid., p. 281
147 "Ah! how nice you would be": CORR., I, pp. 462–63 (December 10, 1866)
147 "You are definitely regarded": *Manet*, exhibition catalogue, p. 520
147 "How about my giving you": CORR., I, p. 459 (November 26, 1866)
147 "I must confess": Ibid., p. 464 (December 10, 1866)
148 "Tell Paul to return": Ibid.

VII. *"La Littérature Putride"*

149 "the true, palpitating": CORR., I, p. 474
149 "My *feuilleton* appeared": O.C., I, p. 225
150 "Have you read all of Balzac": CORR., I, p. 501 (May 29, 1867)
151 "*Les Mystères* is a contemporary": Ibid., p. 475 (February 27, 1867)
151 "If, in any era": Honoré de Balzac, *La Comédie humaine*, NRF (Pléiade), 1962, V, p. 153
152 "Be lenient": CORR., I, p. 505 (June 6, 1867)
152 "Allow me . . . to tell you": Ibid., p. 485 (April 4, 1867)
152 "I labor over certain things": Ibid., p. 486
153 "Your correspondent is mistaken": Ibid., p. 479 (March 7, 1867)
153 "The support this project was given": Ibid., pp. 483–84 (March 25, 1867)
153 "We must turn the novel upside down": Ibid., p. 504 (June 4, 1867)
153 "There are several things I've rearranged": Ibid., p. 513 (July 16, 1867)
154 "Bellevaut will doubtless tell you": Ibid., p. 515

154 "My frightful production of books": quoted by John Lough in *Writer and Public in France*, p. 347

154 "Theater is the only literature": Ibid., pp. 364–65

154–55 "Let's say a play": O.C., X, p. 1271

155 "People down here don't have": CORR., I, p. 527 (October 4, 1867)

155 "It seemed to me much too long": Ibid., p. 529 (October 6, 1867)

156 "I am certain that a masterly work": Ibid., p. 471 (February 12, 1867)

156 "I am very satisfied": Ibid., p. 485 (April 4, 1867)

156 "I am very pleased": Ibid., p. 500 (May 29, 1867)

156 "My father instructs me": Ibid., p. 494

157 "I propose that *Thérèse Raquin*": Ibid., p. 523

157 "Thérèse had never seen a man": O.C., I, p. 541

158 "By killing Camille": Ibid., p. 583

158 "The thin, bony, slightly swollen head": Ibid., p. 579

158 "Now his hand unconsciously traced": Ibid., p. 630

159 "[An old acquaintance]": Ibid., p. 629

159 "dressed her, jerked her right and left": Ibid., p. 647

159 "She used her eyes": Ibid., p. 634

159 "She felt in her moribund flesh": Ibid., p. 636

159 "Their corpses lay all night": Ibid., p. 667

160 "There's a touch of lockjaw": *Thérèse Raquin*, Paris, Garnier-Flammarion, 1970, pp. 53–54

160 "In the past several years": O.C., I, p. 673

161 "Balzac . . . made a Madame Marneffe": Ibid., p. 674

161 "[Zola] sees woman as Manet paints her": Ibid., p. 675

161 "If this represented some individual fantasy": Ibid., p. 676

161 "M. Zola is said to be a young man of talent": Ibid., pp. 674–75

161–62 "Certainly not, one couldn't have Germinie Lacerteux": Ibid., p. 677

162 "beautiful lies, ready-made sentiments": Ibid., p. 678

162 "It would not displease you": Ibid.

162 "Where science is concerned": Ibid., p. 521

162 "He who reads the novel with care": Ibid., p. 520

162 "[My few congenial readers] will recognize": Ibid., p. 522

163 "We visited the Louvre": Mark Twain, *The Innocents Abroad*, New York, New American Library (Signet), 1966, p. 100

164 "A writer for the official bulletin": Burchell, *Imperial Masquerade*, p. 128

164 "My dear Sir, the heart of this garden": Ibid., p. 126

165 "I seldom see Baille": CORR., I, p. 500

165 "I've wanted for quite some time": Ibid., p. 507

165 "Two years in Aix": Ibid., p. 501

166 "Paul has been an epidemic germ": Rewald, *Cézanne et Zola*, p. 71

166 "Paul is for me a veritable Sphinx": Clive Thomson, "Une Correspondance inédite: vingt-sept lettres de Marius Roux à Emile Zola," *University of Ottawa Quarterly*, vol. XLVIII, no. 4, p. 344

166 "The analytic painters, the young school": CORR., I, p. 491 (April 8, 1867)

166 "Paul is a child ignorant of life": John Rewald, *Cézanne. Sa vie, son oeuvre, son amitié pour Zola*, Paris, Albin Michel, 1939, pp. 137–38

166–67 "I cannot give you the address": CORR., II, p. 219 (May 30, 1870)

167 "You are doubtless aware": Toulouse, *Enquête*, pp. VIff.

167 "Alas, you are quite right": CORR., I, p. 470

168 "Your last letter announced": Ibid., p. 512 (July 16, 1867)
168 "You will print in 18 cm. format": Colette Becker, "La Correspondance de Zola, 1858–1870," pp. 167–68
169 "This pains me but as a last resort": CORR., II, pp. 116–17

VIII. THE MASTER PLAN

170 "I hear from other persons besides Lord Cowley": Thompson, *Louis Napoleon*, p. 277
171 "any Frenchman": Claude Bellanger, ed., *Histoire générale de la presse française*, Paris, Presses Universitaires de France, 1969, II, p. 346
171 "What we have is an unprecedented": Henri Mitterand, *Zola journaliste*, Paris, Armand Colin, 1962, p. 86
173 *"Eugène Bastin* is not a novel": O.C., X, p. 735
173 "Poor mankind, dreaming wide awake": Ibid., p. 726
173 "I've saved the best for last": CORR., II, p. 118
173 "Yesterday a friend asked me": O.C., XII, p. 862
174 "I find in Philippe Solari": Ibid., p. 887
174 "Yesterday I saw Duret at Manet's": CORR., II, p. 118 (April 17, 1868)
174 "You think Pelletan": Thomson, "Une correspondance inédite, vingt-sept lettres de Marius Roux à Emile Zola," p. 362
174 "I saw Pelletan this morning": CORR., II, p. 122
175 "Has the salary question": Ibid., p. 124
175 "I must apprise you of my conversation": Ibid., p. 129
175 "I've learned that we shall soon": Ibid., p. 158 (October 7, 1868)
175 "I thank you for confiding in me": Ibid., p. 159
175–76 "You are under siege": Ibid., 126 (May 21, 1868)
176 "[I] would like to launch something big": Goncourt, *Journal*, II, p. 475 (December 14, 1868)
176 "Ah! how many sinister dreams": O.C., XIII, p. 207
177 *"La Belle Hélène* amounts to nothing": Ibid., p. 117
177 "Walk around our working-class slums": Ibid., p. 132
177 "At Toulon mother and child": Ibid., p. 249
177 "I know M. Haussmann": Ibid., pp. 196–97
178 "On some Wednesday morning": Ibid., p. 131
178 "I think I know what troubled you": Ibid., X, p. 758
179 "The Church intends to possess woman": Françoise Mayeur, *L'Education des filles en France au XIXe siècle*, Paris, Hachette, 1979, p. 140
179 "The Prince Imperial, then a boy of twelve": Thompson, *Louis Napoleon*, pp. 291–92
180 "In France there seemed to be bands and banners": Ibid., p. 291
180 "The administration should assemble": O.C., XIII, p. 234
181 "He had me talk at length about myself": Alexis, *Emile Zola*, p. 91
181 "More stay-at-home then than now": Ibid., p. 175
181 "Such scandalous conduct": Robert, "Une polémique entre Zola et *Le Mémorial d'Aix*," p. 6
181 "My father, a civil engineer": Ibid., p. 7
182 "Deliver the letter and plead the cause": CORR., II, p. 152
182 "I ask you first to find out": Ibid., p. 171
183 "She never loved him deep down": O.C., I, p. 715

183 "The lovers could imagine": Ibid., p. 734
184 "She rediscovered him there": Ibid., p. 740
184 "The young woman luxuriated": Ibid., p. 763
184 "The idea of having shared her": Ibid., p. 801
184 "God the Father did not pardon": Ibid., p. 896
185 "Guillaume's marriage": Ibid., p. 760
185 "Long contemplation of his wife": Ibid., p. 769
185 "My child, I have come to regard you": Ibid., p. 878
186 "Let's reason this out": CORR., II, p. 165 (November 14, 1868)
186 "The few lines they would expurgate": O.C., X, pp. 768–69
186 "Attached you will find the note": CORR., II, p. 169 (November 26, 1868)
187 "I don't know if you still review": Ibid., p. 175 (December 7, 1868)
187 "My dear friend, I am immersed": *Manet*, exhibition catalogue, p. 522
187 "made in the mold of his characters": Goncourt, *Journal*, II, p. 475 (December 14, 1868)
187 "Now and again recriminations": Ibid.
188 "No need to indicate here": RM, II, p. 800
188 "how in procreation as in creation": Ibid., V, p. 1697
188 "My work will be less social than scientific": Ibid., pp. 1736–37
189 "block from mind the provinces": Daumard, *Les Bourgeois de Paris*, p. 326
189 "The railroads, exercising a bizarre influence": Maurice Descotes, *Le Public de théâtre et son histoire*, Paris, Presses Universitaires de France, 1964, p. 311
190 "the invasion of women from abroad": Ibid.
190 "Railroads were created. The first rapid fortunes": Alexandre Dumas *fils*, *Théâtre complet*, Paris, Michel Lévy, 1896, I, p. 26
190 "[The whore] has invaded society": Goncourt, *Journal*, I, p. 312 (January 18, 1857)
190 "Characteristic of the modern movement": RM, V, pp. 1738–39
190 "It will burn like matter": Ibid., p. 1741
191 "A novel whose milieu": Ibid., p. 1775
192 "I would like to make your acquaintance": CORR., II, p. 168
192 "I've heard much talk about": Ibid., p. 197 (March 24, 1869)
193 "I have a request to make of you": CORR., II, p. 187
193 "I arrived with a preconceived Flaubert": O.C., XI, p. 135
193 "We are now like women": Goncourt, *Journal*, II, p. 308 (December 20, 1866)
194 "The melancholy of [Aix's] promenades": *"Naturalisme pas mort." Lettres inédites de Paul Alexis à Emile Zola*, edited by B. H. Bakker, Toronto, University of Toronto Press, 1971, p. 3
194 "Around September 15, 1869, at 8 p.m.": Alexis, *Emile Zola*, pp. 90–91
195 "Remember, France has sown the world": O.C., XIII, p. 303
196 "With this frightful war": CORR., II, pp. 223–24
196 "If I left Paris I promised": Ibid., p. 225

IX. WARTIME IMPROVISATIONS

197 "She seems to have been lively and quick-spirited": Lindsay, *Cézanne*, p. 130
198 "She became a burden in social and economic terms": Ibid., p. 131
199 "What if we put out a small paper": CORR., II, 225–26
199 "Roux and I are starting a little newspaper": Ibid., p. 227 (September 21, 1870)
199 "We have received news through a carrier pigeon": Labouchère, *Diary of a*

Besieged Resident in Paris, New York, Harper & Brothers, 1871, pp. 18–19
200 "I soft-headedly thought that a Bonaparte": Bellanger, *Histoire de la presse*, II, p. 360
200 "As of November 1, 1870, we cede to you": CORR., II, pp. 227–28
200 "[Our printer] sorely regrets": Ibid., p. 252
201 "May I invoke my long collaboration": Ibid., p. 230
201 "I observe the revolution march past": Ibid., p. 229
202 "I immediately contacted M. Leuven": Ibid., p. 233 (December 13, 1870)
202 "He offered me Quimperlé": Ibid.
203 "Your letters gave me great pleasure": Ibid., p. 242 (December 15, 1870)
203 "I see I can't win a victory": Ibid., pp. 242–43
203 "I sometimes feel gusts of pride": Ibid., p. 243
203 "second Paris, gay and magnificent": Hippolyte Taine, *Journeys through France*, New York, Henry Holt, 1897, p. 61
203 "It rains continually": CORR., II, p. 240 (December 14, 1870)
203 "[Bordeaux] repels me": Ibid., p. 234 (December 13, 1870)
204 "Roux's telegram made me very happy": Ibid., p. 245
204 "Enclosed are fifty francs": Ibid., pp. 241–42
204 "I must tell you that you're not very good": Ibid., p. 256
204 "If M. Thiers is in Bordeaux": Ibid.
205 "Three days ago, Marie": Ibid., p. 253
205 "He told me that he had received": Ibid., p. 248 (December 18, 1870)
205 "He has a bird's head": Encyclopédie Larousse (nineteenth century), article on Glais-Bizoin.
205 "I have good news": CORR., II, p. 253 (December 20, 1870)
206 "You will leave on the 10:10 p.m. convoy": Ibid., p. 258 (December 21, 1870)
206 "I'm at the end of my tether": Ibid., p. 264
207 "In place of the reactionary": Michael Howard, *The Franco-Prussian War*, New York, Collier Books, 1969, p. 444
207 "I spent all my time queuing up": CORR., II, p. 278
207 "How are you? How did you get through the siege?": Ibid., p. 275
208 "Tell me what shape": Ibid., pp. 279–80
208 "The streets swarmed with officers": Olivier Got, "Bordeaux vu par Zola, 1870–1871," *Revue historique de Bordeaux et du département de la Gironde*, vol. XXII, 1973, p. 110
209 "Noon; a detachment of mounted police": O.C., XIII, p. 388
209 "Today a tragic session": Victor Hugo, *Carnets intimes*, Paris, Gallimard, 1953, p. 108
209 "Would you like me to send you": CORR., II, pp. 276–77
209 "Your proposition is irresistible": Ibid., p. 277
210 "How many bald pates": O.C., XIII, pp. 358–59
210 "Imagine if you will": Ibid., p. 353
210 "When I left the auditorium": Ibid., p. 390
210 "I can't accept your praise": CORR., II, p. 284
211 "At first we provincials": Stewart Edwards, *The Paris Commune, 1871*, New York, Quadrangle, 1977, p. 118
212 "At one end of the square": Goncourt, *Journal*, II, p. 739 (February 27, 1871)
212 "We have always desired freedom": Marquis of Normanby, *Year of Revolution*, London, Longman, 1857, II, p. 205

212-13 "By the time a column of National Guards": Edwards, *The Paris Commune*, p. 139
213 "Everyone was shrieking": Ibid., p. 142
213 "I took over the ministry": Ibid., p. 165
214 "Obscure a few days ago": Ibid., p. 155
214 "I am voting for the reddest of the reds": Ibid., p. 185
214 "a revolutionary and patriotic festival": Ibid., p. 186
214 "a monarchist plot just beyond": *La Commune de 1871*, Paris, Editions de Delphes, 1965, p. 55
214 "The royalist conspirators have *attacked*": Ibid., p. 62
215 "partisan of the regular government": Ibid., p. 70
215 "Once again I almost missed": O.C., XIII, p. 431
215 "Between the dissidents of City Hall": Ibid., p. 436
216 "Meeting follows meeting": Ibid., p. 445
216 "I do not represent my paper": Ibid., p. 448
216 "What will M. Thiers's conduct be": Ibid., p. 452
216 "Toward the end of the session": Ibid., p. 470
217 "Heartbroken, I must tell you": Ibid., p. 471
217 "The communal revolution": *La Commune de 1871*, p. 159
217 "Religious or dogmatic instruction": Ibid., p. 78
218 "the most active auxiliaries": Ibid., p. 238
218 "This Sunday, Paris, without any other means": Goncourt, *Journal*, II, p. 786 (April 30, 1871)
219 "Terror reigns supreme": Rodolphe Walter, "Zola et la Commune," *Les Cahiers naturalistes*, no. 43, 1972, p. 26
219 "Our implacable enemies": Mitterand, *Zola journaliste*, p. 143
219 "At this moment, Prussia postures": Ibid., p. 144
219 "It's a magnificent amphitheater": CN, p. 516
220 "[I saw] a thin column of black smoke": Paul Verlaine, *Oeuvres en prose complètes*, Gallimard (Pléiade), 1972, p. 547
221 "The massacres that were to grow more fearsome": Edwards, *The Paris Commune*, p. 322
221 "I managed to take a walk through Paris": Mitterand, *Zola journaliste*, p. 147
222 "With warm days upon us": *Le Sémaphore de Marseille*, June 3, 1871
222 "I remember a walk I took there": Ibid., June 2, 1871
222 "Measures taken against fugitive insurgents": Ibid., June 5 or 6, 1871 (dispatch of June 2)
223 "I am now back in Batignolles": CORR., II, p. 294 (July 4, 1871)

X. *NULLA DIES SINE LINEA*

224 "everything in the world exists to result in a book": Stéphane Mallarmé, *Oeuvres complètes*, Paris, Gallimard (Pléiade), 1956, p. 378
224 "I had spent three years": RM, I, pp. 3–4
225 "lacked all practical sense": Ibid., p. 45
225 "When Pierre . . . could understand": Ibid., p. 48
225 "The party wall no longer existed": Ibid., p. 55
225 "Félicité was a type": Ibid., pp. 55–56
226 "The Rougon tribe": Ibid., p. 64
226 "Heredity had preoccupied him": Ibid., p. 68

226 "Every party has its freaks": Ibid., p. 128
227 "The year was 1851": Ibid., p. 93
227 "Alone at last": Ibid., p. 228
228 "He thought about horizons": Ibid., pp. 138–39
228 "As if to isolate and seal": Ibid., p. 38
228 "When one leaves Plassans": Ibid., pp. 5–6
229 "The little door . . . had stood forgotten": Ibid., p. 187
229 "In Provence, humble women": Ibid., pp. 14–17
230 "Nothing more awesomely grandiose": Ibid., p. 27
231 "This endless parade of heads": Ibid., pp. 31–32
231 "Miette was becoming a boy": Ibid., p. 32
232 "We were hardly more than a handful": Edmond Lepelletier, *Emile Zola*, Paris, Mercure de France, 1908, p. 266
232 "He doesn't yet have his style down pat": RM, I, p. 1541
232 "I've just finished your torturous": Ibid.
233 "Through *Le Mémorial d'Aix*": CORR., II, pp. 297–98
233 "His demeanor, which combined": Emile Bergerat, *Souvenirs d'un enfant de Paris*, Paris, Fasquelle, 1912, p. 398
234 "Today Zola dines with me": Goncourt, *Journal*, II, p. 898
234 "Versailles recovered its former animation": *Histoire de la Troisième République*, edited by Jean Héritier, Paris, Librairie de France, 1932, p. 58
234 "Go ahead, Gabrielle": MS, Collection Jean Claude LeBlond
235 "Have we not seen laborers": René Rémond, *La Vie politique en France depuis 1789*, Paris, Armand Colin, 1969, II, p. 309
235 "[That flag] has always been for me": D. W. Brogan, *France under the Republic*, New York, Harper & Brothers, 1940, p. 83
236 "Of all the mysteries": Adrien Dansette, *L'Histoire religieuse de la France contemporaine*, Paris, Flammarion, 1965, p. 322
236 "Suspended in midair": Ibid., p. 349
236 "Since assembling in Versailles": Ibid., p. 350
237 "I must tell France the truth": Ibid., p. 342
237 "Until the country's definitive institutions": Rémond, *La Vie politique en France*, p. 306
238 "It is the government of the country": Guy Chapman, *The Third Republic of France*, London, Macmillan, 1962, p. 37
238 "Society is dying of universal suffrage": Goncourt, *Journal*, II, pp. 827–28 (July 11, 1871)
239 "new barbarians [who] threaten": Jean-Marie Mayeur, *Les Débuts de la Troisième République*, Paris, Editions du Seuil, 1973, p. 26
239 "With God's help": Mayeur, *Les Débuts*, p. 27
239 "M. de Gavardie, the man who goes unheard": O.C., XIII, p. 537
239 "Then came the interminable": Ibid., p. 596
240 "At bottom he may be a nice chap": Ibid., p. 714
240 "The Right, on hearing": Ibid., p. 591
240 "What wicked foolishness": Ibid., p. 682
241 "Yesterday I spent two hours": Ibid., p. 709
241 "Return to Paris, for the sake": Ibid., pp. 950–51
241 "rally around the thought": Raoul Girardet (editor), *Le Nationalisme français, 1871–1914*, Paris, Armand Colin, 1970, p. 51
241 "In France, certain things": O.C., XIII, pp. 532–33

242 "Now that the Republic has brought off": Ibid., p. 532
242 "Once a German has taunted us": Ibid., pp. 707-9
242 "What barbarism! What regression!" Flaubert, *Correspondance Gustave Flaubert-George Sand*, Paris, Flammarion, 1981, p. 324
243 "knock[s] me senseless": CORR., II, p. 288 (June 30, 1871)
243 "I'm ashamed at not yet": Ibid., p. 312 (February 2, 1872)
243 ". . . I've still accomplished nothing!": CN, p. 403
244 "The day [the Assembly] is dissolved": O.C., XIII, p. 971
244 "First there's what he calls 'the Sketch' ": Alexis, *Emile Zola*, pp. 163-65
245 "M. Zola makes no drafts": Toulouse, *Enquête*, pp. 272-73
245 "Aristide gets rich through expropriation": B.N., n.a.f., 10282, preparatory notes for *La Curée*, p. 294
246 "What I'm about to write is decidedly": Ibid., p. 298
246 "like a bird of prey": RM, I, p. 359
246 "When he stood by the window": Ibid., p. 362
247 "At thirteen he was already": Ibid., p. 407
247 "The hothouse, which resembled": Ibid., p. 354
247 "[They] loved the new Paris": Ibid., p. 496
248 "[She] grew accustomed": Ibid., pp. 510-11
249 "A new grotto appeared": RM, I, pp. 548-49
249 "The costume ball began: Ibid., p. 557
249 As much can be said of high society's self-made entertainments: Kurtz, *The Empress Eugénie*, pp. 218-219
250 "When they opened the dining room": Ibid., pp. 557-58
250 "In literature, M. Zola belongs": CORR., II, p. 306
251 "This debate isn't yours": Ibid., pp. 303-5

XI. CONFRONTING THE MORAL ORDER

254 "[The theater] is dying": O.C., X, p. 1061
254 "I meekly followed the crowd": Ibid., XII, p. 909
254 "Modern art will not flourish": Ibid., p. 911
255 "At this moment, princes are rebelling": Ibid., XIV, p. 28
255 "Strange family that won't die": Ibid., p. 106
255 "Napoleon I's wardrobe": Ibid., p. 107
255 "History suffices unto the glory": Ibid., p. 108
255 "[I conjecture] that with the assumption": Sigmund Freud, *Civilization and Its Discontents*, New York, Norton, 1962, p. 53
256 "Royalists and Bonapartists feel": O.C., XIV, p. 170
256 "I know people who need you": O.C., XIV, p. 76
256 "The Church neither ignores nor despises": Philip Spencer, *The Politics of Belief in Nineteenth-Century France*, London, Faber & Faber, 1954, p. 240
257 "Françoise Roussel had already done": Ibid., p. 122
257 "When the Jesuit Dufour was found": Ibid., pp. 161-62
258 "[Confessor and penitent] have grown together": Ibid., p. 163
258 "Zola's article on Father Dufour": CORR., II, p. 319
259 "Ah! my dear Ulbach": Ibid., p. 318
259 "Meanwhile there is a political dinner": O.C., XIV, 206-10
260 "Bring Emile Zola to trial!" Mitterand, *Zola journaliste*, p. 172
260 "articles that incite hatred": Ibid.

260 "I'm sorry you haven't been here": CORR., II, p. 324
261 "We didn't have [Zola's] address": Maurice Dreyfous, *Ce qu'il me reste à dire*, Paris, Ollendorff, 1912, p. 283
261 "I can still see him seated": Ibid., p. 285
262 "Here, gentlemen, is what I would like": Ibid., p. 286
262 "That is how two very young men": Ibid., p. 287
262 "For almost twenty-five years": Colette Becker (editor), *Trente années d'amitié. Lettres de l'éditeur Georges Charpentier à Emile Zola*, Paris, Presses Universitaires de France, 1980, pp. 8–9
262–63 "My dear Monsieur Zola. Kindly correct": Ibid., p. 17
263 "I'm pushing ahead with": Ibid., pp. 18–19
263 "It is a colossal pantry": RM, I, p. 1615
264 "The stomach—Paris's stomach": Ibid., p. 1613
264 "Many was the time, in 1872": Alexis, *Emile Zola*, pp. 96–97
264 "The man gave him invaluable information": Ibid.
265 "Florent, who had inherited his mother's capacity": RM, I, p. 641
265 "Accepting the woes": Ibid., p. 644
265 "Lisa believed that one must work": Ibid., pp. 647–48
266 "The young woman dreamed about": Ibid., p. 652
266 "grasps the need for luxury": Ibid.
266 "He listened to her, dumbstruck": Ibid., pp. 694–95
266 "Little by little a kind of dull anxiety": Ibid., pp. 728–30
267 "Red faces stared him down": Ibid., p. 718
267 "Gaiety returned to the huge, sonorous pavilions": Ibid., p. 893
267 "with her thighs trammeled by the burden": Ibid., pp. 650–51
268 "Mirrors all around the shop": Ibid., p. 667
268 "The peace and cleanliness": Ibid., p. 803
269 "Gavard the poulterer": Ibid., p. 792
269 "Every day they'd visit the tripery": Ibid., pp. 774–75
270 "His secret dream was to live forever": Ibid., p. 725
270 "[Lisa] gorged him like a little boy": Ibid., p. 695
270 "He avoided her": Ibid., pp. 812–13
270 "After those seven years": Ibid., p. 727
270 "To Florent she seemed colossal": Ibid., pp. 738–39
271 "His hands in his pockets and whistling": Ibid., p. 623–24
271 "I left my firedogs": Quoted in preface to *Le Ventre de Paris*, Paris, Garnier-Flammarion, 1971, p. 37
272 "It's curious how this pudgy lad": Goncourt, *Journal*, II, p. 1033 (January 25, 1875)
272–73 "It seems to me that I am always the beginner": Alexis, *Emile Zola*, p. 206
273 "one would be hard put to imagine a style": Auguste Dezalay (editor), *Lectures de Zola*, Paris, Armand Colin, 1973, p. 19
273 "The import of his books is this": Ibid., pp. 19–20
273 "I'm a bit like those Muslims intoxicated": RM, I, pp. 1621–22

XII. THE COMPANY OF FIVE

274 "On lovely summer evenings": Alexis, *Emile Zola*, p. 175
275 "I've found him forsaken": Cézanne, *Correspondance*, pp. 141–42

275 "Pissarro may have fathered us all": Joachim Gasquet, *Cézanne*, Paris, Bernheim-Jeune, 1926, pp. 148, 189
276 "We have high hopes for our Cézanne": Camille Pissarro, *Correspondance, 1865–1885*, edited by Janine Bailly-Herzberg, Paris, Presses Universitaires de France, 1980, p. 77
276 "if it's five-legged sheep": Ibid., p. 88
276 "I know that [Pissarro] thinks highly of me": Cézanne, *Correspondance*, p. 148
276 "My wife begs Mme Zola to come fetch": Pissarro, *Correspondance*, pp. 77–78
277 "I should like to describe our dominical sessions": O.C., XI, pp. 129–31
278 "Flaubert had characteristic gestures": Dreyfous, *Ce qu'il me reste à dire*, p. 267
278 "I sought to love you": Flaubert, *Correspondance (1830–1865)*, Paris, Gallimard (Pléiade), 1973–1991, II, p. 549 (April 12, 1854)
278 "In a stentorian voice": Goncourt, *Journal*, II, p. 12 (January 18, 1864)
279 "There are neither beautiful nor ugly subjects": Flaubert, *Correspondance* (Pléiade), II, p. 31 (January 16, 1852)
279 "He must purchase my name": Flaubert, *Correspondance* (Pléiade), III, 224 (June 15, 1862)
280 "My mother has bequeathed Croisset": Flaubert, *Oeuvres complètes*, Paris, Club de l'honnête homme, 1972, XV, pp. 119–20
280 "If we were to hunt about a bit": Flaubert, *Oeuvres complètes*, Paris, Club de l'Honnête Homme, 1972 (February 22, 1873 to Mme Roger de Genettes)
281 "Russia can wait": Ely Halpérine-Kaminsky (editor), *Ivan Tourguéniev d'après sa correspondance avec ses amis français*, Paris, Fasquelle, 1901, p. 21
282 "She is ugly but with a kind of ugliness": Leonard Schapiro, *Turgenev*, Oxford, Oxford University Press, 1978, p. 42
283 "He who has faith has everything": Ibid., 146
283 "During the operation I was thinking": Goncourt, *Journal*, III, p. 252 (April 25, 1883)
284 "Oh, we have hard times to live through": Halpérine-Kaminsky, *Tourguéniev d'après sa correspondance*, p. 57 (May 6, 1871)
284 "Since the first time I saw you": Ibid., p. 48 (May 26, 1868)
285 "It's not that life is more difficult": Ibid., p. 61 (November 26, 1871)
285 "Who is there to talk to now?" Flaubert, *Oeuvres complètes*, XV, p. 36 (August 21, 1871)
285 "[Flaubert] would declare in his booming voice": O.C., XI, pp. 135–36
285 "One must know everything": Flaubert, *Correspondance* (Pléiade), II, p. 544 (April 7, 1854)
286 "Given my general scheme": RM, I, p. 1648
286 "He would prowl through the house": Ibid., p. 919
287 "Marthe noted his bare, rough-hewn head": Ibid., p. 911
287 "Not a sound came from the third floor": Ibid., p. 916
287 "Walking through the salon": Ibid., p. 949
287 "The person in Paris": Ibid., p. 961
288 "He often spoke about charity": Ibid., p. 974
288 "The great, enveloping silence": Ibid., pp. 989–90
289 "The old Rougon grudge": Ibid., p. 1105
289 "Marthe stood spellbound": Ibid., p. 1183
290 "When all was ready": Ibid., p. 1199

290 "The curtains over the windows": Ibid., p. 926
291 "people at the subprefecture": Ibid., p. 928
291 "One no longer feels at home": Ibid., p. 1000
291 "He raised his head, he examined": Ibid., pp. 1011–12
292 "[Madame Faujas] hoisted Ovide": Ibid., p. 1200
292 "The mother gave the child his life": Sigmund Freud, "A Special Type of Object Choice Made by Men," in *Sexuality and the Psychology of Love*, New York, Collier Books, 1963, pp. 56–57
293 "The weakness of woman's brain": Prost, *Histoire de l'enseignement*, p. 268
293 "Of all the avenues that lead to happiness": Ibid., p. 491
293 "A young lady always knows too much": RM, III, p. 66
294 "For a moment I built a whole future": Alexandre Dumas *fils*, *La Dame aux camélias*, Paris, Garnier-Flammarion, 1981, pp. 333–34
294 "The secondary school education of young women": Prost, *Histoire de l'enseignement*, p. 268
294 "the *ancien régime* and its edifice of regrets": Mayeur, *L'Education des filles en France*, Paris, Hachette, 1979, pp. 139–40
294 "France is not a convent": Ibid., pp. 185–86
295 "The mind of the public": Flaubert, *Correspondance Flaubert-Sand*, p. 480 (September 26, 1874)
295 "Today, in literature, the essential thing": Goncourt, *Journal*, II, pp. 976–77 (end of April 1874)
295 "I feel that it's a reproach": Ibid., p. 979 (May 31, 1874)
296 "This very day I've read": Flaubert, *Oeuvres complètes*, XV, p. 303 (June 1, 1874)
296 "I read it, *La Conquête de Plassans*": Ibid., pp. 304–5 (June 3, 1874)
296 "exhale . . . vomit": Ibid., p. 167 (October 5, 1872)
296 "As regards madness": quoted by Dezalay in *Lectures de Zola*, pp. 22–23 (April 20, 1875)

XIII. The Lure of the Stage

298 "Special effects often save": Jean-Pierre Moynet, *French Theatrical Production in the Nineteenth Century*, New York, American Theater Association, 1976, p. 66
299 "The machinist's art uses every resource": Ibid., p. 111
299 "Money is a very big thing": Goncourt, *Journal*, I, p. 1157 (November 1, 1862)
299 "Ah, it is very difficult indeed nowadays": Guy de Maupassant, *Bel-Ami*, Paris, Gallimard (Folio), 1976, p. 167
300 "You shouldn't despise the little things": Eugène Scribe, *Théâtre complet*, Paris, André Aimé, 1841, XXII, pp. 23–24
300 "You will use any weapon": O.C., XII, p. 425
301 "No sooner does he strike an image": Ibid., XI, pp. 640–41
301 "Every great writer begets life": O.C., XI, p. 649
301 "Who in this book can condemn this woman?": Flaubert, *Oeuvres*, Paris, Gallimard (Pléiade), 1958, I, p. 666
302 "shoving reality into a narrow": Ibid., p. 640
302 "His alleged audacities are calculated": Ibid., XII, p. 415
302 "In the middle of the most loudly applauded": Ibid., X, p. 1072
303 "[Laurent Tailhade] was dandled": Ibid., p. 1078

303 "May [the playwright] forswear": Ibid., p. 1077
303 "A *Coward.* The title struck me": Ibid., p. 1073
304 "It is always dangerous": Ibid., XV, p. 121
304 "a purely human drama": Ibid., p. 123
305 "The critical fraternity": Ibid., p. 124
305 "I thank M. Louis Doré": CORR., II, p. 338 (July 13, 1873)
305 "My explicit intention was to write": O.C., XV, p. 223
306 "true and poignant": CORR., II, p. 360
306 "I've reread the play": Ibid.
306 "[Montigny] returned my manuscript": Ibid., p. 359 (July 23, 1874)
306 "I've been silent because": Ibid., p. 366 (October 9, 1874)
307 "The Cluny is a theater": Goncourt, *Journal,* II, p. 1001 (November 1, 1874)
307 "Ten years hence": CORR., II, p. 371
307 "So what if *Les Héritiers*": Stéphane Mallarmé, *Correspondance, 1871-1885,*
     Paris, Gallimard, 1965, II, pp. 50–51
307 "Do you like the atmosphere": O.C., XV, p. 318
307 "idiot paintings": Arthur Rimbaud, *Oeuvres,* Paris, Garnier, 1968, p. 228
308 "This humoristic comedy": Ibid., p. 319
308 "I haven't forgotten you": CORR., II, p. 374
309 "It's certain that I was riding": Flaubert, *Oeuvres complètes,* XV, p. 360
309 "Nothing more delightful": Daudet, *Trente ans de Paris,* pp. 335–36
310 "Once I witnessed": O.C., XI, p. 150
310 "I was summoned back": Goncourt, *Journal,* II, pp. 1134–35 (May 5, 1876)
311 "Zola tells us that in his student days": Ibid., p. 1059 (April 4, 1875)
311 "We chat about how we feel": Ibid., pp. 1221–22 (January 28, 1878)
312 "I'm too scared": CORR., II, p. 383 (February 1, 1875)
312 "The time has come to brace yourself": Halpérine-Kaminsky, *Tourguéniev
     d'après sa correspondance,* p. 55
312 "The more I think about it": Ibid., p. 81
313 "If you have an atlas": Ibid., pp. 213–14
313 "By the 1880s, about a dozen": Ronald Hingley, *Russian Writers and
     Society in the Nineteenth Century,* London, Weidenfeld & Nicolson, 1977,
     p. 158
314 "I thank you for the trouble": CORR., II, p. 357 (June 29, 1874)
314 "Would you like to receive": Florence Montreynaud, "Les Relations de Zola
     et Turguéniev," *Les Cahiers naturalistes,* no. 43, 1972, p. 61
314 "Here is my first article": CORR., II, p. 383 (February 22, 1875)
314 "Thank you for your article": Halpérine-Kaminsky, *Tourguéniev,* p. 221
314 "I am very pleased that you liked": A. V. Knowles (editor), *Turgenev's Letters,*
     New York, Scribner's, 1983, p. 210
315 "If Zola accepts my terms": Montreynaud, "Les Relations de Zola et Tour-
     guéniev," pp. 62–63
315 "The salaries of government functionaries": André Wallon, *La Vie quoti-
     dienne dans les villes d'eaux de 1850 à 1914,* Paris, Hachette, 1981, pp. 136–
     37
316 "I've just received a letter": Halpérine-Kaminsky, *Tourguéniev,* p. 226
316 "My dear Zola": Ibid., p. 240
316 "This means that my monthly contribution": CORR., II, p. 475 (July 27, 1876)
316 "Would you be up to reading": Halpérine-Kaminsky, *Tourguéniev,* p. 235
317 "The story of a man neutered": RM, I, p. 1679

317 "This volume caused him more trouble": Alexis, *Emile Zola*, p. 101
317 "Several mornings in succession": Ibid., p. 102
318 "Indeed, he was of so nervous a temperament": RM, I, p. 1037
318 "He thought about this village": Ibid., pp. 1231–32
319 "The abbé Mouret's devotion": Ibid., p. 1287
319 "[Its lord had] enjoyed it for one season": Ibid., p. 1248
320 "It was like some vision": Ibid., p. 1253
320 "You realize that Le Paradou": Ibid., p. 1256
320 "He couldn't slip into the trance": Ibid., p. 1295
320 "Oh, death, death, venerable Virgin!": Ibid., pp. 1314–15
321 "peace prevented": Ibid., p. 1345
321 "They possessed the forest": Ibid., pp. 1390–91
321 "What few people know": Ibid., p. 1356
321–22 "I see you, I know that you are naked": Ibid., p. 1417
322 "Jesus who died for us": Ibid., p. 1473
322 "I have often thought": Ibid., p. 1506
322 "as if to resuscitate": Ibid., p. 1507
323 "In part three, [Albine]": Ibid., p. 1679
323 "The peasants will be a gray": Ibid., p. 1680
324 "I'm working feverishly": CORR., II, p. 358
324 "Here naturalism of a bestial kind": RM, I, p. 1683
324 "the most immoral": Ibid.
324 "No, [Mouret] is not really": Ibid.
324 "Isn't the abbé Mouret strange": Ibid., p. 1684
324 "There are charming things": Ibid.
324 "intoxicating": Dezalay, *Lectures de Zola*, p. 23
325 *"La Faute de l'abbé Mouret* is doing *very well"*: CORR., II, p. 389

XIV. OCEANIC VISTAS

327 "In some considerable degree": Dreyfous, *Ce qu'il me reste à dire*, p. 177
327 "[My father] had come to know": Jean Renoir, *Renoir, My Father*, Boston, Little, Brown, 1962, pp. 140–41
328 "Because he was witty": Dreyfous, *Ce qu'il me reste à dire*, p. 182
328 "Charpentier arrived yesterday": Flaubert, *Oeuvres complètes*, XV, p. 226
328 "He had the audacity to collect us": O.C., XI, p. 250
329 "Charpentier remains the lovable June bug": Becker, *Trente années d'amitié*, p. 28
330 "The sea, always the sea!": CORR., II, pp. 404–5
330 "We have a superb variety": Ibid., pp. 408–9 (August 13, 1875)
330 "Here are a few figures": Ibid., p. 406 (August 7, 1875)
331 "I myself am astonished": Ibid., pp. 409–10 (August 14, 1875)
331 "You can't imagine anything uglier": Ibid., p. 410
331 "Don't overindulge": Bakker, *Lettres inédites de Paul Alexis*, p. 97
332 "Excellent trip, a splendid night": CORR., II, pp. 469–70
332 "Since I was near the door": Ibid., pp. 478–79 (August 11, 1876)
333 "We're in a veritable desert here": Ibid., p. 479
333 "The really delightful thing is": Ibid.
333 "a jewel, a feudal town": Ibid.

333 "Yesterday the Charpentiers showed me": Goncourt, *Journal*, II, p. 1149 (October 15, 1876)

334 "We spend our days on our backs": CORR., II, p. 474

334 "a novel whose frame is officialdom": RM., II, 1492

335 "The return of Henri V": Ernest Renan and Marcellin Berthelot, *Correspondance*, Paris, Calmann-Lévy, 1929, pp. 435–36

335 "inaugurate a salutary regime": Mayeur, *Les Débuts de la Troisième République*, p. 30

335 "The executive power is entrusted": Rémond, *La Vie politique en France*, II, p. 308

336 "All interest was concentrated": Brogan, *France under the Republic*, pp. 109–10

337 "Fear! That is their great political means": Rémond, *La Vie politique en France*, pp. 311–12

337 "Exactly when during the Second Empire": RM, II, p. 1497

338 "Zola, on entering": Goncourt, *Journal*, II, p. 1048

339 "Strong states derive their strength": RM, II, p. 366

339 "Their presence was an undreamed-of honor": Ibid., p. 211

340 "He regularly imagined": Ibid., p. 150

340 "He cursed himself": Ibid., p. 72

340 "He was afraid that the pain": Ibid., p. 121

341 "Beware of women!": Ibid., p. 35

341 "She exulted": Ibid., p. 342

341 "He found Paris enlarged": Ibid., p. 215

342 "there are no principles": Balzac, *Le Père Goriot*, Paris, Garnier-Flammarion, 1966, pp. 114–15

342 "My idea is to reign": Ibid., p. 112

342 "I am persuaded that the novelist": Alexis, *Emile Zola*, p. 105

343 "[Jourde] told me": CORR., II, p. 399

343 "Our mistake, my friend": Ibid., p. 415 (September 7, 1875)

343 "I don't share Turgenev's harsh view": Flaubert, *Correspondance Flaubert-Sand*, p. 530

343 "I read it straight through": Mallarmé, *Correspondance*, II, p. 107

343 "You no longer look for anything": Ibid., p. 526

344 "We could point out": RM, II, p. 1505

344 "what Zola portrays": Ibid.

344 "generally proper deportment": Ibid.

XV. "If the Good Democrats Expected Sycophantic Drivel . . ."

345 "The father was a peasant": Régine Pernoud, *Histoire de la bourgeoisie*, p. 482

346 "I have always considered": Ibid., p. 409

346 "Workers are outside political society": Adeline Daumard, *Les Bourgeois de Paris*, p. 283

347 "Extreme poverty brings about": Louis Chevalier, *Classes laborieuses et classes dangereuses à Paris pendant la première moitié du dix-neuvième siècle*, Paris, Plon, 1958, p. 162

347 "Everyone has read those admirable pages": Ibid., pp. 510–11

347-48 "The circumstances that oblige workers": Chevalier, *Classes laborieuses*, p. 233
348 "the French language is not fixed": Victor Hugo, *Cromwell*, Paris, Garnier-Flammarion, 1968, p. 97
348 "If you dare, go sit once a week": Maurice Descotes, *Le Public de théâtre*, p. 248
349 "If the effect of democracy": Alexis de Tocqueville, *Democracy in America*, New York, Vintage, II, pp. 85-87
349 "on a three-hour jaunt": Descotes, *Le Public de théâtre*, p. 262
350 "the thinking men who worked indefatigably": Henri Heine, *Chroniques de la Gazette d'Augsbourg*, Paris, André Delpeuch, 1927, pp. 122-23
350 "tearful success": For French edition: *succès larmoyant*
350 "I looked at it with religious awe": Flaubert, *Correspondance* (Pléiade), I, p. 227 (May 1, 1845)
350 "The people have so completely": Robert Baldick, *The Life and Times of Frédérick Lemaître*, London, Hamish Hamilton, 1959, p. 142
351 "Gentlemen, we regret": Ibid., p. 103
351 "To the lamppost with poisoners!": J. Lucas-Dubreton, *Louis-Philippe*, Paris, Fayard, 1938, p. 257
351 "It is not the thought of civilized people": Lucas-Dubreton, *Louis-Philippe*, p. 258
351 "It was especially at street-corner taverns": Henri Heine, *Oeuvres de Henri Heine*, Paris, Eugène Renduel, 1834, IV, pp. 157-58
352 "local deterioration": Dumas fils, *Théâtre complet*, I, p. 26
352 "The struggle these last few days": Roger Price, *1848 in France*, Ithaca, Cornell University Press, 1975, p. 117
352 "Today, clemency equals lunacy": Edwards, *The Paris Commune*, pp. 340-41
352 "To show nature complete": RM, II, p. 1538
353 "Living in the nineteenth century": Ibid.
353 "Unjustified title": Goncourt, *Journal*, I, p. 1067 (April 1862)
353 "a novel whose frame": RM, II, p. 1540
353 "Worker novel—Situated in": Ibid., p. 1542
354 "[My next novel] lies dormant": CORR., II, p. 420
354 "It must be a miracle of exactitude": Ibid., p. 421, and RM, II, p. 1544
354 "Bareheaded women running": RM, II, p. 1548
355 "In its trimestrial bulletin": Ibid., pp. 1553-54
356 "simple sublime": Denis Poulet, *Le Sublime*, Paris, Flammarion, 1887, pp. 67-68
357 "The labors of the day made": RM, II, p. 403
357 "She was like her mother": Ibid., p. 408
357 "to work, to eat one's daily bread": Ibid., p. 410
357 "The clock, in rosewood": Ibid., p. 476
358 "She enjoyed putting her iron down": Ibid., p. 500
359 "The still, with its weirdly": Ibid., p. 411
359 "She thrust her bare pink arms": Ibid., p. 506
359 "Coupeau and Lantier were having": Ibid., p. 611
360 "For the next two years": Ibid., p. 683
360 "Yes, yes, just a bit more": Ibid., p. 789
361 "Death meant to take her": Ibid., p. 796
361 "The first time [Gervaise] went": Ibid., p. 473

361 "The aroma of goose": Ibid., pp. 580–81

363 "night seemed as though": Ibid., p. 764

363 "I have only one regret": CORR., II, p. 456 (May 24, 1876)

364 "If the good democrats": Alexis, *Emile Zola*, p. 110

364 "Only its form has upset people": RM, II, p. 373

364 "There was reason to hope": RM, II, p. 1558

365 "*L'Assommoir* is the portrait": CORR., II, p. 486

365 "I mean to be a novelist plain and simple": Ibid., p. 488

365 "it is as I wish it to be": Ibid., pp. 488–89

365 "The crude and relentless obscenity": RM, II, p. 1561

366 "In politics as in letters": CORR., II, pp. 535–36 (February 10, 1877)

366 "The book is bad. It reveals": RM, II, pp. 1564–65

367 "*L'Assommoir* is certainly not likable": Ibid., p. 1564

367 "The very fury of attacks proves it": Ibid.

367 "Here is a very great work": RM, II, pp. 1567–68

368 "Like you, I've read bits of *L'Assommoir*": Flaubert, *Oeuvres complètes*. XV, p. 510

368 "too much stirring of chamber pots": CORR., II, p. 464

368 "Too many books like this one": Flaubert, *Oeuvres complètes*. XV, p. 540

368 "Zola's *L'Assommoir* is a huge success!": Ibid., p. 544

368 "anemic and summary": Ibid., p. 551

368 "[From my manuscript of *La Fille Elisa*] I read Zola": Goncourt, *Journal*, II, pp. 1160–61 (December 17, 1876)

368 "Zola triumphant resembles a parvenu": Ibid., II, pp. 1173–74 (February 19, 1877)

368 "delete your allusion": CORR., II, p. 471 (July 24, 1876)

369 "I know several people who made a pastime": Dreyfous, *Ce qu'il me reste à dire*, pp. 235–36

369 "I am elated with the numbers": CORR., III, p. 102

XVI. LITERARY FATHERHOOD

370 "Your letter reached me the moment": Halpérine-Kaminsky, *Tourguéniev d'après sa correspondance*, p. 80

370 "*Things aren't going well*": Flaubert, *Oeuvres complètes*. XV, p. 303 (June 1, 1874)

370 "Flaubert was tormented by the melancholy": Daudet, *Trente ans de Paris*, p. 321

371 "On August 1, I at last start": Flaubert, *Oeuvres complètes*. XV, p. 328.

371 "Niggerdom personified": Ibid., XVI, p. 24

371 "B. and P. are wearing me out": Ibid., p. 238

372 "We're short a *mere*": Ibid., XV, p. 398

372 "You know that I am not a poseur": Flaubert, *Correspondance Flaubert–Sand*, p. 500

373 "I cannot tell you how deeply moved": Flaubert, *Oeuvres complètes*. XV, pp. 339–40 (August 29, 1875)

373 "But one must live": Ibid., p. 417 (October 7, 1875)

373 "It was on the rue du Faubourg Saint-Honoré": O.C., XI, p. 129

374 "[Flaubert] received his friends on Sunday": Guy de Maupassant, *Oeuvres complètes*, Paris, Louis Conard, 1910, XIX, pp. 139–43

375 "What was discussed": Leon Edel, *Henry James: The Conquest of London, 1870–1881,* New York, Avon, 1978, p. 221
375 "Well, my friend, what's what": CORR., II, p. 520 (January 3, 1877)
376 "I entered the rue Saint-Georges": Pierre Cogny, *Le "Huysmans intime" de Henry Céard et Jean de Caldain,* Paris, Nizet, 1957, pp. 113–14
376 "Our little group": Alexis, *Emile Zola,* p. 183
376 "I am very busy and couldn't answer": Ibid., p. 514
377 "the inexplicable amalgam": Robert Baldick, *The Life of J.-K. Huysmans,* Oxford, Clarendon Press, 1955, pp. 2–3
378 "I haunted the Latin Quarter": J.-K. Huysmans, "Sac au dos," in *Les Soirées de Médan,* Paris, 1981, pp. 121–22
378 "A skillfully cut jewel": Baldick, *Huysmans,* p. 27
379 "You said it—I am a realist": J.-K. Huysmans, *Lettres à Théodore Hannon (1876–1886),* edited by Pierre Cogny and Christian Berg, Paris, Christian Pirot, p. 1985, p. 35
379 "A writer can be chaste": CORR., II, p. 555
379 "Green pustules and pink flesh": J.-K. Huysmans, *Oeuvres complètes,* Geneva, Slatkine, 1972, II, p. 161
380 "No, we are not sectarians": Ibid., pp. 161–62
380 "What are you telling me?": CORR., III, p. 79 (July 16, 1877)
380 "So you're working": Ibid., pp. 84–85 (August 3, 1877)
381 "If you want my frank opinion": Ibid., II, p. 506 (December 13, 1876)
381 "Would that I were the person": Ibid., p. 554 (April 4, 1877)
381 "our relations with Zola": Alexis, *Emile Zola,* pp. 180–81
382 "In a restaurant destined to become": Cogny, *Le "Huysmans intime,"* p. 133
382 "To tell you the whole truth": Huysmans, *Lettres à Théodore Hannon,* pp. 54–55
382–83 "Alexis gave the strident keynote": Cogny, *Le "Huysmans intime,"* p. 135
383 "weaken," "diminish," or "modify": Léon Gambetta, *Discours et plaidoyers politiques,* Paris, Charpentier, 1882, V, p. 185
384 "The administrative favors": Brogan, *France under the Republic,* p. 129
384 "[Only] the union of the Centres": Ibid., p. 131
384 "You know full well": Jacques Chastenet, *L'Enfance de la Troisième,* Paris, Hachette, 1952, p. 221
384 "Simon showed considerable dexterity": Chapman, *The Third Republic of France,* London, Macmillan, 1962, pp. 169–70
385 "Clericalism? There is the enemy!": René Rémond, *L'Anticléricalisme en France de 1815 à nos jours,* Paris, Fayard, 1976, p. 185
385 "radical modifications of all our great": Rémond, *La Vie politique en France,* p. 354
385 "The chamber, which deems it important": Ibid., p. 353
385 "Considering that the government formed": Ibid., p. 356
386 "Paris is insufferable": CORR., III, pp. 112–13
386 "Two things sustain me": Flaubert, *Oeuvres complètes.* XV, p. 591
386 "In a fit of anger": O.C., X, p. 1373
387 "Today the novelist in me": CORR., III, p. 85
387 "There are days when I'm worried": Ibid., pp. 101–2 (August 21, 1877)
387 "the wrong key": Ibid., p. 113 (September 2, 1877)
388 "She didn't know a single street": RM, II, p. 815
388 "She was very proud": Ibid., p. 850

388 " 'Oh, sir!' she murmured": Ibid., p. 808
389 "Intimacy established itself": Ibid., p. 830
389 "painful and inadmissible": Ibid., p. 872
389 "Every afternoon she'd descend": Ibid., pp. 879–80
389 "She became childlike": Ibid., p. 895
390 "fairy-tale gala": Ibid., p. 900
390 "[The declaration] burned her": Ibid., p. 901
390 "A feeling of joy, born of": Ibid., p. 926
390 "Always in between, spying upon them": Ibid., p. 947
390 "She had lost control of her will": Ibid., p. 999
391 "Paris remained for her that place": Ibid., p. 1029
391 "Tranquil and timeless": Ibid., pp. 1091–92
392 "sensual, wicked woman": Ibid., p. 999
392 "*Ivanhoe* had bored her at first": Ibid., pp. 847–48
392 "Paris, vaster than the ocean": Flaubert, *Madame Bovary*, Paris, Classiques Garnier, 1971, p. 60 (part 1, chapter 9)
392 "On the Right Bank": RM, II, p. 849
393 "Round about them stretched a desert": Ibid., p. 1023
393 "As soon as Hélène and Henri": Ibid., p. 947
393 "She couldn't see anything very definite": Ibid., p. 1030
393 "At the window": Ibid., p. 1031
394 "*Une Page d'amour,* which seems an adventitious work": Becker, in preface to *Une Page d'amour,* Garnier-Flammarion, 1973, p. 34
394 "the responsibility for incest": Jean Borie, *Zola et les mythes,* Paris, Editions du Seuil, 1971, p. 215
395 "You argue that this tree": CORR., III, p. 156 (January 1878)
395 "Since 1868 I have settled": Ibid.
395 "I assuredly do not like everything": Ibid., p. 172
396 "not just something magnificent": Mallarmé, *Correspondance, 1871–1885,* II, p. 172
396 "*Mon bon,* I finished the volume": RM, II, pp. 1624–25
397 "I intended to go see you": Guy de Maupassant, *Correspondance inédite,* edited by Artine Artinian, Paris, Editions Dominique Wapler, 1951, p. 96
397 "I have never met anyone harder to please": Goncourt, *Journal,* II, p. 1229
397 "The critics may say whatever they like": Ibid., p. 1233 (April 23, 1878)
398 "I remember my youth spent in a small town": O.C., XI, p. 300
398 "I believe that a boy": Ibid., p. 301
398 "One of my good friends": Ibid., p. 302
399 "Once I said that our theater was dying": Ibid., p. 305
399 "When we write a novel in which we strive": Ibid.
399 "The great task of our century": Ibid., pp. 305–6
400 "The theory that ascribes ultimate authority": Ibid., p. 313
400 "In literature there can be no other sovereignty": Ibid., p. 315
400 "Seeking new authors in that lean year": Alexis, *Emile Zola,* p. 141
400 "Derision! I heard [the crowd]": CORR., I, p. 192
401 "Yesterday I received your manuscript": CORR., II, p. 546
401 "My name, my place": Ibid., 545 (February 21, 1877)
401 "I just want this business settled": Ibid.
401 "Considered in light of my theater criticism": Ibid., p. 144 (December 2, 1877)
401 "the thing just doesn't seem much good": Ibid., p. 139

402 "He might have gotten away with such antics": O.C., XV, pp. 411–12
402 "Disastrous, *Le Bouton de rose*": Goncourt, *Journal*, II, pp. 1235–36
403 "wildly paternal affection": O.C., XV, p. 327
403 "Not with impunity does one judge": Ibid., p. 329

XVII. A VERDANT PARADISE AND A BLOND HORIZONTAL

404 "Along with embroidery": CORR., III, p. 122 (September 13, 1877)
405 "Balzac says somewhere": Alexis, *Emile Zola*, p. 178
405 "Do you think, oh working class": quoted in *History of the House*, edited by Ettore Camesasco, New York, Putnam's, 1971, p. 258
406 "Paris seemed a hundred leagues away": Alexis, *Emile Zola*, p. 185
406 "I've bought a house, a rabbit hutch": CORR., III, pp. 201–2 (August 9, 1878)
407 "We are lodged here in a verdant": Ibid., p. 189 (July 14, 1878)
407 "Change of program": Ibid., p. 214
407 "Repeat to our friends": Ibid., p. 237
407 "I doubt I shall be back in Paris": Ibid., p. 246
408 "The Charpentiers are the exception": Ibid., p. 223
408 "I'd been intending to offer you": Ibid., p. 231 (October 14, 1878)
408 "As you've gone through something": Ibid., p. 247 (December 14, 1878)
408 "Artists are crossing a dry patch": O.C., XII, pp. 165–66
409 "it's still the slack season": Ibid., p. 167
409 "My dear Zola, the glum *Mirabeau*": Henry Céard, *Lettres inédites à Emile Zola*, edited by Colin Burns, Paris, Nizet, 1958, p. 130
409 "There would be no point": O.C., XII, p. 224
410 "I should like to excoriate": Ibid., p. 178
410 "I'm convinced that seeing M. Dumas": Ibid., p. 188
410 "multiply with terrifying fecundity": Ibid., XI, pp. 221–22
411 "Times have changed": Ibid., p. 237
411 "He is very clearly the breed of novelist": Ibid., p. 230
412 "I admit that I am not excessively fond": Ibid., p. 228
412 "Written correctly": Ibid., p. 241
412 "Would you do me the kindness": CORR., III, p. 250 (December 11, 1878)
412 "Everyone's passing around *Le Figaro*": Céard, *Lettres inédites*, p. 57
413 "Why this diabolical furor?": O.C., XI, p. 249
413 "banalities, accommodations": Ibid., p. 252
413 "You'd think that during the dozen years": Ibid.
413 "I am portrayed as egregiously vain": Ibid.
413 "Well, my good fellow, what will you give me": CORR., III, p. 253
414 "You know that your friend Bardoux": Ibid., 202 (August 9, 1878)
414 "was very nice. My absolute conviction": Ibid., p. 217 (September 19, 1878)
414 "I love you but must, with your leave": Ibid., p. 243 (November 11, 1878)
414 "Ah! if good old Parisians": Ibid., p. 254 (December 23, 1878)
414 "a novel whose setting is the boudoir": RM, II, p. 1657
415 "Under the empire, playboys obtained": O.C., XIV, pp. 120–21
415 "The ladies' grandstand is full": Ibid., pp. 82–83
416 "My dream is of an extraordinary *Nana*": CORR., III, p. 102 (August 21, 1877)
416 "[Zola made us] summon forth memories": Alexis, *Emile Zola*, p. 115
416 "In real life, many prostitutes of Satin's ilk": Céard, *Lettres inédites*, pp. 110–11

417 "She wants to ride horseback like Cora Pearl": CE, pp. 309–10
417 "La Sancy very gay": Ibid., p. 311
418 "Abasement of the naked man": Ibid., p. 312
418 "The Prince of Wales in the dressing room": Ibid., p. 313
419 "Tramping through the mud and splashed": RM, II, p. 726
419 " 'I've had some news' ": Ibid., p. 748
419 "A street urchin came up whistling": RM, II, p. 1101
419 "When *L'Assommoir* appeared, Manet painted": Françoise Cachin in *Manet*, exhibition catalogue, p. 393
420 "For certain rather spicy lines": Ibid., p. 1108
420 "Every pair of opera glasses": Ibid., p. 1119
421 "Around the table the gentlemen in question": Ibid., p. 1173
421 "The guests had stopped eating": Ibid., p. 1181
421 "Ever since the beginning": Ibid., p. 1184
421 "Muffat was . . . not very lighthearted": Ibid., p. 1149
422 "lofty and dark": Ibid., p. 1144
422 "He, who had never seen the Comtesse Muffat": Ibid., 1213
422 "Beyond the dazzling arc": Ibid., pp. 1220–21
423 "Nana was lost in ecstatic": Ibid., pp. 1270–71
423 "For the slightest thing Fontan": Ibid., p. 1295
424 "Some windfalls came their way": Ibid., pp. 1313–14
424 "She had always trembled before the law": Ibid., p. 1315
425 "I'll show your Paris something about great ladyship": Ibid., p. 1346
425 "Nana became a woman of fashion": Ibid.
425 "Nana was bored to tears": Ibid., pp. 1357–58
426 "a sudden blossoming of her nature": Ibid., p. 1375
426 "What lay on the pillow": Ibid., p. 1485
426 "With her, the scum": Ibid., pp. 1269–70
427 "People were already dancing": Ibid., p. 1420
428 If Les Frères Provençaux restaurant served an omelette: Burchell, *Imperial Masquerade*, p. 78
428 "Marvelous thing, wealth!": Goncourt, *Journal* II, p. 347 (May 31, 1867)
428 "if it were possible to give [the people]": Ibid., I, p. 202 (August 28, 1855)
429 "The main body of horses": RM, II, p. 1403
429 "On the seat, without realizing": Ibid.
429 "There came a sound like the roar": Ibid.
430 "Nana could still hear her name": Ibid., p. 1405
430 "A delicate line, curving only slightly": Ibid., p. 1271
431 "We recognize that to publish": RM, II, p. 1687
431 "Enormous curiosity surrounds *Nana*": Céard, *Lettres inédites*, p. 103
431 "Given M. Zola's genre": RM, II, p. 1688
431 "Here's a good story which Huysmans": Ibid.
432 "Except for several coarse words": Ibid., p. 1688
432 "What a dandy row!": CORR., III, p. 396 (October 28, 1879)
432 "the thing that bothers me most": RM., II, p. 1689
432 "Nana is the whore at her rawest": Ibid., p. 1693
432 "goose like Nana, who can't pull herself": Ibid.
433 "The Marquis de Sade believed": Ibid.
433 "In high society, when there's a marriage": CORR., III, p. 407 (November 22, 1879)

433 "I send you herewith the best": Céard, *Lettres inédites*, pp. 121–22 (December 16, 1879)

434 "The book on smallpox came yesterday": CORR., III, p. 422

434 "Since *Nana* interests you": Ibid., p. 432

434 "*Nana* may be seized": Guy de Maupassant, *Chroniques, études, correspondance*, edited by René Dumesnil, Paris, Librairie Grund, 1938, p. 280

435 "My dear Zola, I spent all of yesterday": Flaubert, *Oeuvres complètes*, XVI, pp. 321–22

436 "Millions must be inundating you": Ibid., p. 322

436 "My silence must surprise you": Flaubert, *Oeuvres complètes*, XVI, p. 133

436 "Our friendship broke off": "Jean-Baptistin Baille," Colette Becker, *Les Cahiers naturalistes*, no. 56, 1982, pp. 155–56

437 "In [my last] letter, I told you": Ibid., pp. 124–25

437 "Did you know that I broke my leg": Ibid., p. 134

437 "I cannot say how touched I am": Ibid., p. 121 (January 10, 1879)

437 "Thank you for your telegram": Ibid., p. 137 (February 5, 1879)

437 "Turgenev has just told me that he's leaving": CORR., III, p. 291 (February 8, 1879)

438 "You already know, from my telegram": *Flaubert and Turgenev. The Complete Correspondence*, Edited and translated by Barbara Beaumont, New York, Norton, 1985, p. 156

438 "I *mourn the loss*, with no difficulty": Flaubert, *Oeuvres complètes*, XVI, p. 143

439 "Everyone feels cheerful": Goncourt, *Journal*, III, pp. 67–69 (March 28, 1880)

439 "Zola's happiness is troubled": Ibid., p. 67

440 "No death could cause me": O.C., XI, p. 121–22

440 "one of its most illustrious sons": Ibid., pp. 124–25

441 "We left without partaking": Goncourt, *Journal*, III, p. 73 (May 11, 1880)

441 "Although good-natured, Alexandrine": Denise LeBlond-Zola, *Emile Zola raconté par sa fille*, Paris, Grasset, 1931, pp. 130–31

441 "Mme Chanteau scolded Pauline": RM, III, pp. 961–62

442 "When we arrive, the coffin is in the courtyard": Ibid., pp. 1794–95

442 "People tell me it's unavoidable": CORR., IV, p. 119 (October 20, 1880)

442 "The fear that heart disease would claim him": Ibid., p. 958

443 "At first we thought we'd flee Médan": Ibid., p. 123 (October 30, 1880)

XVIII. "The Fetishism of Mediocrity"

444 "The old man was determined": Brogan, *France under the Republic*, p. 138

445 "For me the idolatry": Goncourt, *Journal*, II, p. 1199 (September 3, 1877)

445 "We must, in our national interest": Rémond, *La Vie politique en France*, pp. 358–59

446 "no imprudence, no dissidence, no mistakes": Chastenet, *L'Enfance de la Troisième*, p. 255

446 "wherever the Jesuit spirit finds a crack": Chapman, *The Third Republic*, p. 190

446 "His attempts to live in a more decorous": Brogan, *France under the Republic*, pp. 144–45

447 "The decrees were duly executed": Ibid., pp. 150–51

447 "You must close the book": in *Histoire de la Troisième République* (Héritier), I, p. 113
448 "Today, although there is still": O.C., X, p. 1380
448 "The Republic will live or": Ibid.
448 "What makes our hearts beat fast": Ibid.
448–49 "In every political problem": Ibid., p. 1384
449 "In France, whenever political men": Ibid., p. 1389
449 "power trembles": Ibid.
449 "Masters grow": Ibid., pp. 1396–97
449 "No one considers us writers and artists": Ibid., p. 1400
450 "It's because there are easy victories": Ibid., pp. 1400–1
450 "If we set aside extraordinary political careers": O.C., X, p. 1372
450 "What do you make of Zola?": Maupassant, *Chroniques*, p. 267
451 "Take a scrofulous person": Ibid.
451 "Is it not frightening": Ibid., p. 1374
451 "M. Zola spoke about": CORR., IV, p. 99
451 "Henceforth, you are dead": Ibid., p. 96
452 "You have behind you": Ibid., p. 98
452 "You add, with an injured air": Ibid., 101
452 "M. E. Zola . . . , while often voicing": Ibid., p. 103
453 "You wish to offer me": Ibid., p. 107
453 "the fetishism of mediocrity": O.C., XIV, p. 436
453 "Your *Figaro* article": Céard, *Lettres inédites*, p. 147
453 "So, my brother republicans": O.C., XIV, p. 441
454 "I am very perplexed": Ibid.
454 "How shall I learn": Ibid., p. 442
454 "After a tumultuous decade": Ibid., p. 443
455 "M. Gambetta is not a passionate lover": Ibid., p. 492
455 "He's still a disguised": Ibid.
455 "Observe his head": Ibid., p. 471
455 "A journalist who made no mark": Ibid.
456 "That is what the disabused paladin": Ibid., p. 650
456 "why not have faith": Ibid., p. 651
456 "In every phase": Ibid., p. 654
457 "I have said it elsewhere": Ibid.
458 "It's simple theft": CORR., III, p. 393 (October 24, 1879)
458 "Hugo, who has been followed through life": O.C., XII, pp. 323–24
458 "I appreciate the dispatch": CORR., IV, p. 117 (October 4, 1880)
458–59 "I am indeed guilty": Ibid., p. 167 (March 30, 1881)
459 "I am seized by a violent distaste": Ibid., p. 174
459 "To any young writer": O.C., XIV, p. 668
459 "We are all children": Ibid.
460 "Can you send me": J.-K. Huysmans, *Lettres inédites à Emile Zola*, Geneva, Droz, 1953, p. 47
460 "Céard, Alexis, and Hennique seconded": J.-K. Huysmans, *Lettres inédites à Camille Lemonnier*, Geneva, Droz, 1957, p. 92
461 "I appreciate the description": CORR., IV, p. 184
461 "As yet I have found nothing": Céard, *Lettres inédites*, pp. 177–78
462 "Huysmans will handle the diocesan": Ibid., p. 181
462 "Would you like me to send": Céard, *Lettres inédites*, p. 60

462 "Could you do me a favor": CORR., III, p. 344
463 "Will you allow me one small observation?": Ibid., pp. 149–50
463 "Your good letter": CORR, IV, p. 112
463 "The newspaper director who wrote me": Ibid., III, p. 215
464 "The Russians are robbing you blind": Ibid., p. 237
464 "Very remarkable. You will without doubt": Ibid., IV, p. 162 (February 28, 1881)
464 "My wish is obviously that you should enjoy": Ibid., 172
464 "Since I'm the culprit here": O.C., XIV, p. 626
464 "If you only knew": Bakker, *Lettres inédites de Paul Alexis*, p. 23
465 "I'm a bit rushed": CORR., III, pp. 345–46
465 "Do you authorize": Ibid., p. 386
465 "Do it. I would suggest": Ibid., pp. 385–86
465 "Your articles on the critical reception": Ibid., p. 415 (December 8, 1879)
465 "Simply a coincidence": *Les Soirées de Médan*, ed. by C. Becker, Paris, Le livre à venir, 1981, p. 299
466 "Naturalist authors, those imbued": O.C., X, pp. 1205–6
466 "We are the true patriots": Ibid.
466 "Dominion over the world": Ibid., p. 1230
466 "The new republican civism pervaded": Girardet, *Le Nationalisme français, 1871-1914*, pp. 70–71
467 "Remain French": Ibid., p. 72
468 "It behooves her, though she herself": Ibid., pp. 77–78
468 "*A Good Frenchman. Composition—Sketch*": Ibid., p. 79
468 "We simply wanted": Maupassant, *Chroniques*, p. 273
469 "If, among working-class people": O.C., XIV, p. 531
469 "By bourgeoisie I mean": Ibid.
469 "As nights were magnificent": Alain Pagès, "Le Mythe de Médan," *Cahiers naturalistes*, no. 55, 1981, p. 32
470 "They allow everything": RM, III, p. 1613
471 "Do you need notes": Huysmans, *Lettres inédites*, pp. 62–63
471 "I send you a meager harvest": Ibid., p. 70
471 "Just as he found": Alexis, *Emile Zola*, p. 127
472 "The courtyard, clean and sad": RM, III, p. 7
472 "No sooner did one of the mistresses": Ibid., 107
472 "Every morning she'd implore him": Ibid., p. 25
473 "For some time, Monsieur Gourd had been prowling": RM, III, p. 247
473 "You must listen to your father": CORR., III, p. 349 (June 24, 1879)
474 "[Adèle managed to cut the umbilicus]": Ibid., p. 371
474 "In any event, the goal of masters": Pierre Guiral and Guy Thuillier, *La Vie quotidienne des domestiques en France au dix-neuvième siècle*, Paris, Hachette, 1979, p. 129
475 "My novel is a work of precision": CORR., IV, p. 217 (August 24, 1881)
475 "We would never have dared": O.C., XII, p. 608
475 "Metaphysical man is dead": O.C., X, p. 1203
476 "It seems that the gentleman": CORR., IV, p. 262 (January 29, 1882)
477 "Well, judgment has been passed!": Ibid., p. 279 (February 14, 1882)
477 "Oh, bourgeois and bourgeoises": RM, III, p. 1630
477 "Facts do not impinge": Dezelay, *Lectures de Zola*, p. 29
477 "If you wish, my novel": RM, III, p. 1633

478 "Make no mistake": CORR., IV, p. 279
478 "My heart goes out to you": Ibid., p. 301
478 "Zola visits me today": Goncourt, *Journal*, III, p. 92 (December 14, 1880)
479 "Zola displays that agitated disquiet": Ibid., p. 182 (July 6, 1882)
479 "Do you know a recurrent dream": Ibid., p. 166
479 "If I didn't have my family": CORR., I, pp. 133–34
479 "Alas, my wife does not feel": CORR., IV, p. 216 (August 7, 1881)
480 "My wife struggles along": Ibid., p. 217 (August 24, 1881)
480 "My wife feels worse than I": Ibid., p. 338 (November 2, 1882)
480 "Returning from Médan": Goncourt, *Journal*, III, p. 182 (July 6, 1882)
480 "I hope my godson": CORR., IV, pp. 323–24 (September 4, 1882)

XIX. GATHERING SHADES

481 "He never left the slightest litter of papers": Ernest Vizetelly, *Emile Zola*, London, John Lane, 1904, pp. 397–98
481–82 "This evening, at Daudet's house": Goncourt, *Journal*, III, p. 451 (May 2, 1885)
482 "You know I am a bit": CORR., V, p. 93 (April 16, 1884)
482 "Everything is immense": Alexis, *Emile Zola*, p. 188
482 "There was indeed a huge couch": Lepelletier, *Emile Zola*, p. 160
482 "*Nana* earned me the most": CORR., V, pp. 328–29
483 "Apropos of what we said": Ibid., p. 380 (March 26, 1886)
483 "My friend, would you perchance": Ibid., p. 409 (June 16, 1886)
484 "We lunch gaily and afterward": Goncourt, *Journal*, III, p. 118
484 "My poor wife and I": CORR., VI, p. 146 (May 26, 1887)
484 "The efficient housekeeper she had always been": LeBlond-Zola, *Emile Zola*, p. 126
485 "On Médan's patron saint's day": Cogny, *Le "Huysmans intime,"* p. 154
485 "Stretched out for entire half days": Henry Céard, "Zola intime," *Revue illustrée*, Paris, no. 3, December 1886–March 1887, p. 145
486 "No one in Médan": CORR., IV, p. 324 (September 5, 1882)
486 "I have had only ignoramuses": Ibid., V, p. 234 (February 2, 1885)
486 "Paris tempts me very little": Ibid., p. 222 (January 18, 1885)
486 "We reestablished ourselves": Ibid., IV, p. 385 (April 28, 1883)
487 "an affection standing guard": RM, IV, p. 160
487 "I know that making Virginie": CORR., III, pp. 106–7 (August 23, 1877)
487 "That foul Busnach": Goncourt, *Journal*, IV, p. 497 (January 1, 1894)
488 "We need accurate decor": Ibid.
488 "The persistence with which certain critics": O.C., XV, p. 796
488 "The day it pleases me": Ibid., p. 783
488 "It's undeniable that certain changes": Ibid., pp. 784–85
489 "We request that you give": CORR., III, p. 310 (April 1879)
490 "strings, couplets": Goncourt, *Journal*, III, p. 7 (January 18, 1879)
490 "I am mired in theater": CORR., IV, pp. 93–94 (August 22, 1880)
491 "I want *Au Bonheur des Dames*": RM, III, p. 1680
491 "for *Pot-Bouille* and other novels": Ibid.
491 "Last Monday we received": in *Le Figaro*, July 25, 1991
492 "There are seventy-three tills": CE, pp. 154–55
493 "oil lamps are hung": Ibid., pp. 159–60

493 "The young women's rooms": Ibid., pp. 162–63
494 "At the Louvre department store": Ibid., p. 226
494 "Clerks strip off their bosses": Ibid.
494 "The book has its *poetic* side": RM, III, p. 1681
495 "Once the house next door": Ibid., pp. 171–72
495 "It was woman for whom": Ibid., p. 461
496 "On a Monday": Ibid., pp. 611–612
496 "The double movement. Octave making a fortune": B.N., n.a.f., 10277–78
497 "Baudu's shop was filled": RM, III, p. 402
497 "grace and tenderness": Ibid., p. 440
498 "Gazing out the window": Ibid., p. 606
498 "A compact wave of heads": Ibid., pp. 491–92
498 "Six o'clock approached": Ibid., pp. 796–97
500 "Exasperated, the Baudu family": Ibid., p. 597
500 "At lunch he asks me": Goncourt, *Journal*, III, p. 166 (April 18, 1882)
500 "What a heavy thing is a pen!": CORR., IV, p. 334 (October 25, 1882)
500 "Madame Marty . . . told herself": Ibid., p. 636
501 "I shall end up loathing": Ibid., p. 309 (June 16, 1882)
501 "I don't know how the devil": RM, III, p. 1702
501 "Since M. Grimm calls the tune": Ibid., p. 231
501 "Every powerful talent": O.C., X, pp. 1281–82
502 "I've plunged into work": CORR., IV, p. 394 (May 20, 1883)
502 "Impossible to do anything good": *Manet*, exhibition catalogue, p. 527
503 "a marmalade": Ibid., p. 355
503 "But that's a problem for some people": O.C., XII, p. 932
503 "Manet has always been the apple of discord": Ibid., p. 966
503 "bad character": Ibid.
503 "The scene unfolds out of doors": Ibid., p. 967
504 "His long struggle against the public's incomprehension": Ibid., p. 1003
504 "All those artists are too easily": Ibid.
504 "M. Zola has just broken with": CORR., III, p. 356
505 "I am stupefied by the article": Ibid., p. 355
505 "Your letter gives me great pleasure": Ibid., p. 356
505 "I was one of the first to defend": O.C., XII, p. 1019
506 "I saw him the evening he lay down": *Manet raconté par lui-même et ses amis*, Geneva, 1945, pp. 179–80
506 "At Proust's request": *Manet*, exhibition catalogue, p. 528
506 "In 1863, the mob": O.C., XII, p. 1042
507 "The opportunity to eulogize him": CORR., IV, p. 411 (September 4, 1883)
507 "There were some grand, aristocratic dinners": Schapiro, *Turgenev*, p. 302
508 "Suddenly I notice that my lips": Ibid., p. 299
509 "What with some of us having": Goncourt, *Journal*, III, pp. 156–57
509 "medical science is virtually helpless": Schapiro, *Turgenev*, p. 319
509 "Imagine a man who is perfectly well": Ibid., p. 321
510 "The religious ceremony flushed out": Goncourt, *Journal*, III, p. 273 (September 7, 1883)
511 "One would have thought": Schapiro, *Turgenev*, p. 331
511 "Turgenev described how": Goncourt, *Journal*, III, p. 60 (February 1, 1880)
511 "When he finished reading aloud": RM, III, p. 1745
511 "I put it aside because": CORR., IV, pp. 442–43 (December 15, 1883)

512 "He had left the *lycée* at Caen": RM, III, p. 811
512 "Lazare confided in his cousin Pauline": Ibid., p. 839
513 "physician of genius": Ibid., p. 848
513 "His letters [from Paris]": Ibid., p. 857
513 "Her nature, which brimmed over": Ibid., pp. 856–57
514 "One evening Lazare told his mother": Ibid., p. 877
514 "She was renunciation itself": Ibid., p. 1129
514 "The sun set in the immense sea": Ibid.
515 "Underneath his feeling of being bereft": Ibid., p. 997
515 "Inseparable from this were ideas of symmetry": Ibid., p. 999
516 "pitched battle between will and doubt": Toulouse, *Enquête*, from Zola's preface, pp. VII
516 "*La Joie de vivre* is *Candide* transported": RM, III, p. 1771
516 "This strange book, which offends": Ibid., pp. 1771–72
517 "I know very well that you don't believe": Ibid., p. 1770
517 "Do me a favor and tell Zola": Ibid., p. 1767
518 "That Zola is a blasted assimilator": Goncourt, *Journal*, III, p. 282 (November 2, 1883)
518 "Tonight, after you left": CORR., IV, pp. 441–42 (December 14, 1883)
518 "Yes, I am somewhat annoyed": RM, III, p. 1768
518 "Take a coach from Brest to Quimper": CORR., IV, p. 410 (August 6, 1883)

XX. "MY RECURRENT DREAM WAS OF BEING INSIDE THE EARTH,
VERY FAR AWAY"

520 "The populace always had": RM, III, p. 1817
521 "The most important matter": Emile Zola, *La Fabrique de Zola*, edited by Colette Becker, Paris, Sedes, 1986, p. 43
521 "Universal suffrage made us": Georges Lefranc, *Les Gauches en France*, Paris, Payot, 1973, p. 292
522 "As stated by the General Council of the IWA": Fernand Braudel and Ernest Labrousse (editors), *Histoire économique et sociale de la France*, Paris, Presses Universitaires de France, 1976, III, p. 821
522 "to undermine society, property": *Procès de l'Association Internationale des Travailleurs*, Paris, Editions d'Histoire Sociale (EDHIS), 1968, p. 195
522 "those who are now disturbing minds": Daniel Ligou, *Histoire du socialisme en France*, Paris, Presses Universitaires de France, 1962, p. 16
523 "It seems monstrous": Ibid., p. 20
524 "In it Guesde addressed such matters": Ibid., pp. 26–27
524 "the nationalization of capital": Ibid., pp. 34–35
524 "Long live the socialist": Ibid., p. 36
524 "Considering that collective appropriation": Alexandre Zévaès, *Les Guesdistes*, Paris, Marcel Rivière, 1911, pp. 9–10
525 "In the provinces, the situation": Chastenet, *L'Enfance de la Troisième*, p. 302
526 "the earth will open": CORR., V, p. 347 (December 11, 1885)
526 "You who are a walking encyclopedia": Ibid., pp. 72–73 (February 13, 1884)
527 "You are very kind, very kind": Ibid., p. 75 (February 19, 1884)
527 "Anzin, outside Valenciennes's fortifications": Zola, *La Fabrique*, p. 376
528 "The downstairs room is entered": CE, p. 450

528 "A fire always going": Ibid., p. 454
528 "We plunged into a gallery": CE, pp. 459–60
528 "My recurrent dream was of being": CN, p. 294
529 "The stable was situated": Ibid., p. 463
529 "I must capture, above all, the topographical": Ibid., p. 456
530 "Strings of empty or loaded wagons kept passing": RM, III, pp. 1161–62
531 "But he *was* surprised by the boy's courage": Ibid., p. 1250
532 "Etienne remained at the level of the fervent neophyte": Ibid., p. 1275
532 "Etienne would begin to talk again": Ibid., pp. 1279–80
533 "The meeting was at the Plan-des Dames": Ibid., pp. 1375–76
533 "From the depths of the forest": Ibid., p. 1380
534 "The women had appeared, nearly a thousand": Ibid., pp. 1435–36
535 "They pointed the bloody little lump": Ibid., p. 1453
535 "day would dawn on the extermination": Ibid., p. 1462
535 "He was . . . overwhelmed by . . . remorse": Ibid., p. 1459
536 "Who was the guilty one?": Ibid., p. 1521
537 "Just as the engineers were cautiously": Ibid., pp. 1546–47
537 "Beneath his feet, the heavy, stubborn hammering": Ibid., p. 1591
537 "They would settle down, elbow to elbow": Ibid., p. 1240
538 "always perfectly polite": Ibid., p. 1306
538 "He would gladly have exchanged": Ibid., p. 1375
539 "You little worm": Ibid., p. 1169
539 "Etienne had listened without moving": Ibid., p. 1245
539 "You goddam traitor": Ibid., p. 1487
540 "The old struggle was beginning yet again": Ibid., p. 1571
540 "Chaval's body": Ibid., p. 1576
541 "The book pokes along": CORR., V, pp. 125–26 (June 14, 1884)
541 "*Germinal* will be serialized": Ibid., p. 196 (December 8, 1884)
541 "Your note pleased me very much": Ibid., pp. 192–93 (December 1, 1884)
541 "We are both exhausted for no good reason": CORR., V, p. 140 (August 12, 1884)
541 "The fear that I may empty myself": CORR., V, p. 242 (March 11, 1885)
542 "Neither with them nor against them": RM, III, p. 1860
542 "gentle, calm, upright": RM, III, p. 1861
542 "Go consult statistics": Ibid.
542 "blind instinct": Ibid., p. 1866
542 "You call *Germinal*": CORR., V, pp. 244–45 (March 14, 1885)
543 "I do not agree that my characters are abstract": Ibid., p. 249 (March 22, 1885)
543 "I wish you had explained": Ibid.
543 "Of all the novels published": RM, III, p. 1862
543 "In their elephantine pace": Ibid., p. 1866
544 "There are books by M. Emile Zola": Ibid., p. 1869
544 "The editorial committee of my paper has instructed me": CORR., V, p. 387
544 "We know no comparable work": Bakker, *Lettres inédites de Paul Alexis*, p. 533
544 "At the risk of being labeled a socialist": CORR. V, pp. 26–27
545 "It is the young whom we must question": Ibid., p. 34
545 "and when the Chamber will have voted": Ibid., p. 331 (November 11, 1885)

546 "The scene had to be seen to be believed": Maurice Barrès, *Les Déracinés*, Paris, Plon, 1924, II, p. 216
546 "One day you will perhaps learn": CORR., V, p. 267

XXI. Rifts and Betrayals

547 "In the show there are surpassingly beautiful": O.C., XII, p. 974
548 "I can't discuss every Impressionist painter": Ibid., pp. 1017–18
548 "My dear Emile, I shall soon": Paul Cézanne, *Correspondance*, pp. 160–61
548 "I agree that I must not be too quick": Ibid., p. 161
549 "I beg you to send Hortense": Ibid., pp. 165–66
549 "Before I left Paris": Ibid., p. 169
549 "I'm in a calmer state of mind": Ibid., p. 172
550 "my good family, considerate of": Ibid., p. 167
550 "Safeguard it, if you don't mind": Ibid., p. 207
550 "I'd like you to do several favors": Ibid., p. 217
550 "[I live] in the most complete isolation": Ibid., p. 223
551 "My old friend, I am terribly sorry": CORR., V, p. 276
551 "minister of state": Ambroise Vollard, *Paul Cézanne*, New York, Crown, 1937, p. 103
551 "He resembles Daudet's description": Ibid., p. 240
552 "Each one talked about the number of copies": Ibid., p. 104
552 "I am very grateful": Cézanne, *Correspondance*, p. 204
552 "A work whose documentation shouldn't present": Alexis, *Emile Zola*, pp. 121–22
553 "Toward the end of my novel": CORR., V, p. 270
553 "How a work of art grows": Ibid., p. 305 (September 23, 1885)
554 "nudities desired and never possessed": RM, IV, p. 50
554 "It was fifteen feet wide": Ibid., p. 33
554 "dream flesh": Ibid., p. 47
554 "She rebelled, as if this naked body": Ibid., pp. 92–93
555 "She'd plant herself in front of the canvases": Ibid., p. 110
555 "He began to paint in the silence": Ibid., p. 115
555 "They contemplated each other, hesitant": Ibid.
555 "The word *plein-air* provoked shouts": Ibid., p. 128
555 "In the disaster of his illusions": Ibid., p. 130
556 "Christine alone existed": Ibid., pp. 147–48
556 "He was haunted by the need to paint": Ibid., pp. 153–54
557 "How fine it would be": Ibid., p. 204
557 "Every rejected canvas": Ibid., pp. 206–7
557 "You see it every day, you pass": Ibid., pp. 216–17
557 "Living on his scaffold for days on end": Ibid., p. 233
558 "They clasped each other in vain": Ibid., pp. 229–30
558 "the very flesh of Paris": Ibid., p. 236
558 "Always at war with reality": Ibid., p. 245
558 "soldier of the uncreated": Ibid., p. 243
558 "She stupefied him": Ibid., p. 347
559 "No, he couldn't accomplish the formula": Ibid., p. 359
559 "Our generation immersed itself": Ibid., p. 357
559 "Pessimism twists people's guts": Ibid., p. 360

559 "It is not only through Sandoz": Ibid., pp. 1391–92
560 "I went to dinner with the Impressionists": Camille Pissarro, *Correspondance,*
1886–1890, edited by Janine Bailly-Herzberg, Paris, Valhermeil, 1986, II, p. 44
560 "My compliments, Emile. It's a story": RM, IV, pp. 1386–87
561 "You kindly sent me *L'Oeuvre*": Ibid., p. 1387
561 "I don't believe it will do us any harm": Ibid., p. 1388
561 "What a beautiful book": Rewald, *Cézanne et Zola,* p. 135
562 "[Sandoz] recalled their efforts, their certainty": RM, IV, pp. 295–96
562 "[Sandoz] had been astonished at first": Ibid., p. 257
562 "My dear Emile, I have just received": Cézanne, *Correspondance,* p. 225
562 "He still embraced Cézanne": Gasquet, *Cézanne,* p. 79
563 "Several low bookcases": Goncourt, *Journal,* IV, pp. 686–87 (December 14,
1894)
563 "You can't ask a man to talk": Vollard, *Cézanne,* p. 105
564 "Women go very well against the background": Ibid., III, pp. 505–6 (November 15, 1885)
564 "It wouldn't be so bad if one could hurry through": Baldick, *Huysmans,*
p. 143
564 "set upon, dismembered, disemboweled": Ibid.
564 "There are no discordant tones in the life": Mme Alphonse Daudet, *Souvenirs*
d'un groupe littéraire, Paris, Fasquelle, 1910, pp. 133–34
565 "You terrify me": CORR., V, p. 282 (July 22, 1885)
565 "I am very distressed, my good Daudet": Ibid., pp. 285–86 (July 25, 1885)
566 "Zola visits me. He frets over the novel": RM, IV, p. 1503
566 "I finished *L'Oeuvre* only this morning": CORR., V, p. 370 (February 23,
1886)
567 "an absolutely flat landscape": Céard, *Lettres inédites,* p. 298
567 "Why don't you give yourself over to some project": CORR., V, p. 371 (February 23, 1886)
567 "It's a little valley four leagues away": Ibid., p. 394 (May 6, 1886)
567 "I'm still working on the plot outline": CORR., V, p. 401 (May 27, 1886)
568 "To the west, a small copse": RM, IV, pp. 367–68
569 "[With the acre or two bought from the lord] began": Ibid., pp. 391–92
569 "Buteau owed this nickname": Ibid., p. 381
570 "Never, whatever the circumstance": Ibid., p. 730
570 "Fouan's coffin seemed so diminutive": Ibid., p. 803
571 "[Jean] suffered above all from the feeling": Ibid., p. 737
571 "Wide-eyed, the old man accepted": Ibid., p. 517
572 "She worked like a slave": Ibid., p. 471
572 "like a dropsical old cart horse": Ibid., p. 792
573 "They stood jostling each other": Ibid., pp. 806–7
573 "In this sunny graveyard": Ibid., p. 808
573 "I've gotten my book off to a so-so start": CORR., V, p. 409
573 "We haven't yet left Médan": Ibid., p. 428
573 "You present *La Terre* in such flattering terms": Ibid., VI, p. 68 (January 4,
1887)
573 "You put my desultory notes to good account": Ibid., p. 70 (January 8, 1887)
574 "It is only two-thirds written": Ibid., p. 100
574 "This book is a deliberately assembled collection": Guy Robert, *La Terre*
d'Emile Zola, Paris, Les Belles Lettres, 1952, p. 444

574 "Any woman who will have soiled her mind": Robert, *La Terre d'Emile Zola*, p. 444
574 "Georgics of debauchery": Ibid., p. 445
574 "Writers, painters, sculptors": *1889: La Tour Eiffel et l'Exposition Universelle*, exhibition catalogue, Musée d'Orsay, 1989, p. 28
575 "He has no taste": Ibid.
575 "at the behest of conscience": RM, IV, p. 1529
575 "To the young it seemed that after leading": Ibid., p. 1527
575 "The jury appeared to be": Ernest Vizetelly, *Emile Zola*, pp. 276–78
576 "Unbelievably lazy when it came to": Ibid.
576 "It is quite true that Zola seems": Ibid., p. 1528
577 "We repudiate these creatures of Zolistic rhetoric": Ibid., p. 1529
577 "But that decadence compromises": Ibid.
577 "What a singular adventure": Céard, *Lettres inédites*, pp. 331–32
577 "Only yesterday evening": CORR., VI, p. 191 (October 13, 1887)
578 "implied nothing of the disdain": Ibid., p. 192 (October 14, 1887)
578 "tortuously affectionate": Goncourt, *Journal*, III, p. 717 (October 15, 1887)
578 "I believe that we two must forget": CORR., VI, p. 195
579 "Am I forbidden to judge freely": Ibid., p. 391 (April 27, 1886)
579 "You tell me that certain Russian papers": Ibid., V, p. 435 (September 16, 1886)

XXII. ANOTHER DREAM

580 "When French youth will have . . . grown up": Jean-Marie Mayeur, *Les Débuts de la Troisième République*, Paris, Le Seuil, 1973, p. 113
581 "constitute a power": Jean Bouvier, *Le Krach de l'Union Générale*, Paris, Presses Universitaires de France, 1960, p. 23
581 "The struggle against foes of their faith": Ibid.
582 "With the king, Bontoux discussed": Ibid., p. 37
582 "The Treasure of Saint Peter": Ibid., p. 32
582 "Gambling fever affected two social classes": Ibid., p. 31
583 "This enterprise was the creation": Ibid., p. 280
584 "The Republican party has shown how well": Girardet, *Le Nationalisme français*, p. 107
584 "While you wander lost": Ibid., p. 110
586 "Gais et contents": Jacques Chastenet, *La République des Républicains*, Paris, Hachette, 1954, p. 181
586 "In France there exist men who seek war": Ibid., pp. 184–85
587 "His popularity was thenceforth based upon the absurd legend": Adrien Dansette, *Le Boulangisme*, Paris, Librairie Académique Perrin, 1938, p. 71
588 "like ecstatic Hindus": Ibid., p. 92
588 "The same brush that tarred deputy Wilson": Chastenet, *La République des Républicains*, p. 198
589 "Exercised over politics and worried": CORR., VI, p. 280 (April 1888)
589 "One noticed early along that workers": Chastenet, *La République des Républicains*, p. 208
590 "If you want my impression": Dansette, *Le Boulangisme*, p. 139
590 "*un bicorne sur un pieu*": Ibid., p. 258
590 "endangering the security of the state": Ibid., p. 274

590 "I cry like a child": Ibid., p. 362
591 "If our parliaments are unpopular": CORR., VI, p. 382
593 "A fellow office worker belonged to a group": André Antoine, *Mes souvenirs sur le Théâtre Libre*, Paris, Fayard, 1921, pp. 15–16
593 "But pent up all day": Ibid., p. 17
593 "A singular place is Paris, a place fraught": Ibid., p. 31
594 "I dined this evening with Paul Alexis": Antoine, *Mes souvenirs*, pp. 101–2
594 "In his column this morning": Ibid., pp. 143–44
594 "It would not be without interest": CORR., VI, p. 349
595 "I have taken the liberty of giving": CORR., VI, p. 285 (May 25, 1888)
595 "I'd like to produce a book": RM, IV, pp. 1625–26
596 "Rest assured that nothing is unforeseen": CORR., VI, p. 350 (November 16, 1888)
596 "It was like growing up far from the world": RM, IV, p. 827
597 "Oh! What I would like": Ibid., p. 854
597 "Every evening, wearing a hair shirt": Ibid., p. 940
598 "Angélique and Félicien walked slowly": Ibid., p. 993
598 "I admit that M. Zola's purity": Ibid., p. 1655
599 "This fairy tale is, at bottom": Ibid., p. 1656
599 "[Jules] Michelet wrote": Ibid., p. 1710
600 "What I already envision, amidst vast plains": Ibid., pp. 1712–13
600 "One will hear, like musical accompaniment": Ibid., p. 1711
601 "I shall study the ambitions": Ibid., V, pp. 1738–39
601 "trains advancing civilization": Zola, *La Bête humaine*, Paris, Garnier-Flammarion, 1972, p. 12
601 "You have requested permission": RM, IV, p. 1730
601 "*The Railroads*, his novel about the activity": Ibid., p. 1713
602 "At first, great trepidation": CE, p. 553
602 "A nightmare procession of women": RM, IV, p. 1044
603 "He experienced peace and happiness": Ibid.
603 "He was standing still, beaten": Ibid., pp. 1046–47
604 "He could have clawed her heart out": Ibid., p. 1015
605 "With a final heave, Pecqueux pushed him over": Ibid., p. 1330
606 "They should have taken water at Rouen": Ibid.
606 "What mattered the victims": Ibid., p. 1331
606 "I've worked like mad at my novel": CORR., VI, p. 413
606 "Never has there been so much blood shed": RM, IV, p. 1749
607 "It's undeniable that the railroad": Ibid.
607 "When Zola speaks of 'the logic' ": Ibid., p. 1747
607 "Here even more than in *L'Assommoir*": Ibid., p. 1748
608 "I am most flattered, my dear confrere": CORR., VI, 455 (March 9, 1890)
608 "foul secretions": Goncourt, *Journal*, III, p. 1159 (April 17, 1890)
608 "My dear Zola, . . . I can only repeat": RM, IV, p. 1751
608 "long admired, and admired unreservedly": CORR., VII, p. 90
608 "My method is invariably as follows": Ibid., VII, pp. 67–68 (June 27, 1890)
609 "rehabilitate him in the eyes": Vizetelly, *Emile Zola*, p. 240
609 "Yes, my dear friend, I accepted": CORR. VI, p. 306
609 "To return to the subject of naturalism": Ibid.
610 "Once I've agreed to be something": Ibid., p. 307 and pp. 32–33
610 "deeply and irremediably committed": Ibid., p. 313

610 "like a jackal sniffing carrion": Ibid.
610 "I consider perfectly ridiculous and out of touch": Ibid., p. 315
610 "It's not quite accurate to say": Ibid., pp. 314–15 (July 30, 1888)
611 "I'm no longer young": Ibid., p. 468
611 "I've just seen Halévy": Ibid., p. 433
611 "The powerful writer was no more abundantly endowed": René Peter, "Zola et l'Académie," *Mercure de France*, January 3, 1940, p. 572
612 "Life knit together the households": Albert Laborde, *Trente-huit années près de Zola. La Vie d'Alexandrine Emile-Zola*, Paris, Les Editeurs Français Réunis, 1963, pp. 87–88
612 "With the complicity of Alexandrine and my mother": Ibid., pp. 88–89
613 "His stomach has melted away": Goncourt, *Journal*, III, p. 763 (March 4, 1888)
613 "I have no clear-cut opinion on the matter": CORR., VI, p. 355
614 "A man of forty, hitherto engrossed": RM, IV, p. 1626
614 "Me; work; literature, which has consumed my life": Ibid., pp. 1626–27
615 "My mother hinted to her cousin": Laborde, *Trente-huit années*, p. 92

XXIII. "I'M ALWAYS DEVASTATED BY THE LIMITED SCOPE OF THE ACCOMPLISHMENT"

616 "I'm still lackadaisical": CORR., VI, p. 376
616 "My dear confrere, haven't I already told you": Ibid. (March 6, 1889)
617 "It's been almost two months": Ibid., p. 387 (May 3, 1889)
617 "the Babylonian immensity": Goncourt, *Journal*, III, p. 999 (July 2, 1889)
617 "There's nothing new here": CORR., VI, p. 389
617 "I am seized with a furious desire": Ibid., p. 414 (August 27, 1889)
618 "The broker arrives at the Bourse": CE, p. 64
619 "Brokers pretend . . . that they lead": Ibid., p. 70
619 "The absolute mystery of it all": Ibid., pp. 92–93
619 "A firm like the Union is but a pretext": Ibid., pp. 106, 112
620 "He would make those millions fructify": RM, V, p. 55
620 "He had a portfolio stuffed with ideas": Ibid., p. 59
621 "In Napoleon's Egyptian expedition": Ibid., p. 78
622 "Strikingly obvious at first glance": Ibid., p. 139
622 "There it was with its gingerbread face": Ibid., pp. 228–29
622 "He got up and gestured heavenward": Ibid., p. 243
623 "Jews are men like other men": Ibid., p. 385
623 "Inextinguishable hatred": Ibid., p. 91
623 "innate knowledge of numbers . . . the natural ease with which they negotiate": Ibid.
623 "Gundermann was decidedly right": Ibid., p. 384
624 "very motley . . . One can't enrich oneself": CE, pp. 91–92
624 "I mustn't forget that at the bottom": RM, V, p. 1244
624 "Where was the Jew during the Revolution": Edouard Drumont, *La France juive*, Paris, Flammarion, 1938, I, pp. 297–99
625 "king of gold": RM, V, p. 22
625 "makes bull and bear markets": Ibid., p. 21
625 "He was, as he himself put it good-naturedly": Ibid., p. 95
625 "Money is decidedly a thankless subject": CORR., VII, p. 83
625 "Nothing, I believe, resists": Ibid., p. 87 (September 12, 1890)

626 "Taken as a whole, the picture seems true": RM, V, p. 1281
626 "blind, unconscious, synthetic entity": Ibid., p. 1278
626 "As this writer has matured and broadened": Ibid., pp. 1282–83
627 "I am nineteen years old [and] would like": CORR., VII, p. 80
627 "What can I say except that": Ibid., VII, pp. 79–80 (August 18, 1890)
628 "Don't despair, I am at work": O.C., XV, p. 521
628 "In asking me to collaborate": CORR., VI, p. 343
628 "Several days ago I found myself": Ibid., p. 441
628 "I didn't discourage": Ibid., VII, p. 77
629 "Yesterday we had our largest take": Ibid., VII, p. 174
629 "It received favorable reviews": Jean-Max Guieu, *Le Théâtre lyrique d'Emile Zola*, Paris, Fischbacher, 1983, p. 44
629 "If, in the score of *Le Rêve*": CORR., VII, p. 174
629 "I have always loathed groups": Ibid., p. 119
630 "The novel, some thirty installments of which": Ibid., p. 220 (November 28, 1891)
630 "We announced a convocation": Ibid., p. 249 (February 16, 1892)
631 "What [waggish confreres who joke about]": O.C., XIV, pp. 747–48
631 "I most certainly would . . . do the Balzac statue": CORR., VII, p. 172
631 "See him as soon as possible": Ibid., p. 171 (July 1, 1891)
632 "I found a Rodin full of joy": Ibid., p. 180
632 "the committee of the Société des Gens de Lettres is regretfully": Judith Cladel, *Rodin*, Paris, Grasset, 1950, p. 211
632 "Right now I cannot consider politics": CORR., VII, p. 149
633 "Indeed I would! Not now": Jules Huret, *Interviews*, Vanves, Editions Thot, 1984, pp. 43–44
633 "a novel that will have the military world": RM, V, p. 1773
634 "[There will be] a study of the army": Ibid., p. 1369
634 "I've started to assemble documents": CORR., VII, p. 126
634 "I recall him more than once suddenly arriving": RM, V, p. 1371
634 "[You will . . . shortly receive]": CORR., VII, p. 138
635 "It was no longer a question": Howard, *The Franco-Prussian War*, p. 189
635 "If you abandon Bazaine, revolution will break out": Ibid., p. 196
636 "They more or less requisitioned": CE, p. 618
636 "In the town, after the battle": Ibid., p. 643
636 "taciturn, churlish": RM, V, p. 1383
636 "On the lawn of my property two barracks": MS, Archives Programme Zola
637 "In the public's eyes": RM, V, p. 1420
639 "At seven o'clock the Prussian king": Ibid., pp. 583–85
639 "In the wavering light": Ibid., p. 687
639 "Destiny swooping down": Ibid., p. 1375
640 "had sunk to the lowly": Ibid., p. 405
640 "Here, surely, was the spirit of brotherhood": Ibid., p. 521
640 "Burning down houses": Ibid., p. 883
641 "Thunderstruck, brought back to his senses": Ibid., pp. 883–84
641 "You want to know if I am satisfied": CORR., VII, p. 244
641 "I penned the last word": Ibid., p. 288
641 "Yesterday I sent you a copy from the printing": Charpentier, *Trente années d'amitié*, pp. 115–16
642 "I hope that people will recognize": CORR., VII, p. 288

642 "Was everybody, except for": RM, V, p. 1444
642 "*La Débâcle* did not for a moment": Ibid., p. 1445
642 "I've just read the article you were good enough": CORR., VII, p. 305 (July 18, 1892)
642 "pluck . . . the necessity of revenge": RM, V, pp. 1448–49
643 "War is inevitable": Ibid., p. 1415
643 "a nightmare, a hideous nightmare": Ibid., p. 1449
643 "What I saw as a combatant": Ibid., pp. 1450–52
644 "You can excuse and legitimize war": Ibid., p. 1462
644 "virile pity": Ibid., p. 1422
644 "after one has closed this massive, tufted book": Ibid., pp. 1423–24
644 "The nightmare needed organizing": Ibid., pp. 1432–34
645 "As for *La Débâcle*, finally": Henry James, *Notes on Novelists*, New York, Scribner's, 1914, pp. 63–64

XXIV. A CELEBRATION AT THE CHALET DES ILES

646 "Many thanks, my dear doctor": CORR., VI, p. 390
646 "Dear Doctor, I shall remain": Ibid., p. 416
646 "daughter of Jeanne Sophie Adèle": Ibid., p. 421
647 "Today, Paul Alexis . . . confirmed the rumor": Goncourt, *Journal*, III, p. 1076 (November 21, 1889)
647 "I must tell you that the famous voyage": CORR., VII, p. 195
648 "My old friend, I would . . . have very much liked": Ibid., p. 194
648 "After the 15th, drop by the flat": Ibid., p. 195
648 "My old friend. Here we are in Spain": Ibid., p. 199
648 "If you have something special": Ibid., pp. 199–200
649 "Thank you, my old friend": Ibid., p. 202 (September 29, 1991)
649 "Old friend, my wife is going absolutely mad": Ibid., p. 217
649 "I did everything to stop her": Ibid., p. 218
649 "Tomorrow you will find life": Ibid., p. 312
650 "My dear little Linette, you do well": Laborde, *Trente-huit années*, pp. 99–100
650 "The enthusiasm was indescribable": CORR., VII, p. 321
651 "Rest assured . . . that I shall never": Ibid., p. 312 (July 1892)
651 "tenderness . . . remorse": Ibid., p. 314 (August 16, 1892)
651 "Tell my little Denise": Ibid., p. 318
651 "I must have a portrait of the three of you": Ibid., p. 413
651 "I would like to have made your youth": Ibid., pp. 412–13 (July 29, 1893)
651 "I am not happy. This division": Ibid., VIII, pp. 143–44
652 "Outside this ring": LeBlond-Zola, *Emile Zola*, p. 189
652 "The common people with their unconscious": RM, I, p. 68
652 "I always wanted to finish": CORR., VII, p. 358
652 "I have loved life": RM, V, p. 1580
654 "I believe that the future of humanity": Ibid., p. 953
654 "I open them": Ibid.
654 "Our affection lacks something": Ibid., p. 994
655 "You must change your life and repent": Ibid.
655 "And what made it more painful": Ibid., p. 1026
655 "Ah, if only he had lived": Ibid., p. 1047

656 "servant . . . handiwork": Ibid., p. 1061
656 "He anathematized cities": Ibid., pp. 1085–86
656 "Is it a laudable task": Ibid., p. 1084
656 "She was like an idol": Ibid., p. 1071
656 "Was it due to his senility": Ibid., pp. 1143–44
657 "messiah . . . savior": Ibid., p. 956
657 "I shall discuss the anxieties": Ibid., p. 1609
658 "I finished *Le Docteur Pascal*": CORR., VII, p. 382
658 "Even if this volume, which is the epitome": RM, V, p. 1617
658 "The death of Charles": Ibid., p. 1617
658 "*Le Docteur Pascal* is a kind of index": Ibid.
658 "The consistent pessimism": Ibid., p. 1621
659 "Through education, by imparting": Ibid., p. 1616
659 "Not only is this love improbable": Ibid., p. 1619
659 "my Clotilde, who has offered me": Ibid., p. 1573
660 "This is not a banquet": Jules Huret in *Le Figaro*, June 22, 1893
660 "We celebrate our silver": Ibid.
661 "colossal" monument: Ibid.
661 "My dear and illustrious friend": Ibid.
661 "Sunshine filtering": Ibid.
661 "There is, in this woman": Goncourt, *Journal*, IV, pp. 421–22 (June 28, 1893)
661 "*I am absolutely lost*": Maupassant, *Chroniques*, p. 419
662 "Two weeks ago on Thursday": J. K. Huysmans, *The Road from Decadence. Selected Letters of J. K. Huysmans*. Edited and translated by Barbara Beaumont, Columbus, Ohio State University Press, 1989, p. 119
662 "Was it not natural that Alexandrine": LeBlond-Zola, *Emile Zola*, p. 185
662 "I don't want you to misconstrue": Laborde, *Trente-huit années*, pp. 101–2

XXV. A DOUBLE LIFE AND A TRILOGY

664 "I rely upon you": CORR., VII, p. 424 (August 18, 1893)
664 "the feeling of respect and admiration": Colin Burns, "Le Voyage de Zola à Londres en 1893," *Les Cahiers naturalistes*, 1986, p. 46
664 "I thought about our dear Paris": Ibid., p. 65
665 "charming and remarkable": Ibid.
665 "We march from ovation": CORR., VII, p. 443 (September 24, 1893)
665 "It is very certain that the British press": O.C., XII, pp. 687–90
665 "This celebration at the Guildhall": Burns, "Le Voyage de Zola à Londres," p. 50
666 "Yes, I demand that once": Ibid., p. 54
667 "I've described [the banquet] for you": CORR., VII, pp. 444–45 (September 24, 1893)
667 "Amidst all the plaudits": Burns, "Le Voyage de Zola à Londres," pp. 58–59
668 "I happened to ask him": James, *Notes on Novelists*, p. 46
668 "the fanatics once more raised their heads": Vizetelly, *Emile Zola*, p. 336
668 "infamous": Ibid., p. 337
668 "As Zola spoke, Madame Zola": Goncourt, *Journal*, IV, p. 443
669 "a long crisis": CORR., VIII, p. 125
669 "I never perceived anything": LeBlond-Zola, *Emile Zola*, pp. 186–87
669 "An indulgent father": Ibid., pp. 189–90

670 "It has pained me all week": Céard, *Lettres inédites*, p. 31
670 "I believe that my father": LeBlond-Zola, *Emile Zola*, p. 187
670 "We were a bit intimidated": Ibid., pp. 188–89
671 "Poor Denise is very taken up": CORR., VIII, p. 275 (November 20, 1895)
671 "I had her go over her Bible history": Ibid., p. 268 (November 17, 1895)
671 "We'd take little walks": Albert Laborde, "Emile Zola à Médan: un entretien avec Albert Laborde," *Les Cahiers naturalistes*, no. 38, 1969, p. 157
672 "The weather is terrible": CORR., VIII, p. 245 (August 8, 1895)
672 "Splendid weather": Ibid., p. 266
672 "I went into the Verneuil woods": Ibid., p. 20
672 "A photographic craze": Ibid., VI, p. 188 (October 8, 1887)
673 "At the end of the century": Jean Sagne, *L'Atelier du photographe, 1840–1940*, Paris, Presses de la Renaissance, 1984, p. 90
673 "Yesterday your uncle tried to develop": Laborde, *Trente-huit années*, p. 114
673 "Framed in its embrasure": CORR., I, p. 375
674 "immense positivist labor": René Ternois, *Zola et son temps*, Paris, Les Belles Lettres, 1961, pp. 144–45
675 "A novel about Lourdes": Ibid., p. 149
675 "This movement astonishes us": Ibid.
675 "The whole town swells": Ibid., p. 150
676 "How many interesting tableaux": Ibid.
676 "Lourdes does wonders for people": Ibid., p. 193
676 The little sisters of the Assumption: Ibid., p. 194
677 "Expressions on their faces": Zola, *Mes Voyages*, edited by René Ternois, Paris, Fasquelle, 1958, p. 33
677 "Men, women, children": Ibid., p. 35
678 "No medical precaution is taken": Ibid., pp. 43–44
678 "The most astonishing facts": Ibid., p. 76
679 "I do not deny the unknown": Ibid., p. 81
679 "What's needed is a man": Ternois, *Zola et son temps*, p. 287
680 "I am very far behind": CORR., VIII, pp. 125–26
681 "natural phenomenon . . . in all ages, in all climes": Ternois, *Zola et son temps*, p. 300
681 "transforming crowds into colossi": Ibid., p. 364
681 "When one closes the volume": Ibid.
682 "German socialists": Ibid., p. 365
682 "we really rub our eyes": James, *Notes on Novelists*, p. 32
682 "occurrences": Ternois, *Zola et son temps*, p. 368
682 "You [Monsieur Zola] represent": Ibid., p. 370
683 "For some time now the whole religious world": Ibid., p. 373
683 "hysteric": Ibid.
683 "It's neither my novel as a whole": Ibid.
684 "Make two volumes": Ibid., p. 246
684 "a door open upon the twentieth century": CORR., VII, p. 324
684 "The outline of *Lourdes* is more or less complete": Ibid., p. 409
684 "is steadily moving toward": Brogan, *France under the Republic*, p. 259
685 "the Republic, *in France*, is simply a form of government": Ibid., p. 264
685 "All that is new is the political form": Dansette, *Histoire religieuse*, p. 460
686 "Do you think perchance": Ibid., p. 469
686 "to deny one's past": Ibid., p. 472

686 "As Chesnelong put it": Brogan, *France under the Republic*, pp. 264–65
687 "Bloody repression is necessary": Ternois, *Zola et son temps*, p. 327
688 "cupidities and appetites": Ibid., p. 190
688 "I am told that as soon as one walks": Ibid., p. 387
689 "Rome must destroy": Ibid., pp. 388–89
689 "With some astonishment I heard Zola's voice": Goncourt, *Journal*, IV, p. 650
689 "I know for a fact": CORR., VIII, p. 170
690 "I must thank Count Joseph Primoli": CORR., VIII, p. 177
690 "I am neither an interviewer nor an interviewist": Ibid., p. 179
690 "small and gray": Zola, *Mes Voyages*, p. 143
690 "Ten a.m., on the Janiculum": Ibid., p. 145
691 "The huge nave, the branches": Ibid., p. 146
691 "Pierre, who arrives there with the memory": Ibid., p. 147
691 "For my Pierre, the day of his arrival": Ibid., p. 200
692 "My Pierre, after seeing": Ibid., p. 159
692 "The Congregation of the Index": CORR., VIII, p. 177
693 "He rises at 6": Zola, *Mes Voyages*, pp. 191–92
693 "In the garden he perambulates": Ibid., pp. 218–19
693 "What strikes me is all this antiquity": Ibid., pp. 229–30
694 "A prisoner yes, but the immense expanse": Ibid., pp. 217–18
694 "It's a curio city which should be put": Ibid., p. 290
694 "Zola gave us a very good dinner": Goncourt, *Journal*, IV, p. 765
695 "As if floored by some apparition": O.C., VII, p. 904
695 "I resolved as usual": CORR., VIII, p. 254
695 "poor old head . . . sometimes very weary": Ibid., p. 266 (November 16, 1895)
696 "The pope is the eternal prisoner": Ternois, *Zola et son temps*, p. 603
696 "and never has he emerged": Ibid.
696 "He has never been realistic": Ibid., p. 605
696 "A novel is essentially a work of imagination": Ibid., p. 607
696 "It's more boring": Ibid., p. 606
696 "bungled compilation": Ibid., p. 608
697 "Everything is decadence": O.C., VII, p. 510
697 "Judging from the latest tips": Becker, *Trente années d'amitié*, p. 124
697 "I can't accomplish as quickly as I should like": Laborde, *Trente-huit années*, p. 110
697 "Dear wife, I've now received": CORR., VIII, pp. 260–61
698 "You know that I purposely": Ibid., pp. 267–68
698 "I absolutely insist upon fetching you": Ibid., pp. 276–77
698 "This week Octave wrote to me": Ibid., p. 263
699 "Thus shall I rest for an entire month": Laborde, *Trente-huit années*, p. 120

XXVI. AND THEN THERE WAS ONE

700 "If, in the score of *Le Rêve*": CORR., VII, p. 174
701 "Late in the day, I have gotten interested": O.C., XV, p. 830
702 "All of you poor people": Ibid., p. 572
703 "The wheat will ripen": Ibid., p. 580
703 "When a despotic, all-powerful genius": Ibid., p. 832
703 "It seems to me on reflection": CORR., VIII, pp. 383–84
703 "Our father visited us in our box": LeBlond-Zola, *Emile Zola*, p. 188

704 "In theory, it doesn't matter whether a text": CORR., VIII, p. 392
704 "If my libretto displeases you": Ibid., pp. 390–91
704 "mysticism did not absorb": Ibid., p. 394
705 "before a rebirth": Ibid., p. 393
705 "Catholicism, Christianity itself": O.C., VII, p. 1180
705 "confusedly . . . affection, truth, and life": Ibid., pp. 1420–21
706 "Life had begotten life": Ibid., p. 1562
706 "Allow the religion of science": Ibid., p. 1561
706 "Snobbism has it that one must talk tough": Emilien Carassus, *Le Snobisme et les lettres françaises de Paul Bourget à Marcel Proust*, Paris, Armand Colin, 1966, p. 411
707 "Wasn't he, Duvillard, the sole victor": O.C., VII, p. 1509
707 "the progress of love": Ternois, *Zola et son temps*, p. 670
707 "While everything around us": Ibid., p. 671
708 "a beautiful book, a bold protest": Ibid., pp. 673–74
708 "Never has M. Zola": Ibid., p. 672
708 "a misunderstood document": O.C., XII, p. 706
708 "For years I have had the conviction": Goncourt, *Journal*, IV, p. 952
708 "A week ago this ex-debunker": Ibid., p. 985
708 "In the name of literary friends": O.C., XII, pp. 705–7
710 "I arrived a bit late for dinner": Yvonne Martinet, *Alphonse Daudet*, Gap, Imprimerie Jean-Louis, 1940, p. 793
710 "Polemicists of very different temperament": *Le Figaro*, December 21, 1897
710 "If I have been chosen to pay Daudet homage": O.C., XII, p. 723
711 "with the genealogical tree of *Les Rougon-Macquart*": Martinet, *Daudet*, p. 781
711 "We were four brothers": O.C., XII, p. 725
711 "I told you that I couldn't vouch": CORR., VIII, pp. 328–29
712 "I have never hidden anything": Toulouse, *Enquête*, preface p. vi
712 "superior degenerates . . . obsessional": Ibid., pp. 279–80
712 "Besides himself, Zola worships": Jean-Denis Bredin, *L'Affaire*, Paris, Julliard, 1983, p. 232

XXVII. *J'ACCUSE*

714 "I have received no word": Bredin, *L'Affaire*, p. 65
715 "[Mercier] told [Hanotaux]": Maurice Paléologue, *Journal de l'Affaire Dreyfus*, Paris, Plon, 1955, p. 4
715 "despair and humiliation": Bredin, *L'Affaire*, p. 20
716 "They put me in the strictest solitary confinement": Alfred Dreyfus, *The Diary of Captain Alfred Dreyfus*, New York, The Peebles Press, 1977, p. 42
716 "The individual arrested has reportedly": Bredin, *L'Affaire*, p. 79
716 "Along with his extensive knowledge": Ibid., p. 89
717 "The Dreyfus Affair sticks to General Mercier's back": Ibid., p. 91
717 "Someone in the ministry of war": Ibid., p. 93
717 "the most urgent moral imperative": Ibid., p. 98
717 "honorable person . . . This man is the traitor": Ibid., p. 97
717 "Not a single judge appears to have suspected": Ibid.
718 "He has no relative, no wife": Ibid., p. 100
718 "The country sees that simple soldiers": Ibid., p. 100

719 "Your brother's cause must be defended": Ibid., p. 133
719 "religious impulse": Ibid., p. 134
719 "Lazare lost no time": Ibid., p. 135
719 "ancestral tradition of humility . . . I know some": Ibid., p. 136
720 "ageless, his body stooped over": Ibid., p. 160
720 "It may be imagined that [the code]": Ibid., pp. 161–62
720 "I could not believe [what *L'Eclair* reported]": Ibid., p. 164
721 "Our circle of action": Ibid., p. 170
721 "[He] had serious financial problems": Ibid., p. 146
722 "keep the two cases separate": Ibid., p. 160
722 "In my opinion it is imperative": Ibid., p. 162
722 "What do you care that that Jew": Ibid., p. 163
722 "What you've said is abominable": Ibid.
723 "The minister has just told me": Ibid., pp. 173–74
723 "I have read that an elected deputy": Ibid., p. 167
723 "Paris. Midnight 35": Ibid., p. 173
724 "good health . . . splendid trip": Ibid., p. 175
724 "more insistent as the hours passed": Ibid., p. 177
724 "*Le Matin, La Patrie, La Libre Parole*": Ibid., p. 192
725 "The sole basis of the accusation": Ibid., p. 200
726 "For several years I have followed": O.C., XIV, p. 779
726 "stupefied . . . in our age of democracy": Ibid., pp. 782–83
726 "Our factual accounts became poetry": Alain Pagès, *Emile Zola. Un intellec-tuel dans l'Affaire Dreyfus*, Paris, Librairie Séguier, 1991, p. 57
727 "Truth is on the march": O.C., XIV, p. 888
727 "Captain Dreyfus was condemned": Ibid., p. 891
727 "How many simple folk have accosted me": Ibid., p. 894
727 "Who doesn't sense that we stand": Ibid., p. 895
727 "turned against a poor wretch": Ibid.
728 "a syndicate to shape opinion": Ibid.
728 "We have witnessed a base exploitation": Ibid., p. 901
728 "Let us hope that tomorrow's action": Ibid.
729 "Set your mind at rest": Paléologue, *Journal*, p. 58
729 "But he would have to obey": Bredin, *L'Affaire*, p. 183
729 "veiled lady": Ibid., p. 195
729 "foreign legation": Ibid., p. 194
730 "I have received these last days": Ibid., p. 196
730 "who, having been informed": Ibid., p. 200
730 "unwitting agent": Ibid., p. 214
731 "I believe that you have in your hands": Ibid.
731 "We must know whether it is true": Ibid., p. 215
731 "the hatred of three hundred hypnotized": Ibid.
732 "respectful . . . homage": Ibid., p. 216
732 "So there exists such a thing": O.C., XIV, pp. 907–9
732 "Republican blood does not yet run": Ibid., p. 915
733 "Today the tactic of anti-Semitism": Ibid.
733 "judicial apotheosis": Ibid., p. 913
733 "implicate such glorious names": Bredin, *L'Affaire*, p. 227
733 "permitted to furnish explanations": Ibid.
734 "If circumstances have permitted me": O.C., XIV, p. 895

734 "I accuse Lieutenant Colonel du Paty de Clam": Ibid., pp. 930–31
735 "The party of justice had been born": Bredin, *L'Affaire*, p. 236
736 "We the undersigned": Pagès, *Emile Zola*, pp. 129–30
736 "noble, militant attitude": Ibid., p. 130
736 "for service rendered to the cause": Ibid., pp. 130–31
736 "the 'syndicate' grows more numerous": Ibid., p. 129
736 "defender of humanity": Ibid., p. 134
737 "May my admiration and enthusiasm": Ibid., p. 138
737 "Please allow a young woman": Ibid., p. 139
737 "Your free words and Your divine anger": Ibid., pp. 138–39
737 "Yesterday evening, my father gave me": Ibid., p. 140
737 "At the end of the nineteenth century": Michel Winock, *Nationalisme, antisémitisme, et fascisme en France,* Paris, Éditions du Seuil, 1982, p. 164
738 "Just who is this Monsieur Zola": Bredin, *L'Affaire*, p. 235
738 "grave misdeeds committed": Ibid., p. 239
739 "bizarre mixture of fanaticism": Paléologue, *Journal*, p. 111
739 "Buttoned tight at the waist": Bredin, *L'Affaire*, pp. 244–45
739 "artisans of the other affair": Ibid., p. 247
739 "Yesterday evening the war ministry": Paléologue, *Journal*, p. 113
739 "superb swordsman": Ibid., p. 112
740 "What do you want this army to become": Bredin, *L'Affaire*, p. 248
740 "We would have been happy": Ibid.
740 "I will repeat the very characteristic words": Ibid., p. 249
741 "He seemed quite calm": Bredin, *L'Affaire*, p. 250
741 "M. Zola speaks, or, rather, reads": George Bonnamour, *Le Procès Zola. Impressions d'audience*, Paris, A. Pierret, 1898, p. 191
741 "Dreyfus is innocent, I swear it": O.C., XIV, p. 939
742 "Down with Zola": Pagès, *Emile Zola*, p. 177, and Bredin, *L'Affaire*, p. 244
742 "On January 17 in Nantes": Bredin, *L'Affaire*, p. 266
742 "Every morning, very early": Alfred Bruneau, *A l'ombre d'un grand coeur*, Paris, Charpentier et Fasquelle, 1932, p. 120
742 "this handful of maniacs . . . I told companions": Pagès, *Emile Zola*, p. 182
743 "not one of us would have come out alive": Bredin, *L'Affaire*, p. 252
743 "Zola's true crime has been in daring": Ibid., p. 254
743 "M. Zola having been convicted": Céard, *Lettres inédites*, p. 30
743 "Arriving in the midst of this tempest": Ibid., p. 32
744 "My mother feared for his life": LeBlond-Zola, *Emile Zola*, p. 242
744 "Why assume that incarceration": CORR., IX, pp. 175–76 (March 18, 1898)
744 "Nothing new here, things continue": Ibid., pp. 166–167
745 "the honor of the country": Bredin, *L'Affaire*, p. 280
745 "A court-martial has just dared": Ibid., p. 281
745 "Since nothing surprises me anymore": Bruneau, *A l'ombre d'un grand coeur*, p. 131
745 "At the entrance to the sumptuous villa": Ibid., pp. 132–33
746 "nothing is above the law": Pagès, *Emile Zola*, p. 222
746 "We were mindful of the peril": Bruneau, *A l'ombre d'un grand coeur*, p. 134
746 "grave misdeeds while in service": Bredin, *L'Affaire*, p. 253
746 "betraying to Scheurer-Kestner": Ibid.
746 "I would have bicycled every morning": Pagès, *Emile Zola*, p. 225
746 "a fool, a peacock": Ibid., pp. 227–28

746 "deeper cause, some sinister blemish": Ibid., p. 228
747 "It stands to reason": Ibid.
747 "I was there, I saw him cry": Ibid., p. 229
747 "How could Louis Philippe have authorized": O.C., XIV, p. 1009
748 "Backed up against the wall": Pagès, *Emile Zola*, pp. 232–33
748 "Save us; save us": Bredin, *L'Affaire*, p. 297
749 "civil personality": Pagès, *Emile Zola*, p. 254
749 "the brambles": Ibid.
749 "Back to Venice": Ibid.
749 "This was the sum total": O.C., XIV, pp. 1138–39
750 "Dear wife. Events compel me": LeBlond-Zola, *Emile Zola*, p. 244
750 "It was done, I was no longer": O.C., XIV, p. 1139
750 "I don't know a word of English": Ibid.
751 "He finally acquiesced": Pagès, *Emile Zola*, p. 259
751 "cellar vents, portholes": O.C., XIV, p. 1140
751 "Except for a few close, loyal friends": Ibid., p. 1141
751 "You will page M. Pascal": Vizetelly, *Emile Zola*, pp. 16–17
751 "I believe that you must, at all costs": O.C., XIV, p. 1167
752 "He was . . . so conspicuous": Ernest Vizetelly, *With Zola in England*, London, Chatto & Windus, 1899, p. 38
752 Details of the "letting": Ibid., p. 116
753 "A very tranquil day": O.C., XIV, pp. 1142–43
753 "A day of great calm": Ibid., p. 1145
753 "I unpacked my manuscripts": Ibid., p. 1149
754 "Today, at 10 o'clock": Ibid., p. 1151
754 "What struck me was the number": Ibid., pp. 1153–54
755 "Day after day I've discussed with dear Desmoulin": CORR., IX, pp. 240–41 (August 3, 1898)
755 "I understand very well": Ibid., p. 256
755 "I am going to have my children": Ibid., pp. 241–42
756 "I believe that luggage is not inspected": Ibid., pp. 1503–4
756 "Jean arrived with the children": Ibid., p. 1505
756 "I needn't tell you anything": MS, Collection Puaux-Bruneau
757 "Charpentier's presence": Denise LeBlond-Zola, *Emile Zola*, pp. 261–62.
757 "Since the Zola affair is back": Henri Guillemin, *Zola, légende et vérité*, Paris, 1979, Editions d'Utovie, pp. 129–30
758 "In 1896, you received": Bredin, *L'Affaire*, p. 304
759 "merely confirmed": Ibid., p. 306
759 "Ah, my dear, how happy I was": Laborde, *Trente-huit années*, pp. 133–34
759 "Tell immediately": O.C., XIV, p. 1159
759 "As was natural, [he] was quite excited": Vizetelly, *With Zola in England*, p. 142
760 "Colonel, there is not a drop of your precious blood": Bredin, *L'Affaire*, p. 313
761 "torn to pieces": Ibid., p. 315
761 "The same day, the minister of justice": Ibid., p. 316
761 "Never have I seen an autumn day more clement": CORR., IX, pp. 329–30
762 "The nervous, passionate man I am": Ibid., p. 371
762 "Zola must remain over there": Owen Morgan, "Zola et l'Affaire Dreyfus:

Quelques documents inédits," *Il terzo Zola. Emile Zola dopo i Rougon-Macquart*, Naples, 1990, p. 438

762 "If my friends judge my return": MS, Archives Programme Zola

762 "I can still see before me": Vizetelly, *With Zola in England*, pp. 189–90

763 "Loulou's English is more than adequate": MS, Collection Larat (November 2, 1898)

763 "For two whole days": MS, Collection Morin-Laborde

764 "Despite the sadness of the situation": MS, Collection Morin-Laborde (November 29, 1898, to Elina Laborde)

764 "As for myself, my poor dear": Laborde, *Trente-huit années*, p. 138

765 "Over here amazement is general": MS, Collection Morin-Laborde, (February 16, 1899)

765 "All along his route": Paléologue, *Journal*, pp. 173–74

766 "Today's election is an insult": Bredin, *L'Affaire*, p. 346

766 "Save France and the Republic": Ibid., p. 347

766 "The Court admits the new facts": Louis L. Snyder (editor), *The Dreyfus Case: A Documentary History*, New Brunswick, Rutgers University Press, 1973, p. 256

766 "This unexpected declaration": Ibid., p. 258 (*Le Matin*, June 3, 1899)

767 "The responsibility which had so long rested": Vizetelly, *With Zola in England*, p. 218

XXVIII. The Fifth Act

768 "to support only governments": Bredin, *L'Affaire*, p. 359

768 "Waldeck, lawyer to Eiffel": Ibid., p. 363

769 "The succession of emotions": Alfred Dreyfus, *Five Years of My Life*, New York, Peebles Press, 1977, p. 238

769 "I saw how Zola": Ibid., p. 240

769 "[They] provided . . . a great hall": Snyder, *The Dreyfus Case*, p. 331

770 "rebirth and salvation": Bredin, *L'Affaire*, p. 369

770 "The choice is clear": Ibid., p. 370

770 "There was in everybody's eyes": Paléologue, *Journal*, p. 194

771 "I recognized these pathetic phrases": Ibid., pp. 195–96

771 "I have not reached my age": Bredin, *L'Affaire*, p. 379

771 "That is just what you should do": Ibid.

771 "But no! The certainty": Ibid.

772 "Ah! my dear, my great and valiant friend": O.C., XIV, p. 1526

772 "His imperious mask": Paléologue, *Journal*, p. 210

772 "With his very first words": Ibid., pp. 215–16

773 "the present French government . . . Concerning such public opinion": Bredin, *L'Affaire*, p. 385

773 "The law does not ask jurors": Ibid., p. 393

773 "extenuating circumstances": Ibid., p. 394

774 "shredding a military judgment": Ibid., p. 396

774 "The government of the Republic": Dreyfus, *Five Years of My Life*, p. 398

774 "nervous fits": MS, Collection Puaux-Bruneau (July 8, 1899)

774 "My good friend, I . . . thank you": CORR., IX, p. 523

775 "That business about extenuating circumstances": MS, Collection Morin-Laborde, partly published in Laborde, *Trente-huit années*, p. 145

775 "Since when have there been": Dreyfus, *Five Years of My Life*, p. 242
775 "It was a strange initiative": Bredin, *L'Affaire*, p. 396
775 "I am in mortal fear": O.C., XIV, pp. 959ff.
776 "there are punishments more severe": Bredin, *L'Affaire*, p. 407
777 "The view that one can save a people": O.C., XIV, pp. 994–95
777 "I played my role as staunchly": Ibid., p. 1002
777 "I think I shall compose four gospels": Emile Zola, *Les Oeuvres Complètes*, Paris, François Bernouard, 1928, XXVIII, p. 694
778 "indulge . . . lyricism": Ibid., p. 692
778 "create the Family": Ibid.
779 "would either be a shameful nonentity": David Baguley, *"Fécondité" d'Emile Zola*, Toronto, University of Toronto Press, 1973, p. 30
779 "For about ten years I have been": O.C., XIV, pp. 785–88
782 "[They] are on the road that leads": Baguley, *"Fécondité" d'Emile Zola*, p. 117
782 "We open the road, we set the example": O.C., VIII, p. 497
783 "They now had nothing for themselves": Ibid., p. 502
783 "[It] seems less a novel than a poem": Baguley, *"Fécondité" d'Emile Zola*, p. 157
784 "Far from being about humanitarianism": O.C., VIII, p. 515
784 "I know what my book's flaws are": Ibid., p. 516
785 "[When Marguerite told me that Georges]": CORR., IX, p. 336
785 "I'm terribly sorry that my remarks": MS, Collection Morin-Laborde
785 "to struggle with dark thoughts": Laborde, *Trente-huit années*, p. 143
785 "five days that marked a happy truce": MS, Collection Morin-Laborde
785 "I envy you your calm": Ibid.
785 "life is ceaseless pain": Ibid., to Amélie, July 30, 1900
785 "We children waited": LeBlond-Zola, *Emile Zola*, p. 277
786 "No, my friend, I shall not go": MS, Collection Puaux-Bruneau
786 "He thought it important": LeBlond-Zola, *Emile Zola*, p. 277
786 "An inveterate noctambulist": Bakker, *Lettres inédites de Paul Alexis*, pp. 25–26
787 "My beloved wife dead": Ibid., p. 450
787 "I am not giving a speech": Ibid., p. 32
787 "perpetuate the memory": Ibid.
788 "It is not true": O.C., VIII, pp. 977–78
788 "During the first four years": Ibid., p. 704
789 "a powerful boost": Ibid., p. 984
789 "Zola, who would achieve communism": Ibid.
789 "once shook crowds with his striking visions": Ibid., p. 985
789 "I have no intention of trying": Vizetelly, *Emile Zola*, p. 498
789 "the poor of spirit . . . holy battalion": F. W. J. Hemmings, *Emile Zola*, Oxford, Clarendon Press, 1966, p. 300
790 "[This] prohibition created a new class": Brogan, *France under the Republic*, p. 360
790 "How do you like the dismissal": MS, Collection Puaux-Bruneau
791 "You're all very lucky indeed": MS, Collection Laborde
791 "I no longer know why we didn't accompany him": LeBlond-Zola, *Emile Zola*, p. 278
792 "We were about to leave the apartment": Ibid., p. 280

793 "Hacquin, I'll tell you how Zola died": Armand Lanoux, *Bonjour, Monsieur Zola*, Paris, Amiot-Dumont, 1954, p. 374

793 "it seems prudent": Hemmings, *Emile Zola*, p. 304

793 "Her face enveloped in a long crepe veil": *Le Figaro*, October 3, 1902

794 "Several political associations have . . . sent": Ibid.

795 "Still young, Zola had conquered glory": Bruneau, A *l'ombre d'un grand coeur*, pp. 196–98

795 "I rely on your tact and leave you free": Lanoux, *Bonjour, Monsieur Zola*, p. 377

796 "Glory to Zola! Honor to the apostle": Vizetelly, *Emile Zola*, p. 523

EPILOGUE

797 "We were at the dawn of life": Rewald, *Paul Cézanne*, p. 211

798 "the love of ugliness": Rewald, *Cézanne et Zola*, p. 161

798 "I can't get over this most recent separation": MS, letter to Jeanne Rozerot, Archives Programme Zola

799 "The line needed reinforcement": *Le Figaro*, June 4, 1908

799 "All at once this shy, solitary man": Ibid., July 5, 1908

800 "[The president and official cortege] had just reached": Ibid.

801 "I shall arrange a lunch": MS, Archives Programme Zola

801 "The demonstrations of homage": Ibid.

802 "If I die before I can see this through": Ibid.

803 "The Fasquelles are having a soirée": Ibid.

BIBLIOGRAPHY

ZOLA'S WORKS, NOTES, AND LETTERS

Oeuvres complètes. Edited by Henri Mitterand. Paris: Cercle du Livre Précieux, 1967, 15 volumes

Les Rougon-Macquart. Edited by Henri Mitterand. Paris: Gallimard (Pléiade), 1960–1967, 5 volumes

Les Rougon-Macquart. Edited by Colette Becker in collaboration with Gina Gourdin Servenière and Véronique Lavielle. Paris: Laffont (Collection "Bouquins"), 1991–1993, 5 volumes

Contes et nouvelles. Edited by Roger Ripoll. Paris: Gallimard (Pléiade), 1976

Carnets d'enquêtes (selections from Zola's preparatory notebooks). Edited by Henri Mitterand. Paris: Plon, 1986

Preparatory notebooks for *Les Rougon-Macquart* and *Les Quatre Evangiles*: Bibliothèque Nationale, département des manuscrits, nouvelles acquisitions françaises 10268–10345

Mes Voyages—Lourdes, Rome. Edited with an introduction by René Ternois. Paris: Fasquelle, 1958. Also published in the *Oeuvres complètes,* vol. VII

Correspondance. General editor B. H. Bakker. Montreal and Paris: Presses de l'Université de Montréal and Editions du CNRS, 1978–1993. Nine volumes have appeared to date, covering Zola's life through the Dreyfus Affair.

Letters written to Zola: Bibliothèque Nationale, département des manuscrits, nouvelles acquisitions françaises 24510–24524

GENERAL SOURCES

The following list is largely restricted to books and articles that bear upon Zola's life and times. An exhaustive bibliography has been compiled by David Baguley in two volumes, *Bibliographie de la critique sur Emile Zola,* vol. I: *1864–1970*; vol.

II: *1971–1980* (University of Toronto Press). There is annual updating in *Les Cahiers naturalistes.*

Albalat, Antoine. *Gustave Flaubert et ses amis.* Paris: Plon, 1927
Alexis, Paul. *Emile Zola, notes d'un ami.* Paris: Charpentier, 1882
———. *"Naturalisme pas mort." Lettres inédites de Paul Alexis à Emile Zola, 1871–1900.* Edited by B. H. Bakker. Toronto: University of Toronto Press, 1971
Allem, Maurice. *La Vie quotidienne sous le Second Empire.* Paris: Hachette, 1948
Amicis, Edmondo de. *Souvenirs de Paris et de Londres.* Paris: Hachette, 1880
Antoine, André. *Mes souvenirs sur le Théâtre Libre.* Paris: Fayard, 1921
Aron, Jean-Paul. *Le Mangeur du XIXe siècle.* Paris: Laffont, 1974
Auriant, L. "Emile Zola et les deux Houssaye. Documents inédits." *Mercure de France,* vol. 297
Baguley, David. "Les Sources et la fortune des nouvelles de Zola." *Les Cahiers naturalistes,* no. 32 (1966)
———. *"Fécondité" d'Emile Zola.* Toronto: University of Toronto Press, 1973
Baldick, Robert. *The Life of J.-K. Huysmans.* Oxford: Clarendon Press, 1955
———. *The Life and Times of Frédérick Lemaître.* London: Hamish Hamilton, 1959
———. *Dinner at Magny's.* London: Gollancz, 1971
Baligand, Renée. "Lettres inédites d'Antoine Guillemet à Emile Zola (1866–1870)." *Les Cahiers naturalistes,* no. 52 (1978)
Barbusse, Henri. *Zola.* Paris: Gallimard, 1931
Barrès, Maurice. *Les Déracinés.* Paris: Plon, 1924
———. *Mes Cahiers, 1896–1923.* Edited by Guy Dupré. Paris: Plon, 1963
Becker, Colette. "Du garni à l'hôtel particulier: quelques aperçus sur la vie et l'oeuvre de Zola à partir des calepins cadastraux." *Les Cahiers naturalistes,* no. 43 (1972)
———. "François Zola et son fils." Ibid., no. 44 (1972)
———. "Un Professeur de Zola: Pierre-Emile Levasseur." Ibid., no. 49 (1975)
———. "Zola à la librairie Hachette." *University of Ottawa Quarterly,* vol. XLVIII, no. 4, October–December 1978
———. "Un Ami de jeunesse d'Emile Zola: Georges Pajot. Lettres inédites." *Les Cahiers naturalistes,* no. 53 (1979)
———. "Quelques documents sur la jeunesse d'Emile Zola à Aix-en-Provence." Ibid., no. 55 (1981)
———. "Jean-Baptistin Baille." Ibid., no. 56 (1982)
———. "La Correspondance de Zola, 1858–1870: trente lettres nouvelles." *Les Cahiers naturalistes,* no. 57 (1983)
———. *Les Apprentissages de Zola.* Paris: Presses Universitaires de France, 1993
———. *Dictionnaire d'Emile Zola.* With Gina Gourdin Servenière and Véronique Lavielle. Paris: Laffont, 1993
Bellanger, Claude, ed. *Histoire générale de la presse française.* Vols. II and III. Paris: Presses Universitaires de France, 1969 and 1970
Bellessort, André. *La Société française sous Napoléon III.* Paris: Librairie Académique Perrin, 1960
Bergerat, Emile. *Les Années de bohème.* Vol. I of *Souvenirs d'un enfant de Paris.* Paris: Fasquelle, 1911
Bernos, Marcel, et al., eds. *Histoire d'Aix-en-Provence.* Aix-en-Provence: Edisud, 1977

Billy, André. *Les Frères Goncourt. La Vie littéraire à Paris pendant la seconde moitié du XIXe siècle*. Paris: Flammarion, 1954

Bonaparte, Napoleon-Louis. *Des idées napoléoniennes*. Paris: Amyot et Plon, 1860

Bonnamour, Georges. *Le Procès Zola. Impressions d'audience*. Paris: A. Pierret, 1898

Borie, Jean. *Zola et les mythes ou De la nausée au salut*. Paris: Editions du Seuil, 1971

Bornecque, Jacques-Henry. *Les Années d'apprentissage d'Alphonse Daudet*. Paris: Nizet, 1951

Boussel, Patrice. *L'Affaire Dreyfus et la presse*. Paris: Armand Colin, 1960

Bouvier, Jean. *Le Krach de l'Union Générale*. Paris: Presses Universitaires de France, 1960

Bouyala d'Arnaud, André. *Evocation du vieux Marseille*. Paris: Editions de Minuit, 1959

––––––. *Evocation du vieil Aix-en-Provence*. Paris: Editions de Minuit, 1979

Brady, Patrick. *"L'Oeuvre" de Emile Zola. Roman sur les arts. Manifeste, autobiographie, roman à clef*. Geneva: Droz, 1968

Braudel, Fernand, and Ernest Labrousse, eds. *Histoire économique et sociale de la France*. Paris: Presses Universitaires de France, 1976

Bredin, Jean-Denis. *L'Affaire*. Paris: Julliard, 1983

Brisson, Adolphe. "Souvenirs littéraires: les débuts d'Emile Zola." *Les Annales politiques et littéraires*, no. 1302

Brogan, D. W. *France under the Republic (1870–1939)*. New York: Harper & Brothers, 1940

Brombert, Victor. *The Intellectual Hero*. Philadelphia: J. B. Lippincott, 1961

Bruneau, Alfred. *A l'ombre d'un grand coeur. Souvenirs d'une collaboration*. Paris: Charpentier et Fasquelle, 1932

Burchell, S. C. *Imperial Masquerade: The Paris of Napoleon III*. New York: Atheneum, 1971

Burns, Colin. "Henry Céard and His Relations with Flaubert and Zola." *French Studies*, vol. VI (1952)

––––––. "Zola et l'Angleterre." *Les Cahiers naturalistes*, no. 12 (1959)

––––––. "Zola in Exile." *French Studies*, vol. XVII (1963)

––––––. "Le Voyage de Zola à Londres en 1893." *Les Cahiers naturalistes*, no. 60 (1986)

Burns, Michael. *Dreyfus: A Family Affair*. New York: HarperCollins, 1991

Bury, J. P. T., and R. P. Tombs. *Thiers, 1797–1877: A Political Life*. London: Allen & Unwin, 1986

Carassus, Emilien. *Le Snobisme et les lettres françaises de Paul Bourget à Marcel Proust. 1884–1914*. Paris: Armand Colin, 1966

Carter, Lawson A. *Zola and the Theater*. New Haven: Yale University Press, 1963

Céard, Henry. "Zola intime." *Revue illustrée*, vol. III, 1887

––––––. *Lettres inédites à Emile Zola*. Edited by Colin Burns. Paris: Nizet, 1958

––––––. *Correspondance inédite, Henry Céard et Edmond Goncourt (1876–1896)*. Edited by Colin Burns. Paris: Nizet, 1965

Cézanne, Paul. *Conversations avec Cézanne*. Edited by P. M. Doran. Paris: Collection Macula, 1978

Chapman, Guy. *The Third Republic of France: The First Phase, 1871–1894*. London: Macmillan, 1962

Charpentier, Georges. *Trente Années d'amitié. Lettres de l'éditeur Georges Char-*

pentier à Emile Zola. Edited by Colette Becker. Paris: Presses Universitaires de France, 1980

Chastel, Guy. J.-K. *Huysmans et ses amis.* Paris: Grasset, 1957

Chastenet, Jacques. *L'Enfance de la Troisième, 1870–1879.* Paris: Hachette, 1952

———. *La République des Républicains, 1879–1893.* Paris: Hachette, 1954

———. *La République triomphante, 1893–1906.* Paris: Hachette, 1955

Chemel, Henri. "Zola collaborateur du *Sémaphore de Marseille* (1871–77)." *Les Cahiers naturalistes,* nos. 14 and 18 (1960 and 1961)

Chevalier, Louis. *Classes laborieuses et classes dangereuses.* Paris: Plon, 1958

Cim, Albert. *Le Dîner des Gens de Lettres, souvenirs littéraires.* Paris: Flammarion, 1903

Cladel, Judith. *Rodin, sa vie glorieuse et inconnue.* Paris: Grasset, 1936

Cogny, Pierre. "Lettres inédites d'Edmond de Goncourt à Emile Zola." *Les Cahiers naturalistes,* no. 13 (1959)

———. *Le "Huysmans intime" de Henry Céard et Jean de Caldain.* Paris: Nizet, 1957

La Commune de 1871. Paris: Edition de Delphes. 1965

Coppée, François. *Souvenirs d'un Parisien.* Paris: Alphonse Lemerre, 1910

Corbin, Alain. *Les Filles de noce.* Paris: Flammarion, 1982

Corley, T. A. B. *Democratic Despot: A Life of Napoleon III.* New York: Clarkson N. Potter, 1961

Crouzet, Marcel. *Un Méconnu du réalisme: Duranty (1833–1880). L'Homme. Le Critique. Le Romancier.* Paris: Nizet, 1964

Dansette, Adrien. *Le Boulangisme, 1886–1890.* Paris: Librairie Académique Perrin, 1938

———. *Histoire religieuse de la France contemporaine.* Paris: Flammarion, 1965

Daudet, Alphonse. *Trente ans de Paris.* Illustrated edition. Paris: Flammarion, n.d. (originally published by Marpon-Flammarion in 1888)

Daudet, Alphonse Mme. *Souvenirs d'un groupe littéraire.* Paris: Fasquelle, 1910

Daudet, Ernest. *Mon frère et moi. Souvenirs d'enfance et de jeunesse.* Paris: Plon, 1882

Daudet, Léon. *Quand vivait mon père.* Paris: Grasset, 1940

Daumard, Adeline. *Les Bourgeois de Paris au XIXe siècle.* Paris: Flammarion, 1970

Débats de la Cour de Cassation. Paris: Stock, 1899

Deffoux, Léon. *Le Groupe de Médan.* In collaboration with Emile Zavie. Paris: Crès, 1920

———. "Emile Zola et la sous-préfecture de Castelsarrasin en 1871." *Mercure de France,* vol. 191 (1926)

———. *La Publication de "L'Assommoir."* Paris: Société Française des Editions Littéraires et Techniques, 1931

Des Cars, Jean. *Haussmann: La Gloire du second Empire.* Paris: Librairie Académique Perrin, 1978

Dezalay, Auguste, ed. *Lectures de Zola.* Paris: Armand Colin, 1973

Dhur, Jacques. *Le Père d'Emile Zola. Les prétendues lettres Combes.* Paris: Société Libre d'Edition des Gens de Lettres, 1899

Dreyfous, Maurice. *Ce qu'il me reste à dire. Un demi-siècle de choses vues et entendues, 1848–1900.* Paris: Ollendorff, 1912

Drumont, Edouard. *La France juive.* 2 vols. Paris: Flammarion, 1938 (originally published by Flammarion in 1886)

Du Camp, Maxime. *Paris: Ses organes, ses fonctions et sa vie dans la seconde moitié du XIXe siècle.* 6 vols. Paris: Hachette, 1879

Dupuy, Aimé. *1870-1871: la guerre, la Commune et la presse.* Paris: Armand Colin, 1959

Duveau, Georges. *La Vie ouvrière en France sous le second Empire.* Paris: Gallimard, 1946

Edel, Leon. *The Life of Henry James.* Vol. 3. Philadelphia: J. B. Lippincott, 1962

Edwards, Stewart. *The Paris Commune, 1871.* New York: Quadrangle, 1977

Emile-Zola, François and Massin. *Zola photographe.* Paris: Denoël, 1979

Flaubert, Gustave. *Oeuvres complètes.* Paris: Club de l'honnête homme, 1972

———. *Correspondance (1830-1869).* Edited by Jean Bruneau. 3 vols. Paris: Gallimard (Pléiade), 1973, 1980, 1981

———. *Correspondance Gustave Flaubert-George Sand.* Edited by Alphonse Jacobs. Paris: Flammarion, 1981

Furst, Lilian. "George Moore et Zola. Une réévaluation." *Les Cahiers naturalistes,* no. 41 (1971)

Gaillard, Jeanne. *Communes de province, commune de Paris. 1870-1871.* Paris: Flammarion, 1971

Gambetta, Léon. *Discours et plaidoyers politiques.* Vols. IV–VIII (June 1873–January 1879). Paris: Charpentier, 1881-1883

Gasquet, Joachim. *Cézanne.* Paris: Bernheim-Jeune, 1926

Gerbod, Paul. *La Vie quotidienne dans les lycées et collèges au XIXe siècle.* Paris: Hachette, 1968

Girard, Marcel. "Positions politiques d'Emile Zola jusqu'à l'affaire Dreyfus." *Revue française de science politique,* vol. V (1953)

Girardet, Raoul. *Le Nationalisme français, 1871-1914.* Paris: Editions du Seuil, 1970

Goncourt, Edmond and Jules de. *Journal. Mémoires de la vie littéraire.* Edited by Robert Ricatte. 4 vols. Paris: Fasquelle et Flammarion, 1956

Got, Olivier. "Bordeaux vu par Zola, 1870-1871." *Revue historique de Bordeaux et du département de la Gironde,* vol. XXII (1973)

Grant, Elliott M. *Emile Zola.* New York: Twayne, 1966

Guieu, Jean-Max. *Le Théâtre lyrique d'Emile Zola.* Paris: Fischbacher, 1983

Guillemin, Henri. *Zola, légende et vérité.* Paris: Editions d'Utovie, 1979

Guiral, Pierre. *Marseille et l'Algérie, 1830-1841.* Paris: Editions du CNRS, 1957

———. *La Vie quotidienne en France à l'âge d'or du capitalisme, 1852-1879.* Paris: Hachette, 1976

Halpérine-Kaminsky, Ely, ed. *Ivan Tourguéniev d'après sa correspondance avec ses amis français.* Paris: Fasquelle, 1901

Hemmings, F. W. J. "Zola, Manet and the Impressionists (1875-1880)." *PMLA,* vol. 73 (1958)

———. *Emile Zola.* Oxford: Clarendon Press, 1966

———. "Emile Zola devant l'exposition universelle de 1878." *Cahiers de l'Association Internationale des Etudes Françaises,* no. 24 (1972)

———. *The Life and Times of Emile Zola.* New York: Scribner's, 1977

———. "Le Père d'Emile Zola et les chemins de fer d'Autriche." *Les Cahiers naturalistes,* no. 55 (1981)

Herbert, Robert L. *Impressionism: Art, Leisure, and Parisian Society.* New Haven: Yale University Press, 1988

Houssaye, Arsène. *Les Confessions. Souvenirs d'un demi-siècle (1830–1880).* 5 vols. Paris: Dentu, 1885

Howard, Michael. *The Franco-Prussian War.* New York: Collier Books, 1969

Hugo, Victor. *Choses vues. Souvenirs, journaux, cahiers.* Edited by Hubert Juin. Paris: Gallimard (Folio), 1972

Huysmans, J.-K. *Lettres inédites à Emile Zola.* Edited by Pierre Lambert. Geneva: Droz, 1953

————. *Lettres inédites à Edmond de Goncourt.* Edited by P. Lambert. Paris: Nizet, 1956

————. *Lettres inédites à Camille Lemonnier.* Edited by Gustave Vanwelkenhuyzen. Geneva: Droz, 1957

————. *Oeuvres complètes.* Vol. II. Geneva: Slatkine, 1972

————. "Emile Zola et L'Assommoir." In *Les Rougon-Macquart,* vol. I. Edited by P. Cogny. Paris: Editions du Seuil, 1961

————. *Lettres inédites à Arij Prins.* Edited by Louis Gillet. Geneva: Slatkine, 1977

————. *Lettres à Théodore Hannon.* Edited by Pierre Cogny and Christian Berg. Paris: Christian Pirot, 1985

James, Henry. *Notes on Novelists.* New York: Scribner's, 1914

————. *The Letters of Henry James.* Vol. I. Edited by Percy Lubbock. New York: Scribner's, 1920

Josephson, Matthew. *Zola and His Time.* New York: Macaulay, 1928

Jourdain, Francis. "Zola outragé et calomnié." In *Présence de Zola.* Paris: Fasquelle, 1953

Jouvenel, Bertrand de. *Vie de Zola.* Paris: Librairie Valois, 1933

Kahn, Maurice. "Anatole France et Emile Zola." *La Grande Revue,* vol. 121 (1926)

Kanes, Martin. "Zola and Busnach: The Temptation of the Stage." *PMLA,* vol. 77 (1962)

————. "Zola, Flaubert et Tourguéniev: autour d'une correspondance." *Les Cahiers aturalistes,* no. 36 (1968)

Kurtz, Harold. *The Empress Eugénie.* Boston: Houghton Mifflin, 1964

Laborde, Albert. *Trente-huit années près de Zola. La Vie d'Alexandrine Emile-Zola.* Paris: Les Editeurs Français Réunis, 1963

————. "Emile Zola à Médan." *Les Cahiers naturalistes,* no. 38 (1969)

Labouchère. *Diary of the Besieged Resident in Paris.* New York: Harper & Brothers, 1871

Lanoux, Armand. *Bonjour, Monsieur Zola.* Paris: Amiot-Dumont, 1954

Lapp, John C. "Taine et Zola: autour d'une correspondance." *Revue des sciences humaines,* no. 87 (1957)

————. "Emile Zola et Ludovic Halévy: notes sur une correspondance." *Les Cahiers naturalistes,* no. 27 (1964)

————. *Les Racines du naturalisme. Zola avant "Les Rougon-Macquart."* Paris: Bordas, 1972

LeBlond-Zola, Denise. *Emile Zola raconté par sa fille.* Paris: Grasset, 1986 (originally published by Fasquelle, 1931)

————. "Emile Zola et l'amour des bêtes." *Les Cahiers naturalistes,* no. 6

LeBlond, Jean-Claude. "Zola acquéreur de biens." *Europe,* nos. 468–469 (1968)

Lefranc, Georges. *Les Gauches en France (1789–1972).* Paris: Payot, 1973

Lepelletier, Edmond. *Emile Zola, sa vie—son oeuvre.* Paris: Mercure de France, 1908

Levillain, Philippe. *Boulanger fossoyeur de la monarchie.* Paris: Flammarion, 1982

Ligou, Daniel. *Histoire du socialisme en France (1871–1961)*. Paris: Presses Universitaires de France, 1962

Lindsay, Jack. *Cézanne: His Life and Art*. New York: New York Graphic Society, 1969

Lioult, Jean-Louis. "Nouvelles précisions sur les années aixoises d'Emile Zola." *Les Cahiers naturalistes*, no. 65 (1991)

Lottman, Herbert. *Gustave Flaubert*. Paris: Fayard, 1989

Lough, John. *Writer and Public in France: From the Middle Ages to the Present Day*. Oxford: Clarendon Press, 1978

Lucas-Dubreton, J. *Louis-Philippe*. Paris: Fayard, 1938

Mallarmé, Stéphane. *Correspondance, 1871–1885*. Vol. II. Edited by Henri Mondor and L. J. Austin. Paris: Gallimard, 1965

———. *Correspondance, 1886–1889*. Vol. III. Paris: Gallimard, 1969

Manet, Edouard. *Manet, 1832–1883*. Edited by Françoise Cachin and Charles Moffett, exhibition catalogue. Paris: Editions de la Réunion des Musées Nationaux, 1983

Marrus, Michael R. *Les Juifs de France à l'époque de l'affaire Dreyfus*. Paris: Calmann-Lévy, 1972

Massis, Henri. *Comment Zola composait ses romans*. Paris: Charpentier, 1906

Mathieu, Caroline, ed. *1889: La Tour Eiffel et l'Exposition universelle*. Paris: Editions de la Réunions des Musées Nationaux, 1989

Maupassant, Guy de. *Chroniques, études, correspondance*. Edited by René Dumesnil, with the collaboration of Jean Loize. Paris: Librairie Grund, 1938

———. *Correspondance inédite*. Edited by Artine Artinian, with the collaboration of Edouard Maynial. Paris: Editions Dominique Wapler, 1951

———. *Correspondance. 1862–1880*. In *Oeuvres complètes*, edited by Jacques Suffel. Geneva: Cercle du Bibliophile, 1973

Mayeur, Françoise. *L'Education des filles en France au XIXe siècle*. Paris: Hachette, 1979

Mayeur, Jean-Marie. *Les Débuts de la Troisième République. 1871–1898*. Paris: Editions du Seuil, 1973

———. *Catholicisme social et démocratie chrétienne*. Paris: Editions du Cerf, 1986

McMullen, Roy. *Degas: His Life, Times, and Work*. Boston: Houghton Mifflin, 1984

Meyer, Arthur. *Ce que mes yeux ont vu*. Paris: Plon-Nourrit, 1911

Michelet, Jules. *L'Amour*. Paris: Hachette, 1859

———. *La Femme*. Paris: Flammarion (Collection "Champs"), 1981

Mistler, Jean. *La Librairie Hachette de 1826 à nos jours*. Paris: Hachette, 1964

Mitterand, Henri. "Zola devant la Commune." *Les Lettres françaises*, no. 732 (1958)

———. "La jeunesse de Zola et de Cézanne: observations nouvelles." *Mercure de France*, vol. 335 (1959)

———. "Emile Zola à Marseille et à Bordeaux de septembre à décembre 1870." *Revue des sciences humaines*, nos. 98–99 (1960)

———. "Emile Zola et *Le Rappel*." *Les Cahiers naturalistes*, no. 15 (1960)

———. "La Correspondance (inédite) entre Emile Zola et Michel Stassioulevitch, directeur du *Messager de l'Europe* (1875–1881)." *Les Cahiers naturalistes*, no. 22 (1962)

———. *Zola journaliste. De l'affaire Manet à l'affaire Dreyfus*. Paris: Armand Colin, 1962

———. *Emile Zola journaliste. Bibliographie chronologique et analytique* (in collaboration with Halina Suwala). Vol. I, 1859–1881. Paris: Les Belles Lettres, 1968

———. *Album Zola* (in collaboration with Jean Vidal). Paris: Gallimard (Pléiade), 1968

———. "Les manuscrits perdus d'Emile Zola." *Les Cahiers naturalistes*, no. 39 (1970)

Montreynaud, Florence. "Les Relations de Zola et de Tourguéniev: documents inédits." *Les Cahiers naturalistes*, no. 43 (1972)

———. "La Correspondance entre Zola et Stassioulevitch, directeur du *Messager de l'Europe* (deuxième partie)." Ibid., no. 47 (1974)

———. "Les Relations de Zola et de Tourguéniev (avec treize lettres inédites de Zola à Tourguéniev)." Ibid., no. 52 (1978)

Moore, George. *Impressions and Opinions.* New York: Scribner's, 1891

———. "My Impressions of Zola." *English Illustrated Magazine*, vol. XI (1894)

———. *Memoirs of My Dead Life.* New York: Appleton and Co., 1911

———. *Confessions of a Young Man: Avowals.* New York: Boni and Liveright, 1923

Moreau-Nélation, Etienne. *Manet raconté par lui-même.* 2 vols. Paris: H. Laurens, 1926

Morgan, Owen R. "Léon Hennique et Emile Zola." *Les Cahiers naturalistes*, no. 30 (1965)

———. "Zola et l'Affaire Dreyfus: Quelques documents inédits." *Il terzo Zola. Emile Zola dopo i Rougon-Macquart.* Naples, 1990

Newton, Joy. "Zola et Nadar." *Les Cahiers naturalistes*, no. 54 (1980)

———. "La Correspondance Zola-Nadar." Ibid., no. 56 (1982)

———. "Zola et Rodin." Written in collaboration with Monique Fol. Ibid., no. 51 (1977)

———. "La Correspondance entre Zola et Rodin." Written in collaboration with Monique Fol. Ibid., no. 59 (1985)

Niess, Robert J. *Zola, Cézanne and Manet: A Study of "L'Oeuvre."* Ann Arbor: University of Michigan Press, 1968

Ory, Pascal. *L'Expo universelle.* Paris: Editions Complexe, 1989

Pagès, Alain. "Le Mythe de Médan." *Les Cahiers naturalistes*, no. 55 (1981)

———. *Emile Zola. Un intellectuel dans l'Affaire Dreyfus.* Paris: Librairie Séguier, 1991

Paléologue, Maurice. *Journal de l'Affaire Dreyfus.* Paris: Plon, 1955

Palmer, Michael B. *Des petits journaux aux grandes agences. Naissance du journalisme moderne.* Paris: Aubier, 1983

Perruchot, Henri. *La Vie de Cézanne.* Paris: Hachette, 1956

Peter, René. "Zola et l'Académie." *Mercure de France*, vol. 296 (1940)

Picon, Gaetan. *1863: Naissance de la peinture moderne.* Geneva: Skira, 1974

Pinckney, David. *Napoleon III and the Rebuilding of Paris.* Princeton: Princeton University Press, 1958

Pissarro, Camille. *Correspondance, 1865–1885.* Edited by Janine Bailly-Herzberg. Paris: Presses Universitaires de France, 1980

———. *Correspondance, 1886–1890.* Edited by J. Bailly-Herzberg. Paris: Editions du Valhermeil, 1986

Ponteil, Félix. *Les Institutions de la France de 1814 à 1870.* Paris: Presses Universitaires de France, 1965

Price, Roger. *The French Second Republic: A Social History.* Ithaca: Cornell University Press, 1972

Prost, Antoine. *Histoire de l'enseignement en France, 1800-1967.* Paris: Armand Colin, 1969

Provence, Marcel. "Cézanne et ses amis. Numa Coste." *Mercure de France,* vol. 187 (1926)

Rebérioux, Madeleine. "Le Socialisme français de 1871 à 1914." In *Histoire générale du socialisme.* Vol. II. Edited by J. Droz. Paris: Presses Universitaires de France, 1974

Reinach, Joseph. *Histoire de l'affaire Dreyfus.* 7 vols. Paris: Fasquelle, 1929

Rémond, René. *La Vie politique en France depuis 1789.* Vol. II. Paris: Armand Colin, 1969

――――. *L'Anticléricalisme en France de 1815 à nos jours.* Paris: Fayard, 1976

Rewald, John. *Cézanne et Zola.* Paris: Editions A. Sedrowski, 1936

――――. *Cézanne. Sa vie, son oeuvre, son amitié pour Zola.* Paris: Albin Michel, 1939

――――. *Paul Cézanne.* New York: Simon & Schuster, 1948

――――. *Paul Cézanne: Correspondance.* Paris: Grasset, 1978

――――. *The History of Impressionism.* New York: Museum of Modern Art, 1973

Richardson, Joanna. *Zola.* London: Weidenfeld & Nicolson, 1978

Rigaud, Joseph. *A propos du cinquantenaire de la mort d'Emile Zola. L'ingénieur François Zola, père du célèbre littérateur. Sa vie, sa famille et son oeuvre.* Aix-en-Provence: Roubaud, 1957

Ripoll, Roger. "Zola et les communards." *Europe,* nos. 468-469 (1968)

――――. "La Vie aixois dans *Les Rougon-Macquart.*" *Les Cahiers naturalistes,* no. 43 (1972)

――――. *Réalité et mythe chez Zola.* 2 vols. (doctoral thesis). Paris: Honoré Champion, 1981

Robert, Guy. "Des Inédits d'Emile Zola. Une polémique entre Zola et *Le Mémorial d'Aix* en 1868." *Arts et Livres,* vol. II, no. 6 (1946)

――――. "*La Terre*" *d'Emile Zola. Etude historique et critique.* Paris: Les Belles Lettres, 1952

Robida, Michel. *Le Salon Charpentier et les impressionistes.* Paris: Bibliothèque des Arts, 1958

Rubenach, Jane. "Une Correspondance inédite entre Emile Zola et Jules Claretie." *Les Cahiers naturalistes,* no. 51 (1977)

Rudelle, Odile. *La République absolue, 1871-1889.* Paris: Publications de la Sorbonne, 1983

Sainte-Beuve. *Correspondance générale.* Edited by Jean Bonnerot. Vols. XIV, XVI, and XVII. Paris: Didier, 1964, 1970, and 1975

Salvan, Albert J. *Zola aux Etats-Unis.* Providence: Brown University Press, 1943

Sanders, James B. "Zola et la censure théâtrale: une chronique inédite en librairie." *Les Cahiers naturalistes,* no. 51 (1971)

Schapiro, Leonard. *Turgenev, His Life and Times.* Oxford: Oxford University Press, 1978

Schom, Alan. *Emile Zola.* New York: Henry Holt, 1987

Serman, William. *La Commune de Paris.* Paris: Fayard, 1986

Sherard, Robert H. *Emile Zola: A Biographical and Critical Study.* London: Chatto & Windus, 1893

――――. *Twenty Years in Paris.* London: Hutchinson and Co., 1905

Snyder, Louis L., ed. *The Dreyfus Case: A Documentary History.* New Brunswick: Rutgers University Press, 1973

Speirs, Dorothy, and Dolores Signori. *Emile Zola dans la presse parisienne, 1882–1902.* Toronto: University of Toronto Press, 1985

———. *Entretiens avec Zola.* Ottawa: Les Presses de l'Université d'Ottawa, 1990

Spencer, Philip. *The Politics of Belief in Nineteenth-Century France.* London: Faber & Faber, 1954

Sternhell, Zeev. *La Droite révolutionnaire, 1881–1914. Les origines françaises du fascisme.* Paris: Editions du Seuil, 1978

Suwala, Halina. "Zola et les conférences de la rue de la Paix." *Les Cahiers naturalistes,* nos. 37–38 (1969)

———. *Naissance d'une doctrine. Formation des idées littéraires et esthétiques d'Emile Zola (1859–1865).* Warsaw: University of Warsaw Press, 1976

Taine, Hippolyte. *Essais de critique et d'histoire.* Paris: Hachette, 1892 (sixth edition)

———. *Nouveaux essais de critique et d'histoire.* Paris: Hachette, 1866 (second edition)

———. *Journeys through France.* New York: Henry Holt, 1897

Ternois, René. *Zola et son temps. Lourdes-Rome-Paris.* Paris: Les Belles Lettres, 1961

———. "Les Zola. Histoire d'une famille vénitienne." *Les Cahiers naturalistes,* no. 18 (1961)

———. *Zola et ses amis italiens.* Paris: Les Belles Lettres, 1967

Thompson, J. M. *Louis Napoleon and the Second Empire.* Oxford: Basil Blackwell, 1954

Thomson, Clive. "Une Correspondance inédite: vingt-sept lettres de Marius Roux à Emile Zola." *University of Ottawa Quarterly,* vol. XLVIII, no. 4

Toulouse, Edouard. *Enquête médico-psychologique sur les origines de la supériorité intellectuelle. Emile Zola.* Paris: Flammarion, 1896

Troyat, Henri. *Emile Zola.* Paris: Flammarion, 1992

Tuchman, Barbara W. *The Proud Tower.* New York: Macmillan, 1966

Vallès, Jules. *Oeuvres complètes.* 4 vols. Edited by L. Scheler and M.-C. Banquart. Paris: Livre Club Diderot, 1969–70

———. *Articles littéraires. Littérature et révolution.* Edited by Roger Bellet. Paris: Editeurs Français Réunis, 1970

Verlaine, Paul. *Oeuvres en prose complètes.* Edited by Jacques Borel. Paris: Gallimard (Pléiade), 1972

Villemessant, Hippolyte de. *Mémoires d'un journaliste.* Vols. III and IV. Paris: Dentu, 1873 and 1875

Vizetelly, Ernest. *With Zola in England.* London: Chatto & Windus, 1899

———. *Emile Zola, Novelist and Reformer: An Account of His Life and Work.* London: John Lane, The Bodley Head, 1904

Vollard, Ambroise. *Paul Cézanne.* New York: Crown, 1937 (originally published in Paris by Crès, 1924)

Walker, Philip. *Emile Zola.* London: Routledge and Kegan Paul, 1968

Wallon, Armand. *La Vie quotidienne dans les villes d'eaux de 1850 à 1914.* Paris: Hachette, 1981

Walter, Rodolphe. "Zola et ses amis à Bennecourt (1866)." *Les Cahiers naturalistes,* no. 17 (1961)

———. "Emile Zola à Bennecourt en 1868: les vacances d'un chroniqueur." Ibid., no. 37 (1969)

———. "Zola et la Commune." Ibid., no. 43 (1972)

Weber, Eugen. *France Fin de Siècle*. Cambridge: Harvard University Press, 1986

Wilson, Angus. *Emile Zola*. New York: William Morrow, 1952

Winock, Michel. *Nationalisme, antisémitisme et fascisme en France*. Paris: Editions du Seuil, 1982

Xau, Fernand. *Emile Zola*. Paris: Marpon et Flammarion, 1880

Zévaès, Alexandre. *Les Guesdistes*. Paris: Marcel Rivière, 1911

———. *Zola*. Paris: Editions de la Nouvelle Revue Critique, 1945

Zola, François. *Questions posées par la direction générale des Ponts et Chaussées relativement aux différents projets de docks et autres travaux présentés au concours pour être exécutés dans le port de Marseille, et leur solution*. Marseille: Typographie des Hoirs Feissat et Demouchy, 1835

———. *Lettre adressée à M. le Maire et à MM. les membres du conseil municipal de la ville de Marseille accompagnant le traité et le projet pour la distribution dans la ville de Marseille*. Marseille: Imprimerie de Poussielgue, 1838

INDEX

873